Connections: A World History

Combined Volume

Edward H. Judge

Le Moyne College

John W. Langdon

Le Moyne College

vango books | Read it. Get it.

New York   San Francisco   Boston   Upper Saddle River
London   Toronto   Sydney   Tokyo   Singapore   Madrid
Mexico City   Munich   Paris   Cape Town   Hong Kong   Montreal

Executive Editor: Charles Cavaliere
Editor in Chief, History: Priscilla McGeehon
Assistant Development Manager: David B. Kear
Production Project Manager: Lynn Savino Wendel
Associate Editor: Emsal Hasan
Editorial Assistant: Lauren Aylward
Director of Marketing: Brandy Dawson
Senior Marketing Manager: Laura Lee Manley
Marketing Assistant: Athena Moore
Senior Managing Editor: Ann Marie McCarthy
Senior Operations Supervisor: Mary Ann Gloriande
Media Project Manager: Brian Hyland
Senior Art Director: Maria Lange
Manager, Rights and Permissions: Zina Arabia
Manager, Visual Research: Beth Brenzel
Image Permission Coordinator: Richard Rodriques
A/V Project Manager: Mirella Signoretto
Permissions Coordinator: Marcy Lunetta
Cover Illustration: Ronald Walko
Full Service Project Management: Kristy Zamagni, Pre-Press PMG

To Susan and Janice

VangoBooks™ is an imprint of Pearson Education
Pearson® is a registered trademark of Pearson plc

Pearson Education LTD
Pearson Education Singapore, Pte. Ltd
Pearson Education Canada, Inc.
Pearson Education–Japan
Pearson Education Australia PTY, Limited

Pearson Education North Asia, Ltd., Hong Kong
Pearson Educación de Mexico, S.A. de C.V.
Pearson Education Malaysia, Pte. Ltd
Pearson Education Upper Saddle River, New Jersey

10 9 8 7 6 5 4 3 2 1

ISBN 13: 978-0-20-565694-3
ISBN 10:   0-20-565694-3

CONTENTS

PART II   Trans-Regional Conflicts and Religious Connections, 200–1200 C.E.

CHAPTER 11

The Origins and Expansion of Islam, 100–750

CHAPTER 12

Religion and Diversity in the Transformation of Southern Asia, 711–1400

CHAPTER 13

African Societies and the Impact of Islam, 1500 B.C.E.–1500 C.E.

CHAPTER 20

The West in an Age of Religious Conflict and Global Expansion, 1500–1650   481

PART IV The Shift from Regional to Global Connections, 1500–1800

CHAPTER 21

The Search for Stability in East Asia, 1300–1800   505

CHAPTER 22

Southern Asia and the Global Shift in Wealth and Power, 1500–1800   533

CHAPTER 27
Industry, Ideology, and Their
Global Impact, 1700–1914   663

CHAPTER 28
Nation Building in North and
South America, 1789–1914   698

CHAPTER 33
World War II and the Holocaust, 1933–1945

CHAPTER 34
East Versus West: Cold War and Its Global Impact, 1945–Present

CHAPTER 35
The Upheavals of Asia, 1945–Present

MAPS

We are two professors who love teaching world history. For the past two decades, at our middle-sized college, we have team-taught a two-semester world history course that first-year students take to fulfill a college-wide requirement. Our students have very diverse backgrounds and interests. Most take world history only because it is required, and many find it very challenging. Helping them to understand it and infecting them with our enthusiasm for it are our main purposes and passions.

This is an exciting time to be teaching world history. In an age of growing global interconnectedness, an understanding of diverse world cultures and their histories has never been more essential. Indeed, it is increasingly apparent that students who lack this understanding will be poorly prepared to function in modern society or even to comprehend the daily news.

At the same time, the teaching of world history has never seemed more challenging. As the amount and complexity of the material increases, students can get bogged down in details and inundated with information, losing sight of the overall scope and significance of the human experience. Conveying world history to college students in a comprehensible and appealing way, without leaving them confused and overwhelmed, is one of the toughest challenges we face.

To help meet this challenge and better connect with our students, we have written a compact, affordable world history text that is tailored to meet their needs. In developing this text, we pursued several main goals:

First, because students often find it difficult to read and process lengthy, detailed chapters, we sought to write a text that is *concise and engaging*, with short, interesting chapters that focus on major trends and developments.

Second, since students often see history as a bewildering array of details, dates, and events, we chose a unifying theme—connections among world societies—and grouped our chapters to reflect the growth of such connections from regional to global.

Third, having seen many students struggle because they lack a good sense of geography, we included 223 maps—far more than most other texts—and provided a number of other features designed to help readers better understand and process the material.

A Concise and Readable Text

Since even the best text does little good if students do not read it, we endeavored above all to produce one that is concise and readable. We addressed ourselves to first-year college students, using a simple, straightforward narrative that tells the compelling story of the peoples and societies that preceded us and how they shaped the world. To avoid drowning our readers in a welter of details, we chose to take an introductory approach rather than an encyclopedic one. With this text, students will become familiar with the most important trends, developments, and issues in world history, and they will gain an appreciation for the vast diversity of human societies and endeavors.

To make our book less overwhelming and more accessible to students, we have limited most chapters to about 10,000 words, and divided each chapter into short topical subsections. By writing concise chapters, we have enabled average students to read them in an hour or so. By keeping subsections short, we have partitioned the text into manageable segments, so that readers can process material before they move on. By furnishing an outline at the start of each chapter, marginal notes that highlight our main theme, and a perspective section at the end, we have kept in sight the overall trends and developments, without interrupting the narrative's basic flow.

Connections in World History

In our teaching we have found that many students find world history confusing and overwhelming, in part because they have no overall framework for understanding it. To help them sort things out, we have focused our text on a central theme of connections among world societies. By stressing this theme, we have sought to maintain a sense of coherence and purpose, and to give our readers a framework that will help them to make sense of history.

Rather than dividing our text into ancient, medieval, and modern eras, an arrangement that works for Europe but has limited value elsewhere, we have instead grouped our chapters into two overlapping ages: an Age of Regional Connections, lasting until about 1650 C.E., and an Age of Global Connections, dating from roughly 1500 to the present. Each age is then subdivided into three sections, reflecting the expansion of connections from regional to global levels. This framework, summarized in our table of contents, is designed to give students the "big picture" of world history that they often lack.

Within each section are chapters that provide both regional and global perspectives, stressing not only each culture's distinct features but also its connections with other regions and cultures. Readers thus can readily appreciate both the diversity and the interconnectedness of human societies.

Within each chapter, on almost every page, are **marginal notations** that summarize material and highlight our connections theme. Readers thus can easily keep sight of the overall context.

An Extensive and Consistent Map Program

Many students approach world history with only a rudimentary understanding of world geography, and maps are a crucial tool in understanding world history. Our text contains a copious abundance of carefully crafted maps, designed within each chapter to build one upon another. With over 220 maps throughout the book, *Connections* offers one of the most extensive map programs of any world history survey textbook.

Each chapter begins with a **foundation map**, positioning chapter events in global context or highlighting a key part of the world under discussion.

We have worked very hard to make the maps clear and to place them where readers can refer to them without turning pages. As much as possible, the maps use colors, fonts, labels, and other markers consistently, so that students will find these features familiar from one map to the next.

Finally, the map captions were carefully written to clarify the maps, to connect them with surrounding text, and to guide the students' attention to the most important elements in that map. Each map caption includes a question to help students consider critical issues.

Features

We have incorporated in our text a carefully selected set of features, each chosen with this basic guideline in mind: Will it help students to better envision, understand, and process the material they are reading?

VISUALS   We provide an ample array of photos and other visuals, selected to illustrate developments explicitly discussed in the text. To ensure that students will connect the text with the images, we have placed them in the margins near the passages that they illustrate.

PRONUNCIATION GUIDES   Since students often struggle to pronounce unfamiliar names and places, we have placed parenthetical pronunciation guides immediately following first use of such names and places in the text.

CHAPTER-OPENING VIGNETTES   Each chapter opens with a vignette designed to capture the reader's interest and introduce the chapter's main themes.

PRIMARY SOURCE DOCUMENT EXCERPTS   To acquaint students with primary sources and illuminate materials covered in our text, we have provided concise excerpts from selected historical sources, in feature boxes placed where the document is discussed in the text.

CHAPTER REVIEW SECTIONS   Each chapter has a comprehensive end-of-chapter review section that incorporates the following features:

- **Putting It in Perspective.** This feature provides a concise overview of the chapter's main themes, highlights key connections, and puts them in historical perspective.
- **Key Concepts.** Key concepts are highlighted in boldface in the text, defined in the text when first discussed and also in an alphabetic glossary, and listed at the end of each chapter with page references to facilitate review.
- **Key People.** Important individuals mentioned in the text are also listed at the end of each chapter, followed by page references to facilitate review.
- **Ask Yourself.** A set of questions at the end of every chapter encourages further reflection and analysis of topics, issues, and connections considered in the chapter.
- **Going Further.** A list of books at the end of each chapter provides resources for teachers and students interested in delving more deeply into topics covered.
- **Key Dates and Developments.** Each chapter contains a comprehensive chronology that lists the key dates and developments, helping students to see at a glance sequence of important events.

A Student-Centered Textbook

For several years, we and our colleagues have used a draft version of our text, with highly encouraging results. Since the book is affordable and portable, we find that most students buy it and bring it to class. Since chapters are concise and engaging, we find that students actually read them before coming to class and thus are better prepared to understand and discuss key issues. Students who completed questionnaires or wrote reviews of our chapters said they found them clear and compelling. By pointing out passages they found dry or confusing, these students also helped make the book more readable. We went to great lengths to create a text that is useful, accessible, and attractive to our students. For they, after all, are the reasons we wrote this book.

Ed Judge and John Langdon

SUPPORT MATERIALS

VangoBooks are innovative course materials created to better meet the needs of today's college students. They are portable, convenient, student-oriented texts that present essential information and issues in a compact form at a much lower price than traditional textbooks. Designed to make world history more meaningful and accessible, this VangoBook comes with an extensive package of support materials for instructors and students.

For Instructors

INSTRUCTOR'S MANUAL   For each chapter of the text, the Instructor's Manual provides lecture outlines, chapter summaries, learning objectives, discussion questions, Connection Questions, and suggestions for audio-visual materials.

TEST-ITEM FILE   Written and extensively class-tested by Connie Brand of Meridian Community College, the Test-Item File Includes over 3000 questions (multiple choice, essay, short answer, true/false, and map questions).

TESTGEN   A computerized test-management program for Windows and Macintosh computers that allows users to customize their own tests, for both traditional and online classrooms. The user-friendly interface enables instructors to view, edit, and add questions. Search and sort features allow instructors to locate questions quickly and arrange them in preferred order. Available online at www.pearsonhighered.com/irc. Contact your local Pearson representative for an access code.

POWERPOINT SLIDES AND DIGITAL TRANSPARENCIES   Available for downloading to adopters of *Connections* from the Pearson instructor resource center (www.pearsonhighered.com/irc). Contact your Pearson representative for an access code.

For Students

VANGOBOOKS.COM   **VangoBooks.com/judge** offers educational tools specifically designed to help students fully understand world history and study smarter. Resources such as documents, audio, video and images are correlated to each chapter in *Connections*. Interactive maps feature engaging simulations to enrich the maps from the text. Multiple Choice and True/False questions from the Chapter Exams provide a great way to prepare for tests, while the Essay section offers a variety of sample essay questions. Test questions and essays can be submitted online for immediate grading.

VANGOCARD FOR WORLD HISTORY   Colorful, affordable, and packed with useful information, Pearson's VangoCard for World History makes studying easier, more efficient, and more enjoyable. Course information is distilled down to the basics, helping students quickly master fundamentals, review a subject for understanding, or prepare for an exam. And because Cards are laminated, they are a durable reference tool. VangoCards can be packaged with the text. Contact your local Pearson representative for details.

RESEARCH NAVIGATOR™   *Available when bundled with the text.* Make the most of your research time with Research Navigator. Understanding the research process is important to success in college. Pearson's **Research Navigator** is the easiest way to start a research assignment or research paper. With access to exclusive databases of credible and reliable source material, including the EBSCO Academic Journal and Abstract Database, The *New York Times* Search by Subject Archive, "Best of the Web" Link Library, and *Financial Times* Article Archive and Company Financials, **Research Navigator** gives students all the tools they need to conduct online research for projects and papers.

■ Extensively revised and updated, the **Primary Source: Documents in Global History DVD** is both a rich collection of textual and visual documents in world history and an indispensable tool for working with sources. Extensively developed with the guidance of historians and teachers, the revised and updated DVD version includes over 800 sources in world history—from cave art to satellite images of the Earth from space. More sources from Africa, Latin America, and southeast Asia have been added to this revised and updated DVD version. All sources are accompanied by headnotes, focus questions, and are searchable by topic or region.

- ■ Titles from the renowned **Penguin Classics** series can be bundled with—*Connections: A World History* for a nominal charge. Please contact your Pearson Arts and Sciences sales representative for details.
- ■ *The Prentice Hall Atlas in World History, Second Edition* includes over 100 full-color maps in world history, drawn by Dorling Kindersley, one of the world's most respected cartographic publishers. Copies of the Atlas can be bundled with *Connections: A World History* for a nominal charge. Contact your Pearson Arts and Sciences sales representative for details.
- ■ CourseSmart **CourseSmart Textbooks Online** is an exciting new choice for students looking to save money. As an alternative to purchasing the print textbook, students can subscribe to the same content online and save up to 50% off the suggested list price of the print text. With a CourseSmart eTextbook, students can search the text, make notes online, print out reading assignments that incorporate lecture notes, and bookmark important passages for later review. For more information, or to subscribe to the CourseSmart eTextbook, visit www.coursesmart.com.

Acknowledgments

In conceiving, composing, and bringing out this book, we are deeply grateful to the many people who helped us along the way. Our senior colleagues Bill Telesca and Fr. Bill Bosch, with whom we first taught world history, shared with us their many decades of experience as teachers and scholars. Our current colleagues, Doug Egerton, Holly Rine, Yamin Xu, and Bob Zens have class-tested a preliminary version of our book, and have provided us with feedback from their students and insights from their expertise in Atlantic World, Amerind, East Asian, and Islamic history. Yamin Xu has also been particularly helpful with the spelling and pronunciation of East Asian names. Connie Brand and her colleagues at Meridian Community College have likewise class-tested our book with their students, and Connie has written an extremely useful test bank.

Expert Content Reviewers

We are teachers of world history, but we are not experts in every area of history. For that reason, we acknowledge with profound gratitude the insightful and thorough critiques provided by a panel of expert reviewers, who read and commented on the following chapters:

David Christian, San Diego State University (Human origins and early societies: Chapter 1)

Karl Galinsky, University of Texas (Greece and Rome: Chapters 6-10)

Leonard Gordon, Columbia University (Southeast Asia: Chapters 3, 12, 17, 22, 29, 32, 35)

Megan Greene, The University of Kansas (Asia: Chapters 4, 14, 15, 21, 25, 29, 32, 33, 35)

William Ochsenwalk, Virginia Polytechnic Institute and State University (the Muslim world: Chapters 11, 12, 13, 15, 17, 22, 30, 37)

Jeffrey Pilcher, University of Minnesota (Latin America: Chapters 5, 18, 19, 26, 28, 36)

Sean Redding, Amherst College (Africa: Chapters 2, 13, 23, 30, 37)

Advisory Council

We greatly appreciate the helpful suggestions offered to us by an Advisory Council of our colleagues and peers that Pearson brought together:

Sanjam Ahluwalia, Northern Arizona University
Robert Becker, Gainesville State College
Brett Berliner, Morgan State University

Rebecca Berry, Wake Tech Community College
David Blaylock, Eastern Kentucky
Beau Bowers, Central Piedmont CC

Ras Michael Brown, Southern Illinois University
Brian Bunk, University of Massachusetts—Amherst
Harry Carpenter III, Western Piedmont Community College
Charles Crouch, Georgia Southern University
Lisa Edwards, University of Massachusetts—Lowell
John Frederick, South Louisiana Community College
Patricia Gajda, The University of Texas at Tyler
Donald Grinde, SUNY, Buffalo
Anthony Gulig, University of Wisconsin Whitewater
Brian Gurian, Harrisburg Area Community College
Anne Hardgrove , University of Texas at San Antonio
Donald Harreld, Brigham Young University
Randolph Head, University of California, Riverside
Padhraig Higgins, Mercer County Community College
Marie Hooper, Oklahoma City University
Michael Houf, Texas A&M University—Kingsville
Michael Jacobs, University of Wisconsin—Baraboo
Ellen Jenkins, Arkansas Tech University
.im. Timothy Jenks, East Carolina University
Robe..rt Kunath, Illinois College
Ben Lie..berman, Fitchburg State College
Susan Ma..neck, Jackson State University
David Joh.. Marley, Vanguard University
Joel McMa..hon, Georgia Perimeter College
..id McQ..ilkin, Bridgewater College
Dav..a Meh..rtens, University of Massachusetts—Dartm.., In
Cristin.. outh..
Scott Mor.. diana University of Pennsylvania

Luke Nichter, Bowling Green State University
Robert Parkinson, Shepherd University
Tracie Provost, Middle Georgia College
David Rayson, Normandale Community College
Scott Reese, Northern Arizona University
Maria Teresa Romero, Saddleback College
Steven Salm, Xavier University of Louisiana
Linda Scherr, Mercer County Community College
David Simonelli, Youngstown State University
Govind Sreenivasan, Brandeis University
Rachel Stocking, Southern Illinois University Carbondale
Michael Swope, Schoolcraft College
Joseph Tse-Hei, Pace University
John Van Sant, University of Alabama
Charles Weber, Wheaton College
Theodore Jun Yoo, University of Hawaii at Manoa
Alex Zukas, National University
Patricia Ali, Morris College
Stanley Arnold, Northern Illinois University
Mary Gross, Marian College of Fond du Lac
Michael Jacobs, University of Wisconsin—Baraboo
Lester Lee, Salem State College
Farid Mahdavi, San Diego State University
Laura Mitchell, UC Irvine
Pamela Sayre, Henry Ford Community College
Gordon Thomasson, Broome Community College (SUNY)
Khodr Zaarour, Shaw University

Reviewers

We also thank the many scholars and teachers whose thoughtful and often detailed comments helped improve our book. Whatever errors remain are, of course, our own:

Sanjam Ahluwalia, Northern Arizona University
Robert Becker, Gainesville State College
Brett Berliner, Morgan State University
Rebecca Berry, Wake Technical Community College
David Blaylock, Eastern Kentucky University
Connie Brand, Mississippi Community College
Beau Browers, Central Piedmont Community College
Ras Michael Brown, Southern Illinois University
Robert W. Brown, University of North Carolina, Pembroke
Brian Bunk, University of Massachusetts—Amherst
Fred Burkhard, University of Maryland, University College
Robert J. Caputi, Erie Community College
Harry E. Carpenter III, Western Piedmont Community College
Abdin Chande, Adelphi University
Nupur Chandhuri, Texas Southern University
Ken Chauvin, Appalachian State University
Yinghong Cheng, Delaware State University
Charles Crouch, Georgia Southern University

Lisa M. Edwards, University of Massachusetts—Lowell
Charles H. Ford, Norfolk State University
John H. Frederick, South Louisiana Community College
Patricia A. Gajda, The University of Texas at Tyler
Donald A. Grinde, Jr., SUNY, Buffalo
Anthony Gulig, University of Washington, Whitewater
Mark Gunn, Meridian Community College
Brian Gurian, Harrisburg Area Community College
Edward M. Hanlon, John Jay College
Donald J. Harreld, Brigham Young University
Paul Hatley, Rogers State University
Randolph Head, University of California, Riverside
Padhraig Higgins, Mercer County Community College
Marie Hooper, Oklahoma City University
Michael Houf, Texas A&M University—Kingsville
Clark Hultquist, University of Montevallo
Ellen J. Jenkins, Arkansas Tech University
Timothy Jenks, East Carolina University
Rhea S. Klenovich, Lakeland College
Robert Kunath, Illinois College

Joseph Tse-Hei Lee, Pace University
Yi Li, Tacoma Community College
Benjamin Lieberman, Fitchburg State College
Valdis Lumans, University of South Carolina, Aiken
Susan Maneck, Jackson State University
Cathlyn Mariscotti, Holy Family University
David John Marley, Vanguard University
Joel McMahon, Georgia Perimeter College
David K. McQuilkin, Bridgewater College
Cristina Mehrtens, University of Massachusetts—
    Dartmouth
David Meier, Dickinson State University
Greg Miller, Hillsborough Community College
Robert Scott Moore, Indiana University of
    Pennsylvania
Luke A. Nichter, Bowling Green State University
Chris Padgett, American River College
Van Plexico, Georgia Perimeter College
Tracie Provost, Middle Georgia College

David Rayson, Normandale Community College
Scott S. Reese, Northern Arizona University
Maria Theresa Romero, Saddleback College
Steven J. Salm, Xavier University of Louisiana
Linda Scherr, Mercer County Community College
David Simonelli, Youngstown State University
Govind P. Sreenivasan, Brandeis University
Anthony J. Steinhoff, University of Tennessee,
    Chattanooga
Elizabeth Stice, University of Hawaii, Hilo
Rachel Stocking, Southern Illinois University,
    Carbondale
William Van Norman, James Madison University
John Van Sant, University of Alabama, Birmingham
Charles Weber, Wheaton College
Theodore Yoo, University of Hawaii at Manoa
Qiang Zhai, Auburn University
Alex Zukas, National University

Numerous others have contributed immensely to this work. Kathryn Buturla, Gwen Morgan, Dan Nieciecki, Adam Zaremba, and the late Marc Ball assisted us with various aspects of our research and writing. Jaime Wadowiec and Vicky Green each read our work, in its early stages and supplied us with a student's perspective on its clarity, structure, coherence, and appeal to readers. Erika Gutierrez, Lisa Pinto, and Janet Lanphier challenged us, believed in us, supported us, and pushed us to expand our vision and broaden our goals. Phil Herbst poured his heart into editing our work, correcting our mistakes, improving our style, sharpening our insights, enlivening our narrative, clarifying our explanations, and pressing us to excel. David Kear further refined our work, strengthened our writing, highlighted our connections theme, and worked assiduously to make our numerous maps the best in the business. Charles Cavaliere likewise worked carefully on our visuals and photos, locating appropriate images to illustrate certain passages and placing these images near the passages they illustrate.

Our biggest debt of gratitude is the one that we owe to our wives. Sue Judge and Jan Langdon sustained, encouraged, and supported us, especially when the going got tough, enduring numerous sacrifices as they shared both our burdens and our joys. We owe them far more than words can express or than we can ever repay. This book is rightfully theirs as much as it is ours.

A Note on Dates and Spellings

In labeling dates, like many other world history teachers, we use the initials B.C.E. (Before the Common Era) and C.E. (Common Era), which correspond respectively to the labels B.C. (Before Christ) and A.D. (*Anno Domini*, "The Year of the Lord"), long used in Western societies. In spelling Chinese names we use the Pinyin system, internationally adopted in 1979, but we sometimes also give other spellings that were widely used before then. (In Chapters 32 and 35, for example, Chinese Nationalist leader Jiang Jieshi is also identified as Chiang Kaishek.) Our spelling of names and terms from other languages follows standard usage, with alternative versions given where appropriate. (Chapter 17, for example, notes that Central Asian warrior Timur Lenk was also called Tamerlane in Europe.)

CHAPTER 1

The Emergence of Human Societies, to 3000 B.C.E.

- Our Earliest Ancestors
- The Origins and Impact of Agriculture
- The Emergence of Complex Societies
- Chapter Review

Early Human Cave Art

Fossils and cultural artifacts, such as these dramatic paintings on cave walls in southern France, provide us with insights into the lives and societies of early humans (pages 8-9).

In July 2001, in a desolate, sun-baked region of the north-central African nation of Chad, a group of professional fossil-hunters, searching for remnants of life in past ages, made an astonishing discovery. There, in the windswept, shifting sands, they came upon a small crusty object that appeared to have teeth. At first they thought it was the fossilized jaw of a pig, but on further examination they concluded that it was the flat-faced skull of a **hominid** (*HAH-mih-nid*), a term scientists apply to human beings and their two-legged pre-human predecessors. Later testing showed that the skull was seven million years old—the oldest hominid fossil yet discovered.

Early Farming and Herding Areas

This discovery, which created great excitement, illustrates both the allure and challenge of studying the distant past. Although hominids have existed for millions of years, humans have left behind written records only for about 5,000 years. Recorded history thus covers only a small fraction of human experience. The preceding ages, encompassing all human existence before the emergence of writing, are often called the prehistoric era, despite the probability that people who lived then kept track of their history by passing on oral accounts. Since these early people left no surviving written records, however, modern scholars who study this era must rely mainly on analysis of fossils and cultural artifacts, augmented by enlightened speculation subject to scholarly debate. Several scholars, for instance, challenged the Chad discovery, claiming that the skull might belong to an ancient gorilla rather than a hominid.

Despite such disputes, the general outlines of our ancestry are reasonably clear. Hominids first emerged in Africa at least five million years ago, and for millions of years most likely survived by eating wild plants. Over many generations, they learned to communicate by spoken language, form small nomadic groups for cooperation and protection, fashion stone tools, hunt wild animals, and use fire, passing on their knowledge and skills to their young. In their quest for food, some hominid groups migrated from Africa to parts of Eurasia. Over time, most early hominid species died out, but one branch of the hominid family survived, evolving within the past half million years into modern humans like ourselves.

Equipped with greater intelligence and communication skills than their hominid forerunners, humans formed larger communities, devised better tools and weapons, learned to hunt more effectively, and occasionally fought with other groups vying for food. Some communities, seeking new food sources, migrated to Australia and the Americas. Some eventually figured out how to raise food, by growing crops and domesticating certain animals. Farming and herding made possible even larger communities, such as cities and states, that established commercial, cultural, and political connections, inaugurating the historical era.

Our Earliest Ancestors

Since no historical records survive from before five thousand years ago, most of what we know of the prehistoric era is based on the work of archeologists and anthropologists, who study early hominids through fossils, cultural artifacts, and genetic comparisons with other animals. Using such sources, scholars surmise that humans are descended from hominids who lived in east-central Africa millions of years ago (and hence that we all have African ancestry). By modern human standards, early hominids were small, standing only three or four feet tall, with brains that were smaller and less complex than ours. But hominids had larger brains than other animals, and voice boxes that could make more complex sounds, enabling them to better communicate what they learned with each other and with their offspring. And hominids walked on two feet rather than four, enabling them to use their arms and hands for creative purposes, such as fashioning and using tools and weapons.

About two million years ago, as hominids grew in dexterity and brainpower, some began to chip and shape pieces of stone into rough-hewn tools. Modern researchers have characterized this activity—the first indication of conscious cultural behavior—as the onset of the Old Stone Age or **Paleolithic** (*pā-lē-ō-LITH-ik*) period, the earliest and longest stage of cultural development, lasting from approximately 2,000,000 B.C.E. until about 10,000 B.C.E. During this extended period, hominids vastly improved their social and communicative skills, learned to hunt in groups that pursued prey from one region to another, and migrated to diverse regions, including northern Africa and parts of Eurasia. In the process they developed diverse ways of life.

Hominids, with improved communication, hunt and migrate in groups

Hominids and Cultural Adaptation

Beginning in the Paleolithic period, hominids diverged from other animals in a significant way. Rather than adjusting to their environment mainly through biological evolution, as most other organisms did, hominids also developed through **cultural adaptation**, the process of using their intellectual and social skills to adjust to their surroundings and improve their chances for survival. Organized into small kinship groups that traveled from place to place, they developed a number of new techniques that they shared with each other and their young, thus transmitting their knowledge and skills to future generations.

With their growing intellectual capacities, hominids increasingly found better ways to make use of and adapt to their environment. From long and sometimes bitter experience, for example, they learned which plants were digestible, which could be harmful or lethal, and which had certain medicinal or intoxicative properties. In time some hominid groups learned how to hunt with the use of crude stone axes, which they used to hurl at their prey and then to strip away the hides for clothing and the meat for food. Later, they learned to use fire for cooking meats and plants to make them more digestible, for warding off wild animals, and for providing nighttime warmth and light.

Hominids use their intelligence to adapt to their surroundings

Furthermore, as their powers of memory and speech improved, hominids transmitted their discoveries to each other and their offspring by sharing ideas and learning from one another. A hominid woman who learned to build a fire, for example, could share

Hominids pass on what they learn to each other and their young

Early hominid tools.

Hominids, connected by kinship, travel in foraging bands

Hominids live in family groups that raise children

Hominid families develop flexible gender roles

this knowledge with the rest of her group, and also teach it to her children. A hominid band returning from the hunt could sit around the fire, cook their meat, share their experiences, and pass on wisdom and practices from earlier generations. One result was that hominids could build upon their knowledge from one generation to the next, and thus could adapt more quickly than other animals. Another result was that separate human societies eventually developed their own **cultures**: unique combinations of customs, beliefs, and practices—including languages, arts, rituals, institutions, and technologies—that distinguished these societies from each other.

Foraging, Family, and Gender

Early hominids apparently were scavengers, moving about in small nomadic groups that survived mainly by gathering wild nuts and berries, feeding occasionally on the carcasses of dead animals. Then, after exhausting the readily accessible food resources in a particular region, the hominid groups moved on. As they learned to hunt they not only increased their consumption of meat, but also killed or drove away their prey, so they still relocated periodically to find new sources of game. Since these groups survived by searching for and scouring food, they are often called **foragers**—those who subsist by gathering wild plant foods and hunting wild animals.

Having no written records of these early foraging societies, modern scholars study them by examining archeological remains, comparing what they learn with the practices of the few foraging cultures that still exist today in Siberia, South Africa, Australia, and the Americas. These sources suggest that Paleolithic peoples traveled in foraging bands, mobile communities of perhaps thirty to sixty people connected by kinship. While large enough to provide their members with sustenance and protection, groups of this size, unencumbered by material possessions, were small enough to easily pack up camp and relocate to find new food sources and adjust to changing seasons or climates. As members of the same **kinship group**—an extended family comprising grandparents, parents, siblings, aunts, uncles, cousins, and other relatives—they were also bound together by familial obligations and affections.

Compared with many other large mammals, which grow to almost full maturity within a few months or years, human children remain physically immature, and thus dependent on older caregivers, for a dozen years or more. They therefore require a high level of protection, nurturing, and supervision, usually provided by their parents and other relatives, for an extended time. Furthermore, unlike many other animals, adult humans frequently form an enduring emotional bond with a specific sexual companion. These traits and conditions help to explain why human parents often stay together to care for their children, and why the central institution of most human societies has been the family.

Family concerns may also help explain why our ancestors probably divided their work along gender lines. Evidence suggests that in foraging societies men usually did the hunting and fighting, while women were more likely to gather plant food, attend to the campsite, and care for the young. This division of labor was by no means rigid: women at times no doubt helped with the hunting or defense, while men at times assisted in tending the hearth and taking care of the children. Nor did the gender roles imply that women were valued less than men. On the contrary, since a group's survival depended on women to bear children, and since gathering plant food supplied a more reliable source of nutrition than hunting wild game, the functions of the women may well have been considered more important than those of the men. A community, after all, could endure the loss of several adult males, but women and children were essential to its long-term survival. Since the men were thus more expendable, under normal conditions it made sense for them to perform the dangerous duties of hunting wild animals and defending the camp against predators and outsiders, and for women to handle the safer yet more essential tasks of minding the campfire, foraging for plant food, preparing meals, and nurturing the young.

Since the foraging band was relatively small and its members were mostly related, its structure was probably quite simple. Although some members might have greater influence as a result of intellect, experience, or personality, there was no real need for government officials or class divisions such as those that would later arise in larger, more diverse societies.

The absence of rank in foraging bands did not mean that everyone was equal, but rather that the adults in the group could collaborate in making decisions, securing the campsite, procuring food, raising the young, and moving to new places. Societies in which the members cooperated—supporting one another, sharing both the burdens and the bounty, and passing on their knowledge to their young—tended to be stable and enduring. Some were also able, when the need arose, to migrate substantial distances to ensure their survival or improve their way of life.

Foraging societies have simple structures based on collaboration

Ice Age Migrations and *Homo Sapiens*

The Paleolithic period corresponded roughly with what geologists call the Pleistocene (*PLĪ-stuh-sēn*) epoch, also called the **Great Ice Age**, an immense stretch of time (roughly 2,000,000 B.C.E. to 8000 B.C.E.) marked by frigid glacial stages when enormous ice masses called glaciers spread across much of the globe (Map 1.1). These prolonged cold spells, or "ice ages," each lasting tens of thousands of years, alternated with somewhat shorter intervals of relative warmth. Although tropical regions did not experience glaciers, their climates fluctuated considerably, bringing major changes in vegetation and animal life.

Induced perhaps by growing populations or by environmental changes that threatened their food supply, many mammals migrated during the Pleistocene epoch to new habitats. Among these mammals were foraging hominid bands, some of which left Africa and traveled to Asia, possibly following herds of wild animals, by about 1.8 million years ago. Much later, by about 800,000 years ago, other groups of foraging hominids made their way to Europe. These hominid migrants used their cultural skills to adapt to their new surroundings, employing local materials such as wood, bamboo, and rock to make shelters, hatchets, and hunting axes.

Ice Age hominids migrate to Eurasia and adapt to new environments

Then, by about 150,000 to 200,000 years ago, as hominid development and migrations continued, there emerged a new species now called *Homo sapiens* (*HŌ-mō SĀ-pē-enz*). This term, which means "wise human," designates the species that includes all modern people, and distinguishes us from other types of hominids that no longer exist.

Some hominids evolve into Homo sapiens, our human species

The complex processes by which our species developed, and the reasons why it prevailed while other hominids died out, are far from being fully understood. Humans, it is clear, have larger skulls, housing larger brains, than earlier hominid species. But so did the people modern scholars call **Neanderthals**, an extinct group of large-brained hominids whose remains were first discovered in 1856 in Germany's Neander Valley, and who existed from roughly 200,000 to 30,000 years ago.

Other hominid groups eventually become extinct

FOUNDATION MAP 1.1 The Great Ice Age, 2,000,000–8000 B.C.E.

In the Great Ice Age, or Pleistocene epoch (2,000,000–8000 B.C.E.), ice covered much of the Earth's land surface during prolonged glacial stages, commonly called ice ages. Notice that the areas in green, which are now under water, were exposed as dry land as sea levels dropped during the last ice age. How might this development have aided human migrations, especially to the Americas?

Regions covered by ice 20,000 years ago	
Land exposed by lower sea levels	

Even the basic outlines of what happened have been subject to dispute. Some experts, for example, formerly asserted that distinct groups of *Homo sapiens* developed independently in separate parts of Africa and Eurasia, evolving from earlier hominids already living there. Most experts, however, now believe that *Homo sapiens* first appeared only in Africa, migrating later to Eurasia and thence to the rest of the world (Map 1.2).

Humans develop enhanced reasoning and communicating skills

In any case, *Homo sapiens* eventually developed greater intellectual and linguistic skills than other hominids and thus were able more effectively to reason, communicate, and cooperate, sharing information with each other and passing it on to future generations. Early humans thereby developed more effective tools and weapons, including needles and fishhooks carved from the antlers and tusks of wild animals and spears that could be hurled at large animals from a safe distance. Using sturdy plant fibers, people also began to fashion ropes and lines that could be tied to hooks and harpoons, used to make nets and traps, and eventually strung onto bows from which to shoot arrows at prey.

As hunting skills improve, human populations and migrations increase

These innovations helped some early humans to hunt more effectively, and thus to acquire warmer clothes and larger amounts of animal meat, which they could now supplement with fowl and fish. Modern scholars speculate that, with access to more and better food, people may have lived longer and been able to support more children. Increasing population no doubt led to growing competition for food, inducing some

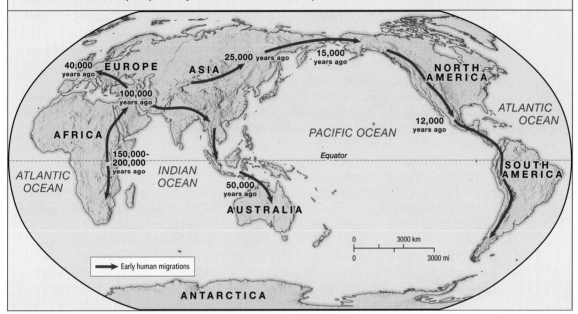

Map 1.2 Humans Inhabit the Continents, 200,000–10,000 B.C.E.

Although prehuman hominids migrated from Africa to Asia over a million years ago, most scholars think that human beings (*Homo sapiens*) first emerged in Africa by about 150,000–200,000 years ago. Note that, about 100,000 years ago, humans began to migrate out of Africa, and that by about 12,000 years ago (10,000 B.C.E.), they inhabited all the continents except Antarctica. What factors prompted early humans to move to distant places?

groups to migrate to new regions in quest of new food sources. Hence, as their hunting skills improved, human societies spread out across Africa and Eurasia. Eventually human hunters depleted the numbers of such mammals as bears, lions, deer, and gazelles, and destroyed the herds of fur-covered mammoths that once roamed across Eurasia.

In their ongoing search for sustenance, some human societies migrated even farther. By 50,000 B.C.E., according to evidence uncovered by archeologists, people had made their way from Southeast Asia to Australia, an impressive feat that entailed venturing out in boats on the open seas. Other humans apparently migrated from northeast Asia to the Americas by at least 12,000 B.C.E., during the last ice age, when the huge glaciers absorbed so much water that sea levels dropped by hundreds of feet, thus exposing a broad land bridge that connected Siberia with Alaska (Map 1.1). From Alaska the migrants spread throughout the Americas, where they found pristine lands that still teemed with mammoths, bears, and gazelles. By the end of the Paleolithic period, in almost every region of the globe that was fit for human habitation, there were human societies.

Human groups migrate to Australia and the Americas

Physical and Cultural Diversity

As humans moved to various lands and latitudes, their bodies adjusted to different climates and conditions. Over time, this biological adaptation apparently produced some modest physical differences. For example, some of the peoples who lived in northern regions eventually developed lighter skin coloration, which was better able to produce nutrients from the scarcer sunlight, and sometimes hairier bodies to protect them from the cold. Those who inhabited hotter regions typically had darker pigmentation, which was better able to protect them from the harmful rays produced by abundant sunshine.

Despite such differences in outward appearance, however, all human beings belong to the same species (*Homo sapiens*), and they can readily mate and produce healthy offspring with those of different coloration and other physical features. Thus the concept of **race**, which divides human beings into categories based on external characteristics, skin color in particular, relies on relatively insignificant distinctions. Indeed, in mapping the human genome, modern scientists have found that genetic variability among humans is remarkably small, providing no scientific basis for racial categorization.

From a historical perspective, far more important than physical diversity has been cultural diversity, resulting from the variety of ways in which separate human societies have adapted over time to their separate circumstances. In a number of ingenious ways, people have adjusted their habits and lifestyles to take advantage of the terrain, vegetation, climate, and wildlife of the regions they inhabit.

Even in Paleolithic times, substantial differences emerged among cultures in various parts of the world. People who lived on warm prairies, including the great grasslands of Africa, wore lightweight clothes made from skins and fibers and dwelt in easily assembled structures made of grasses or skins. Those who lived in colder regions, such as the northern parts of Eurasia and North America, needed more protection from the elements; these people wore rugged hides and furs and resided for months at a time in seasonal camps with warmer, sturdier shelters. Where the terrain was rocky or mountainous, people lived in stone structures and caves; where it was wooded they built their lodgings from branches, boughs, and bones. Those who lived near lakes or rivers teeming with fish had little need to travel for food; they thus built permanent, durable dwellings made of wood and stone.

These early distinctions gradually developed into different ways of life, with societies diverging not only in clothing and shelter, but also in customs, institutions, languages, practices, and beliefs. Consequently, the great diversity among human beings has not been physical but cultural. The study of world history thus focuses mainly on the development of diverse cultures, their similarities and differences, and on the connections and conflicts that have arisen among them.

Paleolithic Cultural and Spiritual Perspectives

As Paleolithic peoples pondered the world around them, and thought about the meaning of life and death, they developed new forms of expression. Paintings, carvings, and burial sites surviving from the Stone Age attest to the various forms of art and ritual practiced by early peoples, seeking no doubt to understand and influence the forces shaping their lives.

In southern Africa, for example, researchers have found rocks adorned with geometric symbols, suggesting that more than 100,000 years ago humans may have been using symbols to express abstract ideas. Other discoveries, on the inner walls of caves in Australia, northern Africa, southern Europe, and southern South America, include impressive illustrations dating from between 35,000 and 10,000 years ago. Using charred sticks, brushes made of ferns, furs, or feathers, and natural pigments from the soil mixed

Margin notes:

Although skin colors differ, humans are all one species

Humans adapt to diverse conditions and develop diverse cultures

Early humans develop symbols and artistic expression

with animal fats, prehistoric artists in these regions created life-sized paintings of large animals in motion (see page 1). Dramatic images of horses, reindeer, bulls, and buffaloes, many of them galloping or gamboling, leave little doubt that the artists who drew them were creative and contemplative human beings who could communicate and conceptualize as we do. Perhaps these artists were simply decorating their caves by portraying scenes from the world around them. Or perhaps, as some scholars have suggested, they were engaged in a magic or religious ritual by which they sought to capture or command the spirits and vitality of the beasts they portrayed, hoping to ensure the success of the hunt.

Other works of art from this era include sketches of humans adorned with paints and animal hides, discovered on cave walls in southern France, and little statues of women with enlarged breasts and reproductive organs, found throughout central Europe. The former may depict people engaged in a community ritual or celebration. The latter, which have been labeled Venus figurines, reflect a fascination with sexual reproduction, and they may have played a role in ancient fertility rites. These and other artifacts seem to suggest that early humans believed in spiritual forces and sought to influence them, employing arts and rituals in efforts to make hunting, gathering, and procreation more fruitful.

Burial practices provide further insights into Paleolithic outlooks. Archeological evidence suggests that people have been burying their dead for at least 100,000 years. At many prehistoric grave sites, found in central Asia, southwest Asia, and central Europe, human remains are often accompanied by tools, clothing, and other ornaments. The burial of such objects with the deceased might simply reflect a desire to show respect and honor for the dead. Or, more intriguingly, it might indicate that early humans believed in some form of life after death, and were equipping their departed loved ones with the essentials for an eternal journey.

Venus figurine.

1908
24,000 BCE

Early humans engage in arts, rituals, and burials

image of fertility

Intercultural Connections and Conflicts

Although separate societies created distinctive cultures, they typically did not develop in isolation from each other. At various times and places, in the process of moving about or expanding their domains, some human groups inevitably came into contact with others. Scholars believe that most foraging groups developed contacts with neighboring societies, leading often to fairly extensive intercultural connections.

At times these connections were no doubt practical, based on agreements to divide up or share lands and other essential resources. At times the links may well have been familial, marked by intermarriage between members of separate communities, forming family ties and mutual interests that bound the communities together. At times connections involved exchanges of goods and information, sometimes over vast areas: in southwest Australia, for example, researchers have found prehistoric artifacts produced several thousand miles away, in that continent's northwest regions. These early connections helped pave the way for more elaborate arrangements, including formal trade agreements and diplomatic relations, that emerged later as societies grew larger.

Connections at times could also result in conflicts, especially when sharing or trading arrangements failed to meet the needs of all involved. If hunting depleted a region's wild game, for example, groups that had earlier shared the hunting grounds might clash,

Early societies form practical, familial, and commercial connections

Early societies engage in conflicts for resources and survival compelling the losers to move elsewhere, where they might forge new connections or come into conflict with other groups. With resources scarce and survival at stake, human societies had to protect their habitats and hunting grounds against intrusions by others, or move to a new region if the outsiders proved stronger. People thus often feared outsiders as potentially dangerous foes.

Connections and conflicts have since been central to human societies

Because the Paleolithic period covered most of the duration of human existence, the behavior patterns that evolved in that era had a lasting effect on later societies. Hence throughout history humans have tended to identify closely with their own cultures, to connect with societies having similar interests, to unite with others in the face of common threats, and to engage in countless struggles for resources (such as land and food) against competing societies. Connections and conflicts among divergent cultures have thus been central components of the human experience.

The Origins and Impact of Agriculture

By the end of the last ice age, about 10,000 B.C.E., people in some regions, prompted perhaps by environmental changes, were beginning to turn from nomadic foraging toward a more settled way of life. In West Asia, in particular, as the warming climate expanded the area covered by grasses and grains, people developed new techniques to gather and process them for food. They made sickles out of flint stone, for example, to cut down the grain and grinding stones to husk and pulverize the kernels. Archeologists who first found evidence of such tools dating from this era designated it as the onset of a New Stone Age. But something far more important was happening than the use of new stone tools. People were beginning to grow their own food.

In Neolithic times people start raising their own food

In the New Stone Age, or **Neolithic** (nē-ō-LITH-ik) period, which lasted roughly from 10,000 to 3000 B.C.E., people not only developed better tools but also domesticated plants and animals, cultivated crops, herded livestock, and established permanent settlements. This transition from foraging to farming, one of history's most momentous developments, has been called the Neolithic or Agricultural Revolution. Although it took several thousand years, when compared to the many millennia of foraging that preceded it, and when measured by its immense long-range impact, agriculture's onset was revolutionary indeed.

The Origins of Farming and Herding

Farming and herding begin in West Asia by 8000 B.C.E.

Based on archeological evidence, including the remains of early farm settlements and tools, scholars have surmised that farming first began in West Asia, between 9000 and 8000 B.C.E., in a crescent-shaped region (sometimes called the "Fertile Crescent") that today encompasses Israel, Syria, and Iraq (Map 1.3). Although experts disagree about specific dates and events, they have provided a general outline of what probably took place.

As climate changes increase wild grains, some people settle in one place

Scholars believe that by 12,000 B.C.E., as the last ice age ended, a warming of the climate and melting of the glaciers had left much of this region—today mostly desert—covered with forests and grasslands. Over the next few millennia, some of the people who lived there began to subsist mainly by harvesting the wild wheat and barley grains that grew in abundance in the grasslands. Since they no longer had to move about in search of wild game and plant food, these people often settled in the same place for a number of years. Unlike nomads, whose need to move around precluded them from having too many children and possessions, the West Asian settlers had little need to limit their families or belongings. With less need to move, and more food to feed their offspring, these settlers could sustain larger families, build more permanent shelters, and accumulate a wider variety of tools, clothes, and other belongings. Their numbers thus began to grow as their mobility declined.

Eventually, however, as the region's population increased, and perhaps as drier weather reduced the abundance of wild wheat and barley that grew there, the supply of wild plant food was no longer sufficient to feed all the inhabitants. Some no doubt responded to this challenge by moving elsewhere to resume their nomadic ways. But others, encumbered by large families and numerous possessions, opted instead to stay put.

Those who stayed put, in order to survive, gradually found new ways to produce more food. They learned that they could enhance the yield of the wild grains by pulling out the weeds that grew up among them. They also discovered that if they took the seeds from the most productive plants and sprinkled them in bare spots elsewhere, new plants would eventually grow there. In time some people found that they could save the seeds and sow them the next year, enabling them to plant and raise their own crops. These first farmers were most likely female, since women were the traditional gatherers of plant foods. Although they could scarcely have foreseen the immense long-term impact of their efforts, the resourceful people who first developed farming rank among the most influential innovators of all time.

Meanwhile, West Asian hunters were also developing another, equally momentous, food production process. They discovered that certain game animals, such as wild sheep and goats, could be captured and kept alive in captivity rather than killed in the hunt. At first this practice merely provided a useful standby food source: by keeping a few live animals, a family or community could kill the creatures and eat the meat from them when other edibles ran out. Eventually, however, people learned that sheep and goats—as well as cattle, pigs, and horses—would mate and reproduce in captivity. These animals thus

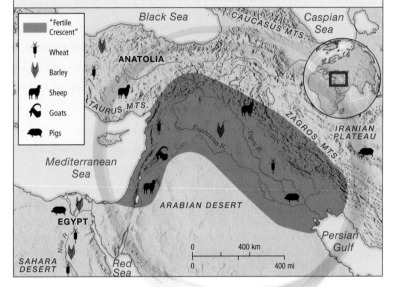

Map 1.3 Agriculture Emerges in West Asia, 9000–8000 B.C.E.

Scholars believe that humans first began to practice agriculture between 9000 and 8000 B.C.E. in a region of West Asia sometimes called the "Fertile Crescent." Observe that this region, extending from the Mediterranean Sea to the Zagros Mountains, included the valleys of the Tigris and Euphrates Rivers. What factors may have aided the rise of farming and herding in this region?

Settlements and food surplus foster population growth

As populations grow, settlers cultivate grain to enhance yield

West Asians start raising, not just hunting, animals

were domesticable: they could be bred and adapted by people to meet the needs of human societies. People could raise their own herds and produce their own meat.

Eventually many other uses were found for domesticable animals. Their fleeces and hides, for example, were used to make blankets and clothes. Their manure served as a fertilizer to replenish the soil and prolong its productivity. The milk provided by cows, mares, and ewes furnished an ongoing food source, readily available without killing the creature that supplied it. In time people also began to use large animals to pull plows and carts, providing enormous advantages for farming, transport, and travel.

Domesticated animals furnish clothing, food, fertilizer, labor, and transport

Agricultural Innovation and Expansion

East Asians and Africans develop distinct forms of farming and herding

Although West Asians were probably the first inventors of agriculture, they were not the only ones. In places far from West Asia, adapting to their own environments and challenges, inhabitants developed different forms of farming and herding, using plants and animals native to their locales (Map 1.4). In the north central African region called the Sudan, for example, where grasslands then covered much of what is now the Sahara desert, people began herding cattle and cultivating sorghum (a starchy grain), perhaps

Map 1.4 Agriculture Develops and Spreads, 9000 B.C.E. – 1000 C.E.

Over thousands of years, through human ingenuity and contacts among cultures, agriculture developed and spread from its early areas of origin to other regions, as indicated by the arrows on this map. Note the large dots that indicate early areas of plant and animal domestication, with boxes indicating early food crops, domesticated animals, and estimated dates. What factors may have contributed to the development and spread of agriculture? Why did people domesticate different plants and animals in different parts of the world?

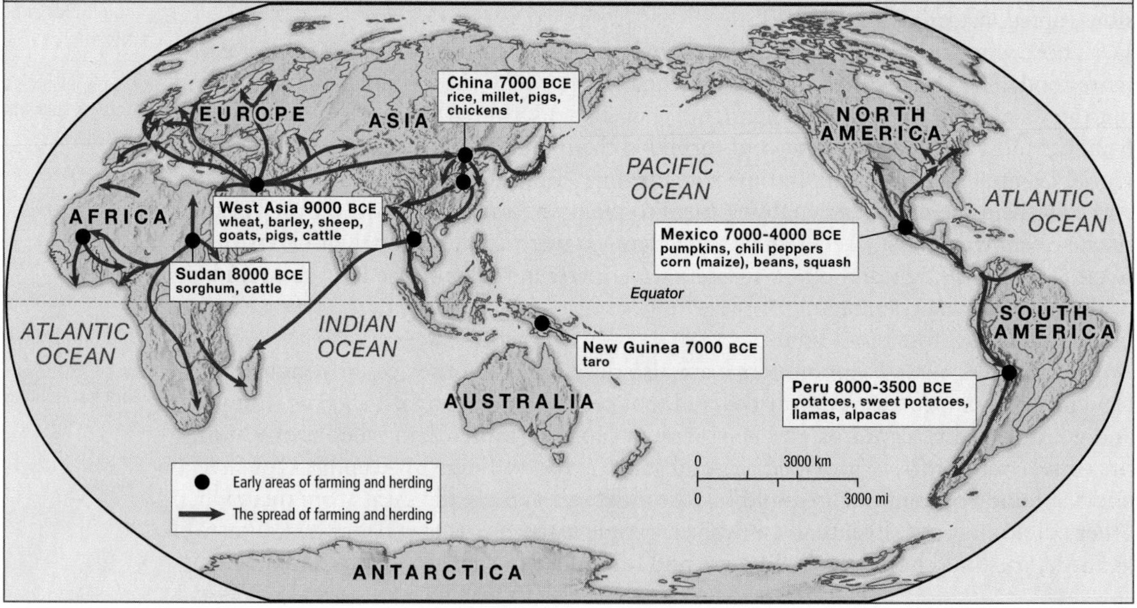

China 7000 BCE
rice, millet, pigs, chickens

West Asia 9000 BCE
wheat, barley, sheep, goats, pigs, cattle

Sudan 8000 BCE
sorghum, cattle

Mexico 7000-4000 BCE
pumpkins, chili peppers
corn (maize), beans, squash

New Guinea 7000 BCE
taro

Peru 8000-3500 BCE
potatoes, sweet potatoes, llamas, alpacas

Early areas of farming and herding
The spread of farming and herding

as early as 8000 B.C.E. In China, in the valleys of the great rivers, settlers started to grow crops of millet and rice, and to domesticate pigs, by about 7000 B.C.E. By this time also, on the island of New Guinea, early farmers were probably growing taro, a starchy root crop, on swamplands they had drained by digging ditches to channel away the water.

Farming and herding also spread through contacts among cultures. By around 7000 B.C.E., for example, agriculture had begun in ancient India's Indus Valley, and by 6000 B.C.E. it had started in Europe and Egypt's Nile Valley. The proximity of these regions to West Asia, and the fact that plants (such as wheat and barley) and animals (such as sheep and goats) domesticated in West Asia were raised in all these regions, suggests that agriculture probably spread there through intercultural connections. In exchanging goods and ideas, early societies also most likely exchanged knowledge about farming and herding.

> Cultural connections spread farming and herding practices

Farmers and herders in these new areas, however, were by no means mere borrowers. They cultivated native food crops (such as oats in Europe and figs in Egypt), domesticated local animals (such as different types of cattle in the Nile and Indus Valleys), and eventually grew fibers (such as flax in Europe and cotton in Egypt and India) that could be woven into lightweight linens and clothes. But crops such as wheat and barley continued to predominate in these regions, especially as people learned to grind the grains into flour, to bake the flour into bread, and (especially in West Asia and Egypt) to brew the barley into a beverage similar to what we now call beer.

> Egypt, India, and Europe develop new crops, foods, and drinks

In the Western Hemisphere, where people had no contact with farmers and herders in Africa and Eurasia, agriculture developed differently, with different crops predominating. In what is now southern Mexico, archeologists have found indications of farming as early as 7000 B.C.E., and evidence that, by 4000 B.C.E., farmers there were growing corn, beans, and squash, the cultivation of which would later spread throughout much of North America. By 3500 B.C.E., and perhaps much earlier, people in what is now Peru were planting potatoes and sweet potatoes (Map 1.4). In the Americas, however, since human hunters had earlier killed off most large domesticable animals, livestock herding was virtually unknown—except in Peru where people raised llamas and alpacas.

> People in Mexico and Peru independently develop farming

The spread of farming was also interwoven with population growth. As farmers and herders produced more food, the size of their societies grew, leading them to cultivate additional lands and to clear away forests for farming. After all, only a small percentage of the plants that grew in the forest were edible, while almost everything that grew in a grain field could be used for human or animal consumption. An acre of crops could feed far more people than an acre of woods.

> Spread of farming promotes population growth and deforestation

Therefore, to increase the land available for farming, people began to cut and burn down trees and bushes, diminishing bit by bit the forests themselves. In the process, they discovered that burned-over forests were extremely fertile, as the ashes from the burned vegetation served as a superb fertilizer. After several years of nourishing crops, however, the soil would be exhausted of its nutrients, and thus produce less food. So the Neolithic farmers simply moved to another region, cut and burned down more forests, and started the process anew. This "slash and burn" practice was in some ways quite destructive: it ravaged the habitats of wild plants and animals and undermined the subsistence of local hunters and gatherers. At the same time, however, it enabled farming societies to expand their food supplies, and helped to spread the practice of farming to additional places.

Foragers, Hunter-Farmers, and Pastoral Nomads

Not all groups of people, however, were quick to take up agriculture. Since raising crops and herds typically took more time and required harder work than hunting and gathering, societies were unlikely to turn to farming unless compelled to do so by some combination of population growth and diminished food supply. Even then, they could do so only where the climate and terrain made farming feasible, where some of the local plants and animals were suitable for domestication, and where people had developed the tools and techniques for planting, harvesting, breeding, pasturing, and storing. As a result, the transition from foraging to farming was a long, uneven process that lasted thousands of years. Clearly farming and herding were not the answers for everyone.

Foraging persists in regions too cold or too dry for farming

Some groups, indeed, never took up farming and continued to live as hunters and gatherers in small mobile foraging bands. In the far northern regions of Eurasia and North America, for example, where it was too cold to grow crops, people sustained themselves largely by hunting and fishing. In the arid plains and deserts of Australia, Africa, and central North America, where there was insufficient water for farming, foraging supported relatively sparse populations.

Societies without large domesticated animals combine farming and hunting

Other groups adopted farming but not herding, especially in the Americas, where there were few large domesticable animals. In eastern and southwestern North America, for instance, even after societies took up farming, hunting and fishing continued to play a key role, providing people with meat and fish to supplement crops of corn, beans, and squash. In many of these societies women did most of the farm work, since the men were often away hunting.

Pastoral nomads in semi-arid lands practice herding but not farming

Still other societies embraced herding but not farming, especially in Central Asia, where the arid climate and sparse vegetation were suitable for grazing animals but not for growing crops. Mobile herders such as these are known as **pastoral nomads**: people who raise livestock for subsistence and move occasionally with their herds in search of fresh grazing grounds.

Pastoral nomads connect and conflict with settled farming societies

Always looking for new pasturelands, without which they could not endure, pastoral nomads occasionally came into contact with settled agricultural societies. Sometimes the nomads clashed with the farming communities, fighting desperate battles for the use of lands that both groups saw as vital. Sometimes, however, the two groups traded, exchanging the herders' hides and fleeces for the farmers' grains and flour. Eventually, ranging across the open expanses between the settled societies, the nomads also served as conduits of commerce and information, conveying goods (such as carpets, cloth, and jewels) and techniques (such as horse breeding and metalworking) to distant and disparate cultures.

Thus, for many millennia, pastoral nomads coexisted uneasily with settled agricultural societies. Equipped by their harsh, itinerant existence with ruggedness and mobility, the nomads often managed to prevail in conflict. In the long run, however, since agriculture could support far more people than nomadic herding or foraging, settled societies eventually gained huge advantages in population, weapons, possessions, and power—enabling them to defeat, attract, or displace almost all nomadic peoples. The future belonged mainly to societies based on farming.

Agricultural Society: Village, Family, and Land

As time went on, the lives of farmers increasingly diverged from those of nomadic peoples. Although both farmers and pastoral nomads centered their societies on families and divided their duties by gender, many differences developed between them.

One key difference was permanence of place. Unlike nomads, who moved from place to place, farmers typically settled in one location. Almost everywhere they dwelt in **farming villages**, small settlements of homes in a compact cluster, surrounded by lands on which the villagers raised food. Village homes were mostly simple structures, fashioned from local materials such as earth, thatch, wood, or stone, and grouped together to facilitate socialization and defense. The lands around the village often included not only farm fields but also pasturelands for grazing livestock. A typical farming village was a permanent settlement: those who were born there usually lived and died there, and their descendants likely did the same for many generations.

Most farmers live in villages and raise food on surrounding lands

Another key contrast was size. Agricultural communities frequently grew much larger than nomadic groups, whose numbers were limited by the need for mobility. A typical farming village, sustained by a steady food supply and stabilized by permanence of place, might include a few hundred people, and sometimes substantially more. Furthermore, as neighboring villages formed connections with each other, creating networks based on mutual protection and support, agricultural societies grew even larger.

Stability and food supply increase the size of farming societies

The growing size of these societies, and the need to parcel out farmlands among families, required a higher degree of structure than was normally present among nomads. Possession of land, scarcely a concern for nomads, became an essential interest in agricultural societies, where people's livelihood depended largely on the land. As families grew larger, they often sought to maintain and expand their access to various lands and to pass this access on to their offspring. Thus, as village families intermarried with each other and with families from other villages, it became increasingly important to keep track of who was descended from whom, in order to determine who would control which lands.

Larger size of farming societies requires greater organization

Family relationships in farming communities therefore tended to be more structured than the informal kinship ties that existed in nomadic societies. Marriages between farming families were typically arranged by the parents of the bride and groom and often sealed by a transfer of assets, such as land or livestock, between the two families. Marriages between members of different agricultural societies, moreover, frequently took the form of an alliance, designed in part to create closer ties or to formalize arrangements for cooperation and support.

Farming societies develop structured families and gender roles

Farmers also diverged from nomads in terms of gender roles and status. In foraging bands, the role of women was crucial to the group's survival, since the women's work supplied the plant food on which the whole group relied and since women often had to manage the group while the men were off on a hunt. Among pastoral nomads, where women were often responsible for tending, breeding, birthing, and milking the livestock, their role was also essential to the society. In many farm communities, however, the men produced most of the food, laboring daily in the fields, while women for the most part stayed behind in the village. Their roles, which typically involved raising children, maintaining the household, and helping in the fields when needed, came to be seen as subordinate to the roles of men.

Women and men doing farm work in the Americas.

In farming societies women bear and raise many children

Family sizes further affected gender roles. In nomadic societies, where mobility was at a premium, large families could be a burden, so parents tended to keep their families small, freeing women to assume many duties outside of child-raising. In agricultural societies, however, where many hands were needed to help work the fields at sowing and harvest times, large families were considered desirable. Expected to bear, nurse, and raise many children, farming village women had limited ability to get much involved in affairs outside the household.

Farming societies are often patriarchal, dominated by men

Gender roles and gender status nonetheless varied among agricultural societies. In the Americas, for example, in farming villages where there was no livestock to provide meats and hides, the men often hunted wild game while women did most of the farming. In such societies, since women were the primary food producers and men were often absent on the hunt, women sometimes played a key role in managing village affairs. And even in Eurasia and Africa, capable women with strong personalities often played a prominent role in running their families and villages. For the most part, however, agricultural societies the world over tended to be **patriarchal** (*PĀ-trē-ARK-ul*), dominated by males who served as heads of household and as community leaders.

The Impact of Agriculture

Farming societies require hard labor and foster disease

Initially, agriculture's impact was not always advantageous. Early farmers and herders, for example, typically had to work much harder than gatherers and hunters. Farmers had to clear the land, till the soil, sow the seeds, tend the fields, pull the weeds, and do their best to shield their crops from insects, animals, and birds. They also had to harvest, process, and preserve the food that they grew, as well as to care for their livestock and protect it from predators. Furthermore, judging by remains found in excavations of early farming villages, Neolithic farmers appear to have been smaller, and probably less healthy, than nomadic foragers. From living in close contact with their pigs and cattle, farmers acquired new illnesses, the forerunners of deadly scourges such as influenza and smallpox. By settling continuously in the same place, they accumulated garbage and waste, which fouled their water and attracted disease-bearing insects and rodents. And, unlike small nomadic groups whose mobility and flexibility provided access to a variety of plant and animal foods, settled farming societies typically relied on a few basic crops to feed many people, leaving them vulnerable to disasters such as floods, droughts, crop failures, insect infestations, and famines.

Settled farming societies produce surplus food

In the long run, however, societies based on agriculture had a crucial advantage: they had the ability to produce surplus food. In good years the farmers could grow more food than they consumed, then store the surplus to meet future needs, initially in pits but later in bins and silos that were raised to protect against flooding.

Surplus food enables some to specialize in nonfarming pursuits

The production of surplus food in turn had enormous implications. It provided agricultural societies with a backup food supply, helping to ensure their survival, even during deadly droughts and famines. It enabled farming families to support more children, allowing their communities to grow into settlements of hundreds or thousands of people, and contributing to an overall increase in human population. And it freed some people in settlements based on farming from the need to provide their own food, allowing them to specialize in other pursuits—including arts, crafts, commerce, religion, warfare, and governance. Agriculture thereby supported and sustained the development of large, complex, regional societies, which would increasingly dominate human history.

The Emergence of Complex Societies

Toward the end of the Neolithic period, beginning in West Asia and North Africa, several factors combined to produce complex societies—large, organized, stable communities in which farm surpluses enabled many people to specialize in occupations other than farming. These societies included towns and cities, sizable permanent settlements supported by surplus food from surrounding farms. To manage their substantial populations, many of these societies formed governments, engaged in trade, organized religions, and extended control over surrounding territories, eventually creating very large and populous regional societies. The rest of this chapter discusses general features of early regional societies; the chapters that follow then examine the development of specific societies, as each was shaped by internal and external connections and conflicts.

Towns, Cities, Occupations, and Religion

By the seventh millennium B.C.E., as food supplies increased, the populations of some West Asian settlements were starting to grow quite large. Jericho (*JER-ih-kō*) in Palestine and Çatal Hüyük (*chah-TAHL hoo-YOOK*) in what is now Turkey, for example, developed into towns—large settlements, home to several thousand people, that served not

Surplus food makes possible the rise of towns and cities

only as residential centers but also as trading hubs (Map 1.5). Jericho, perhaps the world's oldest town, apparently started as a farming village, at some point before 8000 B.C.E., with huts constructed of mud-dried brick around a natural fresh-water spring. By 7000 B.C.E. it had many such homes, was surrounded by a stone defensive wall, and had become an active center of trade. Çatal Hüyük, an even more substantial population and trading center, had also emerged as a sizable town by around 7000 B.C.E. It included numerous houses made of mud brick, shrines to various gods and goddesses, and marketplaces for exchange of various foods and goods.

Over many centuries, the population of some settlements continued to grow. By the fourth millennium B.C.E., near the Tigris (*TĪ-gris*) and Euphrates (*yoo-FRĀ-tēz*) rivers in what is now Iraq, communities such as Ur (*OOR*), Uruk (*OO-rook*), and Lagash (*lah-GAHSH*) had developed into cities—

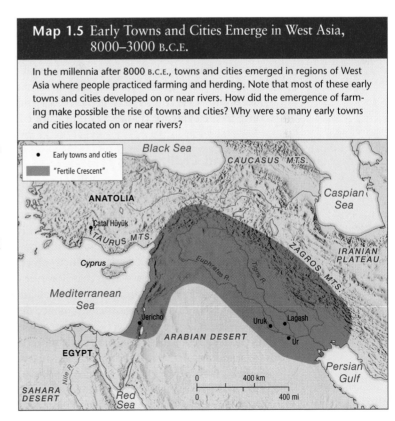

Map 1.5 Early Towns and Cities Emerge in West Asia, 8000–3000 B.C.E.

In the millennia after 8000 B.C.E., towns and cities emerged in regions of West Asia where people practiced farming and herding. Note that most of these early towns and cities developed on or near rivers. How did the emergence of farming make possible the rise of towns and cities? Why were so many early towns and cities located on or near rivers?

very large, complex, densely populated settlements in which many people engaged in occupations other than farming. These early cities, which housed up to 30,000 people, also featured sizable buildings, bustling marketplaces, and extensive fortifications.

City-dwellers specialize in arts, crafts, production of goods, and commerce

Although towns and cities depended on farming, their most influential inhabitants were those who did not farm. With their food supplied by others, these people could specialize in various occupations. Some, for example, were artisans who specialized in tool making, basket weaving, pottery, and carpentry, as indicated by the remnants of their handiwork at archeological sites such as Çatal Hüyük and Uruk. Others no doubt were merchants, who exchanged goods in the urban marketplaces unearthed at these sites. Still others may have been artists and sculptors, as suggested by excavations of shrines and temples embellished with wall paintings and statues of goddesses and gods.

Early potters and pottery in West Asia.

These excavations also reflect the emergence of organized religion. Early peoples, as we have seen, probably engaged in rituals, summoning spirits to help secure food and ensure fertility. As societies grew more complex, these rituals grew more elaborate: people came to worship various gods and goddesses, divine beings believed to embody and control essential forces such as sun and rain, plants and animals, storms, rivers, forests, and fertility. Hoping to please or appease these divinities, priests and priestesses—people who specialized in the performance of religious rituals—conducted ceremonies and sacrifices in city shrines and temples. These religious structures also may have reinforced the authority of rulers, depicting them as divinities or as agents of the gods.

Organized religions and powerful rulers emerge in large complex societies

Other excavations add to the impression that rulers exercised great authority. Fortifications and weapons found at Ur, Uruk, and other early cities suggest that they must have had numerous laborers to build the walls and watchtowers, soldiers to defend against outsiders, and governing officials with the authority to organize and supervise large groups of workers and warriors. Also uncovered at these sites were remains of palaces, and royal tombs in which officials and servants were buried alongside the rulers, adding to the evidence that early cities were run by strong central governments.

States and Civilizations

Before complex societies emerged there was little need for strong central governments. Decisions could be made and conflicts resolved in foraging bands by the group as a whole, and in villages by the patriarchal leaders. If one villager injured another, for example, the heads of households could readily get together to determine punishment and compensation, usually in accord with community customs. Since everyone was acquainted, and frequently related, such informal mechanisms normally sufficed.

Large societies develop complex governance structures

As settlements grew so large that not everyone knew each other, however, residents could no longer rely on family and village leaders to settle disputes or decide issues for the whole community. Large societies hence developed governments, often starting with a single strong leader who, as the need arose, empowered others to assist him. Over time the result was an array of officials who carried out decisions, maintained order, organized food reserves, supervised construction projects, and resolved conflicts among strangers. If one city resident harmed another, the injured party could thus appeal, not to family and friends, but to a government official with the authority to impose punishment and compensation.

A government's main functions, however, were to secure the society's sustenance, ensure the survival of its ruling elite, and defend it against outsiders. Some cities, therefore, secured their food supply by exerting dominion over neighboring villages, using armed warriors to force village farmers to part with a portion of their produce. Some of this food was then used to feed the ruler and officials, as well as other urban residents, and some might be stored as a hedge against future shortages. The ruler and his warriors, in return, protected the villagers from conquest by rival outsiders.

To secure food supplies, cities exert control over neighboring farm villages

By 3500 B.C.E. the rulers of several West Asian cities, including Ur and Uruk, were using this system, commonly called tribute, to maintain their food supplies and control the surrounding countryside. By thus establishing governance over a specific territory, these early West Asian rulers effectively formed **states**—territorial entities ruled by a central government. Several centuries later in North Africa, a legendary ruler called Menes (*MĀ-nāz*) extended his sway over numerous settlements in the Nile valley, creating an Egyptian state that stretched for hundreds of miles.

In governing sizable territories, early rulers form states

Historians have long noted that these early states, and others emerging somewhat later in northwest India and northern China (Map 1.6), all arose in river valleys in semi-arid regions. Many scholars have held that such environments prompted the formation of states, claiming that they were most likely created to organize vast numbers of people to build banks and dikes for flood control and to dig irrigation ditches for

Early states arise along rivers

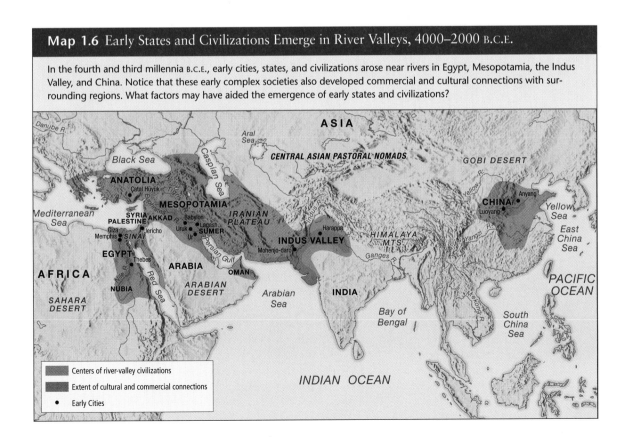

Map 1.6 Early States and Civilizations Emerge in River Valleys, 4000–2000 B.C.E.

In the fourth and third millennia B.C.E., early cities, states, and civilizations arose near rivers in Egypt, Mesopotamia, the Indus Valley, and China. Notice that these early complex societies also developed commercial and cultural connections with surrounding regions. What factors may have aided the emergence of early states and civilizations?

Centers of river-valley civilizations

Extent of cultural and commercial connections

• Early Cities

bringing river water to nearby farm fields. Other scholars, however, citing evidence that irrigation ditches existed before states in West Asia and China, have suggested instead that these societies formed states mainly to manage and control their growing populations. Whatever the case, it is clear that the rivers, by supplying plentiful water for people, crops, and livestock, and by enriching valley soils with periodic floods that left behind fertile silt, facilitated the formation and growth of permanent settled societies.

It is also clear that, by providing a convenient means of transportation, the rivers helped connect these societies up and down the river valleys. Thus, over many centuries, through trade, alliances, and conquests, cities and states along these waterways formed commercial, cultural, and political connections with each other. The result was the emergence of large, complex, regional societies in West Asia and Egypt by 3000 B.C.E., in India not long thereafter, and in China about a thousand years later.

River connections promote the rise of early regional civilizations

These large, complex regional societies are customarily characterized as history's first **civilizations**—a term applied to very large, complex societies, or regional groups of complex societies, with widely shared or similar customs, institutions, and beliefs. Historically, however, the word civilization has also been used to indicate an "advanced" level of social and cultural achievement, and hence by some peoples to claim they are superior to others. People in large, complex societies, for example, have frequently deemed themselves more "civilized" (that is, more culturally advanced) than outsiders, whom they have sometimes disparaged as savages and barbarians. To prevent ambiguity and avoid this kind of cultural bias, we will avoid the latter usage of the word, while noting nonetheless that the emergence of the early civilizations, discussed in the next four chapters, traditionally marks the beginning of the historical era.

Chapter Review

Putting It in Perspective

For tens of thousands of years, early humans lived in small, nomadic bands that were based on kinship and survived by hunting and gathering. Over time, as they adapted to a growing range of challenges and environments, our ancestors migrated to distant lands, eventually spreading throughout the entire world. They devised new tools and weapons, developed distinctive cultural expressions, divided their work along gender lines, formed marriage and family connections, exchanged information and goods, and occasionally engaged in conflicts with each other. Still, as long as they had to forage for food and move periodically from place to place, their societies remained simple and small.

Then came the advent of agriculture. People in some areas started to raise crops and animals and to form permanent settlements, some of which eventually grew into larger, more complex communities. In time some villages grew into towns, and some towns became cities, with large populations of people who specialized in nonfarming pursuits such as commerce, carpentry, tool making, warfare, religion, construction work, and governance. Some of these cities expanded their control over neighboring villages and towns, thereby creating states, which in turn would form the basis of large, complex, regional societies later called civilizations.

Henceforth, although nomadic cultures would long endure in areas unfit for farming, history would largely be dominated by complex, regional societies, and by the connections and conflicts that transpired among them. The first such regional societies, discussed in the next chapter, emerged in the fourth millennium B.C.E. along rivers in West Asia and North Africa.

Reviewing Key Material

KEY CONCEPTS

hominid, 2	Neanderthals, 5
Paleolithic, 3	race, 8
cultural adaptation, 3	Neolithic, 10
cultures, 4	pastoral nomads, 14
foragers, 4	farming villages, 15
kinship group, 4	patriarchal, 16
Great Ice Age, 5	states, 19
Homo sapiens, 5	civilizations, 19

ASK YOURSELF

1. How did hominid development differ from that of other animals? Why did hominids organize into nomadic kinship groups? Why did they divide their work along gender lines?
2. Why did early hominids, and later early humans, migrate to distant lands? Why did human societies develop a wide range of diverse cultures?
3. Why did humans begin to grow their own food? What were the advantages and disadvantages of farming and herding? Why did some societies remain nomadic?
4. How did agricultural societies differ from nomadic ones? What were the major long-range impacts of the emergence and expansion of agriculture?
5. Why did some Neolithic peoples organize cities and states? What were the major features and advantages of these complex societies?

GOING FURTHER

Bellwood, P. *First Farmers: The Origins of Agricultural Societies.* 2005.

Boaz, Noel T. *Eco Homo: How the Human Being Emerged from the Cataclysmic History of the World.* 1997.

Campbell, Bernard G. *Humankind Emerging.* 6th ed. 1992.

Christian, D. *Maps of Time: An Introduction to Big History.* 2004.

Cohen, Mark Nathan. *The Food Crisis in Prehistory: Overpopulation and the Origins of Agriculture.* 1977.

Coulson, D., and A. Campbell. *African Rock Art.* 2001.

Diamond, Jared. *Guns, Germs, and Steel: The Fates of Human Societies.* 1997.

Ehrenberg, Margaret. *Women in Prehistory.* 1989.

Fagan, B. *The Long Summer: How Climate Changed Civilization.* 2004.

Fagan, B. *People of the Earth: An Introduction to World Prehistory.* 11th ed. 2003.

Gamble, C. *Timewalkers: Prehistory of Global Civilization.* 1994.

Henry, D. O. *From Foraging to Agriculture.* 1989.

Johanson, Donald C., and Blake Edgar. *From Lucy to Language.* 1996.

Johnson Allen W., and Timothy Earle. *The Evolution of Human Societies: From Foraging Group to Agrarian State.* 1987.

Leakey, R. *The Making of Mankind.* 1981.

Manning, P. *Migration in World History.* 2005.

Megarry, Tim. *Society in Prehistory.* 1995.

Mellars, Paul, ed. *The Emergence of Modern Humans.* 1991.

Mithen, S. *After the Ice: A Global Human History.* 2004.

Stringer, Christopher, and Robin McKie. *African Exodus: The Origins of Modern Humanity.* 1997.

Sykes, B. *The Seven Daughters of Eve.* 2001.

Tattersall, I. *Becoming Human: Evolution and Human Uniqueness.* 1998.

Walker, Alan, and Pat Shipman. *The Wisdom of the Bones: In Search of Human Origins.* 1996.

Wenke, Robert J. *Patterns in Prehistory: Humankind's First Three Million Years.* 3rd ed. 1990.

Key Dates and Developments

Paleolithic Period/Pleistocene Epoch
2,000,000–10,000 years ago

by 2,000,000 years ago	Early hominids use stone tools
by 1,800,000 years ago	Early hominids migrate from Africa to Asia
by 800,000 years ago	Early hominids migrate to Europe
by 150,000–200,000 years ago	Modern humans (Homo sapiens) emerge in Africa
by 100,000 years ago	Humans in Africa fish, mine, and carve symbols
by 100,000 years ago	Humans begin to inhabit Eurasia
by 50,000 years ago	Humans migrate to Australia
by 35,000–10,000 years ago	Humans produce cave art in Australia, Africa, Europe, South America
by 12,000 years ago (10,000 B.C.E.)	Humans migrate to the Americas

Neolithic Period
10,000–3,000 b.c.e.

by 9000 B.C.E.	Farming begins in West Asia
by 8000 B.C.E.	Farming begins in the African Sudan
by 7000 B.C.E.	Farming begins in India, China, New Guinea, and Mexico
by 7000 B.C.E.	Towns emerge in West Asia
by 6000 B.C.E.	Farming begins in Egypt and Europe
by 3500 B.C.E.	Farming begins in Peru
by 3000 B.C.E.	Cities and states emerge in West Asia and Egypt

CHAPTER 2

Early Societies of West Asia and North Africa, to 500 B.C.E.

- Early West Asian Societies
- Early Northeast African Societies
- West Asia and North Africa: The Phoenician Connection
- The Israelites and Their God
- Chapter Review

The Ziggurat Of Ur

Early West Asian and North African societies produced impressive monuments, such as this massive "ziggurat" temple in the ancient Sumerian city of Ur, amply attesting to the power of their rulers and religions (page 27).

According to legend, King Sargon of Akkad (*AH-kuhd*), regarded as history's first empire-builder, was a man of humble birth. Abandoned in infancy by his mother, who put him in a basket and set him adrift on a river, he was rescued and raised by a gardener. Having thus found favor with the fertility goddess Ishtar, the story continues, Sargon became a local ruler's cup bearer and grew into a great warrior. Assembling an empire in West Asia in the twenty-fourth century B.C.E., he conquered Sumer (*SOO-mehr*), a prosperous region northwest of the Persian Gulf. But rather than destroying its great cities he embraced their culture and later imposed it on other lands he conquered. He also expanded commerce, trading with lands as far away as India and Crete.

Early West Asian and North African Societies

Sargon's story exemplifies the challenge of studying ancient times. Fragmentary records surviving from that era often were compiled centuries after the events described. Many were based on oral traditions, passed on from one generation to the next and typically embellished by heroic legends and accounts of godly interventions. It is thus difficult for historians to determine precisely what occurred. The actual events of Sargon's early life, for example, as well as the boundaries of his realm and even the years of his reign, are open to question—as is the location of his capital city, which has yet to be found. Similar gaps exist in our knowledge of all ancient societies, which is based on fragmentary records and archeological evidence supplemented by the enlightened speculation of scholars. The accounts that emerge are incomplete and often differ in details, but the story they tell is fascinating nonetheless.

Sargon's story also shows how connections were created among cultures. Sometimes warriors conquered cosmopolitan societies and then adopted their culture, as Sargon did when he annexed and emulated the cities of Sumer. Sometimes conquerors imposed their values on the people they vanquished, as Sargon did by spreading his adopted culture to other lands he ruled. And sometimes cultures influenced each other through commerce, exchanging their ideas along with their commodities, a process encouraged by Sargon in his expansion of trade.

Such connections were central to the growth of the complex societies that emerged in West Asia and Northeast Africa more than 5,000 years ago. As we saw in Chapter 1, these societies arose along rivers (the Tigris, Euphrates, and Nile) where farming had long been practiced and where the resulting food supply supported sizable settlements. In each society people lived at the mercy of the rivers that, while sustaining their settlements, could also destroy them. In each society people worshiped many gods and goddesses, believing they could intervene in human lives and hoping to get their help. Through various connections and conflicts, over several millennia, these societies interacted with each other and with peoples in other regions, leaving striking legacies that endure to this day.

Early West Asian Societies

Agriculture, as we saw in the last chapter, first arose in West Asia around 9000 B.C.E. In the following millennia, it came to be practiced extensively in the plains around the Tigris and Euphrates rivers (now part of modern Iraq), where periodic floods deposited rich silt that kept the soil fertile.

By the fourth millennium B.C.E., as farming flourished in this region, its population seems to have grown considerably. Shielded from outsiders by mountains to the north and deserts to the south and fed by ample harvests from fertile farmlands, people there formed increasingly complex societies. Farming villages merged into towns, and some towns grew into cities, with central governments, organized religions, extensive commerce, and eventually even writing systems.

Thus emerged what is traditionally considered the world's first civilization, in a region that the Greeks would later call Mesopotamia (*MESS-uh-puh-TĀ-mē-uh*), a name that means "between the rivers." So impressive were its achievements that later conquerors, including Sargon of Akkad, adopted and imposed its ways throughout West Asia and beyond. Tigris + Euphrates

Towns and cities emerge in Mesopotamia, forming early civilization

Early Mesopotamia: The City-States of Sumer

The largest and most influential of the early Mesopotamian cities, such as Ur, Uruk, and Lagash, had emerged by 3500 B.C.E. in the region called Sumer, near where the Tigris and Euphrates rivers connect (Map 2.1). By 3000 B.C.E. some of these settlements, surrounded by protective walls, were more than a mile in diameter and home to more than 30,000 people. Most of the residents were farmers, living in huts made of sun-baked mud bricks, who went out by day to tend their crops in nearby fields. But other city-dwellers, supported by surplus food supplied by the farmers, specialized in a variety of occupations. Their numbers included artisans, merchants, laborers, priests and priestesses, soldiers, and government officials.

Conflict was common among Sumerian cities, many of which were actually **city-states**, independent urban political domains that controlled the surrounding countryside. Eager to enhance their security and wealth, the larger city-states sometimes sought to swallow up others, provoking periodic wars. Warriors who emerged as leaders in combat typically became the kings and officials of their city-states.

Early Sumerian city-states connect and conflict with each other

Over time the kings amassed great power to command armies, levy tribute and taxes, dispense justice, and organize the building of roads, canals, and dikes. In many places kingship became hereditary, as rulers succeeded in passing on their powers to their sons. Officials helped the kings govern, while priests and priestesses exalted the rulers as descendants of the gods. Royal authority was thus reinforced by religion.

SUMERIAN RELIGION AND WORLDVIEW. The most famous Sumerian ruler was King Gilgamesh (*GIL-guh-mesh*) of Uruk, hero of the *Epic of Gilgamesh*, a magnificent narrative poem from the third millennium B.C.E. In this epic the handsome young king, described as part god and part man, is confronted by Enkidu (*EN-kih-doo*), a former wild man who has been tamed by a prostitute. The two men battle ferociously, but emerge as friends. Together they embark on many adventures and overcome many challenges.

King Sargon and a High Official.

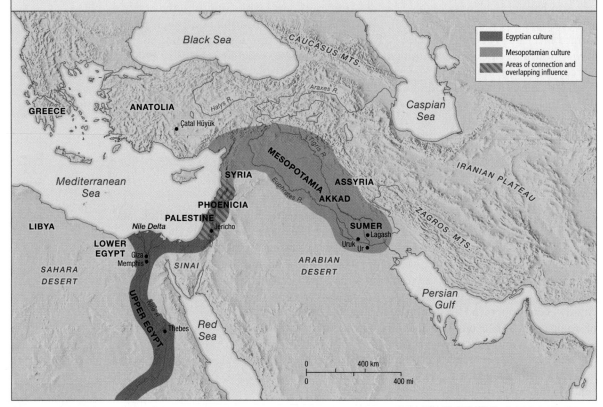

FOUNDATION MAP 2.1 Complex Societies Emerge in West Asia and Northeast Africa by 3000 B.C.E.

By the third millennium B.C.E., complex societies had emerged in Mesopotamia and Egypt and acquired extensive regional influence. Note that the lands on the eastern Mediterranean coast, later called Phoenicia and Palestine, connected Mesopotamia and Egypt, and were eventually influenced by both cultures. How did these connections develop, and how did each culture influence the other?

When fertility goddess Inanna (later called Ishtar) becomes infatuated with Gilgamesh, he brazenly spurns her advances, so in a rage she has her father the sky god send a wild bull to destroy him. Together, Gilgamesh and Enkidu manage to slay the beast. But the gods respond by taking the life of Enkidu, who describes to Gilgamesh the dismal underworld awaiting people after death. Hoping to avoid his friend's fate, Gilgamesh searches for immortality, only to learn that eternal life is beyond his grasp.

The epic exhibits fundamental features of Mesopotamian religion. Like many ancient belief systems, it was **polytheistic** (*PAH-le-thē-ISS-tik*), meaning that people worshiped more than one god. Gods and goddesses personified forces central to agricultural society, such as earth, sun, water, sky, fertility, and storms. Deities such as Ishtar and her father were temperamental figures, portrayed in human form and believed to affect every aspect of life. People who pleased the gods by rituals and sacrifices could hope for assistance and good fortune, but those who (like Gilgamesh and Enkidu) displeased the

Gilgamesh epic illuminates Sumerian religion and worldview

gods could expect retribution. The overall outlook was gloomy: humans had to serve unpredictable and often spiteful gods in this life, with little hope for a better fate in the next life.

Religion nonetheless played a central role in most ancient societies. It supplied an explanation for the forces of nature, and a means by which people could try to influence those forces. It provided a focus for festivals, such as new year holidays at the start of spring, celebrating life's natural cycles with rituals, dances, and songs. Religion also exalted the rulers as divine agents, thus enhancing their authority and helping them to maintain stability and order. Priests and priestesses, typically members of rulers' families or devoted followers, heralded the rulers as godlike beings descended from divinities and performed rituals intended to bring divine favor on the realm.

Religion was crucial to early cultures and rulers

To further enhance their status and the city's prestige, rulers built splendid temples to the gods and palaces for themselves. Beginning around 2200 B.C.E., some cities constructed **ziggurats** (*ZIG-uh-rahtz*), massive brick towers that ascended upward in a series of tiers, typically topped by shrines that could be used for religious ceremonies. Dominating urban landscapes, ziggurats also served as symbols of a city's power and as lookout towers for its defense (see page 23). Governance and religion were thus allied and intertwined, each supporting the other. ✱ *(politics)*

Early religion and governance are intertwined

COMMERCE, INNOVATION, AND CUNEIFORM WRITING. Secured by this alliance and sustained by surplus food, Sumerians made great strides in other endeavors. They promoted interregional commerce, pioneered the use of wheels, learned to fashion metals into tools and weapons, devised ways to keep track of time, performed architectural and engineering feats, and invented writing.

Became center of trade

Although Sumer's farms produced abundant wheat and barley, and its herds of sheep supplied abundant wool, woods and metals were scarce in Sumer—so its cities traded with other lands to get them. As early as the fourth millennium B.C.E., Sumerians were exchanging their textiles and grains for cedar wood and copper from the eastern Mediterranean, gold from Egypt, and gems from what is now Iran. To carry these trade goods, Sumerians fashioned wooden boats for rivers, cargo ships for seas, and wheeled carts to be pulled over land by animals.

Sumerians connect commercially with neighboring cultures

Overland transport was vastly improved by the wheel, an innovation that, although often associated with Sumer, probably originated among nomads to its north. By 3000 B.C.E., Sumerian traders were transporting goods in carts with wooden wheels, and thus introducing wheels to other regions as they traveled. One of history's most useful inventions, wheels were later attached to chariots for warfare, thereby intensifying conflicts as well as contacts among cultures.

Development of wheeled carts improves overland connections

Sumerians also made advances in metalwork. In the late Neolithic period, hoping to improve on their wood and stone implements, some West Asians started fashioning tools out of copper ore. At first they simply pounded the copper into useful shapes; later they learned to heat it until it melted and pour it into clay molds to cool. However, although copper worked well for small tools and ornaments, it was too soft for larger tools and weapons. In the fourth millennium B.C.E., therefore, metalworkers began to mix the molten copper with tin, thereby producing a sturdier metal called bronze. By 3000 B.C.E., Sumerian artisans increasingly used bronze to make swords and shields for soldiers and sometimes knives and axes for farmers.

Development of writing aids governance, commerce, and spread of knowledge

Other innovations, involving calculation and record keeping, are credited to the Sumerians. They developed, for example, a calendar based on cycles of the moon. They devised a computation system, centered on segments of 12 and 60, which is still used for dividing time into hours, minutes, and seconds. And they used their architectural and engineering skills to construct palaces, temples, fortifications, and irrigation systems.

Furthermore, as trade and tribute grew extensive and society became more complex, Sumerians devised shapes and symbols to keep track of financial and administrative transactions. Later, as this system improved, they used it to record their rituals and laws, as well as the legends and exploits of rulers such as Gilgamesh. This momentous invention, which we now call writing, facilitated governance, enhanced commercial connections, and vastly aided the preservation and transmission of knowledge.

The Sumerians wrote by inscribing figures in wet clay, which then hardened into tablets, some of which are still preserved today. They etched their symbols from right to left, using wedge-like characters that scholars now call **cuneiform** (*KYOO-nē-ih-form*), which means "wedge-shaped." At first these characters were merely stylized pictures (pictographs) of people, animals, and objects such as carts, houses, baskets, and bowls. Eventually, however, as characters were added to express ideas (ideographs) and sounds (phonetics), writing became very complex, so schools were set up in palaces and temples to train writing specialists, or scribes. To enter this prestigious profession, relied on by rulers to help manage their realms, students in these early schools endured memorization, recitation, copy work, harsh discipline by teachers, and harassment by older classmates.

Cuneiform writing.

Connections and conflicts help spread writing system

Few Sumerians actually learned to write, but those who did played a crucial role in spreading and preserving their culture. So useful, indeed, was their writing system that it was adopted not just by speakers of Sumer's various languages, but also by outside conquerors seeking to unite and rule the Sumer region.

The Akkadian Conquest and Spread of Sumerian Culture

Conquest played a crucial role in spreading Sumerian culture. Beginning around 2350 B.C.E., the Sumerian city-states were conquered by King Sargon of Akkad, the ambitious ruler whose story is told at the start of this chapter. Sargon went on to conquer most of Mesopotamia, uniting the whole region under his rule and creating one of history's first empires (Map 2.2).

Akkadian conquerors adapt and spread Sumerian ideas

Sargon also established a pattern that repeated itself time and again throughout history: the conquerors learned from the people they conquered and helped to spread their culture. The Akkadians (*ah-KĀ-dē-inz*), for example, adopted the Sumerian calendar, writing system, and methods of computation, introducing them to other regions as Akkad's rule expanded westward. Hence, as a result of Akkadian conquests, Sumerian ideas spread across Mesopotamia and into the lands along the eastern Mediterranean Sea.

The Akkadian empire, which declined after Sargon's death, was overrun around 2230 B.C.E. by nomadic warriors from mountains to the northeast. The Sumerians later regained power, led by the city-state of Ur, which extended its rule over southern Mesopotamia until around 2000 B.C.E. After that the region came under the control of a people called the Amorites (*AM-uh-rītz*), who created their own extensive empire.

later conquered

Map 2.2 Akkadian Empire Unites Mesopotamia in Twenty-fourth Century B.C.E.

King Sargon of Akkad created the Akkadian Empire in the twenty-fourth century B.C.E. and ruled it from his capital, known as Akkad (or Agade), whose ruins and precise location have yet to be found. Note that Sargon's empire embraced all of Mesopotamia and some of the surrounding regions. What steps did Sargon take to connect and unify his realm?

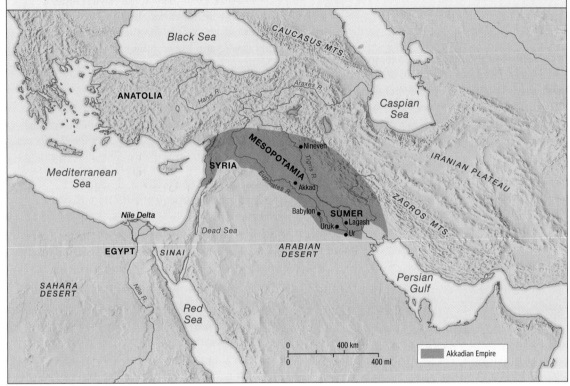

Babylonian Society and Hammurabi's Code

The Amorites, warlike pastoral nomads from Arabia, came to Mesopotamia shortly before 2000 B.C.E. through the region later called Syria, possibly in search of grazing lands for their herds. Through a series of conquests, they gradually extended their control over most of Mesopotamia, which they ruled until about 1600 B.C.E. Like the Akkadians before them, they embraced many aspects of Sumerian society, adapting the ruling and writing systems in order to meet their needs and even settling in cities supported by farming. Since their capital was a city called Babylon (*BAB-ul-ahn*) on the Euphrates River, their empire and culture are often called Babylonian (*bab-uh-LŌ-nē-in*).

Babylonians adapt and spread Sumerian ideas

The most notable Babylonian ruler was Hammurabi (*hah-moo-RAH-bē*), who reigned from 1792 to 1750 B.C.E. and issued the famous law code that now bears his name. **Hammurabi's code**, a compilation of earlier Mesopotamian laws, was carved on a black stone pillar and placed in a temple to promote public knowledge of the law (see "Excerpts from Hammurabi's Code"). The code sought to regulate matters such as trade and contracts, marriage and adultery, debts and estates, and relations among social classes. It assigned penalties based on retribution—the famous principle of "an eye for

Hammurabi's code seeks to regulate Mesopotamian society

Document 2.1 Excerpts from Hammurabi's Code

Hammurabi's Code had 282 articles, mostly assigning punishments for crimes or compensations for commercial and marital infractions. Today these articles provide fascinating insights into Mesopotamian society

6. If any one steal the property of a temple or of the court, he shall be put to death, and also the one who receives the stolen thing from him shall be put to death.

22. If any one is committing a robbery and is caught, then he shall be put to death.

104. If a merchant give an agent corn, wool, oil, or any other goods . . . , the agent shall give a receipt for the amount, and compensate the merchant . . . Then he shall obtain a receipt from the merchant for the money that he gives the merchant.

105. If the agent is careless, and does not take a receipt for the money . . . , he can not consider the . . . money as his own.

106. If the agent accept money from the merchant, but . . . quarrel with the merchant (denying the receipt), then shall the merchant swear before God and witnesses that he has given this money to the agent, and the agent shall pay him three times the sum.

108. If a tavern-keeper (feminine) does not accept corn . . . in payment of drink, but takes money, and the price of the drink is less than that of the corn, she shall be convicted and thrown into the water.

109. If conspirators meet in the house of a tavern-keeper, and these conspirators are not captured and delivered to the court, the tavern-keeper shall be put to death.

129. If a man's wife be [caught having intercourse] with another man, both shall be tied and thrown into the water, but the husband may pardon his wife and the king his slaves.

132. If the "finger is pointed" at a man's wife about another man, but she is not caught sleeping with the other man, she shall jump into the river for her husband.

142. If a woman quarrel with her husband, and say: "You are not congenial to me," the reasons for her prejudice must be presented. If she is guiltless . . . , but he leaves and neglects her, she shall take her dowry and go back to her father's house.

143. If she is not innocent, but leaves her husband, and ruins her house, neglecting her husband, this woman shall be cast into the water.

195. If a son strikes his father, his hand shall be hewn off.

196. If a man put out the eye of another man, his eye shall be put out.

199. If he put out the eye of a man's slave, or break the bone of a man's slave, he shall pay one-half of its value.

200. If a man knock out the teeth of his equal, his teeth shall be knocked out.

SOURCE: *Hammurabi's Code of Laws.* Translated by L. W. King. http://eawc.evansville.edu/anthology/hammurabi.htm

an eye"—in an effort not only to deter crimes but also to limit retaliation by ensuring that the punishment did not exceed the damage done.

Hammurabi's code provides many insights into Mesopotamian society. It reveals, for example, that society was divided into nobles, commoners, and slaves, as different penalties are assigned depending on social status. A noble who knocked out another noble's tooth, for example, was liable to have his own tooth knocked out ("a tooth for a tooth"), but a noble who knocked out a commoner's tooth would only have to pay a fine. A noble who hit a commoner would likewise have to pay a fine, but a commoner who hit a noble would be publicly whipped, and a slave who hit a noble would have an ear cut off.

Property rights, as reflected in the code, were valued very highly. Theft and robbery, for example, were punishable by death. Merchants and artisans could be penalized for providing shoddy goods, but the principle regulating commercial transactions was "let the buyer beware." Tenant farmers were expected to work the land diligently and give the landowner a portion of their crops. Slaves, who were most likely debtors, criminals, or prisoners of war, had limited rights, but they were allowed to own property, marry nonslaves, and even purchase their freedom.

Hammurabi's code regulates commercial and familial connections

Hammurabi's code also sheds light on marriage and gender roles. It shows, for example, that marriages were contractual, typically arranged by the parents. To seal the contract, the groom gave a gift to the bride's father, and her family supplied a **dowry**—a bridal endowment of money or property (preserved today in a custom whereby the bride's family pays for her wedding). The code gave greater rights and higher status to men than to women. A husband, for example, could legally have a mistress, or even take a second wife if his first one failed to bear children. But a woman who cheated or ran off on her husband could be cast into the water to drown.

Women did have some rights: they could buy and sell goods, and even own property, which they were allowed to inherit and pass on to their descendants. Records indicate that some women owned shops or taverns, worked as brewers or bakers, and even served as priestesses or scribes. But records also show that men sometimes sold their wives into slavery, and that women often died before age forty, victimized by infections associated with childbirth or worn out by ceaseless labor.

Men had greater rights than women in Mesopotamia

The law code was not Hammurabi's only achievement. He built fortifications, temples, irrigation channels, and dams that could cut off water to potential enemies downstream—a potent military tool in a region where survival depended on river water. He also centralized the state administration, appointing officials to control the regions of his realm and collect regular taxes from their residents. This practice was more efficient, and less disruptive to the economy, than the old Sumerian tribute system, in which armies were sent out from cities to the surrounding regions to collect tribute by force.

Hammurabi centralizes administration and taxation

For all his accomplishments, however, Hammurabi failed to establish an enduring regime. Following his death in 1750 B.C.E. the Babylonian kingdom declined and was eventually overrun by warlike pastoral nomads using horse-drawn chariots.

Indo-European Migrations

The warriors that challenged Babylon, beginning around 1600 B.C.E., spoke languages now classified as **Indo-European.** Since numerous languages in India, Iran, and Europe share many common features, modern linguists group them as a language family called Indo-European, divided into subfamilies such as Celtic, Greek, Italic, Slavic, Indo-Iranian, and Germanic (the branch to which English belongs). The ancient tongues from which this family evolved differed substantially from Sumerian languages, which form their own language group, and from those spoken by Akkadians and Babylonians, which scholars place in the **Semitic** language family along with Arabic and Hebrew.

The peoples who spoke ancient Indo-European tongues are also called Indo-Europeans. Although their origin is unclear, many scholars think they descended from pastoral nomads who had herded sheep, goats, and cattle since before 4000 B.C.E. on the grassy plains northeast of the Black Sea called steppes (*stepz*).

Indo-European nomads domesticate horses

Among the enduring influences of the early Indo-Europeans was the domestication of horses, which proved immensely useful for both transport and warfare. When hitched to carts, horses hauled tents and supplies, helping people to move about more easily and travel longer distances. When attached to war chariots, developed in Central Asia by 2000 B.C.E., horses enabled warriors to attack and maneuver with great speed, giving them a huge advantage over traditional foot soldiers. When harnessed to military supply wagons, horses conveyed the provisions needed to support an army on the move. Indeed, horses ultimately became the main form of military transport, and remained so until the Second World War in the twentieth century C.E. Long before that, however, horses had aided some of history's greatest migrations.

Indo-Europeans migrate to Anatolia, Europe, Iran, India

In the third millennium B.C.E., perhaps because population growth was outpacing the availability of good pastureland in the steppes, nomads apparently migrated great distances in search of fresh pastures for their herds. Aided and accompanied by their horses, some went southwest to Anatolia (*an-uh-TŌ-lē-uh*), the site of modern Turkey, while others moved south to the Iranian Plateau (Map 2.3). During the second millennium B.C.E., some went further west, dispersing throughout much of Europe, while others migrated east into northern India. Both the widespread use of horses and the wide distribution of Indo-European languages can be attributed to these nomadic migrations.

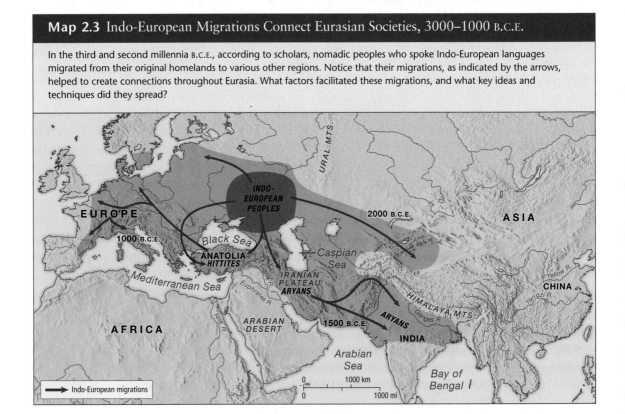

Map 2.3 Indo-European Migrations Connect Eurasian Societies, 3000–1000 B.C.E.

In the third and second millennia B.C.E., according to scholars, nomadic peoples who spoke Indo-European languages migrated from their original homelands to various other regions. Notice that their migrations, as indicated by the arrows, helped to create connections throughout Eurasia. What factors facilitated these migrations, and what key ideas and techniques did they spread?

The Hittite Connection

Among the Indo-Europeans who settled in Anatolia were a people called Hittites (*HIT-tītz*). In the 1590s B.C.E., aided by horse-drawn war chariots and attracted by Babylonian wealth, Hittite armies swept into Mesopotamia, conquering the city of Babylon and ravaging the remnants of Hammurabi's realm. But unrest in their Anatolian homeland soon prompted Hittite armies to withdraw from Mesopotamia. After 1400 B.C.E., however, the Hittites again expanded into Syria and northern Mesopotamia, clashing eventually with Egyptians expanding from northeast Africa (Map 2.4). In these instances, as in so many others, conflict paved the way for cultural connections, as Hittites adopted various aspects of societies they encountered.

Indo-European Hittites settle in Anatolia

But the Hittites did not simply copy other cultures; instead they took features of the cultures they conquered and blended them into their own culture. The Hittites used cuneiform writing, for example, but modified it to fit their own Indo-European language.

Hittites blend Mesopotamian culture with their own

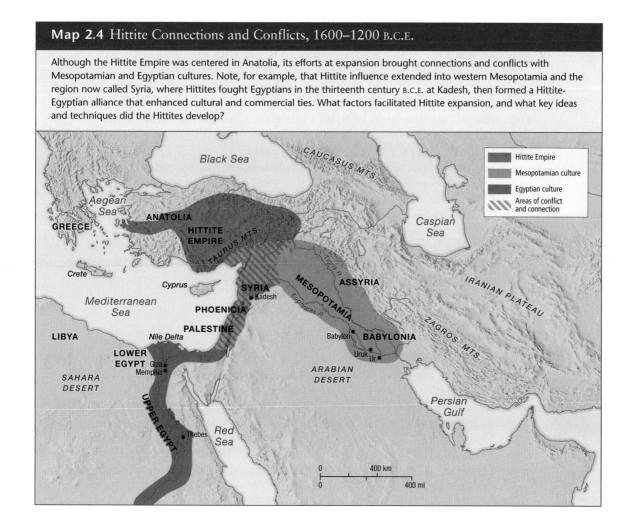

Map 2.4 Hittite Connections and Conflicts, 1600–1200 B.C.E.

Although the Hittite Empire was centered in Anatolia, its efforts at expansion brought connections and conflicts with Mesopotamian and Egyptian cultures. Note, for example, that Hittite influence extended into western Mesopotamia and the region now called Syria, where Hittites fought Egyptians in the thirteenth century B.C.E. at Kadesh, then formed a Hittite-Egyptian alliance that enhanced cultural and commercial ties. What factors facilitated Hittite expansion, and what key ideas and techniques did the Hittites develop?

They worshipped many Mesopotamian gods, but absorbed these gods into their own polytheistic religion, in which the God of Storms was the main divinity. They established law codes in the manner of Hammurabi, but based them on their own pastoral customs, prescribing fines for the killing or theft of livestock—and death for men who had sex with cows or pigs. They adopted farming, but adjusted it to their climate and soil, supplementing grain crops with grapes for making wines and olives from which they made oil.

Hittites develop ironwork, advancing agriculture and warfare

The Hittites also mastered the art of metalwork. At first they cast weapons and farm tools of bronze, as others in West Asia had done for centuries. But copper and tin, the components of bronze, were relatively scarce in Hittite lands. Artisans long had tried making items of iron, a metal abundant in Anatolia and elsewhere, by melting and molding it as they did with bronze, but resulting cast iron goods proved very brittle. By the thirteenth century B.C.E., however, Hittites learned to sear iron until it was red-hot, and then to shape it with hammer strokes before it cooled. Using this process, Hittites forged sturdy iron daggers, swords, spears, and shields, as well as farm hoes and other tools. Within several centuries, despite Hittite efforts to keep iron forging a military secret, it had spread to other lands in Europe, West Asia, and North Africa, and had been developed independently in East Africa. By vastly increasing the availability of inexpensive tools and weapons, the use of iron greatly advanced both agriculture and warfare, enabling far more people than ever before to engage in such pursuits.

Hittites form an agricultural, warlike, patriarchal kingdom

The Hittite kingdom, like most societies centered on agriculture and warfare, was hierarchical and patriarchal. Its various farming villages were united under a warrior king, who was assisted by an influential aristocracy in supervising the soldiers, merchants, artisans, and slaves who made up the rest of society. Women were generally subordinate to men, but they were not entirely subservient: a man could have only one wife, a woman could sometimes reject the husband chosen by her parents, and queens could play important roles as diplomats and priestesses.

Hittites connect and conflict with Mesopotamia and Egypt

Although their political unity was challenged at times by internal strife, by 1300 B.C.E. the Hittites had fashioned an empire that stretched across Anatolia from the Aegean (*ih-JĒ-in*) Sea to upper Mesopotamia, and south along the Mediterranean coast toward Egypt. During the next century, the Hittites clashed and connected with the Egyptians (above). But after 1200 B.C.E. the Hittites succumbed to new invaders, including the **Sea Peoples**, assorted marauders of uncertain origins who ravaged eastern Mediterranean lands, perhaps after being driven by famine from Aegean islands, western Anatolia, and the Black Sea region.

Later Mesopotamia: Assyrians and Chaldeans

Several centuries after the Hittite collapse, much of West Asia was reunited by Assyrians (*uh-SEER-ē-inz*), rugged warriors from the hill country near the northern Tigris River. From the ninth through seventh centuries B.C.E., mounting numerous military campaigns, they gained wealth and power by dominating the productive farmlands and profitable trade routes of West Asia. They created an empire stretching from the Persian Gulf to the Mediterranean Sea, and even into Anatolia and Egypt (Map 2.5). In expanding their domain, the Assyrians acquired a reputation for brutality, overwhelming their foes with well-organized horse-drawn chariot assaults; then torturing, slaughtering, and exiling conquered peoples to prevent rebellions.

But Assyrians also made important cultural contributions. Their magnificent city of Nineveh (*NIN-uh-vuh*), built near the northern Tigris, boasted gardens and zoos, a

An Assyrian warrior on horseback.

Map 2.5 The Assyrian and Chaldean (New Babylonian) Empires, Ninth Through Sixth Centuries B.C.E.

From the ninth through seventh centuries B.C.E., the Assyrians, a people from the hilly region north of the Tigris, conquered a vast empire that included Mesopotamia, Egypt, and surrounding regions. Notice that the Chaldeans, who helped destroy the Assyrian realm in 614–612 B.C.E., created a smaller "New Babylonian" empire. What were the key contributions of the Assyrians and Chaldeans? When and how did the Chaldean empire come to an end?

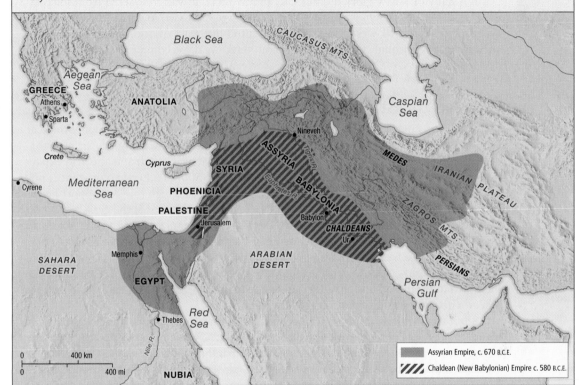

water supply system to conduct fresh water from outlying mountains, and works of art distinguished by brutal realism. Nineveh's royal palace, for example, was adorned with a sequence of sculptured reliefs depicting scenes from bloody battles and lion hunts, arranged so observers could follow the story of the conflict or hunt. And its royal library, unearthed by archeologists in the nineteenth century C.E., housed more than 20,000 clay cuneiform tablets, carried off from Babylon and elsewhere. It thus preserved many centuries of Mesopotamian writings, including the Epic of Gilgamesh.

The Assyrians were hated and feared as few other conquerors had been—and this hatred finally proved their undoing. In 614 B.C.E. the Chaldeans (*kal-DĒ-inz*) from southern Mesopotamia, smarting from Assyrian brutality, allied with the Medes, a people from east of Assyria, to stage a massive assault. The Assyrian empire, which had tyrannized West Asia for almost three centuries, was shattered, and in 612 B.C.E. much of Nineveh was destroyed.

Chaldeans and Medes conquer the Assyrians

The Chaldeans, also called New Babylonians, then became the new masters of Mesopotamia. Under King Nebuchadnezzar (*NEB-oo-kud-NEZ-ur*), who reigned from

604 to 562 B.C.E., the city of Babylon once again rose to greatness, surpassing even Nineveh's size and splendor. Babylon's magnificent city wall, including the splendid Ishtar gate (named for the fertility goddess), was adorned with paintings of yellow and white animals against a bright blue background. And Babylon's remarkable Hanging Gardens, a rising set of stone terraces covered with plants and trees, were counted among the great wonders of the ancient world.

But Babylon's new glory did not last. In 539 B.C.E. it was conquered from the east by the Persians, a people whose history and culture are discussed in Chapter 6. The Persians eventually overran all West Asia and moved into Northeast Africa. There, situated along a river that ran through a desert, they encountered wealthy, complex societies that had developed at the same time as West Asia's early societies.

The Hanging Gardens of Babylon.

Early Northeast African Societies

North Africa is dominated by the Sahara Desert, a hot, dry wasteland roughly the size of modern China or the United States. Only the Nile River, flowing north through the desert from sub-Saharan Africa (Africa south of the Sahara), interrupts the arid expanse. According to scientists, however, between 10,000 and 5000 B.C.E. much of what is now desert was covered by grasslands, with rivers, lakes, and enough rain to support herding and farming. During this era, as noted in Chapter 1, inhabitants of the grasslands started to herd cattle and grow sorghum, while Nile Valley residents learned to raise wheat, barley, sheep, and goats. By 5000 B.C.E., people practiced farming and herding across the northern half of Africa (Map 2.6).

After 5000 B.C.E., however, the climate grew steadily drier. As rainfall became scarce, the grasslands receded and the desert expanded, so farmers and herders had to settle in places where they would have access to water.

As Sahara Desert expands, people move to moister regions

Some settled along the Mediterranean coast, with its mild climate and seasonal rains, where they mainly herded cattle until after 1000 B.C.E., when many turned to commerce as coastal ports and colonies emerged with an expanding sea trade. Others settled in the grasslands that still existed south of the Sahara, especially in the regions around Lake Chad and the Niger River, where they grouped into villages and clans, herded cattle, raised sorghum and yams (a starchy root crop), and traveled the rivers in canoes. Eventually, after 2000 B.C.E., perhaps compelled by a shortage of farmland as the population grew, some of this region's people began migrating to the south and southeast, bringing their agricultural way of life to lands whose inhabitants had hitherto lived by foraging. The migrating peoples, who spoke a variety of related languages now collectively called Bantu (a word simply meaning "people"), may have helped to spread farming and herding across the southern half of Africa during the next three millennia (see Chapter 13).

Bantu migrations spread farming and herding throughout sub-Saharan Africa

Most North Africans, however, settled near the Nile River, where they clustered in farming villages along its fertile floodplains. These villages in time would form the foundations of large, complex, dynamic societies later called Egypt and Nubia.

Many farmers and herders settle in fertile Nile Valley

Egyptian Culture and Society

Nile settlements grow and unite into Kingdom of Egypt

After 4000 B.C.E., as the Nile Valley population grew, towns and villages along the river began uniting into small kingdoms. These kingdoms organized irrigation projects that

Map 2.6 African Environment and the Spread of Farming and Herding, Second Millennium B.C.E. Through First Millennium C.E.

Africa's widely varied environment supported the emergence of farming and herding in grasslands and river valleys, as noted by the labels on this map. Observe that people speaking Bantu languages, as indicated by the arrows, migrated throughout sub-Saharan Africa from the second millennium B.C.E. through the first millennium C.E. What factors facilitated the Bantu migrations, and what ideas and techniques did they help to spread?

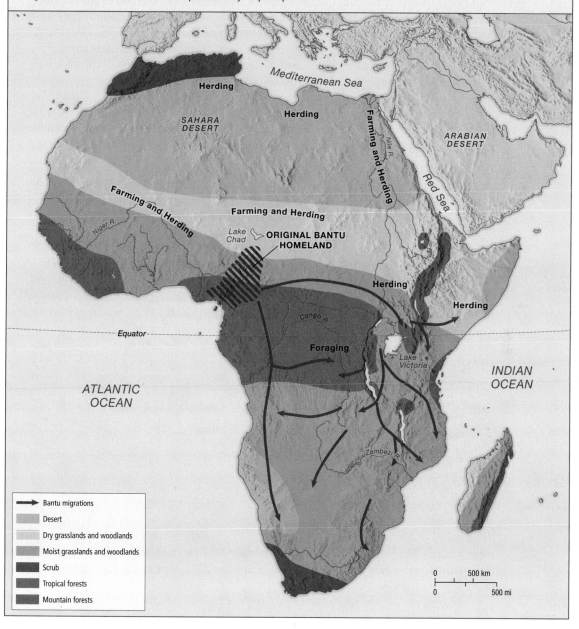

brought river water to farm fields; they also traded with each other and sometimes fought one another. By 3100 B.C.E., through a series of conflicts and conquests, the northern kingdoms had combined into one large Kingdom of Egypt, destined to become one of the ancient world's most powerful and prosperous realms.

In some ways, developments in Egypt paralleled those in Mesopotamia. As in Mesopotamia, smaller states were combined by conquest into larger domains, with powerful rulers, polytheistic religions, writing systems, extensive commerce, and sophisticated technologies. As in Mesopotamia, trade and conquest created connections, with Egyptians adapting ideas and techniques from West Asians and from other Africans.

Egyptians develop connections with West Asians and other Africans

In other ways, however, Egypt differed markedly from Mesopotamia. Separated by seas and deserts from potential foes, and blessed by a river whose annual, soil-enriching floods enabled farmers to produce abundant crops year after year, ancient Egypt was bountiful, powerful, extensive, and predictable, much like the waterway that ran through its midst. Egyptian society seems to have been more stable, and its rhythms of life more regular, than those in West Asia. Egypt's worldview was less gloomy, and its religion more optimistic. And Egypt's women played more prominent roles than women in Mesopotamia.

RELIGION AND WORLDVIEW. Religion was as integral to life in Egypt as it was in Mesopotamia. Egyptians too worshiped many gods, among them the rulers of Egypt. An elaborate system of priests and priestesses perpetuated traditional beliefs, maintained numerous temples, performed sacred rituals, and sought to instill among the people respect for order and obedience to the rulers. In time, belief in the prospect of life after death prompted efforts to preserve and house the remains of rulers and other prominent people.

Central to Egypt's worldview was the concept of *ma'at* (*mah-AHT*), the universe's elemental order, which encompassed truth, justice, harmony, and balance. The rulers, eventually called pharaohs (*FARE-ōz*), were powerful, godlike figures whose main duty was to maintain *ma'at*, without which there would be chaos. They were regarded as descendants of Re (*RĀ*), also known as Amon (*AH-muhn*) or Amon-Re, the sun god and chief divinity, who ruled the heavens much as pharaohs ruled the earth. Religion and governance in Egypt were thus one and the same.

Despite Amon-Re's preeminence, the two most popular deities came to be Osiris (*ō-SĪ-ris*), god of vegetation and the Nile, and Isis (*Ī-sis*), goddess of the earth, who was both his sister and his wife. According to legend, Osiris, a divine early ruler who taught the Egyptians to farm, was slain and cut to pieces by his evil brother Seth, but Isis put Osiris back together and restored him to life. Isis and Osiris thus became symbols of fertility, devotion, and the victory of life over death, inspiring an outlook far more hopeful than that of early Mesopotamian religion.

Seeing life as cyclical, Egyptians come to believe in an afterlife

Sustained by such myths and the cycles of the Nile, whose annual soil-renewing floods were more regular and predictable than floods in Mesopotamia, Egyptians concluded that life itself was cyclical and renewable. They came to believe that death was not the end of life, that Osiris judged the dead by weighing their hearts, and that those whose hearts were light from honorable living would merit eternal life. Religion in Egypt thus reinforced morality, as the prospect of attaining life after death gave people an incentive for honorable behavior.

The prospect of life after death also promoted **mummification**, an elaborate process for preserving the bodies of prominent people after death. First the innards and brains were removed; then the bodies were thoroughly cleansed, packed in a special mineral for several months, tightly wrapped with strips of fine linen, coated with gum, and sealed in a wooden case. Anticipating immortality, those who could afford to do so often had splendid tombs constructed while they were alive, to house their remains and prized possessions after death. No other culture has lavished such care on the bodies of the dead.

HIEROGLYPHIC WRITING AND OTHER INNOVATIONS. Like the early Mesopotamians, ancient Egyptians made momentous contributions to culture, knowledge, and written communication. They produced impressive works of art, decorating their temples and tombs with splendid paintings and sculptures. They charted the constellations, created a sophisticated calendar, and practiced a form of medicine based on natural remedies. They even devised an accounting system and developed mathematics to advance their architectural and engineering skills.

Writing on papyrus aids communication and record keeping

Egyptians also originated a form of writing known as **hieroglyphics** (*HĪ-ruh-GLIF-ikz*). Like Sumer's cuneiform system, it started as a series of pictures and eventually added symbols for ideas and sounds. Like the Sumerians, Egyptians trained scribes to master and use their complex writing system. Unlike the Sumerians, however, Egyptian scribes wrote with ink-dipped reeds on papyrus (*puh-PĪ-russ*), a paperlike material made from plants that grew along the Nile, and then rolled it into scrolls for easy storage or transport. These scrolls, far less cumbersome than the clay tablets used in Mesopotamia, enabled the Egyptians to readily record their legends, rituals, laws, and exploits, providing portraits of their society and recording its history.

Later, however, after Egyptians abandoned early hieroglyphics for other writing systems, no one could read the early records. For many centuries, historians had to rely for knowledge of ancient Egypt on accounts that were written after 300 B.C.E. in Greek. But in 1799 C.E., archeologists with French armies in Egypt discovered the Rosetta Stone, a large black slab on which the deeds of a ruler from the second century B.C.E. were inscribed in early hieroglyphics, a later Egyptian writing system, and Greek. Working from the Greek, which they already knew, linguists learned to read the others and hence to decipher the records of ancient Egypt.

SOCIETY, FAMILY, GENDER ROLES, AND WORK. The records thus deciphered, combined with archeological evidence, reveal that Egypt had a high degree of political and social stratification. They also show that life focused mainly on family and farming, and on the cycles of the Nile.

Egypt's social structure tended to rank people according to status and wealth. Upper classes of priests and state officials lived in luxury; middle classes of merchants, scribes, and artisans enjoyed some prosperity; and lower classes of peasants and laborers worked hard to barely survive. The vast majority of Egyptians were peasants: humble farmers and herders who raised wheat, barley, cotton, cattle, and sheep.

Marriage and family were central to Egyptian society. Although some men practiced **polygyny**, which means they had more than one wife, marriages were mostly monogamous. As in West Asia, husbands provided the homestead while wives brought a dowry and furnishings into the marital union.

Gender roles were well defined but not totally rigid. In lower-class households men mostly worked the fields, but they might also be hunters, miners, craftsmen, or construction workers. Egyptian women mainly did household tasks, such as cooking and making clothes, much like women in West Asia.

Decorated wooden "mummy" case used for the remains of an ancient Egyptian woman.

Women often play key roles in Egyptian society

But women in Egypt seem to have had higher status than women in other ancient cultures. Egyptian women could own and inherit property, seek and obtain a divorce, and engage in such trades as entertaining, nursing, and brewing beer. Furthermore, in contrast to West Asian households, Egyptian families often were matrilineal, with property descending through the female line, and wives in Egypt were recognized as dominant in the home. Egyptian women serving as priestesses played a key role in religion, and a few women even served as rulers. But governance and warfare were, as elsewhere, mainly the work of men.

Nile cycles govern farming, irrigation, and construction

The rhythm of work in Egypt followed the ebb and flow of the Nile, which typically overflowed its banks between July and September. In October, once the waters had receded, the growing season began. With the help of oxen and other farm animals, peasants plowed their fields and planted their crops, then tended them for the next several months, bringing in buckets of water from irrigation canals. The harvest usually started in February, with women and children helping the men to gather crops and thresh grain. Wheat and barley were the principal crops, but Egyptians also grew dates, grapes, and various other fruits and vegetables. In ordinary times, when food was abundant, the government took a portion of the grain to store for use in times of scarcity. Large projects requiring many workers, such as the construction and repair of palaces, temples, and irrigation systems, were normally undertaken after the harvest was over.

The Kingdoms of Egypt

For almost three millennia, with occasional interruptions, Egypt was ruled by a series of kings, who came to be called pharaohs in the fifteenth century C.E. These monarchs governed through a network of agents and officials who enforced royal edicts, collected taxes, dispensed justice, commanded soldiers, and supervised laborers in constructing buildings, monuments, and water-control projects.

The history of ancient Egypt is generally divided into a succession of major eras distinguished by three great "kingdoms" and the periods surrounding them. Although scholars disagree on the precise dates, the approximate durations of these eras are as follows:

The Archaic Period	3100–2700 B.C.E.
The Old Kingdom	2700–2200 B.C.E.
First Intermediate Period	2200–2050 B.C.E.
The Middle Kingdom	2050–1700 B.C.E.
Second Intermediate Period	1700–1570 B.C.E.
The New Kingdom (Empire)	1570–1075 B.C.E.
The Late (Post-Imperial) Period	1075–332 B.C.E.

Ancient Egyptian history can further be divided into dynasties—each a succession of rulers from the same royal family. From the Archaic through the Post-Imperial Periods, historians have identified 31 dynasties in all.

Lower and Upper Egypt united in the Archaic Period

EARLY KINGDOMS AND HYKSOS RULE. The Archaic Period, about which little is known, was the first time that Egypt was unified under a single ruler. Before that, it seems, there had been two separate realms: Lower Egypt, in the Nile River delta in the north, and Upper Egypt, which stretched along the river for hundreds of miles to the south (Map 2.7). Around 3100 B.C.E., the two were combined into one domain by a ruler from the south called Menes (*MĀ-nāz*), who began the first Egyptian dynasty.

Map 2.7 Egyptian Kingdoms and Imperial Expansion, 2700–1075 B.C.E.

During the Old Kingdom (2700–2200 B.C.E.) and Middle Kingdom (2050–1700 B.C.E.), ancient Egypt was a long, narrow country stretching along the Nile River. Notice, however, that during the New Kingdom (1570–1075 B.C.E.), Egyptians created an empire extending south along the Nile into Nubia and northeast into Palestine and Syria, where they clashed with the Hittites in the 1200s B.C.E. How did connections and conflicts with other cultures contribute to Egyptian wealth and power?

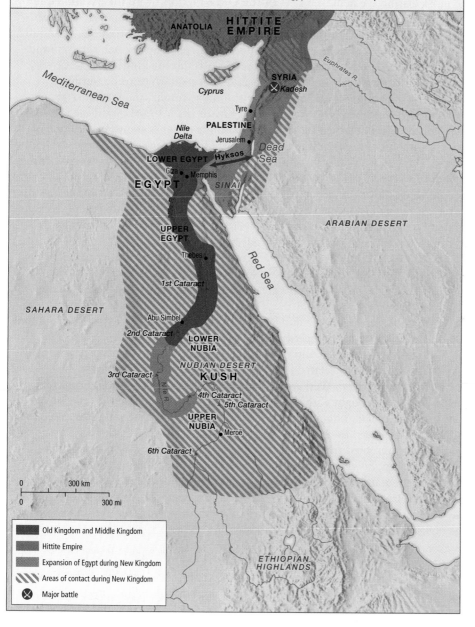

Somewhat more is known about the Old Kingdom, which lasted roughly from 2700 to 2200 B.C.E. During this period Egypt's rulers presided over a mostly peaceful and stable society. Internally they focused on enhancing their power and grandeur, and on creating a centralized state with an effective bureaucracy and tax collection system. Externally they seem to have followed a cautious policy, conducting some trade with other societies, but avoiding aggression and warfare.

The Great Pyramid.

The most distinctive achievements of the Old Kingdom were the pyramids, monumental structures with triangular sides sloping upward toward a point. Used as burial chambers for departed rulers, the pyramids were built mostly between 2700 and 2500 B.C.E., centuries before the Mesopotamian ziggurats (which the pyramids may have inspired). The first pyramid, erected as a tomb for king Zoser (*ZŌ-sur*), was composed of steps ascending toward a 200-foot peak. Not to be outdone, Zoser's successors commissioned ever more grandiose tombs, the largest of which was the Great Pyramid built for the monarch Khufu (*KOO-foo*). Standing almost 500 feet high, it was assembled by tens of thousands of workers using millions of tons of limestone blocks, carefully raised and fitted into place with a series of temporary ramps. The Great Pyramid would later be considered the ancient world's foremost wonder.

The Old Kingdom ended around 2200 B.C.E. with a series of ruinous droughts, followed by an era of civil war and chaos known as the First Intermediate Period. As central authority weakened, individual nobles carved out their own domains and battled among themselves, while bandits and marauders ravaged the land.

Around 2050 B.C.E., however, unity was restored by a powerful ruler named Mentuhotep (*men-too-HŌ-tep*) from Thebes in southern Egypt, beginning the Middle Kingdom. This era brought an increase in trade with other regions, including Mesopotamia, and a growing belief in life after death. Rather than building great pyramids, the kings undertook vast irrigation and land reclamation projects to expand the amount of farmland and enhance the prosperity of their realm.

The Middle Kingdom lasted until around 1700 B.C.E., when a warlike people called Hyksos (*HICK-sōs*), perhaps related to the Amorites who had earlier moved into Mesopotamia, invaded Egypt from West Asia. Using horse-drawn chariots and bronze weapons, which they brought with them from West Asia, the invaders at first proved unstoppable in combat. They conquered all of Egypt, beginning what was later called the Second Intermediate Period.

The Egyptians resented the harsh rule of the Hyksos, whom they deemed culturally inferior. This disdain, however, did not stop Egyptians from adopting Hyksos techniques, including the use of bronze to make improved farm tools and eventually the use of horses in warfare. The Hyksos in turn embraced the complex customs and religion of the great civilization they had come to control. Egyptians nonetheless continued to despise the Hyksos, and ultimately united to expel them.

THE EGYPTIAN EMPIRE. In the mid-1500s B.C.E. the Hyksos were driven out by Ahmose (*AH-mōs*), another great Egyptian unifier from the south, who established the New Kingdom. Unlike its predecessors, the New Kingdom, born of military insurrection, was warlike and expansionist. Within a century its rulers, employing an army equipped with weapons and techniques derived from the Hyksos, had established an Egyptian Empire stretching from Nubia in the south to Syria in the north. In the process emerged two new

Pyramids are built as monumental tombs for Old Kingdom rulers

Middle Kingdom brings increased trade and connections with other cultures

Horses and bronze weapons help Hyksos conquer the Middle Kingdom

Egypt's New Kingdom adapts Hyksos ways to conquer large empire

Egyptian classes: one of professional soldiers who made up the standing army; another of slaves who had been captured as prisoners of war.

The New Kingdom produced some remarkable rulers. One was Hatshepsut (*hat-SHEP-soot*), who became regent for her six-year-old stepson, Thutmosis (*thoot-MŌ-sis*) III, around 1479 B.C.E., and later had the priests proclaim her king. Sidestepping Egypt's long tradition of male rule, Hatshepsut asserted that her father had made her his heir; she dressed in men's clothing, was portrayed on monuments wearing a beard, and often wore one in public. But above all she ruled with vigor and determination, providing Egypt with several decades of stability, commercial expansion, and peace.

After Hatshepsut died around 1458 B.C.E., her stepson Thutmosis III, raised in the army during her rule, emerged as one of Egypt's greatest military leaders. He extended his dominion north to the upper Euphrates, vanquishing various West Asian realms, and south up the Nile, conquering the people known as Nubians. He was the first Egyptian monarch to use the title pharaoh ("great house"), which hitherto had meant the king's palace, and the first known ruler to recognize the potential of sea power, amassing a navy that made Egypt master of the eastern Mediterranean.

In the mid-1300s B.C.E., however, Egyptian power waned when a ruler named Amenhotep (*ah-mun-HŌ-tep*) IV, along with his wife Nefertiti (*nef-ur-TĒ-tē*), attempted a religious revolution. Promoting the worship of a universal deity called Aton (*AH-tun*), the pharaoh changed his own name from Amenhotep ("Amon rests") to Akhenaton (*AH-ken-AH-tun*), or "Aton is pleased." Akhenaton also expelled the temple priests and degraded the traditional gods, provoking a vast resistance among the priests and people. Obsessed with his religious reform, seen by some scholars as an early attempt at **monotheism** (belief in a single god), Akhenaton refused to dispatch soldiers to protect Egypt's Syrian provinces from the marauding Hittites, who were then expanding their West Asian empire. The results for Egypt were a loss of territory, a decline of income from tribute payments, and revolts in the provinces against the pharaoh.

For most of his reign, Akhenaton seems to have ruled jointly with his wife Nefertiti, portrayed in the era's artwork as her husband's equal partner and a woman of great beauty. Late in his reign, however, she disappeared from public life; perhaps she died or fell from favor. Then, when the pharaoh himself died a few years later, the religious revolution ended. The old religion and traditional gods were restored under Tutankhamon (*toot-ahn-KAH-mun*), Akhenaton's youthful successor, today best known as the famed "King Tut" whose fabulous tomb was discovered intact by British archeologist Howard Carter in 1922 C.E.

In the 1200s B.C.E., Egypt's most notable pharaoh was Ramses (*RAM-sēz*) II, the Great, who reigned for more than sixty years. Early in his reign, seeking to regain lands lost under Akhenaton, Ramses fought the Hittites in an epic battle at Kadesh (*KĀ-desh*) in Syria. Although Ramses later claimed victory, his armies neither destroyed the Hittites' power nor drove them out of Syria. So he turned to diplomacy, forming an alliance with his former foes and marrying a Hittite princess to seal the ties. To glorify his kingdom and himself, Ramses ordered the construction of colossal monuments and temples, using an abundance of slave labor.

Under Ramses' successors, however, Egypt was diminished by the attacks of the Sea Peoples, the same raiders who ravaged the Hittites around 1200 B.C.E. A century later, the high priests of Amon-Re seized control of southern Egypt, dividing the empire and making it vulnerable to new commercial and military challenges from abroad. In the eleventh century B.C.E., as Egypt's dominance waned, power in Northeast Africa shifted to the south.

Female ruler Hatshepsut fosters stability and trade

Akhenaton and Nefertiti impose new religion and neglect empire

Statues of Ramses II at Abu Simbel.

Ramses II reinvigorates the empire and allies with the Hittites

Sea Peoples' raids and internal divisions undermine the Egyptian Empire

Nubian Culture and the Kingdoms of Kush

Nubians and Egyptians form commercial and cultural connections

South of Egypt was the region known as Nubia, a name said to mean either "gold" (its most precious product) or "black" (the color of its people). Since at least 7000 B.C.E. Nubians had raised cattle and grain along the upper Nile, forming a series of kingdoms after 4000 B.C.E. Rich in gold and copper, Nubia also provided a link through the desert with lands to the south that produced precious products such as ebony and ivory (Map 2.8). As Egypt grew wealthy and powerful, its rulers often sent caravans and armies to procure these valuable goods, trading and often clashing with the Nubian kingdoms. During the Old and Middle Kingdoms, Egypt dominated northern Nubia; in southern Nubia a kingdom called Kush endured until the fifteenth century B.C.E., when it was conquered and then ruled by Egypt for the next four centuries.

Nubians bearing gifts.

Nubia and Egypt were thus closely linked for over two millennia, during which Nubians combined various aspects of Egypt's culture and religion with their own. They adapted hieroglyphic writing to fit their various languages and blended Egyptian deities, such as Amon-Re and Isis, into the Nubian religion, which featured such divinities as Dedwen, the god of prosperity and incense, and Apedemak (*ah-PEH-deh-mak*), the lion-headed god of war. In some crafts, such as ceramics and metalwork, Nubians were even more skilled than their northern neighbors.

Nubians blend Egyptian culture with their own

With the decline of the Egyptian Empire in the eleventh century B.C.E., the Nubians regained their independence, and eventually formed a new Kingdom of Kush. Effectively imitating the Egyptian pharaohs, the rulers of Kush expanded their dominion commercially and militarily, and in the eighth century B.C.E. they brought all of Egypt under their control. But they came less as conquerors than as restorers, reunifying the realm and assuming all the titles and traditions of Egyptian pharaohs. The Kushites returned the Nile valley to peace and prosperity and helped revive art and architecture in Egypt. For a while it looked as if they might restore the stability and grandeur of days gone by. But in the seventh century B.C.E. they were driven back south by the expanding Assyrians, who briefly controlled the northern Nile. Egypt subsequently regained its independence, only to be swallowed up in the next century by the Persian Empire.

Kingdom of Kush conquers and reunifies Egypt

The Kingdom and Culture of Meroë

Nubians rule from Meroë and develop new cultural distinctions

Up the Nile, as Egypt's influence waned, Nubia continued to flourish, but its cultural and commercial focus gradually shifted southward. In the sixth century B.C.E., its rulers moved south to Meroë (*MER-ō-ē*), a city with ties to sub-Saharan Africa rather than the Mediterranean. Forsaking hieroglyphics, the Nubians devised their own writing system and began to emphasize new religious, cultural, and economic themes. These included increased worship of distinctive Nubian deities such as Apedemak and Dedwen; an enhanced political role for women, indicated by a growing number of female rulers; and increased reliance on camels for transport, rather than horses or donkeys. Iron smelting, invented independently in West Asia and East Africa, spread to Meroë and became a key feature of its economy.

Meroë links Mediterranean world with sub-Saharan Africa

Egyptian influence, although diminished, persisted in Meroë. Its people, for example, continued to entomb their departed rulers beneath sandstone pyramids and to conduct regular commerce with Egypt. Lasting from the sixth century B.C.E. to the fourth century C.E., the Kingdom of Meroë provided the main link between sub-Saharan Africa and the Mediterranean world.

Map 2.8 Egypt, Kush, and Meroë, Second Millennium B.C.E. Through First Millennium C.E.

The Nubian Kingdom of Kush, which flourished up the Nile south of Egypt, had numerous connections and conflicts with Egypt, which it conquered and ruled for a time in the eighth and seventh centuries B.C.E. Note, however, that Meroë, which later emerged farther south along the Nile, was located closer to the Ethiopian Highlands and sub-Saharan Africa, providing commercial and cultural links between these regions and the Mediterranean world. How did these connections influence the commerce and culture of Meroë?

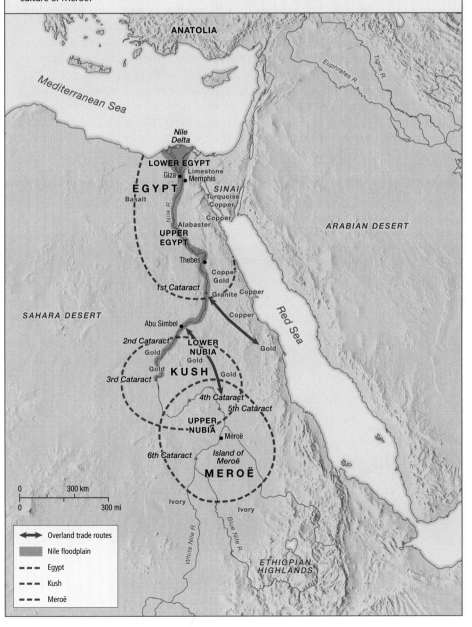

West Asia and North Africa: The Phoenician Connection

Phoenicians form commercial empire linking Mediterranean lands

The Mediterranean world, meanwhile, had been connected into a commercial network with the help of the Phoenicians (*fih-NĒ-shinz*), Semitic-speaking people who lived in what is now Lebanon on the eastern Mediterranean coast. Dwelling by the sea, without large armies or extensive farmlands, Phoenicians turned to sea trade and established commercial cities and seaports. By the twelfth century B.C.E., following the attacks on Egypt conducted by the Sea Peoples, who may have been Phoenician allies, the Phoenicians gained sway over Mediterranean trade from the waning Egyptian Empire. Using hardy wood from the cedar trees of Lebanon, they built state-of-the-art ships with two decks of oarsmen to propel the vessel, a top deck of soldiers to protect cargo, and battering rams to smash enemy craft. Adept at both commerce and warfare, the Phoenicians formed a trading empire, founding city-states and colonies along the coast of North Africa, as well as in what are now Sicily, Sardinia, and Spain. The Phoenicians thus connected West Asia with North Africa and the western Mediterranean (Map 2.9).

Map 2.9 Phoenician and Carthaginian Colonies, Twelfth Through Second Centuries B.C.E.

The Phoenicians, a seafaring people from West Asia, conducted commerce and established colonies around the Mediterranean from the twelfth through eighth centuries B.C.E. Note that they had substantial connections in the western Mediterranean, where their largest colony, Carthage, founded around 800 B.C.E., would later become an independent commercial and naval power. How and why did the Phoenicians acquire such extensive influence?

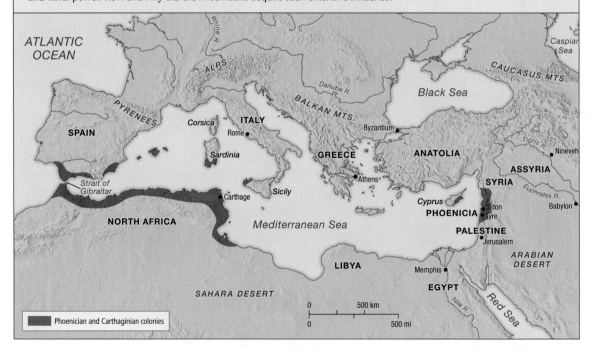

A simplified writing system, developed by Phoenicians, further enhanced connections by easing communications. Employing only 22 symbols, or letters, each for a consonant sound, this system represented spoken words and phrases simply by combining these symbols. Far easier to learn and use than cuneiform or hieroglyphics, whose numerous symbols each represented a word, the Phoenician alphabet greatly aided the spread of writing and reading. As later modified by Greeks (who added vowels) and Romans, it provided a basis for phonetic alphabets eventually adopted throughout the western world—including the one used in writing English today (See Figure 2.1).

Phoenician alphabet advances written communication

Of the colonies founded by Phoenicia, the greatest was the city of Carthage on the North African coast, established around 800 B.C.E. In the following centuries, as Phoenician power waned, Carthage became independent. Building its own commercial empire in the western Mediterranean, Carthage grew into one of the world's largest cities, with a bustling harbor, a metropolitan population of perhaps 400,000, and a city wall more than 20 miles around. An urban republic ruled by its prominent merchants, Carthage dominated its region for centuries, and even sent its vessels into the Atlantic to explore the African and British coasts.

Carthage creates a commercial empire connecting western Mediterranean

HIEROGLYPHIC	REPRESENTS	PHOENICIAN	GREEK	ROMAN
)	Throw stick	∧	Γ	G
ⵣ	Man with raised arms	⟨	E	E
⌣	Basket with handle	∨	K	K
ᴟᴟᴟ	Water	⌒	M	M
⌁	Snake	⟍	N	N
👁	Eye	O	O	O
⌒	Mouth	?	Π	P
ꙮ	Head	9	P	R
⚚	Pool with lotus flowers	W	Σ	S
⊏⊐	House	Ɵ	B	B
⚘	Ox-head	K	A	A

Figure 2.1
Table Comparing Egyptian, Phoenician, Greek, and Roman Characters

The Israelites and Their God

Of all the early West Asians, among the least in power and wealth were the Hebrews, a small group of tribes who spoke a Semitic tongue, herded sheep and goats, fought among themselves, and were often conquered and controlled by others. The Hebrews nonetheless had an enduring religious legacy. For in recording their exploits, customs, and creeds, first in oral and later in written form, some of them produced the Hebrew Bible, one of history's foremost religious and literary works. In the process, they developed a monotheistic faith that would serve as a basis for some of the world's most influential religions: Judaism, Christianity, and Islam.

The Children of Israel

Bible relates stories of Hebrews as Semitic pastoral nomads

The Hebrew Bible provides a striking story of the early Hebrews. According to its narrative, at the urging of his God, the patriarch Abraham left the realm of Ur in Mesopotamia to settle in the land of Canaan (*KĀ-nin*), later called Palestine. After several generations, the sons of his grandson Jacob, who was also called Israel, went to Egypt during a famine to find pastureland for their sheep. There these Hebrews, later called "Israelites" or "children of Israel," were eventually enslaved and spent years in bondage before being led by Moses, a prominent Egyptian born of Hebrew stock, in a flight to freedom called the Exodus (see "Excerpts from the Hebrew Bible"). On their way back to Canaan, the Bible asserts, the God of Israel embraced the children of Israel with his **covenant**, a binding agreement to protect them as his chosen people. He also instructed them to worship him alone, and to keep the Ten Commandments, religious and moral laws that he revealed to Moses. After wandering forty years in the desert, the story goes on, the children of Israel finally returned to Canaan.

A recreation of the ancient walled city of Jerusalem.

Like other ancient narratives, the Bible is based on oral traditions written down centuries after the events portrayed. It contains Hebrew versions of stories found in other narratives, as well as accounts that are not found anywhere else. The Bible tells of a great flood, for example, like one described in the *Epic of Gilgamesh*. And the Biblical account of infant Moses, placed by his mother in the river in a basket and later found by pharaoh's daughter, is similar to the Sargon story told at the start of this chapter. But the Bible's depiction of the Exodus, in which the pharaoh's army drowns in the Red Sea pursuing Israelites who had passed safely through it, is not found in existing Egyptian records. Scholars thus have difficulty determining exactly what took place, and there is much dispute about how much the Bible represents historical fact.

Israelite Hebrews settle in Palestine and create a kingdom

The first non-Biblical reports of the Israelites locate them around 1200 B.C.E. in Canaan, henceforth called Palestine, where they settled in tribes and fought sporadic wars against other local peoples. Among these foes were the Philistines (*FIL-ih-stēnz*), from whom the name Palestine derives, possibly one of the Sea Peoples that attacked the Hittites and the Egyptians. Within a few centuries, the challenge posed by the Philistines, whose military power made them a threat to all their neighbors, compelled the tribes of Israel to combine forces under a warrior king.

Fought with Philistines

The Kingdoms of Israel

King David centralizes power in Jerusalem

The first such king, Saul, proved a better politician than a general: he united the Israelites under his rule but failed to defeat the Philistines decisively before his death

Document 2.2 Excerpts from the Hebrew Bible

The Hebrew Bible contains compelling stories of the Hebrews and their relations with their God, who reportedly delivered them from bondage in Egypt and then gave them commandments, or laws by which to live.

CROSSING OF THE RED SEA. When the king of Egypt was told that the people had fled . . . , Pharaoh . . . made ready his chariot and took his army with him . . . , and he pursued the people of Israel . . . When Pharaoh drew near, the people of Israel lifted up their eyes, and behold, the Egyptians were marching after them; and they were in great fear . . . And Moses said to the people, "Fear not, stand firm, and see the salvation of the LORD . . . " The LORD said to Moses, " . . . Lift up your rod, and stretch out your hand over the sea and divide it, that the people of Israel may go on dry ground through the sea." . . . Then Moses stretched out his hand over the sea; and the LORD drove the sea back by a strong east wind all night, and made the sea dry land, and the waters were divided. And the people of Israel went into the midst of the sea on dry ground, the waters being a wall to them on their right hand and on their left. The Egyptians pursued, and went in after them into the midst of the sea . . . Then the LORD said to Moses, "Stretch out your hand over the sea, that the water may come back upon the Egyptians, upon their chariots, and upon their horsemen." So Moses stretched forth his hand over the sea . . . The waters returned and covered the chariots and the horsemen and all the host of Pharaoh that had followed them into the sea; not so much as one of them remained. But the people of Israel walked on dry ground through the sea . . .

THE TEN COMMANDMENTS. And the LORD came down upon Mount Sinai . . . ; and the LORD called Moses to the top of the mountain, and Moses went up . . . And God spoke all these words, saying,

"I am the LORD your God, who brought you out of the land of Egypt . . . You shall have no other gods before me . . .

"You shall not make for yourself a graven image, or any likeness of anything that is in heaven above . . .

"You shall not take the name of the LORD your God in vain . . .

"Remember the sabbath day, to keep it holy. Six days you shall labor . . . , but the seventh day is a sabbath to the LORD your God; in it you shall not do any work . . .

"Honor your father and your mother . . .

"You shall not kill.

"You shall not commit adultery.

"You shall not steal.

"You shall not bear false witness against your neighbor.

"You shall not covet your neighbor's house; you shall not covet your neighbor's wife . . . , or anything that is your neighbor's."

SOURCE: New Revised Standard Version Bible, copyright 1989, Division of Christian Education of the National Council of the Churches of Christ in the United States of America. Used by permission. All rights reserved. Exodus 14: 5–6, 8, 13, 15–16, 21–23, 26–27, 28–29; 19: 20; 20: 1–3, 4, 7, 8–10, 12, 13–17.

around 1000 B.C.E. This task was left to his successor David, who won many battles, making his kingdom a prominent power in Palestine. King David also collected taxes, created a standing army, consolidated his realm, and established as its capital the city of Jerusalem. As a result, he is often revered as Israel's greatest ruler.

Israelite prominence nonetheless reached its height in the reign of David's son Solomon, lasting from about 960 to 920 B.C.E. Building on his father's foundation of military security, Solomon transformed Jerusalem into a cosmopolitan city. His lavish

Kingdom splits into Israel and Judah after Solomon's death

Israel's people are dispersed, then Judah's are exiled to Babylon

construction projects included a city wall, a royal palace, and an elaborate temple to Israel's God. He also forged connections with other realms, often through marital alliances: according to the Bible his 700 wives included women from Arabia, Phoenicia, and Anatolia, as well as an Egyptian princess.

But Solomon's splendor caused problems. His massive projects, financed by harsh taxes and built by forced labor, offended the proud people whose ancestors, according to the Bible, had fled such servitude in Egypt. The resulting dissent, after Solomon's death, helped split the realm into two kingdoms (Map 2.10). The northern one, called Israel, lasted until 721 B.C.E., when Assyrian conquerors dispersed and assimilated its people, who thereby vanished from history as Israel's "ten lost tribes." The southern kingdom, known as Judah (after one of Jacob's sons), had a more lasting impact: its people, later called Jews (a term derived from Judah), managed despite numerous hardships to preserve their unique religious heritage.

In the early sixth century B.C.E., Judah was conquered by Chaldeans (New Babylonians), who demolished the temple in Jerusalem and exiled the people to Babylonia. Later, following Persia's conquest of Babylon in 539 B.C.E., the Jews were allowed to return to Jerusalem and build a new temple. They remained, however, a part of the Persian Empire, free to practice their religion but lacking political autonomy. Eventually, along with the rest of West Asia, they were incorporated first into the world of the Greeks and then into the empire of the Romans.

The God of Israel

Throughout their ordeals the Israelites developed what became the Jewish faith. Their deliverance from slavery in Egypt and their covenant with Israel's God laid the foundations of their identity as a chosen people. The unity imposed by their kings and the establishment of Jerusalem as their center of worship helped consolidate this identity. Through division, defeat, and Babylonian captivity they struggled to maintain this identity. During times of trouble prophets arose to speak for their God, whose name Yahweh ("I am") was considered sacred, and to remind them of the covenant and laws that bound them to him and to each other. All these experiences were passed on for ages by word of mouth and eventually recorded in the Bible.

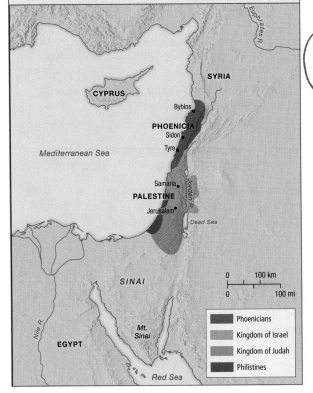

Map 2.10 Israelites and Their Neighbors, Twelfth Through Eighth Centuries B.C.E.

After fleeing Egypt across the Sinai, as related in their Bible, the Israelites settled in Palestine, where they fought the Philistines and others, emerging as a united kingdom by the tenth century B.C.E. Notice, however, that their realm later split into two kingdoms: Israel, whose people were defeated and dispersed by the Assyrians in 721 B.C.E., and Judah, whose people, eventually called Jews, survived later conquest and exile. How and why did the Israelites, a relatively small group of people with little power or wealth, have such an extensive historical impact?

At first the Israelites saw Yahweh as their tribal deity, fearsome and vengeful like other West Asian gods. Eventually, however, the Jews perceived Yahweh as unique. While other gods they knew of could be vengeful and fickle, Yahweh was seen as forgiving and faithful, true to his covenant even when his people turned their backs on him. While other gods were embodied in human forms or graven images, Yahweh was considered a spirit: immortal, invisible, all-powerful, and transcendent. While other gods could be unreasonable and unfair, Yahweh was perceived as just, proclaiming laws based on love of God and neighbor. Above all, Jews came to believe that Yahweh stood alone: he was the one and only God, and all other gods were false.

Jews come to believe in a single, all-powerful God

This concept of a single divinity had enormous potential significance, for it implied that Israel's God was really everyone's God. Centuries later, offshoot monotheistic religions such as Christianity and Islam extended this claim still further, proclaiming that the God of Israel was a universal God whose covenant and laws applied to all humanity. The Hebrew heritage has hence been central to many subsequent societies.

Jewish monotheism will give rise to Christianity and Islam

Chapter Review

Putting It in Perspective

After their emergence in fertile river valleys in the fourth millennium B.C.E., the early societies of Mesopotamia and Egypt developed their cultures and expanded their influence through a complex combination of connections and conflicts. Sometimes these civilizations conquered their neighbors, as in the expansion of Egypt's New Kingdom, imposing on the vanquished the culture of the victors. Sometimes these societies were themselves overrun, by warlike peoples, such as the Akkadians, Amorites, Hyksos, and Assyrians, who then went on to adopt and spread the cultures of those they had conquered. Sometimes other peoples, including the Hittites, Nubians, Phoenicians, and Carthaginians, created connections through both conquest and commerce.

By the first millennium B.C.E., both Mesopotamia and Egypt had lost their independence and come under foreign rule. But these misfortunes also enhanced their influence, which was dispersed far and wide by their successors and conquerors, including eventually the Persians, Greeks, and Romans (Chapters 6, 7, and 8).

Later cultures thereby learned much from ancient West Asia and North Africa. From the Mesopotamians and Egyptians they acquired extensive knowledge in the areas of astronomy, medicine, mathematics, art, sculpture, and architecture. From the Hyksos and Hittites they inherited the use of horses to pull carts and chariots, and the use of metals to make tools and weapons. From the Phoenicians they adopted the use of seafaring ships to maintain distant colonies, and the employment of an alphabet to express their ideas and sounds. From the Jews they eventually inherited monotheism, in the forms of Christianity and Islam. Extensive indeed were the enduring legacies of early West Asian and North African societies.

Reviewing Key Material
KEY CONCEPTS

city-state, 25	Semitic, 31
polytheistic, 26	Sea Peoples, 34
ziggurats, 27	mummification, 38
cuneiform, 28	hieroglyphics, 39
Hammurabi's code, 29	polygyny, 39
dowry, 31	monotheism, 43
Indo-European, 31	covenant, 48

KEY PEOPLE

King Sargon of Akkad, 24   Akhenaton, 43
Gilgamesh, 25   Nefertiti, 43
Enkidu, 25   Tutankhamon, 43
Hammurabi, 29   Ramses II, 43
Menes, 40   Abraham, 48
Zoser, 42   Jacob (Israel), 48
Khufu, 42   Moses, 48
Mentuhotep, 42   Saul, 48
Ahmose, 42   David, 49
Hatshepsut, 43   Solomon, 49
Thutmosis III, 43

ASK YOURSELF

1. What were the main similarities and differences between Mesopotamian and Egyptian civilizations? What circumstances account for the similarities and differences?
2. What key roles did religions play in ancient societies? Why did rulers often portray themselves as descendants and agents of the gods?
3. How did the invention of writing contribute to governance, commerce, religion, law, and the recording of history?
4. How did the religious beliefs of the Hebrews differ from those of their neighbors? What were the main implications of these beliefs? How did these beliefs help the Jews to preserve their identity as a people?
5. How did conflicts and conquests help to spread the achievements of early civilizations? How did cultural and commercial connections contribute to the spread of these achievements?

GOING FURTHER

Aldred, Cyril. *The Egyptians*. Rev. ed. 1984.

Aubet, Maria Eugenia. *The Phoenicians and the West: Politics, Colonies, and Trade*. 1993.

Bahrani, Z. *Women of Babylon*. 2001.

Bertman, S. *Handbook to Life in Ancient Mesopotamia*. 2003.

Blackman, A. *Gods, Priests, and Men*. 1993.

Bottero, J. *Everyday Life in Ancient Mesopotamia*. 2001.

Bright, J. *A History of Israel*. 3rd ed. 1981.

Bryce, T. *The Kingdom of the Hittites*. 1997.

Bryce, T. *Life and Society in the Hittite World*. 2002.

Casson, Lionel. *Everyday Life in Ancient Egypt*. 2001.

Connah, G. *African Civilization: An Archeological Perspective*. 2004.

Crawford, H. *Sumer and the Sumerians*. 2004.

Dalley, Stephanie. *The Legacy of Mesopotamia*. 2006.

David, R. *Religion and Magic in Ancient Egypt*. 2002.

Ehret, Christopher. *The Civilizations of Africa*. 2001

Gil, Moshe. *A History of Palestine*. 1997.

Grant, Michael. *The History of Ancient Israel*. 1984.

Grimal, Nicolas. *A History of Ancient Egypt*. 1992.

Gurney, O. R. *The Hittites*. 2nd ed. 1980.

Ikram, S. *Death and Burial in Ancient Egypt*. 2003.

James, T. G. H. *Pharaoh's People: Scenes from Life in Imperial Egypt*. 1984.

Kemp, Barry J. *Ancient Egypt: Anatomy of a Civilization*. 1989.

Kramer, Samuel N. *History Begins at Sumer*. 1981.

Leick, G. *Mesopotamia: The Invention of the City*. 2002.

Malek, J. *Egypt: 4000 Years of Art*. 2003.

Markoe, G. E. *The Phoenicians*. 2000.

O'Connor, D. *Ancient Nubia*. 1994.

Oates, John. *Babylon*. 1979.

Oren, E. T., ed. *The Sea Peoples and Their World*. 2000.

Postgate, J. N. *Early Mesopotamia: Society and Economy at the Dawn of History*. 1992.

Ray, J. *Reflections of Osiris: Lives from Ancient Egypt*. 2002.

Rice, M. *Egypt's Making: Origins of Ancient Egypt*. 2003.

Saggs, H. W. F. *Babylonians*. 1995.

Shanks, H., ed. *The Rise of Ancient Israel*. 1991.

Shaw, Ian, ed. *The Oxford History of Ancient Egypt*. 2000.

Silverman, David P., ed. *Ancient Egypt*. 1997.

Stiebing, W. H. *Ancient Near Eastern History and Culture*. 2002.

Strouhal, E. *Life of the Ancient Egyptians.* 1992.

Taylor, John. *Egypt and Nubia*. 1991.

Torok, L. *The Kingdom of Kush*. 1997.

Van de Mieroop, Mare. *The Ancient Mesopotamian City*. 1997.

Van de Mieroop, Mare. *History of the Ancient Near East*. 2004.

Welsby, D. A. *The Kingdom of Kush*. 1996.

Key Dates and Developments

West Asia

3500–2350 B.C.E.	Sumerian city-states in lower Mesopotamia
3000–1000 B.C.E.	Indo-European Migrations
2350–2100 B.C.E.	Empire of Akkad in Mesopotamia
2100–1900 B.C.E.	Sumerians again rule lower Mesopotamia
1900–1600 B.C.E.	Babylonians (Amorites) rule in Mesopotamia (*Hammurabi's reign, 1792–1750: Law Code*)
17th–13th centuries B.C.E.	Hittites dominate Anatolia
11th–9th centuries B.C.E.	Phoenicians flourish in Eastern Mediterranean
11th–10th centuries B.C.E.	Kingdom of Israel flourishes in Palestine
10th–7th centuries B.C.E.	Assyrians dominate West Asia
7th–6th centuries B.C.E.	Chaldeans (New Babylonians) dominate West Asia
586–539 B.C.E.	Babylonian Captivity of the Hebrews
6th–4th centuries B.C.E.	Persians dominate West Asia

North Africa

3100–2700 B.C.E.	Archaic Period (*Egypt unified*)
2700–2200 B.C.E.	Egypt's Old Kingdom (*pyramids built*)
2200–2050 B.C.E.	Egypt's 1st Intermediate Period
2050–1700 B.C.E.	Egypt's Middle Kingdom
1700–1570 B.C.E.	Egypt's 2nd Intermediate Period (*Hyksos rule*)
1570–1075 B.C.E.	Egypt's New Kingdom (Egyptian Empire)
13th century B.C.E.	Hebrews leave Egypt (*Moses*)
10th–8th centuries B.C.E.	Egypt under Libyan rule
8th–7th centuries B.C.E.	Egypt under Nubian rule (Kingdom of Kush)
7th century B.C.E.	Assyrians invade Egypt
7th–3rd centuries B.C.E.	Carthage flourishes in eastern Mediterranean
6th–4th centuries B.C.E.	Persians dominate Egypt
6th century B.C.E.– 4th century C.E.	Kingdom of Meroë flourishes along Upper Nile

CHAPTER 3

Societies and Beliefs of Early India, to 300 C.E.

- The Indian Subcontinent

- Harappan India: Early Indus Valley Societies

- Vedic India: The Aryan Impact

- The Religions of India

- Post-Vedic India: Connections and Divisions

- Indian Society and Culture

- Chapter Review

Early Indian Sculpture

India's earliest complex societies, which flourished in the Indus River valley over four thousand years ago (pages 56-59), left behind numerous cultural artifacts, including this sculpture of a bearded man. Based on his stately attire and serene expression, he may have been a ruler or priest.

The **Mahabharata** (*muh-hah-BAH-ruh-tuh*), the world's longest epic poem, tells of a legendary war between related families in ancient India. The epic's most famous segment, the "Song of the Lord" or Bhagavad Gita (*BAH-guh-vahd GĒ-tah*), recounts the reluctance of the warrior Arjuna to fight and kill his own relatives. His chariot driver, a god in human form, explains to Arjuna that, as a member of the warrior caste, it is his sacred duty to fight in battle and fight well. It is permissible to kill in war only if you resolve *not* to spare your kin, since even though the body is slain, the soul will be reborn:

> For certain is the death of the born,
>
> And certain is the birth of the dead;
>
> Therefore that which is inevitable
>
> Thou shouldst not regret.

Thus emboldened by the wisdom of a god, and reassured of the inevitability of both death and rebirth, Arjuna and his kin engage in a lengthy battle that results in extensive slaughter.

Early India

In many ways ancient India, the society that produced the Mahabharata, was similar to Mesopotamia and Egypt. As in those two regions, in India cities emerged near a river where farming had long flourished. Like Mesopotamia and Egypt, India had powerful rulers and priests who served numerous gods and goddesses believed to interact with human beings. Like Mesopotamia and Egypt, India was overrun by outsiders who blended the cultures of the people they conquered with their own culture and spread the combined culture to surrounding regions. As in West Asia and North Africa, such connections and conflicts produced diverse societies that bickered and battled, engaged in commerce, and made major contributions to science, mathematics, literature, and the arts.

As reflected in Arjuna's story, however, India's society was unique in several ways. One was its widespread belief that, as Arjuna was assured, the spirits of those who die are reborn, or reincarnated, into new bodies. While other cultures believed in life after death, usually in another world or a different form of existence, people in India believed that the souls of the dead return to life in *this* world. Another distinction was India's segregation into hereditary occupational groups, such as Arjuna's warrior caste, which people had to stay in until they died and were reborn into another life. Other societies had social classes, but few were as rigid as India's. At the same time, despite the celebration of violence in such epics as the Mahabharata, India also produced belief systems embracing contemplation, passivity, and nonviolence. In a region noted for political fragmentation and almost constant conflict, Indians found hope in the prospect of a better incarnation, security in a rigid social structure, and peace through inner tranquility.

The Indian Subcontinent

India is a subcontinent, a huge land mass substantially separated from the rest of Asia by mountains and seas. To the north are the world's tallest mountains, the towering Himalaya (*HIM-uh-LĀ-uh*) and Hindu Kush (*HIN-doo KOOSH*) ranges. In the south, between the Bay of Bengal and Arabian Sea, is a vast subtropical peninsula that includes the Deccan, an extensive central plateau surrounded by low mountain ranges. Between these regions, stretching across northern India, are broad plains drained by two great rivers: the Ganges (*GAN-jēz*) and the Indus (Map 3.1).

India's geographic diversity promotes political disunity

India's great geographic diversity has fostered political fragmentation, long a dominant feature of Indian society. The challenges involved in vanquishing and ruling so vast and varied a land have deterred or defeated all but a handful of empire builders and leaders. Rare have been the rulers who have managed to unite all of India and keep it united for long.

The terrain and climate have also had other major impacts. The northern mountains have served as both a shield against invasion and a buffer against the icy winds that sweep across Central Asia. But this buffer, along with the subtropical location of much of the subcontinent, also helps to ensure that India has almost relentless heat. Rainfall is seasonal and uneven, with annual monsoon winds bringing heavy rains from surrounding seas in the summer and early fall, especially in the coastal areas and the Ganges valley. Other seasons and other regions, however, tend to be rather dry, and many areas experience recurrent drought.

Ganges and Indus Rivers dominate northern India

In the north, the two great rivers provide abundant water for humans, animals, and the irrigation of crops. The Ganges, rising in the Himalayas, flows south and east to the Bay of Bengal through fertile plains that are favorable for human settlement. Although heavy rains in the Ganges Valley sometimes cause serious flooding, the Ganges has traditionally been viewed as bounteous and benevolent. The Indus River, on the other hand, is far less predictable, prone to significant changes in its depth and course. But it was the Indus, not the Ganges, that gave the subcontinent its name. For it was along the Indus that India's earliest complex societies emerged.

Harappan India: Early Indus Valley Societies

Farming begins in Indus Valley by 7000 B.C.E.

From the majestic Hindu Kush and Himalaya mountains, through the arid plains of what is now Pakistan, the Indus River flows southwest to the warm Arabian Sea. The river usually floods twice a year: once in spring, when melting mountain snow swells the tributaries that feed the river, and once in summer, when the monsoon winds blowing in from the sea bring heavy rains. As in Egypt, the receding floodwaters deposit a rich layer of silt, enabling farmers in the river valley to plant and harvest two crops a year. Thanks partly to this fertility, and partly to farming's eastward spread from West Asia, agriculture came early to the Indus Valley. By 7000 B.C.E., the region was already home to a number of farming villages.

The Early Cities

Towns and cities emerge in Indus Valley by 3000 B.C.E.

As the population increased, the villages grew larger, and by 3000 B.C.E. towns and cities had begun to emerge. As in Mesopotamia and Egypt the growing population, combined perhaps with the need to control the river and irrigate the fields, led to the formation of larger, more complex, and better-organized communities, while farming advances supplied the food surplus needed to support them. Sustained by this surplus, from roughly 2800 to 1700 B.C.E., a cosmopolitan culture with large, thriving cities flourished in the Indus Valley.

The two main cities unearthed by archeologists in the Indus Valley are Mohenjo-Daro (*mō-HEN-jō-DAH-rō*), meaning "Mound of the Dead," and Harappa (*hah-RAP-puh*).

FOUNDATION MAP 3.1 India's Geography and Early Indus Cities, Third Millennium B.C.E.

The Indian subcontinent's main geographic features include the northern mountains that separate it from the rest of Asia, the great Indus and Ganges Rivers that flow from these mountains across northern India, and the vast southern Indian peninsula embracing the Deccan Plateau. Note that India's earliest cities emerged in the northwest, in the Indus River valley, by the third millennium B.C.E. What factors account for the early emergence of agriculture and the rise of cities and towns in this region? Why would this region have more contacts with other cultures than other parts of early India?

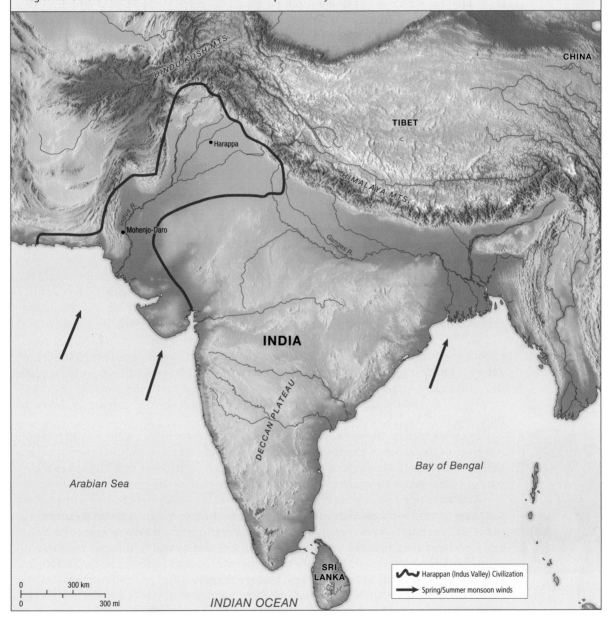

Excavations at Mohenjo-Daro, with citadel in the background.

The entire culture, including these cities and others, is called the Indus Valley or Harappan civilization (Map 3.1).

With 40-foot-thick brick walls, more than three miles around, and populations of 30,000 or more, Harappa and Mohenjo-Daro were similar to cities in ancient Mesopotamia and Egypt. But the early Indus cities were also like many modern ones, with dwellings aligned along straight streets arranged in a grid-like pattern. Working-class districts, with rows of single-room barracks, bordered prosperous neighborhoods of multi-room brick houses with courtyards and bathrooms, served by an ingenious system of pipes that brought water from upriver and deposited waste downstream. Clearly there were disparities between the poor and the rich.

In each city there were temples, marketplaces, and a raised citadel with large buildings probably used by rulers and governing officials. Mohenjo-Daro had a beautiful public bath with a large brick-lined pool, while Harappa had a large grain storage facility, built with a raised floor to protect against floods. These features suggest that each city had a high degree of urban planning and a central authority with the power to carry out large public works projects.

Excavations shed light on early Indus civilization

Farming, Culture, and Commerce

At its height, between roughly 2500 and 2000 B.C.E., the Indus Valley civilization covered over a half million square miles and included hundreds of villages, towns, and cities. Its people raised abundant food, manufactured high-quality goods, devised an elaborate system of symbols, and traded with other societies.

Farming was the foundation of Harappan society. Although wheat was apparently their main food crop, Indus Valley residents also grew rice and barley and herded sheep, cattle, goats, and pigs. Key agricultural achievements included the domestication of chickens and the cultivation of cotton, used to make lightweight clothing suited to the hot climate.

Indus culture centers on farming, fertility, and family

Central to Indus peoples' outlooks were family, nature, and fertility. Numerous carvings and figurines found in their cities, including children's toys and depictions of animals, indicate great respect for family and nature. Religious artifacts, such as phallic symbols and images of large-breasted women, suggest that their worship involved fertility rites. And the sculpture of a stately bearded man, shown on page 54, hints that they may have had a priestly ruling class.

Excavations have also uncovered numerous pottery vessels, as well as farm tools and fine utensils made out of copper and bronze—products that display great metalworking skill. Yet few metal weapons have been found, suggesting perhaps that Harappan societies were less prone to warfare than those of Mesopotamia.

Also uncovered have been numerous square seals, made of soapstone or baked clay, carved with symbols that include depictions of humans, animals, and sacrificial rites. Many scholars have seen these symbols as features of an early writing system, and some speculate that Harappans spoke languages ancestral to those in the Dravidian (*druh-VID-ē-un*) language family that is now dominant in southern India. Other scholars, however, suggest that the symbols are religious, and claim that there is no clear evidence of any Dravidian connection.

One of many inscribed square seals found in the Indus Valley cities.

There is clear evidence, however, that Indus Valley peoples had connections with distant cultures. Harappan clay seals and other Indus artifacts, for example, have been found in the Tigris and Euphrates valleys, while various items made in Mesopotamia have been discovered in India. Especially intriguing are sculptures, excavated at Harappa, that appear to depict Sumerian epic heroes such as Gilgamesh and Enkidu, about whom the Indians must have learned through contact with West Asia.

Indus people connect commercially and culturally with Mesopotamia

The Decline of Harappan Society

In the centuries following 2000 B.C.E., the Indus Valley culture declined. Population seems to have fallen, perhaps on account of climate changes, diseases, or deforestation and soil exhaustion from centuries of intensive farming. There is evidence, too, that movements of the earth's tectonic plates may have unleashed floods and earthquakes that changed the course of the Indus and dried up other rivers in the region, fatally disrupting agricultural and urban patterns. Without surplus food to sustain them, large numbers of people—laborers, merchants, pottery makers, metalworkers, and government officials—apparently left the cities, moving most likely to farming villages so they could raise their own food. By 1700 B.C.E., although farming and herding in the Indus Valley continued, the Harappan cities, with their commerce, governments, and specialized occupations, had been largely abandoned.

Vedic India: The Aryan Impact

As Harappan culture declined, according to many scholars, Indo-European pastoral nomads called Aryans (*AIR-ē-unz*) moved into the Indus Valley from the west and north (Map 3.2). Eventually they spread across northern India, interacting and often clashing with the people who already lived there. Over the next thousand years, from before 1500 B.C.E. until about 500 B.C.E., these connections and conflicts produced a blended culture, distinguished on one hand by political division and conflict, and on the other hand by social stability and control.

Bronze statuette of a dancing girl, found at Mohenjo-Daro.

Indo-European Aryans migrate to north India by 1500 B.C.E.

Aryan Incursions and the Rise of Vedic Culture

The Aryan incursions most likely were part of the general Indo-European migrations described in Chapter 2. Like other early Indo-Europeans, the Aryans were pastoral nomads, herders of cattle and sheep, with metal-tipped weapons and horse-drawn chariots that made them effective warriors. Reputedly light-skinned and ruthless, the ancient Aryans were much later hailed as racial forebears by Nazis and other white supremacists. Scholars, however, reject such racial claims, and instead use terms such as Aryan and Dravidian to designate language groups.

Aryans arrive in India as herders and warriors

At some point before 1500 B.C.E., Aryan speakers started moving into northern India, bringing with them their horses and imposing weapons. There they encountered agricultural peoples, including perhaps Dravidian speakers, with farming villages and fortified towns that may have slowed but did not stop the Aryan advance.

Over several centuries the Aryans prevailed, eventually forming many small contentious kingdoms ruled by warrior kings called rajahs (*RAH-jahz*). As these realms fought one another for regional dominion, regularly raiding one another's herds and attacking each other's domains, conflict and political disunity emerged as central

Aryans prevail over farming peoples of northern India

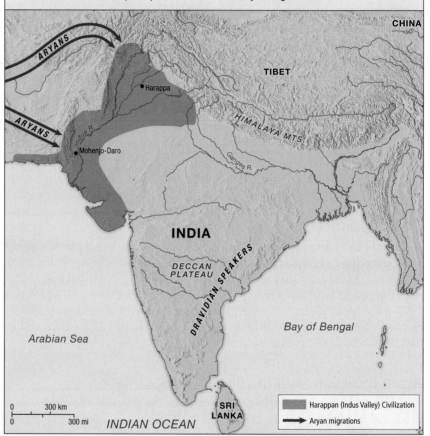

Map 3.2 Aryans Migrate into India, Second Millennium B.C.E.

By 1500 B.C.E., Aryan-speaking peoples had begun moving into India from the northwest, creating historic connections and conflicts with the people who already lived there. Notice that the Aryans came first to the Indus River Valley, birthplace of Harappan civilization, and perhaps interacted with users of Dravidian languages, now spoken mainly in southern India. What were the major impacts on India of the Aryan migrations?

hallmarks of Indian society. But conflict and disunity did not prevent the development of Indian culture.

The culture that developed in Aryan India is often called **Vedic** (*VĀ-dik*), since much of what we know about it comes from Vedas (*VĀ-dahz*), sacred hymns composed by Aryan priests for use in religious rituals. Since the Aryans initially had no writing system, Vedas were composed in oral form, largely between 1500 and 1000 B.C.E., in meters and stanzas that made them easy to remember. Committed to memory, they were passed on by word of mouth for centuries. Only after 800 B.C.E., when a writing system emerged, were the Vedas actually written down.

Although religious in intent, the Vedas provide abundant information about Aryan culture (see "Excerpts from the Rig Veda"). They depict Aryans as people who loved

Document 3.1 Excerpts from the Rig Veda

The Vedas, composed as sacred hymns, provide many insights into ancient Aryan culture. The following excerpts from the Rig Veda reflect Aryan devotion to the war god Indra and Aryan fascination with warfare, competition, and gambling.

WHO IS INDRA?

The god who had insight the moment he was born, the first who protected the gods with his power of thought, before whose hot breath the two world-halves tremble at the greatness of his manly powers—he, my people, is Indra . . .

He . . . who drove the race of Dasas down into obscurity, who took away the flourishing wealth of the enemy as a winning gambler takes the stake—he, my people, is Indra . . .

He who encourages the weary and sick, . . . he who has lips for fine drinking—he, my people, is Indra . . .

He, the mighty bull . . . who with his thunderbolts in his hand hurled down [the enemy] as he was climbing up to the sky—he, my people, is Indra . . .

TO ARMS

His face is like a thundercloud, when the armored warrior goes into the lap of battles. Conquer with an unwounded body; let the power of armor keep you safe.

With the bow . . . let us win the contest and violent battles with the bow. The bow ruins the enemy's pleasure; with the bow let us conquer all the corners of the world . . .

Standing in the chariot, the skilful charioteer drives his prize-winning horses forward wherever he wishes to go. Praise the power of the reins: the guides follow the mind that is behind them . . .

Spare us, O weapon flying true to its mark; let our body be stone . . .

Whoever would harm us, . . . let all the gods ruin him. My inner armor is prayer.

THE GAMBLER'S LAMENT

The dice seem to me like a drink . . . keeping me awake at night . . .

When I swear, 'I will not play with them,' I am left behind by my friends as they depart. But when the brown dice raise their voice as they are thrown down, I run at once to rendezvous with them, like a woman to her lover.

The gambler goes to the meeting hall, asking himself "Will I win?" and trembling with hope. But the dice cross him and counter his desire, giving the winning throws to his opponent.

The dice goad like hooks and prick like whips; they enslave, deceive, and torment . . . They are coated with honey—an irresistible power over the gambler.

SOURCE: Wendy D. O'Flaherty, editor and translator, *The Rig Veda: An Anthology* (New York: Penguin Books, 1984) 160–161, 236–237, 240–241.

wine and music, lived in patriarchal families, worshiped numerous deities, sacrificed animals to the gods, and believed in life after death. As portrayed in the Vedas, Aryans also glorified bravery and warfare, often fighting among themselves as well as against other peoples. The Rig Veda, the oldest and most famous of the Vedas, exalts the Aryan war god Indra, wielder of thunderbolts and destroyer of towns, and asks him to help the nomadic Aryans destroy enemy settlements. The Vedas further suggest that Aryans were fond of competition and gambling, traits that may help explain why they are traditionally credited with inventing both dice and chess.

While thus acclaiming the Aryans, whose very name means "noble," the Vedas disparage the defeated peoples as Dasa (*DAH-suh*), a term meaning "subject" or "slave." This attitude reflects not only the conquerors' contempt for the conquered, but also the disdain of nomadic warriors for settled farming peoples, whom the nomads saw as enslaved to the land and shackled to their villages and towns.

Aryan ways blend with farming cultures to form a complex, diverse society

Eventually, however, as had happened after conquests in West Asia and North Africa, the conquerors adapted ideas and ways from the people they had conquered. In time, for example, Aryans built towns, took up settled farming, and even intermarried with Dravidian speakers and others. Aryan religion became infused with the spirituality of India's farmers, focusing on fertility, stressing nature's cycles of destruction and rebirth, and inferring from these cycles that people's spirits are reborn in a new body after death. As a result of such blending, by 500 B.C.E., India was home to a very complex and multi-faceted society.

The Emergence of Caste

Aryan society, as portrayed in the Vedas, was divided into classes called **varnas**, based on the functions fulfilled by their members in society. At the top were the priests, or Brahmins, who performed religious rituals and sustained sacred legends, and the warriors, or Kshatriya (*kuh-SHAH-trē-uh*), who protected society. At first the warriors apparently were preeminent, but over time the Brahmins, esteemed for their ability to gain favor with the gods, gained superior status. Below the priests and warriors were the commoners, or Vaishya (*VĪSH-yuh*), who performed basic services such as farming, herding, and trading. Below them were the servants, or Shudra (*SHOO-druh*), consisting initially of conquered peoples compelled to menial labor.

Indian society evolves into rigid class system

For centuries after the Aryan incursions, interclass mobility and marriage seems to have been fairly common, blurring class boundaries and diminishing distinctions between Aryans and non-Aryans. As time went on, however, the system became more rigid. Upper-class families, anxious to protect their status, increasingly refused to socialize or arrange marriages with those of lower rank. The classes thus hardened into **castes**, exclusive and restrictive hereditary occupational groupings, based on birth and ranked in hierarchical order. People were expected to fulfill their caste's occupational functions, to marry and share meals within their caste, and to observe its dress and behavioral codes.

Jatis emerge as social-economic subcaste communities

As society grew more complex, numerous regional subcastes, called **jatis** (*JAH-tēz*), emerged. As a rule each jati identified with a certain trade, a specific locale, and often a particular god or goddess. Each jati, embracing hundreds of families, functioned as a community: its members ate, worked, socialized, and intermarried mainly with each other, and cared for one another during times of need. Jatis often vied with each other for higher ranking in the social structure.

Castes also came to be connected with religious notions of purity and pollution. On one end of the spectrum were Brahmins, regarded as pure since they dealt with spiritual rather than bodily functions. On the other end were those who did work that was seen as impure—such as jobs involving contact with dead bodies and human or animal waste. Since touching people who did such work was considered a source of pollution, or spiritual contamination, they were widely shunned as "untouchables," ranking even below the Shudra at the bottom of Indian society.

Family, Status, and Stability

Although Indian society limited freedom and mobility, it provided considerable stability. Grouped by family, occupation, and heredity, people almost always knew their place and what was expected of them. Within the family, for example, women were clearly subordinate to men, and children were strictly subject to their parents. Within the larger society, occupations were determined by caste membership and duties were clearly prescribed. Each caste and subcaste supervised and protected its own members, providing them with security and employment. Deeply rooted in family and status, India's social structure was stratified, hierarchical, and stable.

Yet social interaction and upward mobility were not entirely impossible. Social interaction could occur when people of different castes worshiped together, for example, or when they participated jointly in village festivals and councils. Upward mobility could take place in several ways. One was available to subcastes: an entire jati that excelled in its work could hope to move up within the social hierarchy. Another was available to individuals: those who lived good lives and performed their duties well could hope for a higher standing in their next incarnation, according to India's distinctive religious beliefs.

Jatis and individuals can improve status through good work

The Religions of India

The religious beliefs that emerged in Vedic India, fostered largely by the Brahmin (priestly) caste, are often referred to as the Vedic religion or Brahmanism. Centered on a universal and eternal spiritual source called Brahman, and including a wide array of distinctive gods and rituals, this early religion set forth three basic concepts that have since been central to the Indian worldview: samsara (*sam-SAH-ruh*), dharma, and karma.

Samsara, sometimes called "reincarnation" or "transmigration of souls," was the basic belief that each being has a soul or eternal spiritual core called the Atman, identified with and encompassed in the Brahman, which is reborn into a new body after the old one dies. Each person thus has an ongoing series of lives. **Dharma** represented the faithful performance of the duties that pertained to one's caste or station in life. **Karma** referred to one's fate or destiny in the next incarnation, based on performance of one's dharma in the current life. Those who dutifully carried out their dharma would thereby have good karma and thus be reborn through samsara into a higher status. Those who did not fulfill their dharma would have bad karma and thus likely be reborn into a lower status. A servant who did her job well, for example, could improve her caste status in the next life, while a warrior who fought poorly could be reincarnated into a lower caste.

The Wheel of Dharma, an ancient symbol of Indian Buddhist values.

These three concepts reinforced the social structure. Fearful of acquiring bad karma, and thus undermining their chance for rebirth into a higher caste, lower caste members felt compelled to do their duties, accept their low status, and endure the dominance of priests and warriors. The privileged status of the upper castes was thus also preserved.

Dharma, karma, and samsara reinforce social stability

At the end of the Vedic era, however, around 500 B.C.E., several new religions began to challenge this social structure. Rejecting the concept of caste, Jainism (*JĪN-iz-um*) and Buddhism saw karma and samsara not as the means to a better life but as hardships trapping the soul in an endless cycle of lives. The ultimate goal of these new faiths was to free the soul from this cycle and provide salvation from suffering.

Jains and Buddhists seek salvation from endless cycle of lives

Jainism: Reverence for All Living Things

Jainism was based on the teachings of a wandering religious figure known as Mahavira (*mah-hah-VĒ-rah*), the "great hero," or Jina (*JĪ-nah*), the "conqueror," who lived from around 540 to 486 B.C.E. At the age of 30, according to tradition, he chose a life of **asceticism** (*uh-SET-ih-siz'm*), renouncing all possessions and practicing extreme self-denial, while also promoting pacifism and vegetarianism. His followers, called Jains, believed that all living things—including animals, insects, and plants—possess an eternal spirit and must be treated with reverence.

Jains stress *ahimsa*: nonviolence toward all living things

Jains therefore practiced **ahimsa** (*ah-HIM-sah*), or nonviolence toward all living things. Some Jains even swept the ground ahead of them to avoid stepping on insects and wore face masks to avoid inhaling tiny gnats and flies. By showing profound reverence for life in all its forms, Jains believed they could purify their spirits and eventually attain **moksha** (*MŌK-shah*), or liberation from the cycle of death and reincarnation.

Although Jains, who spurned the inequalities of caste, were widely admired by members of the lower castes, few actually practiced Jainism in its entirety. Most engaged in occupations, such as farming or herding, that at times involved the killing of plants or animals, practices that went against Jainist teachings. Only people such as merchants or scholars, whose trades did not involve such practices, or monks and nuns, who renounced worldly pleasures, could hope to lead a fully Jainist life. Jainist ideals were influential, but few could fully follow them. Jains thus remained throughout the centuries a small religious minority.

Buddhism: The Path to Inner Peace

Buddhism, on the other hand, became one of the world's most widely practiced religions. It grew out of the teachings of Siddhartha Gautama (*sih-DAHR-tah GOW-tah-mah*), a spiritual leader whose influence compares to that of Moses, Confucius, Jesus, and Muhammad. Born into a princely family in the Himalayan foothills of what is now Nepal, Gautama reportedly lived from 563 to 483 B.C.E. According to Buddhist traditions, he enjoyed great comfort in his early life, protected by his parents from all distress. At age 29, however, he ventured outside his palace, eventually encountering an old man, a sick man, and a dead man. Determined to discover the meaning of aging, illness, and death, he left his wife and family to lead an ascetic life. For six years he practiced extreme self-denial, eating sparsely and avoiding most other pleasures. But he found this life no more fulfilling than his earlier self-indulgence.

Siddhartha Gautama gains enlightenment, becoming the Buddha

Finally, while meditating near the Ganges River underneath a tree, Gautama experienced enlightenment, a revelation enabling him to comprehend the secrets of salvation from human suffering. For the rest of his life he traveled throughout northeastern India, gathering disciples, preaching to all who would listen, and sharing the wisdom that had been imparted to him. He came to be known as the Buddha ("enlightened one"), and his followers eventually were called Buddhists.

The Buddha's central teachings, known as the "Four Noble Truths," can be summarized briefly as follows: (1) Life consists of pain and suffering. (2) Pain and suffering are caused by desire. (3) To escape from suffering, one must curb desire. (4) Desire can be curbed by righteous living. To live righteously, one must follow the "Eightfold Path," which entails right thinking, right purpose, right conduct, right speech, right livelihood, right effort, right awareness, and right contemplation. Buddhists are expected to be kind, pure, truthful, and charitable, and to refrain from faultfinding, envy, hatred, and violence—although their adherence to ahimsa is typically less total than that of the Jains. If the faithful absorb these truths and follow this path they can eventually achieve enlightenment, like the Buddha himself, and ultimately escape the cycle of karma and samsara by attaining **nirvana** (*nir-VAH-nah*), a state of infinite tranquility.

These beliefs made Buddhism widely attractive. Like Jainism, Buddhism respected all beings and rejected caste inequalities, thus appealing to people of low social status, such as servants, merchants, and farmers. Unlike Jainism, however, Buddhism counseled moderation: it provided a simple and elegant formula for escape from suffering, not through extreme self-sacrifice or rigid adherence to ahimsa, but through self-awareness, meditation, avoidance of ambition, and pursuit of inner peace.

Buddhism's simple, attractive teachings gain it a wide following

Hinduism: Unity amid Diversity

Challenged by Jainism and Buddhism, which spread slowly throughout India in the centuries after 500 B.C.E., the Vedic religion adapted and endured in the form of Hinduism, an assortment of beliefs and practices that eventually evolved into India's main faith. Unlike Jainism, Buddhism, and other major religions, Hinduism was not based on the revelations of a famous founder or teacher; instead it developed organically in concert with Indian society. Rather than becoming an organized church with a fixed ritual and creed, Hinduism remained a flexible faith with a wide array of divinities, doctrines, and devotions. Supremely adaptable, it readily embraced new gods and new beliefs, including concepts adapted from the Jains and Buddhists.

Traditional Vedic beliefs evolve into Hindu religion

Like their Vedic ancestors, Hindus worshiped a multitude of deities, the most prominent of which was Brahma, seen as the supreme creator and universal being. Other gods and goddesses, however, came to be more widely revered. Shiva (*SHE-vah*), the mighty "destroyer" and "lord of the dance," was a god who embodied the eternal cycle of destruction and renewal. Vishnu (*VISH-noo*), the valiant "preserver" and protector of the world against demonic powers, was a god said to take on different incarnations as needed—including Rama (*RAH-muh*), the ideal man and a model of virtue and reason, and Krishna (*KRESH-nuh*), a benevolent god who involved himself directly in human affairs. Among the main goddesses were Lakshmi (*LUK-shme*), a popular deity identified with wealth and good fortune; Kali, a fearsome divinity linked with violence and death; and Durga, a multi-armed warrior often pictured riding on a lion or tiger. All three were seen as manifestations of a supreme mother goddess, sometimes called Devi (*DA-ve*), a Hindu term for goddess.

Hindu deities Vishnu and Lakshmi depicted in stone sculpture as sensuous lovers.

Unlike Jains and Buddhists, Hindus accepted the caste system, including the notion that an honorable life meant fulfilling one's caste functions. Like Jains, however, Hindus came to believe that they could eventually achieve moksha, gaining an eternal peace akin to the Buddhist nirvana—except that for Hindus this peace involved a union of the personal soul or spiritual core (Atman) with the universal life force (Brahman). Hindus sought to secure this salvation by dedication to their caste duties, devotion to the gods, meditation, and reverence for life.

Hindus come to seek eventual salvation through devotion to caste duties

Although, like Jains and Buddhists, Hindus revered all forms of life, they developed a special veneration for certain places and beings. For example, they regarded the

Hindus revere shrines, pilgrimages, the Ganges River, and cows

Ganges, the source of life-giving waters, as a sacred river, bathing in it for spiritual purification. They treated cows, the source of nourishing milk, as sacred, allowing them to roam undisturbed through towns and villages as symbols of nature's benevolence. They prayed at numerous sacred sites and shrines, making regular pilgrimages to these places. Believing in a rich diversity of divinities, Hindus saw them all as manifold expressions of Brahman—the single, unifying, universal force.

Post-Vedic India: Connections and Divisions

Buddhism's spread and West Asian connections shape post-Vedic India

In the late sixth century B.C.E., several key developments marked the transition from India's Vedic era, traditionally dated as ending around 500 B.C.E., to the post-Vedic era. One was the emergence of Buddhism, a compelling new religion that gained widespread influence throughout India and beyond. Another was the invasion and conquest of northwestern India, between 518 and 513 B.C.E., by the Persians, whose rule of that region vastly increased India's connections with other cultures. In the centuries that followed, both the spread of Buddhism and contacts with outside cultures played key roles in shaping Indian society.

Magadha flourishes south of the Ganges, but India remains disunited

Political disunity continued in post-Vedic India. In the sixth century B.C.E. there were 16 major kingdoms and principalities in northern India alone, including the one where Siddhartha Gautama was born. The dominant kingdom in the north was Magadha (*MAH-guh-duh*), located mostly south of the lower Ganges, in a hilly area laden with visible iron ore deposits. For several centuries Magadha flourished, prospering from its iron mines, agriculture, and control of the Ganges regional trade. But its sporadic efforts to gain sway over its neighbors achieved only limited success.

Conflicts and Contacts with Persians and Greeks

Persian conquest of Indus Valley links India with West Asia

While Magadha flourished in northeast India, new intruders arrived in the northwest. Around 518 B.C.E., forces from the Persian Empire, a realm that had recently expanded across West Asia, began probing the Indus Valley, eventually subjecting it to Persian rule for most of the next two centuries (Map 3.3). Although only this part of India was actually ruled by Persia, most of the subcontinent was affected in some way by the Persian presence. It brought unprecedented trade and contact, not just with Persia but also with cultures in West Asia and North Africa that came under Persian rule. These contacts, for example, enabled Indians to export spices, perfumes, gems, and cotton textiles to the lands of the eastern Mediterranean and in return to receive such goods as wine, tin, and gold.

Alexander invades northwest India, but his forces refuse to go farther

These increased connections, by spreading awareness of India's vast resources and potential wealth, eventually brought new conflicts. In 326 B.C.E. the famed Macedonian warrior Alexander the Great, having overrun Persia with his Greek and Macedonian armies (Chapter 7), invaded India in hopes of bringing its lands and wealth under his control. One Indian rajah tried to halt the intruders with a force of 200 war elephants. But Alexander's soldiers fired flaming arrows, frightening the huge beasts, who then stampeded and trampled the rajah's infantry.

Alexander, however, was unable to follow up on his victory. His men, already far from home, refused to advance any farther, compelling him to turn back toward West

Map 3.3 Persian Empire Connects India with West Asia and North Africa After 518 B.C.E.

For almost two centuries, from about 518 until 326 B.C.E., the Persians ruled northwestern India, enhancing its commercial and cultural connections with West Asia and North Africa. Note, however, that the rest of India, also affected by these enhanced connections, was governed by various independent principalities and kingdoms, most notably the wealthy Magadha realm in the lower Ganges region. What were the major impacts on India of the Persian connection?

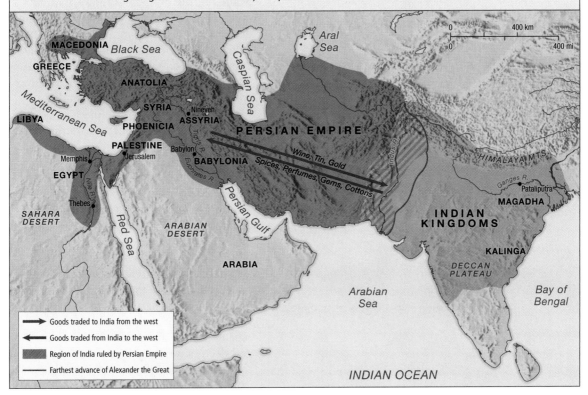

Asia. Although he left behind some officials and soldiers to administer northwest India, they could not perpetuate his control of the region. His unexpected death in 323 B.C.E. created widespread confusion, clearing the way for the formation of India's first full-fledged empire.

The Rise of the Mauryan Empire

In the muddled situation surrounding Alexander's death, Chandragupta Maurya (*chahn-druh-GOOP-tah MOW-rē-ah*), ruler of a minor Ganges Valley principality, saw a chance to expand his power. Having joined in the struggle against Alexander's forces, he adopted some of their military methods to defeat his Indian rivals. By 321 B.C.E. he had gained control of the Magadha kingdom and much of the Ganges basin. He then moved northwest into the Indus Valley, vacated by Alexander's departure, and added it to his domains. In 305 B.C.E. he turned back an effort by Seleucus Nikator (*sih-LOO-kus nih-KAH-tor*), Alexander's former lieutenant and founder of the Seleucid (*sih-LOO-sid*) kingdom in Persia, to retake the

Chandragupta Maurya forms Mauryan Empire in northern India

Map 3.4 Mauryan Empire Unites Much of India, 321–184 B.C.E.

The Mauryan Empire, founded by Chandragupta Maurya, united and connected most of northern India by 300 B.C.E. Notice that by 250 B.C.E., during the reign of his grandson Ashoka, the empire connected much of the subcontinent. How did the Mauryans learn and benefit from contacts with other cultures, and what were the major impacts on India of Mauryan rule?

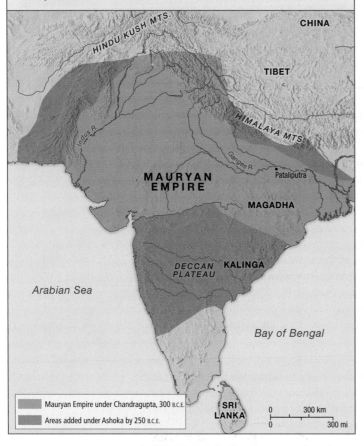

Mauryan Empire under Chandragupta, 300 B.C.E.

Areas added under Ashoka by 250 B.C.E.

Mauryan Empire expands to control much of India

Indus region. In exchange for 500 war elephants, Seleucus agreed to withdraw his forces from northwestern India, leaving this entire region under Chandragupta's rule.

Chandragupta Maurya thus created the Mauryan (*MOW-rē-un*) Empire, uniting much of India in a prosperous and populous domain that lasted from 321 to 184 B.C.E. (Map 3.4). The empire exemplified the benefits of connections among cultures, combining Indian religion and social structure with Persian administrative methods and Macedonian military techniques, while expanding India's commerce with the Mediterranean world.

The Mauryan Empire developed an impressive system of roads and public works, a magnificent capital city at Pataliputra (*PAH-tah-lih-POO-trah*)—now called Patna (*PUTT-nah*)—on the Ganges, and an extensive bureaucracy of officials who administered the realm. The empire also had a huge standing army, reportedly consisting of more than a half million soldiers, and a vast network of spies and special agents to protect its ruler against rebellion or assassination. Imperial laws and decrees were rigidly enforced, and those who defied them were brutally punished. According to legend, however, in his final years Chandragupta embraced Jainism and practiced ahimsa, giving up his throne to become a simple monk.

By this time, around 300 B.C.E., Chandragupta's realm included most of northern India. His policies were continued and extended by his son, who conquered and annexed the vast central Indian plateau called the Deccan. But it was Chandragupta's grandson Ashoka (*ah-SHŌ-kah*), reigning from around 270 until 232 B.C.E., who proved the most memorable of all the Mauryan rulers.

Ashoka's Reign: Buddhism and Paternalism

violent greedy

Ashoka's reign began in violence when he defeated his older brothers in a bloody civil war. Then, like his predecessors, Ashoka embarked on a course of military expansion. In conquering the east coast region of Kalinga, his armies killed many thousands of people. The carnage is said to have so sickened Ashoka that he had a profound change of

heart, renouncing violence and publicly expressing remorse for the misery he had caused. *vegetarian*
He converted to Buddhism, gave up hunting and eating meat, and embraced <u>ahimsa</u>.

Ashoka then used his imperial powers to propagate his new faith. He traveled about preaching Buddhist principles and urged his officials to do likewise. He built numerous Buddhist temples and shrines, patronized Buddhist scholarship and art, and established a number of Buddhist religious communities. He had huge polished stone pillars, carved with his edicts and Buddhist teachings, erected throughout his realm. He hosted Buddhism's Third Great Council, helping thereby to standardize doctrines and resolve religious disputes. According to tradition, he even sent his daughter and son as Buddhist missionaries to the island now called Sri Lanka off India's southern coast. Buddhism, formerly practiced only in parts of northern India, thus spread across the subcontinent and beyond.

Ashoka renounces violence and widely promotes Buddhism

Ashoka also practiced what he preached, creating a benevolent, paternalistic government devoted to the welfare of his subjects, whom he referred to as his children. He dispatched special agents throughout the realm to learn people's needs and ensure that local officials treated them with compassion and respect. To encourage commerce and religious pilgrimages he constructed numerous roads, with rest houses, shade trees, and watering spots along the way. To improve his people's lives, he established hospitals, had wells dug for water, and built irrigation systems. Despite his devotion to Buddhism, he respected and supported other faiths such as Hinduism and Jainism, helping to maintain their shrines and promote their worship. During his long and successful reign he personified the ideal Buddhist king, setting a standard of humanitarian rule that few other monarchs in history would match.

Ashoka's rule, however, was based not just on Buddhism and paternalism, but also on political control, sustained by the empire's large bureaucracy and army. His numerous officials and soldiers collected taxes, enforced his laws, and supervised his public works projects, effectively administering a huge kingdom with numerous people speaking many different languages. Ashoka's authorities used force sparingly, but the threat of its use helped hold his vast realm together. Indeed, Ashoka's promotion of Buddhism and nonviolence, while no doubt sincere, also served to dissuade his subjects from violently resisting his rule.

India After Ashoka: New Connections and Conflicts

Unfortunately for India, Ashoka's successors were neither as humane nor as capable as he. The Mauryan Empire under their rule was weakened by corruption and local revolts, and by financial problems that were worsened by the huge expenses of its bureaucracy and army. As its power steadily declined, so did the territory under its control. The empire finally ceased to exist in 184 B.C.E., when its last ruler was killed by one of his own commanders.

The collapse of the Mauryan Empire began five centuries of political disunity in India. In both the north and the south, a series of small kingdoms emerged. As in the Vedic era, India's great size and diversity once more stood in the way of centralization.

Mauryan collapse initiates five centuries of Indian disunity

Disunity, however, was by no means a disaster. During this era, in spite of their divisions, Indians greatly expanded their contacts with other cultures. Sea lanes linked the subcontinent with Egypt and Arabia across the Arabian Sea, and with southeast Asia across the Bay of Bengal, while land routes connected it through Persia with the West, and through central Asia to China (Map 3.5). Indian monks traveled to southeast and

Indian connections grow with other cultures east and west

Map 3.5 Trade Routes Link India with Other Lands by Late First Millennium B.C.E.

In the centuries of disunity following the Mauryan Empire's collapse in 184 B.C.E., Indians expanded their commercial and cultural connections, using land and sea routes that linked India with other parts of Asia. Notice that, because the Himalaya Mountains were virtually impassable, the main land routes from India to China went north from the Indus Valley, then east through Central Asia along the Silk Road (Chapter 4). Note also that sea routes connected India with diverse cultures to its east and west. What key impacts did these connections have on Indian culture and commerce?

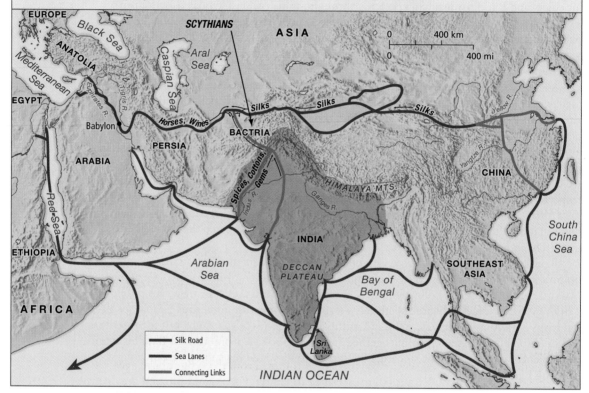

central Asia, and from there to China, preaching the Buddha's message and translating Buddhist writings into different languages. Indian merchants traded extensively with other lands, exporting pepper and other spices, cottons, and precious gems, while importing horses, metal wares, silks, and wines.

Southern India, separate from north, develops regional connections

Meanwhile southern India, separated from the rest of the subcontinent by the Deccan plateau and its adjacent mountain ranges, remained largely indifferent toward the north. Buddhist missionaries often traveled from the north to the south, and merchants conducted trade between the two regions, but given the lengthy and dangerous land travel required, such commerce was not extensive during this period. The kingdoms in the south found it more rewarding to trade by sea, first with the Mediterranean world and later with Southeast Asia. They also warred incessantly with one another and showed no interest in unification.

NORTHERN KINGDOMS AND CONNECTIONS. In the north, around 180 B.C.E., descendants of the soldiers of Alexander the Great established a Greco-Bactrian kingdom in the Indus

Valley and neighboring Bactria (present-day Afghanistan). This regime, looking westward toward Greece, expanded northern India's connections with the Mediterranean world. Beginning around 100 B.C.E., however, the Greco-Bactrians were invaded by Scythians (*SIH-thē-unz*), pastoral nomads driven from their Central Asian homelands (Map 3.5). By 88 B.C.E. the Scythians were entering the Indus Valley, and in 50 B.C.E. they overran that region and destroyed the Greco-Bactrian kingdom.

Scythian rule lasted only a century. By 50 C.E. the Kushans (*koo-SHAHNZ*), the nomadic people who had originally pushed the Scythians out of Central Asia, now drove them from northwest India as well. Forced to move south, many Scythians eventually assimilated into Indian culture, settling in central India, adopting new names, and converting to Hinduism. The Kushans, meanwhile, established in the north a sizable kingdom centered in the upper Indus Valley.

Kushans displace Scythians, driving them south, around 50 C.E.

For almost two centuries, from around 50 to 240 C.E., the Kushans dominated Bactria and parts of northern India. Their kingdom sat astride the trade routes connecting India with China and West Asia, making it a crossroads of both commerce and ideas. From the West, for example, came products such as wines, jewelry, and horses, as well such ideas as the seven-day week, the 60-minute hour, and the solar calendar. From China came porcelain wares and especially silk, a cloth so prized that the main east-west trade route was known as the Silk Road (Chapter 4). From India came spices and cotton cloth, scholars, artists, and poets, and above all Buddhist ideals, which spread from India to Central and East Asia by way of the Kushan Kingdom.

Kushans dominate trade routes connecting India with much of Eurasia

BUDDHISM'S SPREAD AND DIVISION. The most influential Kushan king was Kanishka (*kah-NISH-kah*), whose reign of several decades began at some point between 78 and 144 C.E. A man of broad vision and territorial ambition, he expanded southward toward central India and north into central Asia, creating a large, multicultural kingdom. He is best known, however, for supporting Buddhism and helping to spread it throughout his kingdom and beyond (Map 3.6). Kanishka, who like Ashoka may have been a convert to Buddhism, sent Buddhist missionaries into Central Asia, where they preached the faith to merchants and others in towns along the trade routes. From there Buddhism eventually spread to East Asia, where it later flourished in China, Korea, and Japan. Like Ashoka, Kanishka promoted Buddhist architecture, sculpture, and art. Indeed, the famous popular depictions of the Buddha, seated in meditation with his legs crossed, originated in the Kushan era.

Kanishka expands Kushan Kingdom and widely promotes Buddhism

Kanishka was assisted in his efforts by Ashvaghosha (*ahsh-VUH-gō-shuh*), a gifted Indian dramatist and poet who seems to have been a spiritual advisor to the Kushan king. Raised as a devout Hindu of the Brahmin caste, Ashvaghosha was reportedly a staunch opponent of Buddhism until he was won over in a spirited debate with a noted Buddhist teacher. The author of elegant essays, plays, and poems, including a famous Life of the Buddha written in poetic verse, Ashvaghosha was influential at Buddhism's Fourth Great Council, hosted by King Kanishka, which confirmed the division of Buddhism into two major branches.

Aided by poet Ashvaghosha, Kanishka hosts great Buddhist council

In the centuries before the council, Buddhism as practiced in northwestern India had evolved into an elaborate religion, marked by devotions to numerous divinities and holy persons. Its followers there exalted the Buddha not just as a man who had attained enlightenment but also as a god who could help them gain salvation from suffering. They also venerated various other buddhas and bodhisattvas (*bō-di-SAHT-vuhz*), saintly

Map 3.6 The Kushan Kingdom (50–240 C.E.) and Buddhism's Spread

Over many centuries, Buddhism spread from its birthplace in northern India throughout much of Asia. Notice that the Kushan Kingdom (50–240 C.E.), where Mahayana Buddhism flourished, sat astride the trade routes (shown on Map 3.5) that connected India with Central Asia and China. How did the Kushans contribute to the development and spread of Mahayana Buddhism?

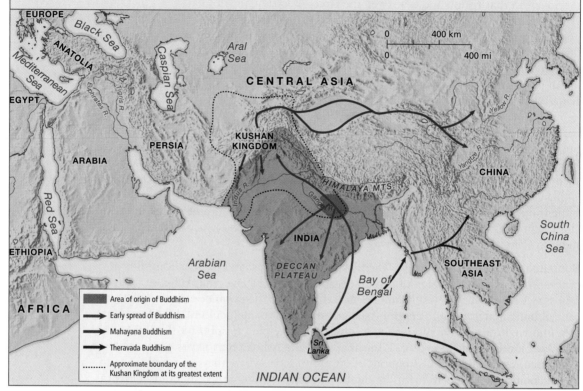

figures who, having gained enlightenment, were moved by compassion to postpone their own nirvana so they could help save others.

Mahayana dominates Kanishka's council, leading to Buddhist split

Devotees of this form of Buddhism called it Mahayana (*mah-hah-YAH-nah*), the "greater vehicle," claiming it saved more people than traditional forms, which shunned such devotions and stressed instead withdrawal from worldly pursuits. Merchants, artisans, officials, and others who were unwilling or unable to set aside their worldly pursuits thus tended to favor Mahayana, which enabled them to seek salvation through devotions and compassion. Mahayana supporters, including Ashvaghosha, dominated the Fourth Great Council, which affirmed their teachings. As the form of the faith embraced by the Kushans and spread by them to Central and East Asia, Mahayana was the main branch of Buddhism that later took hold in China, Korea, and Japan.

Mahayana Buddhism spreads throughout Central and East Asia

Traditional Buddhists, however, rejected the Fourth Council and its teachings. They promoted instead strict adherence to the Buddha's original principles, focusing on righteous living and enlightenment rather than devotions to divinities. Scorned by Mahayana supporters as Hinayana (HĒ-nah-YAH-nah), the "lesser vehicle," traditional Buddhism nonetheless endured in several forms. One, known as Theravada (ter-ah-VAH-dah), the "way of the elders," flourished in Sri Lanka and spread to Southeast Asia, where it remains the main belief system today.

HINDUISM'S EVOLUTION AND ENDURANCE. The reign of Kanishka marked a high point of Kushan power. His successors, less talented than he, failed to consolidate and maintain their hold on the regions he had conquered. By 240 C.E. the Kushan Kingdom had lost most of its lands and had ceased to be an important regional force.

Traditional Theravada Buddhism endures in Southeast Asia

Kanishka's reign also marked a high point of Buddhist influence in India. Divided into competing factions and deprived of its most powerful patron by the Kushan Kingdom's decline, Buddhism began its own slow decline in the Indian subcontinent, even as the faith was spreading to other Asian cultures.

Buddhism's gradual decline in India coincided with Hinduism's gradual evolution into a popular religion. Hinduism competed successfully with Buddhism partly by making the Buddha one of the various incarnations of the Hindu god Vishnu. Above all, however, Hinduism evolved in ways that widened its appeal, softening its asceticism and elitism, while helping it better meet the needs of the lower classes.

Hinduism, competing with Buddhism, evolves into popular faith

As practiced over time by the masses, popular Hinduism invited believers to fully enjoy life within the context of their caste. Although Hindus still had to fulfill their caste's occupational functions, within this framework they were encouraged to seek material success. Merchants or farmers, for example, could pursue prosperity by doing their caste duties honorably and well, thereby improving both their comfort in this life and their status in their next incarnation. Likewise, although Hindus were still expected to associate and intermarry with members of their own caste, within this context they were encouraged to experience the pleasures of social engagement, so central to the community, and the joys of sexuality, so central to the family. While Buddhism, even in its Mahayana form, urged its adherents to curb their worldly desires, popular Hinduism placed the common people under no such restraint.

In addition, as it evolved over the centuries, popular Hinduism also let its followers tailor their devotions to meet their individual needs. Rather than relying on rituals performed by Brahmins, for example, Hindus increasingly sought to develop a personal relationship with a particular god or goddess, typically an incarnation of Vishnu, Shiva, or Devi. By repeatedly invoking the name, singing the hymns, and visiting the shrines of their personal deity, Hindus could hope to create a bond that would help them eventually gain moksha. In the long run, then, Hinduism's ability to meet the daily needs of diverse peoples, combined with its multiplicity of divinities and devotional practices, helped it to adapt better than Buddhism to the needs of Indian society.

Hindus develop devotions to personal divinities

Indian Society and Culture

Except for a short period of peace and unity under Mauryan rule, most of India's early history was marked by conflict and political fragmentation. These conditions, however, did not prevent the emergence of a stable social structure and a flourishing culture. Like ancient Mesopotamia, India showed that society and culture could thrive amid regional diversity, political disunity, and religious discord.

Caste, Family, and Gender

Hindu society centers on caste and family

Hindu society was dominated by the caste system, which influenced almost every aspect of life. Each caste had its own particular dharma, carrying with it rights, obligations, and restrictions. Beyond this was a generalized dharma applicable to all: deference to the Brahmins, devotion to the gods, and reverence for the Ganges and for sacred cattle. Procreation, too, was considered a sacred duty: large families were seen as blessings from the gods, and any attempt to limit family size was frowned upon. Since reproduction was essential to reincarnation, for most people marriage and parenthood were moral obligations. Some Jains and Buddhists might seek sanctity as celibate monks or nuns, but for Hindus the single life was socially unacceptable, and prolonging virginity was considered perverse.

Parents arrange marriages, often when children are quite young

Naturally, to fulfill their dharma, people had to marry within their caste. Unwilling to leave such a crucial concern to romance or personal choice, parents arranged proper unions for their children, sometimes at ages as young as eight or nine, before sexual attraction had a chance to complicate things. Marriages based on romantic love were possible but rare, and generally not regarded as respectable.

Indian society was patriarchal, centered on villages and extended families dominated by males. The villages, in which most people lived, were administered by men, who served on village councils typically composed of male heads of households. The households were largely supported by the labor of the men, who performed the occupational duties associated with their caste, which for most meant farming and herding. Families were governed by their senior males, who exercised ownership of family possessions and authority over the women and children.

In Vedic days the position of women was not entirely subordinate: they could participate equally with men in religious rituals and, within the framework of marriages arranged by their parents, they could have some say in the selection of their spouse. As a rule they could leave home on their own to shop, visit friends or family, and attend celebrations. If they were widowed, they were usually free to remarry, as long as their new husband was a member of the same caste.

Indian society restricts women's rights and roles

During the post-Vedic era, however, the opportunities available to women declined. Women were increasingly barred from religious and social activities, forbidden to remarry after their husbands died, and confined to the home and family. Girls were often engaged before age ten, and then wed at the onset of puberty to men in their twenties, a practice promoting both bridal virginity and male domination. Within the family framework, as in other societies, women might gain substantial influence over household management. But their primary dharma was to serve their husbands; if they performed it with grace and devotion, they might expect a better status in their next incarnation.

then she would commit suicide

The most extreme example of female subordination was **sati** (*suh-TĒ*), a practice whereby widows cremated themselves on their dead husbands' funeral pyre (a pile of wood used to burn a dead body rather than burying it). Although sati, which means "loyal wife," may have predated Vedic India, in Vedic times the widow was allowed to lie briefly on the pyre and then get off before it was set ablaze. By post-Vedic times, however, the practice had returned to its lethal form. Brahmins at first condemned it, but then accepted it as a testament to the eternal sanctity of marriage, and sometimes even promoted it as an exemplary display of a woman's marital fidelity. Although denounced by Buddhists and others, and never practiced extensively, sati survived among some segments of Indian society well into the twentieth century C.E.

The Visual Arts

Early Indian society, while focusing on stability and structure, produced a culture distinguished by its delicacy, intricacy, and subtlety. In areas such as sculpture, art, and architecture, India ranked among the ancient world's most creative and productive societies.

Early Indian sculptors, for instance, produced many superb statues and reliefs, portraying gods and goddesses, animals, and humans in exquisite detail. These sculptors often depicted female figures in alluring and sensuous poses, reflecting a deep fascination with beauty and grace, passion and pleasure, fertility and sexuality.

Later the spread of Buddhism shifted the focus of Indian sculpture and art from the sensual to the spiritual. At first the Buddha's followers, anxious to avoid idolatry, refused to depict him in any lifelike way. In time, however, contacts with Greek culture and the rise of Mahayana Buddhism overcame their concerns. By the second century C.E., sculptors were producing scores of statues of buddhas and bodhisattvas, some of which still adorn the landscapes of southern and Central Asia.

More impressive still was early Indian architecture. Before the coming of the Persians and Greeks, buildings in India were made mainly of wood, but thereafter stone construction became more and more common. During the Mauryan Empire, and especially under Ashoka, artisans erected thousands of shrines and prayer halls, some of them carved into mountainsides and hewn out of solid rock. Even more spectacular were the numerous **stupas**, massive domed edifices constructed of stone, initially built to house relics such as bones of the Buddha and later used as temples for pilgrimage and worship. The faithful flocked to these stupas, and typically prayed while walking around them on a circular path. _Buddha's ashes scattered here._

Buddhism's spread changes Indian art from sensual to spiritual

Persians, Greeks, and Buddhists influence Indian architecture

The Great Stupa at Sanchi in India, commissioned by the Emperor Ashoka.

Science and Mathematics

Early Indian thinkers, like those in West Asia and Egypt, made a number of crucial contributions to science and mathematics. Indian astronomers, for example, accurately plotted the paths of the planets and stars, and even determined that the Earth is a sphere revolving on its axis. And ancient Indian mathematicians devised an early form of algebra.

India's most valuable mathematical innovation, however, was its method of expressing numbers. As early as 250 B.C.E., Indians were using a place-value system of numerical notations, based on the number ten. A thousand years later, Arab scholars adopted this system and then spread it to the West, where the notations were thus called Arabic numerals. This system, far more functional than the cumbersome symbols (such as Roman numerals) used in other ancient cultures, so vastly facilitated numeric computation that it is used almost everywhere today.

Indians develop place-value number system, ancestor of 'Arabic' numerals

Philosophy and Literature: Upanishads and Epics

Like the Epic of Gilgamesh, the Hebrew Bible, and other ancient West Asian works, early Indian literature focused on connections and conflicts between physical and spiritual forces. Its main works were the **Upanishads** (_oo-PAH-ni-shahdz_), philosophical and religious texts composed by learned writers over many centuries beginning in late Vedic

Upanishads reflect
introspective and
intuitive philosophy

times, but it also included superb epic poems recorded in the post-Vedic era. Composed in Sanskrit, an Aryan language used for religious and literary purposes, these works serve as the basic scriptures of the Hindu faith.

Unlike the works of ancient West Asia, however, the Upanishads look inward rather than outward in their search for answers, valuing intuition and flashes of insight over intellectual speculation. They puzzle over such fundamental questions as where we came from, why we are here, how we should live, and where we are going. The answers, consistent with Hindu tradition, seek to connect mortal beings with the immortal and divine. One's spiritual core is Atman, the soul and depth of one's being; the core of the world is Brahman, the life force of all existence. Properly understood, however, Atman and Brahman are identical; thus each individual is one with the divine and cannot be alienated from any manifestation of the infinite. The Upanishads provide guidance for attaining internal peace, rather than an analysis of the external world. They thus exemplify the intuitive introspection often said to distinguish "eastern" thought from the more worldly and analytic "western" approach.

Epics describe the virtues
and ventures of gods
and legendary heroes

A worldly approach was nonetheless reflected in India's two great epic poems, the Mahabharata and the **Ramayana** (*RAH-mah-YAH-nah*), both written in the post-Vedic era based on Vedic oral traditions. The Mahabharata is a massive masterpiece that not only recounts an ancient war, full of legends and godly interventions, but also prescribes proper conduct and devotion to duty. As noted in this chapter's introduction, it includes the splendid Bhagavad Gita, regarded as one of India's most important ethical and spiritual works. The Ramayana describes the wanderings and adventures of Rama, heir to the throne of a northern Indian kingdom caught up in the great war. Later revered as a human manifestation of the god Vishnu, Rama was seen as a model of courage, fidelity, and devotion to family. These virtues were exemplified in the loving relationship between him and his wife Sita (*SĒ-tah*), whose hand he won by bending and breaking her father's great war bow, and who remained loyal to him through many tribulations (see "Ramayana Excerpts: Rama and Sita").

Upanishads and epics
entertain and inspire
Indians over the ages

For centuries these epics were recited from memory at family meals and at roadside inns, delighting and entertaining listeners. Their elegance and directness are enchanting, even to many people today who do not share India's religious traditions.

To Indians for thousands of years, however, these works have been sources of inspiration, not just entertainment. Often incorporated into religious rituals, they have served as guides to proper conduct, illustrated by valiant role models who enact the search for answers to life's most basic questions. Over the ages, millions of people have followed the precepts of the Upanishads and epics, hoping thereby to be cleansed of imperfections and eventually attain moksha.

Indian culture provides
harmony and beauty
amid diversity and
disunity

On the whole, then, early India's culture, developed through interactions among India's diverse peoples, was characterized by complexity and inner depth. It was also shaped by contacts with other cultures, and profoundly influenced by the teachings of Hinduism, Jainism, and Buddhism. It reflected a society that sought unity in the midst of diversity, order in the midst of instability, tranquility in the midst of turmoil, beauty in the midst of bedlam, and virtue in the midst of violence.

Document 3.2 Ramayana Excerpts: Rama and Sita

In these excerpts from the Ramayana, heroic Rama, son of King Dasa-ratha, wins the hand of the princess Sita by bending and breaking the great war bow of her father, King Janak of Videha. Rama and Sita then wed and exemplify the loving, faithful husband and wife.

Rich in royal worth and valour, rich in holy
Vedic lore,
Dasa-ratha ruled his empire in the happy days of
yore . . .
Janak, monarch of Videha, spake his message near
and far,
He shall win my peerless Sita who shall bend my
bow of war,
Suitors came from farthest regions, warlike princes
known to fame,
Vainly strove to wield the weapon, left Videha in
their shame . . .
Stalwart men of ample stature pulled the mighty
iron car
In which rested all-inviolate Janak's dreaded bow of
war, . . .
"This the weapon of Videha," proudly thus the
peers begun,
"Be it shown to royal Rama, Dasa-ratha's righteous
son" . . .
Rama lifted high the cover of the pond'rous
iron car,
Gazed with conscious pride and prowess on the
mighty bow of war.
"Let me," humbly spake the hero, "on this bow
my fingers place,
Let me lift and bend the weapon, help me with
your loving grace."
"Be it so," the rishi answered, "be it so," the
monarch said,
Rama lifted high the weapon on his stalwart arms
displayed,
Wond'ring gazed the kings assembled as the son
of Raghu's race

Proudly raised the bow of Rudra with a warrior's
stately grace,
Proudly strung the bow of Rudra which the kings
had tried in vain
Drew the cord with force resistless till the weapon
snapped in twain! . . .
And the chiefs and gathered monarchs fell and
fainted in their fear,
And the men of many nations shook the dreadful
sound to hear!
Pale and white the startled monarchs slowly from
their terror woke,
And with royal grace and greetings Janak to the
rishi spoke:
Now my ancient eyes have witnessed wond'rous
deed by Rama done,
Deed surpassing thought or fancy wrought by
Dasa-ratha's son,
And the proud and peerless princess, Sita glory of
my house,
Sheds on me an added lustre as she weds a godlike
spouse,
True shall be my plighted promise, Sita dearer than
my life,
Won by worth and wond'rous valour shall be
Rama's faithful wife . . .
With a woman's whole affection fond and trusting
Sita loved,
And within her faithful bosom loving Rama lived
and moved,
And he loved her, for their parents chose her as his
faithful wife,
Loved her for her peerless beauty, for her true and
trustful life,
Loved and dwelt within her bosom though he
wore a form apart,
Rama in a sweet communion lived in Sita's loving
heart!

SOURCE: R. C. Dutt, translator, *The Ramayana: The Great Hindu Epic*, Book I: *The Bridal of Sita*. http://hinduism.about.com/library/weekly/extra/bl-ramayana1.htm

Chapter Review

Putting It in Perspective

By the third century C.E., all the basic elements of Indian civilization were in place. In many ways these elements were a study in contrasts. India's Aryan-inspired literature glorified violence and warfare, but its Jain and Buddhist traditions exalted nonviolence and compassion. India's religious structure accommodated numerous gods, but it also insisted that all beings are one with each other and with the divine in an infinite cycle of life. India's political climate was marked by disunity and conflict, but its social system emphasized stability and control.

These contrasts are hardly surprising, given India's vast size and its great geographical and cultural diversity. Ancient India was not in fact a single society but a wide assortment of societies that interacted through numerous connections and conflicts. These interactions were shaped not only by Harappan, Aryan, and Dravidian influences, but also by peoples who at times ruled parts of India, including especially the Persians, Greeks, Scythians, and Kushans.

Nor is it surprising that ancient India produced no long-enduring empire. In the ancient world, of all the great conquerors and leaders, only a few were able to create and maintain immense, diverse, and populous domains that lasted for centuries. The most successful of these realms, discussed in upcoming chapters, were the empires established by the Chinese, Persians, and Romans.

Reviewing Key Material

KEY CONCEPTS

Mahabharata, 56	asceticism, 65
Vedic, 61	ahimsa, 65
varnas, 63	moksha, 65
castes, 63	nirvana, 66
jatis, 63	sati, 75
samsara, 64	stupa, 76
dharma, 64	Upanishads, 76
karma, 64	Ramayana, 77

KEY PEOPLE

Arjuna, 56	Chandragupta Maurya, 68
Mahavira (Jina), 65	Ashoka, 69
Siddhartha Gautama (Buddha), 65	Kanishka, 72
	Ashvaghosha, 72
Alexander the Great, 67	Rama, 77
Seleucus Nikator, 56	Sita, 77

ASK YOURSELF

1. In what ways were the societies and cultures of India similar to those of West Asia and North Africa? In what ways were Indian cultures and belief systems unique?
2. How did the system of castes develop in ancient India? What were its advantages and disadvantages for the Indian people? How did dharma and samsara help to reinforce the system?
3. What were the basic features and beliefs of Hinduism, Jainism, and Buddhism? In what ways did they support, and in what ways did they challenge, the political and social structures?
4. How and why did Buddhism evolve and divide into separate branches? How and why did Hinduism evolve and endure as a popular religion?
5. What factors made it difficult to achieve and maintain political unity in India? What factors enabled India to flourish despite its political divisions?

GOING FURTHER

Akira, H. *A History of Indian Buddhism.* 1990.
Armstrong, Karen. *Buddha.* 2001.
Auboyer, Jeannine. *Daily Life in Ancient India.* 2002.
Basham, A. L., ed. *A Cultural History of India.* 1975.
Conze, Edward. *A Short History of Buddhism.* 1980.
Flood, Gavin. *An Introduction to Hinduism.* 1996.
Foltz, R. C. *Religions of the Silk Road.* 1999.
Huntington, S. L. *The Art of Ancient India: Buddhist, Hindu, Jain.* 1985.
Kenoyer, Jonathan Mark. *Ancient Cities of the Indus Valley Civilization.* 1998.
Kinsely, David R. *Hinduism: A Cultural Perspective.* 1982.

Klostermaier, K. K. *A Survey of Hinduism.* 1989.

Kulke, Helman, and D. Rothermund. *A History of India.* 3rd ed. 1998.

Masson-Oursel, Paul. *Ancient India and Indian Civilization.* 1998.

McIntosh, Jane. *A Peaceful Realm: Rise and Fall of the Indus Civilization.* 2002.

Pandian, Jacob. *The Making of India and Indian Tradition.* 1995.

Pearson, M. *The Indian Ocean.* 2003.

Possehl, Gregory. *The Indus Civilization: A Contemporary Perspective.* 2002.

Robinson, R. H., W. L. Johnson, and S. A. Wawrytko. *The Buddhist Religion: A Historical Introduction.* 4th ed. 1996.

Sharma, R. S. *India's Ancient Past.* 2005.

Thapar, Romila. *Asoka and the Decline of the Mauryas.* 1961.

Thapar, Romila. *Early India: From Origins to AD 1300.* 2002.

Trainor, Kevin, ed. *Buddhism.* 2001.

Williams, P. *Buddhist Thought.* 2000.

Wolpert, Stanley A. *A New History of India.* 7th ed. 2003.

Key Dates and Developments

by 7000 B.C.E.	Farming in Indus Valley
2800–1700 B.C.E.	Harappan (Indus Valley) civilization
by 1500 B.C.E.	Indo-European Aryans arrive in India
1500–500 B.C.E.	Vedic Age: Vedas, caste system, early Upanishads
563–483 B.C.E.	Siddhartha Gautama (Buddha): founder of Buddhism
540–486 B.C.E.	Mahavira (Jina): founder of Jainism
518–513 B.C.E.	Persian conquest of northwest India
500–300 B.C.E.	Initial compilation of Mahabharata and Ramayana
327–326 B.C.E.	Alexander the Great's invasion of northwest India
321–184 B.C.E.	Mauryan Empire
321–297 B.C.E.	Reign of Chandragupta Maurya
270–232 B.C.E.	Reign of Ashoka
180–50 B.C.E.	Greco-Bactrian kingdom in northern India
50–240 C.E.	Kushan Kingdom; Spread and division of Buddhism

The Origins of the Chinese Empire, to 220 C.E.

The First Emperor's Underground Army

The tomb of China's First Emperor, guarded by a huge underground clay army rediscovered in 1974, attests to the power and grandeur of ancient China. This sketch shows how scholars think the tomb was constructed in the third century C.E.

In 1974, workers drilling a well near the Chinese city of Xi'an (*shē-AHN*) made an extraordinary discovery. Much to their surprise, they found a huge underground chamber filled with thousands of elaborate statues: an army of life-sized clay horses and soldiers armed with real bronze weapons. Nearby chambers, seemingly guarded by this clay army, were later found to contain hundreds of additional artifacts, scores of human remains, and a magnificent bronze mausoleum. Scholars soon determined that this subterranean sepulcher, dating from the third century B.C.E., was the tomb of an ancient Chinese ruler known to history as the First Emperor.

Early Chinese Empire

The realm of the First Emperor centered on a culture that had arisen in northern China several thousand years before his time. Here, as in Mesopotamia, Egypt, and India, early societies emerged along a waterway, in this case the treacherous Yellow River that flows across North China. Farming villages grew into towns, some of which evolved into city-states that expanded into larger domains. Here, as in West Asia and India, moral and religious concepts developed that over the ages would influence millions of people. Here, too, as in other ancient empires, the land was united through the conquests of a mighty ruler, in this case the First Emperor.

Despite such similarities, however, the culture that arose in ancient China was in certain ways distinctive. The Chinese adopted an outlook on governance, for example, that held state officials accountable for public welfare and justified revolts against rulers who failed to maintain it—an outlook most uncommon in the ancient world. The Chinese developed a worldview that conceived reality as a balance of complementary forces, unlike other cultures that perceived life as a struggle between good and evil. The Chinese produced goods, such as paper and silk, found in no other early cultures. And Chinese leaders, building upon the centralized state created by the First Emperor, assembled a professional civil service system to administer one of history's most extensive, populous, and enduring empires.

China's Geographic Diversity

China's geography provides a study in contrasts. The west and southwest are mountainous and bleak. The north is arid and barren, dominated by the Gobi (*GŌ-bē*) desert and Mongolian plateau (Map 4.1). Desolate and forbidding, these regions have remained sparsely inhabited throughout Chinese history. They have also separated China from other societies. Although ancient China had contacts with other cultures, connections were sporadic and hard to maintain.

China's diverse geography impedes early intercultural connections

Eastern China is defined by its two great rivers. In the south is the Yangzi (*YAHNG-DZUH*) River, or Changjiang (*CHAHNG jē-AHNG*), sometimes called "China's

Yangzi and Yellow Rivers irrigate and connect eastern China

FOUNDATION MAP 4.1 China's Geography and Environment, Third Millennium B.C.E.

China's northern deserts and western mountains made connections with other cultures challenging. Note, however, that the great rivers flowing eastward from the mountains aided internal connections and facilitated farming, while seasonal monsoon winds from the South China Sea brought China regular rainfall. How could ease of internal connections and productive farmlands help to form the foundations for a strong Chinese state?

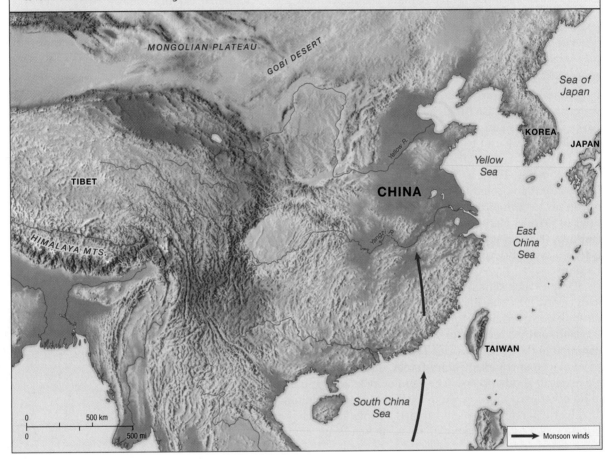

blessing." A broad, deep waterway that seldom floods, it is excellent for transport and reliable for irrigating nearby lands. The climate is warm, the growing season long, and rainfall abundant, as seasonal monsoon winds bring in moisture from seas to the south. The terrain is lush and green, sustaining a variety of fruits, vegetables, and grains. In the north, by contrast, is the Yellow River, or Huanghe (*HWAHNG-HUH*), also known as "China's sorrow." It is shallow, flows through flat plains, and has no regular river bed, so its frequent floods and occasional course changes devastate those who live nearby. In the north the climate is cold and dry, the growing season short, and nature harsh, with recurrent danger of drought, floods, and frost.

Early Chinese Societies

Despite its harsh environment, however, the north was where China's first settled societies emerged. Several factors help to explain this development. One was the profusion of brownish-yellow silt carried by the Yellow River, giving it both its appearance and its name. Deposited through the countryside by periodic floods, this silt was rich in nutrients, regularly restoring the soil's fertility. Farming thus came early to this area, helping to sustain the growing population needed to form cities and states. Another key factor may have been the Yellow River's unpredictability, compelling those who lived nearby to organize into communities large enough to build dikes and channels to control the current.

The Yellow River.

Responding to the benefits and challenges of their environment, from the seventh through second millennia B.C.E. the people of northern China developed a culture that served as the basis for later Chinese societies. They adopted farming and herding, settled with their families in villages, instituted religious rituals, and learned to produce silk. In time they also built towns and cities, fashioned bronze tools and weapons, established a social class structure, created a centralized state, and devised a writing system. As a result, by the second millennium B.C.E., many basic features of Chinese civilization already existed in the Yellow River valley.

Predynastic China

Aided by the silt-enriched soil, people started farming near the Yellow River as early as 7000 B.C.E. As in other agricultural societies, farmers resided in villages and raised food on the surrounding lands. To protect themselves from wind and cold, the villagers lived in pits dug in the ground and covered with thatch roofs. To feed themselves they grew millet, and eventually cabbage and wheat; they also produced fine pottery and domesticated cattle, sheep, goats, and pigs. Later some villagers additionally cultivated silkworms, little short-lived caterpillars that feed on mulberry leaves and spin cocoons of fine soft thread. After painstakingly unraveling these cocoons, Chinese peasants wove the thread into silk, eventually valued as the world's finest cloth.

Farming villages emerge near Yellow River by 7000 B.C.E.

Early Chinese pottery.

According to legend, early China was blessed with heroic benefactors who began its development. Fuxi (*FOO-SHĒ*) supposedly established the family and taught the people how to domesticate animals. Shennong (*SHUN-NUNG*) is said to have invented farming and basic farming tools. Huangdi (*HWANG-DĒ*) is credited with the development of silk, the bow and arrow, boats, and a system of writing. Huangdi is also considered the first of China's predynastic rulers, a series of fabled monarchs who reigned before the rise of ruling dynasties.

Legend also credits the last predynastic ruler, a former poor peasant named Shun, with selecting a man named Yu to harness the floods that disrupted life along the Yellow River. The ingenious Yu purportedly dug channels to divert the floodwaters, thereby creating northern China's other rivers. Shun was said to have been so impressed that he selected Yu to rule after him. Then, when Yu died, the Chinese installed Yu's son as their next ruler. Thus, according to tradition, began the pattern of familial rule, initiating a series of dynasties that would dominate China from then until modern times.

Legend says heroic predynastic rulers initiate Chinese society

Although they are legends, these accounts reveal the perceptions and priorities of the ancient Chinese. They show that the Chinese saw family, farming, writing, river control, and dynastic rule as central elements of their culture. Furthermore, when supplemented

Legends reflect Chinese focus on farming, family, rivers, and rulers by archeological evidence, these stories help historians discern the general features of early Chinese society, especially as it existed under China's first two dynasties.

Xia and Shang Societies

Yu and his son are traditionally regarded as the first two rulers of the Xia (*shē-AH*) dynasty, which reigned in the central Yellow River region from approximately 2200 to 1750 B.C.E. (Map 4.2). Once seen as a figment of folklore, the Xia is now considered China's first historical dynasty, as cities and towns unearthed near the Yellow River appear to have been part of a real Xia realm. One large city called Erlitou (*ER-lē-TŌ*), possibly the capital, had stately palaces and tombs, paved roads, and even a foundry for making bronze tools and weapons.

Map 4.2 China's Early Cities and Dynasties, Second Millennium B.C.E.

China's earliest cities were located in northeast China, around the Yellow River, in lands governed by the Xia Dynasty (2200–1750 B.C.E.) and Shang Dynasty (1750–1122 B.C.E.). Observe, as indicated on the inset map, that some Indo-European nomads apparently migrated to the region west of China by around 2000 B.C.E. What ideas and techniques might the Chinese have learned through contacts with these Central Asian nomads?

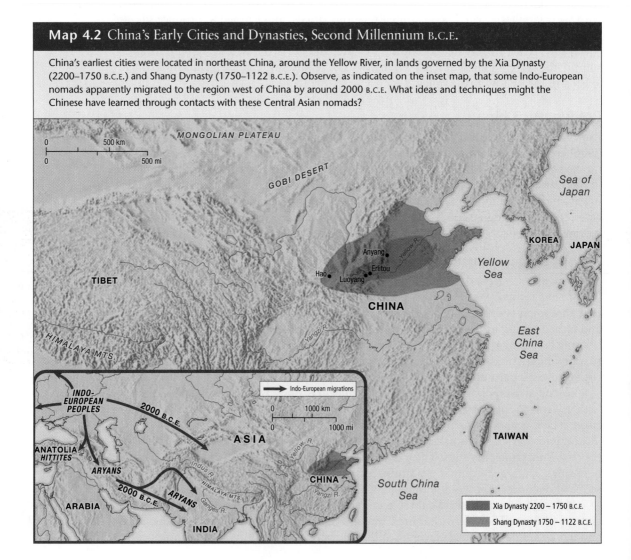

Bronze metallurgy probably came to China by way of the Indo-European migrations, discussed in Chapter 2, which provided early connections among Eurasian cultures. Much as the Hittites moved to Anatolia and the Aryans to India, other Indo-European pastoral nomads moved to what is now northwest China, during the Xia dynasty, with their horse-drawn chariots and bronze weapons (see Map 4.2 inset). The subsequent appearance of such devices in Yellow River societies, and similarities between old Chinese and Indo-European words for wheels and chariots, suggest that China learned of these devices through contacts and conflicts with the nomads.

Central Asian nomads introduce horses and bronze weapons to China

Some Chinese warriors made good use of these vehicles and weapons. In the eighteenth century B.C.E., according to both legend and archeological evidence, the Xia regime was defeated and displaced by a new dynasty known as the Shang (*SHAHNG*), whose warrior nobles were armed with bronze spears, protected by bronze armor, and skilled in the use of war chariots.

Shang dynasty replaces Xia by 1700 B.C.E.

Since the Shang dynasty, which reigned from roughly 1750 to 1122 B.C.E., produced some written records, historians know much more about it than they know about the Xia. Along with evidence from excavations of Shang settlements, especially the capital, Anyang (*AHN-YAHNG*), these records portray a complex, warlike, stratified society.

By Shang times, a number of city-states had emerged in northern China. Although each had its own local ruler, many of these rulers were tied by allegiance, and often also by kinship, to the Shang royal family. These ties brought some political unity to the Yellow River valley.

Shang rule unites and connects Yellow River region

Shang society was stratified into several classes. At the top were the king and his warrior aristocracy, who lived in the city centers in palatial homes, wore fine silk garments, and indulged in food and beverages served in splendid bronze vessels. Below the aristocrats were artisans, who lived elsewhere in the cities in homes made of earth and wood, and who produced bronze vessels and weapons, lacquered wood containers, and fine pottery for the upper classes. Less well off were the peasants, who lived in pit homes in rural villages and worked the fields to supply the society's food. At the bottom of the social structure were slaves, typically prisoners of war, who worked as servants in royal and noble households and as forced laborers in the construction of walls, roads, palaces, and dikes.

Although the leaders of Shang society believed in a supreme deity and numerous lesser gods, the most common form of religion appears to have been **ancestor** worship, veneration of a family's departed relatives and forebears. Based on the belief that the spirits of the dead can influence the gods to help relatives who are still living, this worship involved rituals performed at graves and shrines set up to honor dead kinfolk.

People in Shang times also took part in other religious rituals. On occasion, for example, they seem to have sacrificed domestic animals, and even human slaves, to win divine favor. The early Chinese also studied the sun, stars, and planets, presuming that by doing so they could come to know the will of the gods. In the process they devised a calendar, recorded eclipses of the sun, and invented a form of mathematics.

Remains of early Chinese chariot, with bones of horses and driver.

Chinese Writing

The writing system used in ancient China also evolved out of religious practices. For centuries Chinese oracles—spiritual leaders who sought to communicate with the gods—inscribed little pictures on a tortoise shell or cattle shoulder bone and then heated the

Chinese writing evolves from efforts to receive divine messages

Shang oracle bone.

shell or bone until cracks appeared in its surface. The oracles then followed the cracks to connect the pictures, each of which represented a word, in a sequence believed to convey a divine message. By inscribing pictures denoting the sun, clouds, rain, and upcoming days, for example, and then observing how they were connected by the heat cracks, oracles could theoretically foretell the weather. By using other pictures and symbols, oracles could similarly predict the results of battles, harvests, hunts, and other endeavors.

Shang rulers, anxious to foresee the outcome of their endeavors, made extensive use of these "oracle bones," thousands of which have been rediscovered in modern times. Scholars have been able to decipher the oracle bone symbols, and to determine that they are early versions of modern Chinese characters.

In Chinese writing, each character represents an entire word, not just a single sound as in Western alphabets derived from the Phoenician writing system (Chapter 2). Learning to read and write in China has hence meant mastering thousands of symbols. Because it was not closely tied to the sounds of spoken works, however, the system proved very useful in China, where people in one region often could not understand the dialects spoken in other regions. Since each written character conveyed the same concept no matter what the dialect, people could communicate in writing even if they could not understand each others' spoken words. The written character for horse, for example, conveyed the concept of a horse to people who spoke different dialects, even if the spoken words for horse did not sound the same. Chinese writing thus helped ruling centers communicate with outlying regions, thereby helping to unite a vast and disparate land. As it did elsewhere, writing in China also enabled people to record their history and convey their ideas.

Chinese writing helps to connect a vast and diverse realm

State and Society During the Zhou Dynasty

By the late twelfth century B.C.E., according to traditional accounts, the Shang kings had become oppressive and corrupt, provoking rebellions against them. The victor in these struggles was King Wu, the ruler of Zhou (*JŌ*), a small realm west of the Shang domain. In 1122 B.C.E. he defeated the Shang and started a new dynasty that reigned for more than 800 years in much of northern China (Map 4.3). The Zhou era is traditionally divided into two periods: the Western Zhou (1122–771 B.C.E.), when the kings resided at Hao (near modern Xi'an) in the west, and the Eastern Zhou (770–256 B.C.E.), when they lived further east at Luoyang (*LWŌ-YAHNG*).

The Mandate of Heaven and Dynastic Cycle

Zhou Dynasty replaces Shang regime, calling it corrupt

Composed by Zhou era writers, traditional accounts of the Shang's overthrow tend to discredit the old dynasty and exalt the early Zhou leaders—especially King Wu's brother, the legendary Duke of Zhou. Based on these accounts, after King Wu died in 1116 B.C.E., the duke served as regent for the new king, the late ruler's son, who was too young to rule on his own. The energetic duke reportedly went on to consolidate his family's control and destroy the vestiges of Shang rule, serving as a wise and loyal administrator. When King Wu's son came of age, the duke turned over power to the young king, thus affirming the succession of father to son and setting an example of loyal devotion for future public servants.

Map 4.3 The Zhou Dynasty, 1122–256 B.C.E.

The Zhou dynasty connected much of northern China for centuries, extending its rule throughout the Yellow River region and beyond. Note, however, that in the Warring States Era (403–221 B.C.E.), although the dynasty still existed in name, various nobles with their own large armies acted as independent warlords, fighting among themselves and eventually controlling a very large area. What commercial and cultural developments continued to connect Chinese society despite these divisions and conflicts?

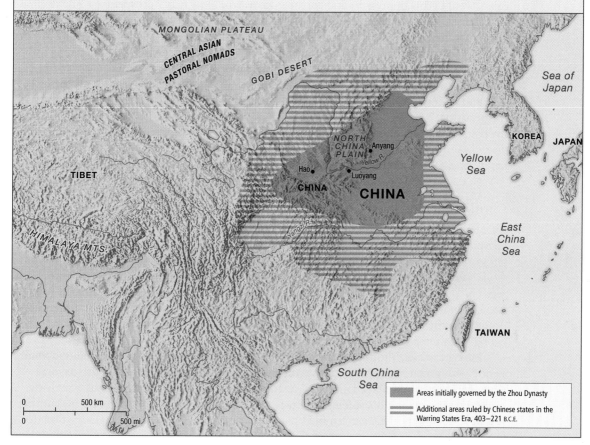

The Duke of Zhou's most important contribution, however, may have been his success at laying the philosophical foundation for Chinese dynastic authority. To justify his family's ouster of one dynasty and creation of another, he is said to have developed the idea of the **Mandate of Heaven.** This concept asserts that, in order to rule China, a dynasty must have the authorization of "Heaven," perceived not as a place but as the main divinity, god of the skies and ancestor of Chinese rulers. This mandate empowered the ruler to reign as "Son of Heaven," but it also required that he govern justly and humanely. If a ruler grew corrupt and oppressive, and if the people were suffering, Heaven would withdraw the mandate and bestow it on someone else, who would then take power and rule with virtue and benevolence. This principle allegedly legitimized the Zhou overthrow of the Shang.

Mandate of Heaven legitimizes Chinese rulers only if just and humane

In claiming this mandate, however, Zhou leaders unwittingly provided both a precedent and a pretext for future rebels to challenge the reigning power, establishing a pattern that would recur throughout Chinese history. This pattern, known as the **dynastic cycle**, had four basic phases. First, a strong leader would arise and conquer all of China, creating a powerful and effective regime. Then he would pass on the rule to his heirs, initiating a dynasty that would reign for some time in stability and prosperity. Eventually, however, the rulers would grow oppressive and corrupt. Taxes would increase, prosperity would decline, and a series of natural and military disasters would signal the loss of Heaven's Mandate. In the cycle's final phase, a new hero would arise to challenge the old dynasty, claiming the mandate for himself and his heirs. If he failed to gain power, he was seen as lacking Heaven's favor; if he succeeded he would found a new dynasty, starting the cycle anew.

The rise and fall of ruling families was not unique to China; Egypt, for example, also had a long chain of dynasties. But the concept of Heaven's Mandate, combined with the persistence of the dynastic cycle, eventually set up expectations that were distinctively Chinese. In China, at least in theory, a dynasty's survival depended on its ability to provide security, stability, and prosperity. If it failed to do so, for whatever reason, it forfeited its mandate, giving the people a right to rebel and replace it.

Conflict, Chaos, and Commerce

This implicit right of rebellion, combined with China's vast dimensions and cultural complexity, made governance a formidable challenge. Rather than trying to control their territories directly, early Zhou rulers developed a decentralized regime in which the regions were governed by subordinates, who received large landholdings in return for their service. These lands were then handed down from father to son, creating a hereditary nobility based on service to the king. But for the kings this system also had a potential drawback: the leading nobles, who had their own lands and armies, might acquire enough power to threaten the regime.

This drawback almost ended the Zhou dynasty in 771 B.C.E., when rebellious nobles joined with nomadic invaders to overthrow a king named You. According to legend, King You sometimes played an extravagant game to entertain a female consort. He lit beacon fires signaling his soldiers to prepare for enemy attack, and then had his consort watch in delight as armies assembled from all directions to meet the imaginary threat. But eventually the soldiers, tired of this game, failed to respond to the beacon fires when real attackers appeared. The capital was overrun, the palace was ransacked, King You was killed, and his lover was captured.

Whatever the truth of this tale—patriarchal societies often have legends blaming women for men's misfortunes—it did help King You's foes justify his removal. But his heir managed to maintain some power by fleeing east to the city of Luoyang, making it his capital and starting a new era now called the Eastern Zhou.

During the Eastern Zhou era (770–256 B.C.E.), many Chinese nobles, acquiring more wealth and power than the king himself, began to act as independent warlords in their own domains. Centuries of chaos and civil war resulted in the Era of Warring States (403–221 B.C.E.), during which all sense of unity and central authority ceased.

As political conflict tore China apart, however, commerce was tying it together. The Eastern Zhou era saw the rise of many new cities, which served as centers of trade, with markets where farmers, artisans, and merchants from near and far exchanged their goods. Roads and canals connecting these cities, built by rulers to move troops and supplies, were traveled by traders transporting such items as metal tools and utensils, lacquered wood plates and boxes, silk, pottery, gems, salt, and lumber. A money economy emerged, using copper coins called cash, with holes in the center so they could be strung together for counting and carrying. China's towns and cities were likewise linked into a large economic system. Although trade between China and faraway lands was difficult and dangerous, by the end of the Zhou era Chinese merchants were trading by sea with Southeast Asia and by land routes crossing Central Asia.

The Central Asian Connection

Central Asia, the vast expanse to China's north and west where the climate was too dry for farming (Map 4.3), was inhabited mainly by pastoral nomads who grazed their herds on its plateaus and plains. Skilled on horseback, the nomads often attacked Chinese settlements to carry off goods and supplies, but they also spread commerce and useful knowledge. Some nomads, for example, exchanged their hides, wool, and horses for Chinese silk, pottery, metalware, and wood products, and then traded what they did not use with others across Central Asia. Direct connections with the nomads, and indirect connections through the nomads with other Eurasian societies, had major impacts on China over time.

Interactions with the nomads, for example, transformed Chinese warfare in the Eastern Zhou era. Chinese armies adopted horseback riding from the nomads, replacing charioteers with mounted riders who could move and maneuver much more quickly. The nomads in turn began using the crossbow, a Chinese invention that could kill with precision from a distance.

Even more momentous was ironworking, a West Asian innovation that spread across Central Asia to China during the Zhou dynasty. Since iron was far more abundant than the copper and tin employed in making bronze, ironworking could be used to produce vast numbers of shields and daggers, enabling rulers to field much larger forces. No longer limited to fairly small forces of bronze-armed noble warriors on horseback, Chinese armies in the Warring States era also fielded tens of thousands of peasant foot soldiers armed with iron weapons.

Ironworking also brought economic benefits to China. Crop cultivation was vastly enhanced by the use of iron-bladed plows, pulled by oxen hitched to a wooden harness, and by iron-bladed spades, used in tilling soil and digging irrigation ditches to expand the amount of farmland. Iron picks and shovels were used in building earthen dams and dikes to protect against floods, earthen walls to defend against nomad attacks, and roads and canals to aid the movement of both armies and goods. Central Asian connections thus helped to expand warfare, farming, and commerce in early China.

The Classical Age of Chinese Philosophy

The Eastern Zhou era, with its ongoing warfare, political turmoil, and economic growth, also produced ideas intended to promote harmony and stability. These ideas laid the basis for China's main belief systems, including especially Confucianism, Daoism, and Legalism.

A metal bell from the Zhou era.

Central Asian nomads connect China with other cultures

Nomads and Chinese adopt horse riding and crossbows from each other

Iron tools and weapons spread to China from west

Iron tools and weapons enhance farming, warfare, and commerce

Historians have noted that this era, from the eighth through third centuries B.C.E., also produced Buddhism, Jainism, and the Upanishads in India, the Avesta (sacred book) of Persia, the major Hebrew prophets, and the foremost Greek philosophers. Although China's great thinkers had no direct contact with those in distant societies, increasing connections among these societies doubtless fed the intellectual ferment that helped inspire some of history's main belief systems.

Confucianism: Noble-Minded Conduct and Familial Respect

Confucius and his disciples.

The central Chinese philosopher was Kongfuzi (*KONG-FOO-DZUH*) or Master Kong the Sage (551–479 B.C.E.). Later known in the West as Confucius, he laid the foundations for China's foremost ethical system. Like other famous moral teachers, including the Buddha and Jesus, Confucius left behind no writings, so it has been hard to separate his ideas from those added later by his followers. His impact nonetheless has been enormous.

Born into a minor noble family in east central China, and raised in humble circumstances after his father's early death, Confucius aspired to a political career. He dreamed of becoming a wise and loyal official who, following in the footsteps of the Duke of Zhou, would help some ruler create a just society based on the wisdom of the past. For years he sought such a post, and briefly held several government positions. Frustrated, however, by administrative indifference to his ideas, he became a wandering teacher, earnestly preaching his convictions to a growing group of disciples.

Confucius aspires to help form a just society

After Confucius was gone, his followers compiled his reflections to produce the *Analects*, a collection of sayings, each typically prefaced by the phrase "The Master said . . ." As a whole, they depict a man deeply troubled by the chaos and corruption of his day, and eager to bring social order and harmony to the violent Eastern Zhou era. The *Analects* envision a society regulated not by rigid enforcement of laws, but by the virtuous behavior of its leaders and citizens. They idealize especially the honorable, "noble-minded" public servant who inspires the people by example and treats them with wisdom, moderation, compassion, and respect. Over the next several centuries, these ideas were elaborated and organized into **Confucianism**, a system of thought that would dominate Chinese public life for more than 2,000 years.

Disciples of Confucius compile his sayings and ideals

Although Confucians recognized the divinity called Heaven, and later built many temples, Confucianism was not so much a religion as an ethical philosophy. Based on the *Analects* and the Five Classics, a set of Chinese literary works compiled over many centuries, Confucian philosophy focused on human behavior rather than divine worship. Its main virtues included:

- *ren (RUN)*, or "humanity," involving compassion, humane conduct, and benevolence;
- *li (LĒ)*, or "ritual," the courtesy, etiquette, and civility by which people should treat one another; and
- *xiao (shē-OW)*, or "filial piety," the devotion that a son owed to his father (and, by extension, that all people owed to their parents, ancestors, and leaders).

In promoting these virtues, Confucianism envisioned a hierarchical society in which all people knew their place, based on mutual respect between rulers and subjects, parents and children, spouses, siblings, and friends (the "five relationships"). Its main premise was that people would irresistibly follow and emulate wise, benevolent leaders. Although

Document 4.1 Excerpts from the *Analects*

In the *Analects*, followers of Confucius recorded his wise sayings and thoughtful exchanges with disciples. Over the centuries, his insights and advice would serve as guides for providing noble-minded public service and leading honorable lives.

The Master said: "Worthy admonitions cannot fail to inspire us, but what matters is changing ourselves. Reverent advice cannot fail to encourage us, but what matters is acting on it . . ."

The Master said: "Above all, be loyal and stand by your words. Befriend only those who are kindred spirits. And when you're wrong, don't be afraid to change."

Adept Lu asked about governing, and the Master said: "Put the people first, and reward their efforts well . . ."

Adept Lu asked: "To be called a noble official, what must a person be like?" "Earnest and exacting, but also genial," replied the Master. ". . . Earnest and exacting with friends, genial with brothers."

The Master said: "The people should be broadly educated by a wise teacher for seven years—then they can take up the weapons of war."

The Master said: "Sending the people to war without educating them first: that is called *throwing the people away*."

The Master said: "The noble-minded seek within themselves. Little people seek elsewhere."

The Master said: "The noble-minded stand above the fray with dignity. And when they band together with others, they never lose track of themselves."

The Master said: "The noble-minded don't honor a person because of something he said, nor do they dismiss something said because of the person who said it."

The Master said: "We're all the same by nature. It's living that makes us different."

Adept Chang asked Confucius: "What makes a person fit to govern?" "Honoring the five graces and despising the four deformities," replied the Master . . . "What are the five graces?" asked Adept Chang. "The noble-minded are generous without expense, hard working without resentment, wishful without greed, stately without arrogance, stern without cruelty . . ." "And what are the four deformities?" asked Chang. "Killing instead of teaching, which is called terror. Expecting results without telling people what you want, which is called tyranny. Issuing vague orders and expecting prompt action, which is called plunder. Grudging and miserly when giving people what they deserve, which is called officialdom."

SOURCE: Confucius, *The Analects*, translated by David Hinton (New York: Counterpoint, 1998) 97, 139, 148, 176, 195, 230–231.

---

elitist in upholding an all-male ruling class of scholars and gentlemen, Confucianism favored noble-mindedness of spirit rather than nobility of birth. Although conservative in championing the virtues and values of the past, Confucianism was progressive in stressing the rulers' duty to provide good government (see "Excerpts from the *Analects*").

The Confucian ethic had momentous implications for the practice of governance. The Master was not a revolutionary in the modern sense, but he clearly detested political oppression, as recorded in this parable: One day the Master came upon an old woman sitting by the mouth of a cave, weeping. When he asked her what was troubling her, she replied, "First my father-in-law, then my husband, and now my son were all killed by a tiger at this place." When Confucius inquired as to why she insisted on living in so dangerous an area, the grieving woman replied, "There is no oppressive government here." Confucius then said to his students, "My children, remember this. It is better to live among tigers than to live under a bad government."[1]

---

[1] James Legge, *The Life and Teachings of Confucius* (London, 1895) 67.

Mencius justifies rebellion against repressive rulers

The Master himself may not have intended his message to be subversive, but many of his followers taught that unjust leaders should be held accountable for their actions. Foremost among them was Mengzi (*MUNG-DZUH*), or Mencius, an eminent Chinese sage who lived from roughly 370 to 290 B.C.E. Mencius held that all humans are equal and good, and that a ruler must both practice and promote the virtue of *ren*. If a ruler failed to do so, Mencius claimed, it was a sign that the ruler had lost Heaven's Mandate, and his subjects had the right to rebel.

Confucianism holds rulers and officials to high moral standards

By holding rulers and officials to high moral standards, the Confucian tradition, over the centuries, promoted good governance and served as a check against tyranny. Some oppressive regimes sought to suppress Confucianism, but their efforts had little lasting success.

Daoism: The Way That Cannot Be Spoken

Daoism urges harmony with nature and avoidance of ambition

Another prominent school of ideas arising in the Eastern Zhou era was **Daoism** (*DOW-iz-um*), a naturalistic philosophy that, unlike Confucianism, had little use for organized social and political institutions. Its main text was the *Daodejing* (*DOW-DUH-JING*), or "Classic of the Way and Its Power," supposedly written in the sixth century B.C.E. by a legendary figure called Laozi (*LAOW-DZUH*), the Old Sage, but probably compiled later from sayings ascribed to him. Centered on the notion of a mysterious, unchanging cosmic force called *Dao* ("The Way"), Daoism was naturalistic in calling on people to live in harmony with nature. It was also passive, and even escapist, urging people to "be bland like melting ice," let go of control, avoid worldly ambition, and accept whatever came their way (see "Excerpts from *Daodejing*"). It delighted in noting that if there were no property there would be no theft, if there were no law there would be no crime, and if there were no fame there would be no disgrace. Beginning as a simple, romantic worldview, Daoism developed into a religion with numerous sacred rituals and shrines.

Unlike Confucianism, Daoism values silence, contemplation, and passivity

Daoism in many ways contrasted with Confucianism. While Confucians relished intellectual and political discourse, Daoists tended to be anti-intellectual and anti-political, focusing instead on silence, contemplation, and passivity. These values were reflected in Daoist precepts, often expressed as paradoxical sayings, such as, "Those who talk do not understand; those who understand do not talk," and, "The way that can be spoken of is not the true Way."

Chinese see Confucianism and Daoism as mutual correctives

Although Confucianism and Daoism might seem contradictory, many Chinese people espoused both. They saw them not as opposites but as mutual correctives, both necessary, each complementing the other. One could, for example, be Confucian in one's public life and Daoist in one's private life. Confucianism produced scholars and politicians, while Daoism inspired artists and poets, but each was essential to the Chinese culture and character.

Yin and Yang: The Balance of Forces in Nature

The balancing and blending of dissimilar concepts, such as those of Confucianism and Daoism, was a crucial characteristic of Chinese culture. This characteristic was reflected especially in another key concept that emerged in ancient China, the notion of **yin and yang**, a principle emphasizing the balancing and blending of natural forces.

Document 4.2 Excerpts from *Daodejing*

Unlike Confucianism, which promoted an active life of public service to others, Daoism advocated simplicity, passivity, avoidance of ambition, and conformity with a silent, shapeless cosmic force called Dao ("The Way"). The following excerpts from Daodejing ("Classic of the Way and Its Power") provide a sampling of basic Daoist ideals.

When you never strive, you never go wrong . . .

Just do what you do and then leave: such is the Way of Heaven . . .

Way is perennially nameless, an uncarved simplicity. Though small, it's subject to nothing in all beneath heaven . . .

Heaven mingling with earth sends down sweet dew, and the people free of mandates share justice among themselves . . .

Way flowing through all beneath heaven: it's like valley streams flowing into rivers and seas . . .

Way is perennially doing nothing, so there's nothing it doesn't do . . .

Uncarved nameless simplicity is the perfect absence of desire, and the absence of desire means repose: all beneath heaven at rest of itself . . .

Bustling around may overcome cold, but tranquility overcomes heat. Master lucid tranquility, and you'll govern all beneath heaven.

When all beneath heaven abides in Way, fast horses are kept to work the fields. When all beneath heaven forgets Way, war horses are bred among the fertility altars.

What calamity is greater than no contentment, and what flaw greater than passion for gain? The contentment of fathoming contentment—there lies the contentment that endures.

You can know all beneath heaven though you never step out the door, and you can see the Way of heaven though you never look out the window.

The further you explore, the less you know. So it is that a sage knows by going nowhere, names by seeing nothing, perfects by doing nothing . . .

. . . To work at Way brings less each day, still less and less until you're doing nothing yourself. And when you're doing nothing yourself, there's nothing you don't do.

To grasp all beneath heaven, leave it alone. Leave it alone, that's all, and nothing in all beneath heaven will elude you . . .

. . . a tree you can barely reach around grows from the tiniest rootlet; a nine-tiered tower starts as a basket of dirt; a thousand-mile journey begins with a single step.

Work at things and you ruin them; cling to things and you lose them. That's why a sage does nothing, and so ruins nothing, clings to nothing, and so loses nothing.

SOURCE: Lao Tzu, *Tao te ching*, translated by David Hinton (New York: Counterpoint, 2000) 10, 11, 35, 40, 54–57, 73.

Rather than seeing life as a conflict between mutually exclusive forces, such as good versus evil and hatred versus love, yin and yang expressed cosmic harmony and unity, with alternating forces supporting and completing each other. Yang represented light, heat, daytime, dryness, and masculinity, while yin signified darkness, coolness, nighttime, moistness, and femininity. Yang was active, aggressive, logical, and rational; yin was passive, nurturing, intuitive, and emotional. Yang was dominant in spring and summer; yin prevailed in fall and winter. Yang was rock and yin was water; yang had strength and yin had stamina; yang was the sun and yin was the moon.

Yin-yang concept stresses natural harmony and balance, not good versus evil

As complementary forces, yin and yang both blended and gave way to each other, just as sun yielded to moon, day yielded to night, and summer yielded to fall. Nature needed both sun and rain, heat and coolness, and, of course, male and female. Society required both reason and emotion, strength and stamina, logic and intuition, action and passivity. Yin and yang represented a natural order based not on conflict and competition but on harmony, symmetry, and balance (see Figure 4.1).

Figure 4.1

Yin-Yang Symbol

The traditional symbol of yin and yang, with the light (yang) side (representing light, heat, daytime, dryness, and masculinity) blending into the dark (yin) side (representing darkness, coolness, nighttime, moistness, and femininity), signifies cosmic harmony and unity, with alternating forces supporting and completing each other.

The notion of yin and yang furnished Chinese people with a framework not only for understanding nature, but also for bringing balance to their everyday lives. Farmers, for example, had to have both strength and stamina, parents needed to be both assertive and nurturing, and the same person might be both a Confucian scholar by day and a Daoist poet by night. Indeed, Confucianism seemed to be rooted in rationality and logic, coinciding with yang, while Daoism relied on intuition and inspiration, corresponding with yin.

Legalism: Regulation, Coercion, and Control

At the end of the Eastern Zhou era, another approach arose that, unlike Daoism, saw harmony and order not as existing naturally in society, but as needing to be imposed on people from above. This approach evolved from the insights of Xunzi (*SHOON-DZUH*), a Confucian scholar who lived from approximately 300 to 230 b.c.e. Witnessing the disorder and violence of the Warring States era, Xunzi concluded that humans are by nature brutal and selfish, and that their ambitions and passions must be curbed by rigorous laws, institutions, rewards, and punishments. Although Xunzi was a Confucian, his disciples Hanfeizi (*HAHN-FĀ-DZUH*) and Li Si (*LĒ-SUH*) expanded his ideas into **Legalism**, a philosophy advocating strict enforcement of stringent laws by a powerful authoritarian state.

Legalism favors strong ruler to impose law, order, and stability

Legalists believed above all in law and order, maintaining that only an authoritarian regime could instill the fear and discipline needed to impose unity and control. If the state was to be strong and prosperous, Legalists asserted, the ruler must possess both the power and the will to enforce strict laws, to punish those who disobeyed, and to suppress all disunity and dissent.

The Birth of the Empire Under the Qin Dynasty

With Legalist backing Shihuangdi creates a huge Chinese empire

In 247 b.c.e., anxious to implement his ideas, the Legalist Li Si became a key official in the state of Qin (*CHIN*), a rising power in northwest China that nine years earlier had overthrown the last Eastern Zhou king. Under Li Si's guidance, a talented, ambitious new Qin ruler set out to create a mighty empire. In one eventful decade, from 231 to 221 b.c.e., he conquered all the other northern states and much of southern China as well (Map 4.4). For the first time ever, almost all of China was united under one ruler. He came to be called Shihuangdi (*SHUR-HWAHNG-DĒ*), that is, the First Emperor, the man whose spectacular tomb was described at the start of this chapter.

Map 4.4 The Qin Empire, 221–206 B.C.E.

In a single decade, from 231 to 221 B.C.E., the state of Qin in west-central China conquered most of the rest of the country, creating China's first empire. Note that the First Emperor, who conquered and ruled all the area shaded on this map, also expanded China's northern fortifications against nomadic invasions, thus creating China's first "Great Wall." How did the Qin Empire, which disintegrated soon after the First Emperor's death in 210 B.C.E., help set the stage for even larger and much longer-lasting Chinese empires?

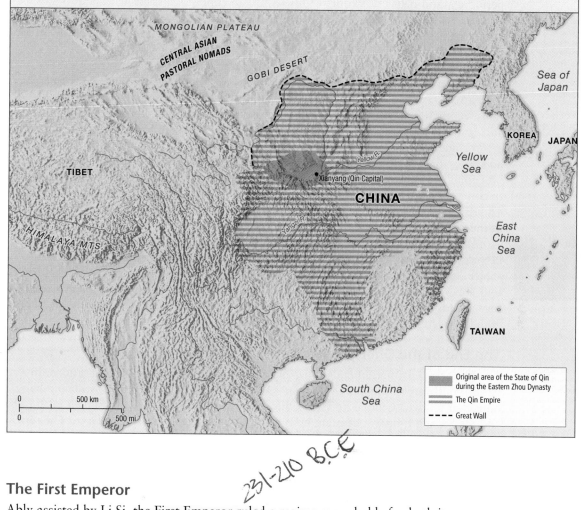

231–210 B.C.E.

The First Emperor

Ably assisted by Li Si, the First Emperor ruled a regime remarkable for both its accomplishments and its brutality. He abolished the conquered states, disarming their forces and executing their rulers. He divided China into provinces and districts headed by officials selected for their talent and loyalty. Rather than appointing his relatives or members of the old nobility, he instead chose able civil servants who were wholly accountable to him. He made the local nobles move to his capital so he could both keep them under close watch and take away their rural lands, causing them also to deplete their wealth by building costly new city homes. Inspired by Legalism and his own

The First Emperor creates a centralized, repressive Qin regime ambitions, he maintained a huge army, a pervasive surveillance system, and a brutal penal code—branding, burning, boiling, or burying alive those who defied his will.

Nothing, it seemed, could escape the First Emperor's determination to regulate Chinese society. To improve command, communication, and commerce, he standardized the written language and laws, coins and taxes, weights and measures, and even the width of roads and axle-width of carts. To intimidate his subjects he made periodic grand inspection tours of his realm. To suppress dissent he is said to have banned the study of philosophy and history, burned the books on those subjects, and buried several hundred scholars alive (ensuring his eventual vilification by later Chinese historians).

Using vast armies of forced laborers, at a huge cost in human lives, the First Emperor constructed massive projects that testified to his magnificence and megalomania. His extravagant palace, for example, measured over 120,000 square feet and could house up to 10,000 persons. Even more colossal was his tomb, whose chance discovery and fantastic features are described at the start of this chapter. His more practical projects included a complex irrigation system, a network of canals connecting China's rivers, and more than 4,000 miles of roads, fifty paces wide, which extended like spokes to link his capital with the regions of his realm. His most renowned achievement, however, was to connect all the fortifications built in the north to protect against nomadic invasions. The resulting structure, 1,400 miles long, later rebuilt and extended, came to be known as the Great Wall of China.

As time went on, and as his inhumane policies alienated his people, the First Emperor grew increasingly paranoid. After several assassination attempts by embittered subjects, he became obsessed with the fear of death. He had oracles and magicians try to find him a formula for everlasting life, and he even sent out a sea expedition to search for "islands of immortality." These efforts apparently failed: in 210 B.C.E., on one of his grand inspection tours, the First Emperor fell ill and died.

The End of the Qin Dynasty

The First Emperor had intended that his dynasty would last 10,000 generations. Instead it outlived him by only four years. His death was followed by provincial rebellions that plunged China into chaos, and by government intrigues that killed both Li Si and the Second Emperor, leading in 206 B.C.E. to the Qin dynasty's collapse. The rebel leaders then battled among themselves until one of them, a former peasant named Liu Bang (*L'YOO-BAHNG*), perceived as a man of the people, emerged victorious in 202 B.C.E. Building upon the centralized state created by the First Emperor, but ruling far more flexibly and humanely, Liu Bang assumed the Mandate of Heaven, starting a dynasty called the Han (*HAHN*) that endured for over 400 years.

The Growth of the Empire Under the Han Dynasty

The Han dynasty (202 B.C.E.–220 C.E.), started by Liu Bang, presided over one of the world's largest and wealthiest domains. In size and population, it matched the vast Roman Empire, then flourishing in the West. The Han Empire also produced a large, effective imperial administration, a sophisticated urban culture and intellectual life, and

The First Emperor standardizes laws, writing, money, weights, and roads

The First Emperor builds huge palace, canals, roads, and first Great Wall

China's Great Wall, now built of brick, began as an earthen barrier under the First Emperor.

The Qin regime is overthrown after the First Emperor dies

The Han Dynasty rules huge powerful empire for centuries

major advances in technology and commerce. The dynasty's impact was so enduring that, even today, the Chinese still call themselves the Han people.

The Early Han: Confucian Bureaucracy and Military Expansion

Liu Bang, later known as Emperor Gaozu[2] (*GOW-DZUH*), achieved considerable success by both extending the Qin state bureaucracy and reducing its severity. During his brief reign (202–195 B.C.E.) he lowered taxes, moderated punishments, and invited Confucian scholars, rigorously repressed by the Qin regime, to serve as state officials. Under his successors, in fact, these scholars came to dominate the bureaucracy, and Confucianism became the official ideology. The result was a ruling synthesis, combining the central authority of Legalism with the humane civility of Confucianism, that would endure for two thousand years—a shining example of China's ability to balance and blend dissimilar forces into a successful system.

Han rulers blend Legalist authority with Confucian civility

In the first few centuries of Han rule the bureaucracy became more formal. Initially, the emperors simply asked local officials to recommend talented young men for government posts. In 165 B.C.E., however, the emperor started examining these candidates to determine which ones were best qualified. Then, to improve the preparation of candidates, in 124 B.C.E. the dynasty established an imperial university at Chang'an (*CHAHNG-AHN*), the capital, not far from modern Xi'an. Later the regime would use written exams, based on mastery of Confucian thought, to decide whom to appoint. These developments laid the groundwork for what would become a key feature of Chinese governance—a professional civil service made up of educated scholars. Elsewhere officials were often warriors trained in military combat; in China they were scholars educated in Confucian civility and ethics.

Han Empire forms the first strong, effective civil service bureaucracy

But China did not lack warriors. After early Han emperors consolidated their realm, Han Wudi (*WOO-DĒ*), the Han Martial Emperor (141–87 B.C.E.), built the Chinese army into an expansive force. In a vigorous series of military campaigns, he extended his control to the south into northern Vietnam, to the north into southern Manchuria and northern Korea, and to the west into distant Central Asia (Map 4.5). He also attacked the Xiongnu (*shē-ONG-NOO*), warlike nomads who had menaced northern China for years, beginning a long struggle that continued under his successors. At its height the Han Empire ruled a vast territory extending more than 3,000 miles east to west and 2,000 miles north to south, embracing almost 60 million people.

The Han Martial Emperor builds a huge army and conquers neighboring lands

Rebellion, Reform, and Ruin

Wudi's many wars, however, and the massive recruitments and harsh new taxes required to support these conflicts, exhausted both China's resources and its people's patience. His successors, less capable than he, were further weakened by repeated Xiongnu raids and internal revolts. The imperial court was racked by intrigues between the emperor's in-laws and his **eunuchs**, castrated males who ran his palace and guarded his many **concubines**, women who served him sexually to ensure that he would have a male heir. As the only males besides the emperor allowed to have contact with his concubines, these men were rendered sexually impotent to ensure that potential heirs born to these

Han Wudi and companions, as pictured by a later artist.

---

[2] Chinese emperors often were awarded a historical name that differed from their given name. *Gaozu*, for example, means *High Progenitor*. The historical name is sometimes preceded by the dynasty name, for example, *Qin Shihuangdi*, *Han Gaozu*. The *first* name is the *family* name in China.

Map 4.5 The Han Empire, 202 B.C.E.–220 C.E.

China's longest enduring empire was that of the Han Dynasty, which reigned for over 400 years, extending its rule west into Central Asia, south into Southeast Asia, and northeast into Manchuria and Korea, forging cultural and commercial connections with these diverse regions. Observe that the Han also conflicted and connected with the Xiongnu, warlike nomads who threatened China from the north. How did the dynasty's territorial expansion, and its conflicts with the Xiongnu, impact developments in China?

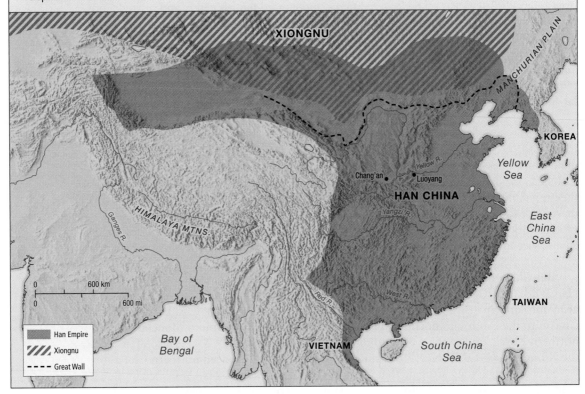

women were really the ruler's sons. Nonetheless, with their management of the palace and regular access to the emperor, talented and ambitious eunuchs often acquired great influence. In the process, they tended to clash with the royal in-laws, who likewise sought to use their position to gain power and wealth.

Palace intrigues among eunuchs and royal in-laws undermine Han rule

In 22 B.C.E., as palace intrigues between eunuchs and in-laws continued to cripple the court, revolts erupted throughout the empire. It looked as if the dynasty was losing Heaven's Mandate. Then, in 9 C.E., a palace coup deposed a child emperor and replaced him with Wang Mang (*WAHNG-MAHNG*), a devoted Confucian who had been on the young ruler's regency council.

Idealistic and egalitarian, Wang Mang launched a series of reforms designed to improve the common people's welfare. He abolished slavery, for example, and tried to take land away from wealthy landlords for use by the poor peasants. He also declared himself emperor, intending to start his own dynasty. But a series of droughts and bad harvests interrupted his plans, and his land transfers sparked fierce opposition among the rich landlords. Then, in 11 C.E., a catastrophic Yellow River flood drowned hundreds of thousands and left millions homeless. As China descended into chaos, various groups began to revolt, demanding the return of the Han dynasty. In 23 C.E., when victorious rebels beheaded Wang Mang and ate the rest of his body, it became clear that they did not think he possessed the Mandate of Heaven.

The Later Han: Revival and Decline

After a few more years of chaos, Han rule was restored under Guangwudi (*GWAHNG-WOO-DĒ*), the Shining Martial Emperor, who reigned from 25 to 57 C.E., initiating an era known as the Later Han (25–220 C.E.). Guangwudi moved the capital east to Luoyang, perhaps because it was near his power base and perhaps also to signify a fresh start. For the next few generations, he and his heirs maintained peace and prosperity, thanks partly to their energetic and conscientious rule, partly to a long stretch of disaster-free weather, and partly to internal strife among the Xiongnu nomads who threatened northern China. In 89 C.E., Chinese generals took advantage of this strife to inflict a crushing defeat upon the nomads, thus ending for a while the chronic Xiongnu threat. In the following decade the generals restored Chinese rule in Central Asia, and one of them even ventured as far west as the Caspian Sea. By 100 C.E. the Han realm had recovered much of its former size and wealth.

The Shining Martial Empire restores Han rule and stability

During the next century, however, dynastic decline resumed. A succession of youthful and short-lived emperors set off a new series of conflicts between their in-laws and court eunuchs. Dismayed by these intrigues, several groups of Confucian civil servants and students sought to rebel in the 160s, only to be tortured and butchered in a wholesale purge. Then came floods and droughts, locust infestations that destroyed the crops, and a deadly epidemic (perhaps smallpox or plague), apparently brought to China by Central Asian nomads, that took millions of lives. The result was massive suffering and population decline, adding to the impression that the Han rulers were losing Heaven's Mandate.

Landlords impose serfdom, sparking mass rebellions

Taking advantage of the anarchy, powerful landlords seized the occasion to subject the villagers to serfdom, a status that bound them to perpetual service on the land. This action in turn triggered peasant revolts, led by a rebel group called the Yellow Turbans, whose head cloths signified solidarity with the earth, traditionally associated in China with the color yellow. Han armies ultimately crushed these revolts, but the generals then took the land for themselves and emerged as regional warlords. After the year 190 C.E., when one of these generals seized Luoyang, deposed the reigning ruler, and slaughtered hundreds of his relatives and eunuchs, all semblance of centralized authority ceased. In 220 C.E., after several more disastrous decades of chaos and civil war, another general forced the last Han emperor to abdicate, officially ending one of China's longest, strongest, and most illustrious dynasties.

Revolts and civil war end Han rule in 220 C.E.

Society, Technology, and the Silk Road

Nonetheless, while the Han dynasty lasted, China boasted one of the world's most stable and productive societies, and many of the world's most useful technologies. As it extended its reach into Central Asia, China also increased its commerce with other cultures along a network of trade routes that came to be called the Silk Road.

Han Society

Han society, like that of other ancient civilizations, was based mainly on village farming and herding. In northern China, where the climate was cool and dry, farmers grew wheat and millet. In the south, where it was warmer and wetter, they mainly raised rice in fields that were flooded to provide continuous moisture. Many peasants also raised chickens and pigs, and some had oxen or water buffalo to help plow the fields. Most agrarian labor, however, was accomplished by human effort.

Patriarchal Chinese families include all living relatives and dead ancestors

Chinese peasants' lives were centered on their families, including not just their parents and children but also the rest of their living relatives and even their departed ancestors, widely believed to be actively concerned with the fortunes of their descendants. Families were ruled by their patriarchs, elder males who made the major decisions, and these men consulted with the spirits of family forebears and conducted ceremonies to venerate both their ancestors and the gods. All family members were expected to obey their elders and superiors.

Women seen as subservient to men in traditional Chinese society

Chinese women, as a rule, were subordinate to men. A bride's father arranged her marriage, typically providing a dowry, and she then became part of her new husband's family. Due to such customs, daughters were often seen by their parents as a burden, to be raised and fed as children only to join and benefit another family as adults. Girls were thus treated as inferior to boys, and young women were trained chiefly to serve as wives and mothers. Wives were required to cook, make clothes, and clean—in Chinese script the character for wife was a woman using a broom. They were also expected to help in the fields when needed and, above all, to bear and raise sons. Women's lives were said to be governed by the "three submissions:" first to their fathers when they were young, second to their husbands when they were married, and third to their sons when they were ultimately widowed.

Chinese women, despite subordinate status, often run their households

Despite their duties and submissions, Chinese women were to some extent protected by Confucian doctrine, which said that fathers, husbands, and sons should treat them with respect and dignity. In addition, Chinese custom made women the household managers, giving those with strong characters an opportunity for influence within the home and family.

Chinese peasants endure poverty and harsh labor

The lives of most peasants were likewise confined. In theory, farmers were highly valued, since the food they grew was vital to survival. Indeed, the Confucian social order ranked farmers higher than merchants, since the former were producers while the latter were viewed as mere traffickers and traders. In reality, however, this ranking meant little. Most peasants lived in poverty, dwelling in villages of wood and bamboo huts, often toiling in service to a wealthy landlord. They worked the fields, tilling, hoeing, and harvesting, with little or no protection from the heat, wind, rain, or cold. Peasants were also expected to pay taxes, to provide the state with periodic labor for building public works projects, and often to serve in the army. Rural life was dreary, with few diversions to break the daily routine.

Urban life provides comforts, entertainments, and diversions

Urban life was far more diverse and sophisticated. Metropolitan areas such as Chang'an and Luoyang, the two great Han capitals, had overall populations of up to a quarter million people, with some 100,000 of them living within the city walls. Wealthy officials and merchants resided in two- or three-story homes made of stucco or wood, with gardens and terraces, plentiful food, and servants to tend their needs. Poorer residents, mostly artisans and laborers, lived in much humbler circumstances, but unlike peasants they had access to urban recreations and diversions. Major cities had palaces, parks, marketplaces, and temples; Chang'an even had a zoo. Entertainment ranged from music, art, and poetry to magic shows, juggling acts, and puppet performances.

Urban life in Han China also had a seamy side. As in modern cities there were gambling houses, brothels, and gangs of youths who roamed the streets. Public executions, designed to deter both crime and disloyalty, typically attracted large crowds. Still, officials posted in small provincial towns, deploring their humdrum existence, often dreamed of reassignment to one of the large, vibrant cities.

Technical and Commercial Creativity

Han cities were also centers of creativity, commerce, and craftsmanship. Here scholars, officials, doctors, inventors, and artisans, freed from the need to farm, developed ideas and techniques that would distinguish Chinese culture as enterprising and ingenious.

Scholars and bureaucrats, for example, exchanged ideas and kept records by writing with small brushes on paper—a product invented in Han China. Astronomers charted the paths of planets and recorded sunspots; other scientists studied acoustics and measured earthquakes. Doctors diagnosed diseases, prescribed herbal remedies and drugs, and discovered the circulation of blood. Physicians also used acupuncture, the insertion of thin needles at various points in the body, to relieve pain and cure ailments, theoretically by restoring the body's yin and yang balance. Farmers benefited from innovations such as wheelbarrows to help carry their loads, water mills to help grind their grain, iron plows to help turn their soil, and harnesses to enhance the labor of their oxen and buffalo.

Commerce and craftsmanship also reflected Chinese ingenuity. Metropolitan markets had a wide array of shops and stalls run by manufacturers and merchants. Their wares were produced by skilled artisans, who worked with bronze, pottery, lacquer, jade, and silk to make tools, utensils, plates, vessels, jewelry, and clothing. These goods might then be purchased directly by people of means or sold to merchants who took the products elsewhere and resold them at a profit. Their travels were aided by a network of canals and roads, complete with suspension bridges. Carts and wagons traversed the roads, while boats plied the rivers and canals, carrying commodities all across China—and, increasingly, beyond (Map 4.6).

Model of a Han era house

Scholarship, science, medicine, and farming flourish in Han China

Networks of roads and canals aid commerce and crafts

The Silk Road and the Sea Trade

As conquest and commerce increased contacts with other cultures, Chinese products came to be highly prized in other lands. Indeed, by the second century B.C.E., several land and sea routes linking the Han Empire with southern and western Asia were already in operation. But long distance trade was risky, due to bandits, storms, and treacherous terrain.

Then, in 126 B.C.E., a Chinese general named Zhang Qian (*JAHNG chē-AN*), after spending many years in Central Asia in the service of the Martial Emperor (Wudi), returned to China with reports of peoples, plants, and products hitherto unknown in the Han Empire. He told of lands far beyond the western wastelands, such as Bactria, Ferghana (*fur-GAH-nuh*), and Persia, with bountiful vineyards whose grapes produced fine wines, as well as splendid horses superior to any in China. He also said that in markets of these regions he had sometimes seen Chinese products, including bamboo canes and silk cloth, no doubt conveyed there along early trade routes.

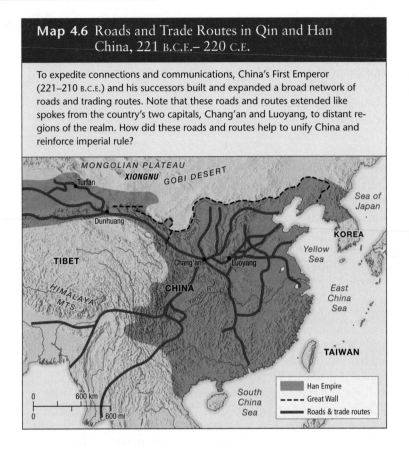

Map 4.6 Roads and Trade Routes in Qin and Han China, 221 B.C.E.– 220 C.E.

To expedite connections and communications, China's First Emperor (221–210 B.C.E.) and his successors built and expanded a broad network of roads and trading routes. Note that these roads and routes extended like spokes from the country's two capitals, Chang'an and Luoyang, to distant regions of the realm. How did these roads and routes help to unify China and reinforce imperial rule?

Chinese conquest of Central Asia boosts commerce with other cultures

Eager to expand his power and wealth, Wudi sent armies into Central Asia, adding cities and realms to his domains and making them tributaries of China. For many of these new subjects this arrangement had advantages, as Chinese soldiers provided protection from bandits, while Han officials sent valuable silk to retain the tributaries' allegiance. The Chinese presence also helped to establish and sustain the long-distance trading network later called the Silk Road.

Silk Road provides commercial connections across Eurasia

The **Silk Road,** named for the precious Chinese fabric often conveyed along its route, was actually a series of trails that connected trading towns across the heart of Asia. The route extended from China westward for thousands of miles across central Asia, with links from there through Bactria into India and through Persia into Mesopotamia and the eastern Mediterranean (Map 4.7). The Silk Road thus provided a commercial connection, though rather tenuous and treacherous, among the various societies of Eurasia and North Africa.

Merchants typically did not travel the whole length of the road; instead they made their way back and forth between certain trading cities, where they could exchange the goods they had brought for goods coming from the other direction. Merchandise was thus transported in a series of stages, passing through many hands along the way. Since

Map 4.7 The Silk Road and Sea Trade, by First Century B.C.E.

The Silk Road, opened by about 100 B.C.E., was a complex series of trade routes linking towns across Asia, providing connections among regions such as China, India, Persia, and West Asia. Note that overland links connected the Silk Road to several sea ports, from which goods were shipped by sea lanes connecting East and Southeast Asia, Indonesia, India, Persia, Arabia, and Africa. What key products were shipped along the Silk Road, and how were they transported? Along with goods, what else did the Silk Road and sea trade convey?

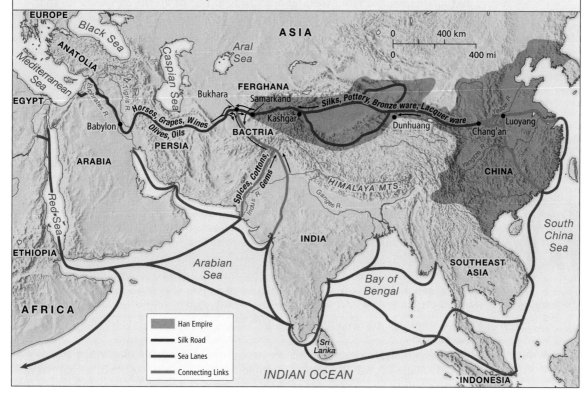

all who handled these items wished to make a profit, and since numerous local princes often imposed tolls and fees, items might well cost many times more at their final destination than they did at their point of origin.

Nonetheless the Silk Road flourished for more than a thousand years, as did the bustling cities and towns that grew up along its route. Located at key passes and junctures, cities such as Dunhuang (*DUN-WAHNG*), Kashgar (*KAHSH-gar*), Samarkand (*SAH-mur-KAHND*) and Bukhara (*boo-KAH-ruh*) bustled with traders, money-changers, camel breeders, and guides, and teemed with markets full of exotic goods. Less celebrated, but no less important, were many smaller settlements along the way, where travelers found rest and recreation as well as food and water for their horses and camels. Some of the cities were independent, with their own ruling princes and dynasties, but many in time came under the protection of larger domains such as China and Persia.

Trading towns flourish along the Silk Road for centuries

Goods from India, China, Europe, and West Asia are exchanged along Silk Road

Traffic on the trade routes typically consisted of items not produced in the country of destination. From the west came fine horses, highly treasured in China, as well as grapes and wines, olives and oils, precious stones and metals, jewelry, and arts and crafts. From the south came Indian cottons, along with cinnamon, ginger, and other Asian spices that were highly valued for flavoring food and for making medications, perfumes, and magic potions. From the east came Chinese pottery, bronze ware, and lacquerware, prized throughout Eurasia. But of all the choice items that made their way westward, perhaps the most treasured were the fine fabrics for which the Silk Road was named. By the first century B.C.E., Chinese silk clothing, with its brilliant colors and exquisite texture, was in fashion among the wealthy as far west as Rome.

Camel caravans transport goods along Silk Road

Cargoes were conveyed along the Silk Road sometimes by horses and wagons, but often by caravans of camels, especially the dual-humped Bactrian variety, whose shaggy hair helped them endure the harsh, windy Central Asian winters. In time camel keepers crossbred these creatures with single-humped Arabian dromedaries, producing a larger and stronger camel that still had a warm shaggy coat. Saddled with bulging sacks, draped on both sides to equalize the weight, and skillfully led by trained guides across mountains and deserts, these ill-tempered but invaluable animals carried loads weighing hundreds of pounds for dozens of miles a day.

Bactrian camel.

Some Chinese merchants, especially those near the southern coast and far from the Central Asian land routes, conducted their trade by sea. But as with the land routes, so along the sea lanes (Map 4.7), merchants and vessels rarely made the entire trip from one end of the line to the other. Instead, Chinese vessels typically traveled the South China Sea to trade with Southeast Asia and the lands later known as Malaya and Indonesia. From there some goods were transshipped, in Malayan or Indian vessels, to India and Sri Lanka, and thence in Persian or Arab crafts to Persia, Arabia, and Egypt. From Egypt some items were resold into the Mediterranean network, eventually ending up in places such as Greece or Rome.

Sea lanes link China with India, Persia, Arabia, Egypt, and Europe

Along with goods, diseases and beliefs were at times conveyed on the Silk Road. Epidemics of smallpox and plague, for example, including deadly outbreaks that ravaged both China and Rome in the second century C.E., spread through Central Asia along the trade routes. In that same century, as we saw in Chapter 3, Buddhist beliefs spread from India to Central Asia, and from there eventually to China along the Silk Road.

Silk Road connections also spread diseases and beliefs.

Despite the importance of the Silk Road and sea lanes, however, the contacts they provided between China and other lands were tenuous and indirect. The Chinese became acquainted with the goods of other regions, for example, but learned little about their people. And the Western societies that valued Chinese goods had little real knowledge of the eastern culture that produced such marvelous merchandise.

Chapter Review

Putting It in Perspective

In many ways, early China was similar to other ancient societies. Like the others, Chinese society began along a river, was based on agriculture, and developed extensive trade networks and large cities. Like the others, it came to be ruled by monarchs who had semi-divine status and governed by means of officials and armies. Like the others, its social structure was stratified, with an aristocratic elite, urban classes of merchants and artisans, and a rural peasantry that made up most of the population.

In other respects, however, Chinese society was distinctive. The Mandate of Heaven, for example, could justify rebellion against rulers who failed to furnish stability and security, a concept unknown in most other early cultures. The Confucian ethic, which held state officials accountable for public welfare, conveyed the relatively rare idea that government should serve society. The notion of yin and yang, with its focus on balance and harmony, provided a perspective that differed from the view of reality as a struggle between good and evil. And the Chinese civil service, with its stress on education and ethics, gave China a government whose officials were trained as scholars rather than as military leaders.

As China's contacts with other cultures grew, it was increasingly influenced by these connections. From Central Asian nomads, the Chinese learned to use chariots and cast bronze, and later to ride horses and forge iron. From the Silk Road and sea trade, the Chinese became acquainted with goods from India, Persia, and West Asia, while Chinese products likewise became available in these places. China nonetheless retained its distinctive character, a land whose products were prized, but whose ways were largely unknown, in expansive societies far to China's west, such as Persia, Greece, and Rome.

Reviewing Key Material

KEY CONCEPTS

ancestor worship, 85
Mandate of Heaven, 87
dynastic cycle, 88
Confucianism, 90
Daoism, 92

yin and yang, 92
Legalism, 94
eunuchs, 97
concubines, 97
Silk Road, 102

KEY PEOPLE

King Wu, 86
Duke of Zhou, 87
King You, 88
Confucius (Kongfuzi), 90
Laozi, 92
Mencius (Mengzi), 92
Xunzi, 94
Hanfeizi, 94
Li Si, 94

Shihuangdi (First
  Emperor), 94
Liu Bang (Emperor
  Gaozu), 96
Wudi (Martial Emperor), 97
Wang Mang, 98
Guangwudi (Shining
  Martial Emperor), 99
Zhang Qian, 101

ASK YOURSELF

1. In what ways was Chinese civilization similar to other ancient civilizations, and in what ways was it distinct? How do you account for these distinctions?
2. What were the advantages and disadvantages of the Chinese writing system? How did it benefit an empire that was vast and linguistically diverse?
3. What were the advantages and disadvantages of the Mandate of Heaven concept and the pattern of dynastic cycle? How did these concepts affect the development of the Chinese empire?
4. How did the concept of yin and yang differ from notions of good versus evil? How did the concept help the Chinese to embrace disparate belief systems such as Confucianism and Daoism?
5. Why did Legalist principles prove effective in creating a vast empire, but ineffective in maintaining it for long? Why did the Han ruling synthesis, combining elements of Legalism and Confucianism, prove so successful and enduring?

GOING FURTHER

Adshead, S. A. M. *China in World History*. 3rd ed. 2000.

Chang, Kwang-chih. *The Archaeology of Ancient China*. 4th ed. 1986.

Clements, J. *Confucius: A Biography*. 2005.

De Bary, T., ed. *Sources of Chinese Tradition*. 2000.

De Grazia, S., ed. *Masters of Chinese Political Thought*. 1973.

Di Cosmo, Nicola. *Ancient China and Its Enemies*. 2002.

Ebrey, Patricia B., et al. *Pre-Modern East Asia*. 2006.

Fairbank, J. K. *China: A New History*. 1992.

Fong, W. *Great Bronze Age of China*. 1980.

Franck, Irene, and D. Brownstone. *The Silk Road: A History*. 1986.

Grotenhuis, E. T., ed. *Along the Silk Road*. 2002.

Hansen, Valerie. *The Open Empire*. 2000.

Hinsch, Bret. *Women in Early Imperial China*. 2002.

Holcombe, Charles. *The Genesis of East Asia*. 2001.

Hsu, Cho-yun, and J. M. Linduff. *Western Zhou Civilization*. 1988.

Keightley, D. *The Origins of Chinese Civilization*. 1983.

Knapp, Ronald. *China's Walled Cities*. 2000.

Li Xueqin. *Eastern Zhou and Qin Civilizations*. 1985.

Loewe, Michael. *Everyday Life in Early Imperial China*. 1988.

Loewe, Michael. *The Pride That Was China*. 1990.

Mote, F. W. *Intellectual Foundations of China*. 2nd ed. 1989.

Needham, J. *Science in Traditional China*. 1981.

Shaughnessy, E. L., ed. *China: Empire and Civilization*. 2005.

Shwartz, Benjamin I. *The World of Thought in Ancient China*. 1985.

Temple, Robert. *The Genius of China*. 1986.

Van Norden, V. W., ed. *Confucius and the Analects*. 2002.

Waley, Arthur. *Three Ways of Thought in Ancient China*. 1983.

Wang, Zhongshu. *Han Civilization*. 1982.

Whitfield, Susan. *Life Along the Silk Road*. 2001.

Whitfield, Susan, ed. *The Silk Roads*. 2004.

Wood, Francis. *The Silk Road*. 2002.

Key Dates and Developments

by 7000 B.C.E.	Farming in Yellow River valley
2200–1750 B.C.E.	Xia dynasty
1750–1122 B.C.E.	Shang dynasty
1122–770 B.C.E.	Western Zhou dynasty
770–256 B.C.E.	Eastern Zhou dynasty
551–479 B.C.E.	Confucius
by 500 B.C.E.	Laozi and origins of Daoism
403–221 B.C.E.	Warring States Era (Mencius, Xunzi)
231–221 B.C.E.	China united by Qin Shihuangdi
221–210 B.C.E.	Reign of Qin Shihuangdi (First Emperor)
202 B.C.E.–6 C.E.	Early Han dynasty
202–195 B.C.E.	Reign of Han Gaozu (Liu Bang)
147–87 B.C.E.	Reign of Han Wudi (Martial Emperor)
by 100 B.C.E.	Origins of the Silk Road
9–23 C.E.	Reign of Wang Mang
25–220 C.E.	Later Han dynasty

Early American Societies: Connection and Isolation, 20,000 B.C.E.–1500 C.E.

- Origins and Arrival of the Amerinds

- The Amerinds of North America

- The Amerinds of Mesoamerica

- South America: Societies of the Andes

- Chapter Review

Pueblo Bonito, Chaco Canyone, New Mexico

Early Americans settled in many different parts of the western hemisphere. Their settlements conformed architecturally to their differing locations, as the ruins of this site in New Mexico are appropriate to a desert canyon setting (page 114).

Early in May 1945, as Soviet troops captured Berlin and ended World War II in Europe, a young Soviet soldier saw that the German National Library was on fire. He was able to save one book from the flames: an exceedingly rare collection of three manuscripts written by the Maya, an American Indian society that had flourished in present-day Guatemala and Mexico before the tenth century C.E. Fascinated by the symbols in the manuscript, the soldier—Yuri Knosorov—returned to the Soviet Union, left the army, and earned a degree in linguistics at Moscow State University.

In 1952 Knosorov quietly published an article entitled "Ancient Writing of Central America." Scholars had been unable to decipher Mayan writing, but his study of it convinced him that the symbols, called glyphs, represented ideas rather than sounds, as experts had previously thought. If true, this would make Mayan writing similar to the hieroglyphic writing of ancient Egypt, and would suggest ways to decipher it. In 1953 his article caught the attention of Tania Proskouriakoff, who had fled the Russian Revolution as an 8-year-old girl in 1917 and had earned a degree in architecture at Penn State. Proskouriakoff had studied Mayan architecture for two decades. She concluded that the figures depicted in Mayan pictorial writing were not gods but ordinary people. This insight, combined with that of Knosorov, led to one of the great intellectual breakthroughs of modern times: the decipherment of Mayan writing. Finally, three decades later, scholars were confidently translating Mayan glyphs and reaching a deeper understandings of Mayan society, one of the most complex of those formed by the peoples known as American Indians. Without the work of Knosorov and Proskouriakoff, much of what this chapter will say about the Maya would have remained unknown.

Areas of Amerind Settlement

Origins and Arrival of the Amerinds

Human life originated in eastern Africa and spread outward to other continents through migration. North and South America, remote from eastern Africa, were the last continents to be populated by humans. When groups of hunting-gathering peoples entered North America through Alaska and pushed southward in search of food and a milder climate, they found abundant wildlife that had never been hunted by humans and therefore did not fear them. Some of these people remained hunter-gatherers, pursuing many mammal species to extinction; others, thousands of years later, turned to agriculture in regions with fertile soils and abundant rainfall.

In most of the Western Hemisphere, human communities remained small and relatively isolated from one another. Some developed towns and even long-range trade networks, and some attempted to combine their societies into larger confederations, but their small populations did not generally require or give rise to complex political and social systems. In two regions, however, complex societies did develop: **Mesoamerica**, which comprises Mexico and northern Central America, and that portion of the Andean mountain range that stretches from Ecuador through Peru to Bolivia and northern Chile. Peoples in these regions were also the only ones able to offer organized resistance against the Europeans who invaded in the sixteenth century of the Common Era.

The Europeans mistakenly thought that the islands of the Caribbean where they first landed were part of the Spice Islands, or eastern "Indies," and so they called the people they encountered *Indians*. This term is still used. In recent years the term *Native Americans* gained popularity with some Indian and non-Indian groups, but it is technically inaccurate, since no human life was "native" to the Western Hemisphere. In this book, we follow anthropological practice in designating these people as **Amerinds** (*AM-uh-rinds*), or American Indians, to distinguish them from the Indians of Asia.

The first humans to reach the Western Hemisphere either walked or traveled in boats from Asia to Alaska. Anthropological evidence clearly points to their Asiatic heritage. Amerind languages are similar in syntax to those of northeastern Asia; Amerinds physically resemble the Mongolian peoples of central Asia, an ethnic group that at one time populated most of northeastern Asia; and, in overwhelming numbers, Amerinds have Type O blood carrying a specific antigen found only in Mongolian peoples.

Amerinds move from the Eastern to the Western Hemisphere

Most Amerinds, however, do not accept these anthropological conclusions regarding their ancestry, preferring native religious accounts that tell of their origins in the Western Hemisphere. Navajo accounts of the Creation, for example, assert that the first American Indians ascended through three subterranean worlds before finally settling in this one, the fourth world. Snohomish lore states that the Creator and Changer began making the world and its peoples in the East, after which he slowly moved westward, creating as he came. The Amerinds, according to the Snohomish, were created in the West, in what came to be called the Americas.

Alternative accounts of Amerind origins

Presuming that the linguistic and biological evidence is correct raises another question: how did the Amerinds cross from Asia to America? At least twice during the Ice Ages of the Pleistocene period, first between 50,000 and 40,000 B.C.E. and again between 26,000 and 8000 B.C.E., tremendous quantities of water were trapped in immense ice caps and glaciers, thus lowering ocean levels by several hundred feet. The Bering Strait, separating Siberia from Alaska, is only 120 feet deep; during the Ice Ages it stood hundreds of feet above sea level, forming a land bridge between Siberia and Alaska. At one point around 18,000 B.C.E. the land bridge was approximately 1,000 miles wide from north to south.

Clovis arrowheads found at sites in New Mexico, Arizona, and Colorado.

The Bering land bridge was used by caribou, reindeer, wooly mammoth, camels, and giant sloths. Some of these species survived in the Western Hemisphere, while others were hunted to extinction by the Amerinds. Since there is archeological proof of human occupation of the Americas beginning between 12,000 and 10,000 B.C.E., most scholars assume that Amerinds crossed around that time, that is, during the second long era in which the land bridge was exposed. There are no cultural artifacts or human bones datable to the earlier era of the land bridge, more than 40,000 years ago. Moreover, the absence of evidence of fur clothing and subterranean (or pit) houses, either in America or in northeastern Asia earlier than 15,000 years ago, supports the more recent dating, as protective clothing and underground dwellings would have been essential to the survival of nomadic groups in the frigid Siberian-Alaskan climate.

Arrows indicate the probable arrival and dispersal routes of the Amerinds. Note the enormous ice sheets that covered much of present-day Canada, and the southward flow of peoples from present-day Alaska through an ice-free corridor. This arrival pattern is the most widely accepted hypothesis, but not the only one: some archeologists suggest that Amerinds may have arrived before the North American glacier began melting and then traveled down the coast in boats rather than moving overland. If the most widely accepted hypothesis is true, why would many Amerinds have continued moving southward, rather than all stopping in the present-day United States?

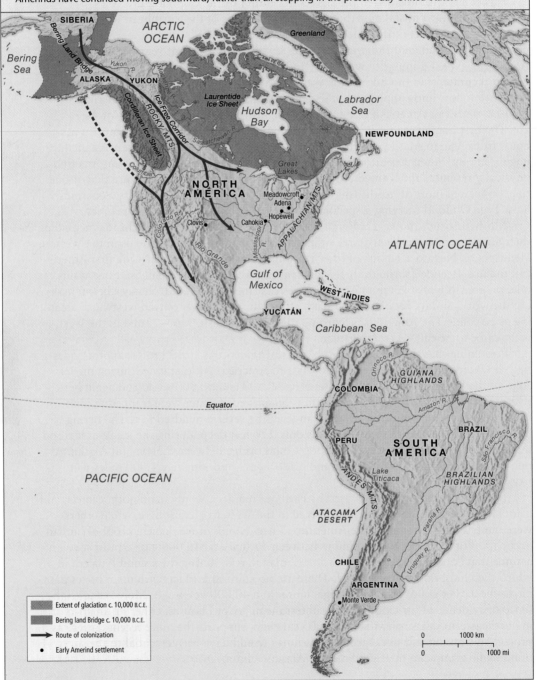

Complicating this theory is evidence of an extensive, impassable barrier of ice separating the area now called Alaska from northwestern Canada between 21,000 and 11,000 B.C.E. Only after that time did the climate warm sufficiently to create ice-free corridors along the continental divide (Map 5.1). Humans could pass through these corridors southward to Mesoamerica and from there to South America. Simultaneously the land bridge flooded and future human migration would have been possible only by boat. Many scholars therefore conclude that people crossed from Siberia to Alaska around 14,000 years ago, remained there for about a millennium, and moved south sometime after 11,200 B.C.E.

Most of the artifacts and skeletal remains found in the Americas are consistent with this explanation. However, DNA evidence from living South American Indians analyzed in 1994 indicates a probable human arrival date between 27,000 and 20,000 B.C.E. Further study in 1997 yielded a date between 41,000 and 31,000 B.C.E., before the peak of the last Ice Age, when the Canadian ice sheets merged. Coast-hopping in boats could have taken Amerinds down the entire Pacific coast of the Americas in fewer than twenty years. Since coastal settlements, if they existed, would have eventually been flooded by melting glaciers, archeological evidence would be unobtainable.

Historians dispute the timing of the Amerind arrival

As these analyses were being published in the late 1990s, dramatic archeological findings at Monte Verde in southern Chile appeared to confirm the existence there of an Amerind village dating to between 14,000 and 10,500 B.C.E. That would place Amerinds at the southern tip of South America before the ice sheets had melted sufficiently to permit human passage. But if the DNA evidence is true, why have no human remains from 20,000–40,000 B.C.E. been found in the Western Hemisphere? Is it because no such remains exist? Or have archeologists not been digging in the right places, or not yet dug deeply enough?

All such speculations are plausible, yet none is supported by convincing evidence. There are other intriguing findings from archeological digs. The Meadowcroft Rockshelter site in southwestern Pennsylvania contains artifacts that may have been fabricated as early as 14,000 B.C.E. Skulls found in Kennewick, Washington, and Spirit Cave, Nevada, suggest that not all Amerinds were of Central Asian origin. Faces reconstructed from these skulls resemble people from the South Pacific islands rather than Mongolia. In the first decade of the twenty-first century, we know that the Amerinds arrived in the Americas from somewhere in Asia. But that is all we know for certain.

The Amerinds of North America

The first people to set foot in North America were nomadic hunter-gatherers. Agriculture appeared about four thousand years later, apparently beginning before 3000 B.C.E. in southern Mexico. The first domesticated plants were probably pumpkins and chili peppers, grown perhaps as early as 7000 B.C.E. Maize (or corn) appeared in central Mexico around 5000 B.C.E. and in southern Mexico 2500 years after that. Between 2000 and 1000 B.C.E., farming villages emerged in central Mexico. Available evidence suggests that the idea of domesticating plants spread northward and southward from Mesoamerica. In North America, farming reached what is now the southwestern United States between 3500 and 2500 B.C.E., the "Eastern Woodlands" of the United States by 1000 B.C.E., and

American agriculture begins in southern Mexico

southern Canada sometime around 500 B.C.E. Agriculture therefore spread north from Mesoamerica over most of North America thousands of years after its appearance in the river civilizations of Asia, delaying the development of North American settled societies for an equivalent period.

Since few North American Amerinds had written languages, what we know of their early societies is based largely on archeological evidence and oral tradition. Scholars have categorized their societies (before the European invasion) into four principal types: hunter-gatherer bands, limited-scale tribal societies, full-scale tribal societies, and complex mound-building and trading societies.

Two Hunter-Gatherer Bands

Hunter-gatherers adapt to environmental conditions

Two North American societal groups, the Arctic and the Great Basin, lacked any genuine political organization. The environments these groups lived in hindered organizational development. In the *Arctic*, where the Eskimo (or Inuit) people lived, frozen, snow-covered ground and brief or nonexistent growing seasons made organized agriculture impossible. Their shelters, made of ice, often melted during the summer, further discouraging permanent settlement. The preinvasion Eskimo lived in small nomadic bands under the informal leadership of whoever happened to be the most proficient hunter. The *Great Basin* societies of Utah and Nevada, such as the Paiute (*PĪ-oot*) and Shoshone (*shō-SHŌ-nē*) peoples, were similarly nomadic, moving about the desert in family units during the lengthy summers and coming together in villages during the winters. Each family had its own leader.

Five Limited-Scale Tribal Societies

Nomadic peoples unite into tribes

More complex political organization emerged in five regions, where societies sometimes coalesced into **tribes**—large associations of villages, bands, or clans that share a common language and often a common leader. But tribes functioned only occasionally—during wartime, for example. Most of the time, these Amerinds associated in individual villages, bands, or clans. Authority was therefore mixed: family elders decided some issues, clan leaders others, and tribal leaders yet others.

In the eastern Canadian *Sub-Arctic* (Map 5.2), the Algonquian (*al-GON-kwē-un*) peoples banded together for the purpose of hunting caribou, a staple of their diet and an animal that, since it traveled in large herds, was best hunted by groups of at least a few dozen people. Hunting thus required that hunting bands combine into tribes, although the affiliation was loose and the tribes had little other impact on everyday life.

Along the *Northwest Coast*, from present-day Oregon north to Alaska, lived diverse maritime peoples whose access to rich food sources encouraged the formation of densely populated fishing villages. These people lived largely by hunting and by fishing the rivers and coastal waters for salmon and seafood, which they preserved by smoking so it would sustain them year round. From the region's great evergreen forests they built splendid wooden homes and carved large dugout canoes and elaborate totem poles that traced their genealogies. Some of their villages combined to form tribes, while others remained fiercely independent. In the neighboring *Plateau* region,

Totem poles from western Canada, carved from Western Red Cedar and depicting real or mythical events.

Map 5.2 North American Amerind Culture Areas, ca. 1500 C.E.

Many Amerind peoples moved through Canada and settled in what is now the United States. The more temperate climate there made agriculture possible, and the Great Plains were filled with buffalo and other large mammals that could be hunted for food and hides. Observe the distribution of peoples across this temperate climate zone: no region was free from settlement. What distinctions in lifestyle might be expected across such a wide area?

INUITS

KUTCHINS

INUITS

INUITS

ARCTIC

Hudson
Bay

INUITS

TLINGITS

SUB-ARCTIC

BEAVERS

CREES

INUITS

CREES

BELLA
COOLAS

KWAKIUTLS

BLACKFEET

CHIPPEWAS

ALGONQUINS

NORTHWEST
COAST

PLATEAU

MANDANS

HURONS

IROQUOIS
(HAUDENOSAUNEE)

NEZ PERCÉS

CROWS

LAKOTAS

EASTERN
WOODLANDS

COOS

SHOSHONES

CHEYENNES

LENI-LENAPES

POMOS

GREAT
PLAINS

MIAMIS

GREAT
BASIN

SHAWNEES

POWHATAN

ARAPAHOS

CALIFORNIA

HOPIS

OSAGES

APACHES

CHEROKEE

NAVAJOS

SOUTHEAST

ATLANTIC
OCEAN

HOHOKAMS

PUEBLOS

COMANCHES

NATCHEZ

APACHES

PACIFIC OCEAN

SOUTHWEST

Gulf of Mexico

MESO-
AMERICA

Caribbean Sea

0   500 km

0   500 mi

113

Anasazi cliff dwelling in the Canyon de Chelly, Arizona territory, photographed in 1873.

encompassing the inland areas of Washington, Oregon, and Idaho, people were originally grouped into individual villages, but eventually learned tribal organization from others to their southeast.

In the *Southwest* there emerged a wide variety of societies, ranging from Navajo and Apache (*NAH-vuh-hō, uh-PATCH-ē*) nomadic bands to the town-dwelling Pueblo (*PWĀ-blō*) Indians, who built walled settlements with central plazas and residences made of adobe (*ah-DŌ-bē*) brick or masonry (see page 107). Flourishing from the second through fourteenth centuries C.E., the early Pueblo peoples, also called Anasazi (*ah-nuh-SAH-zē*), grew maize, squash, and beans using complex irrigation techniques, and produced fine pottery, woven baskets, and cotton cloth. At one point, perhaps for protection, they built cliff dwellings and multistory terraced apartment houses, guarded by watchtowers. Many such cliff houses still survive in Arizona and New Mexico. After 1300, however, Anasazi society declined, probably as a result of drought and invasions by warlike outsiders. In *California*, the Amerinds lived in extended families organized as small tribes.

Four Full-Scale Tribal Societies

Four groups developed full-scale tribal organization, with the tribes functioning continuously. Each tribe was composed of thousands of people ruled by a variety of political chiefs, war chiefs, and religious leaders.

The Cheyenne develop a structured society

The *Plains* Indians included a large number of semi-nomadic tribes that cultivated maize along the region's rivers and hunted the great buffalo herds with bows and arrows. Perhaps the most highly organized among them were the Cheyenne, ruled by a council of 44 chiefs selected on merit. These chiefs oversaw the frequent moves from one camp to another and the tribal buffalo hunt, the success of which depended on teamwork and skill. Men hunted the animals while women repaired bows, made arrows, and sewed garments from the hides. Cheyenne chiefs also exercised day-to-day authority over all matters affecting the tribe. The peoples of the *Prairies*, such as the Sioux, were predominantly agricultural until the availability of horses imported by Europeans revolutionized the art of hunting buffalo. Prairie Indian tribal organization remained centered on village life.

In the *Southeast*, Amerinds formed powerful tribes such as the Cherokee and the Natchez, in which chiefs exercised total authority over their subjects. Some, such as the Natchez, had rigid hereditary castes ranging from "Suns" down to "Stinkards." Others, such as the Choctaws and Creeks, constantly waged war against one another. Southeastern Amerinds blended agriculture with hunting and gathering.

The Haudenosaunee create the Great League of Peace and Power

Finally, in the *Eastern Woodlands*, a variety of farming peoples grew squash, beans, and maize, fished the rivers and streams, and hunted deer in the forests. They typically lived in villages, surrounded by log walls for protection. The Haudenosaunee (*hō-d'nō-SAW-nē*) of what is now New York State lived communally in wooden dwellings called longhouses. Their clans were led by clan mothers, who appointed tribal chiefs. Eventually the Haudenosaunee formed a five-nation alliance called the Great League of Peace and Power, which in turn created a political organization known as the Iroquois Confederacy. This organization made war on other Indian tribes and made alliances with European settlers, but never achieved complete political unity.

Three Complex Societies

Three North American Indian groups developed urban economies and complex governance structures similar in some respects to the early river civilizations of Asia and Northeast Africa. These complex Amerind societies, emerging in the valleys of the Ohio and Mississippi Rivers, were eventually centered in large cities with specialized occupations and extensive trading networks.

ADENA AND HOPEWELL. One of these societies was that of the Adena people of the Ohio River valley, which flourished between 1000 and 300 B.C.E. The Adena constructed small villages near the Ohio River and enhanced them with immense earthworks and mounds. These impressive sites, the most famous of which is the 700-foot-long Great Serpent Mound in present-day Kentucky, were apparently used for ceremonial purposes such as burials. Construction of these mounds would have been impossible without large agricultural surpluses to support the laborers who built them. It seems likely, therefore, that the Adena had specialized occupations, one of the key features of complex societies.

After 300 B.C.E., the Adena were absorbed into what archeologists call the Hopewell culture, centered in Ohio but managing a network of trade contacts with dependent tribes throughout a vast region bounded on the north by Ontario, on the east by New York, on the south by Florida, and on the west by Wisconsin. Hopewell consisted of a series of towns, ranging in size from a few hundred people to a few thousand, each ruled by a chief. Its commercial networks were extensive: graves at Hopewell sites in Ohio contain copper from Minnesota; shells and sharks' teeth from the Gulf of Mexico; obsidian (*ob-SID-ē-un*, a sharp, black stone made of volcanic glass) from Arizona; and grizzly bear teeth from west of the continental divide.

Complex societies emerge in North America

Although agriculture is typically the economic foundation of complex societies, Hopewell was an exception. The natural environment was so rich in fish, game, and plant life that even large towns could prosper through foraging for food. But this subsistence strategy meant that everyone did similar work, and occupational specialties never developed in the way that they did in the river civilizations in Mesopotamia, Egypt, India, and China. The reasons for Hopewell's disappearance around 400 C.E. remain unclear, but the culture's commercial networks survived: seashells from Florida, obsidian from the Rockies, and mica from Tennessee all ended up in Hopewell territory.

A modern photograph of Monk's Mound in Cahokia, where ancient Amerind temples once stood.

MISSISSIPPIAN SOCIETY. Of all the North American Amerind societies, the one most comparable to the Asian and North African river civilizations was that of the people now called Mississippians. Flourishing along and just east of the Mississippi River between 700 and 1500 C.E., their agriculturally-based society benefited from the river's rich deposits of silt, which kept their soil fertile. Their trading networks connected settlements within and beyond their region. The most noteworthy Mississippian center was Cahokia (*kah-HŌ-kē-ah*), the ruins of which lie near the city of East Saint Louis in southwestern Illinois. With between 10,000 and 30,000 inhabitants, Cahokia had a population comparable in size to that of many Eurasian cities, and surpassing that of any other Amerind settlement north of Mexico. Indeed, more people may have lived in Cahokia than in the entire Iroquois Confederacy.

The Mississippian people, like the Adena and the Hopewell, were mound builders. One of Cahokia's many mounds was the largest such structure in all of North America, a colossal earthwork 100 feet high and 1,037 by 790 feet at its base. Cahokia was a

Mississippians develop a river civilization

ceremonial and administrative center, surrounded by residential areas and shops and supported by the cultivation of adjacent fields. In this way it resembled the cities of Mesoamerica. Mississippians, like the Haudenosaunee of the Eastern Woodlands, grew corn, beans, and squash—the "Three Sisters" whose cultivation originated in Mexico—suggesting some level of contact between these regional cultures.

Such a connection is also suggested by archeological evidence. In the only mound that has thus far been excavated at Cahokia, archeologists discovered the carefully positioned bodies of a nobleman and 260 other adults. The number 260 is also characteristic of sacrificial burials found in Mesoamerica, where a 260-day ritual calendar was widely used, dating from centuries before Cahokia. In addition, some of the skeletons found at Cahokia had their front teeth filed. Virtually unknown elsewhere in North America, this practice was widespread in Mesoamerica. It is possible that the skeletons at Cahokia are remains of visitors or traders from Mesoamerica.

The possibility of contact between Cahokia and Mesoamerica cannot, however, be conclusively substantiated, since Cahokia left no written records. The city was devastated by an earthquake around 1250 c.e., and no subsequent Amerind culture built on its foundations. Some evidence suggests that by this time Cahokia was beginning to evolve into a complex society with a variety of occupational roles, including soldiers, officials, artisans, and priests. But its collapse leaves more questions than answers.

Excavation of the Great Mound at Cahokia suggests connections to Mesoamerica

The Amerinds of Mesoamerica

Farther south, in what are now southern Mexico and northern Central America, civilizations developed to levels of social and political complexity unknown in North America. In this region, which scholars today call Mesoamerica, ample rainfall and rich soils supported a series of highly complex civilizations based on agriculture. Archeologists often divide the early history of this region into three periods: Preclassic (1800 B.C.E.–150 C.E.), comprising the Olmec and early Maya societies; Classic (150–900 C.E.), the era of the full-fledged Mayan society; and Postclassic (900–1500 C.E.), consisting first of the Toltec, and later the Aztec society.

The Olmec of the Preclassic Period (1800 B.C.E.–150 C.E.)

The Olmec construct a river civilization

Mesoamerica's earliest complex society was discovered by accident. In the 1930s, British archeologists Matthew and Marion Stirling were excavating ruins presumed to be from the Classic Mayan era (150–900 C.E.), when they realized that the huge carved stone heads they kept finding in swampy, tropical river plains along the Gulf Coast came from an earlier culture. This husband-and-wife team named the newly discovered culture Olmec and excavated three major sites, demonstrating that Mayan civilization was constructed on an Olmec foundation. The center of Olmec culture lay south of the Gulf of Mexico and west of the Yucatan peninsula. Rainfall there averages nearly 120 inches per year, causing the rivers to flood regularly, depositing rich silt in floodplains that extend for miles from the riverbanks. Well suited to tropical agriculture, the Olmec heartland resembled in many ways the areas where the river civilizations of Asia and Northeast Africa began.

OLMEC CITIES. Olmec society apparently emerged about 1800 B.C.E. and lasted until 150 C.E., encompassing the Preclassic Period. The city now called San Lorenzo, founded around 1200 B.C.E., was the most important of a cluster of Olmec cities near the Coatzacoalcos (*kō-AHT-za-kō-AL-kōs*) River (Map 5.3). There the Olmec created immense stone heads and monuments out of basalt mined fifty miles away. The massive stones must have been dragged to the river, floated downstream on rafts, and dragged up from the riverbank to the plateau on which the city is located. In the absence of large domesticable mammals, carts with wheels were unknown.

Enormous stone structures characterize Olmec culture

The human labor involved in the transportation of these stones must have been enormous, since some of the heads of San Lorenzo are more than nine feet high and weigh up to 25 tons. Equally impressive was the carving of the stones—done entirely with obsidian, not metal, tools. Obsidian implements were imported from other parts of Mexico and from Guatemala, indicating that the Olmec state's networks of commerce and trade covered large distances. The jade carvings, cave paintings, and relief sculptures found in this region testify further to the skills of Olmec artisans.

Olmec society creates long-distance trading networks

San Lorenzo was destroyed around 900 B.C.E. by some sort of revolution or invasion, but the Olmec culture survived, relocating its focus northeast to a new city at

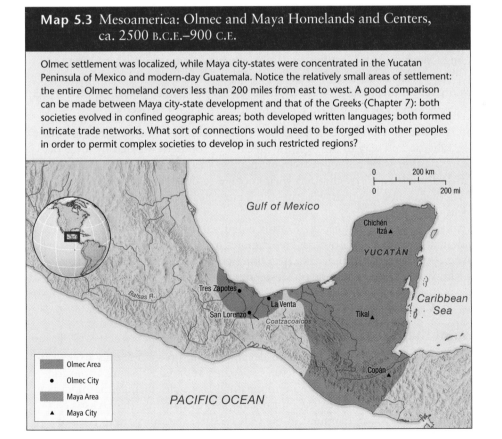

Map 5.3 Mesoamerica: Olmec and Maya Homelands and Centers, ca. 2500 B.C.E.–900 C.E.

Olmec settlement was localized, while Maya city-states were concentrated in the Yucatan Peninsula of Mexico and modern-day Guatemala. Notice the relatively small areas of settlement: the entire Olmec homeland covers less than 200 miles from east to west. A good comparison can be made between Maya city-state development and that of the Greeks (Chapter 7): both societies evolved in confined geographic areas; both developed written languages; both formed intricate trade networks. What sort of connections would need to be forged with other peoples in order to permit complex societies to develop in such restricted regions?

Olmec head carved from basalt and found at La Venta.

The Long Count Calendar demonstrates Olmec mathematical skills

La Venta, about 18 miles south of the Gulf of Mexico. There the Olmec built a mammoth clay ceremonial pyramid in the shape of a volcano, standing 110 feet high. At the Olmec city of Tres Zapotes (*TRĀZ zah-PŌ-tāz*), about one hundred miles northwest of La Venta, archeologists unearthed Stela C, one of the oldest dated monuments in the Western Hemisphere. This tall, stone column bears the date of September 3, 32 B.C.E., or (7).16.6.16.18 in the Long Count calendar used by the Mesoamericans.

THE LONG COUNT CALENDAR. Before the Stirlings' excavations, it was universally believed that the Maya had created the Long Count Calendar, but Stela C suggests its Olmec origin. The Long Count enabled Mesoamericans to date events from a starting point that corresponds to August 13, 3114 B.C.E., in our modern (Gregorian) calendar. Used by both Olmec and Maya, the **Long Count calendar** served a number of purposes, including astronomy, astrology, agriculture, genealogy, and even prophecy, as Mesoamericans believed that the world is repetitively created, destroyed, and re-created at precisely measured intervals. The calendar employed two huge cogwheels, one with 365 notches for the days of the solar year, the other with 260 notches for the days of the "sacred almanac," which embodied the sequence of Olmec and Mayan ritual and ceremonial life. When the wheels were turned, each intersection of two dates would recur only once every 52 years. The world came to an end (and was re-created in fire) approximately every 5,125 solar years. This was called the "great cycle," and since the current cycle began in 3114 B.C.E., the present world is scheduled to end on 21 December 2012 in the Gregorian calendar.

The Long Count calendar testifies to Mesoamericans' convictions concerning the eternity of the world, the endless cycle of life, and the continuity of the traditions on which they organized their societies. Inscriptions on several Olmec objects appear to be early versions of Maya glyphs, but no Olmec writing has been discovered.

THE SPREAD AND COLLAPSE OF OLMEC CIVILIZATION. Some scholars theorize that the Olmec spread their religion and way of life over a wide area of southern Mexico by force of arms. Apparently they were not a peace-loving people. They depicted themselves in sculpture as ferocious warriors, clubbing their enemies to death and torturing their captives. Whether or not this theory is true, the Olmec clearly spread their commerce, art, and ideas through trade.

Eventually, however, the Olmec civilization collapsed. By 300 B.C.E. La Venta had been abandoned, and the population of Tres Zapotes had declined steeply. Well before the Preclassic period ended around 150 C.E., Olmec culture had been absorbed by Amerinds who would evolve into one of Mesoamerica's most complex civilizations: the Maya.

The Maya of the Classic Period (150–900 C.E.)

Time and again in world history, civilizations developed and prospered, only to be conquered by peoples from less complex societies, who then adopted elements of the conquered civilization that they found useful or appealing. Examples include the Akkadian and Babylonian conquests of Sumer, the Hittite conquest of Babylon, the Hyksos conquest of Egypt, and the Aryan conquest of the Indus Valley. But this pattern did not occur in Mexico, as the Preclassic period gradually flowed into the Classic. The Maya, a Mesoamerican people of Guatemala and Mexico's Yucatan Peninsula, did not conquer the Olmec civilization: they emerged in Mesoamerica after the Olmec collapse. They did, however, build on Olmec foundations and eventually transcended Olmec achievements.

AGRICULTURE, TRADE, AND CULTURAL CONTACTS. During the Preclassic period, the Maya developed village-based agriculture. Earlier Mesoamericans had domesticated maize by 2500 B.C.E. and other plants shortly thereafter. Between 7000 and 1500 B.C.E. the world was considerably warmer than it is today, and in much of North America and Mesoamerica the hot, dry weather, combined with excessive hunting by Amerinds, wiped out the giant bison, camels, horses, and mammoths that had once been abundant. Hunting therefore gradually became less important than agriculture, which served as the foundation of Mayan civilization.

The Maya use the Olmec heritage to structure a new society

Mayan agriculture provided a nutritious diet of corn, beans, squash, chili peppers (rich in several vitamins), and tropical fruits. Protein came from wild birds, deer, peccaries, armadillo, and a breed of barkless dog. Sea salt was widely marketed to preserve meat. The Maya, particularly the nobles, also consumed chocolate, drinking beverages made from the cacao bean, the source of chocolate, or snacking on the cacao bean itself.

The cacao bean was traded, as were obsidian, jade, and colorful feathers from a large bird called the quetzal (*ket-ZAL*). Such products were exchanged not only among the Maya themselves, but also with other civilizations in Mexico and Central America. In the process, the Maya established commercial and cultural connections with cultures both more and less socially complex than their own.

The Maya connect Mexico and Central America

Like most other civilizations, the Maya did not evolve in isolation. They were profoundly affected by the Olmec civilization that had existed to their west. From it they learned astronomy and mathematics, developed social and political structures, and adapted a belief system that sought to explain the meaning of human life. And they also had contacts with smaller and weaker groups of people, many of whom they dominated or absorbed.

SOCIETY AND RELIGION. As the Preclassic period became the Classic, Mayan society took shape. It was hierarchical, with a privileged hereditary elite exercising political power. Priests, high-ranking warriors, and wealthy merchants were all nobles. Commoners were free peasants and soldiers, while the lands of the nobles were worked by a group resembling serfs. Below them were slaves, typically commoners captured in battle; although slavery was hereditary, freedom could be purchased by relatives. Politically, the Maya organized themselves as autonomous city-states rather than in a strong central government.

At the top of the hierarchy in each city-state was a sacred king who was both a political and spiritual leader. Kings were brave warriors and shrewd political negotiators who defended the interests of their people. But they also served those interests as spiritual intermediaries between this world and the next. In the Mayan world, political leadership, success in warfare, and religious power were closely linked.

Mayans choose sacred kings as their leaders

The Maya pictured the earth as flat, with 13 layers of heaven above it and nine levels of underworld. An enormous number of gods populated the heavens, while the lower regions were the domain of the nine Lords of Death (see "Excerpt from the Council Book of the Quiché Maya, or *Popol Vuh*"). The Maya were terrified of death, believing that most ordinary people went to the underworld rather than to the heavens, where

Document 5.1 Excerpt from the Council Book of the Quiché Maya, or *Popol Vuh*

The *Popol Vuh*, or "Council Book" of the Maya living in the city of Quiché in southwestern Guatemala, told of the origins and development of Maya civilization. Along with all but four of the thousands of books written by the Maya, it was burned by the Spaniards in the 1520s. Thirty years later, several anonymous members of the Quiché Maya nobility attempted to reconstruct the *Popol Vuh*, using the Latin alphabet rather than the original Maya glyphic writing. Their manuscript was seen in Quiché between 1701 and 1703 by a Spanish friar, Francisco Ximénez, who copied it by hand and added his own Spanish translation. The original manuscript has been lost, and the reproduction and translation prepared by Fr. Ximénez has been in the Newberry Library in Chicago since 1911.

Historians must use such a document with caution. Maya glyphs represented concepts rather than words, and were intended to be used in combination with pictures. Both the glyphs and the pictures were burned in the sixteenth century. How well did the Maya authors remember the precise details of the *Popol Vuh* thirty years after they had last seen it? How accurate was their effort to change glyphs and pictures into words? Was their reconstruction influenced by events connected with the Spanish conquest? When Fr. Ximénez copied their manuscript, did he change it in any way? These questions cannot be answered. Finally, what we have is not the *Popol Vuh* itself, but a document written in the 1550s, decades after the last events described in this chapter. Yet what we have suggests to us how the Maya saw their world, and this excerpt is presented for that purpose.

The excerpt relates the conclusion of the story of the "hero twins," Hunahpú (*hoo-nah-POO*) and Xbalanqué (*zhbahl-ahn-KĀ*), who made too much noise while playing a Maya ritual ball game and were summoned to Xibalbá (*zhih-bahl-BAH*), the Underworld, by the Lords of Death. There they endured many torments and trials, all of which they overcame. But the twins knew that they could not defeat the Lords of Death by force, but could only escape from Xibalbá by trickery. This is the story of their deception.

[The twins disguised themselves as poor orphans and performed amazing dances for the people of Xibalbá.] . . . they worked many miracles. They burned houses

only kings and heroes could live. Special rituals to appease the gods were believed to be capable of holding death back, at least for a while, and also of ensuring the community's prosperity. Rulers and priests led these ceremonies, but ordinary people practiced them too, using their kings as role models.

These rituals involved bloodletting, a practice that connected the temporal and spiritual worlds and allowed departed spirits to materialize in the body of the bloodletter. That person, usually male, pierced some part of his body—often the ear lobe, lip, or penis—with a sharp thorn. Then he drew a knotted cord through the wound to force the blood to run. This type of sacrificial offering was believed to please the gods and bring good harvests, adequate rainfall, victory in warfare, personal happiness, cures for diseases, and many other benefits. Bridging the chasm between worlds brought creation into proper balance, harmonizing the relationship between spirits and mortals.

Maya bloodletting connects two worlds

When the king himself was the bloodletter, he became the portal between the two worlds. The spirits would enter the realm of the living through the wounds he inflicted upon his body. Simultaneously, his own spirit would pass through the wounds into the domain of the dead, where it could influence the gods on behalf of the king's people. The

Document 5.1 *Continued*

as though they were really burning and instantly they were as they had been before . . . they cut themselves into bits; they killed each other; the first one killed stretched out as though he were dead, and instantly the other brought him back to life. Those of Xibalbá looked on in amazement at all they did . . .

Presently word of their dances came to the ears of the Lords of Death, Hun-Camé (*HUHN-kah-MĀ*), or One Death, and Vucub-Camé (*voo-COOB-kah-MĀ*), or Seven Death. Upon hearing it they exclaimed, "Who are these two orphans? Do they really give you so much pleasure?"

"Surely their dances are very beautiful, and all that they do," answered he who had brought the news to the lords.

Happy to hear this, the [lords said], "Tell them to come here, tell them to come so that . . . we may admire them and regard them with wonder."

[So the boys appeared before the Lords of Death, who ordered them,] "Dance! And do the first part in which you kill yourselves; burn my house, do all that you know how to do. We shall give you pay . . ."

Instantly they put fire to the lord's house, and although the lords were within the house, they were not burned. Quickly it was whole again . . . the lords were astounded. "Sacrifice yourselves now, let us see it! We really like your dances!" said the lords . . . And [the twins] proceeded to sacrifice each other. Hunahpú was sacrificed by Xbalanqué, and instantly he returned to life . . .

Then One Death and Seven Death gave their commands. "Do the same with us! Sacrifice us!" they said. "Cut us into pieces, one by one!"

And so it happened that they first sacrificed the one, who was the chief lord of Xibalbá, the one called One Death, king of Xibalbá.

And when One Death was dead, they sacrificed Seven Death, and they did not bring either of them back to life.

The people of Xibalbá fled as soon as they saw that their lords were dead and sacrificed . . . In this way the Lords of Xibalbá were overcome. Only by a miracle and by their [own] transformation could [the boys] have done it.

SOURCE: *Popul Vuh: The Sacred Book of the Ancient Quiché Maya.* English version by Delia Goetz and Sylvanus G. Morley, from the Spanish translation by Adrián Recinos (Norman: University of Oklahoma Press, 1950) 156–160.

---

sacrifice and pain involved in bloodletting would earn the king the respect of the gods and spirits; in return, they would grant favors to him and to his subjects. In a few cases, women became kings, a status that also required them to serve as bloodletters, drawing the knotted cord through their ear lobes, lips, breasts, or genitals.

MAYA CULTURE. The Maya developed a complex and intellectually sophisticated culture. Using an intricate pictographic system of writing, they carved inscriptions on stone pillars and compiled libraries of thousands of books written on long strips of tree-bark paper (see "Excerpt from the Council Book of the Quiché Maya, or *Popol Vuh*"). (The invading Spaniards burned all but four of these books in the sixteenth century.) The Maya also created a numerical system using zero as a number rather than a placeholder, an idea unknown to their contemporaries in the Roman Empire. Their adoption of the Long Count calendar from the Olmec testifies to their belief in recurrent historical cycles, a conviction similar to those held by people in ancient Egypt and China.

The Long Count calendar, the sophisticated numerical system, the intricate glyphic writing system, and the intense interest of the Maya in astronomy led most historians to conclude that they were a contemplative, scientific, and essentially peace-loving people.

Mayans write and store thousands of books

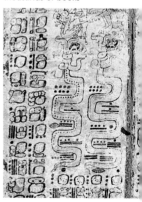

A Mayan calendar showing the phases of the planet Venus.

The Pyramid of the Moon in the city of Teotihuacán.

But that was before Mayan writing was fully deciphered. Following on the work of Knosorov and Proskouriakoff described at the start of this chapter, scholars began to translate Mayan texts in 1988, and what they read overturned that assumption. Writings on bark-paper and in stone indicate that the Maya were warlike and territorial, like many other cultures, both in America and elsewhere. Warfare was a full-fledged institution, with not only sacrifice and the taking of captives to serve as slaves, but also with complex rites of purification and fasting in preparation for battle. Perhaps this Mayan love of combat was ultimately responsible for bringing down one of the great civilizations of the ancient world in the mid-ninth century, at approximately the same time that another notable Mesoamerican culture was collapsing, that of the city of Teotihuacán.

Teotihuacán: Rise and Fall of a Great City-State

The Maya were not the only complex society in Mexico during the Classic period. As early as 300 B.C.E. the city-state of Teotihuacán (*tā-ō-tē-wah-KAHN*) in the Valley of Mexico, just north of modern-day Mexico City, held a population of 10,000. That number grew to 40,000 by 100 B.C.E. and at least 120,000 by 500 C.E. At the height of the Classic period this city may have contained 200,000 people, making it one of the largest cities of its time.

Located near a rich source of obsidian, necessary for making weapons, and trading actively with other cities of central Mexico, Teotihuacán grew into a politically and commercially significant city (Map 5.4). With 600 pyramids, it was central Mexico's preeminent religious and ceremonial center. Along with its pyramids, two thousand apartment complexes and an immense market compound made Teotihuacán the largest and most significant Mesoamerican city-state of the Classic period, and one of the principal cities of the world. It was clearly the focal point of a powerful empire.

Teotihuacán creates a centralized empire

Teotihuacanos, unlike the Maya, did not seem to revere kings as supreme political authorities and intermediaries between two worlds. Indeed, since artistic depictions of the rulers are lacking and no written records have survived, it is not possible to determine precisely how Teotihuacán was governed. It did, however, maintain an army, probably to protect its commercial relationships with other Mesoamerican cultures, including the Maya. The army may also have forced peasants from the surrounding countryside to supply the city's political and religious elites with food.

Teotihuacán maintained commercial connections with Mayan, Zapotec (*za-PŌ-tek*), Mixtec (*MISH-tek*), and other Mexican civilizations. More than 400 workshops unearthed in its ruins indicate that its artisans fabricated exotic ornaments from seashells, onyx, and jade. In exchange, the Maya sent quetzal feathers and the Zapotec sent fragrant incense made from copal gum.

Mesoamerican societies collapse as the Classic period ends

In the late Classic period, however, all of these societies crumbled. Teotihuacán was deserted and burned, possibly as early as 650 C.E., certainly no later than 850. Several Zapotec cities and Mayan states were destroyed around the same time. Epidemic diseases, volcanic eruptions, earthquakes, and invasion by other Amerind tribes have all been proposed as causes. A great war lasting more than 150 years, from 526 to 682 C.E., between two powerful Mayan city-states centered at Tikal and Calakmul, weakened the Maya heartland the way the Peloponnesian War between Athens and Sparta from 431 to 404 B.C.E. (Chapter 7) weakened Greece.

Map 5.4 Teotihuacán: A Mesoamerican Trading Center, 700 C.E.

Teotihuacán took advantage of its central location, its military strength, and its sources of obsidian to establish commercial relationships with many other sites in Mexico, including several Mayan cities. Note the variety of items valued and traded for by the people of Teotihuacán in exchange for obsidian. Which items might have been valued in themselves, and which might have been fabricated into finished products for additional trade?

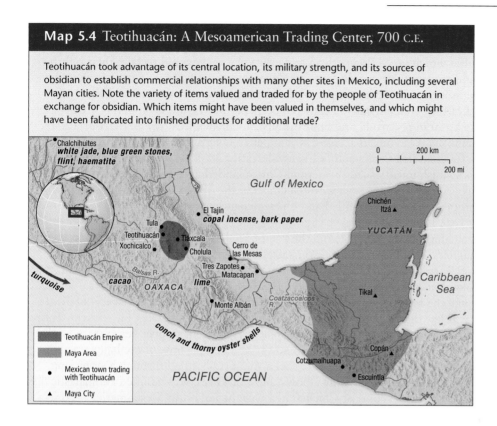

These highly urbanized societies may also have collapsed from internal stresses. An expanding population, coupled with increasing demands by the warrior and ceremonial elites for food and goods, may have overstrained the food supply and embittered the peasantry whose labor supported the entire structure. In this theory, a rebellion of the peasants against the urban center destroyed the great cities, and their inhabitants scattered into small village communities of the kind the Spaniards found in the sixteenth century. Today this theory seems to be the most plausible explanation for the catastrophic end of the great civilizations of Mexico.

The Toltec: Conflict Between Warriors and Priests

This collapse created a power vacuum throughout the Mesoamerican world, which warrior tribes shortly filled. The most successful of these was the Toltec (975 C.E.–1200 C.E.), a people originating in northern Mexico. The Toltec established their capital at Tula, about thirty miles northwest of Teotihuacán, around 960 to 970 C.E. The Toltec ruling elite appears to have been divided between priests and warriors, with each faction struggling to dominate the other. According to legend, an early Toltec priest-king encouraged devotion to the god Quetzalcóatl (*kwet-zahl-KŌ-ah-tul*), or "Feathered Serpent," while the warriors opposed him in the name of a rival deity, Tezcatlipoca (*tetz-cat-lē-PŌ-kah*), or "Smoking Mirror." The two factions quarreled, and the worshipers of Quetzalcóatl were defeated and forced to leave Tula for the east, apparently in 987 C.E.

The Quetzalcóatl legend
is created in
Mesoamerica

According to legend, Quetzalcóatl vowed revenge, claiming that he and his followers would return one day on boats across the Gulf of Mexico. Appearing as white-skinned men, oddities which no Mesoamerican had ever seen, they would reclaim their rightful heritage and redeem their people from bondage. Interestingly, Mayan sources describe the arrival in 987 on the Yucatán peninsula of a man from the west named Kukulcán (*koo-kul-KHAN*), which means "Feathered Serpent" in Mayan; he apparently conquered the Yucatán peninsula and built the city of Chichén Itzá (*chi-CHAIN ēt-ZAH*) for his capital. Was Kukulcán a Toltec worshiper of Quetzalcóatl forced to leave Tula? Murals at Chichén Itzá depict a Toltec army defeating Maya warriors around that time. And when Spanish invaders led by Hernán Cortés landed in ships and marched into central Mexico in 1519, those Maya who remembered the Toltec legend were convinced that the prophecy had been fulfilled and Quetzalcóatl had returned.

The Toltec connect the
Pacific and the Gulf of
Mexico

In the year 1000 C.E. the Toltec capital of Tula served as the hub of a militaristic empire stretching across Mexico from the Pacific to the Gulf. Its warriors dressed themselves as jaguars, coyotes, and eagles; they proudly carried Toltec rule to peoples who would soon learn to hate and fear them. Human sacrifice, an occasional practice in Mayan lands, became more frequent under the Toltec.

Although the brutality and efficiency of its warriors permeated all aspects of Toltec society, the Toltec did not lack appreciation for beauty and grace. In Chichén Itzá, Toltec and Mayan architectural forms merged to create magnificent stepped temples and light, airy hallways bordered by colonnades. The Mayan ritual pastime of the ball game, in which teams competed in an effort to propel a small rubber ball through a stone ring 25 feet above the ground using only elbows, hips, or knees, was adopted enthusiastically by the Toltec. Their ball court at Chichén Itzá was the largest in Mesoamerica, 490 feet long with walls 27 feet high. The game was played for very high stakes, since the captain of the losing team (and sometimes of the winning one as well) was often sacrificed.

Massive stone statues
of Toltec warriors stand
atop the pyramid at
the ruins of Tula de
Allende, Mexico.

The Toltec maintained the commercial connections forged by Teotihuacán and the Maya city-states, expanding them by exporting exquisite metalcrafts, mosaics composed of quetzal feathers, and statuettes and jewelry made from precious gems. Toltec artisans skillfully blended their own methods with techniques learned from Mayan craftsmen. They used turquoise from modern-day New Mexico, gold from Central America, and obsidian and jade from their own realm to create stylized artifacts stunning in their simplicity. Their artistry was so breathtaking that, five hundred years later, the artisans of the Aztec Empire were called *tolteca*.

Toltec craftsman-
ship continues earlier
commercial connections

No doubt the Toltec believed that their militancy would ensure their dominance, but in the 1160s Tula was torn apart and sacked. Its destruction may have been the result of irreconcilable animosity between warriors and priests or of some sort of internal uprising. In the Yucatán, Chichén Itzá gradually decayed, and in 1224 it was abandoned. No one knows why the Toltec empire collapsed, and no empire replaced it until the coming of the Aztecs in 1325.

South America: Societies of the Andes

The civilizations of Mesoamerica were built by only a small fraction of the Amerinds. Many Amerinds never penetrated that far south, remaining in North America, north of the Rio Grande. Many others passed through the region and continued into South

America. Forbidding in terms of topography and climate, South America remains the least explored of the earth's inhabited continents. The migrating peoples who first entered it confronted sweltering rain forests, snow-capped mountain ranges, and waterless deserts. There they created civilizations carefully adapted to such challenging environments.

South American societies must adapt to challenging environments

Hunter-Gatherers and the Chavín Society

At first glance, South America's southeastern corner would seem ideal for human exploitation. The rich grasslands and fertile soils of modern Argentina and Uruguay are ideal for raising cattle, horses, and sheep, and cultivating grains and fruits. But very few Amerinds settled there: they had not yet mastered agriculture, and this area of South America lacked any four-footed mammal larger than a tapir (a pig with a hooked snout). Additionally, these grasslands were covered by vegetation so thick that the land could not be broken without steel plows. Hunter-gatherers were more likely to settle in the immense rain forests of northern Brazil, where wild fruits and vegetables grew in abundance, and tapirs and capybaras (large, short-legged rodents) could be hunted. There the Tapajos (*tah-PAH-hōs*) people eventually developed a hierarchically structured, warlike culture in the central Amazon valley. Archeological exploration of the Tapajos sites is just beginning, and the arrival of humans in that area can only be estimated at between 8000 and 4000 B.C.E. They made the transition to agriculture after that time and were still dominating the region in the sixteenth century.

To the west, the entire Pacific side of South America, the environment is shaped by the Andes Mountains, part of a geologic formation running from Cape Horn, north through Peru, 11,000 miles to the north slope of Alaska. With peaks more than 14,000 feet high, the Andes stand as a barrier to cultural connections across the South American continent. Chile and Argentina would probably have evolved as a single cultural region had not the Andes stood between them. Part of the "Ring of Fire" surrounding the Pacific Ocean, these mountains include many active volcanoes. Earthquakes and mudslides, some of them extremely damaging, are common.

Unlike the rest of the continent, however, the Andean highlands are home to three large, closely related four-footed mammals, the llama, alpaca, and vicuña. Useful for carrying burdens and as a food source, these animals never spread farther north than present-day Colombia because they could not thrive in the heat of lower-lying regions. Hunter-gatherers arrived in the Andean region at some time around 10,000 B.C.E. Four thousand years later, a significant population increase along the seacoast suggests the evolving importance of fishing. Lima beans were domesticated around this time, although the rockiness and aridity of Andean soils delayed the full development of agriculture until irrigation was employed. Sometime after 4000 B.C.E., irrigated fields stimulated the growth of the first Andean society in the Norte Chico region of Peru.

The first Andean society develops in Peru's Norte Chico

Little is known of Norte Chico society, but its principal city, Huaricanga, built around 3200 B.C.E., is the oldest known city in the Americas. Large-scale public buildings were erected there at about the time the Sumerian civilization flourished in West Asia. There must have been some form of centralized government in the Norte Chico, as specialized occupations would have been necessary for the construction of large public monuments. Whatever government did develop was unique, not copied from another society or imported by conquerors.

Map 5.5 Pre-Inca Andean Empires and Culture Areas, ca. 800 B.C.E.–1400 C.E.

Several complex early cultures emerged in what is now Peru. Observe that these South American Amerind societies were intensively concentrated along the spine of the Andes Mountains. South America's challenging topography limited contact between peoples; the Tupi of the Amazon, for example, never learned of the existence of Andean societies, while the Mapuche of southern Chile were cut off from other groups by the Andes and the Atacama Desert. But groups living in this portion of the Andes knew of each other, and their societies developed using knowledge gained from contacts and connections between them. In what ways might life in such a challenging environment have encouraged people to learn from one another?

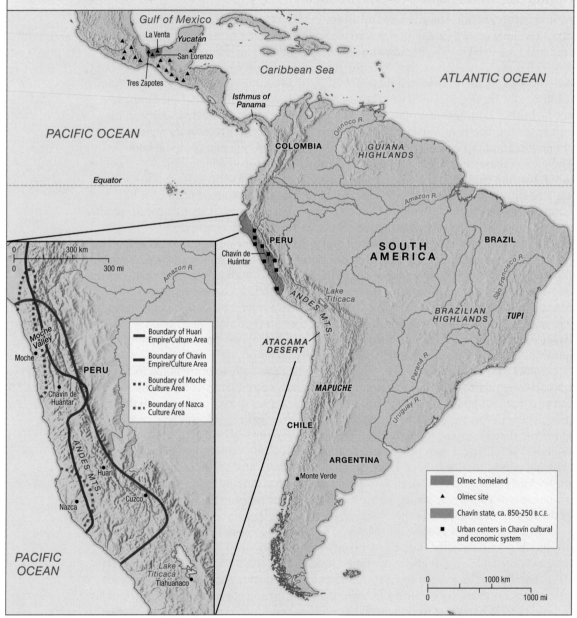

This early society vanished, and an Andean successor state, the Chavín, emerged during what archeologists call the Early Horizon Period (1200–200 B.C.E.). Centered on the ceremonial site of Chavín de Huantar (*cha-VĒN dā WAHN-tar*) in central Peru, it was organized around a polytheistic belief system whose gods were worshiped throughout the central Andes for centuries after Chavín's collapse (Map 5.5). Almost nothing is known of Chavín political structures, but this civilization produced durable textiles, pottery, and metalwork, whose uses reflected Chavín religious convictions.

Isolation was the most significant handicap facing the Chavín empire. Cut off from contact with other South American Indian societies by the Andes and separated from the Olmec civilization of Mexico by 1,600 miles of ocean and 2,000 miles of rugged terrain (Map 5.6), the Chavín people did not have the opportunity to adopt new technologies

The Chavín Empire remains isolated

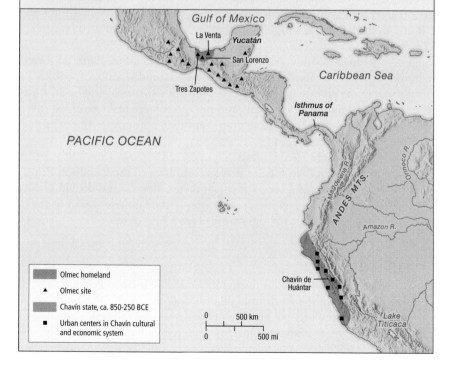

Map 5.6 Geographic Proximity of Olmec and Chavín Homelands, ca. 800 B.C.E.

All pre-Inca Andean societies were profoundly isolated from non-Andean cultures. Notice that the distances between the Chavín empire and the Olmec society of Mexico were simply too great to be traversed readily with available means of transportation. Early American societies knew of the wheel but used it only for children's toys, not for transportation. Even in the twenty-first century C.E., the trip from Olmec lands to Chavín lands cannot be completed by wheeled vehicles because of the absence of roads connecting southeastern Panama with northwestern Colombia. How might such isolation have been a disadvantage to Amerind societies once they were confronted by peoples from less isolated regions?

and ideas. All the Andean societies succeeding the Chavín were similarly isolated. Even today, there is no road connecting Mesoamerica to the Andes because the border between Panama and Colombia remains impassable.

Nazca and Moche Societies

During the Early Intermediate Period (200 B.C.E.–500 C.E.), two post-Chavín societies developed, the Nazca and the Moche. Archeological evidence indicates that they fought each other, but not that they developed commercial or other peaceful connections.

Little is known of Nazca political organization, but its artistic accomplishments continue to impress modern-day observers. Based in southern Peru, the Nazca traced immense patterns on the desert by removing surface debris to expose the underlying strata of rock. These designs, visible only from the air, depict birds, spiders, monkeys, fish, and cats. Some scholars believe that the designs were offerings or signals to the gods; others contend that they were ritualized pathways connecting local shrines. Delicately painted polychrome ceramics and elaborate mummification of the dead also characterized Nazca civilization (as they did the Chavín).

The Moche use irrigation to make agriculture possible

The Moche (*MŌ-chā*) society of northern Peru dominated that region without creating a formal imperial structure. Complex irrigation channels transported water from up to 75 miles away, allowing the Moche to develop a diversified agricultural base that they supplemented with meat from their herds of alpacas and llamas. An elaborate religious hierarchy presided over worship services performed in structures like the Pyramid of the Sun, an adobe building 1,140 feet long and 130 feet high. The first Andean culture to develop accurately representational art, the Moche created ceramic portrait vases and objects of silver and gold. They also took a dim view of medical malpractice: physicians who killed their patients through incompetence were staked out to be eaten alive by birds of prey.

Amerinds use gender as a basis for assigning tasks

Moche women, like women in other early American Indian societies, centered their lives around the home. There they raised fruits and vegetables, tended animals, cooked meals, nurtured children, made clothing, and appeased the gods through rituals. Political life, military service, hunting, and labor on roads and buildings were tasks reserved for men. This gender-based division of labor was so consistent throughout the Americas that scholars have been tempted to speculate, in the absence of concrete evidence, that the Amerinds brought it with them from Central Asia.

The Moche thrived in northern Peru for the first six centuries of the Common Era, finally collapsing under the pressure of a series of earthquakes, floods, and droughts that deprived the ruling elite of its political legitimacy. Apparently the Chinese were not the only people to monitor the environment for signs of Heaven's Mandate.

Tiahuanaco, Huari, and Chimor

The Moche were succeeded by three societies during the Middle Horizon Period (500–1000 C.E.). Two developed in the Andean highlands and one on the Pacific coast.

First of the mountain societies was the Tiahuanaco (*tē-wah-NAH-koo*), named for its impressive capital at 13,000 feet above sea level near Bolivia's Lake Titicaca. The city's population ranged between 30,000 and 40,000, making it the highest large city of the Andes but small in comparison to Teotihuacán. Tiahuanaco's agriculture centered on fields reclaimed from lakeside swamps by means of an immense drainage system. Commercial relationships over long distances were maintained by caravans of sure-footed llamas. Ceremonial buildings were constructed of stones joined together with such artistry and precision that no mortar was necessary; even the blade of a knife could not pass between them. The city of Tiahuanaco featured running water and a closed sewer system.

The second highland civilization of this period was the Huari (*WAH-rē*), located in the mountains of southeastern Peru. This culture developed later than Tiahuanaco and was similar to it technologically and tied to it commercially. In building their commercial enterprises, the two civilizations competed for the copper, lapis lazuli (*LAP-is LAZ-yoo-lē*, a deep blue mineral valued as a gem), obsidian, and turquoise deposits of local valleys. But the Huari culture differed in some ways from that of Tiahuanaco. Huari public buildings were much smaller than those of Tiahuanaco and were built from adobe rather than cut stone. Its capital was larger in area than Tiahuanaco but much less densely populated.

Building Civilizations in the Andean Highlands

Neither of these highland cultures developed elaborate administrative structures, and like all early Andean civilizations, their lack of a system of writing makes it difficult to learn much about them. The Huari collapsed around the year 800 C.E., bringing to an end two thousand years of urban settlements in southern Peru. Tiahuanaco lingered for several centuries, declining slowly well before the arrival of the Europeans. No reasons for the weakening of either culture can be stated with certainty.

On the Pacific coast, the Moche were succeeded by Chimor (*chē-MOR*), a major imperial power that dominated coastal Peru until the emergence of the Inca in the fifteenth century C.E. Chan Chan, constructed in the heart of Moche territory on a huge site directly on the coast, became Chimor's capital and cultural center. The city was notable for its massive ceremonial structures, large warehouses, and extensive one-story living compounds, built without roofs, since rain occurred infrequently along the Peruvian coast. Chimor arose as a successor state to the Moche around 700 C.E., but does not appear to have developed into an expansionistic state before 1300. Once it did, it created the first Andean empire.

A woven polychrome textile panel depicting warriors from Chimor.

Chimor's social structure was hierarchical, topped by a warrior aristocracy supported by priests. Beneath these classes, artisans developed distinctive techniques of pottery-making, textile manufacture, and metalcraft. Close in status to the artisans, merchants organized and carried on commerce with the remotest regions of the empire as well as with other Andean cultures. Peasants, at the bottom of the social hierarchy, supported Chimor's social and economic structure with agriculture, fishing, and livestock raising. This social structure, especially the warrior class and the widespread commercial contacts, indicates that Chimor was intent on spreading its culture and control as far as the imposing mountainous topography of the region would allow.

Chimor creates a warrior society

Indeed, the people of Chimor, known as Chimú, conquered a number of less formidable neighbors, but they do not seem to have oppressed them or treated them as captives. Instead, unlike the Moche and Huari, they deliberately incorporated them into their empire, giving them a stake in the power and prosperity of Chimor. Imperial

Chimor assimilates the peoples it conquers

administration was aided by a far-flung system of roads and bridges that encouraged communication, commerce, and coercion. Given their cultural achievements, the Chimú might well have been far better known today had they not been conquered between 1462 and 1470 by the Inca, who adopted many Chimú practices and policies on their way to becoming South America's most powerful civilization.

Chapter Review

Putting It in Perspective

The first groups of Central Asian nomads who crossed the Bering land bridge and entered the Western Hemisphere were probably very similar to one another in genetic composition, hunting techniques, weaponry, customs, and social life. Their descendants, however, who spread through North and South America through countless generations, diverged from one another in many ways as they adapted to widely varying environments.

In the Arctic and Sub-Arctic regions of North America, brief growing seasons and frozen, snow-covered ground made organized agriculture impossible. The peoples who remained in these regions maintained their hunter-gatherer lifestyles. In the southwestern corner of the present-day United States, arid soils and the absence of huge rivers for irrigation projects similarly limited agriculture. At the same time, agriculture seemed unnecessary in the Pacific Northwest, the Prairies, and the Great Plains, which teemed with abundant fish and game. In the Eastern Woodlands, the Iroquois founded an innovative confederacy based on agriculture, but its small population base prevented the sort of large-scale, complex development found in Mesoamerica. The Mississippi people seemed to be modeling their society on Mesoamerica when they built Cahokia, but its unexplained abandonment ended this experiment.

In Mesoamerica, organizationally complex societies arose, including the Olmec, the Maya, the Teotihuacanos, and the Toltec. In lands with plentiful rainfall, rich soils, a lengthy growing season, and a wide variety of possible crops, these peoples turned from hunting and gathering to agriculture, and agricultural surpluses made possible the development of complex political and social organizations. Mesoamerican civilizations developed elaborate belief systems, advanced mathematical and astronomical knowledge, considerable architectural and engineering skills, and impressive military establishments.

Farther south, the civilizations of the Andes met the challenges of their natural environment. Irrigating the dry soils and carefully shepherding livestock, they constructed a firm agricultural base in an arid environment. With each successive civilization building on the achievements of its predecessors, the Norte Chico, Chavín, Nazca, Moche, Tiahuanaco, Huari, and Chimú societies built temples and public halls, created goods of fabric and metal, threw bridges across raging rivers at dizzying heights, and gradually evolved toward imperial conquest. The later Inca civilization appreciated the accomplishments of the Chimú and adopted many of their practices.

Beginning their development much later than the civilizations that originated in Asia, Africa, and Europe, some Amerind societies had evolved to complex levels of social organization by 1500 C.E. Others, restricted by their environments, continued the ways of their ancestors. Some evolved in isolation from one another, but most had connections and conflicts. Over many centuries, they fought each other, traded with each other, and learned from each other. All did, however, develop in isolation from the cultures and civilizations of the Eastern Hemisphere until 1500 C.E.

Reviewing Key Material

KEY CONCEPTS

Mesoamerica, 109

Amerinds, 109

tribes, 112

Long Count Calendar, 118

KEY PEOPLES

Haudenosaunee, 114

Adena, 115

Hopewell, 115

Mississippian, 115

Olmec, 116

Maya, 118

Teotihuacán, 122

Toltec, 123

Norte Chico, 125

Chavín, 127

Nazca, 128

Moche, 128

Tiahuanaco, 128

Huari, 129

Chimor, 129

Chimú, 129

ASK YOURSELF

1. How did North American Amerinds react to their differing environments?
2. How did Olmec society influence the subsequent development of Maya civilization?
3. How did leadership in Maya civilization reflect the political, spiritual, and military aspects of society?
4. How did the Toltec build on the accomplishments of previous civilizations?
5. How did early South American societies influence one another?

GOING FURTHER

Bruhns, Karen. *Ancient South America*. 1994.

Burger, Richard. *Chavín and the Origins of Andean Civilization*. 1992.

Coe, Michael. *The Maya*. 1999.

Coe, Michael. *The Olmec World*. 1996.

Dickason, Olive. *Canada's First Nations*. 1992.

Fagan, Brian. *Ancient North America*. 2001.

Fiedel, Stuart. *Prehistory of the Americas*. 1992.

Friedel, David, Linda Schele, and Joy Parker. *Maya Cosmos*. 1993.

Keatinge, Richard, ed. *Peruvian Prehistory*. 1988.

Kehoe, Alice. *America Before the European Invasions*. 2003.

Kolata, Alan. *Tiwanaku*. 1993.

Mann, Charles. *1491: New Revelations of the Americas Before Columbus*. 2005.

Moseley, Michael. *The Incas and Their Ancestors*. 2001.

Pasztori, Esther. *Teotihuacán*. 1997.

Pauketat, Timothy, and Thomas Emerson, eds. *Cahokia: Domination and Ideology in the Mississippian World*. 1997.

Sabloff, Jeremy. *The Cities of Ancient Mexico*. 1989.

Schaffer, Lynda. *Native Americans Before 1492: The Moundbuilding Centers of the Eastern Woodlands*. 1992.

Schele, Linda, and David Friedel. *A Forest of Kings: The Untold Story of the Ancient Maya*. 1990.

Sharer, R. *Daily Life in Maya Civilization*. 1996.

Stuart, David. *Anasazi America*. 2000.

Weaver, Muriel. *The Aztecs, Maya, and Their Predecessors*. 1993.

Webster, D. *The Fall of the Ancient Maya: Solving the Mystery of the Maya Collapse*. 2002.

Key Dates and Developments

North American Chronology:

ca. 1000 B.C.E.	Adena society emerges in Ohio River Valley
ca. 100 C.E.	Adena merges with Hopewell society
400	Adena-Hopewell society disappears
700–1200	Anasazi society in southwestern United States
700–1500	Mississippian society along and east of the Mississippi River
1050–1250	Zenith of Cahokian society

Mesoamerican Chronology:

1800 B.C.E.–150 C.E.	Olmec society: The Preclassic Period
1700 B.C.E.	Foundation of San Lorenzo
1200 B.C.E.	Foundation of Tres Zapotes
100 C.E.	Foundation of Teotihuacán
150–900 C.E.	Maya society: The Classic Period
ca. 750	Destruction of Teotihuacán
800–900	Abandonment of Mayan urban centers
ca. 970	Foundation of Tula by the Toltec
ca. 990	Foundation of Chichén Itzá
1156	Destruction of Tula
1224	Abandonment of Chichén Itzá

South American Chronology:

3200–2500 B.C.E.	Norte Chico society in Peru
1200–200 B.C.E.	Early Horizon Period: Chavín society in Peru
200 B.C.E.–500 C.E.	Early Intermediate Period: Nazca and Moche societies in Peru
500–1000	Middle Horizon Period: Tiahuanaco, Huari, and Chimú societies in Bolivia and Peru
1300–1465	Chimú military expansion culminating in rivalry with Inca Empire

CHAPTER 6

The Persian Connection:
Its Impact and Influences,
2000 B.C.E.–637 C.E.

- The Persian Empire

- Persian Governance and Society: Links with Mesopotamia

- Zoroastrianism

- Confrontation with Greece

- The Macedonian Conquest and Its Successor States

- Chapter Review

A Persian Soldier

The sculpted figure of a Persian policeman guards the entrance to one of Persia's royal palaces. This stylized image shows the braided hair and beard worn by Persian men, the long pike considerably taller than a man, and the attitude of vigilance and resolution that Persian emperors expected from their soldiers (page 142).

In 529 B.C.E., a solemn procession filed from northwest India across Afghanistan and onto the plateau of Iran. Its members were carrying the mutilated remains of one of the most powerful rulers of the ancient world. As his body was placed in the sturdy tomb that had been built for him years earlier, priests chanted hymns and recited prayers. Sacrifices were made on his behalf to the fundamental forces of fire and water. Then the tomb was sealed and guards were placed around it to safeguard his royal dignity even in death. Cyrus the Great of Persia had come home.

The Persian Empire

Cyrus, like other kings of his day, was a fearsome warrior. But a list of his military conquests would tell only part of his story. The Persian Empire he founded left a legacy that included an efficient system of government, a tolerant society, a model for fostering commerce and cooperation among many cultures, and a conception of a universal god who rewards those who lead good lives and work for justice. Though often portrayed as foreign and therefore barbaric by the Greeks, Persian civilization was rich in its own right. The empire might well have dominated southwest Asia for centuries had Alexander the Great not arisen in Macedonia and decided to destroy it. Even after its fall, the Persian Empire's legacy profoundly influenced Islamic culture and present-day Iran. The king whom the Persians buried in 529 B.C.E. was an extraordinary ruler who set in motion a series of events and influences that long outlived him.

The Persian Empire

Mesopotamia, Egypt, India, and China all originated in fertile river valleys. Persian society, in contrast, developed on the arid Iranian plateau in southwestern Asia. In that challenging environment, the Persians constructed an empire that at its height would encompass most of southwestern Asia.

Geographic Challenges Confront the First Persians

The Iranian plateau's topography makes it easy to defend

The Iranian plateau, comprising nearly one million square miles, is relatively inhospitable. It contains two immense salt deserts, and the small rivers that cross it are difficult to navigate and offer little water for agriculture. Even entering the plateau can be difficult. It is guarded on the west by the Zagros (*ZAH-grus*) mountains; on the northwest by the Caspian Sea, Caucasus (*KAW-cuh-suhs*) mountains, and Elburz (*el-BURZ*) mountains; on the east by the mountain ranges and arid depressions of Afghanistan; on the southeast by the Baluchi (*buh-LOO-key*) desert; and on the south by the Persian Gulf (Map 6.1). The easiest way to ascend the plateau is from the northeast, where broad corridors through the mountains link Iran to Central Asia.

FOUNDATION MAP 6.1 The Physical Geography of the Iranian Plateau

The geography of the region provides natural defenses for Indo-European peoples settling on the Iranian plateau. Notice that the Zagros and Elburz mountain ranges, the Persian Gulf, the Caspian Sea, and the Baluchi Desert make access to the region difficult for invaders. Sparse rainfall makes the population dependent on irrigation systems that channel runoff from mountain snows that melt in spring. Why might such an easily defensible region have appeared undesirable to earlier settlers?

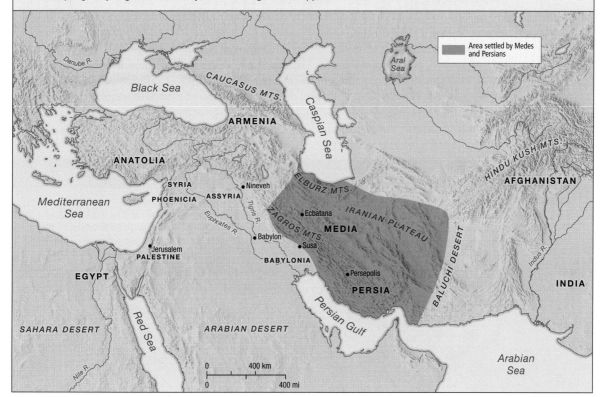

Archeological evidence suggests that people domesticated sheep and goats, and culti-vated wheat and barley, in the foothills of the Zagros mountains at least 10,000 years ago. Little is known of these early Iranians, but artifacts made of obsidian, a mineral not native to the region, indicate the existence of early trading networks. Pastoral nomadism dominated the Iranian plateau, where wide variations in water supply made regular farming impossible. Central Asian nomads arrived on the plateau, through the northwest corridors, about 5,000 years ago.

The Central Asian steppes were no more inviting than Iran, but they were much more difficult to defend against invaders. For thousands of years, hostile tribes had fought each other for control of the region, often contending at the same time with for-midable empires such as China. Winners expelled losers and were then, in turn, driven out. Some of these tribes went to Iran, undismayed by its uncertain water supply, and grazed their herds on the plateau.

Central Asians migrate to the Iranian plateau

The first migrants were influenced by the Sumerian culture they found among peoples living on the plateau (see photo, page 139), but they blended it with their own customs and preferences. Archeological remains indicate that these early immigrants were skilled artists, particularly in ceramics. Then around 1000 B.C.E. an Indo-European tribe from Central Asia migrated down the eastern shore of the Caspian Sea into western Iran. This group was a branch of the Aryans who had earlier moved into India (Chapter 3), and they gave their own name to the plateau they occupied: Iran means "land of the Aryans" (Map 6.2).

The two principal subgroups of Aryan migrants were the Medes (*MĒDZ*), who took up residence in the Zagros Mountains, and the Persians, taking their name from Farsia, the central region of the Iranian plateau. Both spoke the same language, which today is known as Farsi (*FAHR-sē*). They had different accents, but the Greeks, who encountered them during the Greco-Persian Wars, were unable to distinguish between the two and called all of them Persians.

Map 6.2 Indo-Europeans Migrate from Central Asia, 3000–1000 B.C.E.

Between 3000 and 1000 B.C.E., many Indo-European peoples left their homeland in what today is southwestern Russia, relocating in many different directions. One such people, the Aryans, entered the Iranian plateau from the northwest and settled among indigenous peoples already living there. Observe that eventually some Aryans would continue to migrate eastward and settle in India (Chapter 3). How might the knowledge and customs shared by these peoples have forged connections between the widely scattered societies that they created?

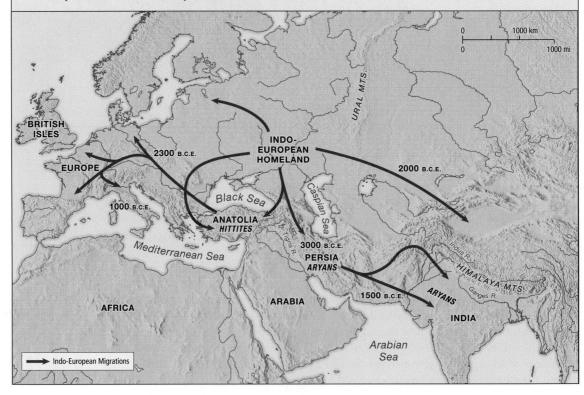

Although they periodically fought against invaders from the Assyrian Empire, the Medes were relatively well protected by the Zagros and established a thriving economy and culture. They mined minerals such as gold, silver, precious gems, marble, iron, copper, and lead, which they used in their artistic endeavors and traded with neighboring cultures.

The melting mountain snows provided the only reliable source of water for agriculture in a land that averages fewer than 12 inches of precipitation per year, so the Medes developed a sophisticated irrigation system. They trapped the waters of the melting snows and diverted them to fields. In one of the many valleys of the Zagros they built Ecbatana (*eck-BAH-tuh-nuh*), the seat of their government and center of their economy. Eventually, however, the Assyrian Empire conquered both the Medes and the Persians, forcing them to pay tribute but never completely subjugating them.

When Babylonia and Assyria erupted into civil war, the Medes and Persians took advantage of the conflict to free themselves from the invaders. First the Median king Cyaxares (*sī-AX-ar-ēs*) strengthened his army, reducing the Persians to the status of vassals. Cyaxares (640–584 B.C.E.) then allied with the Chaldeans against Assyria. But his plans were delayed by the arrival of Scythians (*SIH-thē-ahns*), nomadic warriors from Central Asia, who invaded Iran through the passage between the Caspian Sea and the Caucasus Mountains. Forced to pay tribute to the Scythians, Cyaxares decided to give a banquet for their leaders—at which he got them drunk and killed them. This enabled him to return to his original plan, and by 612 B.C.E. the Medes and Chaldeans had destroyed the Assyrian capital of Nineveh. Cyaxares ruled northern Mesopotamia until his death in 584, while the Chaldeans (or "New Babylonians") ruled in southern Mesopotamia (or "Babylonia"). The Assyrian Empire was shattered, making way for the creation of the Persian Empire.

Cyaxares defeats the Assyrian Empire

Cyrus the Great

The Median kingdom lasted for only a few decades before its Persian vassals started intriguing against it. The Persian ruling family, called the Achaemenids (*ah-KĒ-muh-nids*), married into the ruling house of Media. Cyrus, a child of this union, managed to unify the Persian tribes and wage war against the Median king, who was also his father-in-law. In 550 B.C.E. he captured the king and united the Medes and Persians under the Achaemenid house.

Following his defeat of the Medes, which extended his control from the Persian Gulf to central Anatolia, Cyrus next waged war against King Croesus (*CRĒ-suss*), ruler of a region called Lydia (*LIH-dē-uh*) in western Anatolia. Although Croesus, whose great wealth was legendary, struck first in an effort to expand Lydia eastward, his armies were no match for the Persians. In 547 B.C.E., the Lydian cavalry was poised to strike the Persian infantry when other Persian troops, mounted on camels, counterattacked. The Lydian horses, which had never before seen such animals, panicked and threw their riders into the dust. Cyrus's victory gave the Persian Empire access to the Mediterranean Sea and control of several Greek city-states on the shores of Anatolia, from which it could threaten Greece itself. Although Cyrus made no move against the Greek mainland, the Greeks were unnerved by the proximity of an empire with a large, well-equipped army that enjoyed a reputation for winning. During the following decades they watched the Persians carefully.

Cyrus expands the
Persian Empire to west
and east

Cyrus next moved east, conquering the lands of Parthia and Bactria (modern-day Afghanistan) and extending his dominion from the Aegean (*ih-JĒ-uhn*) Sea in the west to the Hindu Kush mountains in the east. In 539 B.C.E., he invaded southern Mesopotamia, then controlled by the Chaldeans' New Babylonian Empire. By allying himself with various tribes that had struggled against the Chaldeans and portraying himself as their liberator, Cyrus was able to enter the city of Babylon without a fight. The rich Babylonian domains, from Mesopotamia to Palestine, were now under his control. By the time of his death in 530 B.C.E., he had clearly earned the title of Cyrus the Great, one of history's most successful empire builders.

ASSIMILATION AFTER CONQUEST. The importance of Cyrus lay not just in his conquests. For its time, Cyrus's rule was remarkably sophisticated in its approach to subjugated peoples. Conquerors of that era normally pillaged defeated cities and enslaved their populations. Cyrus, by contrast, had a shrewd instinct for governing that allowed him to win the trust of those he defeated. An examination of some of his principles of government illustrates this instinct.

Cyrus the Great leads
through persuasion and
compromise

First, Cyrus demonstrated early in his reign that he would rule through persuasion and compromise rather than force and humiliation. When he conquered the Medes, he granted their leader honors and respect, and he united the Medes with his own people rather than subjugating them. He retained not only Median administrative and military structures but also the Medes who directed them. In this way he won the trust of the Medes and reduced the possibility of rebellion against his rule.

Second, Cyrus treated conquered peoples benevolently, allowing deported peoples to return to their homelands rather than enslaving them. He won the gratitude of the Jews when he freed them from captivity in Babylonia and allowed them to return to Jerusalem. He even encouraged them to rebuild their temple, which the Babylonians had destroyed.

Finally, Cyrus permitted the peoples he defeated to retain their own religions and cultures while simultaneously offering them partnership in the Persian Empire. This two-pronged approach persuaded various ethnic groups to accept his rule; in doing so, they understood that they would not be humiliated and would retain their self-respect. Cyrus also realized that his own people could learn from many of the societies he conquered. At his command, Persians sought out and copied the most useful practices of their new subjects. He also standardized taxes and measurements, codified laws, and fostered commercial and cultural connections within his vast domains.

Cyrus's policies of tolerance were based not so much on benevolence as on pragmatism. He acted in ways he knew would work. He understood that people treated humanely were not likely to rebel. But he also understood the nature of nomadic societies that occupied the Iranian plateau. These groups, often called tribes, usually resisted joining settled societies. They tended to pursue their own interests, migrating at will to various parts of the plateau and following their own traditions and governing methods. Tribal fighters were bound to their chiefs by ties of loyalty cemented by blood relationships and patronage, the voluntary submission of a family or clan to a powerful leader (or patron). Thus chiefs commanded considerable leverage that could be used to support a central leadership, as long as that leadership did not monopolize power or impose its culture on others. In such circumstances, Cyrus acted prudently, accepting conditions he could not change and turning necessity to his advantage by granting autonomy magnanimously.

That magnanimity was not, however, unlimited. Tribal leaders were expected to place their own interests within the context of the empire's larger interests, recognizing that cooperation would benefit everyone. Defense and trade were empire-wide priorities. Permitting the Jews to return to Palestine helped Cyrus assimilate the Phoenician and Palestinian remnants of the Babylonian Empire, and the rebuilding of the temple at Jerusalem was followed by the construction of fortifications designed to protect the western regions of the empire against invasion from Egypt. The Jews were expected to cooperate in this task, and evidence suggests that they did. So did the Babylonians, whose merchants welcomed membership in an empire that offered them secure trade routes to markets in Egypt and Syria. Cyrus's ability to transform conflict into connection thus created an extensive commercial network in Southwest Asia.

Cyrus transforms conflict into connection and cooperation

Persian Governance and Society: Links with Mesopotamia

The Persian Empire, ruled by ambitious, creative leaders, dominated both Iran and Mesopotamia by the middle of the sixth century B.C.E. Then its rulers proceeded to consolidate their hold over their subjects and project Persian influence westward, toward an eventual confrontation with Greece.

From Cyrus to Darius

After the conquest of Babylon, Cyrus presided over the largest empire on earth. He had won the loyalty of most of his subject peoples by treating them humanely. Only one corner of his realm resisted his rule, and the Great King finally overreached himself. The Massagetae (*mahs-ah-JET-ē*), a nomadic people of Scythian origin in northwestern India, were contemptuous of Persian ideals and indifferent to Persian control. In 530 B.C.E., Cyrus, now in his sixties, led his army into the region to subdue these difficult people. The battle went badly for the Persians, and Cyrus himself was knocked from his horse by Tomyris (*tum-Ē-riss*), queen of the Massagetae. She severed his head with a single blow of her sword and returned his mutilated corpse to the Persians, who retreated westward and buried him in the tomb described at the beginning of this chapter.

Cambyses (*kam-BĒ-sēz*), Cyrus's son, succeeded him and wisely decided to leave the Massagetae alone. Instead he invaded Egypt, bringing the Nile Valley under Persian control. But the campaign there took three years and Persians at home, unnerved by Cyrus's defeat and tired of war, revolted in 522 B.C.E. Cambyses (r. 530–521 B.C.E.) rushed back from Egypt to suppress the uprising, but he died along the way. The Persian Empire had never established a routine order of succession, and with three different heirs of the Achaemenid dynasty contending for power, the empire fell into disarray.

The eventual winner was Darius (*duh-RĪ-us*), a 28-year-old soldier who married both Cambyses' grieving widow and a daughter of Cyrus the Great (Persian rulers sometimes married more than one woman for political gain). But he was widely viewed as a

The "Cyrus Cylinder", a damaged clay cylinder completely inscribed with cuneiform writing that shows the influence of Sumerian culture on Persia.

Map 6.3 The Persian Empire Expands, 549–490 B.C.E.

The Persian Empire stretched across portions of three continents on a broad east-west axis. Note that Persia recentered power in southwest Asia eastward away from Mesopotamia, controlling territory from Libya and Macedonia in the west to the Indus valley in the east. The Royal Road facilitated communication and connections across this geographically challenging region, while local governors known as satraps enforced the Persian King's will in areas the monarch himself never visited. What effects would Cyrus the Great's policies of assimilation have had on the peoples of such a vast and diverse region?

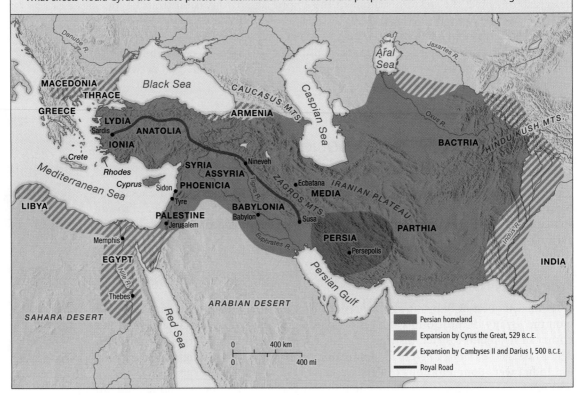

Persian homeland

Expansion by Cyrus the Great, 529 B.C.E.

Expansion by Cambyses II and Darius I, 500 B.C.E.

Royal Road

Darius claims the Persian throne

usurper, and rebellions broke out throughout the empire. Claiming divine support, Darius (r. 521–486 B.C.E.) put down the uprisings by force. It was a bloody beginning for a ruler who would one day be known as Darius the Great.

Prudently, Darius waited a few years before resuming Persia's imperial expansion, using the time to reorganize his army. But he did not wait too long, for he understood that the arrogance he had shown in claiming divine support would have to be justified by victories. In 517 B.C.E., he struck eastward, driving into southwestern India and putting its gold mines to the service of the empire (Map 6.3). His victories in the Indus Valley completed Persia's conquest of three of the four great river civilizations. Only China remained outside his grasp, and it is unlikely that he ever thought of going there. Instead he moved westward, securing Egypt and Libya, and then struck north into southeastern Europe, pressing on as far as the Danube River by 512 B.C.E. With future conquests in mind, he settled down for the time being to solidify his rule.

Administration of the Empire

Cyrus, Cambyses, and Darius had built an enormous empire, many times larger than the Assyrian Empire that Cyrus had overthrown (Map 6.4). Ruling that realm—a vast expanse of many different peoples and cultures—would require a carefully structured bureaucracy. Central control had to be ensured, even as local autonomy was preserved, in order to avoid inefficiency, rebellion, or both.

Darius chose strong central rule. Whereas Cyrus had governed through cooperation backed by the ever-present threat of superior force, Darius emphasized authority. Cyrus had acted benevolently toward defeated rulers and turned them, where possible, into allies. Darius, in contrast, called his enemies "Kings of The Lie" and singled them out for special punishment. More distant from his people than Cyrus and less willing to permit autonomy, Darius grounded his government on the unswerving loyalty of political appointees.

Map 6.4 The Assyrian and Persian Empires Compared, 625–500 B.C.E.

The sprawling Assyrian Empire had dominated southwest Asia, but observe how the conquests of Cyrus, Cambyses, and Darius I dwarf it. Ruling an empire as enormous as Persia was an unprecedented task, requiring administrative innovations such as satrapies. It also required a willingness to grant substantial autonomy to local rulers and leaders, a feature that had characterized Persian governance even before Cyrus. What other policies or institutions might have been devised to permit efficient rule of such an enormous realm?

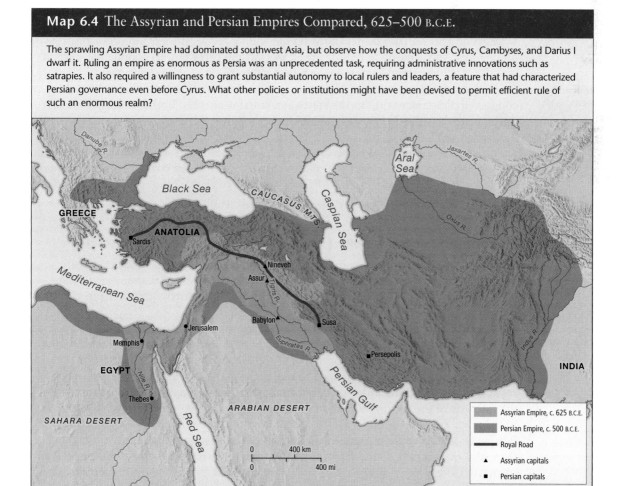

Darius centralizes Persian administration

These concerns led Darius to divide the Persian Empire into twenty provinces, each known in Farsi as a **satrapy** (*SĀ-trap-ē*) and ruled by a governor called a satrap. Most satraps were not Persians but members of the ethnic group they were expected to rule. In this way, Darius strengthened central control while perpetuating the local autonomy characteristic of nomadic society. Linked to the Achaemenids through marriage or birth, satraps were referred to as "the eyes and ears of the Great King."

Selected for their loyalty and their familiarity with local conditions, satraps exercised considerable authority, reinforced by rapid communication. A carefully maintained highway system, dominated by the Royal Road running from Sardis, near the Aegean Sea to Susa (*SOO-suh*), near the Persian Gulf, guaranteed that information would travel quickly. Persia's superb mounted postal service could, under the best conditions, carry a message more than a thousand miles in the course of a week. Foot soldiers, however (see page 133), even if marching at the breakneck pace of 19 miles a day, would take three months to travel the Royal Road. Beyond Susa, the roads eastward to India were less satisfactory, and the terrain rougher.

Darius knew, however, that the swift delivery of a royal message did not necessarily guarantee compliance. The emperor might be master of all he surveyed from his capital, but beyond that horizon he depended on the willing cooperation of subordinates. He needed men, particularly in remote areas, who would carry out his commands without question and who would act in his own best interests. Satraps were the men he chose.

Satraps play a vital role in Persian governance

The satraps were crucial to the prosperity and peace of the empire they served. They conducted diplomacy with border states and warrior peoples. Both inside and outside the empire, they blended persuasion and force as Cyrus and Darius had done. The stability they ensured allowed trade and commerce to thrive. In addition, they were entrusted with the collection of royal taxes. If the satraps failed at this task, the empire would fail. That its fall came with defeat by a military genius, rather than as a consequence of poor administration, is a tribute to the diligence and skill of the satraps as well as to the design of the administrative system developed by Darius the Great.

Mesopotamian Influences: Law, Administration, and Commerce

As Persia expanded and as its bureaucracy grew, its connections with other cultures multiplied. The emperors were particularly attracted by Mesopotamia, birthplace of the Sumerian, Babylonian, and Assyrian cultures and worthy of imitation in several respects.

Hammurabi's Code influences Persian law

Law was one area in which Persians could learn from Mesopotamia. Darius needed a legal system applicable throughout the empire in order to support his administrative structures. Adhering to Cyrus's principle of tolerance for subject peoples, Darius permitted local customs and regulations to remain in place. But he established a system of royal judges to ensure that local laws would be enforced in a manner consistent with the interests of the empire. Deliberately seeking to be known as a lawgiver like the Babylonian king Hammurabi, Darius authorized the compilation and codification of Persian laws. But while Hammurabi's Code survived in numerous cuneiform tablets, Darius's *Ordinance of Good Regulations*, written on parchment (treated sheepskins or goatskins), completely disappeared. In fact, until recent archeological discoveries, some scholars did not believe it once existed. The few indirect references to it found in contemporary Babylonian commercial documents suggest that it was modeled on Hammurabi's Code but altered to apply Persian ethics to both civil and criminal matters.

Persian government was also influenced by Mesopotamia. The Aryans who entered Iran brought with them a simple social structure adapted to life on the steppes of Central Asia. But Cyrus's invasion of Mesopotamia brought Persia into contact with a very complex civilization. Ruling it required levels of organization beyond those present in a nomadic society. The Babylonian Empire had developed a system of provincial governors, many of whose duties were now taken over by Persian satraps and their subordinates, such as tax collectors, police officials, and record keepers. These officials constituted an administrative class of their own, developing codes of conduct specific to their roles in Persian life. In addition, the military occupation of Mesopotamia and its assimilation into the Persian Empire forced the satraps to share power with local warriors, who resented the Persians for their literacy and their knowledge of diplomacy. Soldiers did not generally have these skills, and Persian administrators, responding to their antagonism, gradually became more militaristic.

Persepolis: the east stairway to the great audience hall of Darius I, showing visiting dignitaries bringing tribute.

The conquest of Mesopotamia also brought Persia into contact with western Asia and northwestern Africa. International trade expanded, fostered by the empire's political stability, its control of sea routes, and its well-maintained roads. Persia traded extensively with Syria, Egypt, Greece, and Ethiopia, connecting those regions with Central Asia through Afghanistan. Far more cosmopolitan than its Mesopotamian, Egyptian, and Indian predecessors, the Persian Empire forged connections between cultures separated by thousands of miles.

Possession of Mesopotamia helps Persia create connections

Persian Society and Culture

Contact with Mesopotamia also affected Persian society. To meet the needs of an expanding empire, social classes began to develop in Persian cities. Artisans now needed to fabricate more than saddles and weapons: they created items of metal, fiber, and leather required by an urbanizing society in the process of forsaking its nomadic past. Merchants carried on trade, both locally and over long distances, making use of the Royal Road and Silk Road. Nomads had no need for elaborate systems of irrigation, but settled societies based on arid plateaus did, and the skilled and unskilled workers who built and maintained them were highly valued.

In addition, Persian society included a slave class. Persia had a history of slave-owning—in Central Asia the Aryans had owned slaves—and when invading Persians occupied Mesopotamia, they saw the Babylonians using slaves on large construction projects. Most Persian slaves were prisoners taken in battle, but others were ordinary individuals who, on account of debts, were forced to sell themselves or even their families into slavery to repay their creditors. Slaves were the property of their owners in every sense and could make no decisions (including marriage) without permission. Although some slaves became highly skilled at their tasks and were rewarded with increasing levels of responsibility and respect, most led short lives of hard labor and deprivation.

Persian society develops a class structure

What little is known of Persian family structure suggests a self-reliant society. A Persian man could have more than one wife, provided that he could afford to maintain each of them above the poverty level, a restriction that limited polygamy to the upper classes.

The fact that men were frequently away from home on business or at war meant that elite Persian women normally enjoyed substantial independence. They administered their family estates, organized celebrations, and traveled freely throughout the empire with or without their husbands. Most men and women, of course, lived from one meal to the next and never acquired wealth. These families, on whose labor the empire depended, had little time to contemplate anything other than survival.

Everyone, however—elites, ordinary people, and slaves—benefited from the Persian love of celebration. Festivals were common throughout the empire, particularly once Zoroastrianism took root. That religion, described below, obligates people to seek happiness and considers fasting and penance to belong to the realm of demons. Accordingly, Persians enjoyed feasts filled with music, dancing, and fun. The staple food was barley bread, supplemented by fruits, vegetables, and date or grape wine. Merrymakers on holy days were required to give to the poor and invite even the most destitute to join the revelry. The spring festival of Nō Rōz (*NO ROSE*), commemorating the creation of fire, was celebrated with special foods, the exchange of gifts, and the wearing of new clothes and ornaments. In addition to seven "high feasts," there were many local fairs and frolics. The love of celebrations gave the Persians a spirit of joy that counterbalanced the empire's military might and administrative control.

Persians loved objects made of gold or silver, like this silver figurine of an antelope.

Persians also enjoyed fine jewelry and clothing. Like their Median and Scythian ancestors, they wore a wide variety of bracelets, necklaces, chains, and earrings, often made of gold or silver. Contemporary non-Persian accounts often refer to Iranians as taking great pride in their appearance, and it is likely that their clothing was durable and attractive. Bowls, goblets, and ceremonial vessels were made of brass, gold, and silver, and appear to have been widely used not only by the elite but by many ordinary households.

Much of the empire's cultural inheritance came from the Medes and Persians. The Persians spoke Farsi, which featured a 36-character alphabet, an intricate grammatical structure, and a rich, expressive vocabulary. This language was written not on clay in the Sumerian style, but with pen and ink on parchment.

Another original aspect of Persian culture was architecture. Once the formerly nomadic Persians became sedentary, they made effective use of the column and constructed huge monuments depicting bulls and lions with wings. Persian art that has survived the centuries generally takes the form of sculpture and reliefs carved into the walls of buildings. These monuments reveal a culture sensitive to beauty and aware of its political uses. For example, the emperor, his generals, and courtiers are portrayed as regal, powerful persons of great dignity. Often they are depicted as stylized, mythical heroes, adorned with wings or engaged in single-handed combat with lions or bulls. Delegations from subject kingdoms like Babylonia and Lydia are shown bearing tribute and paying homage to Cyrus or Darius, particularly on the walls of the city of Persepolis (*per-SEH-puh-lis*), the most visually striking of Persia's cities (see photo, page 143).

The emperor maintained official residences in the cities of Ecbatana, Babylon, and Susa, enabling him to rule the empire from whichever city he happened to be living in at the time. During the winter this was usually Susa, centrally located in Mesopotamia; Ecbatana or Babylon served as the capital in the summer. Shortly after his accession to the throne, Darius began building a ceremonial capital at Persepolis, intending to demonstrate his greatness through its massive buildings and sculptures. He died before the work was completed, and his son Xerxes (*ZURK-zēz*) finished the task. Festivals, celebrations, and major imperial functions were held there in an atmosphere that suggested the largest empire of its day would last for thousands of years.

Persepolis survives today only as ruins, but even those fragments are impressive. It contained a series of massive public buildings, including the royal treasury and several superbly designed reception halls. These structures and colossal monuments portrayed the power and ferocity of the Persian Emperor. Anyone witnessing such grandeur would conclude that Persia in 500 B.C.E. was truly the center of the world. But just as Cyrus the Great had been unexpectedly brought down in battle by a small tribe of nomadic Scythians far to the east, his successors would inadvertently lead the empire to destruction in wars with seemingly unimportant people along its western frontier.

A photograph of the ruins of the entrance to the Palace of Darius in Persepolis.

Zoroastrianism

Those assimilated into the Persian Empire participated in a dynamic, expanding state and a flourishing economy. Many also practiced a religion that gave divine sanction to the ambitions of the Persian emperors: **Zoroastrianism** (*zohr-ō-ASS-trē-ahn-iz'm*).

At first the Medes and Persians were polytheistic, worshipping a variety of deities including two powerful gods, Ahura and Mazda (*uh-HOOR-uh* and *MAHZ-duh*). Like other polytheistic peoples, the Medes and Persians incorporated religion into their daily lives, believing that various gods represented natural forces such as wind, rain, and sunlight and praying to the one whose benefits they sought. This belief system changed significantly in the sixth century B.C.E. with the empire's adoption of the ideas of a holy man who had lived centuries earlier on the Iranian plateau.

A Religion of Good and Evil

Zoroastrianism was based on the ideas of the prophet Zoroaster—or Zarathustra (*zah-rah-THOO-strah*), as he is more commonly known today—who apparently lived in Persia sometime between 1300 and 1000 B.C.E. Zoroaster sensed that two powerful Persian gods, Ahura and Mazda, were in fact a single god, whom he called Ahura Mazda. He perceived Ahura Mazda as the universal god of light who had created human beings and given them free will to choose between right and wrong. To explain the existence of evil, Zoroaster maintained that Ahura Mazda had a malignant twin, Ahriman (*AHR-ē-mun*), whom Ahura Mazda had defeated and banished from paradise but who still sought to influence human behavior as lord of the forces of darkness.

Zoroaster's promotion of monontheism—belief in one god—won few converts until he blended it with an ancient cult emphasizing fire worship. Zoroastrians built fire temples to enshrine the light of Ahura Mazda. They conceded that lesser gods existed but characterized some as attributes of Ahura Mazda, while others were manifestations of The Lie, a set of false doctrines propagated by Ahriman to lead people astray.

Once the Persian emperors adopted Zoroastrianism, they gave control of it to the Magi (*MĀ-jī*), the scholar-priests of the Persian world who guarded the temples and compiled Zoroaster's ideas in a sacred text called the *Avesta* (see "Excerpt from the *Avesta*"). The Magi, who later played a role in the Christian story of the birth of Jesus

Zoroaster preaches a monotheistic religion

Document 6.1 Excerpt from The *Avesta*.

The *Avesta*, the Holy Scripture of Zoroastrianism, is a collection of prayers to Ahura Mazda and to lesser spirits and beings.

Purity is the best good. Happiness, happiness is to him: Namely, to the best pure in purity.

Broken, broken be Satan Ahriman, whose deeds and works are accursed. May his works and deeds not attain to us. May Ahura Mazda be victorious and pure.

Let Ahura Mazda be king, and let Ahriman, the wicked holder-aloof, be smitten and broken.

All the evil thoughts, evil words, evil deeds, which I have thought, spoken, done, committed in the world, which are become my nature—all these sins, thoughts, words, and deeds, bodily, spiritual, earthly, heavenly, O Lord, pardon; I repent of them.

In the name of God, the Lord, the Increaser. May he increase in great majesty. I praise and exalt Ahura Mazda, the Brilliant, Majestic, Omniscient, the Perfecter of deeds, the Lord of Lords, the Prince over all princes, the Protector, the Creator of the created, the Giver of daily food, the Powerful, Good, Strong, Old, Forgiving, Granter of forgiveness, Rich in Love, Mighty and Wise, the pure Supporter. May thy right rule be without ceasing.

SOURCE: *The Avesta*, translated by Arthur Henry Bleeck (New York: Gordon Press, 1974) 3–6.

of Nazareth, came to see all creation as a cosmic struggle between the forces of good, led by Ahura Mazda, and the forces of evil, led by Ahriman. At the end of life, each individual would be judged by Ahura Mazda: those who had led lives of goodness and truth would be rewarded with eternal bliss; those who had practiced wickedness and deceit would be doomed to everlasting pain. At the Last Judgment, righteousness would overcome The Lie.

Zoroastrianism influences later monotheistic religions

Many beliefs later important to Judaism, Christianity, and Islam first appeared in Zoroastrianism: the existence of one God of justice and benevolence, the conflict between God and the Devil, the divine judgment of individuals based on their moral behavior, and the notions of heaven and hell. Zoroastrianism was also the source of the cult of Mithras (*MITH-rahs*), a divine-human "god of day" revered as Ahura Mazda's main deputy, which later spread widely in the Greek and Roman worlds. Zoroastrianism survived for more than a thousand years, until, in the seventh and eighth centuries C.E., it was displaced by Islam. Refugees fled to the area surrounding Bombay in India, where Zoroastrianism survives today, practiced by Parsees, the descendants of these refugees.

Social and Political Content

Zoroastrianism delivers a social message

Zoroastrianism was more than theology: it also carried a strong social and political message about how people should conduct themselves. Zoroastrians believe that the entire purpose of the struggle between good and evil is the improvement of life on earth before the Last Judgment, and that individuals will be judged not only by what they have believed but also by what they have done. Thus Zoroastrians feel compelled to engage in government, political affairs, and issues of social justice.

From 521 B.C.E. onward, the Zoroastrian faith was strongly supported by the Persian kings, who liked to portray themselves as Ahura Mazda's earthly agents. Darius the Great had the magnificent Behistun relief carved to depict his triumphs over his enemies through the divine assistance of Ahura Mazda, who appears in the relief as a winged god blessing the proceedings. Zoroastrianism's sociopolitical ethic proved very useful to the

Persian kings: it established a moral order in Persia and designated the Great King as God's vice-regent on earth. To disobey his commands was equivalent to sinning against God and humanity.

Neither Darius nor his successors imposed Zoroastrianism on Persia's subject peoples; to do so would have violated the cultural autonomy that formed the basis of Persian rule. But Darius seems to have believed that Ahura Mazda had bestowed upon him the awesome yet appropriate duty of unifying the known world into a single empire based on justice and peace. In pursuit of that sacred goal, the emperor believed he had to respect the various cultures of the peoples entrusted to his care. He also had to draw them away from The Lie by giving them positions of responsibility (such as satrap) and demonstrating that obedience to the empire carried with it not slavery but opportunity. In this way Zoroastrianism reinforced attitudes that Darius had already learned to value. Or perhaps, given his enormous influence, it was the other way round.

Confrontation with Greece

The Persian Empire first came into contact with Greece when Cyrus completed the conquest of Lydia in 546 B.C.E. Several Greek city-states in the region of Ionia along the western coast of Anatolia thereby fell under Persian domination, since Lydia had previously protected them. The Greeks knew little about Persian culture prior to Lydia's defeat and liked little of what they learned thereafter. Zoroastrian monotheism and musings about social justice baffled polytheistic people who believed that justice for humans was not a high priority for the gods. To the fiercely independent Greeks, Persia's tolerance for its subject peoples seemed only a strategy for making bondage less offensive. For their part, the Persians regarded the Greeks as no more sophisticated or dangerous than the other peoples the empire had subdued. The conquerors of Assyria and Babylon were not intimidated by a land divided into many competing city-states that seemed to lack military potential. For several decades after the defeat of Lydia, the west Anatolian city-states reluctantly accommodated themselves to Persian rule. Then, in 499, the Ionian Revolt began.

The Ionian Revolt and the Persian Response Darius (King)

The uprising in Ionia took Persia by surprise. The Persians had followed their standard policy of working with local leaders, but the Ionian officials with whom they worked discredited themselves with their own people by their collaboration with Persia. The rebellious cities were far away from Susa, and the Greeks, who never understood Persians, apparently thought that this distance would discourage the emperor from retaliating. Almost as an afterthought, the rebels appealed for aid to the Greek city-states across the Aegean Sea. Athens, one of the leading city-states, responded by sending a fleet, which was defeated in 494 B.C.E. The revolt disintegrated and Darius sought to consolidate his victory by directing the city-states of the Greek mainland to submit to Persian domination of Aegean commerce. He was astounded when Athens and Sparta, another important city-state, promptly killed his messengers, an act of sacrilege from the Persian perspective and an insult to the emperor. Deeply offended, Darius prepared for war.

The Ionian revolt brings Persia into conflict with Greece

In 492 B.C.E., a powerful Persian fleet heading for Greece was wrecked near Mount Athos. A second force was dispatched two years later and landed in the Bay of Marathon (Map 6.5). The Persians expected to defeat their enemy easily—an expectation the Athenians in fact shared. Persia's army of 20,000 soldiers outnumbered the Greeks two to one, but in the Battle of Marathon more than six thousand Persians perished, while the Greeks lost only 192 men.

Darius's defeat at Marathon causes Persia to rethink its strategy

The Greeks believed that their victory at Marathon had frustrated Persia's intention to conquer the entire Greek mainland. But to the Persians, Marathon was only a small setback that did nothing to change Darius's strategy of ensuring Persian domination of the Aegean Sea. He had intended merely to punish the Greeks for their revolt, not conquer them; but his loss at Marathon convinced him that conquest was necessary. Darius intended to return with a much larger army but died in 486 B.C.E., before his forces were ready. It was a foregone conclusion, however, that his son and successor, Xerxes, (r. 486–465 B.C.E.) would renew the struggle.

Map 6.5 Conflict Between Persia and Greece, 492–479 B.C.E.

Persia's suppression of the revolts of the Ionian city-states in western Anatolia provoked Greek intervention. Persia responded with two separate invasions of the Greek peninsula. Note that Persia, a land-based empire, was forced by geography to construct a powerful navy in order to fight the Greeks. Persia's inability to conquer Greece meant that Greek civilization would continue to evolve apart from eastern influences, and would eventually form part of the foundation of what came to be known as Western civilization. Had Persia been victorious, what might have happened to Greek society and culture?

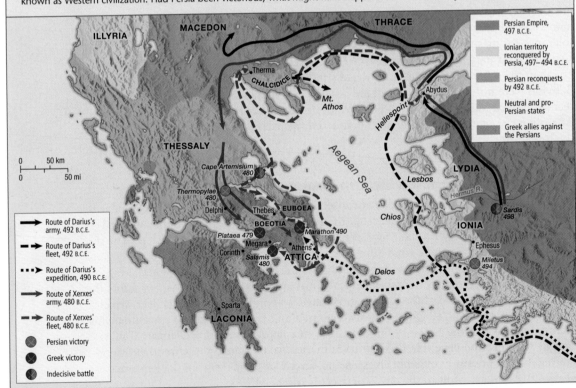

Xerxes and the Invasion of Greece

Xerxes invaded Greece with the explicit intention of subduing its mainland. Although he was confident of victory, he had learned from Marathon not to underestimate his opponents, and in 481 B.C.E. he left Susa at the head of a massive army. The Greek historian Herodotus (*hair-AH-duh-tuss*), who chronicled the Persian Wars, reported that an invading host of 2,641,000 men drank entire rivers dry when camping for the night. This was a wild exaggeration—there probably weren't two million men of military age in all of Persia—but Xerxes could have brought about 250,000 soldiers, enough to frighten the usually quarrelsome Greeks into creating an anti-Persian alliance. Sparta provided leadership on land, while Athens mobilized a formidable navy. At stake in the struggle was the future leadership of Greece, western Anatolia, and the entire Aegean basin.

Greeks put aside their quarrels to unite against Persia

The Persians struck simultaneously by land and sea. At a narrow mountain pass near the town of Thermopylae (*thur-MAH-puh-lē*), 360 Spartans held out for days against more than 10,000 Persians. The Spartans died to the last man, delaying the Persian advance long enough to permit their comrades to mount a successful defense on the plains beyond. Today a plaque at the entry to the pass commemorates the Spartan ideal that inspired such sacrifice: "Go tell the Spartans, stranger passing by/ That here, obedient to their laws, we lie." Shortly thereafter, further dramatic Greek victories forced the Persians to withdraw.

In retrospect it is clear why the Persians lost. First, they faced massive logistical problems in trying to sustain such huge military forces so far from home. Second, their lightly armed soldiers, equipped for mobile fighting on the plains of Asia, were surprised to find the Greek infantry better equipped to fight in the narrow passes and rocky hills of Greece. Finally, the Greeks were more highly motivated than their enemy, because they had more to lose. The Persians could withdraw to fight again, but if the Greeks lost they would lose their independence.

A variety of factors prevent Persia from conquering Greece

Stalemate

Their defeat in Greece astounded the Persians and convinced Xerxes to return home. He had been absent too long for a monarch with such extensive ambitions and responsibilities. Moreover, he faced a rebellion in Babylonia, probably provoked by news of his difficulties in Greece. If he failed to put it down his throne stood in jeopardy.

But the Greco-Persian conflict was far from over. Misinterpreting Xerxes' withdrawal as evidence that the Persians had given up, Athens and its allies landed troops in western Anatolia to pursue the Persians and secure Ionian independence. After nearly three more decades of intermittent warfare, the two sides signed the Peace of Callias (*KAHL-ē-us*) in 448 B.C.E.: Athens agreed to leave Anatolia to the Persians, who in turn promised to stay out of Ionia and the Aegean Sea.

What had begun as the small-scale Ionian Revolt had turned into an unanticipated stalemate, and Persian ambitions were frustrated. Darius and Xerxes had discovered their reach exceeded their grasp: Persia could land forces on the Greek mainland and devastate the countryside, but it could neither conquer Greece nor hold Ionia. The Greeks had seen the benefits of cooperation in the face of a powerful enemy, but they learned little from the experience. Athens and several of its allies, after driving Persia from Ionia, soon took up arms against Sparta.

Greek resistance blocks further Persian expansion

Xerxes returned home in 479 B.C.E., and though he had intended to return to Greece, he never rallied himself for war again. After suppressing the Babylonian rebellion, he was content to live in luxury, gradually withdrawing from affairs of state. Then, in 465 B.C.E., he was assassinated. Thereafter Persia endured a succession of weak rulers who were unable to deal effectively with rebellion in Egypt and rising discontent at home. But in 431 B.C.E., when the Greek city-states went to war with one another, the Persians found themselves with a new opportunity for conquest.

Persian Resurgence

The Peloponnesian War gives Persia a new opportunity

From 431 to 404 B.C.E., Greece was racked by the Peloponnesian (*pell-luh-puhn-Ē-zhē-un*) War. Rival alliances led by Athens and Sparta clawed at one another and left the Greek mainland open to intervention or invasion. At first Persia alternated between supporting one alliance or the other, but eventually it funded the expansion of the Spartan fleet. That fleet enabled Sparta to challenge Athens's longstanding control of the sea and eventually defeat the Athenian alliance, which had been Persia's most persistent antagonist. Artaxerxes (*AR-tuh-zurk-zēz*) II, Persian emperor from 404 to 358 B.C.E., then took advantage of Greek exhaustion and moved to reclaim the Ionian city-states.

Had the Greeks united, it is likely that they could have defeated the Persians, whose army, consisting largely of draftees, was weakened by low morale. But Persian diplomacy and bribery combined with centuries of Greek rivalry to keep the Greeks divided. Finally, in 387 B.C.E., Artaxerxes gained enough leverage to impose a treaty called the King's Peace, withdrawing his forces from Greece in exchange for recognition of his control of Ionia. After 16 years of struggle, Persia had emerged as the real winner of the Peloponnesian War. The Persian city of Susa was now the capital of the Aegean world.

The Macedonian Conquest and Its Successor States

The days of the Achaemenids, however, were numbered. The satraps, sensing the weakening of royal authority, enriched themselves in the provinces at the emperor's expense. Plots, intrigues, and assassinations grew more frequent. Emperor Artaxerxes III (358–338 B.C.E.) proved too distracted by these troubles to pay attention to Macedonia, a new threat to Persian power arising north of Greece (Map 6.5).

The End of the Persian Empire

Persia's failure to fight Macedon leads to the defeat of the Persian Empire

In 341 B.C.E., Persia refused to assist Athens in its war against Philip II of Macedon (*MASS-uh-dun*), preferring to negotiate with the Macedonian leader. It was a short-sighted policy. By 339 B.C.E., Persian troops had been drawn into the war, and in the following year Philip (r. 359–336 B.C.E.) had united all Greece under his leadership. Artaxerxes was poisoned by satraps seeking to weaken the emperor's position, and his eventual successor, Emperor Darius III (336–330 B.C.E.), was not an effective leader. Suddenly vulnerable, Persia stood alone against the new Macedonian power in the west.

Philip would have been a formidable enough adversary even for Cyrus the Great, but his murder at his daughter's wedding in 336 B.C.E. brought to the Macedonian throne his son Alexander III, later known as Alexander the Great, a military genius whose talents have never been surpassed. Alexander, whose story is told in Chapter 7, defeated the Persian army in a series of battles in 334–333 B.C.E. Yet Darius III and his counselors underestimated the abilities of this 22-year-old novice. The Persian Empire had lost many battles but had always won the wars, provided that its leadership had the sense to play for time.

The problem was that the impetuous Alexander had no intention of letting the Achaemenids stall. He sacked Persepolis in 330 and stood over the corpse of Darius III, murdered that summer by his own troops while fleeing from Alexander's advance. The Achaemenid dynasty died with Darius III, but by officiating at his funeral ceremony, Alexander designated himself as that dynasty's rightful heir. The former Persian Empire, which had conquered so many peoples itself, was subjugated under the Macedonian empire of Alexander the Great.

Part of a mosaic illustrating the Battle of Issus, in which Darius III (in chariot) led the Persians to defeat against Alexander the Great.

Persia Under Macedonian Rule

Persian government, always tolerant of subject peoples, was now forced to accept Greek political institutions and culture. Alexander wisely retained most of the local Achaemenid administrative structure, but he encouraged the mixing of Greeks and Persians, taking several Persian wives himself, and significant numbers of Macedonian and Greek soldiers settled permanently in Persia. Alexander's policies appear to have worked well, since no noticeable unrest marred his rule and no rebellions followed his unexpected death in 323 B.C.E. at the age of 33.

Alexander attempts to combine Greek and Persian institutions

Soon thereafter, one of Alexander's generals, Seleucus Nikator (*sell-LOO-kus ni-KĀ-tur*), assumed control over most of the old Persian Empire; the new state was called the Seleucid (*sell-LOO-sid*) kingdom. But in an effort to secure his position with the Macedonian leadership, Seleucus (r. 305–280 B.C.E.) promoted Macedonian officials over Persians and displayed no sympathy for or connection to the Persian culture or language. Soon he lost the support of the Persian nobility on the old empire's eastern fringes. Rebellions broke out there, and by 304 B.C.E. Seleucus was forced to turn control of western India over to Chandragupta Maurya, founder of the Mauryan Empire. Thus the disintegration of the Persian Empire helped create a new empire in India. By 129 B.C.E., the Seleucid kingdom had fallen apart, with two principal successor states emerging: the Greco-Bactrian kingdom, comprising northern Afghanistan and part of northwestern India, and the Parthian empire, extending from Armenia southeastward to the Arabian Sea.

The crumbling of Alexander's empire creates successor states

The Parthian Empire

The collapse of the Seleucid kingdom opened the way for the Parthians, a Central Asian tribe that had moved onto the Iranian plateau during the Achaemenid dynasty. The Parthians ruled formerly Seleucid lands using Persian-style satrapies and administrative flexibility—both essential for governing a region composed of so many different ethnic groups. The Romans, whose empire arose to the west of Persia in the second and first centuries C.E. (Chapter 8), considered the Parthians worthy heirs of the Persians. After Roman armies were routed by the Parthians in 53 B.C.E., Roman Emperor Caesar

Augustus (31 B.C.E.–14 C.E.) refrained from provoking them. Subsequent Roman emperors launched repeated attacks on the westernmost portions of the Parthian empire but never succeeded in conquering Parthian Persia.

Parthian Persia facilitates commerce across Asia

Parthian Persia was a critical crossroad of Asian trade because of its strategic location along the Silk Road (Map 6.6). The Parthians eagerly participated in trans-Asiatic commerce, serving as middlemen between China and Southwest Asia while maintaining safe roads and centers of hospitality for passing merchant caravans from many different cultures. Parthian merchants filled Chinese orders for alfalfa plants, grape vines, and Persia's magnificent Ferghana horses. Their contact with China also promoted the transmission of Indian goods and Buddhist doctrines eastward during the third century C.E. Like the Persians, the Parthians connected East and West. But the Parthians lacked the forceful leadership necessary to win back the westernmost provinces of the old Persian Empire. Following their collapse as a result of internal intrigue in 224 C.E., the imperial throne passed to a people known as the Sasanians (*suh-SAY-nee-uns*).

The Sasanian Empire

Sasanians defeat Rome and rebuild Persia

For the first time in recorded history the Iranian plateau was ruled by a people who were not invaders. The Sasanians had arrived in Fars, just north of the Persian Gulf, even before the Medes and Persians. Now they seized an opportune moment, first to help the Parthians fight the Romans, and then to replace the Parthians and construct their own empire. They fought the Roman Empire for several decades, taking Mesopotamia in 256 under the leadership of King Shapur (*shah-POOR*) I (r. 240–271 C.E.). Four years later, the Roman Emperor Valerian (r. 253–259) personally commanded the Roman legions in a campaign to expel the Sasanians from the Roman province of Syria. Shapur's forces defeated the Romans, however, captured Valerian, and brought him back to Persia as a prisoner. The Sasanians then drove through Syria into central Anatolia.

Shapur stood firmly in the tradition of the Achaemenians, Macedonians, Seleucids, and Parthians, ruling diverse ethnic groups simultaneously through the time-honored recognition of local autonomy. He tolerated the practice of Judaism, Christianity, and Buddhism, but he institutionalized Zoroastrianism as Persia's state religion and made it a powerful ally of the Sasanian monarchy. Shapur's successors were strict Zoroastrians who ended toleration and persecuted those who followed other faiths.

Sasanian Persia builds on the Zoroastrian concern with justice

Zoroastrianism reinforced the Sasanian ruling concept of the circle of equity: there could be no monarch without an army, no army without prosperity, and no prosperity without justice. Zoroastrianism's emphasis on social justice and ethical conduct made it the ideal faith for Sasanian rulers. They insisted that the emperor, who was believed to have been chosen by God, must be obeyed, but he in turn had to ensure prosperity and a just and equitable society. They proclaimed that the circle of equity limited the emperor's authority because that authority depended on his own righteous conduct. But, coupled with traditional Persian respect for local autonomy, it also enabled the Sasanians to claim divine sanction and to compel popular support.

Persia's struggle with Rome continued throughout the Sasanian period, intensifying after Emperor Diocletian's division of the Roman Empire in 284 C.E. (Chapter 9). The eastern portion of the Roman Empire, later called the Byzantine Empire (Chapter 10), fought the Persians for control of Anatolia and eastern Mediterranean trade routes.

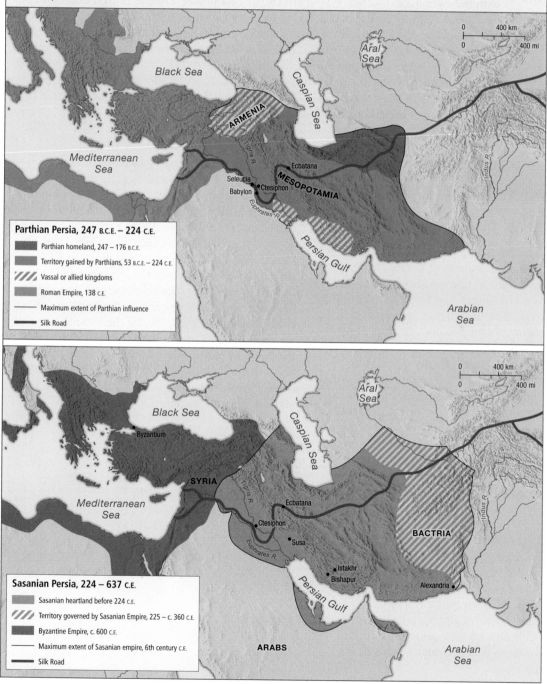

Map 6.6 The Parthian and Sasanian Empires, 247 B.C.E.–637 C.E.

The Parthians and Sasanians occupied pivotal positions in turn. Notice that Persia's location on the Silk Road made it important in trans-Asiatic commerce, while its location at the eastern edge of first the Roman and then the Byzantine Empire connected it to those regimes, making it sometimes a natural partner and sometimes an antagonist. Neither Parthians nor Sasanians were as economically or militarily powerful as Rome or Byzantium, but they were nevertheless significant forces in southwest Asia. Why might Rome and Byzantium have chosen to coexist with these empires rather than trying to conquer them?

Parthian Persia, 247 B.C.E. – 224 C.E.

- Parthian homeland, 247 – 176 B.C.E.
- Territory gained by Parthians, 53 B.C.E. – 224 C.E.
- Vassal or allied kingdoms
- Roman Empire, 138 C.E.
- Maximum extent of Parthian influence
- Silk Road

Sasanian Persia, 224 – 637 C.E.

- Sasanian heartland before 224 C.E.
- Territory governed by Sasanian Empire, 225 – c. 360 C.E.
- Byzantine Empire, c. 600 C.E.
- Maximum extent of Sasanian empire, 6th century C.E.
- Silk Road

Under King Khusrau I (531–579), the Sasanians fought with the Byzantines over Arabia. Both sides cultivated client tribes in southern Arabia, hoping to dominate trade routes between the Red Sea and the Arabian Sea.

Persia's conflict with Byzantium gives the Arabs an opportunity

But one of Khusrau's successors, King Khusrau II (590–628), pushed the quarrel with the Byzantines too far. Taking advantage of a power struggle in Byzantium, between 604 and 619 Khusrau II defeated Byzantine armies in Mesopotamia, Syria, Palestine, Anatolia, and Egypt. At that point the Byzantine Emperor Heraclius reorganized his armies, counterattacked against the overextended Sasanian forces, and, by 628, had pushed them out of all the territories they had conquered. This disaster threw the Sasanian monarchy into disarray and left it open for conquest by Islamic Arab armies between 637 and 651 (Chapter 11). In 651 the last great pre-Islamic Persian dynasty ceased to exist, and Persia became part of a new Arab empire.

Chapter Review

Putting It in Perspective

Starting from an inhospitable plateau in Southwest Asia, the Achaemenid dynasty of Persia created the largest empire the world had yet known. The Persians ruled by a combination of force and flexibility. Though they could be brutal, they were also tolerant and practical, allowing various degrees of local autonomy among the many cultures and ethnic groups that they conquered. By permitting those they subdued to retain their cultural identities while enjoying the benefits of Persian order and prosperity, the Persians won their loyalty. Persia's excellent road system and centralized governmental organization enabled its emperors to govern this huge region effectively. In Zoroastrianism, those emperors had a belief system whose clearly developed social ethic enabled them to cast themselves and their officials as warriors for truth and light against evil and The Lie.

In its efforts to centralize its control and its methods of governing, Persia stood in the company of the great river civilizations. In its attempts to expand rapidly over vast expanses of territory, it outperformed them. But Darius and Xerxes overreached themselves in attempting to subdue the mainland of Greece, and their persistence carried with it repercussions that eventually doomed the Achaemenians.

Alexander the Great's Macedonian Empire conquered Persia, but its founder's early death split his realm into three parts. The former Persian Empire was then ruled by three successor states: the Seleucids, Parthians, and Sasanians. Persia's strategic location across Asian trade routes such as the Silk Road assured its continued economic viability, and Khusrau II's dramatic victories over the Byzantine Empire seemed to signal the reestablishment of the western boundaries of the Achaemenian Empire. But the Byzantines struck back, leaving the Sasanians open to the unanticipated invasion of Arab armies that ended the Persian Empire. Persia's administrative efficiency and social tolerance, both well in advance of similar developments elsewhere in the world, continue to mark its place in world history.

Reviewing Key Material
KEY CONCEPTS

satrapy, 142	Zoroastrianism, 145

KEY PEOPLE

Cyrus the Great, 137	Herodotus, 149
Cyaxares, 137	Artaxerxes, 150
Cambyses, 139	Philip of Macedon, 150
Darius the Great, 139	Alexander the Great, 151
Zoroaster (or Zarathustra), 145	Seleucus Nikator, 151
	Shapur I, 152
Xerxes, 145	Khusrau II, 154

ASK YOURSELF

1. Do Cyrus and Darius merit the appellation "Great"? In what ways were they different from rulers who preceded and followed them?
2. What was distinctive about Zoroastrianism? In what ways did it differ from Hinduism and Buddhism?
3. Why were Persia and Greece frequently at war? Why did the Persians eventually fail to defeat the Greeks?
4. In what ways did the Persian Empire create connections with other peoples and cultures?
5. Why were the Seleucids, Parthians, and Sasanians never able to fully reconstruct the Persian Empire after the death of Alexander the Great?

GOING FURTHER

Allen, Lindsay. *The Persian Empire*. 2005.

Balcer, Jack. *Sparta by the Bitter Sea: Imperial Interaction in Western Anatolia*. 1984.

Boyce, Mary. *Zoroastrians: Their Religious Beliefs and Practices*. 1979.

Briant, Pierre. *From Cyrus to Alexander: A History of the Persian Empire*. 2002.

Brosius, Maria. *Women in Ancient Persia*. 1996.

Cawkwell, George. *The Greek Wars: The Failure of Persia*. 2005.

Curtis, John. *Ancient Persia*. 2000.

Dandamaev, Muhammad. *A Political History of the Achaemenid Empire*. 1989.

Dandamaev, Muhammad, and Vladimir Lukonin. *The Culture and Social Institutions of Ancient Iran*. 1989.

De Souza, Philip. *The Greek and Persian Wars, 499–386 BC*. 2003.

Frye, Richard. *The History of Ancient Iran*. 1984.

Garthwaite, Gene. *The Persians*. 2005.

Herzfeld, E. *Iran in the Ancient East*. 1987.

Holland, Tom. *Persian Fire*. 2005.

Miller, M. *Athens and Persia in the Fifth Century B.C.* 1997.

Sekunda, N., and S. Chew. *The Persian Army, 560–330 BC*. 1992.

Sherwin-White, Susan, and Amelie Khurt. *From Samarkand to Sardis: A New Approach to the Seleucid Empire*. 1993.

Wiesehofer, Josef. *Ancient Persia: From 550 B.C. to 650 A.D.* 1996.

Zaehner, Robert. *The Dawn and Twilight of Zoroastrianism*. 1994.

Key Dates and Developments

ca. 1000 B.C.E.	Medes and Persians settle on Iranian plateau
ca. 1300–1000 B.C.E.	The Prophet Zoroaster preaches that there is one god, Ahura Mazda
612 B.C.E.	Destruction of Nineveh by Median King Cyaxares
550 B.C.E.	Persian King Cyrus unites Medes and Persians under the Achaemenid dynasty
550–530 B.C.E.	Reign of Cyrus the Great
546 B.C.E.	Persia conquers Lydia
539 B.C.E.	Persia conquers Babylonia
530–522 B.C.E.	Reign of Cambyses
525 B.C.E.	Persia conquers Egypt
521–486 B.C.E.	Reign of Darius the Great Construction of Persepolis and the Royal Road The *Ordinance of Good Regulations*
517 B.C.E.	Persia conquers the Indus Valley
512 B.C.E.	Persian forces reach the Danube River (Europe)
499 B.C.E.	Ionia revolts against Persian rule
490 B.C.E.	Athens defeats Persia at Marathon
486–465 B.C.E.	Reign of Xerxes
480–479 B.C.E.	Xerxes invades Greece and is defeated
448 B.C.E.	Peace of Callias: stalemate with Greece
334–330 B.C.E.	Alexander the Great defeats Persia
323 B.C.E.	Death of Alexander; creation of the Seleucid Kingdom
240 B.C.E.–224 C.E.	The Parthian Empire
227–642 C.E.	The Sasanian Empire

CHAPTER 7

Classical Greece and Its Conflict with Asia, 2000–30 B.C.E.

Greek Athletes

Runners in ancient Greece sprint in a race depicted on a glazed Athenian vase. Athletic events, such as the Olympic Games (page 172), were extremely important in Greek culture and were often portrayed on ceramic pieces.

Late in the year 334 B.C.E., an army of Greeks and Macedonians entered Gordium in Anatolia (modern Turkey), capital city of the fabled King Midas whose touch turned all things to gold. Led by an energetic young Macedonian who sought to become a legend in his own right, the army paused at a bridge that symbolically linked Europe with Asia. At the entry to the bridge stood a large wagon designed to be pulled by yoked oxen. The wagon was fastened to the bridge abutment by an immense knot—three feet in diameter—tied around both the yoke and the wagon pole. Popular belief held that the man who could untie this Gordian Knot would conquer Asia.

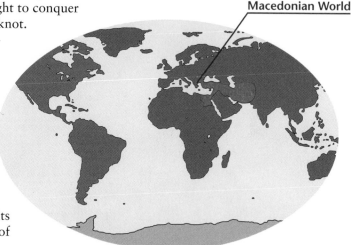

The Greco-Macedonian World

The young commander, who indeed sought to conquer Asia, tried for nearly two hours to untie the knot. Eyewitness accounts disagree over what happened next. Some say that in a rage, he severed the knot with a single stroke of his sword. Others claim that after staring silently at the knot for several minutes, he simply removed the pin connecting the yoke to the pole and slipped the knot off. The first version calls attention to the commander's strength and ruthlessness, the second to his practicality. In either case, the commander—known to history as Alexander the Great—possessed all these traits in abundance. He went on to conquer much of southern Asia.

Centuries before Alexander, numerous small city-states had emerged in the mountains and islands of Greece. Fiercely independent, these city-states had often clashed but occasionally also cooperated. In the fifth century B.C.E., many banded together to fight off Persian invaders, but later they returned to warring among themselves. In the fourth century B.C.E., weakened by wars, they were conquered by the northern armies of Macedonia. United under the leadership of Alexander, the Greeks built a vast empire that included Egypt, Palestine, Mesopotamia, Persia, and northwest India. Although Alexander's empire proved short-lived, it spread Greek culture to all these regions, connecting far-flung realms to what would evolve into Western civilization.

Early Greece

Mesopotamia, Egypt, India, and China emerged in the valleys of great rivers, while Persia developed on the Iranian plateau. In the final millennium before the Common Era, a new society took shape on both the Greek mainland in southeastern Europe and on nearby islands in the Aegean Sea.

Greek civilization developed on a rocky land. An extension of the Balkan Peninsula, Greece has neither fertile plains nor irrigating rivers, and its mountains cut the peninsula into isolated areas. River travel made communication rapid in the civilizations of

Indo-Europeans occupy the Greek Peninsula

FOUNDATION MAP 7.1 Greece and Western Anatolia

The Greek Peninsula has a rugged topography. Greece's mountains impeded communication between settlements only a few miles apart, while its numerous islands and peninsulas further made travel difficult. Note that Greek city-states are separated from each other not only by mountains, but also by the Aegean Sea. What impact did this isolation have upon Greek economic and political development?

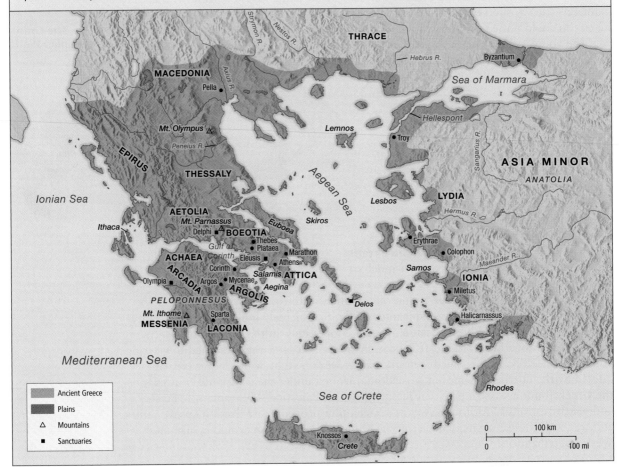

Mesopotamia, Egypt, India, and China; in Persia, the relative flatness of the Iranian plateau made land travel much easier than in Greece. Despite these drawbacks, however, Greece attracted a wave of Indo-European settlers who at some time prior to 1650 B.C.E. migrated there and called it Hellas.

Those early inhabitants proved to be hardy and resilient, able to survive on the sides of rugged mountain ranges (Map 7.1). From their hardships, they created a rich body of heroic legends and epics, which would serve as a basis for Greek religion and culture. As the mountainous terrain proved a barrier to political unification, they organized into many independent city-states with distinctive forms of governance.

Because it lacked a single centralized kingdom, Greek civilization appeared less complex than the other early societies. Eventually, however, it spread through much of the ancient world. During its expansion it changed significantly, as it absorbed elements from the cultures it encountered.

Fresco from the Palace of Knossos, Crete, showing the Minoan sport of bull dancing.

Mycenae and Crete

The early centuries of Greek history are enveloped in myth, but historians and archeologists have gradually uncovered the reality behind the fables. The Indo-European migrants, speaking a language that evolved into ancient Greek, settled on the Greek peninsula before 1650 B.C.E. No records of a previous population exist. The first well-organized Greek civilization on the peninsula is called Mycenaean (*mī-SĒ-nē-an*), after a site named Mycenae, mentioned in ancient Greek legend and excavated in the late nineteenth century C.E. by a German entrepreneur and amateur archeologist, Heinrich Schliemann (*SHLĒ-mahn*). Other early sites were unearthed in subsequent years.

Mycenaean culture seems to have been influenced by a civilization that flourished on the island of Crete, about 60 miles southeast of the Greek peninsula. This culture, called *Minoan* after a mythical Cretan ruler named Minos (*MĪ-nus*), built impressive monuments and government complexes. Minoans possessed a system of writing, now called "Linear A," which scholars have never deciphered. Mycenaeans appear to have borrowed from the Minoans a variety of artistic and architectural techniques, the principles of centralized bureaucracy, and the idea of using a palace as the seat of government. They also appear to have conquered Crete around 1450 B.C.E.

Mycenae developed a diversified civilization. By 1450 it was a thriving center of trade, with satellite cities at Athens and Thebes. Mycenaean metalwork was traded as far west as Sardinia and as far south as the upper Nile. The Mycenaeans used a system of writing similar to the Minoan script; known as "Linear B," it has been translated successfully. Mycenaeans used writing not to describe heroic feats or to create poetry or drama, as the Greeks later did, but to compile inventories of nearly everything made in the kingdom. From these massive lists emerges a picture of a highly centralized government intensely interested in every aspect of the economic life of its people. Its rulers, however, like those of Crete, remain unknown: no representations of them have been uncovered. Only through the *Iliad* do we know the name of the most famous Mycenaean, Agamemnon.

Mycenaeans develop a centralized government

Gold mask of Agamemnon.

The *Iliad* and the *Odyssey*, two epic poems allegedly written in the eighth century B.C.E. by a Greek poet named Homer, may actually have been composed by several writers using earlier traditions. The *Iliad* tells the dramatic stories of the Mycenaean siege of Troy (a city in what is today western Turkey), the quarrel between Mycenae's King Agamemnon and the warrior hero Achilles (*ah-KILL-ēz*), the interaction between gods and men during the battle, and the eventual fall of Troy. The *Odyssey* depicts the adventurous journey home of Odysseus (*ō-DISS-ē-us*), one of the Greek heroes of the Trojan War.

The people depicted in Homeric poetry were long believed to be entirely mythical. Then in 1876 C.E. Heinrich Schliemann, who believed the poems had a historical basis, discovered evidence of a complex culture at Mycenae. Six years later Schliemann unearthed the ruins of Troy, which indicated that the story told in the *Iliad* might be based in fact. Archeological evidence suggests that Troy was destroyed around 1200 B.C.E.,

Schliemann uncovers the history behind Homer

perhaps following the Greek siege described in the Homeric poems. Whatever the pro-portion of myth and reality in these epics, they encouraged the Greeks to perceive them-selves as a warlike, heroic, and resourceful people.

The Polis

Homer's writings were composed during the so-called Dark Age of Greece (1150–700 B.C.E.), a chaotic era during which the Greeks evolved from Mycenaean monarchy to a political form more suited to the regional isolation imposed by terrain. The English word "political" is derived from the Greek word **polis** (*PŌ-liss*), meaning "city-state," referring to a city, its people, and the surrounding countryside that they controlled.

Early Greek city-states were small. The largest, Thebes, contained about 40,000 adult males, who alone were citizens exercising full civil rights. Women, children, slaves, and resident aliens had no such rights. Over the centuries, some city-states extended their domination over large rural areas, which provided them with the population re-quired for economic expansion and military power.

Greek isolation leads to the development of multiple forms of government

The Greeks developed several methods for governing a polis, all of which entered the political vocabulary of the western world. One-man rule was known by Greeks as **monarchy**; rule by a select few, as **oligarchy**; rule by a class of well-born families, as **aristocracy**; and rule by the entire body of citizens, as **democracy**. These four methods were all considered legitimate, differing from **tyranny**, the illegal seizure of power (usually in a time of emergency) by someone who had no right to it and who thereby became a "tyrant" for the duration of the crisis.

Of all these systems, many Greeks thought democracy the least efficient. Since *all* citizens had the right to participate in *every* decision, democracy was cumbersome. It was also impractical: in Athens, for example, votes were cast and counted at a meeting place in the center of the city, so some citizens who lived at a distance were unable to partici-pate. Both then and in subsequent centuries, democracy was considered inappropriate for city-states or countries with large, dispersed populations. These almost always chose one of the other methods of rule.

In the Greek city-states, individualism flourished, voters knew the leaders they elected, and large bureaucracies were unknown. This political arrangement was very different from centralized empires such as Egypt and China, where governments were remote from their subjects. The polis became both a significant force in Greek history and culture and a model for future civilizations to adapt or imitate.

Archaic Greece, 700–500 B.C.E.

Greek techniques of government matured during the era later called the **Archaic Period**. During this time, overpopulation and a shortage of land suitable for farming prompted many Greeks to colonize Sicily, Italy, France, Spain, and North Africa. In this way, Greek culture came to dominate and define the Mediterranean world. At the same time, those remaining in Greece responded to overpopulation through other changes in society and government.

Greek Colonization and the Spread of Greek Culture

Rocky terrain limited the size of Greek farms, and although some crops, such as olives, could be grown on hillsides, the available soil could not support significant population expansion. Midway through the eighth century B.C.E., many city-states began to look to overseas colonization as a safety valve by which to reduce population pressures. In the course of a few decades, Greek settlements were established on the shores of the Black Sea (Map 7.2), on the coast of North Africa in present-day Libya, in southern Italy and Sicily, and in southern Gaul (today France).

The farmlands that the Greeks carved out of these new settlements were not necessarily larger or more fertile than those they left behind, but these new holdings expanded significantly the total amount of land available for cultivation. Since the climate and topography of much of the Mediterranean and Black Sea basins were essentially similar to that of Greece itself, the transfer of Greek agricultural techniques was relatively simple. As in any migration of populations, some settlers went willingly, even eagerly, while others would much rather have remained at home. The city-states gave every willing person the opportunity to go and forced others to leave.

Map 7.2 The Greek Colonies, 750–550 B.C.E.

Faced with an expanding population and limited arable land, Greek city-states exported their surplus people to colonies throughout the Mediterranean basin. Notice that these colonies, which cover a distance of 2,300 miles from east to west, are all located on the shores of the Mediterranean, Aegean, and Black Seas. Colonial expansion by water came naturally to the Greeks, a maritime people who looked at the sea as a highway rather than an obstacle. How might this extensive colonization forge connections between Greeks and other peoples?

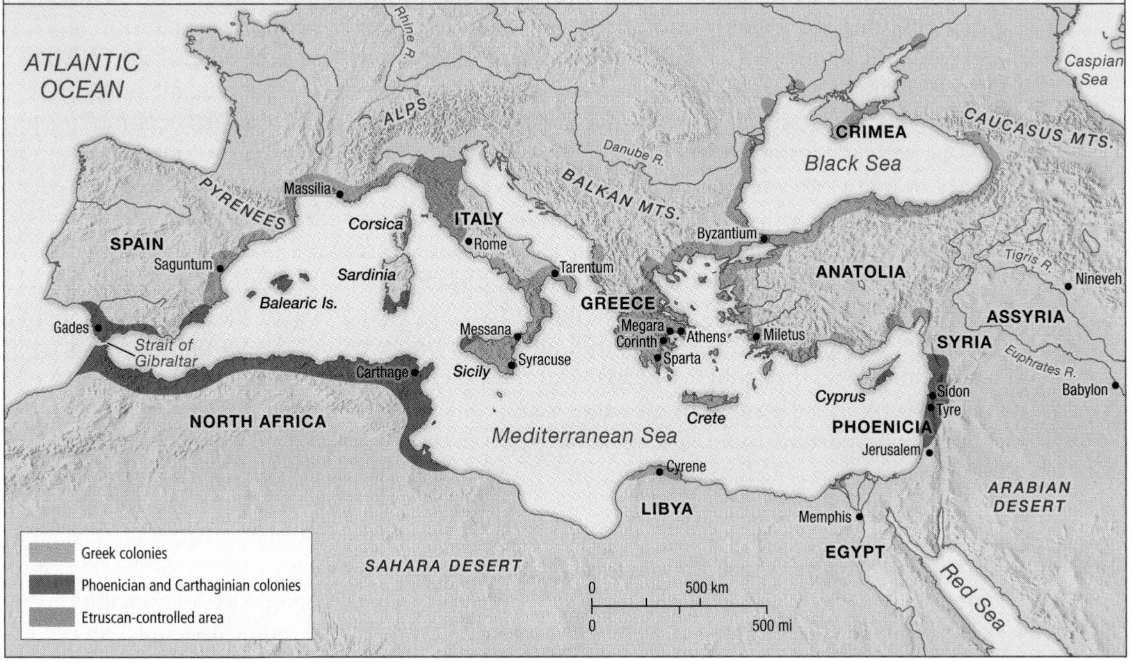

Greeks connect much of
the Mediterranean world

As Greeks spread throughout the region, they carried their culture with them. Greek words, coins, and religious practices were transmitted to areas hundreds of miles away. As the colonists encountered other peoples, they began to build trading networks with merchants in cities on the Greek peninsula itself, linking Greece not only to its new colonies but also to previously unfamiliar cultures. From these peoples, such as the Phoenicians in North Africa, the Greeks learned new methods of plowing fields, new ways to lay out cities, and new ideas about the nature of existence. Colonization proved a two-way street, connecting Greece to parts of Europe, Africa, and Asia in ways that enriched peoples and cultures in all these places. The Mediterranean basin became active and vibrant with the exchange of commerce and culture.

Rivalry Between Sparta and Athens

Most Greeks, of course, remained on their peninsula, dealing with overpopulation and land scarcity in ways other than colonization. Two of these ways are illustrated by two city-states that developed on the peninsula, becoming bitter rivals for influence and power. The first of these, Sparta, created a society organized along militaristic lines and entrusted power to an oligarchy. The second, Athens, chose a limited democracy in which all adult male citizens enjoyed the right to cast votes that counted equally. Later, cooperation between these two states would enable Greece to beat back a dangerous invasion from Persia. But competition between the two cities resumed once the Persian threat disappeared. Eventually divided into two antagonistic armed camps, the peninsula was vulnerable to an equally dangerous invasion from Macedonia, in the north.

SPARTAN MILITARY OLIGARCHY. Sparta expanded its economic base by conquering nearby regions, creating a highly militarized society in the process. Territorial expansion increased the available farmland and food supply, which in turn kept Spartans satisfied and enhanced prospects for peace among its people. Sparta's very name, meaning "The Scattered," suggests its origin as five small villages on the plain of Lacedaemon (*lah-sih-DÁ-mun*), a location so well protected by mountain ranges that Sparta found it unnecessary to build city walls for defense.

Spartans believed that under Lycurgus (*lī-SUR-juss*), a legendary lawgiver who may have lived in the seventh century B.C.E., they had rejected their individuality in favor of the collective mentality of a garrison state. Every aspect of society was directed toward military strength. Boys left home at age 7 to live in barracks, where they spent twelve years in rigorous physical and military training before becoming soldiers. Even after marriage, they took all meals with their regiments. The basic food served was black broth, consisting of pork simmered in blood and seasoned with vinegar and salt; most non-Spartans found it disgusting. Spartan girls were also raised under a strict discipline, for it was believed that regular physical exercise would help them produce strong children.

Sparta creates a
regimented oligarchy

Sparta was not, however, a military dictatorship. All adult male citizens were eligible to attend the public assembly, at which laws were passed and policies made. Execution of the laws was entrusted to Sparta's two hereditary kings, acting with a council of 28 members. The councilors were chosen for life terms by the public assembly. Spartan government was an oligarchy, responsive to the wishes of this assembly.

The regimented organization of Spartan society was not imposed on a reluctant people, but sprang from the needs of daily Spartan life. Spartans had to coax a living from rocky soil and suppress local peoples resentful of Spartan domination. The oligarchs perceived these needs, but the citizens recognized them too. Indeed, the basis of Sparta's rivalry with Athens was neither economic nor militaristic, but political. The Spartans were convinced that regimentation and oligarchy offered the best guarantee of social peace, while Athenians found them offensive.

During this period the Greek city-states frequently fought among themselves. After 550 B.C.E., however, Sparta attempted to minimize conflict by persuading neighboring states to join with it in the Peloponnesian (*pel-uh-puh-NĒ-zhun*) League, so called since most of its members lived on the large peninsula known as the Peloponnesus (*pel-uh-puh-NĒ-suss*). By 510 that alliance had enough power outside the Peloponnesus to force Athens into a form of dependency, thus ensuring its cooperation against possible external enemies, particularly Persia.

ATHENIAN DEMOCRACY. Although the Spartan military oligarchy was unappealing to Athens, its involvement of all adult male citizens in the responsibilities of government was not. During the Archaic Period the Athenian aristocrat Draco (*DRĀ-kō*) developed a legal code, the first of its kind in Greece, to regulate a similar political participation among Athenians. Published in 621 B.C.E., this code was harsh and in parts brutal (hence our adjective *draconian*, meaning "severe"), but it held that the law belonged to all citizens and must exist in written form so that all might consult and understand it. At this time Athens was an aristocracy, although its evolution in the direction of democratic forms had already begun.

Building on this foundation, the chief magistrate Solon (*SŌ-lun*) reformed the Athenian state in the 590s, banning enslavement for debt and guaranteeing basic rights to even the poorest citizens. Solon was a skilled political operator, undermining aristocratic privileges and allowing all citizens to participate in government, while positioning himself as a mediator between aristocrats and commoners. Finally, beginning in 508 B.C.E., the Athenian aristocracy transformed itself into a democracy. An assembly of all male citizens over the age of 18 accepted or rejected proposed laws; a council of five hundred proposed those laws and supervised major governmental committees; and a board of ten officials called *archons* administered the polis, handling all military and legal issues. This type of participatory governance was not radically different from Spartan practice, except for the absence in Athens of hereditary kings.

Excluded from voting, and all other political rights, were women, slaves, and males under the age of 18. Athenian democracy therefore differed significantly from present-day conceptions of democracy, which are based on political equality and on the participation of every citizen above a certain age, regardless of gender or social class. Most important positions in Athens were still held by aristocrats, since ordinary men had neither the leisure nor the money to devote themselves to state service full-time. But however exclusive Athenian democracy was, it offered a clear alternative to the Spartan model. In Athenian democracy, the state existed for the citizen rather than the citizen for the state. The citizen therefore served the state as a matter of self-interest, a principle that has inspired and challenged democracies from Athenian times to the present.

Spartan oligarchy grows out of a shared conviction

Spartan warrior.

Athens evolves from aristocracy to democracy

Classical Greece, 500–338 B.C.E.

The Peloponnesian League provided an initial framework for defending Greece against outside invasion. That defense, however, was sorely tested during the **Classical Period** (500–338 B.C.E.), an era in which classical Greek philosophy, art, and drama were flourishing. Early in that period, the Greeks combined to repel the attacks of the powerful Persian Empire. Later, however, the city-states resumed fighting among themselves, weakening each other and opening the way for the conquest of Greece by Macedonians from the north.

The Persian Wars

As we saw in Chapter 6, the revolt of the Ionian city-states in western Anatolia provoked war between Persia and Greece. Darius I and Xerxes invaded Greece between 492 and 479 B.C.E., but Persian forces were unable to overcome a Greek alliance that included Athens, Sparta, and their respective allies. By 479 B.C.E. Persia had abandoned the struggle and retreated to Anatolia.

Greece gains self-confidence by defeating the Persian invasion

The Persian Wars influenced Greece significantly. Victory boosted its self-confidence and strengthened its identification with accountable government rather than what Greeks saw as arbitrary Persian rule. Yet the image of heroic Greeks resisting Persian invaders ignores the fact that most Greeks failed to fight at all: hundreds of city-states collaborated with the Persians, remained neutral, or tried to ignore the threat. Not all Greeks were convinced of the value of cooperation.

Athenian Dominance and the Spartan Response

Pericles.

The dramatic demonstration during the Persian Wars of the strength to be found in cooperation might have impelled the Greeks toward unity. Instead, however, it promoted division and eventual disaster. With hindsight, the Greeks probably should have left the Persians alone. But in 477 B.C.E. Athens formed the Delian ($D\overline{E}$-*lē-un*) League, an alliance that embarked upon a thirty-year naval campaign aiming to drive the Persians out of the Aegean, secure the independence of the Ionian city-states, and ensure Athenian domination of the region. Indeed, Athens soon dominated the League, forcing its allies to pay tribute and threatening Spartan influence. Spartan skepticism at the prospect of chasing the Persians into Asia, coupled with its fear of Athenian power, ended the fragile collaboration between the two dominant Greek states. The Spartans used their own Peloponnesian League to counter the Delian League. Now Athens and Sparta, without the common danger of Persia to unify them, faced off against each other as heads of rival alliance systems (Map 7.3).

It was not the Spartan militaristic oligarchy but the proud Athenian democracy that created this predicament. The confrontation began during a period considered the pinnacle of Athenian greatness, often termed the Age of Pericles (*PAIR-ih-clēz*). It was named for an Athenian aristocrat who was repeatedly elected to the highest positions in government between 467 and 429 B.C.E. Under his leadership the Acropolis, a hilltop citadel in the midst of the city, was transformed into a magnificent architectural display of Athenian power. Building on its extensive agricultural base, its population of over 300,000, and its large merchant fleet, Athens under Pericles'

Map 7.3 The Delian and Peloponnesian Leagues, 431 B.C.E.

Cooperation between the most powerful Greek city-states prevented the Persian Empire from conquering the Greek Peninsula. But that cooperation did not survive the withdrawal of the Persian threat. Observe that Athens and its allies in the Delian League controlled the area surrounding the Aegean Sea, while Sparta and its Peloponnesian League partners, like Thebes and Corinth, tended to be land-based. Eventually these two alliance systems fought the Peloponnesian War against each other between 431 and 404 B.C.E. How did this conflict make the eventual conquest of Greece by Philip of Macedon possible?

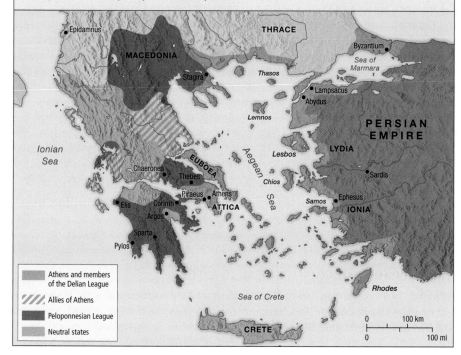

leadership became an economic and commercial power unlike anything previously imagined in Greece.

That sort of domination generated envy and fear in Sparta. Athenians defended their political and economic dominance on the grounds that their city needed to protect its commerce. But Pericles exerted Athenian power throughout the region, putting down uprisings in several smaller cities that resented paying tribute. The city-state that revered liberty and democracy at home had become an agent of expansion abroad. Sparta regarded the Athenian policy of establishing democracies in its satellites as a threat to the continued existence of oligarchic and aristocratic governments and called on its Peloponnesian League.

Pericles builds Athens into a powerful city-state

The Peloponnesian War

In confronting the Peloponnesians, Pericles had to choose between Athenian expansion and retreat. He preferred war, and he was not alone. As Thucydides (*thoo-SID-uh-dēz*), the first major historian to report events accurately and analytically, wrote in his

History of the Peloponnesian War, "The Peloponnesus and Athens were both full of young men whose inexperience made them eager to take up arms." In 431 B.C.E. a commercial dispute led Sparta to demand that Athens give all Greek cities independence. In essence, such a policy would have dismantled the Athenian empire. Athens refused, and the competing alliances went to war. Thucydides concluded, "The thing that made war inevitable was the growth of Athenian power and the fear this caused in Sparta." It was the first thesis statement written by a genuine historian, and the conflict it spoke of is often called "the suicide of Greece."

The Peloponnesian War weakens Greece

The Peloponnesian War (431–404 B.C.E.) devastated Greece, bringing destruction of property, famine, disease, and death. It lasted more than two decades due to a central paradox: because Sparta had a powerful army but no navy, while Athens had a superb navy but a small army, neither found it easy to engage the other. Although Sparta eventually defeated Athens, the duration and severity of the conflict ensured that there would be no real winner—at least not in Greece itself.

Philip of Macedon conquers Greece

Exhausted, the warring city-states fell to an outsider: Philip II of Macedon, who between 359 and 336 B.C.E. turned his primitive realm on Greece's northern frontier into a formidable political and military power. Modifying the phalanx (a closely arrayed formation of troops difficult for infantry to penetrate) by lining it with men wielding pikes 18 feet long, Philip swept down from the north in 338 B.C.E. to defeat the Athenians and Thebans. Greek independence was thus extinguished by foreigners, who took command of the temples and palaces of Athens. These catastrophes might have been avoided had Sparta and Athens not weakened each other in the Peloponnesian War.

The Arts and Philosophy in Classical Greece

Greece in the Age of Pericles was not focused exclusively on politics and war. This was also a golden age of Greek culture. In Greece, the division of the peninsula into separate city-states seems to have fostered an appreciation of the virtues, capabilities, and rights of individual people. Although often inspired by belief in the gods, Greek artistic forms also demonstrate a profound fascination with the human person.

Architecture, Sculpture, and Pottery

Ancient Greek gods and goddesses inspired the magnificent temples of the Acropolis, a hilltop complex of public buildings in Athens. The Acropolis was dominated by the Parthenon, a temple of Athena, goddess of wisdom, for whom the city was named. Avoiding thick walls, Greek architects used a variety of handsome columns, on the Acropolis and elsewhere, to support the roofs of public buildings in a graceful yet functional style.

The Parthenon.

Inside the Parthenon, a variety of lifelike sculptures paid tribute to Athena. Since Greeks believed their gods and goddesses looked and acted like humans, Greek sculpture portrayed them in human form. They were also shown in action rather than in frozen, artificial poses. Greek sculpture was therefore qualitatively different from the comparatively static, stylized depictions of humans in the art of Egypt, Persia, and China. The

Greeks develop increasingly realistic art forms

Greeks also portrayed the human form on their pottery, which combined artistic beauty with utilitarian value. Potters created an extensive array of jars, bowls, urns, vases, cups, and other vessels, glazed in vivid colors and fired in kilns. Decorating these pieces were depictions of men and women in realistic, active poses, some of them heroic (such as in combat against soldiers or wild beasts), some of them ordinary (for example, weaving, cooking, or farming). Greek pottery was prized not only in the peninsula but also throughout the Mediterranean world and in much of Asia. Greek art and architecture mark the beginning of a lengthy transition to styles today's observers would recognize as modern.

Galloping horses pull a chariot across the face of a ceramic Greek vase.

Greek Drama

In Greek literary life, the Classical Period produced four Athenian dramatists whose works remain influential in the present. The earliest of these playwrights was Aeschylus (*ES-kuh-luhs*), who lived from 525–456 B.C.E. He wrote complex plays dealing with people caught in conflict between their personal wishes and the claims of justice and reason. A generation later, Sophocles (*SAH-fuh-klēz*) wrote carefully crafted dramas such as *Antigone* and the *Oedipus* (*an-TIH-guh-nē, ED-ih-pus*) cycle. The works of Sophocles (496–406 B.C.E.) draw a precise line between the divine and the human; when pride causes men and women to think that they can cross that line, the consequences for themselves and their families are tragic.

Oedipus, whose career is described in Sophocles' trilogy of plays, was a fictional ruler fated by the gods to inadvertently kill his father and unknowingly marry his mother. Terrible results flowed from these actions, and Oedipus stood as a warning to those who would doubt the awesome power of destiny (see "Excerpt from Sophocles' *Oedipus the King*"). People may not understand divine law, but they must obey it for the sake of order and rationality in the world.

Greek drama concentrates on human personalities

The third dramatist was Sophocles' contemporary Euripedes (*yoo-RIP-ih-dēz*). Euripedes (ca. 480–406 B.C.E.) focused not so much on the divine, but on the tragic flaw of human beings: the tendency to subordinate reason to emotion. The three eminent tragedians were complemented by Aristophanes (*air-ih-STAH-fuh-nēz*, ca. 445–386 B.C.E.), a comic writer who poked fun at the famous and powerful. In their examination of human personality as well as divine law, of the demands of reason and justice as well as the necessity of action and heroism, these dramatists served as a bridge between the more limited horizons of ancient literature and the psychologically complex plays of later Western culture.

Philosophy

Greek philosophy has been even more foundational than drama to Western culture and thought. Following the "pre-Socratic" thinkers, who inquired into the nature of the universe, philosophers in the early Classical Period, called Sophists, taught rhetoric, mathematics, science, and philosophy to young men throughout Greece.

The Sophists' most influential critic was the great Athenian philosopher Socrates (*SOCK-rah-tēz*, ca. 470–399 B.C.E.), who taught that fulfillment meant attaining the good, the beautiful, and the true through the pursuit of excellence in learning. "The unexamined life is not worth living," Socrates asserted, and he taught his pupils by means of **Socratic dialogue**—rigorous questioning and analysis of ethical issues.

[handwritten annotation: focused on ?'s of ethics + truth]

Document 7.1 Excerpt from Sophocles' *Oedipus the King*

Oedipus, King of Thebes, attempts to find his father's murderer by consulting the blind prophet Teiresias. The tragedy of the play is that Oedipus, who never knew his father, is himself the murderer. Teiresias tries to show him the truth, but Oedipus is proud and contemptuous of those beneath him and will not listen.

TEIRESIAS

Alas, how terrible is wisdom when
it brings no profit to the man that's wise!
This I knew well, but had forgotten it,
else I would not have come here . . .
I say you are the murderer of the king
whose murderer you seek . . .

OEDIPUS

Do you imagine you can always talk
like this, and live to talk of it hereafter?

TEIRESIAS

Yes, if the truth has anything of strength.

OEDIPUS

It has, but not for you; it has no strength
for you because you are blind in mind and ears
as well as in your eyes.

TEIRESIAS

You are a poor wretch
to taunt me with the very insults which
every one soon will heap upon yourself . . .

Eventually Oedipus learns the truth, and, in despair over having inadvertently killed his father and then married his own mother, blinds himself. The *Chorus* of the play deplores the pride which led him to his fate:

CHORUS

If a man walks with haughtiness
of hand or word and gives no heed
to Justice and the shrines of Gods
despises—may an evil doom
smite him for his ill-starred pride of heart!—
if he reaps gains without justice
and will not hold from impiety
and his fingers itch for untouchable things.
When such things are done, what man shall contrive
to shield his soul from the shafts of the God?

The Socratic dialogue was meant to draw students out by pressing them to answer a series of leading questions, such as "Is democracy the most reasonable form of government?"

Socrates' rigorous questioning leads to his execution

Eventually Socrates ran into difficulties with Athenian authorities, who convicted him on charges of undermining the gods and teaching young people to question their elders. At his trial, Socrates refused to apologize for his conduct, claiming that his actions were proper behavior for an educated and inquisitive person. Sentenced to death, he met his fate with dignity and grace, drinking a cup of hemlock (a potent poison) and continuing to converse with his followers until a cold numbness overcame him. But Socrates' teachings guaranteed him immortality. Although he had written nothing himself, his student Plato (427–346 B.C.E.) recorded the master's reasoning and founded his own school of thought.

Born early during the Peloponnesian War and shaped by its social and political turbulence, Plato saw civil society as deeply flawed. Many of his dialogues, including

The Republic, aimed to nudge the Athenian elite toward a more effective form of government for the polis. He contended that the state exists to serve its people, and that only a philosopher-king, a statesman whose education equips him to know the truth, is genuinely qualified to lead. For Plato, democracy was absurd: it gave power not to the most knowledgeable individual but to the most popular. Government should be led by the most competent, he argued, and only an aristocracy that honors learning and the quest for truth can produce competent leaders.

Plato's broad inquiry went beyond considerations of governance to contemplate the nature of reality itself. He argued that the world we experience with our senses is not truly real. Things such as horses, trees, and human beings are but copies of ideal forms of horses, trees, and human beings; copies are all that the human mind is able to perceive. A divide therefore exists between our physical world (an imperfect reflection of reality) and the ideal (or "real") world, composed of unchanging absolutes called Forms. In a famous allegory, or story with a symbolic meaning, he illustrated the two perceptions by asking his readers to imagine a prisoner sitting in a cave with his back to the light (see "Excerpt from Plato's 'Allegory of the Cave' "). All the prisoner can see on the cave walls are the shadows of objects moving and actions taking place behind him. The prisoner thinks that the things he sees are reality, because he knows no better. But they are copies of reality. The task of the educated person is to see with the mind the true

Greek philosophy seeks to understand the world

Document 7.2 Excerpt from Plato's "Allegory of the Cave"

This is part of a dialogue between two philosophers who are considering the reality or unreality of the world we perceive with our senses.

First Speaker: And now, let me show in a figure how far our nature is enlightened or unenlightened: Behold! Human beings living in an underground den . . . here they have been from their childhood, and have their legs and necks chained so that they cannot move, and can only see before them . . . Above and behind them a fire is blazing at a distance, and between the fire and the prisoners there is a raised way; and you will see, if you look, a low wall built along the way, like the screen which marionette players have in front of them, over which they show the puppets.

Second Speaker: I see.

First Speaker: And do you see men passing along the wall carrying all sorts of . . . statues and figures of animals made of wood and stone and various materials, which appear over the wall? Some of them are talking, others silent.

Second Speaker: You have shown me a strange image, and they are strange prisoners.

First Speaker: Like ourselves; and they see only their own shadows, or the shadows of one another, which the fire throws on the opposite wall of the cave?

Second Speaker: True; how could they see anything but the shadows if they were never allowed to move their heads? . . .

First Speaker: And if they were able to converse with one another, would they not suppose that they were naming what was actually before them?

Second Speaker: Very true . . .

First Speaker: To them, the truth would be literally nothing but the shadows of the images.

Second Speaker: That is certain.

reality of the world that our senses perceive, and thus to understand the ideal essence of physical things. This understanding is truth.

Plato's most brilliant student, Aristotle (*AIR-ih-STAH-tul*), revised his mentor's teaching. Aristotle (384–322 B.C.E.) asserted that both the nature and the substance of an object are part of that object and not part of some ideal world. This realism led him to surpass Plato's breadth of inquiry and to become one of the most influential thinkers of all time.

Philosopher, scientist, poet, and student of politics, Aristotle took the entire universe as his field of study. He wrote on physics, chemistry, biology, geography, and cosmology. The classification of political systems discussed earlier in this chapter is Aristotelian, based on his rigorous analysis of 158 Greek city-states. Aristotle proposed that the universe is composed of five elements: earth, air, fire, water, and ether, this last being an invisible medium through which stars and planets supposedly move around the earth. Those celestial bodies, he argued, were impelled by a "prime mover," a force that initiates all motion but that cannot itself be moved.

In his later years Aristotle became tutor to Alexander the Great, molding that Macedonian conqueror into an enthusiast for, and transmitter of, Greek culture. Aristotelian ideas and principles, preserved and transmitted by Muslims and Byzantine Christians, shaped the thought of the medieval Islamic and Christian European worlds.

Classical Greek Society and Religion

Most Greeks, of course, never had the opportunity to learn from Socrates, Plato, or Aristotle. The vast majority were artisans, farmers, slaves, and women whose labors allowed little time for philosophy, and who believed that their destinies were not in their own hands, but were controlled by an assortment of unpredictable gods.

Free Labor and Slavery

Greek civilization relies on agriculture

As with the societies in other ancient civilizations, labor in the Greek economy was organized around both rural and urban activities. Daily life in the countryside was simple and primarily agricultural. Greeks ate grains and fruits, enjoying vegetables and fish on occasion. The goats and sheep they raised provided milk and cheese, while pigs provided the modest amount of meat that Spartans ate every day. In the cities, men earned their living as artisans or skilled laborers. The unskilled worked alongside slaves in manual jobs such as garbage removal and street-sweeping, with the same daily wage going to both the enslaved and the free.

Slavery was common in Greece, as in most of the ancient world. Greek slaves generally shared the material standard of living of their owners, who were not necessarily wealthy. They were paid modest wages for their work, and might eventually save enough to purchase their freedom. Most slaves were foreigners captured in warfare or in slave raids. Well-born prisoners of war were usually ransomed by their families, so slaves tended to come from the ranks of the poor. Criminals, debtors, and orphans were also sometimes forced into slavery, but because most Greeks considered all non-Greeks to be inferior, foreigners were more likely to be enslaved than native Greeks.

Slavery differed in various parts of Greece. In Athens, slaves constituted nearly one-third of the total population. Since male prisoners of war were routinely imprisoned or killed, nearly all Athenian slaves were women. They helped the master with his farm or business, or the mistress of the house with her domestic chores. Legally they were human property. They could be beaten, usually for disobedience or laziness, but not killed. They were clearly inferior to citizens in civil rights and considered inferior also in natural abilities.

In Sparta, slaves were bound to the land that they worked on their masters' behalf, but otherwise enjoyed considerable freedom of action. Although many Spartan slaves were foreigners, others were *helots* (*HĒ-lots or HELL-uts*), named after the nearby town of Helus, which Sparta had conquered. Most Spartan slaves were male, in contrast to the situation in Athens, and the Spartan oligarchy lived in permanent fear of helot revolts. This fear helps explain the intense militarization of Spartan society.

Greek culture rests on a slave foundation

The Status of Women

Greek women enjoyed a status above that of slaves but below that of free men. In Sparta, women were highly valued for their ability to bear and rear healthy young warriors who would defend the city-state and make possible its expansion. In recognition of this status, Spartan women were permitted to voice their opinions on all state issues. Girls there were raised in much the same way as boys, with an emphasis on physical training and horsemanship. Some evidence suggests that Spartan girls as well as boys competed naked in athletic events, and that girls performed ritual dances in the nude before mixed audiences.

Greek women.

Spartan women usually married at 18, later than women in other Greek city-states, while men married in their mid-twenties. Since men remained in the barracks until age 30, young husbands visited their wives secretly at night, and they might father children before ever seeing their wives by daylight. As a consequence, the mother was the dominant figure in Spartan family life. Women could own property and transact business without the consent of their husbands, who spent most of their time in the barracks or away on military campaigns. Women were also guaranteed full civil rights under the law, except for the right to vote, a right no Greek polis ever granted them.

Athenian women, in contrast, were confined to the home, except for infrequent occasions such as celebrations or funerals. As full citizens of a state that relied on substantial male political participation, Athenian husbands possessed nearly total authority over their households and everyone living in them. A woman was protected by her father or male guardian until she married; if divorced or widowed, she returned to him. Virginity before marriage was highly prized for both men and women. After marriage, wives were expected to remain faithful, but a husband's casual adultery, particularly when away from home, was not considered immoral. Wives ran their households, supervised slaves, and wove clothing for family members. Once menopause occurred, Athenian women enjoyed greater freedom, working as midwives, nurses, and seamstresses.

The subordination of women to men was written into Greek law. Protections for women actually protected the rights and interests of their husbands. In Sparta, women were honored as mothers of the next generation of warriors; in Athens, women were

Female status differs in Athens and Sparta

prized for conveying economic and political rights to their male children. Authority in Greece was a male monopoly.

Greek Religion

Asklepios, the Greek god of medicine.

What is now called Greek mythology was originally a belief system reflecting ancient Greek culture. The twelve major Greek gods were said to live on Mount Olympus, the highest mountain in the northwest Peloponnesus. Unlike the divinities in other early civilizations, the Greek gods were not believed to have created the universe; both the universe and the earth were assumed to be eternal. The major Greek gods were believed to have created men and women, but not out of dust and a rib (as in Jewish and Christian tradition), nor out of a clot of blood (as in Islamic belief). Instead they engaged in sexual intercourse with mortals to produce heroic humans whose own offspring then became the human race.

Among themselves, the gods had love affairs that produced additional gods. Zeus, figuratively and literally the "Father of the Gods," sired Ares (*AIR-ēz*), the god of war, by his wife Hera, and six other gods by a variety of women. The children of Zeus also included Apollo, Athena, and Aphrodite (*aff-rō-DĪ-tē*), gods and goddesses of exceptional beauty and varying sexual appetites. Poseidon (*puh-SĪ-dun*), god of the sea, was Zeus's brother, and Demeter (*dih-MĒ-ter*), goddess of grain, their sister. All played significant roles in Homer's *Iliad*, as they intervened on one side or the other during the Trojan War.

Greek deities were clearly more powerful than humans, but they had human traits. They could be greedy, generous, lusty, chaste, envious, kind, angry, and affectionate. Generally the gods on Mount Olympus took little direct interest in humans, but from time to time, out of boredom, they sought pleasure in manipulating human affairs, playing with people on earth as children play with dolls and toys. Other deities, who did not reside on Olympus, lived closer to mortals, affecting their lives each day by rewarding or punishing them. All gods and goddesses were believed to crave worship, adoration, and sacrifices of food and drink, which fearful humans provided to win divine favor.

Greek religion depicts the gods as similar to human beings

For example, every fourth year men and women competed in a great festival of athletic events (see page 156) in honor of the deities they worshiped. These Olympic Games, named for the mountain on which the main gods lived, consisted of nine events, including a chariot race. The Olympic Games attracted participants and spectators from throughout Greece, and all warfare between city-states stopped whenever the games were held. Presumably the gods' enjoyment of these sports made them more kindly disposed toward humans. The ancient games were last held in 395 C.E., but were revived by Europeans in 1896.

Greeks honor the gods in the Olympic Games

The Greek gods live today in Western literature and drama, but in ancient times they were believed to be never far away from their people. That humans served as their puppets did nothing to diminish this closeness. The gods could feel pain (when a god was wounded in battle, his blood ran black), and what kept them immortal was their diet of ambrosia and nectar. They quarreled with each other and took delight in frustrating each other's plans. For Greeks, the gods were not remote beings but a part of everyday life.

The Empire of Alexander the Great

When Philip of Macedon conquered Greece in 338 B.C.E., it is unlikely that the Greeks felt the gods had deserted them. Greeks simply believed that Philip, for all his power and glory, was just one more tool in the hands of the Olympians. When he was assassinated in 336, only two years after his dramatic triumph, his new subjects nodded knowingly to one another: the gods had grown tired of him. The chief murder suspect was his first wife, Olympias, who had been cast aside by Philip in favor of a younger woman, also killed, along with her young daughter, soon after the king's murder. Since these events left Olympias and her 20-year-old son Alexander in control of the kingdom, many Macedonians suspected that Alexander had been part of the plot, though there is no evidence of his involvement. These sorts of intrigue, of course, would have been typical among the gods, and therefore familiar to both Greeks and Macedonians.

Alexander's Conquests

Alexander III of Macedon (336–323 B.C.E.), who quickly succeeded Philip, was a young man of unusual political and military talents. Having been tutored in his youth by Aristotle, he had developed a profound admiration for Greek culture, especially as his native Macedonia was looked upon by the Greeks as a backward frontier area, good only at fighting. Alexander, whose mother claimed descent from Achilles, immersed himself in Homeric poetry and by his late teens had become, in the words of one scholar, "self-confident, endlessly curious, and reckless," much like Achilles himself. After his father's murder, Alexander moved swiftly to ensure the loyalty of the army and to kill anyone questioning his claim to rule. Then he descended upon Greece, destroying the powerful city of Thebes and forcing the Greeks to recognize him as Philip's legitimate successor.

Alexander consolidates Macedon's hold on Greece

After subduing Greece, Alexander resumed the invasion of Persia that Philip had planned. That invasion appeared wildly risky. Persia was not the power it had been under Darius I and Xerxes, but it had a strong army, and its immense size placed any invader at a disadvantage. In addition, Alexander's position at home, resting (unlike his father's) on no domestic achievements whatsoever, was not yet secure. But he was eager for conquest and moved quickly against Persia with a mixed army of Macedonians and Greeks. In 334 B.C.E., at the Granicus (*grun-Ī-kus*) River in northwestern Anatolia, he won his first major victory. After that, as he entered Asia by way of the bridge at Gordium, he cut the Gordian Knot.

Alexander the Great.

Alexander justified his attack on Persia by claiming to be the champion of Greek culture against barbarian values and the instrument of Greek revenge for Xerxes' invasion in 480. Despite all justifications, Alexander's principal objective was heroic conquest, and he was talented enough to achieve it. In battle, Alexander was able not only to plan a sequence of moves but also to anticipate his enemy's likely responses and to be ready with countermeasures. He was also able to change his course of action in the midst of the confusion of battle. Complementing these impressive abilities was Alexander's religious faith. The incident of the Gordian Knot convinced him that the gods had willed that he rule Asia, which he defined as the Persian Empire. Seeing himself as a second Achilles, he had no doubt he would succeed.

Alexander claims to be promoting Greek culture in southwest Asia

Map 7.4 The Empire of Alexander the Great, 336–323 B.C.E.

The armies of Alexander the Great created Greek-based connections across southwest Asia. Note that his enormous empire, constructed in only 13 years, duplicates almost exactly the Persian Empire of Cyrus, Cambyses, and Darius I (Map 6.3). Alexander's conquests placed a permanent Greek imprint on millions of people, while eastern concepts like despotism flowed westward into Greece. What kinds of changes would have occurred during this blending of such varied cultures?

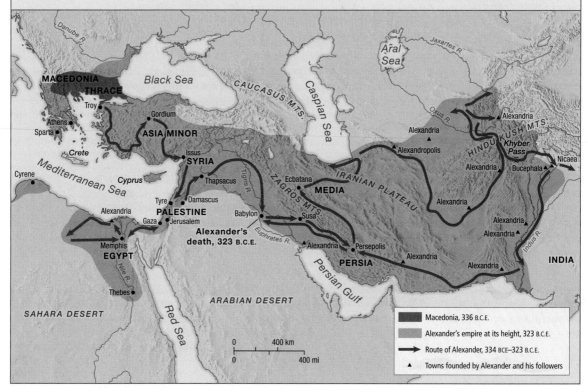

Alexander invades the Persian Empire

Alexander met the Persians in battle at Issus, in southwestern Anatolia, in 333 B.C.E. The Persian Emperor Darius III was an experienced military leader, and his army was more than twice as large as Alexander's. The outcome was in doubt at first, but Alexander personally led a headlong cavalry charge that broke through Darius's bodyguard, forcing the Persian emperor to flee the field. Next Alexander moved south through Syria and Palestine into Egypt, adding to his dominions the rich former realm of the pharaohs, and founding there the city of Alexandria, destined to become one of the world's great cultural centers. This conquest of Egypt secured the Mediterranean coastline so that Persia could not use it as a springboard for invading Greece.

No longer underestimating Alexander, Darius offered to surrender to him all of the Persian Empire west of the Euphrates. To the dismay of his commanders, Alexander rejected the offer. He marched northeast to Mesopotamia, where he again vanquished the Persians, paving the way for his conquest of their entire empire. Storming across Persia, he crossed into Afghanistan and through the Khyber Pass (Map 7.4) into India. By 326

B.C.E. he was east of the Indus River and dreamed of pressing on to the "eastern sea" (which may have been either the Ganges River or the Bay of Bengal), but his men, having been away from home for eight years, refused to continue. Compelled to turn back, Alexander returned to Persia but never saw Greece again.

The Fate and Impact of Alexander's Empire

Ruling the former Persian Empire turned out to be more difficult than defeating it. But Alexander was insightful about how an empire should be run and wise in his decision to retain satrapies and other features of Persian government. Like previous outsiders who had overrun complex civilizations, the Macedonian leadership quickly adopted useful techniques from its new subjects.

Alexander tried to fuse Persian and Greek cultures, taking several Persian wives, encouraging his commanders and officials to do the same, and placing both Greeks and Persians in important political and administrative positions. These moves won him more praise in Persia than in Greece. In Persia, Alexander sought to have his rule recognized as a continuation of the imperial tradition by retaining the satrapies and by officiating at the burial services of Emperor Darius III. In Greece, however, he was still resented as an outsider. Most Greek cities feared Macedon more than Persia, and during Alexander's long absences they frequently rebelled. Accustomed to independence, they resented centralized rule under Macedonian governors and charged (without evidence) that Greeks were being denied privileges that Alexander was granting to Persians.

Alexander adopted Persian governing practices, but he had little use for Persian culture. According to his Greek biographer Plutarch, he considered himself "a governor from God and a reconciler of the world." He hoped that Greek language, literature, philosophy, and art would, through his actions, permeate all of Asia, inspiring its peoples to pursue virtue, excellence, wisdom, and truth. This heroic idealism blended with practicality in his plan to develop the Tigris, Euphrates, and Indus Rivers as commercial waterways linking all of Asia.

Alexander spreads Greek culture eastward

These undertakings promised to be long and arduous, however, and Alexander was an impatient man. His soldiers' unwillingness to proceed eastward from the Indus was a great disappointment to him, for which he compensated by exalting his own greatness and indulging in festivals and celebrations. At one in 323 B.C.E. he reportedly consumed more than a gallon of wine in half an hour. He quickly developed a fever, grew weaker, and died several days later from symptoms consistent with tropical malaria. He was only 33 years old.

Alexander's sudden death threw his empire into confusion. Each of his most important generals seized a portion for himself: Ptolemy (*TAHL-em-ē*) took Egypt, Antigonus (*an-TIH-guh-nuss*) held Greece and Macedonia, and Seleucus Nikator controlled all the rest, from western Anatolia to the border of India. The Seleucid Empire, as we saw in Chapter 6, was the first of a series of successor states to the Asian portions of Alexander's empire. It was followed by the Greco-Bactrians, Parthians, and Sasanians, none of whom were able to reconstitute the Persian Empire that Alexander had conquered.

Alexander's early death dissolves his empire

Although Alexander's empire was no longer unified, the importance of his accomplishments remained. He had defeated the immense Persian Empire, spread Greek culture throughout southwest Asia, and connected Europe, Asia, and Africa in ways that would later benefit the Roman Empire. These connections are delineated later in this chapter.

Alexander leaves a
mixed legacy

At the same time, Alexander's legacy should not be romanticized. Although he championed Greek civilization, he developed no appreciation for the achievements of the Persian Empire he opposed. He demolished one of the great powers of the ancient world without replacing it with a culture that demonstrably improved the lives of its people. In addition, his model of kingship, which exalted an aloof, militaristic, divinely inspired monarch, blended West with East but benefited neither. Finally, Alexander's conquests, for all their brilliance, were personally motivated. Despite his love for Greek culture and his oft-stated desire to fuse the Greek and Persian worlds, he never thought seriously about establishing political and economic institutions that could have helped unify a realm stretching from Macedonia to Egypt and from Greece to India.

Connections and Conflicts in the Hellenistic World

Alexander's diffusion of Greek values and practices eastward was accompanied by the westward spread of values and practices from the civilizations of the East. His penetration of southwest Asia and Egypt created a set of new societies and political entities that were not simply Greek, Persian, Egyptian, or Indian but a blend of them in varying combinations. To distinguish it from the earlier **Hellenic** culture developed by the Greeks, this new culture is traditionally called **Hellenistic**.

Commercial and Cultural Connections

Hellenistic kingdoms
promote commerce
and trade

Nowhere was this convergence of cultures more obvious than in economics. The post-Alexander monarchies of southwest Asia (Map 7.5) used confiscated Persian wealth to construct roads and harbors for the promotion of trade. These improvements kept Mediterranean goods flowing eastward and Asian luxuries moving westward. Foodstuffs were shipped by sea, while luxury goods traveled overland by camel caravans, protected by the Seleucid and Ptolemaic states. Spices from India and silks from China became widely prized in Greece, while exquisite examples of Greek sculpture and pottery were prized in India and China. Greek law and custom became the foundation on which business was transacted. Greece benefited immensely from this commerce, particularly in agricultural commodities: the grain produced in surplus in the eastern Hellenistic monarchies improved the nutrition of people throughout the rocky peninsula who had always lived on the edge of malnutrition. Greek fish, wine, and olive oil were exported to the East in return.

Cultural contact in the Hellenistic world extended beyond trade and commerce. In astronomy, physics, mathematics, and medicine, Greek thinkers profited from the knowledge and techniques of the East. In Egypt, Alexandria grew into a renowned center of learning and inquiry. Most of its population spoke Greek, which rapidly became the tongue of educated people throughout the Hellenistic world. Alexandria remained a predominantly Greek city through the early years of the Roman Empire.

Map 7.5 The Hellenistic Kingdoms, 323–146 B.C.E.

No one knows whether Alexander the Great could have held together the enormous territories he conquered. We do know that after his death at age 33, none of his successors could do so. The division of Alexander's empire into a variety of kingdoms ended the temporary political unity of southwest Asia and created a region in which the only unifying factor was Hellenistic culture. Notice the unequal distribution of lands between Alexander's three successors and their dynasties. Which do you think would prove the most powerful and influential? Why?

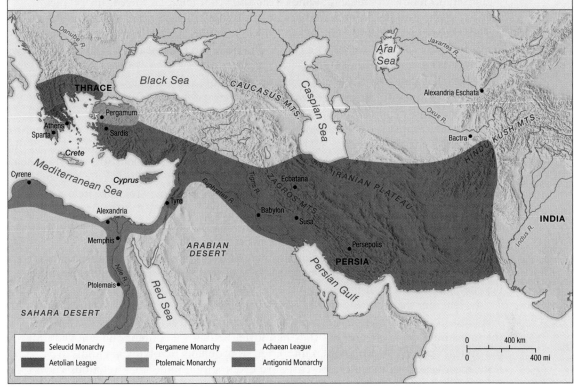

Seleucid Monarchy
Aetolian League
Pergamene Monarchy
Ptolemaic Monarchy
Achaean League
Antigonid Monarchy

Alexandria's library was justly famous, and in 245 B.C.E. its chief librarian, Eratosthenes (*air-uh-TAHS-thuh-nēz*), calculated the circumference of the earth at 24,675 miles—an error of only seven-tenths of one percent. More than 17 centuries before Columbus, he also predicted that a ship leaving Spain could reach India either by sailing around the southern tip of Africa or by sailing west. Educated people throughout the ancient world knew that the earth is round and had a good sense of its size.

Another Hellenistic astronomer, Aristarchus of Samos (*air-ih-STAR-kuss, SĀ-mus*), constructed his ideas on Babylonian foundations. More advanced in his thinking than Aristotle, Aristarchus (310–230 B.C.E.) proposed that the earth revolves around the sun and that the far-off stars orbit neither the earth nor the sun. But Aristarchus's view, though correct, did not prevail. The astronomer Claudius Ptolemy (85–165 C.E.), working in Egypt, endorsed Aristotle's concept of heavenly bodies moving around the earth, and Ptolemy's writings proved so influential that the idea of a heliocentric (sun-centered) system was not taken seriously until the publication of the work of Copernicus nearly 14 centuries later.

Hellenistic science makes significant advances

More influential than Aristarchus was Archimedes (*ark-ih-MĒ-dēz*) of Syracuse (285–204 B.C.E.), a master of mathematics, physics, and mechanical engineering. The creator of the science of hydrostatics (fluid pressure), Archimedes determined that when an object is immersed in a container of liquid, it displaces from the container the precise equivalent of its own volume in liquid. According to legend, he solved this problem while stepping into his bathtub and became so excited that he ran through the streets naked, shouting, "Eureka!" (Greek for "I have found it!"). Less dramatic but equally significant were his discoveries of a compound pulley to raise heavy weights and a screw system to lift water to higher levels.

Alexander the Great's dynamic conquests also affected the pursuit of philosophy in Greece. In response to the changes wrought by Alexander, Hellenistic thinkers sought permanence and stability. Epicurus (*EP-ih-KYOOR-us*) (341–270 B.C.E.), for example, advised that nothing is to be gained by trying to appease the gods, who are indifferent to human problems. As all matter, including the gods, is composed of atoms, he argued, the soul dies with the body. Pleasure is simply the absence of pain. Epicureans therefore held that one should not be troubled by change, resent fate, or try to alter destiny. Zeno (*ZĒ-nō*) refuted this position with a complex philosophy called Stoicism. Release from pain is not an end in itself, he charged, and Epicurean withdrawal into private life is wrong. Stoics must show courage, cultivate wisdom, and do their duty, remaining steadfast in time of crisis even in the face of overwhelming odds. It is not success that matters, but the virtuous pursuit of duty. Neither Epicureanism nor Stoicism became the dominant philosophy of the day. Most people were attracted by one and then by the other, depending on the circumstances.

Eastern mystery religions spread westward

In religion, the two-way flow of ideas benefited the West more than the East. The cults of Greek deities like Apollo and Athena were transported eastward with the spread of Greek culture, but they had little theological content and enjoyed limited appeal among eastern peoples interested in problems involving sin and salvation. Even Greeks who emigrated eastward eventually found Greek religious views sterile. The westward flow, on the other hand, brought eastern mystery religions (also called "salvation religions") to the Greek world, with profound historical consequences.

Mystery religions addressed directly the problems of human weakness, divine redemption, and eternal life. In each of them, a god or goddess either became human or became deeply involved with human beings, teaching his or her followers certain divine secrets or mysteries. Through initiation into these mysteries, new converts, or novices, were believed to become one with the deity, whose sacrifices redeemed the sins of the novices and promised them immortality. Once the initiation was complete, the novice felt "born again" into a new life.

Two of the most important Hellenistic mystery cults centered on the god Dionysus (*dī-uh-NĪ-suss*) and the goddess Demeter. Dionysus was the god of fruitfulness and wine. His festivals, preceded by solemn performance of the mystery rituals he allegedly taught his followers, included choral singing, pantomime, free-spirited sexual activity, and great quantities of wine. Worshippers believed they were linked with deceased ancestors, fellow revelers, and generations of believers yet to be born.

Rituals devoted to Demeter, the goddess of grain, were called the Eleusinian (*el-yoo-SIN-ē-un*) Mysteries because they were celebrated only at Eleusis, a city-state near Athens. Demeter's followers memorialized the cycle of life as represented in the sowing, sprouting, and harvesting of grain. The grain that is scattered on fertile soil germinates, sprouts, and is reaped for bread and future seeding. Similarly, a girl is taken from her parents, is "seeded" through sexual intercourse, and produces offspring. When men and women die, they are buried in the earth and remain part of the cycle of life. New life springs forth from every grave, and those devoted to Demeter look forward to eternal life.

Mithras slaying the sacred bull.

Mystery religions became extremely popular in the Hellenistic world. The cult of Mithras, a Persian god who created the universe by catching and sacrificing a sacred bull, eventually reappeared in Western culture. Devotions to the Egyptian deities Isis and Osiris, involving a god who is slain but then restored to become the judge of humankind (Chapter 2), also became highly influential in Greco-Roman civilization. But in the long run, the main beneficiary of eastern religious influences was Christianity. In the first century C.E., the Apostle Paul preached the message of this eastern-inspired religion to a Greek population already familiar with many of its basic conceptions.

Politics and Governance

Politically, too, the impact of Hellenization was two-sided. Alexander's conquests removed the Persian Empire from world history and spread the Greek language and Greco-Macedonian military techniques into southern Asia. But distinctively Greek forms of government were not transmitted in the same way. Athenian democracy and Spartan oligarchy may have been suitable forms of governance for small, internally cohesive city-states, but they were not suited to sprawling, multiethnic empires. For leaders wishing to rule such diverse states, monarchy seemed to work best, as it permitted the creation of royal dynasties in which the authority of the king was believed to derive from the gods. The royal family thus became the symbol of political unity within the empire, transcending tribal loyalties and language differences.

Hellenistic kingdoms reject democracy and oligarchy

Although monarchy was nothing new to the Greeks—the word itself is Greek—it had belonged to the legendary past. Homer's *Iliad* sang of kings like Agamemnon and Priam, but the Greeks of the fourth century B.C.E. thought that monarchy had been replaced by better forms. Then the eastern empires that Alexander conquered made them appreciate the power of a central authority. Emperors disposed of their subjects like Athenians disposed of used clothing, and they cared little for the opinions of the people. To an ordinary Greek this was tyranny, not monarchy, but to Ptolemy, Seleucus, and their successors it was convenient.

Hellenistic Kingdoms revitalize monarchy

Yet the post-Alexandrian empires were ruled entirely by Greeks, even if the form of government they adopted was eastern. Greeks held every influential political, diplomatic, military, and administrative post. The Hellenistic rulers were anxious to recruit Greeks and Macedonians for their armies and navies, as they believed that relying on local warriors would be politically dangerous. Cities laid out in the Greek style, designed and constructed by Greek architects and engineers, were built throughout the new empires, and Greek immigration into these empires was encouraged.

The political structures of Hellenistic expansion proved strikingly fragile. Although there were too many Greeks for their rocky homeland, there were not nearly enough to staff every important position in southwestern Asia. The Hellenistic kingdoms could not sustain the vigor, curiosity, and enthusiasm of Alexander the Great. They declined slowly for a hundred years and eventually collapsed when challenged by a dynamic new dominion arising in the west, centered on the city of Rome.

Chapter Review

Putting It in Perspective

The Greeks developed sophisticated forms of government, created magnificent works of poetry and drama, formulated enduring answers to fundamental questions about the nature of reality, and made striking advances in scientific inquiry. But their refusal to cooperate with one another ultimately delivered them into the hands of conquerors. Their short-lived alliance against the Persians ran aground on the rocks of Athenian ambitions, and the ensuing Peloponnesian War so weakened them that they fell to Macedonia.

Nevertheless, the accomplishments of Greek culture spread throughout the Mediterranean basin with Greek colonies, and Alexander's soldiers carried them into Egypt and across southern Asia to the Indus valley. Greek learning enriched the lives of hundreds of millions and altered the course of history. Europeans were particularly fascinated by Greek culture. They adapted its methods for governing the polis to their own states. Words such as tyranny, aristocracy, oligarchy, and democracy continue to be used to describe governmental systems throughout the world. Europeans produced their own philosophies, dramas, and architectural forms on foundations laid by Greece. Alexander spread Greek culture eastward, but its long-range influence lay to the northwest, in its appeal to a Europe that did not yet exist in the era of great confrontations and connections between Greece and Persia.

Reviewing Key Material

KEY CONCEPTS

polis, 160
monarchy, 160
oligarchy, 160
aristocracy, 160
democracy, 160
tyranny, 160

Archaic Period, 162
Classical Period, 164
Socratic dialogue, 167
Hellenic, 176
Hellenistic, 176
mystery religions, 178

KEY PEOPLE

Alexander the Great, 157, 173
Homer, 159
Lycurgus, 162
Draco, 163
Solon, 163
Pericles, 164
Thucydides, 165
Philip of Macedon, 166
Aeschylus, 167
Sophocles, 167

Euripedes, 167
Aristophanes, 167
Socrates, 167
Plato, 168
Aristotle, 170
Eratosthenes, 177
Aristarchus of Samos, 177
Archimedes, 178
Epicurus, 178
Zeno, 178

ASK YOURSELF

1. Why were the Greek city-states unable to create a permanently unified state?
2. How did the Persian Wars affect the Greeks, both for good and for ill?
3. How did Greek religion differ from eastern "mystery religions"? What does Greek religion tell us about the Greeks themselves?
4. Describe the connections forged between ancient Greece and other civilizations.

GOING FURTHER

Blundell, Sue. *Women in Ancient Greece*. 1995.

Burkert, Walter. *Greek Religion*. 1985.

Cartledge, P. *Spartan Reflections*. 2001.

Cohen, G. *The Hellenistic Settlements in Europe, the Island, and Asia Minor*. 1996.

Cook, R. *Greek Art: Its Development, Character and Influence*. 1991.

Davies, J. *Democracy and Classical Greece*. 1993.

Demand, Nancy. *A History of Ancient Greece*. 1996.

Donlan, W., S. Pomeroy, J. Roberts, and S. Burnstein. *Ancient Greece: A Political, Social, and Cultural History*. 1998.

Freeman, Charles. *Egypt, Greece and Rome: Civilizations of the Ancient Mediterranean*. 1996.

Hammond, N. *The Genius of Alexander the Great*. 1997.

Hanson, Victor. *The Other Greeks: The Family Farm and the Agrarian Roots of Western Civilization*. 1995.

Kagan, Donald. *The Peloponnesian War*. 2003.

Lawrence, A. *Greek Architecture*. 1996.

McDonald, William, and Carl Thomas. *Progress into the Past: The Rediscovery of Mycenaean Civilization*. 1990.

Miller, S. G. *Ancient Greek Athletics*. 2004.

Murray, Oswyn. *Early Greece*. 1993.

Osborne, Robin. *Greece in the Making, 1200–479 B.C.* 1996.

Patterson, Cynthia. *The Family in Greek History*. 1998.

Shipley, G. *The Greek World After Alexander, 323–30 BC*. 2000.

Walbank, F. *The Hellenistic World*. 1993.

Key Dates and Developments

1100–750 B.C.E.	The "Dark Age"; Homer's writings are composed
750–500 B.C.E.	The Archaic Period
750–550 B.C.E.	Greece colonizes the Mediterranean basin
621 B.C.E.	Draco's legal code in Athens
594 B.C.E.	Solon's reforms in Athens
ca. 560 B.C.E.	Formation of the Peloponnesian League
500–338 B.C.E.	The Classical Period
499 B.C.E.	Beginning of the Ionian revolt against Persia
490 B.C.E.	Athenians defeat Persians at Marathon
480 B.C.E.	Sparta's sacrifice at Thermopylae
	Athenian victory over Persians at Salamis
478 B.C.E.	Formation of the Delian League
461–429 B.C.E.	Age of Pericles at Athens
431–404 B.C.E.	The Peloponnesian War
399 B.C.E.	Trial and execution of Socrates
338 B.C.E.	Philip of Macedon conquers Greece
336–323 B.C.E.	Conquests of Alexander the Great
323–30 B.C.E.	Era of the Hellenistic Kingdoms

CHAPTER 8

The Romans Connect the Mediterranean World, 753 B.C.E.–284 C.E.

Romulus And Remus

A statue of Romulus and Remus being suckled by a she-wolf. This legend encouraged Romans to consider themselves tough, resilient people accustomed to overcoming hardships (page 183).

According to Roman legend, in the early eighth century B.C.E. the daughter of a local king in central Italy was impregnated by Mars, the god of war. Then she was killed by her uncle for having disgraced the family by surrendering her virginity. Just before she died, she gave birth to twin sons, who were left on a roadside to die. But a she-wolf came upon them, and rather than devouring the helpless infants, she nursed them. Eventually the twins were discovered by passing shepherds, who adopted them and raised them as their own.

The twins of this legend were named Romulus and Remus. Their upbringing was unconventional, and their adolescence was tempestuous: Romulus killed his brother and fled from the shepherd family that had raised him. Then in 753 B.C.E., on the banks of the River Tiber in the fertile plain of Latium (*LĀ-shē-um*) in west-central Italy, he founded a village that, according to the story, became the city of Rome.

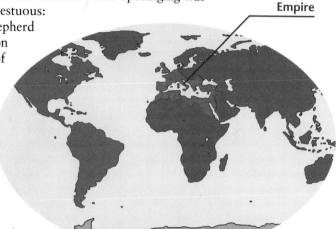

The Roman Empire

Although legendary, this account of Rome's origin reflects the Romans' image of themselves as offspring of the god of war, toughened by the milk of a she-wolf. (see page 182). Proud of their origins, the Romans created influential institutions and helped spread the cultural contributions of ancient Greece and Christianity as they conquered and then managed one of history's most adaptable, effective, and enduring empires.

The Roman Republic to 133 B.C.E.

The true story of Rome's founding is somewhat less dramatic than its legendary one. Archeological evidence dates the initial habitation of Latium, in west-central Italy, to around 1000 B.C.E. Three tribes from central Italy appear to have clustered there, possibly on account of the location's advantages. Built on seven hills surrounding a place on the Tiber River that could be bridged, the developing city enjoyed formidable natural defenses against land-based attacks. At the same time, the 14 miles that separated it from the Mediterranean Sea provided defense against both pirates and naval landings. As the city's later inhabitants also learned, their central location in the Mediterranean basin was close to major trade routes and a good place from which to rule the entire region. Potential competitors, such as Sicily's Syracuse and North Africa's Carthage, were also well located, but, being seaport cities, they were more vulnerable to naval assaults (Map 8.1).

Rivalry with Etruria

At first the Romans were ruled by the kings of Etruria (*ih-TRUR-ē-uh*), a plain northwest of Latium (Map 8.2). The people of Etruria, known as Etruscans, had adapted the Greek writing system to fit their local language, thereby creating what came to be known as the

Etruria creates a trading network in the Mediterranean basin

FOUNDATION MAP 8.1 Rome, Carthage, and the Central Mediterranean

Italy's topography is as rugged as that of Greece, but while Greece remained divided, Rome managed to unite the entire Italian peninsula. The mountains of Greece encouraged the development of independent city-states with different forms of governance. In Italy, Rome's domination of the peninsula, based in large measure on its central location astride principal north-south communication routes, made unification possible. Note that only 350 nautical miles separated Carthage from Rome. Why would Carthage's location, at the southwestern end of the neck of water between Sicily and North Africa, eventually lead to rivalry with Rome?

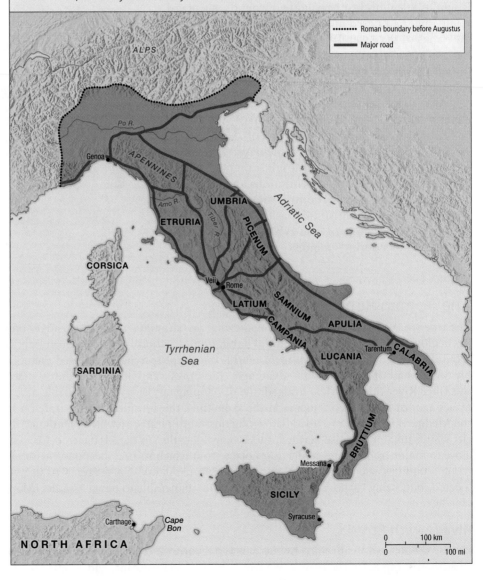

Latin alphabet. They also brought Rome into a Mediterranean commercial network.

What little we know about the Etruscans comes primarily from their cemeteries. Their durable tombs, cut out of solid rock, were filled with exquisite goods made of iron, bronze, and gold. Etruscan pottery and copper and tin metalwork found in these tombs have also been uncovered in North Africa, the eastern Mediterranean, and along the Rhine and Danube Rivers in Europe. Clearly Etruria had a broad trading network that used central Italy's rich tin and copper deposits to advantage. Rome's resistance to Etruscan rule probably was due not only to political and ethnic differences but also to Rome's desire to capture and expand Etruscan trade routes.

In addition to archeological knowledge, we have very few written accounts of Etruria. We do, however, have this suggestive description from the Greek historian Theopompos of Chiops: "Sharing wives is an established Etruscan custom. Etruscan women take particular care of their bodies and exercise often. It is not a disgrace for them to be seen naked. Further, they dine not with their own husbands, but with any men who happen to be present. They are expert drinkers and are very good looking."

Roman legend assigns the early city seven kings, the last of whom was an Etruscan tyrant whose misdeeds provoked the ambitious Romans to revolt in 509 B.C.E. According to Roman tradition, the uprising succeeded, although archeological evidence indicates that the Etruscans did not withdraw from Latium until after their defeat at the hands of a Greek naval force in 474 B.C.E. Nevertheless, the expulsion of the Etruscans was commemorated by Romans for centuries as the end of tyranny and the beginning of rule by a *res publica* (*RĀZ POOB-lick-ah*, or "public possession"). Thus began the Roman **Republic**, a flexible form of government by elected representatives that proved capable of military conquest and administrative efficiency.

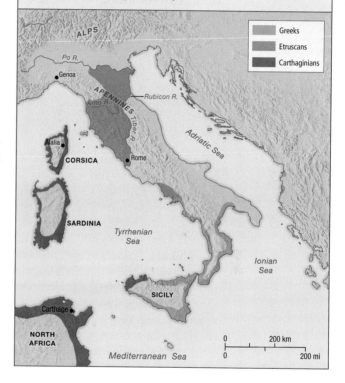

Map 8.2 Italy in 600 B.C.E.

Italy in 600 B.C.E. was heavily influenced by non-Italian peoples. Observe that Carthaginians controlled Corsica, Sardinia, and western Sicily, while Greeks dominated the remainder of Sicily and the southwestern tip of the Italian Peninsula. Etruscans controlled most of Italy north of Rome. Rome's victory over Etruria guaranteed the Romans domination over Italy and laid the foundation for their rivalry with Carthage for control of the Mediterranean. Why would the Greek colonies, as outposts not of a centralized Greek state but of individual city-states, be unable to intervene decisively in the Roman-Carthaginian rivalry?

Rome dominates Italy by defeating Etruria

The Republic and Its Foundation in Law

The government of the Roman Republic was grounded in principles and practices unlike those developed earlier in Greece. Athenian democracy was based on the right of all adult male citizens to debate, deliberate, and vote. This type of government—a direct democracy—was possible in a city-state with a limited population, but Rome was larger than Athens, and it tended to keep growing. The Romans therefore governed themselves through a republic—a system in which all adult male citizens voted not on the issues of the day but for representatives elected to a variety of assemblies that drafted, debated, and passed laws. If the citizens did not approve of the laws, they could vote the representatives out of office in the next election.

The Roman representative assemblies, however, did not have full authority over public affairs. The Republic's principal political institution was the senate, which was an advisory body composed of the most prestigious statesmen of Rome. The senate was dominated by patricians, wealthy landowners who led Rome's military units and who constituted the majority of the educated class. Senators selected new members of the senate, often nominating their own sons or relatives. The senate elected Rome's two consuls, officials who administered the state for one-year terms.

Rome establishes a Republic based on law

The governments of Mesopotamia, Egypt, China, and Persia were based largely on the power and personalities of individual rulers, but Rome's government was based on laws. Rulers in those other civilizations made the laws; in Rome, rulers were subject to the laws. Roman law distinguished between civil and criminal procedures. It aimed at developing solutions that would be fair to all parties in a dispute. In this pursuit it proved remarkably flexible, sometimes relying on precedent, sometimes on concepts of both common and individual good, and sometimes on common sense. As Rome expanded beyond its traditional boundaries, it amplified its civil law into "law of peoples," which applied to Romans and foreigners alike. The "law of peoples," in turn, evolved into **natural law**, a Roman vision of legal principles applicable to all societies regardless of time or circumstance. The necessity of ruling many non-Roman peoples encouraged Roman jurists to develop universally valid legal standards, and these influenced subsequent legal systems and laid the foundations of international law.

This legal system helped regulate a bitterly divisive social contest between patricians and plebeians known as the **Struggle of the Orders**. Common people, or plebeians (*plih-BĒ-uns*), frustrated in their attempts to attain a meaningful voice in state affairs, went on strike in 494 B.C.E. and withdrew from the city, creating their own assembly apart from the senate. This new assembly elected tribunes, or spokesmen who were charged with protecting the plebeians' rights and presenting their concerns to the senate. Even more alarming to the patricians, however, was the plebeians' refusal to serve in the army. Since commoners were the foot soldiers, without whom there would be no army, the patricians were forced to give in. Over the next two centuries they yielded their privileged legal and political positions bit by bit.

The Struggle of the Orders strengthens the Roman Republic

By 471 B.C.E. the patricians accepted the assembly, although its decisions did not enjoy the status of law until 287 B.C.E. In 450 B.C.E., plebeian agitation forced patricians to publish the famous Law of the Twelve Tables (see "Excerpt from the Twelve Tables"), a series of laws displayed on twelve tablets along with regulations governing legal procedure. Published and public laws thus opened the legal system to full use by all free men, breaking the patricians' monopoly. By 342 B.C.E. the patricians yielded further, agreeing to the plebeian demand that one of the two consuls be a plebeian. Gradually, wealthier plebeians moved into the patrician class, which grudgingly allowed them a role in the governing of the Republic. But when the Struggle of the Orders ended in 287 B.C.E., all Roman citizens were equal before the law. Roman practicality and flexibility prevailed,

Document 8.1 Excerpt from the Twelve Tables

The Roman Republic encapsulated its most important laws in the book of Twelve Tables, which the great orator Cicero praised as follows: "Though all the world exclaim against me, I will say what I think: that single little book of the Twelve Tables, if anyone look to the fountains and sources of laws, seems to me, assuredly, to surpass the libraries of all the philosophers, both in weight of authority, and in plenitude of utility." (Cicero, *De Oratore*, I, 44.)

TABLE I

1. If anyone summons a man before the magistrate, he must go. If the man summoned does not go, let the one summoning him call the bystanders to witness and then take him by force.

3. If illness or old age is the hindrance, let the summoner provide a team. He need not provide a covered carriage with a pallet unless he chooses.

TABLE II

2. He whose witness has failed to appear may summon him by loud calls before his house every third day.

TABLE IV

1. A dreadfully deformed child shall be quickly killed.

2. If a father sell his son three times, the son shall be free from his father.

5. A child born after ten months since the father's death will not be admitted into a legal inheritance.

TABLE V

1. Females should remain in guardianship even when they have attained their majority.

TABLE VIII

3. If one is slain while committing theft by night, he is rightly slain.

4. If a patron shall have devised any deceit against his client, let him be accursed.

13. It is unlawful for a thief to be killed by day . . . unless he defends himself with a weapon; even though he has come with a weapon, unless he shall use the weapon and fight back, you shall not kill him. And even if he resists, first call out so that someone may hear and come up.

TABLE IX

4. The penalty shall be capital for a judge or arbiter legally appointed who has been found guilty of receiving a bribe for giving a decision.

TABLE XI

1. Marriages should not take place between plebeians and patricians.

SOURCE: Oliver J. Thatcher, ed., *The Library of Original Sources*, Volume III: *The Roman World* (Milwaukee: University Research Extension Co., 1901) 9–11.

and rather than being plunged into civil war, the Republic evolved into a healthier, stronger system of government.

The equality of all citizens before the law naturally exalted citizenship, a privilege conferred upon all adult males who, by birth or adoption, belonged to one of the three tribes that had founded the city. Roman citizenship entitled the holder to a number of rights, including the right to appeal any official decision to the highest authorities. Citizens of Rome were also safe from unjust imprisonment, and the authorities were required to treat them with respect. The highest positions in the Republic were open to any citizen, regardless of ancestry or wealth.

Like the Persians, Rome tried to assimilate the peoples it conquered, and eventually the benefits of citizenship were employed in this process. The most talented and useful males in tribes or ethnic groups subdued by Rome were offered full citizenship and the opportunity to advance their careers in the service of a great and powerful state.

Rome uses citizenship as a benefit

This practice made Roman citizenship one of the most highly prized distinctions of its day. The proud boast, *"Civis Romanus sum"* (CHIH-vis rō-MAHN-us SOOM, "I am a Roman citizen"), commanded immediate respect throughout the Roman Empire. Some foreigners even sold themselves into slavery to Rome, hoping someday to be freed and become citizens. But Rome's decision to grant citizenship to some foreigners while withholding it from others transformed citizenship from a right into a privilege. The legacy for some modern European nations has been to use citizenship as a reward that can be revoked if a citizen's conduct proves offensive to the state.

Romans were proud of their government and laws. Representative government, the Twelve Tables, equality before the law, and citizenship as privilege combined to make it possible for Rome to rule the Mediterranean basin.

The Punic Wars and Rome's Mediterranean Domination

Rome's domination of the Mediterranean basin was first achieved, however, by its powerful army. The Roman army was divided into legions of approximately 5,000 men each, subdivided into centuries of 100 men, each of which was commanded by a centurion. Every adult male was required to serve in the army for as long as he was needed, and no man was permitted to run for public office unless he had served at least 10 years, thus making military service a springboard for influence in politics. In ordinary times, between 10 and 15 percent of men served in the legions; in emergencies, this figure rose to 25 percent. No society matched this degree of militarization before World War I, and Rome managed it for centuries.

Rome's legions enable it to project its power beyond the Italian peninsula

Rome's army was superbly trained and equipped. Infantry legions were accustomed to 20-mile forced marches, the distance being measured by counting the soldiers' steps: each double (left-right) step was about 5 feet, and 1,000 such steps took them a "mile" (derived from *mille*, the Latin word for "thousand"). Food consisted of bread and vegetables, a diet so ingrained that on one occasion soldiers objected when they had to eat meat instead. Courage was richly rewarded through promotions and honors, while cowards were stoned or flogged to death. If a century broke and ran in the face of the enemy, the penalty was *decimation*: every tenth soldier in the entire legion would be executed.

This combination of harsh discipline and constant training, together with skilled, experienced commanders, gave the legions a degree of self-assurance bordering on arrogance. Like tightrope walkers who remain unafraid because they *know* they will not fall, the armies of the Roman Republic moved steadily from conquest to conquest, losing an occasional battle but never a war. They reacted to defeat with bemusement and returned until they finally won. Magnanimous in victory, they aimed not merely to conquer but also to rule diverse peoples and integrate them into the Roman state.

Rome and Carthage struggle for Mediterranean domination

Rome's principal rival for control of the Mediterranean was the city of Carthage, the former Phoenician colony (Chapter 2) that had become a great naval power on the central North African coast (Map 8.3). Carthage tried for decades to conquer the large island of Sicily, off the tip of southern Italy, which it intended to use as a staging area

Map 8.3 The Mediterranean World at the Time of the Roman Republic, 264–44 B.C.E.

Rome grew from a centrally located city on the Italian Peninsula (Map 8.1) to the dominant power in the Mediterranean basin. Success in the Punic Wars against Carthage removed Rome's military and commercial rival in North Africa and facilitated its conquest of Gaul, Anatolia, and Syria, thereby connecting the entire Mediterranean world. Notice that Rome's conquests and dependencies spanned a distance of nearly 3,000 miles. What impact did the vastness of Rome's holdings by 133 B.C.E. have on its republican institutions?

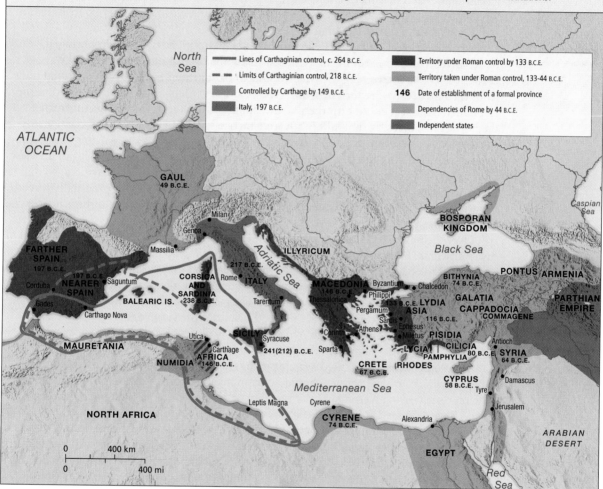

from which to expand into continental Europe. From the Romans' perspective, however, Carthaginian control of Sicily would threaten their control of Italy. From 264 to 146 B.C.E. the two cities fought what would later be called the three Punic (*PYOO-nik*) Wars. In the First Punic War (264–241 B.C.E.), Romans gained control of Sicily by applying land-based military techniques to war at sea. They developed powerful ships with iron-tipped bows designed to ram opposing vessels. In the tumult following a ramming, a gangplank would slide from the bow of the Roman ship onto the deck of its enemy. Foot soldiers would run down the gangplank, board the crippled vessel, and fight what amounted to a land battle on a ship. Given the power of its infantry, Rome usually won such engagements.

Now Rome owned territory outside Italy and would have to defend, tax, and govern it. Within three years, Rome also took control of the Mediterranean islands of Sardinia and Corsica. Sicily, Sardinia, and Corsica were designated as provinces, subordinate regional units, each of which had its own governor and local administration and were not directly subject to the authority of the senate, an arrangement that later contributed to the fragmentation of the Republic.

Hannibal's tactical innovations frustrate but do not defeat the Romans

Carthage fought back, led by Hannibal, a brilliant military tactician outraged by Rome's seizure of Sardinia and Corsica. Hannibal began the Second Punic War (218–201 B.C.E.) by crossing the Mediterranean to southern France, then invading Italy from the north, crossing the Alps with troops and war elephants. It turned out that the elephants' huge feet could grip the narrow, slippery Alpine paths more securely than the hooves of horses. Hannibal's innovative tactics enabled him to surround and crush the Roman legions, but he never marched on Rome itself, probably realizing that subjugating and occupying the city would be beyond the strength of Carthage. From his viewpoint, the most desirable outcome would be Rome's surrender of its provinces, so that its domains would be limited to the Italian peninsula. But Hannibal was eventually forced to return to Carthage when Roman forces conquered coastal Spain, and there he lost the Second Punic War.

Over the next 53 years, the Mediterranean balance of power was firmly reoriented in favor of Rome. During this period, the Republic acquired an extensive empire. The senate authorized the pacification of Spain and the subjugation of Macedon and Greece, placing each of these areas under a Roman governor and, as with the three Mediterranean islands, designating them as provinces. In the Third and final Punic War (149–146 B.C.E.), Rome completely destroyed the city of Carthage, sold the survivors into slavery, and claimed Carthage's empire. North Africa's grain surpluses henceforth fed the masses of Rome.

Rome's triumph preserves its political values

The Punic Wars constituted a major turning point in the history of the Mediterranean basin. Carthage neither shared nor appreciated Rome's devotion to the rule of law, representative government, and equality of all citizens. A Carthaginian victory would have relegated Rome to the status of a historical oddity, a high-minded political experiment that was unable to compete effectively with less sophisticated states. Rome's triumph, on the other hand, helped to preserve these political values, as well as to ensure Rome's domination of the Mediterranean. By 133 B.C.E., the Roman Republic had established nine non-Italian provinces, making it an empire in all but name. Its new status changed it considerably.

Changes in Society and Culture

Victory over Carthage alters Roman society

Rome's domination of the Mediterranean led to changes in social stratification, gender relations, and the institution of slavery. The first change altered Rome's social divisions from political to economic. The wealth that came with conquest obscured the old patrician-plebeian distinction and replaced it with a gap between those who profited economically from expansion and those who did not. The newly rich as likely came from plebeian background as patrician. Now talent, ambition, and good fortune, rather than birth alone, were the means to success. The new gap that developed between the rich and the poor proved more difficult to bridge than the old distinction between patrician and plebeian.

Changes in Roman society also gave women a more elevated status than that found in other societies of the time. Persia and Greece had relegated women to the private life of the family, but in Rome, women routinely appeared in public and presided at meals where both sexes were present. Within the family the patriarch ruled, but clearly women were active participants in decision-making, consulted by their husbands in all matters pertaining to the family's welfare. They enjoyed their own religious rituals, cults, and festivals from which men were excluded.

Outside the home, Roman women enjoyed a significant measure of independence—able to own property, conduct monetary transactions, and even manage businesses. A few women became physicians, practicing gynecology, and many plebeian women became midwives. Even at the highest levels of male-dominated society, women's influence was felt: Roman senators spoke freely of being lobbied by their wives, and under the Empire women, such as the Empress Livia, second wife of Caesar Augustus, exercised considerable indirect power over political affairs. From time to time the Roman assemblies passed laws restricting the rights or mobility of women. These laws sparked formal protests, most notably in 195 B.C.E., when numerous women picketed the senate and forced the repeal of a law forbidding women to ride alone in carriages. Men retained ultimate authority in private and public life, but few of them underestimated or ignored female influence.

Roman women resist male attempts to limit their independence

A third change altered the Roman institution of slavery. Like many other ancient civilizations, Rome enslaved people to labor on behalf of others. In Rome's early days many citizens owned a few slaves, who worked as domestic servants or agricultural laborers. These slaves were almost always from the Italian peninsula, usually captured through warfare with non-Roman tribes. Chronic debt, alcoholism, or mental incompetence could cause even native Romans to become slaves, and in some cases, parents who could not afford to raise their own children sold them into slavery.

A contemporary mosaic shows female Roman students wearing togas.

This situation changed after the Third Punic War. Rome's succession of military conquests brought tens of thousands of captive foreigners to Italy as slaves. It then became a mark of status for a Roman to own many slaves and to employ them not only for manual labor but also as skilled workers, musicians, and tutors.

Slaves, of course, resented their condition. They lacked freedom and were forced to labor for someone else's prosperity or pleasure. While some worked for owners who were decent and compassionate, many others endured brutal punishments. Those who worked in mines or as part of agricultural work gangs experienced particularly harsh forms of servitude. At times slaves rebelled. While slave revolts were not frequent, they terrified the Romans and were suppressed with deadly force, much as the Spartans suppressed the helots. The most famous such revolt, led by a gladiator named Spartacus in 73 B.C.E., involved more than 70,000 slaves and lasted two years. Rome sent a succession of legions to crush the uprising, but Spartacus and his forces defeated all of them but the last. In 71 B.C.E. Spartacus was killed, and thousands of his followers were crucified.

Rome suppresses slave revolts

Slavery in Rome declined after the string of Roman conquests ended, but it never disappeared as long as Rome lasted. The use of forced labor and the fear of slave revolts remained ingrained in Roman life until the empire collapsed.

Dissatisfaction with the Republic

The Roman ability to adapt and synthesize was put to the test once the Punic Wars ended. The governing system of multiple assemblies advised by a senate had to be restructured to serve the needs of an increasingly complex and extensive empire. A tax system was required to fund a permanent standing army and to pay administrators to govern distant provinces. Otherwise, the senate feared, military leaders might rule those lands and use them as a base for challenging senatorial authority. The senate also hoped to organize the entire Mediterranean basin into a vital center of commerce and manufacturing. Yet this wealth encouraged an opulent lifestyle among the Roman elite and growing resentment among the Roman lower classes.

Social Discontent and Decline in Popular Rule

The expanding Roman state faced serious social problems. The Punic Wars had laid waste much of the Italian countryside, and since most of Rome's citizen-soldiers were farmers in civilian life, their frequent absences on military campaigns left their families unable to sow and harvest crops. Upon returning home, many veterans sold their devastated or run-down farms to wealthy buyers, who pieced the lands together to form immense private estates. The veterans then worked for inadequate wages in cities, where they competed with slave labor. Their discontent threatened Rome's stability as their plight threatened its defense: only landowners could serve in the army, and given the harm done to the land and the declining number of landowners, Rome's ability to field its famous armies was threatened.

The Roman Republic faces serious social problems

The senate tried to address the problem by dividing some public lands among the poor, but this practice affected only a small number of families. Ominously, generals began accepting propertyless men into the legions, promising them farms upon their retirement. These men were, quite naturally, more loyal to their commanders than to the senate, and many Romans began to think that the senate had lost touch with the needs of the people.

As Rome's domain expanded, the Republic lost control of events. The more territory it occupied, the more borders it had to defend. The greater the burdens of defense became, the more power was delegated to military commanders. The more powerful military commanders became, the less willing they were to take orders from the senate. As this sequence spiraled out of control, the advocates of republican rule found themselves isolated.

Sulla's dictatorship ends the Roman Republic

In 91 B.C.E. the senate defeated a bill to extend citizenship to all Rome's allies in the Italian peninsula. Many of the disappointed allies revolted, and civil war was waged sporadically until 79 B.C.E., when the Roman general Sulla (*SOO-la*) put down the strife and emerged as **dictator**—a tyrant ruling for the duration of the crisis. His seizure of power effectively ended the Roman Republic, although he tried unsuccessfully to restore it and many of his successors claimed to be loyal to it. But the Republic's usefulness was over: it could no longer control its own generals, as the rise of Sulla indicated, and it had failed to evolve to meet the changing needs of an expanding state. Generals such as Sulla and Pompey, who served in Spain, pretended to bow to the senate's will while effectively ignoring it and making their own policy at the far-flung extremities of empire.

Julius Caesar

With the Republic approaching its end, ambitious generals maneuvered to follow Sulla's lead. After Pompey subdued and colonized Spain, he used that province as a base for advancing his power. Elected consul in 59 B.C.E., he formed a political alliance, the First Triumvirate, with two other prominent generals, Caius Crassus and Julius Caesar. Caesar enjoyed military success in Spain and also in Gaul (today France), which he used as a power base for splitting the Triumvirate. In 48 B.C.E. he defeated Pompey at the battle of Pharsalus. Pompey fled to Egypt and was murdered there. Three years later, Julius Caesar proclaimed himself dictator of Rome.

Julius Caesar ruled Rome for only one year, but he left an enduring mark on world history. Descended from Rome's original aristocracy, he was educated by tutors and studied oratory and rhetoric in Greece. He blended political ambition with military genius in pursuit of his overriding goal: to restore order to the Greco-Roman world. Caesar accomplished a great deal in his one year as dictator: he revised the Roman calendar, made the senate more representative of the citizenry, and gave discharged soldiers and even the urban poor the opportunity to own a bit of land. A masterful literary stylist whose works are still enjoyed two millennia after his death, Caesar spread Roman culture into the lands he helped conquer, such as Spain and Gaul, where he founded colonies. Popular in many quarters for his willingness to implement reforms, he was resented in others for his shrewdness and his betrayal of Pompey. He rewarded his non-Italian supporters with Roman citizenship, ensuring their loyalty but angering many citizens of Rome.

As dictator, Caesar was remarkably magnanimous, granting pardons to many of his opponents and enemies. Within a short time this generosity destroyed him. On March 15, 44 B.C.E. (the famous "Ides of March"), he was stabbed to death in the Roman Forum by several conspirators, two of whom (Gaius Cassius and Marcus Brutus) were among the opponents he had pardoned. Caesar's assassination terminated the brief stability he had created, plunging Rome into renewed civil strife.

Julius Caesar's dictatorship moves Rome closer to empire

The Birth of the Roman Empire

Caesar's assassination was followed by a struggle for power in which his grandnephew and adopted son Octavian (*ock-TĀ-vē-un*) emerged triumphant. Octavian then reshaped the governing institutions of Rome, molding them into a structure that would support his military dictatorship while seeming to remain republican in nature. As Caesar Augustus, Octavian served as a towering transitional figure between the Roman Republic and the Roman Empire.

The Rise of Octavian

Caesar's killers were swiftly defeated by his followers, led by the Second Triumvirate: Caesar's eloquent defender Marcus Antonius, immortalized as Marc Antony in Shakespeare's *Julius Caesar*; the skillful and subtle politician M. Amelius Lepidus; and Octavian, then only 18 years of age. Rome, however, was not large enough for two dynamic leaders such as Octavian and Antony. Lepidus was pushed aside, and Octavian took Rome's western

Tombstone of a Roman soldier.

possessions while Antony took Greece, Egypt, and the east. Caesar had dreamed of uniting Rome and Egypt, hoping to transfer his capital eastward. He had courted the Queen of Egypt, the clever Cleopatra VII, last of the Ptolemaic dynasty that had ruled that land since the death of Alexander the Great. Caesar had acknowledged to friends his paternity of her son Caesarion (*seh-ZAIR-ē-un*), born in 47 B.C.E. Now Antony seemed to have taken Caesar's place, spending the winter of 41–40 B.C.E. with Cleopatra in Alexandria and, in 32 B.C.E., marrying her.

Octavian outmaneuvers the Triumvirate and becomes Caesar Augustus

Octavian resolved to destroy Antony, fearing that if Antony became sole leader of Rome, he and Cleopatra would probably subordinate Italy to Egypt. Cleverly Octavian declared war against Cleopatra rather than Antony, mobilizing Rome's forces in a patriotic struggle to preserve Italian supremacy. Antony and Cleopatra responded by urging eastern princes to fight for their liberation from the tyranny of Rome.

In September 31 B.C.E. Octavian's forces defeated Antony and Cleopatra at the battle of Actium (*ACK-tē-um*). The following year Octavian's armies attacked Egypt itself. Antony, hearing a rumor that Cleopatra had been killed, took his own life by falling on his sword; the Queen of Egypt, after her lover's suicide and her empire's defeat, put an asp to her breast and died from its poisonous venom. Octavian had overcome all his rivals. Returning to Rome in triumph, he was hailed as the man who had ended decades of civil war. In 27 B.C.E. the senate voted him the title **Augustus**, meaning "one who rules with majesty and grandeur." Octavian now called himself Caesar Augustus.

Rome's defeat of Egypt orients its empire eastward

Octavian's victory at Actium shifted Rome's focus toward the east. As Caesar Augustus, Octavian claimed the Egyptian throne and began Egypt's gradual absorption into Roman civilization. Alexandria, which for nearly three centuries had been the world's center of Hellenistic learning and culture, now became subject to Rome. The cultures of the eastern provinces, including Egypt and Syria, were attractive to the Romans. And now with northern Africa and Palestine, Rome's Mediterranean empire was a "Greco-Roman world" and the Mediterranean Sea Rome's *Mare Nostrum* (*MAH-rā NAHS-trum*, "our sea").

From Republic to Empire

At the time, however, Rome seemed the center of the world, and its governance, following fifteen years of turmoil, was a matter of some concern. Ironically Caesar Augustus, the first Roman Emperor (27 B.C.E.–14 C.E.), hated dictatorial rule and wanted to restore the Republic. Although he tried to reinvigorate republican institutions, especially the senate, most of his political innovations enhanced his own authority.

Augustus consolidates an empire while ruling a republic

As commander of Rome's army, Augustus was called *Imperator*, which after his death evolved into "Emperor." But the term *Imperator* was a military title that said nothing about Augustus's position in civil government. In that sphere he ruled not as king or emperor but as one man holding a broad variety of republican offices. He served a succession of one-year terms as consul, giving him influence over those who served one year only. The senate appointed him to several magistracies and conferred on him powers normally reserved to tribunes. Thus, as consul, he spoke to the people on behalf of the government, while as tribune he spoke to the government on behalf of the people. All these positions were republican, but they were not designed to be held by one man. Augustus made himself emperor in everything but name, and in so doing he transformed Rome into an empire while claiming loyalty to the Republic.

The Roman Empire was a work in progress. Spain, Germany, the Balkan Peninsula, and much of southeastern Europe fell to Augustus's legions. Virtually the entire coastline of the Mediterranean was Rome's, giving substance to the claim of *Mare Nostrum*. Rome's control of the waves eased communication between the empire's remotest regions, overcoming the administrative problems that distance might have created. Augustus also constructed fortified camps and connected them to one another with well-built Roman roads. These camps extended Roman rule and brought Rome's culture to many parts of continental Europe.

The distant regions were inhabited mainly by tribal peoples who spoke Germanic languages and whom the Romans labeled "barbarians." As Rome defeated one tribe after another, Augustus and his successors consolidated their control by offering command positions in Roman armies to the highest-ranking Germanic chieftains and Roman citizenship to some of their most important followers. This systematic use of privilege and citizenship to win over the most powerful Germans helped Rome lay the foundations of a truly multiethnic empire while reducing foreign pressure on its extended borders. The result was the **Pax Romana** (*POCKS rō-MAHN-ah*), or "Roman peace." Until his death in 14 C.E., Augustus presided over a stable and prosperous society.

Rome's skillful use of citizenship helps create the Pax Romana

Caesar Augustus, Emperor of Rome.

Greco-Roman Culture

The *Pax Romana* was founded on a number of interlocking factors: military superiority, Augustus's political skills, the integration of foreigners into the empire, and material prosperity. In addition, **Greco-Roman culture**, rich and attractive, helped keep Roman society stable. Rome's familiarity with Greek culture began through contacts with Greek colonies on the Italian peninsula and on Sicily and continued when Rome conquered Greece. For centuries Rome had envied and attempted to imitate Greek arts and letters, in the process preserving Greek literary and philosophical masterpieces and making them known throughout the immense, multiethnic Roman Empire. This cultural transmission was enhanced by the incorporation into the empire of Egypt, especially Alexandria, where a fabulous library contained many Greek manuscripts. Some Greek philosophical schools, such as the Stoics, appealed to the Romans, who appreciated the Stoic insistence on living in harmony with natural forces. Now the "Augustan Age," or age of Augustus, brought forth a dazzling display of poetry that rivaled anything produced by the Greeks. Much of it sang the praises of the *Pax Romana* and of the ruler who created it.

Virgil, one of Rome's most noteworthy poets, lived from 70 to 19 B.C.E., long enough to enjoy the early years of the age of Augustus. Using a Greek literary form, the epic poem, Virgil in the *Aeneid* (*ih-NĒ-id*) narrates the legend of Aeneas (*ih-NĒ-us*), a Trojan warrior who fled from Troy as the Greeks sacked it. In the legend, Aeneas makes his way to Italy, where he acquaints early Romans with the ancient splendor of Greece. The *Aeneid* provides an alternative creation story for the origins of Rome, shifting the Roman self-image away from the tough and ruthless descendants of Mars who were nursed by a she-wolf and toward the refined and enlightened bearers of Greco-Roman culture. Virgil portrayed Rome as the benefactor of the known world, enlightening barbarian peoples and staunchly upholding Greek ideals of the good, the beautiful, and the true. The *Aeneid* remains, with the *Iliad* and the *Odyssey*, one of the world's great epics.

Greco-Roman culture helps build the empire

Ovid (*AH-vid*) (43 B.C.E.–ca. 17 C.E.), a generation younger than Virgil, wrote for a less learned audience. He immortalized Rome's most popular religious and seasonal festivals in verses that nearly everyone who could read could enjoy. But Ovid was surpassed in popular appeal by Virgil's contemporary Horace (65–8 B.C.E.), whose eloquent, soaring odes praised the accomplishments of Caesar Augustus. All educated Romans, and many learned people since that time, memorized Horace's stirring lines celebrating Greco-Roman virtues and exalting the heroic victories of the noble Romans over the so-called barbarians. In Virgil, Ovid, and Horace, Rome had a trio of poets whose work, by incorporating Greek themes and styles, immortalized Roman civilization.

Latin becomes the dominant language of the Roman Empire and of most of Europe

The language in which Roman literature was written and in which Roman ideas were spoken was Latin, the language of Latium. Rome's newly acquired subject peoples continued to speak their own languages, but any who wished to take advantage of Roman contacts had to learn Latin. Gradually, Latin became the common language, first of the educated classes and then of the ordinary people of the Roman Empire. Over centuries, it evolved into many of Europe's languages, including French, Italian, Portuguese, Romanian, and Spanish; these are called "romance languages" because of their Roman origins. The dominance of Latin demonstrated that Rome's conquests were linguistic and cultural as well as military and economic.

Roman aqueduct, Segovia, Spain.

The Romans also made permanent contributions to architecture, and Roman building can still be seen not only in Italy, but also in southern France, Spain, and North Africa. Rome went beyond the graceful pillars of Greek architecture to create enormous domed interior spaces, vaulted ceilings, and arches. Central to these innovations was Rome's invention of concrete, a combination of water, sand, and powdered limestone that provides impressive strength and durability when set. Concrete enabled Romans to create not only buildings of great beauty, but also large sports arenas and utilitarian projects such as bridges and aqueducts. An aqueduct was a long conduit supported by arches that brought fresh water from mountain lakes to lower-lying urban centers, using nothing more than gravity. Many Roman aqueducts still exist two thousand years after their construction, and a few remain in service, a convincing testament to both the durability and the usefulness of Roman architecture.

Challenges to Augustus's Work

When Augustus died in 14 C.E., Rome was undisputed master of Europe, the Mediterranean, and much of Southwest Asia (Map 8.4). To Romans, those were the only useful portions of the known world. No other state of the day could challenge Rome's control of its empire. There were, however, three factors threatening the stability of Augustus's imperial domain.

Augustus's personal authority cannot be passed on to his successors

First, Augustus himself had never formalized his position within the empire. Insisting that the Republic would one day be restored, he called himself *princeps civitatis* (*PRIN-cheps chi-vē-TAH-tis*), "first citizen of the state," a modest title that died with him. His other title, *Imperator*, was purely military in nature, but his control over the army was personal rather than institutional. His generals were loyal to him because of his personal attributes. If future emperors lacked such qualities, the army would not hesitate to destroy them and replace them with more suitable candidates—possibly with one of the generals themselves. In short, Augustan rule was personal rather than institutional.

Map 8.4 The Roman Empire, 138 C.E.

The Roman Empire, using the conquests of the Republic as a foundation (Map 8.3), expanded into Britain, Dacia, Cappadocia, Thrace, Judaea, and Mauretania. Note that the extent of the Empire from northwest to southeast was greater than its extent from east to west. Why would this impressive expansion actually weaken Rome's security and place the continued existence of the Roman Empire in jeopardy?

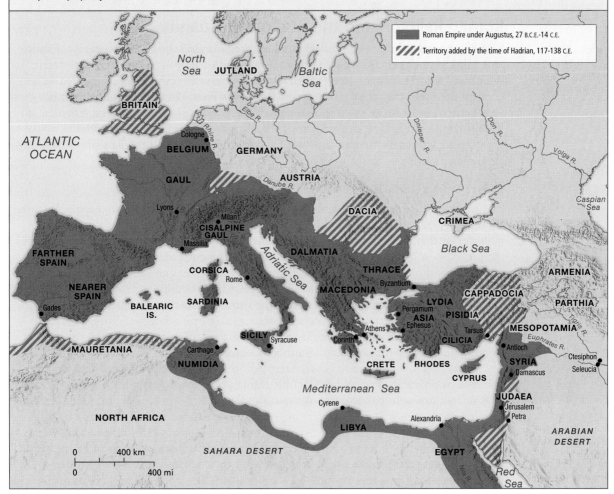

Second, the empire itself had grown too large. Sea travel on the Mediterranean made possible rapid communication between distant points, and Rome's willingness to purchase loyalty with citizenship and privilege helped it hold the borders for many years, even expanding them northward into Britain. But even though the Roman legions constituted an unparalleled fighting force, those borders were too extensive to be held forever by armies of the ancient world. Sooner or later, invaders would press on enough points simultaneously to uncover a weak spot and break through. Skilled leadership could delay but not prevent eventual collapse.

Rome confronts challenges to imperial rule

Finally, Rome's expansion and multiethnic diversity brought it into contact with monotheism, or belief in a single god, which differed substantively from the traditional Roman polytheistic religion. As the new religious beliefs spread throughout the empire, they presented significant challenges to the core values of the Roman world.

Roman Religion and the Rise of Christianity

Polytheism and monotheism embrace conflicting values

Rome's original belief system reflected what it regarded as the civic virtues of tolerance and cultural pluralism, in which various conquered societies were permitted to retain their own cultures. Roman polytheism also permitted the gods of the conquered to be incorporated into the larger pantheon of Roman deities. Monotheism, however, is by its very nature intolerant of what it considers "false gods." The monotheistic religions of Judaism and Christianity, at first merely irritating to the cosmopolitan Romans, actually represented serious challenges to a belief system that had served the Romans well.

Rome's Polytheistic Religion

The religion of Rome, like that of most other ancient cultures, was polytheistic. Its principal gods, such as Jupiter, Juno, Mars, Neptune, and Bacchus, presided over a great many lesser deities, each identified with some natural or human-made force: Mars was the god of war, Neptune of the sea, and Bacchus of wine. Each god had his or her personal cult of devotions and rituals. If the proper ceremonies and sacrifices were offered, the god was appeased and would bless and protect the worshipper. Those who ignored the gods earned their wrath, expressed in the form of natural disasters and personal tragedies. Roman religion was another manifestation of fundamental Roman practicality, based not so much on morality as on a contractual relationship with the gods. Those who fulfilled the contract would be rewarded with good fortune on earth.

Today this sort of religion is often termed "pagan," but actually it served Rome's complex, sophisticated society well, constituting yet another example of the adaptability of Roman culture. In particular, polytheism's tolerance for previously unfamiliar gods enabled the empire to assimilate conquered peoples without forcing them to abandon their beliefs. It was easy for Rome to integrate the religious beliefs and practices of the people it conquered. Foreign gods, such as Mithras of Persia and Osiris of Egypt, were simply added to the Roman array of deities after their native lands were conquered. All that was expected was that conquered peoples would be courteous enough to respect the festivals of the principal Roman gods, such as Jupiter, thereby appeasing those gods and deflecting their wrath from Rome.

Tellus, the Earth, sits with infants and animals, surrounded by personifications of the Four Winds in this relief from the Altar of Peace in Rome.

Jewish Resistance and Eastern Cults

When Rome overran Judaea in the eastern Mediterranean region, however, it discovered that the Jews, who believed in a single, all-powerful God, were intolerant of all other belief systems and unwilling to participate in Rome's rituals. Perplexed by this conduct, the Romans isolated the Jews, a policy that worked fairly well, since the Jews considered themselves the **Chosen People** and prized their separateness. They had no interest in converting Romans to their own faith and simply wanted to be left alone; the more militant among them hoped that Rome would someday be overthrown or simply go away.

The intolerance of the Jews irritated the Romans, and Roman rule embittered the Jews, who revolted on the death in 4 B.C.E. of Herod, a puppet king whom Rome had elevated from among the Jewish people. Augustus sent his legions to put down the insurrection and replaced Herod with an official who reported directly to the *Imperator*. After suppressing the revolt, Rome attempted to make peace with the Jews by assigning responsibility for Jewish religious matters and local affairs to the Sanhedrin (*san-HED-rin*), the highest Jewish judicial body.

Jews and Romans mistrust one another

Nevertheless, Jews continued to resist Roman domination, and especially the taxes that Augustus imposed in order to pay for the Roman legions permanently stationed in Judaea. Some Jewish sects, advocating direct action, not only refused to pay taxes but also engaged in serious though futile efforts to dislodge the Romans. Best known among these groups were the Zealots (*ZELL-uts*), who practiced terrorism and assassination not only against Romans but also against Jews who collaborated with the occupying legions. Other sects revived the traditional Jewish prophecies of the coming of a Messiah who would liberate God's Chosen People from earthly oppression—in this case, from the Roman Empire. John the Baptist, a desert preacher, prophesied that the arrival of the Messiah was near. In contrast to these groups, Jewish apocalyptic sects such as the Essenes (*ESS-ēnz*) concluded that the world would end soon and that pious people should withdraw from public life and prepare for the end.

Simultaneously, interest in eastern mystery religions was spreading across the Roman Empire, affecting not only Jews but polytheists as well. Alexander's conquests had acquainted Greeks with eastern cults that promised personal immortality through the sacrifice of a god who had died and risen from the dead. Mystery cults became widely popular in Greece and the eastern Mediterranean region. Rome's absorption of Hellenism spread familiarity with those cults to all parts of the empire, including Judaea. It was in Judaea that Jesus of Nazareth preached.

Eastern mystery cults spread throughout the Roman Empire

JESUS OF NAZARETH. Born around 4 B.C.E. in Jerusalem, Jesus was raised in the town of Nazareth in the Zealot stronghold of Galilee and was thoroughly familiar with the apocalyptic predictions of the Essenes. But as a man of peace, he disagreed with the Zealots, and his teachings regarding how to live in this world, rather than only preparing for the next, also distinguished him from the Essenes. Jesus, who declared that he did not intend to change Jewish law, was permitted to preach in the synagogue. Like the great Jewish rabbi Hillel (30 B.C.E.–9 C.E.), with whose teachings he was undoubtedly familiar, Jesus taught in texts such as the Sermon on the Mount (see "Excerpt from the Sermon on the Mount") that Jews must love one another as they loved God and treat others as they themselves wished to be treated. A small group of his followers thought he was the Messiah, and Jesus reportedly revealed himself to them as exactly that. But he did not intend to destroy the Roman Empire; he sought to establish a spiritual kingdom, not a political one.

Excavations at Qumran, northwest of the Dead Sea, reveal how the Essenes lived around 150 B.C.E.

Jesus's emphasis on the spirituality of his rule disappointed those Jews who hoped that the Messiah would deliver them by force from Roman bondage. Other aspects of Jesus's teachings alarmed more traditional Jews, particularly those closely connected with the Sanhedrin. To them, Jesus appeared as a radical reformer threatening their established place within the Jewish hierarchy or as a troublemaker who might provoke their Roman rulers.

Document 8.2 Excerpt from the Sermon on the Mount

Soon after the beginning of his public ministry in 26 C.E., Jesus of Nazareth spoke from a mountain to a large crowd. His address, as recounted in the Gospel of St. Matthew, has become known as the Sermon on the Mount. It contains many of his most fundamental teachings.

And seeing the multitudes, He went up on a mountain, and when He was seated His disciples came to Him.

Then He opened His mouth and taught them, saying,

"Blessed are the poor in spirit, for theirs is the kingdom of heaven.

"Blessed are they who mourn, for they shall be comforted.

"Blessed are the meek, for they shall inherit the earth.

"Blessed are those who hunger and thirst for righteousness, for they shall be filled.

"Blessed are the merciful, for they shall obtain mercy.

"Blessed are the pure in heart, for they shall see God.

"Blessed are the peacemakers, for they shall be called sons of God.

"Blessed are those who are persecuted for righteousness' sake, for theirs is the kingdom of heaven.

"Blessed are you when they revile and persecute you, and say all kinds of evil against you falsely for My sake.

"Rejoice and be exceedingly glad, for great is your reward in heaven, for so they persecuted the prophets who were before you . . .

"You have heard that it was said, 'An eye for an eye and a tooth for a tooth.'

"But I tell you not to resist an evil person. But whoever slaps you on your right cheek, turn the other to him also.

"If anyone wants to sue you and take away your tunic, let him have your cloak also.

"And whoever compels you to go one mile, go with him two.

"Give to him who asks you, and from him who wants to borrow from you do not turn away.

"You have heard that it was said, 'You shall love your neighbor and hate your enemy.'

"But I say to you, love your enemies, bless those who curse you, do good to those who hate you, and pray for those who spitefully use you and persecute you,

"that you may be sons of your Father in heaven; for He makes His sun rise on the evil and on the good, and sends rain on the just and on the unjust . . .

And so it was, when Jesus had ended these sayings, that the people were astonished at His teaching . . .

SOURCE: *The Holy Bible,* The New King James Version (1983), Matthew 5: 1–12 and 38–45, 7:28.

Jesus of Nazareth challenges orthodox Judaism

There was nothing politically revolutionary in Jesus's thought, but he was clearly an unsettling figure within Judaism. Pontius Pilate (*PUNCH-us PĪ-lut*), Roman procurator of Judea from 26 to 36 C.E., a tough former legionary turned political official, was indifferent to Jewish religious quarrels and concerned solely with the maintenance of peace and order. The crowds acclaiming Jesus in Jerusalem during the Jewish Passover festival in 29 C.E. alarmed him. To avert civil unrest and possible riot and bloodshed, Pilate condemned Jesus to death by crucifixion.

Paul of Tarsus and the Spread of Christianity

After Jesus' death, the unrest subsided in Jerusalem, where his disciples continued to live. Pilate did not attempt to suppress them, assuming they were just another of the many different Jewish cults. As rumors began to circulate that Jesus had risen from the dead, however, his followers grew increasingly outspoken. They came to be known as Christians, or those who believe that Jesus was the Christ (a Greek word meaning Messiah).

The head of the Christian sect was Peter, a Galilean follower of Jesus and a man of traditional Jewish beliefs who felt that Jesus' teachings were meant exclusively for Jews. The new sect therefore continued to observe Jewish laws and customs, accepting only circumcised males and people who obeyed Jewish dietary regulations. To these it added new practices such as baptism (in which new members were sprinkled with or immersed in water as a symbol of new spiritual birth) and communion (at which believers consumed bread and wine in commemoration of Jesus' Last Supper with his disciples). Without Paul of Tarsus, Peter's sect might have remained a purely Jewish offshoot, ignored by mainstream Jews.

Paul of Tarsus (a town in what is today Turkey) was a Jewish Roman citizen fluent in Hebrew, Latin, and Greek. He helped persecute Christians until, while traveling from Tarsus to Damascus in Syria around 31 or 32 C.E., he experienced a vision that convinced him of the truth of Christian belief. Paul promptly converted to Christianity and, noting that the sect was largely ignored by mainstream Jews, decided to proclaim it to non-Jews, whom the Jews called Gentiles. He taught that Judaism was essentially preparation for the arrival of the Messiah, who by his coming had fulfilled the ancient prophecies and inaugurated a new age. Paul proclaimed that Jesus was not only the Messiah but also the Son of God, and that his teachings were meant for all people on earth.

Traveling and preaching throughout Greece, Turkey, Syria, and Palestine, Paul spread Christianity among the Gentiles. Many, familiar with eastern mystery religions, embraced the new religion. They were drawn to its forgiveness of sinners who repented, its promise of personal immortality, its emphasis on community, its inclusiveness (for example, treating women and slaves as the spiritual equivalents of free men), and its message that each individual had a part to play in the completion of God's work on earth. A small, physically unimpressive man, Paul was a compelling preacher whose devotion and intensity inspired many conversions.

Paul preaches Christianity to the Gentiles

Paul's decision to preach to the Gentiles transformed Christianity from a minor Jewish sect into a distinct and dynamic new religion. Insisting that male converts should not have to endure the Jewish rite of circumcision (the Greeks considered circumcision a form of mutilation), he made it possible for people to become Christians without first becoming Jews. Soon Gentile communities of Christians were larger than the original community of Christians in Jerusalem, which persisted in vainly attempting to convince other Jews that the Messiah had come. When Judaea revolted against Rome in 66 C.E., the Christianized Jews were accused of collaborating with the Romans, and by the close of the first century it was apparent that Christianity's future lay solely with the Gentiles.

Paul's vision of Christianity as a religion speaking to all humanity distinguished the new faith not only from Judaism but also from the other mystery religions. It gave Jesus's message a universal character rather than limiting it to one ethnic group selected by God. The only initiation required was baptism. Within the Roman Empire, Christianity began to challenge polytheism, offering converts a sense of mission and a place in God's plan for the redemption of the world. It also, of course, offered a powerful reward that

Paul's teachings give the message of Jesus a universal appeal

polytheists considered absurd: eternal life. In time, Christianity's strong appeal and consequent spread transformed the Roman Empire, and the teachings of a Galilean preacher became the foundation of one of the principal religions of the world.

ROME'S VIEW OF CHRISTIANITY. Traditional Roman religion, with its intricate rituals and great range of deities, continued to serve most of the empire's citizens. But Rome's integration of the eastern Mediterranean made it relatively easy for Christianity to spread throughout the region. Paul traveled along well-established trading routes to Greece and Anatolia, while other missionaries carried the new faith to Syria and Egypt. In the northern and western reaches of the empire, however, Christianity encountered indifference bordering on hostility. By 250 C.E. fewer than 10 percent of Romans were Christian.

Rome becomes suspicious of Christianity

Nevertheless, imperial authorities were suspicious of Christianity. Its practitioners owed their allegiance to a king who, although his kingdom was spiritual, seemed to rival the emperor. In addition, unlike the public Roman rituals, Christian ceremonies were conducted privately, appearing to be secret and thus potentially subversive. Finally, Christians' intolerance of all other gods and refusal to offer sacrifices to the official Roman pantheon—including deceased emperors, whom Romans openly worshiped—threatened the stability of the state.

By the reign of the Emperor Nero (54–68 C.E.), Christianity had become enough of an annoyance within Rome itself to provoke this unstable and incompetent ruler to atrocities and persecutions. Between 64 and 312 C.E. several imperial persecutions consigned Christians to martyrdom by fire, beheading, crucifixion, or mauling by wild beasts. Sometimes Christians were slaughtered in front of tens of thousands of spectators in the Colosseum, a large stadium in Rome. Those who died during persecutions were considered by Christians to be holy martyrs. Their memories were honored and their heroism used to spread the new religion even further. But as long as the force and power of the state remained arrayed against it, Christianity could never attract more than a small minority of Romans.

St. Mamai of Georgia, a Christian martyred by the Romans, is shown with a cross in one hand while riding a lion, symbolizing his triumph over death and ignorance.

From Golden Age to Disarray

Nero's relentless pursuit of Christians did not obscure his inadequacies as a ruler. He was so ineffectual that the army ousted him in 68, and two years of political turmoil were finally ended by the triumph of Vespasian (*vess-PĀ-zē-un*), a general who abandoned all pretenses of ruling a republic and openly established his own imperial dynasty, the Flavians (*FLĀ-vē-uns*).

The next century was the golden age of Rome. By 180 the emperor had come to be recognized as a guarantor of peace, stability, and prosperity. An enormous commercial network integrated the entire Mediterranean basin and attracted trading partners from Asia and Africa. After 180, however, a combination of epidemic disease, political incapacity, and external pressures weakened the empire and left its continued existence in doubt.

Commercial Connections

Rome's golden age brings prosperity to the Mediterranean and connects the Mediterranean to the wider world

Economic prosperity made it grand to be a Roman citizen during the golden age. The city of Rome itself was exciting. Noisy and cosmopolitan, with a multiethnic population exceeding 600,000, it was the most impressive European city of its time. All citizens received free grain, wine, and oil; those who were not citizens were fed at low, government-subsidized prices. Chariot races, gladiatorial combats, and other athletic contests provided entertainment.

Roman economic productivity increased and Roman commerce dominated the Mediterranean world (Map 8.5). The Roman Empire after Augustus developed a productive agricultural system. The number of small farms increased, many of them worked by retired military veterans who settled in the regions where they had been stationed. The result was the cultivation of large expanses of rich farmland in Gaul, Britain, and central and eastern Europe, ensuring Romans an abundant supply of food.

The Romans also built an enormous interconnected area of free trade and transport. They developed a system of paved, well-maintained roads connecting Rome to all parts

Map 8.5 Rome's Economic Organization of the Mediterranean World, 180 C.E.

The economic linkages forged by Rome united the Mediterranean world into an enormously powerful economic engine. Roman roads, most of them paved with stone, linked cities throughout the empire and connected Rome to caravan routes serving Asia and Africa. Notice that the shipping times indicate how rapidly Roman galleys could cross the Mediterranean. Observe also the large number of products listed in the legend, which demonstrates the complexity of trade within the Roman world. But what does the clustering of legionary headquarters in northern Europe and the eastern Mediterranean suggest about the negative aspects of the extent of the Roman Empire?

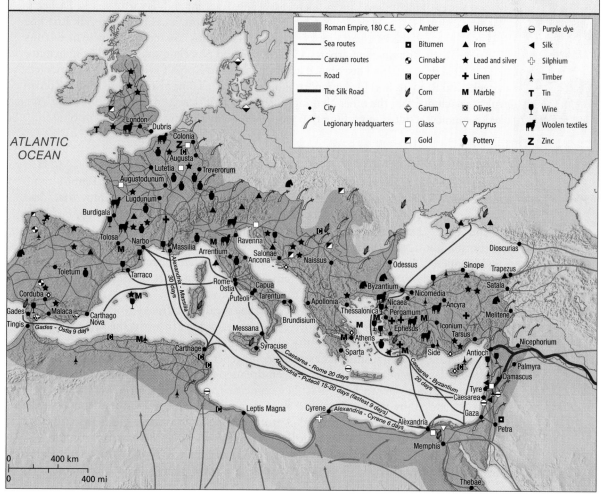

The Roman Colosseum (see page 202).

A modern photo of the Appian Way, part of the network of Roman roads that facilitated travel and commerce throughout the Empire.

"Barracks Emperors" weaken the Roman Empire

of its vast empire. These ensured the regular flow of goods into and out of the city, and of soldiers to frontiers and trouble spots.

Rome's provinces were encouraged to trade not only with the capital but also among themselves. Wine from Gaul and Italy, wool from Britain, olive oil from Syria, and grain from Egypt traveled in Roman ships across the Mediterranean, transshipped at ports connected by land routes to the far-flung reaches of the empire. Prosperity and security stimulated the growth of manufacturing, particularly in northern Europe, which grew to rival Italy itself in the production of glass, pottery, brass, and bronze.

Rome's commercial expansion affected the eastern Mediterranean profoundly. Roman ships cleared the sea of pirates and incorporated it into the empire's commercial network. In addition, Rome used its eastern lands to launch further contact with the Parthian and Sasanian Empires, which had consolidated the remnants of the Persian and Alexandrian empires. This easterly orientation that began after Actium brought Rome into contact not only with Persian and Macedonian successor states but also with India and China.

In the second century C.E., Roman mariners sailed regularly from ports in Egypt through the Indian Ocean to the Indus River, trading goods of Roman manufacture for the varied wares of the Indian subcontinent, especially fragrant and flavorful spices. Earlier, in the first century B.C.E., Han Wudi, China's Martial Emperor, had opened the Silk Road between China and the Parthian Empire; in the course of this commerce, Chinese merchants often met their Roman counterparts. Chinese silk and porcelain sold well in Roman markets, and in 96 C.E. China dispatched an ambassador to Roman Syria, where he observed the Greeks and Romans and filed a report of his impressions. But neither Chinese nor Roman rulers concluded that the other civilization had much of interest to offer, and this intriguing set of contacts resulted in nothing that would alter either's view of the world or of itself.

The Empire in Disarray

Toward the end of the second century C.E., the golden age of the Roman Empire came to an end. The Flavians and their successors, known as the "five good emperors," had ruled efficiently and effectively. They kept the army under control, defended the borders of the empire, reformed and revitalized the bureaucracy, and consolidated their own authority. But during the reign of Marcus Aurelius (165–180 C.E.), the last of the "five good emperors," a deadly epidemic of smallpox drastically reduced the empire's population, eventually even killing the ruler himself. To make matters worse, the incompetence of his son Commodus soon plunged the empire into civil war.

In 235 the empire fell under the rule of the so-called barracks emperors, a succession of generals who typically gained power by force and quickly lost it the same way. Between 235 and 284 more than twenty different emperors tried to rule. The administrative structure that Augustus had established degenerated into military despotism.

Such developments would have been dreaded even under normal circumstances, but it was Rome's misfortune that they coincided with intense pressure on its frontiers caused by the migration of the Germanic peoples, whom the Romans called barbarians. In the second and third centuries C.E., some of these Germanic tribes, originating in northern and eastern Europe, began to force their way across the borders of the Roman Empire, attracted by Rome's prosperity and the fertility of the lands it controlled.

Chapter Review

Putting It in Perspective

Rome, which began in the eighth century B.C.E. as a tiny city in the midst of the Italian peninsula, eventually assembled an empire that surpassed the Persian Empire in size and wealth. Victory over Carthage gave the Romans dominance over the Mediterranean basin, enabling them to build an extensive trading network that would spread their goods and influence. However, Rome's republican form of government, which was admirably suited to the proper functioning of a small city-state, could not satisfy the demands of a far-flung seaborne empire. Roman generals contended for the right to exercise political power, and in 27 B.C.E. Octavian eliminated his opponents and became "the first citizen of the state."

As Caesar Augustus, Octavian managed the transition from republic to empire by perpetuating the institutions of the former while employing the broad powers of the latter. But Octavian's successors never created a coherent philosophy of government with which to supplant the Republic, and Rome's golden age eventually degenerated into misrule as military dictators sought unsuccessfully to defend lengthy frontiers.

Rome's genius lay in winning conflicts and forging the cooperative connections that often grew out of them. Its legions stormed across the Mediterranean world, conquering all rivals and dominating the region for centuries. Its rulers brought the lands and peoples they defeated into a multiethnic realm that rewarded ability with citizenship. Romans rarely rejected a good idea, taking the achievements and even the gods of their subject peoples and making them their own. The very extent of the empire ultimately doomed it, but it lasted for centuries.

Benefiting from Roman cultural connections, Christianity spread across the Roman world and eventually grew into one of the most influential of the world's religions. Paul of Tarsus transformed the message of Jesus of Nazareth from the belief system of a small Jewish sect into a compelling faith that promised salvation and resurrection to all people. Paul's travels and preaching would probably not have been possible had not Rome united the eastern Mediterranean region and had not Paul himself possessed Roman citizenship.

Eventually, however, the Roman Empire's control of the Mediterranean world weakened. The strong leadership of the "five good emperors" gave way after 180 to the military rule of the barracks emperors, which was marked by constant power struggles and assassinations. The Chinese principle of the dynastic cycle explained the inevitability of good rulers being succeeded by bad ones and prescribed a change of dynasties as the proper cure for such troubles. But China was not pressed on all sides by the ambitious invaders who now sensed Rome's weakness and sought to take advantage of it.

Reviewing Key Material

KEY CONCEPTS

Republic, 185
Struggle of the Orders, 186
Natural law 186
Dictator 192

Augustus, 194
Pax Romana, 195
Greco-Roman culture, 195
Chosen People, 198

KEY PEOPLE

Hannibal, 190
Livia, 191
Spartacus, 191
Sulla, 192
Pompey, 192
Julius Caesar, 193
Caesar Augustus (Octavian), 193
Marcus Brutus, 193
Marc Antony, 193
Cleopatra, 194

Virgil, 195
Ovid, 196
Horace, 196
John the Baptist, 199
Jesus of Nazareth, 199
Pontius Pilate, 200
Peter, 201
Paul of Tarsus, 201
Nero, 202
Vespasian, 202
Marcus Aurelius, 203

ASK YOURSELF

1. How did the Roman Republic differ from Athenian democracy? In what ways did the Roman Republic's governing framework respond to the political needs of Romans?

2. How did Rome use citizenship as a tool of governing its pluralistic empire?
3. How was the Roman Republic transformed into the Roman Empire?
4. How did the Roman Empire's organizational structure facilitate the spread of Christianity? What challenges did this new religion present to Rome?
5. Reflect on this statement: "Rome's genius resided in its superb talents for winning conflicts and forging connections."

GOING FURTHER

Beard, W., and M. Crawford. *Rome in the Late Republic*. 1984.
Boren, Henry. *Roman Society*. 1992.
Cameron, Averil. *The Later Roman Empire*. 1993.
Cornell, T. *The Beginnings of Rome*. 1995.
Crawford, M. *The Roman Republic*. 1993.
David, J.-M. *The Roman Conquest of Italy*. 1996.
Dickson, Suzanne. *The Roman Family*. 1992.
Drinkwater, J., and A. Drummond. *The World of the Romans*. 1993.
Dupont, Florence. *Daily Life in Ancient Rome*. 1992.
Eck, W. *The Age of Augustus*. 2003.
Garnsey, P., and R. Saller. *The Roman Empire: Economy, Society, and Culture*. 1987.
Goldsworthy, A. *The Punic Wars*. 2001.
Hildinger, E. *Swords Against the Senate: The Rise of the Roman Army and the Fall of the Republic*. 2002.
Kallet-Marx, R. *Hegemony to Empire*. 1995.
Kamm, A. *The Romans*. 1995.
MacMullen, Ramsay. *Christianizing the Roman Empire*. 1984.
Scullard, H. *A History of the Roman World, 753–146 B.C.* 1993.
Shotter, D. *The Fall of the Roman Republic*. 1994.
Turcan, Robert. *The Gods of Ancient Rome: Religion in Everyday Life from Archaic to Imperial Times*. 2000.
Wheeler, Mortimer. *Roman Art and Architecture*. 1985.

Key Dates and Developments

The Roman Republic

753 B.C.E.	Traditional date for the founding of Rome
509 B.C.E.	Establishment of the Roman Republic
494–287 B.C.E.	Struggle of the Orders
450 B.C.E.	Law of the Twelve Tables
264–241 B.C.E.	First Punic War
218–201 B.C.E.	Second Punic War; Hannibal crosses the Alps
149–146 B.C.E.	Third Punic War; destruction of Carthage
200–133 B.C.E.	Rome's conquest of the eastern Mediterranean
91–88 B.C.E.	Conflict between Rome and its allies
45–44 B.C.E.	Julius Caesar's dictatorship
March 15, 44 B.C.E.	Assassination of Caesar
44–42 B.C.E.	The Second Triumvirate defeats Caesar's murderers
41–30 B.C.E.	Antony and Cleopatra

The Roman Empire to 284 C.E.

27 B.C.E.–14 C.E.	Caesar Augustus's rule as *Imperator* Conquest of Spain, Germany, southeastern Europe
ca. 4 B.C.E.	Birth of Jesus of Nazareth
29 C.E.	Crucifixion of Jesus in Jerusalem
45–58 C.E.	Paul of Tarsus: preaching Christianity in the eastern Mediterranean
54–68 C.E.	Misrule of Emperor Nero
69–180 C.E.	Rome's Golden Age
235–284 C.E.	Rule of the "barracks emperors" Onset of the Germanic migrations

CHAPTER 9

Germanic Societies and the Emergence of the Christian West, 100–1100 C.E.

Emperor Constantine I

Roman Emperor Constantine I, depicted by this statue, legalized Christianity and moved the empire's capital east from Rome to Constantinople. The western part of the empire, including Rome, was then overrun by Germanic peoples who in time developed a new culture, blending Roman, Christian, and Germanic ways to create the Christian West.

In 312 C.E. Constantine (*KON-stun-tēn*), son of a Roman emperor who had died in 306, advanced with an army on the city of Rome to secure his own claim to the throne. His main rival, with a much larger army, was blocking access to Rome at the Milvian Bridge. According to legend, as Constantine prepared for battle, he saw in the sky a symbol of Christ and a phrase proclaiming "In this sign you will conquer." He adopted the symbol as his battle standard and the next day won a great victory.

Constantine went on to become one of the most pivotal Roman emperors. Interpreting his vision and his victory as signs from the Christian God, he legalized Christianity, which had been banned and periodically persecuted since 64 C.E. He moved the empire's capital eastward from Rome to Byzantium, a city he rebuilt as a grandiose New Rome, soon known in his honor as Constantinople. And he defended the realm against Germanic peoples who threatened it from the north.

Constantine's endeavors set the stage for Europe's transformation in the centuries that followed. His legalization of Christianity, and its designation by his successors as the Roman state religion, helped eventually to make it Europe's main faith, embodied in a wealthy and powerful institution called the Church. And his new capital at Constantinople reinforced the empire's eastward orientation at the expense of the west. The prosperous eastern half of the Roman realm, later called the Byzantine Empire, was ruled from Constantinople for another millennium (Chapter 10). But the western half was conquered in the fifth century by Germanic peoples, whose connections and conflicts with the Romans and their heritage eventually produced a new civilization, often called the Christian West, combining Germanic and Roman elements with Christian religious beliefs.

The Christian West

The Germanic Peoples

To the north and northeast of the Roman world lived an assortment of tribal societies, now collectively called Germanic peoples, since most spoke languages belonging to the Germanic branch of the Indo-European language family. These peoples included, among others, the Franks, Angles, Saxons, Lombards, Alemanni (*AH-luh-MAH-nē*), Vandals, and Goths (Map 9.1). Their tribal warrior societies, disparaged by Romans as "barbarian," in time would overwhelm Rome itself, Germanicize the Christian West, and help to shape what came to be known as Western Civilization.

Germanic Society: Kinship and Combat

Early German pastoral nomads live by herding, hunting, and fighting

Initially the Germans were mainly pastoral nomads who lived in northern Europe by herding, hunting, and fighting. They herded cattle to get meat, milk, and cheese for food and hides for making clothes. They hunted deer and other wild game for additional meat

FOUNDATION MAP 9.1 Germans, Celts, and Romans, by the First Century C.E.

In the first several centuries C.E., Germanic-speaking peoples engaged in connections and conflicts with the Roman Empire. Note that Celtic-speaking peoples, displaced from central and western Europe by Germanic migrations, resettled in what are now Scotland, Wales, Ireland, and Brittany. What advantages did Germanic peoples have in their clashes and contacts with the Romans? Why did Germanic invasions and infiltration pose a serious threat to the Roman Empire?

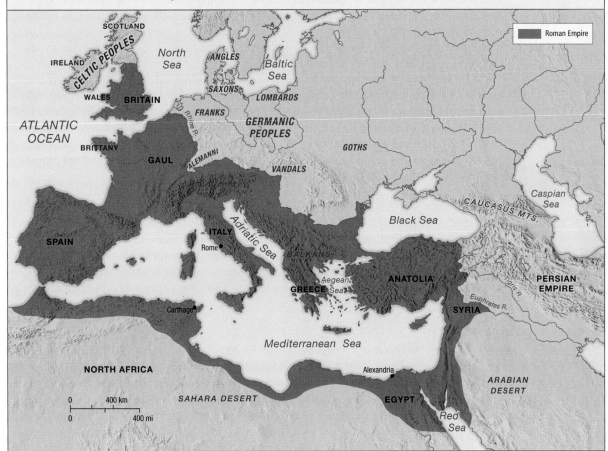

and hides. They made swords and spears from iron, an ore abundant in northern and central Europe, and used these weapons to stage raids and attacks on neighboring peoples. The Germans were not much interested in commerce, preferring instead to get their goods from raids and the spoils of war.

Like many tribal peoples, the Germans based their societies on kinship ties, involving loyalty and patriarchy, rather than on territory or formal institutions. The members of each tribe, linked by family connections, saw themselves as an extended clan with a common ancestry and heritage. These kinship loyalties frequently led to blood feuds: if an outsider killed a member of the tribe, the victim's kinsfolk felt bound to avenge this crime by killing either the murderer or someone from the

Germanic tribal societies feature kinship ties and blood feuds

murderer's clan, an act of vengeance that often triggered battles between tribes. These tribal ties foreshadowed the notion of **nation**, a political community united by its people's sense of common heritage and culture, which later played a prominent role in European history.

The tribes were often organized as chiefdoms, ruled by a chief who was typically elected by an assembly of warriors. Attached to the chief by bonds of mutual loyalty, these warriors were expected to protect him with their lives or die with him in battle. In future centuries some of the chiefdoms matured into monarchies, with the chief becoming a king and his men of war nobles who served on his royal council. Germanic tribal structure thus helped to shape later Europe's stratified societies, dominated by warrior kings and nobles.

Germanic jewelry.

Patriarchal males dominate society, with women in supportive roles

Much as male warriors ran Germanic societies, senior males dominated Germanic families. In these patriarchal households, women were valued mainly for their reproductive roles and service to the male warriors. Men of means and status could have more than one wife, and fathers were free to sell their daughters in marriage to whoever made the best offer. The main role of women was to support the men, who fought the wars that protected the society and secured the food that sustained it—a function and relationship that would prevail throughout much of European history.

Like most other early societies, including the pre-Christian Greeks and Romans, Germans were polytheistic, worshiping numerous gods and goddesses who personified various aspects of the world around them. The main divinities included Woden (*WŌ-dun*), creator of the earth and sky; Tiu (*TĒ-oo*), the god of war; Thor, the god of thunder; and Friia (*FRĒ-uh*), the goddess of fertility and love. Although the Germans later adopted Christianity and abandoned these deities, their names would survive in Anglo-Saxon week days such as Tuesday (Tiu's day), Wednesday (Woden's day), Thursday (Thor's day), and Friday (Friia's day).

Sometimes the Germans called on the divinities to decide legal issues brought before the chief and his assembly. Believing that the gods would protect a guiltless person from harm, the chief might order a trial by ordeal, in which the defendant was put to a test to determine innocence or guilt. An accused woman, for example, might undergo ordeal by fire: if she could walk through flames without being burned, she would be considered innocent. Or, when faced with conflicting testimony, the chief might order an accused man to face his accuser in battle, typically in face-to-face combat with swords. This practice endured into the Christian era, when it took the form of a duel, in which the combatants appealed to "God's judgment" to bring victory for the side that embodied justice and truth.

Germanic Migrations and Their Threat to Rome

Germanic peoples migrate toward Roman frontiers

During the last several centuries B.C.E., while Rome was extending its control over the Mediterranean basin, many Germans began moving south into central and western Europe, driven perhaps by a scarcity of food resulting from population growth. By the first century C.E. they had largely displaced these regions' tribal peoples, who spoke Celtic (*KELL-tik*) languages (another branch of the Indo-European family) and lived mainly by farming. As Celtic tribes resettled in the regions now called Scotland, Wales, Ireland, and Brittany (in western France), the Germans moved toward the Roman frontiers, where they increasingly took up farming and interacted with the Roman world (Map 9.1).

The Germans thus became more settled and agricultural but no less warlike. They came to reside in villages, where they lived in wooden huts and grew grains such as wheat, oats, and barley on the surrounding lands. Women did much of the field work and most household chores, boiling grains to make thick gruel, grinding them into flour for flat baked bread, and fermenting them into lush, hearty beer that has since been a favorite German beverage. The men helped with planting and harvesting but still hunted and herded, made war against other German tribes, staged raids on Roman towns and farmlands, and even fought the famed Roman legions.

The Romans responded to the growing German threat not only by waging numerous battles against the Germanic "barbarians" but also by seeking to assimilate them. Roman leaders recruited many Germans as soldiers, awarded German leaders with command positions, and sometimes even made them Roman citizens. By employing Germanic warriors, the empire secured the services of its most dangerous adversaries. It also, however, brought growing numbers of Germans into the Roman armies. As Germans became a large portion of these armies and bore much of the empire's defensive burden, they began to think that they should enjoy a substantial share of its riches. The pressure on the empire from Germans in its armies was further compounded by war among German tribes. The losers, forced off their lands, typically moved toward the fertile soils and ample wealth of the Roman world.

Romans combat Germans but also recruit them into Roman armies

Beset with internal power struggles throughout much of the third century, the Romans proved unable to control or pacify the Germans, who invaded and raided at will. By the late third century, the Roman Empire was in serious danger.

Germans increasingly invade and raid Roman lands

The Decline of the Western Roman Empire

Beginning in the late third century, to deal with the growing crisis, Roman rulers divided the empire into eastern and western sectors, hoping to make it easier to manage and defend. This division, however, combined with the eastward relocation of the capital from Rome to Constantinople in the early fourth century, mainly strengthened the eastern sector at the west's expense. In the fourth and fifth centuries, while Christianity replaced polytheism as the empire's dominant religion, the western half of the realm was wracked by continued Germanic invasions, culminating in the fall of Rome and the end of the Western Roman Empire.

The Divided Empire and Its Eastern Orientation

In the third century C.E., as noted in the last chapter, a prolonged crisis shook the Roman Empire. Increasing Germanic attacks coincided with a series of military revolts that proclaimed as emperor more than twenty different generals within fifty years (235–284), bringing to power "barracks emperors" more focused on fighting for power than defending the frontiers. Germans repeatedly raided and infiltrated the western parts of the realm, disrupting commerce and provoking social chaos. In the east, taking advantage of the tumult, the Sasanian Persians drove the Romans out of Mesopotamia. The Roman world seemed to be in disarray.

Diocletian divides empire to improve its administration

But desperate times brought forth an exceptional leader in 284, when Diocletian (*dī-uh-KLĒ-shun*), a common soldier who had risen through the ranks, seized power as Roman Emperor. Faced with continual revolts and invasions, he quickly concluded that the empire was too vast for one man to rule alone. So he divided it into two parts, along a line running north and south between Italy and Greece (Map 9.2), keeping himself in charge of the east and naming a co-emperor to administer the west. Later he added a junior ruler to assist each emperor, creating a four-ruler system called a tetrarchy (*TET-rar-kē*). For a while this imaginative reform seemed to work, enabling the leaders to restore order and fight invasions more effectively.

Diocletian's retirement in 305, however, led to a new power struggle, eventually won by Emperor Constantine I (312–337), whose victory in 312 at the Milvian Bridge is

Map 9.2 The Romans Divide Their Empire, Third Through Fifth Centuries C.E.

To better administer and defend the immense Roman realm, Emperor Diocletian (284–305 C.E.) divided it administratively into eastern and western sectors. Notice that Constantinople, the new capital built by his successor Constantine I (312–337), was located in the midst of the empire's wealthier eastern sector. How and why did these developments, combined with Germanic invasions, weaken the west and contribute to the empire's permanent division and disintegration?

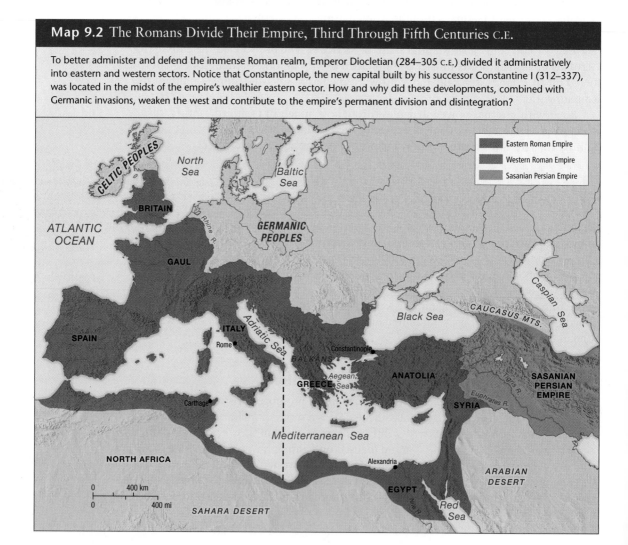

noted at the start of this chapter. He restored the empire's unity, defeating all his rivals and emerging as sole ruler by 324. He also shored up its defenses, enlarging the army and bureaucracy and stationing more forces along the frontiers. Furthermore, as noted above, he moved the capital east from Rome to Byzantium, where he built a splendid New Rome that came to be called Constantinople.

Constantine restores unity and moves capital east to Constantinople

In many respects, the new capital's site was superb. Surrounded by water on three sides, the New Rome would prove much easier to defend than the old Rome in the west. Situated astride the trade routes connecting Europe with Asia, Constantinople flourished for centuries, not only as the seat of imperial authority, but also as one of the world's leading commercial and cultural centers. The new capital's location strengthened the realm's wealthy eastern sector politically and militarily. In reinforcing the empire's eastward orientation, however, the change of capitals further relegated the less prosperous west to a secondary status, setting the stage for its continuing decline under ongoing Germanic onslaughts.

Moving capital strengthens eastern empire but weakens west

The Triumph and Transformation of Christianity

Constantine's reign also heralded the triumph of Christianity, an eastern salvation religion that, in spite of Roman persecutions, had by then attracted a sizable following (Chapter 8). Following his vision and victory in 312 at the Battle of Milvian Bridge, Constantine became an avid supporter of the Christian faith. He did not at once become a baptized Christian, in part because his position as emperor made him the high priest of the polytheistic Roman state religion. But he legalized the Christian faith in 313, took an active interest in its internal affairs, and finally was baptized in 337 on his deathbed, preparing the way for Christianity's later adoption as the empire's official religion.

Constantine legalizes Christianity and plays active role in Church

Constantine's delay in converting to Christianity reflected an abiding Roman ambivalence toward the new religion. Like its parent Judaism, Christianity was monotheistic and intolerant of all other gods and forms of worship. Roman authorities did not demand that Christians adopt polytheism, only that they pay homage to the Roman gods and then worship in their own way as other cults and creeds did. But Christians refused to participate at all in the Roman state religion, in effect defying imperial authority. To many Romans, Christians thus seemed not only narrow-minded and intolerant but also disloyal to the empire.

The Arch of Constantine in Rome.

Still, by the time of Constantine, many Romans were losing faith in the traditional gods, who were supposed to protect the empire in return for Roman performance of the proper rituals. As German invasions continued, it became increasingly obvious that these rituals were not working, and Roman devotion to the old gods steadily declined.

Meanwhile Christianity was gaining influence. Its promise of potential salvation for all, whatever their social status, attracted numerous converts, especially among women and the urban poor. Constantine's military success, achieved in the name of the Christian faith, showed loyal Romans that this new religion could protect imperial interests, perhaps more effectively than the old gods did. His legalization of Christianity hence met little opposition, even among prominent polytheists, whom Christians categorized as pagans ("country-dwellers") since many lived on rural estates. It also helped to advance the Christian faith, to such an extent that in 380 one of his successors, Emperor Theodosius (*thē-uh-DŌ-shus*) the Great, declared Christianity the official religion of the Roman Empire (see "Decree Making Christianity the Official Roman Religion").

Christianity becomes the official Roman state religion

Document 9.1 Decree Making Christianity the Official Roman Religion

In 313 C.E., Roman Emperor Constantine the Great legalized the Christian faith, which his predecessor Diocletian had recently persecuted. In 380 C.E., Emperor Theodosius the Great issued the following decree, making Christianity the Roman state religion and promising to punish those who disagreed with Christian teachings. In less than a century, the empire thus went from persecuting to enforcing Christianity and punishing as heretics those who dared to dissent.

It is our desire that all the various nations which are subject to our Clemency and Moderation, should continue in the profession of that religion which was delivered to the Romans by the divine Apostle Peter, as it hath been preserved by faithful tradition; and which is now professed by Pontiff Damasus and by Peter, Bishop of Alexandria, a man of apostolic holiness. According to the apostolic teaching and the doctrine of the Gospel, let us believe in the one deity of the Father, the Son and the Holy Spirit, in equal majesty and in a holy Trinity. We authorize the followers of this law to assume the title of Catholic Christians; but as for the others, since, in our judgment, they are foolish madmen, we decree that they shall be branded with the ignominious name of heretics, and shall not presume to give to their conventicles the name of churches. They will suffer in the first place the chastisement of the divine condemnation, and in the second the punishment which our authority, in accordance with the will of Heaven, shall decide to inflict.

SOURCE: Henry Bettenson, ed. Documents of the Christian Church, 2nd ed. (London: Oxford University Press, 1963) 22.

Christianity's triumph helped to transform it, in the course of the fourth century, from a persecuted popular movement with little power and wealth into a powerful and wealthy institution widely known as the Church. Theodosius and his successors supported Christian efforts to destroy paganism by banning pagan worship, closing temples to Roman and Greek gods, and even ending the Olympic games, which had been staged to honor Greek gods for more than a thousand years. In return, the Church became a pillar of the Roman state, calling on Christians to fully support the imperial leaders.

Christian Church is structured on imperial lines, under pope in Rome

By this time the Church had also organized itself along Roman imperial lines, with numerous priests who served as its local agents and above them officials called **bishops** who presided over districts known as dioceses (*DĪ-uh-sis-iz*). At the head of this hierarchy was the bishop of Rome, also known as the **pope** (from the Latin word for "father"), a religious leader who headed the Church much as Roman rulers headed the empire and who claimed to be the vicar (or agent) of Christ on earth. Pope Celestine (*suh-LES-tēn*) I (422–432) even asserted that whoever held this office also possessed the "keys of the kingdom of heaven," which Christ had entrusted to his disciple Peter (see "Bible Passage on 'The Keys of the Kingdom' "). The popes saw themselves as successors to Peter, the leader of Christ's disciples, whom Christians considered the first head of the Church.

Thus developed the concept of **papal primacy** (supremacy of the pope), later to become Church doctrine, which held that the pope had authority over the whole Christian Church. Claiming to be vicars of Christ, a poor preacher who said his kingdom was "not of this world," the popes paradoxically headed a Church with great wealth and power in this world. Their claims of papal primacy helped to fuel discord with eastern Church leaders—a discord deepened by the empire's east-west division and by growing German dominance in the west.

Document 9.2 Bible Passage on "The Keys of the Kingdom"

In this passage from the Christian scriptures, Jesus promises to build his Church upon his disciple Peter (whose name means "rock") and to give Peter "the keys of the kingdom of heaven." The popes who later headed the Christian Church, seeing themselves as Peter's successors, would use this passage to assert that they too held the keys to eternal salvation.

Now when Jesus came into the district of Caesarea Philippi, he asked his disciples, "Who do men say that the Son of man is?"

And they said, "Some say John the Baptist, others say Elijah, and others Jeremiah or one of the prophets."

He said to them, "But who do you say that I am?"

Simon Peter replied, "You are the Christ, the Son of the living God."

And Jesus answered him, "Blessed are you, Simon Bar-Jona! For flesh and blood has not revealed this to you, but my Father who is in heaven.

And I tell you, you are Peter, and on this rock I will build my church, and the powers of death shall not prevail against it.

I will give you the keys of the kingdom of heaven, and whatever you bind on earth shall be bound in heaven, and whatever you loose on earth shall be loosed in heaven."

SOURCE: *The Bible*, Revised Standard Version, Matthew 16: 13–19 (New Revised Standard Version Bible, copyright 1989, Division of Christian Education of the National Council of the Churches of Christ in the United States of America. Used by permission. All rights reserved.)

Crisis and Chaos in the West

Christianity's triumph coincided with the empire's disintegration, as Constantine's successors proved unable to preserve its unity or to protect it from Germanic invasions. After Constantine's death in 337, his sons divided the empire anew and fought among themselves, initiating decades of sporadic civil wars and succession struggles. On several occasions the realm was reunified but never for very long. By the century's end, in many respects, it had become two distinct states: an Eastern and a Western Roman Empire, each with its own separate ruler.

Eastern and Western Empires diverge under Constantine's successors

The empire's vast size, moreover, continued to compromise its defenses. The Roman army was capable of defeating either the Germans in the west or Sasanian Persians in the east, but not both at the same time. Since a normal day's march covered only twenty miles, and since two thousand miles separated the western and eastern frontiers, Roman forces could not be moved quickly back and forth. Sooner or later, the empire's enemies were bound to wear it down on one frontier or the other.

The threat in the west proved more serious. Persia in the east, though a formidable foe, was a single state with specific lands and borders to defend; Roman forces there could thus focus their efforts against a well-defined adversary. In the west, however, there were many German tribes, often with ill-defined homelands, who frequently struck the Roman realm in several places at once. Furthermore, with their nomadic roots, the Germans proved highly flexible and mobile: when defeated in battle, they often simply moved elsewhere to attack.

German mobility and flexibility frustrates Roman defenses

Faced with this danger, Constantine's successors sought valiantly to stabilize the west. Some took a forceful approach: Emperor Valentinian I, who ruled the western half of the realm from 364 to 375, ruthlessly imposed and collected heavy taxes for imperial defense, then led large armies north into France (then called Gaul) and Germany to crush Germanic forces. Other emperors pursued the time-tested practice of assimilation, trying to pacify warlike tribes by giving them farmlands on the Roman frontiers while employing their best warriors and generals in the Roman legions.

Attacks from east by Huns drive Germans deeper into Roman lands

Such efforts might have staved off disaster had not a new threat emerged in the east in the late fourth century. Around 370 the Huns, aggressive nomads probably related to the warlike Xiongnu who long had tormented China, swept in from Central Asia and attacked the Goths, Germanic peoples living north of the Black Sea (Map 9.3). The eastern Goths, or Ostrogoths (*OST-ruh-goths*), who lived in what is now Ukraine, fell to the Huns and were ruled by them for the next eight decades. The western Goths, or Visigoths (*VIZ-uh-goths*), who lived in what is now Romania, were driven south into the Balkan peninsula, where they defeated the Roman armies in 378. Theodosius the Great (379–395), the Roman ruler who made Christianity the official religion, bought them off for a time by giving

Map 9.3 Hunnic and Germanic Invasions, 370–500 C.E.

Beginning around 370 C.E., invading Huns from Central Asia drove Germanic peoples to the west and south, leading to further invasion and infiltration of Roman lands. Note that Visigoths invaded Italy and sacked Rome in 410, that Huns invaded the western Roman realm before turning back in the 450s, and that Vandals attacked Rome by sea in 455, setting the stage for the fall of the Western Roman Empire in 476. Why was the Western Roman Empire unable to withstand these onslaughts?

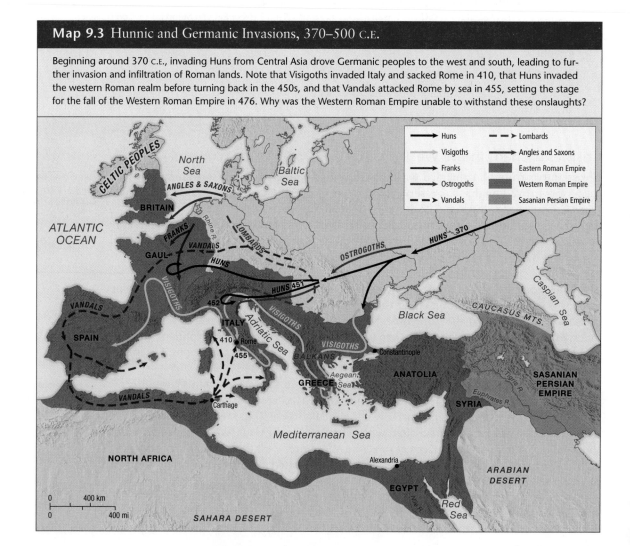

them Roman lands in the eastern Balkans, where they settled and soon converted to the Christian faith.

After Theodosius died, however, the situation changed. His sons, who split the empire (briefly reunified by their father) between them, angered the Visigoths by failing to award a Roman command post to Alaric (*AL-uh-rik*), their brilliant young leader. The Visigoths promptly rebelled, moved south into Greece, and later invaded Italy. For years the Western Roman Empire fought them off, its forces led by Stilicho (*STILL-ih-kō*) the Vandal, a Germanic general who emerged in those days as the empire's best military leader.

Alaric and the Goths strike deep into Roman lands

Alaric and Stilicho, each with Germanic heritage, embodied both the potentials and perils of Roman assimilation efforts. Alaric the Goth, like Stilicho the Vandal, valued the empire and had no desire to destroy it; what Alaric sought was a high Roman post for himself and a secure homeland for his people. Stilicho, who instinctively understood these motives, hoped eventually to ally with Alaric against other Germanic tribes. But the Western Roman Empire's leaders, seeing Stilicho's willingness to work with the Visigoths as a sign of treason, convicted and beheaded him in 408, depriving the realm of its finest commander at an hour of maximum danger.

Angered by news of Stilicho's alleged treason, Romans massacred hundreds of Germans living in the Western Empire, including Germans who served as Roman soldiers and members of their families. Many German soldiers who escaped swore vengeance and joined Alaric, whose army grew to exceed 30,000 men, while the Western Empire found itself without an effective commander. Alaric asked for a permanent Visigothic homeland in return for his army's commitment to defend the empire. The Romans, distrusting the Germans, refused this offer, so in August 410 the Visigoths attacked Rome itself—and for the first time in eight centuries the city fell to foreigners. After sacking the city, Alaric's forces moved south in search of further plunder, but their leader died of an illness later that same year.

Alaric and the Goths sack Rome in 410 C.E.

The pope characterized Alaric's death as divine punishment for the sack of Rome; the Goths attributed it to his having eaten some spoiled meat. Either way, the resulting respite for the Western Roman Empire proved relatively brief. In 434 a warrior named Attila (*uh-TILL-uh*) became leader of the Huns, and in 441 he began to threaten the Eastern Roman Empire. Constantinople bought him off with tribute, and so in 451 he turned against the west.

Alaric dies, but Rome is soon threatened by Attila and the Huns

Attila the Hun, called the "scourge of God," was a brutal man—but then so were most warriors of his day. Unlike Alaric, however, Attila was neither a Christian nor an admirer of the Roman Empire. As the Huns devastated northern Italy, fear spread that they would move south and lay waste to Rome itself. This fate was avoided in 452 when Pope Leo the Great, having ventured north from Rome to the Huns' encampment, met with Attila and apparently persuaded him to withdraw. Possibly Attila learned from his scouts that Constantinople had sent an army to attack the Huns; probably Attila's forces had been weakened by a recent famine and plague. For whatever reasons, the king of the Huns turned away—and died in his sleep the very next year from a severe nosebleed, reportedly after getting drunk to celebrate his own wedding.

Pope Leo dissuades Attila from marching on Rome

The Fall of Rome and End of the Western Roman Empire

Rome had been saved from the Huns, but the position of the Western Roman Empire continued to deteriorate. Germanic tribes continued to invade, often meeting little resistance, driving into Britain, Gaul (France), Spain, northwest Africa, and Italy itself (Map 9.3).

Chaos in the west ruins commerce and regional connections

Interregional commerce, hampered by constant warfare, virtually disappeared in the west, as did collection of imperial revenues. People subsisted in self-contained local economies, with little access to goods or information from other parts of the empire. Commerce continued to thrive in the east, but in the west the connections that knit the empire together increasingly unraveled.

Germans force last western emperor to abdicate in 476 C.E.

The western emperors could no longer control what happened in the provinces or even defend Rome itself. The Vandals sacked the city in 455, marking the beginning of the end. Twenty-one years later a Germanic general called Odoacer (*Ō-dō-Ā-sur*) forced the abdication of a boy named Romulus Augustulus (*ROM-yoo-lus ah-GUS-tyoo-lus*), the last Roman emperor in the west. This action completed the process, begun by Diocletian and Constantine, of reorienting the Roman Empire to the east. In the west, with Rome itself in the hands of the Germans, the empire simply ceased to exist in 476 C.E.

Technically, the Roman Empire did not end in 476: since it continued to function in the east, all that had fallen was its ancient capital and its western provinces. Emperors reigned in Constantinople for almost another millennium, claiming all the while to rule the Roman Empire. Indeed, when Constantinople finally fell to the Turks in 1453, the victorious Turkish sultan promptly assumed the title of "Roman emperor."

Empire continues in the east while popes dominate in the west

Yet two things changed dramatically in 476, and history changed with them. First, by deposing the last western emperor, Odoacer removed from Rome its traditional symbol of imperial authority. This authority soon would be claimed by the popes, who, as bishops of Rome, held the most prestigious position remaining in the west. In succeeding centuries, by asserting secular as well as spiritual authority, the popes would place the Christian Church at the center of Europe's politics as well as its religion. Second, with the Germans in control of Rome, the rulers in Constantinople, later called Byzantine emperors, could no longer assert their authority in the west. Although it would take centuries for Europeans to recognize this reality, the Western Roman Empire was gone, and the future of the west would hence be shaped by its Germanic conquerors.

Early Medieval Europe:
Germanic and Christian Connections

In Europe the period from the fall of Rome through the fourteenth century, since it came between ancient and modern times, is known as the Middle Ages, or **medieval** (*mē-dē-E-vul*) era. In the early part of this era, dominated by Germanic tribes that had overrun the Western Roman Empire, European society was characterized by tribalism and localism. In central and western Europe, with the end of Roman rule, Roman cities, roads, trade, and money fell into disuse. Learning and literacy declined, interregional commerce dwindled, and central administration virtually disappeared.

The end of Western Empire gives rise to Medieval Western culture

In the long run, however, conflict and fragmentation in the west helped foster creative new connections. Europeans gradually developed a new culture, blending Germanic and Celtic customs with Christian beliefs and the remnants of the Roman heritage. For a time in the early 800s, a Germanic empire reunited much of the Christian West. That realm, however, soon disintegrated, and Europe was devastated by new nomadic invasions and raids from the north, east, and south. Nonetheless, by the eleventh century, led by a landed warrior nobility and an energized Christian Church, Europe experienced a political and cultural revival.

The Emergence of Germanic Kingdoms

At the start of the Middle Ages the Germans were still grouped in tribes, united by kinship and custom, and ruled by chieftains typically elected from among the strongest warriors. Although hunting and fighting remained central to their heritage, most tribes by this time had settled into an agricultural life, dwelling in villages while tending their crops and herds. Families remained patriarchal, dominated by male heads of household, with women in supportive roles. Men typically tended cattle and raised grains such as wheat and barley, while women ground the grain, baked bread, and helped work the land. Wealth was measured in cattle and land, often acquired by the warriors, who thus came to form an early kind of rural nobility.

As cultivation increased food supplies that supported population growth, some Germanic groups—including the Ostrogoths and later the Lombards in Italy, the Visigoths in Spain, the Franks in what is now France, and the Angles and Saxons in England—set up kingdoms (Map 9.4). Unlike tribes, which were groups of people,

Germanic peoples set up kingdoms, ruled by dynastic monarchies

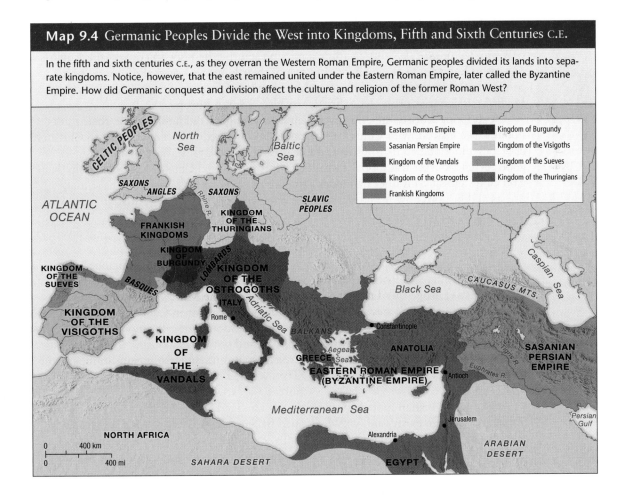

Map 9.4 Germanic Peoples Divide the West into Kingdoms, Fifth and Sixth Centuries C.E.

In the fifth and sixth centuries C.E., as they overran the Western Roman Empire, Germanic peoples divided its lands into separate kingdoms. Notice, however, that the east remained united under the Eastern Roman Empire, later called the Byzantine Empire. How did Germanic conquest and division affect the culture and religion of the former Roman West?

kingdoms were large units of territory ruled by monarchs often chosen from the same royal family, or dynasty. The national monarchies that later grew out of these kingdoms eventually became Europe's foremost form of governance.

The Early Medieval Church: Expansion and Adaptation

The central institution of the early Middle Ages, however, was not the Germanic kingdoms but the Christian Church. Led by the popes in Rome, the Church managed to win the allegiance of the Germans and Celts, to preserve elements of Christian learning from the Roman era, to care for the poor and the sick, and to provide religious unity in the midst of political fragmentation. By maintaining its Roman heritage, while adapting the Christian faith to Germanic and Celtic cultures, the Church also helped to shape a new European society.

Church converts Celts and Germans to Christianity

The Church strove to Christianize the Germans and Celts, usually by working through tribal chiefs or kings. In the mid-fifth century, for example, a bishop from Britain named Patrick, who as a youth had spent time as a slave in Ireland, used this approach to convert that island's Celtic tribes. Around 496 King Clovis of the Franks adopted Christianity, supposedly after his prayers to the God of his Christian wife Clotilda had helped him win a great battle. In 597 a Roman monk named Augustine (*AW-gus-tēn* or *ah-GUS-tin*), heading a mission sent by the pope to convert the Anglo-Saxons in England, began by baptizing one of their kings and several thousand of his people. Later, after Ireland and England had become Christian strongholds, Irish and English missionaries promoted Christianity elsewhere in Europe.

Baptism of Clovis as depicted in a later engraving.

In adopting Christianity, however, Celts and Germans did not abandon their traditional ways. Instead, with Church approval, they converted their old shrines into Christian churches and modified their festivals into Christian holy days. Rather than praying for good fortune to their traditional gods, the people now asked Christian saints to help them gain God's blessings. Rather than conducting trials and ordeals based on tribal ritual, priests and bishops now presided at them in the name of Christ. The Christian faith was thus adapted to fit Celtic and Germanic cultures.

Germanic Western Christianity diverges from Eastern Christianity

In adjusting to these rural, tribal cultures, western Christianity increasingly diverged from the more urbane and cosmopolitan Christian culture of the Byzantine east. Aware of the growing gap, the Church in the west sought to preserve some semblance of Christian learning and Roman culture, especially in Christian monasteries.

Monasteries help preserve faith and learning in west

Medieval Europe thus was shaped by **monasticism** (*muh-NASS-tih-siz-um*), a movement in which especially devout men (called monks) and women (called nuns) withdrew from secular society to live in religious communities (monasteries for monks and convents for nuns), where life was characterized by prayer and self-denial. During the Middle Ages, Christian monasteries played a prominent role in western scholarship, education, agriculture, hospitality, charity, and health care. They worked effectively to spread the Christian faith, and later to reform the Christian Church.

Although Christian monasticism originally emerged in third-century Egypt, its most influential western expression was developed by Saint Benedict (480–543). An earnest and devout young man from a wealthy family, Benedict withdrew from the affluence of urban Rome to live a life of poverty and meditation in the wilderness, in time attracting

Document 9.3 Excerpts from the *Rule* of Saint Benedict

In founding his monastic movement, Saint Benedict (480–543) wrote a Rule, or set of regulations for monks, which his sister Scholastica later adapted for nuns. As reflected in the following excerpts, the Rule prescribed a life of austere humility, based on renunciation of personal possessions (poverty), repression of "desires of the flesh" (chastity), and total submission to superiors such as the abbot who headed the monastery (obedience).

Holy Scripture, brethren, cries out to us, saying, "Everyone who exalts himself shall be humbled, and he who humbles himself shall be exalted" (Luke 14:11) . . .

The first degree of humility, then, is that a person keep the fear of God before his eyes and beware of ever forgetting it. Let him be ever mindful of all that God has commanded; let his thoughts constantly recur to the hell-fire which will burn for their sins those who despise God, and to the life everlasting which is prepared for those who fear Him. Let him keep himself at every moment from sins and vices, whether of the mind, the tongue, the hands, the feet, or the self-will, and check also the desires of the flesh . . .

As for self-will, we are forbidden to do our own will by the Scripture, which says to us, "Turn away from your own will" (Eccles. 18:30), and likewise by the prayer in which we ask God that His will be done in us . . .

And as for the desires of the flesh, let us believe with the Prophet that God is ever present to us, when he says to the Lord, "Every desire of mine is before You" (Ps. 37:10). We must be on our guard, therefore, against evil desires, for death lies close by the gate of pleasure . . .

The second degree of humility is that a person love not his own will nor take pleasure in satisfying his desires, but model his actions on the saying of the Lord, "I have come not to do My own will, but the will of Him who sent Me" (John 6:38) . . .

The third degree of humility is that a person for love of God submit himself to his Superior in all obedience, imitating the Lord, of whom the Apostle says, "He became obedient even unto death."

. . . Let no one presume to give or receive anything without the Abbot's leave, or to have anything as his own—anything whatever, whether book or tablets or pen or whatever it may be—since they are not permitted to have even their bodies or wills at their own disposal; but for all their necessities let them look to the Father of the monastery. And let it be unlawful to have anything which the Abbot has not given or allowed. Let all things be common to all, as it is written (Acts 4:32), and let no one say or assume that anything is his own.

SOURCE: The Order of Saint Benedict, *The Rule of Benedict*. Chapter 7: On Humility (http://www.osb. org/rb/text/rbejms3.html#7), Chapter 33: Whether Monks Ought to Have Anything of Their Own (http://www.osb.org/rb/text/rbejms3.html#7).

similar young men to join him as monks. He eventually founded a monastery on a hill called Monte Cassino and wrote for the monks a *Rule*, or set of regulations for monastic life, which his sister Scholastica (*skuh-LASS-tih-kuh*) later adapted for women. Throughout the Middle Ages, the *Rule* of Saint Benedict would set the standards not only for his followers, known as Benedictines, but also for most other western monastic communities (see "Excerpts from the *Rule* of Saint Benedict").

In keeping with Benedict's *Rule*, monks and nuns took vows of poverty, chastity, and obedience, pledging thereby to forsake personal possessions, abstain from sex, and fully submit to their monastic superior. They lived in communities based on equality and hard work: whether sons of nobles or slaves, monks were expected to labor in the fields and

Abbey of Monte Cassino, on the site of Saint Benedict's first monastery.

Monasteries provide havens for prayer, learning, farming, and charity

live a life of self-denial. They promoted learning by setting up local schools, maintaining libraries, writing books, and copying religious manuscripts. They advanced agriculture by clearing swamps and woodlands and by implementing new farming methods. They provided charity for people in need, hospitality for travelers, and sometimes even health care for the sick. In a fragmented and dangerous world, monasteries provided a safe haven for prayer, learning, farming, and charity. They also promoted Christian beliefs throughout Europe, with significant assistance from the rulers of the Franks.

The Franks and Their Effort to Reunite the West

Frankish rulers expand their realm and help spread Christianity

The realm of the Franks was the most expansive of all the Germanic kingdoms. King Clovis (481–511) not only accepted Christianity but also expanded his domain to include most of what is now France and western Germany (Map 9.4). His heirs, however, proved less capable than he, and by the early eighth century they were largely relying on an official called the mayor of the palace to run their affairs. One such mayor was Charles Martel, who defended the Frankish kingdom against the Muslims, recent conquerors of Spain, by defeating their forces near Tours (*TOOR*) in central France in 732 (Chapter 11). As a result, he gained fame in the west as Europe's savior from Islamic conquest. He also supported Benedictine monks from England, led by Saint Boniface (*BAH-nih-fiss*), in their efforts to Christianize central Europe. In return, Boniface anointed Martel's son Pepin (*PEP-in*) as King of the Franks in 751, helping him take the throne from an ineffective ruler. Charles Martel's descendants, later known as the Carolingian (*kar-uh-LIN-jun*) dynasty (from *Carolus*, Latin for Charles), thus came to rule the Frankish realm.

Charlemagne's conquests reunite much of western and central Europe

These events set the stage for the remarkable reign of Pepin's son Charles (768–814), known to history as "Charles the Great," or Charlemagne (*SHAR-luh-MĀN*). Standing well over six feet tall in an age when most men were much shorter, Charlemagne, who had boundless energy, was the most commanding of all the early medieval warrior-kings. In a pivotal series of conflicts he conquered the Saxons in north Germany, the Lombards in north Italy, and various other Germanic peoples; he also took land from the Muslims in northeast Spain and the Byzantines in east central Europe (Map 9.5). He thereby reunited most of western and central Europe for the first time since the fall of Rome.

Charlemagne's chapel at Aachen.

The symbolic climax of Charlemagne's career was provided by the pope. In 799, attacked by his enemies in Rome, Pope Leo III (795–816) escaped and found refuge in northwest Germany with Charlemagne, who then restored the fugitive pope to the papacy (office of the pope). Leo soon found a dramatic way to show his appreciation, as well as to assert the Church's secular political power. On Christmas Day 800, as Charlemagne knelt in solemn worship during a visit to Rome, the pope suddenly crowned him "Charles Augustus, . . . Emperor of the Romans." It looked as if the Roman Empire had been revived in the west.

But Charlemagne's realm, vast as it was, was still in many ways a Germanic kingdom. Its capital was not in Rome but at Aachen (*AH-ken*) in northwest Germany; its center was not the Mediterranean Sea but the Rhine River; its rulers were not Romans but Franks; and its emperor, for all his talent, was still a semi-literate warrior king. Indeed, Charlemagne's coronation horrified the Byzantine rulers at Constantinople, who regarded their realm as the real Roman Empire and resented the new Germanic imitation of it in the west.

Map 9.5 Charlemagne's Empire Reunites the West, 768–814 C.E.

In his long and eventful reign, Charlemagne, ruler of the Franks, created an empire that reunited much of Western and Central Europe. Notice that he not only conquered the Saxons and Lombards but also subjected some Slavic states to tribute. Note also, however, that his realm was a Frankish, not a Roman, Empire, with its capital in the north at Aachen rather than in Rome. How did Charlemagne differ from the former Roman rulers, and how did his empire differ from the former Roman realm?

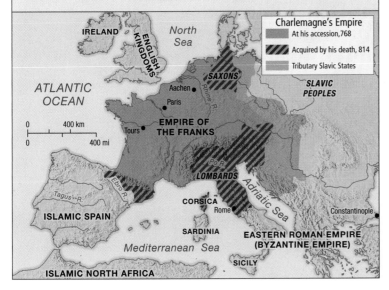

Charlemagne's Empire
- At his accession, 768
- Acquired by his death, 814
- Tributary Slavic States

Undeterred, Charlemagne strove to consolidate and educate his empire. He compelled the Saxons and other polytheists in his realm to adopt Christianity. At Aachen, under the guidance of a learned English Benedictine monk named Alcuin (*AL-koo-in*), he assembled scholars who copied manuscripts, founded libraries, and set up schools at monasteries and cathedrals throughout Europe. Alcuin's curriculum, divided into a *trivium* (*TRIV-ē-um*) made up of grammar, rhetoric and logic, and a *quadrivium* (*kwah-DRIV-ē-um*) of arithmetic, astronomy, geometry, and music, became the standard for medieval European education.

Charlemagne promotes Christianity and learning

Charlemagne's efforts, however, had only a limited impact. Very few people, for example, actually received an education. By this time most people in the west spoke Germanic dialects, which later evolved into languages such as German and English, or regional offshoots of Latin, which developed into languages such as French, Italian, and Spanish. Only the literate elite, mostly monks and Church officials, could read and write formal Latin, which remained the language of learning throughout the Middle Ages.

Regional languages develop, but the Church and the learned use Latin

Furthermore, after Charlemagne died in 814, his Carolingian Frankish Empire did not long endure. In 843 his three grandsons, after fighting among themselves, divided the

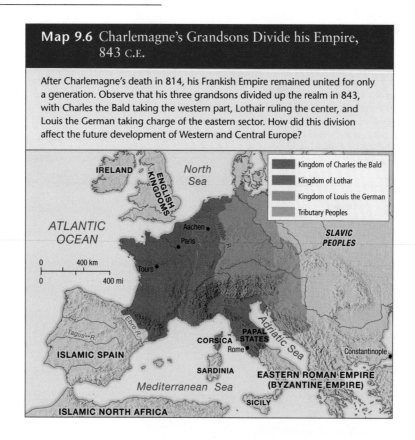

Map 9.6 Charlemagne's Grandsons Divide his Empire, 843 C.E.

After Charlemagne's death in 814, his Frankish Empire remained united for only a generation. Observe that his three grandsons divided up the realm in 843, with Charles the Bald taking the western part, Lothair ruling the center, and Louis the German taking charge of the eastern sector. How did this division affect the future development of Western and Central Europe?

realm into three separate kingdoms (Map 9.6). The middle kingdom soon fragmented still further, while the western one went on to form the basis for medieval France, and the eastern one the basis for medieval Germany.

Vikings, Muslims, and Magyars: Invasions and Connections

Christian Europe after Charlemagne also experienced a series of new invasions. In the ninth and tenth centuries, it was assaulted by outsiders, coming first by sea from the north and the south and later by land from the east. Although these invaders pillaged towns and ravaged the countryside, they also helped to create new connections between Europe and other cultures.

By sea from the north came Norsemen, or Vikings, seafaring warriors who exploded out of Scandinavia in the ninth and tenth centuries, propelled perhaps by a growing population and a scarcity of food. With superior seamanship and shallow-draft ships, using both sails and oars, they dominated the coasts and rivers of Europe, plundering numerous towns for slaves and booty, and even robbing churches and monasteries of their precious vessels and vestments. But the northern invaders were not always destructive. Many settled along the European coasts, trading with Muslims and Byzantines and eventually adopting Christianity. Some Norsemen, known as Normans, took control of the region now called Normandy in northwestern France, from which their successors in 1066 conquered England

Viking ship.

Vikings ravage Europe but create new kingdoms and commerce

Map 9.7 Viking, Muslim, and Magyar Invasions, Ninth and Tenth Centuries C.E.

In the ninth and tenth centuries, Christian Europe was beset by sea and land attacks from all directions. Note that Vikings invaded from the north, ravaging coastlines and plying the rivers from Western Europe to Russia, while the Magyars came by land from the east and the Muslims by sea from the south. How did these incursions, which brought widespread loss and destruction, also help expand commercial and cultural connections between the Europeans and their neighbors?

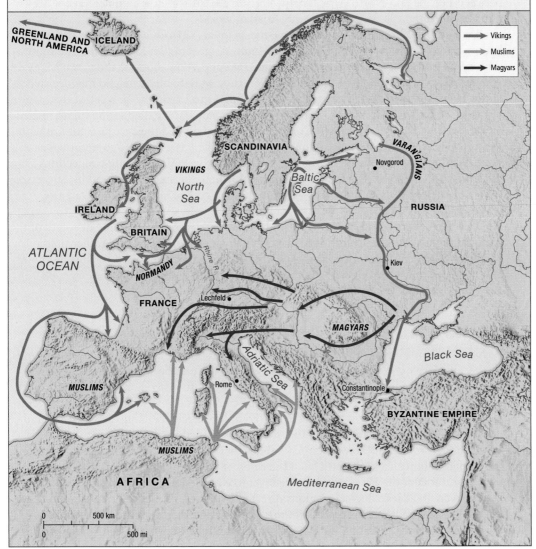

and became its kings and nobles. Other Norsemen, called Varangians (*vuh-RAN-junz*), reportedly served as early rulers of Kievan Rus (*KĒ-ev-un ROOS*), the first Russian state, which forged commercial and religious links with the Byzantine Empire (Chapter 10). Still other Norsemen explored the north Atlantic, founding settlements in Ireland, Iceland, Greenland, and even for a time on the coast of North America (Map 9.7).

By sea from the south in the meantime came Muslims, also known in Europe as Saracens (*SAIR-uh-senz*). In the mid-ninth century, seaborne marauders from Islamic North Africa staged periodic raids along Europe's Mediterranean coast. Unlike the eighth-century Muslim warriors defeated by Charles Martel, who came to conquer lands and spread their faith, the skillful Saracen sailors came mainly to plunder. Indeed, in 846, they pillaged the city of Rome. Still, these Muslim raiders, by plying the sea routes between Europe and North Africa, helped create a basis for later commercial connections between the Islamic and western Christian worlds.

By land from the east a bit later came the Magyars (*MAH-jarz*), warlike tribes that had migrated westward from their Ural mountain homeland. Starting in the late ninth century they struck deep into central Europe. Like the Vikings before them, the Magyars pillaged towns and plundered the land. In 955 they were finally defeated in a decisive battle at Lechfeld (*LEK-feld*) by the forces of King Otto I (936–973), ruler of the eastern Frankish domains in Germany. Eventually the Magyars, later called Hungarians, settled in what is now Hungary, adopted Christianity, and combined their eastern culture with western Christian ideals. Their conqueror, who emerged as a heroic figure known as Otto the Great, was crowned by the pope as emperor in 962. Claiming connections with the Christian Church of Rome and the imperial Roman heritage, Otto and his successors were called Holy Roman Emperors—although they were really Germanic warriors whose realm was mostly German, not Roman.

Germanic warriors in fact proved vital to Europe's recovery from the disasters of the ninth and tenth centuries, but this recovery relied on regional warlords rather than on powerful monarchs who ruled large domains. Their security shattered by outside raiders and invaders, and their hopes for unity dashed by the dissolution of Charlemagne's empire, Europeans increasingly looked to warrior nobles to protect their society.

Europe's Warrior Nobility: Protection, Land, and Power

Responding to the invasions and political fragmentation of the ninth and tenth centuries, Europeans developed a new set of arrangements to restore the security and stability needed for a farming economy. Rather than submitting to a strong central state, as in the days of the Roman and Frankish Empires, they came to depend for their defense on autonomous regional warlords. Connected by complex allegiances and sustained by landed estates, these warlords developed into a hereditary landed nobility.

Although rooted in the warrior assemblies that long had served Germanic chieftains, the landed nobility arose directly from the ruins of the Frankish realm. To administer their vast domain, the Franks had divided it into counties, each managed by a count, and later also created large duchies, regions directed by dukes. As central authority waned in the decades after Charlemagne's death, these counts and dukes eventually became autonomous warlords. Treating their positions as hereditary, they amassed landed wealth and assembled powerful armies.

With the onslaught of outside invaders in the 800s and 900s, lesser lords and landowners were forced to accept the protection of these great warlords and become their **vassals**, subordinate warlords who swore allegiance and pledged military service to a higher lord, their overlord. In return for such allegiance and service, the overlords often gave their vassals grants of land called fiefs (*FĒFZ*). In the absence of strong central government, these warlords exercised political and military power on the local and regional level. Strengthened by their warrior status and sustained by their possession of land, they evolved into hereditary nobles. Typically less than 5 percent of the population, they exercised enormous influence based on their family's rank and status, the extent of their land holdings, the size of their armies, and the number of their vassals.

Warfare was central to the status and family life of the medieval nobility. The lords (noblemen) fought wars, training for combat and hunting between conflicts to sustain their military skills, while the ladies (noblewomen) managed the households, caring for children and supervising servants so the lords could go off to hunt, train, and fight. Noblemen served on horseback as **knights**, armed mounted warriors whose code of conduct entailed strict devotion to their overlords and to the Christian Church. As early as age 7, looking forward to future knighthood, boys in noble families were taught by their fathers to ride horses, to hunt, and to use bows and arrows, swords, shields, lances, and armor. Girls in noble families often also learned to ride and hunt, but they were trained mainly for marriage, motherhood, and household management, duties that typically precluded most women from engaging in combat.

Although later observers characterized the arrangements between lords and vassals as a comprehensive system called feudalism, there was really no set system or consistent feudal order. Instead there were numerous individual agreements, often quite different from each other, creating an extremely complex web of relationships. Many vassals, for example, served several lords, based on separate agreements with oaths of service to each. Most lords in turn served as vassals to higher lords. A count, for example, might be a powerful lord with vast landholdings and numerous vassals of his own, but he might also be the vassal of a duke, who might in turn be the vassal of a king. Thus, during wartime, a count and his vassals could be called into service of a duke who had been called into service of a king. Yet the medieval king, despite his lofty status, was not an absolute ruler: he depended on the support of his vassals, the great lords of his realm, some of whom might have stronger armies than he did.

Role of nobles centers on combat and knighthood

Medieval peasant women helping with the harvest and grinding grain into flour.

Economy and Society: Manors, Lords, and Serfs

The nobles, occupied with military duties, did not raise their own food. Instead their **manors**, or landed estates, were worked by peasant farmers. Typically, each noble owned at least one manor. Some were huge, with a massive castle and vast stretches of forest and field; others were much smaller. But even the lowest noble was the lord of his manor and master of all who dwelt there. The peasants, who lived on the manor in a village and cultivated the surrounding fields, were typically required to give the lord a portion of their crop, and perhaps to labor several days a week on land set aside to feed the lord and his family. The peasants thus supported the lord so he could fight, providing some protection and security in a dangerous world.

Nobles own manors, landed estates, worked by peasant farmers

The peasants, who made up 80 to 90 percent of the population, varied widely in status. Some remained free, and a few even prospered. Most, however, became **serfs**, bound to the manor and under the control of its lord. Without the lord's permission, serfs as a rule could not own or inherit property, leave the manor, or even get married. Unlike slaves, serfs supposedly had rights—they did not have to serve in the army, they were not

Peasant serfs, bound to the manor, provide food and labor for landlords

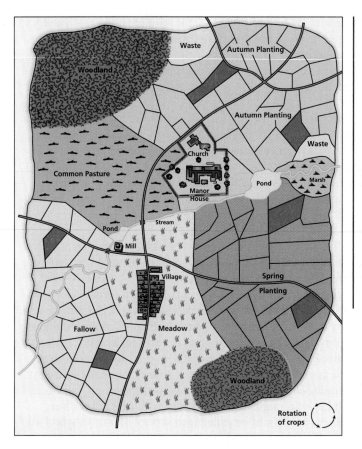

Figure 9.1
Diagram of a Typical Medieval Manor. On a typical medieval manor, the lord who owned it and his family lived in a large manor house, while peasants lived in a village elsewhere on his manor. Each peasant family had a hut in the village and a few strips of land in each surrounding field to farm, as shown by the hut and strips of one family shaded here in red. Each year crops were rotated according to a 3-field system, with one field planted for spring-summer crops, another for autumn-winter crops, and a third left fallow (uncultivated) to regenerate its soil.

supposed to be bought and sold apart from the land, and the lord was expected to provide them with plots of land to farm. In practice, however, there were few restraints on the lord, who could punish his serfs for perceived transgressions by flogging and beating them, sometimes even to death.

Harsh peasant life centers on farming, family, and faith

Peasant life was monotonous and routine, centered on fields, family, and Church. Men were mainly responsible for working the land and tending the herds, the mainstays of economic life. But women typically played numerous crucial roles, grinding grain, baking bread, brewing beer and ale, curing cheese, cooking meals, making clothes, raising children, and often also helping to care for animals, cultivate fields, and harvest crops. Peasants ate mostly dark bread, supplemented by cabbage and carrots, peas and beans, and perhaps eggs and cheese, washed down with wine, beer, or ale. Some peasant families had wood or brick homes that, while modest, had two or more rooms; others lived in one-room windowless huts with dirt floors, thatch roofs, and walls of mud or clay. Peasants received no formal education, rarely traveled beyond the safety of the manor, and had few diversions aside from celebrating baptisms, weddings, and holy days at the village church—their main link to the larger Church and hence to the outside world.

The Decline and Revival of the Western Church

Despite its exalted status in medieval Europe, by the tenth century the Church in the west was in trouble. In some respects, its problems were symptoms of success, since its great wealth and power attracted unscrupulous men to its service, fostering corruption and intrigue. In other respects the decline of the Church was connected with the rise of the regional warlords, who often managed to gain control over local Church offices. The lords used their influence to fill Church positions with their relatives and supporters, at times even selling these positions to the highest bidder. Chosen thus for their loyalty rather than their ability, and provided with little education, local priests were often illiterate and incompetent, while bishops were frequently dishonest and corrupt. In Rome the papacy itself was controlled by powerful local clans, who secured the selection of their family members and agents. A series of scandalous popes led lives of open debauchery, commanding neither influence nor respect.

From Scandal to Reform

In 963 Pope John XII (955–964), an unprincipled young man who had become pope through the influence of his powerful father, was deposed by a council of bishops for crimes including adultery, incest, and murder. Declaring the council illegal, he violently reclaimed his throne, only to die soon thereafter—reportedly either from a stroke that he suffered during an adulterous affair or from a beating inflicted by his lover's furious husband.

Scandals compromise Christian Church in the West

Eighty years later Pope Benedict IX, another immoral young man who became pope through his father's influence, was run out of town by the people of Rome, who replaced him with their own choice as pope. The next five years (1044–1049) saw a rapid succession of popes, as Benedict regained the papacy, sold it to another man, and then later claimed it back. In the meantime, Holy Roman Emperor Henry III placed several of his hand-picked German bishops on the papal throne.

This sorry spectacle actually marked the onset of the Church's revival. The Germans installed by Henry III were the first of a number of reforming popes, many of whom had close connections with Cluny, Europe's most influential monastery. Founded in the tenth century, this French Benedictine monastic institution had been made subject directly and only to the pope in order to keep it free from the control of local rulers and nobles. Its monks over the years had become known for their piety and rigor, and by 1050 they had founded more than sixty daughter houses, all ruled by the mother house at Cluny. Its leaders pushed openly for Church reform, calling for strict priestly **celibacy** (*SELL-ih-buh-sē*), or abstinence from marriage and sex, and an end to **simony** (*SIM-uh-nē*), the sale of Church offices. The Cluniac monks who became pope resolutely attacked Church abuses, restoring the papacy as Europe's preeminent institution. Their efforts were fated to have far-reaching consequences.

Reforming popes enforce priestly celibacy and attack Church abuses

The Great Schism of 1054

Among the most crucial consequences of this papal revival was a reinforcement of a growing rift between eastern and western Church leaders. Ever since Rome had fallen to Germanic tribes, the cosmopolitan Christians of the Eastern Roman Empire had found it hard to accept the supremacy of the Church in the west, increasingly run by Germanic leaders the easterners saw as "barbarians." The four main centers of the eastern Church—Constantinople, Antioch, Jerusalem, and Alexandria—were each led by a patriarch who saw himself as equal to the pope. Although patriarchs might grant the pope senior status as the bishop of Rome, they saw him as "first among equals," regarding him as a senior leader but not as supreme ruler. Over the centuries, in the interests of unity, the eastern patriarchs had usually gone along with the papacy, but they nonetheless resented its claims to overall supremacy.

The papacy's growing strength deepens conflict with Eastern Church

By the eleventh century, however, centuries of friction had worn away any willingness to compromise, and the recent papal scandals had intensified eastern disdain for the papacy and the western Church. Now the new reforming popes, in an effort to attack abuses, were asserting even greater powers and claiming unlimited primacy over the whole Church. The eastern patriarchs found these papal assertions offensive and threatening.

A climax came in 1054, when the patriarch of Constantinople issued an insulting letter to a western bishop that found its way to the dying Pope Leo IX (1049–1054), who then sent envoys to Constantinople to press the patriarch for an apology. Although Leo died several weeks after they arrived, the envoys had several tense meetings with the patriarch and then issued an edict of "excommunication," formally excluding him from Christian worship and from the Christian community. The patriarch responded with a similar edict against the papal envoys.

Conflict in Church brings enduring east-west schism

This episode produced an enduring split between eastern and western Christendom, often called the Great Schism of 1054. Although deepened by longstanding disputes about the wording of the official creed (profession of beliefs) approved during Constantine's reign, the rift was actually rooted in the conflict concerning whether the pope should have total supremacy over the entire Church. The division was not really caused by a single event, but rather by a series of political, cultural, and theological developments occurring over many centuries. The result was the emergence of two separate branches of Christianity: an Eastern Orthodox religion over which the patriarchs presided, and a Western, or Roman Catholic, Church, ruled by the pope in Rome.

The Power of the Popes

Schism frees the popes to focus on reform in West

As divisive as it was, the schism freed the papacy from its involvement in affairs of the eastern Church, thereby allowing subsequent popes to focus on reform in the west and to assert their authority over all other western religious and political leaders. The stage was thus set for conflict between the Roman popes and Europe's secular rulers.

Popes claim supremacy over all secular rulers

In 1059, to ensure that future popes would not be chosen by powerful families or emperors, Pope Nicholas II decreed that new popes must henceforth be elected by a group of specially designated bishops called cardinals. In 1073, the cardinals elected a radical reformer named Hildebrand who had spent time at Cluny. As Pope Gregory VII (1073–1085), he extended the concept of papal supremacy into secular affairs, holding that all lords and princes were his subjects and that he could depose or punish them if he judged their conduct immoral. To free the clerics who served the Church from family attachments and distractions, he made celibacy the rule for all priests and bishops throughout the western Church. He also insisted that only the pope could appoint Church officials.

This attack on corruption and insistence on papal appointment directly threatened Europe's kings and lords, who were used to selecting loyal supporters as bishops in their realms. When Gregory banned lay investiture, a practice in which secular ("lay") rulers conferred on new bishops the symbols of spiritual authority, the German emperor Henry IV openly defied him, refusing to forsake this practice. The pope responded in 1076 by excommunicating and deposing Henry, giving German nobles a convenient pretext to rebel against him. Alarmed but inventive, in January 1077 the deposed emperor went to Canossa in Italy and reportedly stood barefoot in the snow to beg forgiveness of Gregory, who was compelled as a priest to pardon the penitent prince. Henry thus regained his title and later even drove Gregory into exile. But the specter of an emperor humbling himself before the pope nonetheless reinforced the notion of papal authority over secular rulers, paving the way for an even more sensational exercise of papal power.

Pope and emperor clash over right to "invest" bishops

In 1095 Pope Urban II, a former Cluniac monk and disciple of Gregory VII, dramatically proclaimed a great crusade, or holy war, calling on Europe's lords and princes to restore Christian control over the "holy lands" in Palestine where Christ had lived and died. Urban's call touched off a chain of crusades that, although they failed in the long run to achieve their original goal, created further connections and conflicts between the Germanic West and the Byzantine and Muslim worlds (Chapter 16).

Pope Urban II preaches crusade against Muslim rule of 'holy lands'

Chapter Review

Putting It in Perspective

The Germanic migrations, and the resulting division of the Roman Empire, ultimately transformed the west. The German tribes attacked, infiltrated, and eventually triumphed over the Western Roman Empire, replacing it with their own tribal institutions, developing over time into territorial kingdoms. Despite sporadic efforts to restore the empire in the west, central authority waned and Roman institutions fell into disuse. Political, social, and economic life became largely regional and rural, dominated by warlords who also controlled the land. The peasant farmers who tilled the soil eventually sank into serfdom, effectively forsaking freedom in return for security and protection.

The main exception to this decentralization was the Christian Church, which maintained its headquarters in Rome despite the disappearance of the Western Roman Empire. The Church's administrative structure, modeled on that of the old empire, helped to preserve some measure of central authority in the west, while the Church's monasteries helped to sustain some semblance of Latin learning. Indeed, in the absence of other strong central institutions, the Church became Europe's predominant religious and cultural organization, with the popes who led it exercising vast religious and political powers. In converting and incorporating the Germans, however, the Church in the west was altered by their conventions and customs. Eastern Christians hence found it hard to accept the leadership of the Germanicized West, which they considered culturally inferior. Eventually Christianity split into Western and Eastern churches.

In the west, as the warrior nobles and manorial economy helped to restore stability following the Viking, Muslim, and Magyar invasions, a reformed and re-energized papacy asserted its authority over secular rulers. In the east, although the Eastern Roman Empire survived, it too developed new institutions and ideals, forming the basis of what would later be called the Byzantine World.

Reviewing Key Material
KEY CONCEPTS

nation, 210
bishops, 214
pope, 214
papal primacy, 214
medieval, 218
monasticism, 220

vassals, 226
knights, 227
manors, 227
serfs, 227
celibacy, 229
simony, 229

KEY PEOPLE

ASK YOURSELF

1. What were the basic characteristics of the Germanic societies? How and why did these societies connect and conflict with the Roman Empire?

2. Why were the Roman emperors unsuccessful in their efforts to protect the western part of the empire from the Germanic invaders? How did the division of the empire contribute to the fall of the western part?

3. How and why did Christianity become the Roman Empire's main religion? How did this change in status transform the Christian Church?

4. Why did the western Church emerge as the dominant institution in medieval Europe? How did the Church adapt to the Germanic cultures? What factors contributed to divergence and discord between the Western and Eastern churches?

5. Why did Europe's warrior nobility become so powerful in the ninth and tenth centuries? What were the main roles of lords, vassals, manors, and serfs?

GOING FURTHER

Barbero, A. *Charlemagne: Father of a Continent.* 2004.

Brown, Peter. *The Rise of Western Christendom: Triumph and Adversity, A.D. 200–1000.* 2003.

Collins, R. *Early Medieval Europe, 300–1000.* 1991.

Constable, Olivia R. *Housing the Stranger in the Mediterranean World: Lodging, Trade, and Travel in Late Antiquity and the Middle Ages.* 2004.

Coulton, George G. *The Medieval Village.* 1991.

Cruz, Jo Ann, et al. *Medieval Worlds.* 2004.

Duby, Georges. *Rural Economy and Country Life in the Medieval West.* 1990.

Dunn, M. *The Emergence of Monasticism.* 2000.

Edwards, M., trans. *Constantine and Christendom.* 2003.

Fletcher, R. *The Barbarian Conversion: From Paganism to Christianity.* 1997.

Gies, F. and J. *Marriage and Family in the Middle Ages.* 1987.

Hanawalt, Barbara. *The Middle Ages.* 1998.

Haywood, John. *Encyclopedia of the Viking Age.* 2000.

Herrin, J. *The Formation of Christendom.* 1987.

James, Edward. *The Franks.* 1988.

Lawrence, C. H. *Medieval Monasticism: Forms of Religious Life in Western Europe in the Middle Ages.* 1984.

Le Goff, Jacques. *Medieval Civilization, 400–1500.* 1989.

Logan, F. Donald. *The Vikings in History.* 3rd ed. 2005.

Lopez, Robert, et al. *Medieval Trade in the Mediterranean World.* 2001.

Lot, F. *The End of the Ancient World and the Beginning of the Middle Ages.* 2000.

McCormick, Michael. *Origins of the European Economy.* 2001.

McKitterick, R., ed. *Early Middle Ages: Europe, 400–1000.* 2001.

McKitterick, R. *The Frankish Kingdoms Under the Carolingians, 751–987.* 1983.

Pelikan, Jaroslav. *The Excellent Empire: The Fall of Rome and the Triumph of the Church.* 1987.

Power, Eileen. *Medieval People.* 1993.

Reynolds, Susan. *Fiefs and Vassals.* 1994.

Reynolds, Susan. *Kingdoms and Communities in Western Europe, 900–1300.* 2nd ed. 1997.

Riche, P. *The Carolingians: A Family Who Forged Europe.* 1993.

Rosenwein, B. *A Short History of the Middle Ages.* 2002.

Southern, Richard W. *The Making of the Middle Ages.* 1992.

Ward-Perkins, B. *The Fall of Rome and End of Civilization.* 2005.

Wolfram, H. *History of the Goths.* 1988.

Key Dates and Developments

100s–200s	Early Germanic attacks on Roman territory
284–305	Reign of Diocletian (division of the Roman Empire)
312–337	Reign of Constantine (building of Constantinople)
380	Proclamation of Christianity as the Roman state religion
410	Sack of Rome by Alaric and the Visigoths
432	Beginning of Patrick's efforts to Christianize Ireland
451–453	Invasion of Italy by Attila and the Huns
476	Abdication of the last Western Roman Emperor
496	Adoption of Christianity by Clovis and the Franks
529	The *Rule* of Saint Benedict
597–605	Augustine's efforts to Christianize England
732	Defeat of Muslim forces by Charles Martel at Tours
768–814	Reign of Charlemagne, formation of Frankish Empire
843	Division of Frankish Empire by Charlemagne's grandsons
800s–900s	Viking, Magyar, and Saracen invasions
1054	Schism of 1054 (Eastern Orthodox vs. Roman Catholic)
1073–1085	Reign of reforming Pope Gregory VII (Hildebrand)
1095	First Crusade proclaimed by Pope Urban II

The Byzantine World, 284–1240

The Basilica Of Saint Sophia, Constantinople

Interior of the former Basilica of Saint Sophia in Constantinople, a Byzantine church converted to a mosque in 1453. Notice the domed Romanesque architecture (page 244), and imagine the impression such a magnificent building would have made on citizens of Constantinople during the Byzantine Empire.

Justinian, the ailing Roman emperor's nephew and recently appointed co-ruler, prepared to enter a magnificent church on April 4, 527. It was the day of his formal coronation. At his side was his wife Theodora, who would be crowned as empress. The imperial couple was greeted by black-robed priests who prepared them for the ceremony by covering them in clouds of fragrant incense. Once inside the church, Justinian and Theodora proceeded slowly through an immense throng of guests down a long aisle leading to the main altar. Waiting there was another group of priests, robed in cloth-of-gold and wearing jeweled crosses and rings. These priests stood in front of a glittering screen made of gold and silver; on it paintings of holy men and women of early Christianity were displayed. Choirs chanted hymns and prayers as Justinian and Theodora knelt before the priests, beginning the six-hour ceremony.

Byzantine claims in Europe

Kievan Rus

The Byzantine Empire

Justinian was crowned Roman emperor, but his coronation took place hundreds of miles east of the city of Rome. The religious ceremony took place in Constantinople, the "New Rome" founded in the fourth century by Emperor Constantine I. Rome itself was conquered by Germanic invaders in 476, and only the eastern portion of the empire survived. There a new society evolved, preserving Rome's heritage but grounded in its own variant of Christianity and its own conception of the relationship between political and spiritual authority. The realm would be known as the Eastern Roman Empire and later as the Byzantine Empire, after the old city of Byzantium on which the new Constantinople had been built. Situated where Europe and Asia meet, the Byzantine world, often called simply Byzantium, blended elements of East and West but was truly part of neither.

Still, the empire's eastern rulers, however distinct their civilization was becoming, had no intention of writing off the western half. For centuries they would claim it and occasionally succeed in retaking portions of it, though only temporarily. The Byzantine Empire endured without the west for a thousand years. And even after it declined, through centuries of internal and external conflict, its legacy lived on in Russia, which in the tenth century adopted eastern Christianity and joined the Byzantine world.

The Foundations of Byzantine Governance

When Constantine legalized Christianity (Chapter 9), he did not know that he would soon be compelled to resolve its internal disputes and thereby assume leadership in the Christian Church. And when moving his capital east to Constantinople, he scarcely envisioned that the empire's western section would eventually fragment into separate Germanic kingdoms, leaving only the eastern portion intact. But these events set in motion trends that allowed the Eastern Roman Empire to develop separately, with governing structures substantively different from those in the west.

FOUNDATION MAP 10.1 The Early Byzantine Empire, 481 C.E.

After Constantine reoriented the Roman Empire eastward, Germanic tribes gradually overran the western portion of the realm. Following the abdication of the last Western Roman Emperor in 476, only the Eastern Roman Empire, known as the Byzantine Empire, remained. Notice that the Eastern Roman Empire controlled the prosperous commercial region of the eastern Mediterranean. How might this location have assisted the Byzantines in defending the legacy of Rome?

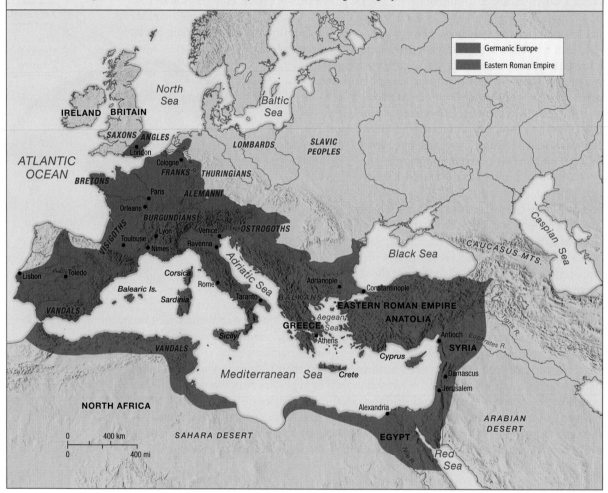

Constantine and the Christian Church

No sooner had Constantine become sole emperor in 324 than he became involved in a serious dispute among Christians. For a decade or so, an Egyptian Christian priest named Arius (*AIR-ē-us*) had been preaching that since God had created Christ, God the Father was older than and superior to God the Son. This perspective differed from the prevailing Christian belief that the Father, Son, and Holy Spirit were three co-equal persons of the Blessed Trinity. Arius's teaching, which his opponents branded a **heresy**—a religious opinion contrary to accepted Church doctrine—left the Christian Church sharply divided. In fact, the Arian Heresy, as it was called, threatened to produce a **schism**, or division of the church into separate, competing churches.

Constantine was perplexed: why should anyone want to quarrel about something that was irrelevant to everyday life and could never be proven or disproven? He instructed the opposing parties to settle the issue amicably. But this advice enraged both sides, provoking Constantine into calling an ecumenical (*eck-ū-MEN-ih-kull*), or worldwide, council of Christian bishops and theologians. It convened in 325 in the Byzantine town of Nicaea (*nī-søĒ-uh*), near Constantinople (Map 10.1), with the emperor himself presiding.

Assuming the role of practical counselor in matters of religion, Constantine intended to enforce uniformity within the Church to which he did not formally belong but with which he sympathized. His presence at Nicaea demonstrated that he was in charge, and he shaped the council's findings in a manner that satisfied the great majority of bishops. The Nicene Creed, a statement of belief drafted by the council that is still recited today in many Christian churches, declared that Christ was "of the same being" as God the Father. A few delegates, including Arius, refused to sign this creed; they were expelled from the council and exiled by the emperor.

Constantine intervenes in Christian affairs

The Union of Church and State

Constantine's forceful intervention in the Council of Nicaea illuminates how governance would develop in the Eastern Roman Empire. While western institutions evolved under the influence of Germanic concepts of kingship, the Byzantines held to and amplified the authoritarian legacy of the caesars. Their political institutions were also derived in large measure from the monarchist principles of Alexander the Great and his successors, in which the ruler was exalted above all. For example, the eastern Roman emperor was referred to as "lord of the world." After the Emperor Theodosius the Great proclaimed Christianity the official religion of the empire in 380, he and future rulers were also called "equal of the Apostles." The interchangeable use of these two titles reflected the combination of secular and spiritual authority in one man.

In Constantinople, the rulers embraced Christianity fervently. The emperor was viewed as God's vice-regent on earth, a sacred person who headed the Church as well as the state and who acted with the fullness of divine as well as human authority. This was the Byzantine concept of **caesaropapism** (*sē-zar-ō-PĀ-pizm*), the vesting of all spiritual and political authority in a single person—a man who served as both caesar and pope. It contrasted profoundly with the position taken by the bishop of Rome, who claimed no political supremacy, but called himself head of the Christian Church (or pope) and used his spiritual authority to curb the ambitions of kings and princes after the Western Roman Empire collapsed in 476.

Caesaropapism unifies spiritual and political authority

In the east, however, a patriarch exercised spiritual leadership over a Christian community equivalent to that exercised by a bishop in the west. Each of the four eastern patriarchs—of Constantinople, Antioch, Jerusalem, and Alexandria—considered himself equal to the bishop of Rome and subject solely to the emperor in Constantinople. They did not recognize the bishop of Rome's claim to lead the entire Christian Church, maintaining instead that overall leadership was vested solely in the emperor.

In the emerging Byzantine world, then, Church and state were united in the person of the ruler. In relocating the capital of the empire, Constantine infused it with the spirit of a new, dynamic faith that half a century later would be proclaimed the empire's official religion. These actions revolutionized both government and society in the Eastern Roman Empire, accelerating the decline of paganism and embedding Christianity in the popular culture. This all-embracing, vigorous Christianity made caesaropapism work and laid the foundations of Byzantine governance.

Early Byzantium: Challenges and Survival

In the two centuries following Constantine's death in 337, the Roman Empire's western section gradually gave way to Germanic pressure, its own internal weaknesses, and the neglect it suffered after the transfer of the capital to Constantinople. But the stability of the eastern part was by no means ensured. First, religious problems continued to distract the empire. In 361 Emperor Julian (361–363) tried to revive paganism and reverse the trend toward Christianization. For his actions he was called "the Apostate"—a person who abandons a religion and returns to a previous belief system. Julian's return to paganism might have led to civil war had he not been killed fighting the Persians in 363. Sasanian Persia constituted a second threat to the empire's stability. Fortunately for the Byzantines, the Sasanian Empire was large and cumbersome, and if it sent too many soldiers against Constantinople, it risked uprisings among the non-Persian peoples along its own eastern frontiers.

Sasanian Persia challenges the Byzantine Empire

For the next century, as Germans overran the western empire, Constantinople survived, for it was too strategically situated and too well defended to be attacked directly. When the Western Roman Empire collapsed in 476, the eastern empire was holding off the Ostrogoths in southeastern Europe. Constantinople could not have dispatched a powerful army to save Rome without endangering itself. Now only the eastern empire remained. Although future emperors would long refuse to acknowledge the loss of the west, their efforts to regain it proved futile.

Justinian and Theodora

Gradually the eastern character of the empire intensified. The Emperor Justinian, who ruled from 527 to 565, exercised power even more forcefully than Constantine had. He was determined to make the most of the awesome powers of caesaropapism.

Born in Macedonia in 482, Justinian became in his mid-thirties the power behind the throne of his uncle, the Emperor Justin. Through Justin he negotiated a reunification of the Christian Church, which had been divided since the Roman pope and patriarch of Constantinople had excommunicated one another in 484. Justinian stood firm in his belief in unity, both religious and imperial: just as there was one God, so must there be one Church and one Roman Empire. When he came to the throne in 527, he was determined to restore and maintain those unities under God, of whose will he considered himself, as a caesaropapist, the chief executive on earth.

Justinian resolves to reunify both Church and Empire

Justinian was a disciplined autocrat—a ruler whose authority was unlimited. He was also a shrewd judge of men and a gifted administrator. In addition, he married a woman whose skills complemented and enhanced his own. Theodora, a comic actress and strip-tease dancer whose parents were circus people, had enthralled Justinian when she performed at his court. He promptly overcame the horrified protests of his counselors and made her his wife. When he was crowned Emperor in 527, he insisted that she be crowned

Empress—a formal designation as co-ruler. With an iron will and outstanding political judgment, Theodora worked tirelessly in the service of her husband and the empire.

In 532, when a violent uprising against his rule threatened his life, Justinian consulted his advisors and decided to flee Constantinople. But Theodora disagreed, arguing that in an hour of peril a ruler must not abandon his responsibilities. Neither emperor nor advisors would ordinarily have taken that sort of rebuke from a woman, but Theodora was Empress, a regular participant in imperial deliberations and a superb politician. Shamed by her courage and logic, Justinian and his advisors remained in Constantinople and put down the rebellion.

Theodora overcomes Justinian's caution

CODIFICATION OF ROMAN LAW.

Justinian and Theodora were autocrats, but they ruled by Roman law and not by whim. With Roman order overturned by Germanic control of the West, Justinian decided to codify and streamline the law. He appointed prominent jurists to compile all the laws of Rome that were still in force; they were published in 529 as the Code of Justinian. This pathbreaking collection of statutes made Roman law the most influential legal system in history. The Byzantine Empire preserved it for centuries, eventually returning it to Western Europe.

Byzantium codifies Roman law

The Code not only preserved Roman law, however, but also inadvertently froze it. Exalted by the Byzantines as a perfect system, Roman law was closed to the possibility of further change. It remains the foundation of the modern legal systems of many Western nations but never displayed the flexibility to adapt and change that would later characterize Anglo-American law (see "Excerpt from the Code of Justinian").

Empress Theodora and attendants.

ATTEMPTS TO REUNITE THE EMPIRE.

Justinian's Code was the foundation of his honest and efficient administration. But his government was in constant financial distress, largely because of its extensive and expensive military commitments. Throughout his reign, Justinian waged war to reunify the Roman Empire.

Reunification was unlikely, however, given the circumstances of the day. By the time of Justinian, two distinct cultures had evolved, the one Byzantine, the other a blend of Roman and Germanic. Their political and religious institutions were so different that permanent reunification could have been achieved only by occupation, and a standing occupation force large enough to secure Rome was too large for the Byzantines to afford. The Germanic tribes that had conquered the western empire were powerful forces in their own right, and in any case Byzantine troops were needed to defend the eastern empire against the Persians on its eastern border.

Nevertheless, Justinian's political and economic realism was overridden by his religious faith. Not only did a Roman Empire without Rome seem absurd, but he was also disturbed by the heretical Germanic kingdom that ruled Rome. Those Germans were Arian Christians, believing that Christ was a divine creature made by God. The Arian Heresy had been condemned at the Council of Nicaea more than a century earlier, and Justinian would not tolerate its presence in Rome.

So for the next three decades the Byzantine Empire waged war, despite lacking forces to fight on its eastern and western frontiers simultaneously. Whenever Byzantium advanced in Italy and reoccupied Rome, the Persians attacked in the east. When Byzantine troops were shifted to the east, the Germans took back the territory they had lost in Italy. The arrival of the bubonic plague in 541—its first recorded appearance in the eastern Mediterranean region—further weakened the Byzantine forces.

Justinian's religious convictions drive him to attack Rome

Document 10.1 Excerpt from the Code of Justinian

"The compilation of Roman law which was enacted under the Byzantine emperor, Justinian I . . . has been without doubt the most important and influential collection of secular legal materials that the world has ever known. The compilation preserved Roman law for succeeding generations and nations. All later Western systems borrowed extensively from it." (Allen Watson, page xxiii)

BOOK ONE, PART I

10. Justice is a steady and enduring will to render unto everyone his right. The basic principles of right are: to live honorably, not to harm any other person, to render to each his own. Practical wisdom in matters of right is an awareness of God's and men's affairs, knowledge of justice and injustice.

11. The term "law" is used in several senses: in one sense, when law is used as meaning what is always fair and good, it is natural law; in the other, as meaning what is in the interest of everyone . . . it is civil law.

BOOK ONE, PART III

31. The emperor is not bound by statutes.

BOOK ONE, PART IV

1. A decision given by the emperor has the force of a statute. This is because the populace commits to him and into him its own entire authority and power . . .

BOOK ONE, PART V

1. All our law concerns [either] persons or things or actions.

3. Certainly, the great divide in the law of persons is this: all men are either free men or slaves.

4. Freedom is one's natural power of doing what one pleases, save insofar as it is ruled out either by coercion or by law. Slavery is an institution . . . whereby someone is against nature made subject to the ownership of another. Slaves are so-called, because generals have a custom of selling their prisoners and thereby preserving rather than killing them.

9. There are many points in our law in which the condition of females is inferior to that of males.

BOOK TWENTY-FOUR, PART II

3. A true divorce does not take place unless an intention to remain apart permanently is present. So things said or done in anger are not effective unless the parties show by their persistence that they are an indication of their considered opinion. So where repudiation takes place in anger and the wife returns shortly afterward, she is not held to have divorced her husband.

BOOK TWENTY-FOUR, PART III

1. An action for the dowry takes precedence at all times and in all circumstances; for it is in the public interest for women to keep their dowries, since it is absolutely essential for women to have dowries so that they can produce offspring and replenish the state with their children.

SOURCE: Allen Watson, trans. and ed. *The Digest of Justinian*, Volume I (Philadelphia: University of Pennsylvania, 1985).

The Byzantine Empire becomes culturally Greek rather than Latin

As the Byzantine Empire became increasingly eastern and less Roman, it became increasingly Greek. Constantine's creation of a new capital had at first expanded knowledge of Latin in the east, since much of the empire's administration was transferred to Constantinople. But Greek remained the spoken language of the Eastern Roman Empire, and gradually it replaced Latin in official transactions. Greek was also more prestigious than Latin: public speeches in Constantinople were normally given in Greek, and it was

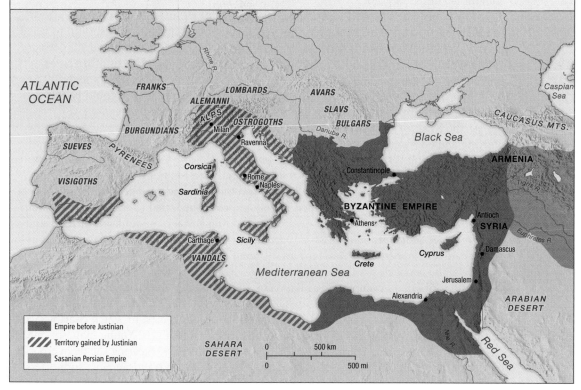

Map 10.2 The Byzantine Empire During Justinian's Reign, 527–565

Justinian, the last of the Latin-speaking emperors, never accepted the loss of the Western Roman Empire. In comparing this map with Map 10.1, note that Justinian's armies reconquered sizable segments of the West. Pressure from other areas, however, made it impossible for Justinian to hold his gains and prevented his successors from undertaking further westward initiatives. Where might this pressure have come from?

the language of instruction in all Byzantine schools except those teaching law. Justinian was the last native Latin-speaking Byzantine emperor.

Justinian's death in 565 was a significant event in the ongoing turning of the empire away from Rome. His successors, lacking his commitment to reunification, did little to realize it. As Rome receded in significance, Byzantine efforts were concentrated against pressures from the Persians in the east (Map 10.2). Then, from the seventh century onward, the Arabs in the south and southeast proved an even more dangerous foe. Eventually, Constantinople had little choice but to let go of the west.

Byzantine Society

During the two centuries from Constantine to Justinian, Byzantine society was prosperous and even wealthy. The Roman emperors brought from the west a privileged imperial court; a large, generally efficient and well-compensated bureaucracy; legions of ambitious entrepreneurs; clever con men on the lookout for every angle; and assorted hangers-on hopeful that some of the glory of the New Rome would rub off on their cloaks.

This transplanted society's showplace was Constantinople, whose population approached 400,000 in the early sixth century C.E. Ships docked in the Golden Horn, the city's inner harbor, bringing treasured goods from Asia and Africa. The city's artisans created splendid wares and textiles. The imperial court glistened with jewels, while visitors admitted to the emperor's presence passed by artificial trees filled with mechanical songbirds crafted in gold.

Constantinople becomes a major trading center

Constantinople's superb location gave it control of the trade routes of the eastern Mediterranean, and its vibrant economy amply justified Constantine's decision to build his new capital there. Grain and cotton from Egypt, spices from India, and silks from China were traded on the docks not only of Constantinople but also of other cities throughout the realm. Transporting goods by sea instead of land made trade in bulk profitable and lowered prices on imported goods enough so that they could be purchased not only by the aristocracy but also by a developing middle class.

As the Byzantine Empire's urban economy expanded, it was run by an increasingly wealthy and confident commercial class. City women enjoyed substantial mobility and freedom of action. Many owned shops, kept the books for merchant houses, and bartered with traders from three continents. But this prosperity rested not only on trade but also on the labors of masses of peasants who worked the land and supplied food and soldiers for the empire. Rural people remained largely impoverished, tied to the land, the production of food, and the reproduction of enough children to keep the ranks of farmers and soldiers filled. Social mobility between farm and city was virtually unknown, and rural and urban people seemed to inhabit two different worlds.

Constantinople.

Byzantines hold celebrations and sporting events in hippodromes

Social life for peasants centered on weekly religious services, religious holidays, and celebrations of family events such as baptisms and weddings. Activities in cities were more varied; many were centered around the Church, but secular attractions were also available. Crowds gathered in large outdoor arenas, known as hippodromes, to watch chariot races, combats between men and wild animals, and athletic competitions. Young male spectators cheered for their favorite teams—the "Blues" or the "Greens"—wearing the team colors, cutting their hair in outlandish styles, and often fighting in the stands against supporters of the opposing side.

By the seventh century C.E., however, Byzantine prosperity had begun to fade. The hippodromes were half empty and the religious pageants lost much of their luster. The decline was due primarily to two invasions—Muslim soldiers from Arabia and microbes carrying bubonic plague. The bacterial threat proved even more deadly than the military one.

Crises of the Seventh Century

The bubonic plague, which repeatedly ravaged the empire, took a dreadful toll. Plague germs are ingested by fleas that suck the blood of infected black rats. The fleas then move from rats to humans and pass on the microbes by biting their new hosts. Before the development of broad-spectrum antibiotics in the twentieth century, mortality rates from the three varieties of plague were very high. Pneumonic plague, spread by a victim coughing directly into the face of an uninfected person, killed 50 percent of its victims; septicemic plague, occurring when a flea transmits the germs directly into a blood vessel, killed 100 percent. But the most common form of the disease was bubonic plague, occurring when a flea bites soft tissue anywhere on the human body. Mortality was about 35 percent fifteen centuries ago and is approximately 20 percent today.

Bubonic plague, which Europeans later called "the Black Death," appeared in the Byzantine Empire in 541 when ships from North Africa inadvertently carrying infected rats docked in Byzantine ports. Victims died horribly, their bodies covered with "buboes," or large nodules filled with blood that turned black. The high fevers, delirium, and intense pain that accompanied the plague terrified the uninfected population; frightened citizens left the sick untended and bodies unburied in the streets. Epidemics hit the urban centers particularly hard, disrupting commerce and culture and causing millions to perish. The empire's population declined drastically, from 17 million in 610 to 7 million in 780, owing not only to the plague but also to incessant wars.

Bubonic plague devastates Byzantium

These wars constituted the second of the Byzantine Empire's crises. Between 613 and 628 the emperor Heraclius (610–641), a devout Christian and tenacious warrior, fought a series of devastating conflicts against the Persians, the age-old eastern enemies of the Byzantine realm. Led in combat by their courageous emperor, who personally slew a number of enemy generals, the Byzantines emerged victorious. Worn down, however, by the recurrent plague and the draining wars against Persia, they soon found themselves hard pressed to resist an even more dangerous foe.

Out of Arabia in the 630s swept formidable desert warriors who spread the world's third major monotheistic religion—Islam—by conquest. The military forces of this vigorous new faith, whose rise is described in the next chapter, quickly overran Syria, Mesopotamia, Palestine, Egypt, and much of North Africa, depriving the Byzantine Empire of many of its richest lands. The Muslims, as practitioners of Islam are known, also subjugated Persia, which had been weakened by its wars against the Byzantines. Constantinople did not fall to Islamic forces until the fifteenth century, but in the seventh century the loss of so many of its most cherished lands impoverished the Byzantine Empire not only materially but also psychologically.

The material losses were especially significant. Commerce withered as Byzantine trade routes with Mesopotamia and Syria passed into Islamic hands. This trade reduction weakened the wealthy, self-confident Byzantine commercial class and coincided with an alteration in the status of women. Theodora had been the first in a series of important Byzantine empresses: seven governed as regents for their young sons, two ruled the empire themselves, and others were quietly yet effectively influential. But in spite of the prominence of such powerful women, the situation for women in general deteriorated after the onset of the plague. As in Persia and Arabia, women were now required to veil themselves in public and to remain at home for most of their lives, their social contacts with men restricted to members of their own families. As Byzantine society became more agrarian and less commercial, women's lives became increasingly confined and their roles increasingly subordinate to those of men.

Islamic expansion weakens Byzantium

The crises of the seventh century did not prove fatal to the Byzantine Empire, however. Recovering from their extensive initial losses, the Byzantines eventually managed to hold back the armies of Islam, establishing the empire as a bulwark against Islamic expansion into southeastern Europe. But Byzantium by this time was considerably weaker, both from the effects of disease and the ravages of foreign wars, than it had been a century earlier. These circumstances amplified the divisions and weaknesses within the Christian Church, making them dangerous to the continued stability of the empire.

Eastern Christianity's Culture and Conflicts

Christianity and Byzantine daily life reinforce one another

The Christian Church dominated the empire's spiritual and cultural life. Spiritually that domination was penetrating and vibrant. As one historian has observed, for the Byzantines, "Christ, his Mother, and the Saints were as real as members of their own families." To be Byzantine was to be deeply Christian and to express that faith in elaborate rituals and observances. Byzantine church services were usually between four and six hours long. The emperor took part in all major worship services held in Constantinople, often marching to church at the end of a procession that could include as many as 50,000 gloriously robed officials. During services, the churches resounded with chants and hymns; clouds of incense perfumed the air. Christianity was the connective tissue of Byzantine life and the worldview that gave life meaning.

The former Basilica of Saint Sophia in Constantinople, with its massive dome surrounded by four graceful Islamic minarets following its conversion into a mosque.

Culturally, Christianity inspired architectural works of exquisite beauty. Beginning around 450, the Church built basilicas, shrines, and monasteries from one end of the empire to the other. Byzantine architecture was noted for its elegant domes, and the emperors ordered the construction of massive ones. For example, the Basilica of Saint Sophia in Constantinople commissioned by Justinian featured an immense dome held up by several smaller ones (see page 234). The ceilings were adorned with elaborate ornamental mosaics depicting scenes from the life of Christ, the lives of the saints, and the principal events of the Jewish and Christian Scriptures. Angels and holy men and women were portrayed in the colorful, stylized paintings, called icons, that hung on the walls. As the exteriors of these domed structures were frequently rather plain, those entering them were often awed by the grandeur inside.

Doctrinal quarrels divide eastern Christendom

Yet despite the devotion of its faithful and the grandeur of its culture, eastern Christendom suffered from serious shortcomings. First, the Church engaged in recurring doctrinal quarrels over the precise nature of Jesus Christ. The Monophysites (*mahn-AH-fizz-ītz*) contended that Christ was purely divine, while the Nestorians asserted that he was actually two persons, one human and the other divine. In 681, at an ecumenical council in Constantinople, representatives of all Christian churches agreed on an official definition: Jesus was one person with two distinct natures, one divine and one human, each the equal of the other. This statement should have settled the issue, and over time it did. But in the short term Monophysitism (*mah-NAH-fizz-ih-tizm*) remained strong in the empire's eastern provinces, such as Armenia and Anatolia, which were crucial to Byzantium as the source of much of its food and most of its soldiers. Not until the eleventh century did the issue of Monophysitism vanish, and then not by agreement among Christians, but rather because these provinces were conquered by Islamic forces.

Iconoclasm creates a passionate controversy

While struggling with the insoluble issue of Jesus's true nature, the empire was also divided by a controversy over icons, the religious paintings of Jesus, Mary, and the saints that were distinctive to Byzantine art. Popular belief held that divine graces flowed through these images to anyone who looked at them with reverence. One of the consequences of this belief was the worship of icons, a form of idolatry and arguably a violation of the Second of the Ten Commandments, which decreed that "Thou shalt not make any graven images." In 726 Byzantine Emperor Leo III banned icons, calling their worship perverse and superstitious. His prohibition provoked a wave of **iconoclasm** (*ī-KAHN-ah-klah-zum*, or image breaking) throughout the empire, resulting in the destruction of many priceless works of art and triggering a bitter dispute that tore the empire apart. A revolt against iconoclasm then broke out in Greece, and in Rome the pope, supporting the use of icons, denounced

Leo. The destruction of icons was prohibited at a Church council in 787, restored by another in 815, and banned again in 843. For two more centuries iconoclasm remained a divisive force in Byzantine life, although it was gradually overshadowed by the growing division between the eastern and western Church.

As explained in the preceding chapter, the Christian Church's most divisive problem was the prospect of a rupture between eastern and western Christendom. Ever since the empire's capital had moved to Constantinople, the two branches of the Christian Church had developed radically different organizational structures. At various times between 476 and 1054, the western papacy attempted to assert its authority over Constantinople; at other times, Byzantine patriarchs and sometimes emperors adopted initiatives designed to enhance their privileges.

From a Byzantine perspective, the struggle was doctrinal as well as political. The Byzantines, in designating the emperor as an equal of the apostles, could not then subordinate him to the pope in theological matters. Church tradition held that questions of doctrine could only be solved by an ecumenical council, at which the Holy Spirit would make its wishes known. Although the pope asserted authority over both the emperor and an ecumenical council, Byzantines could not accept what to them would have amounted to a redefinition of Christianity and of the emperor's role within it. At the same time, from a western perspective, the eastern Church's tendency to debate obscure theological issues was dangerous to Christian unity.

So many issues separated the two branches of Christianity that, when the formal schism finally came in 1054 (Chapter 9), it merely ratified a reality that had existed for centuries. Henceforth, despite occasional short-lived efforts at reconciliation, the Eastern Orthodox Churches, functioning under their own patriarchs and caesaropapist rulers, remained independent of the pope in Rome and the Roman Catholic West.

Icon of St. Michael the Archangel.

The Great Schism divides Christendom

Foreign Conflicts and Byzantium's Decline

Religious issues disturbed the middle years of the Byzantine Empire, but conflicts with foreign powers determined its ultimate fate. These, too, possessed a religious dimension, as Islam's compelling spiritual vision, combined with its relentless armies, posed a persistent challenge to the Christian world.

Muslims fail to conquer the Byzantine Empire

The Arab Conflict

After subjugating Persia by 642, the Arab armies, eager to spread Islam westward, continued their assault on Byzantium. In 655 they destroyed the Byzantine navy, enabling them to besiege Constantinople from 673 to 678. But the Byzantines were able to break the siege with the help of a secret weapon called Greek Fire. A flaming liquid whose precise composition remains unknown, Greek Fire was sprayed on the hulls and sails of enemy ships. Since it was oil-based, any of the substance that missed its target floated on the water, where it spread to other ships and incinerated anyone who fell or jumped overboard. In 678 the perplexed Muslims raised the siege and withdrew, turning their energies in the next decades to completing the conquest of North Africa. Then, moving across the Straits of Gibraltar and through Spain into Europe, they were finally stopped in 732 near Tours, by Franks led by Charles Martel (Chapter 9).

Ruins of the fifth-century walls of Constantinople in present-day Istanbul.

Byzantines fighting the Bulgars.

Although the Byzantine Empire survived the initial Arab onslaught, its territorial holdings were greatly diminished (Map 10.3). Beginning in the mid-800s, however, Byzantine power gradually revived. The Arab threat waned, and in the tenth century, rejuvenated Byzantine armies invaded Syria, destroying the bases from which the Arabs had launched their raids. Later the Byzantines conquered much of Bulgaria and established a strong imperial position in the Balkans. From 843 until 1025 the Byzantine Empire prospered under a series of forceful, farsighted leaders. Its position was stronger than at any time since the age of Justinian.

The Turkish Conquests

Then, between 1025 and 1070, a series of incompetent leaders undermined the strength that the Byzantine Empire had won with such difficulty in the preceding two centuries. This weakness opened the way to a challenge from a nomadic central Asian tribe called the Seljuk (*SELL-yook*) Turks.

During the eleventh century, the Seljuks had gradually been conquering Persia and Mesopotamia. In the process they had become Muslims, and, as part of an overall plan to unify Islamic lands, they intended to strike next at Egypt and destroy the regime there. To do so they would have to move from Mesopotamia to the east and south of the Byzantine Empire, whose eastern Anatolian provinces they coveted but whose existence as the region's major power they had no intention of challenging.

The Seljuk Turks threaten the Byzantine Empire

Adjacent to the Turks' new Mesopotamian territories was Armenia, populated by Monophysite Christians who had been antagonized by Byzantine policies of religious discrimination and crushing taxation. The Turks decided to take advantage of Armenia's dissatisfaction with Byzantine rule, hoping to secure their borders before attacking Egypt. In 1064, led by Sultan Alp Arslan, Turkish forces destroyed the capital of Armenia and penetrated deep into Byzantine Anatolia, where they met only sporadic resistance. Six years later, hoping to prevent further Turkish advances, the Byzantine emperor Romanus IV Diogenes (*rō-MAH-nus dī-AH-juh-nēz*) concluded a truce with the Sultan.

The truce was almost immediately broken by Turkoman raiding parties composed of southwest Asians who spoke a language related to Turkish but who refused to accept Seljuk control. Romanus, erroneously concluding that Sultan Alp Arslan was behind these raids, moved eastward to punish him in 1071. At the same time the Sultan, considering the truce still in force, moved southward against Egypt. When he learned that the Byzantines had broken the truce, however, he turned north to intercept Romanus.

The two armies met on August 26, 1071, at Manzikert in Armenia, where the Byzantines were soundly defeated. The battle proved disastrous for the Byzantine Empire. Romanus was captured, and the new Byzantine emperor, Michael VII Ducas, soon broke the generous treaty that Alp Arslan had granted the Byzantines after Manzikert. Exasperated, the Sultan gave up his plan to attack Egypt and moved forcefully against the empire. By 1080 the Seljuk Turks controlled nearly all of eastern Anatolia.

Defeat at Manzikert severely weakens the Byzantine Empire

The Byzantine Empire still held the coasts of the Mediterranean and Black seas and western Anatolia (Map 10.3). But eastern Anatolia and Armenia had been the empire's source of food and soldiers, and, once lost, these valuable territories could neither be retaken nor replaced. The Turks, who had had designs on eastern Anatolia but had never thought of conquering Byzantium itself, now held the strategic initiative and possessed

Map 10.3 The Gradual Retraction of the Byzantine Empire, 628–1328

By 1200, the Byzantine Empire was considerably smaller than it had been in 481 (Map 10.1). Arabian invasions from the south in the seventh century surprised the Empire's leaders and forced them to divide their forces between Persian and Arab threats. Observe that the Empire was gradually pushed westward, and that it lost all its North African territories to the Arabs. At the start of the thirteenth century, Byzantium's collapse was not assured, but its long-term survival was clearly questionable. How might the loss of these regions have handicapped the Byzantine emperors?

Map A

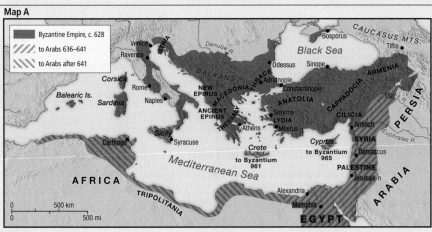

Map B

Map C

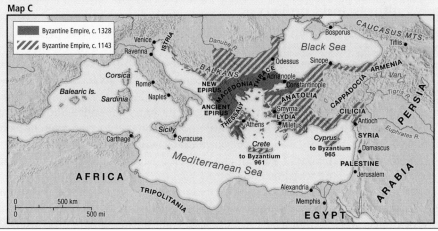

the resources necessary for eventual victory. It came in 1453, when the Ottoman Turks, successors to the Seljuks, completed the Islamic conquest of West Asia and defeated the Byzantine Empire.

Pre-Christian Russia

The Byzantine Empire was largely shattered after Manzikert, but Byzantine influence lived on in the north. There, in 988, the Grand Prince of an area called Kiev had converted to eastern Christianity. His decision meant that even after Byzantium's collapse, its culture and religion would continue in his realm. This area of Byzantine influence eventually grew into an enormous country known as Russia.

Russia's Difficult Climate and Terrain

Russian territory stretches from eastern Europe across northern Asia. Endless forests blanket its northern expanses, while its south is covered with vast treeless plains known as steppes (Map 10.4). Although Russia today possesses thousands of miles of seacoast, throughout most of history it was in effect landlocked. Its long northern coastline borders the Arctic Ocean, ice-bound for much of the year, while access to its Baltic and Black Sea ports, acquired in recent centuries, is controlled by countries that have often been hostile. This landlocked condition inhibited trade routes and frustrated Russia's development for centuries.

Geography impedes Russian development

　　Russia is not only landlocked but cold, the most heavily populated frigid land in the world. Even its southernmost portions lie no farther south than North Dakota. The Gulf Stream, which moderates the climate of continental Europe, touches only a tiny portion of Russia. Siberia, in Asian Russia, is known for its brutally cold conditions, and in the northern part of European Russia the soil remains frozen for more than half the year. This cold severely restricts both the quantity of arable land and the length of the growing season. Central Asian Russia suffers from both severe cold and inadequate moisture, making agriculture impossible there without irrigation. Finally, as nearly all the region's principal rivers flow north or south, rather than east or west, travel across Russia has always been difficult, hindering commerce and the use of its natural resources.

Early Cultures and Conflicts

Sarmatians use the stirrup to conquer and rule southern Russia

Societies appear to have developed earliest in southern Russia, where the cold was less severe. The Cimmerians (*sih-MARE-ē-uns*), linguistically related to the Greeks, ruled the lands north and east of the Black Sea between 1000 and 700 B.C.E. They were conquered by the Scythians, a Central Asian nomadic people who also invaded Persia. Between 700 and 200 B.C.E. the Scythians dominated southern Russia, but their formidable military state collapsed under pressure from another group of nomads called Sarmatians (*sahr-MĀ-shuns*), who then ruled the region until about 200 C.E. Fighting from horseback with heavy armor and long swords, the Sarmatians made good use of stirrups, a Central Asian innovation that secured the feet of a mounted warrior, allowing him to charge and thrust without being knocked from his horse.

　　The Scythians and Sarmatians were related to the Persians. Their occupation of southern Russia brought them into contact with Greek colonies on the northern shore of the Black Sea. They were accomplished metalworkers and outstanding fighters whose kings

Map 10.4 The Topography of Russia

Russia's formidable topography impeded its settlement and development for centuries. Its great rivers flow north-south rather than east-west, dead-ending travelers from its southern regions in the frigid Arctic rather than linking its Baltic and Pacific coasts. Notice that between taiga and desert lie vast expanses of forest and grassy steppes, areas in which large-scale farming has always been difficult. Battling these geographic challenges, the Grand Princes of Kiev laid the foundations of the Russian Empire. How might Russia's location across extreme northern latitudes restrict its development?

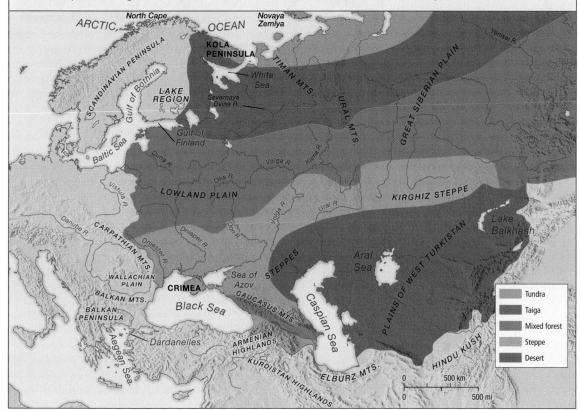

ruled by divine right; the Greeks were skilled fishers and tireless traders who elected their leaders. Neither group made any systematic attempt to conquer the other. Both preferred to reap the benefits of commercial contact and frequent intermarriage, practices that resulted in a blending of their cultures. But both found themselves displaced by the nomadic invasions that were having such a disastrous impact on the Western Roman Empire.

First among the invading nomads were the Germanic Ostrogoths, discussed in Chapter 9, who established a powerful kingdom between the Baltic and Black seas from 200 to 370 C.E. Then the Huns, a fearsome collection of Turkic-speakers, arrived on their way to Central Europe and an eventual confrontation with Pope Leo the Great (Chapter 9). The Avars were next, extending their control over a wide band of southern and western Russia beginning in 558. They threatened both Europe and Byzantium before collapsing in the mid-seventh century. Clearly the southern Russian plain was well-traveled by nomadic peoples heading for the more moderate climes of southwest Asia and Europe.

Nomadic invasions cross Russia

Khazars convert
to Judaism

When the Khazars (*KAH-zars*) moved into the lower Volga region of southwestern Russia in the seventh century, they appeared at first to be simply another invading culture that would dominate the region for a while and then be replaced. But their influence surpassed that of their short-lived predecessors. They abandoned their nomadic heritage and built large towns along the trade routes connecting Asia and Europe. Thus they served as a commercial and cultural crossroads. As one of the first peoples in the world to create a professional, paid army, they developed military skills that helped hold back Islamic armies. But they tolerated Islam, as well as paganism, Judaism, and Christianity, within their borders. In the eighth century they adopted Judaism, an unprecedented conversion based not on conquest but conviction. The legacy of the Khazars to the development of a Russian state was rich and surprising.

But the people who were destined to organize that state and dominate its successors lived well to the north and west of the Khazar realm. These people were the eastern Slavs, members of a linguistic group that today includes the speakers of Russian, Belarussian, and Ukrainian languages. The Slavs were skilled ironworkers and woodworkers, with well-established agricultural patterns that were exceptional in northern lands. One of their tribes, in fact, may have been the "Rus" (*ROOS*) who gave the land its name: Russia.

Kievan Rus Connects to the Byzantine World

The origin of the people who called themselves "Rus" is disputed. Some scholars argue that they were Norsemen from Scandinavia, also known as "Varangians," who allegedly arrived in northwestern Russia around 862 and imposed order on the Slavs who lived there. Other historians contend that the Rus lived in the south and were known to both Arab and Byzantine observers before 862. But one point is not in dispute: late in the ninth or early in the tenth century, the Rus, wherever they originated from, founded the state known as Kievan Rus. By 988 this state had become part of the Byzantine world.

The First Period: Early Rulers and Campaigns

Kievan Russia's history is customarily divided into three periods. The first, lasting from approximately 882 until 972, was the era in which the state was established and consolidated. Its first ruler was Oleg, a prince who gradually extended control over several neighboring East Slavic tribes. They were forced to pay tribute to him in Kiev, his capital, a town on the lower Dnieper (*nē-YEH-pur*) River in southern Russia (Map 10.5). In 907 Oleg went to war against the Byzantine Empire in what seems to have been an inconclusive series of skirmishes. Constantinople did, however, buy off the Rus with a highly generous commercial treaty.

Kievan Rus develops a
centralized state

Oleg's successor, Prince Igor (913–945), conducted a series of campaigns designed to maintain Kiev's domination over its tributary peoples. He also fought a large-scale war against the Byzantines from 941 to 943, during which his forces plundered the suburbs of Constantinople. But Greek Fire kept him from conquering the city, and in 945 he was killed while collecting tribute (always a dangerous undertaking) from one of the East Slavic tribes. His widow Olga assumed his powers, ruling Kiev as regent for their young son Sviatoslav (*svē-AH-tuh-slav*) from 945 to 962.

Olga connects Kiev to
Constantinople

Olga became the first prominent female leader in Kievan Russia, in part by relentlessly enforcing her control over the tributary groups, in part by coming to terms with

Map 10.5 Kievan Rus, ca. 900

While the Orthodox Christian Byzantine Empire contended for supremacy in southwest Asia with the Muslims (Chapter 11), a new Orthodox Christian monarchy was emerging farther north. Grand Prince Vladimir's conversion to Orthodoxy in 988 oriented Kievan Rus to the south and west, turning it away from Asia and toward Europe. Note that Kievan Russia's location, on the western edge of Asia and the eastern fringe of Europe, would have supported a turn in either direction. This made Vladimir's adoption of Orthodox Christianity decisive for future Russian development. Could Kievan Russia have offered any support to the Byzantine Empire in its ongoing struggle with the Muslims?

the Byzantine Empire. She converted to eastern Christianity and traveled to Constantinople, where she met the emperor himself. The two appear to have concluded a cautious alliance, providing Sviatoslav with a degree of security on his southern frontier when he became Grand Prince (or ruler) of Kiev in 962. Although her son did not convert to Christianity, ultimately Olga's efforts on behalf of her new faith were recognized by the Orthodox Church, which canonized her as a saint.

Sviatoslav ruled for only ten years, but they were a pivotal decade for Kievan Rus. In 965 he boldly attacked the Khazars, sacking their capital and fatally weakening their state. But this action was shortsighted, since the Khazars had been useful as a buffer against nomadic Central Asian tribes, particularly the ferocious Pechenegs (*PEH-chen-egs*). Three years later Sviatoslav, as the ally of Byzantium, conquered Bulgaria. The Pechenegs seized upon his absence to besiege Kiev, and in 969 Constantinople suddenly awoke

Sviatoslav's defeat of the Khazars leaves Kiev open to attack

to the dangers of instability on its northern border. The Byzantine Emperor broke his alliance with Kiev, and in 971, after two years of bitter warfare, Sviatoslav withdrew from the Balkans. On his way home in 972 he was killed by the Pechenegs, who boiled the flesh off his skull, then made it into a cup from which they drank in the hope of imbibing his courage. The first period of Kievan Russia's history had come to a discouraging end.

The Second Period: Connections to Christendom

Eight years later, following civil war among Sviatoslav's three sons, Vladimir (*VLAD-i-mēr* or *vlad-Ē-mēr*), the youngest, emerged victorious. His accession as Grand Prince in 980 ushered in Kiev's second and most glorious era, which lasted until 1054. Vladimir did much to unite and consolidate his realm, secure its borders, and enhance both its culture and its commerce. But his most momentous step was conversion to the Christian faith and his insistence that it be adopted throughout his realm. Vladimir's historic conversion took place in 988–989, when Christianity was spreading swiftly into Scandinavia, Poland, and Hungary. As part of a complex set of arrangements with Constantinople, he not only was baptized a Christian but also married the Byzantine emperor's sister.

Vladimir Christianizes Kiev

Russian legend offers an explanation for the conversion. According to popular accounts, Vladimir had summoned to Kiev representatives of the three great monotheistic religions, requiring each delegation to present arguments in support of its beliefs. After the presentations, he and his advisors decided against Judaism because its principles had not prevented the conquest of Judea by the Romans or the more recent defeat of the Jewish Khazars by Kiev itself. Islam was attractive as a dynamic, expanding movement, but its expansion had slowed considerably since the eighth century. A more practical problem was that the Islamic faith forbade the use of alcohol, and Russians could not imagine getting through the harsh winter months without it. Impressed with the majesty and beauty of Byzantine ritual, Vladimir chose Christianity. In so doing, he connected his realm with the Christian world.

It is significant that Russia adopted eastern rather than western Christianity. By 988 those two branches had diverged dramatically from one another, and in 1054, as already noted, the Great Schism formally divided them into two distinctly regional religions. Vladimir's preference for the Byzantine branch, known after 1054 as the Orthodox Church, carried with it three monumental consequences for Russia.

Russia inherits caesaropapism through Orthodox Christianity

First, Russia attached itself to a Christian church that remained firmly anchored in the rituals, practices, and doctrines of early Christianity. Western Christendom, by contrast, had gradually revised many of these traditions, exalting one bishop (the pope) above all others, altering the liturgy of divine worship, forbidding the marriage of priests, and later fragmenting with the rise of Protestantism in the sixteenth century. The rigorous internal questioning and self-criticism characteristic of western Christendom remained alien to Russia, as did the notion of a spiritual authority that was separate from and superior to that of the secular state. The Russians instead inherited the eastern caesaropapist tradition, which closely connected the church and state and placed both under the authority of the ruler of the realm.

Second, the slow weakening and eventual collapse of the Byzantine Empire eventually made Russia, by default, the leader of the Orthodox world. Outside of Russia, the Orthodox Church was increasingly marginalized and reduced to the status of a weak minority faith. Russia thus became the flagship of eastern Christianity.

Finally, Vladimir's choice made his country the beneficiary of the Byzantine cultural heritage. Orthodox Christianity linked Kiev to a rich, dynamic collection of rituals and traditions that enriched its rather spartan Slavic culture. Byzantine art, with its extensive use of gold and vivid depictions of Christian saints and events, left an indelible stamp on Russian symbolism. Orthodox worship services, chanted and sung in a liturgical language developed for Slavic peoples (rather than in Hebrew, Arabic, or Latin, as would have been required had Russia converted to Judaism, Islam, or Western Christianity) played a key role in the development of the Russian language. So did the Cyrillic alphabet, adapted from the Greek with extra letters added to represent Slavic sounds. Over the centuries, these and other influences, flowing from the Byzantine connection, contributed to the formation of a distinctive, energetic, and inspirational Russian culture.

Byzantine culture enriches Kievan society

Vladimir was later canonized a saint in the Orthodox Church. His actions provided a platform for the accomplishments of his successor, Iaroslav (*YAHR-ah-slahv*) the Wise (1019–1054), who governed at the height of Kievan power. Iaroslav's military campaigns against Pechenegs and Poles consolidated a state ranging from the Black Sea to the Baltic. He authorized the preparation of Russia's first legal code, built churches and monasteries throughout the land, and transformed the city of Kiev into a vibrant center of commerce and culture. He also appointed a wise Russian churchman as metropolitan of Kiev, Russia's leading church official, thus giving Russia its first native-born church leader. But his decision to divide his lands upon his death among his five sons condemned Kievan Rus to political turmoil and civil war, starting in 1054. Taking advantage of this instability, a new wave of Turkic-speaking invaders from the steppes, the Polovtsy (*pah-LAHV-tsē* or *pah-lahv-TSĒ*), appeared in the southeast and harassed the Kievan state for decades.

The Third Period: Chaos and Conflict

With this civil war and the subsequent Polovtsy invasion, the third era of Kievan Rus began, a lengthy period of chaos and conflict (1054–1240) during which its very survival was often in doubt. Iaroslav's grandson Vladimir Monomakh (*MAH-nō-MAHK*), who served as Grand Prince from 1113 to 1125, fought constantly to defend the state, primarily against the Polovtsy but also against other invaders from the west and south. Monomakh managed to preserve his realm but was unable to guarantee its long-term survival. His successors quarreled among themselves, sacked Kiev itself, and eventually transferred the capital northeast to the city of Vladimir. Repeatedly raided by the persistent Polovtsy and increasingly detached culturally and commercially from the declining Byzantine Empire, the Kievan realm fragmented into feuding principalities. By the time Kiev fell to the Mongols in 1240, the center of Russia had shifted to the northern forests, affording its people a more defensible position against the seemingly unending stream of invaders moving across the southern steppes.

The Polovtsy invade and weaken Kiev

Economy and Society

Agriculture was the source of Kievan prosperity. Because of Russian geography, the growing season was relatively brief, but the black soil of the region was rich and plentiful. Northern areas produced barley, oats, and rye, while wheat was the principal crop farther south. Farmers divided their lands into two parts, leaving each one fallow, or uncultivated, in alternate years. Eventually this alternation evolved into a three-field system, in which a parcel of land would be sown in one year with a spring crop, in the second year with a winter crop, and in the third with no crop at all. This system enhanced the fertility of the soil and increased food production.

Grain cultivation was supplemented by cattle raising and beekeeping, which supplied candle wax to light homes and honey to sweeten food and drink. Fishing and hunting were also important. Russia was a snowy land, but its vast forests and numerous lakes and rivers contained enough game and fish to feed a population much larger than the one that lived there. The majority of that population, of course, was rural; in Kievan Rus there were many towns but few cities. Most townspeople, including artisans who practiced skills in tanning, metalworking, and woodworking, also worked on the land.

Kiev connects
southwestern Russia
commercially

Townspeople were also merchants. Kiev's location on the Dnieper River north of the Black Sea gave it control of, or easy access to, the principal trade routes of southwestern Russia. The Grand Prince was in some ways the chief merchant as well as the chief executive. Collecting tribute from subject peoples in the form of honey, beeswax, furs, hides, and slaves, he presided over an active and complex trade with Byzantium, Bulgaria, and Baghdad. Relations with Constantinople were commercial as well as cultural and religious.

In addition to directing trade, waging war, and regulating affairs of state, the Grand Prince presided over a social and governing elite centered on his siblings and cousins. His courtiers intermarried with local Kievan nobles to form the **boyar class**, an aristocracy that played a significant role throughout much of Russian history. Most Kievan peasants were free, although some fell into debt so burdensome that they were scarcely better off than the slaves who formed the base of the social structure.

Byzantine Christianity
influences Kiev

From bottom to top, Kievan society was interlaced with Byzantine Christianity. The Orthodox Church offered much more than services on Sundays and holy days. It provided a colorful, enriching series of rituals designed to guide the believer from birth through life to death. It owned and administered early forms of charitable institutions, hospitals, and schools. It dominated Russian art, architecture, and literature, giving each a distinctively Byzantine flavor. In addition, its married clergy sent their children not only back into the Church but into all other walks of life, spiritualizing Kievan society to a degree unmatched in Western Christendom.

The End of Early Russian Civilization

The spiritual richness of Kiev, impressive though it was, could not prevent the state's collapse. A number of factors converged to make that outcome possible. Economically, in the eleventh century, Kiev began to lose its privileged commercial position, as Polovtsy occupation of the south disrupted Kievan connections with both the Byzantine Empire and Islamic southern Asia. Socially, a gradual reduction in peasant status led to serious unrest in the twelfth century. Politically, Kievan Russia failed to develop as a fully centralized state. It was instead a loose federation of principalities, which only unusually talented rulers such as Vladimir and Iaroslav could hold together.

Nomads besiege
Kievan Rus

Recurrent civil strife in turn left Kiev vulnerable to unending attacks by Turkic-speaking nomads such as the Khazars, Pechenegs, and Polovtsy. Although Russia defeated them time and again, they continued to undermine its vitality. In 1240, the Mongols sacked Kiev, ending the third period of early Russian civilization.

Chapter Review

Putting It in Perspective

In the fourth century C.E., when Emperor Constantine legalized Christianity, took a leading role in Church affairs, and moved the Roman Empire's capital eastward to Constantinople, he laid the foundations of the Byzantine realm. After 476, when Germanic forces conquered Rome and ended the empire in the west, the Eastern Roman Empire continued to develop a distinctive society, blending Roman traditions with Greek culture and a vibrant version of the Christian faith that united Church and state authority in the person of the emperor.

Byzantine emperors continued to claim all the western territory they had lost, but their efforts to retake it achieved no lasting success. Far more significant were the achievements of Byzantium itself. Among these were Justinian's Code, which systematized Roman law and guaranteed its survival into modern times. In the area of religion, Byzantine Christianity developed a rich set of rituals that preserved early Christian practices to the present day. And, beginning in the tenth century, Byzantine religion and culture took root in Russia, where they were destined to outlast the Byzantine Empire itself.

Byzantium's culture was splendid, its commercial connections were extensive, and many of its emperors were effective, capable leaders. Some, however, proved to be incompetent or corrupt. A political system that restrained executive power could have survived the mistakes of these emperors, but the Byzantine Empire's caesaropapist heritage exalted the ruler's authority, even if he or she was disastrously ineffective. Although the emperors worked to unify their people religiously, Byzantium's chronic quarrels over doctrinal differences that could not be resolved frustrated their efforts and weakened the empire in the face of its enemies.

In the end the empire's enemies proved its undoing. Drastically diminished by Arab conquests during the seventh century, the realm regrouped and regained a measure of power and prosperity, only to be battered by the Turks beginning in the eleventh century. Both the Arabs and Turks were driven by a compelling, militant new faith that arose in Arabia in the early 600s. That dynamic force, to which we now turn, was known as Islam.

Reviewing Key Material

KEY CONCEPTS

heresy, 236
schism, 237
caesaropapism, 237

iconoclasm, 244
boyar class, 254

KEY PEOPLE

Justinian, 235, 238
Theodora, 238
Constantine, 236
Arius, 236
Theodosius, 237
Julian "the Apostate", 238
Heraclius, 243
Leo III, 244
Alp Arslan, 246

Romanus IV Diogenes, 246
Oleg, 250
Igor, 250
Olga, 250
Sviatoslav, 250
Vladimir, 252
Iaroslav the Wise, 253
Vladimir Monomakh, 253

ASK YOURSELF

1. Why was caesaropapism important in the administration of the Byzantine Empire? How did Justinian and Theodora utilize it?
2. Why was Byzantium unable to reconquer and hold Rome?
3. Could the Great Schism of 1054 have been avoided? Why or why not?
4. How and why did Kievan Rus emerge as a powerful state in Russia? How was Kievan Rus affected by Byzantium?
5. Which features were distinctive about Byzantine civilization? Which of these features were passed on to later cultures?

GOING FURTHER

Agold, Michael. *The Byzantine Empire, 1025–1204.* 1985.

Barnes, T. *The New Empire of Diocletian and Constantine.* 1982.

Grant, Michael. *Constantine the Great.* 1993.

Harvey, A. *Economic Expansion in the Byzantine Empire, 900–1200.* 1989.

Hussey, Joan. *The Byzantine World.* 1982.

Hussey, Joan. *The Orthodox Church in the Byzantine Empire.* 1986.

Kazhdan, A., and Ann Wharton Epstein. *Change in Byzantine Culture in the Eleventh and Twelfth Centuries.* 1985.

Magoulias, Harry. *Byzantine Christianity: Emperor, Church, and the West.* 1982.

Mango, Cyril. *Byzantium: The Empire of New Rome.* 1980.

Martin, Janet. *Medieval Russia, 980–1584.* 1995.

Obolensky, Dmitri. *The Byzantine Commonwealth: Eastern Europe, 500–1453.* 1971.

Pohlsander, H. *The Emperor Constantine.* 1997.

Treadgold, Warren. *A History of the Byzantine State and Society.* 1997.

Vernadsky, George. *Kievan Russia.* 1973.

Ware, Timothy. *The Orthodox Church.* 1993.

Key Dates and Developments

The Byzantine Empire

284 C.E.	Diocletian's division of the Roman Empire
325	Constantine's intervention at the Council of Nicaea
527–565	Rule of Justinian and (until 548) Theodora
529	Code of Justinian
541	Bubonic Plague appeared in Constantinople
681	Council of Constantinople defined the nature of Jesus
726	Leo III's ban on icons and images; Iconoclasm
1054	The Great Schism
1071	Battle of Manzikert Kievan Rus
700–200 B.C.E.	Scythians controlled southern Russia
200 B.C.E. – 200 C.E.	Sarmatians controlled southern Russia
200–650 C.E.	Germanic invasions
7th century C.E.	Arrival of the Khazars
ca. 862	Varangians arrived in northwestern Russia
882–972	Foundation and First Period of Kievan Rus
945–962	Regency and Conversion of Olga
962–972	Rule of Sviatoslav
980–1054	Second Period of Kievan Rus; Vladimir as Grand Prince (980–1019)
988	Conversion of Russia to Byzantine Christianity
1054–1240	Third Period of Kievan Rus
1240	Mongol conquest of Kiev

CHAPTER 11

The Origins and Expansion of Islam, 100–750

- Pre-Islamic Arabia
- The Rise of Islam
- Islam Expands, 632–661
- The Umayyad Caliphate, 661–750
- Society and Culture in Early Islam
- Chapter Review

The Great Mosque At Mecca

The Great Mosque at Mecca during pilgrimage season. The large black structure at the center is the Ka'ba (page 262).

Night was approaching in the Arabian desert. Moving eastward from the Red Sea, a caravan of camels laden with goods hastened to reach the gate of the city before darkness fell. Safely inside, the handlers fed and watered the camels while the merchants shook the dust from their clothing and bought food at a bazaar. Before retiring for the night, they visited the center of the city, an open square filled with shrines and statues. There they performed a series of rituals, thanking their gods for protecting them in the desert and leading them to safety.

The Expansion of Islam, 632-732 C.E.

This was the city of Mecca, a haven for travelers in an unforgiving wasteland. For centuries Mecca had provided food, water, rest, and sanctuary for anyone passing through its gate. Its food sellers, craftsmen, and peddlers prided themselves on making everyone welcome, regardless of the traveler's station in life or religious beliefs. The city's shrines offered every passerby a chance to worship his favorite god. But in the early seventh century, Mecca was changing. In 630, a man who had been born there six decades earlier returned to his home. He brought with him a new, monotheistic faith, preaching belief in one god, Allah, and rededicating Mecca to the worship of that god. In the following centuries that new faith, known as Islam, spread throughout the world. Neither Mecca nor the Arabian peninsula would ever be the same.

Pre-Islamic Arabia

In the sixth century of the Common Era, the world of the eastern Mediterranean had long been a commercial crossroads attracting all sorts of believers, including those who believed in no gods at all. It was a place where not only goods but cultures, languages, values, and customs intermingled. On the fringe of this world lay the Arabian Peninsula, a land of searing heat at the southwestern tip of Asia. Arabia was not a centralized state but home to a collection of tribes and clans. The region was noted for fragmentation and rivalry rather than unity. Yet out of Arabia came Islam, a vigorous, zealous form of monotheism that aspired to unify not only its home peninsula, but the entire world, under a banner of allegiance to one God. Islam excited the entire region, spreading its beliefs, its values, and the Arabic language over much of southern Asia and northern Africa within the next century. Lands once devoted to Greek, Roman, or Persian gods, to Judaism and Christianity, were united as a new Islamic world.

Camels and Commerce

Arabia in the centuries before Islam was an isolated area, even though it lay just south of the eastern Mediterranean basin, one of the busiest places in the world. An immense peninsula bordered by five seas should constitute an ideal location for oceangoing commerce, but Arabia had just two decent harbors. It has no rivers at all, so internal transportation was difficult, and fresh water was almost completely unavailable. Only the southwest receives ample rainfall. The rest of the peninsula consists of imposing mountains and arid, scorching deserts, culminating in the Empty Quarter of the southeast, the largest expanse of uninterrupted sand anywhere on the planet. Much of Arabia was unsettled, traversed only by Bedouin (*BED-oo-win*) peoples, nomads who moved from one oasis to another on camels.

Aptly nicknamed "the ships of the desert," camels were indispensable to what commerce there was in Arabia. Able to carry 500-pound loads for distances up to 25 miles per day, camels can work for as much as three weeks without drinking, taking advantage of their huge stomachs and their ability to retain water until needed. Defiant and ill-tempered, camels were nevertheless crucial to travel, even though a sizable portion of each beast's load had to be reserved for food and no less than a gallon of water per day for the man who guided it. Despite this limitation, camels made trade possible across the forbidding interior of Arabia, and caravans of camels traveled up and down the Red Sea coast.

Camel transport sustained the economic life of both the nomads of the north and the more settled peoples of the fertile, rain-fed southwest. But given the importance of water in a desert land, it is not surprising that southern Arabia grew to dominate the peninsula. City-states developed in that area after 1000 B.C.E., led by kings and fed by slaves. The region also produced luxury goods such as frankincense and myrrh, aromatic substances that appear in Christian accounts of the birth of Jesus. Compensating for lack of harbors, southern Arabians built ships that traveled the waters of the Arabian Sea and Indian Ocean in search of products and profits. By 400 B.C.E. the southerners had created a commercial network that operated in two directions. Southward, their ships of the sea carried imports and exports to and from eastern Africa, Persia, and India. Northward, their "ships of the desert" carried these goods across oceans of sand, linking southern Arabia to Mesopotamia and the eastern Mediterranean. These trade routes connected with one created by the Phoenicians in the Mediterranean to form the longest commercial highway in history. Southern Arabians were primarily responsible for introducing Indian spices to the Mediterranean world, initiating a spice trade whose importance lasted more than a thousand years. In this commercial network northern Arabia was subordinate to the southern city-states, which, protected by the same deserts and mountains that made their existence so precarious, did not fear their northern neighbors.

Camels make commerce possible in Arabia

A camel caravan.

The Collapse of Southern Arabia and the Rise of Mecca

Eventually, however, in spite of the early commercial advantages of southern Arabia, its prosperity collapsed. The Ptolemaic (*tahl-ih-MĀ-ick*) Empire of Egypt, one of the successor states of the vast empire of Alexander the Great, had by 100 B.C.E. established its own commercial route linking Egypt to India by way of the Red Sea. Simultaneously, the Ethiopian kingdom of Axum on the western bank of the Red Sea, which actually owned territory on the Arabian Peninsula, threatened the commerce of the declining Arabian city-states. Finally, the northern Arabians took this opportunity to interfere with overland

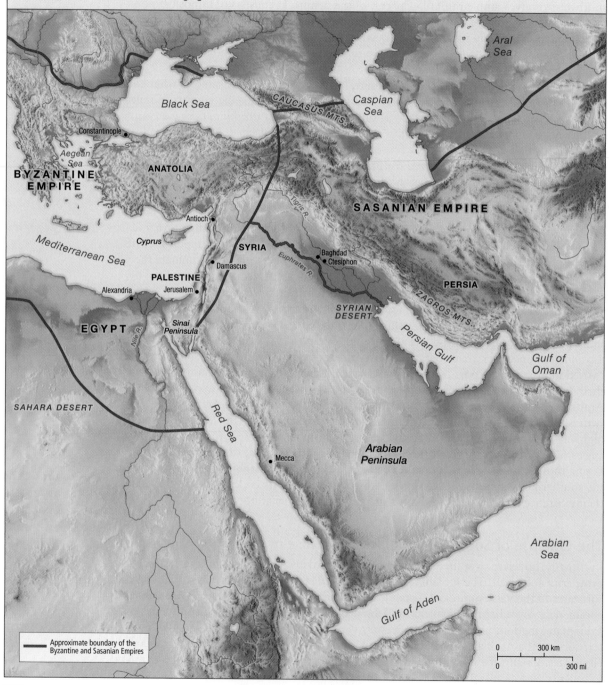

FOUNDATION MAP 11.1 Physical Geography of the Arabian Peninsula

Mesopotamians, Assyrians, Babylonians, Egyptians, Persians, Greeks, and Romans all knew of the existence of Arabia, but none of them considered it important. Its forbidding geography explains this lack of interest. Observe the lack of rivers to channel the small amount of moisture that falls as rain. An enormous limestone plateau jutting into the Arabian Sea, the Arabian Peninsula bakes under intense heat and lacks subsurface supplies of fresh water. How might Arabia have forged connections with other societies if its topography had been less discouraging?

Aral Sea

Black Sea

CAUCASUS MTS.

Caspian Sea

Constantinople

Aegean Sea

ANATOLIA

BYZANTINE EMPIRE

SASANIAN EMPIRE

Antioch

Tigris R.

Cyprus

Mediterranean Sea

SYRIA

Baghdad
Ctesiphon

Euphrates R.

Damascus

PERSIA

PALESTINE

Alexandria

Jerusalem

SYRIAN DESERT

ZAGROS MTS.

EGYPT

Nile R.

Sinai Peninsula

Persian Gulf

Gulf of Oman

SAHARA DESERT

Red Sea

Mecca

Arabian Peninsula

Arabian Sea

Gulf of Aden

Approximate boundary of the Byzantine and Sasanian Empires

0   300 km

0   300 mi

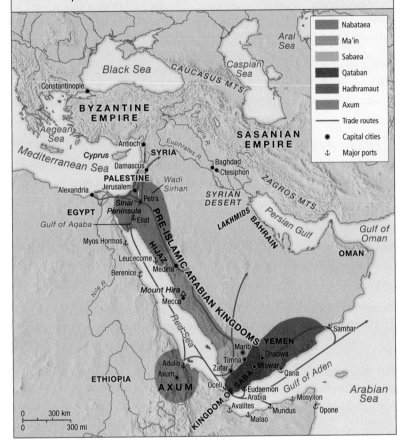

Map 11.2 Arabia and Adjacent Regions, 500 C.E.

Isolated and arid, the Arabian Peninsula in 500 C.E. was divided into states and subdivided into feuding clans. Nearby states like Axum traded with Arabian states but otherwise left them alone. Note that the eastern shore of the Red Sea could serve as a highway for camel caravans linking the Kingdom of Saba to the ports of the eastern Mediterranean. What role could cities like Medina and Mecca play in the development of such commerce?

trade routes, eroding southern control over the peninsula's interior (Map 11.1). By 300 C.E. the southern city-states had lost much of their power and wealth (Map 11.2).

As the city-states weakened, regional powers engaged in a military, commercial, and religious contest for Arabia. At this time the capital of the Roman Empire was being transferred from Rome to Constantinople, while the Sasanians, energized by Zoroastrianism, were revitalizing Persia six centuries after the Greco-Macedonian conquest. Byzantium, inspired by Christianity, also considered the Arabian Peninsula open for commercial exploitation and religious conversion.

Monotheistic beliefs had entered Arabia as early as 70 C.E., when the Roman destruction of the second Temple in Jerusalem initiated a dispersal of Jews throughout

Competing forces contend for Arabia

Southwest Asia. Southern Arabian kings, observing that two of their most dangerous enemies, Byzantium and Ethiopia, were Christian, adopted Judaism in the early 400s. But in 520 an Ethiopian invasion destroyed the southern city-states and established a Christian protectorate. Judaism was weakened through forcible conversion to Christianity, but Ethiopian military domination was never secure, and in the 570s the Ethiopians were replaced by the Persians. Under Persian rule, Judaism, Christianity, and Zoroastrianism were all tolerated in southern Arabia.

The destruction of the southern Arabian states proved to be highly significant, because it ended the southern domination of the peninsula and created a politico-economic vacuum that neither Ethiopia nor Sasanian Persia could fill. The Bedouin nomads of the interior now gravitated toward the less highly developed towns of the north, linking them with the city of Mecca on the western edge of the Arabian desert.

Mecca emerges as a principal Arabian sanctuary

For several centuries Mecca had been a place of sanctuary where both travelers and the bandits pursuing them could rest and refresh themselves undisturbed. It was also a religious center, housing tribal idols from much of the peninsula and offering numerous pilgrims an opportunity to view the Ka'ba (*KAH-bah*), a shrine containing large stone idols (see page 257). As southern Arabia's commercial power vanished following the Ethiopian and Persian invasions, Mecca took on added importance as a resting place for camel caravans traveling up and down the Red Sea coast and across the desert. Making the most of this opportunity, the Quraysh (*kurr-ISH*) tribe, which rose to dominate the city around 500 C.E., became custodians of the Ka'ba, protectors of pilgrims, and traders determined to establish an international commercial dynasty.

The Rise of Islam

As the sixth century drew to a close, the Arabian Peninsula was changing rapidly. The powerful southern city-states were gone, and no central authority had taken their place. Traditional trade routes had been disrupted and new ones were being formed. Monotheistic religions had been introduced but none had succeeded in converting very many. Mecca, now flourishing as a religious and commercial center, seemed to offer a promising new focus for regional control.

Then a boy, born into a minor clan of the Quraysh tribe in Mecca, transformed the changing Arabian Peninsula. He was Muhammad ibn Abd'Allah (*muh-HAHM-ahd ibn abd-AHL-lah*), and he would become one of the most influential figures in history.

The Prophet Muhammad

Muhammad was born in 570, shortly after his father had died. The boy was raised by a grandfather and later by an uncle. He worked on caravans up and down the Red Sea coastline, first as a camel tender and then as a merchant, and at age 25 he married his employer, a wealthy widow named Khadija (*kah-DĒ-jah*). In Mecca he earned a reputation as a responsible businessman and camel merchant, despite his inability to read or write, and as a spiritual person committed to living an ethical life. Often he went to the mountains near the city to pray and meditate. While doing so, in 610 he experienced the first of a series of revelations. He described these revelations as transmitted to his unconscious mind by the Archangel Gabriel, a figure in both Jewish and Christian scriptures. But Muhammad claimed to have felt the words rather than to have heard them, and said that they came directly from Allah, the one and only God.

Allah's name was known to Arabians. He was one of a number of gods whom they worshiped, but no cult was devoted solely to him and his nature was not well defined. He was not the one God worshiped by the few Arabs who had come to believe in monotheism. But Muhammad said that his revelations identified Allah as the only God, and they clarified his nature.

At first the disclosures Muhammad reported concerned God's nature and his relations with humanity. Allah is omnipotent and merciful, Muhammad claimed; he created everything, and it is the duty of everyone to acknowledge his greatness and worship him. He expects the rich to assist the poor and requires that all people live honest, faithful, and upright lives in compliance with specific rituals and regulations. On the Last Day, according to Muhammad, Allah will bring all souls before him and will judge them according to their actions on earth, consigning some to heaven and others to hell.

Muhammad's visions introduce a new religion

Muhammad's definition of God and of people's relations with him clearly paralleled those of other religions with which Meccans were familiar. Jews were uncompromising monotheists who accepted the Mosaic code of ethical conduct and followed clearly defined religious practices. Christians believed in the Day of Judgment and described it in words and images similar to those transmitted to Muhammad. Zoroastrians believed in the eternal struggle between good and evil and in the eventual triumph of Ahura Mazda over the forces of The Lie. But Judaism, Christianity, and Zoroastrianism had failed to win significant numbers of followers in Arabia, possibly because in a land fragmented into tribes and clans, polytheism seemed more reflective of the realities of daily life. Now Muhammad believed that Gabriel had instructed him to do much more than simply believe in a single god. He was to prophesy in the tradition of Moses and Jesus, to speak to men and women on behalf of Allah, to turn them away from the errors of polytheism and lead them to the worship of the one true God.

The Shahadah (see page 266): "There is no God but Allah, and Muhammad is His messenger."

Muhammad sees his mission as the completion of God's revelation

Muhammad's revelations provided a religious explanation for why other monotheistic religions had failed to win the hearts and minds of Arabs. According to Muhammad's account, Gabriel had said that Jews and Christians possessed their own scriptural texts and were recognized by Allah as **People of the Book**. Their books—the Jewish and Christian scriptures—were valid but incomplete and only partially accurate. They had been copied, translated, and revised over the centuries until they no longer contained the fullness and purity of divine revelation. Muhammad's mission was to communicate the totality of God's teaching in its pure and final form. He was to be the last and greatest of the prophets, the Messenger of God.

This charge was a daunting prospect for an illiterate merchant, but Muhammad believed he knew how to proceed with his mission. He recited his revelations over and over to secretaries who recorded his words carefully in Arabic, and many of his followers memorized them. These recitations became the **Qur'an** (*kuh-RAN*, also spelled *Koran*), the sacred scripture of the religion that would soon become known as Islam (*IZ-lahm* or *is-LAHM*), Arabic for "submission" to the will of God. Organized neither topically nor chronologically but roughly by length of recitation (from the longest to the shortest), the Qur'an is a difficult text. But individual believers felt compelled to read it, and it became a powerful force in their lives (see "Excerpts from the Qur'an"). It was also a force in

A hand-copied page from a nineteenth-century edition of the Qur'an.

Document 11.1 Excerpts from the Qur'an

The Prophet Muhammad stated that the Qur'an was the authentic word of God, and was dictated to him by the Archangel Gabriel. It is the Holy Scripture of Islam.

Q 1: 1–7.

In the name of Allah, the beneficent, the merciful.
All praise is due to Allah, Lord of the worlds—
The beneficent, the merciful,
Sovereign of the Day of Judgment.
You alone do we worship; You alone we ask for help.
Guide us to the straight path,
The path of those upon whom You have bestowed favor,
Not of those who have evoked Your anger,
Nor of those who are astray.

Q 2: 190.

Fight in the way of Allah those who fight you
But do not commit aggression.
Indeed, Allah does not like aggressors.

Q 80: 33–42.

But when there comes the Deafening Blast
On the Day of Judgment a man will flee from his brother
And his mother and his father
And his wife and his children,

For every man, that Day will be a matter to occupy him.
Some faces, that Day, will be bright—
Laughing, rejoicing at good news.
And other faces, that Day, will have upon them dust,
Blackness will cover them.
Those are the disbelievers, the wicked ones.

Q 3: 104.

Let there be arising from you one community (*umma*),
Inviting to good, enjoining what is right
And forbidding what is wrong,
And those will be the successful.

Q 29: 46.

And do not argue with the People of the Scripture
Except in a way that is best,
Except for those who commit injustice among them,
And say, "We believe in that which has been revealed to us
And revealed to you.
And our God and your God is one,
And we are in submission to Him."

SOURCE: *The Qur'an.* Saheeh International. (Abul-Qasim Publishing House: Jeddah, Saudi Arabia, 1997).

Muhammad's recitations become the Qur'an

Arab history, as its compilation and eventual publication standardized classical Arabic, and the Qur'an and the Arabic language became the two principal unifying forces within the Arab world.

In 613 Muhammad began to preach publicly outside the circle of his own family and friends. He quickly encountered opposition from the merchant elite of the Quraysh, who probably viewed the Qur'an as a challenge to their own tribal values. They certainly realized that the new teachings would disrupt the polytheistic traditions and genial tolerance of the sanctuary at Mecca, which would rapidly lose its attractiveness as a haven for commercial travelers. The tribal chiefs, moreover, felt that Muhammad's claim to be God's messenger challenged their political authority. The elite tried to buy Muhammad off with an offer of membership in their inner circle. When he refused their bribes, they tried intimidation and then a boycott of his family and associates that prevented them from buying food in local markets. But nothing persuaded Muhammad to give up his religious mission.

From Mecca to Medina

By 619 Muhammad had some one hundred followers in Mecca, a small return on his investment of six years of preaching and teaching. At the same time, the oasis town of Medina (*meh-DĪ-nuh* or *meh-DĒ-nuh*), two hundred miles north, took an interest in his message. Medina was jealous of Mecca's economic domination, and the town was friendly to monotheism, since many of its residents were monotheistic Jews. In 622, after sporadic negotiations, 75 men from Medina invited Muhammad to move there to mediate some internal disputes. Late that summer he, his closest relatives, and their families undertook a nine-day journey known as the *Hijra* (*HĒJ-rah*, sometimes rendered as "flight" or "severing of relationships"). They reached Medina on September 24, 622, making that year the beginning of the Islamic lunar calendar. It was the pivotal event of Islamic history, symbolizing a flight from polytheism to monotheism.

Medina had been divided by religious quarrels among various tribes, some of them polytheistic and some Jewish. Muhammad offered them a monotheistic creed with scriptures in Arabic and a rigorous moral code that he himself would apply as a neutral judge. The polytheistic tribes accepted his arrival and soon converted to Islam, but the Jewish clans resisted despite Muhammad's willingness to incorporate some obviously Jewish practices into his evolving faith. The Jews rejected his claim to stand in the tradition of their great prophets Moses, Elijah, and Isaiah (*ē-LĪ-jah, ī-ZĀ-uh*).

Muhammad establishes an Islamic community at Medina

Faced with Jewish resistance, Muhammad reported receiving a new series of revelations that became part of the Qur'an. These recitations disclosed that the Hebrew patriarch Abraham was a greater prophet even than Moses and that, at God's command, he had built the Ka'ba shrine in Mecca. Muhammad now claimed that Abraham was the father of the Arab people, a pure monotheist whose beliefs had been corrupted by subsequent generations of Jews, just as subsequent generations of polytheists had placed idols in the Ka'ba. Now, Muhammad claimed, Allah had directed him to make Islam a completely independent religion, replacing both Judaism and Christianity because it represented the ultimate revelation of God.

Over the next several years Muhammad carried out this charge, building an **umma** (*OOM-mah*), a purely Islamic community under his leadership. Believers called themselves Muslims, or "those who submit" to the will of God. The foundation of the *umma* was five basic religious tenets; a Muslim is anyone who follows them, and following them, Muslims believe, will guarantee life in paradise with Allah after death.

The **five pillars**, as these tenets are called, were adapted from existing Christian, Jewish, and Arabian practices (see "The Five Pillars of Islam"). Together they constituted a foundation for the *umma*, giving it a religious charter and shared identity. In turn, the *umma* provided a means for social unity in a fragmented Arabia, demonstrating that the belief in a single god carried with it serious political implications. If polytheism had proven attractive to Arabians because its fundamental disunity reflected their daily realities, then monotheism's insistence on obedience to one god had the potential to end social and political disunity.

The umma is founded on the Five Pillars of Islam

Muhammad's construction of an *umma* at Medina gave him a base from which to attempt to convert Mecca. His followers plagued Meccan trading caravans, provoking the

Muhammad strives to convert Mecca

Document 11.2 The Five Pillars of Islam

1. **Shahadah**, or *bearing witness* (by proclaiming that "There is no God but Allah and Muhammad is His Messenger")
2. **Salat**, or *saying prayers* five times daily while facing in the direction of the Ka'ba in Mecca
3. **Zakat**, or *giving alms* to the poor
4. **Sawm**, or *abstaining from food and sex during daylight hours in the holy month of Ramadan* (*RAHM-ah-dahn*)
5. **Hajj**, or *making a pilgrimage* to Mecca during one's lifetime

Meccan commercial establishment into open hostility. In three battles between 624 and 627, Meccans failed to destroy Islam, and Muhammad's survival was widely interpreted as evidence of divine approval of his mission. Then in 628 Muhammad led a large band of Muslims from Medina on a pilgrimage to the Ka'ba. This gesture of reconciliation, designed to show that Islam was an intrinsically Arabian belief system rooted in tradition, persuaded many Arabian tribes to support Muhammad. In 630 he returned to Mecca, bearing gifts and pardons for his former enemies.

With Mecca now supporting him, Muhammad was able to extend his influence over even the most polytheistic Arab tribes. The simplicity of Islam's five pillars made it highly attractive. Compared to Judaism and Christianity, with their complex doctrines, regulations, and rituals, Islam was easy to understand. By the time of his death in 632, Muhammad, now known as the Prophet, had unified most of the peninsula around his inspired leadership and religious vision. He had also provided a spiritual framework within which to resolve the blood feuds that had long devastated the region. These successes in Arabia are best explained by Muhammad's claim to authority not on the basis of tribal ascendancy—unconvincing in such a fractured land—but on the basis of his status as the final messenger of God.

Islam Expands, 632–661

Islam's second generation demonstrated that this new religion would not remain confined to the Arabian Peninsula. Once certain internal leadership questions were settled, Arab warriors burst forth into southwest Asia and the eastern Mediterranean basin. Their advance startled the rulers of the long-established empires of Persia and Byzantium, who had not anticipated either a military or a political challenge from desolate Arabia. Barely three decades after the death of the Prophet, Islamic forces were masters of an extensive empire of their own, held together by contacts and connections that were forged in conflict.

An Agreement Between Leader and Followers

Muhammad's death provoked a crisis in Mecca. But this was not a crisis of spiritual leadership. Obviously no one could succeed him as Prophet, since the Qur'an indicated that Allah would send no more such messengers. Besides, Islam was individualistic, based on a personal relationship between Allah and each believer. There was no self-evident need for continuing spiritual directorship such as that provided in Christianity by popes and patriarchs.

Political leadership was a different issue entirely. To leave the *umma* leaderless would be to undermine all of Muhammad's work in unifying the peninsula. Muslims from Medina, still suspicious of Meccans, decided to select their own head, a move that if implemented would fragment Islam. This threat was averted in a highly contentious all-night meeting that selected the Prophet's father-in-law, the Meccan Abu Bakr, as **caliph** (*KĀ-liff*), meaning "successor of the Messenger of God." As Muhammad's successor, he would lead the *umma*.

Muslims wrestle with the question of leadership

Abu Bakr, like his son-in-law, was a member of the Quraysh clan. His selection established the principle that future leaders must also belong to the Prophet's tribe. Abu Bakr lived only two more years, but that was long enough to convince nearly everyone that the position of caliph should continue. The caliphate, or the territory governed by a caliph, developed into an institution that existed only in the Islamic world. Grounded in the idea that Islam must become more than an individualized, person-to-God relationship, it evolved into a compact binding all Muslims to one another within the *umma*. The caliph's appointment constituted a sort of agreement between leader and followers, imposing a set of obligations on both. Any violation of these obligations was both a political breach of contract and a sin against God.

The Ka'ba in Mecca.

This combination of political and spiritual authority carried with it awesome responsibility. Abu Bakr did not hesitate to exercise the former and live up to the latter. He and his successors believed that, since Muhammad's revelations were true, Islam, as the only true faith, must be spread by the faithful throughout the entire world. The contractual understanding implicit in Abu Bakr's concept of the caliphate helped transform Islam from a purely Arabian version of monotheism into a dynamic faith committed to spiritual and political expansion. Abu Bakr and the other companions of the Prophet thus embarked on a series of small-scale military expeditions that quickly developed into full-fledged campaigns. Islamic expansion, which took place between 632 and 732 mostly through armed conquest, was justified by Islam's claim to be a superior religion and achieved by the superiority of Arabian military tactics. It transformed the futures of Asia, Africa, and Europe.

The first caliph transforms Islam into a faith designed to connect all peoples

JIHAD AND THE TWO HOUSES. Islam's expansion conformed to the Qur'an's commandment to pursue **jihad** (*JĒ-hahd*). Often translated into English as "holy war," jihad is literally translated as "striving" or "struggle." In the Qur'an and in the sayings of the Prophet, it is used in the military context of waging war against unbelievers. Some theologians in Islam's early centuries, and some Muslim reformers in the nineteenth and twentieth centuries, suggested that jihad also should be interpreted as an injunction to wage an inner, spiritual struggle against sin and weak faith rather than solely military conquest for the purpose of spreading the faith. But most Islamic jurists and theologians interpret its original intent as military, as did the Muslim soldiers who conquered lands for Islam under the leadership of the caliphs.

The obligation to wage jihad, whether militarily or peacefully, is grounded in Islam's claim to be a universal religion. For Muslims, Allah's revelations apply not simply to Muhammad and his fellow Arabs but to all humanity. Those who have accepted these revelations are required to work diligently to convert those who remain in error. This obligation remains in force until all peoples have either embraced Islam or come under the rule of Islamic governments. While this struggle lasts, the world is divided into two houses, the House of Faith and the House of Disbelief. Conflict exists between these two

Jihad reflects Islam's claim to universality

houses and will continue until the final triumph of Islam throughout the world. A military interpretation of the commandment of jihad draws a clear, uncrossable line between Muslims and unbelievers and is consistent with the military expansion of Islam's first century. Interpretations that emphasize self-defense, or the individual's spiritual struggle to become holy, have become more prevalent in recent times.

THE CALIPHATE AS EMPIRE. In pursuit of jihad, Abu Bakr began to build an Islamic empire, sending forces in 632 against the Byzantine Empire's frontier posts in Syria and Sasanian Persia's installations in southwestern Mesopotamia. Commanded by Khalid ibn al-Walid (*KAHL-ēd ibn ahl wah-LĒD*), whom the Prophet himself had dubbed "The Sword of Allah," these remarkable fighters, emerging by surprise from the desert wastes on horses and camels, quickly established Islamic rule on non-Arabian soil for the first time. This force, though only a few thousand strong, used the desert to its advantage, withdrawing into it when danger threatened and returning only when it chose.

Islam expands beyond Arabia

In the midst of these military expeditions, Abu Bakr died and was succeeded by his kinsman Umar (634–644), a huge man who was feared and respected rather than loved. Under Umar, Islam's expansion continued (Map 11.3). Two years later, when Khalid's army took the Syrian city of Damascus, the Byzantines in Constantinople realized that this was no typical Arabian raiding party but a serious invasion. Jerusalem fell in 638, and only an outbreak of plague and the formidable mountains of northern Lebanon prevented the Muslims from expanding further. In the same year, another Muslim force attacked Sasanian Persia, conquering it completely by 642 in exploits unmatched since the days of Alexander the Great.

Umar turned next against the Byzantine province of Egypt. Byzantine forces there were defeated in a series of engagements, and the patriarch of Alexandria surrendered the entire province in 642. The Arabians took Tripoli, in Lebanon, the following year. But then geographic challenges—the mountains of northern Lebanon, the unfamiliar deserts of northern Africa (where native Berber warriors held the advantage), and the Iranian plateau—slowed them down. Meanwhile the Byzantine Empire reconquered Alexandria with a naval expedition in 645. Arabs, accustomed to fighting on ships of the desert, now had to learn to fight on ships of the waves. They made the transition, but future conquests took longer than their first ones.

Umar creates a multi-ethnic caliphate

Under Umar the caliphate became an empire composed of many different ethnic groups. In Syria, Persia, and Egypt, he ruled through local officials wherever possible and left agricultural lands in the hands of their owners. Unoccupied lands were awarded to his soldiers, who cultivated them with slaves taken from the conquered peoples. Arabs thus became an elite warrior caste rather than immigrants who assimilated into the peoples and cultures they conquered.

This Islamic empire differed in several ways from the great empires of China, Persia, and Rome. It was significantly larger than any of those realms and too extensive to be governed by one man ruling from one capital. Unable to centralize authority in the caliph, Muslims delegated considerable power to his representatives, or *emirs*, who did not always follow his wishes. Eventually distant lands, such as Egypt and Spain, broke away to form their own caliphates. Most important, the Islamic empire was held together by religious faith, not by centralized authority, as in Persia, or by military superiority, as in Rome.

Map 11.3 Islamic Expansion in Southwest Asia, 632–661

In the century following the death of the Prophet Muhammad, Islamic soldiers poured out of the Arabian Peninsula to conquer lands spanning three continents. Notice that they started with southwest Asia before being blocked in their north-westward expansion by the Byzantine Empire. Spreading the Islamic faith and the Arabic language into the eastern Mediterranean, Mesopotamia, Persia, and the Indus Valley, they forged commercial and cultural connections that endure today. What similarities and differences can you see between the Persian Empire and this new Islamic Empire, which Muslims called a caliphate?

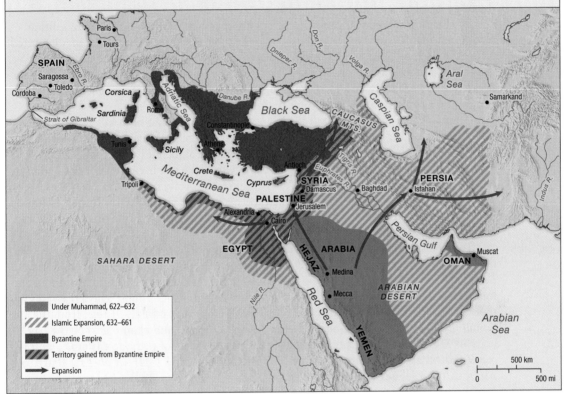

Legend:
- Under Muhammad, 622–632
- Islamic Expansion, 632–661
- Byzantine Empire
- Territory gained from Byzantine Empire
- Expansion

The Arabs were set apart not only by their status as conquerors but by their practice of Islam. Their aim was to take the pure truth of Islam to the world, but in the seventh century they did not force conversion on those they conquered. In fact, Christians and Jews in Arabia were permitted freedom of worship, as long as they submitted to Islamic rule. In Persia, Zoroastrians were initially extended these same rights. Umar considered Islam an Arab religion to be practiced by an ethnic elite, the people to whom Muhammad revealed the Qur'an. Those conversions that did occur were immediately suspect, since Muslims were exempt from tribute. There were, of course, entirely legitimate spiritual reasons for conversion. The appeal of Islam's doctrines and rituals was not confined to the Arabian Peninsula. Many of those who converted considered this new faith a distinct improvement over those it displaced.

Islam serves a conquering Arab elite

The Challenge to a Unified Islam

In 644 Umar was assassinated by a Persian slave. The new caliph, Uthman (*UHTH-mahn*), was chosen over his rival Ali by a committee of six Quraysh electors. Both men were sons-in-law of the Prophet. This election was closely contested, and Uthman's victory left a legacy of difficulties. A member of the Umayyad (*oo-MĪ-yahd*) family of Mecca, Uthman openly appointed his relatives to high positions, thereby alienating many high-ranking Muslims. Ali's defeat drove his followers underground and placed the unity of Islam in doubt.

For the time being, warfare held the empire together. In response to the Byzantine reconquest of Alexandria, the Arab governor of Egypt built an Islamic fleet that captured Cyprus in 649, pillaged Sicily three years later, and in 655 moved against Constantinople. But these successes could not save Uthman from the consequences of his favoritism. Exasperated by his relatives, Arab garrisons in Mesopotamia and Egypt intrigued against him, and in 656 Uthman was stabbed to death while reading the Qur'an.

The murder of Uthman provokes a split within Islam

Uthman's murder scandalized the Islamic world. Umar had been killed by a foreign slave bearing a grudge, but the assassins of Uthman were Muslims, including in their ranks a son of Abu Bakr. They were also kinsmen and associates of Ali, who was promptly elected caliph in his own right. Civil war broke out because Uthman's family was now compelled to avenge him, a duty required by Arabian custom. After massacres perpetrated by both sides, Ali was stabbed to death in 661 by one of his former followers. Muawiya (*moo-AH-wē-ah*), a kinsman of Uthman, was elected caliph after persuading Ali's eldest son to renounce his own claim.

Islam divides into Sunnis and Shi'ites

Two major consequences flowed from this sequence of events. First, Muawiya's selection created the Umayyad Caliphate, a succession of caliphs from the same family that presided over nine decades of Islamic expansion. Second, and far more significant in the long term, the *umma* split permanently into two antagonistic groups. The Umayyads and their followers constituted the majority, calling themselves **Sunni** (*SOO-nē*, from the *Sunna* [*SOO-nah*], or traditional practices of the Prophet) and claiming to be the true heirs of Muhammad and the doctrinally pure practitioners of orthodox Islam. The followers of Ali and his line made up the minority, or *Shi'at Ali* (*SHĒ-at ah-LĒ*, "Party of Ali"), calling themselves **Shi'ites** (*SHĒ-īts*).

Doctrinal differences between the two groups were inconsequential in the beginning, but significant differences in practice emerged. For example, Shi'ite Muslims developed a religious hierarchy, while Sunnis did not. In addition, after Hussein (*hoo-SĀN*), second son of Ali and a grandson of Muhammad, led an uprising against the Umayyads in 680 in Iraq and was slain with nearly all his family, Shi'ites developed a sense of persecution and martyrdom that divided them emotionally from the majority.

The Umayyad Caliphate, 661–750

The split between Sunnis and Shi'ites changed the political nature of the Islamic empire. The Party of Ali never gave up asserting that they were the true heirs of the Prophet and that the Sunnis were usurpers. They constituted a minority within the caliphate, but they spread throughout it, preaching opposition to Sunni Islam in North Africa, Egypt, Syria, Mesopotamia, and Iran.

Muawiya was forced to deal with Shi'ite factionalism in his efforts to rebuild the moral authority of the caliphate. To limit fragmentation, he transformed the caliphate into a centralized authority, convincing its leaders to recognize his son Yazid as his successor before his own death. The elective system thereby died out and was replaced by the dynastic principle. Muawiya hoped that this transformation would settle the issue of succession and block the Shi'ites from power. In practice claimants to the title continued to emerge, particularly when the new caliph was very young. Nonetheless, the centralization of authority kept the Umayyads in power until 750 and helped their eventual successors, the Abbasids (*ah-BAH-sids*)—descended from Abbas, one of the Prophet's uncles—rule for a full five centuries.

The Umayyads centralize political authority in Islam

Umayyad Expansion

Factionalism within Islam slowed but did not stop the empire's dynamic expansionism. Its centralized authority continued the drive for conquest. Muawiya had been proclaimed caliph in Jerusalem, but he promptly moved his government to Damascus, from which he could more readily threaten Byzantine power. His forces moved against Constantinople again in 669, blockading it between 673 and 678 but eventually failing, primarily because of the Byzantines' lethal incendiary weapon, Greek Fire. Events farther east were more encouraging: Muslim armies overran eastern Afghanistan in 664 and penetrated western India as far as the lower Indus valley. In North Africa, they reached the eastern border of Algeria by 670. However, in 680, Muawiya's passing led to a Shi'ite rebellion. When the Shi'ite leader Hussein was defeated and killed, Shi'ite hatred for Umayyad rule intensified.

Islam continues to expand

For a time internal difficulties slowed the Islamic advance. In 682 rebellious Muslim forces besieged Mecca and burned the structure housing the Ka'ba. Yazid died that same year, and his son and heir perished several months later. Another branch of the Umayyad family now assumed power, and a new caliph returned to the centralizing policies of Muawiya. All administration and tax collection throughout the empire were now conducted in Arabic, replacing the Greek and Persian languages for administrative purposes. Local officials were replaced by Arabians loyal to the caliphate, and a professional administrative elite replaced tribal chiefs. By 705, the caliphate rested on firmer foundations and was ready to return to conquest.

The wars that began in 705 differed substantively from earlier Islamic campaigns. With the nearby lands of Syria, Mesopotamia, Iran, and Egypt already in the caliphate, campaigns were undertaken in distant places that involved the cooperation of non-Arabian armies. Islamic forces penetrated deep into western India and stormed across northern Africa while preparing for a mammoth, although ultimately unsuccessful, siege of Constantinople. This new expansionist wave not only spread the faith farther from Mecca but also laid the foundation for Islamic commercial dominance throughout the region, linking the trade routes of the Mediterranean Sea, the Red Sea, the Arabian Sea, and the Indian Ocean.

In 711 a mixed expedition of Arabs and Berbers crossed the strait of Gibraltar and invaded Spain. Within four years this army had pushed organized Christian resistance to the northern mountains of Iberia. For the first time Islam was entrenched on the continent of Europe, and the Muslim advance appeared unstoppable. It appeared to be

Islam moves into southwestern Europe

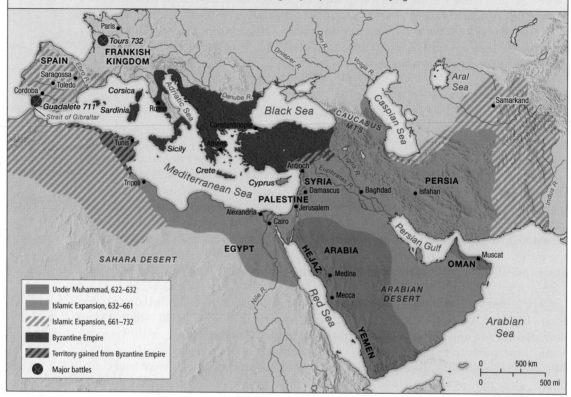

Map 11.4 Islamic Expansion, 661–732

After expanding throughout southwest Asia (Map 11.3), Islamic forces were blocked from entering southeast Europe by the Byzantine Empire. They thereupon swept across North Africa, crossed the strait of Gibraltar, and landed on the Iberian Peninsula in 711. Note that in present-day France, they were defeated at the battle of Tours by a Frankish army headed by Charles Martel. What sort of problems might such a far-flung empire pose for those trying to administer it?

Legend:
- Under Muhammad, 622–632
- Islamic Expansion, 632–661
- Islamic Expansion, 661–732
- Byzantine Empire
- Territory gained from Byzantine Empire
- Major battles

only a matter of time before all of the European kingdoms would fall, after which the Byzantine Empire could be assaulted from Europe as well as Asia.

Collapse of the Umayyad Caliphate

The Franks halt Islam's expansion into Europe

The Islamic impulse had, however, reached its westward limits. Continued Shi'ite claims to the caliphate distracted the empire. Eventually they found support from another branch of the Quraysh, the Abbasids. Although Sunni Muslims, the Abbasid clan advocated the overthrow of the Umayyads and reconciliation between Sunni and Shi'ite. At the same time, a joint Arab-Berber invasion of France was defeated in 732 at the battle of Tours (Map 11.4) by a Frankish army commanded by Charles Martel. Unable to sustain a prolonged campaign so far north of their base in Spain, the invaders retreated south of the Pyrenees, ending a tumultuous century of Muslim expansion.

During that century the Umayyad Caliphate had come to rule immense stretches of territory—from the straits of Gibraltar to the Indus River valley. This political empire had also been unified economically into a Muslim zone of trade and commerce. Culturally, the spiritual principles of Islam and the widespread adoption of the Arabic language glued the far-flung empire together and gave it a sense of religious purpose. Ultimately, the economic and cultural connections forged by a century of Islamic conquest endured long after political unity had crumbled.

Meanwhile the Abbasids were waiting for Umayyad power to decline. By 747 their patience was rewarded. In a ten-year period the Muslims had been defeated by the Khazars (730), the Franks (732), the Turks (738), and the Greeks (740). In addition, the Syrian base of Umayyad rule was running out of soldiers, and the Arabian armies were exhausted. Revolts broke out in Afghanistan, Iran, and Mesopotamia, culminating in the seizure of the caliphate by Abbasid forces in 750. Umayyad rule was over, as was the heroic period of Islamic expansion. The Abbasids would emphasize consolidation over conquest.

Society and Culture in Early Islam

By 750 Islam was the principal belief system of the rulers of a vast empire stretching from Spain in the west, through North Africa to Egypt, including Lebanon, Syria, and the Arabian Peninsula, and east through Mesopotamia, Iran, and Afghanistan into India. Unlike the other two major monotheistic religions, Islam combined a personal relationship with God, a dynamic military impulse, and a political succession based on a family relationship to a divinely inspired prophet. Preaching total submission to the will of God, Islam changed all the societies and cultures it conquered, blending with them to produce an entirely new Islamic society and culture.

Islam connects various peoples into a far-flung empire

Religious Observance: The Mosque

Among the distinctive creations of Islamic culture was the **mosque**, or Islamic house of worship, which architecturally blended the influences of many different societies. Immediately after conquering an area, Muslims marked it as their own by building mosques. Muhammad apparently did not intend to build any sort of temples, emphasizing personal prayer five times a day rather than prayer in communities. But his own home in Medina quickly became sacred space, and the Prophet himself had decided that each such space should orient prayer in the direction of the Ka'ba in Mecca.

Muslims develop a unique house of worship

Mosques include no statues, portraits, or any other depictions of God, angels, or any person living or dead. The interior spaces are simply furnished. There are no chairs or benches for worshipers, and although some mosques contain a pulpit, this feature is not mandated. Walls are covered with artistic geometric designs and with verses from the Qur'an inscribed in Arabic; the rugs that cover the floors are similarly patterned. Minarets, or ornamental towers, are often attached to the sides of mosques so that an Islamic cleric can ascend to call the faithful to prayer at the appointed times of day.

The Dome of the Rock.

In some cases, Muslims took existing churches in Christian lands they conquered and converted them to mosques. Usually, however, they built new structures, using them to demonstrate the supremacy of Islam over the "old" monotheistic faiths of Judaism and Christianity. The magnificent Dome of the Rock in Jerusalem, built by an early caliph, served that purpose by establishing an Islamic house of prayer on a site sacred to all three faiths. That place is the traditional site of King David's altar and King Solomon's temple, making it significant to both Jews and Christians. In Islamic tradition, it is the spot on which Abraham was told by God to sacrifice his son Isaac and from which Muhammad rode his horse into heaven during one holy night. Construction of a mosque on such a site carried the obvious implication that Islam had come to replace what it considered ancient and inadequate forms of worship.

Byzantine and Persian motifs were often incorporated into Islamic architecture, not only in mosques but also in other public buildings and private residences. Arabian culture, being primarily desert based, had few architectural styles of its own and readily adopted those from other lands that it found beautiful. Frescoes and mosaics decorated many such buildings. The overall impression of grace, beauty, and harmony is intended to replicate the ideal qualities of the universe as Muslims believe God designed it. Islamic architecture reflected the God-centered nature of Muslim society.

Legal Uniformity: The Shari`ah

The God-centric nature of Muslim society was probably most completely expressed in Islamic law, considered more important than theology to a practicing Muslim. Although pre-Islamic Arabia had no formal legal structure, the roots of the **Shari`ah** (*SHAH-rē-ah*), the Islamic legal code, are to be found there, and Muhammad himself was more an arbitrator, lawgiver, and judge than a theologian or politician. He endorsed many customs common to the pre-Islamic social order and enshrined them in the Shari`ah, a compilation of religiously sanctioned obligations and duties intended to regulate daily life so that men and women might more easily carry out the will of God in the *umma*. Consequently the Shari`ah differs from secular legal systems, which use punishment to achieve social control. Shari`ah, in contrast, prescribes the pathway to paradise.

Islamic law, in other words, is essentially moral and spiritual, the product of a new religion's concerted effort to turn a nomadic, tribal society away from the things of this world and toward the wishes of God. The Shari`ah accordingly prohibits gambling, intoxication, and the lending of money at interest. It restricts personal revenge and outlaws the blood feud that turned so much of Arabian tribal life into never-ending cycles of murder between rival families. It attempts to strengthen sexual morality and affirm the sanctity of marriage. It provides legal recourse for women, orphans, the disabled, the mentally infirm, the poor, and anyone else who might be termed defenseless within the social structure. In a culture that valued strength, the Shari`ah protected the weak.

Large sections of the Shari`ah are concerned with family life and gender relations. The wife is integrated into her husband's family and guaranteed a portion of his inheritance. Men are required to treat women with honor and respect. The insistence that women be veiled in public and spend much of their lives sequestered in their homes comes not from the Shari`ah but from Byzantine and Persian customs, which are designed in part to promote honor and respect for women. A man may marry as many as four wives, but if he does so, he must treat them equally in terms of financial support, sexual intercourse, household duties, and respect. Women are permitted to practice contraception, initiate divorce proceedings, remarry after divorce, and own property in their own names. Harsh penalties are provided for physical abuse of wives, adultery, and other such crimes.

The Shari`ah was compiled in the eighth, ninth, and tenth centuries C.E. and still forms the basis of civil and criminal law in some Islamic states. It provided legal uniformity throughout the early Islamic world and survived the subsequent deterioration of Islamic caliphates. But altering the Shari`ah in any meaningful way is considered impossible in Islamic society, as Muslims believe it represents the will of God as transmitted by the last and greatest of the prophets.

Thus the same rigidity that helped perpetuate Islamic law's influence also made it increasingly obsolete as Islamic societies modernized and certain traditional practices and beliefs came into question. The status of women under the Shari`ah provides a valid example. While it offered protections for women not available in eighth-century Arabia, it now places women in a position unequal to men. Women may sue for divorce only if they can show cause; a man needs no cause. Women can testify in court, but a man's testimony is weighted more heavily. Women are to be honored and respected but may have only one husband, while a man may have four wives. Penalties for adultery are much more severe for women than for men.

Islamic law treats men and women differently

Tolerance of Other Faiths

Islamic law applied, of course, to all Muslims, and it formed the basis of civil law in all early Islamic states. But not all citizens of such states were Muslims. The dramatic expansion of Islam aimed to convert those unbelievers who were willing to accept Allah's message as delivered by Muhammad, and to subjugate those who would not convert. While conquered peoples were invited and encouraged to embrace Islam, forced conversions were rare and are in fact prohibited by the Qur'an. Non-Muslims were free to practice their religions under conditions imposed by Islamic law, and were required to pay a heavy tax each year. This tax, which was not paid by Muslims, helped underwrite the expenses of the state. Obviously, if everyone converted to Islam, the financial impact on the government would have been negative. That fact made forced conversions both religiously forbidden and fiscally unwise. Tolerance for other creeds was characteristic of most Islamic societies, and Jews in particular often found it more congenial to live under Islamic rule than under Christian governments.

Salat, or ritual worship, mandates a sequence of prayers to be performed five times each day (see page 266).

This level of tolerance, while impressive by the standards of the day, did not mean that people of other faiths accepted Islamic conquest. Christians in particular were horrified at the prospect of domination by rulers practicing a faith they considered heretical. The Byzantine Empire fought desperately to prevent the triumph of Islam, and Charles Martel's victory over the Muslims at Tours caused rejoicing throughout Europe. Although Muslims were required to tolerate other monotheists and treat them decently, they often treated those they conquered with thinly concealed contempt and sometimes with overt hostility. Polytheists and atheists, on the other hand, were barely tolerated, and many converted to Islam in order to improve their condition.

Chapter Review

Putting It in Perspective

As the Umayyad Caliphate passed into history, Islam was only 140 years old. From a set of revelations claimed by an obscure merchant living on a desert peninsula, Islam had evolved into a powerfully attractive monotheistic belief system with many more followers than Judaism or Zoroastrianism and only slightly fewer than Christianity. The Prophet Muhammad had provided a series of ideas that unified the previously fragmented Arabian Peninsula, setting aside tribal rivalries in the name of faith in Allah.

In addition to establishing Arab unity, Islam inspired warriors to spread their faith across thousands of miles of Europe, Africa, and Asia. The new religion offered Spaniards, Berbers, Egyptians, Syrians, Mesopotamians, Persians, Afghans, and many others a set of easily comprehensible beliefs as well as a centralized governing structure that gave Muslims throughout the world a sense of community. The Shari`ah, a complex yet readily accessible religious law, helped ensure legal uniformity throughout the Islamic empire.

In the Golden Age of Islam, just ahead, this dynamic new culture would attain unprecedented heights as a dominant force in much of Africa and most of south Asia.

Reviewing Key Material

KEY CONCEPTS

People of the Book, 263	jihad, 267
Qur'an, 263	Sunni, 270
umma, 265	Shi'ites, 270
five pillars, 265	mosque, 273
caliph, 267	Shar`iah, 274

KEY PEOPLE

Muhammad, 262	Uthman, 270
Khadija, 262	Ali, 270
Abu Bakr, 267	Muawiya, 270
Khalid ibn al-Walid, 268	Hussein, 270
Umar, 268	Charles Martel, 272

ASK YOURSELF

1. How did Islam transcend Arabian tribalism?
2. To what extent were Muhammad's beliefs original? In what ways were they derived from other belief systems familiar to Arabia?
3. Explain Islam's appeal to Arabs and to those they conquered.
4. What was the significance of the office of caliph in Islam's expansion between 632 and 732?
5. How and why do Sunni and Shi'ite Muslims differ?

GOING FURTHER

Armstrong, Karen. *Muhammad: A Biography of the Prophet.* 1992.

Bloom, Jonathan. *Paper Before Print: The History and Impact of Paper in the Islamic World.* 2001.

Bonney, Richard. *Jihad from Qur'an to bin Laden.* 2004.

Denny, Frederick. *An Introduction to Islam.* 1996.

Donner, F. *The Early Islamic Conquests.* 1986.

Esposito, John. *Islam: The Straight Path.* 1998.

al-Hassan, Ahmad, and Donald Hill. *Islamic Technology: An Illustrated History.* 1986.

Hawting, G. *The First Dynasty of Islam.* 1986.

Hitti, Philip. *The Arabs: A Short History.* 1996.

Hourani, Albert. *A History of the Arab Peoples.* 1991.

Ibrahim, Mahmood. *Merchant Capital and Islam.* 1990.

Kennedy, Hugh. *The Prophet and the Age of the Caliphates.* 1986.

Lapidus, Ira. *A History of Islamic Societies.* 2002.

Lewis, Bernard. *The Political Language of Islam.* 1991.

Lombard, M. *The Golden Age of Islam.* 1975.

Ochsenwald, W. *The Middle East: A History.* 2004.

Perry, G. *The Middle East: Fourteen Islamic Centuries.* 1992.

Peters, F. *Muhammad and the Origins of Islam.* 1994.

Renard, John. *Islam and the Heroic Image.* 1994.

Richard, Y. *Shi'ite Islam.* 1994.

Rodinson, Maxime. *Mohammed.* 1971.

Rogerson, B. *The Prophet Muhammad: A Biography.* 2003.

Spellberg, Denise. *Politics, Gender, and the Islamic Past.* 1994.

Watson, Andrew. *Agricultural Innovation in the Early Islamic World.* 1983.

Key Dates and Developments

520 C.E.	Ethiopian incursion into southern Arabia
570	Persian occupation of southern Arabia begins Birth of Muhammad ibn Abd'Allah
610	Muhammad's revelations and the beginning of his preaching
622	The *Hijra*, or emigration from Mecca to Medina of Muhammad and his followers
630	Return of Muhammad to Mecca
632	Death of Muhammad; Caliphate of Abu Bakr (632–634)
634–644	Caliphate of Umar; Muslims take Damascus, Jerusalem, Persia, and Egypt
644–656	Caliphate of Uthman; Muslim naval victories
651	First compilation of the Qur'an
656–661	Caliphate of Ali, marked by blood feuds following Uthman's assassination
661–750	The Umayyad Caliphate, initiated by the murder of Ali; division between Sunni and Shi'ite Muslims
664	Muslim seizure of eastern Afghanistan
670	Muslims' arrival in eastern Algeria
673–678	Blockade of Constantinople
705–715	Islamic conquest of Algeria, Morocco, and Spain
713	Islam in India
732	Umayyad expansion halted by Charles Martel's victory at Battle of Tours
750–1258	The Abbasid Caliphate

CHAPTER 12

Religion and Diversity in the Transformation of Southern Asia, 711–1400

- Islam Expands Eastward
- Islamic Persia and the Abbasid Caliphate
- Cosmopolitan Islam
- The Decline of the Abbasid Caliphate
- The Gupta Empire in India
- The Islamic Impact on India
- India's Influence on Southeast Asia
- Chapter Review

Angkor Wat

The temples of Angkor Wat are reflected in the moat surrounding the temple complex in Siem Reap, Cambodia. Angkor Wat testifies to the influence of Hinduism in portions of Southeast Asia (page 296).

In 711 an Arab ship passed the mouth of India's Indus River, sailing northwest from the island of Ceylon. Laden with spices, silks, and exquisite objects made from metal and jewels, it was bound for a Persian Gulf port at the mouth of the Tigris and Euphrates Rivers. But the ship never arrived at its destination. From an inlet near the Indus, a pirate ship moved swiftly to intercept the Arab craft. The pirates captured the ship, killed the crew, and sailed off to tally the value of their plunder.

Hearing the news, the Umayyad governor awaiting the cargo was furious. How dare these pirates steal from Muslims? The governor probably realized that he could not locate the pirates or recover the cargo, but he could punish the entire region, as a warning that Arab ships were not to be disturbed. He promptly sent 12,000 mounted warriors against the rajahs (kings) of the western Indian region of Sind. Conquest proved easy, and suddenly the Muslims stood on the banks of the Indus, considering how attractive it might be to seize all of India for Islam.

This sequence of events, initiating direct contact between Muslims and Hindus, launched 13 centuries of conflict and connection between practitioners of the two religions.

Buddhism, Hinduism, and Islam Affect South Asia

Islam Expands Eastward

Islam's swift conquests in North Africa and southwestern Asia encouraged its further expansion into Persia, Afghanistan, and India, where its impact was dramatic. The Abbasid Caliphate, which assumed leadership of Islam by overthrowing the Umayyad dynasty in 750, relocated its capital eastward to Baghdad. It then extended its domination over the Iranian plateau and the remains of the Persian Empire. The Abbasids presided over Islam's Golden Age, a flourishing of learning and culture across the Muslim world that, at the time, stretched from west and South Asia across North Africa to Spain. But this vast region was unified only by religion. In the long run, the Abbasids proved no more capable than the Umayyads of imposing centralized governance on such a diverse set of realms and peoples. They themselves fell victim to a series of revolts in outlying provinces, and in 945 a group of Iranian warlords reduced them to the status of a puppet government.

The Abbasids are unable to unify the caliphate politically

Islam was also beginning to penetrate the vast expanses of the Indian subcontinent, which since the collapse of Mauryan rule in 184 B.C.E. had been unified just once, under two centuries of Gupta rule (320–550). The arrival of Islam did not cause disunity but perpetuated it, as Hindus and Muslims persistently fought one another, creating hostility that endures today.

Neither religion was able to prevail over the other, and as India divided between Hindus and Muslims, Hindu priests, Buddhist monks, and energetic merchants carried Indian culture into the mainland societies and islands of Southeast Asia. There a

FOUNDATION MAP 12.1 The Abbasid Caliphate in 800 C.E.

Islam spread so rapidly that its practitioners were unable to develop political institutions that could govern its extensive acquisitions adequately. The Abbasid Caliphate sprawled from Syria to the Indus Valley, but the caliphs never exerted central control over their realm. Notice that their decision to relocate their capital from Damascus eastward to Baghdad testifies both to the importance of the eastern portion of the caliphate and to the difficulty of controlling the western portion. In the absence of political centralization, what techniques could the caliphs use to control their empire?

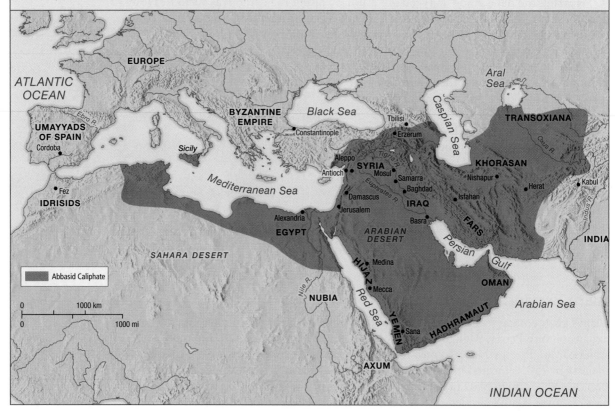

fascinating set of hybrid cultures emerged, influenced by India yet clearly distinct from the customs and traditions of the subcontinent.

Islamic Persia and the Abbasid Caliphate

The caliphate profits from the Persian-Byzantine wars

The Islamic conquest of Iran was made possible by the decline of Sasanian Persia, which had been weakened by its numerous inconclusive campaigns against the Byzantine Empire. Early in the seventh century the Sasanian King Chosroes (*KAHS-ress*) II attacked the Empire, taking Antioch, Damascus, Jerusalem, and Egypt (Map 12.1). But the Byzantines reconstructed their armies and in 622 launched a devastating drive into the Sasanian lands, burning a magnificent Zoroastrian fire temple in 624 and penetrating Mesopotamia three years later. By 633 both Sasanians and Byzantines were exhausted, and at this precise moment Muslim warriors burst forth from Arabia. The Muslims' timing could not have been less convenient for the Sasanians, who were unable to mount an effective defense. Their armies were defeated by Islamic forces in 636, and their empire collapsed in 642.

Persia's conquest by the Muslims marked a dramatic break with its Zoroastrian religious heritage. Although the new rulers tolerated Zoroastrianism, its followers were subject to discrimination and taxation. Many converted to Islam; others moved to western India near Bombay, where their descendants (called Parsees) remain to this day. A few persevered in remote corners of the Iranian plateau. Politically, the once-glorious Persian Empire was now absorbed into the Islamic empire. Muslim conquest marked the end of historic Persia as a powerful, independent political force.

Persian Influences on Islamic Governance and Culture

Although the Persian Empire had ended, its culture survived in an altered form under the alien Islamic regime. Persian culture blended with Islamic ideas of government to form a distinctive new culture exhibiting both Iranian and Arabian elements.

The Muslims proved just as susceptible as the Greeks to the attractions of eastern forms of governance. Persian kings had exercised centralized powers far beyond those held by local Arabian tribal leaders, and the caliphs promptly adopted as much of that authority as they dared. In particular, the caliphs admired the Persian policy of subordinating the religious authority of Zoroastrian priests to the political will of the emperor. Soon interpreters of Islamic law found themselves overruled by political officials who had subordinated themselves to religious authority during the time of the Prophet but intended to do so no longer. The power of the caliphate grew dramatically in the years following the conquest of Persia. This enhancement of the caliph's authority, coupled with the growing importance of Arabic as a common language, provided a degree of unity in this region of the developing Islamic empire.

Persian influences modify Islam

Arabic, of course, had always been the language of Islam. The *Qur'an* required that Arabic be used for all prayers. Thus all converts had to learn Arabic, and many who did not convert realized that knowledge of that language was essential for dealing with their new masters. But the Persian language did not disappear, as Arabs were enchanted by its richness and beauty. Poets and scholars who wrote in Arabic began to adopt Persian expressions, imagery, and syntax; Persian plot lines found their way into Arabic folktales; Persian vocabulary supplemented and enriched spoken Arabic. The result was an Arabic language that grew beyond its roots in the Arabian Peninsula to become a cosmopolitan tongue that Islamic conquerors could use to enhance their influence in Southwest Asia.

The Impact of Shi'ite Opposition

The conquest of Persia took place within the context of the great Sunni-Shi'ite split, which divided the Islamic world after 661. Refusing to accept the Sunni leadership of the Umayyad caliphs, who set up their government in Damascus, Persian Shi'ites had made great progress preaching their beliefs on the Iranian Plateau. This made it impossible for the Umayyads to impose an Islamic Peace on their vast holdings. This failure annoyed merchants, who depended on political stability for their commerce to prosper.

Shi'ites undermine
the caliphate

The people of Persia suffered from additional grievances. Non-Muslims in Iran were required to pay a special tax as the price of religious toleration. Upon conversion, this tax was supposed to disappear, but the Umayyad government, unable to balance its accounts, was reluctant to lift this burden from Persian converts. Moreover, the caliphate inexplicably refused to reinvest any of the income it derived from taxes in Persia itself, where arid conditions required constant, expensive irrigation. These grievances fueled a revolution in 747, led by a man who called himself Abu Muslim. His real name and ancestry are unknown, but his rhetorical and political skills energized Persian malcontents and attracted Shi'ite Arab dissenters.

Abbasids use Persian
connections to
overthrow the
Umayyads

The resulting turmoil squeezed the Umayyads between two angry groups, a situation that worked to the Abbasids' advantage when they overthrew the Umayyads in 750. The Abbasid revolt, which had begun in a northeastern Persian province in 747, was led by Muslims loyal to the family of a man named Abbas, an uncle of the Prophet Muhammad. Its success aided by uprisings in Persia, the Abbasid Caliphate took care to look after the needs of this province. Persia suddenly benefited from tax revenues, and Persian influence rose at the Abbasid court. Although they were themselves Sunni Muslims, the Abbasids strove to placate Persian Shi'ites, hoping perhaps to heal the century-old schism within the Islamic world or at least to ensure their continued domination of that world.

The Rise of Baghdad

The Abbasids reorient
the caliphate eastward

The Abbasids also shifted the focus of the Islamic world eastward. The gateways to Europe through Constantinople and southern Africa through Ethiopia were barred by Christian states hostile to Islam. Northern Asia was mountainous and cold, filled with wolves and unfriendly Turkic tribes. Opportunity for Islamic expansion clearly lay in the east. In 763 the caliphate moved its capital east to a new city, which it built on the site of a tiny village known as Baghdad. Located in eastern Mesopotamia near the site of ancient Babylon, Baghdad's founding embodied the Abbasid transfer of emphasis from western to eastern Islam.

The caliphate's decision to relocate was considered carefully. In addition to being close to the eastern Islamic lands, Baghdad was strategically located at the juncture of the trade routes connecting Syria, Mesopotamia, and Persia. It had easy access to the Tigris and Euphrates rivers in one of the most fertile areas of Mesopotamia. Favored by its location, Baghdad quickly became the largest urban area in the history of western Asia, populated in the early 800s by somewhere between 300,000 and 500,000 people. By comparison, Constantinople at that point contained about 200,000 people. Baghdad proved to be central to the development not only of the Abbasid Caliphate but of Islamic civilization.

Cosmopolitan Islam

Islam now developed a prosperous, cosmopolitan civilization. The Islamic faith had originated in the Arabian Peninsula, grounded in local Arab customs and culture. Its explosive century of expansion, however, had exposed it to a broad variety of ethnic and linguistic groups across southern Asia. For the leadership of Islam, a religion that claimed universality, the next step was both obvious and challenging: it must grow beyond its Arabian origins. To do so, it would have to reach out to people of diverse ancestries, offering them a path to salvation and combining their backgrounds and cultures into a new civilization that would be greater than the sum of its parts. To do otherwise would limit Islam's appeal, restricting it to an ethnic Arabian elite, denying its claim to worship the one true God of all humanity, and perpetuating it as a conquering rather than a constructing faith.

Baghdad enabled the Abbasids to take that next step. They made Islam a universal religion and inspired a golden age of Islamic civilization. Cosmopolitan and diverse, Baghdad welcomed Arabians, Mesopotamians, Syrians, Persians, Indians, Egyptians, Central Asians, Christians, Zoroastrians, Jews, and many others. In this new, vibrant city these people were assimilated into a new, vibrant civilization built on a self-confident, dynamic faith that offered spiritual equality to all who embraced it. Growing into a major industrial and commercial center, Baghdad provided jobs for all who sought them and ample revenues to sustain Abbasid ambitions.

Islam becomes a universal faith

Abbasid Governance

Chief among Abbasid ambitions was correcting the errors of the Umayyads. While the Umayyads had reserved influential positions for Arabs, the Abbasids sought to advance talented people, regardless of ethnicity, to positions of responsibility. The government at Baghdad recruited personnel from throughout the empire with the promise of equality of opportunity in a large empire serving a universal faith. The privileges and elite status long enjoyed by Arabs were abolished. Jews served the caliphate as bankers and financial advisors; Persians as bureaucrats and scribes; Mesopotamian Christians as engineers and diplomats.

Abbasids utilize all conquered peoples

Although Arabs supervised all these groups, they were Arabs completely devoted to the Abbasid regime. Loyalty to the caliph was more important than ethnic ancestry. The exclusively Arab armies were replaced by a skilled force of paid professional soldiers of mixed ethnic background. No longer needed for conquest, they were assigned to maintain internal order, patrol the frontiers, and keep watch on the Byzantine Empire. Their leadership was still Arabian, but their most important characteristic was loyalty.

The Abbasids built on governmental foundations laid by the Umayyads, particularly their centralization of authority. Control was maintained by the Caliph and his advisors. Government bureaus collected taxes, kept records, handled correspondence, and disbursed tax revenues. Judges were charged with applying the Shari`ah, or Islamic law (Chapter 11), to everyday life in every corner of the realm. A *wazir* (*WAH-zēr*) supervised and coordinated the entire politico-legal system in Baghdad. Governors closely tied to the caliph's family ruled outlying provinces with degrees of loyalty proportionate to their distance from the capital. As messages had to be transmitted slowly across the caliphate by either camel or ship, the caliph's operational authority dwindled significantly on the remote fringes of the empire. Although fully centralized political control eluded the Abbasids, the overall extent of centralization in the caliphate was impressive.

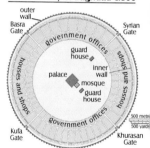

The inner city of Baghdad c.800

A sketch of the inner city of Baghdad around the year 800 C.E.

Commerce and Culture in the Abbasid Caliphate

The administrative stability of the Abbasid era also promoted significant commercial and cultural achievements. Abbasid caliphs nurtured trade routes that crossed both Asia and Africa, while in the caliphate itself they fostered literature and the arts.

Perhaps because Muhammad himself had been a merchant, commercial activity was generally held in higher esteem in Islamic lands than it was in either Christian Europe or Confucian China. The Abbasid caliphs, eager to increase both their own immense wealth and the prosperity of the lands they ruled, lowered trade barriers, promoted the work of artisans and merchants, and encouraged long-distance commerce. A vast network of trade routes stretched by land across both Central Asia and the Sahara Desert, and by water across the Mediterranean and the Red and Arabian seas. Products widely traded included Chinese silks and Indian spices; gold, salt, slaves, and ivory from Africa; steel and leather from Spain; and magnificent hand-woven carpets and textiles from southern and western Asia. Banking and credit helped to finance expensive commercial enterprises. The widespread use of the Arabic language eased business transactions, and Arabic numerals simplified and standardized bookkeeping.

Eager to imitate the Indo-Persian civilizations, which they considered superior to that of the Arabian Peninsula, the Abbasids led their empire into a spectacular cultural renaissance. The Caliph Harun al-Rashid (*hah-ROON al rah-SHED*), who ruled from 786 to 809, built a magnificent palace that reflected both his astonishing wealth and his reputation as a generous patron of the arts. He brought to Baghdad authors, artists, architects, and entertainers from as far away as Morocco in North Africa and Delhi in India, and they made the city a radiant cultural center. Harun's son established in Baghdad an academy called the House of Wisdom. There some scholars translated ancient Greek, Latin, and Sanskrit writings into Arabic, while others laid the foundation for the devotion to keen observation and objective thinking that became characteristic of Arab scientific and intellectual life.

From the eighth through the twelfth centuries, Islamic learning blossomed. In philosophy, Muslims such as Ibn Sina (*ib-un SE-nah*), later known in Europe as Avicenna, translated and wrote commentaries on the works of the ancient Greek philosopher Aristotle, which at this time were unknown in the West. Ibn Sina was also inspired by the discovery of Indian and Greek writings on medicine, which he and other Muslims translated, compiled, explained, and amplified. The Persian scholar al-Khwarizmi (*al kwa-RIZ-me*) analyzed the findings of various classical thinkers, including Claudius Ptolemy, whose detailed conception of an earth-centered universe was later revised by other Muslims, including Ibn al-Haytham (*ib-un al-hi-THAHM*) and Nasir al-Din al-Tusi (*nah-SEER al-den al-TOO-si*). Ptolemy's view of the universe, as modified by Muslim scholars, prevailed until the seventeenth century both in the Islamic world and in the West.

A page from a twelfth-century Islamic manuscript dealing with alchemy.

Inspired by their contacts with India and China, Muslims under the caliphate also proved to be talented innovators. For example, they developed the quadrant, the astrolabe, the celestial globe, and other instruments of navigation. Most of these had been invented by other peoples, but Muslims refined and used them to great advantage. Muslims also excelled at physics and optics, and they developed windmills, watermills, water-clocks, new methods of irrigation, and instruments used in meteorology. Applying Persian and Indian mathematics, al-Khwarizmi devised both algebra and the Arabic numerals that are universally used today.

The production of paper provides an excellent example of Islamic development of an earlier invention. Paper had been invented in China sometime between 200 and 50 B.C.E. When the Muslims encountered this product, they found that it was made of wood-based

Document 12.1 Quatrains from *The Rubaiyat*

Omar Khayyam's collection of quatrains, or four-line poetic stanzas, was translated from Omar's elegant Persian into English by Edward FitzGerald in 1859. This translation made the work accessible to Western readers, and it has since been translated into more than one hundred languages. Omar was a master of astronomy, history, jurisprudence, mathematics, medicine, and philosophy as well as poetry. *The Rubaiyat* reveals his fatalistic fascination with questions of eternal interest: Who are we? Why are we here? Where are we going? What is the nature of our relationship to God?

The moving finger writes; and, having writ,
Moves on; nor all your piety nor wit
Shall lure it back to cancel half a line,
Nor all your tears wash out a word of it.

Oh, threats of hell and hopes of paradise!
One thing at least is certain: **this** life flies.
One thing is certain and the rest is lies:
The flower that once has blown forever dies.

fibers derived from tropical plants like bamboo, hemp, and jute. Papers made from these fibers were not particularly durable, and since these plants did not grow in Islamic lands, Muslims looked for new sources of fiber. They began to use rags made from linen or from cotton cloth, which produce paper that is extremely durable. In 794, the first Islamic paper mill was built in Baghdad. Soon the availability of this paper throughout Muslim lands encouraged scholarly writing in virtually every area of knowledge. Paper made it possible for Muslims to preserve, and eventually transmit, Greek and Byzantine knowledge and culture. When Europe first came into contact with this Islamic knowledge base in the twelfth century, its scholars were both impressed and intimidated.

Works of fiction and folklore also flourished in this era. The most famous of these was probably *The 1,001 Nights*, also known in the West as *The Arabian Nights*. Embellished over the centuries, this assortment of fanciful and fantastic fables eventually came to include such well-known adventure stories as "Sinbad the Sailor" and "Aladdin and His Magic Lamp." Of the many marvelous works of poetry produced in this period, among the best known is *The Rubaiyat*, a collection of verses originally composed around 1100 by a famous scientist and mathematician named Omar Khayyam (see "Quatrains from *The Rubaiyat*").

A Muslim astronomer's depiction of the constellation Sagittarius, copied from the original manuscript in 1730.

Sufis and Fundamentalists

Not everyone in the caliphate participated in the economic and cultural achievements of Islam's Golden Age. Many devout Muslims worried that the Age's emphasis on material prosperity, its encouragement of artistic expression, and its wide-ranging intellectual efforts were undermining the simplicity and spirituality of their faith. As various groups sought different ways to revitalize Islam and return it to its roots, several distinct responses emerged.

One was **Sufism** (*SOO-fizm*). Deriving from Persian influence on Shi'ism, Sufism was a mystic strain of Islam that advocated direct union with God through prayer, contemplation, and religious ecstasy. Sufism developed gradually during the first three centuries of Islamic history. In its early stages, it was characterized by rejection of the

Islamic mysticism seeks direct connection with God

luxury and wealth that Islam had come to emphasize under the influences of Persia and Byzantium. Sufism favored a simple lifestyle, recalling the devout Muslim to the origins of the faith on the austere deserts of the Arabian peninsula. In Arabic, *suf* (*SOOF*) means "wool," and Sufis (*SOO-fez*) wore rough woolen clothing, obviously uncomfortable in the Middle Eastern heat, to symbolize their renunciation of worldly pleasures, a renunciation also practiced by Buddhist and Christian mystics and monks. Later Sufism also came to involve the pursuit of a mystical union with God through elaborate dances and ceremonies. Sufi doctrines varied widely as different brotherhoods of Sufis developed. One principal tradition was centered in Mecca and another in northeastern Persia, although Sufi brotherhoods also became common in India.

Another response to the materialism of the Abbasid Caliphate was the growth of militant Islamic fundamentalism. Unlike the Sufis, who strove mainly to withdraw from the secular world, the fundamentalists sought to combat and repress it. In general, fundamentalists believed that Islam itself had become corrupted by secular influences, and that purification of the Muslim community, or *umma*, was necessary to restore fidelity to the original revelations of Allah transmitted through Muhammad. Like Sufism, Islamic fundamentalism took a wide variety of forms, including Wahhabism, which eventually became the dominant form of Islam on the Arabian Peninsula.

Inspired by a deep suspicion of intellectual pursuits, the fundamentalists who led eleventh-century Spain exiled both the great Muslim scholar-physician Ibn Rushd (*ib-un ROOSHD*), known in the West as Averröes, and the Jewish philosopher Moses Maimonides (*mī-MAH-nih-dēz*), charging them with polluting the Qur'an by trying to reconcile it with modern philosophy. Later Islamic governments in Spain appointed religious courts, instructing them to enforce the Shari`ah against any attempts at secularization.

Fundamentalist resistance to secularization fostered a climate of intellectual repression. As Islamic scientific and technological curiosity was submerged in a rising tide of fundamentalist religious fervor, Islam was poorly prepared to face the cultural and military challenges soon to be posed by the West.

The Decline of the Abbasid Caliphate

Like all the large empires before them, the Abbasids found their vast territory difficult to rule. Communication over the thousands of miles separating Spain from Baghdad was challenging enough under the best of circumstances. Quarrels between rival leaders, disputes between Sunni and Shi'ite Muslims, and tensions between various ethnic groups also interfered with the ability of the Abbasids to govern effectively and frustrated their dream of conquering the world for Islam.

Forces of Disintegration

The glory of Islamic learning could not obscure the disintegration of the caliphate, which set in even before its consolidation was complete. First, Harun al-Rashid (786–809), the most powerful of the caliphs, unintentionally weakened his own system. In attempting to ensure that his older son would succeed him as caliph, he gave his younger son, al-Mamun, a governorship in northeastern Persia. But Al-Mamun used this position to challenge his older brother, initiating four years of civil strife. Al-Mamun won, but the conflict alienated Mesopotamia and the Abbasid armies, both of which had supported the older son. Legitimate succession, a vexing problem in Islamic states since the death of Muhammad's son-in-law Ali, proved to be the first problem to erode the strength of the Abbasids.

Second, al-Mamun gained the crucial backing of the Persian prince Tahir (*TAH-bēr*) only by making Tahir hereditary governor of northeastern Persia. This grant of authority undermined the Abbasid drive for centralization. It also helped create a warlord nobility that rivaled and eventually replaced the caliph and provided a focus for Persian Shi'ite opposition to the Sunni regime in Baghdad.

Third, to increase their power the Abbasids established armies of Turkish slaves from central Asia called Mamluks (*MAM-lukes*). These male slaves, purchased before they turned 13, were converted to Islam and segregated in military barracks. There they studied military tactics, developed loyalty and comradeship, and after several years, became soldiers in the caliph's armies. In theory, every Mamluk was a disciplined servant of the state, without ties to family or region; his loyalty was to the caliph and the army. In practice, Mamluks fought for the caliph only so long as he paid them well and proved a competent leader. Failure in either respect could easily lead to his overthrow, as Mamluks quickly became the state's most efficient warriors. They antagonized the people of Baghdad, most of whom considered them uncivilized foreigners, so the caliphs built a new capital at Samarra (*sah-MAR-rah*) in Mesopotamia in 836 and took the Mamluks with them. The move solved one problem but created another by eroding the caliphate's authority.

The Abbasid Caliphate decays

Finally, a growing disloyalty in the Abbasid bureaucracy accelerated the caliphate's decline. Dominated by factions based on family ties and cronyism, the bureaucrats began to peddle their services and influence to the highest bidders. As the caliphs became less able to maintain control of the central government, discontented factions in outlying areas took advantage of the situation and revolted. In the ninth century, unrest broke out in Egypt, Mesopotamia, and Iran. Occasionally the caliphs were able to restore order, but only through the use of the unpopular Mamluks. As the authority of the central administration disintegrated, the empire itself collapsed.

The Mosque of Ibn Tulun, Cairo.

Although the last caliph did not leave the throne until his murder by the Mongols in 1258, the tenth century marked the end of effective Abbasid rule. One by one, provinces of the empire had broken away. Egypt was taken over by a Mamluk family in 868 and then by the Shi'ite Fatimid dynasty in 969. The governor of Islamic Spain created his own independent caliphate in 929, confirming a separation that had actually begun much earlier. A mass revolt of frontier troops that could not be repressed resulted in the loss of Persia in the ninth century. By 935 the Abbasid caliph had lost control of every province outside the immediate vicinity of Baghdad. After a power struggle lasting nearly a decade, the Buyid (*BOO-yid*) dynasty of Shi'ite Persian warlords seized control of Baghdad in 945. The caliphs were allowed to remain as puppet rulers, but they exercised no authority. The glorious era of Abbasid rule was over.

Abbasid power ends in the tenth century C.E.

Continuity of Islamic Unity and Expansion

Political fragmentation did not, however, destroy the unity of Islam. Despite its multitude of rulers and cultures, the Muslim community was still held together by Shari`ah and the Qur'an. Islamic law provided a code of conduct that differentiated Muslims from all other

Muslims preserve unity through scripture, language, and law

peoples, giving them a common identity. Stipulations that the Qur'an must be read only in Arabic helped to make that language a common means of communication—and a unifying force—across different Muslim cultures. Finally, the pilgrimage to Mecca, a common practice in pre-Islamic Arabia that Muhammad eventually required of all believers, also helped to create cohesion.

The pilgrimage symbolized the equality of all Muslims in the context of their complete submission to Allah. Pilgrims were greeted at the outskirts of Mecca, where they exchanged their clothing for simple white robes in which they entered the holy city. During the entire seven days of the pilgrimage, no distinctions of birth, race, wealth, or position separated one Muslim from another. All wore the same white robes, performed the same rituals, and professed the same unworthiness in the sight of Allah. The pilgrimage also promoted contacts and common values among Muslim pilgrims from diverse cultures, inspiring them to foster these values in their native lands.

Nor did political division put an end to Islamic expansion. Indeed, even as the caliphate declined and the various Muslim factions fought against each other, Islamic faith and Islamic armies were penetrating into India, clashing with the ancient cultures of that immense subcontinent.

An Islamic schematic world map, dating from the Abbasid caliphate and showing the Ka'ba at the center of the world.

The Gupta Empire in India

After the end of the Mauryan Empire in 184 C.E., India remained divided among several states, a subcontinent whose cultural pluralism seemed both the reflection and the principal cause of its political disunity. Then the unexpected happened: a relatively unknown Indian family reunified the north and created the Gupta Empire (320–550), the first centralized Hindu state.

Gupta Rule and Achievements

The Gupta family came from northeastern India, where they controlled the Barabar (*bah-RAH-bur*) Hills, rich in high-quality iron ore. This guaranteed them an ample resource for swords and shields and a favorable cash flow. The dynasty's founder, Chandra Gupta I (320–335), was not related to the man of the same name who established the Mauryan Empire, and little is known about him. The actual architect of the Gupta Empire was Chandra's son, Samudra (*sah-MOO-drah*) Gupta, whose 40-year rule (335–375) gave northern India its first centralized monarchy since the Mauryans five centuries earlier.

Samudra Gupta was encouraged by his father to rule the entire known world. He fell short of that lofty goal but did manage to overthrow no fewer than 20 regional Indian kings, and in the process he gained control of both the Indus and Ganges river valleys. He also conquered several states on the central Deccan Plateau, but chose to rule those kingdoms through vassals. In turn his son, Chandra Gupta II (375–415), extended the empire's power by expelling the Scythians from west central India (Map 12.2). The new empire then exercised direct authority over port cities on the Arabian Sea, enabling it to profit handsomely from trade with western and southeastern Asia. Neither Samudra Gupta nor Chandra Gupta II had any success in subduing the independent Tamil states of south

The Gupta dynasty unifies northern India

India. The size of the subcontinent, as always, posed a formidable obstacle to any would-be unifiers.

Chandra Gupta II is known more for the stability of his reign than for his military success. Accounts by both Hindus and Buddhists describe a period of religious tolerance and peace across northern India, signs of a rare social stability. The Guptas, although Hindus themselves, not only tolerated Buddhists and Jains but also subsidized their religious temples and monasteries. During this time spiritual, artistic, and philosophical culture flowered. Magnificent Hindu temples were constructed throughout the subcontinent, setting the tone for Indian architecture for centuries to come, and a number of schools of classical Hindu philosophy were established. Of these schools, **yoga**, which emphasizes meditation and self-knowledge, is the most widely known and practiced in the West.

The Guptas' preference for Hinduism affected more than philosophy and architecture in northern India. It also affected gender relations. From the Persians, Hindus had adopted **purdah** (*PURR-dah*), the seclusion of married women through their confinement to certain rooms of the house. Under this custom a respectable woman could show her face only within the family, and she had to wear a thick veil when going out in public. In northern India the custom became so vigorous that to ask after the health of a man's wife might be considered impolite. Purdah was not, however, imposed upon Buddhists or Jains, and even Hindus were free to modify it according to local custom.

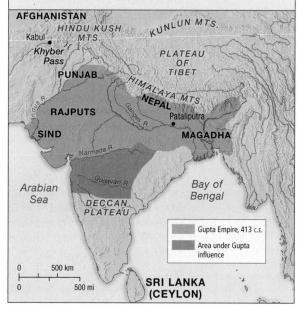

Map 12.2 The Gupta Empire in 413 C.E.

India's size and topography (Map 3.1) deterred centralization, so unified governments were often confined to particular geographic subdivisions of the subcontinent. Note that early in the fourth century C.E., the Gupta Empire unified much of northern India from its base on the Gangetic Plain. Although not as large as the Mauryan Empire (Map 3.4), the Gupta Empire received tribute from areas like the Indus Valley and Nepal, bringing a degree of stability to most of India north of the Deccan Plateau. Why would governments in northern India find it difficult to expand their control southward?

The spiritual and artistic development characteristic of Gupta India was rooted in material prosperity and wealth. Trade with the West flourished, particularly with Byzantium and Rome. Indian perfumes, spices, ivory, and wood were prized in Europe. When Alaric the Goth besieged Rome in 408, part of his ransom for withdrawing his forces included 3,000 pounds of Indian pepper. But commerce with the East was even more extensive and profitable. China coveted Indian ivory, brass, cotton cloth, and unusual animals like mongooses and elephants; in return the Indians received Chinese amber, silk, and oils. Some of the trade went by sea, but ocean routes were vulnerable to weather and pirates; camel caravans traveling the Silk Road through Central Asia were far more likely to arrive intact. In the late Gupta era, however, the opening of trade with resource-rich Southeast Asia made the sea passage worth the risk.

Guptas connect far-flung regions commercially

At home, Gupta prosperity was based on agriculture, which was productive enough to enable peasants to pay significant taxes-in-kind (a portion of their harvest). The subcontinent's climate and soil supported good harvests of wheat, rice, citrus and noncitrus fruits, and sugarcane. Because of Hindu religious prohibitions, Indians rarely ate meat, but dairy products were widely available, and fish constituted a staple in the south. The main obstacle to agriculture was weather, especially the periodic flooding in the Bay of Bengal and long periods of intense heat requiring irrigation. But famine was rare in Gupta India. The government supplemented tax revenues through ownership of all metal and salt mines, which provided a steady, substantial income.

Conflict and Collapse

Chandra Gupta II was followed by Kumara (*kuh-MAH-rah*) Gupta, whose 40-year reign (415–455) witnessed the first signs of trouble. The Central Asian migrations continued, and this time it was not the Scythians but the Huns who came calling. They were a particularly dangerous breed of Central Asian nomads: violent, ruthless fighters who killed frequently and indifferently. Kumara Gupta blocked them at the Khyber (*KĪ-burr*) Pass in the mountains between northern India and Central Asia, through which nomadic tribes seeking the more fertile lands of South Asia had long traveled. This success enabled him to hand the empire intact to his son Skanda Gupta but not to preserve it. Throughout Skanda Gupta's reign (455–467) the Huns were a constant menace, and the treasury could scarcely bear the strain of holding them back.

The Gupta Empire collapses under pressure from the Huns

Once the Huns penetrated northern India, other nomadic tribes followed, disrupting Gupta trade with Central Asia and severely reducing the empire's income. Economic setbacks combined with Hun aggression caused north Indian political unity to crumble. The Huns took the Punjab in 499, conquering Kashmir and most of the plain of the Ganges River shortly thereafter. The Gupta Empire collapsed by 550.

The Huns were not interested in replacing the Gupta Empire with one of their own. They were restless warriors, not empire builders. As the north Indian empire shattered into a series of independent kingdoms, the Huns were content to collect tribute. Some kingdoms paid, while others ignored the Huns and were ignored by them, as was the case in eastern Europe.

Centralized control existed nowhere in the subcontinent. In south India, the Tamil states disappeared, and authority was divided between forest-based tribes and valley-based villagers, both of which were ruled by warrior aristocracies. India drifted in this way for nearly two centuries, with most of its people oblivious to issues of state control and foreign threats. Then came Islam.

The Islamic Impact on India

Islam's initial venture into India occurred almost by accident. The piracy of an Umayyad ship in 711, described at the beginning of this chapter, led directly to Muslim invasion and occupation of the Sind in western India. Those actions established a contact between Muslims and Hindus that altered the economic and cultural frameworks of the Indian subcontinent. Eventually India became part of a sprawling Indian Ocean Islamic trading network, while conflict between Hindu polytheists and Muslim monotheists divided the region for centuries.

Islamic Invasions from Persia

After 711, Muslim raids from the Sind devastated the northern Indian region of Gujarat (*guh-jah-RAHT*), temporarily provoking a unified defense. Northern India successfully resisted further Islamic invasions until 998 when a new threat emerged, this time from Persia.

By this time Persia was divided among three groups of Muslim warlords. The Buyids, who had conquered Baghdad and subordinated the Abbasid caliphs in 945, ruled Mesopotamia and western Persia from then until 1055; the Samanids (*sah-MAH-nids*) controlled eastern Persia from 819 to 999; and the Ghaznavids (*gaz-NAH-vids*) dominated northeastern Persia and Afghanistan from 962 until 1040 (Map 12.3). Baghdad's fall in 945 had opened the frontiers between the Middle East and Central Asia to nomadic Turkish tribes that crossed between these regions at will. In the eleventh century, one of these tribes, the Seljuk (*SELL-jook*) Turks, took both Persia and Anatolia from the weakened Abbasids, adding Turkish customs and genes to an already simmering stew of ethnicities.

Muslims invade India from the west

The Buyids of western Persia legitimized themselves by propping up the caliphs and then governed like the warlords they were. In eastern Persia, the Samanids tried to replicate the early Abbasid bureaucracy. They presided over a cultural renaissance centered on the city of Bukhara (*boo-KAH-rah*), in which Arabic literary and legal forms blended

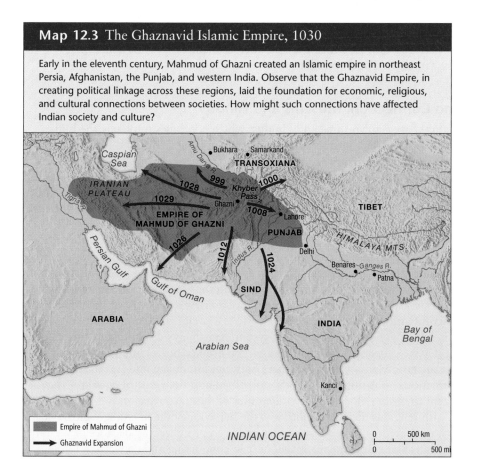

Map 12.3 The Ghaznavid Islamic Empire, 1030

Early in the eleventh century, Mahmud of Ghazni created an Islamic empire in northeast Persia, Afghanistan, the Punjab, and western India. Observe that the Ghaznavid Empire, in creating political linkage across these regions, laid the foundation for economic, religious, and cultural connections between societies. How might such connections have affected Indian society and culture?

with Persian, and Farsi joined Arabic as a language of transmission for Islamic culture. Finally, in northeastern Persia and Afghanistan, the Ghaznavid government of Mamluks took control of both state and bureaucracy, creating a hybrid Persian-Islamic culture while attacking every non-Islamic area within reach. The most attractive area was India.

Mahmud of Ghazni connects Persia, Afghanistan, and India

The Ghaznavids took their name from the Afghan city of Ghazni, just west of the Khyber Pass. From that stronghold they could plunder the trade routes between India and southwestern Asia. Between 998 and 1030 Mahmud of Ghazni (*MAH-mood of GAZ-nē*), known as the "Sword of Islam," led 17 raids on the northwestern Indian region of Punjab. He pillaged its cities remorselessly, destroying magnificent Hindu temples (whose idols, from his Islamic viewpoint, were abominations) and confiscating every jewel, coin, and woman he could find. This plunder enriched Ghazni, which quickly became a major cultural center of the Islamic world. Its glittering mosques and palaces were heavily influenced by Persian architectural concepts. But the empire was founded on bloodshed, rape, and destruction, all carried out in the name of God and in the interest of profit.

An extensive cave/temple complex near present-day Mumbai.

Shortly before his death in 1030, Mahmud annexed the Punjab. The Ghaznavid dynasty now controlled all of northwestern India, including the Indus Valley. But in Ghazni the political situation was deteriorating. Ignoring the advice of his Persian counselors, Mahmud had permitted the Seljuk Turks to use grazing pastures in Ghaznavid territory. The Seljuks responded by making war on the Ghaznavids and by 1040 had expelled them from northeastern Persia. Leaving that region to their enemies, the Ghaznavids relocated to northwestern India, which they plundered relentlessly while generating hatred and bitterness within the Hindu population.

Conflict and Connection: Muslims and Hindus

The deep hostility between Muslims and Hindus, which continues to plague the Indian subcontinent today, is rooted both in the behavior of the Ghaznavids and in religion itself. There was little compatibility between these two belief systems. Islam's rigorous, uncompromising monotheism holds that there is only one God and that all human beings must subordinate themselves to his will in every act of daily life. To Muslims, Hinduism, with its vast number of gods and goddesses, is simply polytheistic idolatry. To Hindus, however, the Muslims' monotheistic conviction is both presumptuous and preposterous.

Muslims and Hindus confront one another in India

Beyond this fundamental fissure, Islam asserts the essential equality and unworthiness of all people who stand before Allah. This view, grounded in ancient Arab tribal customs, gives any Muslim the right to address even the most exalted leader as an equal. Hinduism, in contrast, is based on a rigid caste system that reinforces inequality between different levels of society. To Muslims, a system that assigns a majority of the population to lifelong discrimination is offensive. Since a caste is a social class into which you are born and from which you cannot move, this system has always discouraged conversion to Hinduism: if caste is determined by birth and you are not born Hindu, how can you fit into Indian society? Many other differences between Hinduism and Islam exist, but these two distinctions—the number of gods worshiped and the value of equality—have proved sufficient to ensure more than a millennium of mutual suspicion.

Ghaznavids persecute Hindus in India

Coupled with religious incompatibility was the behavior of the invading Ghaznavids. Their regime was created by slave soldiers who had been brutalized by decades of warfare with Central Asians and who were interested only in conquering and converting foreign peoples, not in assimilating them. Considering Hindus' polytheism, they placed little value on Indian culture, customs, art, or architecture, much of which they destroyed. The Hindus understandably judged all Muslims by the conduct of the Ghaznavids and fought back, often, for example, setting fire to Islamic mosques and burning the worshipers alive.

Consequently, the basic incompatibility between Islam and Hinduism was intensified by atrocities and persecutions on both sides. Yet despite this hostility, from the tenth century onward, Hindus and Muslims shared the subcontinent. Eyeing each other warily, they maneuvered for position. The Ghaznavids retained the advantage until 1186, when they were ejected by another Islamic Turkish tribe, the Ghurids (*GUR-ids*). Hindus put up fierce resistance against the Ghurids, having learned in the eleventh century exactly what Islamic occupation meant for their families and their culture. Buddhists suffered even more than Hindus, in part because their faith's rejection of violence made them reluctant to resist aggression, in part because, like Islam, their faith sought converts and Muslims viewed it as competitive. The Ghurids destroyed Buddhist monasteries throughout India, driving the faith from its native soil. While flourishing in exile in Tibet, Japan, China, and Southeast Asia, Buddhism did not return to India with any significant presence until the 1950s, when India was unified under a secular democracy that granted toleration to all faiths (Chapter 35).

Despite Hindu resistance, the Ghurids eventually triumphed, establishing what came to be known as the Delhi Sultanate. From 1206 to 1526, a succession of sultans tackled the challenge of consolidating an Islamic regime in a region dominated by Hindu culture and beliefs. The result was a society combining both Indian and Islamic characteristics. Although at first the Delhi Sultanate leveled Hindu temples and sought conversions, it soon changed course, staking its stability on values that Hindus and Muslims could share, including loyalty to kings, strong relationships between patrons and clients, and virtues such as service and honor. Delhi's ruling elite was primarily Islamic, but meritorious or wealthy Hindus were permitted to enter it while retaining their faith and customs. No more than a quarter of the northern Indian population converted to Islam, and for three centuries the Delhi Sultanate ruled a predominantly Hindu population through collaboration rather than confrontation.

The Delhi Sultanate attempts to unify India

Delhi brought stability to northern India and at one point was able to expand its holdings into the southern part of the subcontinent. But it could not hold all of India together: the subcontinent was simply too large and too diverse, linguistically and culturally. India continued to be buffeted and battered by internal conflicts and external attacks, and eventually it was conquered by invaders from the north.

The Quwwat-ul-Islam mosque in Delhi, featuring Hindu motifs such as tasselled ropes and bells.

India's Influence on Southeast Asia

Islam was not the only religion to transform southern Asia. As Muslim rule migrated across southwest Asia and India, Hinduism and Buddhism spread into Southeast Asia, bringing India's influence to a vast region already affected by China.

Funan: The First Southeast Asian State

Geographically, Southeast Asia is divided into three subregions: the Southeast Asian mainland (sometimes called Indochina), the Malay (*MĀ-la*) peninsula, and the Indonesian archipelago (*ahr-kih-PEL-ah-gō*), or group of islands. Southeast Asia is a seismically active area,

Geographic and climatic challenges confront Southeast Asia

Map 12.4 Southeast Asia, 800–1400

In Southeast Asia, Islam, Buddhism, and Hinduism coexisted at the crossroads of the Indian and Pacific Oceans. All three religions entered the region on ships carrying goods between India and China. Notice the strategic location of the Indonesian islands, perfectly placed as connectors between these two great oceans. In what ways did the convergence of these three religions, combined with the intense commercial activity typical of Southeast Asia, create unique societies?

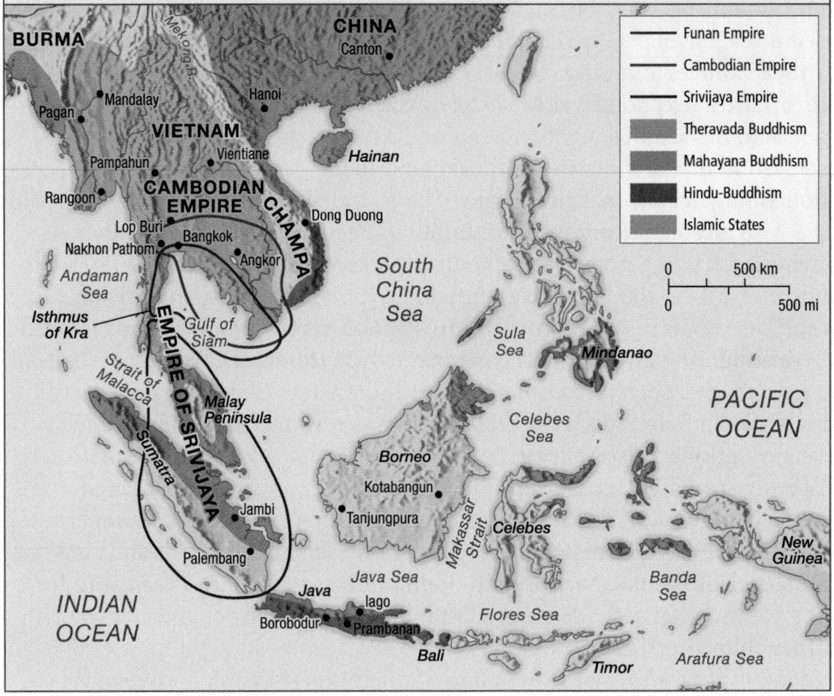

part of the "Ring of Fire" surrounding the Pacific Ocean, and most of the islands are volcanic in origin (Map 12.4). Its tropical climate, abundant rainfall, and highly fertile soils give it great agricultural potential. But this promise has been difficult to realize. As much of the area is covered by teeming rain forests, farmland must be cleared again and again but without removing so much cover that the soil itself washes away. As a result, the large populations of Southeast Asia walk a fine line between survival and catastrophe.

Little is known of the origins of the first inhabitants of Southeast Asia. They had lived there for many centuries before the sustained immigrations from southern China that began around 3000 B.C.E. Many of these original inhabitants remained in the region, becoming the peoples now referred to as Malays. Others moved eastward across the Pacific Ocean or westward across the Indian Ocean, sailing in sturdy double-outrigger canoes built to compensate for strong oceanic swells. They populated many of the islands that dot those seas.

Southeast Asia lay across a trade route widely used in the first centuries of the Common Era to transport goods from China to India and from there to the Mediterranean

Commercial traffic creates Southeast Asian states

basin. Eventually Malay merchants, who controlled oceangoing traffic, added spices from Southeast Asia to their shipments of Chinese silk. As a connection point for traders from both India and China, Southeast Asia eventually absorbed cultural elements from both of its wealthy and powerful neighbors.

In what is today southern Vietnam, the first Southeast Asian state emerged in the first century C.E. Chinese traders referred to it as Funan (*foo-NAHN*). Its point of origin was the Mekong (*MĒ-kong*) River delta, but quickly it expanded southward into the Malay peninsula, enabling it to control trade across the strategically located Isthmus of Kra (*KRAH*). This was a narrow neck of land between the South China Sea and the Bay of Bengal. Merchants preferred to carry their cargoes across it rather than risk the lengthy ocean voyage around the Malay peninsula. Funan's control of this transfer point increased its prosperity as well as its exposure to foreign peoples and cultures.

With the traders came their ways of life. Most of the actual transporting, buying, and selling was done by Indians. Accordingly, Buddhist monks and Hindu priests from India arrived in Funan shortly after the merchants. The learning of these religious men, as well as their familiarity with events outside the region, quickly made them sought-after counselors to local princes, and their religious beliefs and artistic tastes spread readily through the population. As intermarriage increased, a cultural synthesis occurred, featuring the adoption of Sanskrit as a written language and considerable mixing of cuisine and customs. Literary works native to India were also sometimes adopted by Southeast Asians, who added their own villains and heroes to the ancient Vedic sagas. For many years Indian influence was so pervasive that all of Southeast Asia was known as "farther India." The Chinese remained aloof from most of Southeast Asia, but they took a close commercial interest in Vietnam, and Chinese expansionism affected both Vietnam and Thailand.

Indian traders and religious leaders influence Funan

Following Funan's lead, other Southeast Asian states began to consolidate after 600 C.E. In what today is Thailand, for example, the local tribes, fearful of Chinese territorial expansion, unified into a loose confederacy heavily influenced by Buddhism. They maintained a tense, uneasy relationship with the Chinese until both were overrun by the Mongols in 1253. Farther east, another state developed in Vietnam, partly in response to periodic Chinese invasions, some of which were followed by occupation but usually by reduction to tributary status. The country finally expelled the Chinese in the tenth century, but memories of its long, bitter subjugation linger to this day, as does a powerful Chinese influence upon Vietnamese culture. In particular, Confucian social doctrine and the prevalence of a highly educated bureaucracy recruited through merit endured in Vietnam until the middle of the twentieth century, as have many elements of Chinese cuisine.

The Cambodian Empire

Dominating the southern portion of the Southeast Asian mainland was the Cambodian empire. Funan enjoyed well-developed links to the Khmer (*k'MARE*) people, the main ethnic group of modern Cambodia, who originated north of that state along the Mekong river valley in what is today Laos. Around 600 C.E. the developing Khmer state of Chenla absorbed Funan, and over the next two centuries the framework for a Cambodian empire emerged, locating its capital near the inland town of Angkor (*ANG-kor*).

Funan connects to the Khmer people of Cambodia

Cambodia was heavily influenced by Hinduism, although Buddhism was welcomed and amiably tolerated. Strong Hindu influence was seen particularly in the construction

Hinduism influences Cambodia

of religious buildings. Over two centuries an extensive Hindu temple complex was constructed near the Khmer capital at Angkor Wat (see page 278). Dedicated to the Hindu god Vishnu, the elaborate buildings and ceremonial rooms in this temple complex entranced visitors long after the collapse of the state that had built it. Following that collapse, the complex at Angkor Wat was abandoned and forgotten. Only in the nineteenth century was it rediscovered by French explorers.

Hindu influence was also apparent in Cambodian government. The king was assisted, and to some extent restricted, by an intricate Hindu bureaucracy dominated by military leaders and Hindu priests. But the Hindu caste system was never replicated in Cambodia, which retained an unusually egalitarian social structure.

The Cambodian empire slowly expanded south to the Gulf of Siam. It endured until the early 1200s, when it was overthrown and replaced by a Thai tribal regime.

Srivijaya: Coalition and Cultural Blend

The most complex of the early Southeast Asian states was centered not on the mainland, where Funan and the Khmer state were located, but on the Indonesian island of Sumatra (*soo-MAH-trah*). This was the Malay kingdom of Srivijaya (*srē-vē-JĪ-yah*), first described to the outside world by a Chinese Buddhist pilgrim in 671.

Srivijaya is a Sanskrit word meaning "Great Conquest." It appears to have been created as a maritime trading empire, catering to oceangoing traffic between China and India that was bypassing the overland portage across the Isthmus of Kra. As sailors became more familiar with the dangerous passage through the straits between Sumatra and the Malay Peninsula, the time saved outweighed the risks incurred, and the new kingdom prospered while Funan's power declined.

Relief sculpture at the temple complex of Borobodur in central Java, depicting scenes from the life of the Buddha.

Srivijaya becomes a Buddhist commercial empire

The capital of Srivijaya was the Malay port city of Palembang (*pah-lum-BANG*) on the coast of Sumatra. Its rulers, usually called by the Indian term *maharajah*, were accomplished diplomats, stitching together a coalition of Malay maritime principalities through a careful balance of Hindu spiritual leadership, bribery, and intimidation. Although known to history as an empire, Srivijaya was politically decentralized. It never expanded its territorial control even to the neighboring island of Java, preferring to influence principalities there through the same combination of tactics that worked so well on Sumatra.

While the Cambodian empire was grounded in Hinduism, Srivijaya was overwhelmingly Buddhist. The spectacular Buddhist temple complex called Borobodur (*bō-rō-bō-DUHR*), built in central Java between 770 and 825, was constructed with more than two million cubic feet of stone. At the time it was the largest integrated network of buildings south of the equator. A ten-tiered megaplex, it represents the ten levels of increasing enlightenment passed through by the pilgrim on his or her spiritual journey to nirvana. Borobodur testifies to the pervasiveness of Buddhist cultural influence in Southeast Asia, as Cambodia's Angkor Wat testifies to Hindu influence.

Srivijaya blends Indian and Southeast Asian cultures

But whether they adopted Hindu or Buddhist architecture, whether they adopted Sanskrit as a written language or translated Vedic epics into their own tongues, the Southeast Asian states did much more than *adopt* Indian culture. They *adapted* it to their own tastes and purposes, integrating it, for example, with their own customs of spirit worship and tribal rule. Ancient Indonesian deities were transformed into Hindu gods and goddesses, while traditional Indonesian dances and songs were blended with

Indian rhythms and played on Indian instruments. These processes created a series of hybrid, blended cultures unlike any others.

Srivijaya flourished for several centuries, until in 1025 it was weakened by a devastating raid launched by one of its commercial competitors, the southeastern Indian state of Chola (*CHŌ-lah*). After that Srivijaya's fortunes declined sharply, and by the thirteenth century it had disintegrated into smaller maritime principalities. The Javanese king Kertanagara (*kur-tan-ah-GAH-rah*) constructed a short-lived successor state in the late 1200s, but after that no comparable system arose in the Indonesian archipelago until the Dutch East India Company arrived at the beginning of the seventeenth century.

Chapter Review

Putting It in Perspective

Islam's Abbasid Caliphate looked eastward rather than westward, and its willingness to accept a synthesis of Arabic and Persian cultures on the Iranian plateau added greatly to the richness of Islamic civilization. The Abbasids presided over an Islamic golden age in commerce, culture, poetry, and power. But they were unable to unify the Islamic world, owing to the immensity and ethnic diversity of their conquests.

In the eleventh century, the caliphate was superseded by the rule of Central Asian warlords who carried Islam into India. They were no better at unification than the Abbasids. The Indian subcontinent's vastness, diversity of geographic features and cultures, and attachment to Hinduism consistently frustrated both external and internal efforts to impose unification. The Mauryas and the Guptas succeeded for a time, each by creating a centralized empire, but ultimately failed, as did early Muslim endeavors. Between 1206 and 1526, the Delhi Sultanate attempted to create a hybrid Indian-Islamic system, with more success culturally than politically.

The peoples of Southeast Asia were influenced by commercial contacts with China and by the Indian religions of Hinduism and Buddhism. Funan, Cambodia, and Srivijaya developed states that tried to manage the trade flowing between China and India. They succeeded for a time, but eventually dissolved in the face of external invasion or internal ethnic rivalry. Hinduism and Buddhism offered many insights into the nature of human life and the destiny of human souls but few into administrative organization and political power. Eventually, Islam and European imperialism would contend for dominance in Southeast Asia.

Reviewing Key Material
KEY CONCEPTS

Sufism, 285	purdah, 289
yoga, 289	

KEY PEOPLE

Abu Muslim, 282	Moses Maimonides, 286
Abbas, 282	al-Mamun, 286
Harun al-Rashid, 284	Chandra Gupta I, 288
Ibn Sina, 284	Samudra Gupta, 00
al-Khwarizmi, 284	Chandra Gupta II, 288
Omar Khayyam, 285	Kumara Gupta, 288
Ibn Rushd, 286	Mahmud of Ghazni, 292

ASK YOURSELF

1. How did Persia and Arabia influence one another in the seventh century C.E.? What were the consequences of this mutual influence?
2. Why was the Abbasid Caliphate at first so successful in ruling its vast territories? What accounts for its eventual failure and collapse?
3. How did Islam affect India?
4. How did Hindus and Muslims view one another? What impact did their rivalry have on India?

GOING FURTHER

Adshead, S. *Central Asia in World History*. 1993.

Ahsan, Muhammad. *Social Life Under the Abbasids*. 1979.

Bloom, Jonathan M. *Paper Before Print: The History and Impact of Paper in the Islamic World*. 2001.

Bosworth, C. *The Later Ghaznavids*. 1977.

Cady, J. *Southeast Asia: Its Historical Development*. 1964.

Chauduri, K. *Trade and Civilization in the Indian Ocean*. 1985.

Frye, Richard. *Islamic Iran and Central Asia*. 1979.

Hall, K. *Maritime Trade and State Development in Early Southeast Asia*. 1985.

Higham, Charles. *The Civilization of Angkor*. 2001.

Ikram, S. *Muslim Civilization in India*. 1964.

Kwanten, Luc. *Imperial Nomads: A History of Central Asia, 500–1500*. 1979.

Lombard, M. *The Golden Age of Islam*. 2004.

Morgan, David. *Medieval Persia, 1040–1797*. 1988.

Osborne, Milton. *Southeast Asia: An Introductory History*. 1995.

Risso, Patricia. *Merchants and Faith: Muslim Commerce and Culture in the Indian Ocean*. 1995.

Sandhu, Kernial. *Early Malaysia*. 1973.

SarDeSai, D. *Southeast Asia: Past and Present*. 1994.

Schimmel, A. *Islam in the Indian Subcontinent*. 1980.

Sharon, Moshe. *Black Banners from the East: The Establishment of the Abbasid State*. 1983.

Wolpert, Stanley. *India: A New History*. 1997.

Key Dates and Developments

184 B.C.E.	Collapse of the Mauryan Empire in India
50 B.C.E.–50 C.E.	Scythian rule in northwestern India
50–250 C.E.	Kushan rule in northwestern India
78 C.E.	Fourth Great Council of Buddhism, in Kashmir
ca. 100 C.E.	Funan, the first Southeast Asian state
320–550	The Gupta Empire
455–550	Invasion of India by the Huns
ca. 600s	Establishment of the Kingdom of Srivijaya
636	Muslim defeat of the Sasanian Empire
711	Arab rule in the Sind in western India
750	Establishment of the Abbasid Caliphate
770–825	Construction of Borobodur
786–809	Rule of Harun al-Rashid as caliph in Baghdad
ca. 800	Establishment of the Cambodian Empire
800–1000	Construction of Angkor Wat
945	Buyid warlords' seizure of Baghdad
962–1040	Ghaznavid rule in Khurasan and Afghanistan
969	Establishment of the Fatimid Caliphate in Egypt
998–1030	Mahmud of Ghazni's invasion of India
1040	Seljuk Turks' seizure of northeastern Iran
ca. 1100	*The Rubaiyat* of Omar Khayyam
1206	Establishment of the Delhi Sultanate by the Ghurids

CHAPTER 13

African Societies and the Impact of Islam, 1500 B.C.E.–1500 C.E.

Figure Of A Sacred King

This bronze sculpture of a sacred king was created in the Ife region of southwestern Nigeria between the 12th and 15th centuries C.E. Many African kings were sacred personages who served as intermediaries between the tangible world of human beings and the unseen world of the gods (page 304).

It was just past midday on a humid summer's day in West Africa in 685 C.E. In a small village on the border between grassy plains and the desert, in what would later be the kingdom of Ghana, the men were resting in whatever shade was available. They had spent the morning weeding their root crops of sorghum and yams. The women were inside their huts, preparing the midday meal. Children were tending a flock of goats and a few scrawny cattle. Then, from the north, they sighted an animal unlike anything they had ever seen before.

The children spotted it first and ran whooping to fetch their parents. Everyone rushed out to catch a glimpse of this amazing beast, awkward and ungainly, as it slouched across the sands toward the grassland. By the time the village assembled, there was not just one camel in view, but several dozen. They were loaded with cargo and led by men wearing loose-fitting white robes and turbans on their heads. The leader approached one of the men of the village and asked for water. But he spoke a strange tongue, and no one could understand his words.

Muslims had come to West Africa, bringing goods from the eastern Mediterranean, a written language, a monotheistic religion, and many other things. The region was about to change dramatically.

Trans-Saharan trade area

East African city-states

Bantu homeland

Africa Before Islam

Human life first evolved in Africa, but not written history. Although Egypt, Nubia, and the northern coast have recorded histories that date back thousands of years, most of Africa has no form of writing, and thus no written records, before the arrival of Islam. Consequently, most of what we know about early African history is known through legend and folklore, transmitted from one generation to the next by word of mouth, and through the work of modern archeologists and anthropologists.

Absence of written records restricts knowledge of early African history

Compounding the difficulty of knowing early African history is the means by which writing came to most of the continent. As it was introduced primarily by Islamic and Christian traders, invaders, and missionaries, Africa was often seen and interpreted by foreigners, and early African voices were ignored. Foreigners usually judged Africa by the standards and institutions of their own worlds, rather than evaluating the continent within its own frame of reference. These facts make the study of early African history particularly challenging.

Yet this study is also rewarding. African societies were as varied as the continent's geography and climate (Map 13.1). They ranged from the Mediterranean and desert societies of the north to the forest and grassland societies of central and southern Africa and from the wealthy farming and trading empires of West Africa to the commercial city-states of Africa's east coast. In some regions, especially those that came under Islamic influence, sophisticated systems of governance and commerce emerged. Elsewhere

FOUNDATION MAP 13.1 Early Africa, Including Bantu Migrations and Trade Routes, 1500 B.C.E.–1500 C.E.

The African continent, bisected by the Equator, runs north-south through 70 degrees of latitude. This provides it with widely differing climates to accompany its diverse topography. Notice that Africa hosts a lengthy and varied coastline, tropical grasslands, equatorial rain forests, and enormous deserts. How did the Bantu migrations help Africans overcome the isolation this topography would encourage?

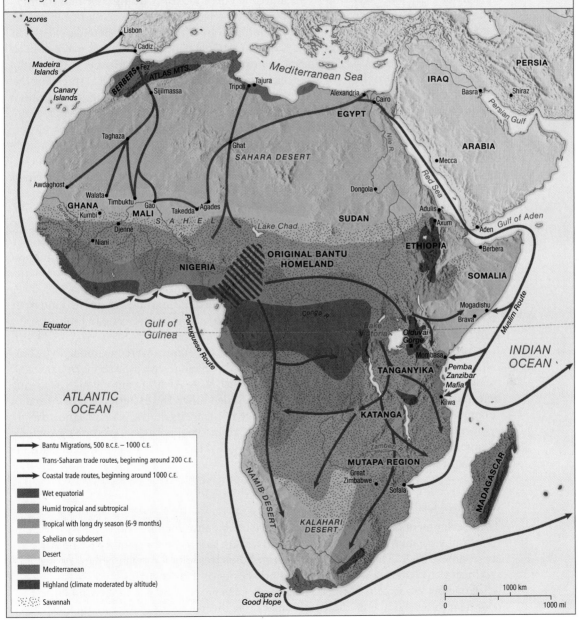

Bantu Migrations, 500 B.C.E. – 1000 C.E.

Trans-Saharan trade routes, beginning around 200 C.E.

Coastal trade routes, beginning around 1000 C.E.

Wet equatorial

Humid tropical and subtropical

Tropical with long dry season (6-9 months)

Sahelian or subdesert

Desert

Mediterranean

Highland (climate moderated by altitude)

Savannah

people lived largely in stateless societies, based mainly on clans and villages, without strong regional governments or rulers.

The Bantu Migrations: Cohesion in Diversity

Despite the geographic breadth and social diversity of African societies, there were connections among them. Between 500 B.C.E. and 1000 C.E., tribes of Africans known as **Bantu** (from their word for "people"), who spoke closely related languages also known by that name, migrated gradually from their homeland in West Africa, near the boundary between what are now Nigeria and Cameroon. Research into the Bantu migrations is made difficult by the absence of written sources mentioned earlier, but many historians believe that over the centuries Bantu peoples moved into eastern, central, and southern Africa, spreading their knowledge of farming and ironworking and a common set of Bantu languages and customs.

Bantu migrations connect African regions

Although no written accounts of this migration exist, many scholars presume that it resulted from pressures on available land and food resources exerted by an expanding population. Bantu peoples had mastered agriculture before the migrations began, and by 500 B.C.E. they had acquired technology sufficient to smelt iron for tools, equipment, and weapons. Thus they were able to clear forests rapidly and cultivate crops efficiently. They dominated and in some cases displaced the foraging societies they encountered as they spread across eastern, central, and southern Africa.

Bantu peoples organized themselves into families and clans. Bantu villages, towns, and cities were governed by ruling councils composed of male heads of families. One of these men, elected chief, spoke for the community in dealings with other Bantu and non-Bantu societies. This decentralized method of rule served the Bantu well until population growth put pressure on resources of land and food. By the fourteenth century C.E., a centralized Bantu kingdom known as Kongo had emerged in Central Africa. The king of Kongo ruled through a multilevel administration to manage resources equitably, dispense justice, and defend the kingdom against external threats.

Muslim travelers connect West and East Africa to the Islamic empire

As the Bantu migrations were ending, Islamic connections were beginning. Muslim merchants from Arabia and North Africa crossed the Sahara with caravans of camels, establishing commercial and cultural contacts with West African empires such as Ghana and Mali. At the same time, Muslim mariners sailed down the eastern coast of Africa, bringing their religion and the Arabic language to local city-states. These Islamic travelers forged links between West and East Africa, connecting both regions to the growing Islamic empire stretching from Spain to south Asia. The connections created by Muslims and Bantu continue to affect Africa today.

Regional Cultural Adaptations

The development of these varied trade, travel, and cultural connections across Africa testifies to the creativity and adaptability of Africans, not to the hospitality of the African environment itself. This immense continent, home to the first human beings, presented significant challenges to the growth and prosperity of their societies.

Covering 20 percent of the land surface of the globe, Africa is the second largest continent (after Asia), a landmass of remarkable diversity in climate and topography. But in all its diversity, Africa, located almost entirely in the tropics and subject to extremes of heat, rainfall, and dryness, has never been an easy place in which to live. Most of its precipitation is seasonal rather than consistent, and in its vast desert regions—the Sahara (the world's largest desert), the Kalahari (*kah-lah-HARR-ē*), and the Namib (*NAH-mib*)—there is virtually no rain at all. Here agriculture is impossible and pasturage for livestock scarce. On both sides of the equator, however, lie dense rain forests with far too much moisture for raising grain crops and herds. Only the valleys of the Nile and Niger rivers, and the grassy regions that stretch across the continent both north and south of the tropical rain forests, offer opportunity for settled societies. Fortunately these grassy areas, known as savanna, constitute more than half of Africa's land surface; without them the continent would be largely empty of people and domesticable animals.

Wide climatic variations challenge African societies

Africans adapted their cultures and societies to these topographical and climatic variations in several ways. In the north, where the weather is relatively mild, the Berbers, Caucasian peoples who had earlier adopted Phoenician culture and language, lived along the Mediterranean coast. They fished, farmed, and engaged in maritime commerce with the Egyptians and Phoenicians and later with the Greeks and Romans. Eventually they also developed a series of trade routes by camel caravan across the scorching Sahara to the south. Even after being conquered by the Arabs, they managed to maintain their way of life and distinct ethnic heritage.

South of the Sahara, but still north of the rain forest, across the region known as the Sudan, stretch endless expanses of savanna. Since perhaps as early as the fifth millennium B.C.E., people in this area have herded cattle and raised crops such as sorghum, millet, and yams. As in most agricultural societies, these people lived in villages, grouping themselves into families and clans and organizing their lives around the care of their crops and herds.

The San people of the Kalahari.

Cattle were prized as symbols of status and wealth and were often offered as part of the bargain in commercial and political agreements. A man's family also offered them to the family of his bride as part of their marital agreement, though upon divorce the bride's family would be obligated to return the cattle. Cow's blood was also prized as a highly desirable beverage. The central position of these animals in the lives of their owners, even in modern times, is attested to by the decision of a small village in Kenya to send 14 cattle to the United States in 2002 as a gesture of condolence for the September 11, 2001, terrorist attacks on the World Trade Center and the Pentagon.

The most influential early residents of the Sudan were the Bantu-speakers. Beginning around 500 B.C.E., perhaps in search of more ample food and water to support their growing population, Bantu peoples gradually moved out of the Sudan into Africa's equatorial savannas and forests, where they raised livestock and cleared the land so they could practice agriculture. Their knowledge of ironworking enabled them to fashion weapons and farming tools that gave them an advantage over the foraging societies they encountered, and they incorporated many of these foragers into Bantu culture. By the time they finally reached southeastern Africa, around 1000 C.E., the Bantu had created a large set of societies, related by language and culture, throughout the continent.

Bantu knowledge spreads over much of Africa

Clans and Kingdoms

Despite cultural and linguistic similarities, the Bantu developed differing social organizations. In the sub-Saharan savanna, kingdoms often emerged as large groups of villages combined under a regional ruler who exercised both spiritual and temporal authority. Farther south, however, although small groups of villages sometimes formed coalitions, societies tended to remain stateless, ruled autonomously by local chiefs and councils. Along the eastern coast a series of city-states emerged, each with an independent ruler. Finally, in the central rain forests and eastern plains, some foraging societies managed to survive as small, nomadic clans.

Clans provide foundation for African life

Africans relied primarily for their protection and survival on their families and clans, which formed the foundation of their social, cultural, and religious life. Although some African societies were matrilineal (in which children trace their ancestry through their mother's lineage), the dominant figure in most families was the male head of household. This patriarchal figure was typically responsible for performing religious rituals, maintaining contact with the spirits of departed ancestors, and serving on the council of the village chief.

African clans unite groups of families

Men who had sufficient means often practiced polygamy, thereby establishing links with a number of families and creating an intricate network of kinship ties and loyalties that bound the community together. For example, a man marrying women from two different families could expect support—such as food in time of drought or assistance during illness or injury—from both. Moreover, the marriages also bound these families in relations of mutual support and hospitality. Polygamy therefore connected families in beneficial ways.

African Traditional Religion

Local rituals that have survived into modern times suggest that most African societies were polytheistic, like their contemporaries in Mesopotamia, India, Southeast Asia, Greece, early America, and elsewhere. Each god represented a different natural force and was believed to perform a different function, bringing, for example, rain, wind, or sun to local people. Many such societies practiced **animism**, the belief that spirits existed that could either help or harm human beings. Many other African societies also appear to have believed in a single god that created the earth and the first human beings. This god, whether endowed with human characteristics, as in Ghana, or considered to be a supreme creative force, as in many Bantu-speaking lands, was extremely powerful and could help or injure humans at will. Africans therefore believed it wise to behave properly and to worship this and all other gods through carefully prescribed rituals.

In some African societies, a caste of priests or prophets performed the rituals. These people were believed to be able to communicate with the gods if the community desired rain, good harvests, or good health. In other African societies, the privilege of contacting the single creator was reserved for the king alone (see page 299). This personal relationship between king and creator was a principal element of royal power as well as a foundation for the eventual development of large empires. Indeed, many African peoples believed that after death the king was rewarded by becoming a lesser god.

An Akuba wooden doll from Ghana, a classic African fertility symbol.

African religion reinforces royal authority

As in China, ancestor worship was widely practiced in early Africa. The spirits of deceased clan or family members were thought to exercise considerable influence over the day-to-day lives of their descendants. Bad luck or accidents were assumed to be reminders that living people must continue to perform ceremonies in honor of the dead. To stop such devotions would be to condemn ancestral spirits to extinction; they survived as spirits only as long as the living remembered them.

When the Muslims arrived in Africa, they found a variety of creeds practiced by the peoples they encountered. Some elements of those beliefs, such as faith in a supreme creator, were similar to Islam and might ease conversion to the creed of the Prophet. Others, such as the king's role in contacting the creator god, would discourage rulers from embracing the new Islamic faith, in which all people were equal before Allah. Still others, such as the Christianity practiced in Ethiopia, held that Jesus of Nazareth was the Son of God and were clearly incompatible with Islam.

Early African Culture

In early Africa, religious beliefs and practices often affected artistic expression, which played many roles in daily life. Literature and poetry, set to music in the form of chants or songs, often performed a religious function. Music and chanting not only accompanied but formed a crucial component of every stage in the lives of Africans: birth, coming-of-age rituals, weddings, political ceremonies, and funerals. Dancing served not only as a pastime but also as a method of communicating with ancestral spirits. Religious incantations and folk legends were transmitted from one generation to the next through music and song.

Architecture, too, fulfilled religious requirements. In most of Africa, ordinary people lived in huts constructed of mud or thatch, the materials most readily available, but religious buildings were constructed of more durable stone. In northeastern Africa, Egyptians, Nubians, and Ethiopians built pyramids and religious monuments out of stone. In southern Africa stone structures seem to have served practical as well as ceremonial purposes. When Muslims arrived in West Africa, they introduced techniques of brickmaking that Africans then used to build palaces and mosques.

African architecture, art, and music reinforce religion

Finally, woodcarving served explicitly ceremonial needs throughout Africa. Elaborate wooden headpieces and masks were carved to depict spirits and gods, and to communicate with them. Often these masks were used in rituals featuring dancing and chanting. The masks helped the clan elders teach lessons to the young and transmit the collective folk wisdom of the people from one generation to the next. With their great beauty and vivid expression, African masks testify to both the artistic talents and the deeply held beliefs of those who created them.

Grass-skirted masks represent the spirits of ancestors among the Kuba people of the Congo.

Islamic Africa and Spain: Commercial and Cultural Networks

Even before Islam created strong commercial and cultural links that tied Africa to the larger world, North Africa was in touch with that world. It had been influenced by the Egyptian and Phoenician civilizations, with their links to the Persians and Macedonians, and was eventually absorbed into the Roman and Byzantine empires. The Romans, however, did little for the region, since their attention was directed largely toward Europe and West Asia. Diocletian's division of the empire in 284 C.E. partitioned North Africa as well: modern-day Morocco, Algeria, and Tunisia remained with the western empire until its collapse in 476 while Libya and Egypt passed under Byzantine rule.

Map 13.2 Islamic North Africa and Iberia, 910

The Sahara Desert cuts North Africa off from the rest of the continent and orients it toward the Mediterranean. When Muslims moved from east to west across the top of Africa, they eventually turned north toward Iberia rather than south toward the desert. Note that by 910, the Iberian Peninsula was divided into an Islamic Caliphate, independent Christian kingdoms, and independent Muslim states. What do these subdivisions suggest about Muslim prospects for conquering Europe from a base in Iberia?

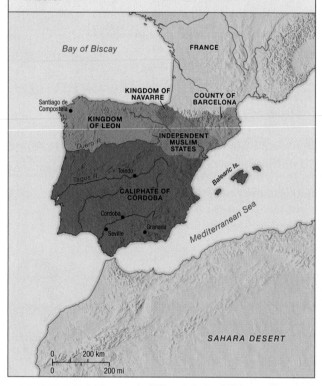

During all this time, however, North Africa remained on the margins of Mediterranean commerce, and its political connections with Rome and Constantinople were fragile. But when North Africa became part of Islamic civilization early in the eighth century, its entire orientation changed.

Islamic North Africa

Between 476 and 639 North Africa was isolated, not greatly influenced by either Germanic Europe or the Byzantine Empire. It was populated largely by Berbers, who pursued their own heritage and scorned outsiders. In the northeast, the Egyptians had a long and rich cultural heritage, but their civilization had been in eclipse for more than a thousand years. Although an outside influence, Christianity flourished in North Africa as a distinctively Egyptian faith—Coptic Christianity—whose Monophysite view of Jesus as a purely divine being was viewed as heresy by both Rome and Constantinople. Byzantine efforts to replace Monophysitism created hostility that Arab armies, bringing Islam, were able to use to their advantage.

When it came, the Arab onslaught was swift, taking North Africans by surprise. Between 639 and 642 the Arabs used a combination of force and generosity to conquer Egypt, whose fertile Nile valley attracted and enriched the Islamic caliphate. More than one million Arabs had moved to Egypt by 750. Most Egyptians converted to Islam, not only for spiritual but for economic and practical reasons, as Muslims were exempt from taxation and free from intimidation or coercion. Within a century fewer than a third of the Egyptians remained Christian.

North African cultures become isolated after the Roman Empire's collapse

Islam connects North Africa and Southwest Asia

Initial Arab plans to move south into Nubia were frustrated by the skills of Nubian archers and a Christian government that had long experience fighting Egyptian attacks. But prosperity and population growth made Egypt an ideal base for expansion to the west. In the next few decades the Arabs moved across North Africa, taking advantage of the fact that the region's various inhabitants feared one another as much as they despised the Muslims. Refusing to cooperate, North African groups fell one by one. By 711, little more than 70 years after the Muslim invasion of North Africa began, the Islamic empire stretched across that entire region, and its soldiers were crossing the Strait of Gibraltar into Spain.

Cosmopolitan Umayyad Spain

The Muslims first arrived in Spain as invited guests. The Germanic king of Spain had died in 709, and in the contest over his succession one contender for the throne appealed to the Islamic *amir* (*AH-mēr*, or governor) of North Africa for help. The *amir* responded by sending an Arab-Berber expeditionary force under General Tariq ibn Ziyad (*tah-RĒK ibn zē-YAHD*), which landed in 711, defeated the other contender, and prepared to go home. But Tariq heard rumors that the legendary treasure of the ancient Jewish King Solomon was hidden in a cellar in Toledo (Map 13.2). He took the city and found nothing but rats in its cellars, but saw to his astonishment that many of the residents welcomed his forces and converted to Islam. The next year the *amir* himself conquered Spain with an army of 20,000 men. About four-fifths of the Iberian peninsula (modern Spain and Portugal) came under Muslim control, while the Christians were pushed into a few surviving kingdoms in the Spanish north. The Muslims called their newly acquired territory *al-Andalus* (*al-AHN-dah-loose*); Spaniards called it Andalusia. For the next five centuries, Spain was closely linked with North Africa and was the westernmost part of Islam's growing commercial and cultural network.

Islam is invited into Spain

The Court of the Lions at the Alhambra in Granada, Spain.

From 711 to 756 Islamic Spain was ruled by the *amir*, who for most of that time reported to the Umayyad caliphate in Damascus. From Spain, the Muslims tried to advance into France, but they were defeated by the Franks at Tours in 732. When the Umayyads were overthrown by the Abbasids in 750, one of the Umayyad family's princes escaped from Damascus and governed Spain from Córdoba (*CŌR-duh-buh*). Al-Andalus thereupon became the last bastion of Umayyad rule during the Abbasid caliphate. This unusual situation lasted for nearly two centuries: Iberia was a long way from Baghdad, the new capital of the Abbasids, and as long as Spain remained loyal to the Sunni brand of Islam, the Abbasids, Sunnis themselves, were willing to leave the Spanish Umayyads in peace.

Umayyad Spain fused Arabic culture and language onto a Spanish and Berber population base. The result was a civilization of distinctive cultural achievements. The Arab occupiers created exquisite irrigated gardens, splendid mosques and palaces like the Alhambra in Granada (*gra-NAH-dah*), elegant fountains and courtyards, and important works of science, poetry, and philosophy. They also married into Spanish families, converted large numbers of people to Islam, and assimilated the local population to a degree unheard of in other Islamic lands. In so doing, they joined with the Spaniards to create a uniquely Hispano-Arab culture, vestiges of which endured for centuries after the collapse of Spanish Islam in 1492.

Islam shapes a distinctive Spanish culture

This cosmopolitan culture emerged gradually from Islamic Spain's flourishing urban centers of Seville (*suh-VIL*), Córdoba, and Granada. Poetry praising warrior virtues and romantic conquests was written either in Arabic or in a Spanish language thick with Arabic words and expressions; the rhyme schemes and meters were Roman. Scholars from throughout the Islamic empire came to Spain, building libraries, studying medicine and mathematics, and translating Aristotle's philosophy and the medical works of the Greek physician Galen from Arabic into Latin, all under the patronage of the state.

Economic prosperity and cultural connections made such achievements possible. Accustomed to sunny, dry climates, Arabs brought to arid Spain methods of irrigation perfected in Yemen and Syria, some based on timed water flow. Soon the Iberian Peninsula was abundant with figs, dates, cherries, pears, pomegranates, and dozens of other crops whose cultivation was imported from the southern and eastern Mediterranean. As Byzantine naval power declined in the western Mediterranean, Islamic Spain established seaborne trading routes with Africa, non-Spanish Europe, and western Asia. This flourishing commerce made the Spanish Umayyads financially independent of Damascus, free to promote not only cultural magnificence but political autonomy. A series of capable governors consolidated the new Hispano-Arab state on a model congenial to the Abbasids, who in turn did not interfere in Spain's affairs.

Spain loosens its ties with the Caliphate

In 909, a political development in Islamic Egypt accelerated Spain's distinctive cultural development. The **Fatimid** (*FA-ti-mid*) family, a Shi'ite dynasty in Egypt, began a six-decade struggle to break away from Abbasid rule and establish a caliphate of their own along the Nile. The Umayyad governor of Spain seized the opportunity provided by this distraction to claim the title of caliph for himself in 929. The unity of the *umma* was now shattered, with three different men claiming to be its true leader. The Islamic state of Spain, now known as the Caliphate of Córdoba, was a separate Sunni Muslim government presiding over a luxuriant hybrid culture unlike any other in the Islamic world.

The Caliphate of Córdoba deepens the connection between Spain and Islam

Although the Caliphate of Córdoba lasted little more than a century, Hispano-Arab culture continued to prosper there. Córdoba's population grew to 500,000, and by the twelfth century the caliphate was noted for its immense paper mills. Its intellectual life blossomed with scholars such as Ibn Rushd (*Ib-un ROOSHD*), known in Latin Europe as Averröes (*uh-VAIR-ō-ēz*), a philosopher and physician who argued that the Qur'an was an allegory requiring rational interpretation and who reintroduced the work of Aristotle and Plato to European readers. Jews and Christians were not only tolerated in Córdoba but also encouraged to contribute their talents to Islamic civilization.

Nevertheless, internal dissent undermined the caliphate: Arabs fought with Berbers, Arab clans intrigued against each other, and by the late tenth century Umayyad control was crumbling. In northern Spain, the surviving Christian kingdoms sensed weakness and began to pressure the Muslims.

Fatimid Egypt

As the Umayyads had managed to survive for centuries in Spain, remote from the Abbasid world, so in Egypt the Shi'ite Fatimids found refuge. Abbasid rule was always stronger in Asia and Arabia than in North Africa, particularly after the capital of their caliphate moved eastward from Damascus to Baghdad in 763. The Abbasids appointed Mamluks, Turkish slaves from Central Asia, to rule Egypt on their behalf, but the resulting Mamluk dynasties proved short-lived. Then between 909 and 969 the Fatimids set forth their claim, not only to the province of Egypt but to spiritual and political authority throughout the Islamic world.

Shi'ism finds a foothold in Egypt

The Fatimids were **Isma'ilis** (*iss-mah-ILL-ēs*), a branch of Shi'ite Islam. Isma'ilis claimed to be the true imams (or direct descendants of Muhammad's son-in-law Ali), and they denied the legitimacy of both the orthodox Shi'ites and the Sunnis. Orthodox Shi'ites believed that the last imam had hidden himself in a cave after 874 and would return one day as the Messiah. Isma'ilis disputed this belief and claimed direct descent from Isma'il, the last publicly seen imam, who died in 760. These doctrinal disputes, like those in Christian Byzantium, plagued the Islamic empire. In Baghdad, the Abbasid Caliphate was in decline, its power eroded by the size and complexity of its empire. Ultimately, it could not hold Egypt.

Having established their own caliphate, the Fatimids moved their capital from Alexandria to Cairo, a new city they founded in 969. For worship of their cult dedicated to the family of Ali, they built magnificent mosques rivaling those at Mecca and Medina, such as the exquisite Al-Azhar Mosque in Cairo. But they left the Egyptian population undisturbed in its Sunni Muslim faith, a political necessity but a spiritual contradiction: if they were indeed the true imams, how could they fail to oppose Sunni doctrine and practice? This tolerance undermined their claim to universal legitimacy and eventually destroyed their caliphate. Lacking adequate support, the Fatimids were defeated first by European crusaders who took Jerusalem in 1099 and ultimately by the Muslim general Salah al-Din (*sah-LAH al-DĒN*), also called Saladin (*SAH-lah-dēn*), who brought together several Muslim states to fight the crusaders. By 1173 Fatimid rule in Egypt was over.

Al-Azhar Mosque, Cairo.

Far from the seats of Islamic power in Damascus, Baghdad, and Mecca, North Africa developed as a series of distant states out of touch with mainstream Muslim spiritual and political evolution. Islam's impact on the continent of Africa was, however, profound. Through commerce as well as conquest, Islam spread from North Africa to the west and south, with consequences that shaped the course of African history for centuries to come.

Fatimid Egypt is defeated by Sunni Muslims

Trade Across the Sahara

The Sahara resembled an ocean of sand, which the Arabs could navigate on camels, their ships of the desert. Muslim caravan trade brought Islam and other changes to West Africa, and Africans, in turn, reached out to the Islamic world.

Early Saharan Trade

In the first millennium B.C.E., long before the arrival of caravans from North Africa, kingdoms had been established in the western part of Africa's vast savanna region known as the Sudan. These early kingdoms were based on villages, each containing families and clans linked by kinship ties. Councils of elders advised the chief in governing each village; the chief represented the village in dealings with regional and provincial leaders, who in turn answered to a king.

West African kingdoms seem to have protected their peoples effectively and saw no compelling reason to expand until the development of north-south trade across the Sahara. The trade was made possible by the arrival of camels from Central Asia some time before 200 C.E. Without them the Sahara would have remained unexplored and uncharted; with them merchant caravans crossed the desert in search of profit.

Once the camel came, Berber tribes such as the Tuareg (*TWAH-reg*), accustomed to an arid environment, set out to cross the Sahara, exploring its vastness and mapping safe, direct trade routes. Financed by Jewish merchants operating out of oases in North Africa, Berber caravans carried salt, dates, and manufactured goods to the Sudan, exchanging these commodities for slaves, gold, ivory, and gum. By the seventh century, commerce by camel across the Sahara was regular and profitable.

Camels make the trans-Saharan trade possible

Islam's Interaction with West Africa

Following the Islamic conquest of North Africa, the trans-Saharan trade became part of a huge commercial and cultural network extending from Persia to Spain. Eager to expand both their faith and their fortune, Muslim merchants replaced the Jewish financiers, and many traders and camel drivers converted to Islam. By the eighth century, trade across the Sahara was generating great wealth, and some caravans included thousands of camels, braving sandstorms, bandits, and withering heat on difficult journeys lasting for months.

Islam influences West Africa profoundly

The effects of the trans-Saharan trade on West Africa were highly significant. First and foremost, it introduced Islam into the region. Berber and Arabian Muslims brought with them not only their faith but their complex cultures. West African rulers and councils became literate in Arabic and began to keep written records. Islamic laws, institutions, and administrative forms also took shape. Muslims brought new goods to trade and taught Africans how to make bricks, enhancing the durability of buildings in societies that had previously used dried mud for walls. Beyond these advantages, West Africa became part of an extensive community of Islamic peoples.

Second, the trade created a tremendous potential market for African gold. Mines established in the areas that are now Ghana, Senegal, and Nigeria, all in West Africa, provided work that raised standards of living across the area. The ready availability of African gold stimulated the economy of the entire Mediterranean basin, and gold became the medium of exchange for the silks and spices of India. Legends of African riches, many of them exaggerated, fascinated both Europe and Asia. Africa seemed to be an exotic realm of cities overflowing with gold, ruled by fabulously wealthy kings. The lure of gold linked Africa, Asia, and Europe.

Trade connects West Africa to Southwest Asia

Third, the camel caravans carried cargoes of slaves, and in this trade Islamic influence was decisive. Upper-class Muslims wanted African slaves for their households; Muslim military commanders purchased them for their armies; local operators of salt and gold mines in West Africa used them for labor. Muslims purchased, transported, and sold the slaves at huge profits. This trade involved moving the captives across the desert to the Middle East, a crossing that was stressful even for well-fed camel merchants but agonizing, and sometimes fatal, for slaves.

African slavery was not exclusively racial, since whites captured in war were also sold. But since there were no whites native to West Africa, the overwhelming majority of slaves were black. Some slaves were sold to owners in Islamic cities in Spain and Portugal during the medieval period, but slaveholding never spread to the rest of Europe. In contrast, it was widely practiced in Islamic lands. Only with Europe's discovery of the Americas in the late fifteenth century did slavery become a race-based global phenomenon.

Trans-Saharan trade urbanizes West Africa

Finally, the trans-Saharan traffic urbanized West Africa and transformed clusters of villages into centralized kingdoms. African merchant families served as middlemen between Muslim traders and African mine owners. These merchants opened caravanserais (*care-ah-VAN-sair-ās*), complexes of inns and markets where camel merchants could sleep, care for their animals, refresh themselves, and conduct their business. Shops and services expanded in these complexes, and urbanization quickly followed. Between the ninth and thirteenth centuries, the populations of cities such as Kumbi (*KOOM-bē*),

Djenné (*jen-NĀ*), and Timbuktu, in what would later be known as Mali, grew to exceed 10,000 inhabitants each. What had been tiny kingdoms expanded as well, as Africans learned more about the sophisticated political systems of the larger Islamic world and adapted some of its features.

West African Kingdoms: Ghana and Mali

The expansion of trade stimulated by the camel caravans enhanced the wealth of West Africa. Its rulers used much of that wealth to construct extensive empires on the foundations of what had been small kingdoms. Two of those empires, Ghana and Mali, provided centralized government and economic organization to a region previously divided along clan and tribal lines.

The Conversion of Ghana

The kingdom of Ghana (not to be confused with the modern republic of the same name) was located in the area north of the Niger and Senegal Rivers (Map 13.3). It was founded by the Sondinke (*sahn-DIN-kā*) people between the second and fourth centuries of the Common Era. By 800, Muslim traders were calling it "the land of gold," and it began

---

Map 13.3 West Africa, 800–1400

The trans-Saharan trade connected West Africa to the Islamic world. Observe, both here and on Map 13.1, that trans-Saharan trade routes connected West Africa to the commercial highways of the Mediterranean Sea. Kingdoms such as Ghana and Mali emerged to organize traffic in salt, gold, and slaves. In addition to money and goods, what did Islamic traders supply in return?

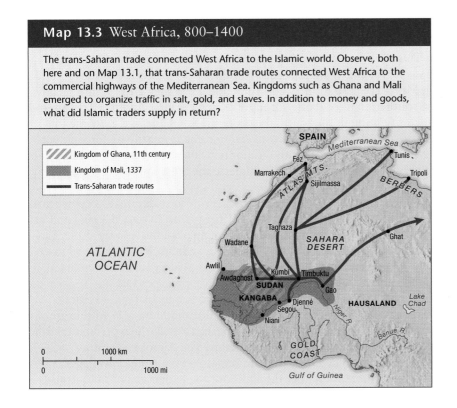

appearing on their maps in 833. Ghana was a prosperous kingdom, located between major sources of gold and salt. Its rulers did not control the gold mines, which were located in a southern forest belt that they could neither penetrate nor influence for long. But they did control the transport of gold from south to north, an extraordinarily profitable trade that made them rich.

At the same time, Berber tribesmen known as Sanhaja (*san-HAH-yah*) conducted a valuable salt trade from north to south. Salt was essential to life in a prerefrigeration age, as it offered an effective method of preserving meat. The continual exchange of salt for gold was carried out in Ghana's capital city of Kumbi, where a swarm of royal officials collected tribute, customs duties, taxes, and revenues.

The Sanhaja brought Ghana not only salt and manufactured goods but Islam. The ruling elite learned Arabic and accepted Muslim aid in organizing an efficient bureaucracy. Few Ghanaians (*GAHN-ē-ans*) converted at first, however. Because the king's authority was religious as well as political, he was reluctant either to convert personally or to urge spiritual changes on his people, most of whom continued to practice animism.

By the tenth century, however, Ghana's kings had become wealthy enough to expand their domain northward until the kingdom dominated an area nearly as large as Texas. In the process they took control of the salt trade routes from the Sanhaja, who simultaneously were being squeezed out of their trans-Saharan trade routes by competition from Berbers to the north. Irritated by these events, the Sanhaja found solace and inspiration in a militantly puritanical sect of Islam called *al-Mirabitun* (*al mē-RAH-bih-TOON*), whose followers were known as **Almoravids**.

The Almoravids believed that to be successful in a war against unbelievers, the faithful Muslim must first conduct an inner struggle to purify his soul against the remnants of unbelief. This Berber movement, considered unorthodox by most Muslims, inspired the religious fervor the Sanhaja needed to fight back. In the 1050s they moved north, conquering Morocco in 1070. Between 1086 and 1106 they crossed into Spain and controlled the southern half of Iberia for more than a century. And in 1076, after more than a decade of fighting in the south, they conquered Ghana and converted its people to Islam. Historians debate whether conversion came primarily by force or persuasion. Available evidence indicates that the Almoravids blended trade, preaching, and military intimidation in a successful effort to Islamicize the most important kingdom in West Africa.

Ghana's conversion altered its society and politics. Prior to widespread acceptance of Islam, the capital city of Kumbi was actually two distinct towns. In one, the king and his people lived and held court in buildings constructed largely from mud; in the other, Sanhaja traders lived and conducted their business in stone dwellings. Kings, believed to exercise divine powers, were considered holy persons, although not gods. Their political authority was grounded in the sense of awe they inspired in their people.

With the coming of Islam, mosques were built all over Kumbi as the two cities merged into one. Stone houses replaced those built of mud, and literacy in Arabic grew dramatically. The sacred role of the king gradually vanished before the worship of Allah, while Islamic prayer and ritual replaced Ghanaian magic. The Almoravids, however, were based to the north and presided over trade routes stretching from central Spain to the Niger River, and they possessed neither the skills nor the temperament to centralize such far-flung holdings. Having undermined the authority of the king, they substituted

Gold and salt make Ghana a powerful kingdom

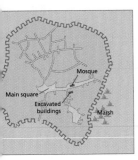

Kumbi.

Almoravids convert Ghana to Islam

Ghana's conversion roots Islam in West Africa

nothing for it. Their camels, sheep, and goats devoured Ghana's pastures and wrecked its agricultural base. As the Almoravids paid more and more attention to their territories in Spain, the Sondinke reasserted their leadership in Ghana itself.

For a time in the twelfth century Ghana seemed to be returning to its former greatness, but the bases of its power had been fractured. Kings, no longer seen as holy men, could not lead their people on the basis of their sacred powers. In addition, Ghana's agriculture never recovered from the Almoravid occupation, and its trade routes had been severely disrupted. Political uncertainty and the failure of the Almoravids to restore central authority prompted trans-Saharan caravans to bypass Ghana. Such routes were less convenient but also less troubled, and this shift in commerce proved fatal to Ghana's prosperity and power.

Trade begins to bypass Ghana

Islamic Mali, 1200–1450

The alteration of trade routes worked to the advantage of the Mandinke (*man-DIN-kā*) people, who had converted to Islam but had not been subjected to the Almoravids. Living close to the Niger in a region more suitable for agriculture than Ghana's northern areas, they controlled the more lengthy central trade routes and seized the opportunity to break free of Ghanaian control. In 1235, following a lengthy struggle among Mandinke tribes, a king named Sundiata (*soon-JAH-tah*) emerged victorious and began to construct a successor state to the ruined kingdom of Ghana. This new state, known as Mali, became even more influential.

The Mandinke people, who were linguistically tied to the Sondinke and who had been part of the kingdom of Ghana, built their successor state on the upper Niger River. Constructed on lines similar to those of Ghana, this new kingdom of Mali enjoyed a rich agricultural base. Rainfall in this sector of West Africa was more abundant in the twelfth century than it is today, and temperature ranges appear to have been less severe. A secure food supply combined with Ghana's traditional position astride the gold-salt trading route ensured population growth and employment opportunities necessary for success.

Mali emerges as Ghana's successor

All that was needed was capable leadership, and the Mandinke were fortunate to have the dynamic Sundiata, who ruled Mali from about 1235 until 1255. Sundiata was one of 12 royal brothers who together were heirs to the throne of the tiny West African kingdom of Kangaba. A neighboring king, Sumanguru, overran Kangaba early in the thirteenth century and murdered 11 of the brothers, sparing only Sundiata, a sickly child who was not expected to live to adulthood.

But Sundiata survived, grew into a strong warrior, and in 1235 defeated Sumanguru in battle. Within a few years Sundiata's forces made Mali the clear winner of the struggle among the Ghanaian successor states. Sundiata's capital in the Niger River town of Niani (*nī-AH-nē*) became both a base for military conquest and a vibrant commercial center. Sundiata's fame spread across Africa, and his immediate successors continued his expansionistic policies and consolidated Mali's wealth. Sundiata's son, Mansa (or "Emperor") Uli (1255–1270), was secure enough to leave his kingdom and become the first of his line to make the pilgrimage to Mecca.

Sundiata builds a powerful kingdom in Mali

Uli achieved that level of security through his consolidation of Mandinke control of the Songhai (*sahn-GĪ*) people and the central Saharan trade routes. Building on Mali's power and prosperity, Kankan Musa (*MOO-sah*), monarch from 1312 to 1337, eventually ruled almost twice the amount of territory once controlled by Ghana. Like rulers in France and China, he selected provincial administrators from within the ranks of his own family, assuring himself of their loyalty and centralizing control more tightly. Those men governed an empire that now commanded the only approaches to the salt deposits in the north, the gold mining district in the south, and the copper mines to the east. Mansa Musa, at the height of his powers, was the most formidable and wealthy ruler in the recorded history of West Africa, before or since.

Mansa Musa put Mali on the map, both literally and figuratively, during his pilgrimage to Mecca in 1324. Passing through Cairo on his way to Arabia, the emperor visited the sultan of Egypt. His caravan of thousands of camels, one hundred elephants, a vast number of servants and courtiers, and an incredible quantity of gold (which he lavished on innkeepers, camel tenders, and princes alike) made a powerful impression on the Arab world. Muslims in southwest Asia marveled at a visit from a monarch whose holdings were equivalent in size to all of Arabia. For his part, Musa learned about the Mediterranean world and Islam's role in it. His pilgrimage was glorified in song and story for centuries.

Mansa Musa connects Mali to Southwest Asia

Mansa Musa's caravan aimed to do more than enable a West African emperor to make the pilgrimage to Mecca and thus fulfill one of the five pillars of Islam. The spectacle must have been intended to strengthen Mali's connections to the principal cities of the Middle East. Indirect evidence indicates that Mansa Musa succeeded. A dormitory was established in Cairo for students from West Africa, and on his return to Mali, the emperor set about making Timbuktu into a center of learning and culture. Poets, mathematicians, astronomers, and theologians came to Mali from across the Arab world, drawn by the prospect of riches and the excitement of building a new empire of knowledge in yet another desert. Aided by an architect from al-Andalus, Musa built new mosques in Timbuktu and Gao (*GAOW*), along with flat-roofed houses in the Mediterranean style. Having become a renowned center of Islamic scholarship, Timbuktu attracted not only permanent residents but also North African visitors such as Ibn Battuta (*ibn bah-TOO-tuh*), who traveled through Mali in 1352–1353.

Mansa Musa on pilgrimage.

Ibn Battuta left a written record of an impressively sophisticated civilization (see "Ibn Battuta's Travels in West Africa"). He found the roads and cities clean and safe. The emperor, he wrote, was a just judge, quick to punish wrongdoers in accordance with Islamic law; and scholars, poets, and scientists made Mali an intellectual oasis. But other accounts suggest that Ibn Battuta, who spoke no African languages and could communicate only with the Arabic-speaking elites, overestimated both the sophistication of Mali and the extent of its practice of Islam. Mansa Musa apparently told visitors in the 1330s that he was reluctant to force the Mandinke to surrender their animist beliefs in spirits and magic. His own authority was derived in large measure from his status as a sacred person, and to disturb animist beliefs might jeopardize the regular mining of gold. A modern view of fourteenth-century Mali might characterize it as a pyramid, Islamic at the apex but animist at the base.

Mali was ruled by a Muslim emperor who claimed to be partly divine and whose immense wealth permitted him to employ a standing army of nearly 100,000 men. That sort of force bought a great deal of social control in West Africa. It did not, however, ensure a long life for Mali. By 1400 the Songhai tribe, which had been subdued by Mansa Uli, was reasserting itself, reviving its long-lost monarchy and pressing for independence.

Document 13.1 Ibn Battuta's Travels in West Africa, 1352

Ibn Battuta spent three decades during the four-teenth century traveling across the Islamic world. This excerpt from his account of his journeys illustrates the challenges of mining salt in West Africa.

From Marrákesh [in Morocco] I traveled with the suite of our master [the Sultan] to Fez, where I took leave of our master and set out for the Negrolands. I reached the town of Sijilmása, a very fine town, with quantities of excellent dates . . . At Sijilmása I bought camels and a four months' supply of forage for them. Thereupon I set out [in 1352] with a caravan including, amongst others, a number of the merchants of Sijilmása. After twenty-five days we reached Tagházá, an unattractive village, with the curious feature that its houses and mosques are built of blocks of salt, roofed with camel skins. There are no trees there, nothing but sand. In the sand is a salt mine; they dig for the salt, and find it in thick slabs, lying one on top of the other, as though they had been tool-squared and laid under the surface of the earth. A camel will carry two of these slabs. No one lives at Tagházá except slaves, who dig for the salt; they subsist on dates, camels' flesh, and millet imported from the Negrolands. The negroes come up from their country and take away the salt from there . . . The negroes use salt as a medium of exchange, just as gold and silver is used [elsewhere]; they cut it up into pieces and buy and sell with it. The business done at Tagházá, for all its meanness, amounts to an enormous figure in terms of hundredweights of gold-dust.

We passed ten days of discomfort there, because the water is brackish and the place is plagued with flies. Water supplies are laid in at Tagházá for the crossing of the desert which lies beyond it, which is a ten-nights' journey with no water on the way except on rare occasions . . . We passed a caravan on the way and they told us that some of their party had become separated from them. We found one of them dead under a shrub, of the sort that grows in the sand, with his clothes on and a whip in his hand. The water was only about a mile away from him.

SOURCE: Ibn Battúta, *Travels in Asia and Africa 1325–1354* (1929) 317–318.

Between 1464 and 1492 the Songhai king, appealing to animism against Islam despite his own status as a Muslim, carried on a relentless military campaign that eventually destroyed the Mali empire. In its place the Songhai king Ali erected a new realm that dominated the region for most of the next century.

The Songhai defeat Mali and create a successor state

Ethiopia's Christian Kingdom

Islam's expansion in Africa was neither steady nor consistent. Unqualified success in converting the north did not guarantee anything more than partial victory in the west. In the northeast, Muslim intentions to expand southward from Egypt and southwestward from Arabia were blocked not by traditional animists but by Christians in Ethiopia.

Human remains at least 1.5 million years old have been found in Ethiopia, and Egyptian writings speak of a civilization there nearly 2,000 years before the Common Era. The Jewish Scriptures record the visit of the Ethiopian Queen of Sheba to King Solomon of Judaea in the tenth century B.C.E. Apparently she came bearing great riches and irresistible charms, for the legend says that after she returned home she bore a son, through whom all

Map 13.4 Ethiopia and the Red Sea Region, 632 C.E.

Ethiopia was converted to Christianity during the earliest days of the Christian faith. It maintained trade relations with various Arabian kingdoms across the Red Sea. Notice Ethiopia's strategic location at the junction of the Gulf of Aden and the Red Sea. What aspects of Ethiopia's location and topography protected it against Islamic incursions after 632 C.E.?

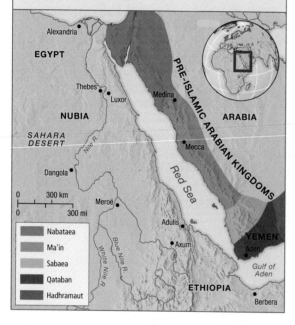

Nabataea
Ma'in
Sabaea
Qataban
Hadhramaut

Ethiopia resists the expansion of Islam

future kings of Ethiopia claimed descent from Solomon. These references to Ethiopian civilization are, of course, indirect. Direct evidence of Ethiopian culture dates from the sixth century B.C.E., recorded in inscriptions and monuments unearthed by archeologists. These indicate settlement by southern Arabians who blended with the African population to create a hybrid Arab-African culture centered on the city of Axum (*ahk-SOOM*) (Map 13.4).

Like other African societies at this time, this civilization practiced a religion based on polytheism and animism. But its religious practice changed between 320 and 340 C.E., when the Ethiopian king Ezana (*eh-ZAH-nuh*) made Christianity the state religion. Converted by Byzantine Monophysite priests from Egypt, Ezana consecrated polytheist temples to the worship of Christ and created a Christian commonwealth in sub-Saharan Africa.

Ethiopia enjoyed abundant rainfall and rich soil, and Axum became a major participant in Red Sea trade. A favorable combination of commerce, agriculture, and cattle-raising enabled this Christian land to prosper despite its isolation from surrounding polytheist communities. Ethiopia's resources were sufficient to encourage its Christian rulers to project Axum's power across the Red Sea into southern Arabia. Thus Ethiopia became involved in Arabian tribal conflicts. In the early seventh century, Arabians periodically crossed the Red Sea to invade Ethiopia, without notable success.

In 615, several of Muhammad's followers who had fled Mecca arrived in Axum, where they were treated with great courtesy. Their presence in Ethiopia improved Axum's relations with Arabia, and they informed Muhammad of Ethiopia's friendship. The Muslims observed that the early forms of Christian ritual still practiced in Ethiopia were in some ways compatible with rules in the Qur'an, but the Prophet instructed the Muslims not to attempt conversions. To this good will was added Ethiopia's military and naval strength, which made it a discouraging target for invasion.

But eventually Islamic expansion cut Christian Ethiopia off from the Red Sea trade and, after Muslims conquered Egypt in 642, from any consistent contact with the Byzantine Empire. Still, surrounded by Islam, Ethiopia for centuries maintained both its political independence and its Christian faith. Rumors of its continued existence fascinated twelfth-century European crusaders. They spread stories of a legendary ruler named Prester John, whose Christian kingdom in East Africa might assist Europeans in seizing the Holy Land from Islamic control. Though the crusaders made no connections with Ethiopia, the land retained its Christian heritage and its strong monarchical rule into the twentieth century.

The City-States of East Africa

Organized settlement along the East African coast is less than two thousand years old.
A few small tools dating to 500 B.C.E. have been discovered, but these seem to have been
used by small nomadic bands of foragers. These hunters traded with Greeks and Romans,
furnishing them with African products such as ivory, rhinoceros horns, fragrant spices, and
black slaves, but they built no permanent ports. Persians and Chinese certainly knew of
East Africa, but they showed no more interest than the Greeks or Romans in colonizing it.
No organized coastal settlements traceable to pre-Islamic times have been found. The history of East Africa changed, however, as first the Bantus and then the Muslims arrived and
blended their cultures with those of the local foragers, as well as with each other.

Development of a Bantu-Arab Culture

When people arrived in East Africa to settle rather than forage, they appear to have come
from two different directions: overland as part of the Bantu migrations from the west and
across the Indian Ocean from Muslim lands. The Bantu came first, arriving from central
Africa with cattle, kings, and castes of both warriors and priests. They also brought their
Bantu language, which eventually combined with Arabic elements and script to develop into
modern-day **Swahili**, a term designating not only the language but also the entire Bantu-
Islamic East African culture. The first recognizable ruins in East Africa date from the ninth
century C.E. and are clearly Bantu, consisting of small agricultural communities of huts and
mud houses, with an occasional stone structure that was probably a religious shrine.

East Africa develops on a Bantu foundation

The Muslims came next, down the coast ("Swahili" means "coasters" in Arabic)
from Egypt and Arabia in small, swift boats called dhows (*DOWS*), settling along the
Somali shoreline and on the Indian Ocean island of Zanzibar. Islamic settlements, usually beginning as Muslim quarters in existing Bantu towns, began in earnest after 1100.
The Arabs turned Bantu towns such as Kilwa, Mombasa, and Malindi into ports attracting oceangoing commerce. This trade in turn encouraged the creation of a series of East
African city-states (Map 13.5).

An Arab dhow.

Muslim expansion into India, the extension of Egyptian influence southward from the
Red Sea, and the conversion of Indonesians to Islam all encouraged the development of
an Indian Ocean community of states and peoples. African traders sailed across the Indian
Ocean not only to India but also to Indonesia, and the traffic flowed in both directions:
Indians settled all along the East African coast, while Indonesians, accustomed to living on
islands, preferred the huge offshore island of Madagascar, which they named Malagasy.

As Islam spread throughout the area, the East African city-states built an Islamic
culture upon Bantu agricultural foundations. In the thirteenth and fourteenth centuries,
great mosques were built at Kilwa, Mombasa, and Mogadishu (*mō-gah-DĒ-shoo*). Ibn
Battuta, visiting the coast in 1331, described Mogadishu as a bustling port filled with
wealthy Muslim merchants and a highly ritualized court life. Recent excavations at
Kilwa have uncovered the foundations of an imposing royal palace, probably built in the
Abbasid Islamic style in the early fourteenth century.

East Africa, like Greece, develops city-states

This Swahili East African culture suggests the power exerted by connections
among differing civilizations. East Africa's strength and prosperity emerged not from

Map 13.5 City-States of East Africa, 1500

East Africa's city-states used the Indian Ocean as a highway across which to market products from the interior of Africa. This connected them to the Muslim-dominated Indian Ocean commercial network and turned their political and mercantile elites Islamic. In southern Africa, Great Zimbabwe developed as the center of an empire built on agriculture, animal husbandry, metalworking, and trade in gold, using Sofala as a port. Note that the trade routes hug the African and Asian coastlines. Why would mariners be reluctant to sail directly across the Indian Ocean, for example, from Goa to Kilwa?

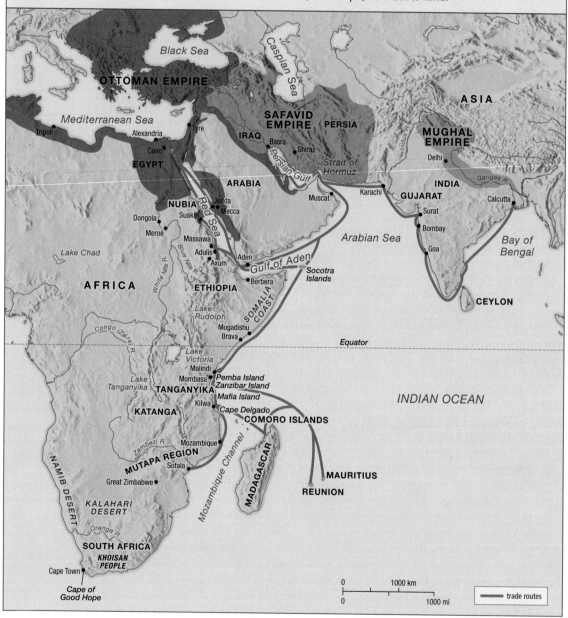

the Bantu or Islamic traditions alone but from their blending, a synthesis that existed nowhere else on earth.

East and West Africa Compared

The societies of West and East Africa were both influenced by the Bantu, but they evolved in very different ways. In economic structure, commercial relations, political organization, and contact with non-African cultures, their differences were more pronounced than their similarities.

East African city-states, located on the coast, were oriented toward oceangoing trade. They depended on inland regions for food, which, given the ample rainfall and fertile soil of the East African savanna, was abundant. In West Africa, by contrast, cities were located inland, in the midst of agricultural regions, rather than on the coast. The Atlantic was uncharted and not usable for trade. West African trade was land-based, traversing the Sahara, while East Africa used the Indian Ocean—charted and easily navigable—as a commercial highway.

In West Africa, this inward-looking organizational structure led eventually to the creation of extensive empires like Ghana, Mali, and Songhai. Each East African city-state, in contrast, had its own council, headed by a king or sheikh, and was jealously protective of its own rights and distinctive trading networks. While West African empires produced gold, salt, and copper, each East African city-state developed a specialty. One produced tools, another cotton goods, and a third perfumes. Some produced gold, but others did not.

In East Africa, the slave trade was not as profitable as it was in the west. But in both east and west, Muslims expanded that trade, shipping black captives to Arabia, Iraq, Persia, India, and China. In India and China, however, the demand for African slaves was limited by the large size and pervasive poverty of native populations, while in southwest Asia Muslims found it easier to get slaves from West Africa, by means of the trans-Sahara trade routes. Slavery nonetheless persisted in East Africa, where slaves were used to provide heavy labor and to transport goods.

East and West Africa develop differently

Slavery becomes important to West Africa

The Bantu Connection: Central and Southern Africa

Of all the regions of Africa, the central and southern zones were least affected by the outside world before the fifteenth century C.E. The spread of Islam, which had such an important impact on other parts of the continent, had minimal influence in the center and south. Instead it was the long-enduring Bantu migrations that provided these regions with some degree of ethnic and linguistic cohesion.

The Bantu Influence

Central Africa consists primarily of tropical woodlands and grassy plains, ideal environments for bands of hunter-gatherers, including the diminutive peoples once referred to as Pygmies but known among themselves by such names as Mbuti. Central Africans such as these lived in the rain forests in groups without formal chiefs, moving from camp to camp to secure food. Farming and herding apparently came to this region with the Bantu migrations. Linguistic evidence indicates that people speaking Bantu languages migrated out of the West African savannas and into Central Africa. Archeological evidence suggests that this migration took place over many centuries, primarily between 700 B.C.E. and 800 C.E.

Bantu influence Central Africa

The Bantu brought herds of livestock, iron-making skills, and experience in raising crops such as millet and yams, which unfortunately did not grow as well in the tropical forests as they did in the savanna. Eventually the Bantu began to depend on bananas, the cultivation of which spread, in the fourth and fifth centuries C.E., from Indonesia through Madagascar and to Central Africa. Many Bantu remained in the region, interacting and intermarrying with its native peoples, while others moved on to the east and south.

Settlements in Central Africa, as elsewhere on the continent, were organized along village lines, with several villages sometimes combining to form a chiefdom and several chiefdoms occasionally constituting a kingdom. Several Bantu states had developed by the thirteenth century, including the kingdom of Kongo, which covered a large area around the Congo River. Within these realms, each village or group of villages was led by a hereditary chief, and the king was typically selected from among the chiefs by a group of electors. Elsewhere in the region, however, the people continued to live in stateless societies, without creating central governments.

For the most part, Central Africa remained agricultural and maintained only limited contact with peoples and civilizations from other parts of the continent. The dense rain forests and woodlands, the intense equatorial heat, and the presence of dozens of tropical diseases, such as encephalitis and yaws, ensured the region's isolation.

Farther south, however, the climate is variable and temperate, free from most of the parasites and insect-borne diseases that plague much of the continent south of the Sahara. The Bantu arrived there in the eighth century C.E., bringing with them their knowledge of ironworking and their agricultural skills. They developed a society in relative isolation. Southern Africa's remoteness from Arabia and Europe protected it from incursion and invasion until the sixteenth century.

Mining dominates the economies of early Southern African societies

Beginning in the twelfth century, governmental systems in Southern Africa appear to have become more sophisticated than those of their predecessors, characterized by more elaborate social stratification and increasing interest in the mining of gold and copper. Numerous prehistoric mines have been located in present-day Zimbabwe (*zim-BAHB-wā*) and in the Transvaal (*TRANZ-vahl*) region of South Africa. At least some of this gold reached the Indian Ocean trade through the East African city-state of Kilwa. The towns and trading centers of southern Africa never attained any degree of political unity, although they were influenced to some extent by Swahili culture. They also maintained commercial connections with an Islamic world that seems to have had little interest in venturing inland to convert their inhabitants.

Great Zimbabwe

The most fascinating of the southern African kingdoms is the unnamed one that built the imposing stone-building complex known as Great Zimbabwe. Although more than 150 stone ruins have been discovered in an area extending from southwestern Zimbabwe into Mozambique, most are fragmentary. But the ruins of Great Zimbabwe, an impressive set of buildings northeast of Johannesburg, South Africa, are comparable to no other ancient sites in Africa. Their rounded stone towers, walls, and battlements suggest raw power similar to that conveyed by the fortifications of medieval Europe.

Great Zimbabwe was constructed over several centuries. Its earlier, less complex structures date from the eighth century, while the most recent buildings were erected between 1700 and 1750. This complex served as the political and ceremonial hub of a far-flung southern African empire, possibly as large as Mali. Like Ethiopia, this empire's prosperity rested upon a combination of agriculture, cattle raising, and commerce; unlike Ethiopia, however, its trade was based on gold. Abandoned gold mining sites abound throughout the region. Regrettably, we know almost nothing of this state's culture, religion, or political organization, since neither the people who built it nor the local Arab and African traders left any written records. In the nineteenth century the ruins of Great Zimbabwe were explored and mapped by a German geologist, who promptly but mistakenly declared that one of its buildings was a copy of King Solomon's temple. Today we know that Great Zimbabwe was built by south Africans from local granite without reference to Solomon's temple or any other non-African architectural achievements. But we know nothing beyond what archeological analysis can suggest.

Great Zimbabwe creates a Southern African empire

Great Zimbabwe.

Chapter Review

Putting It in Perspective

Throughout most of their early history, African societies developed largely in isolation from each other, separated by distance, desert, forest, and heat. Two major developments, however, helped to foster connections among the continent's cultures. One was the great Bantu migration, a process lasting many centuries, which spread herding, farming, and ironworking across Africa's sub-Saharan lands and created some ethnic and linguistic links among their assorted peoples. Another development that built connections was the spread of Islam, which came about much more quickly and brought to Africa's northern, western, and eastern regions both a militant new religion and a common written language. Through Islam, these regions were connected to a vast commercial and cultural network that ranged from Spain to South Asia.

Neither of these developments, however, did much to intrude on the dramatic diversity that has continuously characterized the African continent. Indeed, in many ways, they added new elements to its rich and diverse history. Early Africa was influenced by many different peoples: Arab, Bantu, Berber, Mandinke, Mbuti, Sondinke, Tuareg, and numerous others. Today we enjoy only limited knowledge of the accomplishments of these peoples, and Africa's past is still inadequately understood. Archeology, anthropology, and oral tradition can only supplement the scant written record.

Reviewing Key Material
KEY CONCEPTS

Bantu, 302	Isma'ilis, 308
animism, 304	Almoravids, 312
Fatimid, 308	Swahili, 317

KEY PEOPLE

Sundiata, 313	Mansa Musa, 314
Mansa Uli, 313	Ibn Battuta, 314

ASK YOURSELF

1. Why were the Bantu migrations so important to the cultural development and cohesion of early African civilizations?
2. How did the arrival of the Muslims change North Africa?

3. How did the trans-Saharan trade change both West Africa and the Islamic world?
4. How did the Indian Ocean community affect the economic and political development of East Africa?

GOING FURTHER

Bovill, E. *The Golden Trade of the Moors: West African Kingdoms in the Fourteenth Century.* 1995.

Brooks, George. *Landlords and Strangers: Ecology, Society, and Trade in Western Africa, 1000–1630.* 1993.

Bulliet, Richard. *The Camel and the Wheel.* 1975.

Davidson, Basil. *The Lost Cities of Africa.* 1987.

Ehret, Christopher. *The Civilizations of Africa.* 2001.

Harris, Joseph. *Africans and Their History.* 1998.

Horton, M., and J. Middleton. *The Swahili.* 2000.

Iliffe, J. *Africans: The History of a Continent.* 1995.

Khapoya, V. *The African Experience: An Introduction.* 1994.

Levtzion, Nehemia. *Ancient Ghana and Mali.* 1973.

Marcus, Harold. *A History of Ethiopia.* 1994.

Mbiti, John. *African Religions and Philosophy.* 1990.

Middleton, John. *The World of the Swahili: An African Mercantile Civilization.* 1992.

Pouwels, Randall. *Horn and Crescent: Cultural Change and Traditional Islam on the East African Coast, 800–1900.* 1987.

Reader, J. *Africa: A Biography of a Continent.* 1997.

Sellassie, S. *Ancient and Medieval Ethiopian History.* 1972.

Shillington, Kevin. *History of Africa.* 1995.

Trimingham, J. *A History of Islam in West Africa.* 1970.

Trimingham, J. *Islam in East Africa.* 1974.

Vansina, Jan. *Paths in the Rainforest: Toward a History of Political Tradition in Equatorial Africa.* 1990.

Key Dates and Developments

?3000 B.C.E.–700 C.E.	The Bantu Migrations
320–340	Establishment of Christianity in Ethiopia
639–642	Islamic conquest of Egypt
700–1750	Construction of Great Zimbabwe
702	Islamic conquest of the Berbers
711	Islamic conquest of Spain
800–1100	Zenith of the Kingdom of Ghana
929	Establishment of the Caliphate of Córdoba in Spain
969	Establishment of the Fatimid Caliphate in Egypt
1050–1100	Rise of the Almoravids in Morocco and Spain
1085–1492	The Reconquest in Spain
1100–1800	City-states in East Africa
1235	Sundiata founds the Kingdom of Mali
1324	Pilgrimage to Mecca of Mansa Musa
1352–1353	Ibn Battuta visits Mali
1433	Sack of Timbuktu by the Tuaregs

CHAPTER 14

The Evolution and Expansion of East Asian Societies, 220–1240 C.E.

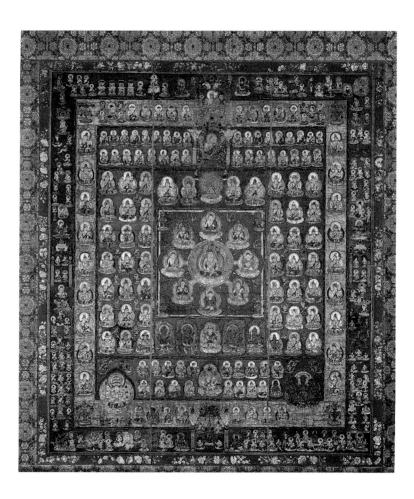

Buddhist Mandala

In the third through seventh centuries C.E., aided by increased connections among Indian, Central Asian, and East Asian societies, Buddhism emerged as East Asia's main belief system. This Buddhist diagram from ninth-century Japan, depicting numerous holy figures, is called a mandala and used as a focus for prayer and meditation.

Although revered as the father of Japanese culture, Prince Shotoku (*shō-TŌ-koo*), regent of Japan from 593 to 622, borrowed many ideas from neighboring China. He actively promoted Buddhism, which recently had spread from China to Japan. He sent Japanese missions to the Chinese mainland, brought Chinese artisans and artists to Japan, and adopted the Chinese calendar for Japanese use. To strengthen his government, he instituted a bureaucratic system based on the Chinese model. He even asserted equality with the Chinese emperor, sending him a letter addressed "from the ruler of the land of the sunrise to the ruler of the land of the sunset."

East Asian Societies

According to Chinese sources, the emperor was not impressed—his reply was haughtily addressed "the emperor speaks to the prince."

Shotoku's story illustrates several important aspects of East Asian history in the centuries following the collapse of China's Han dynasty in 220 C.E. (Chapter 4). One decisive development was the expansion of Buddhism. In the third through sixth centuries, as the Chinese endured a prolonged era of disunity, Buddhism spread from India through Central Asia to China, eventually becoming China's main faith. From China it spread to Korea and Japan, where it was incorporated into the cultures and used by leaders such as Shotoku to enhance their authority.

Another key feature of East Asia in this era was the preeminence of China, reflected in Shotoku's borrowing of Chinese ideas and in the Chinese emperor's refusal to address Japan's prince regent as an equal. In the late sixth century, reunited and reinvigorated after centuries of chaos, China re-emerged as one of history's most powerful and prosperous empires. For the next seven centuries, its cohesion, commerce, technology, and influence were unsurpassed in East Asia. So successful was the Chinese system, and so strong was the Chinese state, that neighboring countries, including Prince Shotoku's Japan, often found it advantageous to imitate Chinese ways. Even the nomadic warriors from the north, who conquered much of northern China in the twelfth and thirteenth centuries, adopted many features of Chinese society.

A third key East Asian reality, embodied in Shotoku's assertion of equality with the Chinese emperor, was the ability of China's smaller neighbors to preserve their cultural autonomy in the face of Chinese preeminence. Vietnam, Korea, and Japan adopted Chinese concepts and conventions but altered them to fit their own cultures, creating in the process their own unique variants of East Asian civilization. And the northern nomadic invaders, after conquering parts of China, used Chinese methods and ideas to organize, govern, and exploit the lands that they had conquered. Connections and conflicts with neighboring peoples thus not only promoted China's preeminence but also in time helped these neighboring peoples hold their own against China.

China's Age of Disunity, 220–589

The foundations of Chinese preeminence had been laid by the end of the Han Empire (206 B.C.E.–220 C.E.), which rivaled the concurrent Roman Empire in size, population, and influence. After the fall of the Han, however, China endured an Age of Disunity (220–589 C.E.) that was in some ways similar to Europe's Early Middle Ages. As in the West, the Chinese Empire was torn apart by internal divisions and nomadic invaders. As in the West, the collapse of imperial authority was followed by a general decline in learning and commerce. And as in the West, where people in these troubled times sought comfort in Christianity, East Asians likewise found a new faith, turning to Buddhism for consolation in the midst of chaos.

The Three Kingdoms Era

The fall of China's Han dynasty in 220 C.E. resulted in the creation of three separate kingdoms in the north, south, and west, none strong enough to defeat the others (Map 14.1). Dominated by powerful families and warlords, these kingdoms engaged each other in an endless series of brutal battles. For most of the century, China was torn apart by civil wars and ravaged by diseases and natural disasters. By the year 280 the population, which had approached 60 million at the height of the Han dynasty, had declined to only 16 million by official counts. It was a terrifying time.

Civil war and devastation mark the Three Kingdoms Era

Despite all the devastation, however, the Chinese later came to see the era as exciting and heroic, full of great exploits and adventures. The *Romance of the Three Kingdoms*, China's most beloved epic tale, was told, retold, and embellished over the ages until it was finally published in its modern form in the sixteenth century. For countless generations, people in China have thrilled to its stories of three heroic blood brothers who, in the declining years of the Han dynasty, joined in the famous "Oath of the Peach Garden" to fight together for their country (see "Excerpts from *Romance of the Three Kingdoms*"). At times they managed to outwit their mortal enemy Cao Cao (*TSOW-TSOW*), a character based on a real Chinese general who seized power in northern China at the end of the Han era. In the long run, however, the three heroes failed to reunite China or preserve the Han dynasty.

The actual Three Kingdoms era (220–280) was disastrous for China. For decades descendants of the real Cao Cao fought against descendants of his foes, wreaking widespread havoc. By 280 a general from the north had managed to conquer the south and west, briefly reuniting the realm under the short-lived Jin (*JĒN*) dynasty. But after he died a decade later his 25 sons vied for power, dividing the domain into numerous warring states. Then one of them unwisely asked for assistance from the **Xiongnu** (*shē-ONG NOO*), warlike Turkic nomads from the Central Asian steppes who had long threatened China from the north. This request gave the Xiongnu, many of whom had entered the empire during its years of division, a new opportunity to overrun northern China. And they did so with a vengeance. By 317 the Xiongnu had laid waste to northern China's great cities, destroyed the imperial library at Chang'an, and driven the Jin emperors out of the north. The Xiongnu rulers also claimed the Mandate of Heaven, thereby asserting that they had divine approval to rule over China (Chapter 4).

Nomadic Xiongnu overrun northern China in early 300s

FOUNDATION MAP 14.1 China's Age of Disunity, 220–589

With the fall of the Han Dynasty, China experienced a long age of disunity, beginning with the Three Kingdoms Era (220–280), depicted in Map A. Notice that, after splintering into numerous small states in the Sixteen Kingdoms Era (304–439), shown in Map B, northern China was reunified under Toba (Northern Wei) rule from 439 to 534 (Map C) but again divided by the mid-500s (Map D), while southern China endured a succession of short-lived regimes known as the Six Dynasties. How did this age of disunity affect China's culture and religion?

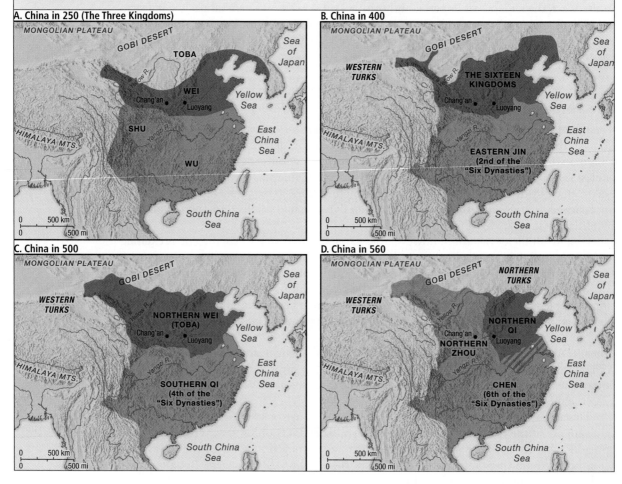

A. China in 250 (The Three Kingdoms)

B. China in 400

C. China in 500

D. China in 560

Division, Invasion, Adaptation, and Migration

For the next century the Yellow River region, birthplace of Chinese culture, endured further ruin as Xiongnu chieftains and other tribal leaders ravaged the land and warred among themselves. This era was known in the north as the time of the Sixteen Kingdoms (304–439) for its rapid succession of short-lived regimes, most of which failed to establish any dynastic continuity. The era finally ended in 439 when the Toba (*TŌ-BAH*), a Mongolian nomadic tribe, gained control over the entire northern region (Map 14.1).

Document 14.1 Excerpts from *Romance of the Three Kingdoms*

Told and retold over the centuries until published in its modern form, Romance of the Three Kingdoms is China's most beloved epic tale. In the following excerpts from early in the story, its three heroes meet, agree to fight as one, and together take the "Oath of the Peach Garden" swearing brotherhood and mutual fidelity.

Empires wax and wane; states cleave asunder and coalesce . . . The rise of the fortunes of Han began with the slaughter of the White Serpent. In a short time the whole Empire was theirs and their . . . heritage was handed down until the days of Kuang-Wu . . . A century later came to the throne the Emperor Hsien, doomed to see the beginning of the division . . . known to history as the Three Kingdoms . . .

The Government went quickly from bad to worse, till the country was ripe for rebellion . . .

Yüan-tê was twenty-eight when the outbreak of the rebellion called for soldiers. The sight of the notice saddened him and he sighed . . . Suddenly a rasping voice behind him cried, "Noble Sir, why sigh if you do nothing to help your country?" Turning quickly he saw standing there a man . . . with a bullet head like a leopard's, large eyes, a pointed chin, and a bristling moustache. He spoke in a loud bass voice . . . "Chang Fei is my name . . . I live near here where I have a farm; and I am a wine-seller and a butcher as well. And I like to become acquainted with worthy men . . ."

Yüan-tê replied, "I am of the Imperial Family, Liu by name, and my distinguishing name is Pei. . . . I would destroy these rebels and restore peace to the land, but alas! I am helpless."

"I am not without means," said Fei. "Suppose you and I raised some men and tried what we could do."

. . . The two betook themselves to the village inn to talk over the project. As they were drinking, a huge, tall fellow appeared pushing a hand cart . . . He had eyes like a phoenix and fine bushy eyebrows like silkworms. His whole appearance was dignified and awe-inspiring. "I am Kuan Yü" said he; ". . . I have been a fugitive . . . for five years because I slew a ruffian who . . . was a bully. I have come to join the army here.

Then Yüan-tê told him his own intentions and all three went away to Chang Fei's farm . . . Said Fei, "The peach trees in the orchard behind the house are just in full flower. Tomorrow we will institute a sacrifice there and solemnly declare our intention before Heaven and Earth . . ."

All three being of one mind, the next day they prepared the sacrifices, a black ox, a white horse, and wine for libation. Beneath the smoke of the incense burning on the altar they bowed their heads and recited this oath: "We three, Liu Pei, Kuan Yü and Chang Fei, though of different families, swear brotherhood, and promise mutual help to one end. We will rescue each other in difficulty, we will aid each other in danger. We swear to serve the state and save the people. We ask not the same day of birth but we seek to die together. May Heaven, the all-ruling, and Earth, the all-producing, read our hearts, and if we turn aside from righteousness or forget kindliness may Heaven and man smite us!"

SOURCE: Lo Kuan-Chung, *Romance of the Three Kingdoms* (Tokyo: Charles E. Tuttle Company, 1959) I: 1, 2, 4–6.

Then, as so often happened after such conquests, the victors adopted features of the conquered society, thus connecting and combining the cultures. To strengthen and sustain their rule, for example, the Toba established a Chinese-style administrative system, staffed it with Chinese officials, and created a new dynasty called the Northern Wei (*WAY*) that restored to northern China a semblance of stability for most of the next century. In the 490s they even moved their capital to Luoyang, which had also been the capital during the Later Han, and made Chinese the official language of their realm.

Nomadic conquerors
adopt Chinese ways,
creating internal strife

In time these cultural adaptations helped to produce new conflicts. The adoption of the Chinese language created serious strife among the Toba warriors, many of whom resented the submersion of their own Mongolian language. Their resentment fueled internal strife, and by the 530s northern China was once again divided into different domains and dynasties.

Turmoil in north
prompts mass migration
to south

Meanwhile, China's ongoing turmoil had prompted a mass migration. As chaos enveloped the north in the third through sixth centuries, thousands of wealthy and educated Chinese families fled to the south. As a result this region, long accustomed to domination from the north, gradually emerged as China's cultural center as well as its most populous and prosperous zone. Largely spared the ravages that befell the north, southern China nonetheless experienced recurrent power struggles throughout the Age of Disunity as six successive short-lived regimes, later called the "Six Dynasties," sought but failed to achieve a long-lasting reign.

Central Asian Connections and the Arrival of Buddhism

During these tumultuous times, a new religion began to flourish in China. Founded in northern India in the sixth century B.C.E. by the man later called the Buddha, Buddhism was based on the belief, embodied in his Four Noble Truths, that one could best avoid life's pain by curbing desire and living righteously. After spreading throughout India, it was later adopted by the Kushans (*koo-SHAHNZ*), who ruled the region to India's northwest from roughly 50 to 240 C.E., and who fostered the Buddhist faith in many Central Asian towns and cities (Chapter 3).

Buddhism spreads to
China from India via
Asian trade routes

By this time there was regular contact between Central Asia and China. Most of the connections were commercial, as merchants traded along the Silk Road established in the early Han dynasty. But over time the trade routes conveyed not just goods but ideas, including religious beliefs. Promoted in Central Asia by the Kushans, Buddhist ideas spread from there along the Silk Road to China, arriving in the Later Han dynasty (Map 14.2).

Buddhism, meanwhile, had split into two branches. Theravada (*ter-ah-VAH-dah*) Buddhism, prevailing in Sri Lanka and Southeast Asia, largely remained true to the simple beliefs originally advanced by the Buddha. But Mahayana (*mah-hah-YAH-nah*) Buddhism, the branch that came to China through Central Asia, had all the trappings of an established religion, with priests, sects, monasteries, convents, and bodhisattvas (*bō-dih-SAHT-vuhz*). Said to be former mortals who had earned the endless peace called nirvana but postponed it to help others get there, bodhisattvas were revered as saviors by Mahayana Buddhists, who sought to follow their examples of mercy, hope, and love.

Statue of the Buddha
from Central Asia, Third
Century C.E.

Mahayana Buddhism fits
with Chinese traditions

Mahayana's features coincided with certain aspects of the Confucian and Daoist traditions, long prevalent in China. Its stress on charity, compassion, and good works, for example, paralleled the Confucian ethic of benevolence, civility, and public service. At the same time, its basic Buddhist emphasis on meditation and curbing desire concurred with Daoism's focus on silence and passivity. Furthermore, like Mahayana Buddhism, Daoism had evolved over time into a complex religion with numerous devotions and divinities, a hierarchical structure of priests and officials, and a network of monasteries and convents. In fact, although Daoism and Buddhism retained their separate identities, to the common people of China they were often indistinguishable from each other. Chinese people could thus adopt Buddhism without forsaking their traditional beliefs.

Map 14.2 Buddhism Spreads to East Asia, Second Through Sixth Centuries C.E.

In the early centuries of the common era, Buddhism expanded from its origins in India throughout the eastern part of Asia. Notice that, while Theravada Buddhism spread across Southeast Asia, Mahayana Buddhism expanded through Central Asia to China, where it took hold during the Age of Disunity (220–589), and eventually spread from there to Korea and Japan. What factors and conditions facilitated Buddhism's spread?

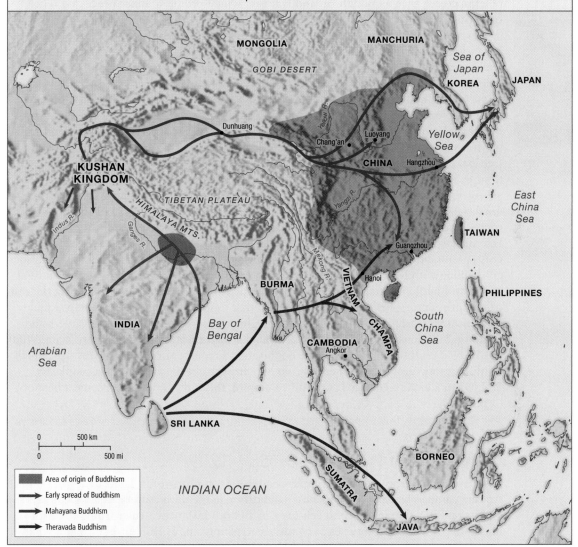

The Spread of Buddhism in China

Initially Buddhism did not make much of an impact in China. As long as the Han dynasty flourished, Confucianism reigned as the official philosophy, and the Confucian bureaucrats who ran the country enjoyed great prestige as preservers of stability and order.

Foreign religions such as Buddhism, dismissed by Confucians as alien cults, attracted little following.

Instability and disunity aid Buddhism's spread

In the Age of Disunity, however, the cultural climate changed. As nomadic invasions and civil wars shattered China's stability, the prestige of the Confucians declined, and Chinese cultural confidence gave way to confusion and anxiety. People began to look for relief in creeds such as Buddhism and Daoism, which promised inner peace and relief from life's burdens.

In the fourth century, then, in the chaotic conditions of northern China, Buddhism began to thrive. With its emphasis on avoiding desire and ambition, the faith was actively fostered by Xiongnu warlords, who hoped to keep power by promoting passivity among the people. Buddhism's premise that life was painful reflected the people's perceptions, while Buddhism's promise of escape from pain consoled them. The faith offered hope of salvation from suffering and the prospect of attaining nirvana, perpetual peace. Buddhism's numerous shrines and temples gave Chinese artists and sculptors opportunities to express creativity, while its monasteries and convents, like the ones in Christian Europe, provided a refuge for those who felt called to a life of contemplation and devotion. By 400 C.E. most of northern China had accepted the new faith.

Buddhist temple in north-western China.

Buddhism comes to southern China from India and from the north

By this time Buddhism had also begun to penetrate the south. Partly it came from northern China, where it was already established, and partly it arrived over land and sea routes from India and Southeast Asia. From 399 to 414 a Chinese Buddhist monk named Faxian (*FAH shē-YAN*) made a historic pilgrimage from China to India, crossing treacherous mountain passes on foot. After spending a decade in India, visiting Buddhist shrines and talking with Indian Buddhists, he returned by sea to southern China with hundreds of Indian Buddhist texts, which he painstakingly translated into Chinese. During the rest of the fifth century, his efforts and those of other monks and missionaries helped make Buddhism increasingly popular in southern China, where it attracted both leaders and common folk. Finally, in 517, it was proclaimed the official religion there by Liang Wudi (*lē-AHNG WOO DĒ*), the so-called Bodhisattva Emperor, a ruler so devout that, much to his advisors' dismay, he twice gave up his throne to become a Buddhist monk. By 589, when China re-emerged as a unified empire, the entire land had become a bastion of Buddhism.

China's Age of Preeminence, 589–1279

History does not repeat itself, but similar patterns do at times recur. There are, for example, striking parallels between China's initial unification in the third century B.C.E. (Chapter 4) and its reunification in the sixth century C.E. In both instances a ruler from the north united the realm after centuries of chaos, establishing a powerful but brief regime that paved the way for a far more eminent, enduring dynasty. In the third century B.C.E., the First Emperor ended the Warring States Era by conquering all of China, founded the short-lived Qin dynasty, and opened the way for four centuries of Han dynastic rule. In the sixth century C.E. a northern general named Yang Jian (*YAHNG jē-AHN*) ended the Age of Disunity by conquering all of China, founded the short-lived Sui (*SWAY*) dynasty, and opened the way for six centuries of Chinese preeminence under the Tang (*TAHNG*) and Song (*SŌNG*) dynasties.

China Reunited: The Sui Dynasty, 589–618

Yang Jian, a general with both Chinese and Toba ancestry, emerged as China's dominant force through crafty opportunism. First he married a wealthy noblewoman, whose status helped him become the main advisor to a northern emperor; then he wed his daughter to that emperor. When that emperor died soon after she bore him a son, Yang Jian arranged to have himself named regent for his own grandson, the infant who inherited the throne. Then, in 581, he deposed the boy monarch and claimed Heaven's Mandate for himself, starting a new dynasty called the Sui. Using skillful propaganda, carefully cultivated Buddhist support, and a well-planned river and land campaign, he conquered one-by-one the several weak states that had survived in the south. By 589, for the first time in centuries, one man ruled all of China.

Yang Jian conquers and reconnects China, initiating Sui dynasty

Yang Jian, who reigned from 581 to 604 as Wendi (*WUN-DĒ*), proved a resourceful emperor. He devised a nationwide law code and restored the civil service system begun by the Han dynasty. He centered his government at Chang'an, earlier the Han capital, and built it into one of the world's great cities. He also began construction of the Grand Canal, a thousand-mile waterway linking the Yellow River in the north with the Yangzi River in the south. Henceforth, since China's great rivers flow from west to east, the canal played a crucial role in connecting the north with the south, transporting troops and grain, and thereby combining the north's military might with the south's agricultural prosperity.

Central rule is restored as Grand Canal links north and south

Yang Jian's son and heir, however, was a disastrous ruler. Yangdi (604–618) has gone down in Chinese annals as a despot who reportedly poisoned his father to hasten his own rule, then alienated his people by imposing harsh taxes and sacrificing millions of laborers' lives to erect an extravagant palace, complete the Grand Canal, and rebuild the Great Wall. He also launched a series of disastrous wars that ruined the economy and prompted widespread rebellions. Then he abandoned his armies and fled to the rural south where he lived in luxuriant debauchery until he was murdered in 618. That same year the powerful Duke of Tang, one of Yangdi's most effective governors and generals, declared himself emperor and assumed the Mandate of Heaven, thereby putting an end to the Sui dynasty.

The Grand Canal.

China Triumphant: The Tang Dynasty, 618–907

The seizure of power by the Duke of Tang ushered in a new regime known as the Tang dynasty (618–907). Under its dominion, China attained new heights in political stability, economic prosperity, military expansion, cultural sophistication, and technological innovation.

The new Tang Dynasty builds on Sui foundations

The Tang era's most successful ruler was Li Shimin (*LĒ SHUR-MIN*), son of the Duke of Tang. After persuading his reluctant father to claim the throne, the 18-year-old Li led a series of skillful campaigns against numerous revolts while holding back the northern nomadic invaders. Then, after ambushing and killing his two older brothers, he forced his father to abdicate and assumed the throne himself at age 26. Bold and energetic, Li then reigned from 626 to 649 as the Emperor Taizong (*TĪ-ZŌNG*).

Nothing seemed impossible to Taizong. He forced the northern nomads to become his vassals and allies, then with their help invaded Central Asia and conquered Turkestan (Map 14.3). He even sent an army to India to arrest a local ruler who had insulted his ambassador. In China he promoted education, patronized the arts, and revitalized the

Map 14.3 China Under the Tang Dynasty, 618–907

Under the Tang Dynasty, China expanded into Central Asia, reopening trade routes and cultural ties with its various neighbors. Observe that the Grand Canal, constructed under the Sui Dynasty (589–618) and expanded under the Tang, linked the Yellow and Yangzi Rivers and the port of Hangzhou, expediting commerce and communication between China's north and south. How did good internal connections contribute to the Tang Empire's power and wealth?

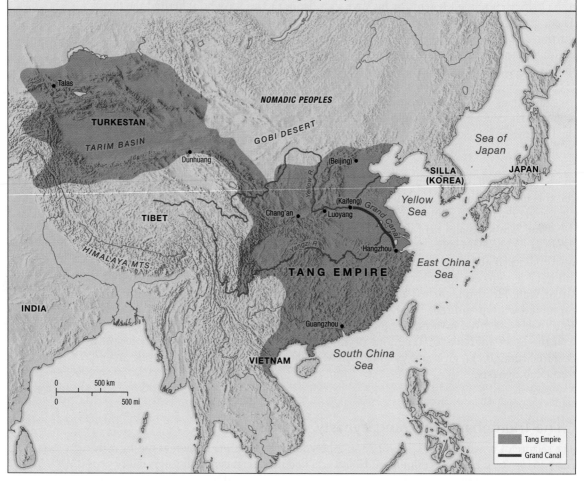

civil service. Although a Confucian, he promoted religious toleration and devotion among the Buddhist and Daoist masses. Revered as a hero, he attained a legendary status among the Chinese people.

Another notable Tang-era leader was Wu Zhao (*WOO-JOW*), later known as Empress Wu. According to traditional accounts, in her youth she was one of Taizong's many concubines and was obliged to enter a Buddhist convent after he died. But she was only 24 and reportedly a reluctant nun. When the new emperor visited her convent, the accounts assert, she seduced him and won his heart. She became his full-time consort and

Wu Zhao rises from concubine status to become Empress Wu

then his official empress. In 660, when his eyesight failed, she took over as informal regent and skillfully ruled the realm, staffing the government with her supporters and killing those who got in her way. In 683, when the emperor died, she had their sons locked in the palace and ruled as regent until 690, when she formally claimed the throne for herself. Finally, in 705, a palace coup forced the aged Empress Wu to abdicate the throne and resume her long-lost calling as a nun.

Although disgruntled male Confucian historians later denounced her as a brutal and shameless opportunist, Wu Zhao actually accomplished a great deal. During her long period of power she granted tax relief, improved the civil service system, decreased the power of the old nobility, fostered military expansion, and promoted economic prosperity.

Not long after Wu Zhao's removal, one of her grandsons took the throne as Emperor Xuanzong (*shu-WAHN ZŌNG*), reigning from 713 to 756. His early reign was a time of peace, prosperity, and cultural achievements, the age of China's most beloved poets and a high point of Chinese art. The emperor himself patronized the arts, lengthened the Grand Canal, reformed the bureaucracy and coinage, and maintained a magnificent court. But in his later years, after falling madly in love with a concubine called Yang Guifei (*YAHNG GWĀ-FĀ*), he neglected his duties and let her relatives run the country. In 751, as the empire drifted without strong direction, its armies were driven from Central Asia by Islamic forces. In 755 a massive revolt led by An Lushan (*AHN LOO-SHAHN*), a Chinese general of Turkish descent, forced the emperor and Yang Guifei to flee from the capital for their lives. Thus began a civil war that brought about the strangling of Yang Guifei, the abdication of Xuanzong, and the devastation of China.

Empress Wu.

The Tang dynasty survived the An Lushan revolt, but it never regained its earlier domination. Local warlords took advantage of the turmoil to reassert their power, while the palace eunuchs guarding the emperor's concubines came to dominate the court. Religious strife broke out as Confucian civil servants came to resent the untaxed wealth of Buddhist monasteries, some of which had acquired vast riches through generous donations. In the mid-800s, as Confucian civil servants worked to suppress Buddhism as a "foreign cult," a Daoist emperor who hated all things foreign ordered thousands of Buddhist shrines and monasteries destroyed. Later that century a famine in eastern China sparked a mass rebellion and convinced many that the Tang regime had lost Heaven's Mandate. Finally in 907, as local warlords carved up the country, one of them overthrew the dynasty, leading to a new age of disunity.

Revolts, religious strife, and famine destroy the Tang dynasty

China in Turmoil: Ten Kingdoms and Five Dynasties, 907–960

Fifty-three years of dynastic disruption followed the end of the Tang era. The south was partitioned into warring states, later called the Ten Kingdoms. The north retained a measure of unity under a string of brief regimes called the Five Dynasties but also lost a number of border provinces to the Khitans (*KĒ-TAHNZ*), a people from Manchuria who emerged as a new nomadic threat. Establishing a capital at what is now Beijing (*BĀ-JĒNG*), the Khitans created an expansive domain called the Liao (*lē-OW*) Empire,

Nomads again move into northern China during turmoil

Map 14.4 Song China and the Khitan Liao Empire, 960–1125

Under the Song Dynasty (960–1279), China enjoyed a renewed era of stability and prosperity. Notice, however, that the northernmost part of China was controlled by the Khitans, a nomadic people from the northeast, whose Liao Empire (907–1125) also ruled much of what is now Manchuria and Mongolia. How did the Song approach to northern nomadic peoples differ from that of the Tang?

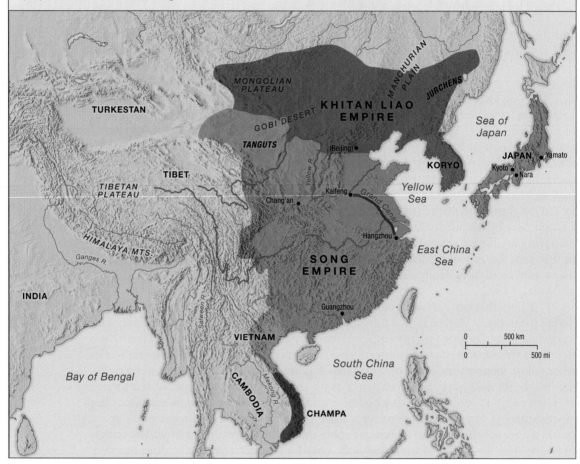

which for the next few centuries ruled Manchuria, Mongolia, and parts of northern China (Map 14.4).

Meanwhile, in 960, a Chinese general named Zhao Kuangyin (*JOW KWAHNG-YIN*) began the reunification of the rest of China. He overthrew the last of the north's Five Dynasties at the urging of his troops, who proclaimed him emperor and pledged him their absolute allegiance. Once they had done so, he compelled his key officers to retire, thus preventing their emergence as warlords and ensuring that none of them could threaten his rule. He then annexed most of the south's Ten Kingdoms, exploiting their peoples' hunger for unity and peace.

China Resurgent: The Song Dynasty, 960–1127

In the process of reunifying China, Zhao Kuangyin founded the Song Dynasty, which lasted from 960 until 1279. In its later years, however, it ruled only the south, and it never matched the size or military success of the Han and Tang dynasties. But it was second to none in political and economic vitality.

Zhao Kuangyin, who reigned from 960 to 976 as Emperor Taizu (*TĪ-DZUH*), took a series of decisive steps. He restored and strengthened the Confucian civil service, promoting professional governance. He banned court eunuchs from holding high state office, preventing conflicts between them and the civil servants. He centralized control over the army, reducing the influence of local nobles and warlords. Toward the end of his life he decreed that he would be succeeded, not by his young son, but by his talented brother, who then completed the conquest of the south to consolidate dynastic control.

Unlike their predecessors, however, the Song rulers made little attempt to conquer or control foreign lands, judging that such ventures in the past had drained the country's resources. In 1004, for example, after a futile effort to subdue the Khitans and win back the border provinces they ruled, the Song made peace and agreed to pay them a large annual tribute. Similar settlements, far less costly than conquest and control, were also arranged with other peoples on China's borders. This policy reversed China's age-old practice of making weaker neighbors pay tribute, but it did enable China to buy peace with tribute in silver and silks.

The Song regime placates neighbors rather than fighting them

Instead of expanding outward, the dynasty focused its energies on controlling China itself. To stop the rise of local warlords and prevent armed revolts, it tightly managed the army, frequently rotating commands among generals to keep them from turning the forces they led into their own personal armies. To limit the power of aristocratic families that had often dominated regional affairs, it enticed some of them to move to the new capital at Kaifeng (*KĪ-FUNG*), where they lived in splendor but had little local power.

The Song regime reduces the power of generals and nobles

To administer the empire, the Song regime consolidated the Confucian civil service bureaucracy. **Civil service exams**, established initially in the Han dynasty and revived under the Sui and Tang, were now standardized and strengthened, requiring of applicants comprehensive knowledge of the Confucian classics. Potential state bureaucrats were required to pass a series of extremely rigorous exams, first on the regional and then on the national level. So competitive were the tests that not even 1 percent of the candidates actually became state officials. Those who did, once in office, had to earn their promotions through performance. As a result, their loyalty was largely to those who had the power to promote them—that is, to the emperor and central government, which hence became more autocratic than ever.

The Song regime strengthens the civil service and exam system

Chinese civil servants typically were quite conservative. Trained in the ancient classics, which many had learned by heart, Confucian bureaucrats were steeped in tradition and devoted to the system that reinforced stability, fostered civility, and brought them great power and prestige. Most came from wealthy families, since they could send their sons to schools or hire tutors to prepare them for the civil service exams. To ensure they had the means to do so, families of state officials often intermarried with those of wealthy landowners. This practice over time helped create a Confucian **scholar gentry**—an educated elite class supported by both official state posts and large rural estates—that tended to be self-perpetuating and resistant to change.

Confucians thwart efforts to reform Chinese economy

As the Song regime searched for ways to cover the costs of its vast army and bureaucracy, however, a key civil servant decided that change was needed. From 1069 to 1085 a reforming official named Wang Anshi (*WAHNG AHN-SHUR*), as the emperor's main advisor, sought to boost state revenues by increasing the wealth of the farmers and merchants who paid the state taxes and duties. He intervened in the economy, establishing price controls and government monopolies, introducing a graduated land tax that increased with the soil's productivity, and providing low-interest loans to peasants so they could increase their harvest by buying seeds and tools. He engaged the state directly in commerce, acquiring products in one area and selling them elsewhere at a profit. He even tried to open up the civil service exams to more talented young men. But his actions horrified other civil servants, who, as members of the Confucian elite, looked down upon merchants, had little use for commerce, and feared that his reforms would upset their domination of the social order. When floods, droughts, and famine, sparking widespread unrest, seemed to show that Heaven did not favor Wang Anshi, his enemies managed get him dismissed and undo most of his reforms.

Commerce makes Song China an economic giant

Wang's enemies could not, however, undo the growing influence of the commercial class. Although Confucians ranked merchants as nonproducers at the bottom of the social scale, merchants helped to bring about huge advances in money and banking, trade and transport, manufacturing, and technology, fostering a Chinese commercial revolution. Combined with vast increases in agricultural output, these advances also promoted urbanization. By the twelfth century the empire had at least fifty large cities, each with hundreds of thousands of inhabitants. With abundant capital and resources, expanding foreign and domestic markets, many miles of roads and canals, merchant ships, textile mills, printed books, advanced military technology, flourishing farmlands, and thriving cities, Song China appeared to have all that was needed for sustained economic and industrial growth, and perhaps even global domination.

China Divided: Jurchens and Southern Song, 1127–1279

Warlike nomads again overrun northern China

In the twelfth and thirteenth centuries, however, China's growth was disrupted again by nomads to the north. In 1114 the Jurchens (*JUR-chenz*), warlike pastoral nomads from Manchuria, staged a massive rebellion against the Khitans and their Liao Empire. Seeing this rebellion as an opportunity to win back for China the northern border provinces under Khitan control, the Song emperor allied with the Jurchens. The result was disaster for the dynasty. In the 1120s, after totally crushing the Khitans, the Jurchens turned violently against their Chinese allies. By 1127 the Jurchens had overrun all of northern China, plundered the capital at Kaifeng, and driven the Song armies deep into the south (Map 14.5).

The Song regime eventually rallied, but it never regained control of the north, where the Jurchens ruled for the rest of the century. The Song rulers could do little more than secure and stabilize the south. Establishing a new capital in 1138 at the bustling

Map 14.5 The Jurchens and the Southern Song, 1127–1279

After overthrowing the Khitan Liao Empire in the 1120s, the Jurchens, nomadic warriors from the Manchurian Plain, attacked the Song Dynasty and overran all of northern China. Note, however, that the Song Dynasty, now called the Southern Song (1127–1279), continued to govern the south, where it ruled over a prosperous realm with thriving commerce until the Mongol invasions of the thirteenth century. How did southern China continue to prosper despite the loss of the north?

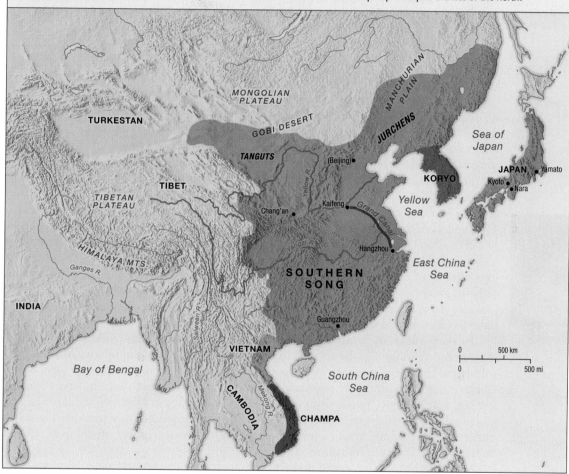

eastern port of Hangzhou (*HAHNG-JŌ*), they maintained their regime in southern China until 1279.

During this era, known as the Southern Song, the regime ruled only half the country. But the half it ruled was probably the most prosperous place on earth. Agriculture and technology continued to advance and flourish; cities and commerce continued to grow and thrive. Although substantially reduced in its size and power, the realm was as rich as ever. Nonetheless, despite its great wealth and technical sophistication, it could not survive the great challenge of the thirteenth century, when first the Jurchens and later the Song fell to the Mongol conquests (Chapter 15).

The Song regime survives and thrives in south until the Mongol conquest

Highlights and Hallmarks of Chinese Society

From the sixth through twelfth centuries, during the Tang and Song dynasties, China may well have been the world's most prosperous and cosmopolitan culture. The empire had extensive trade; innovative technology; inspiring poetry and art; robust religious institutions; large, vibrant cities; and intense intellectual creativity. But many Chinese people, including most peasants and women, derived little benefit from their country's commercial and cultural preeminence.

Commercial and Technological Innovations

Stability, security, roads, and waterways strengthen Chinese commerce

China's commercial preeminence was based on such factors as effective governance, agricultural abundance, and creative innovation. The Tang and Song regimes, with their capable civil servants and soldiers, typically provided the internal stability, effective law enforcement, and security from foreign threats needed for commerce to thrive. They also constructed and maintained the thousands of miles of waterways and highways, including the bustling Grand Canal and the tree-lined roads alongside it, that connected China's productive farmlands with its urban commercial economy.

Government-forged connections also contributed to China's agricultural abundance. Tang and Song domination of northern Vietnam, for example, introduced farmers in southern China to new strains of fast-growing rice developed in the region of Champa (now central Vietnam). Since Champa rice matured in three months, rather than in five like other strains, farmers could double their output by growing two crops in succession, rather than one, each year. Other agricultural innovations, including the use of animal-powered pumps and waterwheels to bring new lands under irrigation, added substantially to China's food supply.

Terraced rice fields in southern China.

Farming advances increase population and commerce

Farming advances in turn helped sustain China's growing population, which rose from under 50 million in the seventh century to over 100 million in the twelfth, and contributed to the rise of commercial farming. As cultivating rice took up less of their time, Chinese farmers additionally produced and sold marketable goods such as silk, cotton, and tea, a distinctive Chinese drink that emerged in the Age of Disunity and later gained global popularity. Most important, perhaps, the growing food supply supported large numbers of merchants, manufacturers, artisans, and inventors, some of whom developed innovations that would transform the world.

Some innovations improved domestic commerce. As copper and silver grew scarce, for example, and as the coins made from them proved cumbersome for interregional trade, enterprising Tang era merchants introduced "flying cash" (mobile money)—paper notes that could be bought in one region and redeemed for face value in another. These notes in turn prepared the way for the use of checks, credit certificates, and government-issued paper money during the Song era. The invention and use of the abacus, a computing device with sliding counters grouped in multiples of ten, also greatly aided commercial calculations.

Giant ships and magnetic compasses enhance international trade

Other innovations enhanced international trade. As bandits and brigands made land trade dangerous along the Central Asian Silk Road (Chapter 4), especially after Tang armies lost control of that region in 751 C.E., Chinese merchants increasingly transported their silks, ceramics, tea, and other goods by sea. Giant ships, sailing from Chinese ports, were equipped by Song times with multiple masts, watertight compartments, and magnetic compasses. The compass was especially influential, enabling ships to stay on course while traveling great distances with no land in sight. Adopted from the Chinese by Arab sailors, and later used by European explorers, the compass eventually helped open an era of global trade and travel.

Additional Chinese innovations also had global impact. Gunpowder, which eventually revolutionized warfare around the world, was originally used in Tang China for fireworks, then by Song armies in grenades, flame-throwers, and crude early cannons. Coal was first used in northern China as fuel, and was later used to smelt iron and make steel, eventually resulting in sturdier weapons and farm tools the world over. Song-era China also developed, among other things, a mechanical clock and cotton textile mills centuries before other societies.

China's most influential invention, however, may have been the printing process. The printing of books, using blocks of wood that were carved for each page and brushed with ink to make impressions on paper, began in Tang China and improved during Song times. Song-era printers also experimented with moveable type, using small blocks of print for each character, but since Chinese writing employs thousands of characters, most Chinese printers found it more efficient to simply make a block for each page. Printing eventually spread westward from China to the Muslim and Christian worlds, sparking a global revolution in information and learning.

Gunpowder and other Chinese innovations will have a global impact

Early carved woodblock used for Chinese printing.

Spiritual, Intellectual, and Cultural Creativity

In China itself, printing was used first to publish Buddhist scriptures and later to record the works of religious thinkers, scholars, philosophers, and poets. By providing writers, artists, and artisans with security and food so they could specialize in diverse pursuits, Tang and Song stable governance and agricultural abundance also contributed to China's flourishing intellectual and cultural life.

Stability and prosperity foster cultural creativity

In the early Tang era, while Buddhism enjoyed broad support from the people and their rulers, several innovative Buddhist sects became very influential. One was **Pure Land Buddhism**, which claimed that humans could not achieve enlightenment by their own works and instead preached salvation by faith in the Buddha of Infinite Light who ruled the Western Paradise, or "Pure Land." Another was **Chan** (*CHAHN*) **Buddhism**, known in Japan as **Zen**, which taught that meditation was the only path to enlightenment, and stressed love of nature, simplicity of life, and individual self-discipline.

In the late Tang era, as noted above, Confucian officials began suppressing Buddhism as a "foreign cult," bringing about both a Buddhist decline and Confucian revival that continued into the Song era. But the "neo-Confucianism" that emerged triumphant was far more complex and theoretical than the simple, pragmatic ethical system devised by Confucius and his followers over a millennium earlier. Responding to the challenge of Buddhism and Daoism, neo-Confucian thinkers grappled with such concepts as the nature of reality and the meaning of life. In contrast to the Buddhists and Daoists, however, neo-Confucians concluded that reality is understood through education and reason rather than through meditation, and that life derives meaning from action and involvement rather than withdrawal. By the twelfth century, when the great philosopher

Confucianism rebounds and synthesizes learning and tradition

Zhu Xi (*JOO-SHĒ*) created a neo-Confucian synthesis stressing tradition, education, and personal morality, neo-Confucianism reigned supreme among the educated elite. Buddhism retained a following but ceased to be China's main faith, while Daoism continued to thrive among peasants, poets, artists, and others who had close connections with nature.

China's most beloved poets, Li Bai (*LĒ-BĪ*) and Du Fu (*DOO-FOO*), flourished in the early Tang era. Li Bai (701–763) was a homeless wanderer and Daoist free spirit, undisciplined and romantic, a lover of nature and wine. He wrote more than 20,000 poems, including the haunting "Drinking Alone by the Moonlight," which contains the following lovely but lonely lines:

Chinese poetry flourishes in the Tang era

alcoholic →

> A cup of wine, under the flowering trees;
>
> I drink alone, for no friend is near.
>
> Raising my cup, I beckon the moon to join me;
>
> For he, with my shadow, will make three men . . .

According to legend, Li Bai's career ended during a drunken nighttime boat ride, when the sentimental poet drowned while trying to embrace the moon's reflection on the water.

Although a great friend and admirer of Li Bai, Du Fu (712–770) was a more refined and sober poet who wrote in structured verse and was known for his Confucian compassion and strong social conscience. Having failed the civil service exams as a young man, he lived for years in poverty and endured many hardships. Some of his poems contrast the wasteful indulgence of the rich with the sufferings of the common people, as reflected in these famous phrases:

> Inside the red gates the wine and meat go to waste;
>
> On the roadside lie the bones of men who died from cold . . .

Turning away from Confucianism, a system that stamped him a failure, Du Fu became a Buddhist and spent his last years as an impoverished pilgrim. On one of his journeys he met a government official who had read and appreciated his poetry. The delighted official took the poet home, wined and dined him, and gave him his own bed to sleep in. Du Fu died the next morning.

Arts and crafts thrive in Tang and Song eras

Chinese arts and crafts likewise flourished in the Tang and Song eras. Tang sculptors produced splendid Buddhist statues to adorn many temples as well as lifelike figures of horses and soldiers to guard the emperors' tombs. Other skilled artisans fashioned fine porcelain vessels and glazed pottery statuettes. Song-era painters refined the technique of working with a flexible brush on silk, creating naturalistic masterpieces ranging from magnificent vistas and landscapes to exquisite studies of birds, insects, bamboo sprigs, and flowers.

Glazed pottery horse from the Tang era.

Urban and Rural Society

China's commercial, cultural, and intellectual life was centered mainly in the cities, especially the imperial capitals, which ranked among the world's largest and busiest metropolitan areas. While urban dwellers enjoyed abundant goods and cultural activities, however, village farmers, who made up most of the population, lived in stark simplicity. Women of all classes were typically subordinate to men.

Chang'an, China's capital during the Tang dynasty, was that era's grandest city, with an overall population of almost two million, half of whom lived within its walls. It was laid out as a rectangle, roughly five by six miles, with wide north-south and east-west boulevards connecting its main gates and other avenues dividing it into a huge grid (Map 14.6). The city was dotted with Buddhist and Daoist temples and monasteries. Its two large markets boasted goods and visitors from all over Asia, as well as performers, musicians, artists, craftsmen, and fashionably dressed shoppers. The emperor's palace sat in the north, behind the Imperial City, a section of Chang'an that served as government headquarters.

Kaifeng and Hangzhou, the Song era capitals, strove to imitate Chang'an's size and splendor. Kaifeng, located near where the Grand Canal connected with the Yellow River, was a commercial hub that had shops, warehouses, shipyards, restaurants, and hotels

China's great cities provide extensive commerce and diverse activities

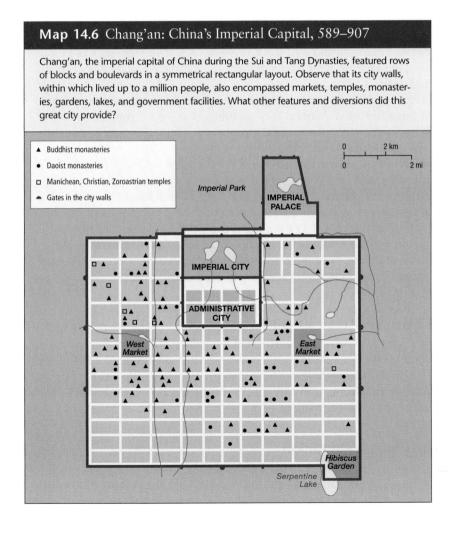

Map 14.6 Chang'an: China's Imperial Capital, 589–907

Chang'an, the imperial capital of China during the Sui and Tang Dynasties, featured rows of blocks and boulevards in a symmetrical rectangular layout. Observe that its city walls, within which lived up to a million people, also encompassed markets, temples, monasteries, gardens, lakes, and government facilities. What other features and diversions did this great city provide?

▲ Buddhist monasteries
● Daoist monasteries
□ Manichean, Christian, Zoroastrian temples
⬢ Gates in the city walls

Imperial Park
IMPERIAL PALACE
IMPERIAL CITY
ADMINISTRATIVE CITY
West Market
East Market
Hibiscus Garden
Serpentine Lake

0   2 km
0   2 mi

but lacked the elegant symmetry of Chang'an. Hangzhou, situated south of the Yangzi River at the canal's other end, was a striking seaport brimming with bridges and waterways, merchants and shops, cabarets and tea houses, entertainers and artisans, public baths and brothels. In the thirteenth century, long after Hangzhou had passed its prime, European observer Marco Polo nonetheless described it as the world's "finest and noblest city."

The peasants, who made up most of China's population, knew little of this urban elegance. Dwelling in rustic rural villages, they rarely traveled farther than the nearest market town. The young men worked the fields around the village, and the elder males reigned as family patriarchs. But women typically ran the household, preparing meals, raising children, tending the chickens and silkworms, and helping in the fields when needed.

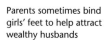

Patriarchal Chinese society subjects women to men

No matter what class they belonged to, women were subject to men: first to their fathers, then to their husbands, and finally (if widowed) to their sons. Parents arranged marriages as compacts between families, often engaging in complex negotiations to decide such matters as the size of the dowry to be supplied by the bride. Society demanded virginal brides and faithful wives, but placed no such requirements on men, who might have mistresses or concubines if they could support them. Property and inheritance laws favored men, as did the education and civil service systems. A few women, such as Empress Wu and Yang Guifei, did exercise great influence, but even they achieved their goals mainly by working through men.

Parents sometimes bind girls' feet to help attract wealthy husbands

Women of means, whose lives were not burdened by physical labor, sometimes paid a painful price for this exemption. Starting in Song times, many girls from urban and well-off rural families underwent **foot binding**, a process in which their feet were tightly wrapped with strips of cloth for years, beginning in early childhood. Foot binding was designed to restrict the foot's growth and achieve a "lily-foot" effect, with toes and heels pointed downward to resemble the bell-shaped lily flower. Since many Chinese men considered women with tiny feet sexually attractive, and since men of means saw it as a sign of wealth and status to have a wife with feet so dainty that she could not work, mothers often bound their daughters' feet to help them attract wealthy husbands. But the process was extremely painful, and the resulting deformation frequently made it hard for the woman to walk without a cane. Foot binding thus became an indicator of social status, distinguishing idle upper class ladies from hardworking peasant women.

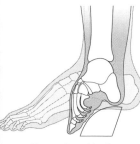

Foot reshaped by foot binding compared to normal foot.

Vietnam and the Chinese Impact

Overshadowed by China's vast size and wealth, the lands on its borders often served as its colonies or tribute-paying vassals, while their societies broadly imitated Chinese ideas and ways. China's neighbors nonetheless managed to preserve key elements of their traditional cultures and even, in time, to secure their political autonomy. Especially successful in these endeavors were the Vietnamese.

Vietnam Under Chinese Dominion

Vietnam occupies the easternmost part of the huge Southeast Asian peninsula, which extends out from southwestern China, west of the South China Sea (Map 14.7). A lush subtropical region with abundant sunshine, rainfall, mountains, forests, rivers, and plains,

Map 14.7 Early Vietnam and Its Expansion in the Tenth Through Fifteenth Centuries

Throughout most of its history, Vietnam was linked with China by strong political, cultural, and commercial connections. Notice, however, that after gaining political autonomy from China in the mid-900s, Vietnam expanded its rule southward in ensuing centuries over the region of Champa. What distinctive social and cultural patterns developed in Vietnam that distinguished it from China?

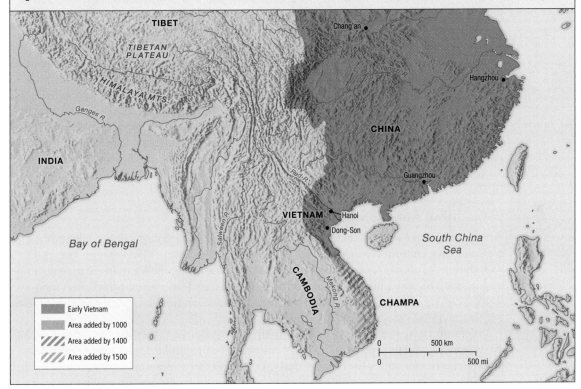

it was one of Asia's first agricultural areas, with early farmers raising yams, rice, chickens, and pigs. In what is now northern Vietnam, a thousand miles from the early centers of Chinese society, people produced fine works of bronze, traded throughout Southeast Asia, and developed a distinctive culture centered on village societies in which women played a leading role.

In 218 B.C.E. this region was conquered by China's Qin dynasty. Although Qin rule ended with the dynasty's demise in 206 B.C.E., the Han Martial Emperor (Wudi) reconquered the Red River valley in 111 B.C.E. For much of the next millennium the region was ruled by the Chinese, who imposed on it their language, writing system, Confucian ideals, and bureaucratic structures. It briefly regained independence under the legendary Trung Sisters, who reportedly rebelled and reigned as independent queens from 39 to 41 C.E., and later during China's Age of Disunity (220–589), when the region was divided, like China itself, among local warlords. It again came under Chinese rule during the Sui dynasty (589–618) and throughout the Tang era (618–907).

Various Chinese dynasties rule northern Vietnam

Vietnam blends Chinese beliefs and ways into its own culture

Thus, unlike the rest of Southeast Asia, which was heavily influenced by India's culture, northern Vietnam was overlaid with Chinese ideals and institutions. While Theravada Buddhism spread through the rest of Southeast Asia, for example, the Vietnamese adopted from China the Mahayana branch of that faith, combining it with Confucianism and Daoism to form a blended belief system called the **Three Religions**. Vietnam also adapted various aspects of Chinese education, urban life, architecture, and administration to fit traditional Vietnamese culture.

Vietnamese women retain a distinctive role and status

As a result of this adaptation, Vietnam retained distinctive social and family patterns, which gave women a relatively prominent role. Among both rural villagers and urban dwellers, Vietnamese women enjoyed a higher status than women in China. A Vietnamese woman, for example, could take an active part in selecting her spouse, receive from his family a wedding endowment rather than giving him a dowry, and have him come to join her family's household rather than going to join his. Thus supported by ongoing connections with their families of origin, Vietnamese women apparently could also seek and obtain divorces, inherit and bequeath family wealth, and even keep their own family names after marriage. These practices, which predated the imposition of Chinese culture, were never completely eradicated by it.

Vietnamese Autonomy

Vietnam becomes autonomous in the 900s

With its distinctive social structure and distance from China's power centers, Vietnam maintained its own cultural identity throughout the many centuries of Chinese rule. Finally, in 939, during the chaotic decades following the fall of the Tang, the Vietnamese managed to regain their political autonomy. Then, in 968, a legendary leader named Dinh Bo Linh (*DIN-BŌ-LIN*), having defeated the other warlords and unified the realm, proclaimed himself Vietnam's first emperor.

Henceforth Vietnam was ruled mostly by native regimes rather than by outsiders, but this autonomy did not mean the end of Chinese influence. Indeed, as China regained its unity and strength under the Song dynasty, Dinh Bo Linh and his successors found it advisable to recognize Song rulers as official overlords and pay them tribute. In response China's rulers largely left the Vietnamese alone, free to develop their own institutions and policies. But Vietnam's rulers continued to imitate practices that had proven successful in China. Borrowing ideas from the great empire to their north, the Vietnamese formed a stable state with its capital at Hanoi, developed a Chinese-style bureaucracy, and eventually even experienced their own succession of dynastic cycles. They also began gradually expanding to the south, incorporating over the next five centuries the various kingdoms that made up the region called Champa, whose culture had hitherto been influenced by India. This process eventually brought the whole eastern coastline of Southeast Asia under Vietnamese rule (Map 14.7).

Vietnam expands southward along Southeast Asian coast

Korea and the Chinese Impact

China's influence was also felt in Korea, the large peninsula that extends from Manchuria toward Japan, across the Yellow Sea from northeast China. Like the Vietnamese, the Koreans developed a distinctive language and culture, then came under Chinese rule in the second century B.C.E. Also like the Vietnamese, the Koreans adapted Chinese ideas and institutions to their local culture. Eventually the Koreans, too, regained their political autonomy, but for centuries they continued to pay tribute to China's emperors.

Early Chinese Influence in Korea

Chinese influence in Korea dates from the third and fourth centuries B.C.E., when refugees from China's Warring States Era migrated to the Korean peninsula, bringing Chinese farming and writing techniques. Later, in 109–108 B.C.E., Han China's Wudi conquered northern Korea, only a few years after he had conquered the Vietnamese. As in Vietnam, he and his Han successors imposed in Korea their Confucian cultural values and administrative system.

Also as in Vietnam, the collapse of China's Han dynasty in the third century C.E. brought to the Koreans both autonomy and division into warring states. Eventually, in the disarray of the fourth century C.E., three rival kingdoms emerged in the Korean peninsula: Silla (*shē-ILL-ah*) in the southeast, Paekche (*PĪK-chā*) in the southwest, and Koguryo (*kō-GOOR-yō*) in the north (Map 14.8). During the next few

Korea is influenced by Chinese migrations and conquest

Three kingdoms emerge in Korea during China's Age of Disunity

Map 14.8 Early Korea and Its Kingdoms in the Fourth Through Tenth Centuries

Korea's culture, commerce, and beliefs were strongly influenced by its connections with China. Observe that, after gaining autonomy from China in the third century C.E., Korea was divided into three rival kingdoms from the fourth through seventh centuries. Then, with Chinese help, Silla emerged predominant until the tenth century, when Koguryo gained control of the peninsula, ruling as the Kingdom of Koryo. In what ways was Korean culture influenced by connections with China? How did Korean society and governance differ from that of China?

centuries, as these three realms fought each other for supremacy, new waves of refugees arrived from China's Age of Disunity, spreading their Buddhist beliefs among the Koreans.

After China was reunified in 589 C.E., both the Sui and the Tang rulers made repeated efforts to reconquer the Koreans but were rebuffed by Koguryo's rugged resistance. In the 660s, however, aiming to dominate all of Korea, Silla joined forces with China to conquer Paekche and Koguryo. Then, having unified Korea with Chinese help, Silla used its united forces to resist full Chinese control, agreeing instead to pay tribute to the Tang regime.

Korea blends Chinese ways and beliefs into its own culture

For the next few centuries Silla ruled Korea as a semi-autonomous tributary of China, broadly imitating its society and culture. During this era Korea, like Vietnam before it, adopted China's writing system, imitated its architecture, and sought to replicate its great cities and civil service bureaucracy. Mahayana Buddhism, with monasteries, temples, statues, shrines, and sects similar to those then flourishing in Tang China, spread across the peninsula. Koreans copied Chinese customs and commodities and even produced ceramics and porcelain ware superior to China's.

In several respects, however, the administrative and social structure of Korea differed from that of China. Governmental posts in Korea remained under the control of local aristocratic families, rather than being staffed through a system of civil service exams. Despite the outward appearance of a Confucian civil service bureaucracy, Korea's regions and provinces continued to be governed mostly by warlords rather than scholar-officials, and its peasants remained in a status similar to serfdom.

Korean porcelain vase from the Kingdom of Koryo.

The Kingdom of Koryo, 935–1392

During the ninth century the deterioration of the Silla regime, accompanied by the decline of China's Tang dynasty, gave the kingdoms of Paekche and Koguryo a chance to reassert their autonomy. But eventually Wang Kon (*WAHNG-KŌN*), a wealthy northern merchant who became a military officer, seized control of Koguryo and reunited Korea by conquering Silla in 935 and Paekche in 936. He then shortened the name of his kingdom to Koryo (*KOR-yō*), from which comes the name Korea, and established a dynasty that lasted until 1392.

Koryo was even more imitative of China than Silla had been. It set up a new capital at Kaesong (*KĪ-SŌNG*), modeled after the great Chinese city of Chang'an, with a similar gridlike pattern and impressive imperial palace. Koryo established a Confucian-style administration with its own civil service exams—but the old aristocracy nonetheless maintained its monopoly of the major posts. And in the eleventh century, after experiencing several invasions by the Khitans, Koryo even built its own version of the Great Wall across the northern part of the peninsula.

Like Vietnam, then, Korea blended Chinese ways with its own distinctive culture. In the meantime, across the sea to Korea's east, another East Asian society adopted Chinese ideas, then diverged from them to become more distinctive from China than Vietnam and Korea.

The Emergence of Japan

Of the various East Asian peoples, Japan's were among the last to develop a complex culture based on farming settlements. Living mostly on four main islands, more than a hundred miles east of the Korean coast, the early Japanese were largely isolated from outside influence (Map 14.9). With a mild climate, abundant rainfall, a scenic mountainous terrain, and ready access to the sea, they lived for centuries on hunting, fishing, and gathering wild food. Rice farming began by the third century B.C.E., along with the use of bronze and iron. By 300 C.E. the land was dominated by native warrior clans called uji (*OO-JĒ*).

A distinctive religion emerged, based on the worship of divine spirits called kami (*KAH-MĒ*), which included not only gods and goddesses of the sun, moon, and earth but also the spirits of ancestors, animals, and natural objects such as rocks, trees, and waterfalls. Worship centered on fertility and purification rites, often performed in a festival atmosphere. Originally nameless, this nature-based Japanese religion was later called **Shinto** (*SHĒN-TŌ*), the "way of the kami." *the way of gods*

By 500 C.E. the Yamato (*YAH-MAH-TŌ*) uji, a powerful warrior clan, had brought approximately two-thirds of Japan under its control, thereby establishing itself as the ruling dynasty. Tracing their descent from the Shinto sun goddess, the Yamato emperors

Japan develops a distinctive religion worshipping spirits in nature

Yamato clan forms a dynasty that claims divine status

Map 14.9 Japan Emerges as an Island Nation in the Sixth Through Twelfth Centuries

Although it borrowed many ideas and features from China, Japan developed as an independent nation with a distinctive culture. Notice that Japan, endowed with a mild climate and mountainous terrain, is located on islands over a hundred miles from the Asia mainland. Nara and later Heian (eventually called Kyoto) served as the early capitals and homes of Japan's emperors, even as others exercised real power in their name. How did Japan's society and governance differ from that of China?

claimed a divine status that helped perpetuate their position. Although others have often ruled in their name, the Yamato heirs have persistently maintained the imperial title, and they still reign today as history's longest enduring dynasty.

Early Borrowing from China

In the mid-sixth century, a new religion came to Japan from China by way of Korea. Buddhism, promoted in Japan by the Soga clan as a compelling new faith from the mainland, was rejected by other clans as an alien cult, eventually resulting in warfare. In 587 the Soga won and later installed their own Prince Shotoku as regent to the Yamato ruler.

Shotoku promotes Buddhism and Chinese ways in Japan

Prince Shotoku, whose exploits are highlighted at the start of this chapter, directed affairs from 593 until his death in 622. Determined to learn from China's experience and to borrow concepts useful for Japan, he sent at least four large missions to China for trade and cultural exchange. He instituted in Japan a Chinese-style bureaucracy, based on ranks that were assigned by merit rather than uji status, thus improving government effectiveness and strengthening the central state at the expense of the warrior clans. He further promoted Buddhism—building temples, supporting monasteries, and issuing precepts urging adherence to Buddhist ideals—so effectively that he would later be revered as a bodhisattva.

Thus began an era of extensive borrowing from China. Over the next two centuries, the Japanese adopted China's writing system and imitated Chinese literature, poetry, philosophy, art, and architecture. The Fujiwara clan, which came to dominate the Japanese court in the 640s, surpassed the Soga in copying China's laws, taxes, roads, and civil service. The city of Nara, erected in 710 as Japan's new capital, was modeled after Chang'an, and Japan's Nara Period (710–784) was marked by imitation of Chinese ways.

Ancient Buddhist temple near Nara, Japan.

The Heian Era: Divergence from China

By 794 a new capital, even more imitative of Chang'an than Nara, was constructed at Heian (*HĀ-YAHN*), later called Kyoto (*kē-YŌ-TŌ*), where the emperors would reside for more than a thousand years. During the Heian Period (794–1185), Japan gradually stopped imitating China, developing instead a distinctive new culture that blended Japanese and Chinese ways.

Japan develops a distinctive culture blending Japanese and Chinese ways

Emperor Kammu (*KAH-MOO*), who built the new capital during his reign (781–806), sought to unite his realm religiously by blending Buddhism, the faith imported from China, with Japan's native Shinto beliefs. He thus promoted various sects that accepted conflicting beliefs as different levels of truth or that depicted Shinto as an early revelation of Buddhist beliefs in Japan.

Japanese women develop a distinctive literature

In the ninth century, a new writing system developed called **kana** (*KAH-NAH*), which used simplified Chinese characters to create a phonetic Japanese alphabet. By 1000 C.E., while men in Japan still struggled to write Chinese, which they considered a superior language, Japanese women, typically denied an education in Chinese, were using kana to produce Japanese prose classics. The most famous is *The Tale of Genji* (*GEN-jē*), a subtle, sensitive portrayal of the refined court life at Heian and the romantic

Document 14.1 Excerpts from *The Tale of Genji*

Murasaki Shikibu's classic tale portrays in exquisite detail the lives and loves of an emperor and his court. These excerpts describe the emperor's love affair with Genji's mother, the birth of Genji, the death of his mother, and the emperor's abiding love for them both.

In a certain reign there was a lady not of the first rank whom the emperor loved more than any of the others. The grand ladies with high ambitions thought her a presumptuous upstart, and the lesser ladies were still more resentful. Everything she did offended someone. Probably aware of what was happening, she fell seriously ill . . .

It may have been because of a bond in a former life that she bore the emperor a beautiful son, a jewel beyond compare . . .

With the birth of the son, it became yet clearer that she was the emperor's favorite. The mother of the eldest son began to feel uneasy. If she did not manage carefully, she might see the new son designated crown prince . . .

When the young prince reached the age of three, the resources of the treasury . . . were exhausted to make the ceremonial bestowing of trousers as elaborate as that for the oldest son. Once more there was malicious talk, but the prince himself, as he grew up, was so superior of mien and disposition that few could find it in themselves to dislike him . . .

In summer the boy's mother, feeling vaguely unwell, asked that she be allowed to go home . . . The emperor . . . begged her to stay, and see what course her health might take. It was steadily worse . . .

So, in desolation, he let her go. He passed a sleepless night.

He sent off a messenger and was beside himself with impatience . . . The man arrived to find the house echoing with laments. She had died shortly past midnight . . . The emperor closed himself up in his private apartments. He would have liked to keep the boy with him, but no precedent could be found for having him away from his mother's house through the mourning . . .

The months passed and the young prince returned to the palace. He had grown into a lad of such beauty that he hardly seemed meant for this world . . . When, the following spring, it came time to name a crown prince, the emperor wanted very much to pass over his first son in favor of the younger, who, however, had no influential maternal relatives . . .

Lacking the support of maternal relatives, the boy would be most insecure as a prince . . . As a commoner he could be of great service . . . The emperor therefore encouraged the boy in his studies, at which he was so proficient that it seemed a waste to reduce him to common rank. And yet—as a prince he would arouse the hostility of those who had cause to fear his becoming emperor. Summoning an astrologer . . ., the emperor . . . concluded that the boy should become a commoner with the name Minamoto or Genji.

SOURCE: Murasaki Shikibu, *The Tale of Genji*, translated by Edward G. Seidensticker (New York: Alfred A. Knopf, 1978) 1–4, 13, 15.

---

affairs of a fictional prince named Genji (see "Excerpts from *The Tale of Genji*"). The tale was composed by a court lady known as Murasaki Shikibu (*moo-RAH-sah-kē SHĒ-kē-boo*), who, while vastly enriching Japanese literature, offered the world what may well be its oldest complete novel.

Political changes in Heian Japan brought further divergence from the Chinese model. The powerful Fujiwara clan increasingly dominated the imperial family, first by forcing the emperors to marry Fujiwara women, then by serving as regents for their offspring. As soon as an emperor had a son by his Fujiwara wife, the clan leaders would force that emperor to retire so they could rule as regents for his infant son who became the new emperor. But this farce only weakened the central government because other ambitious clans, deprived of influence at court, built power bases in the countryside, while smaller landowners submitted to their protection to avoid taxation.

The Rise of the Warrior Class

Peasant serfs and samurai warriors embrace new Buddhist sects

By the twelfth century, although the court at Heian continued to claim authority, Japan was actually dominated by local warlords ruling independent estates. Each warlord developed his own army of warriors, later known as **samurai** (*SAH-MOO-RĪ*), who provided military service to their lords. These warriors were often supported by peasant labor on land given them in reward for military service, similar to the manors of medieval Europe (Chapter 9). In time the samurai became Japan's dominant class, with a unique code of conduct. Rejecting the urbane Heian society, which they saw as decadent and weak, the samurai instead adopted an austere rural culture based on courage, honor, discipline, simplicity, and indifference to pain. Supported by foot soldiers and protected by elaborate armor, the samurai fought on horseback, using bows, arrows, and tempered steel swords. Professing total loyalty to their lords, they were trained to value death over dishonor. In a practice called **seppuku** (*SEP-OO-KOO*), also known as hara-kiri, or "belly-cutting," a defeated warrior could restore his honor by taking his own life without showing pain.

Minamoto clan creates a dominant military leader called the shogun

Regional warlords and samurai warriors come to dominate Japan

This rise of the samurai reduced the peasants to serfdom, forcing them to work the land in servitude to support the warrior class. For comfort many peasants turned to Pure Land Buddhism, the Chinese creed that promised its faithful salvation in the Western Paradise. The samurai, meanwhile, embraced Zen, Japan's name for China's Chan Buddhism, perhaps because its stress on meditation, discipline, simplicity, and self-understanding seemed akin to their warrior code.

The rise of the samurai also brought an end to the political power of the Heian court. In 1185, when the Minamoto (*MĒ-NAH-MŌ-TŌ*) clan defeated the forces controlling Heian in a great naval battle, clan leader Minamoto Yoritomo (*YŌ-RĒ-TŌ-MŌ*) emerged as the country's dominant warlord. In contrast to what often happened in such situations in China, however, he did not seize the throne and end the Yamato dynasty, whose emperors were worshipped as descendants of the gods. Instead, in a move that set a precedent for future conquering warlords, in 1192 he assumed a new post called **shogun** (*SHŌ-GOON*), the commander-in-chief of Japan's armed forces and its real ruler. Thenceforth, while the emperors still reigned in Heian (Kyoto) as religious figures, they lacked political power. Minamoto Yoritomo and his successors as shogun actually ruled from the city of Kamakura (*KAH-MAH-KOO-RAH*), which served as Japan's true political center from 1192 until 1333.

Wooden statue of Buddhist monk from Kamakura era.

Chapter Review

Putting It in Perspective

Despite the disasters of the third through sixth centuries, China survived its Age of Disunity, merging its new Buddhist faith with the basic elements of its ancient society and emerging reunited in 589 C.E. Then, for almost seven centuries, under the Sui, Tang, and Song dynasties, China flourished as one of the world's largest and most cosmopolitan societies. Its officials mastered the art of governing an expansive empire, its merchants and manufacturers produced unprecedented prosperity, and its farmers found ways to feed its rural masses and large urban populations. Its poets, artists, inventors, intellectuals, and religious believers created a culture noted for its elegance, complexity, and technological sophistication.

So successful was China's experience that other East Asian cultures often followed its example, sometimes compelled by Chinese conquest, sometimes encouraged by commercial and cultural connections with China. The Vietnamese, Koreans, and Japanese all copied or adapted features of Chinese society, especially its writing system, Buddhist beliefs, Confucian civil service, art, architecture, and urban organization. Thus, through a series of connections and conflicts, Chinese culture dominated most of East Asia.

Conflicts, however, also undermined China's preeminence. For all its power and wealth, China never fully succeeded in subduing the nomads to its north. The Tang dynasty held them off and sometimes even conquered their homelands. But in the tenth century, after that dynasty's fall, tribal Khitan warriors captured some of China's northern provinces and added them to their Liao Empire. Eventually China's Song dynasty, after failing to defeat these warriors, decided instead to pay them tribute. But in the twelfth century the Jurchens, after the Song rulers helped them conquer the Khitans, overran and dominated the whole northern half of China.

This disaster did not mark the end of China's troubles. For in the thirteenth century the Mongols, an even more expansionist group of nomadic invaders from the north, would conquer the Jurchens and then all of China and most of Eurasia as well.

Reviewing Key Material

KEY CONCEPTS

Xiongnu, 325
civil service exams, 335
scholar gentry, 335
Pure Land Buddhism, 339
Chan (Zen) Buddhism, 339
foot binding, 342

Three Religions, 344
Shinto, 347
kana, 348
samurai, 350
seppuku, 350
shogun, 350

KEY PEOPLE

Prince Shotoku, 324, 348
Cao Cao, 325
Faxian, 330
Liang Wudi, 330
Yang Jian (Wendi), 330
Yangdi, 331
Duke of Tang, 331
Li Shimin (Taizong), 331
Wu Zhao (Empress Wu), 332
Xuanzong, 333
Yang Guifei, 333
An Lushan, 333

Zhao Kuangyin (Taizu), 334
Wang Anshi, 336
Zhu Xi, 340
Li Bai, 340
Du Fu, 340
Trung Sisters, 343
Dinh Bo Linh, 344
Wang Kon, 346
Kammu, 348
Murasaki Shikibu, 349
Minamoto Yoritomo, 350

ASK YOURSELF

1. How and why did Buddhism spread throughout China, emerging as its main religion, during the Age of Disunity? Why did Buddhism decline in China by the middle of the Song era?
2. After China was reunified in 589, what steps did the Sui, Tang, and Song regimes take to maintain its unity and prosperity during the next seven centuries? How did these various regimes respond to the ongoing threat of the northern nomadic peoples?
3. What were the main hallmarks and achievements of Chinese society during the Tang and Song eras? How did the lives of rural peasants differ from the lives of

city-dwellers? How did the roles and rights of women differ from those of men?

4. Why and how did Vietnam, Korea, and Japan emulate Chinese ideas and institutions? How did they blend their own cultures and traditions with ideas and institutions adapted from China?

GOING FURTHER

Adshead, S. A. M. *Tang China.* 2004.

Batten, B. I. *To the Ends of Japan.* 2003.

Benn, Charles. *China's Golden Age: Everyday Life in the Tang Dynasty.* 2004.

Bingham, Woodbridge. *The Founding of the T'ang Dynasty.* 1975.

Cho'e, Yongho, ed. *Sources of Korean Tradition.* 2000.

Davis, Richard L. *Court and Family in Sung China.* 1986.

De Bary, W. T., et al., eds. *Sources of Japanese Tradition.* 2001.

Dien, A. E., ed. *State and Society in Early Medieval China.* 1990.

Ebrey, Patricia Buckley, et al. *East Asia: A Cultural, Social, and Political History.* 2006.

Ebrey, Patricia Buckley. *Inner Quarters: Marriage and the Lives of Chinese Women in the Sung Period.* 1993.

Gernet, Jacques. *Buddhism in Chinese Society.* 1995.

Hymes, R. P. *Way and Byway: Taoism, Local Religion, and Models of Divinity in Sung China.* 2002.

Kim, KiBaik. *A New History of Korea.* 1984.

Liu, J. T. C. *China Turning Inward: Intellectual Changes in the Early Twelfth Century.* 1988.

Mann, S., and Y. Cheng, eds. *Under Confucian Eyes: Writings on Gender in Chinese History.* 2001.

Mason, R. H. P. *A History of Japan.* 1987.

McKnight, B. *Law and Order in Sung China.* 1992.

Nahm, Andrew C. *Introduction to Korean History and Culture.* 1993.

Owen, S. *The Great Age of Chinese Poetry: The High T'ang.* 1981.

Pai, H. I. *Constructing "Korean" Origins.* 2000.

Shaughnessy, Edward, ed. *China: Empire and Civilization.* 2005.

Souryi, P. F. *The World Turned Upside Down: Medieval Japanese Society.* 2001.

Sullivan, M. *The Arts of China.* 4th ed. 1999.

Tao, Jingshen. *Two Sons of Heaven.* 1988.

Taylor, K. W. *The Birth of Vietnam.* 1983.

Temple, Robert. *The Genius of China.* 1989.

Twitchett, D., and M. Loewe. *Cambridge History of China.* Vol. 3. *Medieval China.* 1986.

Varley, H. Paul. *Japanese Culture.* 4th ed. 2000.

Warshaw, Steven. *Japan Emerges.* 1987.

Woodside, A. *Vietnam and the Chinese Model.* 1988.

Wright, Arthur F. *The Sui Dynasty.* 1978.

Key Dates and Developments

China

220–589	China's Age of Disunity
300–500	Buddhism spreads throughout China
581–589	Unification of China by Yang Jian
589–618	Sui Dynasty
618–907	Tang Dynasty
626–649	Reign of Taizong (Li Shimin)
660–705	Dominance of Wu Zhao (Empress Wu, 690–705)
713–756	Reign of Xuanzong
720–770	Poetry of Li Bai and Du Fu
755–766	An Lushan revolt
907–960	Fall of the Tang and renewed disunity
907–1125	Khitans rule northern borderlands (Liao Empire)
960–1279	Song Dynasty
960–976	China Reunified under Zhao Kuangyin (Song Taizu)
1069–1085	Wang Anshi Reforms
1127–1206	Jurchens conquer Khitans and rule northern China

Vietnam and Korea

111 B.C.E.	Chinese conquer northern Vietnam
108 B.C.E.	Chinese conquer northern Korea
220–589	Age of Disunity in China, Korea, and Vietnam
300s–668	Korea divided into three kingdoms
668–935	Korea unified under Silla rule
936–1392	Korea unified under Koryo rule
939	Northern Vietnam gains autonomy from China
968	Din Bo Linh unifies northern Vietnam, becomes emperor
1000–1500	Vietnam expands southward into Champa

Japan

by 300	Emergence of Uji warrior clans
by 500	Emergence of Yamato clan as Japan's imperial dynasty
500–600	Buddhism spreads to Japan
592–622	Prince Shotoku guides Japan, emulates Chinese culture
710–784	Nara era: intensive emulation of China
794–1185	Heian era: emergence of the samurai
1000–1010	*Tale of Genji*, by Murasaki Shikibu
1185–1333	Kamakura era: reign of the Minamoto shoguns
1192	Minamoto Yoritomo becomes shogun

CHAPTER 15

Nomadic Conquests and Eurasian Connections, 1000–1400

Temujin Is Proclaimed
Genghis Khan

In this fourteenth-century illustration, Temujin is proclaimed Genghis Khan as his sons (on the right) and supporters look on. Genghis Khan and his successors created a vast empire that connected cultures across Eurasia.

- The Nomads of Central Asia
- The Rise and Fall of the Seljuk Turks
- The Mongol Invasions
- The Mongol Khanates: Conquest, Adaptation, and Conversion
- The Mongol Impact: Connections and Consequences
- Chapter Review

Around 1162, in the harsh Mongolian region northwest of China, the wife of a Mongol chieftain bore him a son named Temujin (*TEH-moo-jēn*). About nine years later, when members of a rival tribe poisoned his father, Temujin and his mother were left without status or support. Raising her son in great hardship, Temujin's mother taught him that he was divinely destined to avenge his father and become a great ruler. Later, when captured by foes and confined in a heavy wooden collar, Temujin managed to overpower his guard and escape to a nearby river, where he hid until a friendly tribesman released him from the collar. This incident further convinced the young Mongol that he was destined for greatness.

Turkic and Mongol Empires

Temujin grew to be a formidable warrior, single-minded and opportunistic in pursuing power. Returning to his tribe, he eventually asserted himself as its leader, vanquished its neighbors, and killed his father's murderers. He won battles and forged alliances with other Mongol tribes, overcoming their fierce independence to unite them into a powerful military machine. Then, after they proclaimed him "Genghis Khan" (*JEN-gis KAHN*), or "universal ruler," he led them on a quest to conquer the world.

Genghis Khan and his followers were part of a wide array of nomadic herders who had long lived in Central Asia. For ages these peoples, most of whom spoke Turkic or Mongolian languages, had lived sparse lives tending cattle and sheep, moving about in search of grazing grounds and sometimes raiding or invading settled societies to their east, south, and west.

In the tenth through fourteenth centuries, however, Central Asian nomads made a momentous impact on the wider world. Some took control of northern China, forming empires and dynasties there. Others, known as Seljuk (*SELL-jook*) Turks, conquered Islamic Southwest Asia, embraced the Islamic faith, and sparked a series of consequential conflicts with the Christian world. Then the Mongols, led by Genghis Khan and his heirs, overran much of Eurasia, creating the largest land empire the world had ever seen. In time these conquerors adopted many features of the societies they conquered, while expanding commerce and helping to spread ideas, technologies, weapons, and diseases. By conquering and connecting the cultures of Eurasia, Central Asian nomads changed the course of world history.

The Nomads of Central Asia

By 1000 C.E., agriculture had long since become the way of life for most people on the planet. Although it required tedious, time-consuming labor, farming provided greater stability and much more food than hunting or herding alone. It could thus support far more people than could these other forms of subsistence. Agriculture was the economic foundation of the large, complex, settled societies that had arisen in China, India, Persia, Southwest Asia, Europe, and several parts of Africa (Map 15.1).

FOUNDATION MAP 15.1 Areas of Farming and Herding by 1000 C.E.

By 1000 C.E., settled agricultural societies prevailed in places where climate and soil supported farming. Note, however, that in Central Asia, where climate and soil made farming unreliable, most people lived as pastoral nomads, following their herds in search of grazing grounds, and occasionally interacting with the settled agricultural societies to their east, west, and south, as indicated by the arrows. How did these connections influence the societies of both the settled farmers and the nomadic herders?

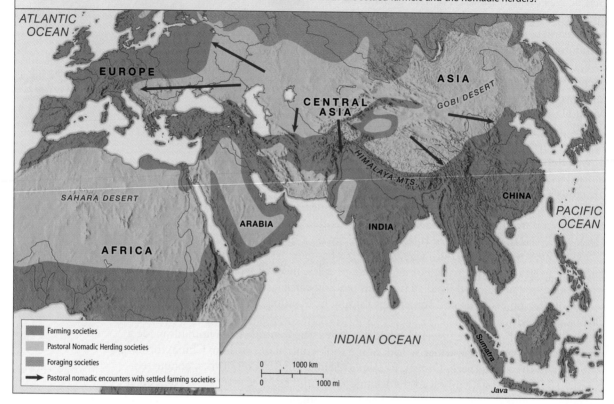

In some areas, however, conditions were not suitable for farming. These areas included the northernmost reaches of Eurasia, where it was too cold; the equatorial rain forests of Africa, where it was too wet; and the arid plains and deserts of Africa and Eurasia, where it was too dry. In these regions, where limited food supplies kept populations low, people lived as nomads, moving frequently and surviving by hunting or herding.

Central Asia connects Eurasian societies

The largest of the regions where nomadic life prevailed was the immense Central Asian expanse, extending for thousands of miles from the semi-arid steppes of southern Russia to the barren Mongolian highlands. Sparsely populated and bleak, battered by harsh winds and brutal winters, Central Asia was both a barrier that separated Eurasia's settled societies and the crossroads of the trade routes that connected them. It thus not only shaped the nomadic lifestyle of its hardy inhabitants but also helped shape the commerce and cultures of the surrounding societies.

Herding and Horsemanship

Herding was the main way of life for most Central Asians. As pastoral nomads—herders who move about in search of fresh grasslands on which to pasture their herds—they set up camps where they found good grounds for grazing, then moved elsewhere when the forage was depleted. The nomads ate mainly meat, milk, cheese, and butter, and clothed themselves largely with fleeces and hides, supplied by their herds. To protect themselves from the winds and rain, they fashioned large tents (known as yurts) from coarse felt made of matted wool and animal hairs. They even collected the animals' manure, using it as fuel for the fires that warmed them and cooked their food.

A Mongol family outside its tent, or yurt.

Some Central Asians raised cattle, many kept goats, and those involved in overland trade used camels, but most of the nomads centered their livelihoods on sheep and horses. Sheep were prized mainly for their meat, milk, and wool, but also because they survived better than cattle on the sparse, coarse vegetation of the steppes. Horses were used for hunting, herding sheep, and pulling carts that carried tents and goods from one campsite to the next. Since mare's milk was preserved by fermenting it into a beverage called kumiss (*KOO-miss*), horses also supplied an important source of sustenance.

Horses were also crucial to the conduct of war. Nomadic life meant frequent movement in search of new pastures, and this movement often led to clashes with neighboring nomads or settled societies. Especially during famines or droughts, when food and adequate grazing grounds were scarce, mounted nomads fought each other for the scarce pasturelands and sometimes traveled into farming regions to raid villages and towns. Survival depended on both mobility and fighting skill.

Nomadic warrior societies depend on horses

Central Asian societies thus were warrior societies. The men spent most of their time in the saddle, learning at an early age to eat, sleep, hunt, herd, fight, and raid on horseback. They trained to ride for days without food or rest, to attack in unison, and to fight with fearless abandon. In these endeavors they were ably assisted by their mounts, sturdy steppe ponies bred and trained for discipline and endurance, with long shaggy hair that protected them from the wind and cold.

The warriors also were greatly aided by the use of stirrups. Developed by Central Asians in the first or second century C.E., these rings that hung from each side of the saddle secured the feet of the riders, allowing them to stand and maneuver while moving at high speed. Mounted warriors could thus load and reload their powerful bows and fire their arrows in any direction with amazing accuracy, even while charging or fleeing at full gallop. Large armies from settled societies, vastly outnumbering the nomadic warriors, might chase them back to the open steppes, only to be annihilated during the pursuit by the well-aimed arrows of the retreating nomads.

Stirrups give Central Asian warriors an advantage

Family and Social Structure

Family and society on the steppes were structured to meet the needs of nomadic life. Gender roles, social status, governance, and religion all showed the stamp of a culture that focused on mobility, resourcefulness, and warfare.

Women played a prominent role in Central Asian societies, managing the camps while men traveled far afield to hunt, raid, and fight. Women tended the campfires and gathered the manure that fueled the flames. They sheared the sheep and goats, and then used the fleeces, along with furs and hides brought back by men from the hunt, to make

Women sustain nomadic societies

essential items such as clothing, mats, rugs, and the large tents called yurts. Women bred the sheep and horses, helped them give birth, milked them, and used the milk to make butter, cheese, and kumiss. And, of course, women bore and nursed the children, caring for and protecting them when the men were gone. Skilled on horseback and adapted to a mobile life, the women could readily move their whole families and households on short notice. Some women on occasion traveled with the men into combat, attending to such necessities as food and other supplies.

Marriages, as elsewhere, were arranged by parents, often to enhance family status or form political ties. As a sign of prestige, prominent warriors typically took several wives, frequently maintaining a separate tent and household for each. The leading warriors also constituted a kind of nobility, but their social status depended more on military prowess than heredity. Status could improve based on acts of bravery or leadership in combat, or decline in the absence of such exploits.

Nomads combine into tribes and federations

Like other nomadic peoples, Central Asians organized into clans and tribes that were small enough to maintain mobility, with no need for complex governance systems. For political and military purposes, however, the nomads sometimes formed larger federations linking many tribes. These federations were typically led by a regional overlord called the **khan,** who exercised broad authority but was expected to consult regularly with a council of tribal leaders and gain its approval for his decisions.

Central Asian spirituality centered for centuries on **shamanism** (*SHAH-mun-izm*), a form of religion in which spiritual leaders called shamans performed elaborate rituals and induced trances in efforts to communicate with spirits, heal the sick, forecast the future, and influence events. Typically consulted by tribal leaders facing major decisions, such as when to do battle or whom to select as khan, shamans often played a crucial role in nomadic cultures. Eventually, however, as Central Asians adopted various forms of Buddhism, Christianity, and Islam through contact with settled societies, shamans lost much of their clout.

Ongons (spirit houses) used by shamans to contact spiritual forces.

Contacts and Conflicts with Settled Societies

Central Asia was bordered on the east, south, and west by the large, complex, settled societies of China, India, Persia, Mesopotamia, Byzantium, and Europe. With numerous farming villages, thriving towns and cities, intricate social structures, organized religions, and sophisticated technologies, these wealthy, populous societies tended to see themselves as "civilized" and the nomads as crude "barbarians." The settled societies, however, often owed their origins, and many of their attributes, to contacts and conflicts with the nomads.

CULTURAL AND COMMERCIAL CONNECTIONS. Over the ages, as noted in earlier chapters, Central Asian nomads had played pivotal roles in forming, connecting, and challenging the settled Eurasian societies. The Indo-Europeans who migrated to India, the Iranian Plateau, Anatolia, and Europe in the second millennium B.C.E. came from Central Asia, imparting and imposing their languages and ways (Map 15.2). So did the Kushans, who ruled northern India from the first to third centuries C.E.; the Xiongnu and other nomads who dominated northern China from the third to sixth centuries C.E.; and the Huns whose attacks on Germans and Romans in the fourth and fifth centuries C.E. foreshadowed the German conquest of the Western Roman Empire. Central Asians over the

Map 15.2 Key Central Asian Nomadic Movements Before 1000 C.E.

Over many centuries, numerous nomadic groups from Central Asia helped to forge Eurasian connections. Observe, for example, that Hittites migrated to West Asia and Aryans to India in the second millennium B.C.E., that Kushans settled in northwest India in the first through third centuries C.E., that Xiongnu penetrated northern China in the third through sixth centuries C.E., and that Huns invaded Eastern and Central Europe in the fourth and fifth centuries C.E. What major impacts did each of these groups have on the development of Eurasian cultures?

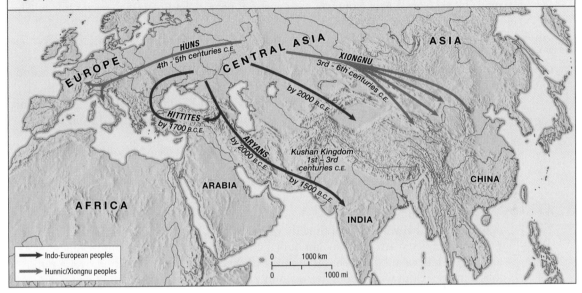

centuries had also spread skills such as ironworking and horsemanship, belief systems such as Buddhism, and diseases such as smallpox from one region to another.

Nomadic attitudes toward settled societies were mixed. On one hand, nomads disdained the sedentary lives of settled villagers and townsfolk. Nomads might be poor, and at the mercy of the elements, but from their perspective at least they were unfettered and free, neither bound to the land and a landlord like a typical peasant, nor crammed into a crowded, fetid city like urban artisans and merchants. Rugged, vigorous, and violent, Central Asians centered their lives on their horses and herds, with little desire to imitate their sedentary neighbors.

On the other hand, to enhance their Spartan lifestyle, the nomads often relied on contacts with settled societies. Some nomads bartered with villagers and townsfolk, offering hides, wool, and furs from their herds and hunts in exchange for such goods as flour, grain, cotton, silk, iron, and salt produced by the settled societies. Some nomads even made their livelihoods by facilitating commerce among settled societies, forming and guiding caravans that carried commodities across Central Asia, along the ancient Silk Road and other overland trade routes.

Nomads trade and interact with settled societies

Other nomads, however, coveting the wealth and abundance of the towns and villages, repeatedly raided them and sometimes even carried off their residents for use or sale as slaves. As long as settled societies were united and strong, they were generally able to resist the nomads by beating them in battles, buying them off with tribute, and building barriers such as China's Great Wall. But when settled societies were divided and weak, their thriving towns and fertile farmlands made tempting targets for the nomads, especially when famine or drought drove the nomads to seek new sources of sustenance.

THE NOMADS IN NORTHERN CHINA. Nowhere was the interaction between nomadic and settled societies more consequential than in northern China. Since around 2000 B.C.E., when horse-drawn chariots and bronze weapons were introduced to this region by nomads from Central Asia, contacts with pastoral peoples had played a crucial role in Chinese history (Chapters 4 and 14).

Nomads help sustain the Silk Road and spread Buddhism

Examples of this interaction are numerous. In the third century B.C.E., to protect his realm against nomadic raids, China's First Emperor linked his northern fortresses to create the first Great Wall. In succeeding centuries, many nomads served as merchants and guides along the Silk Road, the great cross-Asian trade route opened by China's Martial Emperor by around 100 B.C.E. Later, in China's Age of Disunity (220-589 C.E.), nomadic groups ruled northern China and supported Buddhism, a religion spread from India to China via Central Asian merchants and nomads.

In the tenth century C.E., as related in Chapter 14, nomadic Mongols from Manchuria known as Khitans captured several northern Chinese provinces. In the early 1100s, anxious to oust the Khitans, China's Song dynasty aided other nomads called Jurchens, unwittingly enabling them to conquer northern China and rule it for the next century.

Khitans and Jurchens adopt Chinese ways

Northern China nonetheless remained a settled society. The Khitans at first tried maintaining tribal ways, but in time they created a Chinese-style dynasty called the Liao Empire, complete with a Confucian bureaucracy, civil service exams, and Chinese writing. The Jurchens did likewise, calling their dynasty the Jin and presiding over a populous Chinese realm with a complex economy, cosmopolitan culture, and Confucian administration. In China, as elsewhere, nomads who conquered a settled society tended to embrace its institutions, though they were often still seen as alien barbarians by the people they ruled.

The Rise and Fall of the Seljuk Turks

While Khitans and Jurchens penetrated northern China, far to the west and south another nomadic expansion was under way. In the tenth and eleventh centuries, changes in the Central Asian climate, reducing the already fragile food supply, may have pushed some tribes to the brink of starvation. Forced to migrate in search of new food sources, they set in motion a series of chain reactions. When one tribe moved into its neighbors' pasturelands, it often drove them into surrounding regions, where they in turn attacked the local peoples. In time some nomadic groups, compelled by such events to combine with others, began to invade the cities and farmlands of neighboring settled societies.

Driven by such forces, Turkic-speaking tribes from Central Asia infiltrated the Islamic lands of southern Asia. One such group, the Ghaznavids from Afghanistan, penetrated northeastern Persia in the mid-tenth century. By the early eleventh century they were also moving into northwest India, ravaging that region and subjecting it to their rule (Chapter 12). But then they made a monumental mistake: they let another Turkish group from Central Asia move with its herds into Persia.

The Seljuk Conquests

These newly arriving nomads, who would dominate much of Southwest Asia for the next few centuries, were the Seljuk Turks. In the decade following 1025, with Ghaznavid consent, they entered northeastern Persia. Led by heirs of their deceased chieftain Seljuk, they had been chased from Central Asia by other Turkish tribes, who found them too belligerent even for the warlike ways of the steppes. Once in Persia the unruly Seljuks attacked their Ghaznavid hosts, defeating them in 1040 at Dandanqan (*dahn-dahn-KAHN*), a decisive battle that opened southern Asia to waves of Turkish nomads (Map 15.3).

The Seljuks then drove westward, plowing through Persia and into Mesopotamia. Recent converts to Islam, they embraced its dominant Sunni branch and attacked its Shi'ite minority. In 1055 the Seljuks captured Baghdad, claiming to have freed it from the clutches of Shi'ite warlords but actually bringing it under the control of the growing Seljuk domain.

The Great Seljuk Empire

The Great Seljuk Empire, as the new realm came to be known, was consolidated and expanded by Sultan Alp Arslan, who reigned from 1063 to 1072. Bent on extinguishing Shi'ism and reuniting the Islamic world under Sunni sway, he planned to attack the Shi'ite Fatimid Caliphate in Egypt. Seeking first to protect his western flank, however, he came into conflict with the Christian Byzantine Empire, whose armies he defeated in 1071 at Manzikert (Chapter 10). This victory sidetracked the Seljuks, who went on to conquer Syria and Palestine but never made it to Egypt. Instead, with Byzantine lands now vulnerable, the Turks flooded westward into Anatolia, a rich farming region that had been for centuries the heart of the Byzantine Empire.

Seljuks invade Syria, Palestine, and Anatolia

Once in Anatolia, the Seljuks sought to make it a Sunni Muslim stronghold. They restricted Christianity and promoted Islamic immigration from elsewhere in their empire, granting special rights to those who embraced Islam. In the long run these Turkish efforts proved so successful that Anatolia, which had been a Christian bastion for almost a millennium, was transformed into a Muslim land that is today called Turkey.

The Great Seljuk sultans nonetheless centered their empire in Persia. Like others who had earlier ruled this region, the Seljuks fell in love with the Persian culture and adopted many of its features, including its Farsi tongue. Although Arabic was enshrined in the Qur'an and used in Muslim worship, the Seljuk elite communicated in Farsi, while commoners spoke a brand of Turkish peppered with Farsi expressions. Under Turkish and Persian influence, then, Islamic culture continued to evolve away from its Arab roots, while Seljuks were transformed from nomadic marauders into settled rulers of a vast cosmopolitan empire.

Seljuks embrace Persian culture

Thus, rather than ruining Islamic culture, Seljuk rule revitalized it. In this effort the early Seljuk sultans were ably guided by a Persian chief minister, the Nizam al-Mulk (*nē-ZAHM al-MOOLK*), a superb administrator who founded a series of eminent educational institutions and skillfully adapted the structures of the long-dead Persian Empire to meet the needs of the Seljuks. A devout Sunni Muslim, the Nizam also guided Seljuk Sultan Malik Shah (*mah-LĒK SHAH*), who reigned from 1072 to 1092, into unrelenting warfare against Shi'ism.

Fine woven carpet from Seljuk culture.

Map 15.3 Southwest Asia and The Seljuk Turks, 1040–1189

In the eleventh century the Seljuk Turks, nomadic warriors from Central Asia, created a realm they called the Great Seljuk Empire, winning major battles at Dandanqan, Baghdad, and Manzikert. Note, however, that once the empire began to break apart after 1092, a breakaway Seljuk Sultanate of Rūm ruled eastern Anatolia, the Great Seljuk sultans continued to reign in Persia, and a new sultan in Egypt, Salah al-Din, eventually carved out a realm embracing Palestine and Syria. How did the Seljuks help to revitalize Islamic culture?

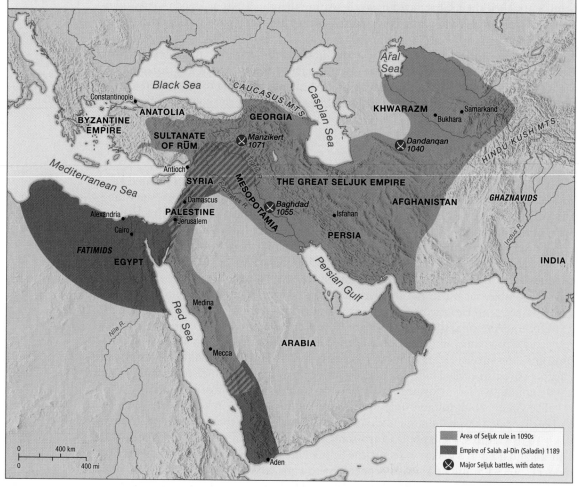

The Shi'ite Assassins strike at Sunni leaders

This anti-Shi'ite drive met fierce resistance from a radical Shi'ite sect known as "the self-sacrificers." Founded in 1090 by a zealot called "the Old Man of the Mountain," this group terrorized the Islamic world for almost 170 years, slaying numerous Sunni leaders, including the Nizam al-Mulk. According to legend, at a secret mountain fortress its members used hashish (*hah-SHĒSH*), a mild narcotic, to fortify themselves for murder by providing a foretaste of the pleasures of paradise awaiting them if they were martyred. This sect of Shi'ite killers came to be known in Arabic as hashashin (*hah-SHAH-shēn*), or "hashish users," and hence in the West as the **Assassins**.

The Fragmentation of the Seljuk Realm

The assassination of the Nizam al-Mulk in 1092, followed quickly by the death of Malik Shah, touched off a succession crisis that split the Seljuk realm apart. In the west several smaller states emerged, while in the east the Great Seljuk sultans struggled for the next century to control what was left of their empire.

The main successor state in the west was the Sultanate of Rūm (ROOM), a breakaway Seljuk regime that controlled much of Anatolia. Since the name Rūm ("Rome") asserted a claim to the Roman heritage, and since the realm of Rūm expanded toward Constantinople, the Byzantine ruler, as Eastern Roman emperor, saw the sultanate as a mortal threat. In desperation he sought aid from the Christian West, appealing to the pope in Rome, who responded by launching a Christian holy war, later called the First Crusade (1096–1099), which defeated Islamic forces in Anatolia, Syria, and Palestine (Chapter 16). When the Muslims finally reconquered this territory in the next century, they were led not by Seljuks but by Salah al-Din (*sah-LAH al-DĒN*), a gifted Sunni Muslim warrior also called Saladin (*SAH-lah-dēn*). He ended Shi'ite rule in Egypt, served as its sultan for two decades (1173–1193), and drove the Christian crusaders out of Palestine. The Seljuk Sultanate of Rum endured in Anatolia, but lost a key battle in 1202 to Georgia, a realm to its northeast skillfully ruled by a talented woman named Tamar.

The eastern remnant of the Great Seljuk Empire lost power in the 1150s, as its local commanders battled each other for the remains of the realm. In this struggle the commanders of Khwarazm (*khwah-RAZ-um*), a Central Asian region northeast of Persia (Map 15.3), eventually emerged supreme. Known as Khwarazm Shahs, they created a large but loose-knit empire that included much of southern Central Asia and northern Persia. Profiting from commerce along the Asian trade routes and an extensive irrigation system that sustained farming on the steppes, Khwarazm endured until 1218 when it was confronted by the Mongols, nomadic warriors whose conquests threatened to engulf all Eurasia.

Tamar, ruler of Georgia, 1184–1213.

Seljuks threaten Byzantium; Christians respond with Crusades

Khwarazm Shahs connect Central Asia and Persia

The Mongol Invasions

In the early thirteenth century, as noted at the start of this chapter, Mongol warriors set out to conquer the world. Genghis Khan and his heirs, leading a coalition of tribes with a combined population of less than two million, terrorized societies from China to central Europe, overrunning realms with far richer resources and many times more people than Mongolia. Although the Mongols did not conquer the whole world, they did conquer much of Eurasia, creating a huge empire that dwarfed all previous realms. In so doing, they forged connections and fostered trade, spreading ideas and technologies that in time enriched and strengthened the conquered settled societies, fortifying them against further nomadic conquests.

The Conquests of Genghis Khan

Beginning in 1206, following the Mongol conference at which Temujin was proclaimed Genghis Khan, he and his armies set out on their campaign of world conquest. First they allied with the Uighur (*WĒ-goor*) Turks to their southwest, a people who would later

Map 15.4 Conquests of Genghis Khan, 1206–1227

After Temujin was proclaimed Genghis Khan by the Mongols in 1206, he and his armies set out to conquer the world. Notice that his empire, carved out by conquest over the next two decades, eventually extended from the Sea of Japan in the east to the Caspian Sea in the west, incorporating much of northern China and all of Central Asia. In what ways did he help lay the foundations for enhanced connections across much of Eurasia?

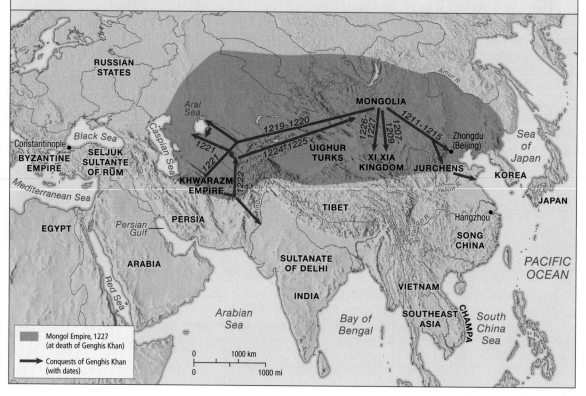

Mongol Empire, 1227
(at death of Genghis Khan)

→ Conquests of Genghis Khan
(with dates)

help the Mongols run their realm (Map 15.4). Then the Mongols moved south against the Tanguts (*TAHN-goots*), Tibetan tribes that had formed a regime called the Xi Xia (*SHĒ shēYAH*) Kingdom in northwestern China. By 1209 the Mongols conquered Xi Xia and forced it to pay tribute but did not yet destroy it.

Mongols lay waste to northern China

The Mongols then moved to their southeast, attacking the Jurchen realm that dominated northern China. From 1211 to 1215 they laid waste to this region, reducing some ninety cities to rubble. In 1215 they attacked the Jurchen capital, a well-fortified metropolis at what is now Beijing, and took it after several months of siege. After finally penetrating its walls, they went on a rampage, plundering its riches, killing its residents, and setting its buildings ablaze. The massacres and fires reportedly went on for a month.

Mongols devastate Khwarazm and Xi Xia

Genghis Khan next directed his efforts far to the west and south. In 1218 he sent emissaries and merchants to meet with the Khwarazm Shah, supposedly to seek diplomatic and commercial ties, but also no doubt to scout this realm and perhaps find a pretext for invading it. The pretext was provided when one of the shah's governors, in a reckless act of defiance, robbed and massacred the Mongol merchants. Responding with ruthless fury, from 1219 to 1221 the Mongols devastated the Khwarazm Empire, ruining its agriculture by wrecking the irrigation system, pillaging the towns along the trade routes, demolishing Persian cities that had come under Khwarazm rule, and slaughtering the inhabitants. Then, because the Xi Xia Kingdom in northwest China had refused to help him conquer Khwarazm, Genghis Khan returned in 1226 to obliterate it and its people.

Genghis Khan died in 1227, allegedly falling off his horse in battle. By then, however, his Mongols had defeated numerous armies, plundered hundreds of cities and towns, killed millions of people, and carved out an empire extending from the Sea of Japan to the Caspian Sea (Map 15.4).

Reasons for Mongol Success

Many factors facilitated the Mongols' amazing military success. These factors included their fighting skills and unity, the lack of a united resistance, their use of reconnaissance and terror, their adoption of ideas and techniques from their foes, and their remarkable leadership.

A Mongol archer on horseback.

Fighting skills. The Mongols' skilled horsemanship gave them an immense advantage in mobility, enabling them to strike without warning, capitalize on enemy mistakes, and quickly change direction in the midst of battle. With their powerful bows and superb marksmanship they could shoot with deadly precision from several hundred yards away, decimating an opposing force before it could fight back, or fire flaming arrows over the walls of a surrounded city. With their courage and endurance they could swiftly cover great distances, maintain composure in combat, and almost always outfight and outlast their foes.

Unity and discipline. Insisting that his generals renounce tribal ties and demanding total loyalty to himself, Genghis Khan centralized his command and instilled iron discipline in his troops. As a result, even when his forces grew to 200,000 and included thousands of Turks and other non-Mongols, they were still able to fight as one and closely coordinate their actions in the course of combat.

Genghis Khan's armies unite Turks and other non-Mongols

Lack of united resistance. Animosities among his enemies, and the previous breakup of China and Persia through invasions by other nomads, enabled Genghis Khan to attack and destroy his targets one at a time. He was also occasionally aided by his enemies' foes: in northern China, for example, Chinese and Khitan residents who resented Jurchen rule helped the Mongols to end it.

Reconnaissance. Rarely did the Mongols attack until they had thoroughly scouted their adversaries. From spies, traveling merchants, and tortured captives, Mongol leaders learned about the composition of enemy forces, the layout of cities, and the design of defenses. This knowledge permitted them to plan their assaults efficiently and carry them out with overpowering effect.

Terror and intimidation. Almost everywhere they went, the Mongols' reputation preceded them, complete with reports of merciless invaders, leveled cities, and wholesale slaughter. And the Mongols cleverly fostered this fear, sparing some victims so they could spread terrifying tales and using others as human shields in subsequent attacks. Employing such methods, the Mongols sowed discord and panic among their foes. At the same time, by pledging not to kill those who offered no resistance and to protect those who had useful skills—such as engineers, artisans, and merchants—the Mongols even got some groups to submit without struggle.

Mongols adopt ideas and techniques from allies and defeated foes

Borrowed ideas and techniques. The Mongols were quick to adopt innovations from the cultures they conquered. From Chinese and Turkish siege engineers, for example, the Mongols learned how to build catapults to heave huge rocks and flaming projectiles over fortress walls, preparing the way for assaults on cities and citadels. From their Uighur Turk allies, the Mongols learned to write, adapting Uighur script to express Mongolian words, compile information, maintain records, and communicate over long distances. From Central Asian merchants and Chinese officials, the Mongols learned how to finance and administer an empire. The most eminent such official was Yelü Chucai (*YEH-LOO choo-SĪ*), a Confucian scholar of Khitan heritage who worked for the Mongols and taught them how to govern. In one of history's most astute acts of statecraft, he convinced them that they could make a fortune by exploiting and taxing northern China's cities and farms—thus derailing a proposal to depopulate the region and turn it into grazing grounds for Mongol herds.

Leadership. A final key factor was their leader himself. Genghis Khan was a masterful military strategist, a talented diplomat, a shrewd opportunist, and a superb leader. Believing that he was destined to conquer the world, he inspired his forces to achieve unprecedented feats. Yet he was also a remorseless man who lived to fight and kill and is said to have claimed that a man's greatest joy was to conquer his enemies, plunder their possessions, ride their horses, and ravish their women. History has furnished few other figures so capable and so cruel.

The Mongol Khanates:
Conquest, Adaptation, and Conversion

Mongol khanates connect Eurasian cultures

The Mongol drive for power did not end with Genghis Khan. After his death, his sons and grandsons continued to seek world domination, expanding Mongol rule across Eurasia. In the process they established four great **khanates**, vast autonomous regions of the Mongol Empire, each ruled by a khan descended from Genghis. These realms included the Khanate of the Great Khan, comprising most of East Asia; the Khanate of the Il-khans, which dominated Persia and Mesopotamia; the Khanate of the Golden Horde, which ruled over Russia; and the Khanate of Jagadai (*JAH-guh-dī*), which controlled Central Asia (Map 15.5). In adapting their rule to these regions, however, the Mongols were themselves transformed, taking on many ways and ideas of the peoples they ruled.

East Asia: Khubilai Khan and His Mongol-Chinese Empire

The richest and most populous khanate was the one ruled by the **Great Khan**. Chosen by tribal council as Genghis Khan's main successor, he was both the direct ruler of all Mongol lands in East Asia and the overlord of the other Mongol realms, whose khans were considered his vassals. As long as the empire remained intact, he was the planet's most powerful person.

Map 15.5 The Four Mongol Khanates Connect Eurasia in the Thirteenth and Fourteenth Centuries

Building on Genghis Khan's conquests, his sons and grandsons further extended Mongol rule, conquering the rest of China, Russia, Persia, and much of Islamic West Asia. Notice that the four huge "khanates" they formed united much of Eurasia, creating and enhancing connections among distant and diverse cultures. How did Mongol rule help to expedite the exchange of goods and knowledge?

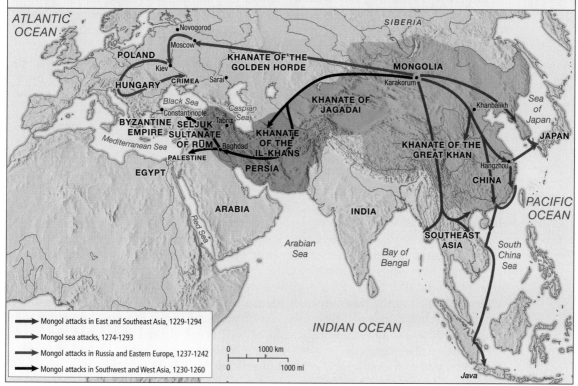

Genghis Khan's son Ögödei (*UH-guh-dā*), elected Great Khan in 1229, vastly expanded the whole Mongol realm, sending armies in the 1230s to invade southwest Asia and Russia. In East Asia he completed the conquest of north China, routing the last remnants of the Jurchen realm that had survived his father's devastation. Then he planned to move against the Song regime in southern China. But Ögödei died in a drinking binge in 1241, leaving his successors to continue his work.

Ögödei's most eminent successor, as a warrior and a ruler, was his nephew Khubilai (*KOO-bih-lī*) Khan. After leading Mongol armies against the Song forces during the 1250s, this talented leader, the ablest of Genghis Khan's grandsons, was chosen as Great Khan in 1260. Over the next two decades, he defeated the Song regime and completed the conquest of China. In 1271 he even claimed the Mandate of Heaven, the divine warrant to rule China, installing himself as its emperor and starting a new dynasty called the Yuan (*yoo-WAHN*). By 1279, when the last Song forces were finally crushed,

Khubilai Khan completes the conquest of China

Khubilai was master of East Asia, ruling as both the Mongol Great Khan and the Emperor of China.

Elsewhere Khubilai was less successful. In 1274 and 1281 he launched against Japan two massive naval invasions, with hundreds of ships and thousands of warriors. But these attacks failed due to Japanese resistance and terrible sea storms the Japanese called **kamikaze** (*KAH-mē-KAH-zē*)—"divine winds" they believed the gods had sent to protect Japan. In the 1280s Khubilai sent armies into Southeast Asia, but they were bogged down by the region's dense rain forests, stifling heat, oppressive humidity, and deadly tropical diseases. In 1293 he dispatched a seaborne force to attack the island of Java, but this force was decisively repelled.

Mongol rulers embrace Chinese ways

In China, however, Khubilai reigned supreme. Unlike other Mongols who disdained China's sedentary society, he embraced many Chinese ways. He moved his capital from Mongolia to northern China, ruling his realm from Khanbalikh (*KAHN-bah-LĒK*), the "city of the Khan," today called Beijing. He adopted China's administrative system, adapted to urban life, and spared China's cities from devastation if they accepted his rule. He encouraged commerce, promoted use of paper money, repaired and expanded highways, and fostered the formation of merchant corporations. He extended the Grand Canal from the Yellow River north to his capital, thus securing the transport of grain and goods along an 1100-mile waterway flanked by a paved road. He practiced religious toleration, became a Buddhist, and even took a Christian woman as one of his four main wives.

Chinese Confucians resent Mongol rule

Despite such efforts, Khubilai and his heirs were deeply resented in China. Many Chinese, regarding their culture as the world's most advanced, saw the Mongol rulers as uncouth barbarians. Chinese Confucians were offended by the Mongols' crude cuisine, their refusal to bathe, their tolerance for non-Chinese religions (such as Christianity and Islam), and the relatively high status they accorded to women. But above all, Confucian scholars resented their own loss of status: although the Mongol regime still employed them as administrators, it reduced their privileges and abandoned their civil service exam placement system, while placing Mongols and other foreigners in most important posts. Within several decades after Khubilai's death in 1294, Mongol rule in China was further weakened by struggles among his successors and by deadly natural disasters.

Southwest Asia: Mongol Devastation and Muslim Resilience

In many ways, Islamic Southwest Asia's experience with the Mongols was similar to East Asia's. In both regions, an assault begun by Genghis Khan was resumed and expanded by one of his grandsons. In both regions, the Mongols overcame strong resistance by a wealthy, cosmopolitan society. In both regions, Mongol forces were eventually turned back, but only after carving out an enormous empire. And in both regions, the Mongols adopted beliefs and practices of the peoples they ruled, but continued to be seen by these peoples as alien oppressors.

Mongols invade Persia and Anatolia

THE MONGOL ASSAULTS ON THE MUSLIM WORLD. The Mongol conquest of Southwest Asia started with assaults on Persia. Ravaged during Genghis Khan's assault on Khwarazm in 1219–1221, Persia got a respite when those armies withdrew. In 1230, however, Great Khan Ögödei sent a sizable force there to complete his father's unfinished business.

Later, after routing local armies and overrunning Persia, the Mongols dispatched armed forays into Anatolia, defeating the Seljuk Sultanate of Rūm in 1243. But at the time they lacked sufficient forces to follow up this victory. Nor were they yet ready to invade Mesopotamia, where the Abbasid Caliphs, claiming spiritual leadership of the Islamic world, reigned in the heavily fortified city of Baghdad.

In the 1250s, however, the Mongols decided to resume and expand their Southwest Asian conquests. While Khubilai led armies against China's Song regime, in Mongolia his brother Hülegü (*hoo-LEH-goo*) assembled a huge force, complete with siege equipment and Chinese technicians, to aid in his intended assaults on Muslim cities and citadels. Hülegü arrived in Persia in 1256 and was joined there by other Mongol forces in the region.

Hülegü conquers Islamic Southwest Asia

The Mongol forces first attacked the Assassins, the Shi'ite murder sect, which by this time had established numerous fortresses throughout the rugged mountains south of the Caspian Sea. One by one the Mongols stormed and demolished these strongholds. By the end of 1257, the Mongols had massacred or captured most of the sect's members, thus eliminating the cult of killers that had long terrorized the Sunni Muslim leaders.

Attackers using a catapult against a walled fortification.

But Sunni Muslims had little time to rejoice. Within weeks the Mongols were threatening Baghdad and insisting, as their price for sparing the city, that the reigning Abbasid Caliph offer them homage and tribute. When Islam's spiritual leader refused to submit, the irate Mongols routed his armies and besieged his city. In February of 1258, after holding out for several weeks, Baghdad fell to the invaders, appalling the Muslim world. Hülegü let his men plunder the city and had the captured caliph trampled to death by horses. Thus ignobly ended the once-great Abbasid Empire.

The next year, while Hülegü headed homeward with some of his troops to take part in a Mongol power struggle, the rest of his army moved west into Syria and Palestine. But the Muslim Mamluks who then ruled Egypt, themselves descended from Central Asian Turks, sent a huge force that decisively defeated the Mongols in 1260 in Palestine. Hülegü later returned to Southwest Asia but died in 1265 without regaining the initiative.

THE IL-KHAN CONVERSION AND TRIUMPH OF ISLAM. Hülegü's heirs, a series of Southwest Asian Mongol rulers known as **Il-khans** (subordinate khans), focused mainly on ruling their own realm. But the Khanate of the Il-khans, which stretched from eastern Anatolia to India's Indus River (Map 15.5), faced serious problems. In their campaigns of conquest the Mongols had ravaged the region, destroying its cities and irrigation systems, killing many of its people and wrecking its economy. As their conquests ceased and they lacked new places to plunder, they made things worse by imposing heavy taxes, effectively pillaging their own empire and ruining its recovery. The coexistence of Mongol and Islamic law created legal chaos, and a string of short reigns by inept Il-khans damaged the regime still further. So did the fact that the Mongol rulers were seen by their subjects as alien, barbaric oppressors.

Eventually, however, like countless earlier rulers of Persia and Mesopotamia, the Mongols were converted by the culture they conquered. Enamored by the splendor of Islamic civilization, they fostered trade, patronized science and scholarship, built cities and schools, and gradually forsook their nomadic ways. Many Mongols became Muslims, including the Il-khans themselves.

Il-khans adopt Islamic ways

The ablest Il-khan was Mahmud Ghazan (*MAH-mood gah-ZAHN*), who focused his brief reign (1295–1304) on rebuilding the region. He converted to Islam, instituted fair taxation, repaired irrigation systems, and returned abandoned lands to cultivation. Though a Sunni Muslim, he tolerated Shi'ites, who had been harshly persecuted under the Abbasid Caliphate.

Rashid al-Din combines Eastern and Western learning

Most of what we know of Mahmud Ghazan, and much of our knowledge of this era, comes from Ghazan's prime minister Rashid al-Din (*rah-SHED ahl-DEN*), an eminent example of the cultural connections fostered by Mongol conquests. Born a Jew, Rashid became a Muslim and worked for the Mongols in places from China to Persia. As a physician familiar with Chinese medicine, he helped bring Chinese knowledge of human anatomy to the Muslim world, whence it later spread to Europe. As a historian, Rashid worked with Eastern and Western scholars to produce the first great history of the world, a monumental work with lavish illustrations (see catapult drawing from Rashid's book on page 369). As an economist and government official, Rashid promoted fiscal and administrative reforms, ably guiding the regime of Il-khan Mahmud Ghazan.

Unfortunately for the Il-khans, Ghazan's reign was cut short in 1304 by his death from an illness at age 32. Instead of consolidating his achievements, his successors indulged in the pleasures of their court, letting corrupt officials run the realm. In 1335, when the last of the Il-khans died without an heir, the empire disintegrated into provinces controlled by ambitious warlords.

As the Il-khan Empire became the first Mongol khanate to vanish, it was clear that the Muslim world had weathered the nomadic onslaught. Both Seljuk Turks and Mongols had brought death and destruction to Southwest Asia, but both had also embraced its culture and religion, and for a time provided good governance, until their realms were fragmented by conflicts among the rulers. Both had actually expanded Muslim horizons, the Seljuks by making Anatolia Islamic and using Persian culture to revitalize Islam, and the Mongols by uniting a Eurasian empire that brought East Asian medicine, scholarship, commerce, and technology to the Muslim lands of Southwest Asia.

Russia: Conquest, Tribute, and the Tatar Yoke

Although the Mongol invasion of Russia, like those of China and Southwest Asia, involved the vanquishing of a vast realm by a grandson of Genghis Khan, the Mongol method of governing Russia differed from that employed elsewhere. For one thing, the Mongols ruled Russia indirectly. Withdrawing their forces after ravaging Russia's city-states, the Mongols demanded tribute and made Russian rulers vassals of the Mongol khan. For another thing, the Mongols who ruled Russia did not adopt Russian ways. Rejecting Russia's Orthodox Christianity and settled agrarian society, they lived in the steppes, remained pastoral nomads, and embraced Islam. Still, by aiding the rise of Moscow as Russia's dominant city, Mongol rule in Russia, which lasted more than two centuries, played a key role in Russia's political development.

Batu Khan conquers Russia

The onslaught began in late 1237 when Batu Khan (*BAH-too KAHN*), grandson of Genghis and cousin of Khubilai and Hülegü, stunned northern Russia by attacking in winter, piercing the dense forests by using frozen rivers as highways for his horsemen. In December his Mongols, whom the Russians called Tatars (*TAH-tarz*), overran Russia's

Document 15.1 Russian Chronicle Account of the Mongol Attack on Kiev

In 1240, having earlier overrun northern Russia, Batu Khan and his Mongols, known by the Russians as Tatars, descended upon the great city of Kiev. This account from the Russian chronicles provides a vivid description of the Mongol assault.

In this year [1240] Batu Khan approached and surrounded the city of Kiev with a great multitude of soldiers. The Tatar force besieged it, and it was impossible for anyone either to leave the city or to enter it. Squeaking of wagons, bellowing of camels, sounds of trumpets and organs, neighing of horses, and cry and sobs of an innumerable multitude of people made it impossible to hear one another in the city. The entire country was overflowing with Tatars. . . .

Batu ordered that many wall-destroying rams be brought to Kiev and placed near the Polish Gate, because that part was wooded. Many rams hammered the walls without interruption day and night and the inhabitants were frightened, and there were many killed and blood flowed like water. And Batu sent the following message to the inhabitants of Kiev: "If you surrender to me, you will be forgiven; if, however, you are going to resist you will suffer greatly and perish cruelly." The inhabitants of Kiev, however, did not listen to him, but calumniated and cursed him. This angered Batu very much and he ordered [his men] to attack the city with great fury. And thus with the aid of many rams they broke through the city walls and entered the city, and the inhabitants ran to meet them. It was possible to hear and see a great clash of lances and clatter of shields; the arrows obscured the light and because of this it was impossible to see the sky, but there was darkness from the multitude of Tatar arrows, and there were dead everywhere and everywhere blood flowed like water.... The Tatars took the city of Kiev on St. Nicholas Day, December 6 [1240].

SOURCE: *Polnoe Sobranie Russkikh Letopisei (Complete Collection of Russian Chronicles)*, X, 115–117. Translation by Basil Dmytryshin, *Medieval Russia: A Source Book, 900–1700* (2nd. ed., New York: Praeger Publishers, 1973), 112–113.

major cities, putting people to the sword and buildings to the torch, spreading terror, death, and devastation. In spring 1238, the Mongols arrived at Novgorod (*NOV-guh-rud*), a prosperous commercial metropolis, but decided not to attack, partly because the spring thaw made the swampy area unfit for a siege, and partly because the city's merchants quickly agreed to pay tribute. The Mongols had learned that they could profit as parasites, not just as plunderers.

Besides, Batu's main aim was to secure his northern flank for an invasion of Europe. In 1240 he began this quest with an assault on Kiev, former capital of Kievan Rus (Chapter 10), sacking the city and leaving behind fields full of skulls and bones (see "Russian Chronicle Account of the Mongol Attack on Kiev"). In 1241 the Mongols moved into Poland and Hungary, where they encountered European knights. Finding arrows useless against the metal armor of these mounted warriors, Batu's marksmen shot the knights' horses out from under them to win several major battles. But early the next year, when Batu learned that Great Khan Ögödei had died, he withdrew his forces to the east to influence the choice of a successor.

Europe thus was spared, but not Russia. Batu and his minions set up a new realm that came to be called the Khanate of the **Golden Horde**. From their capital at Sarai (*sah-RĪ*), amid the steppes and pasturelands north of the Caspian Sea, they commanded a domain that extended from north Central Asia into Eastern Europe. For the next few centuries the Mongols dominated Russia, forcing its city-states to furnish tribute, soldiers, and slaves, while playing their princes off against one another. This era of Mongol domination was known in Russia as the **Tatar Yoke.**

Golden Horde rules Russia indirectly

Still, the Tatars largely let the Russians run their own affairs as long as their main leader would travel to Sarai and humbly seek the khan's formal permission to serve as Grand Prince. At first the khans alternated this office among various Russian princes, so none would gain too much power. Eventually, however, the khans entrusted it mostly to the rulers of a rising metropolis called Moscow. Henceforth, by doing the khan's bidding and acting as his agents in repressing other Russians, Moscow's rulers usually maintained the title of Grand Prince. In time this status would help Moscow become Russia's leading city, and eventually grow powerful enough to challenge Mongol rule.

Central Asia: The Struggle to Maintain the Mongol Heritage

Strife among the Mongols also threatened their empire. Discord stemmed from its size and diversity, which bred conflicts among its various regions, and from its lack of a clear succession system, sparking power struggles among Genghis Khan's heirs. As early as the 1260s, Batu's successors in the Golden Horde clashed with Hülegü's Il-khan regime, while Khubilai fought a four-year battle against a younger brother to prevail as Great Khan.

Khanate of Jagadai seeks to maintain Mongol heritage

In time the struggles among the Mongols tended to converge in Central Asia, in the lands that Genghis Khan had consigned to his second son, Jagadai. Centered among the other three khanates, the Khanate of Jagadai was the empire's hub (Map 15.5). It was also the poorest and least populated khanate, and the one that came closest to maintaining the Mongols' original nomadic warrior lifestyle.

The khanate's devotion to this lifestyle set the stage for conflicts. War and conquest were part of the Mongol heritage, and the empire's expansion had come mainly at the expense of settled societies. But the Khanate of Jagadai, largely surrounded by the other three khanates, could not expand without attacking other Mongols. At first it saw no need to do so and was content to supply the other realms with rugged Central Asian horsemen to sustain their assaults.

Eventually, however, after conquering settled societies, the other khanates adopted new customs and beliefs. The Il-khans embraced Islam, as did the Golden Horde, while Khubilai became a Buddhist, declared himself Chinese emperor, and moved the Great Khan's capital from Mongolia to China. Seeing such changes as a debasement of Genghis Khan's legacy, the rulers of the Central Asian khanate rallied to restore this heritage.

Kaidu combats Khubilai for control of Mongol heritage

Their leader, Ögödei's grandson Kaidu (*KĪ-doo*), was resentful that his branch of the family had lost out in the struggles for succession as Great Khan. In the 1260s he extended his sway over the Khanate of Jagadai, portraying himself as protector of the Mongol traditions. He declared that all true Mongols must live in tents on the steppes and must not degrade themselves by dwelling in cities and towns. Then, in the 1270s, after assembling an army of followers, he attacked the western part of the region ruled by the Great Khan.

Responding swiftly, Great Khan Khubilai sent a strong force to repel the attack. But Kaidu, refusing to admit defeat, stunned the other Mongols in 1277 by invading

MONGOL RULERS AND KHANATES
GREAT KHANS IN BOLD

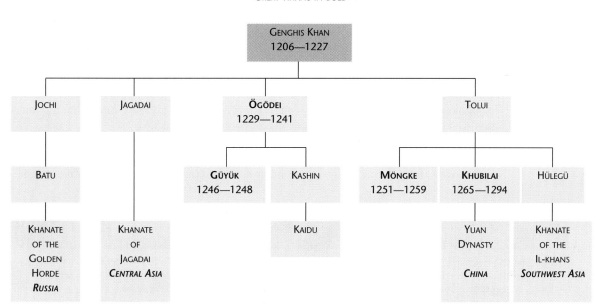

Mongolia itself. Although the next year Khubilai's armies drove back the forces of Kaidu, the Great Khan chose to continue his military efforts elsewhere rather than to stop and finish off his upstart relative. So the conflicts continued for a generation, until Kaidu died in 1301. Left without a leader, his followers reluctantly submitted a few years later to Khubilai's successor, but then fought among themselves sporadically for decades. By the 1340s, as a result, the Jagadai Khanate had split into two smaller realms.

The Mongol empire thus began to unravel, but its impact could not be undone. In conquering much of Eurasia, the Mongols wrought massive ruin, but in ruling it they forged connections that had extensive and enduring consequences.

The Mongol Impact: Connections and Consequences

The initial impact of the Mongol onslaught was widespread devastation. Across Eurasia hundreds of cities and towns were leveled, thousands of farmlands were ruined, and millions of people were killed. According to contemporary counts, the population of China dropped by 40 percent, from around 100 million to about 60 million, during the decades of Mongol invasion and rule. Russia's wealth and talent were depleted by two centuries of the Tatar Yoke. Southwest Asia was hit especially hard, pillaged first by the Seljuk Turks and then by the Mongols. Many of the region's great cities were destroyed, and it took decades for its farms to recover from the damage done to irrigation.

In the long run, however, the main impact of the Mongol era was increased Eurasian integration. By connecting distant and diverse regions under a common rule, the Mongols promoted trade and travel from one end of Eurasia to the other, vastly enhancing the exchange of goods, ideas, and technologies—as well as the spread of diseases—among Eurasian societies.

Trade and Travel: *The Pax Mongolica*

Much as Romans had created a Roman Peace, or *Pax Romana*, promoting commercial and cultural exchanges in the first and second centuries C.E., the Mongols produced a Mongolian Peace, later called **Pax Mongolica** (*PAHX mon-GŌL-ih-kuh*), that advanced the flow of goods and ideas among Eurasian peoples (Map 15.6).

Pax Mongolica facilitates Eurasian connections

The *Pax Mongolica* was not just a fortuitous byproduct of the Mongol invasions; it resulted from deliberate policies pursued by Mongol rulers. To manage their vast realm, the Mongols devised an effective administration, using the Uighur Turks' writing system

Map 15.6 Pax Mongolica Enhances Eurasian Connections in the Thirteenth and Fourteenth Centuries

By connecting much of Eurasia in the thirteenth and fourteenth centuries, the Mongols created a Pax Mongolica, a "Mongolian Peace" that enhanced the exchange of goods and knowledge. Note the land and sea routes that linked numerous cultures, carrying cottons from India; spices from Southeast Asia; timber, furs, and slaves from Russia; silks, porcelains, and teas from China; grapes, wines, and olive oils from Europe; and horses, dates, sugar, and slaves from Islamic West Asia and Africa. Along with increasing commerce, what ideas, knowledge, beliefs, and technologies did Mongol rule help to spread?

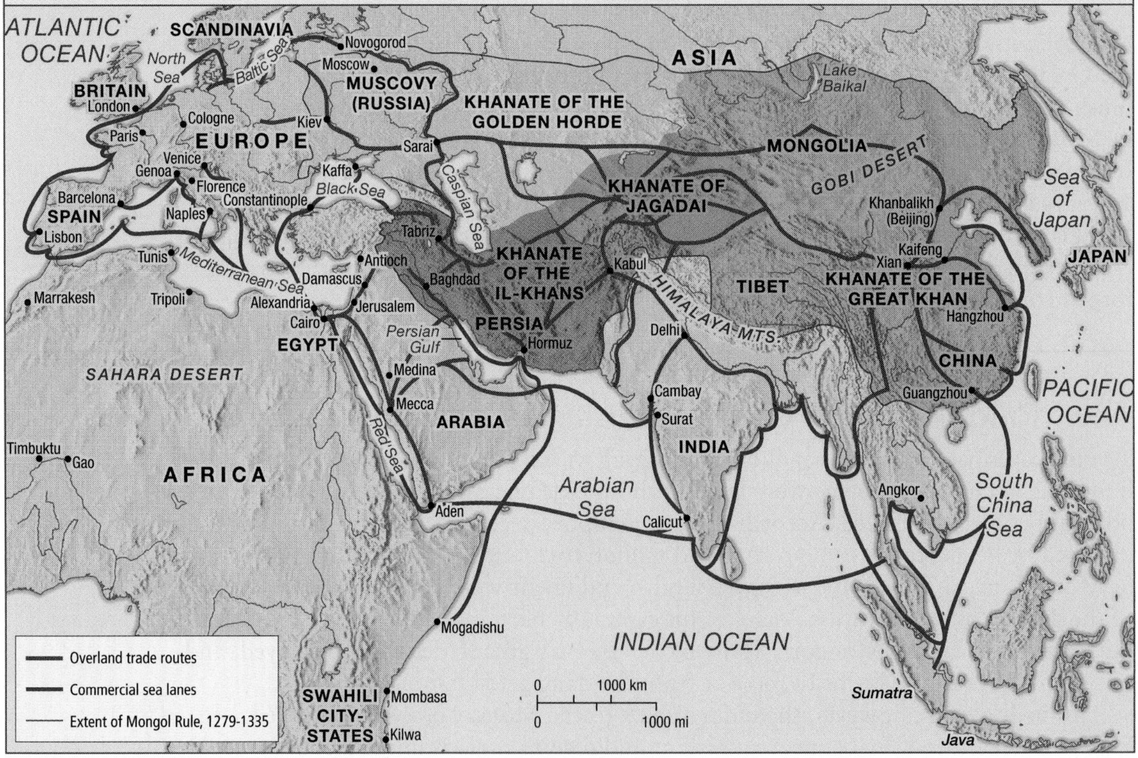

and often employing the Uighurs themselves as civil servants and scribes. To expedite communication, the Mongols created a long-distance postal system, with an extensive network of relay stations, staffed by thousands of riders and ponies capable of carrying messages 200 miles a day. To secure interregional travel and commerce, Mongol forces protected the trade routes with groups of warriors stationed across Central Asia. To enhance diplomatic relations, Mongol rulers dispatched emissaries to distant realms and welcomed embassies from other lands. The Mongols even supplied traveling merchants and dignitaries with an embossed metal seal that served as an early form of passport, to indicate that the bearer's travel was officially approved (see photo on page 376).

Aided and protected by such policies, growing numbers of traders and travelers transported goods and knowledge across Eurasia. Merchants conveyed and exchanged cottons from India; spices from Southeast Asia; timber, furs, and slaves from Russia; silks, porcelains, and teas from China; grapes, wines, and olive oils from Europe; and

Map 15.7 Travels of Marco Polo, 1271–1295, and Ibn Battuta, 1325–1355

The *Pax Mongolica* enabled travelers such as Marco Polo (an Italian Christian) and Ibn Battuta (a Moroccan Muslim) to visit many distant lands. Note that Marco Polo traveled across Eurasia from Italy to China, where he lived for over seventeen years before returning to Europe, while Ibn Battuta's travels took him to numerous cities and places in Africa and Eurasia. How did their vivid descriptions of their travels, and of the lands they visited, help inspire others to create new connections linking Europe, Africa, Asia, and beyond?

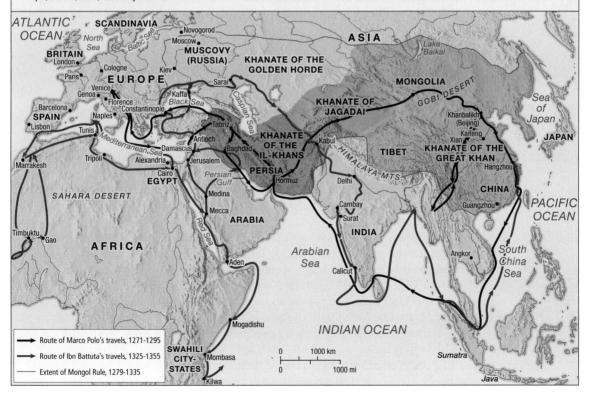

A Mongol "passport."

horses, dates, sugar, and slaves from Muslim domains in Africa and Southwest Asia. Mongol era travelers also spread knowledge by publishing accounts of their visits to widely varied lands.

One such account was that of Marco Polo, an Italian merchant who claimed to have traveled across Central Asia to China (Map 15.7) and to have worked in Khubilai Khan's service from 1275 to 1292. Later, back in Europe, Polo published *Il milione* (The Million), a book describing an immense Chinese empire with huge, prosperous cities, printed books and paper money, flourishing canals and roads, black rocks (coal) that were used as fuel, great ships in bustling harbors, splendid architecture, and fabulous goods. At first he was dismissed as a liar, and even today some critics contend that his accounts were based not on personal experience but on tales heard from other travelers, amplified by his imagination. Nonetheless, whatever their source, his stories helped inspire a fascination with the East among the peoples of Europe. This fascination, along with accounts of Asian wealth and a growing Western appetite for eastern goods such as spices, ceramics, textiles, and teas, led later Europeans to embark on epic voyages that would transform the world (Chapter 19).

Another influential travel account was the *Rihlah* ("Travels") of Ibn Battuta (*IB'n bah-TOO-tah*), a Muslim from Morocco who between 1325 and 1355 journeyed some 75,000 miles across the Mongol khanates and beyond. He reported visiting the reigning Mongol Il-khan, the Golden Horde headquarters at Sarai, various trading towns on the Silk Road, and numerous other settlements in India, Southeast Asia, China, Europe, and Africa. His detailed recollections, dictated after his return, provided his readers, and subsequent historians, with remarkably accurate descriptions of these diverse regions and societies.

Travels of Marco Polo and Ibn Battuta enhance cross-cultural connections

Exchanges of Ideas and Technologies

Eager to exploit the talents of their conquered subjects, the Mongols moved people with special skills—such as architects, engineers, miners, metalworkers, and carpenters—all over the empire. Intrigued by the diverse ideas of the peoples they ruled, many Mongol rulers also welcomed travel by scholars and religious figures.

Such practices helped to disseminate ideas and technologies. Buddhist, Muslim, and Christian communities, for example, emerged in many new places, exposing societies all over Eurasia to their religious ideas. Muslim knowledge about mathematics and astronomy spread eastward to China, where Khubilai Khan employed Persian scholars to help build a new observatory, and westward to Europe, where such knowledge eventually helped inspire a scientific revolution. Chinese expertise in medicine and anatomy was likewise spread westward by traveling scholars and officials, most notably Rashid al-Din. From China also came two enormously influential technologies: printing and gunpowder weaponry.

Mongols help spread religious and scientific ideas

By the time of the Mongol conquests, the Chinese technique of printing on paper from carved wooden blocks had spread to the land of the Uighur Turks, in Central Asia southwest of Mongolia. Allied with the Mongols, and employed throughout their empire as artisans, scribes, and officials, Uighurs then helped spread printing westward across Eurasia. Although printing was initially shunned by Muslims, who deemed that sacred texts must be recopied devoutly by hand, Il-khan officials in Persia introduced printed paper money in 1294—then withdrew it when people rioted against what they saw as

Mongols and Uighur Turks help spread process of printing

worthless pieces of paper. In the 1300s, printed playing cards and holy pictures were introduced into Europe, aided no doubt by diplomats and clerics who had seen them in eastern travels during the *Pax Mongolica*. These printed cards and pictures foreshadowed the development in Europe of woodblock artwork and movable-type printing presses during the next century (Chapter 16).

More direct was the Mongol role in proliferating gunpowder weapons. During the Tang dynasty (618–907 C.E.), the Chinese had learned to combine saltpeter (potassium nitrate) with sulfur and charcoal to create a powder that, when ignited, burned very quickly or exploded. This substance, later called gunpowder, soon proved useful in mining, clearing forests, building canals, and staging fireworks displays. Eventually China's warriors also used it in crude arrow weapons and in bombs that were thrown or catapulted in battle. In the 1200s such devices helped China to slow—but not stop—the Mongol assault.

The Mongols quickly saw the value of such weapons. While fighting the Jurchens in north China (1211–1215), Genghis Khan's forces learned from Chinese allies how to build catapults and gunpowder bombs, which later Mongol armies used in their attacks on Islamic Southwest Asia. By the late 1200s, also with Chinese help, the Mongols learned to cast thick metal firepots and then pack them with gunpowder and a large rock or metal ball. Once ignited, the exploding powder propelled the projectile with enough force to smash holes in enemy walls. Thus were born the first cannons.

Others, too, were capable of copying their foes. Battered by Mongol assaults, Muslims soon learned to make gunpowder weapons, and Europeans, experienced in forging metal pots and church bells, were not far behind. By the 1300s both Muslims and Christians were using gunpowder cannons, and by century's end some European armies had handheld firearms.

Although cumbersome and inaccurate, these early cannons and firearms gradually transformed warfare. Initially gunpowder helped nomadic warriors seize the walled cities of settled societies. But guns eventually gave an edge to the settled societies, which had the resources, mines, and artisans to produce them in far greater numbers than could the nomads. In time the use of firearms neutralized the nomads' advantages—their horsemanship, courage, and speed—by enabling enemy armies to shoot at them from a distance. The Mongols thus helped to spread a technology that later contributed to their undoing.

> Mongols help spread gunpowder weapons

Asian warriors firing arrows from tubes.

The Plague Pandemic

The Mongols also helped to spread a disease that contributed to their undoing. In the mid-1300s Eurasia was swept by a pandemic of **bubonic plague**, a deadly contagion typically carried from rodents to humans by fleas. Unaware of how it spread, people at the time had little chance to protect themselves from this terrible affliction, which brought painful inflammations followed by chills, vomiting, fever, diarrhea, and delirium—often leading to death in three or four days.

The outbreak began in southwest China (Map 15.8), where rats and people had been beset by the plague sporadically for centuries. In the 1330s and 1340s, probably aided by traveling Mongol soldiers whose supply wagons may have harbored infected rats and fleas, the plague spread to other parts of China, where numerous people had already been weakened by floods and famines.

> Mongol connections help spread plague throughout China

Map 15.8 The Plague Pandemic of the Fourteenth Century

In connecting most of Eurasia by conquest and commerce, the Mongols also helped facilitate the spread of disease. Compare this map with Maps 15.6 and 15.7, noting that the plague, having ravaged parts of China, moved westward along trade and travel routes that the Mongols used to connect their vast Eurasian empire. In what ways did the Mongols, and connections they helped develop, contribute to the plague pandemic? How did the plague help to end Mongol rule in China?

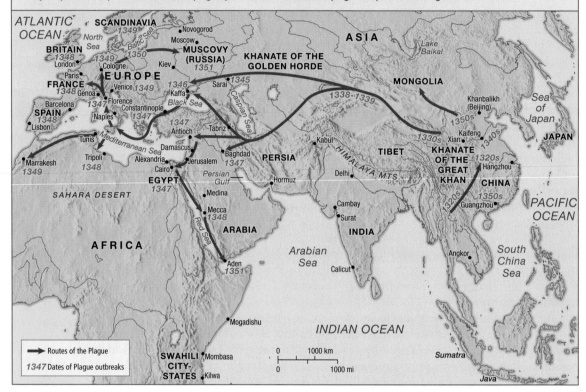

Meanwhile, aided by increased caravan traffic promoted by the Mongols, the plague moved westward across Central Asia, spread by fleas that fed on the blood of squirrels, rats, marmots, dogs, and humans. The deadly contagion ravaged not just caravans and towns along the trade routes but also encampments of nomadic herders and Mongol warriors scattered across the steppes.

Mongol connections help spread plague to Egypt and Europe

By 1346, the plague had reached the Black Sea's northern shores, where it afflicted Mongol soldiers besieging the city of Kaffa, a fortified trading port controlled by the Italian Republic of Genoa. According to some accounts, in one of history's earliest attempts at biological warfare, Mongols catapulted corpses of plague victims over the town walls into the surrounded city, evidently intending to infect its defenders. Fleeing Genoese ships, apparently harboring infected rats, carried the plague to Egypt and to Europe, where perhaps a third of the population perished in an epidemic that Europeans called the Black Death (Chapter 16).

The plague pandemic thus ravaged the peoples of Eurasia and northeast Africa, killing tens of millions and leaving behind a trail of death and devastation. It induced widespread panic, disrupted commerce, and created chaotic conditions that contributed to the disintegration of the Mongol Empire.

The End of the Mongol Era

By the 1330s, when the plague pandemic began, the Mongol Empire was already in decline. In Southwest Asia, as we have seen, the Khanate of the Il-khans dissolved after its last ruler died with no heir in 1335. In Central Asia, the Khanate of Jagadai, torn by internal discord, split into eastern and western khanates during the 1330s and 1340s. In China, Mongol rule was beset by dynastic strife: as Khubilai's descendants vied for power, often by intrigues and assassinations, eight different emperors reigned between 1307 and 1333.

Then catastrophe struck China. In the mid-1330s, deluged by crop-destroying floods, northern China endured a calamitous famine. In the 1340s, before the region recovered, another famine ensued. Faced with widespread starvation, the government strove to repair the dikes and dams, only to have them burst again. Meanwhile, huge amounts of paper money printed to finance the repairs deeply debased the currency. In the midst of these disasters came the plague from southwest China, ravaging much of the country and intensifying the crisis. By the 1350s many Chinese were joining mass revolts against the Mongol regime. To them the disasters had an obvious explanation: the Mongol dynasty had lost the Mandate of Heaven.

Mongols lose the Mandate of Heaven

These disasters and this perception bolstered rebel leaders, especially Zhu Yuanzhang (*JOO yoo-wahn JAHNG*), a poor peasant orphaned as a youth when his parents starved to death in a famine. While other rebels looted the countryside, Zhu amassed an army of supporters. In 1356, as China descended into chaos, he captured Nanjing, one of China's largest cities, and made it his capital. During the next decade he defeated other rebels, gaining control of the entire Yangzi valley. Finally he moved north with his huge army to confront the Mongol emperor, who promptly fled to Mongolia. In 1368 Zhu claimed Heaven's Mandate as the emperor Hongwu (*HONG WOO*) and founded a new dynasty called the Ming (Chapter 21). Mongol rule in China thus came to an end.

The Mongol Empire never recovered from its loss of China. In the late 1300s, a Turkic warrior called Timur (*tĕ-MOOR*) Lenk tried to reunite the Mongol realm, but his ruinous attacks on other Turks and Mongols instead opened the way for new Islamic empires (Chapter 17) and for Russian independence (Chapter 25). For several centuries surviving Mongol khanates would stage sporadic raids on settled societies such as Russia and China. But armed with gunpowder weapons, knowledge of which the Mongols had helped spread across Eurasia, the settled societies with their large armies would increasingly manage to keep the mounted steppe warriors at bay. The age of the great nomadic empires was over.

Chapter Review

Putting it in Perspective

The nomadic invasions of the tenth through four-teenth centuries shook the very foundations of Eura-sia's settled societies. In a remarkable series of assaults, the nomads of Central Asia, with small populations and simple societies based on herding and horsemanship, devastated the large armies, fer-tile farmlands, and cosmopolitan cities of their far more populous and prosperous neighbors. The Khi-tans, and later the Jurchens, moved into northern China, the cradle of Chinese civilization. The Seljuk Turks overran most of Southwest Asia, seizing the historic heartlands of the Islamic and Byzantine worlds. Then came the Mongols, mightiest of all the nomads, who not only overran the Jurchen and for-mer Seljuk domains, but also conquered all of China and much of Eurasia as well.

In the long run, however, the nomadic con-quests transformed the nomads and facilitated the triumph of the settled societies. Over time the victo-rious nomads adopted many features of the con-quered cultures, including governance structures, economic patterns, and religious beliefs. Thus, by the time their empires were finally overthrown, the former nomads had themselves become more settled and cosmopolitan, largely forsaking their original tribal and itinerant ways. Furthermore, by forcibly uniting large parts of Eurasia under their rule, the Seljuk Turks and Mongols fostered connections that in time would strengthen the settled societies. Indeed, by expediting the growth of east-west commerce and the spread of technologies such as gunpowder and printing, the nomadic conquests eventually enhanced the wealth and power of both the Muslim and the Christian worlds.

Reviewing Key Material

KEY CONCEPTS

khan, 358
shamanism, 358
Il-khans, 369
Golden Horde, 371

Assassins, 362
khanates, 366
Great Khan, 366
kamikaze, 368

Tatar Yoke, 372
Pax Mongolica, 374
bubonic plague, 377

KEY PEOPLE

Genghis Khan, 355
Alp Arslan, 361
The Nizam al-Mulk, 361
Salah al-Din, 363
Tamar of Georgia, 363
Yelü Chucai, 366
Ögödei, 367
Khubilai, 367

Hülegü, 369
Mahmud Ghazan, 370
Rashid al-Din, 370
Batu, 370
Kaidu, 372
Marco Polo, 376
Ibn Battuta, 376
Hongwu, 379

ASK YOURSELF

1. Why did the peoples of Central Asia rely mostly on herding and horsemanship rather than on farming? What was the impact of this reliance on their societies and governance?
2. How and why were the Seljuk Turks able to conquer most of Southwest Asia? How were they transformed from destructive marauders into rulers of a cosmopoli-tan empire?
3. What factors account for the incredible success of the Mongol campaigns of conquest? Why did the Mongols fail to conquer Japan, Southeast Asia, Egypt, and Europe?
4. Why did the nomadic conquerors so often adopt the features, structures, and beliefs of the cultures they conquered?
5. What were the benefits and disadvantages of the *Pax Mongolica*? What were its long term impacts on the Mongol Empire and on the large Eurasian settled societies?
6. How did Mongols compare, in their tactics, policies, and impacts, with earlier rulers of multicultural em-pires, such as Persians, Macedonians, Romans, Muslim Arabs, and Seljuk Turks?

GOING FURTHER

Adshead, S. A. M. *Central Asia in World History.* 1993.
Allsen, Thomas. *Commodity and Exchange in the Mongol Empire.* 2002.

Allsen, Thomas T. *Culture and Conquest in Mongol Eurasia.* 2001.

Amitai-Preiss, R., and D. Morgan, eds. *The Mongol Empire and Its Legacy.* 2000.

Bartlett, W. B. *The Assassins: The Story of Islam's Medieval Secret Sect.* 2001.

Chase, Kenneth. *Firearms: A Global History to 1700.* 2003.

Dardess, J. W. *Conquerors and Confucians.* 1973.

De Hartog, Leo. *Genghis Khan, Conqueror of the World.* 1989.

De Hartog, Leo. *Russia Under the Mongol Yoke.* 1996.

Farmer, Edward L. *Early Ming Government.* 1976.

Frank, A. G. *Re-Orient: Global Economy in the Asian Age.* 1998.

Golden, P. *Introduction to the History of Turkic Peoples.* 1992.

Grousset, Rene. *The Empire of the Steppes.* 1970.

Khan, Paul, ed. *The Secret History of the Mongols.* 1984.

Martin, H. D. *The Rise of Genghis Khan and the Conquest of North China.* 1971.

Mokyr, Joel. *The Lever of Riches: Technological Creativity and Economic Progress.* 1990.

Morgan, David. *Medieval Persia, 1040-1479.* 1988.

Morgan, David. *The Mongols.* 1986.

Ostrowski, D. *Muscovy and the Mongols.* 1998.

Ratchnevsky, Paul. *Genghis Khan: His Life and Legacy.* 1991.

Rossabi, M. *Khubilai Khan: His Life and Times.* 1988.

Severin, Tim. *In Search of Chinggis Khan.* 1992.

West, Elizabeth E. *Mongolian Rule in China.* 1989.

Key Dates and Developments

1025–1040	Seljuk Turks enter Persia
1055	Seljuk Turks conquer Baghdad
1071–1076	Seljuks defeat Byzantines, take Syria and Palestine
1092–1194	Seljuk Empire disintegrates
1114–1127	Jurchens defeat Khitans and conquer northern China
1206	Temujin proclaimed Genghis Khan
1211–1215	Mongols defeat Jurchens and ravage northern China
1219–1221	Mongols conquer Khwarazm and ravage Persia
1237–1241	Mongols invade Russia and central Europe
1255–1260	Mongols invade Southwest Asia, take Baghdad in 1258
1274, 1281	Japan rebuffs Mongol invasions with help of storms
1275–1292	Marco Polo reportedly resides in China
1279	Khubilai completes conquest of China
1325–1355	Ibn Battuta travels across much of Asia and Africa
1335	Il-khan regime collapses in southern Asia
1340s	Plague pandemic spreads across Eurasia
1368	Mongols ousted from China; Hongwu begins Ming dynasty
1380–1405	Timur Lenk ravages much of Asia

CHAPTER 16

The Resurgence of the Christian West, 1050–1530

- Conflicts and Connections Between Europe and Islam

- The High Middle Ages

- The Decline of the Middle Ages

- The European Renaissance

- Chapter Review

The Cathedral And Baptistry Of Florence

In the eleventh through sixteenth centuries, the Christian West experienced a political, economic, and cultural resurgence, as reflected in the splendid architecture of Renaissance Florence.

In 1095 the Byzantine Empire, a shrunken remnant of the once-great Roman realm, was in serious trouble. A few decades earlier the Seljuk Turks, after conquering much of Southwest Asia and converting to Islam, had seized the empire's eastern provinces and its most valuable farmlands. The Turks had also overrun Syria and Palestine, conquering a region revered as a Holy Land by Christians, Muslims, and Jews. Seeking to shore up his defenses, the Byzantine ruler, as leader of the Christian East, asked the Christian West for help in fighting the Islamic Turks. It proved to be a fateful request.

Christian West

Crusade Areas

Pope Urban II (1088–1099), as head of the Western Church, responded with a grandiose plan to retake the Holy Land for Christianity. At Clermont, France, in late 1095, he called for Christian warriors to drive out the "accursed" Turks. "Wrest that land from the wicked race," he urged, according to one account of his speech, "and subject it to yourselves." Inspired by religious zeal, dreams of wealth and territory, and a papal promise of "the imperishable glory of the kingdom of heaven," thousands of European Christians heeded his call.

Thus began the crusades, a series of Christian holy wars directed mainly against Muslims, heralding a resurgence of the Christian West. For centuries, captained by feudal warlords and piloted by predatory Church leaders, Western Christians had lagged behind Muslims in power, wealth, learning, and technology. But in the eleventh century, energized by increasing prosperity and reforming popes, the West began to rebound. The crusades not only reflected this resurgence but also enhanced it by bolstering Western commercial and cultural growth.

Europe's High Middle Ages, coinciding with the crusades, witnessed a flowering of the cultural, political, economic, and religious elements that underlie what is now called Western Civilization. Ravaged in the fourteenth century by famines, plagues, schisms, and wars, the West rebounded again. By the fifteenth century, enriched by conflicts and contacts with Muslim societies, it was undergoing a cultural and technological Renaissance and emerging as one of the world's most expansive civilizations.

Conflicts and Connections Between Europe and Islam

The West's resurgence was rooted in conditions that arose in the eleventh century. By then, the Viking and Magyar invasions that plagued Europe in preceding centuries had ceased. Agricultural advances, combined with a warming of the climate, were helping to bring prosperity and population growth. The Great Schism of 1054, by cutting the ties of the Roman popes to Eastern Christianity, freed them to focus on strengthening their supremacy in the West. And a series of ambitious popes began to institute reforms, curtail corruption, and expand the power and prestige of the Western Church.

Seljuk conquest of West Asia leads to Muslim-Christian conflicts

Meanwhile, both the Muslim and Byzantine worlds had problems. In the previous few centuries, the splintering of the Abbasid Empire, and the growth of diverse groups within Islam such as Shi'ites, Sufis, and Almoravids, had undermined Islamic unity. During the 1040s and 1050s, the Seljuk Turks conquered the Muslim heartland, taking Baghdad in 1055 and making the Abbasid caliphs puppets of the Turkish sultan. Although the Seljuks themselves became Muslims, their conquests further fragmented the Islamic world. Then Byzantium made the fateful mistake of engaging the Seljuks in combat, suffering a disastrous defeat at Manzikert in 1071. Within a decade the Turks had taken Palestine, Syria, and eastern Anatolia, opening the way for expanded encounters between Europe and Islam.

Christians and Muslims in Iberia

As Turks took control in the East, Christians were already moving against Muslims in Iberia, the peninsula that now embraces Portugal and Spain, most of which had been under Islamic rule since the early 700s. In the eleventh century, as strife broke out among Iberian Muslims, small Christian kingdoms surviving in the North began working for **Reconquista** (*rā-kahn-KĒS-tah*), or Christian reconquest of Iberia (Map 16.1). In 1063 Pope Alexander II (1061–1074) supported their effort by sending in French and Norman soldiers; he also sanctified it by pardoning their sins, setting a precedent for future popes who would likewise grant spiritual rewards to Christians who fought against Muslims.

Led by Castile and Aragon, Christians expel Muslims from Iberia

Over the next few centuries, forces led by the Spanish Christian kingdoms of Castile (*cass-TĒL*) and Aragon (*AIR-uh-GŌN*) gradually pushed the Muslims back. In 1085, Castile and its allies captured Toledo, an Islamic cultural stronghold in central Iberia. In the Northeast, Aragon captured several Muslim cities, most notably Saragossa in 1118. Fearing that Islam might be pushed out of Europe entirely, Muslims from North Africa intervened in Iberia, but a united Spanish Christian army defeated them in 1212. Christians took Córdoba in 1236, Valencia in 1238, and Seville in 1248, while Portugal freed itself from Islamic rule by 1250. Although Muslims held the southern province of Granada until 1492, by the mid-1200s most of Iberia was under Christian control.

Contacts with Iberian Muslims enhance Western learning and technology

Conquests and connections with Muslims in Iberia brought many benefits to the Christian West. By taking Toledo, a major center of Islamic learning for over three centuries, Christians gained access to its large library of works in Arabic on science and philosophy. Once translated into Latin, these works greatly aided the advancement of Western scholarship. Eventually, Europeans also learned how to make paper and forge fine steel swords through contacts with Muslims in Iberia.

Conquests in Iberia also built Western confidence in religious warfare. Conducting war in God's name, as the Muslims had often done, was now the approach used by Christian crusaders in seeking to take the Holy Land from the Islamic Turks.

The First Crusade: "It Is God's Will!"

Pope wants crusade to take Holy Land and end strife in Europe

In 1095, a decade after the Christian conquest of Toledo, Pope Urban II called for Christian invasion of the Holy Land (see "Excerpts from Pope Urban II's Speech at Clermont, 1095"). Although he was responding to a Byzantine appeal for help, Urban clearly had

FOUNDATION MAP 16.1 Christians Reconquer Spain from Muslims, 1080–1492

From the eighth through eleventh centuries, Muslims ruled much of Spain, building there an impressive Islamic culture. Observe, however, that in the eleventh through fifteenth centuries, supported by the papacy and led by the Christian kingdoms of Castile and Aragon, Spanish Christian forces steadily defeated and drove out the Muslims. What benefits did Christian Europe gain from the legacy of Muslim rule in Spain?

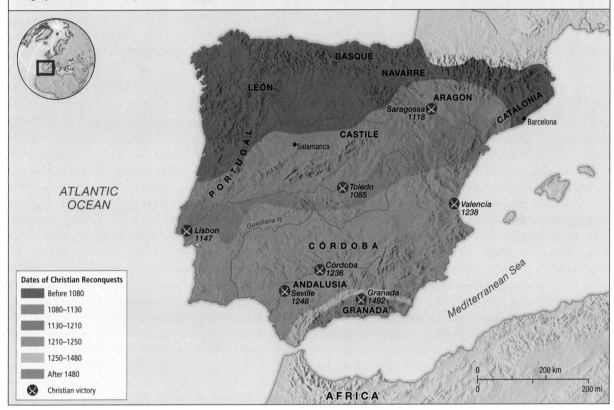

Dates of Christian Reconquests
- Before 1080
- 1080–1130
- 1130–1210
- 1210–1250
- 1250–1480
- After 1480
- ⊗ Christian victory

some additional goals. He hoped to bring peace to Europe, ending wars among its peoples by uniting them in a common cause. He wanted to enlarge Christendom through warfare fueled by faith, against the Muslims, who had shown the world how effective that combination could be. He aspired to enhance the papacy's power, and perhaps even restore its leadership over the Eastern Church.

The response to Urban's appeal was dramatic. As he preached his crusade, he was reportedly greeted by shouts of "It is God's will!" Within months, knights and foot soldiers from Italy, France, and Germany assembled into armies and headed for Constantinople, where they converged in 1097 to continue their eastward march.

The First Crusade (1096–1099) was a stunning success for the West. Benefiting from divisions among Muslims and the recent breakup of the Seljuk Empire, Christian warriors conquered the lands around the eastern Mediterranean (Map 16.2), creating four small "crusader states" and even capturing Jerusalem in 1099. But the Christians also engaged

Crusaders conquer Holy Land but also commit atrocities

Document 16.1 Excerpts from Pope Urban II's Speech at Clermont, 1095

In 1095, at the Council of Clermont in France, Pope Urban II issued a ringing call for a great crusade to retake the Holy Land from the Islamic Seljuk Turks, whom he demonized as an "accursed race" and accused of vicious atrocities. He called on Christian warriors to put aside their conflicts with each other and unite in a common cause that would bring them eternal glory.

From the confines of Jerusalem and the city of Constantinople a horrible tale . . . has been brought to our ears, namely, that . . . an accursed race, a race utterly alienated from God, . . . has invaded the lands of those Christians and has depopulated them by the sword, pillage and fire; it has led away a part of the captives into its own country, and a part it has destroyed by cruel tortures; it has either entirely destroyed the churches of God or appropriated them for the rites of its own religion . . . On whom therefore is the labor of avenging these wrongs and of recovering this territory incumbent, if not upon you?

. . . Let the deeds of your ancestors move you and incite your minds to manly achievements . . . Let the holy sepulchre of the Lord our Saviour, which is possessed by unclean nations, especially incite you, and the holy places which are now treated with ignominy and irreverently polluted with their filthiness . . .

Let none of your possessions detain you, no solicitude for your family affairs, since this land which you inhabit, shut in on all sides by the seas and surrounded by the mountain peaks, is too narrow for your large population; nor does it abound in wealth; and it furnishes scarcely food enough for its cultivators. Hence it is that you murder one another, that you wage war, and that frequently you perish by mutual wounds. Let therefore hatred depart from among you, let your quarrels end, let wars cease, and let all dissensions and controversies slumber. Enter upon the road to the Holy Sepulchre; wrest that land from the wicked race, and subject it to yourselves. That land which as the Scripture says . . . was given by God into the possession of the children of Israel . . . is now held captive by His enemies, and is in subjection to those who do not know God, to the worship of the heathens . . . God has conferred upon you above all nations great glory in arms. Accordingly undertake this journey for the remission of your sins, with the assurance of the imperishable glory of the kingdom of heaven.

When Pope Urban had said these and very many similar things . . . , he so influenced . . . the desires of all who were present that they cried out, "It is the will of God! It is the will of God!"

SOURCE: Robert the Monk, *Historia Hierosolymitana* (Medieval Sourcebook: Urban II, Speech at Council of Clermont, 1095), http://www.fordham.edu/halsall/source/urban2-5vers.html

in butchery and bigotry: unruly bands of "peasant crusaders," seeing the crusade as a war against all non-Christians, massacred Jews in Germany, and Christian soldiers pillaging Jerusalem slaughtered defenseless Muslims.

The Muslim Response and the Later Crusades

In time, however, the crusaders' conquests and brutal behavior motivated Muslims to combine their efforts and launch retaliatory attacks. By 1144 they had amassed a large army and reconquered one of the crusader states. Pope Eugenius III quickly authorized a Second Crusade (1147–1149), led by the German Emperor and the King of France. This time, however, the crusaders lost. After almost getting into battle against Byzantines near Constantinople, they were badly beaten by Islamic Turks in Anatolia, and thus failed to recover any lost ground.

Map 16.2 Crusades Create New Connections and Conflicts, 1095–1300

The crusades, which began as bitter conflicts between Christians and Muslims, also involved attacks by Western Christians upon other Christians. Notice that the First Crusade, in which Christians gained control of the Holy Land and set up "crusader states," was followed by others meant to regain control after Muslim-led counterattacks. Note, too, that the Fourth Crusade never made it to the Holy Land; instead its Christian crusaders sacked the great Christian city of Constantinople. How did the Crusades, which ultimately failed to maintain Christian rule in the Holy Land, bolster connections between Muslims and Christian Europeans? What impacts did these connections have on Western culture and commerce?

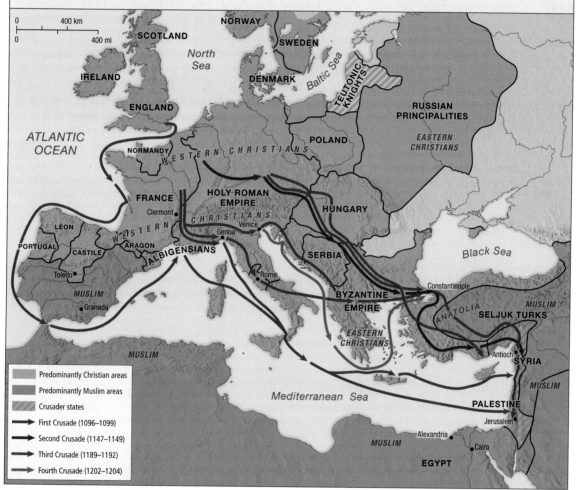

A few decades later, the West lost even more ground. The brilliant Muslim warrior Salah al-Din, known in Europe as Saladin, founded a new dynasty in Egypt in 1173. He quickly conquered Syria and Arabia, uniting them with Egypt into a formidable realm, and then attacked the remaining crusader states. In 1187 his forces took Jerusalem, refraining on his orders from sacking the Holy City. The work of the First Crusade was thus largely undone: most of the Holy Land was again under Muslim control.

Muslims under Salah al-Din retake most of Holy Land

Salah al-Din (Saladin).

Fourth Crusade pillages Constantinople and ousts Byzantine ruler

Later crusades target other Christians not aligned with Rome

At once Europe's three leading rulers—German Emperor Frederick Barbarossa (*bar-buh-RŌ-sah*), English King Richard I the Lionheart, and French King Philip II Augustus—organized a Third Crusade. The Muslims under Saladin prepared to defend their lands, while Byzantines braced for another threat to their region's stability.

The Third Crusade (1189–1192), planned as a multi-pronged land and sea assault, was a disaster for the West. Frederick, by then in his late sixties, drowned on his way to the Holy Land while crossing a river with his armor on. Richard and Philip quarreled constantly, until the latter, citing his poor health, returned to France in 1191. Richard soldiered on, and even defeated Muslim hero Saladin in several battles, but he failed to retake Jerusalem, which henceforth remained under Islamic control.

A decade later, noting weakness and division within the Byzantine Empire, Pope Innocent III (1198–1216) called for a Fourth Crusade (1202–1204), hoping not only to undo the conquests of Saladin, who had died in 1193, but also to reunite Eastern and Western Christianity. Driven more by greed than by faith, however, the Germans, Normans, and Venetians who organized this crusade diverted it against Constantinople. Dismayed at their decision to plunder Christians instead of attacking Muslims, Innocent condemned the crusaders in 1202, but he could not control them. In 1204 they sacked the great city, forcing the Byzantine emperor to flee, and replaced his regime with a Western-dominated Latin Empire that lasted until 1261. The Byzantine realm was then restored and endured until 1453, but it never regained its former size or strength.

Later crusades, forsaking the original quest for control of the Holy Land, were directed against targets other than Muslims. From 1209 to 1229, for example, crusaders in southern France annihilated Albigensians, radical Christian spiritualists who defied Church teaching by denouncing as evil all aspects of the physical world, including sex and material possessions. In succeeding decades the Teutonic Knights, a military religious order founded by earlier crusaders, conquered surviving pagan lands near the eastern Baltic Sea (Map 16.2) and invaded Russian regions settled by Eastern Christians. By 1291, when Muslims finally captured the last Christian outpost in the Holy Land, the initial crusading ideals had long since disappeared.

Islamic Impacts on Western Commerce and Culture

Crusades ultimately fail to meet original goals

Increased contact with other cultures expands European horizons

In the long run, then, the crusades were a failure, at least in terms of their original goals. Muslim control of the Holy Land, although interrupted by the early crusaders, was ultimately restored. Europe remained divided into feuding states, whose leaders focused more on fighting each other than on battling Muslims. The split in Christianity widened, as the crusaders' sack of Constantinople, plundering its cathedrals and its great library, bred lasting bitterness toward the West in the Eastern Church. And brutal assaults against Jews in Europe opened the way for centuries of anti-Jewish abuse.

But the Christian holy wars had unforeseen consequences for Europe and the world. The crusades spurred the growth of European credit and banking, as popes and rulers borrowed heavily to finance these costly ventures. The crusades boosted Western commerce, helping such Italian states as Genoa and Venice gain greater access to east-west trade, long dominated by Muslims. By exposing Europeans to textiles and spices from China, India, and Indonesia, this trade in time inspired Western voyages of exploration, which led in turn to Europe's exploitation of Africa and the Americas. And by giving

Westerners a taste for cane sugar from West Asia and North Africa, this commerce eventually prompted Europeans to grow their own sugar on plantations worked by slaves, vastly expanding the African slave trade.

The crusades and *Reconquista*, combined with the translation of Arabic works into Latin, also exposed Europe to the ideas of eminent Muslim scholars. From the writings of mathematician al-Khwarizmi, for example, the West was introduced to algebra, Arabic numerals, and Egyptian astronomy, laying the foundations for the later growth of European science. Through the work of physician and philosopher Ibn Sina, known in the West as Avicenna, Europeans learned about Greek and Indian medicine and ancient Greek philosophy, contributing greatly to the development of Western medicine and scholarship.

Exposure to Muslim scholarship advances Western learning

New technologies from the Muslim world also enhanced the West's resurgence. Water mills and windmills, which helped farmers drain swamps and grind grain, came to Europe through Islamic Spain. So did the production of paper, a key component of inexpensive printed books, later developed in Europe. Navigational innovations, such as the triangular "lateen" sail (which could be moved from side to side to let sailors tack into the wind) and the astrolabe (a device for navigating by the sun and stars), were introduced to Europe through contacts with Muslims. So were gunpowder weapons, spread westward from East Asia by Mongols and Turks (Chapter 15). In time such technologies helped European nations become global powers.

Exposure to technologies from Muslims advances Western wealth and power

Thus, for all the atrocities and havoc they produced, the crusades and *Reconquista* enhanced connections that contributed to European growth. The Arabic origins of numerous Western words—including cotton, coffee, sugar, tariff, musket, admiral, algebra, and zero—amply attest to the impact of such connections on European commerce, technology, and science.

Water mills in Islamic Syria.

The High Middle Ages

The era surrounding the crusades, which is known in the West as the High Middle Ages (roughly 1050 to 1300), is often seen as the high point of Medieval European culture. It brought advances in almost every area of European endeavor: agriculture expanded, towns and trade grew, monarchies strengthened, religion thrived, universities emerged, scholarship blossomed, and architecture flourished.

Agricultural Advances

Much of this era's economic growth began with agricultural advances, aided by improvements in climate and adoption of new technologies. Between 1050 and 1200 Europe's climate warmed considerably, creating a longer growing season and shorter, milder winters. Farmers were able to plant more crops and cultivate more land, often by clearing swamps and forests. Heavy plows made of wood and iron, introduced earlier but widely adopted mainly in the High Middle Ages, enabled farmers to turn over the earth instead of just scratching its surface, loosening the soil to vastly improve its fertility. The horse collar, a harness that fit around an animal's shoulders rather than its neck, enabled beasts of burden to pull plows and carts with the full weight of their bodies. Water mills and windmills helped farmers use the forces of nature to grind grain and drain swamplands.

Many Western farming advances were pioneered in Asia and Africa

These innovations were hardly unique to Europe. For centuries the Chinese had used heavy plows and water mills, East Asians and North Africans had employed efficient horse harnesses, and Persians had utilized windmills. But in the High Middle Ages interregional contacts and commerce, enhanced by the crusades and *Reconquista*, helped acquaint Europeans with such devices, which combined with the warming climate to increase the quantity and quality of food. As more food and better diets improved the health of childbearing women and helped more children survive to adulthood, Europe's population grew much larger.

The Growth of Towns and Trade

Increases in food and population help expand towns and trade

As the overall population increased, so did the number of people who lived in towns, often working as artisans or merchants, supported by the growing food supply. Towns had walls to protect them and marketplaces where artisans and merchants could exchange their goods—such as tools, furnishings, pottery, or clothing—for food brought in by local farmers. As more towns emerged, interregional trade increased, and a money economy replaced simple barter.

Long distance commerce was also stimulated by the crusades, which expanded European contacts with the East and interest in eastern goods, and by the Mongol conquests, which increased trade and travel across Eurasia (Chapter 15). European seaports, led by Genoa and Venice, imported eastern goods, while banking arose in cities such as Florence to finance commercial ventures. By the thirteenth century, Europe had many urban settlements, ranging from small fortified towns to sizable cities—such as London, Paris, Venice, and Florence—of fifty thousand people or more.

Urban occupations form guilds to protect their interests

In many towns and cities, the people in each occupation—such as merchants, carpenters, masons, shoemakers, or weavers—formed **guilds**, associations to promote their commercial and professional interests. Guilds had long flourished in Chinese and Byzantine cities, but in the West they had largely been absent since the fall of Rome. Their reemergence in the High Middle Ages reflected not only Europe's increasing economic complexity, but also its growing commercial contacts with eastern civilizations.

Guilds as a rule fixed prices, wages, and standards, thereby protecting their members from competition while assuring their customers of quality. Guilds also provided training, as masters in each craft took on young apprentices. Apprentices typically worked with their masters for several years to learn the trade, then became journeymen who labored for wages, and perhaps eventually masters with their own shops or businesses. Some merchant guilds became so influential that they virtually controlled their towns.

Medieval towns were often unpleasant places. They were typically filled with vermin and waste, which served as breeding grounds for disease, and often torn by strife between merchants selling goods from other places and local craft guilds seeking to shield their members from such competition. Apprentices were often exploited, and sometimes even cruelly abused, by their masters. Women were frequently confined to occupations, such as clothes making and domestic service, that were far less prestigious and profitable than crafts and guilds controlled by men.

Medieval walled town.

The Rise of Royal Authority

As towns grew in power and wealth, they sought freedom from the local warlords, who over the centuries had developed into a landed nobility. Some towns strove to assert their own autonomy, while others allied with kings who, eager to expand their power by reducing that of the nobility, were often willing to work with townsfolk against local nobles. The kings issued charters, granting towns the right to establish their own governments and law courts. In return, instead of paying dues to the local noble warlord for protection, these towns now paid taxes to the king, enabling him to hire officials and soldiers so he could rely less on nobles to administer and defend the realm. Under royal protection, the towns also often became havens for peasants escaping their noble landlords, further undermining the influence of the landed nobility.

Towns help strengthen monarchs over landed nobles

The crusades and other foreign wars also motivated monarchs to increase their authority. To organize and finance such complex, costly ventures, kings found it useful to centralize their administrative and tax-collecting systems. In so doing, they not only made their governments more effective, but also made themselves more powerful and wealthy.

Different monarchs used different means to centralize their power. In France, for example, King Philip II Augustus (1180–1223) expanded his control by appointing for each province officials called baillis (*bī-YĒ*) to exercise authority and collect taxes in the name of the king. To ensure their loyalty, he made sure that the baillis had no ties to the provinces they governed and were paid good salaries directly by him. In England, King Henry II (1154–1189) focused on law and order, creating an extensive judicial system that was run by the central government rather than by local lords, thereby enhancing justice, stability, and royal authority.

Monarchs gain power by controlling courts and local officials

Other rulers were hampered by strong opposition from nobility. Henry's son King John (1199–1216), for example, having fallen deeply in debt, was forced in 1215 to accept the **Magna Carta**, a "Great Charter" that affirmed the nobles' rights, placed the king firmly under the law, and barred him from raising new taxes without their consent. In Germany, Emperor Frederick Barbarossa (1152–1190) had to concede broad political and military autonomy to the local princes in return for their recognition of him as overlord.

The general trend of governance in the High Middle Ages was nonetheless toward centralized monarchies. The growth of European populations and economies increased not only the size of royal treasuries and budgets but also the need for more powerful and effective central governments, strengthening the authority of the kings.

The Revitalized Roman Church

Despite the growing power of the monarchs, the Roman Church continued to thrive as Europe's central institution. As Pope Urban II had hoped, his leadership in launching the crusades enabled his successors for the next few centuries to act as political overlords as well as spiritual leaders. Furthermore, since most western Christians saw the Church as the key to their salvation, many donated lands and riches to it in hopes of gaining God's favor. Church wealth and power reached a peak under Pope Innocent III (1198–1216), the initiator of the Fourth Crusade. With huge revenues and a powerful bureaucracy, he crushed heresies, meddled freely in politics, arranged royal marriages, and decided disputes among rulers.

Roman Church and papacy dominate medieval Europe

Map 16.3 Europe in the High Middle Ages, 1050–1300

Europe's High Middle Ages, lasting from roughly 1050 to 1300, witnessed the emergence of cities, universities, and monarchies in Western and Central Europe. Note that the Holy Roman Emperors, whose realm looks impressive on the map, did not manage to fully centralize their power, so the empire was home to many small states that exercised considerable autonomy, while recognizing the emperor as their nominal overlord. How did the growth of cities, commerce, learning, and monarchies help to transform Europe in the High Middle Ages?

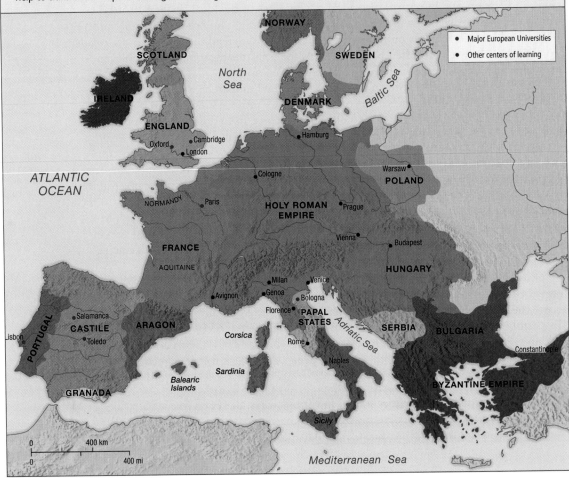

New religious orders also revitalized the Church. The Cistercians, founded in 1098 in what is now eastern France, set up monasteries in remote woods and wastelands to avoid worldly corruption. Under the dynamic leadership of Saint Bernard of Clairvaux (*clār-VŌ*) (1090–1153), who promoted the Second Crusade, the Cistercians acquired vast influence; by 1200 they had more than 500 monasteries. The Dominicans, founded in 1215 in southern France by Saint Dominic (1170–1221), took a different approach: rather than withdrawing from society as monks, they instead became *friars*, living in the world as beggars and becoming Europe's great preachers and teachers.

Another famous order of friars was founded by the era's most beloved Christian saint. After a dissolute youth as the son of a wealthy merchant, Francesco Bernadone (*bār-nah-DŌN-ā*) (1182–1226) had a radical change of heart. He gave up his possessions, dressed in rags, and lived in stark simplicity, ministering to the poor and outcast, and even to animals and birds. His Christ-like compassion attracted many followers, including the future Saint Clare, who started an order of Poor Sisters. He also won the trust of Pope Innocent III, who in 1209 approved what became the Franciscan order: a community of preachers, missionaries, and teachers devoted to the ideals of gentle, faithful Francesco, later revered as Saint Francis of Assisi (*ah-SĒ-zē*).

Cistercians, Dominicans, and Franciscans revitalize Roman Church

Yet the Church's wealth and power also attracted ambitious men who engaged in rampant corruption, and the use of crusaders to fight the Church's foes set a precedent for the use of force against other groups. Jews, for example, forbidden to own land in many countries, frequently worked in towns and cities as artisans, bankers, and merchants. Although they contributed greatly to medieval commerce, their efforts often drew abuse from their Christian competitors and neighbors, many of whom believed false rumors that Jewish religious rites used the blood of young Christians. Christians who dissented from Church teachings, denounced as heretics by Church leaders, typically faced violent suppression, sowing the seeds for great religious conflicts in the sixteenth century (Chapter 20).

European Christians persecute Jews and dissenters

Intellectual and Cultural Developments

Also sown in the High Middle Ages were seeds of scholarship and learning. Confucian academies had long prepared young men in China for civil service, and Muslims had set up learned academies that gathered great scholars in one place. Building on such ideas, Europeans in the High Middle Ages developed the **university**, an educational institution in which scholars from various fields helped students become experts and then granted them degrees to certify their expertise. A university typically consisted of several colleges, each of which served as a sort of educational guild, providing training, setting standards, and accrediting those who mastered their field.

Universities emerge as centers of medieval learning

Medieval European universities started in various ways. In 1088 some students in Bologna (*buh-LŌN-yah*), an Italian town that had become a center for the study of Roman law, formed an association to hire and set standards for teachers. In Paris, around 1170, teachers at the cathedral school formed an instructor's guild and later organized into faculties of arts, law, medicine, and theology. Thus began the Universities of Bologna and Paris; others soon arose at Oxford and Cambridge in England, Naples in Italy, and Salamanca (*sah-lah-MAHN-kah*) in Spain (Map 16.3).

Paris, meanwhile, became a center of **scholasticism**, a system of study combining Christian faith with ancient Greek philosophy, especially that of Aristotle. Contacts with the Muslim world acquainted Paris scholars not with only the works of al-Khwarizmi and Ibn Sina but also with the works of such intellectual giants as Ibn Rushd (Averroes), the great Spanish Muslim thinker, and Moses Maimonides (*mī-MAH-nuh-dēz*), the noted Jewish philosopher who was also Saladin's court physician (Chapter 12). Building on their work, which reconciled Aristotle's pagan philosophy with Muslim and Jewish monotheism, Thomas Aquinas (*uh-KWĪ-nuss*) (1225–1274), a Dominican teacher at the

Medieval scholasticism is based on Greek and Muslim thinking

University of Paris, synthesized Aristotle's ideas with Christian theology. Arguing that scholars must use both faith and reason to learn about God and the world, Thomas became medieval Europe's dominant thinker. His writings, especially his monumental summary of theology, the *Summa Theologica* (*SOO-mah thā-uh-LŌ-jē-kah*), served for centuries as the main foundation of Western thought.

Gothic churches arise as the dominant medieval architecture

As Thomas used reason to reveal God's truth, the French monk Suger (*soo-ZHĀ*) used architecture. As head of a monastery at Saint-Denis (*san-duh-NĒ*) near Paris from 1122 to 1151, Suger constructed a new church, developing a new architectural style soon copied across much of Europe. Earlier churches were bulky and dark, their heavy roofs supported by thick stone walls with round arches and small windows. But the new **Gothic architecture** produced soaring churches with pointed arches and towering walls, braced by external support beams called flying buttresses, which freed vast expanses of wall for stained glass windows that bathed church interiors in radiant light. Cities and towns spent fortunes and decades erecting these majestic cathedrals, which embellished and transformed the European landscape.

Gothic cathedral of Notre Dame in Paris.

Exaltation of Women and Marriage

Cathedral construction in the twelfth and thirteenth centuries coincided with a growing devotion to the Virgin Mary, mother of Jesus Christ. Mary emerged as the Church's foremost saint, revered as the mother of God and honored by festivals, prayers, paintings, statues, and shrines. Many Gothic churches, including famous French cathedrals at Paris, Chartres (*SHART*), and Reims (*RĒMZ*), were named Notre Dame (*nō-truh-DAHM*) ("Our Lady") in her honor.

The cult of Mary in turn reflected an idealization of women. Among knights a code of chivalry extolled gallantry and loyalty to one's lady as well as one's lord. Male poets and minstrels called troubadours praised women as wondrous beings who inspired their men to feats of ardor and courage, while a new literature called "romance" exalted courtly romantic love on the part of men toward their ladies.

Medieval Church idealizes women and marriage

Marriage, too, was exalted, defined by the Church as a sacrament, a vehicle of God's grace, and carefully protected by Church law. Marriage to close relatives was banned, as were divorce and remarriage; children born outside of marriage were deemed "illegitimate" and barred from entering the priesthood or receiving their parents' inheritance. Women were expected, like the Virgin Mary, to be loyal wives and mothers, devoted to the service of husband and family.

Some women, in this service, acquired substantial influence. Wives of nobles, for example, frequently managed their estates, as the men were often away on military duties. And royal women at times exercised real power: Eleanor of Aquitaine (*AK-wih-tān*) (1122–1204), having gone on crusade as wife of French King Louis VII, later governed England during the absences of her second husband, King Henry II, and crusading son, Richard the Lionheart.

Such women, however, were exceptions. Lower-class women played important roles—brewing ale, baking bread, making clothes, raising children, caring for the sick, and helping with the harvest—but socially and legally they were subject to men. And the institutional Church, despite its exaltation of womanhood and marriage, was entirely run by celibate males.

The Decline of the Middle Ages

By 1300, the basic structure of Western civilization, with its thriving commercial cities, maturing national monarchies, powerful Christian Church, and Christian-centered intellectual and social institutions, was firmly in place. But in the years that followed this structure was badly shaken. Battered by Church decline, famine, plague, and constant warfare, Europe's medieval civilization started to unravel, creating a climate of foreboding and fear.

The Avignon Popes

The deterioration of medieval Europe began with the decline of the Church. As national monarchs increased in power and wealth, they were much less willing to accept papal dominance. A crisis began in 1294 when France's King Philip IV the Fair (1272–1307), on the verge of war against England, imposed heavy taxes on the French clergy. Pope Boniface VIII (1294–1303), forbidding him to do so without papal consent, ordered the priests not to pay. But the king struck back, suspending all shipments of church revenues to Rome. Faced with this resistance, the pope for a time backed down.

In 1302, however, Boniface renewed the conflict by issuing an edict declaring that all rulers, indeed all humans, are subject to the pope. Philip retaliated by sending his agents to kidnap the pope, thereby shocking all Europe. The aged and ailing Boniface was soon freed by supporters, but died the next year a broken man.

Clash between pope and king of France creates crisis

The Church's crisis nonetheless continued. In 1309 a new pope, pressured by Philip the Fair, moved from Rome to Avignon (*AH-vēn-YŌN*), a papal enclave bordering southern France. Thus began a long period (1309–1377), often called the Church's Babylonian Captivity (recalling the Biblical Jewish exile in Babylon), during which eight popes in succession lived at Avignon rather than Rome. Although not under direct French control, they were clearly under French influence, undermining their credibility and offending most of Europe.

Famine, Plague, and Social Unrest

While thus deprived of effective spiritual leadership, Europeans were hit with several horrific disasters. A changing climate, marked by colder weather and heavier rains, wreaked havoc with the food supply, already endangered by population growth. Catastrophe struck in 1315–1317, when floods in the North led to deadly famine in which tens of thousands died, while others ate farm animals and seed crops to survive. Further crop failures in 1333, 1337, and 1345–1347 left the population weak, malnourished, and susceptible to disease.

A plague victim.

Then, in fall 1347, a merchant ship returning to Genoa from Kaffa on the Black Sea landed in Sicily with a deadly cargo. In its hold were rats infested with the plague that had recently ravaged much of Asia (Chapter 15). Carried by fleas from rats to humans (bubonic plague), or spread by the coughing of afflicted people (pneumonic plague), the disease devastated Europe from 1347 through 1351. Death toll estimates range from 25 to 45 million people, roughly 30 to 60 percent of Europe's population. Since victims, who often died in three to five days, were covered with dark swellings, the plague at the time was commonly called the "Black Death."

Commerce helps spread bubonic plague from Asia to Europe

Map 16.4 Europe Ravaged by Plague Pandemic, 1347–1351

Known in Europe as the "Black Death," the plague pandemic killed perhaps 30–60 percent of Europe's people, depopulating cities, disrupting commerce, and traumatizing European society. Compare this map with Map 15.8, observing that the plague, having swept westward across Eurasia thanks to Mongol-developed connections, spread from the Black Sea port of Kaffa by ship through Constantinople to Sicily and southern Italy in 1347, then ravaged much of the rest of Europe during the next few years. What key impacts did the plague pandemic have on European society?

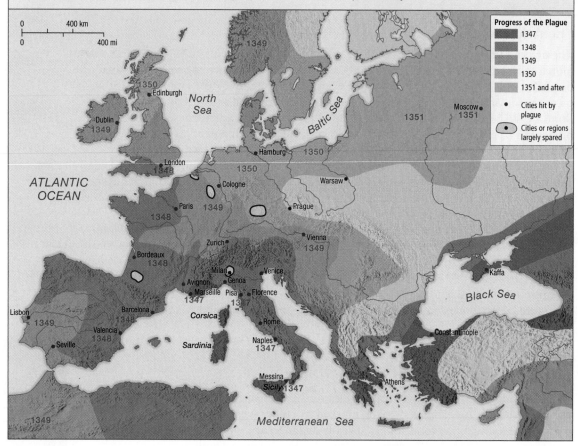

Progress of the Plague
- 1347
- 1348
- 1349
- 1350
- 1351 and after
- • Cities hit by plague
- ⊙ Cities or regions largely spared

The plague, spread by fleas on rats, kills millions in cities and towns

The cities, where people were crowded together and streets were full of sewage and rats, were hit especially hard (Map 16.4). Victims, whose bodies gave off a vile stench, often were left uncared for, as others refrained from assisting them for fear of catching the disease. Hoping to save themselves, thousands fled the cities, helping to spread the plague to the countryside.

Unaware of what caused the disease, many people saw it as divine punishment for the sins of Church and society. Some joined groups of flagellants (*FLAJ-uh-luntz*), people who whipped themselves with chains and leather straps in hopes of gaining God's mercy. Others, however, assuming their time was short, indulged in the pleasures of food, drink,

Document 16.2 Excerpts on the Plague from Boccaccio's *Decameron*

The Decameron, an entertaining literary work by early Renaissance author Giovanni Boccaccio, is a collection of tales supposedly told by people who had fled from Florence to a nearby villa while the plague was ravaging that city in 1348. At the start of his narrative, Boccaccio provides a graphic description of the plague and its impact on the people of Florence.

In the year 1348 . . . , that most beautiful of Italian cities, Florence, was attacked by a deadly plague. It started in the East either through the influence of the heavenly bodies or because God's just anger with our wicked deeds sent it as a punishment to mortal men; and in a few years killed an innumerable quantity of people . . . The symptoms were not the same as in the East, where a gush of blood from the nose was the plain sign of inevitable death; but it began both in men and women with certain swellings in the groin or under the armpit. They grew to the size of a small apple or egg, more or less, and were vulgarly called tumours. In a short space of time these tumours spread . . . all over the body. Soon after this the symptoms changed and black or purple spots appeared on the arms or thighs or any other part of the body . . . These spots were a certain sign of death . . . most people died within about three days . . .

The violence of this disease was such that the sick communicated it to the healthy who came near them . . . To speak to or go near the sick brought infection and a common death to the living . . .

From these . . . occurrences, such fear and fanciful notions took possession of the living so that almost all of them adopted the same cruel policy, which was entirely to avoid the sick and everything belonging to them . . .

Some thought that moderate living and avoidance of all superfluity would preserve them from the epidemic. They formed small communities, living entirely separately from everybody else. They shut themselves up in houses where there were no sick . . . Others thought just the opposite. They thought the cure for the plague was to drink and be merry, to go about singing and amusing themselves . . . , laughing and jesting at what happened. They . . . spent day and night going from tavern to tavern . . .

Others again held a still more cruel opinion . . . They said that the only medicine against the plague stricken was to go right away from them. Men and women, . . . caring about nothing but themselves, abandoned their own city, their own houses, their dwellings, their relatives, their property, and went abroad or at least to the country around Florence . . .

Thus a multitude of sick men and women were left without any care . . . Owing to the lack of attendants for the sick and the violence of the plague, such a multitude of people in the city died day and night that it was stupefying to hear of, let alone to see.

SOURCE: Giovanni Boccaccio, *The Decameron,* translated by Richard Aldington, 1949, 1–4.

and sex. Some tried witchcraft or magic; others secluded themselves from human contact (see "Excerpts on the Plague from Boccaccio's *Decameron*"). Still others attacked the Jews, blaming them for the tragedy.

Even when the plague was gone, its impact remained. Trade was disrupted, as ports turned away ships and towns excluded outsiders. With few workers left to till fields, farms often went untended. Grotesque folk art showed skeletons doing a "Dance of Death," reflecting a general sense of doom.

The plague disrupts trade and farming and fosters a sense of doom

The shortage of workers forced employers to pay higher wages, leading many landlords to let peasants own some land to keep them from leaving the manor for better pay elsewhere. Some nobles tried passing laws to keep wages down and the peasants in place, only to have these efforts spark rebellion. French peasants, often called "Jacques" (*ZHAHK*) by their lords, went on a rampage called the Jacquerie (*zhah-KRĒ*) in 1358, looting and burning manor houses and killing a number of nobles. The lords responded ruthlessly, slaying some 20,000 rebels. In England, villagers and townsfolk alike joined a 1381 Peasants' Revolt led by a rebel called Wat Tyler, who demanded equality for all, claiming God had not created a privileged class of "gentleman" nobles. "When Adam delved and Eve span," asked the rebels, recalling the Bible's first humans, "who was then the gentle man?" Although these and other similar revolts were crushed, the labor shortage improved workers' wages and helped many peasants escape serfdom.

The Great Western Schism

The Church divides, with two and later three competing popes

Compounding Europe's chaos, the Church's ongoing crisis got even worse. In 1377, aiming to end the scandal, the reigning pope moved back from Avignon to Rome, then died the following year. Intimidated by a Roman mob, the cardinals elected in his place an Italian, Pope Urban VI, who boldly attacked Church abuses. Threatened by his reforms, a number of cardinals, most of them French, later reconvened and declared his election invalid. They chose as their pope the French king's cousin, who set himself up at Avignon. But Urban VI in Rome refused to step down, so now there were two competing popes. This Great Western Schism (1378–1417) scandalized all Europe, dividing it between supporters of Avignon and Rome. Hoping to resolve the crisis, in 1409 a council at Pisa deposed both popes and chose a new one, but the other two defied it, producing a three-way split.

Finally, a Council at Constance (1414–1418) ended the schism by persuading two of the three popes to step down and resume their former status as cardinals. The third, unreconciled, fled to a Mediterranean island, from which he excommunicated the rest of the Christian world. Despite this lonely defiance, a newly-chosen pope called Martin V (1417–1431) was able to rule from Rome with general support. But by then the papacy's status had been badly damaged.

Europe in Disarray

In the midst of all these crises, France and England added to the chaos by fighting a series of conflicts called the Hundred Years War (1337–1453). It began with a dispute over who should be king of France and was fought mainly on French soil. Gunpowder cannons and firearms, knowledge of which by then had reached Europe through the Mongols and Muslims, were forged and used by both sides in this conflict, adding to the devastation.

By the 1420s, after winning some substantial victories, the English held large parts of France and seemed on the verge of triumph. But the tide turned in 1429 when a French teenager named Joan of Arc, believing God had summoned her to drive the English from France, inspired French soldiers with a new sense of purpose and pride. As a result, although the English later got hold of Joan and executed her as a heretic, when the war finally ended in 1453 they had lost almost all their possessions in France.

Political conflict also troubled Central Europe. Its nominal overlords, the Holy Roman Emperors, failed to centralize their power, leaving Germany divided into numerous small states while five great families competed for the position of emperor. The Golden Bull, an edict issued in 1356 by Emperor Charles IV, provided some stability by designating seven

An English longbow, as used in the Hundred Years War.

key regional leaders as electors who would choose each new emperor by majority vote. But it also recognized the autonomy of the various local rulers, leaving the empire still divided and weak. In 1438 the electors chose as emperor the head of Austria's Habsburg (*HAHPZ-boork*) family, beginning a succession of Habsburg rulers who held the imperial title almost continuously until 1806. The Habsburgs increased their possessions through strategic marriages, but failed to create a centralized German state.

The European Renaissance

During the fourteenth century, even as Europe was racked with disasters, foundations were laid for a cultural revival, known as the Renaissance ("rebirth"), which lasted until the sixteenth century. It began in Italy, where growing commercial wealth amid ruins of Roman grandeur inspired efforts to restore the culture of the classical age. Based initially in Florence, an Italian city-state and wealthy banking center, the Renaissance eventually brought a new vitality to culture and society throughout Europe.

In the Renaissance, as in the High Middle Ages, connections with other cultures were crucial to European cultural renewal. The Renaissance was rooted in Europe's rediscovery of ancient Greek and Roman art and thought, advanced by contacts with Islamic and Byzantine artists and scholars. It was funded largely by wealth acquired through commerce with Eastern cultures and by the banking system that supported such trade. And it was enhanced by technologies such as paper and printing, developed in China and spread westward through the Muslim world.

Contacts with Muslims, Byzantines, and Asians help enhance Renaissance

In the Renaissance, as in the High Middle Ages, religious themes and the Church played a central role. But the Renaissance focused on life in this world rather than life after death.

Roots and Attributes of the Renaissance

Early in the fourteenth century, Florence produced two pivotal figures who helped lay the foundations for the Renaissance. One was the painter Giotto (*JAW-tō*) (1267–1337), whose portrayals of saints and biblical scenes pioneered **artistic realism**. He created portraits that were lifelike, showing detail, depth, and perspective, overcoming the flatness and stylized rigidity of earlier medieval art. The other was the writer Dante Alighieri (*DAHN-tā ah-lig-YĀ-rē*) (1265–1321), whose poetic masterpiece, the *Divine Comedy*, portrays him as a pilgrim traveling through hell, purgatory, and heaven. Full of Christian devotion, the work also uses biting satire, mocking many popes and rulers by depicting them in hell. Composed in Italian rather than in Latin, it pioneered **vernacular literature**, written in the everyday spoken language of the common people.

Crucifix painted by Giotto.

A generation later, Florence supplied the two great writers who began the Renaissance. Scorning medieval European culture as Germanic and crude, Francesco Petrarch (*PĀ-trark*) (1304–1374) worked to revive the literature of ancient Rome. He collected ancient Latin texts, wrote letters to famous ancient Romans, composed accounts of their lives, and even penned a Latin epic poem. Yet he also used the vernacular, writing beautiful love sonnets in Italian to a woman named Laura who perished in the plague. Petrarch's contemporary, Giovanni Boccaccio (*bō-KAH-chō*) (1313–1375), likewise wrote in Italian vernacular. Boccaccio is best known for *The Decameron* (*dē-KAM-uh-ron*), a collection of 100 stories

Petrarch and Boccaccio begin literary Renaissance

told by ten people to amuse themselves while secluded in an estate outside Florence to escape the plague (see "Excerpts on the Plague from Boccaccio's *Decameron*," page 397). Witty, racy, and bawdy, dealing with intrigue, adventure, and sex, the stories are designed to entertain, not to enlighten. Boccaccio depicted people as they really *were*—charming, crude, and corrupt—not as they *should be*.

Vernacular literature spreads from Italy to northern Europe

Soon engaging vernacular literature also appeared in the North. In English verse, Geoffrey Chaucer (1340–1400) wrote the *Canterbury Tales*, an assortment of lively, earthy stories told by thirty people from all walks of life traveling together on pilgrimage. In French, Christine de Pisan (*pē-ZAHN*) (1363–1430) wrote biographies, poems, and works about women, challenging her era's gender barriers. Many Latin texts were also translated into French, German, English, and Czech.

Classicism, secularism, and individualism characterize Renaissance humanism

Another key feature of Renaissance culture was **humanism**, an outlook emphasizing the value of humans and their activities. Renaissance humanism incorporated *classicism*, *secularism*, and *individualism*. Spurning as Germanic the culture of the Middle Ages, it revered the classical culture of ancient Greece and Rome. Altering the medieval focus on faith and spirituality, it celebrated secular ideals and worldly beauty, even when dealing with religious themes. Rejecting the medieval emphasis on humility and community, it stressed individual pride and achievement.

The Italian Renaissance

In fifteenth-century Italy the Renaissance expanded and flourished. Remains of the ancient Roman world, which surrounded Italians, sustained their desire to revive their region's past glory. The wealth of merchants and city-states, acquired mainly through commerce, enabled them to enhance their prestige by patronizing the arts. And an influx of artists and scholars from the Byzantine Empire, which fell to the Turks in 1453, added to the depth and diversity of Italy's cultural renewal.

Renaissance Italy was politically divided, with the Kingdom of Naples in the South, the Papal States (lands ruled by the pope) in the center, and various independent city-states in the North. The leading city-states—Venice, Milan, Genoa, and Florence—were wealthy commercial centers that ruled the lands around them (Map 16.5). Although organized as republics, each was run from behind the scenes by prominent wealthy families. To gain

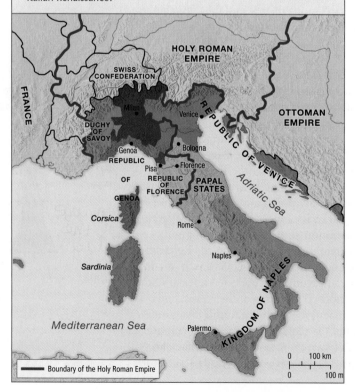

Map 16.5 Political Divisions in Fifteenth-Century Italy

During the Italian Renaissance, Italy was distinguished by artistic expression and by political disunity. Note Italy's division into a variety of city-states, duchies, republics, and kingdoms, with the Papal States in the center, ruled by the pope in Rome. How did commercial and cultural competition among these small states help to bolster the Italian Renaissance?

prestige and enhance civic pride, these families promoted art and culture, often competing to outdo each other.

RENAISSANCE FLORENCE. Florence again led the way. For much of the fifteenth century it was dominated by the Medici (*MED-ih-chē*), a rich banking family that used its fortune to fund the creation of paintings, sculptures, palaces, and churches by the great masters of the day. Many wealthy merchants did likewise, while guilds held contests to decide which artists, sculptors, and architects to commission for major projects.

In 1401 a contest was held to decide who would design the bronze doors of the Florence Baptistry (page 382), a chapel used mainly for baptisms. The winner, Lorenzo Ghiberti (*gē-BAR-tē*) (1378–1455), spent decades creating two sets of majestic doors, made up of panels depicting Biblical scenes, sculpted and cast in bronze. The loser, Filippo Brunelleschi (*broo-nuh-LESS-kē*) (1377–1446), went on to gain fame as an architect, designing chapels and cathedrals for the Medici, the city's cloth merchants, and other wealthy Florentines. Models of perspective and symmetry, his works are relatively small, constructed on a human scale in the spirit of the Renaissance, unlike the towering medieval Gothic churches built for exaltation of God.

Donatello (*dō-nah-TELL-ō*) (1386–1466), a student and rival of Ghiberti, emerged as the city's leading sculptor. A master of anatomy, Donatello created the West's first major nude statue since Roman times, depicting the Hebrew hero David in bronze. His starkly realistic works also included a monumental equestrian bronze sculpture of a Venetian warrior, capturing the power and dignity of horse and rider, and a marvelous wooden statue of a gaunt and aging Mary Magdalene, a friend of Jesus believed by some to have been a repentant prostitute.

The standard for Florentine painting was set by Masaccio (*mah-SAH-chō*) (1401–1428), a youthful artist who improved on the realism of Giotto. Masaccio used perspective, shadows, and light to create a three-dimensional effect, conveying his subjects' personalities through striking stances and expressions. He also mastered the art of **fresco**, or painting on walls when the plaster was still wet so the colors would penetrate it. Later Sandro Botticelli (*bō-tih-CHELL-ē*) (1445–1510), not satisfied merely to depict reality, sought to transcend it by creating beauty, using bright colors, fanciful themes, and sensuous depictions of female anatomy in works such as *Spring* and *Birth of Venus*.

Renaissance Florence also produced several outstanding writers. One was Leon Battista Alberti (*al-BAIR-tē*) (1404–1472), whose treatises *On Building* and *On Family* set the era's standards on architecture and virtue. A multi-talented architect, athlete, scholar, sculptor, and statesman, he embodied the ideal of the well-rounded Renaissance man. Another was Niccolo Machiavelli (*MAH-kē-uh-VELL-ē*) (1469–1527), whose classic work, *The Prince*, devised as a ruler's guidebook for unifying Italy, separated politics from ethics. Focusing not on how statesmen *should* act but on how they *do* act, and not on what is *right* but on what *works*, *The Prince* pragmatically advises rulers to use deceit and violence when necessary to achieve their goals. *ends justify means*

THE HIGH RENAISSANCE. In the early 1500s, envious of Florence's success, ambitious popes such as Julius II (1503–1513) and Leo X (1513–1521) hired prominent artists, architects, and sculptors to help restore Rome as Christendom's greatest city. Thus began the Roman or High Renaissance, an era dominated by three great figures: Leonardo, Raphael, and Michelangelo.

Sketch for a helicopter by Leonardo da Vinci.

Leonardo da Vinci emerges as universal genius

Raphael expresses female beauty and classical harmony

Michelangelo displays superhuman talent as a sculptor and artist

Leonardo da Vinci (1452–1519) started as a painter in Florence, but clashed with the Medici and left in 1482 for Milan, whose ruling family gave him greater freedom of expression. There he produced his first masterpiece, *Virgin of the Rocks*. In this portrait of a serene mother and children among plants and boulders, Leonardo displayed a gift for depicting both nature and human psychology. While in Milan he also painted on a convent wall his monumental *Last Supper*, an emotional drama that peers into the apostles' hearts as each reacts to Jesus's disclosure that "one of you will betray me." Leaving Milan in 1499, Leonardo traveled about Italy, spent time in Rome, and then settled in France under royal patronage. In 1503–1506 he created the world's most famous portrait, a beguiling psychological study of *La Gioconda* (*lah jō-KON-dah*), better known today as *Mona Lisa.*

Considered one of history's greatest artists, Leonardo was also a scientist, sculptor, naturalist, engineer, musician, and inventor. Possessing boundless curiosity, he studied plants, anatomy, optics, mathematics, currents, clouds, and birds' wings. He sketched plans for devices, such as helicopters, submarines, and tanks, whose actual invention lay centuries in the future. He was a visionary and universal genius.

Raphael (*RAH-fī-EL*) (1483–1520), most beloved of Renaissance painters, was known for his exquisite madonnas (portraits of the Virgin Mary) and depictions of female beauty. Born in Urbino, he spent time in Florence before 1508, when Pope Julius II brought him to Rome to decorate the papal palace, known as the Vatican because it sits on Vatican Hill. Raphael's *School of Athens*, a huge fresco mural in the Vatican study, is a full expression of the Renaissance spirit. It depicts classical Greek philosophers, some of them painted in the likeness of Renaissance figures, in a setting of harmony and symmetry. In the center are Plato, flanked by theoretical philosophers and pointing upward toward idealism and inspiration, and Aristotle, flanked by logicians and rationalists, with his arm outstretched downward toward realism and moderation.

If Raphael captured the Renaissance spirit, Michelangelo (1475–1564) transcended it. Raised and trained as a sculptor in Florence, he moved to Rome at age 21 and soon caused a sensation with his *Pietà* (*pē-ā-TAH*), a magnificent marble statue of the Virgin Mary cradling the dead body of her son Jesus. In 1501 Michelangelo was called back to Florence to create a statue of David, the Biblical giant-killer, to symbolize the city's resistance to tyranny. In three years he produced a work of superhuman proportions, an imposing 17-foot likeness of a muscular youth, giant, defiant, and nude.

With singular audacity, in 1508 Pope Julius II summoned the great sculptor to Rome and hired him to paint the ceiling of the Vatican's Sistine Chapel. Lying on his back atop scaffolding near the ceiling, Michelangelo labored four years to produce in fresco a work of colossal genius, an immense set of murals depicting Bible scenes from *Creation* to the *Flood*. In 1536 he added another fresco, the somber and imposing *Last Judgment*, on the chapel's altar wall. In his later years, as he continued to create masterpieces of sculpture, Michelangelo also served as chief architect for Saint Peter's Basilica in Rome, a monumental edifice whose construction had begun in the reign of Julius II.

Politically, the High Renaissance was a time of turmoil and foreign intervention in Italy. Trouble began in 1494 when Milan, on the verge of war against Naples and Florence, asked France for help. Seizing the opportunity, the French invaded and conquered much of Italy, leading the pope to seek assistance from Spain. The next three decades were marked by foreign intervention and internal war, culminating in 1527, when Rome

Michelangelo's David.

was sacked by foreign forces supposedly sent to help the pope. After this attack the Italian Renaissance subsided. As the Spanish opened the Atlantic, eroding Italy's commercial leadership, and as the Protestant movement challenged Rome's religious primacy, Italians lost their undisputed leadership of Western fortune, faith, and culture.

The Northern European Renaissance

Northern Europe, meanwhile, had its own Renaissance, which differed from the Italian in several key respects. First, it was less classical: northerners studied Greco-Roman classics but did not try to imitate ancient culture. Second, it was less secular: it promoted Christian morals, studied early Church fathers, criticized abuses in the Church and society, and abhorred the worldliness of Renaissance popes. Third, it built upon medieval culture rather than rejecting it. Finally, it was less lavish and more practical, partly because northerners had less wealth, and partly because they were offended by Italian extravagance and indulgence.

The northern Renaissance proves less classical and worldly than the Italian

FOUNDATIONS OF THE NORTHERN RENAISSANCE. In the 1400s, two key figures laid the foundations for the northern Renaissance. One was Jan van Eyck (*YAHN van ĪK*), the first in a series of superb artists from Flanders, a region (now part of Belgium) where commercial towns such as Bruges (*BROOZH*), Ghent, and Antwerp enjoyed prosperity and civic pride like that of northern Italy. Van Eyck (1395–1441) mastered the use of oil paints, which produced vivid colors and dried slowly, giving the artist time to paint with patience and precision. He also perfected the realism introduced by Giotto, meticulously portraying the appearances and lifestyles of his subjects. His masterpieces, including the Arnolfini portrait and the Ghent altarpiece, display unsurpassed attention to detail and light.

Northern artist Jan van Eyck perfects realism, perspective, and detail

The other founding figure of the northern Renaissance was the German inventor Johannes Gutenberg (*GOO-ten-berg*) (1400–1468), who began a communications revolution. European books had long been copied by hand onto costly animal-skin parchment, making them expensive and rare. The use of paper and printing from carved wooden blocks, developed initially in China, had spread to Europe in the 1300s by way of the Mongols and Muslims. But this printing process still involved much time and expense, since a whole block had to be carved for each page. In the 1450s, however, Gutenberg began making books by using **movable type**, small metal blocks for each letter, arranged in a frame to print one page and then rearranged and reused to print others. Multiple copies of each page were made by inking the type and pressing it on paper, using a **printing press** similar to the presses used to crush grapes for wine. The use of the movable type printing press spread quickly, vastly increasing the number of books and decreasing their cost. It thereby advanced the spread of ideas and knowledge, at first among the educated elite, but eventually among the masses too.

Gutenberg's movable-type printing press fuels communication revolution

An early printing press.

NORTHERN WRITERS AND ARTISTS. In the early 1500s, as the Renaissance moved north, the printing press helped spread the views of several outstanding writers. One was Dutch humanist Erasmus (*ih-RAZZ-muss*) (1466–1536), the era's most influential thinker. After leaving the monastery where he spent his younger years, Erasmus lived and wrote in various places, winning universal respect as a man of insight, tolerance, and honesty. Dismayed by the Church's elaborate ritualism and scholasticism's rigid formalism, he promoted instead a simple, humane piety called the "philosophy of Christ." His works included *Handbook of the Christian Knight* (1503), a guide to moral living in a corrupt

Northern writers criticize corruption; artists stress innovation

society, and *The Praise of Folly* (1509), a witty, stinging satire that ridiculed the hypocrisy of monks, bishops, lawyers, and scholars.

Another key writer of the northern Renaissance was Erasmus's friend Thomas More (1478–1535), a prominent English lawyer, statesman, and humanist. In 1516 More published *Utopia* ("nowhere"), a fictional journey to an imaginary island where people held property in common, worked together for the common good, and avoided poverty and war by using good sense and reason. By thus portraying his vision of an ideal society, More implicitly criticized by contrast the violence, corruption, and injustice of the society in which he lived. A man of talent and conviction, he later served as Lord Chancellor, England's highest official post, and eventually died a martyr for refusing to forsake the Roman Church.

Many northern artists were influenced by van Eyck's realism and use of oil paints, the style and technique of Italian painters, and the development of printing. One was Hans Holbein (*HŌL-bīn*) the Younger (1497–1543), a German portrait painter who worked in Switzerland and England, producing lifelike portrayals of such figures as Erasmus and More. Another was Albrecht Dürer (*DOOR-ur*) (1471–1528), son of a German goldsmith, who became Germany's most innovative artist. Inspired by visits to Italy, he combined Italian techniques of proportion and perspective with a northern talent for detail similar to van Eyck's, creating such paintings as *Adoration of the Magi* and *The Four Apostles*. But Dürer is best known for his woodcuts (carvings on wooden blocks) and engravings (etchings in copper), used to print multiple copies of the same work. These were then either sold as separate prints or used to illustrate books, making his art available to ordinary people. Although they lacked color, prints such as *The Four Horsemen of the Apocalypse* and *Knight, Death and the Devil* were genuine artistic masterpieces.

[handwritten note: another world / perfect world]

The Four Horsemen of the Apocalypse.

Social and Political Effects

The Renaissance was mainly an urban phenomenon, affecting primarily the cities, where three distinct social groups emerged. At the top were the patricians, wealthy merchants and bankers who dominated urban politics, lived in conspicuous extravagance, and hired artists and architects to exalt their status. In the middle were artisans and shopkeepers, typically members of guilds, who lived in reasonable comfort and often had some education. At the bottom were paid laborers, who subsisted on irregular wages, and the unemployed, who lived in dire poverty. Many cities were great centers of culture, but crowded conditions and lack of sanitation also made them breeding grounds for filth, squalor, stench, and disease.

Renaissance transforms warrior nobility into a cultured upper class

In the countryside, the Renaissance had less of an impact. Still, the landed nobility, originally a crude warrior class, began to assume a sense of refinement and gentility. According to the *Book of the Courtier* (1528), by Baldassare Castiglione (*kah-stēl-YŌ-nā*), the ideal gentleman should be classically educated, widely read, accomplished in arts and music, eloquent in speech, dignified in manner, and graceful in style. Ladies too might exhibit these traits, as education for noble and patrician women became increasingly common. But women were still largely excluded from public affairs, expected instead to be capable household managers and charming hostesses with good social skills.

Peasant life remains harsh, but serfdom declines

Although peasants, who still made up about 90 percent of the population, were affected least by the Renaissance, they did experience some important changes. The labor shortages created by fourteenth-century famines and plagues, along with growing opportunities and attractions in the cities and towns, helped to improve the lives of the common people. Many landlords sought to keep their peasants from leaving by granting them their own land, or by replacing compulsory labor with rent payable in cash. As a result, during the Renaissance serfdom declined, especially in Western Europe. In time, the increased availability of printed books also promoted growing public awareness and literacy among the lower classes.

Politically, the Renaissance advanced the formation of strong national monarchies (Map 16.6), as capable rulers increased both their own power and the unity of their

Renaissance monarchs further consolidate power

Map 16.6 Europe in the Late Fifteenth Century

During the fifteenth century, while the Renaissance engulfed Italy and spread to the rest of Europe, monarchs continued to consolidate their realms and expand their powers. Note, for example, that the marriage of the rulers of Castile and Aragon, and their completion of the *Reconquista* by ousting the Muslims from Granada, would lay the basis for a united Spain, soon to emerge as Europe's wealthiest power. How did growing commercial connections, and the growing strength of European monarchies, help to bolster Europe's power and wealth, despite its political divisions?

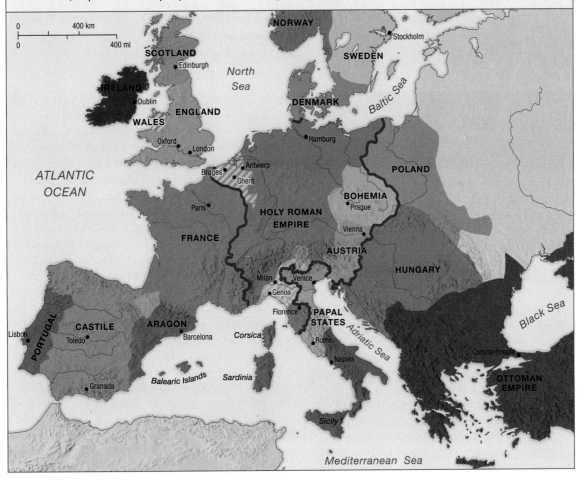

realms. In France, King Louis XI (1461–1483) imposed heavy taxes on the peasants and townsfolk, enlarged the royal army to avoid reliance on the nobles, and extended his direct control over various lands in the North, East, and South. In England, King Henry VII (1485–1509) put an end to three decades of dynastic strife, built up the royal treasury by managing his income frugally, and used his royal council to impose justice and control unruly nobles. In central Europe, Emperor Maximilian I of Habsburg (1493–1519), although unable to centralize control of the Holy Roman Empire, vastly expanded his family's domains by arranging astute marriages for himself and his son.

Castile and Aragon united; Spanish Inquisition and sea voyages begin

But the biggest political success came in Spain, a land long divided into separate states and ravaged by the *Reconquista*. Here the marriage of two monarchs, Isabella of Castile (1474–1504) and Ferdinand of Aragon (1479–1516), linked the two largest realms. To consolidate control and enforce Christian rule they used the Spanish **Inquisition**, a judicial institution that prosecuted people it identified as heretics—including many Jews and Muslims who outwardly converted to Christianity but privately practiced their old faith. In 1492 Isabella and Ferdinand completed the *Reconquista* by conquering Granada, the last Muslim outpost in Spain, and expelled most Jews from their domains. That same year a sea admiral named Columbus, sailing in Isabella's service, embarked on the first in a series of voyages that eventually gave Spain the world's largest empire, made it Europe's greatest power, and altered the course of world history.

Chapter Review

Putting It in Perspective

The West's resurgence was partly due to developments in Europe. The warming of its climate, the ingenuity of its farmers and artisans, and the ambition of its merchants and bankers all contributed to Europe's economic expansion, which supplied the resources to fund expensive enterprises. Energetic popes who reformed and revived the Roman Church, and determined monarchs who turned weak regimes into strong central governments, provided the leadership and stability needed for cultural growth. Talented scholars, artists, architects, and writers splendidly nourished this rebirth. Even the disasters of the fourteenth century, although they disrupted the West's resurgence, failed to derail it for long.

Europe's revitalization, however, also resulted from its contacts and conflicts with Islamic peoples, and its willingness to adopt from them whatever it found useful. From the Muslims, for example,

Europe borrowed the concept of combining warfare with religious zeal, launching its own set of Christian holy wars, or crusades. From Islamic scholars, Europe became acquainted with its own Greco-Roman legacy, and learned to combine its Christian faith with this classical heritage. Through Mongols and Muslims, Europe learned about gunpowder, paper, and printing, Chinese inventions that added greatly to Western power and influence. And it was also through the Muslims that Europe acquired a taste for the fine goods of the East and the wealth to be gained through eastern commerce. These tastes in time sent Europeans on great sea voyages aimed at taking control of this trade from the Islamic world.

But Europe's resurgence was not a sign of Muslim weakness. Indeed, the Muslim expulsion of Christian crusaders from the Holy Land and Western adaptation of Muslim innovations attested to Islamic preeminence. And, as we shall see in the next chapter, while Europe was having its Renaissance, Muslims were conquering Constantinople, rebuilding Persia, and subduing the Indian subcontinent, creating three great empires of their own.

Reviewing Key Material

KEY CONCEPTS

Reconquista, 384
guilds, 390
Magna Carta, 391
university, 393
scholasticism, 393
Gothic architecture, 394
artistic realism, 399

vernacular literature, 399
humanism, 400
fresco, 401
movable type, 403
printing press, 403
Inquisition, 406

KEY PEOPLE

Pope Urban II, 382, 384
Salah al-Din (Saladin), 387
Emperor Frederick
    Barbarossa, 388
King Richard I the
    Lionheart, 388
King Philip II Augustus,
    388
Pope Innocent III, 388
King Henry II, 391
Saint Bernard of
    Clairvaux, 392
Saint Dominic, 392
Saint Francis of Assisi,
    393
Thomas Aquinas, 393
Suger, 394
Eleanor of Aquitaine, 394
King Philip IV the Fair,
    395
Pope Boniface VIII, 395
Wat Tyler, 398
Joan of Arc, 398
Giotto, 399
Dante Alighieri, 399
Petrarch, 399

Boccaccio, 399
Chaucer, 400
Christine de Pisan, 400
Ghiberti, 401
Brunelleschi, 401
Donatello, 401
Masaccio, 401
Botticelli, 401
Alberti, 401
Machiavelli, 401
Pope Julius II, 401, 402
Leonardo da Vinci, 402
Raphael, 402
Michelangelo, 402
Jan van Eyck, 403
Gutenberg, 403
Erasmus, 403
Thomas More, 404
Hans Holbein, 404
Albrecht Dürer, 404
Castiglione, 404
Emperor Maximilian I
    of Habsburg, 406
Isabella of Castile, 406
Ferdinand of Aragon, 406

ASK YOURSELF

1. Why did Pope Urban II initiate the First Crusade? Why were the later crusades undertaken? What benefits and damages did Europe incur as a result of the crusades and *Reconquista*?

2. What factors contributed to Europe's political, economic, and cultural development during the High Middle Ages?

3. What factors led to the disasters and crises of fourteenth-century Europe? What were the social, economic, cultural, and political repercussions of these disasters and crises?

4. What were the main characteristics of the Renaissance? How did the spirit of the Renaissance differ from that of the High Middle Ages? How did the Northern European Renaissance differ from the Italian?

5. In what specific ways did contacts with the Muslim world influence Western commerce, culture, learning, and technology during the High Middle Ages and Renaissance?

GOING FURTHER

Asbridge, Thomas. *The First Crusade: A New History*. 2004.

Bartlett, Robert. *The Making of Europe, 950–1350*. 1993.

Brotton, J. *The Renaissance Bazaar: From the Silk Road to Michelangelo*. 2002.

Burke, P. *The European Renaissance: Centres and Peripheries*. 1998.

Cantor, Norman. *In the Wake of the Plague: The Black Death and the World It Made*. 2001.

Cohn, Samuel. *The Black Death Transformed*. 2003.

Curry, A. *The Hundred Years' War*. 1993.

Finucane, R. C. *Soldiers of the Faith*. 1983.

Gottfried, Robert S. *The Black Death*. 1983.

Hale, J. R. *The Civilization of Europe in the Renaissance*. 1994.

Hay, D., and J. Law. *Italy in the Age of the Renaissance*. 1989.

Herlihy, D. *The Black Death and Transformation of the West*. 1997.

Holmes, George. *Europe: Hierarchy and Revolt, 1320–1450*. 2000.

Jardine, L. *Worldly Goods: A New History of the Renaissance*. 1996.

Jordan, W. C. *Europe in the High Middle Ages*. 2003.

Kedar, Benjamin Z. *Crusade and Mission: European Approaches Toward the Muslims*. 1988.

Kelly, John. *The Great Mortality: An Intimate History of the Black Death*. 2005.

King, Margaret L. *Women of the Renaissance*. 1991.

Madden, Thomas. *A New History of the Crusades*. 2005.

Mollat, M., and P. Wolff. *The Popular Revolutions of the Late Middle Ages*. 1973.

Mundy, J. H. *Europe in the High Middle Ages, 1150–1309*. 3rd ed. 1999.

Nauert, C. G. *Humanism and the Culture of Renaissance Europe*. 1995.

Oakley, F. P. *The Western Church in the Later Middle Ages*. 1980.

O'Callaghan, Joseph F. *A History of Medieval Spain*. 1975.

Phillips, J. R. S. *The Medieval Expansion of Europe*. 1988.

Powell, James M. *Innocent III: Vicar of Christ or Lord of the World?* 2nd ed. 1994.

Renouard, Y. *The Avignon Papacy, 1305–1403*. 1970.

Riley-Smith, J. *The Crusades: A Short History*. 1987.

Rosenwein, Barbara. *A Short History of the Middle Ages*. 2002.

White, John. *Art and Architecture in Italy, 1250–1400*. 3rd ed. 1993.

Key Dates and Developments

1070s	Seljuk Turks defeat Byzantines and conquer Holy Land
1085	Spanish Christians capture Toledo from Muslims
1096–1099	First Crusade
1144	Suger begins first Gothic church at Saint-Denis
1147–1149	Second Crusade
1189–1192	Third Crusade
1202–1204	Fourth Crusade
1267–1273	Thomas Aquinas writes *Summa Theologica*
1309–1377	Popes reside at Avignon
1310–1320	Dante composes the *Divine Comedy*
1337	Hundred Years War begins
1347–1351	Black Death devastates Europe
1348–1353	Boccaccio composes *The Decameron*
1378–1417	Great Western Schism divides Western Church
1430s	Jan van Eyck flourishes in Flanders
1434–1492	Medicis rule Florence: height of Florentine Renaissance
1453	Fall of Constantinople; end of Hundred Years War
1456	Gutenberg publishes Bible printed with movable type
1492	Spanish Christians take Granada; Columbus's First Voyage
1503–1506	Leonardo da Vinci creates the *Mona Lisa*
1508	Pope Julius II brings Raphael and Michelangelo to Rome
1513–1516	Machiavelli's *The Prince* and More's *Utopia* published
1527	Sack of Rome by German and Spanish troops

CHAPTER 17

Culture and Conflict in the Great Islamic Empires, 1071–1707

- The Conquests of Timur Lenk
- The Cosmopolitan Ottoman Empire
- Safavid Persia: A Shi'ite State
- The Mughal Empire: A Muslim Minority Rules India
- Chapter Review

Ottoman Compass Points

A sixteenth-century Ottoman illustration of the 32 points of the compass. At that time the great Islamic empires still dominated trade routes across the Indian Ocean, but Europeans were challenging them for commercial control (page 420).

The morning of May 29, 1453, dawned overcast and warm on the outskirts of Constantinople, the capital of the Byzantine Empire. Shortly after sunrise, the Ottoman Turkish sultan, Mehmed II, ordered his Muslim troops to storm the city. A large cannon made for the sultan by a Hungarian metallurgist pounded away at the city's thick walls. Shortly before noon a hole was torn in one of the walls, and jubilant attackers piled through the breach into Constantinople. The last Byzantine emperor died in hand-to-hand combat, and by early afternoon Mehmed's forces were in possession of a Christian city that Muslims had sought to conquer for more than eight centuries.

Mughal India

Safavid Persia

The Ottoman Empire

As the battle raged around him, Mehmed II calmly rode his horse into the Hagia Sophia (*Hā-jē-ah sō-FĪ-ah*), the Church of the Holy Wisdom, and claimed it for Islam as a mosque. According to legend, the Orthodox Christian priests chanting divine services at the time quickly gathered up the sacred objects on the altar and vanished into the marble walls of the church's sanctuary, from which they will return to finish the services when the Muslims are expelled from Constantinople. Oblivious to this possibility, Mehmed surveyed his conquest, gave orders to limit the looting and pillaging, and contemplated the collapse of the last outpost of Christendom in the old Roman East.

All three of the great Islamic empires of the fifteenth through seventeenth centuries—the Ottoman, the Safavid (*SAH-fah-vid*), and the Mughal (*MOO-gull*)—were created through conflict, but they were connected to each other in many ways. Each was established by nomadic Turks from Central Asia. Each dynasty constructed its new empire on the foundations of existing Asian civilizations, adapting its previously nomadic life to the framework of settled agricultural urban societies. Each empire was spiritually and culturally Islamic. And each was influenced profoundly by a Turkish empire that rose and fell with astonishing speed: the empire of Timur Lenk.

The Conquests of Timur Lenk

Timur was born in 1336 into a Muslim family of Turks in Central Asia. His father, a mid-level government official in the service of the Mongols, claimed descent from Genghis Khan. Timur, who limped from wounds received in battle as a young man, was contemptuously called Timur Lenk, "Timur the Lame," by the Persians he conquered. Europeans corrupted this nickname to Tamerlane (*TAM-ur-lān*). Considering himself a worthy heir to Genghis Khan, Timur set out to conquer Asia, and in the process connected several parts of it, although his lack of patience for administration ensured that his empire would not survive him for long.

Timur's Strengths and Good Fortunes

Timur followed his father by serving the Mongols, although as a cavalry captain rather than as a government official. Charismatic and cruel, he compensated for his limp by turning himself into a master horseman and soon won the allegiance of the Turkish mercenaries with whom he rode. The Mongol leadership of the Jagadai Khanate in Central Asia was torn apart by rival factions, and Timur skillfully allied with one and then the other, pretending to serve each of them while actually serving only himself. By 1360 he had gained control over the lands between the Oxus (*OX-us*) and Jaxartes (*jacks-AR-tēz*) rivers in Central Asia (Map 17.1). Over the next three decades he mobilized a fearsome

FOUNDATION MAP 17.1 The Empire of Timur Lenk, ca. 1405

The extent of Timur's conquests, undertaken in a time without electronic communication or rapid transit, suggests the difficulty of ruling such vast and varied domains. Compare the location of Timur's empire with the Persian Empire of Cyrus and Darius I (Map 6.3). Then remember that nearly two millennia earlier, Darius had ruled even more extensive lands effectively through satraps. Why didn't Timur institute the sort of efficient administration that characterized the Persian Empire?

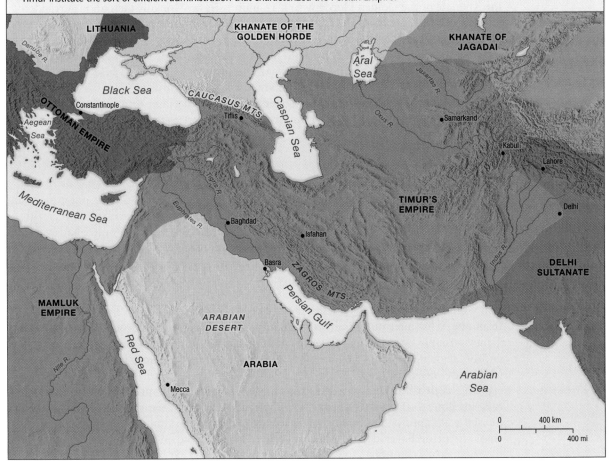

force of mounted cavalry in a series of campaigns designed to conquer every region he could reach.

Timur owed his military successes in part to his personal abilities, in part to the quarrels and weaknesses of his enemies, and in part to luck. Some of that good fortune was an ongoing shift in weather patterns, beginning decades before his birth, that brought ample rains to areas of Central Asia which had previously been arid. New and extensive pasturelands supported the horses and livestock of Turkish nomads who, under Timur's leadership, went from there to conquer large parts of Asia.

Timur Lenk conquers large parts of Asia

In 1370 Timur established his capital in the Central Asian city of Samarkand (*sah-mur-KAHND*), from which the Mongol Khanate of Jagadai had controlled the region. In 1380 Timur's forces descended upon Persia and ravaged the countryside. They then crossed the Iranian plateau and subdued Baghdad. This conquest took 13 years, largely because Timur himself was, for most of that time, in Central Asia, consolidating his base with decisive victories over the Mongols in their own heartland. By the final decade of the fourteenth century he was poised to move further.

In 1395 Timur's mounted archers invaded the region of the lower Volga, destroying the Khanate of the Golden Horde within 18 months. The Mongols thereupon surrendered an empire stretching from the Caucasus Mountains northeastward to Siberia. Two years later Timur turned toward India, devastating the Punjab in the West and sacking Delhi. He enslaved numerous Indians to build him a great mosque at Samarkand, while behind him he left desolate cities stalked by hunger and disease. The severed heads of Hindus were piled into immense towers as testimony to his visit, but Indian Muslims fared no better: some were among the 100,000 prisoners he massacred after capturing Delhi. As the fourteenth century drew to a close Timur marched to the eastern Mediterranean, where he encountered the Ottoman Turks.

Attack on the Ottomans

The Ottoman Turks, successors to the Seljuks in the Balkans, were at that point planning what they hoped would be a decisive assault on the Byzantine Empire. Sultan Bayezid (*BĪ-yeh-zēd*) I, who considered himself the heir to the Great Seljuk Empire, had worked for a decade to consolidate the Ottoman realm, and, using the Balkans as his base, he hoped to join Europe with Asia by taking Constantinople and western Anatolia. His plans alarmed Christian Europe at his back, but he had not reckoned on Timur's presence on the Byzantine Empire's eastern frontier. Suddenly it seemed that the potential confrontation would involve three enemies, not just two. When King Charles VI of France emerged from one of his intermittent bouts of insanity to send messengers urging Timur to save Constantinople by striking at Bayezid's Ottomans from the East, Timur needed no further encouragement. He moved against Bayezid, who led his forces into battle near Ankara (*AIN-kah-rah*) in 1402.

Timur's attack diverts the Ottomans from Constantinople

The battle of Ankara was disastrous for the Ottomans. Timur's well-disciplined, carefully integrated armies routed Bayezid's powerful but poorly organized troops. The sultan himself was captured by Timur and treated with contempt. Timur used Bayezid as a footstool and made Bayezid's favorite wife strip naked to serve midday and evening meals to the conqueror's entourage. Imprisoned in a cage so small that he could not stand, sit, or lie down, Bayezid soon died.

Constantinople had been saved from Ottoman assault, but Timur's victory gave no comfort to the Christians. Who or what could stop Timur from turning his attentions on Europe? As it turned out, only his own restless nature. He had taken every acre of land once owned by the Mongols who had ruled him—except China. There the Ming dynasty had claimed the Mandate of Heaven and ousted the Mongol Yuan dynasty in 1368. Timur moved east to prepare his forces for the largest invasion of his career, but while doing so he drank much more wine than his 69-year-old constitution could absorb, and he died of alcohol poisoning in 1405.

Timur as Warrior and Administrator

In many respects, Timur Lenk was an impressive figure. Illiterate but not ignorant, his insatiable curiosity led him to surround himself with scholars with whom he debated questions of religious doctrine, natural science, and history. A skillful chess player, he was also in real life a master of both battle and diplomacy, employing every means imaginable to defeat his opponent. His nomadic upbringing provided him with a flexibility of perspective that enabled him to seize the most favorable opportunity, whenever it presented itself. Timur's reputation for ferocity terrified everyone in his path and proved useful in securing his remarkable sequence of victories. Yet Timur presented himself as a unifier who attacked only those who had been disloyal to Islam.

The interior of the chapel at the tomb of Timur Lenk in Samarkand, in present-day Uzbekistan.

Some of the very qualities that made Timur a magnificent warrior also made him a poor statesman. The tactical flexibility that served him well in battle equipped him poorly for administration. He never cared to rule the lands he conquered, appointing his sons and grandsons as provincial governors while setting forth at once in search of more military glory. His governors were supposed to act only in Timur's name, but because he was almost never in contact with them they were forced to act on their own. This prevented the creation of durable institutions that might have helped his empire endure.

Timur is unable to consolidate his empire

Timur might have been a builder as well as a destroyer, but his temperament inclined him in other directions. He beautified Samarkand but spent almost no time there, preferring his tents and the back of his horse. His atrocities sealed his reputation. When he died, nothing could hold his lands together. Like a powerful windstorm from the steppes of Central Asia, he leveled everything in his path and then vanished, leaving others to rebuild what he had destroyed.

The Cosmopolitan Ottoman Empire

Like the rest of Asia, the Muslim world had been badly battered by the nomadic invasions of the eleventh through fourteenth centuries. The Seljuk Turks, the Mongols, and Timur Lenk had brought war and destruction, but none proved able to hold their huge empires together. Even though they conquered Islam, they were also assimilated by it.

Islam appealed strongly to these nomads. The simplicity of its monotheism, the hope of paradise offered by its five pillars, and the rigor and consistency of its legal code all resonated with tribal peoples uninterested in the sort of complex doctrinal disputes that fascinated Byzantines. The nomads were accustomed to settling quarrels directly, physically, and permanently.

Islam appeals to nomadic civilizations

Consequently, although nomadic rule in southern Asia could be exploitative and devastating, it did not destroy Muslim culture. Mahmud of Ghazni's conversion to Islam could not save the Il-Khan Empire from dissolution in 1335, but it did perpetuate the hold of the Islamic faith. Timur conquered in the name of Islam, not as its enemy. And Mongol advances in southwest Asia were stopped by Egypt's Muslim Mamluk rulers, who in turn were conquered by invaders from Anatolia known as the Ottoman Turks.

Ottomans and Byzantines

In the late thirteenth century, a Turkic-speaking nomadic group led by a man named Osman (oz-*MAHN*) arrived in Anatolia, fleeing westward from the Mongols. They came as polytheists but were eventually converted to Sunni Islam by the Seljuk Turks, who granted them lands in Anatolia along the Byzantine frontier. These grants placed the Ottoman Turks, so named because they were followers of Osman, in an advantageous position that they were quick to exploit. When the Seljuk state collapsed and the Mongols withdrew, the Ottoman Turks took over as champions of the Muslim cause against the Byzantine Empire.

The Ottomans oppose the Byzantine Empire

That once-great realm was now in ruins. Even after 1261, when the Byzantines recaptured their capital from the Western Crusaders, they were beset by insurrections and civil wars, and they never managed to recover their Balkan provinces of Bulgaria, Serbia, and Macedonia, which the Bulgars had taken. Their glorious capital of Constantinople was in decline, its wealth squandered and its trade with the East having passed into the hands of the Italian commercial republics of Venice and Genoa.

The real winners of the Fourth Crusade were the Ottoman Turks, who had stood by while Christians killed one another. Early in the fourteenth century, in an effort to recover its Balkan possessions from the Bulgars, Byzantium decided to ally with the Turks. Thus Turkish forces, rather than having to fight their way into Europe, came as invited guests. Then they quickly took advantage of Byzantine weakness to construct a network of vassal principalities in the Balkans. When the Serbs and Bosnians rose up against Ottoman rule in 1387, the capable Sultan Murad (*MEW-rahd*) I defeated the rebels at the Battle of Kosovo (*KŌ-sō-vō*) in 1389. This outcome provoked the Europeans to mount a multinational anti-Islamic crusade, which the Ottomans defeated seven years later.

The Pax Ottomanica stabilizes southwest Asia and the Balkans

These Balkan victories gave the Ottomans a territorial base in Europe and allowed them to consider their strategy for administering the area. Murad, who had led them into Europe, was an exceptional ruler who refused to impose Islamic or Ottoman forms of government in the Balkans. He was convinced that new systems must be developed that would take into account local conditions and cultures and permit daily life to continue as it had. With this conviction he laid the foundation of a religiously and ethnically pluralistic society that would create a stable *Pax Ottomanica*, or "Ottoman peace," similar in some ways to the *Pax Romana* created centuries earlier by the Roman Empire. Like the Romans, Murad granted citizenship to all foreigners who were willing to work for his administration.

The primary concern of Murad and his successors, however, was to advance Islam. Several Ottoman officials once told a Byzantine visitor that the westward expansion of the faith had been ordained by Allah, and the Ottomans were the "sword" of that advance. The Byzantine Empire could continue to exist, if its citizens converted to Islam.

The Ottoman goal was not to destroy that empire but to assimilate it into Islamic civilization. In reality, of course, the Byzantine realm had been decaying for centuries, so its absorption into the Muslim world would be of far less value than Murad had hoped.

Murad was slain by a Serb at Kosovo in 1389, and succeeded by his son Bayezid I, who possessed few of his father's leadership abilities. Bayezid continued Murad's policy of granting citizenship to able foreigners, but in other respects he was a warrior, not a statesman. By early 1402 he was ready to besiege Constantinople, but just as his armies were preparing to move, he had to send them back to Anatolia to deal with a momentous threat from the East: Timur Lenk.

Timur's defeat of the Ottomans at Ankara saved the Byzantine Empire, but only temporarily. Once Timur was gone, the Ottomans regrouped. Two successive sultans tried to capture Constantinople and failed. But eventually the Ottoman Turks succeeded and went on to absorb Byzantium into their own immense cosmopolitan empire, one that spanned three continents and endured for more than 400 years.

Timur's attack on the Ottomans eases the pressure on Byzantium

Mehmed the Conqueror

Mehmed II.

The final conqueror of Byzantium was a new sultan named Mehmed (*MEH-med*) II who came to the Ottoman throne in 1451, determined to take Constantinople. By May 29, 1453, he had succeeded, as this chapter's opening story describes (see "Mehmed the Conqueror Takes Constantinople, 1453"). Changing the name of the Byzantine capital from Constantinople to Istanbul, he claimed it for the Islamic faith. The Byzantine Empire had been replaced by an Islamic Ottoman realm.

Constantinople's fall threw Western Christendom into despair. Europe was now threatened directly by the Ottoman Turks from the Southeast, and the flow of east-west commerce was completely in Islamic hands. For Mehmed the Conqueror, however, the events of 1453 fulfilled the will of Allah, who had ordained that His sultan rescue the Roman Empire from unbelievers. Mehmed was now both the legitimate Roman emperor and successor to Constantine the Great, and Ottoman *Padishah* (*PAH-dih-sha*), a Persian word meaning "God's deputy on earth" and used by the Ottomans to mean "imperial sovereign." The Byzantine tradition of caesaropapism, in which the same man exercised both political and religious authority, was of great use to Mehmed and his successors.

The ambitious Mehmed sought to make the Byzantine Empire part of an Ottoman Empire and a platform for Islam's conquest of all Europe and Asia. This was a tall order, but Mehmed saw himself as selected by Allah to achieve the worldwide unity of Islam. He expanded the administrative policies of Murad I, transforming the Ottoman state into a powerful empire prepared to draw on the talents of all its citizens, regardless of their attitudes toward Islam.

Mehmed II intends to restore the Roman Empire

The Ottoman State and Society

Having destroyed the last vestige of Imperial Rome, the Ottoman Empire evolved from an Asian-based Turkish political and social system into a multi-ethnic, intercontinental state. In doing so, it combined previously unrelated administrative methods derived from

Document 17.1 Mehmed the Conqueror Takes Constantinople, 1453

Kritovoulos, a Greek, was not present at the siege of Constantinople, but soon thereafter visited it and entered the service of Mehmed II, who eventually appointed him governor of the island of Imbros. "He admired the Sultan's military prowess and ability, even while mourning the loss of the City and the downfall of the last vestige of the Byzantine Empire (page viii)." His description of the conquest of Constantinople is based on the personal testimony of hundreds who took part in it.

Sultan Mehmed, who happened to be fighting quite near by, saw that a palisade and a part of a wall that had been destroyed were now empty of men and deserted by the defenders . . . He shouted out, "Friends, we have the City! We have it! They are already fleeing from us! They can't stand it any longer! The wall is bare of defenders! It needs just a little more effort and the City is taken! Don't weaken, but on with the work with all your might, and be men and I am with you!"

So saying, he led them himself. And they, with a shout on the run and with a fearsome yell, went on ahead of the Sultan, pressing on up to the palisade . . . Now there was a great struggle there and great slaughter among those stationed there . . . There the Emperor Constantine, with all who were with

him, fell in gallant combat . . . Then a great slaughter occurred of those who happened to be there . . . men, women, and children, everyone, for there was no quarter given. The soldiers fell on them with anger and great wrath. For one thing, they were actuated by the hardships of the siege. For another, some foolish people had hurled taunts and curses at them from the battlements all through the siege. Now, in general they killed so as to frighten all the City, and to terrorize and enslave all by the slaughter . . .

After this the Sultan entered the City and looked about to see its great size, its situation, its grandeur and beauty, its teeming population, its loveliness, and the costliness of its churches and public buildings and of the private houses and community houses and those of the officials . . . When he saw what a large number had been killed, and the ruin of the buildings, and the wholesale ruin and destruction of the City, he was filled with compassion and repented not a little at the destruction and plundering. Tears fell from his eyes as he groaned deeply and passionately: "What a city we have given over to plunder and destruction!"

SOURCE: Kritovoulos, *History of Mehmed the Conqueror*, translated by Charles T. Riggs (Princeton: Princeton University Press, 1954) 70–77.

Turkish, Persian, and Byzantine traditions into a new governing form connecting aspects of three of the dominant cultures of Asia.

THE OTTOMAN GOVERNMENT'S UNIQUE SYNTHESIS. Ottoman government was based on the sultan's exclusive right to rule, a concept drawn from Persian tradition and amplified after 1453 by Byzantine caesaropapism. The sultan was supported in this effort by the four "pillars of empire," a Turkish image taken from the four poles that had traditionally held up the sultan's tent. The first pillar of the government was the **grand vezir** (*veh-ZĒR*), chief minister to the sultan; the second pillar was the judiciary; the third was the treasury; and the fourth consisted of administrators who drew up the sultan's edicts. These pillars existed to enhance the sultan's authority, not to limit it.

The Ottomans blend diverse traditions into a new governing system

But Mehmed II and his successors were not entirely free to rule as they wished. As a Muslim, the sultan was required to conduct himself in accordance with the Shari'ah or Islamic law, based upon the Qur'an, Islamic custom, and the sayings of the first four caliphs. In significant political decisions, he was expected to seek a **fatwa** (*FAHT-wah*), a legal opinion from the highest Islamic legal authority, sanctioning his course of action. Yet seventh-century Islamic law was not always applicable to issues arising in a fifteenth-century Muslim state.

Turkish tradition proved helpful in resolving this problem. The sultan in his role as Padishah enjoyed the right to issue commands and regulations on ordinary governmental matters without interference from the Islamic legal establishment. These state laws, called **urfi** (*UR-fē*), could be shaped in response to modern issues and problems that the Shari`ah could not possibly have foreseen. Urfi could, for example, be used to authorize the lending of money at interest despite religious objections to the practice. In one form or another, the Turkish principle that state law takes precedence over religious law remained in use for centuries in most Islamic nations.

This practical synthesis of diverse concepts meant that the Ottomans behaved differently from other Islamic states. First, their approach to their enemies was shaped by practical considerations rather than by religious zeal. Living side by side with Greeks in the Balkans convinced them of the essential humanity of their opponents and the impracticality of dealing with them harshly. Ottoman willingness to blend governmental traditions enabled them to develop a hybrid system well suited to ruling the assorted cultures and ethnic groups that made up their diverse domain.

Ottoman law book.

Second, the Ottoman system of landholding differed significantly from both Arab and European practice. The nomadic origins of many Islamic societies lived on in the high value placed on land as belonging to the tribe, and the low value placed on individual ownership. European societies, in contrast, placed a high value on individual land ownership, and medieval systems of inheritance encouraged the development of landed nobilities. In Ottoman territory, however, all land belonged to the state. Newly conquered land was distributed by the sultan to his soldiers as a reward. These land grants promoted the growth of a professional standing army. But the land grants could not be handed down from father to son; upon a soldier's death, his land reverted to the state. This system prevented the creation of a landed aristocracy that could challenge or even rival the sultan himself. Instead, what evolved was a meritocracy, in which each succeeding generation was rewarded according to the value of its service to the state.

OTTOMAN SOCIETY. The Ottoman state apparatus was thus a unique blend of Turkish, Persian, Byzantine, and Islamic influences. Unique as well was the society on which it rested. The Ottoman ruling class of about 350 people was composed exclusively of slaves belonging to the sultan. Almost all of them were former Christians who converted to Islam. This elite status was also nonhereditary; these slaves and their descendants could never become a more formal and permanent nobility that might one day rival the sultan. Promotion was based solely on merit and demotion was possible in cases of poor performance. Parallel to this ruling class was the corps of **Janissaries** (*JAN-is-sair-ēz*), a ten thousand–member infantry, also composed of slaves who were Christian-born converts to Islam and totally dependent on the sultan. Armed with gunpowder weapons, the Ottoman armies were superior to all they encountered until the late seventeenth century.

Janissaries help Ottoman armies dominate southwest Asia

In Ottoman society, as in Ottoman governance, privilege was thus based on performance, not ancestry. A household servant might rise to the rank of grand vezir, while a vezir might fall to the status of a blacksmith, all without any loss of dignity. Since all were slaves of the Padishah, all served at his imperial pleasure in whatever post it pleased

Flexibility is a feature of Ottoman society

him to place them. This arrangement was a Turkish-Persian-Islamic hybrid, which at its height proved remarkably effective.

For the sultan, the arrangement carried with it a flexibility that proved particularly useful in a multiethnic empire. Ottoman rule did not depend on overwhelming military force to keep conquered peoples in line. Instead, subject peoples might join and move up in Ottoman administration. This possibility minimized internal unrest. The adaptability of these political and social structures helps explain why the Ottoman Empire survived into the twentieth century.

Suleiman the Magnificent

Selim I claims the title of Caliph

Mehmed the Conqueror lived up to his name, solidifying Ottoman control over Anatolia and moving northwest from Istanbul deeper into southeastern Europe. The next two sultans, Bayezid II (r. 1481–1512) and Selim (*seh-LĒM*) I "The Grim" (r. 1512–1520), concentrated on warfare in the East and South. Selim ruled for only eight years, but in that time he managed to conquer Syria, Palestine, Egypt, and North Africa, defeating the Mamluks in Egypt and beginning a series of attacks on Persia's new Safavid regime. He also improved the Ottoman navy, which now threatened Christian shipping in the Mediterranean. Most significant, he claimed the title of Caliph, vacant since 1258, thereby completing the transfer of Islamic leadership from Arabs to Turks (Ottoman sultans remained Caliphs until 1924). By the end of Selim's reign, the Ottomans ruled about two-thirds of the territory of the old Eastern Roman Empire. All that was left for them to conquer was central and western Europe.

THE OTTOMAN EMPIRE AS A FORCE IN WORLD AFFAIRS. Selim was succeeded in 1520 by his 26-year-old son Suleiman (*SOO-lē-mahn*). Islamic seers, pointing to the sacred number ten, predicted glorious victories for the new ruler: Suleiman was the tenth Ottoman sultan, and he began his reign at the start of the tenth century after Muhammad's move to Medina in 622. Suleiman was also an intellectual, eager to absorb Turkish, Persian, and Byzantine culture and to participate in the European Renaissance's revival of Greek and Roman learning. Suleiman saw himself as a unifier, the leader who could unite East and West under the banner of the Prophet. His 46-year reign extended Ottoman power into central Europe and across the Mediterranean, terrifying Christian Europe and establishing the Ottoman Empire as a decisive force in international affairs (Map 17.2).

Suleiman moves against Europe

The Ottomans struck first into Hungary, slaughtering Hungarian forces at Mohács in 1526. But Suleiman's resources were inadequate for the permanent governance of a hostile country so far from Istanbul, on the other side of the rugged and treacherous Balkan peninsula. Selim had been able to control southwest Asia and North Africa with relative ease, as the inhabitants of those areas had been Muslims for centuries. But central Europe was intensely Christian and unwilling to submit to Islamic rule. Suleiman burned Budapest and marched his armies home for the winter, leaving Hungary open to the influence of the Austrian Habsburgs. That Catholic royal family immediately began to fortify central Europe against the Turkish threat.

Three years later, in May 1529, Suleiman led an immense army to attack Vienna. But the rains were so persistent that summer that the Turks could not bring up their heavy siege artillery over Austria's primitive roads. In October, as winter approached and the

Map 17.2 The Ottoman Empire in 1566

Comparison with Map 17.1 indicates that the Ottoman Empire at the death of Suleiman the Magnificent was much larger than that of Timur Lenk. Notice that the Ottoman Empire connected parts of three continents and included ethnic groups as diverse as Egyptians, Syrians, Mesopotamians, Turks, Greeks, and Bosnians. What methods did the Ottomans develop to rule such far-flung domains and so many distinct peoples?

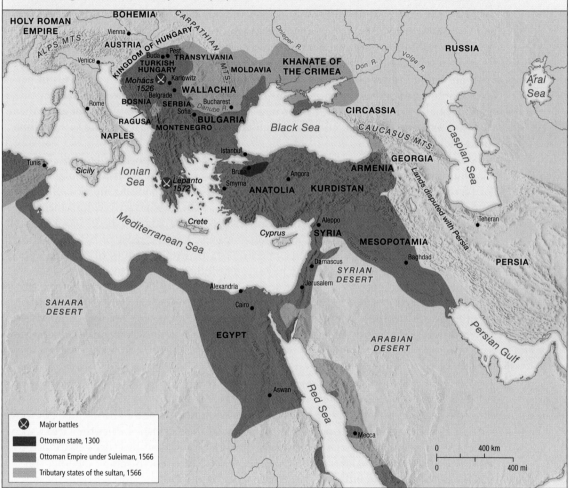

Major battles

Ottoman state, 1300

Ottoman Empire under Suleiman, 1566

Tributary states of the sultan, 1566

cavalry could not feed its horses, Suleiman returned to Istanbul in frustration. In 1532 he tried again, this time failing even to reach Vienna because of poor weather and Hungarian and Croatian resistance. Now, at one of history's turning points, Suleiman concluded that, given distance, weather, terrain, and the hostility of the population, Vienna and central Europe lay beyond the reach of military conquest launched from Istanbul.

Grudgingly, Suleiman turned his attention toward the East. Over the next three decades he fought Safavid Persia for possession of Mesopotamia, sent his powerful navy to raid the eastern Mediterranean, and periodically returned west to extend his control

Suleiman turns eastward

further into Hungary. He also played a major role in European affairs, allying with France against the Habsburgs and supporting Protestants against Catholics during the Reformation. In 1566, on his seventh campaign into Europe, he died in his tent, having failed to unify East and West but having succeeded in making the Ottoman Empire a world power.

SULEIMAN THE LAWGIVER. Despite his constant campaigning, the Sultan was often at home; and if to Europeans he was "Suleiman the Magnificent," to his subjects he was "Suleiman the Lawgiver." Like western monarchs, he was not above the law but subject to it, although his exalted status allowed him a considerable range of action. Given the centrality of the Shari`ah within Islamic culture, he could not have created a new legal structure, but he did adapt the law to the conditions of his immense multi-ethnic empire. His subjects lived on three continents and were free to profess non-Islamic faiths, and while not all of them were subject to the Shari`ah, all were accountable under the urfi, which the sultan alone could declare.

Suleiman adapts Islamic law to Ottoman needs

Suleiman worked diligently to guarantee that laws would apply equally to all. Corporal punishment was replaced by a system of fines, although forgers and perjurers might still have their right hands cut off. The Sultan also strengthened mechanisms for the enforcement of Islamic law, viewing the church-state relationship as one in which two complementary strands reinforced royal authority—a typically caesaropapist perspective.

Was Suleiman the Magnificent an absolute monarch in the sense of having unlimited power? Certainly his authority, dignity, and legal status would seem to fit this description. But Suleiman himself would probably have seen absolutism as a curious contrivance of nonbelievers, of little use to an Islamic sovereign. He was Allah's deputy on earth, the Ottoman Padishah, a ruler for whom the distinction between spiritual and political authority was not a source of tension but of power. Clearly superior, in his own mind, to any monarch in the West, Suleiman would have been unlikely to consider their forms of governance applicable to his lands.

Suleiman.

Europeans challenge the Ottomans economically

A Faltering Empire

After the death of Suleiman, Ottoman fortunes remained favorable for a time. Although in 1571 a multinational European navy demolished the Turkish fleet at the Greek strait of Lepanto (*leh-PAHN-tō*), the vessels were quickly rebuilt, and the Turks continued to dominate the eastern Mediterranean (see page 409). More worrisome in the long run was the takeover of the Indian Ocean spice trade by the Dutch and French in the seventeenth century, costing Istanbul dearly in terms of lost customs duties. That shortfall could not be made up: Ottoman revenues could be expanded only by conquering additional territory, and the empire's failure to advance into Europe meant that its income would stagnate during a period of rapid inflation fueled by gold and silver shipments from the western hemisphere.

This fiscal challenge might have been addressed by competent leadership, but that was in short supply. Suleiman had been trained as a soldier and as a governor of a province before becoming sultan, but his successors had no such experience; they were brought up in the harem to protect them from rivals. Bred to luxury and debauchery, they often became alcoholics and drug addicts. The grand vezirs took over to keep the empire running, but since they governed at the sultan's pleasure, one gesture from him could end either a career or a life.

Poor decisions hurt the empire tremendously. For example, in 1683 the grand vezir Kara Mustafa (*KAH-rah moo-STAH-fah*) led an immense army to once again besiege Vienna, in an effort to accomplish what Suleiman had already concluded was impossible. The Turks were again defeated, this time by a multinational Christian force led by King Jan III Sobieski (*YAHN sō-B'YEH-skē*) of Poland. Istanbul was forced in 1699 to sign the Peace of Karlowitz, recognizing that Hungary and Transylvania belonged to Austria. For the first time Ottoman expansion had been not only stopped but rolled back. The defeat suggested an uncertain future for the empire, especially as its failure to overcome Christian Europe was paralleled by failures to meet challenges to its leadership within the Islamic world from empires farther east.

The Ottoman Empire declines and is unable to respond to Europe's military challenges

Safavid Persia: A Shi'ite State

Ethnic, linguistic, religious, and geographic diversity characterized the Islamic empires from Istanbul to Delhi. Yet Islam provided a powerful faith-based appeal that helped unify its followers. The five pillars offered each Muslim a framework for living a righteous life. The Qur'an, amplified by the sayings of the Prophet, guided the faithful to a deeper understanding of Allah's will. Islamic law, as developed in the Shari`ah, was interpreted differently in different states but furnished a common code of conduct in civil and criminal matters. Mosques and minarets were found in all Islamic communities, although built in various architectural styles. And while Sunni observances differed from Shi'ite services, Islam offered a common tradition that enabled Muslims of all lands and ethnicities to transcend their differences. Nowhere was this more apparent than in Persia.

A late seventeenth-century Islamic map of the world.

Shi'ite Islam as a Unifying Force

The Iranian plateau had for centuries endured the ravages of raiders and nomads from Central Asia, but the combination of Genghis Khan and Timur Lenk brought devastation on a scale previously unknown. Invading armies obliterated towns, erecting huge columns of skulls to mark their former sites. All told, the population of Persia was reduced by 90 percent. Both Genghis and Timur were accompanied by large bands of Turks, who converted to Islam upon arrival in Persia and who eventually rebuilt it once the Mongols had moved on to other conquests.

The rebuilders, who called themselves the Safavid movement, were established by a Kurd named Safi al-Din (*SAH-fē al-DĒN*), who lived from 1252 to 1334. Claiming descent from the fourth caliph, Ali, and through him from the Prophet Muhammad, Safi founded an order of Turkish Sufi mystics who believed that post-Mongol Persia must be rebuilt on a foundation of purified Islamic devotion and militancy. In opposition to the turmoil and exploitation of Mongol conquest, the Safavid movement preached a positive message of rededication and strength. The order spread across Persia, quickly becoming the most powerful spiritual force in the land.

The Safavid movement rebuilds Persia

Map 17.3 The Safavid Empire in Persia, 1600

A shared Islamic faith connected the peoples of southwest Asia, but differing brands of Islam and other areas of conflict divided them. Notice the geographic location of the Safavid Empire, positioned as a buffer state between the Ottoman Empire (to its west) and the Mughal Empire in India (to its east). The Safavids' adoption of Shi'ite Islam separated Persia from both its Sunni Muslim neighbors, while the natural barriers of the Zagros Mountains and the Hindu Kush discouraged those neighbors from interfering in Safavid affairs. What commercial advantages might this central location have offered the Persians?

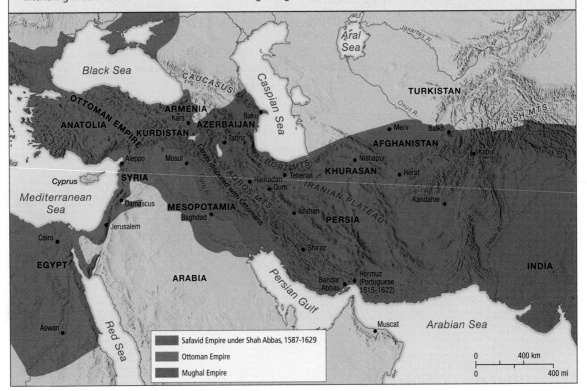

After Timur Lenk ravaged Persia late in the fourteenth century, many survivors looked to the Safavids as the most cohesive opposition force. When Timur's empire broke up early in the fifteenth century, Safavism turned from preaching to political action. In 1501, forces led by Safi's descendant Ismail (*IS-mah-ĒL*) conquered the Persian city of Tabriz (*tah-BRĒZ*) (Map 17.3). Ismail proclaimed himself **shah** (or king) of Persia, a position he held until his death in 1524. He also proclaimed Shi'ite Islam the state religion of Persia.

Safavids use Shi'ism to unify Persia

Ismail's 1501 proclamation was highly significant. Persia had been nothing more than a geographic expression, without any independent political identity, since the Arab conquest had reduced it to dependent status. As the Abbasid Caliphate disintegrated, Persia had been torn by the ambitions of warlords and invaders. Now Ismail, by establishing Shi'ism, gave his subjects a new sense of identity and unity that distinguished Persia from its cosmopolitan, Sunni Ottoman neighbor and created what would later be known as the modern state of Iran.

Ismail's accession to the throne was noted immediately in Istanbul. A revived Persian Empire would have been dangerous enough for the Ottomans, but the Safavids were also Shi'ites. Shi'ite Muslims believe that Ali was the legitimate successor to the Prophet and that his murder in 661 constituted a wrong that has never been avenged. Sunni Muslims, who have been in the majority in the Islamic world since that time, are in Shi'ite eyes usurpers who have no right to guide the faithful.

Shi'ism divided Persia from its Sunni neighbors east and west. Its rituals underscored that division. Regular commemorations of Sunni persecutions of Shi'ites are important parts of the Shi'ite Muslim calendar, and they intensify with a two-week observance of the murder of Ali's son Hussein by Sunni assassins in 680. Then as now, pilgrims marched tearfully through the streets, whipping themselves and chanting dirges in honor of the martyr.

A Safavid battle tunic.

Developments in Persia were profoundly disturbing to the Sunnis who ruled the Ottoman Empire. They worried that hundreds of thousands of Shi'ites living under Ottoman rule might be sympathetic to the Safavids. In addition, the Safavid dynasty was of Turkish origin and commanded considerable support in Anatolia. For their part, the Safavids were similarly worried about possible Ottoman intervention, especially because many Persians—perhaps a majority—were Sunnis. Open warfare broke out when Selim I became Ottoman sultan in 1512. Two years later the Ottomans defeated the Persians and occupied Tabriz, but were unable to force the Safavids from power. The attack initiated a bitter, centuries-long struggle during which Sunnis were persecuted in Iran while Shi'ites were hunted down in Anatolia. The animosity between the two Islamic factions deepened.

Sunnis worry about the attractiveness of Safavid Shi'ism

At one point it appeared that Shi'ism might prevail. Shah Abbas (*ab-BAHS*), who reigned from 1587 to 1629, developed a modern army on the Ottoman model. After defeating the Central Asian Uzbeks (*OOZ-becks*), a nomadic people who had occupied portions of eastern Persia, the shah turned against the Ottomans and captured Baghdad. He also allied with the English, who helped his army expel the Portuguese from the Persian Gulf port of Hormuz (*hōr-MOOZ*) in 1622. Commercial rivalries between European powers enabled the shah to shrewdly play one against another. By the end of the shah's reign, Shi'ite Persia seemed to have little to fear from either Europeans or Ottomans.

Persia avoids dependence on either Europe or the Ottoman Empire

Shah Abbas was also sensitive to the need for a strong economy. He encouraged the rapid expansion of trade in both carpets and tiles, items of exquisite beauty soon prized around the world. Transferring his capital to the centrally situated city of Isfahan (*ISS-fah-hahn*), Abbas gained freedom from persistent Ottoman raids and was able to rebuild the city into a commercial center and an architectural wonder. Isfahan's every detail was meticulously planned, from the enormous central square (used for polo matches, festivals, and ceremonies) to the exquisite royal mosque and the luxurious summer palace. The shops in the royal bazaar were centrally located for ease of taxation. Isfahan's grandeur and beauty enhanced Safavid legitimacy and epitomized the validity of Shi'ite Islam.

The Shah Mosque in Isfahan, considered by experts to be the supreme perfection of Islamic architecture.

Following the death of Shah Abbas in 1629, Safavid fortunes declined rapidly. He was succeeded by incompetent, pampered rulers who were unable to defend an empire that needed cleverness to survive. While the Ottomans reconquered Baghdad, Afghans and Uzbeks seized large regions of Persian territory in the East, and Russian Cossacks began to press the empire from the North. Persia remained independent not through its own strength, but because the Ottoman and Mughal Empires were declining as well.

Regional and Islamic Influence on Family and Gender Roles

In Safavid Persia, as in the Ottoman and Mughal empires, societies were shaped as much by regional customs as by Islamic ideals. In each society, for example, practices affecting family and gender, such as the seclusion of women in the home, were often rooted in regional rather than Islamic traditions.

The Qur'an had established family and gender roles in Islamic Arabia (Chapter 11), strengthening the patriarchal nature of Arabian society but also enhancing the status of women. Both genders were entitled to human dignity and personal privacy. Women were granted explicit property rights and were protected from impoverishment in case of divorce. These rights and protections had not previously been available to them.

Local practices negatively affect the status of women in Islamic countries

Persian women.

As Islam spread beyond Arabia, however, the status of women was impaired by local customs that often overrode Qur'anic requirements. In Persia, for example, male domination and female seclusion had for centuries been embedded in legal and cultural systems. Marriages were arranged by the fathers or male guardians of the brides-to-be. Brides lived with their husband and his relatives, an arrangement that gave them little security should the marriage fail. Persian men, citing local practice, frequently refused women their rights as Muslims to inherit property left them by previous husbands or other relatives. The Shari`ah allowed women to buy and sell property, but in Persia these actions could be taken only through male agents. Although the Qur'an spelled out certain rights for women, these were limited, and in some cases canceled, by Persian traditional practice.

The seclusion of women and their segregation from public life must be placed in context, however. In traditional family-based Islamic societies, the private sphere was typically much more important than the public. Girls could not be educated *outside* the home in Safavid Persia, but *inside* it they were taught the Qur'an and the sayings of the Prophet, at least in middle- and upper-class families. Most economic activity involved the family, and here women exercised considerable influence away from public view. In the Ottoman Empire, women could hold business partnerships and employ tax collectors. In Mughal India, unlike Safavid Persia, women played the primary role in arranging the marriages of their daughters. Men were clearly dominant, but women in the Islamic empires did not define themselves as a separate interest group. They played an indispensable role in family life, in societies in which the family was the center of almost all activity.

The Mughal Empire: A Muslim Minority Rules India

East of Persia, other Muslims struggled to extend their dominion over India and its Hindu population. In the northern part of the subcontinent, the main Islamic rulers were the Delhi sultans, who had established their regime in 1206. For the next few centuries, while the Mongols overran most of the rest of Asia, these sultans tried to spread their control across the Indian subcontinent. Although they ultimately failed, the third of the great Islamic empires was eventually constructed on foundations they laid.

The Delhi Sultanate in India

In the 1220s Genghis Khan complicated the Delhi sultans' situation by chasing Central Asian tribes out of their homelands and into northern India. The reigning sultan, Iletmish (*ill-LET-mish*), prudently refused the refugees' offers of alliance and encouraged them to turn westward into Persia. He thus prevented a Mongol invasion of India. By the time of his death in 1236 Iletmish had consolidated all of north India under the Delhi Sultanate (Map 17.4).

A sensible and enlightened ruler, Iletmish did what he could to reconcile India's Hindu majority to Islamic rule. He left the Hindu rajahs alone as long as they paid tribute on time and supported him against the Mongols. He also proved to be a good judge of talent, openly preferring his daughter Radiya (*rah-DĒ-yah*) as his successor because she was clearly more capable than his sons. But when Iletmish died in 1236, her succession was opposed by her brothers and by a group of influential military officers. Radiya battled against this coalition but finally lost in 1240 and died at the hands of Hindus while fleeing Delhi.

Radiya's defeat plunged the Delhi sultanate into a series of coups and intrigues that ended in 1266 with the assumption of power by the Mamluk slave Balban (*bahl-BAHN*), who had been one of the sultanate's most effective generals. He reorganized the army and government in an effort to hold off the persistent Mongols. Balban's death in 1287 was followed within a decade by the rule of Sultan Ala al-Din (*AH-lah-al-dēn*), an imaginative, skillful, and ruthless leader who expanded the sultanate southward, both to extend its holdings and to raise the money and troops required to defend the North against the Mongols. In 1298 he captured the west Indian state of Gujarat and its vast treasury enriched by the Arabian Sea trade. Then he crossed the Deccan plateau into southern India and managed to occupy the tip of the subcontinent. India, it seemed, had at last been united under Muslim control.

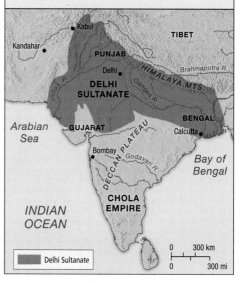

Map 17.4 The Delhi Sultanate in India, 1236

The Delhi Sultanate was India's best hope for defense against the Mongols. Observe that the Sultanate stretched from the banks of the Indus River eastward across the Himalaya Mountains, thereby blocking Mongol penetration of the Indian subcontinent. What factors eventually undermined the regime and opened the door for Mongol invasion?

But Ala al-Din's unifying rule did not last. His successors proved capable of organizing victories over the Mongols but not of holding India together. The subcontinent was simply too large and too diverse, linguistically, culturally, and geographically, to be consolidated by groups with considerable talent for warfare but little for administration.

Ala al-Din temporarily unites all of India

The Sultanate's authority crumbled rapidly. In 1338, a Sufi sect contributed to the defection of the northeastern state of Bengal from orthodox Muslim rule. In 1347, Muslim nobles formed an independent kingdom on the Deccan plateau. In South India, the Hindu states that Ala al-Din had conquered broke away to form the Vijayanagar (*vē-jā-YAH-nah-gahr*) Empire, and in 1390 Gujarat in West India left as well. These losses weakened Delhi so profoundly that it was unable to resist the catastrophic invasion of Timur Lenk.

Following Timur's atrocities in the late fourteenth century, what remained of Indian unity collapsed. The Delhi sultanate was reduced to the status of a North Indian

Timur Lenk destroys Indian unity

principality, and several of its former tributaries now became powerful in their own right. In the fifteenth century, no single state dominated. In 1405 Timur's son established the Timurid (*tee-MOOR-id*) dynasty in India, but it lacked the organized military force necessary for effective imperial rule, and the states of northern India generally ignored it.

Further fragmenting the Indian subcontinent was the emergence of a new **Sikh** (*SĒK*) religion in the late fifteenth century. In the Punjab, centuries of conflict between Hindu and Muslim had deeply scarred the population. There a Hindu mystic named Nanak (*NAH-knock*), inspired by a spiritual experience, worked to develop a synthesis of the two antagonistic religions. Impressed by Islamic monotheism, he accepted the idea of the unity of God, blended it with the Hindu mystical notions of samsara, dharma, and karma, and rejected the Hindu caste system in favor of the Islamic principle of the equality of all believers. Nanak's synthesis, known as Sikhism, still thrives in the Punjab, centered on its holiest site, the Golden Temple at Amritsar (*ahm-RIT-zar*). But his dream of reconciling Hinduism with Islam failed. Rejected by most members of these two opposing creeds, Sikhism became yet another force working against the unity of India.

Sikhs attempt to blend Hinduism with Islam

The Golden Temple.

Babur: Founding the Mughal Empire

India in 1500 was a land in turmoil, divided by religion, culture, and politics. Into this situation came a Muslim invader from Kabul, Babur (*BAH-boor*), whose name means "the Panther," a Turkish-Mongol descendant of both Timur Lenk and Genghis Khan. His ancestry alone was enough to make him feared throughout the subcontinent. Calling himself "the Mughal" (Mongol), Babur committed himself to conquest. In 1524 he was invited into the Punjab by a faction seeking his help in overthrowing the local sultan. Babur accepted the invitation and then quickly overran the Punjab and appointed his own officials to rule it. His Indian allies promptly broke ties with him, but Babur secured pledges of cooperation from a number of noble families in Delhi and advanced on that city in the spring of 1526, intent on overthrowing its sultan.

Babur creates the Mughal Empire

On April 21, 1526, Babur's forces faced the spears and elephants of Sultan Ibrahim (*ib-rah-HĒM*) of Delhi at the battle of Panipat (*PAH-nē-paht*). Although his troops were outnumbered by about two to one, his horsemen were more mobile than the infantry of his opponents, and his cannon blew sizable holes in the elephants. By noon he had won the battle and founded what would be named, after him, the Mughal Empire, the greatest Islamic state in Indian history (Map 17.5).

Four years later, Babur died. His son Humayun (*hoo-MAH-yoon*) proved to be a useless leader, more interested in casting horoscopes and indulging in opium than in ruling an empire. Babur's Afghan generals were dissatisfied, and one of them, Sher Khan Sur (*SHĒR KAHN SOOR*), challenged the new emperor and defeated him in 1539 and 1540. But Sher Khan died young in 1545, and Humayun seized this opportunity to regain the power that had never much interested him. By 1555 he was once again in command of northern India. The following January, however, after smoking at least one opium pipe too many, Humayun slipped on the steps of his private observatory and fractured his skull. This accident left the Mughal Empire in the hands of his 13-year-old son Akbar (*OCK-bar*), whose name in Arabic means "great." As matters turned out, he deserved the title.

Akbar's Reign of Cultural Accommodation

Akbar remained under the tutelage of regents until taking control of his empire at age 20. He was an active man, a formidable hunter and fighter, but illiterate throughout his life. He is reported to have advised others that since the Prophet himself could neither read nor write, it would be a good idea for each family to raise at least one illiterate son. In addition to his total lack of formal education, he appears to have been an epileptic, suffering from seizures and dramatic mood swings that baffled his courtiers. None of these conditions, however, prevented his becoming one of history's finest rulers.

Akbar could not read, but he could learn from the past. He understood not only that India was huge and incurably pluralistic, but also that no government could endure without the cooperation of the Hindu majority. Accordingly, Akbar initiated a program that would reconcile his Islamic regime with the Hindu population. Beginning with a personal gesture, he sent an unmistakable signal by marrying a Hindu princess, who bore him three sons. In 1562 he prohibited the enslavement of prisoners of war and their families, as well as all efforts to forcibly convert them to Islam. One year later he abolished all taxes levied on Hindus making pilgrimages to shrines and temples. In 1564 he canceled a tax imposed on non-Muslims. After fewer than three years of formal rule, Akbar had shown himself to be uncommonly generous, tolerant, and sensible. He was the first Muslim ruler to win significant support from Hindus throughout the subcontinent.

Tolerance and conciliation were not, of course, the only tactics Akbar employed. He also used force to solidify his power. Under Akbar the Mughal Empire tripled in size. Its land mass was one-third that of the Ottoman Empire, but its population of 150 million was six times as large. Yet full integration of southern India proved impossible. Akbar could win battles in the South, but once he returned to the North, southern opposition surfaced and reversed his achievements.

In the rest of India, however, Akbar was master of a competent bureaucracy that administered the Mughal Empire. He divided his domain into 12 provinces, subdividing each into districts. Each province was ruled by a governor directly accountable to the emperor. Akbar himself selected the highest officials, a majority of whom were Muslims born outside of India, but a large minority were drawn from other religious, ethnic, linguistic, and regional groups (15 percent, for example, were Hindus). In addition to demonstrating tolerance and inclusiveness, this policy brought the best qualified Indians into his service, giving them responsible roles in the Mughal Empire as an alternative to leading rebellions against it.

Akbar provides an administrative structure for the Mughal Empire

This bureaucracy also collected taxes. Most Indians were peasants, paying taxes not in money but in produce and livestock. Tax collection was handled at the local level,

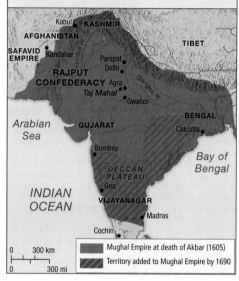

Map 17.5 The Mughal Empire in India, 1690

Building on the foundations laid by the Delhi Sultanate, the Mughals dominated northern and northwestern India, but the size and topography of the subcontinent prevented them from extending their control further. Note that the central Deccan Plateau, a center of resistance to Muslim rule, sealed the Mughals off from southern India's coast until the late seventeenth century. What weaknesses in Mughal rule made this formidable-looking empire vulnerable to eventual foreign incursions?

Mughal Empire at death of Akbar (1605)
Territory added to Mughal Empire by 1690

where the revenue agents, following Akbar's orders, could assess local agricultural conditions. In years in which the harvest was ruined by insects or bad weather, or in which animals were afflicted by outbreaks of disease, agents were directed to use tax revenues for humanitarian relief. Since the highest-ranking tax collectors were Hindus sympathetic to the peasants, the emperor's wishes were unfailingly carried out. Moreover, in legal disputes involving Hindus on both sides, Hindu rather than Islamic law was used, and the decisions of Hindu courts were final unless the losing party appealed to the throne.

These policies meant that Hindus were not only better off under Akbar than under any previous Muslim ruler, but also better off than many would be in centuries to come. Indeed, the emperor's tolerance of Hindus began to worry orthodox Muslims. When, after 1581, Akbar put down several revolts in Muslim regions in the North, he increased his popularity among the Hindu majority. Akbar himself practiced Sufi rituals, with additional practices adapted from Hindus, Jains, Sikhs, and Christians.

Under Mughal rule India's culture became increasingly Persian. Akbar made Farsi the language of administration and Islamic law, offending orthodox Muslims who believed that Arabic, the language of worship, should also be the language of state business. Akbar also encouraged the creation of poetry and literature in the Farsi, Urdu (*UHR-doo*), and Hindi (*HIN-dē*) languages, rather than insisting on the exclusive use of Arabic or Turkish. In addition, Sufism, the basis of Akbar's ritual observances, was essentially a Persian doctrine, and fashions and etiquette at the Mughal court also owed more to Isfahan than to Baghdad or Delhi.

Akbar was not typical of sixteenth-century Islamic rulers. In some ways he resembled an absolute monarch; in others, an enlightened despot—one whose absolute rule is tempered by learning and a commitment to the service of his subjects. In his willingness to incorporate aspects of other cultures into a Mughal synthesis, Akbar can with some justice be called modern. But the end of his reign was troubled by a vicious struggle for succession. Akbar's son Salim (*sah-LĒM*) rebelled in 1601, and after four years of turmoil the emperor died, probably a victim of poison. The impatient Salim then became emperor of the most powerful empire in the history of India, and one of the most formidable in the entire world.

The Great Mughals

Prince Salim's reign ushered in the era of the Great Mughals. With much of South Asia unified under their control, there seemed to be no threats to the empire. Salim celebrated his coronation by taking the name Jahangir (*zhah-hahn-GĒR*)—"World Seizer"—and by continuing his father's efforts to create in India a new unified civilization with Islamic, Hindu, and Persian components.

NUR JAHAN AND SHAH JAHAN: LIGHTING THE WORLD. In 1611 the Persian strand became dominant as Jahangir married a 34-year-old widow from Persia whom he renamed Nur Jahan (*NOOR jah-HAHN*), "Light of the World." She was quick-witted and politically skilled, and since Jahangir possessed neither of these attributes, she quickly became the true sovereign. Through her and her Persian relatives, Safavid style and culture left an enduring mark on India.

Nur Jahan saw to it that her father became Jahangir's chief minister and arranged for the marriage of her niece, Mumtaz Mahal (*MOOM-tahz mah-HAL*), to Shah Jahan ("Emperor of the World"), Jahangir's son by an earlier marriage. She then supported Shah Jahan for the imperial succession. Jahangir, preferring to spend his time drinking wine, making love, and writing Persian poetry, was more than willing to turn military affairs over to his crown prince. By 1622, however, Nur Jahan had become jealous of her stepson, and when she ordered him to undertake a risky expedition to Kabul, he refused and rose in revolt. When Jahangir died in 1627, Shah Jahan exiled Nur Jahan to Lahore, where she lived out her life on a sizable pension.

Nur Jahan becomes the real ruler of the Mughal Empire

That solution was typical of Shah Jahan, who seldom hesitated to spend money. He lavished gifts on his harem of 5,000 women and on Mumtaz Mahal, his wife, who bore him 14 children prior to her death in childbirth at the age of 39. Inconsolable, Shah Jahan immortalized her with the construction of her magnificent tomb, the Taj Mahal (*TAHZH mah-HAHL*), a masterpiece fusing Persian artistic form with Indian craftsmanship and materials. He also built the Pearl Mosque at Agra (*AH-grah*), a sparkling jewel of white marble and a monument to Muslim rule in northern India.

But for all his spendthrift ways, Shah Jahan was not generous to his subjects. Rather than suspending taxation to ease famine and the burden of natural disasters, as Akbar had done, Shah Jahan grudgingly passed out a handful of rupees. This policy prompted recurring revolts on the central Deccan plateau, an area inhospitable to agriculture and a never-ending drain on money and manpower for the Great Mughals. Instead of relief efforts, Shah Jahan sent armies, causing additional resentment.

Shah Jahan builds monuments but neglects his subjects

In the early 1640s Shah Jahan began construction of a new capital at Delhi, the seventh and last such city to be built on that site, which he immodestly named Shah Jahanabad (see "François Bernier Comments on Conditions in Delhi"). The city was laid out on an immense scale and included two spectacular building complexes, the Red Fort and the Jama Masjid (*JAH-mah mahs-JĒD*) Mosque. All this construction required enormous sums of money, which Shah Jahan obtained by increasing tax rates by 50 percent. Thus although he left an architectural legacy that dazzles visitors to the present day, he was neither popular nor competent in his own time, and when he fell ill in 1657, his sons saw their opportunity. They intrigued against each other for a year, and in 1658 the winner was the militant orthodox Muslim Aurangzeb (*ore-RAHNG-zebb*), who ruled as Alamgir (*AH-lahm-gēr*) I ("World Conqueror") for 49 years.

The Taj Mahal.

AURANGZEB'S REIGN: REBELLION AND DISUNITY.
Aurangzeb's combination of cunning, ruthlessness, piety, and administrative brilliance made him the most formidable of the Great Mughals. Joyless and puritanical, he spent many hours in prayer and ended the extravagant ways of his father, both in architecture and in the harem. He also ended Akbar's policy of tolerance for non-Muslims, increasing their taxes, denying them building permits for temples, and requiring Hindus to pay double taxes for food. Those who protested these harsh measures were trampled by elephants. As taxes increased and starvation threatened, revolts broke out in various parts of the empire.

Aurangzeb reverses Akbar's policy of tolerance

Under Aurangzeb's tyranny, Sikhs in the Punjab transformed their peace-loving faith into an instrument of rebellion and evolved into a militant community, the "army of the pure." All Sikh males were baptized with the surname Singh (*SĬNG*), or "Lion." Sikh men vowed to wear beards and carry sabers for mutual recognition. Easily outnumbering them,

Document 17.2 François Bernier Comments on Conditions in Delhi

François Bernier, a French traveler in India in the mid-seventeenth century, commented upon the suitability of Indian buildings to the tropical climate.

In treating of the beauty of these towns . . . I have sometimes been astonished to hear the contemptuous manner in which Europeans in the Indies speak of [Delhi] and other places. They complain that the buildings are inferior in beauty to those of the Western world, forgetting that different climates require different styles of architecture; that what is useful and proper at Paris, London, or Amsterdam, would be entirely out of place at Delhi; insomuch that if it were possible for any one of those great capitals to change place with the metropolis of the Indies, it would become necessary to throw down the greater part of the city, and to rebuild it on a totally different plan . . .

The heat is so intense in [Delhi] that no one, not even the King, wears stockings; the only cover for the feet being slippers, while the head is protected by a small turban, of the finest and most delicate materials. The other garments are proportionately light. During the summer season, it is scarcely possible to keep the hand on the wall of an apartment, or the head on a pillow. For more than six successive months, everybody lies in the open air without covering—the common people in the streets, the merchants and persons of condition sometimes in their courts or gardens, and sometimes on their terraces, which are first carefully watered. Now, only suppose the streets of [Paris] transported hither, with their close houses and endless stories; would they be habitable? or would it be possible to sleep in them during the night, when the absence of wind increases the heat almost to suffocation? Suppose one just returned on horseback, half dead with heat and dust, and drenched, as usual, in perspiration; and then imagine the luxury of squeezing up a narrow dark staircase, there to remain almost choked with heat. In the Indies, there is no such troublesome task to perform. You have only to swallow quickly a draught of fresh water, or lemonade; to undress; wash face, hands, and feet, and then immediately drop upon a sofa in some shady place, where one or two servants fan you . . .

SOURCE: François Bernier, *Travels in the Mogul Empire, A.D. 1656–1668*, translated by Archibald Constable (Delhi: S. Chand, 1968) 240–241.

Mughal armies held them off, but the Sikhs retained their hatred for Islamic political authority and remained a dangerous force.

Aurangzeb encountered further opposition from Hindus on the Deccan plateau, where Shivaji Bonsle (*shē-VAH-jē BAHNS-lē*) founded the Hindu **Maratha** (*mah-ruh-TAH*) nationalist movement to resist Mughal rule. Shivaji was a pioneer in **guerrilla warfare**—raids by small roving bands of warriors that aim to disrupt armies rather than defeating them in open battle. He once killed an opposing Muslim general during apparent surrender talks. Irreconcilable to the Mughal Empire, the Marathas' ferocious Hindu nationalism represented exactly the sort of reaction that Akbar's policy of tolerance and respect had been designed to avoid.

At enormous cost, Aurangzeb unifies India

Aurangzeb reacted vigorously, realizing that the many different forces arrayed against him were as suspicious of one another as they were of Mughal rule. His armies isolated the Sikhs in the Punjab and plundered the Deccan. By 1700 Aurangzeb had unified India to an extent undreamed of even by Ashoka. But his was a grim victory, costing more than two million lives, wasting tremendous sums of money, and despoiling virtually the entire subcontinent. His armies left behind empty cities and devastated farmlands, dooming central India to famine and disease for years to come.

Few mourned Aurangzeb when he died in 1707. His ill-conceived policies had created a vast empire while at the same time impoverishing it, and the opposition his brutality had provoked actually strengthened Indian regionalism and disunity. These developments occurred just as India began to notice the danger posed by visitors from Europe.

Chapter Review

Putting It in Perspective

From the thirteenth through sixteenth centuries, the Islamic world underwent two profound transformations. In the thirteenth it was devastated and divided by Mongol conquests. In the fourteenth, when it seemed to be recovering from these onslaughts, it was hit by a new wave of invaders led by Timur Lenk. Once again the Islamic world was shattered; once again it was rebuilt.

Those who led this second period of rebuilding—the Ottomans, Safavids, and Mughals—were themselves the descendants of Mongolian and Turkish nomads from Central Asia, and thus relative newcomers to the regions they ruled. With the flexibility of outsiders, they were able to combine cultures, creating hybrid systems that drew from various traditions. Consequently, by the sixteenth century, the realms that their descendants ruled were among the most powerful and prosperous on the planet. But these empires also faced dangers that became apparent in the next century.

One danger came from within. The size, multiethnicity, and religious diversity of their domains bred tensions and conflicts that challenged both state and society. Exceptional rulers such as Suleiman and Akbar were able to balance competing interests and treat all subjects fairly, thus maintaining broad support. Other rulers, however, far less talented and tolerant, either sought to impose uniformity by force or withdrew into the pleasures of royal palaces and ignored the needs of their realm. Either way, the results were often mass discontent, and sometimes regional rebellion.

Another threat came from outside. The Europeans, having adopted ideas and technology from the Chinese and Muslims, were searching for new sea routes to connect the East and West. This largely commercial quest led them to engage the Muslim world in a long and bitter conflict over commerce. It also brought them in contact with some extraordinary empires that had arisen in the Americas, in total isolation from the rest of the world.

Reviewing Key Material

KEY CONCEPTS

Pax Ottomanica, 414	shah, 422
grand vezir, 416	Sikh, 426
fatwa, 416	Maratha, 430
urfi, 417	guerrilla warfare, 430
Janissaries, 417	

KEY PEOPLE

Mehmed II, 410	Radiya, 425
Timur Lenk, 410	Ala al-Din, 425
Bayezid I, 415	Nanak, 426
Murad I, 415	Babur, 426
Selim I, 418	Akbar, 426
Suleiman I, 418	Jahangir, 428
Kara Mustafa, 421	Nur Jahan, 428
Jan III Sobieski, 421	Mumtaz Mahal, 429
Safi al-Din, 421	Shah Jahan, 428
Shah Ismail, 422	Aurangzeb, 429
Shah Abbas, 423	Shivaji Bonsle, 430
Iletmish, 425	

ASK YOURSELF

1. What blended features made Ottoman government and society unique? Why were these features developed?
2. How did the Safavids use Shi'ite Islam as a governing tool in Persia?

3. How did the Mughals manage to rule India despite their status as members of a religious minority? What did Akbar do to reconcile his Islamic regime to the Hindu population?

4. In what ways did each Islamic empire blend Islamic practices with the cultures of the people under its rule? How were social structures, family, and gender roles influenced by this blending?

GOING FURTHER

Basham, A. *A Cultural History of India.* 1975.

Chandler, Neelan. *Socio-Economic History of Mughul India.* 1987.

Etil, Esin. *The Age of Sultan Suleyman the Magnificent.* 1987.

Faroqhi, Suraiya. *The Ottoman Empire and the World Around It.* 2004.

Goffman, Daniel. *The Ottoman Empire and Early Modern Europe.* 2002.

Golden, Peter. *An Introduction to the History of the Turkic Peoples.* 1992.

Goodwin, Jason. *Lords of the Horizon: A History of the Ottoman Empire.* 1999.

Hansen, W. *The Peacock Throne: The Drama of Mogul India.* 1972.

Ikram, S. *History of Muslim Civilization in India and Pakistan.* 1989.

Imber, Colin. *The Ottoman Empire, 1300–1650.* 2002.

Itkowitz, Norman. *The Ottoman Empire and the Islamic Tradition.* 1980.

Kafadar, Cemal. *Between Two Worlds: The Construction of the Ottoman State.* 1995.

Keyvani, Mehdi. *Artisans and Guild Life in the Later Safavid Period.* 1982.

Kunt, Metin, and Christine Woodhead, eds. *Süleyman the Magnificent and His Age.* 1995.

Lambton, Ann. *Continuity and Change in Medieval Persia.* 1988.

Marozzi, Justin. *Tamerlane.* 2004.

Monshi, E. *History of Shah Abbas the Great.* 2 vols. 1978.

Richards, John. *The Mughul Empire.* 1996.

Savory, Roger. *Iran Under the Safavids.* 1980.

Soudawar, A., and M. Beach. *The Art of the Persian Courts.* 1992.

Wheatcroft, A. *The Ottomans.* 1993.

Key Dates and Developments

1206–1397	The Delhi Sultanate
1360–1405	Conquests of Timur Lenk
1389	Battle of Kosovo; Ottoman Rule in the Balkans
1453	Constantinople falls to Mehmed the Conqueror; end of the Byzantine Empire
1501	Shah Ismail proclaims Shi'ism in Safavid Iran
1526	Ottoman victory at Moháćs (Hungary) Battle of Panipat; Mughal Empire begins in India
1529	Suleiman fails to take Vienna
1556–1605	Akbar rules Mughal India
1571	Ottoman fleet defeated at Lepanto
1587–1629	Rule of Shah Abbas in Iran
1605–1707	The Great Mughals in India
1683	King Jan III Sobieski defeats Ottomans at Vienna
1699	Peace of Karlowitz

The Aztec and Inca Empires, 1300–1550

Machu Picchu

In the fifteenth century C.E., the Inca Empire constructed this fortress city of Machu Picchu, high in a remote area of the Andes Mountains. The Inca overcame this formidable terrain to create an empire extending for more than 3,000 miles north to south (page 441).

Throughout the city, the women arose before dawn. They laid fresh wood on the fires and warmed up a simple meal of tortillas stuffed with beans. Then they awakened their husbands and children for breakfast. The sun was just barely above the horizon when the men left to work in the fields or started their work at home, making weapons, tools, or goods to be offered for sale. After cleaning the family's dishes and utensils, the women left to sweep the streets and to collect the neighborhood's garbage and waste. At midmorning they would carry the refuse to the water's edge, where it would be loaded into canoes and transported to the mainland. Perhaps some of them would pause to talk among themselves, or simply to gaze out over the placid surface of Lake Texcoco toward the mountains in the distance.

The Inca Empire

The Aztec Empire

These were the women of Tenochtitlán (*teh-nōsh-tit-LAHN*), capital of the Aztec Empire and one of the most unusual cities of the world. Built on a group of islands within a lake in the Valley of Mexico, eight thousand feet above sea level, Tenochtitlán was the center of a civilization that by 1500 was less than two centuries old. Its women worked diligently to keep the city clean, a critical task in a tropical metropolis surrounded by fungus-bearing water. They raised the children and maintained the households for their husbands, most of whom worked as farmers or artisans for eight months and devoted the remaining four to military combat on behalf of the empire. As farmers, the Aztecs cultivated a wide variety of nutritious crops; as artisans, they created quetzal-feather mosaics of exceptional beauty; as warriors, they constructed a powerful state that awed and intimidated all other Amerinds who knew of its existence. Yet within a generation, the realm in which these Aztecs lived and worked was invaded and conquered, not by other Amerind peoples but by a foreign people from another hemisphere.

The Great Amerind Empires

In 1500 C.E., the Amerind civilizations were very new and very isolated. Their newness was due to the relative lateness of the Amerinds' transition from hunting and gathering to agriculture. Before the development of agricultural and urban economies, there had been no need for governments and states with the power to organize labor for public works, such as draining swamps and building walls around cities. All these processes had happened earlier in the river civilizations of ancient Asia and Africa. Also delaying the development of Amerind social organization was the scarcity of large four-footed mammals that could be domesticated for meat and—more important to the economy—for work in pulling plows or heavy loads. These kinds of animals had lived in the Americas before humans arrived, but most had been hunted to extinction shortly thereafter. These and other factors meant that in 1500 early American societies were in earlier stages of development than those inhabiting the Eurasian landmass.

Amerind societies were also isolated compared to Eurasian societies, which had both suffered and benefited from extensive connections among cultures. The economic and technological advantages enjoyed by Europeans in 1500 had been copied or adapted from Persia, Greece, Carthage, Arabia, India, and China—societies that Amerinds did not know existed. European social and governing structures had been influenced by Greece, Rome, the Germanic invasions, and institutionalized Christianity. In contrast, the Aztec and Inca Empires had developed in isolation, cut off not only from any knowledge of the older societies of the eastern hemisphere but also from each other. Because of this isolation, Amerinds lacked immunity to Eurasian diseases, familiarity with Eurasian technology, and acquaintance with Eurasian governing structures.

Isolation delays the development of early America

Three Amerind civilizations, however, had evolved more rapidly than others, despite their isolation. They had created class systems that proved capable of technological innovation, including the construction of cities more extensive in scope and more refined in conveniences than most cities in Asia and Europe. The oldest of the three, the Maya culture of what are now Mexico and Guatemala, had achieved substantial complexity before 800. But a combination of undetermined circumstances had first weakened and then destroyed this civilization in the next few centuries. By 1500 millions of Maya were living in extremely primitive conditions in the rain forests. Their great cities had long been abandoned, and even the ruins remained unknown until the nineteenth and twentieth centuries.

The other two cultures had achieved significant cultural complexity only one or two centuries before 1500. In central Mexico, the Aztec people organized themselves around a warrior elite, conquered neighboring tribes through intimidation or force, and built the spectacular city of Tenochtitlán to serve as their empire's capital. Farther south, the Inca people of Peru pieced together an empire that stretched thousands of miles from north to south, linked by an intricate network of roads and bridges crossing the Andes mountains. They had assimilated other ethnic groups using techniques like those practiced in earlier millennia by Persia and Rome.

Aztec and Inca empires develop in relative isolation

The Aztec and Inca empires each considered itself the greatest on earth, a claim attributable at least in part to its complete lack of knowledge of comparable societies. Eurasian and African societies could learn from each other, but the Aztecs and Inca never had that opportunity. Europeans could, by contrast, learn of Chinese inventions such as gunpowder and paper and adapt them to their own purposes, but Amerind societies could not. Their newness and their isolation constituted fatal disadvantages early in the sixteenth century, when European invaders suddenly arrived by sea.

The Aztec Empire

According to the Aztecs' own creation story, they originated on an island called Aztlán (hence the name *Aztecs*) off the Pacific coast of Mexico, but left that island in 1111 to search for the land promised them by their most important god, Huitzilopochtli (*hwē-tsē-lō-PŌSH-tlē*), or Southern Hummingbird. From 1270 until 1319 they occupied Chapultepec (*chah-PULL-tā-peck*) Hill on the western fringe of what is today Mexico City. By 1325 they had moved onto an island in Lake Texcoco (*tesh-KŌ-ko*), on which Huitzilopochtli had told them they would find an eagle perched on a cactus and devouring a snake—the

An Aztec representation of the founding of Tenochtitlan in 1325 C.E.

The Aztecs' creation story portrays them as a wandering people

symbol in the center of the modern Mexican flag. The Aztecs, who called themselves Mexica (*mē-SHĒ-kah*), named the valley surrounding Lake Texcoco after themselves, calling it the Valley of Mexico. On the islands in the lake they built Tenochtitlán.

Tenochtitlán: City in the Lake

The Aztecs quickly recognized the advantages of building a city on islands. The lake was full of fish and birds to eat, and Aztecs used its waters to cultivate their crops. Instead of irrigating, they layered mud and lake plants to build large, latticework platforms, called **chinampas** (*chē-NAHM-pahs*), on which they planted their crops. Then they floated the entire structure on the surface of the lake. Nourished by the mud and plant matter, the roots of the crops sucked up the lake water and produced huge quantities of fruits, vegetables, and grains. Chinampas could be strung together to form rectangles of land on the lake, complete with intersecting waterways. With inexhaustible moisture and a tropical climate, conditions that permitted the cultivation of two successive crops each year, the chinampa system proved capable of sustaining a large population at high levels of nutrition.

The Aztecs build their capital in a lake

Building a city in the middle of a lake carried with it two additional benefits. First, cargo could be moved by canoe, both within the city on canals and between the city and the mainland. Since Mexico lacked wheeled carts (and the large animals required to pull them), water transport was quicker and less exhausting than packing loads on the backs of people. Second, the location provided valuable strategic protection for an assertive, ambitious people who made enemies easily. The city was connected to the shores by three causeways, each 25 to 30 feet wide, separated at intervals by drawbridges that could be raised to cut off the advance or retreat of hostile forces. To invade Tenochtitlán successfully, an enemy would need to construct a fleet of canoes on the lakeshore. The only other way to penetrate the city was to be invited in.

As a location for a city-state, therefore, Lake Texcoco was an unusual but not irrational choice. Nor were the Aztecs alone in their new surroundings: about a dozen other Amerind towns sprang up along the shoreline, and three of them extended into the lake. By 1500 there were some 50 cities in the Valley of Mexico.

Few cities anywhere in the world could compare with Tenochtitlán. Its center was dominated by a great double temple dedicated to Huitzilopochtli and Tlaloc (*TLAH-lock*), the god of rain. Its many canals were spanned by sturdy bridges. In contrast to other cities of the time, it was also immaculate: there was good drainage, sewage and garbage were hauled away in barges, and every day a crew of a thousand women swept down and washed public streets. Estimates of its population range from 80,000 to 250,000, but even at 80,000, it would have been one of the largest cities in the world. By contrast, in 1500 Seville, the most populous city in Spain, contained 40,000 people.

Exploitation and Human Sacrifice

Tenochtitlán was also the heart of one of the world's most oppressive realms. Following a succession of capable and aggressive leaders, the Aztecs established an empire in 1468 under Motecuzoma I (*mō-teh-koo-ZŌ-mah*), whose name was later corrupted into Spanish as Montezuma. Although destined to last only half a century, this empire (Map 18.1) was hated profoundly by all neighboring tribes for its ruthlessness.

FOUNDATION MAP 18.1 The Aztec Empire in 1519

Notice the empire's location, west of the old Mayan city-states. The Aztecs were a subgroup of the Chichimec tribe of northern Mexico, and their empire represents an intrusion of the Chichimecs into the fringes of the Mayan homelands. Notice also the existence of connections between central Mexico and the Mayan homelands three hundred years before the arrival of the Aztecs, who built trading relationships on preexisting networks. How would the compactness of central Mexico and the Yucatan Peninsula have contributed to contacts between Aztec and Maya?

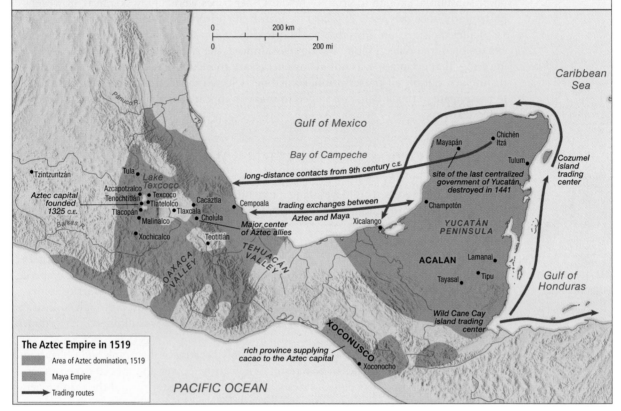

Aztec ruthlessness derived from a **cosmic mission theory** that justified a program of human sacrifice. According to this theory, the sun, the source of all heat and light and therefore of all life, grows weary during its journey across the heavens. It must be sustained by the repeated offering of a life-giving elixir, found only in beating human hearts. For this purpose, human beings were sacrificed on a regular schedule, their hearts torn from their bodies by priests and offered to the sun while still beating. Failure to perform this essential ritual was believed to doom the entire world to perpetual darkness and extinction. Human sacrifice was practiced by other early Amerind cultures, but usually only on important ceremonial occasions or in dire emergencies, such as drought or earthquake. For the Aztecs, human sacrifice was a routine program that allowed elites to legitimize their position and ensure social control.

Aztec religion provides a mechanism of social control

The cosmic mission theory justifies Aztec expansion

The cosmic mission theory was, in fact, a political and religious hoax devised by the ruling elite of the Aztec Empire. Warriors and priests both had a stake in it: warriors obtained prisoners of war for the slaughter, while priests sacrificed the victims in the proper manner. Both classes used the theory as a mechanism of social control, employing it to keep Aztec commoners subservient to the regime and to terrorize subject peoples. If ordinary Aztecs doubted its validity (and there is no reason to assume that they did), their doubt was never substantial enough to produce revolt. Other tribes were highly skeptical, however, particularly since they were expected to furnish the prisoners of war, but they could do little to alter the situation. This theory also provided a spiritual justification for the perpetual expansion of the Aztec Empire by conquest. Indeed, the Aztecs had so terrorized neighboring tribes that conquest was not always necessary to secure prisoners of war. The tribes themselves, out of self-preservation, sometimes selected the victims, who were then forced to participate in mock combats staged to make it appear that they had been captured by Aztec warriors.

Society and Culture

The Aztec Empire was founded on blood. But this obsession with human sacrifice did not prevent the Aztecs from developing a carefully stratified society with a standard of living that many throughout the world would have envied.

Human sacrifice.

Aztecs develop a complex social stratification

Social Classes and Gender Roles. At the top of Aztec society was the ruling class, or *Tecuhtli* (*teh-COOT-lē*), drawn from the leading generals, high officials of Tenochtitlán, chiefs of outlying districts, judges in the capital, and priests. This class elected the emperor, a nonhereditary position. The emperor was almost always a distinguished warrior; only once was a priest elected, and even he had been a general too. Thus, although sons of the *Tecuhtli* were nobles by right of birth, leadership in the empire was ultimately determined by success in warfare.

The lords of Mexico were wealthy men, but only because of their rank and obligations. Aztec society considered riches to be a result of increasing power and official expenses, not a method of obtaining that power. Priests lived in chilling austerity, and the leading generals and political officials spent money on everything and everyone except themselves. This meritocracy offered the chance for social mobility. Commoners could rise into the *Tecuhtli* through exceptional skill in combat, while nobles could descend to common status just as readily through incompetence or cowardice. And the empire paid a great deal of attention to the training of both its leaders and its workers: no Mexican child, whatever his or her rank or wealth, was denied an education.

The love of profit for its own sake that was rejected by the nobility was embraced by the *Pochteca* (*pōsh-TECK-ah*), the merchant caste. Utterly inbred, with marriage restricted to those within the caste and with fathers passing businesses on to their sons, the merchants spent their lives on the road selling manufactured goods and luxury items throughout Mexico and Central America. On their continuous journeys they dispensed justice within their own ranks, defended themselves against bandits without the help of warriors, and prayed without the intercession of priests. They sold jewelry, household implements, and elegant mosaics made of quetzal feathers. The Aztec Empire relied on the Pochteca for its material needs and left them alone.

Below the Pochteca were the *Tolteca* (*tōl-TECK-ah*), a caste of artisans practicing trades such as goldsmith, jeweler, salter (a specialist who preserved food by salting it), and quarryman. Here too skills remained within families. This caste had its own chiefs, who represented Tolteca interests within the highest councils of the empire.

Most Mexica were commoners, or *Macehualtin* (*MAH-sā-wahl-tēn*). Full citizens of the Aztec Empire, they enjoyed certain civil rights. Men could own land, send their children to school, share in the spoils of conquest, vote for local chiefs, and if they were intelligent and courageous, rise out of their class to become honored and wealthy. On the other hand, if a *macehual* did nothing to distinguish himself in the first years of his adult life, he was subject to weighty obligations, including communal labor and the payment of taxes (from which nobles were exempt).

At the bottom of the social structure were the *Tlatlacotin* (*TLA-tla-cō-tēn*), or slaves. They were owned by others, but were housed, clothed, and fed like ordinary citizens. They could sell their labor in their spare time, accumulate savings, buy land or houses, or even buy slaves for their own service. Marriage between a slave and a free person was permitted, and all children of such unions were born free. Unlike the Atlantic trade that later enslaved Africans, slavery as practiced in the Aztec Empire was based not on race but on bad conduct. Enslavement was a punishment for certain crimes or for chronic indebtedness. It also served as a form of welfare: people who were unsuited by temperament to earning a living, who drank too much, or who were mentally or emotionally unstable could sell themselves into slavery in order to obtain food, clothing, and shelter. Giving up the rights and duties of freedom, they were able to survive.

> Slavery in Aztec Mexico had no racial basis

While men in Aztec society engaged in the governance of the empire and its expansion through battle, women were almost completely confined to domestic roles. The remarkable cleanliness of Tenochtitlán and other Aztec cities was largely women's responsibility. Women also wove the elaborate costumes, cotton armor, and everyday clothing worn throughout central Mexico. Marriage and childbearing were expected and were welcomed with joyful festivities. An unmarried woman was an oddity attributable to some sort of mental or emotional defect. Some women served as physicians and accumulated extensive knowledge of herbal remedies and medical procedures.

LAW, HEALTH, AND DEATH IN AZTEC MEXICO. Governing this complex society was a highly effective legal system. There were no lawyers; judges examined defendants directly and used a wide variety of methods to determine the truth. Judges were drawn from the finest graduates of Aztec schools and took up their posts after years of success as warriors.

In keeping with a society that used the cosmic mission theory as a form of social control, punishment for offenses was harsh. Acts considered serious crimes, such as treason, homicide, espionage, adultery, and homosexuality, were punishable by death, a sentence that was carried out immediately. Minor crimes such as theft were punishable by slavery or mutilation. A judge found to have delivered a false verdict based on bribes or favoritism would be executed. No citizens could take the law into their own hands; nor was there any need to do so, since the administration of justice was so swift and severe. The Aztec Empire wanted to control its people, not rehabilitate them, and it succeeded.

> Aztecs develop a legal system based on punishment

Despite its harshness, life under the Aztecs had its advantages. Cleanliness was a cultural expectation, people bathed several times a week, and Aztec medical practices were advanced for their era. Healers knew how to set broken bones and treat dental cavities.

> Aztecs practice sophisticated medical procedures

The Aztec goddess Coatlicue.

Aztec concepts of the afterlife reinforce the cosmic mission theory

Occasionally they even performed brain surgery. Like their medical counterparts elsewhere, they did not understand the causes of diseases, but they developed effective cures and medicines, many of which are still used in Mexico today.

But no medicine, however effective, could stave off death indefinitely, especially in a society so obsessed with hurrying it along through war and sacrifice. When the end arrived, all Aztecs understood that it was ordained by fate, part of an unavoidable pattern of birth, death, and afterlife. Warriors who fell in battle were reborn as colorful hummingbirds; women who died in childbirth were transformed into goddesses. The hummingbirds escorted the sun from its rising to its zenith, while the goddesses accompanied it from its zenith to its setting. Farmers who were struck by lightning or drowned (the latter a frequent occurrence in a city built in the midst of a lake) were led by Tlaloc, the god of rain and water, to a paradise of flowers, springs, and gardens. These beliefs mirrored the cycles of nature itself: the sun comes up each morning after passing the night in the Underworld; corn dies in autumn and is reborn in spring; the luxuriant wild plants of Mexico do the same.

For those unfortunates who died an ordinary, undistinguished death, however, the outlook was much less attractive. Their destination was Mictlan (*MICK-tlahn*), the Underworld, presided over by the god and goddess of the dead. This ghoulish couple ruled a cold, dark realm of dust and bones, seated on thrones surrounded by spiders and owls. The prospect of this afterlife made death in battle welcome rather than something to be feared. In contrast, the sacrificial victims, whose beating hearts nourished the sun, became one with it and lived forever as part of the source of heat and light that made life on earth possible.

The Inca Empire

The Inca civilization of western South America developed even later than Aztec society. Covering a much larger range of territory than Aztec Mexico, the Inca Empire extended from what is today northern Ecuador into central Chile, some three thousand miles from north to south. It also differed from the Aztec realm in many other ways since, although these two empires existed at the same time in the same hemisphere, the barriers to travel between them were so great that they developed in isolation from one another.

A Unified Empire

The Inca's creation story portrays them as a people emerging from the earth

The Inca create an extensive empire in difficult terrain

The Inca creation story asserts that the Inca people emerged around the year 1200 from three caves 18 miles southeast of the city of Cuzco (*COOZ-kō*), Peru. Other Amerind peoples lived in the region, including the Huari, the Chanca, and the Chimú. The Inca did not at first challenge any of them, gradually building Cuzco and developing their political and social institutions. During this time the Inca were apparently ruled by seven legendary emperors, about whom nothing can be known with certainty. But the eighth ruler, Viracocha (*vē-rah-KŌ-chah*) Inca, laid the foundations of an empire. Between 1400 and 1438 he expanded Inca control over a 25-mile radius from Cuzco, reaching as far south as Lake Titicaca (*tih-tē-KAH-kah*) (Map 18.2).

Viracocha was followed by two remarkable rulers who enlarged the small Inca domain into one of the world's biggest empires. Pachacuti (*pah-chah-COO-tē*), who ruled from 1438 to 1471, gave the realm its official name, **Tahuantin-Suyu** (*tah-wahn-tin*

SOO-*yoo*), the Empire of the Four Quarters. He also made his native language, Quechua (*KEH-chwah*), the language of official business and organized the administrative structure of what was becoming a very large state (see page 433). By the time of his death in 1471 the Inca ruled all of present-day Peru. Then Topa Inca Yupanqui (*TŌ-pah IN-kah yoo-PAHN-kwē*), who ruled from 1471 to 1493, extended the empire to the north and south, defeating the Chimú kingdom in Ecuador and conquering the northern half of Chile. Together, given the territory they amassed, he and Pachacuti are ranked with Alexander the Great and Genghis Khan among history's great empire builders.

The Inca conquered in an unusual way, always announcing their attacks in advance and never using force except when persuasion failed. Once defeated, a conquered population was assimilated into the empire through the process of **mitima** (*mē-TĒ-mah*), or resettlement and integration. Within a generation, families resettled in Inca towns had lost their original cultural identities and become Inca, a transition made smoother by the complete absence of discrimination against them.

In 1493 a new ruler, Huayna Capac (*HWAH-nah KĀ-pack*), consolidated Inca gains and focused on the administration of the empire. Further territorial advance was blocked—to the East by the Andes mountains and the dense rain forests of their eastern slopes, and to the South by the Mapuche (*mah-POO-chā*) Amerinds, warlike and hostile to outsiders. Still, at the beginning of the sixteenth century the Inca Empire, just one hundred years old, encompassed a great expanse of land and a great many peoples, much like ancient Rome and the concurrent Ottoman Empire.

Society and Economy

Inca society contained fewer distinct social classes than did Aztec society. At the top of its political pyramid stood the emperor, called the **Sapa** (*SAH-pah*) **Inca**, a man who claimed to rule by divine right because of his direct descent from the sun god, Inti (*ĒN-tē*). He was worshiped as divine during his lifetime; after death he was carefully embalmed and mummified, and became a god like his ancestor, Inti. Because he claimed divinity, the Sapa Inca was compelled to keep the royal line pure; he could not defile it through marriage to a mortal. Thus he always chose one of his full sisters as his principal wife. From among her sons, he chose his heir. The practice usually brought the most competent son to power but also set

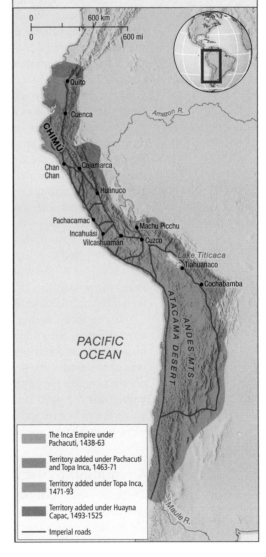

Map 18.2 The Inca Empire, 1438–1525

The Inca Empire of Tahuantin-Suyu was carved out of the Andes Mountains between the highlands of Quito and the Atacama Desert. Note the empire's shape, dictated by Andean geography: it was three thousand miles north to south at its longest point, but only four hundred miles east to west at its widest. The Aztec Empire enjoyed the advantage of compactness (Map 18.1), while the Inca Empire struggled successfully with geographic disadvantages. How did the Inca overcome those disadvantages?

brothers against one another. When the Sapa Inca died suddenly without designating a successor, a brutal power struggle followed.

The Sapa Inca exercises enormous power, even after death

The Sapa Inca's authority was so great that some of it actually survived him. After death, the emperor's body was embalmed with fragrant resins and dried in the sun in the arid highlands around Cuzco. Then his mummy was enshrined in one of the palaces in which he had lived. Servants attended the mummies of each successive Sapa Inca, deciding when to offer him food and drink, occasionally taking one mummy to visit another or to visit living people in their homes. On great ceremonial occasions, or if the empire faced challenges or dangers, all the mummies would be assembled in the great squares of Cuzco. People would pay them homage, and the ruling Sapa Inca would formally consult them, asking their advice on affairs of state. Thus the emperors were revered after death as living spirits equal to most of the other gods of the empire.

Below the Sapa Inca, the empire was governed by a two-class nobility, the Inca Caste and the Curacas (*coo-RAH-kahz*). The Inca Caste was composed of blood relatives of the Sapa Inca, usually numbering several hundred people. Curacas were all other governmental officials and their families. Both components of the nobility were exempt from taxes and were supported by produce from government-owned fields tilled by commoners. Sons of the nobility were the only Inca subjects to be educated, in contrast to the Aztec practice of universal education for boys and girls. Since there was no written language, instruction was entirely oral.

Inca nobility dominates a free people

Beneath the Sapa Inca and the nobility, all were commoners and all were free; slavery was unheard of in Tahuantin-Suyu. Commoners provided all the labor for public works. Since no money existed and payments in kind were unknown, commoners paid taxes through labor service. This duty furnished recruits for the army, laborers in mines and on public works, and messengers who traveled the remarkable system of imperial roads.

The Inca base their society on agriculture

Most commoners were farmers, and Inca agriculture was highly advanced, benefiting from centuries of development by earlier societies in the region, and supported by extensive irrigation. Peasants grew a wide variety of crops, most significantly the potato, which they had developed through selective breeding from a hard, unappetizing nut-like root into one of the world's most nutritious foods. Later, after the Spanish conquest of Peru, the potato was taken to Europe, where it became the staple crop of areas such as Ireland and Poland and was eventually grown almost everywhere.

In the Inca Empire, as in Aztec Mexico, most men spent their days farming, while most women, who played exclusively domestic roles, spent their days doing farm chores, housework, and cooking. Married life was the normal state, and the raising of children was considered woman's sacred task. Sexual intercourse before marriage for both genders was relatively common and not frowned upon, although some women selected for highly favored positions at Inca religious shrines remained virginal for life. These virgins wove the elaborate garments worn by Inca idols, swept and beautified the shrines, and were forbidden to speak to men.

Adaptation to the Andes

The Inca connect their empire by a network of roads and bridges

The Inca were ingenious in adapting to their physical environment and in keeping the empire connected. The extensive network of roads and bridges that they built made it possible to carry a message from one end of the empire to the other in about 12 days. Since the

Sapa Inca ruled from the centrally located capital of Cuzco, he rarely had to wait more than six days for the latest news from outlying areas. The roads were smoothly paved with great blocks of stone and lined with retaining walls. Even in the narrowest mountain passes, a dozen men could walk along them side by side. Across the dizzying gorges formed by swiftly flowing Andean rivers, the Inca threw suspension bridges made of thick fibers and secured at each end by stone pylons. In a kind of postal system, a succession of sure-footed runners traveled these roads and bridges. The messages they carried, in the absence of writing, were composed of a series of knots in cords dangling from a piece of wood called a **quipu** (*KĒ-pooh*).

Physically, the Inca had evolved over the years to meet the demands of their harsh environment. To handle the stress caused by the lack of adequate oxygen at high elevations in the Andes, their lung capacity was 40 percent greater than that of sea-level dwellers, with much denser capillary beds. Their bodies also contained 25 percent more blood of very high viscosity, with a far greater number of oxygen-carrying red corpuscles. To handle that sort of load, their hearts were enlarged by 40 percent, and their bodies tended to be short and compact, with low centers of gravity. These characteristics are still found today in the Andean peoples of Ecuador, Peru, and Bolivia.

A Quipu.

Governance and Religion

Politically, Tahuantin-Suyu was the product of centuries of South American cultural development. Before the Inca became the dominant force in Peruvian life, Peru had experienced a long tradition of centralized political control that made possible extensive public works, road-building, and intervalley irrigation systems. Ceramics and metallurgy were mastered, and commercial relations linked the farthest reaches of the Pacific coast. On this foundation the Inca built new concepts of military organization, colonization, and total state control. Their well-trained ruling class possessed the foresight and skill needed to manage so extensive an empire.

The Inca Empire was divided into four provinces (the "four quarters"), each ruled by a governor from the noble Inca Caste. Each significant city was ruled by a lieutenant who reported directly to the provincial governor. Below these leaders were hereditary governing positions filled by Curacas. These local officials, the basic governing personnel of the empire, handled matters such as taxation, public works, minor crimes, complaints, and institutions such as the imperial mass marriage, announced periodically by the Sapa Inca in order to ensure a ready supply of children for the empire. During this ceremony, all single men and women would line up opposite each other, after which the Curaca assigned mates on the basis of physical condition. For obvious reasons, the day before the imperial mass marriage was usually filled with weddings.

Tahuantin-Suyu's division into four provinces somewhat reduced the imperial power of the Sapa Inca. Although this power was theoretically absolute, in practice it was exercised by many governors and local officials. These men were given considerable latitude in the interpretation and execution of imperial commands, provided that their loyalty was beyond dispute. To guarantee that loyalty, the Sapa Inca occasionally sent from Cuzco a special official known as the *Tocoyricoc* (*tō-COY-rē-cōke*), or "he who sees all." This official was actually an informer charged with reporting on the loyalty and competence of the governor and on the general state of affairs within the province. He was

The Inca centralize their far-flung empire

Inca buildings in the former imperial capital of Cuzco. Stones were fit together with such precision that mortar was unnecessary.

usually a close relative of the Sapa Inca, fearless and incorruptible, and the ever-present possibility of his arrival helped keep administrators honest.

Inca religion is polytheistic and tolerant

Inca religion, like Aztec religion, was founded on sun worship. It combined nature worship and magic, all centered on Inti, the sun god. Behind the sun, and indeed behind all things, stood Viracocha, Creator of the Universe; but he was invisible to men and women, while Inti appeared in the heavens every day. The Inca worshiped other deities, too, such as the Storm God. Like the ancient Persians and Romans, they tolerated the gods of those they conquered, insisting only on a place of honor for Inti in all rites and festivals. Such tolerance was essential to the practice of mitima.

These gods were believed to be pleased by sacrifice, usually of food, coca leaves (later to become the base for cocaine), and animals. In serious emergencies, such as drought or earthquake, or on important occasions, a pure white llama or a beautiful child might be killed to win the gods' favor. But the Inca never developed any equivalent of the Aztec Empire's "cosmic mission theory" to justify human sacrifice.

Aztec and Inca on the Eve of Invasion

Aztec and Inca political systems develop similarly to those of Europe

For all their differences, the Aztec and Inca Empires had in common certain institutions that affected their encounters with Europeans. First, authority resided in an emperor whose power was absolute. No assemblies or councils existed to restrict his decisions, and unquestioning obedience to the emperor was demanded. Theoretically, the emperor could respond quickly to emergencies, and at the head of an army of dedicated warriors, he would be difficult to defeat. But if either empire were ever defeated, the stress on unquestioning obedience to leaders would make it easier for the conqueror to rule. Unconditional obedience was readily transferable from one set of masters to another.

Second, in considering the clash of civilizations that began with the European invasions, the youth and isolation of the Aztec and Inca Empires proved to be disadvantages. The invaders came from societies whose extensive intercultural contacts had furnished them with methods, technologies, animals, and immunities unknown in the Americas. It was not a fair contest. The early American civilizations, remarkably rich in their cultural development in comparison with other cultures in the hemisphere, were about to meet their match. No one can say how the Aztec and Inca societies, so highly developed in comparison with other cultures in the western hemisphere, might have evolved had Europeans never arrived.

The Invasion and Conquest of Mexico

Montezuma II (1502–1520), emperor when the Spanish arrived, was the first priest to rule the Aztec Empire. Thirty-four when elected, he was a valiant warrior as well as a pious man. He was fascinated by magic and omens, or signs about the future, and by 1519 had come to prefer contemplation and diplomacy to action. These priestly tendencies did not, however, make him gentle: he terrified both his court and the general public and was the most feared ruler in the history of Tenochtitlán. His commitment to consolidating his empire rather than continuing to expand it was based not in weakness but in realistic calculation.

Unlike the Inca, the Aztecs had never attempted to integrate conquered peoples into their culture. Their empire was held together by coercion and fear, not by any form of assimilation that might have developed loyalty in the defeated. Therefore it was not surprising that during the reign of Montezuma II two inferior but significant regional powers challenged the supremacy of Tenochtitlán. In the west, the Tarascan (*tah-RAHS-cahn*) Empire united several ethnic groups hostile to Aztec expansion into a small but heavily fortified realm defended by skilled archers. In the east, the **Tlaxcallan** (*tlash-CAHL-lahn*) **Confederacy** knitted together several city-states that spoke Nahuatl (*na-WHA-tl*), the language spoken by the Aztecs and some of their neighbors, into a potent alliance that could have badly injured the Aztec Empire in an all-out war. Cautiously, Montezuma II encircled both sets of enemies as part of a long-range strategy that would yield results in decades rather than years. By 1519 the Aztecs had made substantial progress on both fronts, despite a persistent series of omens that worried their ruling elite and left the emperor perplexed.

The Aztecs base their rule on coercion

The Arrival of the Spaniards

In 1517 disturbing events took place in Mayan territory well to the East of Tenochtitlán. Bearded men with white skin, riding in what appeared to be mountains floating on the sea, began to come ashore on the Yucatan peninsula. More such events took place the following year, accompanied by omens in Tenochtitlán itself. A comet streaked across the sky at midday, temples burned for no apparent reason, and an invisible wailing woman cried out every night. These events were mysterious and unsettling to a people accustomed to searching for messages from the gods. As the Aztecs eventually learned, the strangers in floating mountains were Spaniards in sailing ships following those who had first come to the Caribbean 25 years before, looking for a sea route from Europe to Asia.

Aztecs are perplexed by the arrival of the Spaniards

The Spaniards who came in 1517, however, were no longer looking for Asia; instead they were inspired by tales of gold and glory to be found in Mexico itself. Their leader, Hernán Cortés, was an ambitious Spanish lawyer who left Spain to seek his fortune in the Caribbean. Fifteen years later, in 1519, Cortés accepted a commission from the governor of Cuba to lead an expedition to Mexico to determine the location and strength of a large and reportedly fabulously wealthy empire. He sailed for Mexico with 550 men, including a number of Africans and Cuban Amerinds, and 16 horses.

In the early spring of 1519, as Cortés was arriving in Mexico, the reports reaching Montezuma became more precise and factual. From the Gulf of Mexico, peasants reported sighting white men catching fish with nets and rods. Montezuma and his advisors decided to have the coast and the strangers watched; in the meantime, their arrival was kept secret from the people.

In the summer of 1519, news arrived that the strangers were moving inland. Aztec officials met them and spoke with them through a 15-year-old Mayan girl whom the Spaniards had baptized Marina and who spoke both Nahuatl and Spanish. The Spaniards rode on huge animals and carried and dragged long-barreled sticks that could be made to explode, discharging fire and noise. At this point the ruling elite began to consider the possibility that these people, or at least their leaders, might be gods.

Aztec legend stated that Toltec god-king Quetzalcóatl (*kwet-zahl-KŌ-ah-tul*), expelled from Tula (Chapter 5), had vowed to return one day from his eastern exile and

Dona Marina and Cortes.

The legend of
Quetzalcóatl affects
the Aztec view of the
Spaniards

reclaim Mexico for himself. He and his forces would appear in boats in the guise of light-skinned men. Given the apparently supernatural capabilities of these strangers' boats, animals, and weapons, the possibility that Quetzalcóatl was returning could not be ruled out. Even if they were mere mortals, their arrival could not be prevented: their boats could land anywhere without warning, and their weapons seemed deadly. Under such unprecedented circumstances, watchful waiting seemed the only sensible course.

The Spaniards insisted on meeting with Montezuma. In response, the emperor sent them more than a hundred porters carrying luxurious gifts normally sacrificed to gods. Included with these presents was Montezuma's order that the Spaniards remain in the East and advance no farther inland. The Aztec emperor was trying either to gain favor with a vengeful god or to deal with powerful invaders in a way that would ensure the survival of Aztec power. In either case, the empire was clearly in danger.

Spaniards exploit Aztec
perplexity

Cortés knew nothing of the legend of Quetzalcóatl, but, upon listening to Marina's translations and advice, he realized that Montezuma considered him some sort of god and feared him. He also interpreted the emperor's gifts as an offer of vassalage and therefore a sign of weakness. In Europe, vassalage involved an oath of personal loyalty that gave the lord contractual rights over the actions of the vassal. In Mesoamerica, however, vassalage involved the payment of tribute in return for being left alone. This was a very significant distinction. By interpreting Montezuma's actions in a European context, Cortés seriously underestimated the power of the empire he would encounter. He ignored Montezuma's instructions, accepted the gifts, and pressed on.

Encounter Between Aztecs and Spaniards

Cortés moved his forces west and concluded alliances with peoples such as the Totonacs (*tō-TŌ-nacks*) and Tlaxcaltecs (*tlocks-CAHL-tecks*), who paid tribute to the Aztec Empire. These Amerinds believed Cortés' promises of liberation from Aztec dominance and sent thousands of warriors to accompany the Spaniards inland. In Tenochtitlán, warriors were still engaged in the harvest; otherwise Montezuma would have had hundreds of thousands of warriors ready to defend the empire. Instead, Montezuma arranged for the Spaniards to be escorted into the city, where, without their allies, they would be far more vulnerable.

A 1524 map of
Tenochtitlan.

Tenochtitlán's size
intimidates the
Spaniards

Nothing had prepared the Spaniards for what they saw on November 8. The road to Tenochtitlán was straight, 11,500 feet above sea level, flanked by two immense active volcanoes; the altitude, solitude, and strangeness of it all began to unnerve the Spaniards. But even this impression paled when compared to the sight of the city itself. Not only was it spectacularly beautiful, it was colossal, with at least 80,000 inhabitants, the capital of an empire of more than a million people. Cortés suddenly realized the magnitude of his miscalculation. He had dismissed as exaggerations Amerind stories of the size and glory of Tenochtitlán, interpreting them in the contexts of his familiarity with Europe and of the modest size of the Mexican towns he had encountered thus far. Now he stood before an Amerind metropolis significantly larger than anything he had ever imagined, at the head of an army of a few hundred men. The success of his mission and the lives of his men hung by threads (see "Entry of the Spaniards into Tenochtitlán, November 8, 1519").

Document 18.1 Entry of the Spaniards into Tenochtitlán, November 8, 1519

Bernal Díaz del Castillo, one of the men who accompanied Cortés to Mexico, wrote an eyewitness account of that expedition fifty years after it occurred. Here he describes what the Spaniards saw and felt as they entered Tenochtitlán, which he refers to as "Mexico" or "the city of Mexico."

Early next day we left Itzapalapa with a large escort . . . and followed the causeway, which is eight yards wide and goes so straight to the city of Mexico that I do not think it curves at all. Wide though it was, it was so crowded with people that there was hardly room for them all . . . and we could hardly get through the crowds that were there. For the towers and the passages were full, and they came in canoes from all parts of the lake. No wonder, since they had never seen horses or men like us before!

With such wonderful sights to gaze on we did not know what to say, or if this were real that we saw before our eyes. On the land side there were great cities, and on the lake many more. The lake was crowded with canoes. At intervals along the causeway there were many bridges, and before us was the great city of Mexico. As for us, we were scarcely four hundred strong, and we well remembered the . . . many other warnings we had received to beware of entering the city of Mexico, since they would kill us as soon as they had us inside. Let the interested reader consider whether there is not much to ponder in this narrative

of mine. What men in all the world have shown such daring? . . .

When we came near to Mexico, at a place where there were some other small towers, the great Montezuma descended from his litter . . . many more lords walked before the great Montezuma, sweeping the ground on which he was to tread, and laying down cloaks so that his feet should not touch the earth. Not one of these chieftains dared to look him in the face. All kept their eyes lowered most reverently . . . And as they accompanied their lord we observed them marching with their eyes downcast so that they should not see him, and keeping close to the wall as they followed him with great reverence. Thus space was made for us to enter the streets of Mexico without being pressed by the crowd.

Who now could count the multitude of men, women, and boys in the streets, on the roof-tops and in canoes on the waterways, who had come out to see us? It was a wonderful sight and, as I write, it all comes before my eyes as if it had happened only yesterday . . .

So, with luck on our side, we boldly entered the city of Tenochtitlán or Mexico on 8 November in the year of our Lord 1519.

SOURCE: Bernal Díaz del Castillo, *The Conquest of New Spain*, translated by J. M. Cohen (London: Penguin Publishers, 1963) 216–219.

Operating in Cortés' favor, however, was Montezuma's behavior. Meeting the Spaniards face to face should have convinced the emperor that they were men, not gods. But even after they entered the capital, in the narrow streets where they could have been trapped, the emperor publicly embraced Cortés and continued to lavish gifts upon him. In the next months, the Aztec military elite pressed for the destruction of the strangers, but Montezuma's subservience prevented any such action. Cortés recognized that he held the advantage, and he soon placed the emperor under a form of house arrest in his own palace.

Montezuma's acceptance of this treatment remains inadequately explained. Some historians assert that he continued to believe that Cortés was divine, but the Spaniards did not behave like servants of a Mexica god. They were horrified at the practice of human sacrifice, especially the Aztec custom of presenting their guests with delicious food liberally sprinkled with human blood. They smashed images of Aztec gods and generally behaved in a manner indicating their complete disgust with Mexican culture. This was a strange way for gods to behave. Other historians speculate that Montezuma may have been clinging to whatever measure of power he could still exercise while hoping that events would turn out in his favor. Had he refused to cooperate with the Spaniards, he would have been taken by force, the imperial elite would have split among potential successors, and the Aztec empire would be leaderless in its hour of maximum danger. This explanation is more likely than that he still considered Cortés to be Quetzalcóatl.

The Aztecs finally fight the Spaniards

But if Montezuma hoped to preserve his authority by cooperating with the Spaniards, he was soon disappointed. His subservience to Cortés eroded his support among both the elite and the common people. It vanished completely in May 1520, when the Aztecs took the offensive at last. They surrounded the Spaniards in central Tenochtitlán, and Cortés proved unable to negotiate his way out of the city. Cortés then ordered Montezuma to direct the Aztecs to stop fighting. Cortés did not understand that the emperor ruled *with*, not *over*, the nobility that was now attacking the Spaniards, and could not simply tell his nobles what to do. Montezuma tried anyway but was killed as he attempted to address Aztec forces from the roof of a palace, apparently by a rock thrown by one of his own people.

The End of the Aztec Empire

Denied food and water, under assault from every side, the Spaniards eventually broke out of Tenochtitlán at midnight on June 30, 1520, during a heavy downpour. Some were killed by Aztecs attacking from canoes, but Cortés escaped with most of his men. The Spaniards fought their way through the neighboring hostile regions to Tlaxcaltec lands, which gave them refuge and an opportunity to regroup.

Smallpox cripples the Aztecs

Aztec forces did not launch a full-scale attack against the retreating invaders, in part because their armies were not at full strength due to agricultural duties, but primarily because of political instability. During the fighting in Tenochtitlán, the imperial elite replaced Montezuma with his younger brother Cuitlahuac (*quit-LAH-wock*), who had argued from the first that the invaders must be killed. But within three months Cuitlahuac was dead of smallpox. An infected Spanish soldier carried the disease, and because the peoples of the western hemisphere had never been exposed to European diseases and had no immunity to them, this smallpox outbreak killed more than a third of the population of central Mexico in less than a year.

Smallpox is a disease that kills through high fever, dehydration, and debilitation. The dying suffer terribly, and the survivors often are disfigured by scarring from pustules. The Aztecs concluded that this unknown plague was either a sign of the wrath of their gods or a punishment sent by the gods of the Spaniards. Certainly, since the strangers did not suffer from the disease (having survived it in childhood, they had immunity), their gods were protecting them. In any case, to the Aztecs the epidemic clearly demonstrated Spanish superiority. It also, of course, killed many warriors and made others unfit for battle.

The Aztecs find a strong leader in Cuauhtemoc

In February 1521, however, Cuauhtemoc (*kwow-TĀ-mock*), the son of a former emperor, succeeded Cuitlahuac and rallied his forces to attack the Spaniards. The Aztecs fought in closely packed ranks, using archery, spears, and swords with edges of polished

Document 18.2 Two Elegies on the Fall of the City of Tenochtitlán

Immediately after the fall of Tenochtitlán to the Spaniards, the surviving Aztecs reacted with shock and grief. Both emotions are vividly captured in these excerpts from two elegies, or memorial poems, written by survivors.

FIRST ELEGY

Broken spears lie in the road;
we have torn our hair in our grief.
The houses are roofless now, and their walls
are red with blood.

Worms are swarming in the streets and plazas,
and the walls are splattered with gore.
The water has turned red, as if it were dyed,
and when we drink it,
it has the taste of brine.

We have pounded our hands in despair
against the adobe walls,
for our inheritance, our city, is lost and dead.
The shields of our warriors were its defense,
but they could not save it.

SECOND ELEGY

Our cries of grief rise up
and our tears rain down,
for Tlatelolco [*tlah-tā-LAHL-kō*, a city adjacent to Tenochtitlán] is lost.
The Aztecs are fleeing across the lake;
they are running away like women.

How can we save our homes, my people?
The Aztecs are deserting the city:
the city is in flames, and all
is darkness and destruction.

Weep, my people:
know that with these disasters
we have lost the Mexican nation.
The water has turned bitter,
our food is bitter!
These are the acts of the Giver of Life.

SOURCE: Miguel Leon-Portilla, editor, *The Broken Spears: The Aztec Account of the Conquest of Mexico*, translated from Nahuatl into Spanish by Angel Maria Garibay K., and from Spanish into English by Lysander Kemp (Boston: Beacon Press, Little, Brown, 1962).

obsidian. The Spaniards countered with cannon, muskets, and swords fashioned from Toledo steel. Their metal armor was much more protective than Aztec armor made of cotton, and their horses terrified Aztec foot soldiers.

Spanish firearms killed 25 Aztecs for every one Spaniard killed by the Aztecs, but with more than one hundred thousand warriors in his armies, Cuauhtemoc's forces could sustain such losses. The Aztecs won a number of engagements and sacrificed captured Spaniards, but in late July Cortés received reinforcements from Cuba. The Aztecs' desperate subjects, now believing that the Spaniards would win, flocked to their ranks by the tens of thousands.

Cuauhtemoc requested peace talks in early August, seeking to learn how much tribute the Spaniards would demand as the price of surrender. But it quickly became apparent that Cortés was interested only in total victory, not in turning the Aztecs into vassals of the Spanish Empire. Trapped in the midst of the lake, the Aztecs fought to the end. They finally surrendered the ruins of Tenochtitlán on August 13, 1521. The Spanish invaders took possession of the city and buried the dead. The most powerful empire in the history of Mesoamerica had been destroyed (see "Two Elegies on the Fall of the City of Tenochtitlán").

Spanish firepower.

Reasons for the Spanish Victory

Several factors account for Spain's victory

Spain's victory in this epic confrontation of European and Mesoamerican civilizations can be explained by a number of factors. First, the Toltec legend of Quetzalcóatl distracted and confused the Aztecs before Cortés entered Tenochtitlán. Second, the Spaniards arrived in early November, when many warriors, who might have been able to hold off the invaders, were busy with the harvest. Moreover, Spanish military technology was clearly superior and, together with European tactical insights, gave the invaders a significant, although not decisive, advantage. Smallpox proved even more significant. This contagious disease weakened the Aztec population and nearly eliminated its elite, but had no effect on the Spaniards. As it also killed most of the political elite of the Spaniards' native allies, it gave Cortés the opportunity to name loyal commanders in their place. Cortés' leadership tactics were also important, especially compared to the indecisiveness of Montezuma. And although each side misinterpreted the actions and motives of the other, Aztec misinterpretations proved the more serious and weakened their resistance.

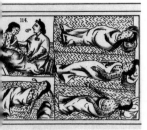

Smallpox victims.

All of these factors gave the advantage to the Spaniards. Overriding them all, however, was the Aztec policy of enslaving, persecuting, and sacrificing the people it conquered. Had the Aztecs assimilated those they defeated and sought to gain their loyalty, Cortés would never have been able to enlist more than one hundred thousand Amerind warriors as his allies, and without them he could not have conquered the Aztec Empire.

The Invasion and Conquest of Peru

The collapse of the Aztec Empire, a momentous event in Mexico, went unnoticed in Peru. The Inca, unaware of Mesoamerican civilizations, would have been more surprised by news of the existence of the Aztecs than by their defeat.

Upheavals Among the Inca

Europeans begin to encounter the Inca Empire

Huayna Capac, who became Sapa Inca in 1493, at first concentrated on consolidating his empire. Then in the early 1520s he began to extend Inca control into northern Ecuador. While fighting there, he received word that a raiding party of Amerinds had crossed into present-day Bolivia in search of tools and jewelry. Huayna Capac sent a detachment of soldiers to drive the raiders back into what is now northern Argentina and fortify the frontier. He did not know that their war leader was a Portuguese adventurer named Aleixo (*ah-LĀ-shō*) García. Had he known, he would not have understood what the arrival of Europeans signified.

The Sapa Inca continued his campaign in Ecuador. Several months later, in 1526, he received terrifying news: an unknown plague was sweeping through Cuzco, killing the strong and weak alike. By forced marches he returned to his capital and soon fell ill himself. The plague, the symptoms of which suggest smallpox, may have been introduced into Tahuantin-Suyu by merchants from Colombia, who had been exposed to Europeans, or by soldiers fighting the raiders from Argentina, who had taken in Europeans like García. Whatever its source, it killed the Sapa Inca and threw his entire empire into disarray.

Before he died, Huayna Capac had time to consider two matters of supreme importance. First was a series of disturbing reports from the coast. Bearded men were floating southward on the waves, riding in a house of gleaming white. Huayna Capac believed that these visitors, together with the unexplained plague, foretold great trouble for the empire. Second, he changed his mind about which son should succeed him. His principal wife being childless, he had originally designated Huascar (*WHASS-car*), a son by one of his other wives, as his successor. But when the fever came upon him, Huayna Capac selected another son, Ninan Cuyochi (*NĒ-nahn coo-YŌ-chē*). The Sapa Inca soon died, and a few days later Ninan Cuyochi died as well. Huascar now claimed the throne, but the fact that his dying father had passed him over emboldened yet another brother, Atahuallpa (*ah-tah-WHALL-pah*), to contest his right to rule. Huascar seized power in Cuzco, while Atahuallpa did the same in Quito, the empire's second largest city. Tahuantin-Suyu descended into civil war.

Smallpox throws the Inca Empire into disarray

Huascar was tactless, willful, and immature, and he alienated so many in Cuzco that the empire's capital gradually lost the will to defend him. Atahuallpa, by contrast, earned the allegiance of the two foremost war chiefs of the realm and conducted himself in battle with dignity and courage. The rugged terrain ensured a long, difficult struggle, but when conflict ended early in 1532 the empire was in the hands of Atahuallpa. One year earlier he had first learned of an actual landing by the Spaniards, who followed the orders of a man named Francisco Pizarro (*pē-ZAH-rō*). Pizarro, a Spanish adventurer, had set sail from Panama in 1531 with about 180 men to conquer what they had heard was a rich land to the South.

Atahuallpa wins the civil war and becomes Sapa Inca

Encounter Between Inca and Spaniards

When Pizarro's forces reached the Inca city of Tumbez, they seized it and learned at once that the Inca Empire had been torn by civil war for four years. The Spaniards, unlike the Inca, understood clearly what smallpox was and knew that they had little to fear from it. They also understood that a physically weakened population distracted by internal turmoil was exactly what Cortés had encountered and conquered in Mexico in 1521.

Spaniards understand the usefulness of smallpox in conquering Amerinds

Atahuallpa reacted to the seizure of Tumbez with a mixture of caution and interest. He concluded, incorrectly, that the newcomers were interested in taking sides in the civil war; if so, they might be worth meeting. After he captured Huascar and ended the civil war, he sought information concerning the invaders.

Unlike the Aztecs, the Inca had no Quetzalcóatl legend to distract them, and the fact that several Spaniards had been killed at Tumbez indicated that they were not gods but humans. The Sapa Inca sent an envoy to assess the situation. This man reported that Pizarro had landed with a very small number of men, that his horses were nothing more than large dogs, that his soldiers lacked fighting spirit, and that he himself could defeat them with two hundred warriors. Now feeling that he could easily rid his domain of these outsiders, Atahuallpa sent them several virgins, escorted by a war chief who promised them silver and gold if they agreed to return home.

Atahuallpa underestimates the Spaniards

In the eyes of the Inca, Pizarro reacted strangely. He accepted the women but declined to leave, marching inland instead. At Tumbez he had killed the governor and other high officials, replacing them with Inca who swore loyalty to him. Yet he continually sent messages to Atahuallpa acknowledging the latter's rights as ruler of

Map 18.3 Pizarro's Third Expedition to Peru, 1531–1533

Pizarro did not simply invade the Inca Empire without familiarizing himself with the terrain and its inhabitants. He was well aware of the imposing size of the empire and the challenging terrain his soldiers would have to cross. Observe that the length of his route was nearly fifteen hundred miles, forcing him to expose his forces to the possibility of hostile assault over a distance four times the width of the Iberian Peninsula, where he was born. His third expedition placed his forces unexpectedly in the midst of an Inca civil war. How did Pizarro use that conflict to disrupt the Inca Empire?

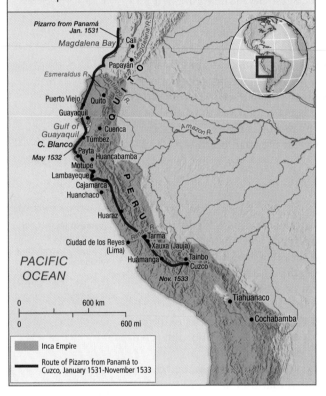

Tahuantin-Suyu. The Sapa Inca sent word to Pizarro of his recent victory over Huascar and pointed out that the visitors were far from home in a foreign and hostile land. Still the Spaniards continued inland by a route leading to the provincial city of Cajamarca (*kah-yah-MAR-kah*), populated by several thousand Inca and guarded by a large fortress. Pizarro hoped to capture or kill the Sapa Inca and take over the Inca Empire without engaging in a long military campaign like the one Cortés had waged against the Aztecs.

Cajamarca and the End of the Inca Empire

Atahuallpa's attitude and tone differed substantially from Montezuma's approach to Cortés in Mexico. However, the Sapa Inca was no less confused about the Spaniards' intentions than Montezuma had been, and he held a much lower estimation of their military potential. Still, the Spaniards might be useful as allies in pacifying the areas previously held by Huascar, and their recognition of his authority suggested that they could become his vassals and eventually be assimilated into the empire through mitima. In any event, they could not be allowed to march around the countryside unsupervised. Atahuallpa resolved to go to Cajamarca (Map 18.3) and see them for himself.

Atahuallpa arrived ahead of the Spaniards, residing at a compound built around warm springs a short distance from the city. On November 15, 1532, the Spanish entered Cajamarca. The Sapa Inca and his courtly entourage entered the city the following afternoon, as two thousand Inca swept the road before him. Carried on a litter, he was greeted by a single black-robed Spanish priest, who directed him to submit to two men called Jesus Christ and the King of Spain. Declaring that there was only one god in the heavens and that all Inca idols were to be destroyed, the priest presented Atahuallpa with a small black book of Christian devotions. The emperor examined it curiously, but since no one in a culture lacking writing could interpret the symbols on its pages (or even realize that they were intended to be read), he assumed the book was a flimsy idol and threw it on the ground. The priest then retrieved it and fled toward one of the houses surrounding the square, calling out in Spanish.

Document 18.3 An Inca Account of the Conquest of Peru

Diego de Castro Titu Cusi Yupanqui, the son of Manco Inca and the nephew of Atahuallpa, was born in 1530, two years before Pizarro's victory over Atahuallpa at Cajamarca. Titu Cusi became Sapa Inca of the unsubdued state of Vilcabamba in 1560. In 1570, he dictated to a Spanish missionary this account of the conquest.

At the time when the Spaniards first landed in this country of Peru and when they arrived at the city of Cajamarca, my father Manco Inca was residing in the city of Cuzco. There he governed with all the powers that had been bestowed upon him by his father Huayna Capac. He first learned of the Spaniards' arrival from certain messengers who had been sent from there by one of his brothers by the name of Atahuallpa, who was older but a bastard . . . They reported having observed that certain people had arrived in their land, people who were very different from us in custom and dress, and that they appeared to be Viracochas (this is the name that we used to apply to the Creator of All Things). They named the people as such because they differed very much from us in clothing and appearance and because they rode very large sheep with silver feet (by which they meant horseshoes). Another reason for calling them so was that the Indians saw them alone talking to white cloths as one person would speak to another, which is how they perceived the reading of books and letters . . .

When my uncle [Atahuallpa] was approaching Cajamarca with all of his people, the Spaniards met them at the springs of Conoc, one and a half leagues from Cajamarca . . . After having heard what they had to say, my uncle attended to them and calmly offered one of them our customary drink in a golden cup, but the Spaniard poured it out with his own hands, which offended my uncle very much. Having seen how little they minded his things, my uncle said, "If you disrespect me, I will also disrespect you." He got up angrily and raised a cry as though he wanted to kill the Spaniards. However, the Spaniards were on the lookout and took possession of the four gates of the plaza where they were, which was enclosed on all its sides.

The Indians were thus penned up like sheep in this enclosed plaza, unable to move because there were so many of them. Also, they had no weapons as they had not brought any, being so little concerned about the Spaniards . . . The Spaniards stormed with great fury to the center of the plaza, where the Sapa Inca's seat was placed on an elevated platform . . . After they had taken everything from him, they apprehended him, and because the Indians uttered loud cries, they started killing them with the horses, the swords or guns, like one kills sheep, without anyone being able to resist them. Of more than ten thousand not even two hundred escaped . . .

SOURCE: Titu Cusi Yupanqui, *An Inca Account of the Conquest of Peru*, translated by Ralph Bauer (Boulder: University Press of Colorado, 2005).

Atahuallpa instructed his entourage to punish the Spaniards. But just then musket fire burst forth from the houses, and great numbers of Spaniards, some on horses but most on foot, poured into the square. The perplexed Inca elite stood transfixed until the Spaniards fell upon them with swords and began cutting off their arms and heads. Then the panicked survivors tried to escape, but the Spaniards killed freely, as none of the Inca in the imperial entourage were armed. After the Inca guarding his litter were killed to the last man, Atahuallpa was taken prisoner. Learning what was happening in Cajamarca, the thousands of armed Inca warriors outside the city, who could certainly have intervened, fled in terror (see "An Inca Account of the Conquest of Peru").

The Spaniards attack the Inca at Cajamarca

Pizarro deceives
Atahuallpa

Having learned from his envoys that the Spaniards lusted for gold and silver, Atahuallpa offered at once to pay a huge ransom for his freedom. Pizarro demanded that two large rooms be completely filled with precious objects, one room with silver and the other with gold. He was soon presented with an amazing treasure: 26,000 pounds of pure silver and 13,420 pounds of 22-carat gold. To make this plunder portable, the Spaniards melted down priceless Inca artworks of great beauty and value, turning them into bars of gold and silver. But Atahuallpa had erred in assuming that he could trust Pizarro. Once the ransom was paid, the Sapa Inca was tried on charges of raising armies to overthrow Spanish rule, murdering his brother Huascar, and marrying his own sister. He was strangled in 1533.

In deciding to kill the Sapa Inca, Pizarro had reasoned treacherously but well. The Inca Caste, after so many years of infighting, was profoundly divided. Civil war, smallpox, and the Cajamarca ambush had killed most of the experienced leaders of the empire. By 1535 the conquest was complete. The Inca Empire had offered no significant resistance.

Reasons for the Spanish Victory

Spain's victory in this confrontation with this greatest of all Amerind empires can be explained by a number of factors. First, the demonstrated success of Spanish weaponry and tactics in Mexico, coupled with Inca ignorance of what had taken place there, gave Spain a decisive advantage at Cajamarca in 1532. As in Mexico, smallpox proved advantageous, killing the Sapa Inca in 1527 and touching off a civil war over the succession that Pizarro interpreted accurately and exploited skillfully. Third, Atahuallpa underestimated the Spanish, especially following the mistaken reports of his envoy. Then, after Cajamarca, the Inca practice of mitima worked to Spain's advantage, as the Inca, assuming the Spaniards would assimilate them as equals, did not resist. Most significant, perhaps, was Pizarro's deception. Pizarro led Atahuallpa to believe he would be freed upon payment of a huge ransom, and so the Sapa Inca did not order his massive armies to attack the invaders. When the extent of this deception became obvious, the Spaniards had been heavily reinforced.

In Peru as in Mexico, Spanish greed for gold and silver led bold men to take risks that, in retrospect, seem incredibly dangerous. But the invaders capitalized on every advantage that came their way, destroying the two greatest Amerind empires in the western hemisphere. On the ruins of those empires, other Spaniards would build a European empire of their own.

Chapter Review

Putting It in Perspective

The civilizations built by the Aztecs and Inca developed in distinctive environments, totally isolated from each other and from the eastern hemisphere. Both were based on political hierarchies headed by emperors and dominated by warrior elites, settled economies balanced between agriculture and trade, and polytheistic religions. These two civilizations created large cities, extensive transportation networks, and intricate social structures. Neither had yet completed its second century of existence when the Spaniards arrived.

Aztec Mexico was clearly the more coercive of the two. Raising human sacrifice to the level of a divine obligation and conducting it with mechanistic efficiency, Tenochtitlán terrified all those who lived in central Mexico. Disdainful of other Amerind cultures, the Aztecs sought not to govern them but to dominate and exploit them. Many of their vassals welcomed the prospect of Spanish rule. The possibility that the Spanish could be more oppressive than the Aztecs seems not to have occurred to the elites of central Mexico.

Tahuantin-Suyu was no less ruthless in its expansion than Tenochtitlán, but it developed into a militaristic empire that aimed to gain the loyalty of conquered peoples rather than slaughter them. The Inca practice of mitima gave subject peoples a stake in the empire. Human sacrifice, while not unknown, was practiced primarily during emergencies or on important occasions.

When Atahuallpa was captured at Cajamarca, the Spaniards found it easy to rule the general population of the empire. Most Inca appear to have believed that the newcomers would integrate all peoples into their new empire with some degree of equality. Like the Aztecs, however, the Inca interpreted new experiences in terms of old customs and were mistaken regarding the conquerors' intentions. They faced a situation completely unlike anything they had ever imagined: conquest by aliens from another world.

Reviewing Key Material

KEY CONCEPTS

chinampa, 436	Sapa Inca, 441
cosmic mission theory, 437	quipu, 443
Tahuantin-Suyu, 440	Tlaxcallan Confederacy, 445
mitima, 441	

KEY PEOPLE

Montezuma I, 436	Hernán Cortés, 445
Viracocha Inca, 440	Cuitlahuac, 448
Pachacuti, 440	Cuauhtemoc, 448
Topa Inca Yupanqui, 441	Huascar, 451
Huayna Capac, 441	Atahuallpa, 451
Montezuma II, 444	Francisco Pizarro, 451

ASK YOURSELF

1. How did the cosmic mission theory shape Aztec society?
2. How did the Inca and Aztec empires differ in their attitudes toward conquered peoples?
3. In the encounters between Europeans and Amerinds, what difference did it make that Amerind civilizations had developed more recently than European civilization?
4. How did Aztec and Inca ignorance of the existence of European civilization handicap them in responding to European invasion?

GOING FURTHER

Bankes, G. *Peru Before Pizarro.* 1977.
Berdan, Francis. *The Aztecs.* 1989.
Cameron, Ian. *Kingdom of the Sun God.* 1990.
Canseco, Maria. *History of the Inca Realm.* 1999.
Caso, Alfonso. *The Aztecs: People of the Sun.* 1988.
Clendinnen, Inga. *Aztecs.* 1991.
Conrad, Geoffrey, and Arthur Demarest. *Religion and Empire: The Dynamics of Aztec and Inca Expansionism.* 1984.
Davies, Nigel. *The Aztecs.* 1989.
Day, Jane. *Aztec: The World of Montezuma.* 1992.
Disselhoff, Hans. *Daily Life in Ancient Peru.* 1967.
Fagan, B. *The Aztecs.* 1984.
Gillespie, S. *The Aztec Kings.* 1989.

Haas, Jonathon, et al. *The Origin and Development of the Andean State.* 1987.

Hassig, Ross. *Aztec Warfare: Imperial Expansion and Political Control.* 1988.

Henning, E., and J. Raney. *Monuments of the Inca.* 1982.

Leon-Portilla, Miguel. *The Aztec Image of Self and Society.* 1992.

Lockhart, J. *We People Here: Nahuatl Accounts of the Conquest of Mexico.* 1993.

Mason, J. Alden. *Ancient Civilizations of Peru.* 1988.

McIntyre, Loren. *The Incredible Inca and Their Timeless Land.* 1978.

Metraux, Alfred. *The History of the Incas.* 1970.

Murra, John. *The Economic Organization of the Inca State.* 1980.

Padden, R. C. *The Hummingbird and the Hawk.* 1967.

Silverblatt, Irene. *Moon, Sun, and Witches: Gender Ideologies and Class in Inca and Colonial Peru.* 1987.

Soustelle, Jacques. *Daily Life of the Aztecs on the Eve of the Spanish Conquest.* 1955.

Sullivan, W. *The Secret of the Incas: Myth, Astronomy, and the War Against Time.* 1996.

Townshend, Richard. *The Aztecs.* 1992.

van Zantwijk, Rudolf. *The Aztec Arrangement: The Social History of Pre-Spanish Mexico.* 1985.

Key Dates and Developments

ca. 1111	The Aztecs move into central Mexico
ca. 1200	Inca ascendancy begins in the central Andes
1325	Foundation of Tenochtitlán
1400–1438	Inca expansion under Viracocha Inca
1438–1471	Pachacuti founds Tahuantin-Suyu
1440	Aztecs dominate the Valley of Mexico
1471–1493	Topa Inca expands the Inca Empire
1502–1520	Reign of Montezuma II
1519	Cortés leads an expedition from Cuba to Mexico
1521	Fall of Tenochtitlán
1527	Death of Huayna Capac; civil war in Tahuantin-Suyu
1531	Pizarro leads an expedition from Panama to Peru
1532	Capture of Atahuallpa at Cajamarca

CHAPTER 19

Global Exploration and Global Empires, 1400–1700

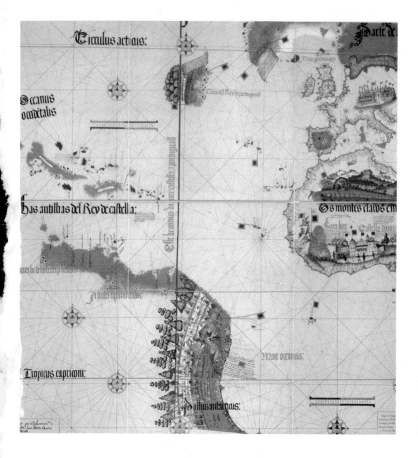

Portuguese Claims
In Africa And Brazil

A sixteenth-century map shows Portugese claims in Africa and Brazil. Few would have predicted that tiny Portugal would lead the way in European exploration of the globe (see page 459).

Morning dawned foggy and damp, but by 8 AM the Portuguese sun was burning off the mist. Already merchants, artisans, vendors, and shoppers were moving toward the docks in Lisbon. It was a typical day in early September 1600, and a fleet had arrived the previous evening from the Indian Ocean. Now its ships were being unloaded and the docks stacked with exotic plants, animals, minerals, and manufactures. Those who arrived early would have first pick from the cargoes.

Cramming the docks of Lisbon was a staggering variety of commodities from four continents. From Europe itself came wheat, wool, brassware, glass, weapons, tapestries, and clocks. North Africa provided dates, honey, barley, and indigo, as well as ornate metalwork. West Africa contributed gold, ivory, musk, parrots, and slaves. East Africa sent ebony, coral, salt, and hemp. Arriving from India were calico, pepper, ginger, coconut oil, cinnamon, cloves, and nutmeg. Southeast Asia furnished sandalwood, resins, camphor, and saffron. From Macao came porcelains, silks, and medicinal herbs. Finally, Brazil supplied sugar, brazilwood, and monkeys from the Amazon. Lisbon in 1600 was the commercial focus of Europe, a cosmopolitan connector of products and peoples from throughout the world.

The Portuguese Empire

The Spanish Empire

Lisbon's prosperity was a relatively recent development. Prior to 1453, world trade focused on the Mediterranean, where Italian city-states like Venice and Genoa competed with Muslim merchants for cargoes and profits. But Mehmed the Conqueror's dramatic victory at Constantinople, which at first appeared to expand Islamic wealth and power significantly, actually weakened existing Muslim trade networks. By stimulating Europeans to seek overseas routes to the Indies and the Spice Islands, the fall of Constantinople reoriented European trade in a westward direction, to the eventual benefit of the eager buyers who swarmed over the Lisbon docks in 1600.

The Iberian Impulse

The Iberian interest in sea voyages is largely anti-Muslim

Portugal was an unlikely location for a commercial nexus. The Iberian peninsula, home to Spain and Portugal, sits at the far southwestern edge of the Eurasian landmass, separated from the rest of Europe by the Pyrenees mountains. From the eighth through twelfth centuries most of Iberia was linked to the Islamic world by Muslim rule. By the mid-1200s, however, fired by an anti-Muslim crusade called the *Reconquista*, the Christian kingdoms of the North had retaken most of the region. In 1479 the two main Spanish kingdoms, Aragon and Castile, were linked by the marriage and joint rule of their respective monarchs, Ferdinand and Isabella, laying the basis for a united Spain. By 1492, when they finally expelled the Muslims from Granada in the South, this couple ruled most of Iberia—except for the kingdom of Portugal along the Atlantic coast.

By this time both Spain and Portugal, far from Europe's centers of commerce and wealth, were embarking on great sea voyages that would soon enlarge European ideas about the geography of the globe. Determined to bypass the Muslims, who controlled the land links and profitable trade with East Asia, both Iberians and Italian city-states searched for an all-water route to India, the Spice Islands, and China, regions that Europeans called collectively the East Indies. The Portuguese, who had been exploring southward along the Atlantic coast of Africa since the early 1400s, finally found a sea route in 1498, arriving in India by way of the Indian Ocean after sailing around Africa. Six years earlier the Spanish had funded an ill-conceived effort to reach East Asia by sailing west across the Atlantic. In the process, and by accident, they discovered what seemed to them a "New World," and they went on to create a western hemispheric empire that rivaled even that of the Mongols in size and significance.

Like the Mongols, the Iberians had a warrior culture, bred by centuries of *Reconquista*. Like the Mongols, they used technologies adopted from other civilizations, such as gunpowder weapons and navigational tools from Asia. Like the Mongols, they killed untold thousands through combat, slaughter, and the spread of infectious diseases, gaining wealth and power by exploiting and enslaving millions. And like the Mongols, they created conflicts and connections among cultures.

Iberians and Mongols share more similarities than differences

Unlike the Mongols, however, the Iberians zealously imposed their faith on the people they ruled. And unlike the Mongols they created new societies, destined to endure even after the Iberian empires were gone.

Portuguese Overseas Exploration

Given the small size and relative poverty of Portugal, it is surprising that this kingdom started the European drive for overseas exploration (page 457). But the forces it set in motion had an immense impact.

Like other European nations, Portugal suffered a drastic fourteenth-century population decline from the Black Death and the famines and epidemics associated with it. Depopulation of villages and poorly producing farmland left much of the landed nobility seriously short of revenue. Some tried to compensate for these shortages by turning to plunder. In 1415 Portuguese raiders captured the Moroccan seaport of Ceuta (*THĀ-oo-tah*), but Portugal's small population and limited resources made it impossible for it to conquer all of Morocco in a land war.

Portugal initiates seaborne exploration

The sea offered an alternative route to plunder, however. Portugal was a nation of farmers and fishermen with a lengthy Atlantic seacoast. Following the conquest of Ceuta, Prince Enrique (*awn-RĒ-kā*), the third son of the king of Portugal and therefore unlikely to inherit the throne, decided to pursue his own interests by organizing maritime expeditions to chart the western coast of Africa. Starting in 1418, these expeditions sought to determine how far south Muslim rule prevailed in Africa and where the Christian faith could be advanced at the expense of Islam (Map 19.1). The Portuguese also wanted to develop trade relations with African Christians, including the mythical Christian kingdom of Prester John, sought by Europeans since the crusades. Slowly, Portuguese explorers and traders moved ever farther south along Africa's west coast. They covered fifteen hundred miles, reaching as far as present-day Sierra Leone by the time Prince Enrique died in 1460. Later generations called him Prince Henry the Navigator.

Henry the Navigator initiates Portuguese expansion

When the Ottoman Turks had taken Constantinople, they had stunned Christian Europe and disrupted its merchants. The Muslims were now in control of the eastern Mediterranean, the meeting point of three continents and the focus of world trade for centuries. While they had no intention of closing the traditional land-sea trade routes to Christians, they intended to raise the fees for safe passage to levels that would enrich the

FOUNDATION MAP 19.1 European Global Exploration Routes, 1415–1522

Note the principal voyages of European exploration, all undertaken for differing reasons. Vasco da Gama's journey to India built on several decades of Portuguese exploration of the western coast of Africa. Columbus's westward expedition was designed to reach first Japan and then the Spice Islands by a route that Columbus believed to be shorter than sailing around Africa. Magellan's circumnavigation of the globe was intended to demonstrate that Columbus could have established a commercially viable connection to Asia had America not been in his way. Why did that conclusion prove incorrect?

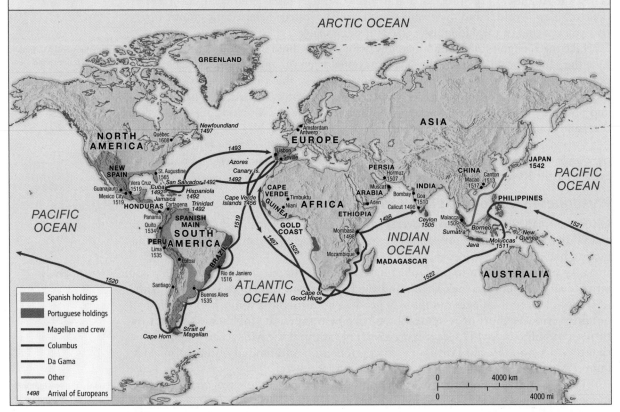

Constantinople's fall intensifies Portugal's maritime quest

Ottoman Sultan and cut deeply into European profits. Their middlemen squeezed European merchants even more by marking up the prices of spices and luxury items as much as 1,000 percent. These burdens were enough to convince several Western nations to search for alternative routes to the East Indies.

Because of Henry's expeditions, Portugal had a sizable lead in this search. Its ships reached the equator in 1471 and discovered that, contrary to legend, the ocean there did not boil. They also found that the heat decreased as they sailed farther south. In 1487, Portugal's King João (*ZHWOW*) II dispatched a land expedition across Africa to search for Prester John and for a connection to the Indian Ocean and a sea expedition to search for a route around Africa. The land expedition failed to find Prester John but did reach India. The sea voyage, commanded by Bartholomeu Días (*DĒ-ahz*), rounded the Cape of Good Hope at Africa's southern tip and could have gone on to India had not the sailors insisted on returning home. When Días sailed into Lisbon in 1489, he reported that Portugal had found a way to undercut the Muslim traders, since cargoes could be shipped by sea for a fraction of the cost by land. Present in Lisbon when Días arrived was a Genoese navigator named Cristóbal Colón, whose proposal for a voyage to find a route to the Indies by sailing westward across the Atlantic had been previously rejected by João II. The Latinized version of this navigator's name was Christopher Columbus.

Columbus's Enterprise of the Indies

An experienced mariner and cartographer, Columbus knew that the earth was round, and he calculated the distance from Portugal to China at fewer than 5,000 miles. He was right about the shape of the earth but wrong about its size. His calculations of one degree of longitude at the equator were off by 15 miles, a mistake that caused him to think that the circumference of the earth was 18,750 miles rather than 25,000. His sources for the size and locations of Asian lands were also inaccurate. But he was able to make a plausible argument that Europeans could reach East Asia by sailing west, across the Atlantic, on voyages that would be shorter than those Europeans had already sailed and less expensive than going around Africa to the Indies. Moreover, since the journey would be east to west instead of north to south, the winds, currents, and climatic changes encountered along the way would be less troublesome. In 1484 Columbus presented his **Enterprise of the Indies**, a detailed plan for a westward maritime expedition, to João II, and asked for Portuguese financial support.

Columbus's errors lead to unwarranted optimism

João referred this request to a committee of experts, who agreed with Columbus that the world is round—a well-known fact by 1484—but considered his estimate of the earth's circumference ridiculously small. This committee projected the distance from Portugal to Japan at 13,100 miles, a highly accurate prediction that placed East Asia well beyond the range of any expedition that expected its sailors to carry their own food and drink. Rather than reconsider his estimate, Columbus tried his luck with King Isabella of Castile (although female, Isabella was officially a *king*, and she insisted on being called by that title). She established a similar committee that reported similar findings. Columbus was about to try the Portuguese court again when Días returned to Lisbon in 1489 with good news about the route around Africa. Recognizing that Portugal would pursue that route for trade, Columbus sought support from Venice and Genoa. But these city-states, with established interests in existing routes through the eastern Mediterranean, turned him away.

Still convinced that his calculations were right, Columbus went back to Isabella in 1492 and was rejected again. However, as he was preparing to leave for Paris to try to interest the French, he was called back to Isabella's court. Her finance minister, Luís de Santander (*loo-ĒSS dā sahn-tahn-DARE*), had scolded his sovereign for lack of imagination and offered to finance the Enterprise himself by loaning funds to Isabella. If Columbus were mistaken, Santander argued, he would die on the voyage and a small investment would be lost; but if, against the odds, he turned out to be right, Castile would have a more direct route to the Indies than either Portuguese or Islamic merchants.

Isabella now gave the Enterprise more careful thought. She and her husband Ferdinand, kings of Castile and Aragon respectively, hoped to instill a militant, crusading Catholicism in all the Spanish kingdoms and unite them under the rule of their daughter Juana. A new route to the Indies would not only make this unified Spain rich, they reasoned, but also make it possible to convert hundreds of millions of Asians to their faith. They decided that the potential rewards were worth the risks. Isabella accepted Santander's offer,

Isabella finances Columbus's gamble

Document 19.1 Columbus Describes His First Encounter with People in the Western Hemisphere, 1492

The Enterprise of the Indies sighted land before dawn on October 12, 1492, and Columbus went ashore after dawn broke. He recorded the events in his own words, including his assumption that his expedition was then very close to Asia.

As I saw that [the native people] were very friendly to us, and perceived that they could be much more easily converted to our holy faith by gentle means than by force, I presented them with some red caps, and strings of beads to wear upon the neck, and many other trifles of small value, wherewith they were much delighted, and became wonderfully attached to us. Afterwards they came swimming to the boats, bringing parrots, balls of cotton thread, javelins and many other things which they exchanged for articles we gave them, such as glass beads, and hawk's bells; which trade was carried on with the utmost good will. But they seemed on the whole to me, to be a very poor people. They all go completely naked, even the women, though I saw but one girl. All whom I saw were young, not above thirty years of age, well made, with fine shapes and faces; their hair short, and coarse like that of a horse's tail, combed toward the forehead, except a small portion which they suffer to hang down behind, and never cut. Some paint themselves with black, which makes them appear like those of the Canaries, neither black nor white; others with white, others with red, and others with such colors as they can find. Some paint the face, and some the whole body; others only the eyes, and others the nose. Weapons they have none, nor are acquainted with them, for I showed them swords which they grasped by the blades, and cut themselves through ignorance. They have no iron, their javelins being without it, and nothing more than sticks, though some have fish-bones or other things at the ends. They are all of a good size and stature, and handsomely formed. I saw some with scars of wounds upon their bodies, and demanded by signs the cause of them; they answered me in the same way, that there came people from the other islands in the neighborhood who intended to make them prisoners, and they defended themselves. I thought then, and still believe, that these were from the continent [of Asia]. It appears to me, that the people are ingenious, and would be good servants; and I am of opinion that they would very readily become Christians, as they appear to have no religion. They very quickly learn such words as are spoken to them. If it please our Lord, I intend at my return to carry home six of them to your Highnesses, that they may learn our language.

SOURCE: Christopher Columbus, *Journal of the First Voyage to America* (New York: A. and C. Boni, 1924) 24–26.

Columbus's first encounter with Indians.

gave Columbus letters of introduction to the Emperor of China, and sent him on his way with three ships, the *Niña*, the *Pinta*, and the *Santa Maria*. Columbus sailed from Palos (*PAH-lōs*), Spain, on August 3, 1492, and made landfall on an island, most likely in the Bahamas, in what is today the Caribbean Sea on October 12 (see "Columbus Describes His First Encounter with People in the Western Hemisphere, 1492"). It was a voyage of fewer than three thousand miles.

Columbus assumed that he had reached islands off the eastern coast of Japan, but the inhabitants did not wear Japanese clothing (indeed, they wore no clothing at all), did not speak Japanese, and did not seem to know anything about Japan. The plant and animal life was unlike anything seen in Asia, and when Columbus returned to Spain in 1493 with samples of what he had found, the general conclusion was that he had landed in an unknown part of the world. Columbus, however, did not agree. He mounted three more expeditions in search of Japan, dying in Spain in 1506 without ever knowing what part of the world he had reached.

Columbus may have been mistaken concerning the nature of the lands he encountered, but Isabella was not. She repaid Santander handsomely and made the discoveries her personal property. Then she appealed to Pope Alexander VI for recognition of Castile's claims to the Indies and its exclusive right to the westward passage. In Christian Europe at that time, such matters were routinely referred to the Vatican. Alexander, a Spaniard, divided the entire world known to Europeans between the two Iberian nations, drawing an imaginary line from pole to pole 450 miles west of the Azores and the Cape Verde Islands (though they are not at the same longitude). Ignoring the rights of the inhabitants whose lands he gave away, he granted everything east of the line to Portugal

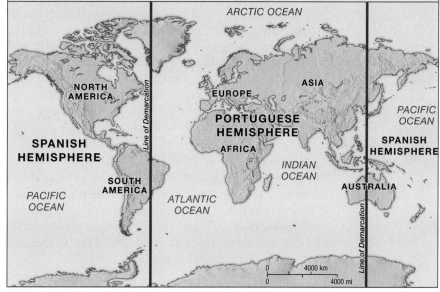

Map 19.2 The Treaty of Tordesillas and the Line of Demarcation, 1494

Observe that the line drawn by the Treaty of Tordesillas not only divided the western hemisphere between Portugal and Spain; it went around the world and bisected the eastern hemisphere as well. One can only imagine the reactions of the Japanese and Chinese emperors and the various rulers of India, had they known that their lands had been assigned to two European nations by a treaty of whose very existence they knew nothing. Europe had progressed from exploring the world (Map 19.1) to dividing it. Why did Europeans believe they had a right to divide the world in this way?

and everything west to Castile. The Portuguese, who had not yet actually sailed all the way to India, were outraged and threatened war.

Subsequent negotiations between Portuguese and Spanish in 1494 resulted in the **Treaty of Tordesillas** (*taur-dā-SĒ-yahss*), an agreement that drew the Line of Demarcation 1,675 miles west of the Cape Verde Islands (Map 19.2). Both sides pronounced themselves reasonably dissatisfied but proceeded to claim their halves of the world. The other European powers, not having been consulted, saw no need to comply; nor did Muslims, who paid no attention to the pope. Still, although the Europeans did not yet know about South America, the treaty's main effect would be to give most of it to Spain, while leaving to Portugal the large eastern section later known as Brazil.

Pope Alexander VI divides the world between Portugal and Spain

Portugal and Spain claim the entire world

The Voyage of Magellan

The Spanish followed up on the voyages of Columbus by creating an American empire, first colonizing several Caribbean islands and later conquering the Aztecs in Mexico and the Inca in Peru (Chapter 18). Some, however, continued to believe that profitable trade routes to Asia could be found by sailing westward from Spain.

Thus, while Cortés was conquering Mexico, a Portuguese mariner known as Ferdinand Magellan (*mah-JEL-lin*), sailing in the service of Spain, was finally accomplishing what Columbus had set out to do. By now it was obvious that the Americas were not part of Asia: in 1497 and 1498 English expeditions had explored the coast of North America, and in 1513 a Spaniard named Balboa had seen another great ocean on the far side of the American continents. But although ancient Polynesians knew the width of the Pacific, no European yet knew this, and the dream of sailing westward from Europe to reach the riches of Asia lived on.

Magellan proves it impractical to sail west from Europe to the Spice Islands

In pursuit of this dream, Magellan set out from Spain in 1519 with five ships and about 280 men. They headed for South America, where for a year they probed the coast for a passage, finally sailing through what is now called the Straits of Magellan in November 1520. For the next four months, with only three ships left, they crossed the seemingly endless Pacific, eating leather and ship rats once supplies ran out. In March 1521, the near-starving survivors reached the Philippines. They claimed the islands for Spain, but the next month Magellan and many of his men were killed in a conflict with the Filipino peoples.

Eventually, in September 1522, one ship with 18 men made it back to Spain, having sailed around the globe. Their voyage had proven that it was indeed possible to reach Asia by sailing west from Europe. But it had also revealed that the trip was three times the distance Columbus had calculated, and that given the distance and dangers involved it was not really worth the trouble.

The Portuguese Seaborne Empire

Magellan's circumnavigation of the globe.

The Portuguese, meanwhile, were finding that using their new sea routes was very much worth *their* trouble. The Treaty of Tordesillas granted half the world to Portugal, and Lisbon set out to make the most of it. Portugal's kings soon placed its new oceanic empire on firm foundations: knowledge of currents, winds, and coastlines; superb sailing vessels; and first-rate seamanship. The curiosity of Prince Henry the Navigator turned out to have tremendous commercial benefits.

Empire in the Atlantic Ocean

Vasco da Gama connects Portugal to India

A generation after Prince Henry's death, King João II authorized the establishment of a fortress and trading post in the Gulf of Guinea in 1482. The next year a Portuguese explorer named Diogo Cão (*COWM*) found the mouth of the Congo River, eventually establishing good relations with the Kongo Kingdom (Chapter 23). Other Portuguese pressed on toward India, as King Manoel (*mahn-WELL*) I commissioned a mariner named Vasco da Gama to sail all the way around Africa to India. In 1497 da Gama left Lisbon, reaching the Cape of Good Hope after 93 days, then rounding it and sailing up Africa's east coast and across the Indian Ocean to India (see "Vasco da Gama's Expedition Observes the Spice Trade, 1498"). This was the greatest seafaring feat in European history to date. As a follow-up, King Manoel dispatched a 12-ship fleet under the command of Pedro Alvares Cabral (*PÁ-dro AHL-vah-rez kah-BRAHL*) in 1500. Blown off course by a violent storm, Cabral made landfall on an "island" in the western Atlantic, naming it the "Isle of the True Cross" and claiming it for Portugal before continuing on to India. It was not an island at all—it was Brazil.

Portuguese sailors bump into Brazil

Manoel decided to assess the value of Brazil as an intermediate base for future voyages to India. In 1501 he sent a three-ship expedition to the new land, with Amerigo Vespucci (*ah-MARE-ih-gō vess-POO-chē*) aboard as cartographer and chronicler. In this capacity on a future trip Amerigo named the entire hemisphere after himself: America. The expedition explored two thousand miles of coastline, leading Manoel to suspect that

Document 19.2 Vasco da Gama's Expedition Observes the Spice Trade, 1498

Vasco da Gama's first voyage to India enabled the Portuguese to observe the nature and extent of the spice trade. This excerpt from the journal of one of the sailors charts the course of that commerce. Notice the emphasis placed on the dangers of overland travel, the frequent payment of customs duties, and the enormous income the Sultan of the Ottoman Empire derived from those duties. All of these facts led the Portuguese to seek a sea route to the Indies in the first place.

From this country of Calecut, or Alta India, come the spices which are consumed in the East and the West, in Portugal, as in all other countries of the world, as also precious stones of every description. The following spices are to be found in this city of Calecut, being its own produce: much ginger and pepper and cinnamon, although the last is not of so fine a quality as that brought from an island called Ceylon, which is eight days journey from Calecut . . . Cloves are brought to this city from an island called Malacca. The Mecca vessels carry these spices from there to a city in [Arabia] called Jiddah, and from the said island to Jiddah is a voyage of fifty days sailing before the wind, for the vessels of this country cannot tack. At Jiddah they discharge their cargoes, paying customs duties to the Grand Sultan. The merchandise is then transshipped to smaller vessels, which carry it through the Red Sea to a place . . . called Tuuz, where customs duties are paid once more. From that place the merchants carry the spices on the back of camels . . . to Cairo, a journey occupying ten days. At Cairo duties are paid again. On this road to Cairo they are frequently robbed by thieves, who live in that country, such as the Bedouins and others.

At Cairo, the spices are embarked on the river Nile . . . and descending that river for two days they reach a place called Rosetta, where duties have to be paid once more. There they are placed on camels, and are conveyed in one day to a city called Alexandria, which is a seaport. This city is visited by the galleys of Venice and Genoa, in search of these spices, which yield the Grand Sultan a revenue of 600,000 cruzados in customs duties . . . [about $15 million in 2006 dollars].

SOURCE: *A Journal of the First Voyage of Vasco da Gama, 1497–1499*, translated by Eric Axelson (Cape Town: Stephan Phillips Ltd., 1998) 77–78.

this was not an island after all. It also brought back samples of a type of brazilwood, a tree whose wood could be used to produce a red dye for textiles. This wood gave Brazil its name and Portugal a reason to explore the area further, since it was really too far west to be of any use as a way station en route to India. Later, the Portuguese learned that they could make a fortune growing sugar in Brazil, provided they settled it with colonists and African slaves. But for the moment, the eastern hemisphere seemed far more attractive.

Empire in the Indian and Pacific Oceans

The Treaty of Tordesillas, amplified by a papal edict of 1514 forbidding other European powers to interfere with Portuguese possessions, enabled Portugal to avoid European competition in the eastern hemisphere for most of the sixteenth century. Its superior gunnery, vessels, and seamanship held off its occasional Asian enemies. But the Portuguese seaborne empire was less an empire than a network of commercial ports and fortifications, designed not for settlement but for trade.

Portugal builds an empire based on commerce

Vasco da Gama's voyage to India opened the Indian Ocean to Portuguese traffic. In 1500, after Cabral bumped into Brazil, one of his ships located Madagascar. The Portuguese established trading posts in India and connected them with their newly founded station at Kilwa in East Africa.

In 1505 the first Portuguese **viceroy**, or vice-king, arrived in India, and beginning in 1510 the second viceroy, Afonso de Albuquerque, began developing the system of fortified posts at strategic locations that guaranteed Portuguese domination of Indian Ocean trade. Albuquerque conquered Goa in 1510 and made it Portugal's headquarters in Asia. During the next five years his forces took Malacca, the Moluccas, and Hormuz. Portuguese seamen reached China shortly thereafter, and in 1557 they established a trading post at Macao.

Goa became the principal port of western India. The Portuguese controlled the Persian Gulf from Hormuz, and their installation at Malacca dominated the passageway from the Indian Ocean to the South China Sea. Fortified Portuguese trading posts were located all along the East African coastline and the seacoasts of India and Ceylon.

Albuquerque's strategy helps Portugal dominate the Indian Ocean

Portugal's Commercial Empire in 1600

The Portuguese created their far-flung empire skillfully, employing their navigational expertise to master the seas and sail them at will. They guarded their knowledge jealously, refusing to share it with competitors. They carefully selected important strategic locations that would help them dominate Indian Ocean trade, and occupied those locations through a combination of diplomacy and intimidation. Once installed there, they protected their positions by negotiating trading rights in contracts that benefited local merchants as well as themselves, giving those merchants a stake in Portuguese success. This strategy enabled a nation with a tiny population of less than two million people to develop a commercial network that spanned the entire globe.

The Portuguese were responsible for establishing regular oceanic trade across vast spaces: between the Atlantic and Indian oceans, between West Africa and Brazil, between southwest Europe and West Africa, and between the north and the south Atlantic (Map 19.3). These sea routes regularized connections between these regions and enhanced commercial and cultural contacts between societies.

Portuguese ships carry goods across enormous distances

Portuguese vessels carried spices from the Indian Ocean to Europe, and while this was a valuable trade route, Portuguese shipping lanes from one part of Asia to another were even more profitable. The Portuguese sold Chinese silk not only in Europe but also in India, the Moluccas, Borneo, Timor, and Hormuz. Cloth from India, spices from the Moluccas, minerals from Borneo, and sandalwood from Timor were distributed throughout the Portuguese empire, as Portuguese ships connected these sites not only to Lisbon but to one another.

A modern-day replica of a Portuguese caravel.

In addition to goods, Portuguese sailors and merchants also carried diseases from one region of the world to another. Malaria spread rapidly across the tropics as mosquitoes bred prolifically in the water carried on Portuguese ships. Asians and Africans, because of prior contact with Europeans, were generally immune to the most drastic effects of Old World diseases, but the Amerinds of Brazil were devastated by smallpox, influenza, and measles. More than a century after Cabral reached Brazil, smallpox remained lethal enough to wipe out the entire Amerind population of Sao Luís in northern Brazil in 1621.

Portuguese commerce connects Asia to Europe

In addition to the transmission of germs, goods, and people, the Portuguese also spread European culture and practices throughout their empire, and scattered bits of information about Asian, African, Amerind, and Brazilian cultures everywhere they went. Building and artistic materials such as rare woods, gems, dyes, and metals were shipped from Asia, Africa, and Brazil to Europe, where they were used in churches, libraries, jewelry, paintings, and furniture. The Portuguese built European-style churches in India and churches with Asian motifs in Brazil. Amerind art was widely sold in Brazil, Africans purchased colorful

Map 19.3 The Flow of Commerce in the Portuguese World, ca. 1600

The Portuguese impulse to expand overseas created commercial connections linking four continents. Note that a bewildering variety of goods, some of which are depicted in the chapter opener, flowed into Lisbon from across the globe. Customs, rituals, languages, clothing, and ideas moved not only to and from Lisbon, but between each of the ports depicted on the map. The result was a vast increase in cosmopolitanism and knowledge from one end of the Portuguese world to the other. Why did this Portuguese challenge worry the Islamic world?

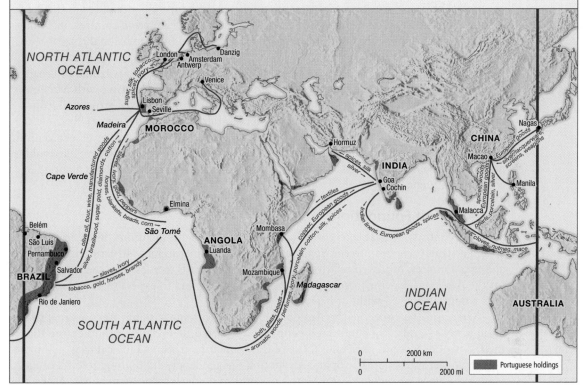

Amerind textiles, and Brazilian-inspired furniture graced parlors in Portuguese homes. The Portuguese seaborne empire facilitated widespread transmission of styles and tastes.

This transmission operated in several directions simultaneously. European clothing was introduced in Africa and Brazil, with sometimes comical results: top hats were widely worn by foremen of labor gangs in Rio de Janeiro, and for a brief period, Portuguese-style baggy pants were all the rage in Nagasaki. Brazilian tobacco was smoked in Portugal and coveted in Africa, where *arrobas*, bundles of tobacco twisted into ropes and soaked in molasses, became so popular that they were used as currency. West African foods and words entered the culture of eastern Brazil, and the African slaves transported to Brazil by the Portuguese became devoted converts to Portuguese Catholicism while retaining many rituals and songs from their African religions. The cross-fertilization of cultures produced by the Portuguese seaborne empire was as stimulating, and penetrating, as the connections generated by conflict and conquest among the many great land-based empires of previous centuries.

The Spanish and Portuguese Empires in America

Once the great Amerind empires had fallen to the Spaniards, Spain began to consolidate what had become the largest territorial possession in human history. From California to the tip of Cape Horn, Spain controlled everything except Portuguese Brazil (Map 19.4). Subduing Mexico proved relatively easy after the conquest of Tenochtitlán. In Peru, however, the Inca found ways to neutralize Spain's mounted cavalry, and although they were unable to expel the invaders, they created an independent Inca kingdom high in the Andes that lasted until 1572. Elsewhere the weaker, less centralized Amerind cultures, including the vestiges of the once-imposing Maya civilization, offered only occasional resistance to their new masters.

Iberia colonizes America

At the same time, the Portuguese began to recognize the economic potential of Brazil. Their eastern seaborne empire involved cooperation and profit-sharing with Muslim traders, but Brazil was entirely theirs, and they used it to profit from the growing European taste for sugar. Unlike Spanish America, with its centralized Amerind societies, Brazil was home to native cultures that lived in the inaccessible interior and had not developed central institutions. These cultures fled from the Portuguese rather than resisting them, but could not provide the labor required for sugar cultivation. Nor, given their small population, could the Portuguese.

The Amerind Foundation

Spain, in contrast, was able to construct its empire on the foundations of Amerind societies. Particularly helpful to the Spanish effort was the hierarchical structure of the Aztec and Inca Empires. It proved relatively easy for the Spaniards to substitute the king of Spain for the Aztec or Inca emperor at the top of the hierarchy and to expect that the king's orders would be obeyed without hesitation.

Iberians build empires on existing Amerind societies

Aztec and Inca polytheism also contributed to this submission. Accustomed to a large array of gods, the conquered peoples interpreted their defeat as indicating that their own gods were weaker than those of the Spaniards. It seemed logical to worship the gods who were stronger. The Spaniards, noting this tendency, did nothing to discourage Inca and Aztecs from considering Catholic saints and angels as powerful gods. Mary, the mother of Jesus, actually had a parallel in Aztec religion, in which one female goddess was the mother of all the gods. Through this blending of Christian and Amerind traditions, the defeated societies were encouraged to accept their fate and embrace the new European faith.

Slave Labor

Once Mexico and Peru had been pacified, Spaniards began arriving steadily from the mother country, drawn to the Americas by the prospect of wealth in gold and silver or in sugar production. For labor in the mines and the fields, they expected to use Amerinds, but Amerinds were not easily enslaved for these purposes. First, smallpox and other European diseases to which Amerinds had no acquired immunity killed large numbers of them. Moreover, those who survived had greatly reduced life expectancies, either owing to Spanish cruelty or because they simply found unrelenting labor unendurable in the absence of the religious significance it had had under the Aztec and Inca Empires. Third, many Catholic missionaries to the Americas, particularly the Franciscans and the Jesuits,

Map 19.4 The Iberian Empires in the Western Hemisphere, 1750

Spain and Portugal, two small countries on the Iberian Peninsula on the southwestern fringe of Europe, constructed enormous empires in the western hemisphere. European languages, customs, and products spread throughout these empires, while American, African, and Asian resources, customs, and cultures moved through Iberia into Europe. But notice that large portions of South America—the Amazon basin, the interior of Brazil, and Patagonia—remained untouched by Europeans. Why?

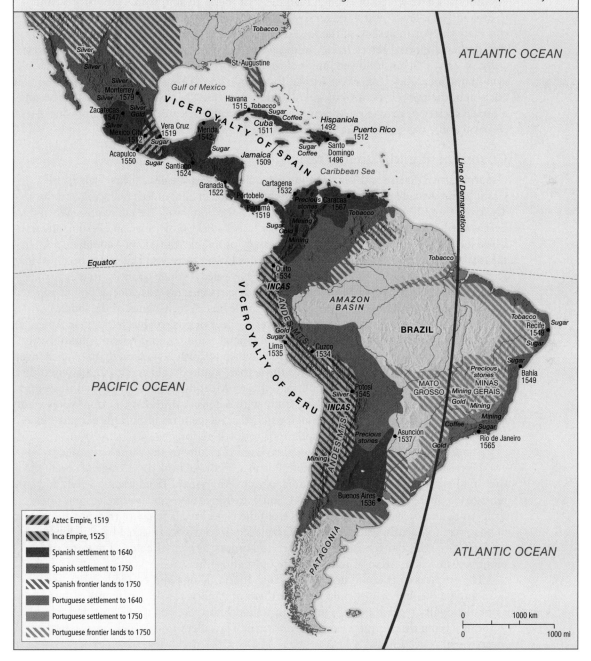

Aztec Empire, 1519

Inca Empire, 1525

Spanish settlement to 1640

Spanish settlement to 1750

Spanish frontier lands to 1750

Portuguese settlement to 1640

Portuguese settlement to 1750

Portuguese frontier lands to 1750

protested strongly against the enslavement of Amerinds. They argued to the king that Amerinds were people with souls, not draft animals.

The missionaries' genuine concern for the well-being of the Amerinds, however, did not extend to Africans, many of whom were soon imported as slaves. With Amerind workers unavailable, the American colonies needed a labor force accustomed to tropical conditions. There were not enough men in all of Iberia to supply this labor force, and if there had been, few could have survived manual labor in tropical climates for very long.

Here the Portuguese took the lead. Having experienced serious labor shortages in Brazil, they imported slaves from trading posts that they had established along the west coast of Africa. Spain followed, and before long Portuguese and Spanish ships were carrying human cargoes from West Africa, thousands upon thousands of slaves to be sold at auction in the port cities of Central and South America. Iberian America quickly became a mixed society of people of Amerind, European, and African descent who produced a physical and cultural blending unlike anything in the eastern hemisphere.

Spaniards replace Amerind labor with African slaves

Government and Administration

Governing such diverse and distant empires required new strategies. At first Isabella of Castile, who owned Spanish America outright by virtue of Santander's financing and the Treaty of Tordesillas, simply appointed her chaplain to administer the entire area. When this overworked priest died in 1503, one year after Isabella herself, her husband Ferdinand established a Board of Trade to oversee the increasingly profitable transatlantic commerce. After the final unification of Spain in 1516 under Carlos I (who three years later also became Holy Roman Emperor Charles V), the Americas were governed through councils. Rather than delegate responsibility to a number of ministries or departments (as was done in France and England), authority was assigned in 1524 to a single board, the **Council of the Indies.**

The Council of the Indies supervised every aspect of governance in Spanish America, including legislative, judicial, commercial, financial, military, and religious matters. It approved all significant expenditures, decided which Spanish laws should apply unchanged in the New World, drafted revisions for those that required adjustment, and advised the king on everything pertaining to colonial affairs. Meeting in Seville between three and five hours daily, it was a hardworking body with extensive authority. Formal votes were not unheard of, but usually the Council reached agreement on important matters before submitting its unanimous recommendations to the king for review.

But distance proved to be the most significant difficulty facing those who tried to govern the western hemisphere. Sailing from Portugal to Brazil took an average of seventy to one hundred days; from Spain to Panama, about seventy-five. Troublesome winds and currents made the return trip even longer. Atlantic crossings were always unpleasant, often dangerous, and occasionally fatal. Ships from the Americas, laden with treasure and exotic goods, were frequently set upon by pirates, although convoys protected by warships eventually reduced this danger. Royal messages and orders, as well as colonial reports, took months to cross the Atlantic and were often lost altogether.

The empires thus could not be run from Iberia. Kings and councils might issue laws and edicts, but who would enforce them in America? Clearly agents of unquestionable loyalty were required, men who would know the royal will instinctively, without having to ask questions at every turn. The rulers found such agents in their viceroys, or "vice-kings."

Viceroys were responsible for the execution of the king's orders on virtually every aspect of colonial administration. Until 1717 there were two viceroyalties in Spanish America: New Spain (from California south to Panama, including the Caribbean), and Peru (from Panama south to Cape Horn). In the eighteenth century Peru was subdivided into two additional viceroyalties because of its overwhelming size.

Portuguese America developed in a less centralized fashion. King João III in 1534 divided the eastern seaboard into 12 hereditary captaincies, varying in width between 100 and 270 miles and extending indefinitely into the uncharted interior. The proprietors were responsible for the recruitment of settlers and the economic development of their captaincies. The system never worked effectively, and in 1549 João III placed Brazil under the direct administration of a governor-general, whose duties were similar to those of a Spanish American viceroy. This action accelerated development and attracted thousands of Portuguese settlers to Brazil.

Whether Spanish or Portuguese, these vice-kings were men of talent and expertise, but the principal qualification for the post was loyalty to the king. They had to make decisions in the king's best interests even when the king's orders might be impractical or irrelevant to conditions in the New World. Under such circumstances, the Spanish viceroy could delay implementation or initiate a reassessment of the situation by invoking the Spanish legal maxim, "I obey but I do not enforce." Portuguese governors-general acted similarly, but without the maxim. A wise monarch would consider such an opinion carefully before overruling his representative.

But the kings of Spain and Portugal were customarily suspicious, and viceroys, like the officials who served under them, were always subject to the *residencia* (*rez-ih-DEHN-sē-ah*). This was a thorough audit of all the appointee's dealings during his term of office. It was conducted by a royal bureaucrat sent from the mother country, and it restrained those who might otherwise have been tempted to engage in illegal activity or abuse of power.

All authority came from the king. Neither Spanish nor Portuguese America contained any broadly based institution providing representation within the government for ordinary people. Spain itself had such a body, called a *cortés*, but because it was a representative institution that restricted royal power, Spanish kings refused to introduce it into the New World. The only truly representative body in the Spanish Empire was the town council, which maintained roads, policed the streets and markets, and regulated local affairs. Only through the town council could the residents of these empires play any role in their own governance. But the authority of town councils was limited to the towns themselves. The extensive centralized powers exercised by the Iberian kings over their American empires helped them hold those distant territories for more than three centuries.

Spain and Portugal find different ways to administer their empires

Viceroys and governors-general administer in the king's name

The Plaza de Armas in Cuzco, Peru, displays sixteenth-century Spanish colonial architectural style.

The Colonial Church

Iberian expansion was driven not only by a quest for gold and glory, but also by the desire to save the souls of New World peoples, who had never before heard the message of Jesus Christ. That ambitious goal was pursued by the Spanish and Portuguese branches of the Roman Catholic Church.

Ferdinand and Isabella, calling themselves "the Catholic kings," had completed the *Reconquista* by 1492 and had made Catholicism an element of Spanish nationality that helped bring unity to their diverse kingdoms. In the New World Catholicism would

Iberian empires are shaped by Catholicism

help assimilate conquered peoples into either Spain's or Portugal's colonial order. The pope supported this effort, granting the Iberian monarchs extensive rights over the appointment of bishops, the activities of religious orders, and the organization of all Catholic undertakings in the western hemisphere. In return, the kings assumed responsibility for supervising the Church in its evangelical, educational, and charitable efforts overseas.

At first these efforts were directed by the Franciscan, Dominican, and Augustinian religious orders. They concentrated on converting the Amerind chiefs, who then saw to it that their people would be baptized. To preach to the newly converted and teach them the elements of the faith, the friars learned native languages and promoted the widening use of dominant Amerind languages as a means of centralization.

The Amerinds reacted to conversion in a variety of ways. Some were enthusiastic, eager to worship the new gods who had proven themselves stronger than the old. Others converted for practical reasons, considering it both wise and useful to adopt the belief system of the conquerors. Still others rebelled, like the Inca of the central Andes, who objected to the destruction of their mummies and idols. Considering this destruction to be sacrilegious, bringing natural disasters and diseases, these Inca rebels returned to their ancient beliefs in the 1560s. Their action provoked a stern response from the viceroyalty of Peru, which worked vigorously over the next decade to eliminate the movement.

A Spanish American catechism from the colonial period.

By 1549 in Brazil and 1572 in Spanish America, priests from the Jesuit order arrived in the New World, and they quickly became the most influential of all. They soon dominated the conversion campaigns, emphasizing similarities between native belief systems and Catholicism, and bringing Amerinds together in settlements to permit mass conversion. They also defended their native followers against many who wished to enslave them. As did the other orders, the Jesuits grew prosperous through their access to native labor. The Church thus became wealthy, but it earned the resentment of colonial elites. In a land without a banking system, the Church became the principal source of funds for agricultural or commercial investment. It also became the largest property owner in the New World and a powerful manufacturer of pottery, fabrics, and leather goods.

The Catholic Church dominates commerce and education

Education in the colonies was handled exclusively by the Church. It operated all primary and secondary schools, educated Amerinds as part of the conversion process, and founded institutions of higher education such as the Universities of Mexico (Mexico City) and San Marcos (Lima), both established in 1551. In Brazil, however, the Portuguese Church did not establish a university until the nineteenth century. Before that, Brazilians seeking a university degree had to pursue it in Europe.

Religious orders for women expanded during the colonial period and played a major role in social and economic life. Convents attracted Spanish women who wanted to manage their own affairs, obtain a good education, and live lives of piety and service. Some women entered convents in order to escape the burdens imposed by husbands and children, or to lead well-protected lives. Most, however, took their vows seriously and contributed greatly to colonial life. Much more important in Spanish than in Portuguese America, convents owned substantial properties, provided funds for investment, and cultivated literary and artistic pursuits. Through its male and female orders, its strong belief in the importance of its work, and its active involvement with the Amerinds, the colonial Church exercised a powerful influence over Iberian America.

Society in the Iberian Empires

The people of Spain and Portugal were predominantly white, although there were a few people of African descent. But Spanish and Portuguese America contained a great many racial and ethnic groups, and in the New World a new social order emerged.

A Spanish American family of mixed races. The man is European, the wife is African, and the child is mestizo.

THE IBERIAN-AMERICAN SOCIAL HIERARCHY. At the top of the social ladder were white Spaniards and Portuguese, who tended to consider free people of other races as undesirable **mestizos** (*mes-TĒ-zōs*). Mestizos were people of mixed descent, often the result of unions between the invading Iberians—almost all of whom were male—and Amerinds or Africans. Only 5 percent of these unions were marriages, and children born outside of marriage were discriminated against. In Spanish America, whites excluded such people from artisan guilds in the 1540s, from the priesthood in 1555, and from any position carrying with it the possibility of social advancement. After 1550 the government discouraged interracial relationships, with little effect. Mestizos were not, of course, exclusively the product of Iberian-Amerind or Iberian-African unions; Amerinds and Africans interacted as well. The result has been a racial mixture found nowhere else on earth.

Race mixing shapes Iberian colonial societies

As time went on, increasing numbers of Africans were imported to make up for the high death rate among slaves. The Spanish and Portuguese did not encourage slave family formation, as it proved far less expensive to buy and transport Africans than to raise African children from infancy to adulthood. Male and female slaves were customarily housed separately. Slaves performed all sorts of physical labor and menial services, ranging from domestic chores and handicrafts to the difficult and life-shortening occupations of miner and field hand.

Iberia had long had slaves, both from Islamic areas and from sub-Saharan Africa, and neither Spaniards nor Portuguese considered black Africans a slave race. For Iberians, enslavement was a matter of social class or wartime misfortune, and it was thus possible for slaves to purchase their freedom. Still, slavery was a brutal, degrading institution, and even those able to buy their way out of it found their lives severely restricted. Many officials and most Iberians treated all Africans as slaves, even if they were legally free.

Africans, whether free or unfree, lived on the margins of society in the Iberian empires, as did Amerinds. Africans were subjected to a superficial assimilation, and they hid their own culture and customs away from the view of white people. Amerinds converted to Catholicism in large numbers, but most proved less adaptable than Africans to the Iberian colonial way of life. Thus many Spaniards and Portuguese valued Africans over native peoples as workers.

Africans and Amerinds occupy inferior social positions

In their own villages, however, Amerinds maintained independent, largely self-sufficient lifestyles. They kept their traditional social structures, permanently distinct from those of their Iberian conquerors. Spaniards and Portuguese forced Amerinds to work through labor exchanges, in which Amerind villages were compelled to provide a specified number of adults for forced labor for a specified number of days each year. The Amerinds adapted themselves to market structures and unwillingly interacted with the Iberian agricultural world. But they played little or no role in colonial town or city life, leaving skilled labor to mestizos and free Africans.

Social class in Iberian America was not based primarily upon skin color, although race was certainly an important factor. Portuguese and Spanish societies were organized according to a European structure of three estates: clergy, nobility, and commoners. The

Iberian colonial societies are organized according to European structures upper levels were reserved for high-ranking bishops and nobles, although Spanish colonial nobles tended to be lower-ranking dignitaries who had earned their ennoblement through military service during or after the Spanish conquests in America. The highest-ranking Spanish nobles had no motivation to go to America, except occasionally as a viceroy or general.

Colonial nobles distinguished themselves from commoners largely by their ownership of great estates. On those lands the nobles built lavish manor houses and presided over large numbers of laborers, servants, and slaves. Most Spaniards in America, of course, were commoners, and they earned their livings as shopkeepers, clerks, overseers, doctors, lawyers, notaries, accountants, merchants, craftsmen, or manual laborers. Some were wealthy, others were poor, but all were European in origin.

Mestizos, excluded from many lines of work, often had to make their living by their wits and skills. By the early 1600s many had found niches as silversmiths, wheelwrights, tailors, and carpenters, but most worked as servants or unskilled laborers. Free Africans and Amerinds were even less fortunate. Constrained by descent and skin color, they could never move into the commoner class.

Iberian whites dominate colonial societies

Among whites of Iberian descent, one additional distinction was made—between peninsulares (*pehn-ihn-soo-LAH-rāz*) and criollos (*crē-YŌ-yōs*). **Peninsulares** were white people born in the Iberian peninsula (hence their name). They monopolized the highest offices in church and state and looked down on **criollos**, white people who had been born in the western hemisphere. The names of these groups varied in Portuguese America, but the principle remained the same. The distinction arose with the efforts of Iberian kings to fill the most important positions in their empires with men of social stature whom they knew well. But over time, peninsular status came to be required even for mid-level colonial positions, and eventually the poorest Iberian-born newcomer considered himself the social superior of people whose families had been born and prospered in America for generations. This unfair treatment angered criollos, alienating many who might otherwise have remained loyal to their king but who later gladly joined independence movements.

Women play significant economic roles in the Iberian empires

THE ROLE OF GENDER. Gender distinctions were particularly evident in the Iberian colonial economy. Elite white women usually married, raised large families, and as widows administered the estates of their late husbands. But they could not engage in professional or commercial activity, and those who were frustrated by patriarchal restrictions frequently entered convents in order to gain at least limited autonomy. Middle- and lower-class white women worked at a wide variety of occupations, including spinning thread, taking in laundry, sewing, peddling goods, selling food, and serving as free domestics in the homes of the elite. Amerind women dominated the town marketplaces as sellers of fruits, vegetables, fish, and meat. Free African women were restricted to domestic service and cooking in inns and marketplaces. Most free women performed some type of paid labor during much of their lives. Survival in Iberian America below the level of the elites was not easy, and women's incomes, however meager, were badly needed.

Amerinds and Europeans in North America

Before the sixteenth century, the peoples of North America were largely isolated from the rest of the world. Influenced only by occasional trade with the Mesoamerican cultures that flourished to their south, the numerous tribes and nations of North American

Amerinds had over the ages developed their own distinctive cultures, values, beliefs, and institutions, without having to deal with outside interference (Chapter 5).

Then, in the sixteenth century, explorers from Europe began to map the continent's coastlines and rivers, looking for gold and a passageway to Asia. In the seventeenth century, having found neither, Europeans started settling in North America, exploiting its resources and farming its lands. In the process, the intruders from abroad displaced the Amerinds, whose numbers were already diminished by European diseases.

Coalitions and Contacts

North America lacked large empires like those that existed in Mexico, Peru, and throughout the eastern hemisphere. Most North Americans lived in village-based societies that typically included no more than a few thousand people, and even the larger nations probably numbered only in the hundreds of thousands. Usually these societies were ruled by powerful kings or chiefs who exercised both religious and political authority. They presided over rituals aiming to establish harmony with the spirits of nature, and also over councils made up of prominent warriors and advisors.

Occasionally some societies combined for protection, but rarely did they surrender their autonomy. In the 1500s, for example, the Haudenosaunee (*HOW-din-ō-SAW-nā*) people of what is now upstate New York organized themselves into a League of Five Nations, later called the Iroquois (*EAR-uh-kwoy*) Confederacy. According to oral tradition, a legendary figure called the Peacemaker, along with a mighty chief known as Hiawatha, persuaded regional leaders to end their constant warfare and join together for the common good. But the League, despite an intricate governance system, was more of an alliance than a union: each of its five members (Seneca, Cayuga, Onondaga, Oneida, and Mohawk) remained a sovereign nation.

The Haudenosaunee create an alliance of Amerind nations

The North American Amerinds were thus politically divided and culturally diverse, but they were not isolated from each other. Using the continent's extensive river systems, they could attack their enemies, travel to distant hunting and fishing grounds, conduct long-distance trade, and maintain a network of contacts with other societies.

North American Amerinds preserve their autonomy

Through contacts with Mexico, some North Americans knew that there was a powerful and wealthy empire to their south. They could not know, however, that there also existed across the ocean mightier and wealthier empires, whose warriors carried weapons against which the Amerinds had no defense and diseases against which they had no immunity. They did not anticipate the catastrophe to come.

The Coming of the Europeans

Not long after the first voyage of Columbus, Europeans looking for a new route to Asia began arriving in North America. In 1497 Italian mariner Giovanni Caboto explored the northeast coast, staking a claim for his English employers, who called him John Cabot. In 1500 Portuguese explorers reached Newfoundland; soon fishermen from Portugal, England, and France were fishing the cod-rich waters off the northeastern banks. They also made contact with the coastal Amerinds, who proved willing to trade their food and furs for European trinkets and tools.

A 1607 map of the northeast coast of North America, drawn by the French explorer Samuel de Champlain.

In the following decades, while the Spanish conquered the Aztecs and built an empire in Mexico, French and English explorers farther north found neither gold nor a climate in which sugar would grow. Lacking such financial incentives, Europeans in the sixteenth century made little effort to colonize the north.

Map 19.5 European Exploration and Colonies in North America, 1607–1763

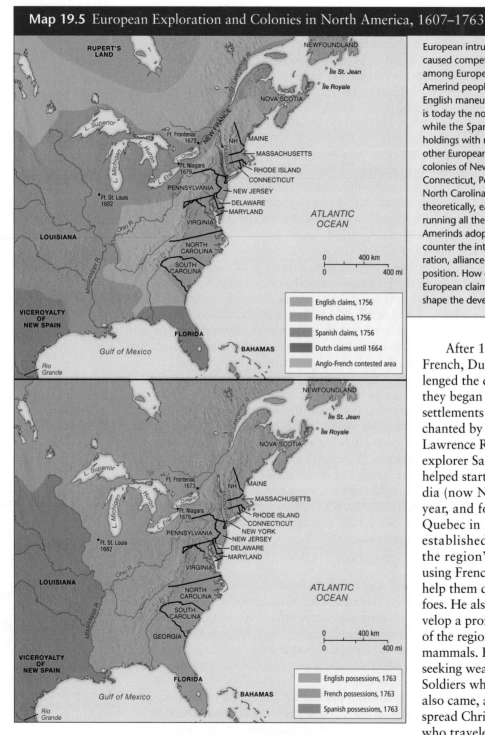

European intrusion into North America caused competition for territory, both among European nations and with Amerind peoples. The French, Dutch, and English maneuvered for advantage in what is today the northeastern United States, while the Spaniards amassed massive holdings with minimal opposition from other Europeans. Note that the English colonies of New Hampshire, Massachusetts, Connecticut, Pennsylvania, Virginia, and North Carolina had no western borders; theoretically, each of them claimed land running all the way to the Pacific Ocean. Amerinds adopted a variety of strategies to counter the intrusions, including collaboration, alliance-building, and outright opposition. How did these conflicting European claims and Amerind strategies shape the development of North America?

Legend (top map):
- English claims, 1756
- French claims, 1756
- Spanish claims, 1756
- Dutch claims until 1664
- Anglo-French contested area

Legend (bottom map):
- English possessions, 1763
- French possessions, 1763
- Spanish possessions, 1763

After 1600, however, as the French, Dutch, and English challenged the dominance of Spain, they began to establish permanent settlements in North America. Enchanted by a voyage up the Saint Lawrence River in 1603, French explorer Samuel de Champlain helped start a small colony in Acadia (now Nova Scotia) the next year, and founded a settlement at Quebec in 1608. Eventually he established good relations with the region's Huron Amerinds, using French forces and firearms to help them defeat their Iroquois foes. He also helped the Hurons develop a profitable trade in the furs of the region's many fur-bearing mammals. French traders followed, seeking wealth from the fur trade. Soldiers who fought the Iroquois also came, as did Jesuits who spread Christianity, and explorers who traveled the Great Lakes and down the Mississippi River. By the century's end the French had claimed these regions as a colony called New France (Map 19.5), based mainly on the fur trade with the Amerinds, most of whom were unaware that their lands were now supposedly subject to someone called the King of France.

Meanwhile other Europeans were arriving. In 1607 about a hundred hearty Englishmen, searching for gold and adventure, founded an outpost called Jamestown (named for King James I) in a region they knew as Virginia (named for Elizabeth I, the "Virgin Queen"). In 1609 an explorer named Henry Hudson, sailing in the service of the Dutch, traveled up the great river that now bears his name, seeking a new passage to Asia. He found no such route but did discover a region rich in furs. In the 1620s the Dutch founded the colony of New Netherland, which four decades later was seized by the English and renamed New York. In 1620 about fifty self-styled "Pilgrims" and fifty other English voyagers arrived at a place they named Plymouth, in a region soon called New England. Within a few decades thousands of other English Puritans, seeking religious freedom, had joined them in forming a Massachusetts Bay Colony. Other English religious groups followed: Catholics created a Maryland colony in the 1630s, and Quakers founded Pennsylvania in the 1680s. By 1700 there was a string of English colonies along the Atlantic coast.

Europeans establish colonies in North America

Disease and Demographic Decline

The coming of the Europeans brought disaster to the North American Amerinds. Like their Spanish rivals to the South, the French, Dutch, and English brought deadly diseases to which the Amerinds had no immunity. The European colonists also brought agricultural techniques involving large farm animals, metal tools and plows, and crops that required the clearing of huge tracts of forest. With a concept of possession that let individuals claim land parcels as their property and exclude all others, they constantly expanded the amount of land under cultivation. Over time these practices, combined with growing numbers of European immigrants, destroyed the Amerinds' way of life.

At Jamestown, for example, the colonists at first related well to the local Powhatan (*POW-uh-TAHN*) peoples, who provided the newcomers with corn, meat, and fish that helped the colony survive. But as more settlers arrived from England and the Powhatans were ravaged by European diseases, the relationship changed. The peoples clashed, the Amerinds attacked, and the English responded by seizing Powhatan lands. Then, rather than planting food, the colonists grew tobacco, which the Amerinds had taught them how to cultivate, and shipped it for sale to England, where smoking became the rage. Within decades the whole region was covered by tobacco plantations, and the surviving Amerinds were forced off their lands.

European diseases devastate Amerind societies

At Plymouth the colony initially survived with the aid of Massasoit (*mass-uh-SŌ-it*), chief of the Wampanoag (*wahm-puh-NŌ-ug*) nation, who in 1621 agreed to help the Pilgrims if they would support his people in battles against tribal foes. Soon, however, clashes occurred between the disease-ravaged Amerinds and growing English communities, which rapidly claimed increasing amounts of land for farms and used firearms when necessary to enforce their claims. In 1675, desperate to save the Wampanoag way of life, Massasoit's son Metacom (*MEH-tuh-kahm*), whom the colonists called King Philip, attacked the Europeans. A brutal war followed, during which the English slaughtered thousands of Amerinds and sold the survivors into slavery. After Metacom was captured and beheaded in 1676, the Plymouth colonists displayed his head on a pole for 25 years. "King Philip's War" effectively ended Amerind resistance, leaving most of New England in European hands.

The English Captain John Smith is condemned by a Powhatan chief.

To the West, the Dutch and English settlers brought both tragedy and triumph to the Iroquois Confederacy. On one hand, as elsewhere, the colonists brought disease, such as a smallpox epidemic that killed perhaps half of the Iroquois population in the 1630s. On the other hand, the Dutch and English gave the Iroquois firearms to help them fight the Hurons and the French, enabling the Confederacy to carve out an empire extending from the Hudson River to the Great Lakes.

In contacts between Europeans and Amerinds, the Amerinds are at a disadvantage

Elsewhere along the coast, similar events occurred. Sometimes Europeans allied with Amerinds to fight common foes, and sometimes Europeans slaughtered Amerinds or drove them off their lands. Sometimes the Amerinds held off the Europeans for awhile, but in the long run their way of life collapsed in the face of European diseases, European weapons, and the spread of European settlement.

The Columbian Exchange

The initial contact between European and American civilizations involved not only conflict and conquest but connection. Since the two hemispheres had been separated from each other since the submersion of the Bering land bridge more than ten thousand years earlier, many varieties of living things had developed in each hemisphere that were totally unknown in the other. The eastern hemisphere had wheat, grapes, horses, cows, sheep, goats, and pigs; the western hemisphere had potatoes, tomatoes, maize, cacao, and tobacco. When people from the two hemispheres encountered one another, their connections involved an interchange of crops and animals. In reference to Christopher Columbus, scholars call this process the Columbian Exchange.

The Columbian Exchange brings benefits as well as devastation

Some exchanges of crops improved the quality of life in both hemispheres. The impact was immediately obvious in the western hemisphere. Before long wheat and grapes were being grown for the first time in the New World, to make the bread and wine that were central to the European diet and religion. Farm animals brought in by the Iberians provided transport, labor, and food, and they flourished in the Americas.

For the eastern hemisphere, corn (maize), potatoes, tomatoes, peanuts, and manioc (*MAN-ē-ok*)—a starchy root plant, now grown widely in Africa and Brazil, also called *cassava* or *tapioca*—proved hardy and rich in nutrients. Eventually becoming staples in Europe, Africa, and Asia, they later helped foster a global population explosion. Other American plants, like cacao (the basis for chocolate) and, particularly, tobacco, were also sought by people around the world.

African women preparing manioc.

Microorganisms were an additional part of the Columbian Exchange. Syphilis, for example, a debilitating venereal disease that first showed up in southern Europe in the 1490s, was probably introduced by sailors returned from the New World. But the exchange of diseases proved far more devastating for the Amerinds. Smallpox, measles, and chicken pox, to which most Europeans had been subjected as children and thus developed immunities, ran rampant through unprotected Amerind populations. About 30 percent of children who came down with smallpox died, and 90 percent of adults. As a result, Amerind farming was interrupted, social structures shattered, villages depopulated, and entire regions abandoned. Smallpox weakened Aztec and Inca resistance to the Spaniards. Throughout the Spanish possessions in the western hemisphere, smallpox and measles ravaged Amerind communities off and on throughout the sixteenth century, reducing those communities by as much as 90 percent.

There are no reliable statistics on pre-1492 Amerind populations, but scholars estimate that the Americas contained between 15 million and 125 million people. In 1600, Spanish estimates indicated a population of one million Amerinds in the viceroyalty of New Spain (Mexico, Central America, and the Caribbean islands). It is clear that European diseases destroyed the overwhelming majority of the Amerind peoples in the greatest demographic catastrophe in history.

Chapter Review

Putting It in Perspective

Tremendous consequences flowed from the Iberian overseas expansion of the fifteenth century. Under different circumstances, China might have discovered a sea route around Africa, or Japanese mariners might have sailed east and found the Pacific coastline of North America. But it was the Europeans whose curiosity and seamanship broadened human geographic knowledge and extended the horizons of the entire world. When they found previously unknown lands, they conquered and exploited them, motivated by a combination of greed and religious faith.

The clash of civilizations in the New World changed forever societies that had previously been isolated from outside influences. Amerind societies largely collapsed in the face of conquest and disease. In their place the Iberians imposed new governance systems, religious beliefs, and social structures. They created a new economy, based on the cultivation of cash crops by imported slave labor. Finally, they transplanted their whole way of life, bringing plants, animals, foods, and diseases common in Europe but hitherto unknown in the Americas.

The political and economic impacts were immense. The Spanish and Portuguese, and later the French, Dutch, and English, were set on a course to become world powers, surpassing the great Asian and Islamic empires. The Atlantic Ocean soon replaced both the Indian Ocean and the Mediterranean Sea as the center of world commerce. Eventually, Europe led the world in power and prosperity, in large part due to its exploitation of Africa and the New World.

But the most direct Iberian legacy was the new culture created in the conquered lands. The Spanish and Portuguese empires ended in the early 1800s, but their legacy lives on today. Though modern Latin American societies remain intensely hierarchical, the peoples of these societies, displaying a broad variety of outlooks and customs, celebrate this cultural synthesis as their unique contribution to the human experience.

Reviewing Key Material

KEY CONCEPTS

Enterprise of the Indies, 461
Treaty of Tordesillas, 463
viceroy, 466
Council of the Indies, 470
residencia, 471
mestizos, 473
peninsulares, 474
criollos, 474

KEY PEOPLE

Prince Henry the
  Navigator, 459
João II, 460
Bartholomeu Días, 460
Christopher Columbus, 461
Isabella of Castile, 461
Luís de Santander, 461
Ferdinand of Aragon, 461
Pope Alexander VI, 463
Ferdinand Magellan, 463
Vasco da Gama, 464

Manoel I, 464
Pedro Alvares Cabral, 464
Amerigo Vespucci, 464
Afonso de Albuquerque, 466
João III, 471
John Cabot, 475
Samuel de Champlain, 476
Henry Hudson, 477
Massasoit, 477
Metacom, 477

ASK YOURSELF

1. Why did Portugal take the lead among European nations in promoting overseas expansion?
2. Why did the Iberian nations enslave Africans and transport them to their empires in the western hemisphere?

3. In what ways did the Spanish and Portuguese empires differ from each other? In what ways were they similar?

4. How did the conflicts between Iberian and American civilizations forge connections that changed them all?

GOING FURTHER

Boorstin, Daniel. *The Discoverers.* 1985.

Boxer, C. R. *The Portuguese Seaborne Empire.* 1971.

Burkholder, Mark, and Lyman Johnson. *Colonial Latin America.* 2000.

Burns, E. Bradford. *A History of Brazil.* 1998.

Callaway, Colin. *New Worlds for All: Indians, Europeans, and the Remaking of Early America.* 1997.

Crosby, Alfred. *The Columbian Exchange: Biological and Cultural Consequences of 1492.* 1972.

Diffie, W., and G. Winius. *Foundations of the Portuguese Empire, 1415–1580.* 1979.

Liss, Peggy. *Mexico Under Spain.* 1984.

Lockhart, James, and Stuart Schwartz. *Early Latin America.* 1982.

Parry, J. H. *The Discovery of South America.* 1979.

Pearson, M. *The Portuguese in India.* 1987.

Pescatello, Ann. *Power and Pawn: The Female in Iberian Families.* 1976.

Ramírez, Susan. *The World Upside Down: Cross-Cultural Contact and Conflict in Sixteenth-Century Peru.* 1996.

Russell-Wood, A. J. R. *The Portuguese Empire, 1415–1808.* 1998.

Scammell, Geoffrey. *The First Imperial Age: European Overseas Expansion, 1400–1700.* 1989.

Schaeffer, Dagmar. *Portuguese Exploration in the West and the Formation of Brazil, 1450–1800.* 1988.

Schnaubelt, Joseph, and Frederick van Fleteren. *Columbus and the New World.* 1998.

Smith, Roger. *Vanguard of Empire: Ships of Exploration in the Age of Columbus.* 1993.

Stern, Steve. *Peru's Indian Peoples and the Challenge of Spanish Conquest.* 1993.

Tracy, J. *The Rise of Merchant Empires: Long-Distance Trade in the Early Modern World, 1350–1750.* 1990.

Key Dates and Developments

1415	Portugal captures Ceuta from the Muslims
1415–1460	Expeditions financed by Prince Henry the Navigator
1489	Bartholomeu Días rounds the Cape of Good Hope
1492	Christopher Columbus reaches the Caribbean islands
1494	Treaty of Tordesillas divides the world between Portugal and Spain
1498	Vasco da Gama reaches India
1500	Pedro Alvares Cabral lands in Brazil
1516	Carlos I becomes King of Spain
1519–1521	The Cortés expedition overthrows the Aztec Empire
1519–1522	The Magellan expedition circumnavigates the globe
1524–1532	Pizarro's three expeditions to Peru
1524	Establishment of the Council of the Indies
1532	Capture of Atahuallpa at Cajamarca, Peru
1549–1572	The Jesuits arrive in the New World

The West in an Age of Religious Conflict and Global Expansion, 1500–1650

Executing A Peasant Rebel

In the sixteenth century, while Western nations forged global connections, Western society was wracked by divisive religious and social rebellions. Here a leader of the German Peasants' Revolt is shown being burned at the stake.

On April 18, 1521, the Imperial Diet, an assembly of the Holy Roman Empire's leading princes and nobles, met at the bishop's palace in the German town of Worms (*VOHRMSS*). There, on the previous day, the Diet had ordered a monk named Martin Luther to retract his writings, which defied the authority of the Roman Catholic Church. Now, in the emperor's presence, the Diet reassembled to hear Luther's response. His bold reply, delivered that day, echoed throughout Europe for decades: "Unless I shall be refuted by . . . the scriptures or by manifest reason (for I believe in neither the Pope nor in the Councils alone . . .) I am not able to retract . . ."

European Colonies and Claims

The Christian West

Angered by this defiance, Holy Roman Emperor Charles V, then barely 21 years old, issued a stinging rebuke. A single monk must not be allowed to deny what Christianity had held for more than a thousand years. To defend the Catholic faith, Charles declared, he was prepared to use "all my possessions, my friends, my body, my blood, my life, and my soul."

Thus were drawn the battle lines of a great religious conflict that divided the Western world for centuries.

At first this conflict was mainly a struggle among European Christians. Backed by Germans who feared imperial power and resented Church corruption, Luther boldly defied both emperor and pope. His success led others to do likewise, creating new religions and sparking revolts that fragmented Western Christendom.

Soon, however, the struggle was entwined with developments worldwide. In 1521, even as Charles vowed at Worms to defend the Catholic cause, his subjects were conquering distant lands such as Mexico and the Philippines, laying the foundations of a global Spanish empire. In ensuing decades, as officials and religious orders spread Catholicism throughout that empire, Charles and his heirs exploited its wealth to fight their European foes.

The result was a century of religious strife, accompanied by zealotry and witch hunts. But these conflicts were also accompanied by increased global trade, new kinds of commerce and production, expansion of learning and literacy, and changes in family life. By the seventeenth century, although Europe was still torn by religious and political strife, its monarchs, missionaries, and merchants had extended their reach around the world.

The Protestant Reformation

In the early 1500s almost all Western Christians still belonged to the Catholic Church. Headed by the pope in Rome and administered by a hierarchy of bishops and priests, the Church had long been a source of authority and unity in the West. Soon, however, this authority was challenged, and this unity shattered, by religious rebellions that divided Western Christendom into differing denominations. Collectively these rebellions are called the Protestant Reformation.

Roots of the Reformation

The Reformation of the sixteenth century was rooted in two key concerns. One was corruption in the Roman Catholic Church, the institution most Europeans looked to for salvation. The other was political unrest in the Holy Roman Empire, an assortment of central European states, loosely united by their rulers' recognition of its emperor as their overlord (Map 20.1).

Renaissance Europe had sophisticated culture, but death and disease still surrounded its people, whose main concern was thus eternal salvation: When they died would their souls go to heaven or hell? Most believed that the Catholic Church held the keys to eternal salvation, providing the rules and rituals they needed to make it to heaven. Chief among the rituals were the **sacraments**, sacred rites believed to bestow the graces needed for salvation.

The most important sacraments were baptism, Eucharist, and penance. To make it to heaven, one first had to undergo baptism, the ritual use of water that brings membership in the Church. Then one had to lead a virtuous life, doing good works and avoiding serious sins. Those who committed such sins and died with them unforgiven were damned

Church corruption and political unrest help spark the Reformation

FOUNDATION MAP 20.1 Europe in the Sixteenth Century

From 1519 to 1556, Europe's most powerful ruler was Holy Roman Emperor Charles V, heir to the Habsburg family's many possessions. Note that these possessions included Spain, Austria, the Netherlands, and much of Central Europe and Italy, as well as a growing Spanish American empire. Who were his major friends and enemies in the rest of Europe? Why did the Protestant Reformation pose a threat to his power?

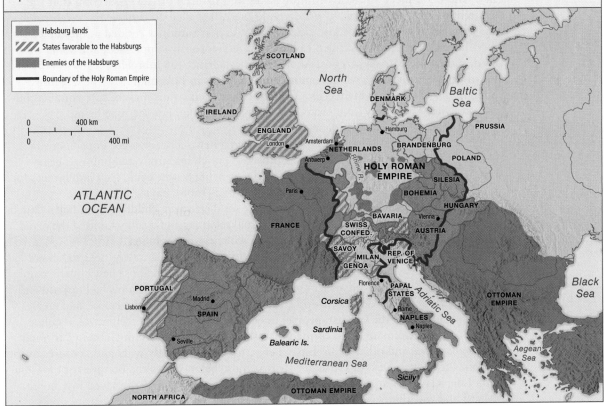

Sketch of Friar John Tetzel selling indulgences.

Sale of indulgences and other abuses increase Church corruption

Scandalous Renaissance popes discredit papacy

to eternity in hell. But through Eucharist (also called Communion), the consumption of consecrated bread and wine, believed by the faithful to be Christ's body and blood, Christians could gain grace to avoid sin. And through penance, the confession of one's sins with sincere repentance to a priest, Christians could have their sins forgiven.

After that, however, sinners still had to atone for the wrong they had done. If they died without doing so, the Church taught, they would have to endure **purgatory**, a place of suffering that purified the soul so it could enter heaven. But people could also atone for their sins while still alive. Through certain prayers and sacrifices, such as fasts, pilgrimages, and charitable works, a person could earn an **indulgence**, a remission of the punishment still due for sins that had been forgiven through penance, to reduce or eliminate suffering in purgatory. Eventually, when popes started granting indulgences for *financial* sacrifices, such as donations to the Church, it began to look as if people could buy their way into heaven.

This sale of indulgences was one of several abuses that contributed to Church wealth and corruption. Others included simony (*SIH-muh-nē*), the sale of Church offices and benefits, and pluralism, the practice by which some clerics held multiple church offices, typically to enhance their income. Furthermore, while high Church officials such as popes and bishops lived lavishly in sumptuous palaces, poorly educated parish priests were often neither sober nor chaste.

Over the years, various individuals had dared to condemn such abuses. One was John Wyclif (*WICK-liff*) (1330–1384), theology professor at England's Oxford University, who denounced the sale of indulgences and Church offices. Asserting that the Church must set an example of poverty and piety, he called on civil rulers to reform it and seize its possessions. He also declared that divine authority resided in the Bible, not the Church. His followers, called Lollards, were vigorously suppressed, and some were even burned to death as heretics. Another Church critic was John Hus (1369–1415), rector of Prague University, who promoted similar ideas in Bohemia (now the Czech Republic). In 1415 he was invited to a Church council with a promise of safe conduct, but then convicted of heresy and burned to death at the stake. For the time being, the Church thus silenced its dissidents.

In time, however, Renaissance popes supplied a new set of scandals. Pope Sixtus IV (1471–1484), for example, sold Church offices to enrich his family and imposed heavy taxes on the Papal States. He also proclaimed that living people could gain indulgences for souls already in purgatory. Pope Alexander VI (1492–1503), having gotten his post through bribery, used Church wealth to indulge his illegitimate children, including a daughter with whom he was alleged to have had sexual relations and a son who used the papal armies in an effort to create his own kingdom. The next pope, Julius II (1503–1513), a vain and violent man, led wars to enlarge the papal domains and sold indulgences to finance extravagant projects—including the construction in Rome of a grandiose new church, Saint Peter's Basilica, replacing an ancient one built by Constantine that Julius had torn down.

Political unrest in Central Europe, the Reformation's other root cause, had meanwhile spread among the German people. Irked by Italians who saw themselves as culturally superior, many Germans also resented the use of money collected in Germany, through indulgence sales and other Church payments, to fund the costly wars and ventures of the Renaissance popes. Devout Germans, such as those belonging to the Brethren of the Common Life, a lay movement stressing piety and simplicity, were also dismayed by Church wealth and worldliness.

Furthermore, the heads of Germany's numerous states were anxious to protect their local autonomy against the ambitions of their overlords, the Holy Roman Emperors. Austrian Archduke Maximilian of Habsburg, elected emperor in 1493, seemed intent on ending this autonomy by transforming the empire into a centralized monarchy. By arranging favorable marriages for himself and his son, he also assured that his grandson, the future Emperor Charles V (1519–1556), would inherit not only Austria, the Netherlands, Sicily, Sardinia, and much of Central Europe and Italy (Map 20.1), but also Spain (where he was King Carlos I) and its American empire. Alarmed, many German princes and nobles resolved to resist any further Habsburg ambitions.

The Lutheran Revolt

Statue of Martin Luther in Wittenberg, Germany.

Into these troubled waters waded Martin Luther (1483–1546), a devout German monk obsessed with fears of death and eternal damnation. As a young man he had prepared to study law but, when caught in a violent storm, vowed instead to enter a monastery if God let him survive. He lived to join the Augustinian order and became an exemplary monk, repeatedly fasting, praying, and confessing his sins. But he still felt unworthy of salvation and feared he was doomed to hell. A 1510 trip to Pope Julius II's Rome only intensified his fears: how could a Church so worldly and corrupt help him save his soul? In confronting this question, Luther plunged Western Christendom into turmoil.

At the University of Wittenberg (*VIT-in-bãrg*), in the central German state of Saxony, Luther studied scripture and became a doctor of theology, finally developing a doctrine that eased his torment. No one, he concluded, is worthy of salvation. It is not something one can *earn* by doing good works. It is rather a *gift* from God, who freely bestows his saving grace on those who have faith in him. We do not gain grace by doing good, reasoned Luther; we do good because we have grace. We are "justified," in Luther's words, not by our deeds but by God's grace, which we receive through faith.

The doctrine of "justification by faith alone," which Luther grounded on the writings of Saint Paul, implicitly threatened the Catholic Church. For if faith alone brought salvation, who needed sacraments and indulgences? Indeed, who needed the Church?

Luther asserts that faith alone, not the Church, brings salvation

Trouble arose in 1517 when a friar named John Tetzel traveled through Germany selling indulgences to help build the new Saint Peter's in Rome and pay the debts of a corrupt archbishop who had purchased his post. The crafty friar, assuring donors that coins put in his coffer would earn indulgences to ease the suffering of their departed loved ones, allegedly used slogans like "As soon as the coin in the coffer rings, the soul from purgatory springs!" Appalled, on October 31 Luther responded by issuing his **Ninety-five Theses**, a set of propositions challenging the Church's power to forgive sins and grant indulgences. Legend says he posted his theses on the Wittenberg castle church door.

The theses circulated widely, winning Luther fame and support among disgruntled Germans and religious reformers, while evoking Rome's anger. In a 1519 debate he defended the views of John Hus and denounced the Church for Hus's execution. In 1520 Luther published an *Address to the Christian Nobility of the German Nation*, urging German nobles to cast off Rome's control and seize Church property, artfully appealing to their Germanic pride and zest for wealth and power. The pope responded with a papal *bull* (edict) condemning Luther's views as heresy.

Luther urges German nobles to reform the Church and seize its property

Undeterred, Luther burned the papal bull and continued his assault. God's truth was found, he said, not in Church teachings but only in the Bible, which people must read and interpret themselves. He denied all sacraments except baptism and Communion, finding no biblical basis for the rest. He renounced not just indulgences but also belief in purgatory, pilgrimages, fasts, papal authority, and even monastic life. Proclaiming a "priesthood of all believers," he rejected priestly celibacy and encouraged clergymen to marry.

In truth, then, Luther was not just a reformer who attacked *abuses* the Church could conceivably correct, but also a rebel who denounced *doctrines* the Church regarded as inspired by God. Luther essentially denied the authority and divine mission of the Church. And this no pope could accept.

The Rising Tide of Rebellion

Soon Charles V, the new Holy Roman Emperor, grew alarmed about the danger Luther posed to both Church and empire. In 1521 he summoned Luther to face the Imperial Diet. Ordered to repudiate his views, as noted at the start of this chapter, the religious rebel held firm. Then, denounced by the emperor as a heretic, he was secretly taken to the castle of Saxony's ruler, Frederick the Wise, a German prince dismayed by Church corruption and determined to resist the emperor's growing power. There Luther hid for a year and began translating the Bible into German.

The printing press and German nobles help spread Luther's ideas

Aided by the new printing press, developed by German inventor Johannes Gutenberg in the 1450s (Chapter 16), and by German nobles eager to expand their wealth and power at Church expense, Luther's ideas spread quickly. Central Europe was soon divided between Lutherans, who adopted these new ideas, and Catholics, who remained loyal to the emperor and pope.

The situation quickly became more complex. By denying the Catholic Church's authority and urging people to interpret the Bible on their own, Luther opened the way for others to dissent, further fragmenting Christendom into additional sects. In 1522, for example, a dissident priest named Huldrych Zwingli (*TSVING-lē*) began his own movement in Zurich, Switzerland. More extreme than Luther, he rejected anything not literally found in the Bible, including the belief that Christ is present in Communion bread and wine. Soon zealots called *Anabaptists* (or Rebaptizers), since they baptized adults (rather than infants) as a sign of conscious faith commitment, split with Zwingli and started communities throughout central Europe.

Other religious rebels called for radical social reforms, helping to inspire a violent Peasants' Revolt against German nobles in 1524–1525. Although Zwingli supported this uprising, Luther did not. Heavily reliant on noble support, and anxious to keep his religious movement from becoming a social rebellion, Luther urged the authorities to "smash, strangle, and stab" the rebels, who were thenceforth slaughtered by the thousands.

Diverted by other conflicts, emperor and pope cannot stop "Protestants"

Meanwhile neither emperor nor pope could stem the Lutheran tide. Charles V was resisted by an alliance of German Lutheran princes, called "Protestants" after 1529, when they formally protested his efforts to curb their religion. He was also diverted by wars against the Ottoman Turks, who conquered much of Hungary in 1526 and besieged Vienna in 1529 (Chapter 17), and even the Catholic French, who so greatly feared his power that they sided against him with the Protestant German princes and Islamic Turks. Several successive popes, faced with calls for a Church council that could work at resolving the religious issues, resisted convening one for fear that it might also act to reduce papal powers. And a growing conflict with England's king further hampered the papacy.

Henry VIII and the English Reformation

England's Reformation, unlike Luther's, was rooted in royal affairs, not doctrinal disputes. John Wyclif, it is true, had earlier sown seeds of religious unrest in England, and Luther's ideas attracted much interest there. But English humanist Thomas More, though critical of Church corruption, explicitly condemned the Lutheran creed. And King Henry VIII (1509–1547) was a staunch Catholic who in 1521 issued a *Defense of the Seven Sacraments*, for which the pope proclaimed him "Defender of the Faith." England seemed safely within the Roman Catholic fold.

Anne Boleyn.

But things began to change in 1527, when Henry aspired to end his long marriage to Catherine of Aragon, a Spanish princess by birth. She had borne him six children, but only one, their daughter Mary, survived. As he and his wife got older, Henry feared he would have no male heir, leaving the realm in crisis after he died. Besides, he had fallen in love with youthful Anne Boleyn (*boo-LIHN*), one of his wife's attendants.

The Church did not permit divorce, but it could grant an annulment, a ruling that the marriage was never valid. Since Catherine had first wed Henry's older brother and then had married Henry after his brother died, and since the Bible stated that a man who took his brother's wife would die childless (Leviticus 20:21), Henry saw his lack of a son as a sign that God disapproved of his marriage to Catherine. He thus appealed to Rome to have the union annulled.

The request put Pope Clement VII (1523–1534) in a difficult bind. He did not want to anger Henry and risk losing England from the Church. But Catherine was the aunt of Emperor Charles V, whose soldiers occupied Rome, and whose help the Church sorely needed against Luther and the Turks. And Charles opposed the annulment: Catherine's marriage was his family's link to England, which he hoped to strengthen by wedding his son Philip to Henry's daughter Mary, who would one day be queen if there were no male heir. Besides, since a prior pope (Julius II) had permitted Henry to wed his brother's widow, an annulment would admit that popes erred, as Lutherans asserted. So Clement delayed his decision.

As Henry's case moved slowly through the papal courts he grew increasingly impatient. By 1533, his mistress Anne was pregnant, so Henry could wait no longer. In order to legitimize his expected heir, he promptly married Anne and got the Archbishop of Canterbury (England's highest cleric), a Lutheran sympathizer named Thomas Cranmer, to annul Henry's marriage to Catherine without waiting for Rome. Anne was then crowned queen, and a few months later gave birth: not to the desired son, but to a girl who was named Elizabeth.

Having acted on his own, in defiance of the pope, the king now completed the break. In 1534 he persuaded Parliament to pass an Act of Supremacy, naming the monarch "supreme head of the Church of England" and cutting all ties with Rome. Then, over the next five years, he closed the English monasteries and seized their property, selling much of it to local nobles. Henry thus solidified his support, since to keep their new lands the nobles would have to back him against the pope. But he also disbanded eminent institutions that had served as centers of learning and charity for centuries.

> The English ruler becomes head of the "Church of England"

Henry's legacy was further tarnished by several other events. In 1535, his former friend Thomas More, the highly respected humanist, was beheaded for refusing to support the Act of Supremacy. In 1536 the unfortunate Anne, having twice failed to produce a son, was accused of adultery and likewise beheaded. A third wife finally bore Henry a boy but perished while giving birth. The king went on to wed three more times before dying in 1547.

Despite his break with the Roman Church and attacks on its English supporters, Henry VIII was not a religious rebel. He remained true to most Catholic teachings, and resisted adopting the new practices promoted by Luther and other Protestants. Not until after Henry's death did the Church of England undergo significant doctrinal change.

Calvin and the Elect

In Switzerland, a new religious rebel expanded the Reformation. John Calvin (1509–1564), raised in France and trained as both a lawyer and a theologian, was initially attracted by Lutheran ideas. But in 1533 he reportedly had a conversion that crystallized his views in a flash of light. He concluded that faith, for Luther the key to salvation, was a gift that God gave only to certain people. And he concluded that the Catholic Church was not just a corrupt institution that needed reform, but an evil institution that should be destroyed.

Calvin settles in Geneva, which becomes key Protestant center

In 1536, having earlier fled to Switzerland to escape a crackdown on Protestants by French authorities, Calvin published the *Institutes of the Christian Religion*, soon the central work of Protestant theology. That same year he agreed to settle in the Swiss town of Geneva, which under his influence soon became the center of the Protestant world.

Calvin's teachings focused on **predestination**, the notion that God long ago decided each person's eternal fate. Some are destined for heaven, others are doomed to hell, no matter what they do. Earlier Church thinkers such as St. Augustine had promoted predestination, but had not gone as far as Calvin in dismissing free will and personal choice. Like Luther, Calvin believed that no one could earn salvation, but unlike Luther he concluded that God saved only **the elect**—those God had chosen beforehand for salvation.

John Calvin.

Although God alone knew who the elect were, Calvin's followers assumed that people like themselves, who led lives of faith and virtue, were among the elect. But for them faith and virtue were *results* of their salvation, not causes. Unlike Catholics, who led good lives in order to save their souls, Calvinists led good lives as a sign that they were already saved. For Catholics salvation came *after* one's life and was based on how one had lived; for Calvinists salvation came *before* one's life and determined how one would live.

Calvinists were also **puritanical**, promoting a strict moral code and "pure" religious practices. They held simple worship services, focused on sermons and Bible readings rather than elaborate rituals, in unadorned buildings rather than grandiose churches. Calvinists abhorred the ornate altars, vessels, statues, and stained-glass windows that adorned Catholic churches.

Calvin's Geneva becomes model of Protestant Christian community

The Calvinist model of a Christian community was Geneva, widely seen as the Protestant answer to Rome. Reformers came from all over Europe to take part in Geneva's religious life and learn from Calvin himself. A religious commission, under Calvin's influence, supervised moral behavior, prohibiting offenses such as gambling, dancing, and drinking. Graver crimes, such as blasphemy, adultery, and witchcraft, were punished by secular leaders, who sometimes used torture and executions. Geneva thus became a very sober and austere community.

The Spread of Protestantism

Geneva also served as a Reformation headquarters, sending disciples hither and yon to spread the Calvinist creed, which took root in parts of Northern and Central Europe. Lutheranism, meanwhile, spread from Germany to Scandinavia, and the Church of England eventually embraced many Protestant beliefs (Map 20.2).

One of Calvin's followers was John Knox, who spent several years in Geneva and then took the new faith home to Scotland, where it later became Presbyterianism. Communities of Calvinists likewise emerged in Bohemia, Hungary, and Poland; in the Netherlands, where they constituted the Dutch Reformed Church; in France, where they were called Huguenots (*HYOO-guh-notz*); and in England, where they were known as Puritans. Calvinist churches were largely independent of each other: rejecting the authoritarianism of popes and bishops, they formed no centralized international institution like the Catholic Church.

Lutherans and Calvinists form smaller churches, not a large centralized church

Nor did the Lutherans develop a single centralized church; instead, they relied on secular rulers to adopt the new faith and impose it on their domains. Many rulers did so, not only because they liked Luther's ideas but also as a way to confiscate the property of the Catholic Church and gain control of religion in their realms. Supported by such rulers, Lutheranism spread quickly across northern Germany and Scandinavia, becoming the main faith throughout the Baltic region.

The Church of England, too, was controlled by the monarchs, who after the death of Henry VIII eventually made it more Protestant. Under Henry's sickly son, King Edward VI (1547–1553), Archbishop Cranmer brought in Protestant theologians,

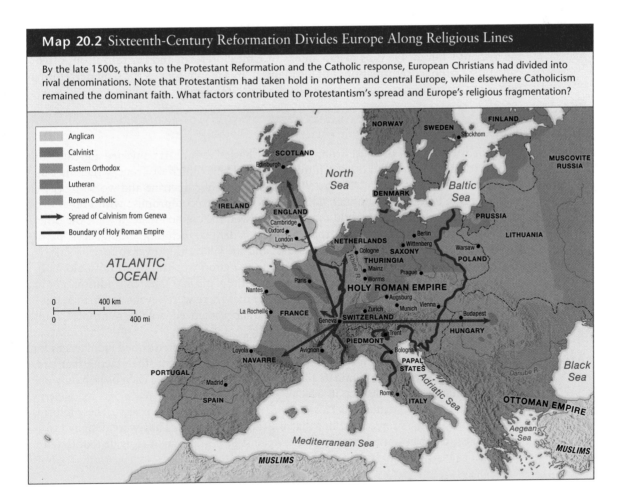

Map 20.2 Sixteenth-Century Reformation Divides Europe Along Religious Lines

By the late 1500s, thanks to the Protestant Reformation and the Catholic response, European Christians had divided into rival denominations. Note that Protestantism had taken hold in northern and central Europe, while elsewhere Catholicism remained the dominant faith. What factors contributed to Protestantism's spread and Europe's religious fragmentation?

Legend:
- Anglican
- Calvinist
- Eastern Orthodox
- Lutheran
- Roman Catholic
- → Spread of Calvinism from Geneva
- — Boundary of Holy Roman Empire

simplified liturgies, allowed priests to marry, and imposed his own *Book of Common Prayer* as the norm for church services. Queen Mary (1553–1558), the Catholic offspring of Henry's first marriage, tried to restore full Catholicism, executing Cranmer and several hundred Protestants. But her efforts were undone by Queen Elizabeth I (1558–1603), the Protestant daughter of Henry's second marriage. Determined to secure her throne by avoiding religious strife, Elizabeth pursued a middle path that aimed at satisfying most of her subjects. The English (or Anglican) Church thus combined Catholic-style liturgies and rituals performed by bishops and priests with the Protestant theology introduced under Cranmer.

By the 1560s, then, Protestantism in various forms had spread throughout northern and central Europe and into parts of France and Eastern Europe (Map 20.2). But by then the Catholic Church, which still prevailed in the South, had launched an effective counterattack and extended its influence far beyond Europe.

The Catholic Counterreformation

In the 1540s, after several decades of inability to stem the Protestant tide, Rome finally mounted a vigorous response. Pope Paul III (1534–1549), the earnest successor to the hapless Clement VII, called a general council to initiate Church reforms, authorized tribunals to prosecute Protestants for heresy, and approved new religious orders that reinvigorated the ancient Church. He thus began an era of Church reform and revitalization, often called the Catholic Reformation, but also labeled by Church foes as the Counterreformation, since it involved a counterattack against Protestantism.

The Council of Trent

The Council of Trent reaffirms Catholic teachings and sacraments

In 1545, after years of pressure from Emperor Charles V, Paul III convened a great council of Catholic bishops and other Church leaders. The Council of Trent, which met in 1545–1547, 1551–1552, and 1562–1563, shaped Catholic doctrine and worship for the next four hundred years. Although Charles V wanted it to compromise with Lutherans, and some bishops hoped it would limit papal power, the council instead went the other direction. It affirmed many things that Protestants denied, including indulgences, papal supremacy, priestly celibacy, the Latin Mass, and the Church's power to forgive sins. It insisted that salvation was based on *both* faith *and* good works, not on faith alone. It declared that divine revelation was found in *both* the Bible *and* Church tradition, not in scripture alone. It reasserted the Church's stance that there were seven sacraments, not just the two (baptism and Communion) that Luther recognized. And to reinforce Church unity, the council affirmed the pope's preeminence.

The Council of Trent also enacted some reforms. Although it affirmed indulgences for pious deeds and prayers, for example, the council forbade their *sale*, the practice that had triggered Luther's revolt. To eliminate pluralism, the council allowed each bishop only one diocese, or administrative district, in which he must reside. To improve the quality of clergy, it ruled that each diocese must have a *seminary*, a training school for priests. These reforms did not win back the Protestants, but that was not their intent. They were designed to purify and strengthen Catholicism for battle against Protestantism, a struggle that lasted far longer than anyone at Trent could foresee.

The Roman and Spanish Inquisitions

The Counterreformation's tactics were sometimes extreme. In central Italy and Spain, where Catholics were in control, they employed Inquisitions, church tribunals mandated to investigate, arrest, and prosecute people suspected of heretical beliefs. In Rome the Inquisition operated under the Holy Office, a council of six cardinals formed in 1542 by Pope Paul III. It was authorized to fine, imprison, and sometimes even execute people it convicted of promoting false doctrines. Starting in 1559, it also published an *Index of Forbidden Books*, a list of works that Catholics were forbidden to read without special permission. Officially designed to protect the faithful from heresy, the *Index* in time banned many works, including even novels such as *Les Miserables* and *The Hunchback of Notre Dame* (Chapter 27), perceived as offensive by the Church.

The Spanish Inquisition, which functioned largely under the rulers of Spain, had been set up in 1478 to investigate Jews and Muslims who had outwardly converted to Catholicism. Now it also targeted people suspected of Protestant views. To extract confessions, inquisitors sometimes used tortures such as the rack, which stretched the victim's body, and the thumbscrew, which crushed the victim's thumbs. Those found guilty of heresy were often burned to death.

Spanish Inquisition persecutes Muslims, Jews, and Protestants

Using closed trials, secret informers, tortures, and executions, the Inquisitions enforced Catholicism and virtually eradicated Protestantism in Italy and Spain. But elsewhere their main effect was to increase anti-Catholic hostility among Protestants, who sometimes employed similar methods against their religious foes.

New Religious Orders

Amid this tumult, the Catholic Church enjoyed a spiritual revival, led by dynamic individuals and new religious orders. Even before the Reformation, the Brethren of the Common Life, an association of devout laypersons and clergy who led simple lives in imitation of Christ, had spread through northern Europe. In Italy, a similar group called the Oratory of Divine Love stressed works of charity and devotion as antidotes to worldly corruption. In the 1530s an Italian woman named Angela Merici (*muh-RĒ-chē*) created the Ursuline (*UR-suh-lĭn*) order, a community of nuns who educated Catholic girls throughout Italy, France, and the Americas. But the most influential new order was begun by a Spanish nobleman named Ignatius Loyola (1491–1556).

An heir to Spain's crusading tradition, Ignatius was a soldier until 1521, when he was crippled in battle by a cannonball. During a long, painful recovery he read books about Christ and Christian saints. Deeply inspired, he then embarked on a spiritual crusade. He withdrew to a cave, where for months he prayed and lived alone in great austerity, depriving himself of all physical comforts. There he developed the Spiritual Exercises, a four-week regimen of prayer and meditation designed to prepare one for selfless discipline in service to God and Church.

After a pilgrimage to the Holy Land and brushes with the Spanish Inquisition, in 1528 Ignatius enrolled at the University of Paris, where he attracted a group of like-minded men. In 1537 they formed a "Company of Jesus," and in 1540 Pope Paul III formally approved them as the Society of Jesus.

The Jesuits, as they were soon known, became Catholicism's most zealous champions. Highly selective, they accepted only men of talent and discipline. Organized on military

Ignatius of Loyola.

lines, they vowed strict obedience to their superiors and the pope. Refusing to withdraw and live as monks or beggars, they served in the world as educators, missionaries, preachers, and political advisors.

Jesuits work to globalize and strengthen Catholicism

As educators, the Jesuits combined Renaissance humanism (Chapter 16) with Catholic ideals, promoting both secular learning and religious faith, while creating a network of schools and universities that eventually became a worldwide educational system. As missionaries, they worked tirelessly to convert the peoples of the Americas, Africa, and Asia to Catholicism, helping to transform their European faith into a global religion. As preachers to European Christians and political advisors to Catholic rulers, they led an intensive anti-Protestant campaign, helping to stem the Protestant tide and even restoring parts of Central Europe to the Catholic fold. They gained a reputation for both eloquence and political intrigue, making many enemies and adding to the climate of religious and political strife.

Religious and Political Strife in Europe

In the wake of the Reformation, Europe was ravaged by a century of religious and political conflicts. Bolstered by the riches of their Spanish overseas empire, the Catholic Habsburgs strove to impose their power and faith by force on Protestant regions. The Protestants, however, staunchly defended their new religions and political autonomy, perpetuating the fragmentation of Western Christianity.

The Spanish Catholic Crusade

In 1556 Emperor Charles V, longtime Catholic champion and ruler of the Habsburg realms, retired to a monastery. Deeming his domains too vast for one ruler, he split them between his brother and his son. His brother Ferdinand received the Habsburg lands in Austria, Bohemia, and Hungary, and succeeded Charles as Holy Roman Emperor. His son Philip got the rest, including Spain and its American empire, the Netherlands, Sardinia, Sicily, and parts of Italy. As King Philip II he ruled these lands from 1556 to 1598.

The wealth of its American empire makes Spain a global power

By this time Spain was Europe's mightiest country, owing largely to its American empire. The conquest of the Aztecs and Inca, with their enormous riches (Chapter 18), had been followed in 1545 by the discovery of vast silver deposits near Potosí (*pō-tō-SĒ*), in what is now Bolivia. These immense resources, exploited by Spaniards using Amerind (American Indian) and African slaves, soon supplied Spain's king with almost limitless wealth. And Philip was determined to use this fortune to further the Catholic cause.

A zealous Catholic, he launched a crusade to reinforce his religion throughout his realms and win back for his Church the lands it had lost. In Spain he used the Inquisition to suppress Protestantism. In America he used missionaries to foster his faith and officials to enforce it; so successful were they that Spanish America became a Catholic stronghold. In the Mediterranean he used his navy to challenge the Ottoman Turks, joining forces with Venice and the pope to defeat the Turkish fleet near the coast of Greece at the Battle of Lepanto in 1571. Elsewhere, however, Philip ran into problems.

Philip's first setback came in England, where he was wed to the Catholic Queen Mary. With her help he hoped to bring England back to Catholicism, and perhaps into his empire. But in 1558 she died in a cholera epidemic, and her Protestant successor Elizabeth, spurning his marriage proposals, soon became a formidable foe.

His next setback was the Dutch Revolt, a rebellion in the Netherlands against his heavy-handed rule. In 1566, alarmed that he might impose the Inquisition on them, Dutch Calvinists rebelled, attacking Catholic churches, smashing sacred vessels, statues, stained-glass windows, and artwork. Enraged by this "Calvinist fury," Philip tried to reassert control by executing rebels and confiscating lands of Calvinist nobles. By 1579 he had sub-dued the Netherlands' southern Catholic provinces, which henceforth became the Spanish Netherlands (and today constitute Belgium). But the northern Protestant provinces then declared independence as the United Provinces of the Netherlands. This new nation, often called Holland (after its main province), continued to fight Spain for a generation.

English and Dutch combat Spain's anti-Protestant campaign

In 1585, fearing that Spain might prevail and then use the Netherlands as a base from which to attack her country, England's Queen Elizabeth sent money and troops to aid the Dutch. Philip, in turn, prepared to invade England. Tension increased in 1587, when Elizabeth approved the execution of her cousin Mary Stuart (Mary Queen of Scots), the Catholic claimant to the English throne. The next year Philip dispatched the Invincible Catholic Armada, a fleet of 130 huge ships, with orders to land in the Netherlands and escort the Spanish army to England to begin the assault.

Its ships emblazoned with crosses and Catholic banners, the Armada set sail in May 1588. In July it met the English fleet in the English Channel. The result was a disaster for Spain. The English, whose ships were smaller and faster, harassed the Armada's huge vessels and kept them from landing. A fierce gale, which the English dubbed the "Protestant Wind," blew the Spanish ships off course, and further storms did even more damage as the Armada's remnants, trying to return to Spain, sailed around Scotland and Ireland. Some survivors, shipwrecked in Ireland, were killed; others settled there and married Irish women.

English ships confront the Spanish Armada.

The defeat of the Spanish Armada in 1588 by no means ended the fighting, which con-tinued until 1604. But it did help the English and Dutch to foil Philip's Catholic crusade, to continue their Protestant course, to challenge Spain for control of the seas, and hence to found their own colonies in North America.

The Wars of Religion in France

From 1562 to 1594, as Catholic Spain battled Dutch and English Protestants, France was torn by internal conflicts called the Wars of Religion. By then, although France remained mostly Catholic, about 7 percent of its people—including about 40 percent of its nobles—had become Calvinists. Known as Huguenots and led by the Bourbon family, they fought Catholic factions in a complex struggle for religious and political power. Catherine de Medicis (*MED-ih-chē*), the influential mother of three Catholic kings who reigned from 1559 to 1589, tried to preserve her family's power by reconciling hostile factions. In 1572, however, fearful of growing Protestant strength, she helped plot the massacre of several thousand Huguenots gathered in Paris for a wedding. But even this atrocity could not save Catherine's clan. In 1589, following her death and the murder of her last royal son, the head of the Huguenot Bourbons inherited the throne as King Henri IV.

The struggle nonetheless continued. French Catholics, refusing to accept a Protestant king, blocked Henri's efforts to enter Paris and assume the throne. So Henri, pragmatically concluding that "Paris is worth a Mass," formally became a Catholic in 1593, thereby gaining acceptance in Paris as king in 1594. Betrayed by their champion, the Huguenots resisted Henri's rule until 1598, when he won them over with religious toleration, issuing the Edict of Nantes (*NAHNT*). This historic document gave French Protestants full civil

Calvinist King Henri IV becomes Catholic and enforces toleration

rights, the freedom to hold worship services in their own manors and towns, and the right to fortify these towns with their own troops. It also helped make Henri IV, already known for his charm and dashing demeanor, one of France's most popular kings. But Henri's tolerant edict did not please everyone: in 1610 he was murdered by a fanatical Catholic. Religious animosities did not die easily in France.

The Thirty Years War

Nor did they die easily in Germany, birthplace of the Reformation, where Lutherans and Catholics had for decades observed an uneasy truce. In 1608 the Calvinists, having made inroads in parts of the Holy Roman Empire, joined with Lutherans in an alliance called the Protestant Union. The next year the Austrian Habsburgs, backed by the wealth of their Spanish cousins, created a rival coalition called the Catholic League, setting the stage for a calamitous conflict known as the Thirty Years War (1618–1648).

Catholic Habsburg rulers battle Central Europe's Protestant nobles

This conflict began in 1618 with an incident called the "Defenestration of Prague" (*dē-FEN-ih-STRĀ-shun*: the act of throwing someone out a window). Protestant nobles in Bohemia, angered by Habsburg efforts to restrict their rights, threw two imperial agents out of a high palace window. Despite their survival—credited by Catholics to divine intervention and by Protestants to the fact that they landed in a dung heap—the fragile peace was shattered. Emperor Ferdinand II (1619–1637), aided by the Catholic League and his Spanish relatives, crushed the Bohemians and other Protestant forces, moving steadily to bring all Germany under Catholic control. By 1629 he was on the verge of triumph, and the Protestant cause seemed lost.

Then, however, two powerful outside forces intervened on the Protestant side. One was Gustavus Adolphus (*gus-TAH-vus ah-DOLL-fus*), Sweden's Lutheran king, who feared for his country's safety should northern Germany come under Catholic control. A talented warrior, he defeated the Habsburgs in several key battles before dying in combat in 1632. The other force was Cardinal Richelieu (*RISH-lih-YOO*), France's chief minister, who first supplied aid to the Protestants, and then had his country join the war on their side in 1635.

As a cardinal in the Catholic Church, Richelieu seemed an unlikely supporter of German Protestants. But his main loyalty was to France, which already faced Habsburg Spain to its South and the Spanish Netherlands to its North. Bent on blocking Habsburg unification of Germany to the East, he aided Protestants as a way to keep Germany divided and weak.

The last phase of the war, from 1635 to 1648, resulted in mass devastation. France and Spain, both deeply involved in the German conflict, battled each other as well. Armies crisscrossed central Europe, assaulting each other and brutalizing the people, while disease and famine stalked the land. The German population was greatly diminished, and wolves roamed the streets in desolate towns and villages.

Although France and Spain fought on until 1659, the German nightmare ended in 1648 with the Peace of Westphalia (Map 20.3). Each German state remained virtually independent, with rulers free to conduct their own diplomacy and decide whether their realms should be Catholic, Lutheran, or Calvinist. The Holy Roman Empire was left with only nominal authority, and it no longer included the Dutch, the Swiss, or the Italians. The Habsburgs remained emperors in name, but their efforts to unify Germany and restore Catholicism throughout Europe had failed. After decades of destructive warfare, Europe remained divided along religious lines.

Map 20.3 Peace of Westphalia Leaves Central Europe Divided, 1648

In 1648, at the end of the Thirty Years War, the Peace of Westphalia left Europe divided along religious lines, while the various states in the Holy Roman Empire retained and enhanced their autonomy. Notice the empire was also diminished by the loss of Switzerland, the Dutch United Netherlands, and the northwest Italian states. Why did the Habsburgs fail in their efforts to unite Central Europe under Catholic Habsburg rule? How did this failure bolster the power of France?

The Globalization of Western Christianity and Commerce

Europe's fragmentation was, paradoxically, accompanied by global expansion. In the sixteenth and seventeenth centuries, as Europe was torn by ruinous religious and political strife, European Christianity and commerce spread across the globe, aided by enterprising missionaries, officials, and merchants.

Catholicism's Global Expansion

Catholics at first took the lead, based on the efforts of empire builders and religious orders. The Spanish and Portuguese, who justified imperial expansion by claiming they were carrying Christ's message to distant lands, systematically imposed their faith on the people they conquered (Chapter 19). Thus in the American colonies, where Iberian Catholics controlled governance and commerce, and where Catholic priests and nuns ran numerous missions and schools, most people adopted the religion of their rulers through coercion, convenience, or conviction.

The Jesuits, joined and often rivaled by other Catholic orders, including Franciscans and Dominicans, also strove to implant Catholicism in Asia. Their work was begun by Francis Xavier (*ZĀ-vē-ur*), one of the first Jesuits, a former Paris roommate of Ignatius Loyola. Arriving in India on a Portuguese ship in 1542, Xavier worked for several years among that country's poor pearl fishers, then traveled to Malaya and the Spice Islands, founding various missions before returning to India. From 1549 to 1551 he lived in Japan, whose culture he greatly admired, and converted thousands to the Catholic faith. In 1552 he set out to begin the conversion of China but grew ill and died on an island off the Chinese coast.

Xavier's deep respect for Asians, and his tireless efforts to understand their languages and cultures, set an example for thousands of Jesuits who followed in his footsteps. Jesuits learned local languages, adapted local customs, and blended Catholic teachings into local cultures, rather than simply seeking to impose European ways. Their success in Asian countries was nonetheless often limited by resistance from local religions and rulers. Still, spread by the Jesuits and their fellow missionaries, preachers, and teachers, Catholicism became a global faith, with thousands of missions, parishes, and schools, and millions of followers, around the world (Map 20.4).

Merchant Capitalism and Global Trade

As some Europeans globalized their religion, others were transforming the global economy. Western merchants, eager to enhance their incomes, worked to gain control over the production of goods and to establish worldwide trading networks. European governments, seeking to increase state wealth, encouraged the growth of overseas commerce and the exploitation of colonies.

For many centuries, Chinese, Muslim, and European merchants had conducted interregional trade, engaging in many practices—such as credit, banking, and marketing of goods—later associated with **capitalism**, an economic system based on competition among private enterprises. But merchants usually did not manufacture the goods they sold. These goods were typically produced by artisans, who owned their own tools and workshops, purchased raw materials such as metals, leather, wool, wood, and wax, and used their labor and skill to make these materials into finished products. The artisans then sold the finished goods to customers or merchants, often at prices fixed by artisans' guilds. Merchants were mostly middlemen: traders who bought goods in one place, took them to another place, and sold them at a profit.

From the fifteenth century onward, however, European merchants increasingly sought to enhance their profits by gaining control of production. They bought mines, woodlands, and herds of sheep and cattle, thereby acquiring their own raw materials. They also bought tools and equipment, then hired their own workers so as not to be dependent on artisans and guilds, many of whom in turn organized their own enterprises. Thus arose a dynamic new class of capitalists: entrepreneurs who created and ran enterprises that produced and sold their own goods.

In this system, later called merchant capitalism, the merchant entrepreneur owned the means of production—tools, machines, and raw materials—and decided how much to produce and to charge for finished goods. The producer worked for the merchant and was paid a fixed wage or a prearranged price for each piece made. The finished products were thus owned by the entrepreneur, who arranged for their transport and sale, setting

Map 20.4 Globalization of Western Christianity and Commerce, 1500–1750

While Europe was torn apart by religious conflict, Europeans were extending their sway over the Americas and parts of Africa and Asia. Note that Europeans not only helped connect these regions by commerce, but also spread their Christian religions, with the Spanish, French, and Portuguese imposing Catholicism, the Dutch and English promoting Protestantism, and the Russians fostering their Orthodox faith in expanding across northern Asia. How did the spread of Christianity and commerce help to bolster Europe's wealth and power?

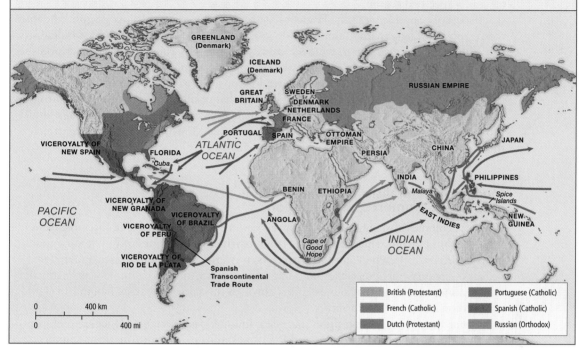

prices so as to be competitive in a free market based on supply and demand. Over time, independent artisans were largely replaced by wage laborers, employed and paid by wealthy merchant capitalists.

In expanding production and trade, merchant capitalists often found allies in their national monarchs. Rulers increasingly realized that, as commerce grew, so did their revenues from taxes and tariffs. They could then use these revenues in hiring armies to fight their wars and officials to administer their realms, thus expanding the power of their government. Rulers therefore instituted policies, later referred to as **mercantilism,** that aimed to create a favorable balance of trade, a condition in which a country's trading exports exceeded its imports in value. Since the nation as a whole would thus sell more than it bought, fortune supposedly would flow into the realm, and into the royal treasury.

Mercantilist policies typically included government support of enterprises engaged in overseas trade. In the fifteenth and sixteenth centuries, Portuguese voyagers backed by the government set up numerous trading posts on African and Asian coasts, creating a commercial empire that made one of Europe's smallest kingdoms into one of its richest (Chapter 19). By 1600, eager to gain some of this wealth, England and the Netherlands had begun to follow suit.

In these countries, and later in France, government support for overseas trade was provided through **charter companies**, trading associations protected by royal monopoly. Since overseas trade involved risks and expenses beyond what one investor could bear, merchants in these countries pooled their resources to form a large company in which many owned shares. To support the company and protect it from competition, the country's ruler then issued a charter giving the company a monopoly of trade between that country and a specified region.

English and Dutch East India Companies dominate east-west trade

Especially notable were the English East India Company, which monopolized commerce between England and India starting in 1600, and the Dutch United East India Company, founded two years later, which dominated trade between the Netherlands and the East Indies. For the next two centuries, these companies and others, with large fleets of merchant vessels, maintained profitable trading posts in various parts of the world, gaining vast riches for themselves and their rulers. Global trading networks supplied European consumers with products from distant lands, such as silks, spices, sugar, coffee, tea, and tobacco, while the revenues this trade produced helped European monarchs centralize their governments and increase their royal powers.

Colonies, Commerce, and Religion

Overseas colonies also enhanced a country's commerce and power. The foremost example was Habsburg Spain, which used silver from its American colonies to buy luxury goods in Asia for resale elsewhere, and to finance its powerful armies and navies, making it sixteenth-century Europe's richest and mightiest realm. Another example was Portugal, which gained wealth in that same century through the sale of sugar, grown in Brazil and other colonies using African slaves.

Other Europeans, seeing these successes, imitated the Iberians. Hence, in the seventeenth century, the French, Dutch, and English established North American colonies. The French set up trading posts in eastern Canada and the Mississippi Valley, bartering with Amerinds for animal furs that sold for a fortune in Europe, and the Dutch did likewise in the Hudson Valley of what is now New York State. The English established a Virginia colony that prospered in time from tobacco, a crop that Amerinds taught them to grow, which was sold in Europe for a big profit. The French, Dutch, and English also set up colonies on Caribbean islands that, imitating the Spanish West Indies and Portuguese Brazil, profited greatly from production and sale of slave-grown sugar. By the late 1600s, bolstered by wealth from their commerce and colonies, England, France, and the Netherlands had replaced Spain and Portugal as Europe's dominant political and economic powers.

French Jesuit baptizing Amerind convert.

These developments also had profound religious implications. France, like Spain and Portugal, promoted Catholicism in its colonies, aided by Jesuits and other French priests who worked among French settlers and Amerinds. Dutch Calvinists established settlements in the Hudson River region, while English Calvinists known as Puritans, fleeing persecution in their native land, moved in large numbers to what became New England starting in the 1620s. English Catholics colonized Maryland in succeeding decades, while Anglicans and other English Protestants populated additional new English North American colonies. By the mid-1600s, like Europe itself, North America had a variety of Christian denominations (Map 20.4).

The French, Dutch, and English impose their religions in their colonies

Western Society in an Age of Religious and Economic Change

As Europeans spread their creeds and commerce to diverse lands and peoples, religious divisions and global expansion were transforming Europe's society. On one hand, religious strife led to suffering and fear; on the other hand, global expansion helped foster growing prosperity.

Warfare, Disease, and Witch Hunts

The era of religious upheaval brought hardship to many Europeans. Religious leaders and warriors, fueled by righteous fury, engaged in persecutions and bloodshed, claiming they were doing God's will. Bands of armed fighters, feeding on the chaos of religious conflict, often roamed the countryside, looting, pillaging, and raping at will. Dislocation and devastation frequently followed in their footsteps.

Adding to anxieties in the sixteenth century was a pandemic of syphilis, a sexually transmitted disease whose victims initially suffered sores and rashes, and later often blindness, insanity, and death. Some experts think syphilis was a virulent form of an earlier European ailment; others assume that European sailors brought it from the Americas after contracting it from Amerinds. Either way, it spread misery and fear in Europe, where it was called the great pox (to distinguish it from smallpox) or the "French disease" (as it was often blamed on French soldiers).

Even more unsettling were the witch hunts of the sixteenth and seventeenth centuries. During this era, over a hundred thousand Europeans, most of them women, were placed on trial for witchcraft, supposedly for using supernatural powers to make evil things happen. Perhaps fifty thousand people were executed for this alleged crime.

Various factors contributed to the witch hunts. One factor was the Reformation, which led Catholics and Protestants alike to persecute heretics and to accuse dissenters of doing the devil's work. Luther, Calvin, and the Catholic Church all favored burning witches. A second factor was the misery bred by religious war, leading many to seek scapegoats for the suffering. A third factor was the syphilis pandemic, causing miscarriages, stillbirths, blindness, and insanity, easily ascribed to satanic influence.

A fourth factor was a pamphlet called *Malleus Maleficarum* (*MAH-lā-oos MAH-lā-fē-CAH-room*), "The Hammer of the Wicked." First published by two Dominican friars in 1486, and circulated widely over the next two centuries, it sought to supply an explanation of witchcraft. It alleged that witches made pacts with the devil, sealed by sex with him, which empowered them to make evil things happen to others. Although witches could be male or female, this book portrayed them mainly as women, whom it considered weaker than men and more easily won over to evil. Witches were said to meet their devils at assemblies called synagogues or sabbaths, thereby indirectly linking witchcraft to Jewish worship.

Those accused of witchcraft were usually women, typically single or widowed, aging, and poor, who often had no family to protect them and thus were easy targets. Older women, beyond childbearing age, were sometimes seen as burdens on society and accused of erratic behavior. Aging might bring on deeper voices and a haggard appearance, leading fearful neighbors to label them "hags." Women's customary roles as midwives and healers also left them open to blame when infants or sick people died. Such circumstances, and depictions of women as tools of the devil going back to the biblical Eve, reinforced the tendency to associate witchcraft with women.

War and global contacts help produce syphilis pandemic

Disease, devastation, and religious conflict help to promote witch hunts

Women accused of witchcraft being hanged.

Document 20.1 Excerpt from a Witchcraft Trial

Witchcraft trials were held throughout European countries and their colonies in the sixteenth and seventeenth centuries. In the seventeenth-century indictment excerpted below, couched in the formal legal language of the day, a woman named Rose Cullender is charged with using "incantations" and "enchantments" to harm a certain Ann Baldinge. Rose is identified as a widow, and Ann is identified as spinster, a term commonly used for women who never married, since many earned their living by spinning thread.

The King's sworn officers maintain upon their oaths that Rose Cullender, late of Lowestoft in the aforesaid county, on the 1st day of February in the 14th year of the reign of our lord Charles . . ., being a common witch and "enchantress" and not having God before her eyes but moved and seduced by the instigation of the Devil did . . . violently, unlawfully, diabolically, and feloniously use, practice, and employ certain evil and diabolical "fascinations"—in English "witchcrafts"—and "incantations"—in English "enchantments"—on one Anne Baldinge, spinster, then and there living in the peace of God . . . , and by the aforesaid evil and diabolical witchcraft and enchantments then and there did feloniously bewitch and enchant her, by which evil and diabolical witchcraft and enchantments . . . the aforesaid Ann Baldinge from the . . . 1st day of February of the above mentioned year to the day of the holding of the inquisition at Lowestoft . . . has languished and languishes still and is greatly wasted in her . . . body and is consumed to the injury of the same Anne Baldinge and in the breach of peace of the said lord King . . . and also in breach of peace of the form of the state given forth and provided for such cases.

SOURCE: Gilbert Geis and Ivan Bunn, *A Trial of Witches: A Seventeenth-Century Witchcraft Prosecution* (London and New York: Routledge, 1997) page 39.

Women depicted as witches were blamed for numerous misfortunes, such as accidents, illnesses, sudden deaths, bad weather, infertility, and sexual impotence. Charges were typically brought by someone who had suffered a loss or by professional witch hunters who made a career of identifying witches (see "Excerpt from a Witchcraft Trial"). Many of the accused were tortured, often until they confessed or implicated others to save themselves. The convicted might be burned to death, hanged (in England), banished, or imprisoned. Some of them may actually have tried witchcraft, but most were no doubt innocent victims of fear, superstition, and witch hunts.

Social Effects of Economic Expansion

Urban middle classes benefit from global commerce

Less dramatic, but far more enduring, were changes wrought in Western society by capitalism and global trade. The main beneficiaries were the growing middle classes who lived in towns (burgs) and cities, and hence were called *burghers* or *bourgeoisie* (*boorzh-wah-ZĒ*). They included merchants and bankers who profited from increased trade; doctors, lawyers, and others who prospered by serving wealthy people's needs; and artisans and manufacturers who raised prices on their products as more wealth became available.

Global trade helped prosperous townsfolk live well, enjoying cottons, furs, tea, coffee, sugar, spices, and later tobacco and chocolate, imported from the Americas and Asia. Towns and cities sported rows of tidy townhouses, along with markets, plazas, taverns, inns, banks, and shops. Wealthy bourgeois even challenged nobles for social and political preeminence. But many wage laborers were hurt by rising prices that increased faster than their incomes. And the urban poor, roughly half the townsfolk, lived in squalid slums full of vermin, beggars, criminals, prostitutes, drunks, and gangs.

The nobles, descendants of medieval lords and owners of rural estates, also were affected by the changing economy. Many came to live in cities, where they dwelt in elegant townhouses and enjoyed luxuries provided by global trade, while leaving hired stewards to manage their estates. To enhance their incomes some nobles even invested in commercial concerns or married their children to sons and daughters of wealthy bourgeois parents. In Western Europe, where access to the sea trade enhanced the size and wealth of the bourgeoisie, the nobles' power declined as monarchs and merchants shaped strong political and economic institutions. In Central and Eastern Europe, however, where lack of access to such commerce kept the urban middle classes small and weak, the nobles remained the dominant political and economic force.

Initially the peasants, some 80–90 percent of the population, were little affected by the economic changes. They lived in isolated villages, with little access to the wonders of the wider world. Occasionally they might travel to a town to visit its markets or attend an annual fair. As a rule, however, they rose with the sun, worked the fields by day, and retired to their villages after dark. In Eastern Europe most peasants were still serfs, bound in service to their landlords; but even in the West, where most were legally free, peasants were subject to burdensome taxes and dues.

By the 1600s, however, capitalist commerce was beginning to affect many peasants. To get around dealing with town artisans and guilds, merchants started lending, or "putting out," equipment and raw materials (such as weaving looms and wool) to peasant families, who used them to make products (such as clothing) in their own huts and cottages. The merchant capitalist paid them a fixed price for each item produced and then sold these items at a lower cost than guild artisans charged for such products. This "putting out" system, later called **cottage industry** or the "domestic system," not only lowered merchants' costs and the price of goods produced but also increased peasant incomes, further reducing the landlords' leverage over local villagers.

New "cottage industries" tie rural villagers into global economy

Family, Gender, Education, and Diet

Religious and economic change also affected family patterns, gender roles, education, and diet. Arising in the 1500s, these effects became increasingly visible in the following century.

In the 1500s, as in eras past, the basic unit of Western society was the patriarchal family, headed by men regarded as masters of their households. Noblemen acted as lords of the family estate and often also as military officers or government officials. Middle class men ran the family business or practiced the family trade, while peasant men farmed the strips of land allotted to their family in fields around their village. As household heads and providers, men expected to be waited on by their wives and to make key decisions for their children, including assignment of family duties and selection of spouses.

Although thus considered subservient to men, women played central roles in family life. They raised children, baked bread, prepared meals, and made clothes, often joining in social circles to support and learn from other women. Women also functioned as midwives and caregivers, delivering babies and treating illnesses with folk remedies passed on from previous generations. Lower-class mothers breast-fed their own infants, while wealthy women often hired a "wet-nurse" to breast-feed theirs. Peasant women sustained their families mainly on dark bread and soups made from peas, beans, cabbages, and carrots, supplemented sometimes by eggs, butter, and cheese. Meat meals, white bread, and sweet pastries, standard fare in the upper classes, were rare among the common people.

Peasant couple at market (engraving by Albrecht Dürer).

Women typically have little freedom or choice

Yet women had little control over their own lives. Parents arranged their marriages, often with more concern for enhancing family status than for their daughters' happiness. Women who wound up with drunken, abusive, or unfaithful husbands had little choice but to endure their plight. Since childhood diseases killed 20–30 percent of all children, women commonly bore at least six or seven children to ensure that some would survive to adulthood.

By the 1600s, despite considerable continuity, some basic family patterns were changing. Increased incomes from commerce and cottage industry, for example, helped many married couples maintain separate households, rather than living as in the past with their extended families. **Nuclear families**, made up of only parents and children, gradually became the norm. And, although their parents still had to approve their marriages, young people increasingly chose their own spouses, often after years of courtship, waiting to wed until their mid-twenties when they could support themselves. Divorce and remarriage, banned by the Catholic Church, were often allowed among Protestants, especially in cases of adultery or abuse.

Printing press and religious schools boost literacy and learning

Learning and literacy, too, were becoming more common. The great increase in the number of books produced by the printing press, combined with the Protestant emphasis on individual reading of the Bible, accelerated the spread of education. Protestant pastors and Catholic religious orders set up schools to teach reading and writing, not only to the offspring of merchants and nobles but also to growing numbers of lower-class children. Although such schools were intended mainly for males, prosperous parents increasingly managed to educate their daughters too, enabling them in time to play a larger role in social and cultural life.

Diets are enhanced by new foods such as potatoes from the Americas

European diets also evolved as new foods from the Americas were added. In the seventeenth century, European farmers began growing crops developed by Amerinds, such as corn (maize), which originated in Mexico, and potatoes, which came from Peru. Potatoes proved especially useful, since they took less space to cultivate than grain crops such as wheat or rye, were easier to preserve, and could feed more people. Europe's global expansion thus enhanced not only its prosperity but also its food supply.

Changes in the Role of Religion

Religion's role was likewise altered in the age of religious conflict. Before the Reformation, since most Europeans sought salvation through the Church, religion was central to society. The Church provided sacraments and religious education, collected and distributed donations for the poor, and kept records of births, deaths, baptisms, and marriages. It also offered festival occasions, including baptisms, weddings, and holy days such as Christmas and Easter. It even condoned midwinter Carnival festivities—also called Shrovetide, Mardi Gras (*MAR-dē GRAH*), or Fasching (*FAH-shing*)—during which people dressed in costumes and ate and drank excessively in preparation for Lent, a 40-day period of fasting and sacrifice leading up to Easter.

After the Reformation, changing outlooks slowly started altering religion's role. Since Protestants needed no Church for salvation, their faith was often private and plain, marked by Bible reading in the home and simple Sunday services. Their sober moral code also frowned on such excesses as Catholic pre-Lenten festivities, while their certainty of salvation removed the need for Lenten fasts and sacrifices.

Religious wars, witch hunts, and economic change diminish religion's role

Religious wars and witch hunts also provoked disenchantment with religion, while growing prosperity left Europeans less focused on death and salvation. In Protestant areas, and even Catholic lands, the saints, shrines, monasteries, pilgrimages, and fasts that earlier meant so much grew less important. Freed by Luther and Calvin from the need to earn salvation, many Protestants focused their energies on material success—and many ambitious Catholics did too.

Most people continued to worship and pray, but their lives were less centered on religion than before and they were less inclined to look to religious leaders for guidance. Europe's age of religious upheaval, begun by efforts to enhance religion and diminish the wealth and worldliness of the Roman Church, instead diminished the role of religion and enhanced the wealth and worldliness of European society.

Chapter Review

Putting It in Perspective

In the early sixteenth century, hoping to reform the Catholic Church, reduce Church corruption, improve public morals, and strengthen piety among the people, religious reformers started a rebellion known as the Protestant Reformation. They were supported in their efforts by many political leaders, alarmed at the growing power of the Habsburg family, and by numerous other people who resented the extravagance of popes and bishops, financed by the donations of the faithful.

But the Reformation's outcome was not what its originators intended. Europe's religious unity was shattered, generating all sorts of new beliefs and competing Christian churches, as religious strife and religious zeal fueled wars, inquisitions, persecutions, and witch hunts. Central Europe was left divided and weak, thwarting Habsburg efforts to transform the Holy Roman Empire, including Germany and much of Italy, into a centralized state. And Europe as a whole was left divided among diverse states, each with its own religious institutions and issues.

Despite this destruction and division, however, Europe's wealth and influence expanded. The worldwide spread of Western Christianity, the growth of global commerce and capitalism, the exploitation of the Americas, the flourishing of the bourgeoisie, and advances in literacy and learning all boded well for Europe, especially for European countries that bordered the Atlantic. By the late seventeenth century, profiting from connections created by global expansion, the West was emerging from its religious strife more prosperous and powerful than ever.

Reviewing Key Material

KEY CONCEPTS

sacraments, 483	puritanical, 488
purgatory, 484	capitalism, 496
indulgence, 484	mercantilism, 497
Ninety-five Theses, 485	charter companies, 498
predestination, 488	cottage industry, 501
the elect, 488	nuclear families, 502

KEY PEOPLE

Martin Luther, 485	John Knox, 489
Emperor Charles V, 485	King Edward VI, 489
John Wyclif, 484	Queen Mary, 490
John Hus, 484	Queen Elizabeth I, 490
Pope Sixtus IV, 484	Pope Paul III, 490
Pope Alexander VI, 484	Angela Merici, 491
Pope Julius II, 484	Ignatius Loyola, 491
Maximilian of Habsburg, 485	King Philip II, 492
Friar John Tetzel, 485	Mary Stuart (Queen of
Frederick the Wise, 486	Scots), 493
Huldrych Zwingli, 486	Catherine de Medicis, 493
King Henry VIII, 487	King Henri IV, 493
Catherine of Aragon, 487	Emperor Ferdinand II, 494
Anne Boleyn, 487	King Gustavus Adolphus, 494
Pope Clement VII, 487	Cardinal Richelieu, 494
John Calvin, 488	Francis Xavier, 496

ASK YOURSELF

1. Why did Martin Luther challenge the authority of the Catholic Church? Why did his challenge become a revolt against the Church, rather than a reform movement within the Church?
2. Why did Luther's challenge result in the formation of many new Christian sects? How did the challenges of John Calvin and Henry VIII differ from Luther's challenge?

3. How did the Catholic Church respond to the Protestant challenge? Why were the popes and the Habsburg rulers unable to crush the Protestants?

4. What circumstances led to the globalization of Western Christianity and commerce? What roles did missionaries, merchants, and monarchs each play in this process?

5. What factors account for the economic and social changes in Europe during the age of religious upheavals? Why were women, especially aging women, so often the targets of witch hunts?

GOING FURTHER

Asch, Ronald. *The Thirty Years' War.* 1997.

Bainton, R. *The Reformation of the Sixteenth Century.* Rev. ed. 1985.

Barstow, A. *Witchcraft: A New History of European Witch Hunts.* 1994.

Braudel, F. *Capitalism and Material Life, 1400–1800.* 1973.

Brendler, G. *Martin Luther: Theology and Revolution.* 1991.

Brodrick, James. *The Origin of the Jesuits.* 1971.

Cameron, E., ed. *Early Modern Europe: An Oxford History.* 1999.

Davidson, Nicholas S. *The Counter-Reformation.* 1987.

Dunn, R. S. *The Age of Religious Wars, 1559–1715.* 2nd ed. 1979.

Duplessis, R. *Transitions to Capitalism in Early Modern Europe.* 1997.

Holt, M. P. *The French Wars of Religion, 1562–1629.* 1995.

Kamen, H. *Empire: How Spain Became a World Power.* 2003.

Kittelson, J. M. *Luther the Reformer.* 1986.

Levack, Brian. *The Witch-Hunt in Early Modern Europe,* 2nd ed. 1995.

Lindberg, C. *The European Reformations.* 1996.

MacCulloch, Diarmaid. *The Reformation: A History.* 2005.

Mattingly, Garrett. *The Armada.* 1959, 1988.

McGrath, A. *A Life of John Calvin.* 1990.

Oberman, Heiko A. *Luther: Between God and the Devil.* 1989.

Olin, J. C. *The Catholic Reformation: From Savonarola to Loyola.* 1993.

O'Malley, J. W. *The First Jesuits,* 1993

Ozment, Steven. *Protestants: The Birth of a Revolution.* 1992.

Parker, G. *The Thirty Years War.* 2nd ed. 1997.

Parker, T. H. L. *Calvin: An Introduction to His Thought.* 1995.

Pettegree, A., ed. *The Early Reformation in Europe.* 1992.

Thomas, Keith. *Religion and the Decline of Magic.* 1971.

Warnicke, R. *Women of the English Renaissance and Reformation.* 1983.

Wier, Allison. *The Life of Elizabeth I.* 1999.

Wiesner, M. E. *Women and Gender in Early Modern Europe.* 2nd ed. 2000.

Key Dates and Developments

Date	Event	Date	Event
1517	Luther's Ninety-five Theses initiate Reformation	1545	Pope Paul III convenes Council of Trent
1519	Charles V becomes Holy Roman Emperor	1556	Charles V retires; Philip II becomes King of Spain
1521	Luther appears before Diet of Worms	1562–1594	Wars of Religion in France
1525	German nobles crush Peasants' Revolt	1566	Dutch Revolt begins
1527	King Henry VIII begins to seek annulment	1588	Spanish Armada defeated
1529	Ottoman Turks besiege Vienna	1598	Edict of Nantes in France
1533	Henry VIII defies Rome and marries Anne Boleyn	1600	English East India Company founded
1534	Parliament makes Henry VIII head of English Church	1602	Dutch United East India Company founded
1536	Calvin publishes Institutes of the Christian Religion	1618	Defenestration of Prague begins Thirty Years War
1540	Pope Paul III approves Society of Jesus (Jesuits)	1648	Peace of Westphalia ends Thirty Years War

The Search for Stability in East Asia, 1300–1800

Imperial Lion In The Forbidden City

This splendid bronze lion in Beijing's Forbidden City, a magnificent complex of palaces and courtyards built in the 1400s for the Chinese emperor, is a powerful symbol of China's historical quest for strength and stability.

In 1587 Japan's leading general, Toyotomi Hideyoshi (*TŌ-yo-TŌ-me he-da-YŌ-she*), took several steps to restore stability and reinforce traditional values. In July, fearful that the spread of Christianity by foreigners from the West was undermining age-old Japanese beliefs, he ordered Christian missionaries evicted from Japan. In August, concerned that widespread possession of weapons was promoting internal unrest, he conducted a Great Sword Hunt, aiming to confiscate the arms of all nonsoldiers. In November, exalting his country's time-honored customs, he staged a Grand Tea Ceremony at Kitano shrine in Kyoto, personally serving tea in exquisite porcelain vessels to more than eight hundred people. The simple art of serving tea, long used in Japan to foster discipline and respect, blended elegance with order, tradition, and tranquility.

East Asia

After decades of conflict and foreign meddling in Japan, Hideyoshi was eager to restore unity and order. His anti-Christian edict was not strictly enforced, his Great Sword Hunt did not end violence, and his Grand Tea Ceremony lasted only a day, yet together they signaled his resolve to stabilize Japan and secure its traditions. Following his lead, Hideyoshi's successors developed a stable regime, vigorously persecuted Christians, and cut off most contacts with the West until the 1800s.

Meanwhile, seared by the Mongol-induced upheavals of the thirteenth and fourteenth centuries, China too sought to promote stability and reinforce traditions. In China, as in Japan, internal warfare and outside influence created instability. In China, as in Japan, Jesuit missionaries and Western ideas gained influence at times. In China, as in Japan, rulers responded by strengthening control and resisting foreign influence, until finally forced by outsiders to do otherwise.

From the fourteenth through eighteenth centuries, East Asia's leading states thus sought stability, a condition combining security from foreign and domestic threats with consistency and structure. Change was welcome only in the context of traditional order; even innovators such as Hideyoshi portrayed themselves as restorers rather than as rebels. While other societies forged global connections, Japan and China chose to focus on regional stability. This focus provided substantial political and economic security, but it did not fully eliminate outside influence.

The Search for Stability in Japan and Korea

In theory, Japan's ruler was its emperor, a hereditary monarch, revered as a god, who reigned in Kyoto, the capital (Map 21.1). Beginning in 1192, however, Japan was actually run by a shogun, commander of its samurai armies, who exercised power in the emperor's name (Chapter 14). To complicate matters, in the next century the shoguns became puppets of the Hojo, a warlord family whose leaders ruled Japan as regents for the shoguns.

FOUNDATION MAP 21.1 Sixteenth-Century East Asia

In the fifteenth and sixteenth centuries, as in earlier eras, China was East Asia's largest and wealthiest power. Note that China under the Ming dynasty dominated the region, fostering stability and prosperity, while Korea and Vietnam paid tribute to China, looked to it for protection, and imitated its ways. Japan, racked by civil war and foreign intrusion, regained unity and stability by the early 1600s. In what ways did Korea, Vietnam, and Japan maintain their distinctiveness despite China's regional domination?

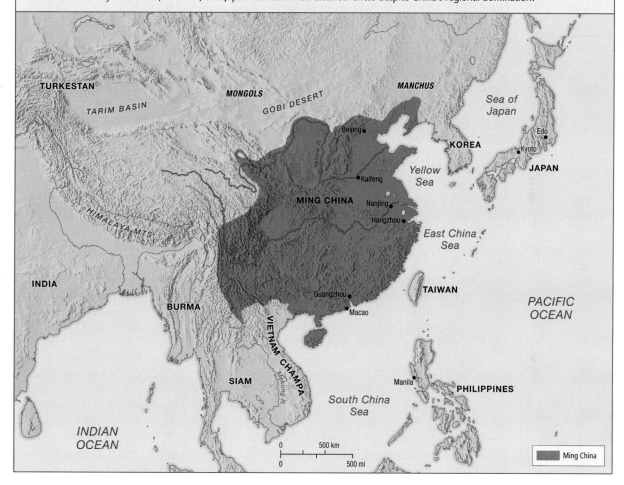

Ironically, Japan's success at repulsing Mongol invasions in 1274 and 1281 (Chapter 15) undermined this system. Having bravely resisted the Mongols, many Japanese samurai, members of the warrior class, expected grants of land as reward, following the usual custom. But no land had been conquered, so there was none to distribute. Furthermore, as samurai divided their family estates among their various heirs, individual landholdings grew smaller, leaving many warriors impoverished and embittered. Blaming their plight on the shoguns and the Hojo regents who controlled them, resentful samurai supported various **daimyo** (DĪM-yō), hereditary regional warlords who dominated parts of Japan. By the 1330s, Japan was ripe for rebellion.

Rebellions, Warring States, and Intruders

When young Emperor Go-Daigo (*gō-DĪ-gō*) came of age to rule in 1331, the Hojo regents tried to force him to retire, as was their practice, so they could continue to exercise power in the name of a new child emperor. But Go-Daigo refused to step down. Instead, backed by resentful samurai, he rebelled. In 1333 General Ashikaga Takauji (*AH-shē-KAH-gah tah-kah-OO-jē*), sent by the Hojo to crush the revolt, switched sides and helped it succeed, ending Hojo rule. But when Go-Daigo refused to appoint him shogun in return for his service, Ashikaga Takauji seized Kyoto and installed a new emperor who did so, thus initiating the Ashikaga Shogunate (1336–1573). Defiantly, Go-Daigo then fled south, set up a mountain headquarters, and began a new rebellion. Although Go-Daigo himself died in 1339, the conflict continued under his successors until 1392, when Ashikaga forces compelled Go-Daigo's grandson to return to Kyoto as a puppet emperor.

By this time, however, the government in Kyoto had little real power, as regional daimyo exploited the chaos to increase their power. From 1467 through 1477, a new civil war between two branches of the Ashikaga family destroyed all sense of central control, initiating an era of regional warfare called the Age of Warring States (1467–1568), similar to China's earlier Warring States Era (Chapter 4). During a century of almost constant conflict, many Japanese daimyo acted as independent rulers, battling each other with their own armies and vassals. Some daimyo also functioned as sea lords, forming pirate companies to raid the Chinese coast.

In the 1540s, while wars still raged among the daimyo, a new source of instability came to Japan. In the south appeared strange foreigners, equipped with deadly weapons that Japanese called "lightning sticks." Although the Chinese had developed gunpowder weapons centuries earlier, Japan's warriors were not directly introduced to firearms until 1543, when Portuguese sailors arrived by sea armed with muskets. Before long, Portuguese and Spanish merchants were trading regularly with various daimyo, bringing guns and other items to exchange for Japanese goods.

A different sort of threat appeared in 1549 with the arrival of Christian missionaries, led by Francis Xavier (*ZĀ-vē-ur*), the first of many European Jesuits who came to Asia to spread their Catholic religion (Chapter 20). Although at first coolly received, the Jesuits won favor by adapting to Japanese ways. Soon several daimyo, hoping perhaps to gain firearms and fortune from trade with the Europeans, adopted Christianity and imposed it on their people. In the ensuing decades, as Spanish Franciscans and other Western missionaries came to compete with Jesuits for converts, several hundred thousand Japanese became Christians. The new faith was professedly peaceful, but some in Japan saw its growing strength as a threat to their Shinto and Buddhist traditions, and its loyalty to a distant pope as a menace to their autonomy.

Sixteenth century map of Japan with European ship off the coast.

Foreign intrusions add to Japan's instability

Some Japanese warlords, meanwhile, equipped their armies with cannons and muskets, hoping to conquer their rivals and unify Japan. Two talented warriors, Oda Nobunaga (*Ō-dah nō-boo-NAH-gah*) and Hideyoshi, ultimately proved successful.

The Unification of Japan

Oda Nobunaga (1534–1582), son of a minor daimyo, set out in the 1560s to unite Japan under his control. He built a powerful army, equipped it with Western firearms, placed it under command of a military genius named Hideyoshi, and used it to conquer rival daimyo in central Japan. Then Oda moved on Kyoto, promising not to pillage the city as previous warriors had done, and captured the capital in 1568 (Map 21.2).

Next Oda's forces moved westward, using the new weapons to defeat other daimyo. In 1573 he deposed the last Ashikaga shogun, ending for a time the position of shogun. By 1582, Oda Nobunaga controlled 32 of Japan's 68 provinces and was well on the way to uniting all Japan. That year, however, he was ambushed by one of his generals and committed suicide to avoid being captured. Someone else would have to finish unifying Japan.

Oda Nobunaga and Hideyoshi work to unify Japan

The person best suited to do so was the man who commanded Oda's armies. Hideyoshi (1536–1598), son of a peasant soldier, was a small, homely man with no class status, no family name, no wealth, and little education, but with exceptional military skills that had made him Oda's leading general. In the eight years following Oda's death in 1582, Hideyoshi managed to defeat or gain allegiance from all remaining warlords, completing the country's unification. The emperor awarded him the title of chief minister and gave him a family name, Toyotomi.

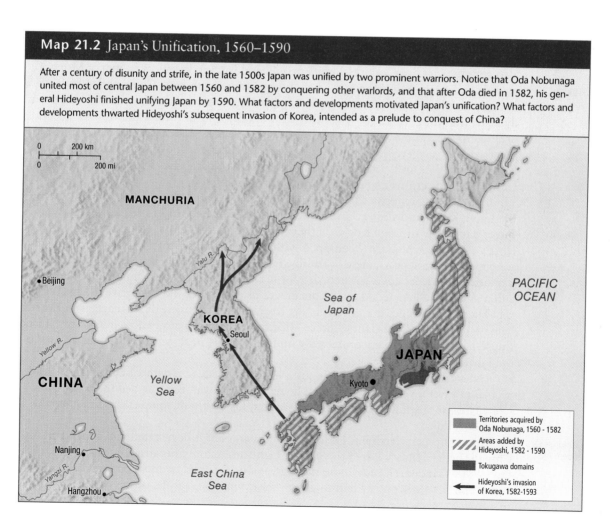

Map 21.2 Japan's Unification, 1560–1590

After a century of disunity and strife, in the late 1500s Japan was unified by two prominent warriors. Notice that Oda Nobunaga united most of central Japan between 1560 and 1582 by conquering other warlords, and that after Oda died in 1582, his general Hideyoshi finished unifying Japan by 1590. What factors and developments motivated Japan's unification? What factors and developments thwarted Hideyoshi's subsequent invasion of Korea, intended as a prelude to conquest of China?

Legend:
- Territories acquired by Oda Nobunaga, 1560 - 1582
- Areas added by Hideyoshi, 1582 - 1590
- Tokugawa domains
- Hideyoshi's invasion of Korea, 1582-1593

Hideyoshi took steps to consolidate control. He conducted a national survey to gather data on the size and yield of all cultivated lands, so as to improve the collection of taxes. He let defeated daimyo keep substantial lands, turning former foes into allies. Furthermore, as noted at the start of this chapter, he ordered the expulsion of Christian missionaries and disarmed Japan's nonmilitary population, thereby moving to secure internal stability. By 1590, although officially he still served the emperor, Toyotomi Hideyoshi was master of Japan.

Hideyoshi resolves to conquer China

Hideyoshi's ambitions, however, were far from fulfilled. According to legend, in 1592 he visited the shrine of Minamoto Yoritomo (*mē-nah-MŌ-tō yō-rē-TŌ-mō*), a warrior who four hundred years earlier had also unified Japan, and told his departed predecessor of some astonishing plans. "You and I are the only ones who have been able to unite all Japan," he allegedly informed Yoritomo's spirit. "Now I intend to go much further than you did—I intend to conquer China!" That same year he began his quest by landing forces in Korea.

Korea and the Japanese Invasion

Hideyoshi.

The fortunes of Korea, a longtime Chinese vassal state, were traditionally tied to those of China. In the thirteenth century, for example, when the Mongols overran China, they also conquered Korea, oppressing its people and forcing its rulers to marry Mongol women and adopt Mongol ways. Then, when Mongol rule over China ended in 1368, a struggle arose in Korea between its Mongolized monarchy and admirers of China's new dynasty, the Ming. In 1388, when the Ming finally sent in forces, the Korean general ordered to repel them instead overthrew his own rulers. Later this general, named Yi Song-gye (*YĒ sung-yeh*), founded a new regime called the Yi dynasty, which reigned in Korea from 1392 until 1910. The Yi rulers restored Korea's ties with China, copying its Confucian institutions and paying it annual tribute.

In the 1590s, as Japan's Hideyoshi pursued his expansionist dreams, these ties benefited both Korea and China. First the Koreans rejected Hideyoshi's request to let Japan's forces pass freely through Korea on their way to China. Then, in 1592, when he sent to Korea a 160,000-man army equipped with firearms and samurai swords, the Koreans sought help from their Chinese overlords. Having learned through spies that the Japanese planned to use Korea as a springboard for invasion of China, the Chinese eventually sent half a million soldiers to aid their Korean vassals. This force did not arrive in time to prevent Hideyoshi's armies from overrunning Korea, but the Chinese did manage, with Korean help, to push back the Japanese forces. Meanwhile Korea's navy, whose innovative **"turtle ships"** had decks that were protected with iron plating, dealt several stunning defeats to the Japanese fleet.

Hideyoshi then tried to bargain, offering to divide Korea with China. In 1597, however, after several years of futile talks, he renewed the war. But it ended the next year when Hideyoshi fell ill and died, distressed that his dream of conquering China would never be fulfilled.

Japanese invasion leaves Korea dependent on China

Korea thus survived, but Hideyoshi's invasion left it devastated and dependent on China. The Yi dynasty lasted three more centuries, mainly because China's rulers sustained the Yi monarchs as tribute-paying vassals. Beset by its location between China and Japan, Korea typically had to accept the dominance of one or the other.

Japan under Tokugawa Rule

Hideyoshi's death left Japan in the hands of a regency council, governing for his 5-year-old son Hideyori (*hē-dā-YŌ-rē*). The council's most powerful member, Tokugawa Ieyasu (*TŌ-koo-GAH-wah Ē-ā-YAH-soo*), an astute old warlord with large estates in eastern Japan (Map 21.2), quickly became dominant. Several western daimyo opposed him, but by 1603 he defeated all his rivals and compelled the emperor to appoint him shogun, thereby both restoring that office and making him Japan's real ruler. As shoguns, Tokugawa Ieyasu and his heirs ruled the unified, stable state conceived by Oda Nobunaga and created by Hideyoshi.

Tokugawa Ieyasu, lacking Hideyoshi's keenness for foreign conquest, focused on consolidating Japan's hard-won stability. Determined to start his own dynasty, in 1605 he formally retired and had his son, Tokugawa Hidetada (*hē-dā-TAH-dah*), named shogun. The aging Ieyasu nonetheless continued to exercise great influence until his death in 1616. In 1614 and 1615, Tokugawa forces attacked Hideyori, seeing Hideyoshi's son, now an adult, as a potential threat. When Hideyori fled and committed suicide, the Tokugawa triumph was complete.

The Tokugawa Shogunate begun by Ieyasu lasted until 1868. It sought to maintain stability, partly by keeping the daimyo and their samurai under its control, and partly by isolating Japan from the outside world. But the Tokugawa years were not static. Indeed, they brought significant changes to Japanese society, including the emergence of a new urban culture.

Castle in Himeji, Japan, built under Hideyoshi and Tokugawa Ieyasu.

The Tokugawa Shoguns

In the Tokugawa era, although the emperor still reigned in Kyoto, the shogun actually ruled Japan from the city of Edo (*Ā-dō*), today called Tokyo. Living in a palace larger than that of the emperor, Ieyasu's successors as shogun headed a regime that embraced the daimyo but centralized power in the shogun's hands.

The shogun directly ruled much of Japan, including its three main cities, Kyoto, Edo, and Osaka. He ruled the rest indirectly, through more than 250 daimyo vassals, who fell into three groups: *related daimyo* (Tokugawa relatives), *house daimyo* (loyal vassals raised to daimyo status by Ieyasu and his successors), and *outer daimyo* (heirs of former independent warlords). The lands of the outer daimyo, many of whom resented Tokugawa rule, were mostly on Japan's periphery, away from the centers of power (Map 21.3).

The shoguns used some clever devices to keep their vassals in line. Daimyo were required to provide soldiers for the shogun's army, laborers for his projects, and officials for his regime. All were obliged to spend half their time at Edo, under the shogun's watchful eyes, and while they were gone their families had to live there, in effect serving as hostages to ensure against revolt. These obligations reduced the daimyo's powers by making them court aristocrats rather than warlords, and impoverished many by requiring them to support more than one household.

The Tokugawa regime, aware of Spanish rule in the Philippines to the South, also took steps to end Western influence in Japan. In 1612–1614, fearful that Japan's growing number of Christians (by then about three hundred thousand in a population of perhaps 12 million)

Shoguns strive to curtail Western connections

Map 21.3 Tokugawa Japan, 1603–1868

Although Japan's emperors continued to reign in Kyoto as religious figures, the Tokugawa shoguns actually ruled Japan from Edo beginning in 1603. Observe that they ruled much of Japan (Tokugawa domains) directly, but that other parts they governed indirectly through daimyo vassals who were either related to the Tokugawa (related daimyo), awarded daimyo status by the Tokugawa (house daimyo), or descended from other warlords (outer daimyo). What steps did Tokugawa shoguns take to reinforce their rule and minimize outside influence?

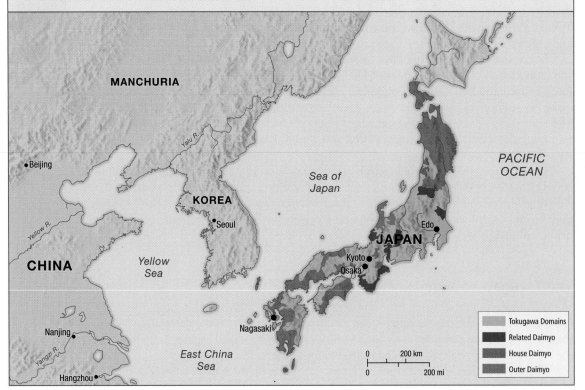

could facilitate foreign interference, the regime began enforcing Hideyoshi's edict expelling European missionaries. It forced Japanese Christians to renounce their faith, sometimes by stepping on a Christian cross or picture of Jesus Christ, and by 1660 executed more than three thousand who refused to do so. In the 1630s it forbade Japanese people to travel abroad or contact outsiders. A Christian revolt in 1637–1638, sparked by oppression and taxation, reinforced the regime's hostility to the foreign faith. After crushing the revolt, in 1639 the regime evicted all Europeans except the Dutch, whose focus seemed to be commerce, not conversion, allowing them to trade at a tiny island near the port of Nagasaki. Japan thus embarked on over two centuries of self-imposed isolation.

Japan's isolation was nonetheless incomplete. Commerce continued with Korea and China, as many outer daimyo, based in coastal domains, pursued both piracy and legitimate trade. The Dutch presence near Nagasaki also supplied some contact with the West, as some Japanese who dealt with the Dutch learned their language and ways. The spread of this knowledge, which the Japanese called **Dutch learning**, acquainted some in Japan with Western approaches to art, science, shipbuilding, weaponry, music, and medicine, even in an age of isolation.

The Evolution of Japanese Society

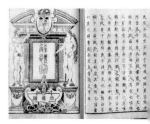

Anatomy text translated from Dutch in Tokugawa Japan.

Tokugawa rule brought unity, stability, and security, but it did not prevent change. In the seventeenth and eighteenth centuries, each of Japan's social classes—samurai, peasantry, and urban dwellers—was slowly transformed.

The samurai continued to constitute Japan's upper class. By tradition they were loyal, proud, and oblivious to pain, but two centuries of peace slowly dulled their fighting edge. With no one to fight, they became civil servants rather than combat warriors. Required to live at the castles of their lords, the samurai lost their old rustic frugality, as castle towns grew into urban centers that fostered indulgence in such pleasures as sex and sakē (*SAH-kā*), an alcoholic beverage made from fermented rice. The warriors still brandished samurai swords and trained in the martial arts, supplementing their skill with the bow and sword by adding techniques of **jujitsu** (*joo-JIT-soo*), a form of hand-to-hand combat that used holds, blows, and throws to disable a foe. But they focused no longer on warfare.

Stability and urban culture modify samurai ways

The peasants, in theory, were esteemed as food providers, but in practice many were harshly oppressed. In earlier times they had supported the samurai by serf labor; now they did so through high taxes, raised from 30 to 50 percent of their rice crop as ruling class ways of life grew ever more lavish. Some farm families became desperately poor, sparking several peasant revolts in the 1700s. Others turned from growing rice to raising cash crops such as mulberry leaves (which fed the caterpillars that spun the thread for silk) and tobacco (the use of which had grown popular in Japan after its arrival from the Americas via the Portuguese and Dutch). Rural Japan thus came to include both prosperous peasants owning large farms with fertile fields and landless families who rented marginal farmlands and lived in poverty.

As increasing commerce spurred the growth of towns and cities, merchants and other urban dwellers thrived. Trade expanded from simple barter, involving mainly rice and tools, to complex commerce that included housewares, textiles, brewing, banking, and lending. Banking houses and businesses gained substantial influence, as daimyo and samurai who lived beyond their means grew deeply indebted to merchants and bankers. The population of Osaka, Japan's commercial center, increased to more than four hundred thousand, while that of the shogun's city of Edo grew to almost a million.

Tokaido Highway, the main trade route connecting Edo with Kyoto and Osaka.

Urban Culture and the Roles of Women

As cities and towns grew larger, Japan's urban culture became increasingly sophisticated. Merchants and other townsfolk, born without prestige, strove to secure it through education and promotion of literature and the arts. Anxious to preserve their superior social status, samurai often did the same.

Learning therefore flourished, though mainly among men. Private schools were established in cities, towns, and Buddhist temples, as merchants, samurai, and even wealthy peasants increasingly sought to educate their sons. As a result, by the nineteenth century Japan had more than ten thousand schools and almost 50 percent male literacy.

Document 21.1 Examples of Haiku Poetry

Haiku, a form of poetry originating in seventeenth-century Japan, consists of 17 syllables arranged in three lines of five, seven, and five syllables. Imitated in other languages, it is an art form that expresses a great deal in a very few words. Here are some English examples focusing on the beauty and simplicity of nature.

Beginning of spring—
the perfect simplicity
of a yellow sky

Chrysanthemums bloom
in a gap between the stones
of a stonecutter's yard

Caterpillar's web—
invisible to passers
caught in its weak trap

rain at the window—
how many more ants before
the end of summer?

the cat fluffs his fur
and tries to avoid the cold
of his own shadow

loving its whiteness
I walk around the birch tree
to the other side

when the tide goes out
all the minnows leave the pool
it's cloudy weather

On a creekbed rock
a salamander resting;
its tail in water

oars flash in the sun;
at the center of the lake
two men cease to row

before the rainstorm
warm breezes turn leaves over
to the silver side

SOURCE: Clark Strand, *Seeds from a Birch Tree: Writing Haiku and the Spiritual Journey* (New York: Hyperion, 1997), 13, 19, 23, 27, 30, 40, 50, 51, 71, 92.

Along with emerging urban culture, rising literacy helped promote growth in literary and artistic works. Book publishing prospered, producing a vast popular literature ranging from the religious to the erotic. **Haiku** (*HĪ-koo*), concise 17-syllable poems organized in three successive lines of five, seven, and five syllables, became a stylish rage (see "Examples of Haiku Poetry").

Arts and crafts flourished with realistic paintings of vibrant urban life and exquisite works of porcelain and lacquered wood. Multicolored prints, made by using dozens of intricately carved woodblocks that each imprinted one hue, helped reproduce masterpieces at reasonable cost.

"Floating world" breeds indulgent urban nightlife

City life was a study in contrasts. On the surface aristocrats were models of samurai discipline and Zen Buddhist virtue, while businessmen were diligent, sober, and frugal family men. But urban amusement areas, often called the **floating world** (to reflect the fleetingness of earthly pleasures), offered these men an indulgent nightlife in teahouses, restaurants, theaters, fashion shops, and brothels. Puppet shows and **kabuki** (*kah-BOO-kē*), a form of drama in which elaborately made-up and costumed men performed both male and female roles with exaggerated and seductive gestures, were also in vogue.

For all its cosmopolitan privileges and pleasures, however, Tokugawa culture did little to enrich the lives of women. In Japan, as in most societies during this era, parents arranged marriages to improve their family's status, often with little regard for their daughter's desires. Wives were subject to their husbands, expected to stay home, raise children, and take care of household chores. Peasant women might also help the men in the fields or engage in the tedious work of producing silk.

Even the wives of the wealthy were largely considered servants by their husbands. Required for the most part to stay hidden in the home, a woman was expected to wait on her husband and discreetly serve him and his guests. Sexual infidelity by women was strictly forbidden, and harshly punished if discovered. Men of means, however, were typically free to have mistresses or patronize the brothels of the floating world. And many samurai warriors, despite their strict moral code, engaged in a variety of heterosexual and homosexual liaisons.

Not all women, however, were confined to the home. In cities and towns, some were employed to make clothing, while others waited on men in restaurants and teahouses. Some women, sold during childhood into servitude by destitute parents, eventually became singers, dancers, musicians, and courtesans, later known as geisha (*GĀ-shuh*). In such roles they could live in comfort and gain some social status—but only as a consequence of serving the pleasures of men.

Women in tradition gowns play Japanese musical instruments.

The Search for Stability in China

China, like Japan, struggled to find stability in the fourteenth through eighteenth centuries. Degraded by decades of Mongol rule and battered by famine and plague, the Chinese finally expelled the Mongols in 1368. A new dynasty, known as the Ming ("Brilliant"), revived China's pride and independence, restoring the strength and splendor of ages past. Reacting to the trauma of foreign rule, however, in the Ming era (1368–1644) the Chinese also turned inward, favoring their own time-tested ways above outside ideas and connections.

The Ming Ascendancy

In the early Ming dynasty China was probably the world's mightiest and wealthiest empire. With the Mongol rulers gone and stability restored, farming and commerce flourished, while China's million-man standing army, equipped with cannons and gunpowder grenades, was East Asia's dominant military force. Surrounding lands such as Korea and Vietnam, and even for a time Japan, were compelled to recognize Chinese supremacy and to pay regular tribute for the right to trade with China.

Chinese domination connects East Asia

Zhu Yuanzhang, the peasant rebel leader who drove out the Mongols and began the Ming dynasty, devoted his reign (1368–1398) to enforcing China's security and his personal power. Using his huge army, he pushed north into Mongolia, destroying Mongol fortresses and dividing their forces; he also extended his rule westward into Central Asia and eastward into Korea. Ruling from Nanjing, he reinstituted the civil service system of the Tang and Song eras, restoring the imperial university and civil service exams and reviving the role of the Confucian scholar-bureaucrats. Determined to run his own government, he abolished the post of chief minister and personally read hundreds of reports each day. Since he aptly titled his reign Hongwu (*HONG-WOO*), meaning "vast military power," he is called the Hongwu Emperor.

As successful as he was, however, Hongwu was no innovator. Rather than creating a new China, he sought to resurrect the old China of the Tang and Song eras. Rather than maintaining ties with the Muslim and Christian worlds, established across Eurasia under the Mongol Empire, he persecuted foreigners and all who had worked with the Mongols. Recalling his own peasant roots, he tried to help the lower classes, abolishing slavery and taxing the rich to provide land and seed for the poor. But in the long run he failed to narrow the gap between rich and poor. His huge standing army drained the economy, and the conservative Confucian bureaucracy became more powerful than ever. The emperor himself, after surviving an attempted coup, grew paranoid. Instituting a secret police that made heavy use of spies and torture, he executed thousands of alleged conspirators. Hongwu thus left a legacy of conservatism and cruelty, creating a regime that was almost as repressive as the Mongol one it replaced.

Aerial view of the Forbidden City.

Hongwu's fourth son, who seized power in 1402 and reigned until 1424 as the Yongle (*YONG-LUH*) Emperor, shared his father's focus on military might. To fortify the north against the Mongols, he rebuilt China's Great Wall in its modern form: compacted earth enclosed by brick and stone, roughly 20 feet wide, 25 feet high, and four thousand miles long. To ensure the flow of food and supplies from south to north, he dredged, repaired, and widened the Grand Canal. He led five campaigns against the Mongols in the North and extended his control into Vietnam in the South. He also moved the capital back north to Beijing, where he converted Khubilai's old imperial compound into the magnificent Forbidden City, whose great red walls, gold-tiled roofs, marble courtyards, and lavish palaces have ever since symbolized China's mystery, majesty, and might (see page 505).

Yongle also worked to make China a great naval and commercial power, building huge fleets of large sailing ships and sending out vast expeditions to foreign lands, hoping thereby to increase China's trade and tribute. The most extensive expeditions were led by Zheng He (*JUNG-HUH*), a former court eunuch and talented Muslim mariner, commissioned by Yongle to explore the whole known world. From 1405 to 1433, in seven great voyages with fleets of up to 70 ships and crews of up to thirty thousand men, Zheng He sailed to the Philippines, Southeast Asia, India, Persia, Arabia, and even down Africa's east coast (Map 21.4). His crews brought back exotic animals such as ostriches, zebras, and giraffes, as well as extensive knowledge of foreign countries (see "Excerpts: Zheng He's Inscription on His Voyages," page 518). But the voyages found nothing to change China's perception that its ways and goods were superior to all others.

Zheng He sails to many Asian and East African lands

Indeed, Zheng He's expeditions, which came decades before the Portuguese and Spanish voyages of exploration (Chapter 19), reaffirmed China's sense of superiority, especially in such areas as commerce, technology, and ocean travel. Unimpressed, however, by contacts with distant cultures they saw as inferior, subsequent Ming rulers, focused on fending off the Mongols and maintaining internal stability, launched no follow-up voyages. Ming China had vast wealth and advanced technologies, but its rulers did not opt to explore further and create connections with the rest of the world. That path, instead, was pursued by Europeans.

Map 21.4 Zheng He Explores the Eastern World, 1405–1433

In the early 1400s, decades before the great Portuguese and Spanish sea voyages, the Chinese government commissioned Zheng He, a Muslim from southwestern China, to lead huge fleets on expeditions to what China called the "Western Oceans." Notice that his voyages took him to numerous Asian and East African lands, including Southeast Asia, India, and many parts of the Muslim world. What were the purposes of Zheng He's voyages, and what did they accomplish?

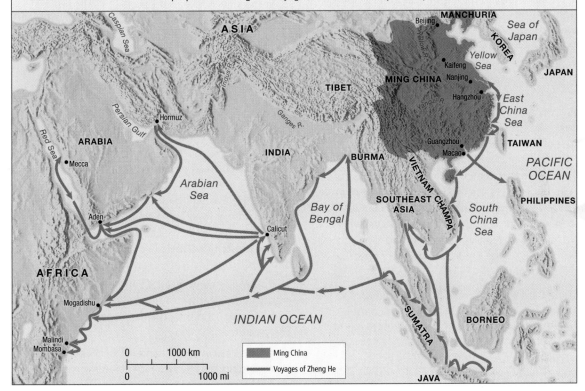

Sources of Ming Stagnation

Intent on preserving their resources for defending their northern borders, China's leaders thus curtailed the great sea expeditions and focused inward. A series of weak and short-lived emperors, supported by conservative advisors, were content to preserve past traditions and maintain the status quo. Trade and commerce continued to grow, as Chinese merchants forged commercial networks throughout Southeast Asia. But in relying on time-tested practices rather than innovation, the dynasty slowly lost its vigor and stagnation set in.

Various factors contributed to Ming stagnation. One was the drain of responding to the continued Mongol threat. The move to Beijing and rebuilding of the Great Wall fortified northern defenses but exhausted China's resources, since the new capital's northern location left the regime more vulnerable to Mongol attack. Regional rivalries were accentuated between the North, which had political and military power, and the South, which had prosperous commerce, fertile farmlands, and most of the population.

Ming rulers curtail overseas connections

Document 21.2 Excerpts: Zheng He's Inscription on His Voyages

On the seventh of his momentous voyages, while waiting for favorable winds at a port in southeast China, the great Chinese Muslim sea admiral Zheng He summarized his exploits in an inscription that was carved in stone, excerpts of which are provided below.

The Emperor . . . has ordered us . . . at the head of several tens of thousands of officers and flag-troops to ascend more than one hundred large ships . . . From the third year of Yongle [1405] till now we have seven times received the commission of ambassadors to countries of the western ocean . . . We have traversed more than one hundred thousand li [over 30,000 miles] of immense water spaces and have beheld in the ocean huge waves like mountains rising sky-high, and we have set eyes on barbarian regions far away hidden in a blue transparency of light vapours, while our sails loftily unfurled like clouds day and night . . . traversing those savage waves as if we were treading a public thoroughfare . . .

I. In the third year of Yongle [1405] commanding the fleet we went to [Calicut] and other countries. At that time the pirate Chen Zuyi had gathered his followers in . . . [Palembang], where he plundered the native merchants. When he also advanced to resist our fleet, supernatural soldiers secretly came to the rescue so that after one beating of the drum he was annihilated . . .

II. In the fifth year of Yongle [1407] commanding the fleet we went to [Java], [Calicut], [Cochin] and [Siam]. The kings of these countries all sent as tribute precious objects, precious birds and rare animals . . .

III. In the seventh year of Yongle [1409] commanding the fleet we went to the countries [visited] before and took our route by the country of [Ceylon]. Its

king . . . was guilty of a gross lack of respect and plotted against the fleet . . . [The plot] was discovered and thereupon that king was captured alive . . .

IV. In the eleventh year of Yongle [1413] commanding the fleet we went to [Ormuz] and other countries. In the country of [Samudra] there was a false king . . . who was marauding and invading his country . . . We went thither with the official troops under our command and exterminated some and arrested [other rebels], and . . . captured the false king alive . . .

V. In the fifteenth year of Yongle [1417] commanding the fleet we visited the western regions. The country of [Ormuz] presented lions, leopards with gold spots and large western horses. The country of [Aden] presented [giraffes], as well as the long-horned animal [oryx]. The country of [Mogadishu] presented [zebras] as well as lions. The country of [Brava] presented camels . . . as well as camel-birds [ostriches] . . .

VI. In the nineteenth year of Yongle [1421] commanding the fleet we conducted the ambassadors from [Ormuz] and the other countries . . . back to their countries . . .

VII. In the sixth year of Xuande [1431] once more commanding the fleet we have left for the barbarian countries in order to read to them [an Imperial edict] and to confer presents.

We have anchored in this port awaiting a north wind to take the sea, and . . . we have thus recorded an inscription in stone.

SOURCE: Teobaldo Filesi, *China and Africa in the Middle Ages*, translated by David Morison (London: Frank Cass, 1972), 57–61. http://www.hist.umn.edu/hist1012/primarysource/source.htm

A second situation that undermined the Ming was the growing influence of the eunuchs, castrated males who ran the imperial court. Although Hongwu had decreed that these men, emasculated to prevent sexual contact with the emperors' concubines, must not hold high posts or ranks, they were the ruler's constant companions and often his closest advisors. Some eunuchs used this status to gain power and wealth, intriguing against government officials and subverting their authority. In 1449 a group of influential eunuchs even talked the rash young emperor Yingzong (*YING ZONG*) into leading an ill-fated attack at Datong (*DAH-TONG*), where there was a pass in the Great Wall, against a group of Mongols who had refused to pay tribute. The result was a disaster: the Chinese army was cut to pieces and the emperor himself was captured.

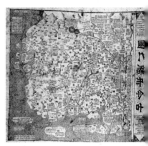

Chinese map of East Asia in the 1550s.

Although the Mongols were later driven back, and returned the hapless emperor even though China refused to pay ransom, the defeat at Datong began a long decline in Ming military power. The North was left exposed to periodic Mongol raids, while the South hated paying high taxes to support the inept Beijing regime. Fortunately for China, the Mongols were temporarily diverted by their own internal conflicts. But in 1550 the Mongols reunited, then penetrated the Great Wall, pillaged the outskirts of Beijing, and terrorized northern China for years thereafter.

A third important element of Ming decline was the behavior of the rulers themselves. Attended by a vast array of eunuchs, cooks, and concubines who indulged their every whim, many Ming emperors had little concern or capacity for governance. They buried themselves in the pleasures of the court, indulging their appetites for food, sex, and drink, and amusing themselves with elaborate forms of entertainment and religious ritual. One ruler had such a liking for the women and food of Korea that he sent officials to that country to bring him back maidens and cooks. Another became so engrossed in his own pleasures that he failed to fill official positions when they became vacant, leaving numerous key posts unoccupied and much state business undone. A third never even learned to write, but focused his energies on woodworking, while his favored eunuch amassed enormous wealth and influence.

A final factor in the Ming decline was the traditionalism and anticommercialism of China's civil service. In the Ming era, as in the past, the imperial administration was staffed with civil servants drawn largely from the sons of landed gentry. In order to pass the extremely rigorous civil service exams, these scholar-bureaucrats, known in the West as **mandarins** (a Portuguese version of a Southeast Asian term for government ministers), immersed themselves in the study of ancient Confucian classics. Steeped in the values of the past, and protective of a system that gave them power and prestige, the Confucian officials resisted innovation and disparaged commerce. Certain that China's ways and goods were superior to all others, many mandarins saw little value in contact or trade with outsiders. With Confucian disdain for avarice and greed, they scorned merchants as parasites who profited from selling goods they had not made, and ranked merchants below farmers and artisans who produced useful things. Since most gentry incomes came from agriculture and most state revenues came from land taxes, many bureaucrats saw little to gain from commerce, either for themselves or for the government.

Confucians resist innovation and outside commerce

Domestic and Foreign Trade

Yet commerce flourished during much of the Ming era. Even as the dynasty declined, China's economy thrived, strengthened by expanded agricultural production and extensive trade.

Farming, as in ages past, was the backbone of China's economy. The growing cultivation of Champa rice, a fast-growing, drought-resistant crop that came to China from

Farming advances support population growth

Southeast Asia during the Song dynasty (Chapter 14), vastly increased the food supply. As a result of seed breeding and experimentation, by Ming times farmers in south China could raise a rice crop in two months or less, enabling them to grow three or four crops a year instead of one or two. With ample food available, China's population, which may have fallen to 60 million in the Mongol era, rebounded to at least 100 million by 1500, and grew to around 150 million during the next century.

Food surplus also spurs commerce and urban growth

The food surplus also enabled more people to move to the cities and towns, the country's main centers of commerce. By the late Ming era, despite dynastic decline, China had at least a dozen cities with metropolitan populations of a million or more. Merchant and craft shops lined the streets, conducting brisk trade in items such as porcelain and stoneware, copper and iron tools, silk, and cotton cloth. The country-side, moreover, had numerous market towns, where peasants went to exchange their produce for seeds, tools, and clothing. Commerce was so profitable that many court eunuchs, and even some mandarins, engaged in business ventures, despite the official Confucian disdain for such mercantile activities.

Although officially discouraged, foreign trade also expanded. Neighboring countries typically paid tribute to the Chinese emperor, partly for military protection and partly for the right to send trade missions to China. Ming regulations limited the size and number of such missions, restricting them to certain ports, but traders from Southeast Asia and Indonesia often ignored these restrictions, as did many Chinese merchants. The resulting commerce, featuring mainly silk and porcelain products from China and spices from Indonesia, grew substantially in the sixteenth century, aided by the efforts of aggressive intruders from Europe and Japan.

Ming porcelain vase.

Intruders from Europe and Japan

Westerners are permitted to trade at Macao

From the South came Europeans, whose great sea voyages around Africa to Asia (Chapter 19) were driven by dreams of lucrative trade with wealthy Asian societies (Map 21.5). First to arrive were mariners and merchants from Portugal, who reached south China in 1514. Their disrespect for Chinese laws, the stench of their unwashed bodies, and their purchase of Chinese children as slaves led many in China to view the Portuguese as crude "ocean devils." They enraged Ming officials by firing their ships' cannon near the great port city of Guangzhou (*GWAHNG-JŌ*), which the English later called Canton, and building an island fortress off the nearby coast. In 1522 Chinese forces drove the Portuguese out, killing a number of them. But the Portuguese persisted, and in 1557 they were allowed to set up a trading post at Macao (*mah-COW*), on a small peninsula south of Guangzhou, in return for paying annual tribute. During the next few centuries, as Dutch and English merchants joined in the Asia trade, Macao served as a central outlet for commerce between China and the West.

Manila galleons link Asia with Spanish America

The city of Manila in the Philippine Islands also emerged as a major trading center. Founded by Spain in 1571, six years after the Spanish opened a round-trip route between Mexico and the Philippines, Manila became the focal point of trade between Asia and America. For more than two centuries, until 1815, ships filled with Chinese silks and porcelains made annual trips across the Pacific to Acapulco on the Mexican coast, where their precious cargoes were sold for Spanish silver mined in the Americas. The goods were bought by wealthy Spanish colonists or sent to markets in Europe, while the ships,

Map 21.5 East Asian Commerce in the 1500s and early 1600s

In the late Ming era (1500s and early 1600s), China conducted extensive commerce with numerous other nations. Note that the Chinese exported such products as tea, silks, ceramics, cottons, and paper, while receiving such commodities as silver, swords, gems, horses, herbs, and spices. Note also that Portuguese merchants conducted commerce at Macao, connecting China's commerce with Europe, and that Japanese pirates plundered Chinese ships and raided China's eastern seacoast. How did such commerce bolster Chinese concepts of cultural and technical superiority?

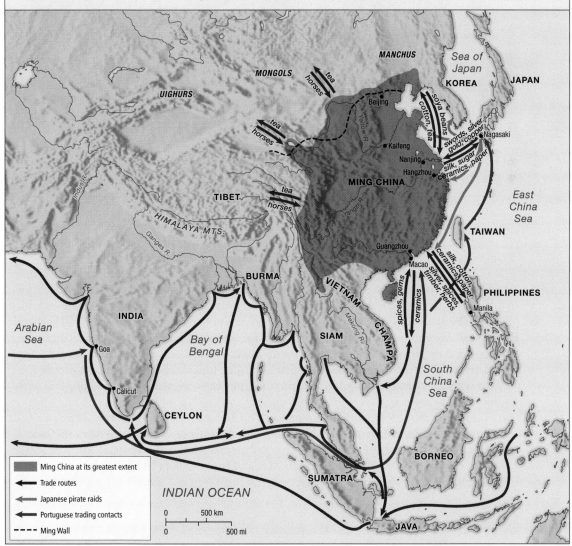

known as Manila galleons, made the return trip full of silver coins to purchase more Chinese products (Map 21.6). Silver thus flowed into China, enriching many merchants but also causing price inflation: as silver became more plentiful, it also became less valuable,

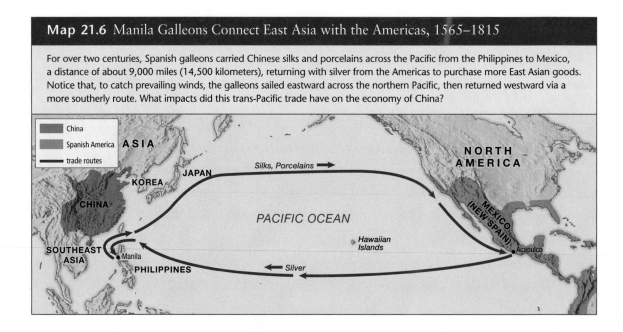

Map 21.6 Manila Galleons Connect East Asia with the Americas, 1565–1815

For over two centuries, Spanish galleons carried Chinese silks and porcelains across the Pacific from the Philippines to Mexico, a distance of about 9,000 miles (14,500 kilometers), returning with silver from the Americas to purchase more East Asian goods. Notice that, to catch prevailing winds, the galleons sailed eastward across the northern Pacific, then returned westward via a more southerly route. What impacts did this trans-Pacific trade have on the economy of China?

and more and more silver was needed to buy the same goods. As goods thus became more expensive, many Chinese consumers experienced serious hardships.

From the East, meanwhile, came Japanese sailors and soldiers, also eager to tap into China's great wealth, but increasingly defiant and unwilling to pay the tribute required for official trade. Instead they turned to plunder. As Japanese pirates ravaged Chinese merchant vessels, ships full of Japanese samurai landed in China to pillage towns and villages and then quickly exit by sea. By the mid-1500s these attacks had become an organized industry, sponsored by Japanese warlords who set up raiding companies, hired many Chinese to participate as pirates, and made huge profits. The Ming fought back by prohibiting trade with Japan, but this ban only prompted even more Chinese to engage in smuggling or join with the Japanese raiders.

Then, in the 1590s, came Japan's assault on Korea, planned by Hideyoshi as a prelude to invasion of China. A massive Ming army of half a million men helped deter the Japanese assault, but the venture's huge cost further drained China's treasury, already depleted by the extravagance of rulers, court eunuchs, and thousands of Ming relatives supported by the state.

Calamity and Rebellion

By the early 1600s, the Ming dynasty was in trouble. Although the war with Japan had exhausted the government and drained its resources, the emperors and their enormous entourage continued to live lavishly, still oppressing the masses with burdensome taxes. At the same time, a conspicuous cooling of the climate, which shortened the growing season and dramatically decreased the harvest, seemed to signal that the regime was losing Heaven's Mandate.

In 1628, as northern China was swept by deadly famine, bands of starving peasants and unemployed soldiers began to ravage the region, creating widespread chaos. Several years later, a fired postal clerk named Li Zicheng (*LĒ zuh-CHUNG*) joined his uncle's robber band and led it in a rebellion. In time, with the help of supportive scholars, he became a popular hero, a benevolent bandit who reportedly raided the rich to feed the starving poor.

1628 famine leads to chaos and rebellion

Calamitous developments aided the rebels' cause. In 1639, lacking the resources to restore order, the Ming regime raised taxes even higher, further angering the people and compelling even more of them to join the robber bands. That same year, a clash between the Chinese and the Spanish in Manila resulted in a suspension of trade that for a time stopped the flow of silver from America. As silver grew scarce in China, many Chinese people quit buying goods or paying taxes, causing sharp drops in prices and state revenues. As floods, droughts, and smallpox epidemics amplified the human disaster, support for Li Zicheng increased. In 1644 he captured Beijing, while the despondent Ming emperor hanged himself on a nearby hill. As with the origins of the Han and Ming dynasties (Chapters 4 and 15), it looked as if a commoner—a man of the people—had gained the Mandate of Heaven.

The Qing Empire

The fall of the Ming dynasty in 1644 resulted, however, not in a new Chinese dynasty led by Li Zicheng but in China's conquest by the Manchus, a nomadic people who came from the region northeast of China known as Manchuria. Called in by Ming loyalists to help drive out the rebels, the Manchus proceeded to form their own dynasty, the Qing (*CHING*), adapting themselves to Chinese ways and ruling through China's bureaucracy. Creating an empire that included all of China and some neighboring lands, Qing rulers ushered in a new Chinese era of stability and prosperity, lasting until decline set in during the late 1700s.

The Manchu Conquest

In the early 1600s the Manchus, descendants of the Jurchens who had ruled northern China for about a century before the Mongol conquests, created a powerful regime in Manchuria. Their brilliant leader Nurhachi (*NOOR-HAH-chē*), who started like Genghis Khan (Chapter 15) by avenging his father's murder, developed an imposing army, united most of Manchuria, and proclaimed himself khan in 1616. After Nurhachi died in 1626, his work was carried forward by his son Hong Taiji (*HONG TĪ-JĒ*), known in China as Huang Taiji, who before his own death in 1643 had started moving into northern China.

The Manchu expansion had only just begun. When Li Zicheng's forces took Beijing in 1644, an ambitious Ming general named Wu Sangui (*WOO sahn-GWĀ*), rather than surrendering to the rebels, called on the Manchus for help. This invitation was all the Manchus needed to move in. With the aid of Wu's forces, the Manchus attacked and overran the Chinese capital, expelling and later destroying Li Zicheng's army. But the Manchus had no intention of restoring the Ming dynasty. Instead they installed Hong Taiji's young son as the new Manchu emperor of China.

Ming general calls in Manchus to help resist rebels

Thus began a new dynasty called the Qing, meaning "Pure," that would reign from 1644 until 1912. At first, however, it ruled only the North, while an aspiring new Ming emperor sought to hold onto the South. But the former Ming general Wu Sangui, now a Manchu vassal, gradually defeated the remnants of the Ming, killing their last ruler in 1662. This left Wu and two other Chinese warlords in command of southern China, which they ruled as Manchu vassals until 1673. Then, turning against the Manchus, the three southern warlords joined forces in a massive revolt that lasted until 1682.

Kangxi and the Consolidation of Manchu Rule

By the time of this rebellion the Manchus had a talented new ruler. Only 20 years old when the revolt began, the Kangxi (*KAHNG-SHĒ*) Emperor (1662–1722) possessed extraordinary talent, intelligence, and vigor. Not confined like many Ming rulers to the comforts of his court, Kangxi led his armies in battle, deftly planning strategy, dividing the rebel coalition, and proving a brilliant general. Wu Sangui persisted in opposition, and even made plans to claim Heaven's Mandate for himself, but the old warlord finally grew feeble and died in 1678. Kangxi then annihilated the heirs of Wu Sangui while simultaneously crushing a Mongol revolt in the north. By 1682 the gifted young Manchu was master of all China.

Yet one pressing problem remained. In the mid-1600s, as revolt and civil war gripped China, much of its southeast coast, and later the island of Taiwan, was dominated by Zheng Chenggong (*JUNG CHUN-GONG*), a pirate of Chinese and Japanese ancestry known by Western merchants as "Koxinga." After Koxinga's death in 1662 his pirate empire, ruled from Taiwan by his son, continued to torment China. At one point, hoping to undermine this realm by depriving it of plunder, the Manchus tried depopulating China's southeast coast by forcing its people to move inland. Finally, in 1683, having fully crushed the rebel warlords and subdued the south, Kangxi sent forces to occupy Taiwan and end the pirate regime. The Manchu conquest was complete. As in the Mongol era, China was once again ruled by outsiders from the North.

But the foreigner Kangxi proved a splendid Chinese emperor. Although he forbade intermarriage between Manchus and Chinese and gave precedence in his government to Manchu officials, he also fostered harmony between Manchu and Chinese civil servants, demanding honesty and talent from both. A frugal and effective administrator, he managed simultaneously to lower taxes and improve bureaucratic efficiency while initiating numerous public works such as flood control and water conservation projects. A man of enormous energy, he rose daily before dawn and dealt with stacks of official reports. During his reign he undertook many great hunting and military expeditions, and he made six elaborate grand tours of his realm to ensure that it was well governed. He gained a reputation as one of history's ablest and wisest rulers.

Kangxi strengthens and expands China's borders

Kangxi's foreign ventures were equally effective. After several times sending forces north to confront unruly Russians infringing on his domain, in 1689 he negotiated a treaty with Russia that defined the borders between the two empires. Later he led his armies into western Mongolia, mastering that region and vastly diminishing the Mongol menace that had plagued China for centuries. He expanded into Tibet, sending forces in 1720 to subdue that land, bringing under Manchu dominion the leader of Tibetan Buddhism, known as the Dalai Lama (*DAH-lī LAH-mah*).

An admirer of China's culture and a man of great curiosity, Kangxi generously patronized intellectual and cultural pursuits. Under his sponsorship scholars produced, among other things, an official history of the Ming era and a comprehensive literary encyclopedia. In certain areas of study, such as mapmaking, mathematics, and astronomy, he was even willing to use the services of scholars from outside of China. Foremost among these foreigners were Jesuits from Europe.

Beijing observatory, center of astronomy in Ming and Qing China.

The Jesuits in China: Cultural Connections and Controversy

The Jesuit presence in China was part of a global effort to spread the Catholic faith (Chapter 20) begun by Francis Xavier in the 1540s in India, Indonesia, and Japan. In 1582 an Italian Jesuit named Matteo Ricci (*mah-TĀ-ō RĒ-chē*), a gifted intellectual and linguist, arrived in China, where he lived until his death in 1610. Ricci and his successors worked hard to make a good impression: they learned the Chinese language, adopted Chinese dress, befriended Chinese scholars, translated Western books into Chinese, corrected Chinese maps and calendars, and even predicted an eclipse. The Jesuits also studied Chinese literature and philosophy and observed Chinese medical practices, including the technique, later used in the Ottoman Empire and Europe, of infecting people with a mild form of smallpox to help them develop immunity. By the time of Kangxi, Jesuits were welcome at the emperor's court, serving as astronomers, architects, mapmakers, engineers, and interpreters. In 1689, Jesuits even helped to negotiate China's treaty with Russia, as they had the background and linguistic skills to communicate with both sides.

Jesuits blend Chinese and Western learning

But Jesuit adaptation to Chinese ways ultimately caused problems. In seeking to spread their faith, the Jesuits presented Christian ideals as similar to those of Confucius (equating, for example, Christian compassion with the Confucian virtue of humanity, or *ren*), and even took part in Chinese rites involving ancestor worship. This blending of traditions antagonized many Chinese scholars, who saw it as corrupting their own beliefs and practices. It also upset other Christians, especially Franciscan and Dominican missionaries, who complained to the pope in Rome that the Jesuits were compromising Catholicism by taking part in Chinese rituals. Kangxi backed the Jesuits and even gave them supportive documents to take back to Rome. But in 1704 the pope denounced Catholic participation in Chinese rites, formally banning it in 1715. Kangxi's successors, influenced by disgruntled Confucians and by a later pope's extension of the ban in 1742, actively suppressed Christianity in China, thus undoing the work begun by the Jesuits.

Blending of ideas upsets Confucians and Christians

The Height of the Qing Regime

After Kangxi died, his fourth son seized power in a coup against his brothers and reigned as the Yongzheng (*YONG-JUNG*) Emperor (1723–1735). Harsh and despotic, he repressed all signs of dissent and imposed strict censorship, especially against works that might be critical of Manchu rule or his seizure of the throne. At the same time, Yongzheng enforced efficiency and discipline, effectively combating corruption and paving the way for the long reign of his son, the Qianlong (*ch'YEN-LONG*) Emperor.

Like his grandfather Kangxi, the energetic Qianlong (1736–1795) was both a champion of cultural pursuits and an effective warrior. A capable scholar, poet, and painter in his own right, Qianlong ordered the compilation and printing of a massive collection of

Qianlong.

Qianlong subdues
Mongols and expands
Qing power

classical Chinese writings. He also assembled in his palace a huge collection of artworks and lavishly supported the work of artists, architects, and scholars.

Qianlong likewise excelled at military expansion (Map 21.7). In the 1750s he subjugated the Mongols, completing the work of his grandfather and ending the age-old

Map 21.7 Manchu Expansion Creates the Qing Empire, 1600–1800

Expanding from their homeland in Manchuria, the Manchus created a vast empire, ruling China as the Qing Dynasty from 1644 to 1912. Notice that, after early Manchus conquered most of China, later Qing rulers extended their sway over Mongolia, Xinjiang, and Tibet. What factors enabled the Manchus to conquer and rule such a vast, populous, and wealthy realm? For what purposes did other neighboring lands pay tribute to Qing China?

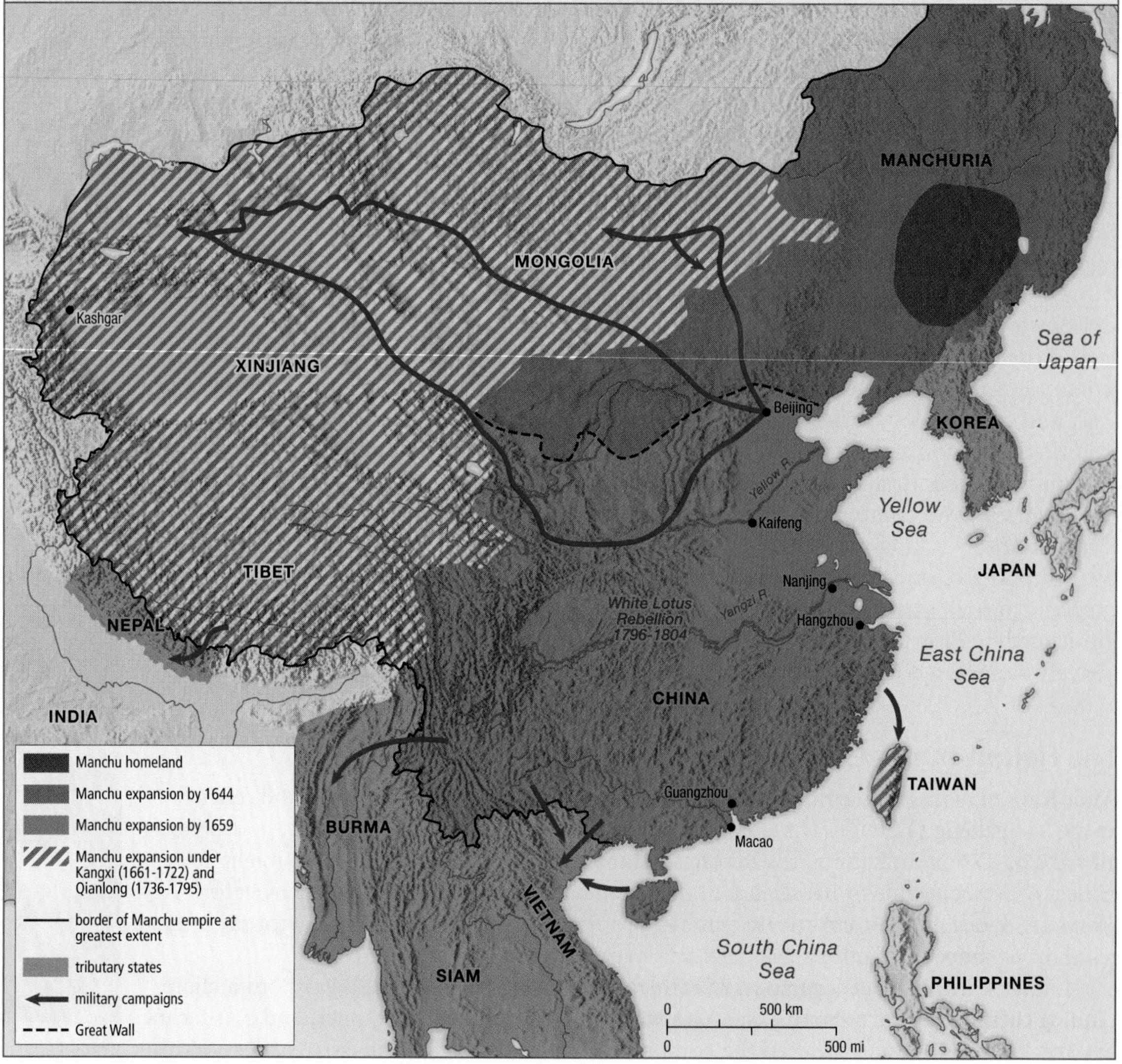

Legend:
- Manchu homeland
- Manchu expansion by 1644
- Manchu expansion by 1659
- Manchu expansion under Kangxi (1661-1722) and Qianlong (1736-1795)
- border of Manchu empire at greatest extent
- tributary states
- military campaigns
- Great Wall

White Lotus Rebellion 1796-1804

threat to China from the northern nomads. He annexed the vast province of Xinjiang (*SHIN-J'YAHNG*), or Chinese Central Asia, thereby extending China westward to its current borders. He also repressed rebellions in Taiwan and southwest China, and sent armies southwest to Nepal and Burma (now Myanmar), forcing them to accept the Manchus as overlords.

Artist's depiction of one of Qianlong's military victories.

For most of his reign, Qianlong was an excellent ruler, but he lived too long for the good of his realm. In his last years, as the rapidly growing population taxed the empire's resources, the aging ruler came under the sway of a handsome court guard named Heshen (*HUH-SHUN*). Using his favored status to acquire vast wealth through corruption, Heshen allegedly amassed for himself almost two tons of silver. Combined with rising poverty and taxes, this corruption helped trigger the White Lotus Rebellion (1796–1804), a massive peasant uprising in Western China led by the White Lotus Society, a religious cult promising the removal of the Manchus and the return of the Buddha. It took the government fully eight years to put down this rebellion, in part because Heshen pocketed much money earmarked to suppress the rebels.

Corruption and misrule spark rebellion in the 1790s

In 1795, in a conspicuous display of Confucian filial piety, Qianlong formally retired so his reign would not last longer than that of his grandfather Kangxi. But the retired ruler continued to influence affairs until his death in 1799, by which time the Qing dynasty, riddled with corruption and faced with internal rebellion, had clearly begun to decline.

Vietnam Under Chinese Sway: Expansion and Foreign Influence

One repercussion of Manchu decline was increased foreign meddling in the lands on China's periphery. In the late 1700s, for example, taking advantage of Chinese weakness and Southeast Asian strife, the French intervened in Vietnam, a vassal state of China that long had blended Chinese institutions with its own native culture (Chapter 14).

The strife in Southeast Asia stemmed from several centuries of Vietnamese autonomy and territorial growth. After occupying Vietnam in the early 1400s, China had withdrawn its troops in the face of Vietnamese resistance, letting Vietnam henceforth run its own affairs, as long as it sent tribute payments to China. In the 1470s, responding to sea raids from the Champa region south of Vietnam, the Vietnamese had invaded that land, beginning a steady southward expansion that continued for the next three centuries (Map 21.8). Led by the powerful Nguyen (*'n-GIH-un*) family, they eventually pushed south of Champa into Cambodian territory, conquering the Mekong River delta in 1757, thereby extending their control over Southeast Asia's entire eastern coast.

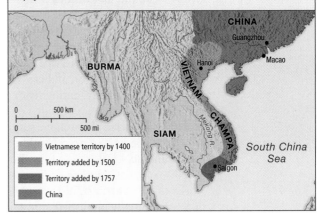

Map 21.8 Vietnam Expands Southward, 1400–1757

In the fifteenth through eighteenth centuries, the Vietnamese extended their rule southward, over the people of Champa and beyond. Note that by the mid-1700s, after incorporating the Mekong River delta in 1757, Vietnam controlled the entire eastern coast of Southeast Asia. What factors account for Vietnam's southward expansion? Why did Vietnam's emperors continue to pay tribute to China?

Vietnamese territory by 1400
Territory added by 1500
Territory added by 1757
China

Tay-Son rebellion takes over all of Vietnam

But Vietnam's expansion was resented by the people of Champa, mostly Buddhist peasants who cultivated Champa rice. In 1771, three brothers called Tay-Son (the name of their native village) led a massive peasant revolt beginning in the Champa region. Fueled by resentment of the Vietnamese regime and its Chinese overlords, the Tay-Son Rebellion drove out the Nguyen from Champa and eventually overran all Vietnam, proclaiming one of the brothers its new ruler in 1788. From China Qianlong sent forces to repress the revolt, but even they were soon driven out.

French connection helps defeat Tay-Son and create new Vietnamese dynasty

Nguyen Anh, of the ousted Nguyen family, appealed to the French for help. Competing with the British and Dutch for Asian influence, the French were quick to comply. With French assistance, Nguyen Anh eventually defeated the Tay-Son and proclaimed himself emperor of a united Vietnam. But the French, having gained a foothold, later expanded their influence, and the Nguyen dynasty (1802–1945) in time became a puppet regime dominated by France (Chapter 29), adding a French Catholic element to Vietnam's blend of Chinese and Southeast Asian cultures.

Chinese Culture and Society in the Ming and Qing Eras

Chinese culture in the Ming and Qing eras was often characterized by contrast. Elite education and scholarship, promoted by the government and embodied in its civil service, were very conservative and conventional, reflecting the regime's focus on stability and control. Popular culture, however, was often original and unorthodox, reflecting the aspirations and experiences of the Chinese people.

Chinese society likewise was marked by divergence. Urban life was often sophisticated and complex, filled with a varied array of comforts, amusements, opportunities, and challenges. Rural life, by contrast, tended to be rough and routine, dominated by farming and the family. Expanding commerce and agricultural production brought prosperity to urban and rural areas alike, but increasing population in time created serious problems for both.

Civil Service, Scholarship, and the State

Confucian civil service supplies stability and learning

As in earlier eras, society and learning in Ming and Qing China were dominated by the government and its Confucian scholar-bureaucrats, who functioned as an educated elite. In village or town schools, and often under private tutors, boys studied the Confucian classics to prepare for civil service exams held on the county, province, and national levels. Since the multi-stage examination process removed all but the brightest and most orthodox candidates, it gave the civil service a very high level of learning and stability, but it also tended to discourage innovation and creativity. Even those who challenged the dominant neo-Confucian philosophy, dating from the Song era, did so to refine it rather than supplant it.

The emperors, who presided in Beijing over the highest level of the civil service exams, grandly patronized elite scholarship. As noted above, Kangxi sponsored an extensive literary encyclopedia and an official history. Qianlong went even further, employing about three hundred scholars and four thousand scribes for more than ten years to assemble the 36,000-volume *Complete Collection of the Four Treasuries*, a compilation of China's great works of literature, art, history, philosophy, science, and medicine. Seven sets of the collection were initially published, and Qianlong ordered a library built to house each set.

Not all major Chinese works, however, were included in the collection. Qianlong, like other emperors, had censors suppress and bureaucrats destroy any works they deemed subversive, especially those in any way critical of the Qing regime. Official scholarship for the most part was orthodox and conventional.

Popular Culture and Commerce

In contrast to official scholarship, popular culture tended to be creative and unconventional. Although Confucian scholars frowned on fiction as subversive and frivolous, several novels gained great popularity, aided by the spread of printing and literacy in Ming and Qing times. *Romance of the Three Kingdoms*, compiled and published in various forms during these two dynasties, was based on the age-old often-told saga of three third-century blood brothers (Chapter 14). *The Water Margin* (also translated as *All Men Are Brothers*) tells of 108 honest outlaws, driven to crime by an unjust government, who harm only the rich and powerful while helping the poor and oppressed. Although this novel was suppressed as seditious by the imperial authorities, it was widely cherished among common folk (as well as by twentieth-century Chinese Communists). *The Dream of the Red Chamber*, written in the 1700s, is often regarded as China's greatest novel: with vivid psychological insight it recounts the decline of a prominent family, interweaving numerous poignant and tragic subplots. These three novels, and various other works, attained the status of classic literary treasures.

Guangzhou (Canton), one of China's great centers of culture and commerce.

Culture and commerce flourished mostly in China's great cities, including Beijing, Hangzhou, Guangzhou, and Nanjing, which were home to millions. Wealthy urban families adorned their homes with majestic landscapes and vivid still-life paintings, colorful silk tapestries, exquisite blue and white Ming vases (see page 520), and multi-colored porcelains from the Qing era. Entertainment districts featured teahouses and theaters, bustling markets displayed vast arrays of goods, and streets were typically crowded with peddlers, artisans, and workers. Merchants and craftsmen who dealt in the same product often clustered in the same district, combining in guilds to regulate prices and trade.

Commerce and culture thrive in China's cities

The country's countless market towns, although less urbane and affluent than the cities, were nonetheless central to the Chinese economy. They linked the peasant masses with the outside world, providing farmers with a place to sell their surplus, purchase household goods, and engage in such amusements as drinking, smoking (a habit derived from the Americas), and card playing (a practice that spread with printing from China to the West).

Market towns connect rural masses with wider world

Village Farming and Population Growth

Even the peasant villages, although generally much smaller and less sophisticated than the cities and towns, advanced China's prosperity by producing plentiful food. As faster growing Champa rice continued to expand output in lush moist regions, harvests in less fertile areas were enhanced by new crops such as sweet potatoes and corn, cultivated initially by Amerinds and brought to China by European traders via Macao and the Philippines. Improved irrigation using water pumps, the mechanized sowing of seeds, the planting of northern wheat as a winter crop in the South, and the massive use of fertilizers (including human waste, or "night soil," brought daily from the cities by bucket brigades) contributed to an era of agricultural abundance.

New crops from abroad enhance China's food supply

As food supply increased, China's population, which had more than doubled in the Ming era, doubled again to more than 300 million by the late 1700s. At first this increase, associated with prosperity and growing agricultural output, created few concerns; indeed, it enlarged both the market and the work force for China's expanding economy. Eventually, however, the growing population caused problems: urban crowding and high crime rates afflicted China's swelling cities, while in rural areas, as China's woodlands were relentlessly cleared to make room for new cultivation, deforestation led to soil erosion and flooding. By the end of the eighteenth century the increase in people was outpacing the food supply, reviving in China the poverty of the past.

The Functions of the Chinese Family

In cities, towns, and villages, in good times and in bad, the patriarchal family remained China's basic social unit: the main provider of training for the young, health care for the sick, and material support for the aging. Elder males formally headed the households—making decisions, enforcing discipline, leading the family in ancestor worship, and arranging marriages—while women typically managed the household in service to their husbands and families. Raising girls, who would one day leave home to serve their husband's family, was often deemed a burden: as in ages past, poor peasant families sometimes sold their daughters into servitude, while urban parents subjected their daughters to foot binding, since tiny feet were considered helpful in attracting wealthy husbands (Chapter 14). For the most part, China's families were sources of stability, reinforcing ancient traditions and resistant to change.

In hard times rural masses become sources of change

Still, during times of misfortune and turbulence, when long-suffering peasants were pushed beyond their limit, rural families and villages sometimes served as sources of rebellion and change. They had done so during the 1640s, as Li Zicheng's rebels helped to overthrow the Ming dynasty. They did so in the 1790s, as the White Lotus Rebellion seriously challenged the Qing regime. And they would do so time and again in the nineteenth and twentieth centuries.

Chapter Review

Putting It in Perspective

In the sixteenth through eighteenth centuries, despite occasional upheavals, the countries of East Asia ranked among the world's most prosperous and stable. Japan, united by talented warlords and then led effectively by Tokugawa shoguns, achieved a significant measure of stability and prosperity. China, despite internal rebellions and rule by outsiders from Manchuria, substantially expanded its great power and wealth. Korea and Vietnam, although they had less power and wealth, nonetheless enjoyed substantial security as vassals and tributaries of China.

Both Japan and China, in seeking stability and security, tried to limit outside influence. Both traded with the Westerners who showed up in the sixteenth century, but Japan eventually restricted this trade to a single Japanese port, and China incorporated it into its tribute system, by which outside countries had long paid tribute for the right to do business with China. Both Japan and China for a time welcomed Jesuits and other Christian missionaries, but both eventually suppressed Christianity as disruptive of traditional beliefs.

In the long run, however, East Asian efforts to resist change were not entirely successful. Although their economies continued to be based on village farming, both Japan and China experienced increased foreign and domestic commerce, significant urban growth, and the development of urban cultures. Japanese unity was achieved by warlords using firearms, and Japan's intellectual life was influenced by Dutch learning, both of which were brought to Japan by mariners and merchants from the West. Meanwhile, crops from the Americas and Southeast Asia advanced China's agricultural growth, Spanish silver from the Americas added to China's wealth, and Jesuits from Europe made important contributions to Chinese scholarship and diplomacy. Thus, even as they sought to maintain stability by limiting foreign influence, East Asian societies were affected by connections with other cultures.

Reviewing Key Material

KEY CONCEPTS

daimyo, 507
turtle ships, 510
Dutch learning, 513
jujitsu, 513

haiku, 514
floating world, 514
kabuki, 514
mandarins, 519

KEY PEOPLE

Go-Daigo, 508
Ashikaga Takauji, 508
Oda Nobunaga, 508
Hideyoshi, 509
Yi Song-gye, 510
Tokugawa Ieyasu, 511
Zhu Yuanzhang
  (Hongwu), 515
Yongle, 516
Zheng He, 516
Li Zicheng, 523
Nurhachi, 523

Hong Taiji, 523
Wu Sangui, 523
Kangxi, 524
Zheng Chenggong
  (Koxinga), 524
Dalai Lama, 524
Matteo Ricci, 525
Yongzheng, 525
Qianlong, 525
Heshen, 527
Tay-Son brothers, 528
Nguyen Anh, 528

ASK YOURSELF

1. What factors brought disunity to Japan in the fifteenth and sixteenth centuries? How was Japan reunified?

2. Why did the Tokugawa shoguns persecute Christians and isolate Japan from outsiders? What were the benefits and drawbacks of these policies?

3. What factors and developments led to the fall of the Ming dynasty and establishment of Manchu (Qing) rule in China?

4. How did China's Manchu rulers (Qing dynasty) seek to achieve stability and limit foreign influence? Compare and contrast these efforts with those of Japan's Tokugawa shoguns?

5. Compare and contrast the culture of China in the Qing Era with that of Tokugawa Japan. How do you account for similarities and differences?

GOING FURTHER

Berry, Mary Elizabeth. *Hideyoshi*. 1982.

Brook, T. *The Confusions of Pleasure: Commerce and Culture in Ming China*. 1998.

Chan, Albert. *The Glory and Fall of Ming China*. 1982.

Chase, Kenneth. *Firearms: A Global History to 1700*. 2003.

Cohen, Warren. *East Asia at the Center*. 2000.

Crossley, Pamela K. *The Manchus*. 2002.

Ebrey, Patricia B., et al. *East Asia: A Cultural, Social, and Political History*. 2006.

Elison, G., and B. L. Smith, eds. *Warlords, Artists, and Commoners: Japan in the Sixteenth Century*. 1981.

Elliott, Mark C. *The Manchu Way*. 2001.

Gordon, Andrew. *A Modern History of Japan: From Tokugawa Times to the Present*. 2003.

Hall, J. W., et al., eds. *Japan Before Tokugawa*. 1981.

Hempel, Rose. *The Golden Age of Japan*. 1983.

Huang, Ray. *1587, A Year of No Significance*. 1981.

MacDonald, D. S. *The Koreans*. 1990.

Matsunosuke, N. *Edo Culture: Daily Life and Diversions in Urban Japan, 1600–1868*. 1997.

Mungello, D. E. *The Great Encounter of China and the West, 1500–1800*. 2nd ed. 2005.

Nakane, Chie, and Shinzaburo Oishi, *Tokugawa Japan*. 1990.

Palis, J. B. *Politics in Traditional Korea*. 1991.

Reid, Anthony, ed. *Sojourners and Settlers: Histories of Southeast Asia and the Chinese*. 2001.

Spence, J. D. *Emperor of China: Self-Portrait of K'ang Hsi*. 1974.

Spence, J. D., and J. Wills, eds. *From Ming to Ch'ing.* 1979.

Stanley-Baker, J. *Japanese Art.* 1984.

Sullivan, M. *The Arts of China.* 4th ed. 1999.

Tong, James W. *Disorder under Heaven: Collective Violence in the Ming Dynasty.* 1991.

Totman, Conrad. *Tokugawa Ieyasu.* 1983.

Varley, H. Paul. *Japanese Culture.* 4th ed. 2000.

Wakeman, Frederick. *The Great Enterprise: Manchu Reconstruction of Imperial Order in Seventeenth Century China.* 1985.

Warshaw, Steven. *Japan Emerges.* 1987.

Whitmore, J. *Vietnam.* 1985.

Woodside, A. *Vietnam and the Chinese Model.* 1988

Key Dates and Developments

1331–1392	Go-Daigo's rebellion in Japan
1336–1573	Ashikaga Shogunate in Japan
1368–1644	Ming dynasty in China
1392–1910	Yi dynasty in Korea
1467–1568	Age of Warring States in Japan
1471–1757	Vietnamese expansion south to Mekong Delta
1514	Portuguese arrival in southern China
1543	Portuguese arrival in southern Japan
1562–1590	Unification of Japan by Oda Nobunaga and Hideyoshi
1582–1610	Work of Jesuit scholar Matteo Ricci in China
1592–1598	Japanese invasions of Korea
1603–1868	Tokugawa Shogunate in Japan
1639	Eviction of Westerners from Japan
1644	Fall of Beijing: first to rebels, then to Manchus
1644–1912	Manchu Rule (Qing Dynasty) in China
1661–1722	Reign of Kangxi in China
1704–1742	Papal banning of Jesuit participation in Chinese Rites
1736–1795	Reign of Qianlong in China

Southern Asia and the Global Shift in Wealth and Power, 1500–1800

Batavia In The 18th Century

The commercial port of Batavia in the Dutch East Indies is shown in this eighteenth century drawing. The Dutch United East India Company helped transfer wealth and commercial domination from Southern Asia to Europe (page 547).

In the stifling early morning heat of June 23, 1757, Siraj-ud-Daulah (*sir-AHJ ud-DOW-luh*), ruler of the East Indian region of Bengal, surveyed his fifty thousand soldiers as they prepared for battle on an open field near the village of Plassey. Looking across the field at the tiny forces of his British opponent, Siraj was confident of victory. The British possessed modern weapons, technologically superior to those manufactured in Asia, but Siraj had purchased some for his own men. The 2,800 troops commanded by the young British officer, Robert Clive, could hardly expect to defeat such a large Bengali host.

Across the field, Clive had long since reached the same conclusion. Weeks earlier, recognizing that he was unlikely to win on the battlefield, he had opened secret negotiations with local Hindu bankers interested in preferential trading agreements with Britain. These wealthy men helped Clive convince Siraj's commanding general to betray his master. So when this general approached Siraj on the morning of June 23, it was not to ask for instructions. Instead, he informed the Bengali ruler of his decision to support the British. Faced with this treachery, Siraj had no choice but to retreat. Clive would later be hailed in England as the "victor of Plassey."

Southern Asia

Victory takes many forms, of which success in battle is only one. Economic influence and technological innovation can also prove decisive, as southern Asia's ruling Muslims discovered when challenged by outsiders from Europe in the seventeenth and eighteenth centuries. Europe's success in its confrontations with these Islamic empires integrated the Indian Ocean into a global trading network and set in motion a tremendous transfer of wealth and power from Asia to Europe.

Confrontation: Europe and Islam in Southern Asia

In 1600, nearly all of southern Asia, from Anatolia to Indonesia, was dominated by Islam. The three great Islamic empires—Mughal India, Safavid Persia, and the multinational empire of the Ottoman Turks—ruled huge and populous domains, while Muslim merchants exercised commanding influence on trade and culture in Malaya and Indonesia. Connected by Islamic culture and linked by flourishing overland and Indian Ocean trade, these regions together constituted one of history's mightiest and wealthiest civilizations (Map 22.1).

Europeans challenge Islamic dominance in southern Asia

By 1800, however, Islamic preeminence in southern Asia had yielded to the Europeans, whose economic and technological strength helped reorient the global balance of wealth and power. Indian Ocean trade had always been regional rather than global. It was more profitable than Mediterranean trade even before the Ottomans took Constantinople in 1453, and in the early 1500s it dwarfed the emerging Atlantic trade. But when the Europeans moved into the Indian Ocean with monopolistic trading companies, they connected Atlantic, Mediterranean, and Indian Ocean commercial networks into a global trading system. Commercial power thereupon became global rather than

FOUNDATION MAP 22.1 Islamic Asian Empires in 1600

As the seventeenth century began, Islam's position in the world seemed unshakable. Notice that the great Islamic empires consolidated in the sixteenth century spread across southern Asia, southeastern Europe, and northeastern Africa. Using the Indian Ocean as a commercial highway, Muslims dominated oceangoing trade in the eastern hemisphere. The Arabic language, colored and enriched by Persian, united the Muslim faithful in a spiritual and cultural community spanning thousands of miles. What advantages and disadvantages can you identify for these empires?

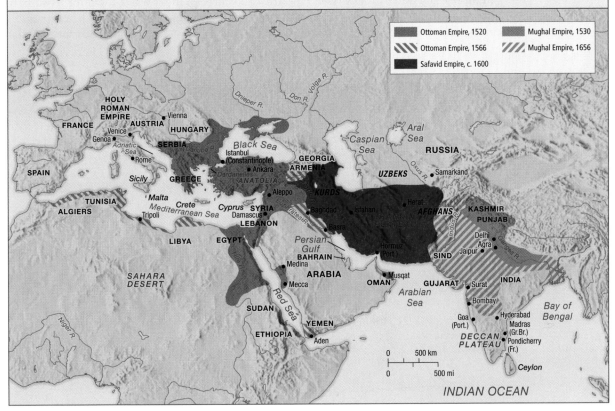

regional, and wealth flowed *out* of the Indian Ocean region through the trading companies and *into* Europe. The great Islamic empires of southern Asia lost this struggle for economic power.

The Indian Ocean Trade

During the sixteenth century, and in the centuries immediately preceding it, the Indian Ocean basin served as the world's main center of maritime trade. Riding the seasonal monsoon winds, which generally blow to the south and west from November to March, and to the north and east from April to September, Arab and Persian sailors carried on a lively commerce connecting India, Persia, Arabia, the city-states of East Africa, and Europe. Farther east, Chinese and Southeast Asian ships carried merchandise back and forth from India to Southeast Asia and the East Indies, and through the Straits of Malacca to the South China Sea and southern China.

The Indian Ocean connects world trade networks

Indian Ocean commerce was highly specialized, with each region typically supplying products that were locally raised, manufactured, or mined (Map 22.2). East Africa, for example, supplied ebony, ivory, slaves, and especially gold, mined in southeastern Africa and shipped from the great port of Kilwa. Arabia and Persia provided horses, figs, dates, and incense, as well as fine woven tapestries and carpets. India was known for its superb cotton textiles as well as for various dyes (including indigo), leather goods, carpets, knives, and assorted spices, including especially cinnamon and pepper. Southeast Asia

Map 22.2 Trade Routes Across the Indian Ocean, 1600

Hindu, Muslim, and Chinese traders crisscrossed the Indian Ocean using trade routes that had been established for centuries. Their familiarity with and systematic exploitation of these routes guaranteed their wealth and power. Note that the Indian Ocean's central position linked the Pacific Ocean with the Mediterranean/Red Sea trade. Why did the arrival of the Europeans in the sixteenth century challenge this established network?

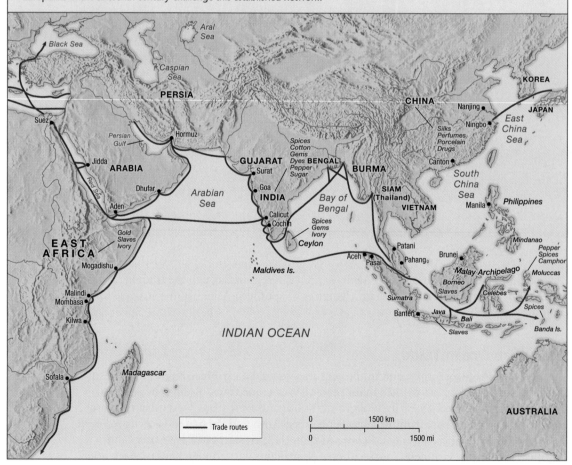

and the East Indies produced rubies, gold, tin, sandalwood, camphor (a waxy substance with a strong aroma used as an insect repellent, embalming oil, and medicine for fighting colds and fevers), and spices such as cinnamon and ginger. The Moluccas (now Maluku), a group of islands in the eastern East Indies, were famous for their nutmeg and cloves; Westerners called them the Spice Islands. And Chinese products, such as porcelains and silks, were valued throughout the Indian Ocean basin and in Europe.

A seventeenth-century drawing of the port of Hormuz.

To handle all this trade, thriving seaports had grown up along Asia's southern coast. These commercial centers included Aden at the mouth of the Red Sea, Hormuz at the entrance to the Persian Gulf, Cambay in northwestern India, and Calicut on India's southwestern seaboard, known as the **Malabar Coast**.

Farther east, Malacca, on the straits connecting the Indian Ocean with the South China Sea, served as the region's greatest commercial center. Although Muslim merchants and mariners conducted much of the commerce, many of these cities were religiously and culturally diverse, with Hindus, Buddhists, Jews, and others engaging in crafts and commerce.

The Islamic empires of southern Asia derived substantial benefits from the Indian Ocean trade. It not only added immensely to the wealth of their realms but also helped fill the treasuries of their rulers, who charged a variety of licensing fees, taxes, and customs duties on artisans, merchants, and shippers. To a certain extent, then, the wealth and power of the Muslim world derived from Islamic domination of the Indian Ocean trade.

Islamic empires rely on Indian Ocean trade

Ironically, one of Islam's greatest triumphs—the conquest of Constantinople in 1453 by the Ottoman Turks—set in motion events that eventually undermined this domination and the fortunes of Islamic southern Asia. For in the late fifteenth century, to avoid paying the huge fees and markups imposed by the Ottomans on goods coming through Constantinople from the East, Portuguese sailors had begun seeking an all-water route around Africa to southern Asia. In doing so they initiated the European voyages of discovery (Chapter 19) and challenged Muslim control of the Indian Ocean.

Shifting Balances of Power and Commerce

Europe's voyages of discovery quickly produced conflict with the hitherto dominant Islamic societies of southern Asia. The newcomers were interested mainly in trade, but also used their warships to project their power in the Indian Ocean. Sixteenth-century European warships were engineered to include powerful cannons whose shot could penetrate the hulls of enemy ships. Mounted on wheeled carriages to make them quickly interchangeable with one another, so that if one failed another could easily be brought up, these cannons revolutionized naval warfare. European nations such as England and Holland developed iron-smelting industries to produce large numbers of naval cannons. The Islamic navies of southern Asia found themselves at a great disadvantage, one that the Europeans were quick to exploit.

European technology puts Muslims at a disadvantage

At first the European traders and merchants came mainly from Portugal, which established trading posts in the Moluccas, Macao, Timor, and elsewhere (Map 22.2). But soon the Portuguese had to share the region with commercial enterprises from England and Holland (also called the Dutch Republic or United Provinces of the Netherlands). Channeling the talents of their ambitious middle classes, these countries constructed large maritime trading empires. Using advanced weaponry, improvements in navigational instruments, and superb organizational skills, they accumulated unprecedented wealth. Although these newly arrived entrepreneurs came mainly to seek riches, and frequently fought one another, eventually they had a profound political and economic impact on India, Indonesia, and mainland Southeast Asia.

The Dutch seize Asian trade routes from Portugal

Portugal's Indian Ocean outposts survived into the twentieth century, but by the middle of the seventeenth its hold on the Southeast Asian trade had been seized by the Dutch. During the next two centuries the Dutch gradually established territorial sovereignty over Indonesia, which they called the Dutch (or Netherlands) East Indies. France and Britain competed for influence in the Indian subcontinent, and by 1763 the British emerged victorious. British domination of India gave London effective control of the Indian Ocean, with naval and military bases in East Africa, the Red Sea, the Persian Gulf, and the Malay archipelago. France, removed from the subcontinent, expanded elsewhere in the nineteenth century, eventually dominating much of North Africa and the Southeast Asian mainland.

Atlantic commercial routes become more valuable

At the same time, however, the focus of the global economy was shifting away from the Indian Ocean. As Europe's trade with the Americas became more profitable than its trade with the East, the busiest commercial routes shifted to the Atlantic. Traffic in Asian luxury goods, which had stimulated Europe's initial explorations in the 1400s, was now surpassed by exponential growth in the Atlantic trade, involving slaves from Africa and sugar, silver, tobacco, and coffee from the Americas. A modern mercantile system was in place, as Europe's colonies supplied their mother countries with the raw materials from which to fabricate finished goods. The mother countries then sold those goods on the open market, using the profits to increase their investment in their colonies and obtain more raw materials. Mercantilism enabled England and Holland to seize the dominant commercial status previously enjoyed by the Islamic world. Global networks, controlled by the English and Dutch, linked Indian Ocean trade with the Atlantic trade. The Indian Ocean commerce itself, however, was clearly in decline, and the Islamic trading centers were dominated, directly or indirectly, by Europeans.

Islamic empires decline as their commercial networks are lost

From the sixteenth to the eighteenth century, as commerce and control of the global economy shifted to the land- and sea-based empires of Europe, the Islamic realms declined in power and influence. Mughal India dissolved into several competing provincial states and came increasingly under British control. The trading states of Indonesia became, for the most part, economic appendages of Holland. Safavid Iran, deserted by a multitude of tribes that had once been its vassals, was plagued by Afghan, Russian, and Turkish invaders. The Ottoman Empire became politically decentralized, militarily weak, and vulnerable to attacks from Austria and Russia. For Islamic southern Asia, the transition to a global economy, and the consequent shift in the global balance of power, had a highly negative impact.

Transformation of the Indian Subcontinent

The Indian subcontinent was the first southern Asian region to be affected by the European expansion. In 1497–1498, Portuguese explorer Vasco da Gama's voyage round the southern tip of Africa brought him to India's Malabar Coast, where he established commercial contacts in the port of Calicut. In the centuries that followed, increasing numbers of merchants and traders from Europe made their way to India, bringing Western wealth, products, weapons, and ways. By the end of the eighteenth century, as the Mughal Empire declined, much of the subcontinent came under European control.

Europeans Arrive in India

When da Gama's two ships entered Calicut harbor in 1498, their appearance perplexed virtually everyone in the port. The admiral explained that he had been sent to develop a southern trade route that would bypass the ancient land connection now dominated by Muslims and preyed on by Mongols. That explanation made a certain amount of sense to the Hindu traders of Calicut, and as the Portuguese had been instructed to pay any price for spices, Indian traders quickly stopped asking questions and started counting their profits. Competing Arab and Chinese merchants, long established in the region and aware of actual values, thought the Portuguese were fools. But when da Gama returned to Portugal, he sold his cargo for 3,000 percent more than the entire cost of his expedition. Soon hundreds of Portuguese ships were sailing regularly to India, and other Europeans eagerly pushed their way into this highly profitable trade. They created a baffling new challenge for India's Muslim rulers.

PORTUGUESE AND MUSLIM RIVALRY. Portuguese seamen soon realized that, although their sea route cut out the land-based Ottoman middlemen, they were now competing for spices with seagoing Muslim merchants in the Indian Ocean. In 1501 Portuguese navigator Pedro Alvares Cabral brought six ships to Calicut after being blown off course along the way and landing accidentally on the coast of Brazil. He left 54 Portuguese merchants in India, directing them to buy spices at the lowest prices possible and store the goods until the next ships arrived. On his way back to Portugal Cabral captured and looted an Arab merchant ship, provoking Muslims to kill all the Portuguese he had left behind in Calicut. In 1502 Vasco da Gama returned with a powerful fleet, pulverized the port of Calicut with his cannons, and sliced off the ears, noses, and hands of eight hundred Muslim seamen. Indian Muslims then left the Portuguese alone. But the Portuguese government in Lisbon realized that it would have to protect its traders, so in 1509 the Portuguese king appointed Dom Afonso d'Albuquerque as his viceroy in the East.

> Portugal intrudes on Indian Ocean trade

View of Goa in the middle of the 17th century.

Albuquerque, a passionate Catholic who despised Islam, built bases on the Persian Gulf, the Red Sea, and the Straits of Malacca. At his suggestion, Portugal seized the island of Goa on India's Malabar Coast; it served as Lisbon's Indian headquarters from 1510 until 1961. By cutting in half the taxes of every Hindu on the island, the Portuguese won local support against the Muslims. Albuquerque devised a number of bizarre schemes to destroy Islam, most of which—such as stealing the remains of Muhammad or damming the Nile so Egypt would starve—were beyond the capacity or interest of the Portuguese Empire. But he did succeed in making his king fabulously wealthy, as Portuguese imports at bargain prices generated a huge increase in European demand for spices.

Portugal's power was brief, however. While the Hindus of South India welcomed the Portuguese as traders and as potential allies against Islamic rule, in the 1560s several central Indian Muslim sultanates declared *jihad* against the Hindus. They defeated the

> Islamic states strike back against Portugal

South Indian Hindu kingdom of Vijayanagar, depriving Portugal of the South Indian trade and jeopardizing its Malabar Coast position.

Shortly thereafter, King Philip II of Spain inherited the Portuguese crown, creating a union between Spain and Portugal that lasted from 1580 until 1640. Philip, like Albuquerque a devoted Catholic, promptly closed the Portuguese port of Lisbon to Protestant shipping. Protestant nations such as Holland and England, previously content to buy their spices from Portugal, now had reason to seek their own sea routes around Africa to India. The Portuguese tried using their bases in Angola and Mozambique to blockade the relatively narrow passage around the Cape of Good Hope, but blockading was an inexact science and their efforts failed. Moreover, after England destroyed the Spanish Armada in 1588 (Chapter 20), the Iberian threat to Dutch and English shipping was substantially diminished.

THE ENGLISH AND DUTCH EAST INDIA COMPANIES. In 1600 and 1602, the English and Dutch governments each created a large commercial enterprise and gave it a national monopoly over trade with India. Before long these ventures, known respectively as the English (later British) East India Company and the Dutch United East India Company, were vigorously pursuing this trade. The problem was that India was not particularly interested in expanding commerce with Europe. The Portuguese were valued customers because they paid in gold, but the Dutch and English companies wanted to create a balance of trade in which they would pay for spices with money that the Indians would then return to them in exchange for manufactured goods. India neither wanted nor needed anything made in northern Europe at that time and was already selling enough spices to Portugal to satisfy its need for gold. But after a demonstration of English naval power in 1612, when one English ship defeated four Portuguese galleons, India's Mughal Emperor was convinced that dealing with London was worth his time.

The Mughal Emperor also turned to England for protection from pirates, asking its navy to escort the annual pilgrim ship to and from Mecca. As one of the Five Pillars of Islam, the pilgrimage to Mecca played a vital role in unifying Muslims throughout the world, and the Mughal Empire sponsored an annual ship to transport the faithful. Previously the Portuguese navy had provided the escort, but now, in return for trading privileges, England took over.

England was willing to cooperate commercially with Holland against Portugal, but the Dutch shortsightedly shut the English out in Indonesia. They kept the Indonesian trade for themselves and eventually established a colony there known as the Dutch East Indies. England, in turn, excluded the Dutch from India, thereby laying the foundation of what would become by the nineteenth century a vast British Empire.

England and Holland contend for trade routes

Meanwhile the English were finding ways to build further connections with India. Since India was unwilling to buy English goods, the English East India Company tried to reduce its gold payments by establishing factories in the region. Recognizing that the Indian cotton cloth known as **calico** (since it came from Calicut), already fashionable in England, could also be used in the spice trade, the English built a textile factory on the east coast of India, paying Indian weavers in gold to make calico cloth. The cloth was then traded for spices in the Moluccas and other islands. Using calico, the English were able to get three hundred times the spices that the gold they paid the weavers could have bought. At the same time the English, by using inexpensive local labor, reduced the cost of calico in the English home market and tied India more closely to England itself.

THE MUGHAL RESPONSE. By this time India's Great Mughal rulers were beginning to notice European activities. The Mughal Empire had earlier been able to control Arabian Sea traffic into Indian ports, but now the English dominated those waters. Also worrying the emperor was London's construction of Fort Saint George beside the East Indian seaside village of Madras (*MAH-drahs*), a sleepy town that would soon become, with Calcutta and Bombay, one of the three principal British ports in India. Obviously the English intended to protect their trade, but a fort constructed for protection, the Mughals realized, could also be used for domination.

The Mughals were uncertain of the precise nature of the threat and didn't know how to handle it. India for centuries had been invaded by land (the Mughals themselves were simply the last in a long line of Central Asian conquerors), but the Europeans had not come by land and did not seem to be invading. They apparently had no desire to move entire populations to India, as previous invaders had done; rather they sought economic relations, to which the empire had no objection. What was worrisome, however, was the military and naval power of the Europeans and the English construction of Fort Saint George. For the moment the Mughals watched and waited. They did not realize that once the Europeans had gained a foothold on the coasts of the subcontinent, it would be nearly impossible to expel them.

Monogram of the Dutch East India Company.

British intrusions perplex the Mughals

DIFFERING EUROPEAN INTERESTS IN SOUTH AND SOUTHEAST ASIA. Regimes throughout South and Southeast Asia were similarly perplexed about European intentions. Their confusion was compounded by sharp differences in motivation among various European groups.

One difference concerned geographic focus. The Portuguese, who arrived first, were interested in the entire region, hoping to turn the Indian Ocean into a Portuguese-controlled commercial zone. Later arrivals, however, focused more narrowly. The Dutch were primarily concerned with Southeast Asia, the English and French with India. It took nearly a century for local rulers to appreciate fully the implication of this difference: if Europeans were interested not only in commercial relations but political control, dividing up the region would make individual parts of it easier to conquer.

A second difference concerned religious attitudes. The Catholic Portuguese and French intended not only to make money but to save souls. Catholics viewed Indians, both Hindus and Muslims, as highly civilized people who needed the Gospel preached to them by missionaries of the universal Roman Catholic Church. The Protestant English and Dutch, on the other hand, were principally interested in doing business. Protestantism rejected the concept of a universal church structure, so establishing a Protestant Church of England in India made little sense, except to serve the spiritual needs of transplanted English subjects. The Dutch, as Calvinists, were even less interested in encouraging conversion: since Calvinism held that everyone on Earth was predestined either to heaven or to hell, there seemed to be no point in laboring strenuously in vain efforts to change what God had already decided.

Europeans have differing motives for entering South and Southeast Asia

These differences among Europeans were at first not clear to South and Southeast Asian rulers. When the differences became clear, the motivations behind them remained difficult to understand. And when those motivations became clear, it was too late to dislodge the Europeans.

The Mughals in Decline

As the English were establishing a foothold on the coasts of India, the Mughal Empire was weakening from within. The oppressive Aurangzeb, who reigned from 1658 to 1707, destroyed the Mughal legacy of tolerance and benevolence established earlier by Akbar (Chapter 17). Aurangzeb's militant Muslim policies alienated Hindus and Sikhs who had previously supported the regime, and he drained the imperial treasury to put down rising opposition from these groups. His son and successor, Bahadur Shah (*BAH-hah-dūr SHAH*), already 63 when he inherited the throne, spent his brief five-year reign fighting his younger brothers and the persistent Sikhs. After the death of Bahadur Shah in 1712, central control of the empire deteriorated as separate groups competed for power. The chaos ended in 1719 when the Sayyid (*SĪA-yēd*) brothers, two influential and ruthless courtiers, killed the inept emperor and became the powers behind the throne.

The Sayyids selected the weak but cultivated Muhammad Shah as emperor. His lengthy reign (1719–1748) was culturally beneficial: Hindus and Muslims drew closer to one another, primarily through their common use of the **Urdu** (*UR-doo*) language, a Hindu tongue written with the Persian alphabet and employing many Persian terms. Urdu poetry flourished at Delhi, and the Mughal court began to tolerate Hindu deities and myths as cultural curiosities, though not as gods deserving of worship.

But Muhammad Shah's rule further weakened the empire's political unity. He tried but failed to restore confidence in central authority, and some of his policies actually strengthened his adversaries. For example, he sought to gain the loyalty of the **Marathas** (*mah-ruh-TAHZ*), a staunchly Hindu people of central India, by recognizing their autonomy and granting them taxation authority. In the short term, the Marathas ceased their opposition, but in the long term these concessions helped them become a powerful force in their own right. To counterbalance the Marathas, Muhammad Shah then tried to win the loyalty of local princes, or **nawabs** (*NĀ-wabs*) (corrupted into English as "nabobs") by granting them taxation privileges in their own regions. The nawabs took the tax advantages but did not prove loyal. Gradually the Mughal Empire dissolved into independent states, owing nominal rather than real allegiance to the emperor in Delhi.

As Mughal power in India declined, Persia was invaded by the Afghans. Nadir (*NAH-dēr*) Shah, the Persian ruler, asked Muhammad Shah for help, but the Mughal emperor, who was fighting the Marathas, refused. Exasperated, the Persians moved against Afghanistan on their own and then continued across the Indus River to punish the Mughals. In 1739, they sacked Delhi and captured Akbar's legendary Peacock Throne. Carrying it back to their capital at Isfahan (*ISS-fah-hahn*), they made it the throne of all Iran's shahs until 1979.

The Persian sack of Delhi marked the end of Mughal centralized authority, although the empire officially continued into the nineteenth century. Abandoning the policies of Akbar, which had made it great, the empire gradually fell apart. Afghans, Iranians, Sikhs, Marathas, and minor Muslim states fought over what remained, and petty rajahs and nawabs played roles well beyond their financial means and political capacities. For many Muslims, these startling developments called into question not only Islamic political power but also the future of Indian Islam.

The Crisis of Islamic India

Islam had conquered India but had never converted it. Hinduism remained the subcontinent's dominant faith, and India's caste system defied repeated Islamic efforts at social leveling. Muslims had successfully installed their own political systems, but religiously and culturally India remained Hindu, a fact impossible to ignore when Mughal authority collapsed. This political crisis caused soul-searching among Indian Muslims.

Ever since waves of Muslim cavalry poured forth from the Arabian Peninsula in the seventh century C.E., Islam had identified closely with Arab and Persian cultures. This connection had enabled most Muslims, from West Africa to Indonesia, to consider themselves part of a cosmopolitan cultural world centered in Southwest Asia. But the Indian subcontinent had always been different. There Islam was the religion of the ruling elites, not the common people. India's complex and rich Hindu culture resisted Arab-Persian influences and offered a viable alternative to the faith and customs of its Muslim conquerors. Most of the Indian population retained its pre-Islamic ways. Even where elements of Islam were assimilated into the local culture—such as in the Punjab, where Sikhism offered a popular synthesis of Hinduism and Islam (Chapter 17)—Muslims viewed the result as a corruption of the pure monotheism of the Prophet.

Indian Islam faces a crisis

Elsewhere, in Afghanistan and Anatolia for example, Muslim conquest had brought in large numbers of Islamic immigrants. But few Muslims emigrated to India, and those who did had to work hard to avoid being assimilated into the Hindu masses. They therefore isolated themselves in the top political structures of the Delhi Sultanate and the Mughal Empire, structures that remained closed to Hindus. Their only success in converting Hindus was among the lower castes, a development that made Indian Islam even less attractive to well-born Hindus.

The collapse of Mughal authority brought Indian Muslims face to face with a disturbing possibility: they might no longer be able to practice their religion in India. No longer in power, they feared being absorbed into Hindu culture. Many viewed emigration or political separation from Hindu India as their only practical alternatives. This crisis of confidence troubled Indian Islam from 1739 until 1947, when India was divided into separate Hindu and Muslim states.

Delhi's Golden Mosque, built by Muhammad Shah in 1722.

British and French Rivalry in India

Meanwhile, a new group of Europeans was making inroads in India, ready to take advantage of Mughal decline. In 1664 France founded the French East India Company, which from 1674 was headquartered at Pondichéry (*pawn-dih-share-RĒ*), 85 miles south of the English East India Company's base at Madras (Map 22.3). As the French began to challenge the English, Anglo-French trade became intensely competitive. By 1739 both Madras and Pondichéry had grown to cities of fifty thousand inhabitants as their respective companies jockeyed for position.

Europeans take advantage of Mughal decline

This Anglo-French rivalry took on a new dimension in 1740, when Britain and France went to war against each other in the War of the Austrian Succession (1740–1748). This war was fought not only in Europe but in each nation's colonial possessions. In 1746 the French, led by Joseph-François Dupleix (*zhō-SEFF frahn-SWAH doo-PLAY*), governor of

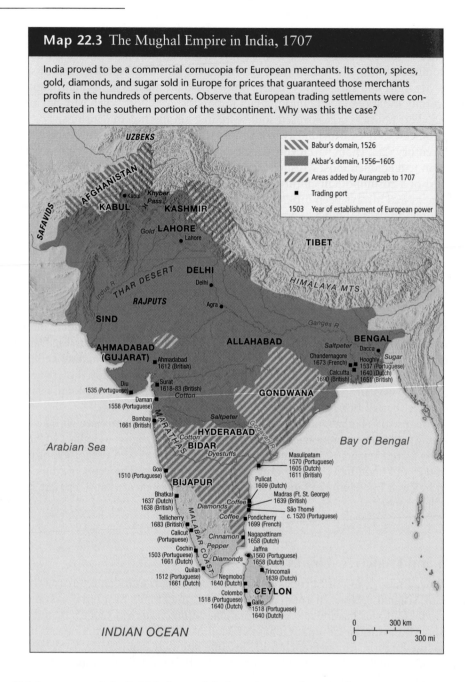

Map 22.3 The Mughal Empire in India, 1707

India proved to be a commercial cornucopia for European merchants. Its cotton, spices, gold, diamonds, and sugar sold in Europe for prices that guaranteed those merchants profits in the hundreds of percents. Observe that European trading settlements were concentrated in the southern portion of the subcontinent. Why was this the case?

Pondichéry, captured the British fort at Madras. Among those in the garrison who were expelled was a 21-year-old bookkeeper named Robert Clive.

Clive had at one point become so bored in his job with the British East India Company that he allegedly attempted suicide, only to have the gun he was using misfire. The fall of Madras suggested to him that it might be more exciting to shoot French soldiers than to shoot himself, and the following year he enlisted in the British forces. In 1748 the English regained Madras, pushing the French back to Pondichéry as the war in Europe closed. Clive returned to Madras, watched Dupleix work at Pondichéry, learned from him, and became his rival.

Using a combination of military force, bribery, and behind-the-throne manipulation, Dupleix extended French civil authority throughout southern India by early 1751. But in 1751 Clive, now a captain, struck a deal with Maratha leaders, and led a joint English-Maratha force that defeated the French. Thereupon the French East India Company re-called Dupleix, who had been appointed, the company contended, to make a profit, not to create a French empire in India.

Britain, by contrast, backed Clive and his ambitions for empire. War resumed in 1756 (the Seven Years War), and in 1757 Clive won the victory at Plassey, as described at the beginning of the chapter. By 1763 Britain had conquered nearly all of France's Indian possessions, establishing a foundation for British domination of the entire subcontinent. In 1765 Clive became governor of Bengal, with enough money to buy off the nawabs and enough soldiers to defend the Company's assets.

Britain outmaneuvers France in India

The British thereafter expanded their influence in India, gradually transferring power from the Company to the British government. Following Clive's policy, they sent out a few tough and competent Englishmen to oversee British rule through Indian leaders. During the next century, India became the "jewel in the crown" of the British monarchs—the cornerstone of England's worldwide empire and a principal element in its prosperity. Once again, the Indian subcontinent was unified under foreign rule.

Muslims and Europeans in Southeast Asia

Unlike India, Southeast Asia proved to be a place where Islam could continue to expand. Located at a crossroads of international trade, it was of interest to both Muslims and Europeans. But the large number of islands in the Indonesian and Malayan archipelagos, and the imposing mountain ranges and rain forests of the Southeast Asian mainland, all proved obstacles to the development of political unity across the region.

Coexistence Between Muslims and Hindus

Beginning in 632, Muslim armies conquered North Africa, the Iberian peninsula, and substantial portions of South Asia. The expansion of Islam into Southeast Asia, however, was carried out by merchants rather than warriors. The Indonesian kingdom of Srivijaya controlled the Straits of Malacca (Chapter 12), and therefore also the flourishing seaborne trade between China and India. Srivijaya was a Hindu kingdom, unlike the Buddhist societies of the Southeast Asian mainland, and might have been expected to resist Islam with the same intensity demonstrated by Hindus in India. But Indonesia gradually accepted Islam as its dominant belief system. A number of factors made this outcome possible.

First, while Muslims came to India as conquerors, they came to Southeast Asia as commercial partners. Islamic merchants settled in Indonesia and the Malay archipelago, established businesses that enriched the communities in which they lived, and married

Muslims and Hindus prove compatible in Indonesia

Map 22.4 Southeast Asia and Indonesia, 1500–1700

Southeast Asia's strategic location at the juncture of the Indian Ocean, the Pacific Ocean, and the South China Sea made it an indispensable thoroughfare for Eastern Hemispheric trade. The region produced spices in abundance and boasted several useful natural harbors. Notice the enormous number of islands in the Malayan, Indonesian, and Philippine archipelagos, making the development of centralized government extremely difficult. How would this geographic handicap leave the region vulnerable to European intrusion?

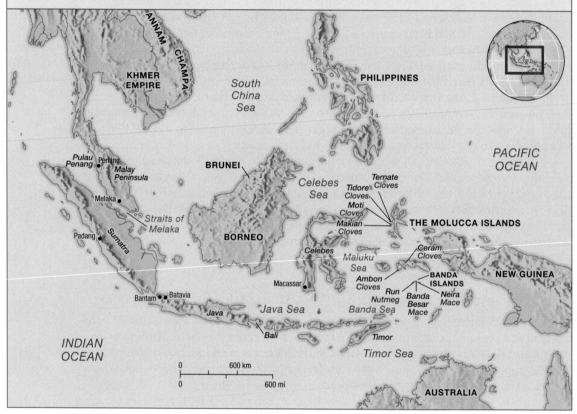

into the families of local elites. Several rulers converted to Islam in the expectation that it would improve their position with regard to rival Hindu states in central Java (Map 22.4). Conversion was also useful for trade, as Muslim connections could bring the India-China trade into Islamic trading networks across the Indian Ocean. Since there were no atrocities of the kind committed against Hindus in India, Muslims were not demonized in Southeast Asia.

Second, Islam appealed to the common people of the region by advocating the essential equality of all believers in the sight of Allah. Since Southeast Asian Hindus did not practice the caste system that so offended Muslims in India, they were not conditioned to lives of inequality and discrimination. Their attitudes toward society were therefore already consistent with those of Islam. Islam's radical leveling, derived from the horizontal social structure of the Arabian Peninsula and from the Prophet

Muhammad's message that all were slaves before God, attracted the lower classes without threatening elite interests.

Finally, Islam was transmitted to Southeast Asia by Sufi mystics rather than by orthodox Muslims. Sufis practiced a form of **pantheism**, the belief that God is present in all things, both animate and inanimate. Since Hinduism is not only polytheistic but pantheistic, Indonesians and Malays found Sufi Islam compatible in this respect with their own beliefs. Sufis also worshiped saints and believed that they could heal the sick, doctrines and practices abhorred by orthodox Muslims but widely practiced in pre-Islamic Southeast Asia.

These conditions eased the spread of Islam across the region beginning in the thirteenth century. When Iskandar, the ruler of Srivijaya, was overthrown by princes from central Java around 1400 and driven from Palembang, he converted to Islam and founded the trading state of Malacca. Soon it was a center of Islamic culture, and the prosperous connections it built with China, Java, and India helped disperse this culture across the region. By the time the Portuguese arrived in 1511, Islam was the most widely accepted belief system in Malaya and Indonesia.

Islam dominates Malaya and Indonesia

The Chronicles of Java.

The European Intrusion

The Portuguese conquest of Malacca in 1511 forced Muslims to move into the interior forests of Sumatra, Java, and Borneo, thus accelerating the geographic spread of the faith. Other Muslims traveled up the Malay Peninsula and established sultanates there. Once the ordinary people of those regions were introduced to Islam, significant numbers of conversions followed. The Malay sultanate of Johore (*jeh-HOR*) and the Javanese kingdom of Mataram (*mah-TEHR-rum*)—both Muslim realms—developed into formidable rivals of the Europeans by 1650. By that time Portuguese commercial dominance had been supplanted by the Dutch.

Having gained independence from Spain through a prolonged and bitter revolt in the late 1500s (Chapter 20), the Calvinist Dutch found themselves denied access to Lisbon's pepper and spice markets by the Catholic kings of Spain, who also ruled Portugal from 1580 to 1640. Accepting this exclusion as the price of liberty, the Dutch promptly sailed for the East Indies and waged naval warfare against the Portuguese. Through their Dutch United East India Company they founded Batavia in 1619 (see page 533); in 1949 it was renamed Djakarta (*juh-KAR-tuh*) and is now Indonesia's capital. In 1641 they joined with Johore to capture Malacca from the Portuguese, and in 1658 they took Palembang. By this time the Portuguese were in full retreat from Southeast Asia, pulling back to the Indian Ocean, where their struggles against the Ottomans and the British were also going badly. The Portuguese were expelled from the Persian Gulf in 1650, and from East Africa (with the exception of Mozambique) by 1696.

The Dutch challenge Portuguese commercial supremacy

Dutch supremacy in Indonesia, like the earlier Portuguese impact, stimulated Islamic expansion rather than blocking it. The introduction of European culture, with values so alien to those of southern Asia, provoked a flight to Islam as a form of reaction against the Dutch intruders. Islamic institutions and culture formed the backbone of Indonesian resistance to European domination for the next three centuries. Additionally, Sufi pantheism produced a synthesis of Hindu and Islamic practices that was particularly notable in the Javanese state of Mataram. In Malay and Indonesian villages, Islam blended easily with local beliefs that demons, spirits, and natural powers manipulated all aspects of daily life.

Although the European commercial empires continued to control trade and exclude rival powers, they had minimal impact on local culture and customs. At the close of the eighteenth century, Southeast Asian Muslims were unconcerned that the Dutch East India Company fell victim to British competition and the French conquest of Holland in 1795. They assumed that the change from Dutch domination to British would have no greater impact on their daily lives than had the replacement of the Portuguese by the Dutch in the seventeenth century.

European domination changes from commercial to colonial

But their assumptions were mistaken, for events in Europe had a direct impact on Southeast Asia. After the king of Holland collaborated with the British against the French occupation of his country (Chapter 26), Britain took control of Java and Malacca for their military value in a global war against France. When the Napoleonic Wars ended in 1815, a victorious Britain returned the East Indies to the Dutch but kept Malaya for itself. This new configuration of European influence was not only economic but also political and territorial. Southeast Asian Muslims, long accustomed to Dutch and British *commercial* exploitation, suddenly found themselves subjects of European *colonial* empires.

The End of Safavid Persia

Islam's conquest of Persia in the seventh century C.E. had enriched the new monotheistic faith with the splendor of Persian language and culture. That enrichment survived the rise and fall of dynasties and a whole series of invasions across the Iranian plateau. In the late sixteenth century, the Safavid Shah Abbas I (1587–1629) reconstituted a strong Persian state as a rival to the neighboring Ottoman Empire (Chapter 17). From his capital at Isfahan, he presided over a golden age of commerce, refinement, and reform. His reign marked the height of Safavid Persia's success. By the mid-eighteenth century, this Persian dynasty was gone.

Safavid Centralization and Decline

The successors of Abbas I centralize the Safavid Empire

The death of Abbas I began the empire's decline. His immediate successors, Safi (*SAH-fe*), who ruled from 1629 to 1642, and Abbas II, who ruled from 1642 to 1666, ended the decentralized provincial administration under which the empire had thrived and replaced it with repressive centralization. This concentration of power at the center caused increasing corruption and inefficiency at the local level, as governors responsible directly to the Shah neglected rural roads and defenses in order to please their royal master by maximizing imperial tax revenues. Surrounded by envious neighbors searching for any evidence of Safavid weakness, Persia grew increasingly vulnerable.

At the same time, Safi decided to confine all the royal princes within the harem, hoping thereby to minimize the possibility that the heir would be challenged by his brothers. But Safi thereby lost the opportunity to train his successor for rule. Traditionally, the heir to the Peacock Throne served an apprenticeship as governor of the strategically and economically valuable province of Khurasan. There he would learn the practical arts of governance from provincial chiefs and royal advisors, in a setting in which the errors typically made by an inexperienced young man would not prove serious. His brothers were traditionally appointed to lesser posts, providing them with valuable administrative experience but also with power bases from which they often challenged the heir upon their father's death.

These rebellions by younger brothers were what Safi hoped to prevent, but by ordering that all princes remain secluded he produced a succession of emperors after Abbas II who preferred the pleasures of the harem to the duties of statecraft. Authority passed to the court eunuchs and the mothers of competing princes, who intrigued constantly against one another and ignored the legitimate needs of the state.

One of the most important of those needs was imperial defense. By 1700 the Safavid army had suffered from the effects of decentralization and the obsession with a revenue surplus. It was disintegrating into regiments led by officers jealous of competing authorities, and in response to this weakness various provinces of the empire rose in revolt. Taking advantage of this civil unrest, Afghan rebels captured Isfahan in 1722. Their success encouraged the Russian and Ottoman empires to attack Persia. Two years later southern Iran was firmly under Afghan control, while the Turks and Russians dominated the North (Map 22.5).

Afghans, Turks, and Russians attack Persia

Map 22.5 Safavid Persia in 1736

Safavid Persia's pivotal location between the Ottoman and Mughal Empires prevented the creation of a unified Sunni Muslim state across southern Asia in the sixteenth, seventeenth, and eighteenth centuries. Note that the Ottoman Empire could never penetrate any further into Persia than the western edge of the Zagros Mountains. But also notice the presence of Russia on Persia's northern border. How might this fact call into question the survival of the Safavid dynasty?

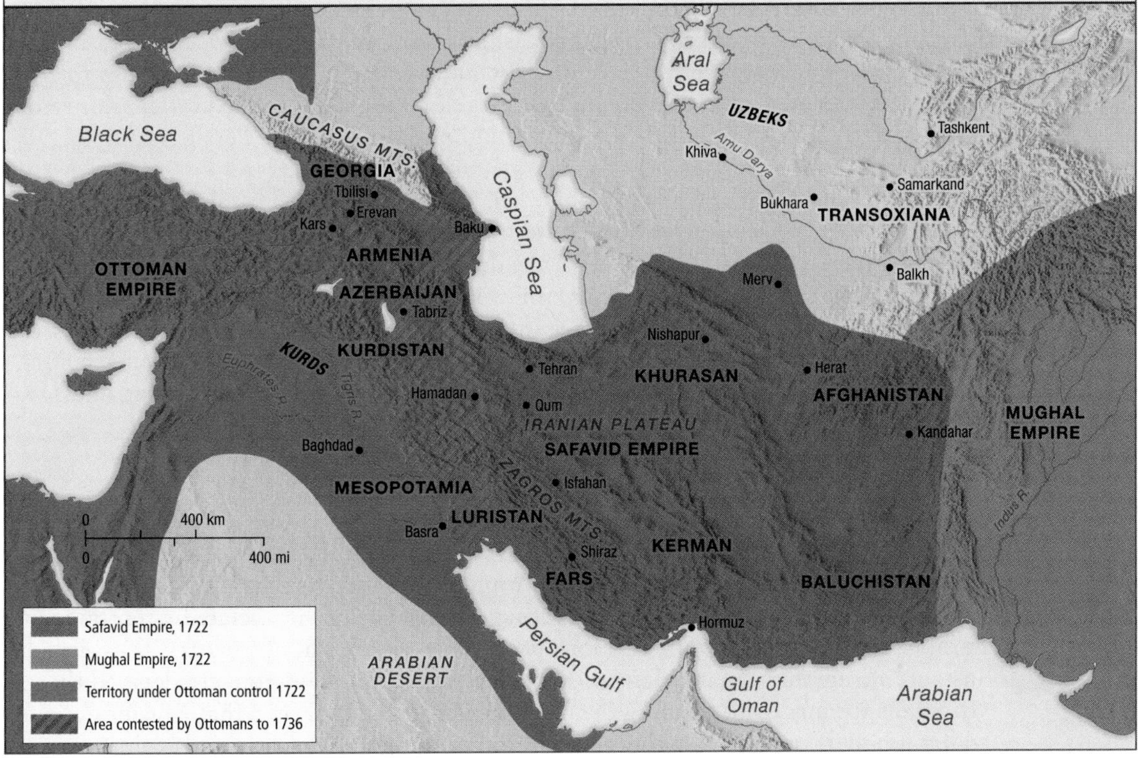

Under such circumstances, the dynasty could not survive. Nadir Shah, a Persian military commander of Turkish ancestry, deposed the last Safavid emperor in 1736 and drove the Turks and Russians off the Iranian plateau. Nadir, a Sunni Muslim ruling a Shi'ite empire, tried unsuccessfully to unify Persia religiously by reconciling Sunni and Shi'ite Muslims. In 1739 he sacked Delhi and threw the Mughal Empire into disarray. But after he was assassinated in 1747, his kingdom fell apart. By 1779 a new regime, the Qajar (*kah-JAR*) dynasty, consolidated its power in Isfahan. The Qajars ruled Persia until the twentieth century.

Shi'ite Islam After the Safavids

The end of Safavid rule carried with it sobering implications for Persia's future. Shi'ite Islam, despite Nadir Shah's efforts, refused to support the new regime. Under the Qajar dynasty, Shi'ism transformed itself into an inward-looking spiritual movement concentrating on the eventual reappearance of the **Twelfth Imam** (also called the Hidden Imam), a messianic leader whose return Shi'ites believed would create a religious kingdom and usher in a period of prosperity and peace enduring until the Last Judgment. The Shi'ite clergy, through its religious schools, became the principal adversary of any dynasty that claimed the right to rule Persia, reserving that right for the Twelfth Imam and, in his continued absence, for the clergy itself.

Shi'ite Islam opposes centralized government in Persia

At the close of the eighteenth century, then, Shi'ism was moving in a direction contrary to that of secular state control. Shi'ite religious reformers insisted that society and government be organized according to genuine Islamic principles, that the Shari`ah replace civil and royal legal codes, and that only religious scholars and teachers lead the *umma*. In the face of growing Russian and British interest in the strategically located Iranian plateau, Shi'ism reasserted itself as the best guarantee of spiritual and moral strength. If the state could no longer defend Persia, Islam itself must do so.

These events separated Persia from other modernizing Muslim cultures. In most such cultures, modernization began with Western economic contact that escalated into colonial and imperial control. But in Persia, the desertion of the dynasty by the religious establishment preceded the introduction of European influence, which therefore proved to be largely economic and indirect. The spiritual authorities, never fully understood by the Europeans, considered themselves the only genuine caretakers of Persian Islamic culture. They stood in opposition to both internal and external political forces, hoping one day to seize the state for themselves.

Cover of a Persian book, circa 1800.

The Ottoman Response to Europe's Challenge

The Ottomans had for centuries been a formidable power, but by 1700 they had lost the initiative. As the tide increasingly turned against them, they belatedly responded to Europe's challenge by adapting to European ways. In Arabia, however, Wahhabism, an austere Muslim movement, blamed Islam's decline on lax devotion, condemned the Ottomans for modeling themselves after unbelievers, and warned that Muslims could triumph only by rigidly adhering to the Prophet's original message.

Document 22.1 A European Visitor Describes Arabia

John Ovington, an English merchant and traveler, traversed the Indian Ocean in 1689. On his journey he stopped in many Islamic countries, including Arabia, which he describes here.

Muscatt is a city in Arabia the Happy, which lies to the eastward of that kingdom, situated upon the Persian Gulf . . . It abounds with many useful and beneficial commodities, with several kinds of drugs, with balsam and myrrh, incense, . . . dates, gold, frankincense and pearl, and maintains a constant trade of rare and valuable goods to Persia, Egypt, Syria, the Indies, etc. . . .

These Arabians are very courteous in their deportment, and extreme civil to all strangers; they offer neither violence nor affront to any; and though they

are very tenacious of their own principles, and admirers of their own religion, yet do they never impose it upon any, nor are their morals leavened with such furious zeal, as to divest them of humanity, and a tender respect. A man may travel hundreds of miles in this country, and never meet with any abusive language, or any behavior that looks rude. And if you happen to be loaded with any money in your travels, you need no arms to defend your person, nor any guards to secure your purse; for you may sleep with it in your hands in the open fields, or lay it by you with safety as you repose yourself in the king's highway.

SOURCE: John Ovington, *A Voyage to Suratt in the Year 1689* (London: J. Tonson, 1696) 187, 192.

The Ottomans Lose the Initiative

In 1683, the Ottomans' last great invasion of central Europe had taken their forces to the gates of Vienna, where they were stopped by a multinational coalition of Christian powers led by the king of Poland. Then, suddenly and unexpectedly, the Christian powers seized the offensive, setting out to reconquer southeastern Europe from the Ottomans and push them back to Constantinople.

Although it was unable to expel the Ottomans from Europe, the multinational Christian coalition did recapture most of Hungary. In 1699, the Peace of Karlowitz transferred these lands from the Ottomans to the Austrian Habsburgs, sealing the failure of Islam's thousand-year quest to conquer Europe for the faith. The Habsburgs had stood for two centuries on the front lines opposing the Muslim advance, and their success in doing so accelerated the erosion of Ottoman power. But while the Safavid decline had led to collapse in only one century, the Ottoman slide took more than two, in part because of the Ottoman Empire's greater power and wealth, and in part because its multicultural, tolerant nature minimized internal dissatisfaction.

The Ottoman Empire begins to decline

The Ottoman position with respect to Europe had been deteriorating even before 1699. Within a half century after the conquest of Constantinople in 1453, which consolidated Islamic control over the profitable trade routes connecting Asia with Europe by land, the sea voyages of da Gama and Cabral had opened the Indian Ocean to Portuguese vessels. As European traders increasingly bypassed the Muslim-dominated land routes, Ottoman income from trade and taxes declined. Unwilling to accept this loss of income, in the sixteenth century the Ottomans competed vigorously against Portugal for Indian Ocean trade. But by the beginning of the seventeenth century, England and Holland had pushed both the Portuguese and the Ottomans aside (see "A European Visitor Describes Arabia"). The efforts of the energetic British and Dutch East India Companies drew commerce to the European sea routes across the Atlantic and Indian Oceans, and trade on the Muslim land routes across Eurasia decreased further. As Ottoman commerce became increasingly marginalized, the Ottoman sultan's cash flow fell steeply. These commercial conditions contributed greatly to the empire's economic decline.

Ottoman central authority grows weaker

This decline also stemmed from a gradual weakening of Ottoman central authority. In the seventeenth century the Ottomans, like the Safavids, had begun to seclude young princes within the harem, depriving them of the possibility of training in administration and politics. Sultans became less competent, while courtiers and provincial governors grew more powerful as greater authority was delegated to them.

Finally, the termination of Ottoman expansion with the Karlowitz treaty of 1699 accelerated the empire's decline. As there were no newly conquered lands for the Ottoman armies to loot, the absence of plunder produced riots in the army over pay and a breakdown of discipline in the sultan's elite corps of Janissaries. Individual generals who could satisfy their soldiers' desires for payment by diverting tax revenues gained power at the expense of Istanbul and undermined the empire's defenses at the same time.

Russia threatens Ottoman security

After 1699, Russia transformed itself from a potential area of Ottoman conquest into a grave threat to that empire's continued existence. Having taken Azov (*ah-ZOFF*) in the Crimea from the Turks in 1696, Russian Tsar Peter the Great modernized his forces and prepared for more extensive campaigns against them. While briefly fighting on Sweden's side in 1710–1711 in the Great Northern War, the Ottomans managed to trap Peter's army and force him to return Azov; in the next decades they reclaimed some of their earlier territorial losses. But Peter went on to defeat the Swedes in 1721, and Russia's emergence as Eastern Europe's dominant power eventually undercut the Ottoman position there.

The entertainment room of Topkapi Palace in Constantinople (Istanbul), with a large throne on the left from which the sultan could observe the proceedings.

In 1768, the Russians renewed their advance. After invading Ottoman territories in the Crimea and the Balkan Peninsula, and annihilating the Ottoman navy off the Turkish coast in 1770, they secured access to the Black Sea through the Treaty of Kuchuk Kainarji (*koo-CHOOK kā-NAR-jē*) in 1774. Two decades later, the Russians once again triumphed over the Ottomans, this time taking the entire northern Black Sea coast. All these losses troubled the sultan greatly, not only in themselves but for what they meant. With Russia clearly capable of conquering the Turks, the Ottomans could no longer think of European powers as their inferiors. By 1800 the combination of commercial decline, decentralization, military losses, and Russian pressure had reduced the onceimposing Ottoman Empire to a condition that would later lead a Russian tsar to label it "the sick man of Europe."

Ottoman Reform and Cultural Synthesis

The Ottomans' difficulties in competing with Europeans commercially and militarily forced the rulers to recognize that the empire had to change to survive. But early in the eighteenth century, many highly placed officials believed that the empire had nothing to learn from unbelievers. Ottoman deterioration, they felt, could be reversed only by strengthening Ottoman practices and insights. Battlefield defeats, the sultan's advisors told him, were caused by the failure of Ottoman armies to follow the time-tested techniques of the past; they had nothing to do with the superiority of European weaponry. In the face of such obstinacy, serious reform seemed impossible. Centuries of hostility had isolated the Ottomans from the West and left them largely ignorant of the scientific, technological, commercial, and industrial advances that had transformed Europe since the boyhood of Suleiman the Magnificent.

When Russia's naval victory in 1770 destroyed the entire Ottoman maritime high command, some saw a chance to reform the navy without entrenched resistance from admirals. In the 1780s, the Ottoman government imported Western experts to assist in creating modernized military units. Sultan Selim III (1789–1807), building on these beginnings and pressured by defeat in war with Austria and Russia in 1792, created a new European-style military force with modern weapons and training. But it never exceeded ten thousand soldiers at a time when the French were placing hundreds of thousands of men under arms. Once again the old army remained hostile to the new.

The Ottomans innovate by turning westward

But Selim's military schools for his modernized forces introduced Western knowledge into the empire, and his European military experts ended Istanbul's isolation from the West. During the nineteenth century, extensive reforms based on Western models changed the empire significantly. Contempt for western accomplishments gave way to grudging respect. European fashions in art, architecture, and clothing inspired Ottoman syntheses. Decentralization permitted healthy increases in local autonomy without compromising the Ottoman state as a whole. The empire once again appeared formidable and cohesive. It might be sick, but it was far from being dead.

Decentralization strengthens the Ottoman Empire

Wahhabism in Arabia

The Ottoman Empire controlled most but not all of southwestern Asia. Central Arabia lay outside its domain, but not outside the feelings of disgust and shame sweeping the Islamic world at the sight of Muslim weakness. In Arabia in the 1740s, a young religious scholar named Muhammad ibn abd-al Wahhab (*wah-HAHB*) concluded that all Islamic states, and especially the Ottoman Empire, had strayed from the path of strict observance of the teachings of the Prophet. In doing so they had incurred the wrath of Allah. Only by returning to this strict observance, al-Wahhab preached, could Islam triumph over unbelievers, whose ranks included (in his opinion) not only Jews, Christians, and polytheists, but also most Muslims.

Wahhabism transforms Arabia

Wahhabism, the austere, deeply puritanical brand of Islam preached by al-Wahhab and still practiced in Saudi Arabia today, contended that the sultan's authority derived neither from God nor from the *umma*; indeed, the sultan had no legitimate claim to power at all. Both the Ottoman religious elite and the entire state apparatus were un-Islamic by nature. Veneration of holy people, living or dead, was idolatry, as were pilgrimages to sacred shrines and gravesites. Sufi mysticism was reprehensible nonsense. The teachings of al-Wahhab, troubling to many Muslims, made him an outcast in Arabia until 1744, when he forged an alliance with the house of the Amir Ibn Saud (*sah-OOD*), who immediately established a small central Arabian state on Wahhabist principles.

Al-Wahhab died in 1791, but by the early nineteenth century Ibn Saud's grandson had taken Mecca and Medina and, following al-Wahhab's opposition to pilgrimages to gravesites, had destroyed all sacred Muslim tombs located there—including, to the horror of orthodox Muslims, the tomb of the Prophet himself. Wahhabist raids on Shi'ite holy sites in Iraq left faithful Shi'ites frantic and finally exhausted Ottoman patience. By 1818 Wahhabism was suppressed by force, but in the twentieth century it seized control of the Arabian Peninsula and created Saudi Arabia.

Medina in the 18th Century.

Chapter Review

Putting It in Perspective

By the end of the eighteenth century, the global balance of power and prosperity had clearly shifted away from the Muslim world. Islamic southern Asia, which had long drawn strength and wealth from its control of the land and sea routes connecting East and West, declined as European countries seized control of the Indian Ocean trade and then intruded, commercially and militarily, on southern Asia itself. Of southern Asia's three great Islamic empires, India's Mughal Empire was largely inoperative, Persia's Safavid empire was gone, and the multicultural Ottoman Empire was clearly in decline.

As the Muslims struggled to meet the Western challenge, two very different responses had emerged. One approach, pursued by the Ottoman Turks, was to adopt some Western ways, seeking to modernize their economic and military structures along European lines. The other response, pursued by Wahhabists and Shi'ites, was to reject Western ways and restore traditional Islamic practices, seeking to preserve and purify their faith so as to draw strength from their seventh-century religious roots.

Neither approach proved effective in slowing the Islamic world's political and economic deterioration. By the eighteenth century, the center of the global trade network had shifted from the Indian Ocean to the Atlantic, where Europe was deriving vast power and wealth from its connections with Africa and the Americas. These connections were both immensely profitable and exploitative, for in the Atlantic world, prosperity was increasingly linked with slave labor transferred by ship from Africa to the western hemisphere.

Reviewing Key Material

KEY CONCEPTS

Malabar Coast, 537	nawabs, 542
calico, 540	pantheism, 547
Urdu, 542	Twelfth Imam, 550
Marathas, 542	Wahhabism, 553

KEY PEOPLE

Siraj-ud-Daulah, 534	Joseph-François Dupleix, 543
Robert Clive, 535, 544	Shah Abbas I, 548
Vasco da Gama, 538	Shah Safi, 548
Pedro Alvares Cabral, 539	Shah Abbas II, 548
Afonso d'Albuquerque, 539	Peter the Great, 552
Philip II, 540	Selim III, 553
Aurangzeb, 542	Muhammad ibn abd-al
Muhammad Shah, 542	Wahhab, 553
Nadir Shah, 550	Ibn Saud, 553

ASK YOURSELF

1. How did control of the Indian Ocean trade benefit Islamic southern Asia? How were Europeans able to gain control of this trade?
2. Why were the Mughals unable to mount an effective resistance to Europeans in India?
3. Why were Muslims and Hindus able to coexist peacefully in Southeast Asia, but not in India? What were the implications for the two regions of these differences in coexistence?
4. How did Shi'ism shape the character of post-Safavid Persia?
5. How and why did Wahhabism develop as the dominant strain of Islam in Arabia?

GOING FURTHER

Alam, M. *The Crisis of Empire in Mughal North India.* 1986.

Bayly, C. A. *Indian Society and the Making of the British Empire.* 1988.

Bose, Sugata, and Ayeshia Jalal. *Modern South India.* 1998.

Boxer, Charles. *The Dutch Seaborne Empire.* 1989.

De Schweinitz, Karl. *The Rise and Fall of British India.* 1989.

Ikram, S. M. *History of Muslim Civilization in India and Pakistan.* 1989.

Inalcik, Halil, and Donald Quataert, eds. *An Economic and Social History of the Ottoman Empire, 1300–1914.* 1994.

Keay, John. *The Honourable Company: A History of the English East India Company.* 1991.

Keay, John. *India: A History.* 2000.

Legge, John D. *Indonesia.* 1965.

Morgan, David. *Medieval Persia, 1040–1797*. 1988.
Morris, Jan. *Pax Britannica*. 1980.
Palmer, A. *The Decline and Fall of the Ottoman Empire*. 1992.
Prakash, Om. *The Dutch East India Company and the Economy of Bengal, 1630–1720*. 1985.
Richards, John. *The Mughal Empire*. 1993.

Savory, Roger. *Iran Under the Safavids*. 1980.
Shaw, Stanford. *History of the Ottoman Empire and Modern Turkey*. 1976.
Spear, Percival. *Twilight of the Mughuls*. 1951.
Wheatcroft, A. *The Ottomans*. 1993.
Woodruff, Philip. *The Men Who Ruled India*. 1954.

Key Dates and Developments

ca. 1400	Iskandar founds the trading state of Malacca
1510	Portugal seizes Goa
1511	Portugal conquers Malacca
1600	Establishment of the British East India Company
1602	Establishment of the Dutch East India Company
ca. 1650	Mataram and Johore dominate Southeast Asian trade
1658	Dutch expel Portuguese from Indonesia
1664	Establishment of the French East India Company
1699	Peace of Karlowitz
1739	Nadir Shah sacks Delhi; the Mughals lose control
1740–1748	War of the Austrian Succession
1744	Alliance between al-Wahhab and Ibn Saud in Arabia
1747	Collapse of Safavid Iran
1756–1763	Seven Years War
1757	Clive's victory at Plassey
1774	Treaty of Kuchuk Kainarji
1779	Qajar rule in Iran
1792–1807	Sultan Selim III reforms the Ottoman Empire
1795	France conquers Holland; Britain moves into Southeast Asia
1818	Ottomans suppress Wahhabism in Arabia

Africa and the Atlantic Slave Trade, 1400–1800

Njinga Of Ndongo

In the fifteenth through nineteenth centuries, African realms were ravaged and transformed by the Atlantic slave trade. In this famous image Anna de Sousa Njinga, ruler of the realm of Ndongo, meets with Portuguese officials while using a servant as a throne to maintain her royal dignity.

In 1482, the central African kingdom of Kongo received some unexpected visitors. Portuguese sailors, searching for a route from the Atlantic to the Indian Ocean, sailed up the Congo River, and later met Kongo's king, known as the manikongo ("lord of Kongo"). Intrigued by his visitors' technology and goods, and perhaps hoping for their help against his local foes, the manikongo opened trade with the Portuguese. He even sent his royal prince to Lisbon to study their language and religion. These ties proved useful in 1491, when Portuguese forces, their banners emblazoned with Christian crosses, helped the manikongo crush a local revolt. Impressed by the power of the Europeans' faith—or at least by the power of their firearms—both the king and the prince soon converted to Christianity.

The prince, who later became Manikongo Nzinga Mbemba (*'n-ZIHN-gah 'm-BEM-bah*), also known by his Christian name as King Afonso I (1506–1543), eventually had reason to regret the Portuguese connection. Despite his devotion to the Christian faith, his people resisted conversion, and profit-minded Portuguese began to carry off Kongolese men to work as slaves on overseas sugar plantations. In 1526 he wrote to the king of Portugal, complaining that the slave traders "are taking every day our natives" and that "our country is being completely depopulated." But the slave trade continued to grow, as Afonso could not even stop his own subjects from trading captured Africans for European guns and goods.

The Kongo story is but one example of the transformation that began in coastal Africa during the fifteenth century. As Europeans arrived by sea, Africans often welcomed them, engaging at first in commercial and cultural exchanges based on mutual interests. But as Europeans started sugar plantations—first on islands off the African coast and later in American colonies—these exchanges increasingly centered on the capture and sale of slaves. For Europeans the slave trade, and the sale of goods produced in the Americas by African slaves, brought wealth, comfort, and growing global power. In Africa, however, the Atlantic slave trade fueled violence and greed, upset traditional economic patterns, disrupted family life, and transformed the political landscape. Although the sale of slaves also enriched and empowered some Africans, it condemned millions of others to brutal bondage.

Major Slave Destinations

Major Sources of Slaves

Africa's Diverse Societies

In the early fifteenth century, before the European intrusion, Africa's many cultures reflected its geographic diversity (Map 23.1). Most Africans, however, belonged either to urban cultures that centered on commerce and Islamic faith, or to village societies that focused on farming and worshipped local gods and spirits.

FOUNDATION MAP 23.1 Fifteenth Century African Connections

Africa's challenging environments often made maintaining connections difficult. Note, however, that in the fifteenth century, as in centuries past, Muslim trade routes connected Islamic West Asia and North Africa by land across the Sahara Desert with West Africa's wealthy kingdoms, and by sea with East Africa's commercial city-states. In the middle of that century, Portuguese voyages down Africa's west coast began to create new connections that eventually would link West, Central, and South Africa with Europe and the Americas. How were Africa's connections shaped by its climate and geography?

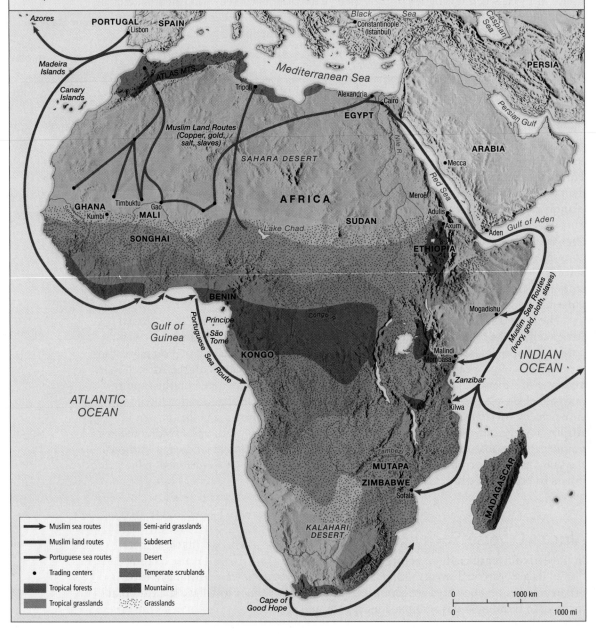

Legend:
- → Muslim sea routes
- — Muslim land routes
- → Portuguese sea routes
- • Trading centers
- Tropical forests
- Tropical grasslands
- Semi-arid grasslands
- Subdesert
- Desert
- Temperate scrublands
- Mountains
- Grasslands

North Africa was fully incorporated into the Islamic world, connected by sea with the Mediterranean basin and by camel caravan trade routes with West Africa across the Sahara Desert. Egypt, where farming flourished in the Nile Valley, was North Africa's most populous and prosperous realm, linked commercially and culturally with both Islamic West Asia and sub-Saharan Africa.

Trade and Islam link North Africa and West Africa

West Africa was partially Islamic. Its thriving cities were typically Muslim commercial and cultural centers, but most of its people lived in farming villages and worshipped diverse local deities. Mali, West Africa's most powerful kingdom, had long prospered from its rich gold mines and its role in the lucrative trans-Sahara trade.

East Africa's coast was lined with bustling commercial city-states that were deeply influenced by Islamic faith, Indian Ocean trade, and Swahili culture, which blended Arabic and African features. In the East African interior, however, farmers and hunters retained their traditional worship of spirits in nature, while to their north Ethiopians still practiced an ancient form of Christianity.

East African culture blends Arabic and African features

Central and South Africa, not yet influenced by either Muslims or Christians, were populated mostly by farmers and herders who worshipped various nature spirits and gods. These regions included numerous **stateless societies**—independent villages and federations of villages ruled by local patriarchs and chiefs—as well as several sizable states. One was the kingdom of Kongo, a prosperous agricultural realm near the mouth of the Congo River. Another was the kingdom of Zimbabwe (*zim-BAHB-wā*), south of the Zambezi (*zam-BĒ-zē*) River, which supplemented its cattle-based wealth with gold mined for sale along Africa's east coast.

Like their counterparts in Asia and Europe, then, fifteenth-century Africans lived in a broad range of societies. Some people were educated and cosmopolitan city-dwellers, connected by faith and commerce with others in distant lands. Most, however, were farmers and herders, unaware of the world beyond their own clans and villages. In the centuries that followed, numerous African societies were disrupted and transformed by the emergence of a global economy based on overseas commerce. Central to that commerce was traffic in human beings.

Slavery and the Slave Trade in Africa

Since ancient times, many societies throughout the world had practiced some form of **slavery**, an institution in which some people owned other human beings and used them for their labor. Often slaves were prisoners of war or victims of raids who were forced to serve their captors. Some were criminals or debtors placed in bondage to pay off crimes or debts; others were children sold into servitude by destitute and starving parents. Some slaves were domestics, or household servants; others worked on farms, in mines, or on construction projects building roads and other public works. All slaves, however, were at the mercy of their masters, who ranged from benevolent to inhumanly harsh.

In Africa, as elsewhere, slavery had emerged in ancient times, both in the Nile Valley and in the vast grasslands that stretched across the continent south of the Sahara Desert. With the opening of trans-Sahara trade routes by the second century C.E. and formation of Muslim trade networks five centuries later, African slaves became an important commercial commodity, not just in Africa but throughout much of the Islamic world (Chapter 13).

African Slavery

Some African societies measure wealth in slaves

Scholars disagree as to how widely slavery was practiced in Africa: some say it was extensive, and others claim it was relatively rare. Most likely the use of slaves in Africa, as in other parts of the world, was common in some regions and uncommon in others. By the tenth century, however, slavery was common enough in some parts of Africa that prosperous people measured their wealth in slaves—rather than in land or in livestock, which served as standards of wealth in other societies.

African slavery was often harsh, involving long hours of forced labor, but it was not necessarily a permanent condition. Slaves in Africa were typically prisoners of war, but debtors, widows, paupers, or outcasts might also be driven into bondage by social pressures or economic need. Slaves were often able to buy or earn their freedom; they could also marry free people and have free children. Although Africans were usually enslaved by a clan other than their own, slaves were not set apart by their appearance, since their skin color and other physical features differed little from those of their African owners.

The Trans-Sahara Slave Trade

The opening of caravan routes across the Sahara Desert by the second century C.E. added a new dimension to African slavery. Along with copper, gold, and salt, slaves became a central feature of the trans-Sahara trade. Merchants traveled from the Mediterranean world to purchase slaves in West Africa; then they transported them across the desert and sold them in North Africa.

Islamic connections expand the trans-Sahara slave trade

The Islamic conquest of North Africa in the seventh century expanded the trans-Sahara slave trade, incorporating it into the larger Muslim world that eventually extended from Spain to India. In time Muslim merchants transported as many as ten thousand African slaves a year to destinations in Islamic lands. The city-states of East Africa, once they came under Muslim control, also became involved in the trading of slaves.

African Slaves in the Islamic World

In Islamic lands the most common form of slavery was domestic servitude, in which slaves served in the homes of wealthy families, tending to their personal needs. The majority of these slaves were women, who typically performed household duties and sometimes also served as concubines. Widely perceived as exotic commodities purchased from distant lands, Africans were highly prized as slaves in many Islamic countries, often serving as a symbol of their owner's wealth and prestige.

Wealthy Muslims prize African women as domestic slaves

The lot of these enslaved Africans was difficult, but their servitude was not necessarily perpetual or hereditary. When a slave woman had a child by a Muslim master, for example, by Islamic tradition she and her child typically became free. Furthermore, since Islam discouraged the enslavement of Muslims, slaves could sometimes secure their own freedom, or at least that of their children, by adopting the Islamic faith.

Still, although Islam asserted the equality of all human beings before God, the presence in many Islamic lands of numerous black African slaves led some Muslims to link dark skin with servitude. One of those who did so was the writer and traveler Ibn Khaldun (*ib'n khahl-DOON*), who wrote in the fourteenth century that black Africans tended to accept servile status because they had a "low degree of humanity." Depicting slaves as less than human no doubt helped many Muslims—and later many Christians—to sidestep religious teachings telling them to treat fellow humans with dignity and respect.

But slavery in the Muslim world was not based mainly on skin color. In addition to enslaving Africans, Muslims also enslaved hundreds of thousands of captives from among the Mediterranean peoples of Southern Europe and the Slavic peoples of Russia and Eastern Europe. Indeed, over the centuries, so many Slavs were captured and sold into servitude that the word *slave* itself probably derives from the ethnic term *Slav*.

Muslims import slaves from Europe and Russia

By the fifteenth century, commerce in African slaves was long established. Particularly in West Africa, rulers and traders often acquired captives from local people or neighboring lands, then sold them to Muslim merchants for transport to faraway places. So accustomed were West Africans to such commerce that their leaders and merchants did not hesitate to sell slaves to Europeans, who in the mid-fifteenth century began to appear in sailing ships along the West African coast.

The Atlantic Slave Trade

The European visitors who first arrived in West Africa did not come to purchase slaves. The Atlantic slave trade, like the European conquest of the Americas (Chapter 19), was an unforeseen outgrowth of European efforts to discover an all-water trade route from Western Europe to southern and eastern Asia.

Portuguese slave trading post at El Mina on the Gulf of Guinea.

The Africans and the Portuguese

In the early fifteenth century, decades before Europeans arrived in the Americas, the Portuguese had started sailing south along the coast of Africa in search of a sea route to Asia. As they sailed farther with each successive voyage, they set up trading posts along the coast to do business with Africans. By mid-century, West African merchants were trading their gold, salt, ivory, and pepper for such European items as firearms, cloth, ironware, and copper goods. By the 1480s, African kingdoms along the Gulf of Guinea (*GIH-nē*) and in west central Africa had likewise opened trade with the Portuguese. Thus, by 1497–1498, when Portugal's Vasco da Gama finally sailed all the way around the tip of Africa and northeast to India, various peoples along Africa's coast had established contact with visitors from Europe.

At first, eager to bypass the Muslim merchants who controlled the trans-Sahara trade, West Africans gladly did business with the newcomers who arrived by sea. These newcomers brought attractive new goods, including guns, textiles, and tools, and frequently offered better terms than the Muslim overland traders. Pleased to have a

Africans trade with Portuguese for new goods and guns

new outlet for their products, and above all to get European firearms, African leaders bartered with the Portuguese and welcomed their trading posts.

The commerce thus created, at least in the beginning, appears to have been based on mutual interest and respect, each side treating the other as a valued trading partner. But as the coastal commerce came to center increasingly on African slaves, this mutual interest and respect began to disappear.

Sugar and the Slave Trade

Almost from the outset the Portuguese trafficked in slaves, shipping their first human cargoes from West Africa in the early 1440s. These newest victims of the ancient trade came to be used, not as household servants like most slaves sent to Muslim lands, but as field laborers on sugar plantations.

Slave plantations support growing sugar trade

By this time demand for sugar was increasing rapidly. Popularized in the Christian West through contacts with Muslims during the crusades and Spanish Reconquista (Chapter 16), sugar provided huge profits to its suppliers. In the fourteenth and fifteenth centuries, sugar cultivation was attempted in Spain and Portugal and on Mediterranean islands. But sugar cane, which requires vast amounts of sunshine and water, a 12-month growing season, and intensive labor, was not well suited to Europe. So in the latter half of the fifteenth century, profit-minded Portuguese set up sugar plantations off the African coast, on tropical islands such as Madeira (*mah-DĀ-rah*), São Tomé (*SOU'n too-MĀ*) and Principe (*PRĒN-sē-pē*) (Map 23.1). To work these plantations they used African slaves, who were accustomed to living and working in a very hot climate.

It was not until the sixteenth century, however, with the European colonization of the Americas, that the Atlantic slave trade really took off. The Portuguese colony of Brazil, with abundant sunshine and rainfall, proved an ideal place to grow sugar cane, and thousands of workers were needed to cultivate, harvest, and process it. Portugal, with a small population and its own labor shortage, simply could not supply enough workers to fill the growing need. Portuguese paupers and convicts sent to Brazil to work on sugar plantations usually perished quickly due to heat, humidity, and tropical diseases. Efforts to use Amerinds as laborers likewise proved futile, as they perished in vast numbers from diseases such as smallpox carried by Europeans (Chapter 19).

Sugar plantation, Brazil.

But Africans were accustomed to hot climates and resistant to tropical diseases, so the Portuguese soon began transporting large numbers of them from the west coast of Africa to Brazil's sugar plantations. Before long West Africa, the Gulf of Guinea coast, and the Congo River region had all become major sources of slaves. In the 1570s Portugal built a large trading port named Luanda (*loo-AHN-duh*) a few hundred miles south of the Congo River, establishing there a colony that came to be called Angola. By the 1600s Angola had become a major source of slaves, and slaves had become the main item of commerce on the West African coast.

Brazilian sugar plantations import African slaves

The Atlantic Trading System

Portugal's domination of the slave trade did not last. As other Europeans saw the huge profits supplied by slave-grown sugar, they too began to get into the act. By the seventeenth century, the Spanish, French, English, and Dutch had set up sugar plantations on

Caribbean islands, which, like Brazil, had the abundant sunshine and rainfall needed to grow sugar. At first the Portuguese supplied these plantations with most of their African slaves. After 1650, however, the English and the Dutch, and later the French, also played key roles in shipping slaves.

The Atlantic commerce that developed has been described as a **triangular trade** (Map 23.2). From bustling European ports such as Lisbon, Nantes, Amsterdam, and Liverpool, ships sailed to Africa bearing guns and textiles, and sometimes also alcohol and tobacco products. There, at coastal trading posts, traders aboard the European ships exchanged these goods for slaves. Then the ships, callously laden with human cargo, crossed the Atlantic to the slave centers of the Americas. There the captives were sold and the ships were loaded with goods—such as sugar, coffee, tobacco, and rum (an alcoholic liquor distilled from sugar cane)—produced in the Americas by slaves. Finally the traders returned to Europe, where they sold these goods at huge profit, a portion of

Triangular trade links Europe, Africa, and the Americas

Map 23.2 The Atlantic Slave Trade in the Sixteenth Through Eighteenth Centuries

In the sixteenth through eighteenth centuries, European merchants developed a lucrative Atlantic trading system centered on African slaves. Notice that Europeans shipped guns and other products to Africa, traded them there for slaves, then transported the slaves to the Americas to produce sugar, coffee, tobacco, and other goods, which were sold back to Europe at immense profits. Why were slaves so central to this commerce? How did this commerce contribute to Western Europe's wealth and power?

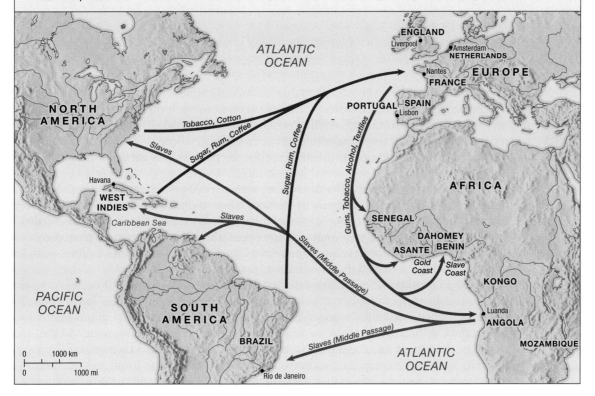

which could be used to buy goods for their next trading trip to Africa. This commerce was controlled mainly by Europeans, who supplied the ships and pocketed most of the profits, but many African slave traders profited as well.

In the seventeenth and eighteenth centuries, the slave trade exploded. Overall volume increased exponentially, from about 300,000 captives shipped from Africa during the 1500s, to more than six million in the 1700s. Although sugar was the main commodity produced by slave labor, African slaves also worked in silver and gold mines and on coffee plantations in Spain's American empire, and on tobacco (and later cotton) plantations in England's North American colonies. By the time the slave trade was curtailed in the nineteenth century, an estimated eleven to twelve million people had been shipped as slaves from Africa to the Americas, and another one to two million had died along the way. More than four million Africans went to Brazil, and another six million to destinations in the Caribbean. About half a million (less than five percent) went to English North America, which would later become the United States.

The Capture and Transport of Slaves

The victims of these slaving ventures suffered a fate that defies imagination. Their hardships began with their capture in Africa, increased during their transport to the coast, and intensified further with their sale to Europeans and shipment across the Atlantic.

African rulers trade captives for wealth and guns

Some of the captives were already slaves who had been sold by their African masters; others were people seized by slave hunters hired by African merchants or local rulers. Most, however, were probably captured soldiers who had been enslaved as prisoners during African wars. African rulers, who generally sought to avoid enslaving and selling their own people, instead enslaved and sold their captive prisoners to acquire wealth and guns.

Captives typically were shackled and chained together, then marched to the coast in long processions. Many either died of exhaustion or took their own lives on the way; others arrived at coastal trading posts dispirited, famished, and diseased. Since relatively few Europeans traveled into Africa's interior, where tropical heat and diseases threatened their lives, this first part of the process was carried out mostly by Africans.

Loading plan for a slave ship

Once the captives reached the coast they were herded naked into wooden cages, examined to determine if they were fit for hard labor, and then sold to Europeans, who branded them with hot irons and crowded them on ships for transport overseas. As the middle part of their three-part journey—from Africa's interior to its coast, from there across the sea to the Americas, and from American ports to plantations or mines—this oceanic crossing was called the **Middle Passage** (Map 23.2).

Packed into ships in layers like freight, with scarce room to move or even sit up, as many as six hundred captives might be carried in a vessel barely 100 feet long. Their skin was rubbed raw by the wooden planks on which they lay and the chains that bound them during the three- to six-week voyage. The air stank with sweat and the stench of the tubs of urine and excrement into which they relieved themselves. Typically between 10 and 20 percent of the captives died on the trip, some from malnutrition, some from suffocation, some from the stifling heat, and some from the diseases that spread unchecked among them. Ship captains, who routinely overcrowded their vessels to ensure a big profit despite the high death toll, callously disposed of corpses on the way by casting them overboard. Some captives also jumped overboard, ending their lives to escape their unbearable fate.

African Slaves in the Americas

Slave market in Rio de Janeiro, Brazil.

When survivors of the Middle Passage arrived in the New World, their situation scarcely improved. At slave markets in port towns such as Havana in the West Indies or Rio de Janeiro in Brazil, merchants and plantation owners poked and prodded the Africans, carefully inspecting them as if they were farm animals up for sale. Once purchased, the slaves were transported to plantations or mines, where they were subjected to relentless hard labor and often physical abuse.

In contrast to the slaves in Islamic lands, many of whom were women, most of the Africans shipped across the Atlantic Ocean were men. Selected for their size and strength, the field slaves who labored on sugar plantations were often simply worked to death. Most of them died within five or six years, usually from exhaustion or disease, but sometimes also from beatings inflicted by their masters. Rebellions by slaves were typically put down with European firearms, and escape attempts by slaves also frequently proved futile, since runaways were easily recognized as slaves because of their black skin.

In spite of all these hardships, Africans endured in the Americas. On plantations they formed their own communities, supporting each other and adapting their African cultures to their new surroundings. When compelled by their owners to adopt Christianity, for example, slaves found ways to make this religion their own. They incorporated African spiritualism, music, and dance into their Christian worship, and frequently assigned to Christian saints some traits of African gods. Some runaway slaves, often called **maroons**, fled to the wilderness and established independent communities, where they lived by farming and hunting, maintained many African customs, and forcibly resisted recapture. Despite oppression and abuse, transplanted Africans and their descendants, later collectively called the **African diaspora**, managed not only to adapt to their new homelands but also to create their own new cultures (Chapter 30).

Africans adapt their cultures to life in the Americas

Riches, Race, and Racism

Slavery and the slave trade brought substantial economic benefits to Europe. Slave labor helped exploit the abundant resources of Europe's American colonies, thereby contributing vastly to Europe's wealth and power. Indeed, cheap raw cotton supplied by slave plantations later helped support an Industrial Revolution that catapulted Western Europe to world domination (Chapter 27).

African slavery in the Americas also enabled many Europeans to indulge in new pleasures and comforts. Thanks largely to the Atlantic trading system, middle class Europeans were increasingly able to enjoy such commodities as sugar, coffee, tobacco products, and comfortable cotton clothing—undeterred by the fact that they were supplied through the suffering of African slaves.

To rationalize the inhuman treatment of so many millions of people, many Europeans and European Americans depicted Africans as inferior beings, or even as a subhuman species. Africans were portrayed as primitive pagans who had little capacity for government, education, or advancement, and who willingly accepted slavery because they lacked intellect and ambition. Some Europeans even asserted that the captives were no worse off as slaves than they had been as villagers in their native Africa.

In time such attitudes, along with encounters among diverse cultures fostered by the opening of the Atlantic, nurtured the notion of **race**. This concept divided human beings into categories called "races," based on external appearance, especially skin color. Like earlier notions of nobility and caste, race had little biological basis; it rested instead on arbitrary classifications that some groups used to assert their superiority over others. The result was the rise of **racism**, the belief that race was the main determinant of human traits and abilities, with white Europeans often claiming a greater capacity than others for intellectual and cultural advancement. In the nineteenth century, racial thinkers codified these concepts into an elaborate pseudo-scientific system, later used by German Nazis and others to rationalize the suppression and destruction of people they deemed undesirable.

Race reinforces European suppression of Africans in America

Long before these developments, however, the Atlantic slave trade had come to be based on race and rationalized by racism. Race reinforced the enduring suppression of Africans in the Americas, where the parents' slave status was almost always inherited by their children, dooming each new generation to live and die in bondage. And even when some Africans in the Americas managed to gain their freedom, they were still often targets of racial discrimination. The racial slavery that emerged in the Americas was thus more harsh and dehumanizing than the traditional slavery long practiced in Africa and the Islamic world.

The Transformation of Africa

The Atlantic slave trade's impact on Africa varied from place to place. The coastal areas where the commerce was conducted, and the nearby lands where the slaves were captured, were the regions most directly affected. Because of their proximity to the Americas, the states of West Africa and the Guinea Coast, as well as the central African regions of Kongo and Angola, supplied the largest number of slaves. Eventually, as these areas were depleted of able-bodied men, by the nineteenth century even East Africa became a source of captive laborers bound for the Americas.

Guns and trade shift power from Africa's interior to its coast

In the sixteenth through eighteenth centuries, as Africa's coastal kingdoms gained weapons and riches from their commerce with Europe, power and wealth shifted away from the continent's interior to its seaboard. This change was especially apparent in West Africa, where the cities and states of the interior, whose wealth depended on the trans-Sahara trade, declined as commerce shifted from the Sahara to the Atlantic. But the impact of the Atlantic trade was also felt elsewhere in Africa. New African powers emerged, their wealth enhanced by the sale of slaves and their might by guns acquired from Europeans in exchange. European countries also set up colonies on the African coast. By the nineteenth century, when the slave trade was outlawed, many parts of Africa had been politically and economically transformed.

The Reorientation of West Africa

The West African interior, made up mostly of extensive grasslands stretching south from the Sahara Desert, had long been one of Africa's wealthiest regions. From the thirteenth through fifteenth centuries, the kingdom of Mali had dominated the grasslands of the western Sudan, along the Senegal (*SEN-ih-gahl*) and upper Niger (*NĪ-jur*) rivers (Map 23.1). Profiting from the trans-Sahara caravan trade in gold, salt, ivory, and slaves, and from the resulting commercial and cultural connections with the rest of the Islamic world, Mali had amassed extensive power and prosperity (Chapter 13).

In the centuries that followed, however, West Africans increasingly sold such commodities to European traders who arrived by sea, rather than to Muslim merchants who came across the desert in camel caravans. The consequent growth of the shore trade, and the corresponding decline of the overland trade, reoriented West Africa's economic focus and shifted its political balance of power from the interior to the Atlantic and Gulf of Guinea coasts.

The city of Timbuktu, a center of trans-Sahara trade.

THE SONGHAI AND KANEM-BORNU EMPIRES. The transformation of West Africa began with the rise and fall of Songhai (*SAWN-GĪ*), a newly emergent regional power that conquered the declining Mali kingdom in the fifteenth century (Map 23.3). Armed with a swift horse cavalry and a fleet of river boats, a Songhai ruler named Sonni Ali (*saw-NĒ ah-LĒ*), who reigned from 1464 to 1492, overran Mali and brought under his control the whole upper Niger River region. His successor Askia Muhammad al-Turi (*ah-SKĒ-ah moo-HAH-muhd ahl-TOO-rē*), reigning from 1493 to 1528 as Muhammad I Askia, further expanded the Songhai Empire. Under him it became a vast, prosperous realm that extended well over a thousand miles from east to west, controlling the region's gold and salt mines and its trans-Sahara trade. Intent on imposing his Islamic faith, Askia appointed Arab Muslims as judges and officials, imported Islamic scholars and lawyers, and used his immense treasury to build a multitude of mosques.

In the early sixteenth century, under Askia's capable leadership, the great Songhai Empire was West Africa's largest, wealthiest, and mightiest state. It had strong armies, stable institutions, a cosmopolitan culture, and a flourishing trade in gold, salt, and slaves. To those who dwelt or did business in its thriving cities, it would hardly have seemed possible that Songhai's days were numbered.

Songhai Empire connects much of West Africa

But numbered they were. The empire's strength began to decline after 1528, when Askia Muhammad al-Turi was murdered by one of his sons. The state was weakened by further succession struggles, often involving intrigues and assassinations, and by the steady shift of trade from the Sahara to the coast. Stability was restored for a while in mid-century, but in the 1580s a new succession crisis led to full-fledged civil war.

Meanwhile, Morocco, an independent Muslim realm on Africa's northwest coast fortified by commercial connections with nearby Spain and Portugal, sought to expand its share of the trans-Sahara trade. Armed with European cannons and firearms, and aided by Spanish and Portuguese mercenary soldiers, the Moroccans took advantage of Songhai's turmoil. In 1591 they crossed the desert with a vast camel caravan and battled the Songhai army at Tondibi (*tawn-DĒ-bē*), a town north of Gao, the Songhai capital. Although outnumbered ten-to-one, the Moroccans used their guns to great advantage. They crushed the Songhai forces, then sacked the great cities of Gao and Timbuktu, reducing the Songhai Empire to a modest domain.

Morocco battles Songhai for trans-Sahara trade

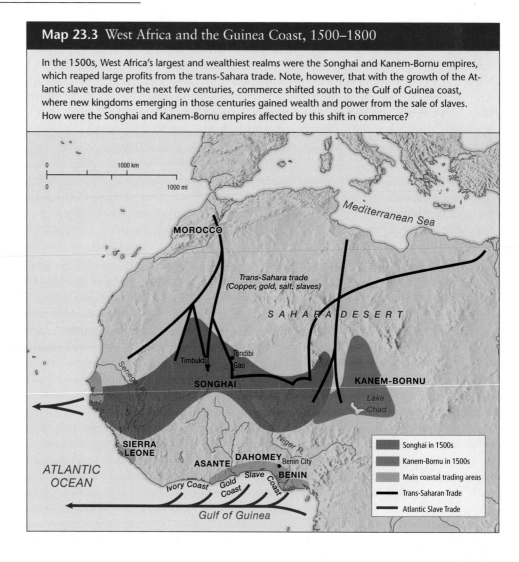

Map 23.3 West Africa and the Guinea Coast, 1500–1800

In the 1500s, West Africa's largest and wealthiest realms were the Songhai and Kanem-Bornu empires, which reaped large profits from the trans-Sahara trade. Note, however, that with the growth of the Atlantic slave trade over the next few centuries, commerce shifted south to the Gulf of Guinea coast, where new kingdoms emerging in those centuries gained wealth and power from the sale of slaves. How were the Songhai and Kanem-Bornu empires affected by this shift in commerce?

Songhai declines as trading patterns shift

Although Songhai's fall was not directly caused by the growth of the Atlantic slave trade, the shift in trade patterns benefited coastal countries such as Morocco, while undermining the once-vibrant economy of the West African interior. Over the next few centuries, as the interior's commerce further declined, its urban centers gradually turned into obscure backwaters. By the 1800s, when French explorers and soldiers arrived in the dusty remnants of these once-great cities, the tales they heard of bygone empires with fabulous wealth and heroic kings seemed too fantastic to believe.

Idris Alawma unites Kanem-Bornu and expands Islam's role

As Songhai declined, new regional powers arose. To the east, in the region around Lake Chad, a dynamic Muslim warrior named Idris Alawma (*id-RĒS ah-LAW-mah*), aided by firearms and a camel cavalry, united the local kingdoms of Kanem (*KAH-nem*) and Bornu (*BOR-noo*) into a modest empire, which he ruled from around 1570 to the early 1600s. Taking advantage of Songhai's decline, he enhanced the wealth of his realm by expanding its participation in the trans-Saharan trade. A devout Muslim, he also took great pains to implant his faith, building numerous mosques, replacing local customs and laws with Islamic courts and judges, and vigorously combating adultery and obscenity.

The Kanem-Bornu Empire survived its founder for almost a century. Then, around 1700, weak rulers and extended famine combined to reduce its power. Like Songhai before it, Kanem-Bornu also suffered from the declining importance of the trans-Saharan trade, as commerce shifted southward from the Sahara to the Gulf of Guinea Coast, which increasingly served as a source of goods and slaves for the Atlantic trade.

THE SLAVE TRADE'S IMPACT ON THE GUINEA COAST. South of Songhai, near the Guinea Coast, the sweeping grasslands of the western Sudan give way to dense tropical forests. This region's dominant power, largely untouched by outside influence until the Portuguese arrived in 1485, was the kingdom of Benin (*beh-NĒN*), centered on the mouth of the Niger River (Map 23.3). The kingdom's magnificent capital, known today as Benin City, had miles of walls and moats, a sumptuous palace, guilds of artisans and artists, and rows of splendid houses along wide clean streets that were virtually free of clutter and crime. Unchallenged by Islam, whose reach had not extended that far south, the oba (or king) of Benin also served as head of the local religion; by the 1600s the obas were even deemed by their people to have supernatural powers. Using their exceptional authority, they sought to protect their realm from European exploitation, restricting but not fully banning the overseas slave trade. Although Benin subsequently declined, the hundreds of exquisite iron, ivory, brass, and bronze sculptures and plaques that it left behind testify both to its cultural wealth and to the remarkable skill of its artisans and artists.

Benin rulers resist European exploitation

Bronze sculpture from Benin.

New African powers emerge from the Guinea Coast trade

To the west of Benin, along the Gulf of Guinea, were lands that Europeans dubbed the Slave Coast, Gold Coast, and Ivory Coast, based on their principal exports. In the seventeenth and eighteenth centuries, some African kingdoms in this region achieved great wealth and power, largely by trading African slaves, gold, and ivory for European firearms. Especially prominent were Asante (*ah-SAHN-tā*), which derived great wealth both from its goldfields and from the sale of slaves, and Dahomey (*dah-HŌ-mē*), whose powerful armies were equipped with muskets and fortified by formidable women who served as palace guards and soldiers.

These riches and weapons then enabled the rulers to expand their own realms and acquire more slaves, establishing a ruthless but very effective cycle. To hold their own, neighboring states had little choice but to get their own guns by trafficking in slaves. As a result, although trade with Europe brought wealth and power to some African kingdoms on the Guinea Coast, those who reaped the greatest rewards were the ones most willing to collaborate with Europeans by selling African people into bondage.

The Depopulation of Central Africa

Central Africa, a hot, humid region encompassing both the Congo River basin's equatorial rain forests and the great tropical grasslands to their south, had little contact with the larger world prior to the 1480s. Central African people were mostly farmers, living mainly in small states and stateless societies centered on villages and clans, although one large state, the Kongo Kingdom (Map 23.4), had emerged by the fourteenth century. The

Map 23.4 West Central Africa and the Slave Trade in the Fifteenth Through Eighteenth Centuries

In the fifteenth through eighteenth centuries, West Central Africa served as a major source of slaves bound to work on sugar plantations, first on offshore islands such as Principe and São Tomé, and later on plantations in the Americas. Note that millions of Africans were captured in the interior, transported to the coast in chains, and then crammed into ships and brutally transported across the Atlantic. Why did some Africans capture and sell other Africans into slavery?

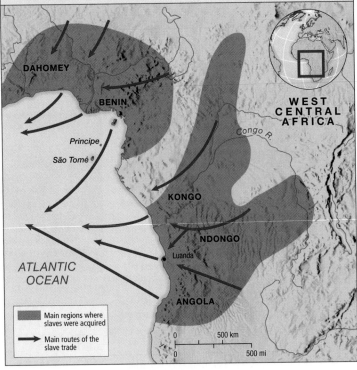

European intrusion, which began with the arrival of Portuguese explorers in the last few decades of the fifteenth century, in time had a devastating impact on the entire region, especially on the areas closest to the Atlantic coast.

CHRISTIANITY, SLAVERY, AND THE KONGO KINGDOM. Of all the peoples of Africa, none received Europeans more warmly than those in the Kongo Kingdom, and none suffered more severely for their efforts. Prior to 1482, this central African realm was largely isolated from the outside world, unaware that Europe even existed. In that year, however, Portuguese navigator Diogo Cão (*dē-Ō-gō COW*), also called Diogo Cam, searching for a waterway connecting the Atlantic and Indian Oceans, sailed up the Congo River.

As related at the outset of this chapter, the Kongolese king, known as the manikongo, established good relations with the Portuguese, and the Kongo's crown prince even went to Lisbon to learn Portuguese ways. After returning to Kongo he became a Christian and, as King Afonso I (1506–1543), the new manikongo sought to convert his people to the Catholic faith. With firearms provided by his Portuguese friends, he also endeavored to increase his power and expand his kingdom.

In the long run his efforts failed. Although many members of the Kongo elite embraced the new religion, most Kongolese people continued to worship their traditional gods. Furthermore, the Portuguese traders who came to Kongo were more interested in profiting from commerce than in spreading their faith. As Kongo lacked gold and other valuable trade goods, they turned their attention mainly to procuring slaves.

Kongo king embraces Portuguese commerce and Christianity

At first Afonso himself provided the slaves, most of whom were prisoners captured in battles won by using guns supplied by the Portuguese. In time, however, the Portuguese began bypassing Afonso, buying slaves from Kongolese warlords and conducting slave raids that carried off Kongolese subjects. Turning against the slave trade, in 1526 the Christian manikongo wrote to the king of Portugal, asking for help in stopping the enslavement of the Kongolese people (see "Excerpts of Letters from the King of Kongo to the King of Portugal").

Portuguese buy slaves from warlords, bypassing manikongo

Document 23.1 Excerpts of Letters from the King of Kongo to the King of Portugal

In 1526 the king of Kongo, Nzinga Mbemba, also known by his Christian name as Afonso I, wrote several letters to the king of Portugal asking for help in suppressing the slave trade, which was destroying his kingdom. The excerpts below provide a poignant African perspective on the impact of the slave trade and the behaviors of Europeans and Africans involved in this enterprise.

Sir, Your Highness should know how our Kingdom is being lost in so many ways . . . , since this is caused by the excessive freedom given by your agents and officials to the men and merchants who are allowed to come to this Kingdom . . . , doing a great harm not only to the service of God, but the security and peace of our Kingdoms and State as well.

And we cannot reckon how great the damage is, since the mentioned merchants are taking every day our natives, sons of the land and the sons of our noblemen and vassals and our relatives, because the thieves and men of bad conscience grab them wishing to have the things and wares of this Kingdom which they are ambitious of; they grab them and get them to be sold; and so great, Sir, is the corruption and licentiousness that our country is being completely depopulated. . . . That is why we beg of Your Highness to help and assist us in this matter . . . , because it is our will that in these Kingdoms there should not be any trade of slaves nor outlet for them. . . .

Moreover, Sir, in our Kingdoms there is another great inconvenience which is of little service to God, and this is that many of our people, keenly desirous as they are of the wares and things of your Kingdoms, which are brought here by your people, and in order to satisfy their voracious appetite, seize many of our people . . . , and take them to be sold to the white men who are in our Kingdoms. . . .

And as soon as they are taken by the white men they are immediately ironed and branded with fire, and when they are carried to be embarked, if they are caught by our guards' men the whites allege that they have bought them but they cannot say from whom, so that it is our duty to do justice and to restore to the freemen their freedom, but it cannot be done if your subjects feel offended, as they claim to be. . . .

SOURCE: *An African Voice of Protest: Letters to the King of Portugal*, compiled by Sara Lyons Watts. http://www.wfu.edu/~watts/w04_Africa.html

Disillusioned with the Portuguese, Afonso also restricted the activities of Christian missionaries, whom he had initially welcomed. But the traffic in slaves continued, largely because neither Afonso nor his successors could prevent their people from dealing directly with the Europeans. By the century's end, as both their subordinates and their enemies openly defied them, the manikongos had clearly lost much of their clout.

In the next century, desperate to free themselves from Portugal's domination, the manikongos allied themselves with the Dutch, who were beginning to move in on the African trade. In 1665, however, the Portuguese defeated the Kongo forces and beheaded the manikongo. After that, the once-powerful Kongo Kingdom steadily disintegrated into smaller domains, mostly controlled by African warlords who were willing to cooperate with the Portuguese. By that time, however, the bulk of the slave trade had shifted to the south, where Portugal had created a colony called Angola.

THE ANGOLA SLAVE COLONY. To the south of the Kongo Kingdom, among a people called the Mbundu (*'m-BOON-doo*), a centralized state known as Ndongo (*'n-DAWN-gō*)

King of Kongo receives Dutch ambassadors.

emerged in the late fifteenth century. Since its ruler was called the *ngola* (*'n-GAW-lah*), the Portuguese, who were beginning to arrive in the region, referred to it as Angola.

Portuguese start a slave colony called Angola

In the sixteenth century this realm was raided regularly by intruders from Kongo, who carried off the Mbundu as slaves and sold them to Portuguese traders. In time, however, as Brazil's sugar fields expanded and the demand for slave labor grew, the Portuguese increasingly sought to secure new sources of slaves. In 1571 they decided to make Angola their colony, and four years later, on its coast, they founded the port of Luanda.

Njinga of Ndongo resists European domination

But Portuguese attempts to exploit the interior met with fierce opposition. Beginning in the 1620s, Anna de Sousa Njinga (*AH-na duh SOO-suh 'n-JIHN-gah*) emerged as the ruler of Ndongo, after her father was deposed as king. Since the realm had no experience with female monarchs, Njinga of Ndongo, as she is commonly called, took on the attributes of a king (see page 556). She dressed as a man, commanded her armies in combat, and reportedly even traveled with her own set of male concubines, clothed as women to stress her kingly status. She also engaged in the slave trade, using it to equip her troops with European firearms, and stubbornly fought Portugal's efforts at colonial expansion. In these struggles she allied for a time with the Dutch, who temporarily gained control of Luanda from 1641 until 1648.

Despite Njinga's resistance, however, the Portuguese ultimately prevailed. First they drove out the Dutch, and then, in the 1650s, they forced Njinga to sign a treaty granting Christian missionaries access to her lands. After her death in 1663, the Portuguese extended their control over the interior, finally conquering the Kingdom of Ndongo in 1683.

Angola's population depleted by slave trade

The result was catastrophic for the Mbundu peoples. Angola emerged as Portugal's primary source of servile labor, supplying an estimated three million slaves, most of them taken to Brazil. These captives constituted more than a quarter of all the slaves shipped across the Atlantic during the duration of the slave trade. Countless Mbundu villages were pillaged of their young males; not until the nineteenth century did the region's population recover. Angola remained under Portuguese rule until 1975.

The Contest for East Africa

East African cities thrive on Indian Ocean commerce

On the other side of the African continent, the situation differed substantially (Map 23.5). Africa's east coast had long been dominated by prosperous Swahili city-states such as Mogadishu (*mo-gah-DE-shoo*), Mombasa (*mōm-BAH-sah*), Zanzibar, and Kilwa. Built on coastal islands and peninsulas, these thriving commercial cities controlled the nearby mainland and carried on a lucrative Indian Ocean trade with Arabia, Persia, and India. Although the city-states had not united into a strong political empire, each exercised considerable commercial power, trading local products such as ivory, ebony, leopard skins, and cotton for porcelains, glassware, pottery, and cloth from the east. The coastal cities also dealt in slaves, brought to them from the interior, and gold, mined in southern Africa and transported up the coast to Kilwa, which by the fifteenth century had emerged as the wealthiest and grandest of the Swahili states.

COMMERCE, CHRISTIANITY, CONFLICTS, AND COLONIES. At first East Africa was little affected by the Atlantic trade. Although Vasco da Gama had stopped there on his way to India in 1498, the Portuguese who followed him in the next few centuries showed

View of Kilwa.

little interest in using this region as a source of slaves for the Americas. The Americas, after all, were a long way from East Africa, which already had a thriving Indian Ocean trade that the Portuguese were eager to exploit. Not until the nineteenth century, when the slave trade was banned and curtailed by ships that patrolled the West African coast, would captives from East Africa be shipped in large numbers to the Western Hemisphere (Chapter 30).

The European impact on East Africa was nonetheless profound. In the early 1500s, in an effort both to expand Christianity and to gain control of the Indian Ocean trade, the Portuguese bombarded the Swahili ports, subjected some of them to tribute, and eventually erected imposing stone fortresses at places such as Kilwa and Mombasa. A substantial part of the coastal trade thus temporarily fell under Portuguese domination.

Portuguese domination, however, did little to advance either Christianity or commerce in East Africa. The Swahili cities, managed by Muslims for centuries, steadfastly refused to adopt the Christian faith. Offended, no doubt, by the Christian militancy and domineering trade policies of the Portuguese, many Africans in the interior refused to do business with them. Shipping and commerce steadily dwindled until 1698, when Arab raiders from Oman in eastern Arabia combined with local Africans to drive out the Portuguese. The Omani Arabs then established a thriving commercial center, complete with flourishing slave markets, on the island of Zanzibar. This center then dominated East African trade until the mid-nineteenth century, eventually furnishing numerous captives for the overseas slave trade.

In southeast Africa, the main attraction for the outsiders was the gold that had long been mined in the kingdom of Zimbabwe, located in the African interior south of the Zambezi River (Map 23.5). In the fifteenth century that kingdom had split apart, with much of it eventually coming under the control of a series of rulers who took the title Mwene Mutapa ('m-WĀ-nā muh-TAH-pah), meaning "master conqueror." In time they established a federation

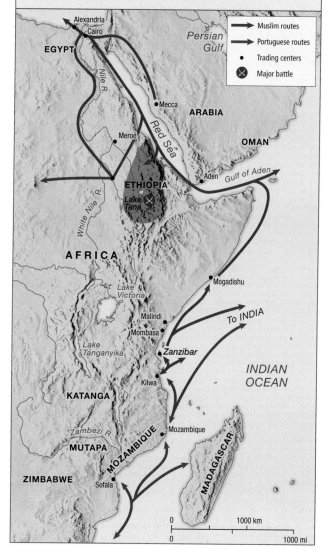

Map 23.5 East African Commerce and Connections, 1500–1800

For centuries, East Africa's coastal city-states were linked with southern Asia, culturally and commercially, by Muslim sea routes. Note, however, that in the sixteenth and seventeenth centuries, the Portuguese forcefully intruded in this region, subjecting some of the city-states to tribute, establishing connections with Christian Ethiopia, and eventually creating in southeast Africa a colony called Mozambique. How did the Portuguese intrusion affect East African commerce? How did East Africans respond to the Portuguese intrusion?

of tribute-paying states, known as the Mutapa kingdom, whose wealth was based, like that of Zimbabwe, on the lucrative gold trade.

In the early sixteenth century, lured by the glitter of this gold, profiteers from Portugal began moving inland, rather than simply conducting coastal trade as they had elsewhere in Africa. After setting up a naval base in 1505 at a place on the coast called Mozambique (*mō-zahm-BĒK*), they soon established settlements along the Zambezi River. These efforts brought them into contact and conflict with the Mutapa kingdom, whose people for decades resisted all efforts to conquer and Christianize them.

In 1575, however, in a bid to acquire European weapons, the reigning Mwene Mutapa signed an agreement allowing the Portuguese to mine his gold in return for providing him with firearms. Eventually, as its rulers made further concessions, the Mutapa realm was reduced to the status of a Portuguese vassal state. In the 1630s, when a revolt arose against the foreign overlords, Portugal crushed the rebels and extended its control over the entire region.

Mozambique becomes a large Portuguese colony

Thus there developed in southeast Africa a large Portuguese colony known as Mozambique. Eventually, in addition to providing gold, it also became a significant source of slaves. Like Angola in the west, it would remain under Portugal's sway until 1975, long after both the Atlantic slave trade and Portuguese prowess were gone.

THE BATTLES FOR ETHIOPIA. No African domain was more distinctive—or more fascinating to European Christians—than the empire of Ethiopia, which bordered on the southern Red Sea across from the Arabian Peninsula. In the fourth century the Ethiopians had adopted Coptic Christianity, a creed that was considered Monophysite (*muh-NOFF-ih-sit*), or "single-nature," holding that Jesus Christ was only divine, rather than both human and divine as other Christians believed (Chapter 10). Since that time the Ethiopians had clung resolutely to their traditional faith, even after they were cut off for centuries from the rest of Christendom by Islamic expansion. Although they were mostly farmers, Ethiopians did conduct commerce, including some traffic in slaves, with the Muslim world.

In the twelfth century, European crusaders were enthralled by rumors of a wealthy Christian kingdom in the East, allegedly led by a powerful king-priest known as Prester John, said to command a sizable army capable of crushing the Muslims. Three centuries later, despite the obvious improbability that he could still be alive, Portugal sent expeditions to East Africa to search for this mythical Christian monarch. So intoxicating was the legend that, when a Portuguese mission arrived in Ethiopia in 1520, its connection with that ancient Christian kingdom evoked as much excitement in Europe as Columbus's voyages to the Americas had elicited in the 1490s.

Christian Ethiopians defeat Muslims with Portuguese help

At first the new connection proved fortunate for Ethiopia. In 1529 and 1531, a neighboring Muslim warlord attacked and laid waste to the realm, forcing many Christians to adopt Islam. But the Ethiopians appealed for help to the Portuguese, who in time sent an expedition to the rescue. Although the head of this mission, Vasco da Gama's son, was captured and beheaded by Islamic forces, a joint Ethiopian-Portuguese force finally vanquished the Muslims east of Lake Tana in 1543 (Map 23.5).

Later, however, the European ties proved troublesome, especially when Jesuits came to Ethiopia seeking to replace its Coptic Christian faith with the "dual-nature" Roman Catholic version, which held that Jesus Christ was both human and divine. In the 1620s, the Jesuits even managed to convert the emperor, who then tried to impose his new faith on his subjects. But the Coptic Christians rebelled, ousting this ruler in 1632, and soon thereafter his successor expelled the Jesuits and most other outsiders. Henceforth, through centuries of chaos and regional conflict, the Ethiopians maintained both their independence and their Coptic creed, resisting the intrusions of both Muslims and European Christians.

South Africa and the Dutch

The southernmost part of Africa, remote from both Europe and Asia, was initially spared from outside intrusion. Its indigenous inhabitants spoke unique languages, now called **Khoisan** (*KOY-sahn*), distinguished by clicking sounds. The Khoisan-speaking peoples were mostly farmers and herders, although some still lived in hunter-gatherer societies. Their lives remained undisturbed, even when the Portuguese began sailing around South Africa in the late 1400s, because at first the Europeans did not try to colonize the region.

In 1652, however, on the southeast coast, the Dutch East India Company set up a way station for Dutch ships traveling back and forth between Europe and the East Indies. That settlement, later called Cape Town (Map 23.6), gradually grew into a small colony, as the mild South African climate and rich soil attracted a number of settlers from the Netherlands.

South African colony helps Dutch connect with the East Indies

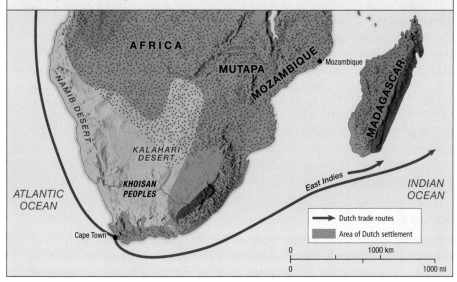

Map 23.6 South Africa and the Dutch Incursions, 1652–1806

Due to its great distance from both Europe and Asia, South Africa was largely spared from out-side incursions until the mid-seventeenth century. Observe, however, that in 1652 the Dutch set up an outpost at Cape Town to serve as a stopping point for ships en route to and from the East Indies, and that Dutch farmers called Boers eventually came from Europe to settle on surrounding lands. What impact did the Dutch settlers have on Khoisan-speaking African peoples who had long lived in this region?

Dutch fort at Cape Town.

The arrival of the Dutch eventually proved disastrous for South Africans. At first the immigrants lived mostly near the coast, but as time went on Dutch settlers called Boers (*boorz*), a Dutch term meaning "farmers," began moving north into the interior, using their guns to defeat and displace the Africans who lived there. The Khoisan speakers were driven off their lands, and most were either enslaved or exterminated.

The Dutch controlled South Africa until 1806, at which point the colony passed into British hands. By then it had become a racially stratified society, dominated by Dutch South Africans who called themselves Afrikaners.

The Impact on Africa of the Atlantic Slave Trade

Although each region of Africa was affected differently by the European intrusions, the overall impacts on the continent were extensive and profound. Traditional trade patterns were disrupted or destroyed, replaced by exploitative systems that typically favored those who trafficked in slaves. Historic states and kingdoms were weakened and undermined, while rulers who seized slaves and sold them for firearms grew in power and wealth. Wars, rebellions, and slave hunts abounded, as ruthless and ambitious Europeans and Africans sought to fill the insatiable demand for servile labor in the Americas.

Demographic Dislocation

Notice announcing a shipment of African slaves.

The demographic dislocation caused by these events was monumental. During the course of the Atlantic slave trade, which flourished from the sixteenth through the early nineteenth centuries, sub-Saharan Africa may well have lost more than fifteen million people. As noted above, eleven or twelve million were shipped as slaves to the Americas, one to two million more died along the way, and another several million were transported to North Africa and Asia, mostly by Muslim merchants.

Historians differ in assessing the impact of these losses. Some believe that they were catastrophic, contributing greatly to Africa's destitution and the destruction of its traditional cultures. Others contend, however, that in the long run the decline was offset by the impact of nutritious new crops, such as sweet potatoes, peanuts, and maize, brought over from the Americas. Especially important in this regard was **cassava** (*kuh SAH-vuh*), also called manioc (*MAN-ē-ock*), a large hardy plant from the American tropics, whose edible portion grows below the ground, much like a carrot or potato. Cassava can be cooked or eaten raw, ground into flour for bread, processed into tapioca and starch, and even used to make an alcoholic drink. Brought to Africa from Brazil, most likely by Portuguese traders, it was widely adopted by African farmers because of both its hardiness and its ability to feed more people per acre than most other major crops. Such new crops, according to some historians, helped to substantially increase Africa's food supply and thus over time its population, offsetting its vast loss of people to the Atlantic slave trade.

New crops from the Americas help offset population loss

Disruption of Family Life

Thus, unlike the Amerinds, whose population never fully recovered from the demographic disaster of the sixteenth century (Chapter 19), many African societies in time regained the population they had lost as a result of the European intrusions. Nothing, however, could offset the suffering of the slaves or the disruption of families decimated by the loss of their loved ones.

In Africa, as elsewhere, the lives of most people centered on their families and clans. Although some people dwelt in cities and pursued specialized professions, most Africans were farmers and herders, living with their kinfolk in small villages, and raising crops or grazing livestock on the surrounding lands. Men did most of the heavy field work, but women and children often helped with the sowing and tilling. A man's prestige was typically based on his physical prowess, while a woman's status was based on her bearing of children.

Africans typically connected in families and clans

As in most agricultural societies, African marriages were arranged by the parents, and wives were generally subject to their husband's authority. **Polygyny**, the practice by which a man has more than one wife at a time, was relatively common in some parts of Africa, even before the advent of the Atlantic slave trade. In Africa, as elsewhere, the bride's family often gave the groom a dowry. In some African cultures, however, the husband's kin were expected to provide a **bridewealth**—a payment from the groom to the parents of the bride to compensate them for the loss of their daughter and assure them that he would treat her well. This practice suggests that women there were highly valued.

The Atlantic slave trade ravaged many millions of African families. During the centuries of its operation, families were robbed of the labor and talents of many of their most productive members. Since American plantations demanded mostly men, the population remaining in West and Central Africa was predominantly female, disrupting the traditional gender balance. In these regions polygyny persisted, and probably even expanded, since the number of available brides for a long time exceeded the supply of available grooms. In East Africa, conversely, polygyny was less pronounced, since much of this region's slave trade was conducted with the Muslim world, where female slaves were frequently preferred.

Atlantic slave trade ravages African families

African Slaves and the Global Shift in Wealth and Power

In the fifteenth and sixteenth centuries, when Portuguese sailors were laying the foundations for the Atlantic slave trade, the Muslim world and China were the main centers of commerce, wealth, and power. Indian Ocean trade, conducted mainly in Muslim ships, linked East Africa, Arabia, Persia, India, Southeast Asia, and the East Indies, while other land and sea routes connected this commerce to China, North Africa, West Africa, and Europe. The Chinese dominated trade in East and Southeast Asia, with other countries paying tribute to China for the privilege of partaking in its commerce.

In the sixteenth through eighteenth centuries, however, Europeans not only intruded into Indian Ocean commerce but also opened sea routes across the Atlantic and Pacific Oceans, creating history's first truly global networks of regular connections (Map 23.7). The Atlantic Ocean, hitherto the western edge of international commerce, gradually became its center. And the nations of Western Europe, hitherto small states that dwelt on the periphery of international trade, now became the primary carriers of oceanic commerce, the rulers of great world empires, and the main centers of a global economy. As trade shifted westward from the Indian Ocean to the Atlantic, wealth and power shifted westward to the Europeans.

Commerce expands from regional to global networks

Map 23.7 Seventeenth- and Eighteenth-Century Commercial Networks

By the mid-seventeenth century, the Atlantic slave trade was part of a growing global commercial network. Notice that the Portuguese, Spanish, and Dutch in this century dominated global trade routes, though the English and French had also set up colonies and were taking part in this trade. Which of this network's key commodities, as listed on this map, were produced through the labor of African slaves?

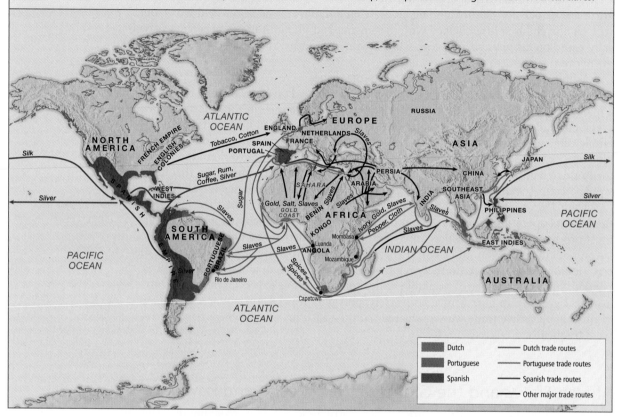

African slaves enhance Europe's commercial wealth

Central to this process were African slaves, who produced much of the sugar, rum, and coffee, mined much of the silver, and later grew much of the tobacco and cotton that fueled Europe's growing global commerce. This commerce in turn helped produce the wealth that sustained the armies, navies, weapons, and bases that projected European power across the globe and paid the officials who ran Europe's global dominions. By 1800 Europe was on its way to world domination, based in part on the servitude and suffering of countless African slaves.

Chapter Review

Putting It in Perspective

The European intrusion in Africa, and the resulting Atlantic slave trade, forged connections and sparked conflicts among cultures that had hitherto been unaware of one another. Diverse societies in Europe, Africa, and the Americas were linked together in an exploitative enterprise that brought great wealth and power to some and enhanced the material comfort of many, while subjecting millions of others to misery. The ancient practice of slavery, typically oppressive and often cruel, was transformed into something that was even more onerous and ominous: a system of subjection that was racial, perpetual, and hereditary. African societies were also transformed, with power and wealth going mostly to those Africans who sold other Africans into bondage. The soil and resources of the Americas were exploited by Europeans, using the labor of unprecedented numbers of captive slaves. And even Europe, though materially enriched, was morally diminished by its leading role in one of history's most infamous atrocities: the forced relocation and brutal exploitation of millions of human beings.

Indeed, in the long run, the slave trade's social impacts may have been the most destructive of all its effects. Millions of victims were torn from their homelands and taken to distant lands under relentlessly cruel conditions. Millions perished in the process; others survived to endure harsh lives in alien surroundings, with their descendants also sentenced to continued enslavement. Others, meanwhile, profited from these endeavors, and even sought to excuse their actions by denying the humanity of those whose lives were destroyed. And even after the commerce in slaves and slavery itself were ended, a bitter legacy of racism and resentment continued to infect the societies of Africa, Europe, and the Americas, connected for centuries by the Atlantic slave trade.

Reviewing Key Material

KEY CONCEPTS

stateless societies, 559
slavery, 559
triangular trade, 563
Middle Passage, 564
maroons, 565
African diaspora, 565
race, 566
racism, 566
Khoisan, 575
cassava, 576
polygyny, 577
bridewealth, 577

KEY PEOPLE

Nzinga Mbemba (Afonso I), 557, 570
Ibn Khaldun, 561
Askia Muhammad al-Turi (Muhammad I Askia), 567
Sonni Ali, 567
Idris Alawma, 568
Diogo Cão, 570
Njinga of Ndongo, 572

ASK YOURSELF

1. How did the Atlantic slave trade originate? Why did Europeans use slaves from Africa to work their sugar plantations?
2. How did slavery in the Americas differ from the slavery practiced in Africa and the Muslim world?
3. What were the main impacts of the Atlantic slave trade on West Africa, Central Africa, and East Africa? Why did it have such a different impact on each of these regions?
4. Why did triangular trade patterns emerge in the Atlantic basin? What were the benefits and detriments of this trade for people in Europe, in Africa, and in the Americas?
5. How did the Atlantic Slave Trade contribute to a global shift in wealth and power?

GOING FURTHER

Ajayi, J., and M. Crowder, eds. *A History of West Africa*. 1985.
Balandier, G. *Daily Life in the Kingdom of Kongo*. 1968.
Barendse, R. J. *The Arabian Seas: The Indian Ocean World of the Seventeenth Century*. 2002.

Birmingham, D., and P. Martin, eds. *History of Central Africa.* 1983.

Conniff, M. L., and T. J. Davis. *Africans in the Americas.* 2002.

Curtin, Philip D. *The African Slave Trade: A Census.* 1969.

Edgerton, Robert B. *Warrior Women: The Amazons of Dahomey and the Nature of War.* 2000.

Ehret, Christopher. *The Civilizations of Africa: A History to 1800.* 2001.

Ellis, David. *The Rise of African Slavery in the Americas.* 2000.

Engerman, Stanley, et al. *Slavery.* 2001.

Harris, J. E., ed. *Global Dimensions of the African Diaspora.* 1993.

Horton, M., and J. Middleton. *The Swahili: The Social Landscape of a Mercantile Society.* 2000.

Inikori, J., and S. Engerman, eds. *The Atlantic Slave Trade.* 1992.

Isichei, Elizabeth. *A History of African Societies to 1870.* 1997.

Klein, Herbert S. *The Atlantic Slave Trade.* 1999.

Klein, Herbert S. *The Middle Passage.* 1978.

Lovejoy, Paul. *Transformations in Slavery: A History of Slavery in Africa.* 2000.

Manning, Patrick. *Slavery and African Life.* 1990.

Mariners Museum. *Captive Passage: The Transatlantic Slave Trade and the Making of the Americas.* 2002.

Middleton, J. *The World of Swahili: An African Mercantile Civilization.* 1992.

Mintz, Sidney W. *Sweetness and Power: The Place of Sugar in Modern History.* 1985.

Northrup, David. *Africa's Discovery of Europe, 1450–1850.* 2002.

Northrup, David, ed. *The Atlantic Slave Trade.* 2002.

Oliver, Roland. *The African Middle Ages, 1400–1800.* 2003.

Robertson, Claire, and M. Klein. *Women and Slavery in Africa.* 1983.

Rodney, W. *How Europe Underdeveloped Africa,* 1981.

Searing, J. F. *West African Slavery and Atlantic Commerce, 1700–1860.* 1993.

Segal, R. *The Black Diaspora.* 1995.

Shillington, K. *History of Africa.* Rev. 2nd ed. 2005.

Solow, Barbara. *Slavery and the Rise of the Atlantic System.* 1991.

Thomas, Hugh. *The Slave Trade: The Story of the Atlantic Slave Trade, 1440–1870.* 1997.

Thornton, J. *Africa and Africans in the Formation of the Atlantic World, 1400–1800.* 1998.

Key Dates and Developments

1300s	Kongo Kingdom emerges		1575	Mutapa kingdom allows Portuguese to mine gold
1400s	Mutapa Kingdom emerges		1591	Moroccans crush the Songhai Empire
1440s	West Africans begin selling slaves to Portuguese		1623–1663	Njinga reigns in Ndongo
1468–1473	Sonni Ali defeats Mali and creates the Songhai Empire		mid-1600s	English and Dutch move in on the Atlantic trade
1482–1483	Kongo Kingdom first visited by Portuguese		1652	Dutch begin Cape Town settlement in South Africa
1503–1507	East African cities attacked by Portuguese		1698	Arabs from Oman drive Portuguese out of East Africa
1520	Ethiopia visited by Portuguese mission		1700s	Height of Atlantic slave trade
1529–1541	Muslims and Portuguese struggle over Ethiopia			
1570s	Angola colony started by Portuguese			

CHAPTER 24

Absolutism and Enlightenment in Europe, 1600–1763

- The Age of Absolutism
- Europe's Intellectual Revolution
- Absolutism and Enlightenment
- Chapter Review

The Hall Of Mirrors, Palace Of Versailles

The Hall of Mirrors in Louis XIV's magnificent palace at Versailles (page 582). This photo captures the wealth and power of the man who became Europe's most famous practitioner of royal absolutism.

As the first rays of the morning sun reflected off dozens of rectangular mirrors lining the long ceremonial hallway at the palace of Versailles, France's King Louis XIV was already awake. In the royal bedroom, as he dressed, he was attended by a dozen people, some of whom were his trusted servants. Others, however, were among the most distinguished nobles of France. The duke of Rohan tied the king's shoes, the count of Nevers handed Louis a freshly powdered wig, while the prince of Condé helped His Majesty into a richly brocaded jacket. Then Louis XIV, outfitted for the morning's affairs, led his distinguished retinue into a large meeting room adjacent to the Hall of Mirrors (see page 581).

Europe

It was an ordinary day in the summer of 1685. Though the ritual of dressing might suggest that a momentous ceremony was about to take place, it was only one of many rituals performed each day as the king went about his daily business of rising, eating, working, playing, and sleeping. Ostentatious and elaborate, the ceremonies were intended to underscore the king's dominance over his nobility as well as his grandeur. They were an integral component of **royal absolutism**, a system of governance in which the ruler's authority is said to come directly from God and thus cannot be limited or challenged by any human institution. Developed most extensively in France, this system was also the model for Austrian, Prussian, and Russian rule in seventeenth-century Europe.

Even as Louis reigned supreme, however, the foundations of absolutism were under challenge. As scientists overturned long-held beliefs about the physical universe, other thinkers began to question prevailing ideas of governance, social justice, economics, and gender roles. The result was an intellectual revolution, based on the assertions that authority and belief must be challenged by reason, that society must be structured by logic rather than by tradition and religion, and that governing authority comes not from God but from the people being governed. Initiated in Europe by a small, educated elite, this revolution opened the way for global advances in science and technology and for people the world over to participate more fully in their society's political and economic life.

The Age of Absolutism

Although monarchies had governed Europe for centuries, royal power had been limited by forces such as hereditary aristocracies and church hierarchies. In the seventeenth century, however, the French monarchy managed to undermine the power of aristocracy and church to establish a governance system based on royal absolutism. Europe's other monarchies, envious of France, sought to do likewise. The Austrian and Prussian monarchies achieved considerable success, but English rulers were compelled to share governing authority with Parliament.

The French Model of Absolute Government

Seventeenth-century French absolutism was a form of government in which no institution could check the power of the king (Map 24.1). This did not mean the monarch could do anything he wished; he was restricted by the kingdom's fundamental laws, derived from centuries of custom. For example, he could not change the national religion from Roman Catholicism to another faith, levy new taxes without the consent of representatives of society, or have someone executed without following legal procedures. The fundamental laws could not be changed, and the king was bound by them, as were all his subjects.

In practice, however, as long as the king respected the fundamental laws, he was nearly all-powerful. A French legislature existed in theory, but only the king could call it into session and even then he was not bound by its decisions. No legislature was summoned between 1614 and 1789. There was a judiciary, but its members were appointed by the king, who controlled their salaries and had the power to exile them for life. Technically royal edicts, to be valid, had to be registered by judicial tribunals known as parlements (*pahr-luh-MAWN*), but in practice the king could compel the parlements to do his will. By the close of the seventeenth century, the French monarchy exercised immense power.

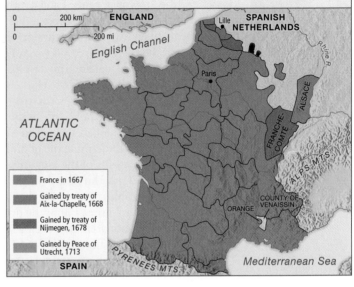

FOUNDATION MAP 24.1 France in 1715

A French proverb tells us, "The natural borders of France are these: the Rhine, the Alps, and the Pyrenees." Louis XIV dedicated much of his 72-year reign, and much of France's blood and treasure, to transforming that saying into reality. Notice that most of his acquisitions moved France in the direction of the Rhine River. Why was Louis XIV unable to achieve his goal of expanding France to its "natural borders"?

Legend:
- France in 1667
- Gained by treaty of Aix-la-Chapelle, 1668
- Gained by treaty of Nijmegen, 1678
- Gained by Peace of Utrecht, 1713

Fundamental laws set boundaries on the power of French kings

ROOTS OF FRENCH ABSOLUTISM. This accumulation of power was an outgrowth of the French Wars of Religion. Following this turmoil between 1562 and 1594, France's government was revived by King Henri IV, a former Huguenot who converted to Catholicism in 1593 once he saw that France would not accept a Protestant king. Five years later he guaranteed Huguenots' rights in the Edict of Nantes (Chapter 20). But Henri, a charming and outgoing back-slapper, governed France largely by the force of his attractive personality. It remained to be seen if a less appealing and talented monarch could rule France effectively.

In 1610, when Henri was succeeded by Louis XIII, the French monarchy was tested. Nine years old, sickly and shy, and dominated by his unpopular Florentine mother, the new king never developed a taste for state affairs. Instead he appointed a series of chief ministers to run the government. His early selections proved inept, but his last, Cardinal Richelieu (*RISH-lih-yoo*), turned out to be exceptionally competent. The cardinal devoted his 18 years in office to constructing the foundations for an absolute monarchy.

Richelieu's main goal was to strengthen the monarchy to such a degree that even an incapable ruler would not harm the country. To achieve this goal he sought to remove all obstacles to royal authority, thereby reducing the prospects for unrest should the king prove weak. The main obstacles were the Huguenots and the nobility.

Although he was a cardinal in the Catholic Church, Richelieu was no religious zealot; he was willing to allow Huguenots freedom of conscience and worship, guaranteed them by the Edict of Nantes. However, the edict had also granted them two hundred "places of safety," fortified towns in central and southern France protected by Protestant militia. To Richelieu, these places of safety were a threat to the monarchy: if Protestant forces invaded France, the fortified towns might support the enemy. So he convinced Louis XIII to annul this portion of the edict. The result was a Huguenot rebellion in 1627, supported by Protestant England. Richelieu led an army to crush the revolt, and a 1629 settlement allowed the Huguenots to retain their civil and religious rights, but not their places of safety.

Richelieu also had no desire to destroy the French nobility; he was an aristocrat himself. But he wanted the nobles to support a strong monarchy and place the country's welfare above their own interests instead of promoting a weakened monarchy that they could manipulate. To undermine the nobility's power, Richelieu removed some of its privileges. He sent direct agents of the king throughout the country to assert the monarchy's control over local affairs, thus depriving nobles of much of their influence over ordinary citizens. To undercut noble control over the nation's defense, the cardinal also suggested a permanent, or "standing," army, but at the time, France's treasury could not bear the expense. For the next French monarch, however, a standing army was both essential and financially possible. This ruler, King Louis XIV (1643–1715), came to epitomize royal absolutism.

Louis XIV was only five years old when his father died in 1643, and Richelieu had died five months earlier. On Louis XIV's behalf, the Queen Mother ruled as regent while Cardinal Jules Mazarin (*mah-zah-RAN*) served as chief minister. Regencies were always dangerous for a monarchy, as its foes might try to take advantage of inexperienced leadership. In this case a conspiracy of French nobles who hated Richelieu's policies used an extended war with Spain as a pretext to move against Mazarin and reverse the trend toward absolutism. This rebellion, known as the **Fronde** (*FRAHND*), lasted from 1648 to 1653.

The Fronde drove Mazarin into exile in Switzerland, but the conspirators failed to intimidate the young king and the Queen Mother into supporting them. They had placed the royal family under house arrest and threatened their lives, but had no plan for how to proceed in the absence of royal support. Reluctant to harm or overthrow the king, they ruled France so badly that the exiled Mazarin found it easy to raise money to hire a mercenary army in Switzerland. This army then liberated the royal captives and defeated the conspiracy.

Despite the Fronde's ultimate failure, the experience left a powerful impression on Louis XIV. Traumatized by the danger to himself and his mother, he emerged embittered at the nobility and convinced that its power must be broken. He allowed Mazarin to remain chief minister and learned statecraft from him until the cardinal's death in 1661. Then, at age 23, Louis XIV began 54 years of directing French affairs himself, strengthening the monarchy by centralizing the government.

LOUIS XIV AND THE CONSOLIDATION OF ABSOLUTISM. Centralization of authority required a large bureaucracy. The king stood at the top of it, setting overall policy, sometimes

Richelieu.

intervening actively in decision-making but often leaving daily business to his ministers. Louis XIV appointed ministers to head various government departments, with each minister reporting to the king individually. Through such one-on-one sessions the king maintained direct personal control over the operation of each department.

This degree of personal control was unprecedented in French history, and it gave Louis the means to undermine the power of the nobility. He reserved positions in government for commoners, whose advancement would depend upon him alone and whose loyalty to him would therefore be unquestioned. Nobles were never placed in influential positions that might enable them again to conspire against the king or obstruct the development of absolutism.

The nobles' opposition to this system was a threat to Louis, who addressed it with a carefully crafted program centered on construction of a magnificent palace in the Paris suburb of Versailles (*vehr-SIGH*). Completed in 1682, it stood as testimonial to the greatness of Louis XIV, who now called himself the "Sun King." With accommodations for ten thousand people, gorgeously manicured grounds, a reflecting pool arranged to catch the rays of the sun on the summer solstice, and a fabulous Hall of Mirrors, the palace of Versailles even today remains so breathtaking that it is easy to overlook the political cunning behind its beauty.

Versailles was crucial to Louis's plans, because nowhere else in France could so many aristocrats be housed in luxurious surroundings. Nobles who lived there received honorary positions entitling them to wait upon His Majesty and look important while doing so. But while carrying rich allowances and boundless dignity, these positions provided no power. Moreover, by assembling the greatest aristocrats of the realm in one place, the king could have them spied on by his servants, who were ordered to report instances of treasonous behavior. The technique was similar to that of Japan's Tokugawa shoguns, who forced their daimyo to live in Edo (Chapter 21). The effect was to strengthen Louis's ability to exercise real power.

The French nobility was thus increasingly isolated from French governance, and Louis worked tirelessly to accomplish just that. Presiding over Europe's wealthiest country, he appointed the astute Jean-Baptiste Colbert as minister of finance, charging him with organizing the economy so as to maximize tax receipts. Colbert shared Louis's conviction that absolutism could not be realized without the foundation provided by a powerful economy and commercial dominance. The creation of a strong urban middle class would enrich the kingdom while providing the monarchy with a consistent revenue stream with which to implement royal policies. When Colbert succeeded, in part by encouraging overseas expansion through monopolistic trading companies (Chapter 22), Louis took the increased revenues and built the permanent army of Richelieu's dreams. The king could not prevent nobles from becoming officers, but he made sure that his war ministers were commoners. Moreover, Louis perfected Richelieu's system of direct royal agents, depriving aristocrats of most of their influence in local politics. Small wonder the nobility detested absolutism.

Louis XIV's efforts to subject France to his royal will extended into the religious sphere. His best-known motto, "I am the state," was complemented by "One faith, one law, one king." Although a staunch Catholic, Louis also believed that the French Church should be somewhat independent of Rome. Louis thus clashed with the pope, who at one point secretly excommunicated him. Louis also outraged much of Western Christendom

Louis XIV moves against the nobility

Louis XIV.

French commercial dominance proves crucial to absolutism

Louis XIV sees religion as a component of absolutism

in 1683 by refusing to send French troops to Vienna to fight the Ottoman Turks, who were invading Europe from the southeast.

Louis had no reservations about defying Rome or allowing the Ottoman threat to weaken his enemy Austria, but he was inflexible about Protestantism. Considering the Huguenots heretics who must be removed from his kingdom in accordance with the motto, "One faith, one law, one king," in 1685 he revoked the Edict of Nantes and insisted that all Huguenots convert to Catholicism. The result was a series of forced conversions, as well as a mass emigration of Huguenots to Prussia, Holland, or British North America in search of religious freedom. Louis's Huguenot policy damaged France economically, since many who fled were merchants or artisans. In the end, Louis's efforts to enforce "One faith, one law, one king" demonstrated that even an absolute monarch could not have everything his way.

Yet Louis achieved much during his lengthy reign. He consolidated his authority as an absolute monarch and made France Europe's dominant power. But he also fought four wars that nearly bankrupted France, largely because he never got around to reforming its taxation system. This failure, even more than his intolerance of the Huguenots, threatened absolutism itself and eventually, in 1789, led to revolution.

Absolutism in Central Europe

Absolute monarchies develop elsewhere in Europe

France's power was the envy of other rulers, particularly in Central Europe, where the sprawling Holy Roman Empire dominated a region that included numerous small German states, the Netherlands, Austria, Bohemia, Switzerland, and parts of northern Italy. Its emperor, almost always from Austria's Habsburg family, was not absolute. He was elected by prominent local rulers who were largely autonomous in domestic matters. In the seventeenth and eighteenth centuries, however, absolute monarchies arose in Central Europe's two most powerful states: Austria and Prussia.

AUSTRIA'S MULTINATIONAL ABSOLUTISM. The Peace of Westphalia, which ended the Thirty Years War in 1648, destroyed the hopes of the Austrian Habsburgs to transform the Holy Roman Empire into a centralized German Catholic state (Map 24.2). Although they continued, with one exception, to be elected as emperors, they had little control over most of the more than three hundred states that made up this so-called empire. But the Habsburgs were still hereditary rulers in Austria and Bohemia, and were routinely elected kings of Hungary, most of which had been under Ottoman control since the 1520s. The Habsburgs sought to regain Hungary and to tighten their domination over the areas they ruled directly, hoping to transform south central Europe into an absolute monarchy.

Habsburgs attempt to build a multinational form of absolutism

Initially the Habsburgs had mixed success. They created a standing army, but were nearly destroyed by the Ottoman Turks, who besieged Vienna in 1683. The Austrian capital's rescue by the King of Poland's multinational army marked a major turning point in Habsburg fortunes, as Austrian armies went on to drive the Turks out of Hungary by 1699. In the process, the Habsburgs compelled the Hungarian nobles to accept them as hereditary rather than elective monarchs. It appeared that a new empire was taking shape in south central Europe.

This empire was actually three distinct realms ruled by the same person. Austria, Bohemia, and Hungary each had its own separate assembly, its own language (respectively

Map 24.2 Growth of Austria and Prussia, 1648–1763

The Thirty Years War (1618–1648) prevented the Austrian Habsburg dynasty from reversing the Protestant Reformation and establishing Catholic religious and political control of Central Europe. Responding to this disappointment, the Habsburgs reemphasized their Austrian roots and worked toward the development of absolute monarchy. Note that their territorial gains in wars with the Ottoman Empire moved the Habsburg monarchy southeast, away from Germany and toward the Black Sea. How did the Great Elector of Prussia, Frederick William, react to Austria's southeastward orientation?

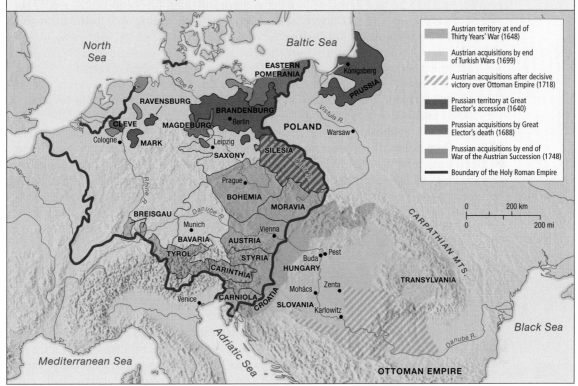

German, Czech, and Magyar), and its own laws and customs. Despite Habsburg efforts to run the empire from Vienna, the Bohemian and Hungarian nobles jealously protected their national identities and privileges, and in 1703, when they felt their privileges threatened, the Hungarians revolted.

In response, the Habsburgs acknowledged that each realm must be governed by its own fundamental laws and customs, and they promised that as hereditary monarchs they would diligently respect those different traditions. In return, they would rule as absolute monarchs, unconstrained by other institutions. Fearful of the growing power of Prussia, Russia, and France, the Bohemian and Hungarian nobles eventually accepted this arrangement. Thus, by the early eighteenth century, a multinational form of absolutism was emerging in the Habsburg domains.

PRUSSIAN ABSOLUTISM: NOBILITY AND MONARCH. Another type of absolutism originated to Austria's north in Brandenburg, a medium-sized state centered on the city of Berlin. Its ruler was a member of the Hohenzollern (*HŌ-un-ZAH-lurn*) family, which in 1618 also inherited the duchy of Prussia southeast of the Baltic Sea. Although the two lands were separated by more than one hundred miles, they formed the nucleus of a new great power that would rise to prominence on the might of its army.

Prussia builds absolutism around its army

In 1640, 20-year old Frederick William von Hohenzollern became ruler of Brandenburg-Prussia. Dismayed by the weakness of his divided state, he set out to strengthen his armies. By 1648 he had developed an eight thousand–man force, and then used it to annex eastern Pomerania, connecting Brandenburg to the Baltic Sea. In the following years, to strengthen his armies further, he agreed to give his nobles, known as **Junkers** (*YOONG-kers*), complete control over their peasants and exemption from taxes in return for loyal military service. As a result, most Junker families furnished officers to the army, while the rest of the people were forced to pay very heavy taxes and the peasants were reduced to full serfdom. Before he died in 1688, Frederick William had brought his scattered lands under centralized rule and created a forty thousand–man army.

By the early eighteenth century Prussia was moving rapidly toward absolutism. The Hohenzollern policy of cooperating with the Junkers in establishing serfdom gave these nobles a stake in a powerful monarchy. In exchange for tax exemptions and peasant labor services, they willingly granted the Hohenzollerns extensive political authority, although their control of the officer corps gave them significant leverage against the monarch. No legislature could check the kings of Prussia, but the army certainly could, a fact no Hohenzollern ruler could forget. Prussian absolutism, unlike the French version, was consolidated in a partnership between nobility and ruler.

SOCIAL BASES OF EUROPEAN ABSOLUTISM. Absolutism in Austria and Prussia differed from that of France, largely due to differences in the ability of nobles to control the peasantry. France, where most peasants were free, had a strong middle class made up of educated urban professionals and wealthy merchant capitalists. These townsfolk helped the monarchy offset the nobility, serving as state officials and providing the ruler with money for hiring armies and bureaucrats. Austria and Prussia, by contrast, lacked strong middle classes, so their monarchs had to rely on nobles to collect the taxes, staff the bureaucracies, and run the armies. In return for such services, the nobles were given full authority over their peasants.

Absolutism in Austria and Prussia is based on the aristocracy and serfdom

The result in Austria and Prussia was a mixture of absolutism with aristocracy: monarchs controlled the central government and exercised vast power, but nobles enjoyed extensive privileges. With no real constraints on how they ran their estates, nobles had almost total control over the peasants who lived there. While peasants in France were legally free, those in Austria and Prussia were serfs. Technically they were not slaves, since they were attached to the soil and were not supposed to be bought and sold apart from the land and their families. In practice, however, they might as well have been slaves. They could not marry, or even leave the estate, without their lord's consent. They were typically forced to work three to six days a week on the lord's lands, or in some places to give him a share of their own crops. They were subject to the whim of the lord, who was free to impose penalties such as flogging that could lead to injury or death.

Austrian and Prussian peasants lived in villages on the lord's estates. Their communities were patriarchal, dominated by village elders and male heads of households. A village assembly composed of such men usually decided which families worked which fields, paid which taxes, or provided military recruits. Marriages were arranged by parents; the wife was subject to her husband and typically at his mercy. Men's drunkenness and abuse of their wives were common, pleasures and diversions were few, and everyone lived at the mercy of the weather, the crops, and the landlord.

A vast gulf existed between upper and lower classes in Austria and Prussia. They often spoke different languages: educated nobles conversed in German, while peasants spoke local dialects. Rulers and nobles typically lived in luxury, while the vast majority of people were illiterate, impoverished, and subservient.

Despite its superficial similarity, then, absolutism in Austria and Prussia was not the same as in France. In France, where nobles were weak and peasants were free, the monarch's power rested on the shoulders of a strong urban middle class, but in Austria and Prussia executive power was based on the aristocracy and serfdom.

Prussian soldiers.

The English Alternative to Absolutism

In England the monarchs, like those in France and Central Europe, sought to construct an absolute monarchy in the seventeenth century. They were blocked, however, by Parliament, a medieval legislature with a House of Lords made up of prominent nobles and a House of Commons representing wealthy commoners. In England, unlike elsewhere, the nobles and middle classes worked together to restrict the ruler, creating thereby a **limited monarchy** that served as an English alternative to absolutism.

PARLIAMENT VERSUS THE KING. England's Parliament was a representative body summoned by monarchs whenever they needed money and soldiers. King Henry VIII (1509–1547) had skillfully manipulated Parliament during the English Reformation, and his daughter Queen Elizabeth I (1558–1603) had also done so during her conflicts with Spain (Chapter 20). Yet Parliament could and did restrict the power of the monarch, and it prevented the emergence of royal absolutism in England.

In Elizabeth's reign, Parliament was increasingly dominated by wealthy members of the House of Commons rather than by nobles in the House of Lords. This shift reflected the growth of English commerce, which brought prosperity to merchants, bankers, and other commoners. Many such people purchased land in the country, established themselves as landed gentry, and represented rural constituencies in Parliament. Literate and vocal, they demanded influence proportional to their economic status.

England's Parliament limits the monarch's power

In 1603, Elizabeth I died unmarried and childless. The throne passed to King James VI of Scotland, son of her executed cousin Mary Stuart, thus initiating England's Stuart dynasty. Ruling in England as King James I (r. 1603–1625), he aimed to establish an absolute monarchy. But James was a spendthrift and a foreigner whose Scottish mannerisms irritated the English. A smart man who was not particularly practical, he repeatedly requested money from Parliament to finance recurring wars with Spain and interventions abroad on behalf of endangered Protestants. These requests were a source of tension between king and Parliament.

James's son Charles I (r. 1625–1649), frustrated with these fiscal restrictions, sought ways to bypass Parliament and make his own laws. Distrusting the Stuarts, Parliament responded by refusing to approve new taxes, instead drawing up a "Petition of Right" that denounced the king's forcing wealthy people to lodge soldiers in their homes and

Financial disputes frustrate English kings' ambitions for absolute monarchy imprisoning his subjects without due process of law. Religion complicated the tension, as many members of Parliament were Calvinist Christians who did not belong to the Anglican Church or recognize the authority of the king as its head. These **Puritans** considered Anglicanism too much like Roman Catholicism, and they developed their own simplified church. In sum, the Stuart kings stood for absolutism and Anglican supremacy; Parliament stood against both.

Charles I rules without Parliament

In 1629, after four tense years, Charles and Parliament deadlocked. Since Parliament could meet only when called by the king, Charles sent it home and ruled without it until 1640. This **Eleven Years' Tyranny** violated centuries of English custom and alienated many. Charles hoped to apply in England the modern ideas of absolute monarchy that were evolving in France, but Parliament stood firm in asserting the medieval right of a legislative body to authorize taxation. These were important differences, and they may have been ultimately irreconcilable, but the failure of executive and legislature to engage in honest dialogue over such crucial matters eventually plunged England into civil war.

In his struggle with Parliament, Charles began in a strong position but made major mistakes. When he raised revenues by reviving old taxes, many considered this an effort to tax without parliamentary consent. When he attempted to impose the Anglican Church in Calvinist Scotland, where he was also king, he prompted a revolt by the Scots. To raise money to put down this revolt, he was forced to recall Parliament in 1640. By this time the possibility of reasoned discussion had ended.

THE ENGLISH CIVIL WAR AND PURITAN REVOLUTION. The new Parliament, which sat from 1640 to 1660, gave Charles the funds he requested but took action to restrain him. It impeached two of his close advisors, one of whom was executed. It passed a law requiring Parliament to meet every three years with or without the king's call, and another law prohibiting dissolution of Parliament without its own consent. These actions asserted new rights never before claimed by Parliament. When, in 1641, it drew up a list of grievances suffered during Charles's reign, the king ordered the arrest of five of its leaders. Parliament refused to hand them over, whereupon Charles withdrew to the north of England, assembled an army, and prepared for civil war.

Parliament's assertion of new rights forces a civil war

The king drew his soldiers (known as Cavaliers) from the rural north and west, while Parliament's forces (called Roundheads because of their short haircuts) came from the more urban and commercial regions in the south and east. To gain Scottish support, Parliament made Calvinist Presbyterianism the official religion of England, Scotland, and Ireland. Oliver Cromwell, a parliamentary leader, developed the Ironside Army, a military force driven by a nearly fanatical Puritanism. The Ironsides became the conflict's finest soldiers, forcing Charles in 1646 to surrender to the Scots, who turned him over to Parliament the next year.

Had Parliament wanted simply to remove Charles, it could have selected another family to rule England. But Cromwell and the army wanted more than a change of dynasty; they wanted a Puritan Revolution. Fearing that a new king, to reclaim the monarch's religious authority, might restore the Anglican Church, they decided to try Charles for treason, execute him, and abolish the monarchy. Many in Parliament refused to go along with such extreme measures, so Cromwell purged it, reducing it to a Rump Parliament of about sixty members. This minority condemned and beheaded Charles I in 1649.

For the next four years, Cromwell governed with the Rump Parliament. In 1651 he invaded Ireland, massacring Catholics in retaliation for the butchering of Protestants in the northern region of Ulster ten years earlier. Protestant landlords were installed throughout the island, and the Catholic Church was driven underground. That same year Cromwell won naval engagements against the Dutch and Spanish, asserting English maritime commercial supremacy in the North Atlantic.

In 1653, Cromwell dismissed the Rump and effectively became a dictator, known as the Lord Protector. He was challenged, however, by extremist forces released by his own revolution. Levellers stood for expanded voting rights, a written constitution, and equal rights for all men. Quakers preached pacifism, rejecting formal worship in favor of personal testimony inspired by one's mystical "inner light." Fifth Monarchy Men saw the end of the world approaching and yearned for the rule of Christ, whom they saw as the fifth monarch in a sequence including Sennacherib of Assyria, Cyrus the Great of Persia, Alexander the Great, and Caesar Augustus. Facing such divisive factions, Cromwell found no support among Anglicans, who despised him for displacing their church, or among royalists, who hated him for killing their king. His death in 1658 made it possible for the army in 1660 to restore the monarchy, much to almost everyone's relief.

Cromwell fails to consolidate a republic

Oliver Cromwell.

Charles II restores the Stuart dynasty

THE STUART RESTORATION AND GLORIOUS REVOLUTION. A decade without a king convinced the English that, whatever its flaws, monarchy was a vital unifying institution. So they restored the Stuarts in the person of King Charles II (r. 1660–1685), son of the beheaded Charles I. Eager to keep his own head, Charles II generally respected parliamentary rights, while Parliament restored the Anglican Church and acknowledged the new king's authority. Tall, handsome, and courteous, he quickly earned the nickname "the merry monarch" for his love of parties and the theater, his reluctance to take himself too seriously, and his extensive familiarity with ladies' bedrooms. Even those who opposed his policies found him hard to dislike.

The great irony of Charles' reign was the religious question. His father, an Anglican, had faced a Parliament dominated by Puritans; now the Parliament was solidly Anglican, but Charles' sympathies lay with Catholicism (although he did not convert until he lay dying in 1685). Aware of these sympathies, in 1673 Parliament passed the Test Act, requiring that all office holders be Anglicans. The first to resign as a consequence was the Lord High Admiral, James, the king's younger brother, a declared Catholic and next in line for the throne, since Charles had no legitimate children. If and when James became king, renewed religious turmoil seemed a certainty.

Charles II's attitude toward Catholicism was tempered by his political realism. Although he admired the French monarchy of Louis XIV, who had sheltered him in the 1650s, Charles was too realistic to try copying it in England. He never provoked Parliament beyond its endurance, and Parliament, fearful of an openly Catholic king, cooperated with him while hoping he would outlive his younger brother. He did not.

When Charles II died in 1685, his Catholic brother became King James II. A man of limited intellect, James antagonized even his allies by his clear favoritism toward Catholics and his blundering dealings with Parliament. James, however, was already in his 50s, and most expected that the throne would eventually pass to his Protestant daughter Mary, wed to the Dutch leader William of Orange. But when, in 1688, James's second wife gave birth to a son, England faced the prospect of a continuous line of Catholic kings.

Parliament takes action against Catholic absolutism

James II actually thought he could restore Catholicism, but Parliament resisted. Its leaders went to Holland and offered to help his daughter Mary seize the English throne. But her husband William, eager to lead England into an alliance against Louis XIV, insisted on becoming king. Once it was agreed that William and Mary could reign jointly, in 1689 they invaded England with a sizable army.

These developments culminated in the **Glorious Revolution**, a cooperative effort by Parliament and the invaders to overthrow James II. The king was removed with very little bloodshed. Unable to find support in England, he fled to Ireland and raised a Catholic army, which was defeated in 1690 by the new King William III. James then fled to France, where he and his heirs launched claims to the English throne for decades.

The Bill of Rights defines England as a constitutional monarchy

In 1689, Parliament passed a **Bill of Rights**, a written document specifying the rights that William and Mary were required to endorse as conditions of their rule. No taxes could be levied without parliamentary approval; the monarchs could not ignore or violate any law passed by Parliament; no one could be imprisoned without due process of law. These conditions created a contractual relationship between the ruler and Parliament, defining England as a limited monarchy.

To many Europeans, the English alternative of limited monarchy seemed an outmoded, ineffective concept, reflecting old medieval notions of power shared between king and nobles. But the notion that government has a contractual duty to ensure people's rights, embedded in the English alternative, was soon regarded as a modern, progressive concept, owing to an intellectual revolution that was challenging many beliefs about science and society.

Europe's Intellectual Revolution

In the sixteenth and seventeenth centuries, while Western society was still in the turmoil of religious upheavals and witch hunts, innovative European thinkers, their horizons broadened by discoveries in the Americas of plants, animals, and human societies previously unknown in Europe, began an intellectual revolution. Using new approaches and techniques, they achieved dramatic breakthroughs in science and advanced new ideas about governance, human rights, economics, and gender roles. At first the new concepts, confined mainly to the educated elite, had little effect on common people's lives or thinking, still largely shaped by family, farming, and faith. In time, however, Europe's intellectual revolution had a profound and global impact.

The Scientific Revolution

European thinkers challenge ancient beliefs

For many centuries, scientific understanding in the West derived largely from ancient thinkers—Egyptians, Mesopotamians, and Greeks—as developed and expanded by Islamic scholars of the eighth through twelfth centuries. In the sixteenth and seventeenth centuries, however, European thinkers advanced new ideas that challenged these old beliefs. The new science they developed was based on the discovery of mechanical laws said to govern the physical universe.

THE SPREAD OF SCIENTIFIC KNOWLEDGE. Prior to the seventeenth century, Western understanding of the universe was based mainly on a system devised in the fourth century

B.C.E. by the eminent Greek philosopher Aristotle. Among other things, this system put the Earth at the center of the universe, surrounded by transparent paths on which the sun, moon, planets, and stars revolved. In the second century C.E., however, observing that the planets did not orbit the Earth in unchanging paths as suggested by Aristotle, the Egyptian astronomer Claudius Ptolemy (*TAH-luh-mē*) proposed that the planets moved around the Earth on separate and irregular paths. For centuries thereafter, astronomers mainly sought to perfect Ptolemy's system by making minor adjustments in it.

The legacy of Aristotle and Ptolemy, lost to the West in the early Middle Ages, was reclaimed and built upon by Muslim thinkers in the eighth through twelfth centuries (Chapter 12). Ibn Sina and Ibn Rushd, for example, expanded upon Aristotle's works, while al-Khwarizmi and Ibn al-Haytham modified Ptolemy's system. As contacts with the Islamic world brought such knowledge to Europe, Western scholarship mainly sought to elaborate and refine it.

Islamic thought makes Europe's scientific revolution possible

NEW SCIENTIFIC PERSPECTIVES. In the 1500s, however, a Polish monk named Nicholas Copernicus (*kō-PUR-nih-kus*) dared to challenge this approach. Others eventually followed, including German astronomer Johannes Kepler, English statesman Francis Bacon, and French mathematician René Descartes (*dā-CART*).

Troubled by the cumbersome complexity of Ptolemy's system, and perhaps inspired by Persian scholar Nasir al-Din al-Tusi's revised thirteenth-century model (Chapter 12), Copernicus advanced the radical notion that the Earth might not be the center of the universe. Perhaps, he argued in a work published in 1543, the paths of planets seem irregular because they orbit the sun, not the Earth, which is itself a planet circling the sun. The other planets do not really change directions; from the Earth they just seem to do so, since the Earth is moving too. At first almost everyone rejected the Copernican hypothesis. Christian leaders, Catholic and Protestant alike, saw it as denying their basic belief that humans are the center of God's creation. Common sense, moreover, seemed to show that the Earth could not be moving; if it were, things would fly off. Since scientists as yet had no instruments to test the hypothesis, and since its presumption of circular orbits failed to fully clarify the movements of planets, it was not generally accepted.

A 1667 representation of the Copernican view of the universe.

The Copernican system revolutionizes science

In the early seventeenth century, however, Johannes Kepler revised the hypothesis by proposing that planetary orbits are elliptical, not circular. He also suggested that there is a precise mathematical relationship between a planet's speed and its distance from the sun: the closer it gets to the sun, the faster it travels. These observations revived the Copernican hypothesis and prepared the way for further discoveries.

In England, Francis Bacon, a lawyer and statesman with practical scientific interests, called for a new approach to scientific study. In his *Novum Organum* (*NŌ-voom or-GAH-noom*), roughly meaning "New Methodology," Bacon challenged scholars to focus on observing reality rather than simply analyzing the works of past thinkers, a practice he saw as merely perpetuating old beliefs. To understand reality, he insisted, scientists must set aside traditional preconceptions and examine the world anew, using an empirical approach involving extensive observation and rigorous experimentation. He thereby helped lay the groundwork for the modern scientific method.

Like Bacon, René Descartes called for creation of a new science based on observation and experimentation. Unlike Bacon, however, Descartes foresaw that the new science would be grounded in mathematics, relying heavily on measurement, quantification, formulas, and

Title page from *Novvum Organum.*

equations. Descartes, moreover, developed a new system of understanding that was not based on the work of Aristotle or any other thinker. In his most important work, *Discourse on Method* (1637), Descartes subjected all previous knowledge to systematic doubt, concluding that the only thing he could be sure of was his own existence: he reasoned that since he was able to think, he must in fact exist. Beginning with the statement *cogito ergo sum* (*KŌ-jē-tō AIR-gō SOOM*), "I think, therefore I am," he devised a new philosophy dividing all reality into two main entities: "thinking substance," or the subjective realm of the mind and spirit, and "extended substance," or the objective world of matter. By separating the study of material things that can be measured from spiritual things that cannot, he helped to separate science from religion and philosophy; by stressing mathematics, he inspired the search for mechanical laws that govern the material universe.

GALILEO'S DISCOVERIES AND NEWTON'S SYNTHESIS. This search for mechanical laws was decisively advanced by Galileo Galilei (*gal-ih-LĀ-ō gal-ih-LĀ-ē*), an Italian scientist who discovered new laws of acceleration and motion, and verified the Copernican hypothesis. The search was then carried further by the English scientist Isaac Newton, who blended the discoveries of Galileo and others into an overall synthesis depicting the universe as a mechanism that operates in accordance with mathematical laws.

Galileo grounds science in observation rather than revelation

Using his own inventions, such as the pendulum and telescope, to improve his measurements and observations, Galileo combined creative thinking with experimentation and mathematical logic, thus blending the approaches used by Copernicus, Bacon, and Descartes. Using a pendulum to time balls of different weight rolling down inclined planes, for example, Galileo observed that falling bodies actually pick up speed as they fall and that they accelerate at the same rate no matter what they weigh. He concluded that the rate of acceleration of falling bodies is a constant that can be expressed in a precise mathematical formula.

Building on the work of Copernicus and Kepler, Galileo probed the heavens with his telescope. He observed, among other things, craters on the moon, thousands of previously unknown stars, and moons that orbited Jupiter. These discoveries demolished old beliefs that the heavens are perfect and finite, and that all heavenly bodies orbit the Earth. In his classic *Dialogue on the Two Chief World Systems* (1632), Galileo ridiculed those who held these old beliefs, asserting instead that his observations validated the hypotheses of Copernicus and Kepler.

Galileo's view of the moon.

Galileo thereby brought upon himself the wrath of the Catholic Church, which in 1616 had condemned the Copernican hypothesis as contrary to Church teachings. Imprisoned and tried at age 68 by the Roman Inquisition, the Church's main agency for combating heresy, Galileo was forced to renounce his views. Devastated by the experience, ailing and later blind, he spent the rest of his days under house arrest, where he nonetheless continued his mechanical experiments. But the impact of his work could not be suppressed. As others used their own telescopes and did their own mathematical calculations, they reached the same conclusions that Galileo reached. Their new science was based on observation and measurement, not on revelation or religious authority.

Later in the seventeenth century, Isaac Newton assimilated and consolidated the work of Galileo and others, creating a new synthesis to explain how the universe functioned. In 1687 he published a monumental work called *The Mathematical Principles of Natural Philosophy*, often simply called the *Principia* (*prin-CHĒ-pē-uh*), from its Latin title. In it he showed that the force causing Galileo's falling bodies to accelerate at a constant rate was the same force that held the heavenly bodies in place and defined their orbits. He further concluded that this force, called gravity, can be measured and described in a concise mathematical formula, based on the mass of the objects involved and the distance between them. The universe, it appeared, was one huge mechanism that functioned according to natural laws, which were valid everywhere and always.

Newton explains the functioning of the universe

Newton's ideas were breathtaking and profound. His earlier work in optics had already marked him as a genius; now his discovery of the law of gravity raised him to the level of a new Aristotle. The poet Alexander Pope, a contemporary of Newton, paid him the supreme tribute: "Nature and nature's laws lay hid in night; God said 'Let Newton be,' and all was light."

The Enlightenment

The scientific achievements of the seventeenth century, along with growing global knowledge of varied lands and peoples, created great ferment among European intellectuals. By observing societies in Africa, Asia, and the Americas, they had become open to new ways of thinking and being. By challenging traditional ideals, and by systematic observation and analysis, they had begun to develop a new kind of science. Now thinkers in areas such as politics, justice, economics, and gender roles sought to make similar advances. Their efforts produced the **Enlightenment**, a European intellectual movement inspired by boundless faith in human reason. Enlightenment thinkers sought to use reason to achieve progress in all areas of human endeavor.

The European Enlightenment values reason above tradition

NEW PERSPECTIVES ON GOVERNANCE. Rational reassessment of human governance was initiated by Thomas Hobbes, an English supporter of absolutism, who in 1651 published a book called *Leviathan*. Horrified by King Charles I's beheading in 1649, Hobbes argued vehemently on behalf of absolute monarchy. He based his case, however, not on religious authority but on secular reasoning, arguing that a single absolute power was essential for a stable society. According to Hobbes, humans are by nature selfish and violent, and human life in its original state was "solitary, poor, nasty, brutish and short," with each individual engaged in a chaotic "war of all against all." To escape this condition, he claimed, people surrender their freedom to the state in return for security and order, creating an unwritten contract between ruler and subjects.

Title page of *Leviathan*.

Although Hobbes championed absolute power, his idea of a contract implied that the ruler had a duty to maintain order and protect the public welfare. But would the contract still apply if the monarch failed to do so? According to Hobbes it would: the danger of violence and chaos was so great the monarch's power must be unconditional, even if the actual ruler was incompetent, corrupt, or tyrannical.

Later thinkers took a different approach to Hobbes's concept of contract. One was John Locke, an immensely influential English thinker. In *Two Treatises of Government* (1689), Locke argued that all people are born with natural rights, which he identified as life, liberty, and property, and that government is obligated to protect these rights. If it fails to do so, and instead proves abusive or despotic, it has broken the contract, and the people have the right to unseat it, forming a new government that better meets their needs. Governments, he implied, get their authority from the people they rule. Locke's

Hobbes and Locke focus on contractual government

Document 24.1 John Locke—Excerpts from The Second Treatise of Civil Government

Writing just before the Glorious Revolution in England, John Locke set forth an inspiring vision of a civil society in which government is legitimate only insofar as it protects the life, liberty, and property of the individual and enjoys the confidence of those who are governed.

The state of nature has a law of nature to govern it which obliges every one; and reason, which is that law, teaches all mankind who will but consult it that, being all equal and independent, no one ought to harm another in his life, health, liberty, or possessions . . .

Men being, as has been said, by nature all free, equal, and independent, no one can be put out of his estate and subjected to the political power of another without his own consent. The only way whereby any one divests himself of his natural liberty, and puts on the bonds of a civil society, is by agreeing with other men to join and unite into a community for their comfortable, safe, and peaceable living one amongst another, in a secure enjoyment of their properties and a greater security against any that are not of it . . .

The great and chief end, therefore, of men's uniting into commonwealths and putting themselves under government is the preservation of their property . . .

. . . when the government is dissolved, the people are at liberty to provide for themselves by erecting a new legislative, differing from the other by the change of persons or form, or both, as they shall find it most for their safety and good . . .

SOURCE: John Locke, *The Second Treatise of Civil Government* (New York: Vintage Books, 1947), 123, 168–169, 184, 232.

Treatises seemed to justify the Glorious Revolution of 1688–1689, in which the English replaced a despotic ruler with new ones pledged to defend the people's rights. Locke also advanced the philosophy of knowledge. In his *Essay Concerning Human Understanding* (1690), he rejected the long-held assumption that people are born with ideas. Influenced by Ibn Tufayl (*too-FILE*), a twelfth-century Muslim who wrote about a person growing up alone on an island, Locke asserted that at birth all minds are like a blank slate, or *tabula rasa* (*TAHB-yoo-lah RAH-sah*), and that ideas are shaped by environment and experience. In stark contrast to prevailing notions of nobility and race, Locke held that all humans are equal at birth; what each becomes is determined by interaction with the surrounding world (see "John Locke—Excerpts from *The Second Treatise of Civil Government*").

Locke's ideas had a huge impact. European political philosophers, and later revolutionaries in the Americas and France, found inspiration in his notions that humans are born equal with natural rights, that governments have a duty to protect these rights, and that people are entitled to change or remove a regime that fails to do so. In 1776, in the American Declaration of Independence, Thomas Jefferson used Locke's views to inspire and justify the American Revolution (Chapter 26).

Another new perspective on governance was provided by Baron Montesquieu (*MONT-usk-yoo*), a French aristocrat who in 1748 published *The Spirit of Laws*. Using an empirical approach, he examined various political systems to determine what worked best. He concluded that no system was ideal and that the best form of government for any given state depended on its size, climate, economy, and traditions. Democracy, for example, seemed best for small city-states with homogeneous populations, while monarchy was best for large, diverse empires.

Document 24.2 Montesquieu—Excerpts from *The Spirit of Laws*

In 1748, the Baron de Montesquieu suggested that the separation of the executive, legislative, and judicial powers of government is essential to the maintenance of liberty and the avoidance of tyranny.

In every government there are three sorts of power: the legislative; the executive in respect to things dependent on the law of nations; and the executive in regard to matters that depend on the civil law.

By virtue of the first, the prince or magistrate enacts temporary or perpetual laws, and amends or abrogates those that have been already enacted. By the second, he makes peace or war, sends or receives embassies, establishes the public security, and provides against invasions. By the third, he punishes criminals, or determines the disputes that arise between individuals. The latter we shall call the judiciary power, and the other simply the executive power of the state . . .

When the legislative and executive powers are united in the same person, there can be no liberty; because apprehension may arise, lest the same monarch or senate should enact tyrannical laws, to execute them in a tyrannical manner.

Again, there is no liberty, if the judiciary power be not separated from the legislative and executive. Were it joined with the legislative, the life and liberty of the subject would be exposed to arbitrary control; for the judge would be then the legislator. Were it joined to the executive power, the judge might behave with violence and oppression . . .

As in a country of liberty, every man who is supposed to be a free agent ought to be his own governor; the legislative power should reside in the whole body of the people. But since this is impossible in large states, and in small ones is subject to many inconveniences, it is fit the people should transact by their representatives what they cannot transact by themselves . . .

SOURCE: Charles de Secondat, Baron de Montesquieu, *The Spirit of Laws*, translated by Thomas Nugent (Chicago: University of Chicago Press, 1952), 69–71.

Montesquieu nonetheless preferred a mixed system that drew on the best features of each form of government. Here his model was Britain, which to him seemed to have a fortunate combination of monarchy (the king), aristocracy (the House of Lords), and representative democracy (the House of Commons). Since the power of each was balanced by the other two, he concluded, this arrangement could prevent the sort of unchecked absolutism that had emerged in his native France. Montesquieu's ideas about the balance and separation of power (see "Montesquieu—Excerpts from *The Spirit of Laws*") later influenced the framers of the United States Constitution.

Montesquieu describes a government in which power resides in separate institutions that balance one another

THE PHILOSOPHES: PROGRESS AND SOCIAL JUSTICE. Montesquieu was one of the eminent French thinkers called **philosophes** (*FĒ-luh-ZŌF*) who dominated the Enlightenment in the eighteenth century. Philosophes espoused **deism,** a rational religion that viewed God not as a divinity involved deeply in human affairs but as a kind of master mechanic or "great watchmaker" who created the universe as a vast machine, established the laws by which it operates, and then mostly left it alone. But above all philosophes believed in reason and progress. They were convinced that society would steadily improve if great thinkers applied reason and scientific rigor to the study of human affairs and then published their work so others could build on it.

The spirit of the philosophes was exemplified by the great *Encyclopedia*, edited by the energetic philosophe Denis Diderot (*dē-deh-RŌ*). In a mammoth undertaking, Diderot and his colleagues gathered detailed articles by experts in numerous fields, from art to astronomy to political theory, and then published them in 28 large volumes (1751–1772) to make them available to all. Convinced of the power of education and publicity, the editors expected thereby to advance all areas of human endeavor.

But a philosophe called Voltaire, widely considered the Enlightenment's dominant figure, disputed this optimistic view. Raised in a middle-class French family and like Montesquieu an admirer of British ideas, Voltaire published works promoting the perceptions of Newton and Locke. Brilliant, sarcastic, and self-righteous, Voltaire was a passionate advocate of tolerance and freedom, an outspoken critic of France's monarchy and the Catholic Church, a crusader against injustice, and a champion of persons who had been abused by the wealthy and powerful.

For example, Voltaire's most famous work, *Candide* (1759), was written in response to a cataclysmic earthquake and tsunami that in 1751 had destroyed much of Lisbon, taking some thirty thousand lives. Subtitled *Optimism*, the book is a biting satire of the early Enlightenment's faith in progress. As the hero Candide and his beloved Cunegunde are exposed to war, torture, rape, disease, corruption, natural disaster, and religious persecution, Candide's teacher Dr. Pangloss repeatedly assures them that this is "the best of all possible worlds." This caricature was a none-too-subtle attack on such thinkers as German philosopher Gottfried Leibniz (*LĪP-nits*), who claimed that all events were necessary parts of God's overall design, and English poet Alexander Pope, who declared in his *Essay on Man* (1734) that "Whatever is, is right." To Voltaire, there was much that was wrong in the world, and a pressing need to combat injustice, ignorance, and oppression.

Like Voltaire, Jean-Jacques Rousseau (*roo-SŌ*), a Swiss-born French author and composer, was a champion of freedom and justice, but his ideas differed from those of other Enlightenment thinkers. Unlike Hobbes, who claimed that people were by nature selfish and violent, Rousseau believed that in the "state of nature" they were honest, unselfish, and free, and that greed, corruption, and oppression were introduced by organized society. Unlike Locke, who regarded property ownership as a natural right, Rousseau saw private property as a source of inequality and evil.

Rousseau's most famous work, *The Social Contract* (1762), began with the ringing phrase "All men are born free, but everywhere they are in chains" and went on to advocate a communal society based on harmony, equality, and virtue. Whereas Hobbes had depicted a contract *between* ruler and ruled, Rousseau envisioned one *among* all members of society. Whereas Locke had stressed individual rights, Rousseau stressed the common good as embodied in the "general will." Government's job was to determine and fulfill this will, not only responding to the desires of the majority but embracing the genuine needs of all people (see "Jean Jacques Rousseau—Excerpts from *The Social Contract*"). Later, believers in democracy and advocates of socialism found inspiration in Rousseau's ideas about community and equality.

The Enlightenment's leading economic thinkers, known as **physiocrats**, included the Frenchmen François Quesnay (*kā-NĀ*), a former court physician at Versailles, and Anne-Robert Turgot (*toor-GŌ*), France's comptroller general in the 1770s. Convinced that increased production and trade would enhance national wealth, they sought to free producers and merchants from artificial restraints imposed by governments and guilds. The physiocrats thus promoted **laissez-faire** (*leh-sā FARE*), a French term meaning "let do" (that is, "let them do as they choose"), a policy that governments should not intervene in economic affairs.

laws of supply & demand

Illustration from the *Encyclopedia*.

Voltaire and Rousseau argue for liberty

Voltaire.

Document 24.3 Jean Jacques Rousseau—Excerpts from *The Social Contract*

In 1762, Jean Jacques Rousseau addressed the problem of the tension between the rights of the individual and those of the community. He found the answer in the concept of a social contract, by which people voluntarily submit to collective government, and in doing so, ensure their individual freedoms.

The problem is to find a form of association which will defend and protect with the whole common force the person and goods of each associate, and in which each, while uniting himself with all, may still obey himself alone, and remain as free as before. This is the fundamental problem of which the *Social Contract* provides the solution . . .

. . . each man, in giving himself to all, gives himself to nobody; and as there is no associate over whom he does not acquire the same right as he yields others over himself, he gains an equivalent for everything he loses, and an increase of force for the preservation of what he has . . .

Each of us puts his person and all his power under the supreme direction of the general will, and, in our corporate capacity, we receive each member as an individual part of the whole . . .

This public person, so formed by the union of all other persons formerly took the name of *city*, and now takes that of *Republic* or *body politic*; it is called by its members *State* when passive, *Sovereign* when active, and *Power* when compared with others like itself. Those who are associated in it take collectively the name of *people*, and severally are called *citizens*, as sharing in the sovereign power, and *subjects*, as being under the laws of the State . . .

SOURCE: Jean Jacques Rousseau, *The Social Contract*, translated by G. D. H. Cole (Chicago: University of Chicago Press, 1952), 391–392. The Physiocrats: Economic Freedom.

These ideas were systematized and expanded by the Scotsman Adam Smith, the "father of modern economics," who in 1776 produced his classic *Inquiry into the Nature and Causes of the Wealth of Nations*. Smith condemned mercantilism, the prevailing practice in which governments established colonies and regulated commerce to produce a favorable balance of trade. Instead he claimed that, if the economy were left alone, the forces of self-interest and competition would work as an "invisible hand" to increase overall prosperity. Consumers would naturally seek to buy quality goods and services at reasonable prices. Producers and merchants who met these objectives would prosper. Those who could make and sell good shoes, for example, at lower prices than competitors, would attract more customers and make more money, a powerful incentive for other producers to meet customers' needs. Supply and demand rather than government, he argued, should regulate production and prices. As demand increased it would drive prices up, but ambitious producers would soon respond by increasing supply, and prices would go down. Over time, quality would improve, prices would fall, and the public welfare would be secured. In promoting such ideas, Smith shaped modern arguments for free-market capitalism.

Adam Smith describes modern economic principles

GENDER AND THE ENLIGHTENMENT. With its focus on challenging traditional beliefs and securing people's rights, the Enlightenment also inspired discussion of what was then a revolutionary concept: the notion that women should have equal rights with men. Some philosophes, including the Marquis de Condorcet (*kōn-dor-SĀ*), argued that depriving women of such rights was irrational and unjust. Others, however, including Rousseau, saw it as unnatural for women to participate in public affairs.

Despite the persistence of such attitudes, some talented women played prominent roles in the Enlightenment. Condorcet's wife, Sophie, for example, translated Adam Smith's works into French and hosted a **salon**, a regular gathering where eminent thinkers and writers mingled with political and social leaders. Madame Geoffrin (*zhaw-FRAHN*), who used her husband's wealth to help finance Diderot's *Encyclopedia*, also held frequent influential salons. The Marquise du Chatelet (*shah-teh-LĀ*), Voltaire's longtime companion, was a gifted scientist and mathematician who translated Newton's *Principia* and other key works into French. And Madame de Pompadour (*pawm-pah-DOOR*), mistress of France's King Louis XV, was a dominant force in political and diplomatic affairs, a friend of the philosophes, and a generous patron of literature and the arts.

Women play an active role in the Enlightenment

While these eminent French women benefited from ties with influential men and hosted salons attended mostly by males, in England some notable women rejected the patriarchal rules of their male-dominated society. Lady Mary Wortley Montagu (*MAHN-tug-yoo*), for example, refused to enter a marriage arranged by her father and promoted the radical notion that women should choose their own husbands. Mary Wollstonecraft, regarded today as a forerunner of modern feminism, was an ardent champion of sexual freedom and women's liberation from male domination. Determined to make her own way in life, she educated herself through extensive reading; then she worked as a governess and teacher before becoming a translator and publisher. In 1792 she published *A Vindication of the Rights of Women*, an impassioned and articulate call for equal education of women and men. Her work, and a "Declaration of the Rights of Woman," published in France in 1791 by a writer called Olympe de Gouges (*aw-LAMP duh GOOZH*) (Chapter 26), were early milestones in the modern women's rights movement.

Absolutism and Enlightenment

Enlightened Absolutism develops in Central and Eastern Europe

Although absolutism by the eighteenth century was Europe's main form of governance, the Enlightenment generated an important shift in the attitudes and actions of some rulers. Intelligent monarchs, no longer content to base their authority mainly on religion and tradition, now sought to portray themselves as benefiting their people and to justify their power as a means for bringing enlightenment and reform. These monarchs met and corresponded with philosophes, published their own ideas, and sought to better the lives of their people through progressive reforms. This linking of absolutism with enlightenment, known as Enlightened Absolutism, flourished in Prussia and Austria as well as in Russia (Chapter 25). In England and France, however, where the monarchs lacked the interest and ability to carry out reforms, Enlightened Absolutism never took hold.

Absolutism and Enlightenment in Prussia and Austria

In the early eighteenth century, few European lands seemed less enlightened than Prussia. Its ruler, Frederick William I (1713–1740), was a crude, militaristic drillmaster king who loved his army above all else and had no use for enlightenment. Dressed in uniform rather than royal robes, he was known to patrol the streets of Berlin and beat the lazy and idle with his cane. But his son Frederick, heir to the throne, was a bright, sensitive lad who enjoyed poetry and drama, admired French philosophy, composed music, and even played the flute. These attributes, combined with his homosexual inclinations and indifference to the army, earned Frederick little but abuse from his father the king. Dismayed by this treatment, at age 18 the prince made plans to flee to England, but he was arrested and forced by his father to watch the beheading of the young man who was his accomplice and lover. The prince henceforth gave in, performed various military duties, and quietly looked forward to inheriting the throne.

Upon his father's death, King Frederick II (1740–1788), later called Frederick the Great, distinguished himself as an enlightened monarch. A friend of Voltaire and other philosophes, and an intellectual in his own right, Frederick undertook extensive reforms, calling himself the "first servant of the state." To promote justice, he codified the laws and reformed the court system. To advance industry and commerce, he built roads and canals while lowering taxes on goods shipped within Prussia. To improve his people's welfare, he drained swamps, expanded agriculture, built schools, and promoted religious toleration. Reluctant, however, to offend the landed nobles whom he needed to lead his armies, he did not end serfdom, leaving peasants in bondage to their landlords.

Ironically, given his youthful disdain for the army, Frederick also proved an exceptional warrior. In a series of brilliant campaigns, he more than doubled the size and population of his country, earning a reputation as a military genius. He succeeded in establishing Prussia as one of Europe's great powers, mainly by fighting against the Austrian Habsburgs.

The Habsburgs, meanwhile, were trying to hold together their multinational empire in the absence of a male heir (Map 24.3). Since Maria Theresa, the 23-year-old monarch who inherited the Habsburg lands in 1740, was female, other rulers presumed her to be weak. In December 1740, Prussia's Frederick II boldly invaded the mineral-rich Habsburg province of Silesia; then France and others joined his war against Austria. Since the war was induced by a woman's succession to the Austrian throne, it came to be called the War of the Austrian Succession (1740–1748).

Maria Theresa proved more formidable than her foes had foreseen. In 1741 she took her newborn son (the future Emperor Joseph II) to Hungary and made a dramatic speech, holding him aloft for the Hungarian nobles to see and convincing them to pledge their support to both their beautiful young queen and their future king. Although unable to retake Silesia, she managed to turn back French and Bavarian efforts to create a puppet state in Bohemia.

Once the war ended in 1748, Maria Theresa set out to strengthen her realm. She and her advisers modernized and centralized the bureaucracy, unified the administration of Austria and Bohemia, and compelled their nobles to pay taxes. To better the lot of her subjects, she established an elementary school system and enacted reforms that reduced the nobles' power and improved the welfare of their serfs. Yet as a staunch Catholic who resisted religious toleration, she did not entirely qualify as an enlightened monarch.

Her son Joseph, however, fully fit this description. After his mother's death in 1780, Emperor Joseph II, dismayed by the suffering of his subjects, issued a series of radical decrees intended to impose Enlightenment ideals throughout Habsburg lands. In 1781 he abolished serfdom, empowered peasants to buy their own land, and even let them choose their own spouses. Later, despite vehement opposition from the pope, he proclaimed religious toleration and freedom of worship for his subjects. He also instituted freedom of the press, civil rights for Jews, equality before the law, and equality of taxation.

These actions did not always achieve the positive effects that Joseph intended. The nobles agitated against them, destabilizing the realm and confusing the peasants Joseph

Frederick the Great rules by Enlightenment principles

Schönbrunn Palace in Vienna, the summer residence of the Habsburgs.

Joseph II imposes the Enlightenment on Austria

Map 24.3 Europe in 1763

By 1763, Europe was clearly a continent in transition. The relentless expansionism of Louis XIV died with him in 1715, and France lost substantial territory overseas during the Seven Years War (1756–1763). Observe that the medieval Holy Roman Empire was becoming obsolete in an era of strong, absolute national monarchies, and was now the subject of a struggle for control between Austria and Prussia. What might this trend toward absolute monarchies mean for a multinational state like the Ottoman Empire?

was trying to help. As rebellions against his reforms broke out in several regions, Joseph grew discouraged. He died disillusioned in 1790, after which his successors rescinded most of his reforms.

Unenlightened Monarchy in England and France

Ironically, neither England nor France—the Enlightenment's two main centers—experienced enlightened or effective monarchy in the eighteenth century. England, with a strong Parliament that could govern in the absence of a capable ruler, nonetheless grew wealthier and stronger. France, with no such institution to make up for a weak ruler, drifted toward bankruptcy and political chaos.

The English monarchy was transformed by several key events in the early eighteenth century. In 1701, twelve years after removing King James II, Parliament passed an Act of Settlement excluding him and his Catholic heirs from the throne. In 1707 an Act of Union formally merged England and Scotland into the Kingdom of Great Britain. In 1714 the death of Queen Anne, the last non-Catholic member of the Stuart family, brought an end to the dynasty.

Anne was succeeded by a distant Protestant cousin, the ruler of a small German state called Hanover, who became King George I (1714–1727). As foreigners, he and his son King George II (1727–1760) relied heavily on their British ministers. From 1721 until 1742, the gifted politician Robert Walpole, the main leader of the House of Commons, effectively ran the government. The precedent he set established a crucial position, later called the **prime minister,** in which the same person serves as leader of both Parliament and the royal government, with both legislative and executive authority. The monarch, of course, was still head of state, but that role came to be largely ceremonial. Indeed, when King George III (r. 1760–1820) tried to play an active role in government, he ran into stiff opposition and eventually was labeled a tyrant by many of his subjects in Britain and North America.

The British Parliament asserts control of policy

Meanwhile absolutism in France, so dynamic under Louis XIV, deteriorated once he was gone. Having outlived his oldest son and grandson, the Sun King was succeeded in 1715 by his 5-year-old great-grandson, who became King Louis XV (r. 1715–1774). While the new king was still a boy, France was ruled by a regent, who let the nobles regain much of the power they had lost under Louis XIV. Later, when Louis XV came of age, he proved a lazy and weak-willed ruler who made several attempts at reform but withdrew when he met opposition from the nobles. Lavish spending, costly wars, and failure to fix a financial system that exempted the nobles from taxation led the French government increasingly toward bankruptcy, creating the crisis that triggered the French Revolution of 1789.

France drifts toward bankruptcy

Chapter Review

Putting It in Perspective

In the seventeenth and eighteenth centuries, Western and Central Europe experienced great changes in approaches to government and society. Absolutism triumphed as the preferred form of government, and science and reason came to dominate all forms of intellectual thought.

Absolutism's triumph was based on interactions among monarchs, nobles, and wealthy middle classes. In France, absolutism triumphed because the monarchy, relying on support from the wealthy middle classes, managed to undermine the nobles' power while expanding their prestige. In Austria and Prussia, where there was no strong middle class, absolutism triumphed because the nobles supported it as a way to promote state power; in return, monarchs allowed the nobles to keep their privileges and control the peasants. In England absolutism did not triumph, largely because the nobles and wealthy middle classes, as represented in Parliament, worked to limit the monarchy and force it to share power with Parliament.

The ascendancy of science and reason, meanwhile, was based on the challenges of innovative thinkers to prevailing views about science and society. These thinkers not only described laws that govern the universe but also provided new perspectives on governance, social justice, economics, and gender roles. In the short run, these perspectives prompted some rulers to become enlightened reformers; in the long run, they helped inspire the American and French revolutions of the late eighteenth century as well as the industrial and technological revolutions in the nineteenth and twentieth centuries.

Reviewing Key Material

KEY CONCEPTS

royal absolutism, 582

Fronde, 584

Junkers, 588

limited monarchy, 589

Puritans, 590

Eleven Years' Tyranny, 590

Glorious Revolution, 592

Bill of Rights, 592

Enlightenment, 595

philosophes, 597

deism, 597

physiocrats, 598

laissez-faire, 598

salon, 600

prime minister, 603

KEY PEOPLE

Louis XIV, 582, 584

Henri IV, 583

Louis XIII, 583

Cardinal Richelieu, 583

Cardinal Mazarin, 584

Jean-Baptiste Colbert, 585

Frederick William von
   Hohenzollern, 588

James I, 589

Charles I, 589

Oliver Cromwell, 590

Charles II, 591

James II, 591

William III and Mary, 592

Claudius Ptolemy, 593

Nicholas Copernicus, 593

Johannes Kepler, 593

Francis Bacon, 593

René Descartes, 593

Galileo Galilei, 594

Isaac Newton, 594

Thomas Hobbes, 595

John Locke, 595

Baron Montesquieu, 596

Denis Diderot, 597

Voltaire, 598

Jean-Jacques Rousseau, 598

Adam Smith, 599

Madame de Pompadour, 600

Lady Mary Wortley
   Montagu, 600

Mary Wollstonecraft, 600

Olympe de Gouges, 600

Frederick William I, 600

Frederick the Great, 601

Maria Theresa, 601

Joseph II, 601

Robert Walpole, 603

Louis XV, 603

ASK YOURSELF

1. Why and how did France become an absolute monarchy in the seventeenth century? Why was the French model so attractive to rulers in Central Europe?

2. How did absolutism in Austria and Prussia differ from that in France? How did Central European society differ from that in the West? What impact did these differences have on governance?

3. What personal, political, social, and religious factors contributed to the failure of absolutism and development of limited monarchy in England in the seventeenth and eighteenth centuries?

4. What combination of circumstances and insights led to the great scientific advances of the seventeenth century? How and why did these advances contribute to the quest for new perspectives on governance and society?

5. What were the central ideals of the Enlightenment, and how did they relate to governance, society, economics, and gender? How and why did eighteenth century monarchs act as enlightened rulers?

GOING FURTHER

Anchor, Robert. *The Enlightenment Tradition.* 1987.

Ashley, M. *The House of Stuart: Its Rise and Fall.* 1980.

Beik, W. *Absolutism and Society in Seventeenth-Century France.* 1989.

Bergin, Joseph. *The Short Oxford History of Europe: The Seventeenth Century.* 2001.

Doyle, William. *The Old European Order.* 1978.

Dunn, John. *The Political Thought of John Locke.* 1990.

Fichtner, P. S. *The Habsburg Monarchy, 1490–1848.* 2003.

Gay, Peter. *The Enlightenment: An Interpretation.* 2 vols. 1966–1969.

Henry, J. *Scientific Revolution and Origins of Modern Science.* 1997.

Hunt, Margaret, and M. Jacob. *Women and the Enlightenment.* 1984.

Jacob, J. R. *The Scientific Revolution.* 1998.

Kenyon, J. P. *Stuart England.* 1978.

Koch, H. W. *A History of Prussia.* 1978.

Ladurie, Emmanuel Le Roy. *The Ancien Regime: A History of France, 1610–1774.* 1998.

Le Donne, John. *Absolutism and Ruling Class.* 1991.

Manning, B. *The English People and the English Revolution.* 1976.

McKay, D., and H. Scott. *Rise of the Great Powers, 1648–1815.* 1983.

Miller, John. *Absolutism in Seventeenth-Century Europe.* 1990.

Munck, Thomas. *The Enlightenment: A Comparative Social History, 1721–1794.* 2000.

Outram, D. *The Enlightenment.* 1995.

Rosenberg, Hans. *Bureaucracy, Aristocracy, and Authority: The Prussian Experiment, 1660–1815.* 1966.

Scott, H. *Enlightened Absolutism*. 1990.
Shennan, J. H. *Liberty and Order in Early Modern Europe*. 1986.
Speck, W. A. *The Revolution of 1688*. 1988.

Wiesner, Merry E. *Women and Gender in Early Modern Europe*. 2000.
Wilson, P. H. *Absolutism in Central Europe*. 2000.
Wolf, John B. *Louis XIV*. 1966.

Key Dates and Developments

Absolutism in France

1610–1643	Reign of King Louis XIII
1624–1642	Cardinal Richelieu as first minister
1643–1715	Reign of King Louis XIV
1643–1648	Ministry of Mazarin
1648–1653	Rebellion of the Fronde
1653–1661	Ministry of Mazarin
1661–1715	Active reign of Louis XIV
1682	Completion of the palace at Versailles
1685	Revocation of the Edict of Nantes
1715–1774	Reign of King Louis XV

Limited Monarchy in England

1603–1625	Reign of James I (first Stuart monarch)
1625–1649	Reign of Charles I
1629–1640	Eleven Years' Tyranny
1642–1647	English Civil War
1649	Execution of Charles I
1649–1658	Rule of Oliver Cromwell
1660–1685	Reign of Charles II
1685–1688	Reign of James II
1688–1689	The Glorious Revolution and Bill of Rights
1689–1702	Reign of William III (and Mary, until 1694)
1701	Act of Settlement
1702–1714	Reign of Queen Anne (last Stuart monarch)
1707	Formation of the Kingdom of Great Britain
1714–1727	Reign of King George I
1721–1742	Governance of Robert Walpole
1727–1760	Reign of King George II

Absolutism in Austria and Prussia

1640–1688	Reign of Frederick William, Great Elector in Brandenburg
1648	Peace of Westphalia (End of Thirty Years War)
1683	Lifting of the Siege of Vienna
1699	Expulsion of Ottoman Turks from Hungary
1701–1740	Reign of King Frederick I in Prussia
1740–1788	Reign of King Frederick II the Great in Prussia
1740–1780	Reign of Maria Theresa in Austria, Hungary, Bohemia
1740–1748	War of the Austrian Succession
1780–1790	Reforms of Joseph II in Austria, Hungary, Bohemia

Europe's Intellectual Revolution

1543	Publication of the Copernican hypothesis
1620	Francis Bacon's *Novum Organum*
1632	Galileo's *Dialogue on the Two Chief World Systems*
1637	Descartes's *Discourse on Method*
1651	Hobbes's *Leviathan*
1687	Newton's *Principia*
1689	Locke's *Two Treatises of Government*
1748	Montesquieu's *The Spirit of Laws*
1751–1772	Diderot's *Encyclopedia*
1751	Lisbon earthquake
1759	Voltaire's *Candide*
1762	Rousseau's *Social Contract*
1776	Adam Smith's *Wealth of Nations*

CHAPTER 25

Russia's Eurasian Empire: Convergence of East and West, 1300–1800

■ Russia's Eastern Orientation

■ Russia's Western Reorientation

■ Chapter Review

Saint Basil's Cathedral, Moscow

Saint Basil's Cathedral, built on the edge of Moscow's Red Square to celebrate Russian expansion in the 1550s, is a striking symbol of Russia's Eurasian culture, combining and connecting contrasting features of Eastern and Western cultures.

In spring of 1697 there appeared in Europe a 250-member traveling entourage from Muscovy, a vast eastern domain, alien to most Europeans, that stretched across northern Eurasia from Poland to the Pacific. The Grand Embassy from Muscovy, as the entourage was known, spent 16 months visiting such countries as Prussia, Holland, England, and Austria, and creating quite a stir. Many Europeans, having never seen Muscovites, were appalled by their heavy drinking and uncouth behavior. In England, for example, the Muscovites stayed three months in an elegant mansion, which they virtually destroyed. They drank around the clock, smashed the fine furniture, tore apart the feather beds, used the prized paintings for target practice, and ran drunken races with wheelbarrows through the splendid gardens and hedges.

Russian Empire

The member of this embassy who attracted the most attention was a young Muscovite who called himself Peter Mikhailov (*mik-HĪ-loff*). Handsome and strong, he stood six feet seven inches tall and spoke with a booming voice punctuated by wild arm gestures and nervous twitches of the head. Word soon spread that he was really Peter Romanov, Muscovy's all-powerful tsar, who had come to Europe looking for ways to strengthen and enrich his country, while traveling with the embassy under an assumed name as an apprentice shipbuilder. Largely unknown outside Muscovy, he would later gain renown as Russian Emperor Peter the Great, a ruler who seemed larger than life in both stature and deeds.

Peter's Grand Embassy not only accentuated the gulf between "crude" Muscovites and "sophisticated" Westerners, it also marked a major turning point in Russian history. Hitherto, although it had contacts with Europe, Russia's political and cultural orientation had generally been Eastern, not Western. In the tenth through twelfth centuries, Russians had adopted Byzantine culture and Eastern Christianity. In the thirteenth and fourteenth centuries, they had been ruled by Mongols from the East. In the fifteenth century, led by the principality of Moscow, they had thrown off Mongol rule and formed a realm called Muscovy (the lands controlled by Moscow) that expanded eastward in the next two centuries all the way to the Pacific. Now, on the eve of the eighteenth century, Peter had decided to reorient his country and culture toward the West. In the century that followed, he and his successors transformed their huge realm into a great world power, blending elements of East and West, known as the Russian Empire.

Russia's Eastern Orientation

Throughout its early history, Russia's political and cultural orientation was determined by its location on the edges of both Europe and Asia, and by its conversion in the tenth century to the eastern form of Christianity, practiced in the Byzantine Empire. Battered by nomadic invasions across the Eurasian steppes, then conquered and ruled for several centuries by

Mongols, Russians clung to their Byzantine heritage, including Eastern Orthodox Christianity. In the fifteenth century, as the Ottoman Turks destroyed what was left of the Byzantine Empire (Chapter 17), Russia re-emerged from Mongol rule as an independent principality under the dominion of Moscow, which claimed both the Byzantine legacy and leadership of the Orthodox world. Over the next few centuries, it expanded to the South and East, asserting control over the Eurasian steppes and all of northern Asia (Map 25.1).

The Byzantine and Mongol Heritage

Orthodox Christianity orients Russia eastward

Kievan Russia's conversion in the tenth century to Eastern Christianity (Chapter 10) had far-reaching consequences. Not only did it bring Russians the richness of Orthodox ritual; it also infused their agrarian Slavic society with Byzantine political and cultural ideals, including the caesaropapist tradition in which a ruler held both religious and

FOUNDATION MAP 25.1 Russian Expansion, 1300–1800

Territorial expansion and East-West connections have been central themes of Russian history. Notice that the Principality of Moscow, a small Russian state under Mongol sway at the start of the fourteenth century, expanded in all directions over the next five centuries, resulting by 1800 in a mammoth Russian Empire that stretched from Eastern Europe to the Pacific. How was Russia affected by connections with both East and West?

Legend:
- Principality of Moscow, 1300
- Expansion, 1300-1462
- Expansion, 1462-1533
- Expansion, 1533-1598
- Expansion, 1598-1689
- Expansion, 1689-1800

secular authority. Eastern Christianity also divided Russia from its western neighbors—Poles, Lithuanians, Germans, and Swedes—who embraced Western, Catholic Christianity and European culture. But it did not furnish Russians with lasting political unity. Indeed, by the twelfth century, the Russian lands were divided among contentious principalities, leaving them open to conquest by the Mongols during the thirteenth century.

The Mongol conquest, by making Russia part of a vast pan-Asian empire, further reinforced Russia's eastern orientation. Adapting to Mongol rule, the Russians retained their Orthodox faith and Byzantine heritage, maintaining a cultural identity that distinguished them from both their Asian conquerors and their European neighbors. As long as the Russians were willing to submit, the Mongols let them keep their faith and culture, thus making Mongol rule more acceptable to Russians than the threat of conquest by the Catholic West. Indeed, in the early 1240s, while pledging allegiance to the Mongols from the East, Russian Grand Prince Alexander Nevskii defiantly battled Catholic Swedish and German invaders from the West.

Mongols reinforce Russia's eastern orientation

The Rise of Moscow

In the fourteenth century, partly through collaboration with Russia's Mongol rulers, Moscow emerged as Russia's leading city and the headquarters of the Russian Orthodox Church. Using this strength and status, Moscow eventually overcame the Mongols, united Russian lands under its rule, and claimed the Byzantine legacy.

In the early 1300s the princes of Moscow, exploiting its position as a trading center among other Russian cities, began increasing their power and wealth by working with the Mongols. Prince Ivan I, who ruled Moscow from 1325 to 1340, helped the Mongols crush a rival Russian city, collected tribute from other Russians for the Mongols, and in 1328 got the Mongols to proclaim him Grand Prince, the overlord of other Russian princes. He also persuaded Russia's **metropolitan**, the head bishop of the Russian Orthodox Church, to settle in Moscow, rather than moving from city to city as his recent predecessors had done. Moscow thus became, and henceforth remained, Russia's religious center.

Moscow emerges as Russia's religious center

Ivan I's successors mostly retained the title of Grand Prince and support of the church while steadily expanding the lands under Moscow's control. Aided by a commanding stone wall built in 1367 around the **Kremlin**—a fortified area in central Moscow housing churches, palaces, and government headquarters—Moscow also warded off attacks from the West by Lithuania and Poland. Alarmed by Moscow's growing power, in 1380 the Mongols sent an army to suppress it, but the Mongol army was ambushed and defeated by Moscow's Grand Prince Dmitri. The Mongols returned to sack Moscow in 1382, forcing it again to pay tribute, but the city nonetheless continued to grow and to act with increasing autonomy.

The Kremlin in the 1400s.

In the next century Grand Prince Ivan III, known as Ivan the Great, used war, intimidation, diplomacy, and bribery to annex most other Russian regions, tripling Muscovy's size (Map 25.2) during his long reign (1462–1505). He won over the **boyars**, Russia's landed warrior nobles, by granting them lands and privileges in return for their allegiance to Moscow. And he refused to pay tribute to the Mongols, who in 1480 finally sent an army against him. At a river southwest of Moscow, the Mongols camped on one side and Russians on the other. As winter came and the river froze, Ivan had his forces pack up for retreat, fearing a Mongol assault across the ice. Assuming, however,

Ivan the Great unites Russian lands and ends Mongol rule

Map 25.2 Expansion of Muscovy, 1300–1533

From 1300 to 1533, while first assisting and later rebelling against their Mongol overlords, the rulers of Muscovy extended their sway over a vast area. Note that the Muscovite realm more than tripled in size during the reign of Grand Prince Ivan III (1462–1505), also called Ivan the Great. What methods did Ivan and other Muscovite rulers use to conquer, absorb, and connect the other Russian principalities?

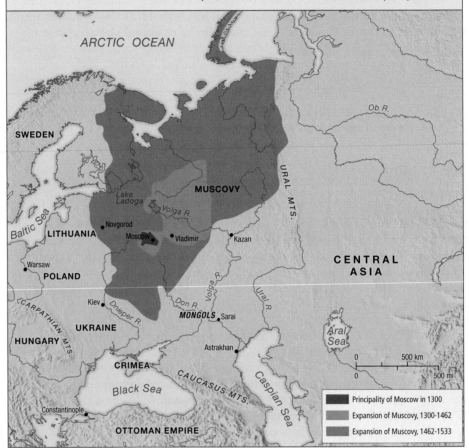

that Ivan was preparing an attack, and alarmed by reports of Russian raids elsewhere, the Mongols instead withdrew. This odd episode ended Mongol rule in Russia and marked the emergence of Muscovy as a fully independent power.

Ivan also worked to make Moscow heir to Constantinople. In 1453, shortly before his reign began, the Ottoman Turks had conquered that city, for centuries the center of Byzantine culture and Eastern Orthodox Christianity. As the Turks converted Constantinople into a Muslim metropolis, Moscow became by default the main city in the Byzantine Orthodox world. In 1472, to enhance this status, Ivan married Zoe Paleologus (*ZŌ-ē pā-lē-AH-luh-gus*), niece of the last Byzantine emperor, who took the name Sofia and called herself empress. Ivan himself started using the term **tsar**, a

Russian version of the title "caesar" used by Roman and Byzantine emperors, to designate his role as Russia's ruler. In the Kremlin he built a new palace and three great cathedrals, staging elaborate ceremonies to stress his majestic status.

In 1510, five years after Ivan's death, a leading Russian cleric advanced the notion of Moscow as the Third Rome. In this view, after Christian Rome fell to the Germans in 476, Constantinople, the Second Rome, became the center of the true Christian faith. Then, when Constantinople fell to the Turks in 1453, Moscow became Christianity's new center and thus was the Third Rome. Religious in origin, this concept later had political overtones, implying that Russian tsars, not Ottoman sultans, were the rightful successors to the Roman and Byzantine emperors.

Moscow claims the heritage of Constantinople

Ivan the Terrible and His Impact

The first Moscow ruler actually crowned as tsar was Ivan III's grandson, Ivan IV, who reigned from 1533 until 1584. Inheriting the throne at age three, he was first dominated by his mother, who died when he was eight, and then by prominent boyars who fought each other for power. In his formative years, the orphaned prince witnessed brutal intrigues in which these boyars arrested and executed each other; at age 13 Ivan ordered the killing of one of them himself. He grew to hate the leading boyars and developed an apparent cruel streak: he is said to have tortured pet dogs by throwing them from the palace roof and to have trampled townsfolk during drunken horseback rides with wild young friends. His erratic behavior, in which drunken revelry and cruelty alternated with piety and repentance, terrorized and convulsed his country later in his reign.

IVAN'S REFORMS AND EASTWARD EXPANSION. In January 1547, still only 16 years old, Ivan staged an elaborate ceremony in the Kremlin during which he was majestically crowned tsar, symbolically aligning himself with the Roman and Byzantine caesars. The next month he married a young woman named Anastasia, from a minor boyar family called the Romanovs, who was able for a while to calm his stormy temperament. After a devastating fire killed thousands of people in Moscow that June, Ivan publicly repented, promised to rule with compassion, and created a chosen council of advisors to assist him.

Ivan IV is crowned tsar, linking him to caesars

For the next 13 years, from 1547 to 1560, Ivan mostly kept his promise. With the help of his chosen council, he enacted reforms combating corruption in government and church, reducing boyar power, and strengthening the central government's authority. A new law code improved judicial procedures, held local governors liable for subordinates' misdeeds, and imposed strict penalties for crime and corruption. A new fiscal system taxed farmland based on its productivity, replacing a widely abused old system whereby local boyars and officials gathered taxes at will, then sent some revenues to Moscow while keeping the rest themselves.

Ivan also reformed the Muscovite military and used it to expand his realm. He created Moscow's first standing army, with central control, an elite royal guard, and gunpowder weapons such as muskets and cannons. He used his army to attack the Mongols, whose lands had by Ivan's time split into smaller khanates. Using cannon fire to pierce fortress walls, in 1552 his armies overran the Khanate of Kazan to Moscow's East, and in 1556 they conquered the Khanate of Astrakhan in the steppes to the Southeast (Map 25.3).

Muscovite cavalry.

These conquests had a momentous impact on Russia's future development. They doubled the size of the Muscovite domain, opened up the Volga River to Russian trade

Muscovy expands into Mongol and Muslim lands

Map 25.3 Expansion Under Ivan IV and Feodor I, 1533–1598

Tsar Ivan IV (1533–1584), also called Ivan the Terrible, inherited a large domain made up mainly of Russian-speaking peoples conquered and connected by his forebears. Observe, however, that Ivan IV expanded much farther to the East and Southeast by conquering the Mongol Khanates of Kazan and Astrakhan in the 1550s. Then, beginning in the 1580s under Ivan and his son Feodor I (1584–1598), Cossack adventurers invaded the Mongol Khanate of Sibir, adding it to Muscovite domains and opening the way for Russian expansion eastward across northern Asia. How did the conquest of these regions, populated mainly by non-Russians, change the nature of the Muscovite realm?

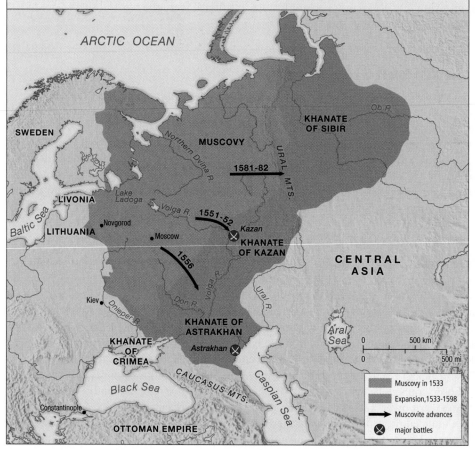

and transport, and removed the main obstacle to eastward expansion across Central Asia and Siberia. They also made Muscovy a multicultural realm, bringing numerous non-Russians, including many Muslims, under Russian rule. Ivan IV's admirers started calling him Ivan *Groznyi*, roughly meaning Ivan the Formidable, later imprecisely translated as Ivan the Terrible.

In gratitude for his military success, Ivan had a cathedral to the Virgin Mary built at the edge of Red Square, a large plaza in central Moscow next to the Kremlin Wall. Completed in 1560, it eventually came to be called Saint Basil's Cathedral, after a wandering ascetic who dared criticize Ivan's later brutality. Composed of nine octagon-shaped red structures, topped with bright candy-colored domes and golden crosses, it has stood ever since as a symbol of Russia's mystery and majesty (see page 606).

IVAN'S REIGN OF TERROR. Ivan's productive years ended in 1560, with the death of his beloved Anastasia, a personal tragedy that soon became Russia's tragedy as well. Deprived of his wife's restraining influence and sickened by suspicion that she had been poisoned, he began attacking members of his chosen council and their associates. Some were arrested and executed; others fled into exile. In 1565 he unleashed a seven-year reign of terror, enforced by an elite cadre of six thousand thugs who, dressed in black and riding at night on black horses, destroyed homes and killed families of boyars Ivan deemed disloyal. In 1570, hearing rumors of a plot against him in Novgorod, he traveled with his forces to that city and conducted an orgy of violence, subjecting thousands of its people to drowning, stabbing, spearing, roasting, or beheading (see "Ivan the Terrible's Attack on Novgorod," page 614).

Ivan's last two decades were disastrous. Thousands of terrified peasants fled to the southern steppes, undermining Muscovy's agrarian economy and causing sporadic starvation. Ivan's armies, earlier so successful in the East against Kazan and Astrakhan, now proved inept in the West, losing a series of ruinous wars to Sweden, Lithuania, and Poland. Then, three years before his own death, Ivan killed his oldest son (and heir) with a cane in a fit of rage. This tragic episode led eventually to a dynastic crisis, known as the Time of Troubles, in which Russia would be torn apart by famine, civil war, and foreign invasions.

Ivan IV terrorizes Russia and loses in the West

THE TIME OF TROUBLES. Ivan was succeeded in 1584 by his surviving son Feodor (*fē-YŌ-dur*), a pious but inept man, known as Feodor the Bellringer, who personally tolled Moscow's many church bells every morning. Feodor I's reign (1584–1598) nonetheless proved productive, owing mainly to his talented advisor Boris Godunov (*GŌ-doo-NOFF*). Godunov sent armies to defeat the Swedes, regaining some territory lost by Ivan IV, while continuing the eastward expansion begun during Ivan's reign. Above all, Godunov compelled the patriarch of Constantinople, overall leader of the Orthodox Church, to install Moscow's metropolitan as the Church's fifth patriarch, making him one of its five main leaders. This action officially recognized Russia's central status in the Orthodox world; it also acknowledged the autonomy of the Russian church, making it a separate branch of the Orthodox faith.

Moscow gains stature in the Orthodox world

Despite such successes, however, a bizarre episode during Feodor's reign foreshadowed troubles to come. In 1591 his nine-year-old half-brother Dmitri, Ivan the Terrible's only other surviving son, was found in a courtyard bleeding to death from a knife wound. Although the death was ruled an accident, many suspected that Dmitri was murdered on the orders of Boris Godunov, so that Boris himself could become tsar after Feodor's death. This impression was enhanced in 1598 when Feodor died and Boris became tsar, elected as such by a **Zemskii Sobor** (*z'YEM-skē saw-BOR*), a specially convened "Assembly of the Land" made up of delegates from Muscovy's various classes.

Boris's short reign (1598–1605) was beset by poor harvests and widespread famine, seen by many Russians as God's punishment for young Dmitri's murder. Resentment converged in 1604 around an adventurer from Poland who claimed to be Dmitri, asserting that he had somehow escaped the earlier murder attempt and was now returning to claim his role as tsar. Known to history as False Dmitri I, he promised his supporters ten years of freedom from taxes; he also raised a ragtag army that was enlarged by defections from

An adventurer from Poland briefly rules in Russia

Document 25.1 Ivan the Terrible's Attack on Novgorod

In 1570, having heard rumors that Novgorod's archbishop was conspiring with Muscovy's Polish-Lithuanian enemies, Tsar Ivan IV took his army to that city to punish it for alleged treason. The following Russian chronicle excerpts, which call the tsar Ivan Vasilevich (Ivan son of Vasily), provide a graphic example of why he is also called Ivan the Terrible.

On January 6 of the same year [1570] . . . , the illustrious Tsar and Grand Prince Ivan Vasilevich, lord of All Russia, arrived in Great Novgorod . . .

On Saturday, the day after his arrival, the illustrious Tsar and Grand Prince Ivan Vasilevich, lord of All Russia, gave the order that the abbots, clergy, and monks, who had previously been brought to the place of execution, should be beaten to death with clubs . . .

On Sunday, the 8th of January, the Tsar went to the Church of St. Sophia with his troops to attend High Mass . . . After the divine service, the Tsar, accompanied by his courtiers, princes, and warriors, went to Archbishop Pimen's palace for dinner. The Tsar sat at the table and began to eat. Soon afterwards, he stopped and turned to his princes and boyars. As was his custom, he shouted to his men in a loud voice shaking with anger. The Tsar commanded his men to plunder the Archbishop's money box, his entire court with all the neighboring buildings, cells, and rooms, and to seize his courtiers and attendants and place them under guard until further notice . . .

Thereupon, the Orthodox Tsar and Grand Prince Ivan Vasilevich, lord of All Russia . . . , held court in the suburbs . . . where he had encamped upon his arrival. The Tsar commanded that the powerful boyars, the important merchants, the administrative officials, and the citizens of every rank be brought before him, together with their wives and children. The Tsar ordered that they be tortured in his presence in various spiteful, horrible, and inhuman ways. After many various unspeakable and bitter tortures, the Tsar ordered that their bodies be tormented and roasted with fire in refined ways . . . He ordered that each man be tied to a sled, be dragged to the Volkhov bridge behind the fast-moving sleds, and be thrown into the Volkhov River from the bridge. The Tsar ordered that their wives and children be brought to the Volkhov bridge where a high platform had been erected. He commanded that they be chained on the arms and legs, and that the children be tied to their mothers and then be thrown from the platform into the waters of the Volkhov River. Meanwhile the Tsar's men, the nobles and soldiers, moved about in small boats on the Volkhov River, armed with spears, lances, hooks, and axes. When the people, men and women of all ages, surfaced, they were stabbed with hooks, lances, and spears, or they were struck with axes. In a horrible manner they were submerged without mercy in the depths of the river, and abandoned to a terrible and bitter death.

Because of our sins, this unspeakable shedding of Christian blood, caused by the excessive anger of the Tsar, continued uninterrupted each day for five weeks or more . . .

SOURCE: *Polnoe Sobranie Russkikh Letopisei* (Complete Collection of Russian Chronicles), III, 254–262. Translation by Basil Dmytryshin, *Medieval Russia: A Source Book, 900–1700*, 2nd ed. (New York: Praeger Publishers, 1973) 237–238.

Boris's forces. In April 1605, when Boris suddenly died, the remaining Muscovite armies refused to support his 16-year-old son, Tsar Feodor II, who reigned only six weeks. Instead they supported False Dmitri I, who was welcomed in Moscow in June as the rightful ruler, replacing young Feodor, who was murdered. The next year, however, after "Tsar Dmitri" angered Muscovites (who hated Poles and despised the Catholic Church) by marrying a Polish Catholic woman, ambitious Russian boyars declared him an imposter and killed him. Then, dramatically displaying their hostility toward the Catholic West, they hacked apart his body, burned the pieces, loaded the ashes into a cannon, and fired it westward toward Poland.

Dmitri's grisly demise, however, did not solve Russia's problems. Instead, for the next five years, Russia descended into chaos. A council of boyars claimed power, naming one of their own as tsar. But the prospect of boyar rule sparked a mass peasant revolt, followed by the emergence of another imposter (False Dmitri II) and by Polish and Swedish invasions that took advantage of the turmoil to seize Russian lands. In 1610 the Poles conquered Moscow and subsequently sought to install their king as the Muscovite tsar.

Faced with the prospect of a Polish Catholic ruler, however, the Russians finally united in a national revival. Led by the 85-year-old Patriarch of Moscow, they raised a National Army that drove the Poles out of the city in late 1612. Then they called a new Zemskii Sobor, which in early 1613 elected as tsar a 16-year-old boy named Michael Romanov, great-nephew of Ivan IV's beloved first wife Anastasia, and son of Filaret (*FĒ-lar-YET*), a prominent Russian churchman who was imprisoned in Poland. Thus began the Romanov dynasty, which ruled Russia until 1917.

Russian national revival rejects Polish rule

The Early Romanovs and the Russian Church Schism

Although the election of Tsar Michael I traditionally marks the end of the Time of Troubles, in 1613 Russia's future still looked very uncertain. A weak young man chosen mainly because others found him non-threatening, Michael ruled jointly with the Zemskii Sobor for the next several years, as Muscovy fought off the Swedes, Poles, and various groups of Russians who rejected Romanov rule. Only in 1619, after a truce with Poland allowed the return of Michael's father Filaret, did it seem clear that the new regime would survive.

For the following 14 years, Michael ruled jointly with his father, who assumed the position of patriarch upon his return to Moscow. As co-rulers, the father-son team of patriarch and tsar gave a new twist to the Byzantine tradition of uniting church and state. Filaret modernized the army and restored regular tax revenues, so by the time he died in 1633 his son Michael sat securely on the throne.

The Romanovs rule Muscovy and expand it westward

Michael was succeeded in 1645 by his own 16-year-old son, who became Tsar Alexis I (1645–1676). Reputedly a kind and gentle man, Alexis nonetheless had a violent reign marked by rebellions and conflicts, including a lengthy war with Poland (1654–1667) that enabled Muscovy to annex eastern Ukraine (Map 25.4). But the biggest crisis of Alexis's reign was a schism in the Russian Orthodox Church.

The schism was triggered by the policies and personality of Patriarch Nikon (1652–1666), an authoritarian churchman who dominated the young tsar and for a time even served as co-ruler, much like Patriarch Filaret in the preceding reign. Convinced by Greek theologians that errors had crept into Russian church rituals, Nikon forced through changes in many popular devotions, including the way to make the sign of the cross and the number of communion wafers to use at Orthodox masses. Many Orthodox Russians, having long regarded the old rituals as central to salvation, saw Nikon's reforms as a threat to their eternal souls.

Before long millions of **Old Believers**, those who rejected Nikon's changes in Russian Orthodox practices, were openly defying church and state leaders, whom they saw as one and the same. In an effort to pacify the religious rebels, Nikon was removed as patriarch in 1666, but since his reforms were left intact the revolt went on. Some Old Believers seized a monastery in the North, then for eight years held off Muscovite forces sent against them. Other Old Believers, rather than submit to a church and government they saw as directed

Schism divides the Russian Orthodox Church

Map 25.4 Muscovite Expansion to the West, 1654–1667

Aided by Cossacks in southern Ukraine who rebelled against Polish rule, Muscovite forces moved into Poland in the mid-1650s. Notice that the long war against Poland resulted in Muscovy's annexation of some territory to its west and southwest, including eastern Ukraine (to the Dnieper River) and the city of Kiev. What key roles did Cossacks play in Muscovite expansion?

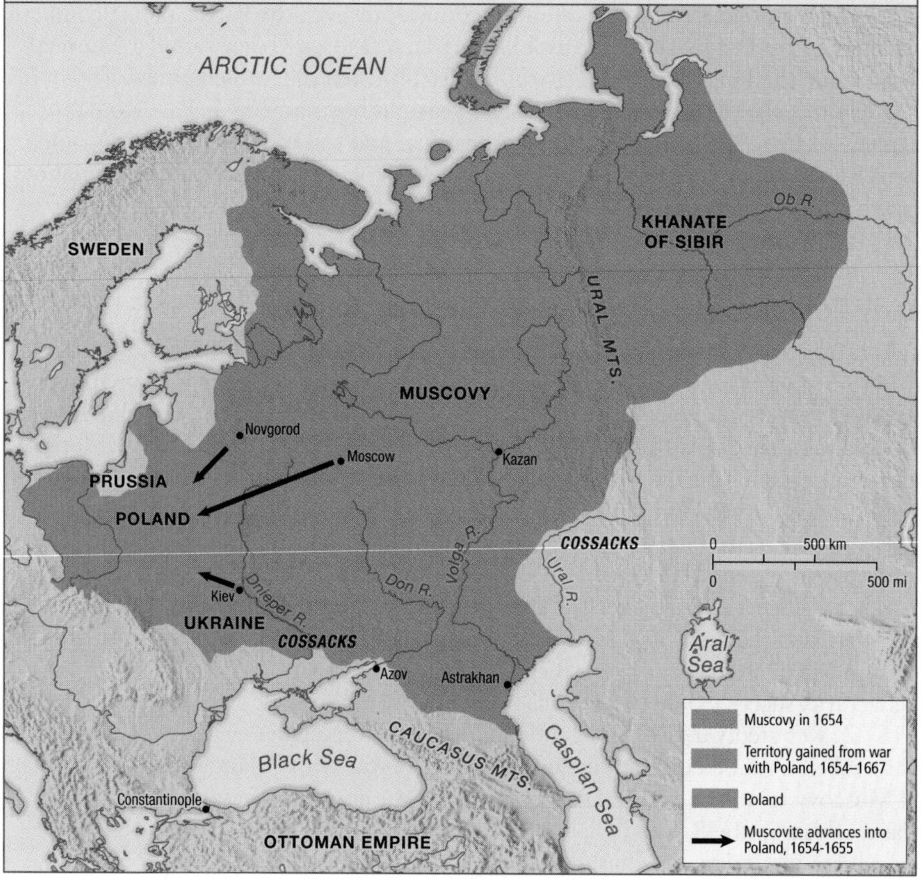

by the devil, resorted to communal suicides, burning themselves to death in boats set ablaze while floating on Russian rivers. Fueled by such zeal, the Old Belief persisted, growing to have millions of supporters, while church and state leaders eventually concluded that efforts to end it were futile.

Muscovite Culture and Society

The passions aroused by the Russian Church Schism reflected the central role of the Orthodox Church in Muscovite culture and society. Another key feature of this society was serfdom, which was firmly entrenched in Russia by the seventeenth century. These institutions affected almost every aspect of Muscovite life.

ORTHODOX AND ASIAN INFLUENCES. Orthodox Christianity permeated Muscovy's culture. Muscovite music was church music, sung slowly and solemnly by all-male choirs without instrumental support, producing a tone sounding joyous to Russians but somber to many outsiders. Muscovite architecture was church architecture, exhibited in numerous ornate churches with onion-shaped domes, gilded crosses, and inner walls covered with elaborate frescoes. Muscovite artists produced mostly **icons**, stylized wooden paintings, typically depicting Christian holy persons, venerated as sources of grace and religious education and often displayed on an iconostasis (icon wall) separating the altar from the congregation in Orthodox churches. Muscovite writers and record keepers were frequently Orthodox monks, who compiled chronicles that serve as the main sources of information about early Russia.

Orthodox influence shapes Muscovite culture

Another key work composed by a cleric was the **Domostroi** (*DAW-muh-STROY*), or "Household Order," a manual advising Russians on family life. Attributed to an Orthodox priest on Ivan IV's chosen council, the *Domostroi* counseled men to discipline their wives and children severely, beating them to instill obedience, and instructed wives to rely on their husbands for advice and support. It also prescribed that diseases, as punishments from God for sins, should be treated mainly by prayer, fasting, and religious rituals (see "Excerpts from the *Domostroi*," page 618).

As reflected in the *Domostroi*, households in old Russia were patriarchal, as in other agrarian societies. Each Russian peasant village typically was run by an assembly of male elders, the patriarchs of each household. Women were excluded from village leadership and often from all public life. In Muscovy, as in India and Persia, women were secluded in the home: they were not supposed to go out in public unless accompanied by a man.

An iconostasis with five rows of icons in a Russian Orthodox Church.

The religious character of Muscovite society was also reflected in the influence of **holy fools**, radical religious ascetics who renounced all worldly goods, wore few clothes, and spoke in seemingly nonsensical phrases deemed prophetic by many Russians. Unlike religious hermits who lived in wilderness caves, holy fools often lived in or near cities, brazenly urging urban dwellers to change their sinful ways. Some warned of cataclysms such as the Time of Troubles; others boldly scolded rulers such as Ivan the Terrible and Boris Godunov. According to legend, Blessed Basil, the holy fool for whom Saint Basil's Cathedral is named, once handed Ivan a piece of bloody meat to signify that the tsar was a great butcher of Russians. Although often persecuted for such actions by agents of the tsar, the holy fools persisted into the mid-1600s, when they were formally suppressed by the Orthodox Church.

Despite the pervasiveness of Orthodox influences, however, some popular aspects of Russian culture came from Asian countries outside the Orthodox world. For example, chess, Russia's favorite game, was an import from Persia; its Russian name *shakhmaty* ("checkmates") comes from Persian words meaning "the shah (king) is helpless." The balalaika (*bal-uh-LĪ-kuh*), a Russian stringed musical instrument, apparently derives from an earlier instrument used in Central Asia. Also from Central Asia came forms of Russian dancing in which people dance alone, not with partners. The abacus, a calculating device on which beads are moved along wires, was adopted from China, as was tea, which became Russia's most widely consumed beverage.

Asian influences affect Muscovite culture

Alcohol was also widely consumed in Muscovite Russia, often in the form of vodka, a potent liquor first distilled in the fourteenth century. Russians gained a reputation for excessive drinking, as exhibited in the story at the start of this chapter. But alcohol also helped Russians endure their long, dark, frigid winters and the rigors of peasant serfdom.

Document 25.2 Excerpts from the *Domostroi*

The Domostroi ("Household Order") sought to give Russians a strict set of patriarchal rules. Men were to run their households firmly, disciplining their wives and children, beating them if they disobeyed, but only in private. Wives were to keep a clean house, rely on their husbands, and avoid drunkenness and gossip. Illness was to be treated mainly by prayer and holy practices.

How to instruct children and save them by fear: Punish your son in his early years and he will comfort you in your old age . . . Do not spare your child any beating, for the stick will not kill him, but will do him good; when you strike the body, you save the soul from death . . . If you love your son, punish him often . . . Raise your child in fear and you will find peace and blessing in him. Do not smile with him, do not play with him, for having been weak in little things you will suffer in great ones . . . Do not give him his will in his youth, but crush his ribs while be is not grown yet, or else he will harden and cease to obey you . . .

How to keep your house clean and well-ordered: In a good family, where the wife is careful, the house is always clean and well-arranged; everything is in order, put away in its right place, cleaned and swept. It's like going into paradise. All this is the wife's job . . . If she complies and does everything as it should be done, she deserves love and favor; but if she fails . . . to do the work . . . , let her husband discipline her and scare her in private; and after he should relent and speak kindly. Behave

likewise with . . . children: punish their offenses, beat them for their faults, then relent . . . But if wife, son, or daughter pay no heed to word or instruction . . . , if they refuse to do what they are told . . . they should be whipped according to their offense. Beat them in private, not in public; punish, then relent and say a loving word . . .

How Christians Are to Cure Diseases and All Kinds of Ailments. If God send any disease or ailment down upon a person let him cure himself through the grace of God, through tears, prayer, fasting, charity to the poor, and true repentance. Let him thank the Lord and beg His forgiveness, and show mercy and undisguised charity to everybody . . . Frequent the miracle-working and holy places, and pray there with a pure conscience. In that way you will receive from God a cure for all your ailments.

The Wife Is Always and in All Things to Take Counsel with Her Husband. In all affairs of everyday life, the wife is to take counsel with her husband, and to ask him, if she needs anything . . . By all means let her abstain from drinking liquor, for a drunk man is bad enough, but a drunk woman has no place in the world. A woman ought to talk with her lady-friends of handiwork and housekeeping . . . And if there is anything she does not know, let her politely inquire about it . . . Let not a woman rail at anyone, or gossip about others . . .

SOURCES: From *The Domostroi*, adapted by Dr. John Slatter (used with permission); *Excerpts from THE DOMOSTROI* (mid-16th century) http://www.dur.ac.uk/a.k.harrington/domstroi.html

SERFDOM AND COLLECTIVE LIABILITY. In the fifteenth through seventeenth centuries, Moscow's growing power was accompanied by growing peasant serfdom. Most Russian peasants were subjected to harsh servitude, bound to the land and dominated by their landlords.

In early Russia, peasants apparently lived in autonomous villages, raising crops such as wheat, oats, and barley, and animals such as cattle and sheep, in the surrounding fields. In expanding their realm and fighting its foes, however, Moscow's grand princes often bribed or rewarded noble warriors by giving them tracts of lands encompassing peasant villages and fields. To support these warriors, who thus became their landlords, peasants were expected to supply labor and food, in return for which the warrior landlords furnished military defense. Initially peasant families were free to move elsewhere, provided they were not in debt to their landlord.

In the fifteenth century, however, to aid landlords by reducing the disruption of peasants moving during growing season, peasant moves were limited by law to a two-week period in late fall after the harvest. Then, during Ivan IV's reign of terror and the chaotic Time of Troubles, as thousands of peasants fled south to escape tyranny and famine, rulers began declaring "forbidden years," in which no peasants could leave their lord's estate at any time. By the early 1600s, almost every year was a forbidden year. Finally, in 1649, this prohibition was made permanent: peasants and their descendants were bound in perpetuity to their landlord's estate.

Russian peasants are gradually subjected to serfdom

A Russian peasant woman's outfit.

Peasants were thus reduced to total serfdom, a status that in Russia differed little from slavery. With few restraints to deter them, landlords could beat their serfs, subject them to burdensome labor, control every aspect of their lives, and even rape serf women. The serfs themselves called serfdom the "rule of the *kmut*" (*k'MOOT*), a flogging device made of strips of knotted leather used to lash peasants to punish them or keep them in line.

Serfdom was reinforced by **collective liability**, a practice whereby all members of a community were jointly responsible for taxes, for various other obligations, and for the actions of everyone in the community. Villagers, for example, were collectively taxed: if one village family either ran away or could not pay its share, the rest had to make up the difference. Similarly, if a runaway serf were returned to the village, the other villagers had to make sure this person did not flee again; if the returned fugitive did escape again, the rest could be severely punished. Villagers were also jointly responsible for services to their landlord, and were obliged to turn in fellow villagers suspected of crimes.

Collective liability connects Russian serfs

Although it reinforced serfdom, collective liability also strengthened community, fostering cooperation and mutual support. Distinct from Western concepts of individual rights and duties, it served as a cement that helped hold together the vast, diverse Russian society.

THE COSSACKS. To escape the confinement of serf society, many Russians fled south to join the **Cossacks,** an assortment of frontier adventurers dwelling in the steppe lands north of the Black and Caspian seas (Map 25.5). The original Cossacks were mostly peasants who, during Ivan the Terrible's reign or the Time of Troubles, fled to the South beyond the reach of landlords and Muscovite rulers. There, on the wild steppes, the escapees and their descendants formed fiercely independent, self-governing societies based on mutual sharing. The Cossacks were a colorful lot, hard-drinking and hard-fighting, living in fortified camps, and frequently hiring themselves out as soldiers and adventurers.

Always eager for a fight, the Cossacks were often disruptive. In the Time of Troubles, for example, they fought on behalf of the False Dmitris and joined peasant revolts, adding to the era's instability. Decades later, many Cossacks supported a revolt led by Stenka Razin (*rah-ZĒN*), a charismatic Cossack who moved north up the Volga River in 1670 with a growing rebel force, butchering landlords and freeing serfs, until crushed in 1671 by a large Muscovite army.

But the Cossacks also performed useful services for Russia. In 1612, for instance, after contributing to Muscovy's turmoil, they joined with the National Army in driving out the Polish invaders. In 1654, after leading an earlier rebellion against Polish rule in eastern Ukraine, the Cossacks turned to Moscow for support, triggering the long war that brought this region under Muscovite rule. And in a series of adventures stretching

Cossacks help unite eastern Ukraine with Muscovy

Map 25.5 Muscovite Expansion in the Seventeenth Century

In the seventeenth century, thanks largely to Cossack adventurers, Muscovy expanded eastward to the Pacific. Observe that, after Cossacks conquered the Khanate of Sibir in the 1580s, other Cossack groups moved across Siberia in the 1600s, establishing settlements along the way, and making Muscovy a huge Eurasian empire rich in timber and furs. What factors contributed to the Cossack expansion across Siberia? How did this expansion help to bring about Russian conflicts and connections with China?

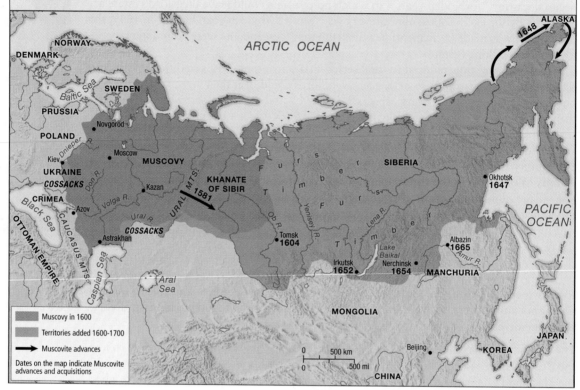

over a century, Cossack groups conquered Siberia, expanding Russia eastward across Asia to the Pacific Ocean (Map 25.5).

Russia's Expansion Across Asia

Far to the East of Moscow, extending across northern Asia from the Ural Mountains to the Pacific, is a vast region called Siberia, a name derived from the Mongol term *Sibir* (*sih-BEER*), meaning "sleeping land." Sparsely populated and bleak, known for its bitter winters and short, hot summers, it consists mainly of forests and plains drained by three great rivers flowing north to the Arctic Ocean. The severe climate ruled out farming in all but the southernmost regions, so early Siberians were pastoral nomads who lived by hunting and herding cattle or reindeer. But Siberia's great forests also teemed with fur-bearing mammals, such as mink, ermine, and fox, whose valuable pelts were a potential source of wealth for Russian trappers and traders. Attracted by such riches, and by the lure of adventure in an untamed land, groups of Cossacks in the 1580s began moving east into Siberia. By the 1700s, after clashing with the Chinese and crushing the Siberian peoples, the Russians ruled the whole vast region.

THE COSSACK CONQUEST OF SIBERIA. The Russian conquest of Siberia was initiated not by the state but by the Stroganovs, a wealthy merchant family anxious to protect and expand its lucrative trade in animal furs from the great Eurasian forests. In 1581–1582 a band of Cossacks, financed by the Stroganovs and led by a soldier of fortune named Yermak, attacked the Khanate of Sibir, a Mongol realm across the Ural Mountains a thousand miles east of Moscow. Using firearms, Yermak's forces initially defeated the larger armies of the Sibir Khanate. A few years later, however, Yermak drowned in battle in Sibir while crossing a river, apparently weighted down by a suit of armor sent him as a gift by Ivan the Terrible. Even a well-meant present from Ivan proved deadly.

Scene from Irkutsk, a Siberian settlement founded by Cossacks in 1652.

Eastward expansion continued under Boris Godunov, who as Tsar Feodor I's advisor in the late 1580s sent Muscovite troops to complete the conquest of Sibir, and as tsar in 1604 ordered the construction of a fortress farther east at Tomsk. Although Boris's death in 1605 and the ensuing Time of Troubles delayed the eastward drive, Siberia nonetheless played a key role in restoring Russian stability. A large loan from the Stroganovs in 1613 and a tax in furs on Siberian residents helped rebuild the Muscovite treasury under Romanov rule.

In the 1620s and 1630s, eastward expansion resumed, as Cossack groups again set out across the Siberian wilderness, founding fortified settlements along the way. One group reached the Pacific, more than four thousand miles from Moscow, in 1639. Another traveled far to the Northeast, and in 1648 went by boat through the straits that separate Siberia from Alaska. A third moved toward Manchuria, eventually coming into contact and conflict with the Chinese Empire.

Cossacks help connect Siberia with Muscovy

CONNECTIONS AND CONFLICTS WITH CHINA. In the 1640s and 1650s, these Cossacks set up fortresses in the region northwest of Manchuria, plundering local peoples and clashing with Manchu outposts. The Manchus, then in the process of extending their rule over China (Chapter 21), treated the Cossacks as an annoying nuisance, sending forces on several occasions to drive them out and destroy their strongholds. But each time Manchu forces left, the Cossacks returned to reoccupy and rebuild their fortresses.

Sporadic clashes continued for several decades, while cultural and linguistic barriers hindered attempts at diplomacy. Envoys sent from Moscow refused to perform the kowtow, an East Asian bow of respect that involved touching one's forehead to the ground, asserting that the gesture was beneath their dignity. This refusal offended the Manchus and Chinese, as did letters delivered from Moscow to Beijing, written in a blunt Russian style that came across to China's rulers as arrogant and belligerent.

Cossacks connect and conflict with Manchus and Chinese

Finally, in frustration, the Kangxi Emperor, greatest of all China's Manchu rulers, sent a large force in the 1680s to drive out the Russians for good. This force destroyed a Russian fortress at Albazin, killing most of its defenders and prompting the Russians to negotiate anew. Moscow this time sent a seasoned diplomat who could speak Latin to the outpost of Nerchinsk near the Manchurian border. China's negotiators included a few French Jesuits, friends of Kangxi from Beijing, who could also speak Latin and thus help to bridge the cultural and linguistic gap. By tactfully softening the language of both sides in the translation process, and by warning the Russians of more Chinese troops on

French Jesuits help arrange treaty between Russia and China

the way, the Jesuits finally facilitated an agreement in 1689. The Treaty of Nerchinsk established a border between Russian and Chinese territory and gave Russians the right to send trading caravans to Beijing. One of history's most successful and enduring accords, it remained in effect (with some modifications) for the next 170 years.

THE EXTENSION OF RUSSIAN RULE. Russia's eastward expansion did not end at Nerchinsk, or even at the Pacific. In the 1700s, Russian explorers crossed from Siberia to Alaska and later moved down the American west coast as far south as northern California. Although their presence in California proved temporary, the Russians held Alaska until 1867, when they finally sold it to the expanding United States of America.

Moscow extends governance over Siberia

Meanwhile Moscow extended governance over its new Siberian lands, home to several dozen distinct nationalities, mostly nomadic societies. Determined to control this immense but sparsely inhabited region, to populate it with Russians, and to continue collecting its rich fur revenues, the Muscovite regime sent out governors, soldiers, and tribute collectors and even encouraged Russian farmers to resettle there.

In many ways, the Russians ruled Siberia harshly, using their muskets to shoot Siberian peoples who resisted or rebelled. Russian attacks and diseases such as smallpox, spread by Russian expansion, killed perhaps half the native population, paralleling the impact of European expansion in the Americas (Chapter 19). Later the Russians also used Siberia as a place to exile criminals and political dissidents.

In other respects, however, the Russians were relatively lenient. They did not extend serfdom to Siberia, for example, nor did they force the Orthodox faith on Siberians—especially since those who converted to Orthodoxy were exempt from the tax in furs. As a result, despite its later reputation as a vast prison camp, Siberia was actually one of Russia's freest regions: a place where people who sought a new life could go to put some distance between themselves and Moscow's autocratic regime.

Russia's Western Reorientation

In the eighteenth century, even as their subjects were expanding and settling an enormous eastern empire, Russia's rulers were reorienting their country and culture toward the West. The transition was begun by Tsar Peter I and continued by his successors, especially Empresses Elizabeth I and Catherine II. Under these rulers Western values and views were imposed upon the realm, while Russia's borders were expanded far to the South and West.

Peter the Great: Westernization and War

Peter in his youth connects with Westerners near Moscow

Tsar Peter I, later called Peter the Great, officially began his reign in 1682. Since he was only ten years old, however, the state was run for the next 12 years by regents—first his older half-sister, then his mother—leaving the young tsar uninvolved in government affairs. Restless and precocious, Peter spent much of this time in Moscow's German suburb, an enclave on the city outskirts housing visiting foreigners, mostly Europeans, whom Russians collectively called Germans. From these foreigners Peter heard about Europe's great cities, technologies, armies, and ocean fleets. He dreamed of seeing them firsthand, and he hoped to make Muscovy a great power with cities, technologies, armies, and fleets matching those of the West. He also hoped to expand Muscovy to the South, at the expense of the Ottoman Turks, to gain year-round warm-water ports on the Black Sea. And so it was that in 1697, after coming of age and taking charge of the government, he embarked on his Grand Embassy to the West, discussed at the start of this chapter. He did so partly to acquire Western technology and knowledge, and partly to gain Europe's support for a war against the Turks.

As a springboard for westernizing Russia, Peter's trip was a success. Concealing his true identity by using an assumed name, he visited cities and seaports, worked as a shipbuilder in Holland, observed European habits and styles, witnessed the workings of Western governments, and enlisted over 750 experts to help him modernize his land.

Peter the Great.

Then, in the decades after returning to Russia in 1698, Peter enacted an array of westernizing reforms. Some were cosmetic, such as making his nobles smoke tobacco, shave their beards, and wear European clothes. Others were substantial: he adopted the western calendar, simplified the Russian alphabet, founded schools, introduced the printing press, and started a newspaper. Peter expanded Russian industry and commerce, created Russia's first navy, and restructured his army and government along Western lines. He instituted a **service state**, requiring all nobles to serve in either the military or the bureaucracy and replacing the old boyar status with a new noble standing based on government service. To structure it he imposed a **Table of Ranks**, a 14-level organizational ladder, requiring state officials and military officers to work their way up the ranks through promotions based on performance rather than on heredity or prestige.

Peter brings Western ideas and ways to Russia

The most vivid symbol of Peter's new Russia was his splendid new capital, Saint Petersburg, whose construction began in 1703. Built on swampy islands at the mouth of a river in northwestern Russia, with sturdy stone and stucco structures designed by Western architects, it cost thousands of laborers their lives. As a seaport on the Gulf of Finland, an arm of the Baltic Sea, Saint Petersburg connected Russia with the great cities of Europe, among which it soon came to be counted. Peter called the city his "window on the West," signifying his country's European future and its break with its Muscovite past.

Peter builds Saint Petersburg as a "window on the West"

Peter likewise achieved his goal of expanding Russia, but not in the way he originally intended. The European powers, with their own problems and goals, refused to join him in war against the Turks. Instead they persuaded him to battle Sweden for lands along the eastern Baltic Sea. The result was the Great Northern War (1700–1721), a pivotal struggle pitting Muscovy, Poland, and Denmark against the Swedes, later joined by the Turks.

At first the war went dreadfully for Peter, as Sweden's young King Charles XII proved a brilliant warrior. With his forces outnumbered five to one, Charles routed the Russians in 1700 at Narva, a town on the Gulf of Finland (Map 25.6), humiliating Peter and making him the laughingstock of Europe. Then, however, disdaining Muscovites as unworthy foes, Charles failed to follow up his victory with an invasion of Russia. Instead he spent six years fighting Poland and forcing it out of the war.

Peter the Great's Palace in St. Petersburg.

Mortified by the Narva defeat, Peter used this time to rebuild his forces, impose training and discipline, improve arms and equipment, and construct a Baltic Fleet. He was ready, then, in 1708, when the Swedes finally invaded, and in 1709 he defeated them decisively at Poltava (*pol-TAH-vah*) in eastern Ukraine. King Charles escaped to Turkey, then regrouped and fought on until his death in 1718, but Peter was ultimately victorious. The Treaty of Nystad (*NĪ-stad*) in 1721 sealed Peter's triumph by giving him control of the Gulf of Finland and the Baltic lands today called Estonia and Latvia. Peter was proclaimed Russian Emperor, transforming the Tsardom of Muscovy into the Russian Empire, henceforth regarded as one of the world's great powers.

Great Northern War connects Russia to Baltic Sea

Map 25.6 The Great Northern War, 1700–1721

Eager to expand his realm to the West and connect it more closely to Europe, Peter the Great went to war against Sweden in 1700. Notice that, after suffering a disastrous defeat at Narva in 1700, he rebuilt and enhanced his forces while Swedish armies fought in Poland, then defeated the invading Swedish armies at Poltava in 1709. Note also that the war resulted in Russian acquisition of lands along the eastern Baltic. How did this war contribute to the emergence of the Russian Empire as a great European power?

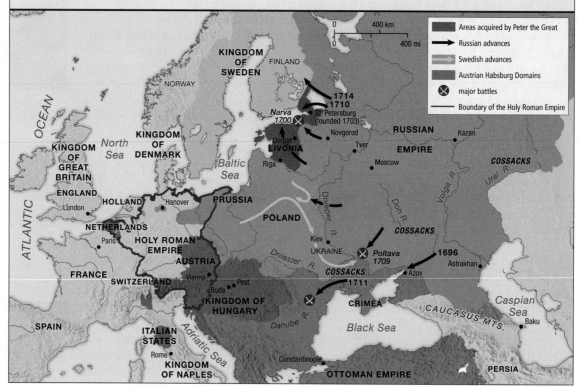

Peter's reign, however, had a darker side. An often cruel man, he imposed heavy taxes on the peasants and alienated the nobles by forcing them to work their way up the Table of Ranks. He also undermined the Russian Orthodox Church, refusing to allow the selection of a new patriarch after the old one died in 1700, and then placing Church administration directly under state control. He melted down church bells to make cannons for his armies, and he conducted an ongoing "Drunken Synod" in which he and his drunken friends dressed as clerics and held mock rituals that ridiculed religious leaders and liturgies.

Such practices made Peter many enemies, including his oldest son Alexis, who secretly plotted with disgruntled nobles and churchmen against his father. When Peter discovered his son's treachery, he had Alexis tried and tortured, as a result of which the young man died in prison in 1718. Having thus, like Ivan the Terrible, destroyed his own heir, the remorseless Peter enacted a new law letting the ruler ignore heredity and designate his own successor.

But Peter never got around to naming an heir. In November 1724, according to some accounts, he was sailing in the Gulf of Finland when he saw a small boat that ran aground in a storm. Plunging into icy waters to rescue the panicked victims, he caught a fever that aggravated earlier abdominal pains. In January 1725, when his condition had worsened to the point of death, he called for a tablet and wrote the words "Give everything to. . . ." Then he dropped the pen, lapsed into a coma, and died the next morning.

Peter destroys son and fails to name a successor as Russian Emperor

Peter's failure to designate an heir almost undid his legacy. For the next 16 years, Russia was weakened by succession struggles and a series of short reigns reminiscent of the Time of Troubles. But Peter's new state proved strong enough to weather these crises, and his legacy was finally ensured in 1741, when his able daughter Elizabeth seized the Russian throne.

Elizabeth I: Culture, Elegance, and Conflict

Like her father, Empress Elizabeth I (1741–1762) was an admirer of the West, and she was determined to continue his westernizing ways. She lacked his boundless energy, however, and was interested more in culture and elegance than in industry and technology. Glamorous, carefree, and single, she is said to have acquired more than fifteen thousand French dresses before her credit was cut off.

Elizabeth's reign brought important cultural accomplishments. She began to transform Saint Petersburg, for example, into a cultural center, attracting artists, architects, and performers to the city. She hired an Italian architect to build there a magnificent Winter Palace, which today houses the Hermitage, one of the world's great art museums. She also sponsored the creation of the University of Moscow, founded in 1755 with the help of Michael Lomonosov (*luh-muh-NŌ-soff*), a universal genius who brought Western science and scholarship to the heart of Russia. She even abolished capital punishment, a penalty often imposed by previous rulers, but did little to improve the status of Russian serfs, enhancing instead the nobles' rights and powers.

Elizabeth brings Western culture to Russia

In foreign affairs, Elizabeth saw Prussia's Frederick the Great as a serious threat to both Central Europe and Russia. So in 1756 she went to war, along with Austria, Sweden, and France, in an effort to defeat Frederick and divide up the Prussian domains. In the ensuing Seven Years War (1756–1763), Frederick fought heroically, displaying military genius against overwhelming odds; but he could not overcome the combined might of his foes. Elizabeth's Russian armies routed the Prussians in several key battles and at one point even captured and sacked Berlin, the Prussian capital. By late 1761, facing utter defeat, Frederick contemplated suicide.

Then came a stunning reversal of fortune. In early 1762, on the verge of victory and in apparent good health, Elizabeth suddenly died. She was succeeded by her nephew, who became Tsar Peter III. An emotionally unstable young man who idolized Frederick the Great, Peter pulled Russia out of the war and instead allied with the Prussians. Frederick regrouped his forces and regained lost ground, while Russia was denied a great military triumph.

Elizabeth's death ends Russian march into Prussia

Catherine the Great: Enlightenment and Expansion

Russia's withdrawal from the Seven Years War saved Frederick the Great but doomed Peter III, enraging his forces by depriving them of victory. In summer 1762 he was deposed and later killed in a plot led by some of his guard officers, allied with his wife, a German princess from a tiny central European state. Although she was not Russian, she quickly seized power and ruled for 34 years as Empress Catherine II (1762–1796), one of Russia's most successful rulers.

Catherine the Great, as she came to be known, was an extraordinary empress. Brilliant, energetic, and ruthless, she set out to modernize Russia's culture, education, economy, administration, and laws. Although assisted by male advisers and indulged by many male lovers, she was clearly the driving force behind Russia's ongoing enlightenment and expansion.

Catherine's charter expanding rights of Russian nobles.

Catherine brings the European Enlightenment to Russia

A gifted intellectual and diligent monarch who sought both to enhance culture and implement reforms, Catherine saw herself as a shining example of the enlightened absolutism then fashionable in the West (Chapter 24). She brought Western scholars, musicians, architects, and art to Russia, corresponded with Europe's leading thinkers, and even wrote her own treatises and plays. Inspired by the ideals of the European Enlightenment, in 1767 she composed a *Nakaz* (*Instruction*), a treatise on governance so filled with notions of liberty and equality that it was banned in France by that country's absolutist regime. In Russia she took steps to extend religious toleration, restrict the use of torture, and begin an education system.

Her passion for reform, however, began to wane in 1773, when southeastern Russia was rocked by a massive peasant revolt. It was led by Emelian Pugachev (*POO-gah-CHOFF*), a Cossack adventurer who promised to abolish serfdom, taxation, and military service and even said he was Peter III returning to reclaim his throne. After several failed attempts, Catherine finally managed in 1774 to crush the Pugachev rebellion, but only by using armies that she had to bring home from abroad. Thereafter, unsettled by the rebellion, she focused as much on expanding her power as on improving her subjects' lives. Her later reforms were aimed mainly at strengthening her administration and expanding the rights of the nobles, thus reinforcing serfdom and leaving the peasants even worse off than before.

Catherine expands Russia to the West and Southwest

Catherine's foreign ventures proved far more effective. In a stunning series of diplomatic and military successes, she expanded her empire westward, adding immensely to the Russian realm at the expense of Poland and the Ottoman Empire, long the dominant powers in Eastern Europe (Map 25.7).

She began in 1764 by engineering the election of Stanislaw Poniatowski (*PON-yah-TOFF-skē*), her friend and former lover, to the Polish throne. Then from 1768 to 1774 she fought a successful war against the Ottoman Turks, fulfilling the dreams of Peter the Great by conquering for Russia extensive lands on the Black Sea's northern shore. In the midst of the war, Prussia's Frederick the Great, eager to acquire a slice of Poland that separated the two main parts of his kingdom, suggested that Austria and Russia join him in exploiting Polish weakness. The result in 1772 was the First Partition of Poland, which gave Prussia territory in the North, Austria part of the South, and Russia some long-sought lands from eastern Poland (Map 25.8).

Catherine plots to revive the Byzantine Empire

But Catherine was not satisfied. She and Gregory Potemkin, the most favored of all her lovers, later devised an elaborate "Greek Project" aimed at crushing the Ottoman Empire and replacing it with a restored Byzantine Empire, reviving the historic realm that the Ottoman Turks had destroyed in 1453. She even had her second grandson named Constantine, intending that one day he would rule this new realm from Constantinople.

To further her aims, Catherine cleverly sought support from Emperor Joseph II, head of the Austrian Habsburg realms. In 1787, she had him join her in touring Russia's new Black Sea provinces, where her favorite Potemkin had constructed numerous settlements

Map 25.7 Expansion Under Catherine the Great, 1762–1796

Empress Catherine the Great, a woman raised in Central Europe, further enhanced Russia's westward orientation through a new series of connections and conflicts. Observe that, by defeating the Ottomans in two major wars (1768–1774 and 1787–1792), and dividing up Poland with Austria and Prussia, she added to the Russian Empire a vast stretch of eastern Europe, home to numerous non-Russian nationalities. What benefits and problems did this expansion bring to the Russian Empire?

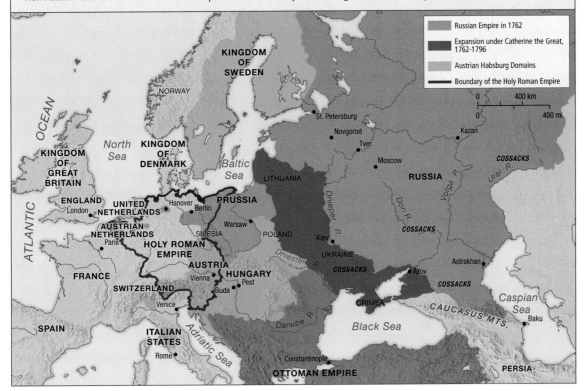

to showcase the prosperity Russia supposedly brought to a region recently taken from the Turks. Impressed by these "Potemkin villages," some of which were little more than temporary façades, and swayed by Catherine's promises of success, Joseph agreed to join her in a new war against the Ottoman Empire.

In the second Russo-Turkish war (1787–1792), Russia won major victories but failed to achieve the ambitious goals of its empress. Sweden, prompted by Britain and Prussia, declared war on Russia, creating a diversion in the North. Joseph II died in 1790, after which his successor, perceiving the Russians as more dangerous than the Turks, pulled Austria out of the war. In 1791 Catherine's beloved Potemkin also perished, leaving the empress distraught and curtailing her interest in the Greek project that he had helped her conceive.

That same year Poland's King Stanislaw Poniatowski, tired of being Catherine's puppet, approved a new constitution designed to make his country more autonomous. Seeing this move as a threat to her dominance of Poland, Catherine ended her war with the Turks in 1792, taking a bit more territory while freeing her forces for use against the Poles. Then, siding with Polish nobles eager to regain rights reduced by the new constitution, she sent a

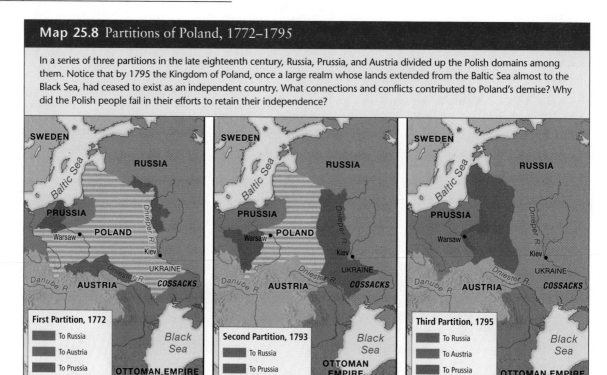

Map 25.8 Partitions of Poland, 1772–1795

In a series of three partitions in the late eighteenth century, Russia, Prussia, and Austria divided up the Polish domains among them. Notice that by 1795 the Kingdom of Poland, once a large realm whose lands extended from the Baltic Sea almost to the Black Sea, had ceased to exist as an independent country. What connections and conflicts contributed to Poland's demise? Why did the Polish people fail in their efforts to retain their independence?

huge army into Poland and forced the king to revoke that constitution. The next year, she and the Prussians conducted a Second Partition of Poland, each taking much land and leaving only a rump Polish state behind (Map 25.8).

Russia, Austria, and Prussia divide up Poland

The enraged Poles united at last in 1794 in a rebellion led by Tadeusz Kosciusko (*tah-DĀ-yoosh kos-CHOO-skō*), a Polish patriot whose love of freedom had earlier led him to fight in the American Revolution. Valiant but hopeless, the Polish uprising was crushed by Russia and Prussia, which then joined with Austria in the Third Partition of Poland (1795), dividing up all that was left of that country. Catherine died the next year, having expanded her adopted country far to the West and Southwest, bringing much of Eastern Europe under Russian rule (Map 25.7).

Russia's Eurasian Society

In less than a century, then, in an extraordinary series of developments, the Tsardom of Muscovy, with its eastern-oriented Byzantine Orthodox culture, had been transformed into the Russian Empire, infused with Western ways. Having gained in that century vast territories stretching from the Black Sea to the Baltic, the Russian realm now extended deep into Europe, embracing dozens of non-Russian nationalities and millions of Catholics, Protestants, and Jews. Russia's underlying culture nonetheless remained Eastern and Byzantine, characterized by serf agriculture and Orthodox Christianity. The result was a blended culture, combining elements of East and West in a complex, conflicted society that can rightly be called Eurasian.

COMMERCE, CULTURE, AND GENDER ROLES. Russia's westward and southward expansion during the eighteenth century was accompanied not only by population growth—from thirteen million at the time of Peter the Great to thirty-six million by the century's end—but also by huge economic, cultural, and social changes. While vastly enlarging its territory and population, Russia also gained an expanded and diversified economy, a complex new urban culture, and an increasingly open society with greater opportunities for women.

Russian society blends East and West

The empire's enlargement helped spur economic growth, partly by bringing Ukraine's rich "black earth" agricultural region fully under Russian rule and partly by giving Russia access to trade through the Baltic and Black seas. The fertile new farmlands not only helped Russia to better feed its growing population; they also provided surplus grain for Russians to sell abroad, adding to the empire's already lucrative fur and timber exports. Russian iron goods and textile manufacturing likewise expanded immensely, with numerous new factories employing thousands of workers. Although many were servile laborers, effectively enserfed to factories rather than to landowners, others increasingly were wage laborers, paid for their labor much like workers in the West.

Russian trader.

Changes in education and culture were equally significant. Eager to update his country's science and technology, Peter the Great sent hundreds of Russians to study abroad in the West, opened Russian schools that focused on mechanics and navigation, adopted Arabic numerals in Russia, and founded the Russian Academy of Sciences—eventually one of the world's leading academic institutions. Stressing culture more than technology, Empresses Elizabeth I and Catherine the Great imported Western architects and artists, promoted poetry and drama, and fostered the growth of literature and ballet—areas in which Russia later gained global preeminence. The University of Moscow, started with Elizabeth's support, offered degrees in medicine, philosophy, and law and published a newspaper for Moscow's literate elite. Noting that Russia still largely lacked primary and secondary schools, Catherine founded schools to train Russian teachers and laid the foundations for a network of elementary schools. She even broke precedent by starting Russia's first state school for women, later called the Smolny Institute.

Russian learning and culture emulate the West

Russia's westernization also brought other changes in the role of women. Peter the Great ended female seclusion, a longstanding Muscovite practice probably derived from Persia, and insisted that women be present and involved in public affairs. He also made it possible for women to rule Russia: although Muscovy at times had been governed by female regents, Peter's wife Catherine, who briefly succeeded him as Empress Catherine I (1725–1727), was Russia's first female ruler and the first of four empresses who ruled Russia in the eighteenth century.

An early Russian newspaper.

The fourth of those empresses, Catherine II, the Great, embodied in her person a greatly expanded political role for women, showing that she could exercise power as skillfully and ruthlessly as any male ruler had done. Dominating Russia with the forcefulness of an Ivan the Terrible or Peter the Great, she proved both more capable and more ambitious than most of her male predecessors. After disposing of her husband, for example, she refused to serve simply as regent for her young son, insisting instead on being empress in her own right. Enlightened and sophisticated, she nonetheless proved relentless in crushing unrest, enhancing her own authority, and expanding both the borders and the power of her adopted country. Her willingness to indulge herself with a number of different lovers, although it gained her a scandalous reputation, was simply another way in which she shared the passions and practices of many male monarchs.

Russian women gain from Western influence

The changes in Russian commerce, culture, education, and gender roles, however, applied largely to urban centers such as Saint Petersburg and Moscow. Rural Russia, with its patriarchal villages and oppressive system of serfdom, remained essentially unchanged from earlier eras. Culture and education were largely the province of the upper classes who lived in cities, attended operas and ballets, kept up with Western ideas and fashions, and spoke to each other in French as well as Russian. The illiterate peasant masses, fortified by faith and often also with alcohol, still toiled in drudgery through Russia's short summers and dark winters, much as their Muscovite ancestors had done.

RELIGIOUS AND ETHNIC DIVERSITY. By the late eighteenth century, however, the empire's masses were far more diverse in culture and religion than in Muscovite times. By the end of Catherine the Great's reign, nearly half her subjects were non-Russians, as the huge realm now included dozens of different languages and cultures. Many of her subjects were non-Orthodox as well, including the millions of Catholics, Protestants, Jews, and Muslims who lived in the newly conquered lands.

Russian Empire incorporates numerous cultures and religions

These new subjects created problems for the Russian state. Some, including many Poles and Ukrainians, deeply resented Russian rule and dreamed of having their own independent homelands. Catherine responded with a combination of religious toleration and political repression, allowing non-Russians in Poland and elsewhere to worship as they chose but stifling all strivings toward political autonomy and, as she did in Poland in the 1790s, crushing anti-Russian rebellions.

Equally vexing was the status of the Jews, millions of whom lived in regions annexed by Russia from Poland. In previous centuries, fleeing persecution in Central Europe and elsewhere, many Jews had moved to the Polish Kingdom, where they were allowed to maintain their distinctive customs and communities. The Kingdom of Poland, which then included Lithuania, Belarus, and Ukraine, had thus become the main homeland of European Jews. Now, suddenly, this homeland was part of Russia, where few Jews had hitherto lived, in part because of laws designed to protect the Orthodox faithful from exposure to alien cultures and beliefs. Acting to sustain this situation, Catherine's government restricted Jews to the newly conquered regions where they already lived. The result was the formation of what came to be called the **Pale of Jewish Settlement** (Map 25.9), a broad band of lands along Russia's western borders where Jews were allowed to reside but were increasingly subjected to legal limitations and abuses.

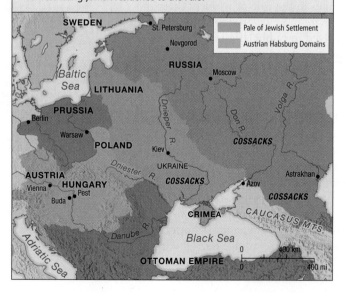

Map 25.9 The Pale of Jewish Settlement, 1783–1917

In expanding westward the Russian Empire came into possession of lands that were home to millions of Jewish people. Then, through a series of edicts beginning in 1783, the Russian government restricted Jewish residence to these conquered lands. Note that these lands, which came to be called the Pale of Jewish Settlement, included much of Poland and all of Ukraine. Why had so many Jews come to live in these regions? What reason did the Russians give for restricting Jewish residence to the Pale?

Chapter Review

Putting It in Perspective

The Tsardom of Muscovy, emerging from Mongol rule in the fifteenth century, was centered on the city of Moscow, the Russian Orthodox Church, and peasant village agriculture, increasingly subject to serfdom. As the realm expanded to the East and South, conquering all of Siberia and a large segment of the steppes, it brought those regions' peoples under Muscovite rule and incorporated their cultures.

In the eighteenth century, however, Muscovy was transformed by its rulers into the Russian Empire, with governance systems, military forces, new technologies, and cultural features modeled on those of the West. The new Russian capital, Saint Petersburg, elegantly showcased the country's new Western orientation, and the Russian Empire's eighteenth-century conquests extended its rule over numerous non-Russians in the West.

Beneath the surface of Westernization, however, Russia's Muscovite foundations remained largely intact. In the multitude of rural serf estates, with their patriarchal villages and households, and in the innumerable Orthodox churches, with their elaborate rituals and pious worshipers, Muscovite Russia lived on in the heart of the Russian Empire. The result was a realm that encompassed vast expanses of both Asia and Europe, with a blended society embracing many elements of both East and West, yet belonging fully to neither.

Reviewing Key Material

KEY CONCEPTS

metropolitan, 609	Domostroi, 617
Kremlin, 609	holy fools, 617
boyars, 609	collective liability, 619
tsar, 610	Cossacks, 619
Zemskii Sobor, 613	service state, 623
Old Believers, 615	Table of Ranks, 623
icons, 617	Pale of Jewish Settlement, 630

KEY PEOPLE

Ivan the Great, 609	Peter the Great, 622
Zoe (Sofia) Paleologus, 610	Elizabeth I, 625
Ivan the Terrible, 611	Michael Lomonosov, 625
Boris Godunov, 613	Catherine the Great, 626
Michael Romanov, 615	Emelian Pugachev, 626
Filaret, 615	Stanislaw Poniatowski, 626
Alexis I, 615	Gregory Potemkin, 626
Nikon, 615	

ASK YOURSELF

1. How and why did Muscovy expand from a small principality into an immense Eurasian realm?
2. How did the Orthodox Church influence Muscovite politics, culture, and society, and why was this influence so pervasive? How and why did Muscovy seek to claim the heritage of the Byzantine Empire?
3. How and why did serfdom develop in Muscovite Russia? How did the practice of collective liability reinforce serfdom? How did serf rebellions and Cossacks, many of whom were from families that had fled serfdom, impact Russian history?
4. How and why did Peter the Great work to Westernize Russia? How did he transform his country into one of Europe's great powers?
5. How did Elizabeth I and Catherine II continue and expand on Peter's work? What were the main impacts of Westernization and westward expansion on Russian culture and society?

GOING FURTHER

Alexander, John. *Catherine the Great: Life and Legend.* 1989.

Avrich, Paul. *Russian Rebels, 1600–1800.* 1972.

Blum, Jerome. *Lord and Peasant in Russia from the Ninth to the Nineteenth Century.* 1961.

Bobrick, B. *Fearful Majesty: The Life and Reign of Ivan the Terrible.* 1987.

Brennan, James F. *Enlightened Despotism in Russia.* 1987.

Bushkovitch, Paul. *Peter the Great.* 2002.

Clyman, T., and J. Vowles. *Russia Through Women's Eyes.* 1996.

Coughlan, Robert. *Elizabeth and Catherine.* 1975.

Crummey, Robert. *The Formation of Muscovy, 1304–1613*. 1987.

De Madariaga, I. *Catherine the Great: A Short History*. 1996.

Dukes, Paul. *The Making of Russian Absolutism, 1613–1801*. 1990.

Evtuhov, Catherine, et al. *A History of Russia: Peoples, Legends, Events, Forces*. 2004.

Kappeler, A. The Russian Empire: A Multiethnic History. 2001.

Massie, Robert. *Peter the Great: His Life and World*. 1986.

Michels, G. *At War with the Church: Religious Dissent in Seventeenth-Century Russia*. 2000.

Perrie, M. *Pretenders and Popular Monarchism in Early Modern Russia: The False Tsars of the Time of Troubles*. 1995.

Poe, M. T. *A People Born to Slavery: Russia in Early Modern European Ethnography, 1476–1748*. 2000.

Pouncy, C. *The Domostroi: Rules for Russian Households in the Time of Ivan the Terrible*. 1994.

Thomson, G. S. *Catherine the Great and the Expansion of Russia*. 1985.

Key Dates and Developments

1240–1480	Mongol Rule in Russia
1328–1340	Reign of Moscow's Ivan I as Grand Prince
1453	Conquest of Constantinople by Ottoman Turks
1462–1505	Reign of Grand Prince Ivan III, the Great
1533–1584	Reign of Tsar Ivan IV, the Terrible
1598–1613	The Time of Troubles
1610–1612	Polish occupation of Moscow
1613	Michael Romanov elected tsar
1652–1666	Reforms of Nikon and Russian Church Schism
1682–1725	Reign of Tsar Peter I, the Great
1697–1698	The Grand Embassy to Europe
1700–1721	The Great Northern War
1703	Founding of Saint Petersburg
1721	Proclamation of the Russian Empire
1741–1762	Reign of Empress Elizabeth I
1762–1796	Reign of Empress Catherine II, the Great
1768–1774	First Russo-Turkish War
1772	First partition of Poland
1787–1792	Second Russo-Turkish War
1793–1795	Second and Third Partitions of Poland

The Atlantic Revolutions, 1750–1830

LA DESTRUCTION DE LA STATUE ROYALE A NOUVELLE YORCK

Toppling The Statue Of King George III In New York

British North American colonists topple the statue of King George III in New York City shortly after the beginning of the American Revolution. Denounced in the Declaration of American Independence as a tyrant, George III's decision to use hired foreign mercenaries to suppress the rebellion earned him the hatred of many colonists (page 639).

The French winter of 1788–1789 was unusually cold, but political discussion throughout the land was heated. Members of France's three classes—clergy, nobility, and commoners—gathered in churches, manors, shops, and taverns to elect delegates to the **Estates General**, a nationwide assembly summoned by the king for the first time in 175 years, to discuss the country's financial crisis. France was alive with rumors: the king would ask for new taxes; the clergy and nobility would resist; the absolute monarchy would be transformed into a limited, constitutional one; or the whole exercise would prove futile.

United States
France
Haiti

At the gatherings, each voter was asked to state his grievances, hopes, and demands. Their comments were recorded in small notebooks that the delegates elected to the Estates General took with them to Versailles. Collectively, the notebooks convey excitement and high expectation as the people of France spoke out to determine their destiny.

Across the Atlantic, others were also determining their destiny that winter. In the French slave colony of Saint-Domingue (*SAN dō-MANG*), later known as Haiti, two competing sets of delegates were chosen for the French Estates General, setting in motion a series of events that would become the Haitian Revolution. Farther north, former British colonists, having recently won the American Revolution (1775–1783), held the first elections for their new United States government.

On both sides of the Atlantic, then, in the late eighteenth century, people were taking steps toward governing themselves. Although their situations differed substantially, the goals in each case involved greater freedom and equality, and the efforts to achieve them eventually involved violence.

The Background of the Atlantic Revolutions

Enlightenment ideas and warfare prepare the way for the Atlantic revolutions

Two very different developments laid the foundation for the Atlantic revolutions. One was the European Enlightenment, which produced a number of new ideas about government and society, including the notion that people have a right to decide their own form of government. These ideas eventually influenced societies around the world (Map 26.1). The other was Britain's victory over France in the Seven Years War, creating conditions that helped set in motion the American, French, and Haitian revolutions.

New Ideas About Government and Society

During the European Enlightenment, prominent thinkers developed political and social ideas challenging the foundations of absolute monarchy and hereditary nobility. English philosopher John Locke, for example, argued that governments get their

FOUNDATION MAP 26.1 The North Atlantic World in 1750

By 1750, three Western European countries—Spain, France, and Britain—had claimed much of North America, often ignoring the cultures, traditions, and prior arrival of North American Amerinds. Notice that these colonial possessions had to connect with their mother countries across the North Atlantic. Those were difficult and often treacherous sea routes. How would this fact affect the chances that European powers could hold their colonial possessions over the long term?

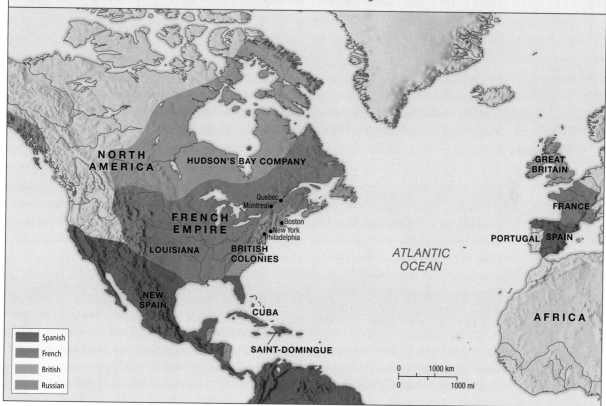

authority, not directly from God, but from the people they rule. People have funda-mental rights, he asserted, and governments have a duty to protect these rights; any regime that fails to do so can be replaced by its subjects. France's Baron Montesquieu proposed limits on absolute authority, advocating a separation of powers in which the ruler's power is checked by institutions that keep it from becoming oppressive. Swiss-born Jean-Jacques Rousseau, a passionate proponent of both liberty and equal-ity, envisioned a society in which all members were free and equal in rights, working together for the common good.

Europe's Enlightenment advances ideas of freedom

These ideas did not cause the Atlantic revolutions, which arose from specific circum-stances in America, Europe, and Haiti. But the new ideas did undermine the basic prem-ise of absolutism, in which the ruler exercised unlimited power coming directly from God, and the premise of aristocracy, in which upper classes had rights and privileges not shared by common people. In time the new ideas inspired and justified revolutions around the world that aimed to secure the people's rights and freedoms.

The Seven Years War

From 1689 to 1763, while Locke, Montesquieu, Rousseau, and others were advancing their ideas, Britain and France fought four major wars. Waged in Europe, North America, and the North Atlantic, involving colonial territories and Atlantic commerce, these were North Atlantic wars, not just European struggles.

Seven Years War becomes a global conflict

The first three wars produced only minor territorial changes, but the fourth was decisive. Known in Europe as the Seven Years War (1756–1763), it was an effort by France, Austria, and Russia to combat the expansive ambitions of Britain and its ally, Prussia. In America, where growing British colonies sought to expand into regions claimed by France and inhabited by Amerinds (American Indians), British colonists called it the French and Indian War. Since fighting also occurred in India (Chapter 22), this multifaceted conflict was actually a global war.

The North American phase of this war at first went badly for Britain. In 1754, in an effort to block the westward expansion of Britain's colonies into the Ohio River valley, the French built a stronghold called Fort Duquesne (*doo-KAN*) in what is now western Pennsylvania. The British sought to drive out the French, but in 1755 British forces were ambushed and slaughtered by the French and their various Amerind allies. In the next few years the French won further victories in Europe and America.

A powder horn of the type used during the French and Indian War.

Responding to this in 1756, Britain's King George II appointed William Pitt, a brash but brilliant politician, to serve as prime minister. By sending able soldiers to America while relying on Prussia to tie down the French in Europe, and by setting up a naval blockade to stop French ports from shipping supplies and soldiers to America, Pitt soon placed Britain in a more favorable position. In 1759 the British captured both Quebec, the capital of New France, and Fort Duquesne, which they renamed Fort Pitt (later Pittsburgh) in honor of the architect of victory. When the conflict ended in 1763, France was forced to surrender almost all of its American empire, keeping only a few small islands and the Caribbean colony of Saint-Domingue. Britain's triumph was complete, and French humiliation was immense (Map 26.2).

The American Revolution

Britain's sweeping victory in the Seven Years War transformed the situation on both sides of the Atlantic. It altered Europe's **balance of power**, a situation in which no one nation would be strong enough to impose its will on the others. France, sensing that this balance of power had been changed in Britain's favor, was resentful and eager for revenge. The war ended the French threat to Britain's colonies, reducing their need for British military protection and thereby decreasing the colonists' dependence on their mother country. At the same time, it greatly increased Britain's state debt, leading its officials to seek ways to make colonists pay a share of the financial burden. And it brought France's former colonies under British rule, potentially putting them and their Amerind inhabitants at the mercy of British colonists eager for new landholdings.

Map 26.2 Territorial Changes in North America Resulting from Seven Years War, 1756–1763

In losing the Seven Years War, France lost most of its North American empire, keeping only a few small islands and the Caribbean slave colony of Saint-Domingue. Britain took over French Canada and French claims east of the Mississippi River, while Spain took French claims to the west of that waterway. Note that to prevent clashes between its colonists and Amerinds, Britain issued a 1763 proclamation prohibiting its colonists from moving west of the Appalachian Mountains. How did British colonists react to this Proclamation of 1763?

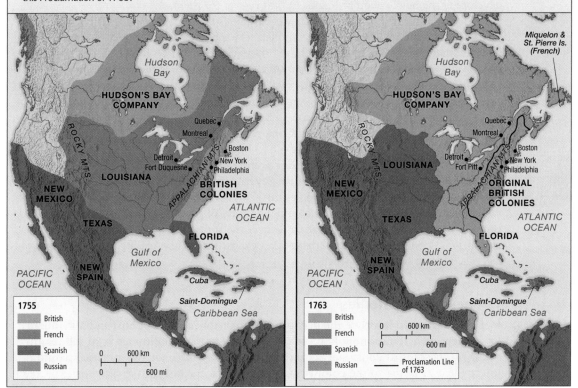

Tensions Between Britain and Its Colonists

Up to this point, tensions between Britain and its colonists had been few. Under British protection, with low taxes and ways of getting around British trade restrictions, the colonies had grown and prospered. The northern ones were dotted with thriving farms and cities, while the South was covered with prosperous plantations, worked by more than half a million African slaves. The colonists had elected their own assemblies (modeled in part on Britain's parliament) and had grown accustomed to running their own affairs.

In 1763, however, relations began to deteriorate, due to a conflict called Pontiac's Rebellion and Britain's subsequent efforts to halt colonial expansion. In the Midwest a group of Amerind nations, trading partners with the French for decades, rebelled at the prospect of living under British rule. Chief Pontiac, head of the Ottawa nation, led a five-month siege against the British at Detroit, while other Amerinds attacked and destroyed

Amerinds rebel at the prospect of British rule

Britain's various frontier outposts. The British responded with deception and atrocity. During what were supposed to be peace talks at Fort Pitt, they gave the Amerind negotiators a "gift" of blankets infested with smallpox. This instance of biological warfare produced an epidemic that, combined with the force of British arms, put an end to the uprising.

Meanwhile, to prevent future clashes between colonists and Amerinds, in 1763 the British issued a proclamation closing the frontier and forbidding colonial settlements west of the Appalachian Mountains. This edict angered many colonists, who had dreams of developing the newly acquired lands in that region for themselves.

British attempts to raise taxes anger colonists

Equally disturbing to the colonists were Britain's attempts to raise revenue. The Seven Years War had doubled Britain's debt and left its people burdened by heavy taxation. Recognizing that colonists paid few taxes even though they relied on British troops for protection, in 1765 Parliament passed a Stamp Act, taxing colonial documents and newspapers by requiring that they be stamped with a royal seal. Since this tax was not approved by their colonial assemblies, many colonists perceived it as "taxation without representation"—a denial of their rights as English subjects to be consulted in such matters. Nine of the 13 colonies sent delegates to a Stamp Act Congress that declared the tax illegal. The Congress declared a boycott of British goods, hoping to force repeal of the tax. Ominously for Britain, the colonies for the first time were uniting in a common cause.

Funeral procession for the Stamp Act following its repeal.

In response to the protest, the British government did repeal the stamp tax but insisted on Parliament's right to tax the colonies. In 1767 Parliament passed the Townshend Acts, which increased customs duties on colonial imports of glass, lead, paper, paint, and tea. But the colonists, having won the struggle over the stamp tax, imposed another boycott, and in 1770 London removed all these taxes except the one on tea. By this time, however, feelings on both sides had hardened.

Clashes in the Colonies

Colonists rebel against Parliament's tea taxation scheme

In 1773, aiming to improve the declining fortunes of the British East India Company, Parliament gave it a monopoly on tea sales to the colonies, allowing it to sell tea directly off its ships to consumers in ports such as Boston. Since this practice would lower the cost of tea to the colonists, company officers and British officials expected little resistance. But the colonists saw the plan as a scheme to conceal the tea tax while undercutting colonial merchants, who could no longer compete with the company's inexpensive tea. When company ships docked in Boston, colonists disguised as Mohawk Indians climbed aboard on a December evening and dumped the tea into the harbor.

The British reacted to this colonial protest, known as the **Boston Tea Party**, by enacting in 1774 the Coercive Acts, called by the colonists Intolerable Acts, closing the port of Boston, and turning elected Massachusetts officials into royal appointees. These measures further angered and united the colonists. In 1774 a Continental Congress, with delegates from 12 colonies, met in Philadelphia. It declared the acts illegal and called on Massachusetts to form a rival government. The British government then declared Massachusetts to be in a state of rebellion. In April 1775, British troops sent to confiscate weapons clashed with colonial militia at Lexington and Concord near Boston.

Even after this fighting, many colonists still hoped to avoid a break with the mother country. They simply wanted respect for their rights and for Britain to once again leave the colonies alone. But a Second Continental Congress, convening the next month, created a continental army, and King George III (1760–1820) decided to crush the rebels by sending in German hired troops (see page 633).

Finally, in July 1776, the Congress issued a Declaration of Independence in the name of all 13 colonies, linking them together as the "United States of America" and transforming the colonial conflict into a revolution. Drafted by Virginia's Thomas Jefferson and reflecting the concepts of John Locke, the Declaration eloquently proclaimed the revolutionary ideals of individual rights and government by the people:

The Boston Tea Party.

> We hold these truths to be self-evident, that all Men are created equal, that they are endowed by their Creator with certain unalienable Rights, that among these are Life, Liberty, and the Pursuit of Happiness—That to secure these Rights, Governments are instituted among Men, deriving their just Powers from the Consent of the Governed, that whenever any Form of Government becomes destructive of these Ends, it is the Right of the People to alter or to abolish it. . . .

The Declaration gave the colonists an inspiring cause to fight for. In time, it changed the way people around the world viewed governance. The American Revolution had begun.

The Revolutionary War

The colonists, of course, needed more than words to fight Great Britain, one of the world's foremost powers. With their separate assemblies and barely trained militias, the colonies lacked coherence and experience. Britain, on the other hand, had vast resources, a well-trained army, and a splendid navy that ruled the seas. Britain also had support from numerous **Loyalists,** colonists who opposed the revolt against their mother country, and Amerinds, who feared that a colonist victory would reopen the frontiers, bringing masses of settlers into Amerind country.

The British are supported by Loyalists and Amerinds

The colonists also had advantages, however. First, they were fighting on familiar terrain and had learned from the Amerinds to harass British positions while avoiding open-field battles, at which the British excelled. Second, the war was unpopular in Britain, whose people were weary of high taxes and prolonged conflicts. Third, British troops were fighting far from home with no real war aim except to crush the colonists. And finally the French, humiliated by defeat in the Seven Years War, decided to take revenge and restore the balance of power by assisting the rebels.

In the early fighting, British forces took the initiative, seizing New York City in 1776. The plan was for them then to move north to Albany, where they would link up with another British army moving south from Canada. This maneuver would have cut the New England colonies off from the rest, dividing the rebels. The British commander in New York, however, instead moved south to attack Philadelphia, the rebels' capital city. Unsupported, the British army coming from Canada was soundly defeated in fall 1777 by colonial forces at Saratoga, north of Albany (Map 26.3).

British lose the early initiative with defeat at Saratoga

The Battle of Saratoga changed the war's momentum. Now convinced that the colonists could win, France joined the war on their side in 1778. On land the colonial commander, General George Washington, proved very capable, while at sea Captain John Paul Jones and the small United States Navy did surprisingly well. In 1781, after several years of stalemate, Washington forced the surrender of a British army at Yorktown, Virginia, with the help of

French soldiers and navy help the colonists defeat the British

Map 26.3 United States of America in 1783

In 1783, having lost the American Revolution, Britain ceded to its former colonies all of its claims south of Canada and east of the Mississippi River, thereby forsaking its Amerind allies by consigning their lands to the expansive new United States of America. Many British Loyalists fled to Canada (British North America), where they became rivals of the descendants of the earlier French settlers. Observe that while the Ohio country (present-day Ohio, Michigan, Indiana, Illinois, Wisconsin, and Minnesota) remained unstructured, states like Virginia, North Carolina, and Georgia claimed land as far west as the Mississippi River. What issues would need to be resolved before additional states could be added to the United States of America?

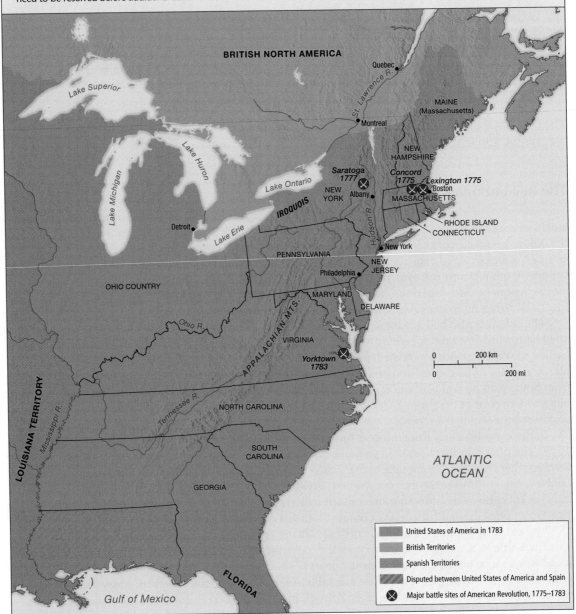

French forces. Extended negotiations followed, and the Treaty of Paris formally ended the conflict in 1783.

The Consequences of the American Revolution

Surrender of British forces at Yorktown.

The obvious winners of the revolution were the colonists, who gained independence and all lands east of the Mississippi River, south of British Canada, and north of Spanish Florida (Map 26.3). These were exciting times for the former colonies, now connected as autonomous states under Articles of Confederation drawn up during the war. But the new confederation, although called the United States, soon found it lacked the unity needed to deal with collective problems.

To remedy this situation, a convention at Philadelphia in 1787 drafted the Constitution of the United States, a document based on Enlightenment principles and Montesquieu's notion of separation of powers. It created a federal republic in which the states and national government shared power. The national, or federal, government had an elected executive called the president, a two-house legislature called Congress, and an independent judiciary headed by a Supreme Court. In 1789, after ratification by the states, the new constitution went into effect. War hero Washington was elected the first president.

The apparent losers were the British, whose humbling defeat cost them their most prosperous North American colonies. But Britain's loss was not as devastating as it appeared. In the wake of the war, some 60 thousand Loyalists relocated from United States territory to Canada, counterbalancing that colony's French Catholics with English-speaking Protestants, thus consolidating Britain's hold on its newest and largest possession. And British trade with America actually increased, as commercial and cultural ties continued to link the mother country with its former colonies. Indeed, slave-grown raw cotton from the United States provided an important raw material for the industrial revolution in Britain, adding immensely to that country's wealth and power (Chapter 27).

Far more severe were the losses of North American Amerinds, whose hopes of preventing white settlers from moving west of the Appalachians were crushed when the British signed the peace treaty giving these lands to the new American nation. The victors ruthlessly punished those Amerinds, including many who had fought on the British side: their villages and farms were deliberately destroyed and their people scattered. But even Amerinds who did not fight the colonists were similarly treated. As more and more white settlers, now calling themselves Americans, expanded across the continent, the original Americans were largely dispossessed. Drastically diminished by diseases, and driven from their ancestral homelands, the Amerinds who survived were eventually forced to live on reservations—marginal lands set aside for them by the United States government. There some strove to retain a hint of their heritage, with mixed results.

Amerinds are displaced and dispossessed by the new United States

The most surprising losers were the rulers of France, which fought on the winning side. Aside from the satisfaction of helping to beat Britain, the French government gained little from the war but debt, already enormous as a result of the earlier Atlantic wars. Essentially, France was bankrupt. Within a few years, its efforts to address this financial crisis by taxing its nobles set off another revolution. This struggle, monumental in its impact, justified the destruction of the monarchy in France with some of the same ideals that had inspired the American Revolution.

Debts from war in America deepen France's financial crisis

The French Revolution

France, indeed, was beset by serious problems. Its monarchy was wasting away under King Louis XVI, a well-meaning but barely competent ruler who would rather repair clocks than handle state affairs. Its treasury had been bankrupted by costly foreign wars, including the American Revolution. Its ability to raise revenues to pay down its debts was hampered by a tax system that exempted the wealthiest two classes—the clergy, or First Estate, and the nobility, or Second Estate—who together controlled more than half of the country's landed wealth. The burden of taxation thus fell on the peasants and bourgeoisie, who made up the Third Estate and who resented the privileged position of the other two classes.

France, however, was a wealthy country, whose flourishing farmlands and thriving businesses made it the envy of Europe. France had the resources to resolve its fiscal crisis, if only the tax system could be changed.

The Estates General and the Onset of Revolution

Louis XVI summons Estates General to deal with fiscal crisis

As described at the start of this chapter, in 1788 Louis XVI, faced with impending French bankruptcy, summoned the Estates General, an assembly of delegates from all three estates, to meet the following spring. Since the Estates General could restrict the king's power, no king had convened it since 1614; but since it alone could change the tax system, Louis had little choice. He wanted the nobles to give up their tax exemptions and they were inclined to do so, but only in return for a greater role in governance. The Third Estate's leaders likewise wanted more authority, but they sought a written constitution that would guarantee the political participation of all the people.

In May 1789, amid great excitement, the Estates General assembled at Versailles, in the grandiose seventeenth-century palace built by King Louis XIV. But the Third Estate, constituting 98 percent of the population, had only half the delegates. Moreover, since the king and first two estates insisted the estates must meet separately, as in the past, with each estate having one collective vote, the Third Estate could easily be outvoted 2 to 1 by the clergy and nobility. When the Third Estate delegates protested this traditional system and refused to meet separately, they took the first step toward revolution.

A commoner awakens on a pile of weapons, frightening a clergyman and an aristocrat.

Faced with this bold opposition, Louis XVI wavered. On June 17, sensing his weakness, the Third Estate declared itself the National Assembly of France and invited the other two Estates to join. Only a few clergy from the First Estate actually did so, but the Assembly nonetheless claimed to speak for the entire French people. Three days later, barred from their meeting hall by order of the king, the Assembly delegates crossed the street to an indoor tennis court and there swore the **Tennis Court Oath**, vowing not to go home until France had a written constitution.

On June 27, after many more clergy and even some nobles joined the National Assembly, Louis appeared to give in, ordering all three estates to meet together as one. But his order was only a delaying tactic. During the next two weeks he summoned loyal soldiers from outlying areas to Versailles to disperse the Assembly. By July 10 they began to arrive.

In Paris, a mob attacks the Bastille

In Paris, only seven miles from Versailles, news of the troops' arrival touched off riots. To protect the Assembly and themselves, mobs of citizens sacked arsenals and stole firearms. On July 14, about 25 thousand of them surrounded a prison called the **Bastille**, a large medieval fortress where guns were supposedly stored. When the prison commandant panicked and lowered the drawbridge, the crowd surged into the courtyard, sending the guards fleeing and killing the commandant. The rioters then started tearing down the prison stone by stone.

When word of the Bastille's fall reached Versailles, the king panicked. Assuming that a mob big enough and well-armed enough to seize such a fortress could easily overwhelm his troops, he came to Paris on July 17 and endorsed what was now called the French Revolution: the end of absolutism and its replacement by a government in which power would be shared between the king and the National Assembly. On August 4, in a frenzy sparked by news of peasant uprisings against noble landowners throughout rural France, the Assembly formally abolished all class privileges. On August 26 it issued a Declaration of the Rights of Man and the Citizen, proclaiming that "Men are born and remain free and equal in rights." Nothing, however, was said about rights for women (see "Excerpts from Declaration of the Rights of Man and the Citizen").

The National Assembly issues a Declaration of Rights

In September, considering these developments far too radical, the king once again ordered troops to Versailles. Paris reacted violently. On the cold, rainy morning of October 5, six thousand women, unable to buy bread because of supply shortages, marched the seven miles to Versailles to confront the king. The **March of the Women** threatened physical harm to the royal family, forcing the king to move with his family to the Tuileries (*TWĒ-luh-rēz*) Palace in Paris, where he was kept under house arrest to stop him from trying to reverse the revolution. Many nobles, aghast at such spectacles and angered at their loss of status, fled the country and plotted against the revolution from abroad.

Women march to Versailles and force the king to go to Paris

The Constitutional Monarchy and Its Demise

Meanwhile, with mixed success, the National Assembly confronted major challenges, including France's financial crisis, the opposition of many Catholic clergy, and the resistance of a treacherous king.

The Assembly turned first to France's immense debt. Since land was the main source of wealth in France, the Assembly promptly confiscated the property of nobles who had fled the country and all the land used by the Catholic Church for nonreligious purposes. The aim was to auction these lands and use the proceeds to pay France's debts while also creating a class of small landowners who would have a stake in supporting the new government. But selling so much land would take years, so in the meantime the assembly issued bonds called *assignats* (*ah-SĒN-yaht*), which could be used as money and redeemed after the lands were sold. Unfortunately, however, by increasing the amount of money in circulation, the issuing of the *assignats* resulted in runaway **inflation**, a situation in which money declines in value and prices of goods and services rise. This weakened the French economy further and caused suffering in the general population, especially among poor people.

An assignat.

Having taken the Church's income-producing property, the Assembly then made the clergy civil servants with salaries paid by the government. This action ensured their financial well-being but also required them, like other civil servants, to swear an oath of allegiance to the state. Some clergy took the oath, but many refused to swear support for a revolutionary government. Thus the Church split into friends and enemies of the revolution.

The Assembly subordinates clergy to the state, alienating many in the Church

Document 26.1 Excerpts: Declaration of the Rights of Man and the Citizen

After the fall of the Bastille (July 14, 1789) and the revocation of the privileges of the nobility (August 4, 1789), the National Assembly drafted, approved, and published a declaration of rights, inspired to some extent by the English Declaration of Rights of 1689 (Chapter 24) and designed to safeguard the liberties of the French people against arbitrary actions by the executive power. Excerpts from this declaration follow.

APPROVED BY THE NATIONAL ASSEMBLY OF FRANCE, AUGUST 26, 1789 The representatives of the French people, organized as a National Assembly, believing that the ignorance, neglect, or contempt of the rights of man are the sole cause of public calamities and of the corruption of governments, have determined to set forth in a solemn declaration the natural, unalienable, and sacred rights of man, in order that this declaration, being constantly before all the members of the Social body, shall remind them continually of their rights and duties; in order that the acts of the legislative power, as well as those of the executive power, may be compared at any moment with the objects and purposes of all political institutions and may thus be more respected, and, lastly, in order that the grievances of the citizens, based hereafter upon simple and incontestable principles, shall tend to the maintenance of the constitution and redound to the happiness of all. Therefore the National Assembly recognizes and proclaims, in the presence and under the auspices of the Supreme Being, the following rights of man and of the citizen:

Articles:

1. Men are born and remain free and equal in rights. Social distinctions may be founded only upon the general good.
2. The aim of all political association is the preservation of the natural and imprescriptible rights of man. These rights are liberty, property, security, and resistance to oppression.
3. The principle of all sovereignty resides essentially in the nation. No body nor individual may exercise any authority which does not proceed directly from the nation.
4. Liberty consists in the freedom to do everything which injures no one else; hence the exercise of the natural rights of each man has no limits except those which assure to the other members of the society the enjoyment of the same rights. These limits can only be determined by law.
5. Law can only prohibit such actions as are hurtful to society. Nothing may be prevented which is not forbidden by law, and no one may be forced to do anything not provided for by law . . .
7. No person shall be accused, arrested, or imprisoned except in the cases and according to the forms prescribed by law. Any one soliciting, transmitting, executing, or causing to be executed, any arbitrary order, shall be punished. But any citizen summoned or arrested in virtue of the law shall submit without delay, as resistance constitutes an offense . . .
9. As all persons are held innocent until they shall have been declared guilty, if arrest shall be deemed indispensable, all harshness not essential to the securing of the prisoner's person shall be severely repressed by law.
10. No one shall be disquieted on account of his opinions, including his religious views, provided their manifestation does not disturb the public order established by law.
11. The free communication of ideas and opinions is one of the most precious of the rights of man. Every citizen may, accordingly, speak, write, and print with freedom, but shall be responsible for such abuses of this freedom as shall be defined by law.
12. The security of the rights of man and of the citizen requires public military forces. These forces are, therefore, established for the good of all and not for the personal advantage of those to whom they shall be entrusted . . .
17. Since property is an inviolable and sacred right, no one shall be deprived thereof except where public necessity, legally determined, shall clearly demand it, and then only on condition that the owner shall have been previously and equitably indemnified.

SOURCE: *Declaration of the Rights of Man—1789* **(The Avalon Project at Yale Law School, 1996–2007)** http://www.yale.edu/lawweb/avalon/rightsof.htm

In 1791, having created serious inflation and divided the Church, the Assembly issued France's first written constitution. It gave the king an absolute veto and the authority to appoint ministers and conduct diplomacy, but it also forced him to share power with an elected Legislative Assembly. A strong, clever king could have dominated such a government, but Louis XVI was neither strong nor clever. Rather than accept the constitution, he decided to escape to the lands of the Holy Roman Emperor, Leopold II, brother of Louis's queen, Marie Antoinette. There Louis hoped not only to find sanctuary but also to convince Leopold to invade France and restore its absolute monarchy.

In June 1791, the king, queen, and their two children fled Paris under cover of darkness and headed for the border. However, since Louis was identifiable from his images on French money, and since he insisted on stopping at a place where he could sleep on a comfortable feather bed, he was recognized and arrested about twenty miles from the border. The royal family was returned to Paris.

The flight of the king was disastrous for the Constitution of 1791. Louis and his ministers tried to pretend it was all a misunderstanding, but no one believed them. Clearly France was a constitutional monarchy ruled by a king who opposed the constitution. Then, fearing that other monarchs might invade France to stop the spread of revolution before it reached their countries, the Legislative Assembly in the spring of 1792 called for war against Austria and Prussia. Louis gladly approved, hoping for a French defeat that would restore him to absolute power.

Beset by inexperienced leadership, since many of its former officers were nobles who had fled the country, France's army at first fought poorly. In August 1792, interpreting French defeats as a sign that Louis was conspiring with the enemy, radical workers in Paris stormed the Tuileries Palace, almost killing the king and his family. Louis survived, but a search of his apartments revealed that he had indeed been collaborating with France's foes. The discovery dealt a deathblow to the constitutional monarchy.

War with Austria sparks a new uprising

The National Convention and the Reign of Terror

The Assembly now summoned a National Convention to meet in September to draft a new constitution. Formally abolishing the monarchy, the Convention moved to put Louis on trial for treason. At the same time, French armies finally halted the Austrians and Prussians well inside France's borders, giving the Convention time to try the king.

A new National Convention abolishes the French monarchy

Louis XVI's trial reflected the new governance concepts embodied in the Enlightenment and American Revolution. Under the old concepts, the people served the king, who was thus considered incapable of treason because that crime was defined as "an act against the king." Under the new concepts, however, the government served the people, whom Louis had betrayed by conspiring with France's enemies. The only real suspense, then, involved the method of punishment. By a vote of 361 to 360, the Convention condemned Louis to death. On January 21, 1793, Louis was executed by **guillotine**, a scaffold devised to release a heavy blade that instantly beheaded its victims. His queen, Marie Antoinette, was guillotined later that year.

Having thus renounced one-person rule, the Convention formed committees to run the government. Most notable was the **Committee of Public Safety**, a group of officials given broad powers to protect France from enemies foreign and domestic. Initially led by

Execution of Louis XVI.

moderates, who failed to deal forcefully with these foes, by July 1793 it was under the control of an outspoken radical named Maximilien Robespierre (1758–1794).

The Committee of Public Safety issues a mass call-up to service

To deal with foreign foes, the Committee enacted a *levée en masse* (*luh-VĀ awn MAHSS*), calling the whole country into service: "The young men shall go to battle; the married men shall forge arms and transport provisions; the women shall make tents and clothing and serve in the hospitals." This mass call-up created a new type of army: untrained and inexperienced, but huge and enthusiastic, it dwarfed the small, professional armies of France's enemies. The *levée* also drafted many talented men who would not otherwise have enlisted, providing effective officers to replace the nobles who had fled. By 1794, the new army had driven the forces of Austria and Prussia out of France.

To deal with internal foes, Robespierre and his Committee established revolutionary tribunals to try anyone suspected of being an enemy of the Revolution. Before long these tribunals were conducting a **Reign of Terror**, condemning suspects by the thousands to the guillotine, crassly called the "national razor." By mid-1794 hundreds of thousands of people had been executed, including some of the country's most notable politicians. No one in France seemed safe.

The Thermidorian Reaction terminates the Reign of Terror

By this time, however, with the Austrians and Prussians in retreat, and with most counterrevolutionaries either executed or in exile, the terror had outlived its usefulness. In July, known as Thermidor (the month of heat) on a new calendar created by the revolutionary regime, Robespierre was denounced by the Convention and sent to the guillotine himself. A "Thermidorian Reaction" followed, with conservative elements hunting down and killing his supporters. The Revolution's most radical phase was over.

The Role of the Lower Classes

Along with these political upheavals, the French Revolution also involved social rebellion: a struggle by the common people to transform French society, historically structured unequally. To achieve "Liberty, Equality, Fraternity," the rallying cry of the French Revolution, the lower classes fought to destroy noble power and privilege, a struggle that proved difficult, traumatic, and bloody.

In seizing the Bastille in July 1789, the lower classes demonstrated that a determined mob could overcome the power of the king. The next month, peasants rose in revolt across rural France, burning the records of noble class privilege and sometimes the nobles' manors. Meanwhile middle-class townspeople, also determined to destroy class privilege, seized control of provincial city governments. In October, the Women's March to Versailles showed that even poor urban women could force change by taking revolutionary action.

The working class sans-culottes assert their power

Revolutionary leaders, seeing the danger of defying the masses, hastened to show solidarity with the *sans-culottes* (*SAHN coo-LAHT*), the urban working poor, "without culottes," who wore ordinary trousers instead of the culottes (knee-breeches) worn by nobles. In 1792, as foreign armies neared Paris, the *sans-culottes* arose to arrest the king and install a more radical government. By 1793, as inflation ravaged France and food grew scarce under wartime conditions, these destitute men and women blamed their situation on conspirators and traitors. The *sans-culottes* cried out for vengeance, and the Committee of Public Safety, itself determined to destroy France's internal enemies, obliged the lower classes with the Reign of Terror.

But the lower classes were not unanimous in demanding radical change. Louis XVI's execution provoked a massive peasant uprising in western France, where Catholic farmers were appalled at the murder of a ruler they regarded as anointed by God. Many of the Reign of Terror's worst atrocities, including the mass butchery of captured peasant rebels, were committed in response by revolutionary soldiers, told by their leaders that the rebellious peasants were subversives and foreign agents.

The Directory and the Rise of Napoleon

The Thermidorian Reaction following Robespierre's fall ended the Reign of Terror, but not the financial crisis. After rampant inflation sparked a working-class uprising in Paris in May 1795, the National Convention dispersed, and a new two-house legislature chose a five-man Directory to run the country.

Hampered by weakness and corruption, the Directory sought to unite France against its foreign foes. These now included Britain and Spain, which had joined Austria and Prussia against France. The new coalition posed a grave threat to the new French army, which had great size and enthusiasm but lacked outstanding leaders.

Then the Directory found Napoleon Bonaparte, who proved to be the leader France needed. Born in 1769 on the Italian island of Corsica, which had come under French control in 1763, he had been sent as a young man to military school in France. He learned to write French superbly but always spoke it with a thick Italian accent. A loner and outsider, a man who relied on immense brainpower rather than noble ancestry, he was commissioned an artillery officer in 1788. The wars against Austria and Prussia that began in 1792 provided ample opportunity for promotion based on talent, and few soldiers ever have been as talented as Napoleon. By late 1793 he was a 24-year-old general, and a rising star.

Desperate for able generals, the Directory appointed him in 1796 to lead an invasion of northern Italy (Map 26.4), which was then dominated by Austria. Surprising the Austrians by crossing the Alps mountains in early spring, Napoleon defeated them in 1796–1797 and seized northern Italy from Austrian control. Then he created three northern Italian republics under French puppet regimes, exceeding his authority and alarming the Directory. Napoleon was an obviously exceptional soldier, but he was also a politically clever and ambitious man. That combination of qualities made him dangerous.

Yet the Directory continued to find Napoleon useful. In September 1797, when French royalists, after winning recent elections, conspired with British agents to overthrow the French republic, the Directory called on General Bonaparte. He sent a subordinate to occupy Paris and overturn the election results, an action that gave the military a central role in French politics. When French leaders considered military action against Britain, once again they turned to Napoleon.

Sent north to examine the possibility of invading Britain across the English Channel, Napoleon decided that France lacked the naval power to do so. If the British fleet caught a French armada at sea, France could lose both army and navy in a single battle. Instead he proposed invading Egypt as the first step toward an eventual French invasion of British India. The Directory gladly agreed: if Napoleon succeeded, it could take the credit; if he failed and was killed, it would be rid of a formidable rival.

Napoleon's invasion of Egypt in 1798 was a tactical triumph. He defeated Egyptian armies in the Battle of the Pyramids near Cairo, and then marched his victorious forces

Clothing of a *sans-culotte.*

The new Directory tries to unite France in war

Napoleon conquers and dominates northern Italy

Napoleon.

Bonaparte conquers Egypt while the British defeat the French navy

Map 26.4 Napoleon's Campaigns in Italy and Egypt, 1796–1799

In seizing northern Italy from the Austrians in 1796–1797, Napoleon Bonaparte proved himself France's ablest general. By conquering Egypt the next year he enhanced his reputation, despite the fact that his forces were trapped there when the British destroyed his fleet at Aboukir Bay. Notice Napoleon's willingness to travel more than a thousand miles to attack the British in Egypt, rather than traveling twenty miles to cross the English Channel and attack them in Britain itself. What accounts for this behavior?

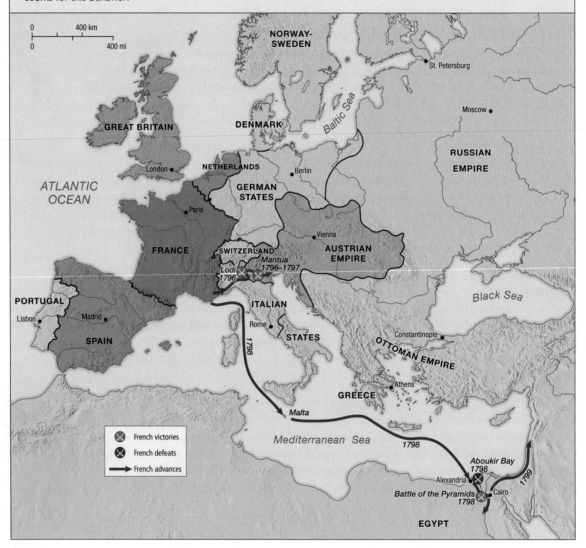

throughout the region (Map 26.4). He also advanced the science of Egyptology: archeologists accompanying him discovered what came to be known as the Rosetta Stone (Chapter 2), a slab inscribed in ancient times with Greek and Egyptian writing that enabled linguists to decipher Egyptian hieroglyphics. But the campaign against Britain was a strategic disaster. In the Battle of the Nile (1798), British Admiral Horatio Nelson destroyed the French fleet at Aboukir (*ab-oo-KEER*) Bay near Alexandria, stranding Napoleon's army. With escape impossible, the next year Napoleon abandoned his troops, riding horseback across North Africa and eventually sailing for France.

The Rosetta Stone.

The Consulate: Consolidation of the Revolution

Arriving in France at the same time as news of his first victories in Egypt, Napoleon received a hero's welcome. While the Directory was furious that he deserted his troops, it was about to lose its authority. Conspirators seeking a stronger government turned to Napoleon, and in a comic-opera coup, in which Napoleon was knocked unconscious, his brother rallied the troops to overthrow the Directory. It was replaced with a three-person executive body called the Consulate, which Napoleon would dominate as First Consul. The plotters hoped the new regime could restore order, preserve the revolution's reforms, and defeat France's enemies.

Napoleon did not disappoint them. Abroad, he defeated the anti-French coalition, forcing England to make peace in 1802. At home, he eased the financial crisis by creating the Bank of France, a private corporation empowered to issue currency and regulate the amount of money in circulation. *Assignats* were abolished and inflation controlled. He affirmed the revolutionary land settlement, letting peasants keep lands acquired from nobles who had fled France, thereby winning the devoted support of the rural masses. His codification of French Laws, known as the **Napoleonic Code**, ensured the integrity of private property while guaranteeing all male citizens equality before the law.

To implement these changes, Napoleon established a central bureaucracy, staffed by well-paid officials who depended on him for their positions and promotions. He also created a new nobility based on merit instead of heredity, granting titles as rewards for service, and opening careers to the most talented people.

Napoleon also healed the split in the French Catholic Church. Personally indifferent to religion, he nonetheless saw the Church as a social cement that could bind the nation together. In 1801 he and the pope signed a *Concordat*, a treaty granting French Catholics freedom of worship. In return, the Vatican recognized the French clergy's status as civil servants. The Church was thereby enlisted in service to the state.

Napoleon's Concordat enlists the Catholic Church in the service of the state

Increasingly, however, Napoleon subverted the revolution's democratic spirit. He never stood for election, instead asking voters to approve his actions in votes held after the fact, and he largely disregarded France's elected assemblies. Disdaining free speech and a free press, he used censorship, propaganda, and police spies to ensure support for his regime, arresting numerous real and imagined foes. The Consulate, which lasted from 1799 to 1804, thus marked both the consolidation and the end of the revolution. Napoleon fulfilled many of its fondest hopes, but also converted its hard-won democracy into a military dictatorship.

The Revolution and the Rights of Women

Napoleon's disdain for democratic ideals was likewise reflected in his attitude toward the rights of women. In this attitude, however, he was no different from the revolutionary governments preceding him.

Women gain little despite their key role in the revolution

Almost from the beginning, women had played a crucial role in the French Revolution, joining the crowds that propelled it forward, and radicalizing it by marching to Versailles in October 1789. Still, the various revolutionary regimes, controlled by middle-class men, did little to advance women's status. Some early reforms increased their rights to inherit property and obtain a divorce, but no actions were taken to permit women to hold government office or to vote in national elections. Liberty and equality, as enshrined in the ideals and actions of the French Revolution, were thus reserved mainly for men.

Attempting to call attention to this disparity, Olympe de Gouges (*aw-LAMP duh GOOZH*), a talented writer of political pamphlets, wrote a Declaration of the Rights of Woman and the Female Citizen in 1791. Amplifying the 1789 Declaration of the Rights of Man and the Citizen, de Gouges's document advocated equal rights for people of both sexes. "Woman is born free and lives equal to man in her rights," she declared; "male and female citizens, being equal in the eyes of the law, must be equally admitted to all honors, positions, and public employment according to their capacity and without other distinctions besides those of their virtues and talents" (see Excerpts from Declaration of the Rights of Women and the Female Citizen).

De Gouges is guillotined for her loyalty to the king

Although Olympe de Gouges's arguments were democratic, her political sympathies were monarchist. Daughter of a butcher, neither her success as a self-made actress and journalist nor her impassioned feminism diminished her loyalty to the king. Her disturbing blend of monarchism and feminism made her suspect in the eyes of male revolutionary leaders. In 1793, after strongly criticizing Robespierre and his Committee of Public Safety, she was guillotined for treason.

The Directory and the Napoleonic Code sustain women's subjugation

The governments that followed the Committee of Public Safety proved even less flexible toward women. The Directory, focused mainly on restoring stability and defeating France's enemies, was neither interested in nor capable of radical reforms. Then Napoleon rolled back women's rights to their prerevolutionary status. The Napoleonic Code actually increased the subjugation of women, depriving them of the right to own property, execute written agreements, and maintain bank accounts—restrictions that endured in France until 1947.

The Haitian Revolution

Women in France were not the only French subjects lacking freedom and rights. Much worse was the condition of the African slaves who worked the plantations in France's Saint-Domingue colony.

American and French revolutionary ideals inspire opposition to slavery

The ideals of liberty and equality that were enshrined in the American and French revolutionary declarations implicitly challenged the age-old institution of slavery. In a hierarchical society, with rights and privileges determined by hereditary status, slavery could be accepted. But in a system based on freedom and equal rights, slavery contradicted core values. Thus, as ideals of liberty and equality spread around the world, so would a movement to end slavery. It began in the 1790s in Saint-Domingue, where slaves, inspired by the revolutions in America and France, decided to liberate themselves.

Document 26.2 Excerpts: Declaration of the Rights of Woman and the Female Citizen

Following the publication of the Declaration of the Rights of Man and the Citizen, Olympe de Gouges, a skillful author of political pamphlets and a well-known figure in Parisian social circles, took exception to that document's implication that human rights were reserved for men alone. Her refutation of that position remains one of the most eloquent assertions of female rights ever written.

THE RIGHTS OF WOMAN Man, are you capable of being just? It is a woman who poses the question; you will not deprive her of that right at least. Tell me, what gives you sovereign empire to oppress my sex? Your strength? Your talents? Observe the Creator in his wisdom; survey in all her grandeur that nature with whom you seem to want to be in harmony, and give me, if you dare, an example of this tyrannical empire . . .

Man alone has raised his exceptional circumstances to a principle. Bizarre, blind, bloated with science and degenerated—in a century of enlightenment and wisdom—into the crassest ignorance, he wants to command as a despot a sex which is in full possession of its intellectual faculties; he pretends to enjoy the Revolution and to claim his rights to equality in order to say nothing more about it.

DECLARATION OF THE RIGHTS OF WOMAN AND THE FEMALE CITIZEN For the National Assembly to decree in its last sessions, or in those of the next legislature:

PREAMBLE Mothers, daughters, sisters [and] representatives of the nation demand to be constituted into a national assembly. Believing that ignorance, omission, or scorn for the rights of woman are the only causes of public misfortunes and of the corruption of governments, [the women] have resolved to set forth a solemn declaration the natural, inalienable, and sacred rights of woman in order that this declaration, constantly exposed before all members of the society, will ceaselessly remind them of their rights and duties; in order that the authoritative acts of women and the authoritative acts of men may be at any mo-

ment compared with and respectful of the purpose of all political institutions; and in order that citizens' demands, henceforth based on simple and incontestable principles, will always support the constitution, good morals, and the happiness of all.

Consequently, the sex that is as superior in beauty as it is in courage during the sufferings of maternity recognizes and declares in the presence and under the auspices of the Supreme Being, the following Rights of Woman and of Female Citizens.

ARTICLE I Woman is born free and lives equal to man in her rights. Social distinctions can be based only on the common utility.

ARTICLE II The purpose of any political association is the conservation of the natural and imprescriptible rights of woman and man; these rights are liberty, property, security, and especially resistance to oppression.

ARTICLE III The principle of all sovereignty rests essentially with the nation, which is nothing but the union of woman and man; no body and no individual can exercise any authority which does not come expressly from it (the nation).

ARTICLE VI The law must be the expression of the general will; all female and male citizens must contribute either personally or through their representatives to its formation; it must be the same for all: male and female citizens, being equal in the eyes of the law, must be equally admitted to all honors, positions, and public employment according to their capacity and without other distinctions besides those of their virtues and talents.

ARTICLE X No one is to be disquieted for his very basic opinions; woman has the right to mount the scaffold; she must equally have the right to mount the rostrum, provided that her demonstrations do not disturb the legally established public order.

(continued)

Document 26.2 (*continued*)

ARTICLE XVII Property belongs to both sexes whether united or separate; for each it is an inviolable and sacred right . . . no one can be deprived of it, since it is the true patrimony of nature, unless the legally determined public need obviously dictates it, and then only with a just and prior indemnity.

POSTSCRIPT Woman, wake up; the tocsin of reason is being heard throughout the whole universe; discover

your rights . . . Regardless of what barriers confront you, it is in your power to free yourselves; you have only to want to. . . .

SOURCE: Olympe De Gouges, *Declaration of the Rights of Woman, 1791.* http://www.library.csi.cuny.edu/dept/ americanstudies/lavender/decwom2.html. From Darline Gay Levy, Harriet Branson Applewhite, and Mary Durham Johnson, eds., *Women in Revolutionary Paris, 1789–1795* (Urbana, Ill.: University of Illinois Press, 1980) 87–96.

The Saint-Domingue Slave Colony

The French import many African slaves to work Saint-Domingue plantations

In the 1600s, the western part of the Caribbean island of Hispaniola, a Spanish colony since the time of Columbus, came under French control and was named Saint-Domingue (Map 26.5). In the 1700s, eager to make a profit, French investors set up plantations there, producing sugar, coffee, cotton, cacao, and indigo. Since the island's Arawak Indians had died from European diseases, the French imported African slaves to work the plantations.

After 1763, when defeat in the Seven Years War cost France its North American empire, Saint-Domingue emerged as the most important and profitable French colony. By the time of the French Revolution, it had more than three thousand plantations, accounting for well over half of French colonial investments. Its half million slaves made up almost 90 percent of its population; the rest of its inhabitants were divided between white French colonists and **people of color**—a term applied to former slaves and persons of mixed racial heritage, legally free but treated by the whites as social inferiors.

The Revolt of Toussaint Louverture

Events in France triggered Saint-Domingue's revolution. When the Estates General was summoned in 1789, the colony's white settlers and people of color each sent separate delegations, the former hoping for greater independence from France, the latter seeking greater equality with the white colonists. During the next few years of turbulence, as French radicals sided with Saint-Domingue's people of color, the tensions between them and the white colonists turned into all-out civil war.

The French Revolution sparks the Saint-Domingue slave rebellion

In 1791, as the colony's free people fought each other, the slaves of Saint-Domingue seized the opportunity to rebel. Led by François-Dominique Toussaint, who called himself Toussaint Louverture (*too-SAN loo-vair-TOOR*), the rebels soon gained the advantage, helping themselves to the lands of the former slave owners. Toussaint, a former domestic slave, had been taught to read and write by a Catholic priest, and quickly developed superb organizational and leadership skills. Escaping slaves flocked to his camps, and within two years he had constructed a cohesive, well-disciplined fighting force of 20 thousand men.

Map 26.5 Saint-Domingue and the Haitian Revolution, 1791–1804

Inspired by events in North America and France, and inflamed by brutal repression, slaves in France's Saint-Domingue colony rose in rebellion and beat back invasions by the British and French, finally proclaiming in 1804 the independent nation of Haiti. Note that Haiti occupies only 25 percent of the island of Hispaniola, sharing it with the Spanish colony of Santo Domingo (the present-day Dominican Republic). How did the success of the Haitian Revolution affect Spain's empire in the western hemisphere?

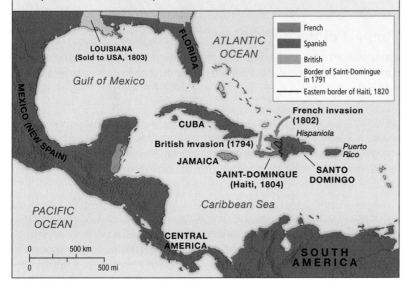

In 1793 two of France's European enemies intervened in the Saint-Domingue rebellion. The British feared that the slave revolt threatened their Caribbean holdings (especially Jamaica, with its 300 thousand slaves), while the Spanish, who still controlled the eastern part of Hispaniola, hoped to take the whole island. Toussaint and his slave army were willing to support any regime that abolished slavery, but it soon became clear that neither invader cared much about abolition.

Britain and Spain intervene in Saint-Domingue

Toussaint's forces now allied with France, judging that their best hope for emancipation lay with the mother country, governed in 1793 by the radical National Convention. Their combined forces defeated the Spanish in 1794, but the British hung on, sickening and dying from yellow fever and malaria. They finally withdrew in 1798 after suffering 100 thousand casualties. Toussaint then had the delicate task of governing Saint-Domingue, supposedly on behalf of France, while preparing to oppose any French efforts to restore slavery. In France, after the Convention was dissolved in 1795, its successors, first the Directory and then Napoleon's Consulate, were far less supportive of abolition.

An assembly controlled by Toussaint proclaimed a constitution in 1801, making him governor-general for life and abolishing slavery. But it did not declare independence from France. By remaining a French colony, though a largely autonomous one, Toussaint hoped to avoid French intervention.

Toussaint Louverture.

Napoleon, however, was by this time convinced that only the restoration of slavery and full French authority would make the colony profitable again. He was so contemptuous of the abilities of black soldiers that he assumed a small French army could defeat them in a few weeks. The British, of course, having lost 100 thousand soldiers in Saint-Domingue during the previous decade, could have told him otherwise. French soldiers died by the thousands of yellow fever and malaria, and also encountered serious problems of supply and logistics. Napoleon counted on Jamaica and the United States to provision his expeditionary force, but both were suspicious of his motives, fearing he intended to expand French holdings in the Caribbean.

The Success and Impact of the Revolution

Dessalines defeats France and declares Haiti independent

For a time the French appeared to be winning. Defeated by invading French forces in 1802, Toussaint was arrested and sent to France, where he died the next year in a frigid prison. But his successor, Jean Jacques Dessalines (*des-sahl-LĒN*), was a relentless killer who hated Europeans and gave the French no mercy. When Britain declared war on France in 1803, plundering French possessions in the Caribbean as it did so, Napoleon decided to cut his losses in the western hemisphere. He sold to the United States the Louisiana territory, a vast stretch of central North America recently reacquired by France from Spain, and pulled his forces out of Saint-Domingue after suffering some 40 thousand casualties. The French had proven as vulnerable as the British to tropical diseases and the military skills of the former slaves. On January 1, 1804, Dessalines declared independence, renaming the new nation "Haiti," an Arawak word meaning "mountainous," succinctly describing the terrain.

Haiti was the second colony, after the United States, to break from its mother country. But the Haitian Revolution differed from the revolutions in North America and France: it was more social than political, and it was clearly racial, pitting black slaves against white slave owners as well as people of color against both. Moreover, its focus on land usage related more to the rebels' African origins (since most had been farmers in Africa) than to French notions of liberty and equality. The Haitians wanted to center their lives on the land rather than on abstract political ideals. Toussaint misunderstood the strength of this desire, and when he invited white planters to return and distributed confiscated plantations to his black generals, he lost the support of his ex-slave soldiers. It took a man like Dessalines, who understood those desires and worked ruthlessly to fulfill them, to consolidate Haiti's revolution.

The Haitian Revolution fuels global antislavery and liberation movements

The revolution's success transformed not only Haiti. It also gave momentum to Britain's growing antislavery movement, and served as a warning to Spanish and Portuguese America and to slaveholders in the United States. In Haiti, victory proved disappointing. The previously prosperous colony of Saint-Domingue lost nearly all its educated elite in the revolutionary wars. Its sugar, cotton, and coffee production were largely destroyed by warfare, leaving the new nation without the financial and educational resources needed to rebuild. In Britain, Haiti's liberation energized the antislavery movement led by William Wilberforce, a devoutly Christian Member of Parliament, who fought the slave trade with moral and religious fervor. In 1807, Parliament passed his bill banning the African slave trade, and Britain's Royal Navy then pressured other nations to stop trafficking in human beings. The United States banned the trade in 1808.

Although France first abolished, then restored slavery, increasingly the institution was condemned. By the end of the nineteenth century it had been abolished throughout the world. Finally, the Haitian Revolution, combined with the earlier American Revolution, helped inspire independence movements throughout Latin America (Chapter 28).

The Napoleonic Empire

Napoleonic forces in battle.

Haiti's independence, important as it was for the Americas, had little impact on its former mother country. Even as he was reluctantly giving up his hopes for France's colonial empire in the Americas, Napoleon was building a French Empire in Europe. With his exceptional military skills and his powerful French army, he defeated France's enemies and conquered much of the continent. In the process, he proclaimed himself emperor. Eventually, however, his ambitions grew beyond his capacity, leading to his personal downfall and the end of his empire.

The Formation and Expansion of the Empire

Napoleon built his empire on military genius, especially his ability to make the most of mobility, deception, and surprise. His armies often appeared where no one expected and performed maneuvers few other forces could match. In the smoke and chaos of battle, Napoleon unfailingly chose the right time and place to attack the enemy's lines. Needing only three hours' sleep a night, he consistently outworked his opponents; possessing an exceptionally nimble mind, he constantly outthought them. His remarkable memory for names and details gave him an added advantage, which he embellished by cheating whenever possible. Fighting Napoleon was no fun.

By 1804, after five years as First Consul, Napoleon had not only stabilized France and consolidated its revolution; he had also defeated most of its enemies and expanded its borders. France by then controlled most of Italy, the Netherlands, and Germany as far east as the Rhine River (Map 26.6). As the all-powerful ruler of a growing territorial empire, Napoleon decided that he needed a title to match his actual status. So in 1804, in an elaborate ceremony at Notre Dame Cathedral in Paris, he crowned himself Emperor of the French. Fifteen years after the onset of revolution, and 11 years after the execution of Louis XVI, France again was a monarchy.

Napoleon expands French rule and crowns himself emperor

France again also terrified its neighbors. In 1805, alarmed by Napoleon's seemingly boundless ambitions, Austria, Russia, Sweden, and Britain formed a new coalition against him. That October, Britain's fleet destroyed the French navy in the Battle of Trafalgar, off the Spanish coast near Gibraltar. Admiral Nelson engineered his nation's greatest naval triumph before dying in combat.

The British destroy French naval power at Trafalgar

No one, however, could figure out how to beat Napoleon on land. His talented subordinates, most of whom had been forced to join the army by the *levée en masse*, helped him win a crushing victory at Austerlitz, in east-central Europe, in December 1805. There Napoleon, outnumbered by Russian and Austrian forces, maneuvered his armies brilliantly to divide and conquer his foes. The next year he established control over much of Central Europe, defeating Prussia, occupying Berlin, and abolishing the Holy Roman Empire. In 1807 he routed the Russians again, and then concluded a treaty of alliance

Napoleon defeats Austria, Russia, and Prussia to dominate Europe

Map 26.6 The Napoleonic Empire, 1804–1814

Having crowned himself emperor in 1804, Napoleon in the next few years defeated the forces of Austria, Prussia, and Russia, making him the master of Europe. But a British naval triumph that destroyed his fleet at Trafalgar in 1805, a debilitating campaign in Spain that began in 1808, and a disastrous invasion of Russia in 1812 eventually proved his undoing. Compare the size of Napoleon's empire with that of the Roman Empire (Map 8.4). Do you see any similarities in the eventual collapse of both these empires?

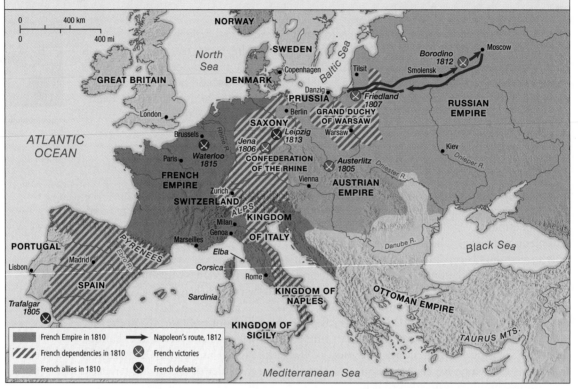

with Tsar Alexander I. As the year ended, the 38-year-old Corsican upstart was the master of Europe.

Yet Napoleon had been unable to conquer Britain, whose naval triumph at Trafalgar had discouraged invasion by France. The French emperor turned to commercial warfare, and in 1806, hoping to undermine Britain's economy by cutting off its commerce, created the **Continental System**. Essentially a Europe-wide boycott of British goods by countries under French influence, the system damaged the British economy but failed to destroy it. Smugglers evaded the boycott, while Britain managed to gain new markets in Latin America, following one of Napoleon's worst blunders: invasion of Portugal and Spain.

When Portugal, linked with England since 1386 in one of history's most enduring alliances, refused to join the Continental System, Napoleon dispatched an invading force. It occupied Lisbon in 1807, while Portugal's royal family escaped to Brazil on British ships. Napoleon next tried to make Spain a puppet monarchy under his brother Joseph, but the French occupation of Madrid in 1808 was challenged by guerrilla forces loyal to Spain's Borbón dynasty. Joseph's coronation in turn prompted revolts in Spain's American colonies, which had no loyalty to this French usurper.

Britain took advantage of Napoleon's Spanish blunder. First, it shipped goods to Spanish America, capturing markets abandoned by Spain because of the war at home, thus helping Britain survive the Continental System. Second, it sent troops to help Spain's guerrillas fight the French, tying down Napoleon's best troops in a drawn out, debilitating conflict.

The Russian Campaign and the Empire's Collapse

In 1810, however, Napoleon's Spanish mistake seemed only a minor annoyance. Confident in his control of Europe, he turned to domestic matters, divorcing his wife Josephine, with whom he had no children, and marrying Maria Louisa von Habsburg, daughter of the Austrian emperor. The marriage was designed to build ties between Austria and France; it also gave Napoleon an heir, born in 1811 and titled the "King of Rome." Yet just as the Bonaparte dynasty seemed secure, Russia reopened its ports to British trade. Tsar Alexander was upset that Napoleon had spurned a Russian candidate for marriage and troubled by the Continental System's damage to Russia's economy, for Britain had been Russia's main trading partner. Napoleon responded by preparing for war. In June 1812 he invaded Russia with a Grand Army of 600 thousand men.

> Troubled Russia resumes ties with Britain

The Russian campaign proved disastrous for Napoleon. His Grand Army was not nearly as powerful as it appeared. With more than 200 thousand seasoned French troops tied down fighting in Spain, Napoleon had had to draft two-thirds of his soldiers from his satellite nations throughout Europe. Reluctant to lay down their lives for France, many eventually deserted. Moreover, the Grand Army's sheer size actually worked against it. As always, Napoleon sought to come to grips with his foes and destroy them. Tsar Alexander's generals, noting that the Russians were outnumbered three to one, disobeyed his orders to fight Napoleon and retreated into Russia's interior. Had the Grand Army been smaller, the Russian generals would have had to stand and fight.

The retreat proved strategically sound, as Napoleon was drawn ever deeper into Russia. By September his forces occupied Moscow, but this did not force Tsar Alexander to surrender, as he was safe in the capital, Saint Petersburg. Then fires, which may have been deliberately set, burned much of Moscow to the ground. With no place to house his forces for the winter, Napoleon began withdrawing in October, retreating over the same route by which he had arrived. Lacking adequate food, and beset by harsh weather, his men died by the thousands from cold, hunger, and disease. The Grand Army that crossed back into French-controlled Europe in December had only 20 thousand men.

> The French occupation of Moscow is followed by Napoleon's calamitous retreat

But Napoleon was not beaten. He raced back to Paris and raised another army, rejecting an Austrian peace plan and thereby prompting Austria and Prussia to join with Britain and Russia. The new alliance then declared a war of liberation from French rule. In 1813, in the Battle of the Nations at Leipzig, Germany, the allies soundly defeated the French. In April 1814, Napoleon gave up his throne and was exiled to Elba, a Mediterranean island. King Louis XVIII, younger brother of the guillotined Louis XVI, was restored to the French throne by the victorious alliance (Louis XVI's only son, Louis XVII, disappeared in 1795 and was never found).

In early 1815, however, while allied leaders were meeting at Vienna to restructure Europe, they were interrupted by startling news: Napoleon had escaped from Elba and returned to France. Louis XVIII sent soldiers to arrest him, but they deserted to their former emperor. Louis then unwisely sent a whole army corps under one of Napoleon's former generals, who turned the entire corps over to his old leader. Napoleon then informed the king: "Sire, there is no need to send me more troops; I have enough."

Louis XVIII fled, and Napoleon reclaimed his throne, but his new reign lasted only a hundred days. The allies regrouped and Napoleon marched north to meet them. At the Belgian town of Waterloo, on June 18, 1815, he was once again defeated. This time the allies sent the former emperor to the remote South Atlantic island of Saint Helena, where he died six years later of stomach cancer at age 51.

Restoration and Rebellion

Final victory over Napoleon enabled allied leaders at Vienna to complete a comprehensive peace settlement. Resolved to restore stability to a continent torn by decades of revolution and war, they worked to reestablish the old order that had existed before 1789. Although they developed plans to use force to suppress any future revolutions, they proved unable to extinguish the new ideas about equality and freedom that the Atlantic revolutions had released.

The Congress of Vienna and the Congress System

Ably directed by Austria's foreign minister, Prince Klemens von Metternich, the Congress of Vienna (1814–1815) based its deliberations on three principles. First was *legitimacy*, the right of former rulers or ruling families to regain the positions they lost in the Napoleonic Wars. Second was *compensation*, the reimbursement of nations that had sacrificed lives and resources to defeat Napoleon. Third was an effort to maintain peace by establishing a *balance of power*, a situation in which no one nation would be strong enough to impose its will on the others, or to dominate Europe as France had under Napoleon.

The Congress of Vienna redraws European borders

To implement these principles, the Congress redrew the map of Europe (Map 26.7). France was returned to its 1789 borders, deprived of all the lands it had gained since the revolution. In Spain, and throughout the Italian peninsula, regimes that had ruled before Napoleon were restored to power. The Holy Roman Empire, abolished in 1806, was replaced by a new Germanic Confederation. Prussia received some German territory west of the Rhine River, and Russia gained control of Finland.

Aiming in part to balance France's power by forming a strong nation to its North, the Congress created a Kingdom of the Netherlands, uniting Belgium (formerly the Austrian Netherlands) with the Dutch Netherlands under Dutch rule. The Congress also reconstituted Poland, earlier partitioned among Russia, Prussia, and Austria (Chapter 25), but agreed to let Russia's tsar serve as Poland's king, effectively making it a Russian satellite.

To further sustain stability and peace, Metternich persuaded the Congress to establish an ongoing mechanism known as the **Congress System**. It called for Europe's main powers to hold periodic meetings to deal with pressing problems and thus to preserve order by preventing wars and revolutions. Congresses were held at various European cities in 1818, 1820, 1821, and 1822; among other things they authorized armed interventions by Austria in Naples and by France in Spain to crush rebellions and restore royal rule.

Map 26.7 Europe in 1815

Seeking to restore stability in Europe and establish a balance of power, the Congress of Vienna in 1815 returned France to its prerevolutionary borders, restored regimes that had been ousted by Napoleon, and created a Germanic Confederation in place of the old Holy Roman Empire. A Kingdom of Poland was restored in name but was still ruled by Russia's tsar. Observe that both Germany and Italy were fragmented, while the rest of Europe was composed of unified states. What difficulties would this pose for nineteenth-century Germans and Italians?

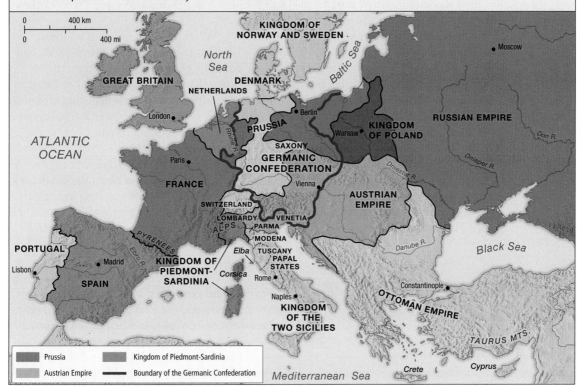

Renewed Attempts at Revolution

In 1821, however, a Greek rebellion against the Ottoman Turks began to divide the powers. In Britain and France, the western parliamentary monarchies, the revolt was seen as a heroic bid to liberate Greece, the cradle of Western culture, from Islamic rule. But the eastern absolute autocracies—Austria, Prussia, and Russia—fearing the appeal of freedom, opposed all efforts at revolutionary change. Even Russia, despite its view of the Turks as foes and the Greeks as fellow Orthodox Christians, initially opposed the revolt, and by mid-1822 the Turks seemed to have suppressed it. But the rebels persisted, and the situation changed.

Revolt in Greece creates tensions among the powers

In December 1825 a group of young Russian army officers from the Napoleonic Wars, viewing their country as backward and repressive in comparison with the Western European countries they had marched through while conquering France, rebelled upon the death of Tsar Alexander I, hoping to force his successor to grant a constitution. Their brief insurrection, the "Decembrist Revolt," was crushed by loyal troops.

Western ideals prompt a failed rebellion in Russia

The new tsar, Nicholas I, reacted by striving for the next 30 years to maintain the old order in Russia through police state mechanisms and military force. In Greece, however, he was willing to intervene to advance Russia's interests.

The Greek Revolt succeeds with support from Russia and the West

Hoping that a liberated Greece would be Russia's friend and client, Nicholas broke with Austria and Prussia to support the Greek rebels. In 1827 the Russian, French, and British navies challenged the Turks, and the next year Russian armies attacked them. The resulting Russo-Turkish War of 1828–1829 brought independence to Greece and inspired revolts in 1830 in France, Belgium, and Poland.

Revolution spreads in 1830 to France, Belgium, and Poland

France's revolt was an aftershock of the 1789 revolution. Realizing that its ideals could not be wholly obliterated, King Louis XVIII, who reigned from 1814 to 1824, had issued a charter affirming such rights as liberty, equality, property, and freedom of religion. In July 1830, however, his reactionary successor, King Charles X, issued ordinances aimed at undermining these rights. The result was an upheaval in Paris deposing Charles. But instead of ending the monarchy, the July Revolution brought to power a royal cousin, King Louis Philippe, who reigned from 1830 to 1848 as a moderate. Remembering the Reign of Terror, the French were not ready to try another republic.

The other two revolts, like the one in Greece, were efforts to gain freedom from foreign rule. The Belgians rebelled in August 1830 against the Kingdom of the Netherlands; the revolt succeeded, and Belgium soon became independent. The Poles, also seeking independence, arose in November against Russian rule, but Nicholas I's army ruthlessly crushed their revolt. The struggle between the old and new orders unleashed by the Atlantic revolutions was by no means over.

Chapter Review

Putting It in Perspective

The Atlantic revolutions, although they occurred in North America, Europe, and Haiti, had implications and repercussions far beyond these regions. Distinctive as these revolutions were, by challenging such entrenched institutions as monarchy, aristocracy, colonialism, and slavery, they helped introduce a new vision of society, centered on ideals of political liberty and social equality.

The American Revolution, and subsequently the United States Constitution, established the precedent that people could decide their own form of governance, discarding structures they deemed oppressive and creating new ones that better served their needs. In freeing themselves from colonial rule, Americans set an example for freedom-seeking colonies in Latin America, and later throughout the world. And in forming a republic with elected officials accountable to the people and governing institutions limited by separation of powers, the United States proved that Enlightenment principles could be put into practice.

The French Revolution showed not only that kings could be overthrown and nobles disinherited, but also that common people could play a key role in shaping their own destiny. In fighting for liberty and equality, the rebels undermined monarchy and aristocracy, first in France and later throughout Europe and Latin America. Napoleon curtailed democratic freedoms and formed a military dictatorship, but he also promoted equality under law and careers based on talent, spread these concepts across Europe by his conquests, and opened the way to Latin American liberation by invading Portugal and Spain.

The Haitian Revolution demonstrated not only that the American and French experiences could be repeated elsewhere, but also that slaves could liberate themselves by organizing to expel their oppressors. African slaves also proved they could defeat European armies, while skillfully playing off Europeans against one another. In blending European ideas of freedom and equality with African concepts of land use, the Haitians took significant steps toward ending both colonialism and slavery.

The Atlantic revolutions, nonetheless, marked only the onset of a long struggle between the old and new orders. Monarchs and aristocrats, backed by supporters of stability and tradition, sought forcefully to restore their status after Napoleon's defeat. But their efforts were soon challenged by a new wave of rebellions, and ultimately subverted by an industrial revolution, already under way in Britain, that in time would revolutionize the entire world.

Reviewing Key Material

KEY CONCEPTS

Estates General, 634
balance of power, 636
Boston Tea Party, 638
Loyalists, 639
Tennis Court Oath, 642
Bastille, 642
March of the Women, 643
inflation, 643
guillotine, 645

Committee of Public
   Safety, 645
Reign of Terror, 646
sans-culottes, 646
Napoleonic Code, 649
people of color, 652
Continental System, 656
Congress System, 658

KEY PEOPLE

William Pitt, 636
Thomas Jefferson, 639
George Washington, 639
King Louis XVI, 642
Marie Antoinette, 645
Maximilien Robespierre, 646
Napoleon Bonaparte, 647
Olympe de Gouges, 650

Toussaint Louverture, 652
Jean Jacques Dessalines, 654
William Wilberforce, 654
Horatio Nelson, 649
Tsar Alexander I, 656
Prince Klemens von
   Metternich, 658

ASK YOURSELF

1. How did the ideals of the Enlightenment, and Britain's victory in the Seven Years (French and Indian) War, contribute to the American, French, and Haitian revolutions?
2. In what ways were these three revolutions similar, and in what ways did they differ? What impact did each of them have on events in the other two countries?

3. What roles did the working classes and women play in the French Revolution? How did they help make it increasingly radical from 1789 to 1794?
4. In what ways did Napoleon advance the ideals and consolidate the accomplishments of the French Revolution, and in what ways did he violate its ideals and undermine its accomplishments?
5. How did Napoleon rise from obscurity to become the master of Europe? How and why was he eventually defeated? How did his conquerors try to restore Europe's peace and stability?
6. How do the Atlantic revolutions compare and contrast with earlier rebellions elsewhere, such as the major lower-class revolts in China (Chapter 21) and Russia (Chapter 25)? Why did the Atlantic revolutions have a greater global impact?

GOING FURTHER

Bailyn, B. *Ideological Origins of the American Revolution*. 1992.
Bergeron, Louis. *France Under Napoleon*. 1981.
Bonwick, C. *The American Revolution*. 1991.
Connelly, O. *The French Revolution and Napoleonic Era*. 3rd ed. 2000.
Countryman, Edward. *The American Revolution*. 2003.
Doyle, W. *The Oxford History of the French Revolution*. 1989.
Eccles, William J. *France in America*. 1990.
Ellis, Geoffrey. *Napoleon*. 1997.
Englund, S. *Napoleon: A Political Life*. 2004.
Fick, Carolyn. *The Making of Haiti*. 1990.
Furet, François. *The French Revolution, 1770–1814*. 1996.
Furet, François. *Interpreting the French Revolution*. 1981.
Graymont, Barbara. *The Iroquois in the American Revolution*. 1972.
Hampson, Norman. *Prelude to Terror*. 1988.
Hobsbawm, Eric. *The Age of Revolution, 1789–1848*. 1996.
Holtman, Robert. *The Napoleonic Revolution*. 1967.
Hunt, Lynn. *Politics, Culture, and Class in the French Revolution*. 1986.
James, C. L. R. *The Black Jacobins: Toussaint L'Ouverture and the San Domingo Revolution*. 1989.
Landes, J. *Women and the Public Sphere in the Age of the French Revolution*. 1988.

Lefebvre, Georges. *The Coming of the French Revolution.* 1989.

Levy, D., et al., eds. *Women in Revolutionary Paris.* 1979.

Liss, P. K. *Atlantic Empires: The Network of Trade and Revolution, 1713–1826.* 1983.

Lyons, M. *Napoleon Bonaparte and the Legacy of the French Revolution.* 1994.

Nash, Gary. *Urban Crucible: The Northern Seaports and the Origins of the American Revolution.* 2006.

Norton, Mary Beth. *Founding Mothers and Fathers: Gendered Power and the Forming of American Society.* 1996.

Norton, Mary Beth. *Liberty's Daughters: The Revolutionary Experience of American Women, 1750–1800.* 1980.

Rudé, George. *The Crowd in the French Revolution.* 1968.

Rudé, George. *The French Revolution.* 1996.

Schama, S. *Citizens: A Chronicle of the French Revolution.* 1989.

Shapiro, B. *Revolutionary Justice in Paris, 1789–1790.* 1993.

Tackett, T. *When the King Took Flight.* 2003.

Wills, Gary. *The Unknown American Revolution.* 2005.

Key Dates and Developments

1756–1763	Seven Years War (French and Indian War)
1763	Pontiac's Rebellion; proclamation closing the frontier
1775–1783	American Revolutionary War
1787–1789	Composition and Ratification of U.S. Constitution
1789	Outbreak of French Revolution
1791	Flight and capture of Louis XVI
1791–1803	Haitian Revolution
1792	Onset of French wars against European powers
1793	Execution of Louis XVI
1793–1794	Committee of Public Safety's Reign of Terror
1795–1799	The Directory
1796–1799	Napoleon's victories in Italy and Egypt
1799–1804	The Consulate
1804	Haiti declares independence
1804–1814	The Napoleonic Empire
1806	Creation of the Continental System
1807–1808	Invasions of Portugal and Spain
1812	Invasion of Russia
1814	Napoleon's defeat and exile to Elba
1814–1815	Congress of Vienna
1815	Napoleon's return and defeat at Waterloo
1821–1829	Greek rebellion against Ottoman Turks
1825	Decembrist Revolt in Russia
1830	French, Belgian, and Polish Revolts

Industry, Ideology, and their Global Impact, 1700–1914

Cotton Mill Machinery

Industrial machines, such as these power looms used to mass produce cotton textiles, played a crucial role in the Industrial Revolution, which transformed the lives and labor of people all over the world.

On April 20, 1812, in the English town of Middleton, several thousand angry men assembled at a textile factory that had recently started replacing its workers with steam-powered machines. Determined to destroy the machines that were taking their jobs, the men began throwing rocks through the factory windows. Armed guards, employed by the factory owner, soon appeared and fired into the crowd, killing three men and dispersing the rest. But the next day, enraged by the bloodshed, the angry men reassembled. Carrying a straw dummy they called "General Ludd," a mythical leader who supposedly headed their movement, they attacked and set fire to the factory owner's home. Then guards again dispersed them, killing five more men.

Early Industrial Regions

The Middleton disorder was one of many that occurred in England between 1811 and 1816, as workers called **Luddites** attacked factories and broke machines they blamed for taking their jobs. They were reacting to **industrialization**, a momentous shift from a rural agrarian economy, in which people lived off the land and made goods by hand, to an urban manufacturing economy, in which goods were made in urban factories by machine.

For many millennia, since the advent of agriculture, most people lived by farming or herding. Work was performed by human or animal power, and most people had to raise food in order for all to survive. Goods, such as clothing and tools, were produced by hand in homes or artisans' workshops. Most people lived in villages or towns; only a small minority lived in cities.

By the early 1800s, however, society in England was changing. New farming methods enabled fewer people to produce more food, while new machines and energy sources greatly accelerated the manufacture of goods. People increasingly worked in factories and lived in the cities that grew up around them rather than in farming villages. This process, later called the Industrial Revolution, spread from Britain to Europe and America, transforming their societies, generating radical new political and social ideas, and giving Western nations the power and wealth to dominate the world. Other nations, responding to this domination, eventually embraced the new methods and ideas, altering lives and labor the world over.

The Industrial Revolution in Britain

Industrialization is by no means inevitable. To industrialize, a society needs not only the talent and desire to do so, but also certain key assets. These include a large labor force, ample food to sustain it, abundant raw materials, machines to make them into finished goods, energy to run the machines, receptive markets, reliable transportation, and capital to fund industrial ventures. Before the nineteenth century, various societies, including China, India, and France, had at times acquired many of these assets and developed thriving commercial economies. But their economies remained primarily agrarian. Not until the 1800s did economies develop in which most people worked in industry or commerce rather than raising their own food. The first place to develop such an economy was Britain.

Agricultural Advances and Population Growth

Britain's ample food supply was based on agricultural methods earlier developed in the Netherlands. Rather than leaving part of the land untilled each year to let the soil regenerate, Dutch and British farmers employed crop rotation, alternating grains such as wheat and barley with soil-enriching crops such as turnips and clover, thereby using all the land every year. By feeding the turnips and clover to sheep and cattle, and selectively breeding these animals to produce larger livestock, farmers simultaneously increased the meat and dairy supply. More and better-fed animals also produced more manure, which was used to fertilize the grain crops, enhancing their yield. These techniques, along with draining of swamps to increase farmland, helped Britain quadruple its food production in the eighteenth and nineteenth centuries.

The new techniques helped subvert the age-old system in which peasant families pastured animals and farmed strips of land near their villages in open communal fields, often surplus lands of large landowners who let peasants use them. By the 1700s in Britain, these fields were increasingly closed off to peasants by large landowners who used fences or hedges to enclose the land, initially to pasture their sheep and later to implement the new farming methods on a larger scale. When local peasants objected, the large landowners often got Parliament (which they controlled) to pass laws approving these **enclosures**. Thus denied access to communal lands, many peasants became wage laborers, often working for large landowners engaged in large-scale commercial farming for profit. These workers formed a growing **proletariat**: a large class of landless laborers, many of whom eventually moved to cities to work in urban factories.

Thus enlarged by farmers driven off the land, Britain's urban labor force was also increased by rapid population growth. From 1750 to 1850, despite extensive emigration to America, the British population grew from roughly six million to more than twenty million—a growth attributed largely to declining childhood mortality. New crops and farming methods provided a stable food supply and healthier diet, and public health advances, such as **vaccination** to immunize people against diseases such as smallpox, helped more children survive to become adults and have children of their own.

The new farming methods, meanwhile, decreased the need for farmers and farm workers, since large-scale farms could now produce more food with fewer workers than before. Combined with rising population, the reduced need for farmers added to the numbers of landless poor people willing to work in factories for very low wages. Many such people also came from Ireland, where widespread cultivation of the potato, imported from the Americas in the sixteenth century and capable of feeding more people using less land than grain crops, had also supported a huge population increase. Together these developments supplied a low-cost labor force for Britain's Industrial Revolution.

Population growth and new farming methods enlarge British labor force

Cotton and Its Connections

Britain itself had many raw materials needed for industrialization. Especially significant were rich deposits of iron, used to build industrial machines and later railways and bridges, and coal, used to smelt iron and power steam-driven machines. But one key resource came not from British mines but from India, Egypt, and American slave plantations.

In the 1700s, British production and use of cotton textiles rapidly expanded. This boom arose partly from convenience and taste: cotton clothes were lighter, cooler, easier to clean, and more comfortable than traditional wool or flax (linen) garments, while dyed and printed calico (cotton cloth from India) was more colorful and attractive. But the boom resulted mainly from mechanization: sturdy cotton fibers worked much better than fragile wool or flax in new machines designed to spin thread. And these machines were central to the Industrial Revolution.

For several centuries, in Western Europe, cloth had been produced through the "putting out" system, often called cottage industry (Chapter 20). Merchant capitalists supplied spinning wheels and weaving looms, along with raw wool or flax, to peasant cottages, where in winter when farm work was light, women spun the fibers into threads that men wove into cloth. This system benefited peasants, who were paid a set price for each piece of cloth produced, and merchant capitalists, who sold it at a profit.

Cotton from India helps to transform British textile production

In the eighteenth century, however, cotton transformed this system. In the 1720s, to protect their business from the growing demand for cotton clothes, Britain's wool producers got Parliament to outlaw calico imports from India. So the British East India Company instead shipped Indian raw cotton, whose fibers—softer yet tougher than raw wool—soon proved ideal for use in machines. In 1733, British machinist John Kay invented the flying shuttle, a hand-powered device that sped up weaving but also created an imbalance, since now it took several spinners (mostly women) to supply enough thread for one weaver (usually a man). In 1767, to correct the imbalance, English weaver James Hargreaves invented another hand-powered device he called the spinning jenny (after his wife), allowing one woman to spin many threads at a time.

Two years later British industrialist Richard Arkwright patented the water frame, a water-powered spinning machine, and in 1779 young inventor Samuel Crompton devised the spinning mule, a cross between the spinning jenny and water frame. Powered by mill wheels turned by river currents, water frames and spinning mules were far more productive than hand-powered spinning wheels and jennies, but they were also large, complex, and expensive. The workers who ran them could no longer work at home: they had to go to mills and factories built along rivers and owned by wealthy people who could afford such machines. This shift from home to factory production marked the onset of the industrial age.

A water frame.

British demand for cotton sustains American slave plantations

Britain's cotton industry took off, undercutting producers in India and elsewhere whose hand-woven cottons could not compete in quantity or price with machine-made cloth. By 1800, output of cotton textiles in Britain increased 800 percent, and by 1830 they accounted for fully half the value of all British exports. This boom sparked a huge demand for raw cotton from America, where the cotton gin, invented in 1793 by Eli Whitney to mechanically separate cotton seeds from fibers, had boosted supplies of raw cotton and cut costs. By increasing the profitability of cotton cultivation, however, the cotton gin also increased the demand for slave labor on American plantations, where slaves from Africa were ruthlessly exploited to furnish the fibers for England's Industrial Revolution.

The Steam Engine and Its Impact

But industry needed more energy than slaves or paid workers could supply, as well as machines more flexible than water-driven ones that had to be placed along rivers. These needs were met by the steam engine, a coal-powered steam-driven machine invented in

1712 by Thomas Newcomen to pump water from mines and improved in the late 1700s by Scottish engineer James Watt.

By 1800 steam engines were used not just in mines but also in factories and foundries, revolutionizing iron production. By using steam-powered bellows to produce a hotter burn, iron-makers could smelt with coke (made from coal, which was plentiful in England) rather than charcoal (made from wood, which was growing scarce), thereby enhancing both quality and fuel supply. By using steam-driven hammers and rollers, manufacturers could now shape iron for countless uses, including improved steam engines and other machinery. Factories using these engines were built in towns and cities, which grew rapidly as more people moved there from rural areas to find work (Map 27.1).

Steam engines transform iron production and transportation

Steam engines also provided a new means of transport. As an island nation with a large ocean fleet, navigable rivers, and numerous canals built mainly in the 1700s, Britain was already well equipped to ship goods and resources by water. But land transportation was still very slow and costly. In 1801, however, a mechanical engineer named Richard Trevithick invented a steam-powered carriage, and by the 1820s George Stephenson, another English engineer, developed a locomotive that ran on sturdy rails forged in the new iron foundries. In 1825, when a rail line linked Stockton coalfield to the town of Darlington, the railway era was born. Within decades, Britain was crisscrossed with railroads on which trains carried freight efficiently—and passengers at exhilarating speeds approaching a mile a minute. The blend of speed and power captured the public fancy, and railways became the sinews and symbols of the industrial age.

The new engines even transformed water transport. By the 1840s, British steamships with metal hulls were replacing sailing ships on the seas, while steamboats were traveling up and down inland rivers. No longer dependent on winds and currents, vessels now ran on fixed schedules, greatly reducing the duration and uncertainty of water travel.

Industrial Britain: Workshop of the World

As a prosperous country with a global empire extending from Canada to India and Australia, Britain already had large markets for its goods at home and abroad. But industry, by producing abundant low-cost goods, opened new mass markets. Historically, for example, unless they were wealthy, families made their own clothes, and underwear was a luxury reserved for the rich. Now, as textile mills produced more and more

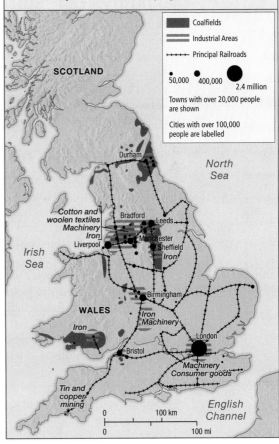

FOUNDATION MAP 27.1 Industrial Development in England by 1840

England took advantage of many assets to become the first industrialized nation. Notice that its compact railway network linked coalfields with industrial areas encompassing factory towns. Why did these factory towns grow dramatically as industrialization progressed?

Low-cost cotton textiles generate mass markets

cheap cotton, more and more people could afford more and more clothes, vastly increasing both market size and industrial profits.

These profits in turn expanded capital for industrial investment, supported by England's strong banking and credit institutions. Unlike Chinese scholar-gentry and French aristocrats, who often scorned commerce as beneath them, many British nobles invested in industry, using profits from their agricultural estates. Merchants and bankers seeking greater wealth and power also invested in industry. Their resources, along with vast fortunes made in textile mills, helped finance the huge start-up costs of iron and railway industries. Industrialization thus produced not only unprecedented wealth but also a powerful new class of industrial capitalists.

In 1851 an Exhibition of the Works of Industry of All Nations opened in London, with hundreds of machines and gadgets displayed in a huge Crystal Palace built of iron and glass. Millions came to marvel at Britain's industrial accomplishments. By this time Britain had the strongest economy on earth, producing over half the world's iron and cotton goods and two-thirds of its coal. Once scorned by Napoleon as a "nation of shopkeepers," industrial Britain had become the "workshop of the world."

The Crystal Palace.

Industry's Early Spread and Social Impact

Britain's industrial superiority, so evident in 1851, did not last long. Eager to duplicate British success, industries elsewhere imported British capital and machinery, copied British ideas, and hired British engineers. Envious of Britain's wealth and power, governments in other lands created and assisted industries, built railways to enhance commerce, and imposed tariffs (surcharges on foreign imports) to protect their new industries from foreign competition. By the second half of the nineteenth century, industry was expanding in Western Europe and North America and altering economies in much of the rest of the world.

Industrialization in Europe and North America

First to industrialize after Britain was the southern Netherlands, which in 1831 became the kingdom of Belgium. Longtime leaders of craftsmanship and banking, Belgians benefited from early agricultural advances, large coal and iron deposits, and ready access to workers and technology from nearby Britain. Starting in the 1830s, Belgium's government built railways, while Belgian banks provided credit to finance industrial ventures. Despite its small size, for most of the nineteenth century Belgium ranked second to Britain in industry.

Industrialization spreads to Belgium and France

France, long Europe's wealthiest nation, initially lagged behind. In the late 1700s and early 1800s, France lacked both the political stability and the large iron and coal supplies needed to industrialize. But in the mid-1800s government subsidies for railways and industries, iron and coal discoveries in Alsace-Lorraine in northeast France, and an influx of workers from Britain fueled French industrial expansion. By 1900, France was one of Europe's industrial leaders.

German customs union fosters industry and national unity

German industry at first was hampered by disunity: the dozens of independent German states each had their own tariffs and economic policies, hindering trade and preventing the development of a national German economy. A customs union, or *Zollverein* (*TSAWL-fuh-rīn*), initiated by Prussia in 1818 and expanded across Germany in 1834, reduced this problem by eliminating tariffs among many German states. Later, after political unification in 1871, Germany industrialized rapidly. Government support for railways (built partly to aid troop movements), a compulsory education system that provided a literate workforce, and laws enabling corporations to collaborate in setting prices and production quotas boosted Germany's industrial output. By the early 1900s, it surpassed even that of Britain.

By that time many other nations, including Italy, Austria, Russia, and Japan, were starting to industrialize (Map 27.2). But world industrial leadership was shifting to North America, where a new industrial giant was surpassing all the others. The United States of America, a huge nation that by 1850 had expanded across the continent, had enormous assets and boundless industrial potential. In the early 1800s, as the North began to industrialize, the South remained largely agrarian, prospering on slave-grown cotton for British textile mills and blocking federal government support for northern industries (Chapter 28). The ensuing civil war (1861–1865), won by the North, opened the way for stunning industrial growth. Aided by vast natural resources, a government that now fully supported industry, and a huge labor force expanded by massive immigration from Europe, U.S. manufacturing soared. So great was its growth that by 1914 the United States was far and away the world's industrial leader.

Industry spreads to Italy, Austria, Russia, Japan, and North America

Map 27.2 The Global Spread of Industry by 1914

Having begun to industrialize in the eighteenth century, Britain attained enormous wealth and power in the nineteenth century. Note, however, that other regions, anxious to emulate this wealth and power, also began to industrialize, and that by 1914 many other regions were industrialized or undergoing industrial development. How and why did the growth of industry help to expand global commerce?

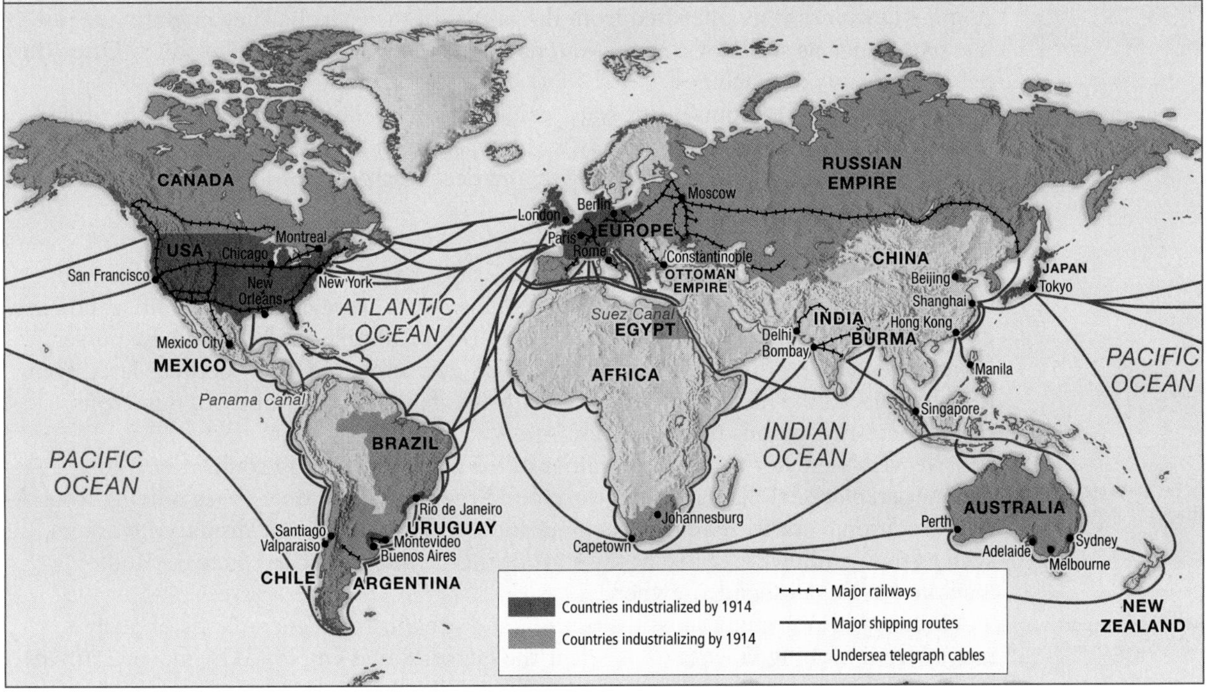

Mechanization and Urbanization

Industry transformed society everywhere it took hold. The lives of common people, centered for centuries on farms and families, came to be dominated by machines, located largely in urban factories. As more and more people moved to cities to take factory jobs, age-old working and living patterns were disrupted and displaced.

One key aspect of industry was mechanization. Machines increasingly replaced people and steam replaced muscle power in manufacturing goods. The machines were marvelous mechanisms, multiplying the number of goods produced while reducing their cost. But machines were also large and expensive, too big for the average home, and far beyond the average family's means. Machines were thus built and installed in factories, rather than homes and workshops, so workers had to go to factories to do their jobs.

Pre-industrial work.

For ten thousand years, since the origins of agriculture, most people's life and labor had been governed by the rhythm of the seasons and the rising and setting of the sun. Farmers and artisans could work at their own speed and to some extent set their own schedules. Work, home, and family were intertwined, with little separation or compartmentalization.

But the factory system subjected workers to a burdensome new discipline. They had to be at work by a set time each morning, often before daybreak, when the work whistle sounded. They worked long hours at repetitive tasks, with machinery dictating their pace, and coal-fired steam engines fouling the air they breathed. Work was hazardous, injuries were common, and breaks were few until the evening whistle blew. Machines seemed to run the workers' lives.

Machines come to dominate factory workers' lives

Workers also lost connection with the things they made. Traditional artisans and villagers could take pride in what they produced with their hands, but factory workers running machines were alienated from the results of their work. They might make just one part—such as soles for a shoe—and never see the whole finished product. Often they felt like servants to machines.

The machines, of course, furnished employment, as the new factory system provided jobs for millions. Work was long, pay was low, and conditions were often dangerous. But in an age of rapid population growth and declining need for farm labor, workers had little alternative.

Nor did they have job security. Machinery created many jobs, but it also took some away. In the 1780s, for example, as early British spinning machines produced abundant thread, handloom weavers who made thread into cloth were in great demand. As their pay and status grew, thousands rushed to join this profitable trade. But a new power loom, invented by Edmund Cartwright in 1785 and improved a few decades later, eventually displaced the handloom weavers. As wages fell and jobs vanished, numerous proud, once-prosperous men were destitute.

Machines create new jobs but displace skilled artisans

Weavers were not the only casualties of the industrial age. In trade after trade, machines replaced skilled artisans, who found they could no longer earn a living from their traditional crafts. Blaming machines for their situation, some displaced workers, such as the Luddites described at the start of this chapter, attacked factories and machines in England and elsewhere.

Towns and cities grow as masses move there for factory jobs

Industry also brought mass dislocation and urbanization. As millions of people moved from farming villages to live near the factories that employed them, small towns grew into cities around these factories. In the 1770s, Britain had four cities with over

50 thousand people; by the 1850s it had more than thirty. Manchester, a booming new factory town, grew in these years from 25 thousand to 500 thousand people. By 1900, over half the English people lived in cities and towns, compared to one in six a century earlier. As industry spread to Europe and North America, and later to Asia, Latin America, and Africa, other countries, too, experienced mass urbanization.

Conditions in early factory towns were appalling. Families were crammed into tenements or shacks, often in one room, with dozens sharing an outhouse. Narrow, muddy streets and tiny courtyards teemed with garbage and sewage, which attracted rats and bred disease. Water from street-side pipes was often impure, and air was polluted with soot and steam from the factories.

Family and Society in the Industrial Age

Industry's impact on family and society was immense. As millions of people raised in rural villages were uprooted and relocated in crowded and alien cities, age-old social and family structures started to break down.

Industry disrupts and divides families

Long accustomed to working as a unit in their cottages and fields, family members now labored separately in factories or mines—often on different shifts, 12–14 hours a day, six days a week. Men, traditionally expected to support their families, typically took the better-paying jobs such as weaving and metalwork. But many early industries hired women and children, since they would work for much less than men. Women, as traditional spinners of thread, were employed in large numbers in early textile mills, usually at very low wages. Children, whose small size made them useful in narrow mineshafts and cramped factory settings, were paid even less.

Women workers in a British cotton mill.

Industry thus disrupted the functioning of families. Unlike rural mothers who mostly worked at home, mothers employed in factories could not take breaks to rest during pregnancy, nurse babies, tend children, or care for household needs. Fathers working long hours in factories were often unable or unwilling to help with the young ones. Many working-class parents, rather than leaving their children untended, sent them to work in mines or mills, sometimes at ages as young as seven or eight. Eventually, however, the social dynamics of industrial cities, where poverty and affluence existed side by side, inspired efforts to curtail such abuses.

Poverty and squalor had long existed in the countryside, and many historians hold that urban workers were initially no worse off—and eventually much better off—than their rural cousins. But country folk, scattered in small villages, had little contact with others in their situation, and were largely invisible to urban elites. Now industrial cities highlighted the gulf between rich and poor, creating a new class-consciousness among both "haves" and "have-nots." Crowded in squalid cities with thousands in the same predicament, workers and their families identified as an exploited class—the urban proletariat. Increasingly aware of their vast numbers, they banded together in country after country to improve their lives, forming labor unions, organizing strikes, and staging demonstrations to enforce their demands.

Crowded in cities, workers identify as an exploited class

Though residing in the same cities, the workers and the urban middle classes—often called the bourgeoisie—seemed to live in different worlds. In working-class areas, drunkenness, gambling, and promiscuity were common among the poorly fed and poorly educated people. In middle-class neighborhoods well-fed people lived in tidy, well-furnished homes,

Young boy at work in a textile mill.

Urban squalor prompts bourgeoisie to support urban improvements

husbands went to work in suits, wives stayed home to manage the household, and children attended fine schools.

Since they shared the same towns, however, rich and poor could not ignore each other. Envious of middle-class comforts and politicized by emerging labor movements, workers pushed for urban reforms. Appalled by the squalor surrounding them and fearful of urban crime and diseases, many members of the bourgeoisie eventually supported such reforms.

Over time, as a result, urban conditions improved. Underground sewers, water sanitizing systems, indoor plumbing, and garbage collections helped curb filth and disease. Electric generators, developed in the 1830s by England's Michael Faraday, eventually provided clean, efficient power for trams and trolleys to transport urban dwellers and—after the invention of the incandescent lamp by America's Thomas Edison in 1879—electric streetlights to light their way at night. Police forces protected people from crime, school systems educated their children, and urban parks and playgrounds met their recreational needs. Although slums, crime, and pollution continued to plague industrial cities, by the early 1900s many were becoming quite livable.

Urban street scene.

Factory conditions also improved. Governments passed laws to limit work hours, improve safety, ensure regular pay, and correct abuses. Wages steadily increased, while mass production of low-cost goods made them increasingly affordable to working-class families, helping millions to lead more comfortable lives.

Urban advances and factory reforms improve working class lives

Women, however, gained little. Indeed, as women's employment in factories came to be seen as exploitative and threatening to the family, women's work outside the home became increasingly unfashionable. Especially in urban middle classes, but even among working classes as men's salaries improved, husbands came to consider themselves failures if their wives worked for wages. Labor thus divided along gender lines, with husbands going to work by day while wives stayed home to tend the children and household. This arrangement freed women from the need to get jobs, but also deprived them of the chance to do so, leaving wives financially dependent on their husbands.

Industry exploits and marginalizes women

New Ideas and Ideologies

Faced with the transforming effects of the Atlantic and Industrial Revolutions, Europeans sought new ideas to explain the new realities. Supporters of the old order, determined to retain past structures and ways, were called **conservatives**—also called the *right* because of where their delegates sat in France's National Assembly. Advocates of change—also called the *left* for the same reason—developed new **ideologies**, systems of thought intended to explain and transform society in accordance with certain political, social, and cultural ideals. Dominant among them, in Europe and later elsewhere, were liberalism, socialism, nationalism, and romanticism.

Liberalism and Socialism

Liberalism, as its name implies, was based on the concept of liberty. Its political values, arising out of the Enlightenment and Atlantic Revolutions, called for constitutional governments (limited monarchies or republics) with restricted powers, elected legislatures, and safeguards protecting people's rights. It stressed individualism and individual rights, championed career advancement based on talent rather than birth, and generally reflected the values of the bourgeoisie. Early liberals typically did not favor full democracy: they advocated voting rights for middle-class men who had some wealth or property and education, but not necessarily for women or for working-class men.

In economics, liberals were disciples of Scottish economist Adam Smith (Chapter 24) and promoters of free-market capitalism. To them competition was the key to prosperity, encouraging manufacturers to produce high-quality goods at low prices to outsell competitors in an open market. Liberals thus urged governments to take a hands-off, *laissez-faire* approach to the economy, letting the forces of supply and demand regulate production and prices. Some liberal economists even saw poverty as inevitable: Thomas Malthus claimed population always grew to the point where there was not enough food for everyone, while David Ricardo's "iron law of wages" said population growth always drove down workers' pay to bare survival levels. Liberals' support for limited government, elected assemblies, individual rights, and free market economies placed them in opposition to authoritarian governments everywhere.

Socialism was in many ways the antithesis of liberalism. While liberals favored liberty, socialists stressed equality, asserting that freedom meant little to those who had no means to enjoy it, and advocating more equitable allocation of society's wealth. Repulsed by the gulf between rich and poor, socialists sought to redistribute income, improve workers' wages, enrich their lives, and enhance their political power. While liberals prized individualism, socialists valued community, with people sharing resources and duties. While liberals praised competition, socialists extolled cooperation, encouraging collective work for the common good and rejecting capitalism as promoting selfishness and greed. While liberals advocated *laissez-faire* governance, socialists demanded public welfare policies to support the poor.

Some early socialists tried forming model communities based on these ideals. Robert Owen, a wealthy British industrialist who had worked as a child in a textile mill, created a model factory town at New Lanarck in Scotland, paying good wages and providing workers with decent housing, schools, and stores that sold low-cost goods. Later he founded a short-lived cooperative community at New Harmony in Indiana. Charles Fourier (*foor-YĀ*), an eccentric French idealist, promoted "phalansteries," communities of 1,620 people, with each member doing a job he or she enjoyed. Although such communities rarely lasted long, they reflected a widespread reaction against the worst aspects of industrialization.

Other socialists, called **Communists**, promoted violent overthrow of the existing order. In 1844 Friedrich Engels, son of a wealthy German industrialist, published *The Condition of the Working Class in England*, a fierce critique accusing capitalists of mass exploitation and murder. Four years later he joined with Karl Marx, son of a German lawyer, to write the *Communist Manifesto*, a ringing, radical pamphlet urging "workingmen of all countries" to unite in a "communist revolution" (see "Excerpts from the *Communist Manifesto*").

According to Marx and Engels, societies pitted rich against poor in ongoing class struggles. The basis of any society was its economy, so the class controlling the economic resources also controlled the political, legal, religious, and military institutions. In preindustrial Europe, for example, the economy was based on agriculture, so the main resource was land. Those who controlled it—the nobles—were the government officials, judges,

Liberals promote political and economic freedom

Socialists promote political, social, and economic equality

Karl Marx.

Document 27.1 Excerpts from the *Communist Manifesto*

According to the Communist Manifesto, first published in 1848, the industrial revolution divided society into two hostile classes: the bourgeoisie, a small group of very wealthy people who controlled the means of production, and the proletariat, a huge and growing group of very poor people who worked in urban industry and were exploited by the bourgeoisie. The Communists' goal was to help organize the proletariat into a revolutionary class that would overthrow the bourgeoisie and create a new political and social order.

A spectre is haunting Europe—the spectre of communism . . .

It is high time that Communists should openly . . . publish their views, their aims, their tendencies, and meet this nursery tale of the spectre of communism with a manifesto of the party itself . . .

The history of all hitherto existing society is the history of class struggles. Freeman and slave, patrician and plebian, lord and serf, guild-master and journeyman, in a word, oppressor and oppressed, stood in constant opposition to one another . . .

The modern bourgeois society . . . has not done away with class antagonisms. It has but established new classes, new conditions of oppression, new forms of struggle . . . Our epoch, the epoch of the bourgeoisie, possesses, however, this distinct feature: it has simplified class antagonisms. Society as a whole is more and more splitting up into two great hostile camps . . . — bourgeoisie and proletariat . . .

The bourgeoisie . . . has played a most revolutionary part . . .

The bourgeoisie has subjected the country to the rule of the towns. It has created enormous cities, has greatly increased the urban population . . . , and has thus rescued a considerable part of the population from the idiocy of rural life . . .

The bourgeoisie keeps more and more doing away with the scattered state of the population, of the means of production, and of property. It has agglomerated population, centralized the means of production, and has concentrated property in a few hands . . .

The bourgeoisie . . . has created more . . . colossal productive forces than have all preceding generations together. Subjection of nature's forces to man, machinery, application of chemistry to industry and agriculture, steam navigation, railways, electric telegraphs, clearing of whole continents for cultivation . . .

Modern bourgeois society, . . . a society that has conjured up such gigantic means of production and of exchange, is like the sorcerer who is no longer able to control the powers . . . he has called up by his spells . . . [N]ot only has the bourgeoisie forged the weapons that bring death to itself; it has also called into existence the men who are to wield those weapons—the modern working class—the proletarians . . .

At this stage, the laborers still form an incoherent mass scattered over the whole country . . .

But with the development of industry, the proletariat not only increases in number; it becomes concentrated in greater masses, its strength grows, and it feels that strength more . . .

The advance of industry . . . replaces the isolation of the laborers . . . by the revolutionary combination . . . What the bourgeoisie therefore produces, above all, are its own grave-diggers. Its fall and the victory of the proletariat are equally inevitable . . .

. . .

The immediate aim of the Communists is . . . : Formation of the proletariat into a class, overthrow of the bourgeois supremacy, conquest of political power by the proletariat . . .

In short, the Communists everywhere support every revolutionary movement against the existing social and political order . . .

The Communists disdain to conceal their views and aims. They openly declare that their ends can be attained only by the forcible overthrow of all existing social conditions. Let the ruling classes tremble at a communist revolution. The proletarians have nothing to lose but their chains. They have a world to win.

Proletarians of all countries, unite!

SOURCE: Karl Marx and Frederick Engels, *Manifesto of the Communist Party* (1848), http://www.anu.edu.au/polsci/marx/classics/manifesto.html

church leaders, and military officers. But in industrial economies, the main resources were factories, and economic life was centered in cities. So the bourgeoisie became the dominant class, taking charge of politics, law, and religion. But the bourgeoisie inadvertently promoted its own demise: by bringing the workers together in factories and cities to exploit them, it united them as an exploited class. Eventually this huge new class, the urban proletariat, would overthrow the bourgeoisie, establish a proletarian dictatorship, and create a classless socialist society.

Communists promote working class revolution

Communism, also called Marxism, provided a compelling explanation for industrial Europe's economic, social, and political turmoil, and a vision of a brighter future for the exploited masses. It gained many followers, attracting idealists, radicals, and workers. The *Manifesto* claimed, in 1848, that Europe was haunted by the specter of Communism. That specter eventually haunted the whole world.

Nationalism and Romanticism

Far more pervasive than communism was **nationalism**, an intense devotion to one's own cultural-linguistic group, and to its embodiment in a unified, independent state. In the 1780s, a German Protestant pastor named Johann Herder, reacting against widespread emulation of the French Enlightenment, asserted that Germans must develop their own national identity. Each nationality, he declared, had its own unique *Volksgeist* (*FŌLKS-gīst*), or "people's spirit," rooted in its language, literature, customs, and culture. Although Herder did not regard one nation's spirit as better than others, later German thinkers viewed the German *Volksgeist* as nobler than the rest.

Meanwhile, the French Revolution, in undermining monarchy, helped to transfer people's allegiance from the person of the ruler to the abstract concept of the nation. *La Marseillaise* (*mahr-sā-YEHZ*), a stirring new French anthem composed in 1792, appealed to the people not as subjects of the king but as "children of the fatherland," urging them to unite in shedding the "impure blood" of "savage" foreign invaders. Although Napoleon, a Corsican by birth, banned this anthem when he became French emperor, he fostered France's national pride by conquering most of Europe. Then, to his dismay, other Europeans rallied national pride to fight against him. Russian resistance to his 1812 invasion was called the Great Fatherland War, and his 1813 defeat at Leipzig was known as the Battle of the Nations.

The Industrial Revolution, by moving rural people to cities and towns, promoted not only working-class consciousness but also national awareness. People increasingly identified with their nation, rather than their clan or village, as public education, newspapers, and popular elections expanded their knowledge of national issues. Politicians soon found they could win mass support with forceful foreign policies and patriotic rhetoric.

Nationalists idealized the nation-state, a political domain embracing all who shared a common language, heritage, culture, and ethnicity. Thus, among Germans and Italians, whose lands were divided into numerous small states, nationalism manifested itself as a crusade for unification. Among subject nationalities, such as Irish, Hungarians, and Poles, it took the form of a quest for liberation. The goal, however, was the same: self-rule for each national group in a unified, strong, and independent homeland.

Nationalists promote unified, independent national states

Romanticism, like nationalism a reaction against the Enlightenment, was a cultural movement pervading Western art, literature, poetry, and music in the late 1700s and

Romantics stress
emotion, passion,
heroism, nature, and
beauty

early 1800s. Rejecting the Enlightenment's intense rationalism, romantics stressed emotion, passion, exuberance, heroism, and the beauty of nature. French novelist Victor Hugo wrote works such as *Les Miserables* (lā mē-zeh-RAH-bl') and *The Hunchback of Notre Dame*, full of sweeping drama and pathos. German painter Caspar Friedrich captured on canvas the wonder and power of nature, while French artist Eugène Delacroix (oo-ZHEN deh-lah-KWAH) dramatized the passion and heroism of the masses in paintings such as *Liberty Leading the People*. In music, the age's dominant figure was German composer Ludwig von Beethoven (BĀ-tō-ven), whose work deeply stirred the romantic soul. His Third Symphony, the *Eroica* (ā-RŌ-ē-kah), written for Napoleon, glorified heroism, while his Sixth celebrated nature. And the stunning climax of his splendid Ninth Symphony was a rousing choral rendition of the *Ode to Joy*, an exuberant romantic verse by German poet Friedrich Schiller.

Although primarily cultural, romanticism was sometimes linked with nationalism and revolution. The brothers Jacob and Wilhelm Grimm, to promote German national heritage, collected and published German folk stories as *Grimms' Fairy Tales*. Walter Scott, in novels and narrative poems, celebrated heroes and events of Scotland's past, thereby evoking Scottish national pride. William Wordsworth, England's exuberant poet of nature, spent a year in revolutionary France and later wrote: "Bliss was it in that dawn to be alive, But to be young was very heaven!" And his countryman Lord Byron, a talented poet and satirist, died in Greece while striving to help it gain national independence.

English novelist Mary Wollstonecraft Shelley blended ideology and industry. Her mother, Mary Wollstonecraft, author of *Vindication of the Rights of Women*, was a forerunner of modern feminism (Chapter 24). Her husband, Percy Bysshe Shelley, was a romantic poet whose works included "Ode to the West Wind," which exalted the power of both nature and revolution (see "Excerpts from 'Ode to the West Wind' "). And Mary Shelley herself wrote *Frankenstein*, the tale of a scientist who creates from lifeless matter an uncontrollable monster, symbolizing both the promise and peril of industry and technology.

A sonata by Beethoven.

Liberty Leading the People, by Delacroix

The European Impact of Industry and Ideology

The Atlantic and Industrial Revolutions, and the ideologies they spawned, created in Europe a cataclysmic clash between past and future. Despite conservative efforts to preserve the past, the forces of change, relentless as the wild West Wind in Percy Shelley's poem and frightful as Frankenstein's monster in Mary Shelley's novel, could not be completely contained.

Reform and Revolution in Europe, 1832–1849

In Britain, where industrialization caused mass dislocation and upheaval, Parliament sought to prevent rebellion by enacting reforms. The Reform Act of 1832, passed under pressure from the king, who was frightened by urban riots, shifted seats in the House of Commons from depopulated rural areas to new industrial towns and extended voting

Document 27.2 Excerpts from "Ode to the West Wind"

Like many romantic poems, Percy Bysshe Shelley's "Ode to the West Wind" glorified the forces of nature. Shelley, however, also used this imagery to glorify the forces of revolution, which, like the wild west wind, bring both destruction and renewal, destroying the old order to make way for the new.

I

O wild West Wind, thou breath of Autumn's being,
Thou, from whose unseen presence the leaves dead
Are driven, like ghosts from an enchanter fleeing,
Yellow, and black, and pale, and hectic red,
Pestilence-stricken multitudes: O thou,
Who chariotest to their dark wintry bed
The wingèd seeds, where they lie cold and low,
Each like a corpse within its grave, until
Thine azure sister of the Spring shall blow
Her clarion o'er the dreaming earth, and fill
(Driving sweet buds like flocks to feed in air)
With living hues and odours plain and hill:
Wild Spirit, which art moving everywhere;
Destroyer and Preserver; hear, O hear! . . .

IV

. . . Oh! lift me as a wave, a leaf, a cloud!
I fall upon the thorns of life! I bleed!

A heavy weight of hours has chained and bowed
One too like thee: tameless, and swift, and proud.

V

Make me thy lyre, even as the forest is:
What if my leaves are falling like its own!
The tumult of thy mighty harmonies
Will take from both a deep, autumnal tone,
Sweet though in sadness. Be thou, Spirit fierce,
My spirit! Be thou me, impetuous one!
Drive my dead thoughts over the universe
Like withered leaves to quicken a new birth!
And, by the incantation of this verse,
Scatter, as from an unextinguished hearth
Ashes and sparks, my words among mankind!
Be through my lips to unawakened Earth
The trumpet of a prophecy! O Wind,
If Winter comes, can Spring be far behind?

SOURCE: Roger Ingpen and Walter E. Peck, *The Complete Works of Percy Bysshe Shelley* (New York: Gordian Press, 1965), II: 294–297.

rights to urban middle classes. The Factory Acts of 1833 and 1847 restricted child labor and corrected other abuses, relieving some of the workers' distress.

Tensions nonetheless remained. In 1838, a coalition of liberals and industrialists began to press for repeal of the Corn Laws, which protected landed nobles from foreign competition by restricting grain imports from abroad. By keeping food prices high, however, these laws compelled industrialists to pay higher wages so workers could feed their families, leading to a clash of interests between the old agrarian and new urban economies.

Parliament's landed nobles at first resisted reform, but their efforts were undermined by disaster in Ireland, where the potato crop had become the primary source of sustenance. In 1845 and 1846 a blight that devastated this crop led to mass starvation. At least a million Irish people perished, while two million others fled to America or to Britain's factory towns. Faced with this human catastrophe, and fearful that it could raise prices and cause starvation in England, in 1846 Prime Minister Robert Peel got Parliament to revoke the Corn Laws, thus allowing both England and Ireland to import cheap foreign grain. Since bad Irish roads hindered grain distribution, this liberal victory did not at once end the famine, but it did advance free trade, henceforth a central principle of Britain's liberal economy.

Irish famine brings mass starvation and prompts migration to America

Chartists promote full
political democracy

Meanwhile the working class was pushing for electoral power. In 1838 a "People's Charter," drafted by reformers later called Chartists, promoted **universal male suffrage** (voting rights for all men), secret ballots, annual elections, equal electoral districts, an end to property qualifications for membership in Parliament, and pay for its members so workers could afford to serve. But Britain's bourgeoisie, having recently won some power, were not prepared to share it with proletarians. Three times in the next ten years the Charter was sent to Parliament, with petitions bearing from one million to five million signatures. Each time it was rejected, and in 1848 it was discredited when Parliament declared most of the signatures invalid. The spirit of Chartism nonetheless endured: over the next six decades, most of its demands were enacted into law.

France, meanwhile, with its own parliamentary monarchy, was also becoming an industrial society. King Louis Philippe (1830–1848), backed by the bourgeoisie, acted like one of them. Wearing a business suit and black coat, he walked to work from his apartment and backed policies supporting French industry. Aware that industry needed literate

French reforms advance
education and curb child
labor

workers, his government enacted an Education Law in 1833, requiring each community to have a school. A Child Labor Law of 1841 banned factory work by children under 8 and obliged working children between 8 and 12 to also attend school. Such reforms, however, failed to prevent revolution.

In 1848, liberal and nationalist revolutions rocked France and Central Europe (Map 27.3). Governments toppled like buildings in an earthquake, while riots raged in the streets of major cities. For a while it seemed that liberalism and nationalism would triumph, but in time most revolts were crushed by conservatives who controlled the armies, while the middle classes were stunned into submission by the brutal spectacle in the streets.

The first revolt came in France, where economic depression and high unemployment fueled discontent among workers. In February 1848, facing mass protests, Louis Philippe summoned the National Guard to keep order. But the guards, drawn mostly from the working classes, rioted against the regime that excluded them from power. Intimidated by the rioters, the king abdicated and the legislature declared a republic based on universal male suffrage.

1848 French Revolution
produces Second
Republic

The Second French Republic, like the first one in the 1790s, was turbulent. Prompted by socialist minister Louis Blanc, it started state-funded National Workshops to employ the jobless and held elections for an assembly to draft a new constitution. But conservatives, who won these elections because voters resented new taxes imposed by the new government, soon ended the workshops, leading to renewed worker riots in Paris. After the bloody repression of these riots, the assembly approved a constitution creating a powerful presidency. In December 1848, voters elected to this office Napoleon's nephew, Louis-Napoleon Bonaparte, whose name reminded them of France's glory days.

Nationalist revolts in
Central Europe are
defeated

France's uprising sent shock waves throughout Central Europe, where nationalism more than liberalism triggered upheavals. Inspired by events in Paris, Hungarians, Italians, and Czechs in the Austrian Empire rebelled for independence, while students and workers fought soldiers in Vienna, the imperial capital. But Austria was not yet industrialized, so its working class was too small to sustain the revolt. The army soon crushed all rebels except the Hungarians, who fiercely resisted until Austria's rulers finally asked Russia for help. Fearful that revolution might spread to his country, the Russian tsar sent 100 thousand troops, repressing the Hungarian rebels in 1849.

Map 27.3 Europe and the Revolutions of 1848

1848 was a revolutionary year in Europe. Observe that, after a revolution in Paris replaced the French monarchy with a republic, other revolts broke out all over the continent—especially in Central Europe, where Italians and Germans sought unification, while Czechs, Hungarians, and northern Italians sought independence from Austrian rule. Why were conservative forces able to quell most of these revolts? To what extent were the goals of these revolts eventually achieved, despite their short-term failure?

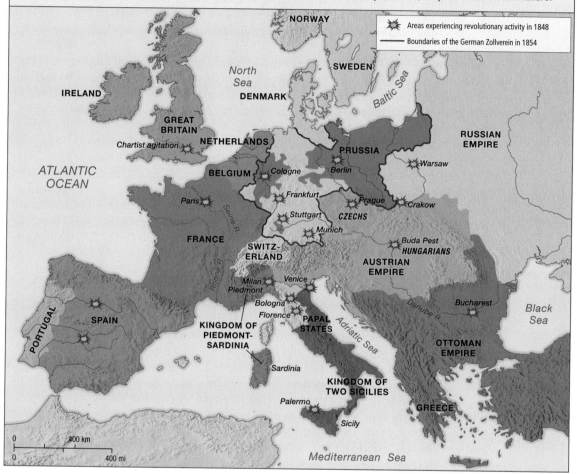

In the German states, rebels fought for a united Germany under a liberal constitution. After riots in Berlin forced the frightened King of Prussia to promise a constitution, the German states sent delegates to an assembly in Frankfurt to discuss unification. The Frankfurt Assembly drafted a liberal constitution for a unified German Empire, offering the post of emperor to the Prussian king. But the conservative king, disdaining the liberal delegates, pointedly declined "to pick up a crown from the gutter," and later sent Prussia's army to disperse the assembly.

Liberalism, Nationalism, and Industrial Growth, 1850–1914

Such setbacks, however, destroyed neither liberalism nor nationalism. From 1850 to 1914, as industry and ideology spread westward, they would make inroads all across Europe.

PROSPERITY AND REFORM IN BRITAIN. In the mid-1800s Britain was the world's main industrial power. It also stood as an example of successful governance, as Parliament prudently enacted reforms to avoid the sort of uprisings that shook much of Europe. But in the early 1900s Britain's stability was shaken by unrest among its workers, its women, and its Irish subjects.

British dominate global trade and enhance global connections

Between 1850 and 1880, Britain was an industrial giant, producing 50 percent of the world's iron, steel, and cotton textiles, 66 percent of its coal, and 40 percent of its machinery. English entrepreneurs and contractors built railways, tunnels, and bridges, not only in the British Isles but also in South Asia, Latin America, and Africa. Until the century's last decades, when Germany and the United States emerged as formidable competitors, Britain dominated global markets in chemicals, machine tools, and electrical goods.

Britain's great industrial age coincided with the reign of Queen Victoria (1837–1901), who gave her name to the "Victorian Era" and to values then prevalent in British society. Victorian morality focused on family and formation of individual character. Bible reading, prayer, Sunday worship, and strict parental discipline taught Britons to believe that God was on their side and that they must serve him by leading righteous lives. These values were typically fostered by mothers, who dominated home and family life, while men dominated the world of work outside the home.

Victorian values combat poverty and immorality

Victorians praised, and often practiced, sobriety, diligence, and hard work. The upper and middle classes, perceiving the poor as drunken and dissolute, attributed these conditions to poverty itself and sought to alleviate them with charity and philanthropy. Organizations such as the Salvation Army and Methodist Church tried to turn the poor to God by providing social assistance. Victorians taught their children to play fair, serve others, control their sexual desires, and always behave in a morally upright manner.

Victorian morality thus helped reduce poverty and unrest in England's industrial cities. Private charity and government reforms helped improve working class conditions, while growing prosperity raised living standards for all but the very poor. As workers grew increasingly assertive in demanding democratic rights, Parliament passed the Reform Act of 1867, tripling the size of the electorate by extending voting rights to urban working-class males. Then, aware that electoral success now depended on working-class votes, Parliament legalized labor unions in 1871 and four years later permitted workers to picket during strikes. The subsequent growth of labor unions helped improve wages and working conditions dramatically. British workers now had an alternative to Marxist revolution: peaceful reform through parliamentary action, collective bargaining, and strikes. And Parliament had learned it could maintain stability by meeting working-class demands.

Labor unions improve workers' lot, but unrest rises after 1900

As the century waned, however, signs of instability resurfaced. Britain's economic growth slowed, as Germans and Americans overcame its lead and took over some of its trade. After rising 35 percent between 1870 and 1900, real wages in Britain fell by 8 percent from 1900 to 1914, triggering unrest among industrial workers. From 1911 to 1914, led by radical labor leaders, workers staged a series of massive strikes, bringing modest gains in wages and working conditions but seriously disrupting Britain's troubled economy.

Meanwhile supporters of **women's suffrage**, a movement that had been working for years to gain women the right to vote, were losing patience with the legislative process. Dismayed that Parliament extended the vote to most adult males while persistently refusing it to females, some women turned to violence. Beginning in 1910, activists known as suffragists, led by Emmeline Pankhurst and her daughters Sylvia and Christabel, planted bombs, vandalized museums, set fires, and staged hunger strikes when arrested. In 1913, to dramatize her crusade, a suffragist threw herself under the racing horses' hoofs at England's famous Epsom Derby. These methods called attention to the suffragist cause, but British women did not get the vote until after the Great War.

Even more unsettling was the **Irish Home Rule** movement. Angered by centuries of British rule, Irish Nationalists, mostly Catholic, demanded domestic self-governance. Britain's Liberal Party eventually took their side, and finally got an Irish Home Rule Bill through Parliament in 1914. But the Protestant majority in northern Ireland rebelled against the prospect of being ruled by Ireland's Catholic majority, and by summer 1914 Ireland was verging on civil war. The outbreak of the Great War that August (Chapter 31) delayed resolution of the issue. But in 1921 most of Ireland became an independent Irish Free State, while Northern Ireland remained part of Britain's United Kingdom.

Suffragist parade.

EMPIRE AND REPUBLIC IN FRANCE. The years 1850 to 1914 were difficult for France. Its government alternated between republic and empire, while its industrial growth, although impressive, lagged behind that of Britain, Germany, and the United States. And a series of diplomatic and military setbacks cost France the dominant position it had enjoyed in continental Europe since 1648.

The unwitting agent of France's undoing was Louis-Napoleon Bonaparte, nephew of the great Napoleon. As president of the Second French Republic (1848–1852), he consolidated control by pleasing business leaders and Catholics, while also showing sympathy for workers. He presented himself as a compassionate idealist with moderately socialistic views, devoted to stability and peace. But the constitution did not permit re-election, so in December 1851, after a skillful propaganda campaign depicting him as the only alternative to radicalism and chaos, he overthrew the Second Republic. The next year he formed a Second Empire with himself as Emperor Napoleon III (not Napoleon II, since the heir to that title, Napoleon I's son, had died in exile in 1832).

Napoleon III then enacted a comprehensive modernization program, based on state support for business and industry. His government subsidized telegraph lines and canals, regulated railways, limited Sunday labor, cleared slums, beautified Paris, and enacted Europe's first pure food and drug laws. His efforts fueled a decade-long economic boom, in which French productivity grew more rapidly than that of any other nation.

Like his uncle Napoleon I, Napoleon III was repressive. He curbed freedom of the press, banned public political debate, and manipulated legislators by adjusting their pay. His regime was a dictatorship, led by a man who suppressed dissent and enacted popular reforms. As long as prosperity lasted, however, he enjoyed broad support.

But prosperity did not last. By 1862 the American Civil War was depriving French textile mills of cotton from southern states and restricting the rich U.S. market for French exports, hurting both France's economy and its emperor's popularity. His reputation was also hurt by the Maximilian Affair, a rash attempt to create a French satellite empire in Mexico under Austrian archduke Maximilian. Fought by Mexican patriots and weakened by French problems supporting an army overseas, the Mexican empire fell in 1867 after the United States, no longer distracted by its civil war, pressured Napoleon III to withdraw his forces.

A far more fatal blunder was Napoleon's failure to block Prussia's move to create a unified Germany. Assuming that Austria would defeat Prussia in an 1866 war, he failed to support Austria and then watched victorious Prussia unite all northern Germany. Belatedly realizing his mistake, Napoleon led his army against Prussia in the Franco-Prussian War (1870–1871). But he was captured in combat, ending the Second French Empire. Paris demonstrations soon led to creation of a Third French Republic, but it surrendered in 1871. Prussia established a unified German Empire, which annexed France's rich Alsace-Lorraine region and replaced France as Europe's dominant power.

> *Franco-Prussian War ends Second Empire and brings in Third Republic*

Defeat left France in turmoil. Radical socialists in Paris created a revolutionary government, the Paris Commune, which governed the city from March until May of 1871, when the forces of the Third Republic crushed it, killing more than 25 thousand revolutionaries. Over the next twenty years, monarchists intrigued against the Third Republic, which excluded them from important government positions. In the 1890s, a prolonged crisis over the conviction of Alfred Dreyfus, a French military officer accused of spying for Germany, deepened the divide between his defenders, mostly liberals, and the military, supported by conservatives and the French Catholic Church. The fact that Dreyfus was Jewish fueled prejudices and passions, and it took 12 years to clear this innocent man.

> *France's Third Republic survives despite serious crises*

Inflamed by the Dreyfus Affair, a series of anti-military ministries governed France from 1898 to 1906, persecuting officers and enacting anti-Catholic legislation. But by 1910, a "nationalist revival" renewed support for the military, as France faced the growing power of unified Germany.

NATIONAL UNIFICATION IN ITALY AND GERMANY. In the 1800s both Italy and Germany, for centuries divided into numerous rival states, emerged as unified nations. Italian and German liberals and nationalists fought to form strong united stable nations. They were joined by industrialists, who hoped unified governments would aid commerce by ending internal trade restrictions and building roads and railways, and by strong leaders in prominent states who wanted to rule the whole nations.

Italy's unification was led by Count Camillo di Cavour, who served from 1852 to 1861 as prime minister to Victor Emmanuel II, king of Piedmont-Sardinia (northwest Italy's Piedmont region plus the island of Sardinia). Cavour's main obstacle was Austria, which controlled the north Italian states of Lombardy and Venetia. Knowing that Piedmont-Sardinia could not by itself defeat Austria, Cavour secretly courted France's Emperor Napoleon III, promising him lands (Savoy and Nice) in return for French help. Together they fought Austria and liberated Lombardy in 1859. But when Prussia threatened to intervene against France, Napoleon III pulled out of the war. Although Austria thus for the time being kept Venetia, the next year several small duchies joined Piedmont-Sardinia and Lombardy in a northern Italian federation (Map 27.4).

> *Cavour and Garibaldi combine to unify Italy*

The initiative then passed to Giuseppe Garibaldi, a flamboyant Italian nationalist who had fought for Uruguayan independence in the 1840s, for an abortive Roman Republic in 1848–1849, and for Piedmont-Sardinia in the war against Austria. He recruited a thousand Italian volunteers, mostly under age 20, to sail to Sicily and fight for Italy's unification from the South.

Map 27.4 Italian and German Unification, 1815–1871

Following the failed revolutions of 1848, inspired in part by Italian and German nationalism, the Kingdom of Piedmont-Sardinia took the lead in unifying Italy, and the Kingdom of Prussia played a parallel role in uniting Germany. Notice that both unification efforts took place in stages, and that by 1871 both Italy and Germany were unified. Which countries were the big losers in these efforts, and why?

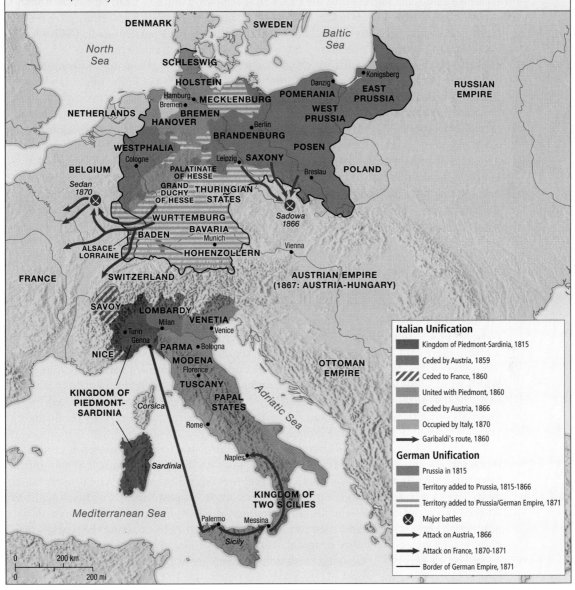

Italian Unification

- Kingdom of Piedmont-Sardinia, 1815
- Ceded by Austria, 1859
- Ceded to France, 1860
- United with Piedmont, 1860
- Ceded by Austria, 1866
- Occupied by Italy, 1870
- Garibaldi's route, 1860

German Unification

- Prussia in 1815
- Territory added to Prussia, 1815-1866
- Territory added to Prussia/German Empire, 1871
- Major battles
- Attack on Austria, 1866
- Attack on France, 1870-1871
- Border of German Empire, 1871

Garibaldi's invasion captured the imagination of Italian nationalists, who flocked to join his forces, known as Redshirts for their colorful dress, after they had won several battles. By September 1860 they had taken Sicily and southern Italy. Garibaldi then planned to march on Rome, where the pope ruled the Papal States that dominated central Italy. But since a French garrison protected Rome, Cavour intervened to prevent war with France. He sent Piedmontese forces into the Papal States, moving south to head off Garibaldi while carefully avoiding Rome. Blocked by Cavour's maneuver, Garibaldi gracefully gave the lands he had conquered to Victor Emmanuel II, who became King of Italy in 1861 when an all-Italian parliament proclaimed a unified Italian kingdom under Sardinia-Piedmont's constitution. Venetia was added in 1866, when Italy joined Prussia in defeating Austria, and Rome in 1870, when France withdrew its garrison during the Franco-Prussian War. The pope was left with less than a square mile on Rome's Vatican Hill.

As a constitutional monarchy with an elected parliament, Italy moved toward democracy and prosperity. By 1914 electoral reforms had extended the vote to most adult males, while expanding industry brought growing wealth to northern Italian cities. But worker unrest, as elsewhere, accompanied industrial growth, while poverty plagued the rural South. And, as self-described "prisoners in the Vatican," the popes refused to recognize the new nation until 1929, when Italy agreed to pay the papacy for the lands it had lost.

Otto von Bismarck.

Germany's unification was led by Otto von Bismarck, a six-foot-five-inch man of towering talent and gargantuan appetite, who became Prussia's prime minister in 1852. An ultraconservative who hated parliaments, he quickly clashed with Prussia's, which had rejected a bill to strengthen and reform the Prussian army. Backed by the king and army, he enacted the army reform anyway, igniting a constitutional crisis that outraged liberals and nationalists. But he knew they would forgive him if he could, in his words, use "blood and iron" to achieve what parliamentary speeches and votes could not: the unification of Germany.

Bismarck uses Prussian army to unify Germany

In 1866 he used the Prussian army against Austria, defeating this other major German power in the Seven Weeks War. He then united all northern German states in a North German Confederation led by Prussia. South German states remained outside the union, so Bismarck in 1870 provoked a conflict with France, foreseeing that the South would join with the North in a war against France. In the Franco-Prussian War of 1870–1871, the south German states and North German Confederation, led by Prussia's modernized army, joined forces to defeat France. In January 1871, Bismarck proclaimed a united German Empire.

Bismarck runs unified Germany, which becomes industrial power

As chancellor to Prussia's king, who was also now the German Kaiser (emperor), Bismarck governed Germany for the next two decades. In foreign affairs, having unified Germany through war, he now pursued peace, forming alliances to isolate France, which by itself was not strong enough to defeat Germany. In domestic affairs he first sought to weaken German Catholics and socialists, neither of whom he trusted. Then he made peace with the Catholics and tried to outflank the socialists by enacting the world's first comprehensive social security program. Yet Germany's Social Democratic Party, supported by an expanding working class, continued to grow, becoming the country's largest party—and the world's largest socialist party—by 1912.

Meanwhile, Germany's economic growth made it the envy of Europe. By 1914, Germany led the world in production of chemicals, electrical goods, and machine tools, and it ranked second in global economic output only to the United States. Workers' wages and buying power doubled between 1871 and 1914. But they still worked an average of

57 hours a week, lived in dark and cramped slum housing, and suffered from high levels of illness, alcoholism, and family violence.

NATIONALISM AND COMPROMISE IN THE AUSTRIAN EMPIRE. Europe's other German power, the Austrian or Habsburg Empire, embraced a dozen major nationalities with four fundamental faiths (Map 27.5). For centuries it had thrived by adapting to changing circumstances, but in the 1800s nationalism eroded the aging empire, inspiring its subject nationalities to glorify their own cultures and eventually seek independence. Notable was the Slavic

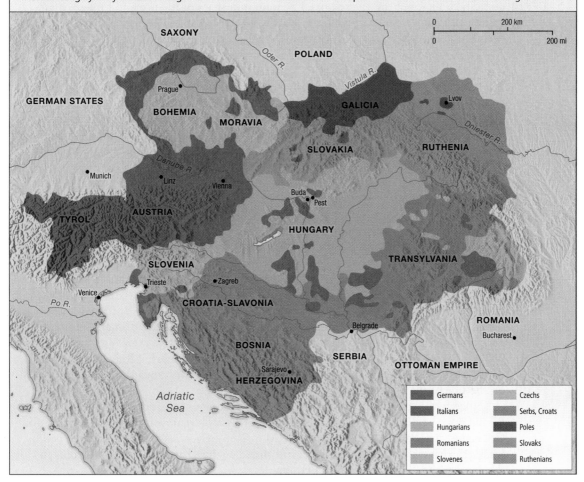

Map 27.5 Ethnic Composition of the Austrian Empire, 1850

Although it was ruled by Austrians, who were Germans, the Austrian Empire was a truly multinational realm. Notice that most Germans lived in the hereditary Habsburg lands west of Vienna, while the rest of the empire was composed of many different nationalities with their own languages and customs. After Austria's defeat by Prussia in 1866, the Austrians were forced to share power with the Hungarians, who were given control of the eastern part of the realm, creating the Dual Monarchy of Austria-Hungary. Why did this arrangement irritate other nationalities and help bolster nationalist movements among them?

Revival, a movement among Slavic peoples in Eastern Europe (including Poles, Czechs, Slovaks, Slovenes, Serbs, Croats, and Ruthenians) to revive their cultural heritage, long submerged by Europe's dominant French and German cultures.

After Austria survived the revolutions of 1848–1849, including nationalist revolts by Czechs, Hungarians, and northern Italians, Emperor Francis Joseph (1848–1916) sought to reassert control by suppressing liberalism and nationalism while trying to transform his diverse domains into one solid centralized state. His regime promoted modernization, subsidizing industries and railways, fostering free trade within the empire, reforming the judicial system, and ending serfdom wherever it still existed.

Austrian Empire's efforts to modernize fail to halt its erosion

But these efforts were undone by external events, especially Italian and German unification. In 1859, as noted above, Austria lost Lombardy in northern Italy to Piedmont-Sardinia, which was aided by France. Then, defeated by Prussia in the Seven Weeks War of 1866, Austria was shut out of German unification and lost Venetia as well. This defeat also compelled Austria to accept the **Compromise of 1867**, granting Hungarians their long-sought autonomy by dividing the Habsburg realm into coequal self-governing Austrian and Hungarian sections. Each had its own constitution, parliament, ministries, and domestic policy, but they were linked by joint ministries of finance and foreign affairs, a combined military, and a common monarch, Francis Joseph. The Austrian Empire thus became the Dual Monarchy of Austria-Hungary.

Compromise with Hungary preserves empire amid growing nationalist unrest

The Compromise of 1867 fully satisfied no one. The Habsburg regime survived, but only through power sharing. Hungary gained autonomy, but fell short of full independence. The empire's other nationalities, emboldened by nationalist triumphs elsewhere in Europe, became ever more determined to gain autonomy. And, as Hungarians imposed their language and rule on national minorities in their part of the empire, these minorities came to despise Hungarians even more than Austrians. The Habsburgs held the empire together by promoting judicious reforms and economic progress—until it disintegrated at the end of World War I.

REFORM AND REACTION IN THE RUSSIAN EMPIRE. Russia in 1850 was Europe's most conservative power, reacting strongly against liberalism and nationalism inside and outside its borders. During his long reign (1825–1855), Tsar Nicholas I had used force to repress rebellion, crushing a Polish revolt in 1830–1831, helping the Ottomans defeat an Egyptian rebellion in 1832–1833, and crushing the Hungarian revolt against Austria in 1849. By 1850 Nicholas, widely considered Europe's handsomest and harshest monarch, had earned his reputation as the "Gendarme of Europe."

The tsar's brutality in stifling dissent, however, unsettled other European powers, which came to see Russia as more dangerous than the declining Ottoman Empire. In 1853, when the Ottomans rejected a Russian attempt to dictate their internal policies, Nicholas provoked war. The next year France and Britain, fearing Russia might win, take Constantinople, and then dominate the eastern Mediterranean, entered the contest on the side of the Ottomans.

Since fighting occurred mainly in the Crimea, a peninsula jutting from southern Russia into the Black Sea, the conflict, pitting Russians against the British, French, and Ottomans, was called the Crimean War (Map 27.6). Even Austria, recently rescued by Russia's crushing of the Hungarian revolt, sided against Russia, leading Nicholas to call the conflict the "War of Austrian Betrayal."

Russian serf women at harvest time.

The Crimean War (1853–1856), eventually lost by Russia, left a complex legacy. It inspired Britain's Florence Nightingale and other English women, appalled by high death rates resulting from disease and inadequate care, to modernize and professionalize the practice of nursing, which later provided career opportunities for women. It introduced new rifles that loaded at the breech rather than the muzzle to permit quicker re-firing. It reinforced changes in the Ottoman Empire, discussed in Chapter 30. And it prompted the next Russian tsar to institute momentous reforms.

Tsar Alexander II, who succeeded Nicholas in 1855 and ended the war the next year, soon decided to abolish serfdom in Russia, where 25 million peasants still lived in bondage to landlords. He was prompted by Russia's defeat, showing that an army of serf soldiers was unfit for modern war, and by concern that an economy based on serf labor could not compete with the industrial West. The global antislavery movement (Chapter 30) and persistent serf revolts in Russia also helped persuade him to end serfdom "from above" to avoid its abolition by rebellion "from below."

The terms of the Emancipation Edict, signed by Alexander in 1861, were complex. To ensure that freed peasants could support themselves, the edict provided them with land. To maintain the

Map 27.6 The Crimean War, 1853–1856

In 1853, portraying itself as protector of Orthodox Christians under Ottoman rule (including Romanians and Bulgarians), Russia went to war against the Ottoman Empire. Fearing Russia would win control of the straits (Bosporus and Dardanelles) that connected the Black Sea with the Aegean and Mediterranean Seas—and thus threaten key routes linking Europe with Asia—Britain and France joined the Ottoman side in 1854. Note that the war was fought mainly in the Crimea, a large Black Sea peninsula under Russian rule, and that Piedmont-Sardinia, hoping to win French support in Italy, also joined the anti-Russian coalition. How did Russia's defeat in this war help to inspire major reforms in the Russian Empire?

support of noble landlords, the state compensated them with long-term bonds for the lands they ceded to peasants. And to reimburse the state for these bonds, peasants were required for 49 years to pay annual taxes known as redemption dues.

Defeat, revolts, and economic weakness prompt Alexander II to end serfdom

Other reforms followed, as the Russian regime sought to deal with its newly freed subjects. In 1864 it created in each county and province a ***zemstvo*** (z'YEMST-vuh), an assembly elected to manage such needs as roads, schools, medicine, and emergency food supplies. Later that year a new judicial system was established, with independent judges and trials by jury—concepts borrowed from the West. And an 1874 military reform, modernizing Russia's armed forces, reduced terms of service from 25 years to 6 and mandated basic education for soldiers.

Russia's Great Reforms peacefully provided 25 million serfs with freedom, land, legal rights, and local governance, while it took a bloody civil war to free four million American slaves. But the reforms raised expectations that could not be met. As living standards failed to improve and population growth left many families without enough land to feed themselves, discontent and poverty plagued the rural masses, while in the cities radical youths formed revolutionary groups.

Great Reforms transform Russia but fail to end unrest

In 1879, a group of young rebels called the "People's Will" sought to spark a revolution by killing the tsar. Initially they failed: explosives they placed under a bridge did not detonate when the tsar's carriage crossed, and a bid to kill him as he traveled by railway exploded the wrong train. In 1880, a rebel employed at the tsar's Winter Palace blew up its dining room with dynamite at dinner time, but that day the tsar was not there. In 1881 rebels threw a bomb at his carriage, but it bounced off and exploded in the road behind him. When he got out to survey the damage, however, they threw another bomb at his feet, and this one finally took the life of the acclaimed Tsar Liberator.

Tsar Alexander III promotes repression and industrialization

Rather than sparking a revolt, however, Alexander II's murder brought a forceful reaction from his son, Tsar Alexander III (1881–1894). The new tsar crushed the revolutionaries and rolled back his father's reforms, asserting state control over *zemstvos* and judges. He oppressed Jews and other non-Russians in his realm, hoping to suppress their nationalist aspirations. He also promoted industrialization by appointing the talented Sergei Witte (*VIT-tuh*) as Minister of Finance in 1892. Over the next decade, using huge sums borrowed from abroad, Witte subsidized industries and built railways to help Russia exploit its vast resources.

Georgian Peasants in southern Russian Empire.

By the early 1900s, then, Russia had a growing industrial proletariat, a free but destitute and discontented peasant class, and large numbers of oppressed non-Russians. This volatile mix soon resulted in revolutions (Chapter 31).

The Global Impact of Industry and Ideology

Although mechanized industries and secular ideologies arose first in Europe, eventually they affected the whole world. Armed with new technologies, inspired by new ideologies, and eager to find resources and markets for their new industries, Western nations in Europe and North America came to dominate the globe. The rest of this chapter discusses the foundations of Western domination and the main ways non-Western nations responded. Succeeding chapters examine in depth the impact of industry and ideology on the Americas, Asia, and Africa.

Industry, Technology, and Global Trade

Industrialization provided both the impetus and means for Western global domination. Industry's demand for resources and markets spurred European economic and political expansion, while advances in technology helped Westerners impose their will on the rest of the world.

Quest for industrial resources spurs global trade

As European nations industrialized and competed economically, they increasingly looked beyond Europe for resources, markets, and investment opportunities. Eager to secure their own supplies of cotton, coal, and iron, and eventually other industrial resources such as rubber, chromium, nitrates, and petroleum, Western industrialists sought to secure access to the resources of Asia, Africa, and the Americas. And as competition saturated domestic markets, European investors used their surplus wealth to seek potential profits overseas.

These efforts were aided by new steel and transportation technologies. The Bessemer steel-making process and Siemens-Martin "open-hearth" method, developed in the 1850s and 1860s, made steel more flexible and durable and less expensive. World steel production increased by 5,600 percent between 1870 and 1900, with 75 percent of it produced in the United States, Germany, and Britain. The steel boom in turn revolutionized transport and trade, as cheap, high-quality steel was used to make rails, railway cars, ships, bridges, and eventually automobiles.

Railway construction benefited immediately. In the second half of the nineteenth century railways were built extensively in the United States, Canada, France, Germany, Russia, Japan, Mexico, Argentina, and elsewhere. New lines connected previously isolated regions, helping to unite nations. They also aided commerce by linking producers with markets, providing farmers and manufacturers with speedy, efficient, low-cost transport for their products.

Shipping also profited immensely. Steel-hulled ships using steel propellers powered by increasingly efficient engines grew in size and range of service. Soon freight, mail, and passengers were being transported to far-flung areas of the world in voyages lasting days instead of weeks. In 1869 the Suez Canal opened, linking the Mediterranean Sea with the Red Sea and Indian Ocean; 45 years later the Panama Canal connected the Atlantic and Pacific Oceans across Central America. By 1900, a network of steel telegraph cables laid under the seas enabled trading companies and governments to exchange information rapidly with distant lands.

Such developments transformed the terms and nature of global trade. Railways moved goods and produce quickly and cheaply to ports, from which steamships moved them almost as quickly around the world. Quicker transport lowered prices dramatically, making many goods affordable to global consumers for the first time. Europeans, for example, developed a liking for Argentine beef and wool from Uruguay and New Zealand, while exports of European manufactured goods enhanced industrial profits. Britain's huge shipping companies moved goods for nations that lacked maritime resources, and British bankers financed railways and harbors around the world. Never before had remote regions been so closely connected.

Railways, steamships, canals, and cables enhance global connections

The Great Global Migrations

Connections forged by industry, railways, and steamships also facilitated history's largest mass migration of peoples (Map 27.7). In the 1800s Europe's population increased from roughly 188 to 432 million, continuing an expansion begun in the previous century. But actual growth was even greater, since more than 60 million people left Europe between 1815 and 1930. Most of the migrants went to North and South America, Australia, and New Zealand. North America's population grew more than tenfold in these years.

Most migrants were young, ambitious men and women eager to improve their lot through hard work in spacious lands offering seemingly unlimited opportunities. By contrast, Europe was overcrowded, its industrial growth having created not only jobs but also teeming, sooty slums that bred disease and crime. Urban steel mills spewed smoke that darkened the sky and caused respiratory diseases, while chemical plants making textile dyes, fertilizers, and explosives poisoned rivers and lakes, exposing people to toxic materials that increased cancer rates. It was little wonder that many people chose to leave.

Some migrants, such as Russian Jews, fled persecution and oppression; others, like Irish Catholics, left to escape poverty and hunger. Some, like southern Italians and German Catholics, departed because they disliked the results of national unification. Others,

Italian immigrants at Ellis Island, New York.

Growing population and industry spark mass global migrations

Map 27.7 Global Migrations, 1815–1930

During the nineteenth and early twentieth centuries, in history's greatest global mass migrations, tens of millions left their homelands to settle in distant places. Notice that most of the migrants left Europe to settle in the Americas, but that some also went to Australia and New Zealand, while several million Asians also migrated, often to work on railways, in mines, or on plantations. What factors and circumstances inspired so many people to migrate?

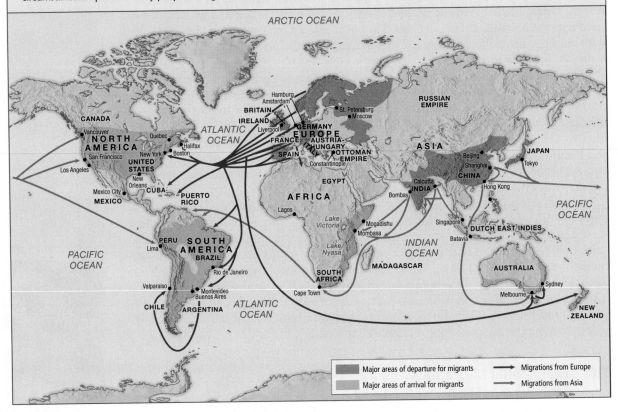

like Italian and Spanish peasants, commuted between South American and European harvests, which came in opposite seasons. Some migrants returned after months or years abroad, but most never went back.

Migrants left Asia as well, but in far smaller numbers than from Europe—about 3 million between 1815 and 1920. Asians became laborers on South American plantations, at North American railway construction sites, and in South African gold mines. In all such places they encountered racial discrimination and settlement policies that favored whites. Opportunities for Asians were better in Southeast Asia's British, French, and Dutch colonies, where "overseas Chinese" often began as petty retailers and worked their way into profitable business careers.

European and Asian migrations enhance global cultural connections

The great migrations established new cultural connections. South America became much more European in culture and ethnicity, while the United States became less exclusively English and Protestant with the arrival of Irish, Italian, German, and Slavic Catholics, as well as Russian Jews. Millions of migrants brought "old country" concepts

Map 27.8 European Imperial Expansion by 1914

In the nineteenth and early twentieth centuries, Europeans came to dominate the globe. Observe that, by 1914, European powers ruled most of Africa and southern Asia, while people of European heritage dominated the Americas, Australia, and New Zealand. Even China was penetrated by Western economic interests, while Japan copied and adapted many Western ways. In what ways did industrial growth and mass migrations also contribute to Europe's global domination?

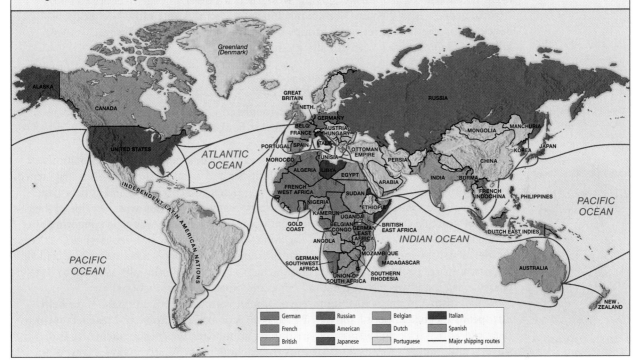

and customs to their new homes, while their letters and occasional return visits to Europe acquainted curious relatives there with new social and political ideas from the Americas. This cross-fertilization would continue long after the great migrations subsided.

Industry, Technology, and Imperialism

As global commerce and competition grew, European nations, eager to enhance their wealth and power, sought ever more forcefully to expand their economies and secure their raw material sources. In the process they practiced **imperialism**, using military force, or the threat of force, to establish colonies in Africa, India, and Southeast Asia and to open up countries such as China to Western commercial exploitation (Map 27.8).

Imperialism was aided by new technologies giving Europeans the means for economic exploitation and political control. Steamships enabled them to transport goods and people all over the globe, independent of seasonal winds that hitherto governed sea travel. Steam-driven vessels also took Westerners up rivers into the interiors of Asia and Africa, helping them access resources and assert military control. Development of dynamite in the 1860s by Swedish scientist Alfred Nobel (who later endowed the Nobel

Prizes) helped Westerners exploit natural resources by blasting mines and cutting roads and railways across harsh terrain. Telegraph lines and undersea cables aided their administration of distant colonies.

Industry, technology, and weaponry advance imperialism

New weapons, however, were the main aids to Western imperial aggression. The breech-loaded rifle, developed in 1843, was far more accurate and quicker to reload than the muzzle-loaded musket, giving Westerners a powerful edge over Asian and African armies. And the new Maxim machine guns, remarkable rapid-fire weapons developed in the 1880s, let small groups of Europeans, shooting from safe distance, kill Asians and Africans with appalling efficiency.

Nationalism, Liberalism, and Racism

Belligerent popular nationalism fuels imperialism

European ideologies also inspired and rationalized global domination. Europeans came to see imperial expansion as a matter of national pride and a means of spreading Western ideals.

In the 1800s growing nationalism reinforced European rivalries, as Western nations competed to show the superiority of their institutions and armies. Liberal reforms heightened the competition: as more Europeans gained voting rights and education, and as newspapers increased public awareness of international affairs, many people took warlike pride in their countries' colonial conquests. This belligerent popular nationalism was called **jingoism,** after a song sung in English pubs asserting "We don't want to fight, but *by jingo* if we do, we've got the men, we've got the ships, we've got the money too!" Jingoism was especially evident in Britain, where people wanted to "paint the map red" (the color usually assigned to British possessions), but it was also present in France and other European nations.

"The White Man's Burden"
Pears' Soap

Racist ad for soap to teach cleanliness to non-white peoples.

Liberalism and nationalism, moreover, joined with Christian compassion to help Europeans idealize imperial activity. Western missionaries, doctors, and teachers went to Asia and Africa seeking to spread Christianity, administer Western medicine, suppress slavery, and "uplift" Asians and Africans by teaching them Western ways. "The White Man's Burden," an 1899 poem addressed to Americans by Britain's Rudyard Kipling, illustrates this combination of idealism and arrogance, depicting imperialism as a blend of compassion, duty, and service (see "Excerpts from 'The White Man's Burden'").

Science, too, supplied some support to European imperialism. In 1859 British biologist Charles Darwin published *The Origin of Species*, promoting his theory that evolution occurs through a process of natural selection, in which organisms best adapted to their environment are most likely to survive and reproduce. Soon thinkers called Social Darwinists applied this notion of "survival of the fittest" to human societies, portraying human progress as a product of struggle between the strong and weak. Europeans then used these ideas to rationalize their expansion as part of a global struggle for survival and progress.

Social Darwinism and racism rationalize imperialism

Such rationales were reinforced by racism, developed by some Europeans into a pseudo-science. In the 1850s a French aristocrat, Joseph-Arthur, comte de Gobineau (*gaw-bē-NŌ*), published a four-volume *Essay on the Inequality of Human Races* that classified humans into distinct races, claimed races should never be mixed, and ranked white Europeans as a superior "Aryan" race. Others would later use his ideas to explain and justify Europe's global domination.

Document 27.3 Excerpts from "The White Man's Burden"

In his 1899 poem, "The White Man's Burden," addressed to the Americans who had recently taken the Philippine Islands from Spain, Rudyard Kipling idealized imperialism by portraying it as a form of service to colonized peoples. His poem, however, betrays a Western attitude of superiority and condescension, depicting colonized peoples as sullen, childlike, slothful, unappreciative heathens.

Take up the White Man's burden—
Send forth the best ye breed—
Go bind your sons to exile
To serve your captives' need;
To wait in heavy harness,
On fluttered folk and wild—
Your new-caught, sullen peoples,
Half-devil and half-child.

Take up the White Man's burden—
In patience to abide,
To veil the threat of terror
And check the show of pride;
By open speech and simple,
An hundred times made plain
To seek another's profit,
And work another's gain.

Take up the White Man's burden—
The savage wars of peace—
Fill full the mouth of Famine
And bid the sickness cease;
And when your goal is nearest
The end for others sought,
Watch sloth and heathen Folly
Bring all your hopes to nought . . .

Take up the White Man's burden—
Ye dare not stoop to less—
Nor call too loud on Freedom
To cloke [cloak] your weariness;
By all ye cry or whisper,
By all ye leave or do,
The silent, sullen peoples
Shall weigh your gods and you . . .

SOURCE: Rudyard Kipling, *The White Man's Burden* (1899), http://www.wsu.edu:8080/~wldciv/world_civ_reader/world_civ_reader_2/kipling.html

Responses to Western Domination

Non-Western responses to Western domination ranged from resistance to cooperation to wholesale imitation. Each response involved painful choices and consequences.

One response, resistance to Western influence, was most evident in regions with long-established complex societies, such as China, India, and many Muslim lands. Such societies, where Westerners were often seen as "barbarians" or "infidels," initially opposed European intrusion, fighting to maintain traditional institutions and economies.

Asian and Muslim societies initially resist Western impact

These societies soon found, however, that Western weaponry and technology, combined with the West's insatiable quest for raw materials and markets, made resistance futile. During the Opium Wars of 1839–1842 and 1856–1860, for example, China's armies and institutions, long dominant in East Asia, proved unable to defeat Western forces and prevent the infusion of Western goods and ideas (Chapter 29). It became apparent that nations failing to industrialize would fall far behind the West in power and wealth, leaving them increasingly vulnerable to Western economic penetration and imperial control.

A second alternative, attractive to countries rich in raw materials required by Western industry, was to seek wealth by selling their resources to industrial nations. This response was evident first in regions that produced raw cotton, such as Egypt, India, and the southern United States, and later in areas with other useful raw materials. Nitrates, for example, used in making fertilizers and explosives, brought prosperity to Chile in the late 1800s. Rubber, used in vehicle tires and drive belts for machines, brought substantial income to

Asian, African, and American regions supply industrial resources

A busy port in Chile in the early 1900s.

Non-Western nations adapt industry and ideologies to resist Western rule

Brazil and later to exploiters of Central Africa and Southeast Asia. Chromium, used in making stainless steel, an alloy whose resistance to heat and corrosion eventually made it a key component of most machines and weapons, did the same for Turkey, southern Africa, and India. And the export of petroleum, used initially to lubricate machines and later to fuel them, eventually brought wealth to the Persian Gulf and other oil-rich regions, especially after petroleum surpassed coal as the world's main energy source in the twentieth century.

This alternative, however, also had major drawbacks. Frequently the fields and mines producing these resources were owned and exploited by Europeans, who paid local workers minimal wages, used the profits to benefit European industry, and flooded local markets with cheap goods that undermined local artisans and traditional commerce. Unless and until these countries gained control of profits from the sale of their resources and used these profits to build their own industries, they remained economic subordinates of the West, serving mainly as suppliers of raw materials for Western industrial nations.

A third alternative was **Westernization**, the adoption by non-Western nations of Western-style industries, technologies, institutions, and ideologies. In time this would prove the only choice that gave these nations sufficient wealth and power to maintain or regain freedom from Western control. But Westernization created a painful predicament, since it involved transforming and even undermining the society's own traditional ideas and institutions.

Some societies adopted only ideas and institutions they found useful in opposing Western domination. In the early 1800s, for example, Latin Americans used liberalism and nationalism to support and validate their fight for freedom from Spanish and Portuguese rule (Chapter 28). Decades later in India, British-educated Indian professionals began a movement, also based on Western-style liberal and nationalist ideals, to press for Indian independence from British colonial control (Chapter 29). Latin America and India, however, were slow to adopt Western industries and technologies, and thus could not compete with Western wealth and power.

Other countries, eager to compete with Western power and wealth, opted for wholesale Westernization. First to do so was Egypt, led from 1805 to 1848 by a rebellious Ottoman viceroy named Muhammad Ali, who used profits from Egypt's cotton exports to build Western-style industries and armies, while also using liberal and nationalist ideals to push for freedom from the Ottoman Turks (Chapter 30). But the British, determined to retain their supremacy in the textile industry, supported the Ottomans against him and forced him to remove tariffs protecting Egypt's industries from competition with low-cost British goods. Egypt thus remained, like India, a supplier of raw cotton for England's textile mills.

More successful in imitating the West was Japan. Forced in the 1850s by Americans and Europeans to open ports to Western trade, Japan responded by adapting Western industries and ways to meet its needs. It also adopted nationalist ideals, a liberal constitution, and Western-style imperialist expansion, emerging as a key regional power by the early 1900s (Chapter 29).

Chapter Review

Putting It in Perspective

Industrialization promised abundant wealth, inexpensive goods, and marvelous machines, while accompanying ideologies offered bright visions of liberty, equality, and national self-rule. But the transition proved terribly traumatic, as early industry also fostered dislocation, destitution, and violence.

These impacts came first to Europe, where the industrial age was born. Conservatives fought to retain control, haunted by fears of revolutionary instability. But the engines of innovation, as loud and relentless as machines in the great mills, pushed the West ever forward into the unknown. Buoyed and buffeted by liberalism, nationalism, and industrial change, societies across the continent were transformed. In Western Europe, long led by Britain and France, the forces of change brought industrial growth, social stress, and political liberalization. In Central Europe, long divided into many small states, these forces promoted Italian and German unification and Germany's emergence as Europe's leading economic and military power. In Eastern Europe, long ruled by large multicultural empires, the forces of change proved divisive: as subject nationalities pushed for greater rights and self-rule, Austrian Habsburgs compromised to keep their realm from crumbling and Russian rulers tried repression and reform in hopes of avoiding upheaval.

Meanwhile, the forces that transformed Europe were affecting the rest of the world. Industry spread to North America and eventually to other regions. Rapid and efficient global trade expanded worldwide connections. The great migrations forged new links among world cultures and continents. And imperialism extended Western rule over much of Asia and Africa. Envious of Europe's affluence, alarmed by its power, intrigued by its technology, and inspired by its ideals, other world cultures increasingly had to endure Western domination or adopt Western methods and machines.

Reviewing Key Material

KEY CONCEPTS

Luddites, 664	nationalism, 675
industrialization, 664	romanticism, 675
enclosures, 665	universal male suffrage, 678
proletariat, 665	women's suffrage, 681
vaccination, 665	Irish Home Rule, 681
conservatives, 672	Compromise of 1867, 686
ideologies, 672	*zemstvo*, 687
liberalism, 672	imperialism, 691
socialism, 673	jingoism, 692
Communists, 673	Westernization, 694

KEY PEOPLE

Richard Arkwright, 666	Napoleon III, 681
James Watt, 667	Alfred Dreyfus, 682
Richard Trevithick, 667	Camillo di Cavour, 682
Friedrich Engels, 673	King Victor Emmanuel II, 682
Karl Marx, 673	Giuseppe Garibaldi, 682
Johann Herder, 675	Otto von Bismarck, 684
Mary Shelley, 676	Emperor Francis Joseph, 686
King Louis Philippe, 678	Florence Nightingale, 687
Emmeline Pankhurst, 681	Tsar Alexander II, 687

ASK YOURSELF

1. What assets are needed for industrialization? How did Britain possess each of these assets in the late eighteenth century? How and why did industrialization spread to Europe and America?
2. How did industrialization affect the lives and work of ordinary people? What were the main impacts of industrialization and urbanization on family and society?
3. Describe and explain the new ideologies that arose in Europe during early industrialization. What were the short-term impacts of these ideologies in Europe?
4. How and why did Britain avoid revolutions in the nineteenth century, while France experienced several such upheavals?
5. Why did nationalism promote unification in Central Europe but disunity in Eastern Europe? How and why did liberalism and nationalism threaten both the Austrian and Russian Empires?

6. How did industry and technology facilitate global migrations and Western imperialism? What other factors fostered imperialism, and how did they do so? What choices and consequences did non-Western nations face in dealing with the Western challenge?

GOING FURTHER

Abernethy, D. B. *Global Dominance: European Overseas Empires*. 2000.

Anderson, Benedict. *Imagined Communities*. 1991.

Ashton, Thomas S. *The Industrial Revolution, 1760–1830*. 1997.

Bayles, Derek. *The Risorgimento and Unification of Italy*. 1982.

Broers, M., *Europe After Napoleon: Revolution, Reaction, and Romanticism, 1814–1848*. 1996.

Cranston, M. *The Romantic Movement*. 1994.

Curtain, Philip. *The World and the West*. 2000.

Feuchtwanger, E. *Bismarck*. 2002.

Fisher, D. *The Industrial Revolution*. 1992.

Flanders, J. *Inside the Victorian Home: A Portrait of Domestic Life in Victorian England*. 2004.

Himmelfarb, Gertrude. *The Idea of Poverty: England in the Early Industrial Age*. 1984.

Hobsbawm, E. J., and T. Ranger. *The Invention of Tradition*. 1990.

Hobsbawm, Eric J. *The Age of Revolution*. 1996.

Inkster, Ian. *Technology and Industrialization*. 1998.

Koditschek, T. *Class Formation and Urban Industrial Society*. 1990.

Lincoln, Bruce. *In the Vanguard of Reform*. 1982.

Lindemann, A. *A History of European Socialism*. 1983.

Marks, R. *The Origins of the Modern World: A Global and Ecological Narrative*. 2002.

Mayeur, J.-M., and M. Reberioux. *The Third Republic from its Origins to the Great War, 1871–1914*. 1984.

McMillan, John. *Napoleon III*. 1991.

Milward, A., and S. Saul. *The Economic Development of Continental Europe, 1780–1870*. 1973.

Mommsen, Wolfgang. *Imperial Germany, 1871–1914*. 1995.

Morgan, K. *The Birth of Industrial Britain*. 1999.

Pflanze, Otto. *Bismarck and the Development of Germany*. 2nd ed., 3 vols., 1990.

Pilbeam, P. *The Middle Classes in Europe, 1789–1914*. 1990.

Pollard, S. *Peaceful Conquest: Industrialization of Europe*. 1981.

Pomerantz, K. *The Great Divergence: China, Europe, and the Making of the Modern World Economy*. 2002.

Sheehan, James. *Germany, 1770–1866*. 1989.

Sked, Alan. *The Decline and Fall of the Habsburg Empire*. 1989.

Sperber, J., *The European Revolutions, 1848–1851*. 1994.

Stearns, Peter. *The Industrial Revolution in World History*. 1993.

Stern, Fritz. *Gold and Iron: Bismarck, Bleichröder, and the Building of the German Empire*. 1979.

Taylor, B. *Eve and the New Jerusalem: Socialism and Feminism in the Nineteenth Century*. 1983.

Tilly, Louise A. *Industrialization and Gender Inequality*. 1993.

Tilly, Louise A., and Joan W. Scott. *Women, Work, and Family*. 1978.

Uglow, Jenny. *The Lunar Men: Five Friends Whose Curiosity Changed the World*. 2002.

Key Dates and Developments

1600s	Onset of Dutch and English agricultural advances
1733	John Kay's flying shuttle
1767	James Hargreaves' spinning jenny
1769	Arkwright's water frame and Watt's steam engine
1785	Edmund Cartwright's power loom
1801	Richard Trevithick's steam-powered carriage
1811–1816	Luddite unrest in England
1825	George Stephenson's steam locomotive; Darlington-Stockton railway
1832	Parliamentary Reform Act in Britain
1834	Customs Union (*Zollverein*) among German states
1838–1848	Chartist movement in Britain
1840–1930	European imperialism and global migration
1845–1846	Irish potato famine; British Corn Laws repealed
1848	Communist Manifesto
1848	Revolutions in France, Austria, Hungary, Italy, Germany
1851	Crystal Palace exhibition in London
1852	Creation of the Second French Empire
1853–1856	Crimean War
1859	Austro-Sardinian War
1860–1861	Formation of the Kingdom of Italy
1861–1874	Emancipation and Great Reforms in Russia
1862–1867	French intervention in Mexico
1865–1914	Post–Civil War American industrial boom
1866	Austro-Prussian Seven Weeks War
1867	Compromise: Dual Monarchy of Austria-Hungary
1867–1884	Reform Bills in Britain
1870–1871	Franco-Prussian War, onset of France's Third Republic
1871	Formation of German Empire
1871–1890	Bismarck governs Germany as chancellor
1894–1906	Dreyfus Affair in France
1911–1914	Suffragist protests in Britain
1912–1914	Irish Home Rule Crisis in Britain

CHAPTER 28

Nation Building in North and South America, 1789–1914

The Constitution Of The United States Of America

In 1787, the recently independent United States replaced its Articles of Confederation with a Constitution designed to strengthen the authority of the central government (page 700). This document, with its accompanying 27 amendments, proved to be not only an extraordinarily durable charter of authority, but an effective protector of the rights of the people against government intrusion in their lives.

In September 1789 George Washington, first president of the United States, received a curious gift from the Marquis de Lafayette, his French comrade-in-arms from the American Revolutionary War. Inside a box of polished hardwoods, lying on a red velvet lining, was a large, rusty key. This, it turned out, was the key to the Bastille, the notorious Paris prison and symbol of royal tyranny, destroyed the previous July 14 in one of the defining moments of the French Revolution. At once the president understood the symbolism: the American Revolution, which had unlocked the door of liberty for English colonists in America, had inspired Lafayette and others in France to unlock that door for their own people. Who better to keep the key than the first president of the new American republic?

North America

South America

Two decades later, on a warm April evening in 1810, a Spanish-American aristocrat named Simón Bolívar (*sĭ-MŌN bō-LĒ-vahr*) sat at his desk in Caracas, Venezuela. Most of Europe was controlled by Napoleon, Spain was occupied by French troops, and the Spanish Empire in America was hanging by a thread. Bolívar opened a worn, leather-lined portfolio. Inside were two copies of the same document, one in English and one in Spanish: the Constitution of the United States. Having found the inspiration that would help him deal with the massive problems confronting South America, Bolívar took up his pen and began to write. The notes he made that evening would form the basis of his speech to an open town meeting in Caracas a few weeks later, a speech that would launch his remarkable political and military career.

Inspired by ideals of liberty and constitutional governance, in the nineteenth century the peoples of the Americas, led by revolutionaries such as Bolívar, fought to achieve independence from European colonial powers and then labored to build new nations and modernized societies. They looked to ideals that originated in Europe, and to the experience of the United States, where independence from colonial control had produced a nation whose founding documents implemented those ideals. But in Latin America, the revolutions were regional. Independence came in different ways at different times, and nation building began in different places under different circumstances. The result was a series of new nations rather than a unified continent, or a federation like those of the United States and Canada. The degree of success that the new nations of North and South America achieved depended largely on their ability to overcome social and geographic divisions, establish effective economies, and build enduring political and social institutions. Generally, those nations that founded their futures on laws and institutions achieved considerable success; those controlled by forceful personalities proved less fortunate.

The Trials and Triumphs of The United States

In 1783, after the American Revolution, the United States of America was an assortment of 13 semi-independent states, connected by a weak central government under Articles of Confederation. Of its three million people, living mainly near the Atlantic coast, about 20 percent were slaves, and most of the rest were of British ancestry. Amerinds, living mainly in the interior, belonged to their own nations, a status soon recognized by treaties. There was little industry: most Americans were farmers, and only about 5 percent of the population lived in cities.

By 1914, on the eve of World War I, the United States was a huge, prosperous nation, spanning the continent from Atlantic to Pacific, with a strong central government. Home to more than 100 million people, including many from southern and eastern Europe, Africa, Latin America, and Asia, the country had become the world's industrial leader, with almost half its people living in cities. Slaves had been freed, and many Amerinds had been forced onto government-controlled reservations. America's remarkable transformation involved four major processes: unification, expansion, industrialization, and immigration.

Unification and Consolidation

The first step toward unification was adoption of a federal constitution. By the mid-1780s leaders of the new republic had recognized that the government created by the Articles of Confederation was too weak to deal with the nation's problems and enforce its laws. So in 1787, in Philadelphia, a constitutional convention met to create a new form of government. After extensive debate and several key compromises, it produced an impressive result. The United States Constitution (see page 698), which went into effect in 1789 while revolution raged in France, established a strong federal government with authority to conduct war and foreign relations, regulate trade, impose taxes, and enforce laws. It was led by a powerful official called the president, who served as head of state, chief executive, and commander-in-chief of the military forces.

The U.S. Constitution provides for strong executive power

The president's power was extensive but limited. It was shared with a two-house legislature called Congress, which was responsible for making laws, and an independent judiciary led by a Supreme Court to interpret those laws. Federal power was also restrained by substantial authority reserved to the states, and by a Bill of Rights, adopted in 1791 as the constitution's first ten amendments, which guaranteed specific liberties for all citizens and explicitly stated that all powers not delegated to the federal government belonged to the states themselves, or to the people. In practice, the constitution's division of powers between the authority of the federal government and the rights of the states created a tension between the two. It was not clear in the nation's early history whether it would develop into a single country with a strong federal union or into an association of autonomous states. After the southern states, which claimed the right to withdraw from the Union, lost the Civil War of 1861–1865, the issue was resolved in favor of a strong federal union. Tensions between states' rights and federal powers nonetheless continue to the present day.

Expansion and Social Division

The expansion of the United States began in 1803, when, unexpectedly, Napoleon Bonaparte offered to sell the Louisiana Territory to the young republic. He was eager for funds and flexibility to pursue his war against Britain and frustrated by French inability to crush the Haitian revolt (Chapter 26). Louisiana, recently obtained by France from Spain, was as large as the original United States, but its vast treeless plains, while vital to Amerinds for food and other resources, were of dubious value to France. Only later, long after President Thomas Jefferson's government had purchased Louisiana from France for 15 million dollars, did it become apparent that the "Great American Desert," now called the Great Plains, contained some of the world's most productive farmland.

The Louisiana Purchase, which doubled the size of the United States, was only the beginning of American expansion (Map 28.1). In 1819, beset by rebellions throughout its Latin American empire, Spain gave in to American pressure and agreed to cede Florida and establish a clear boundary between U.S. and Spanish territory in the West.

In practice this boundary meant little to Americans. In the 1820s, settlers from the southern states began moving into Texas, a vast, sparsely populated part of the new nation of Mexico, which won independence from Spain in 1821. At first Mexicans welcomed the newcomers, who were attracted by cheap land good for growing cotton, but by the 1830s

FOUNDATION MAP 28.1 The Expansion of the United States, 1783–1853

The new American republic spread westward and southward throughout the first half of the nineteenth century, eventually connecting the center of the North American continent "from sea to shining sea." Notice that these acquisitions more than doubled the territory of the original United States. Although the newly acquired lands had once been claimed by European nations like Britain, France, Spain, and Russia, very few people of European descent lived in them. What challenges would this pose for territories seeking eventual admission as new states of the American Union?

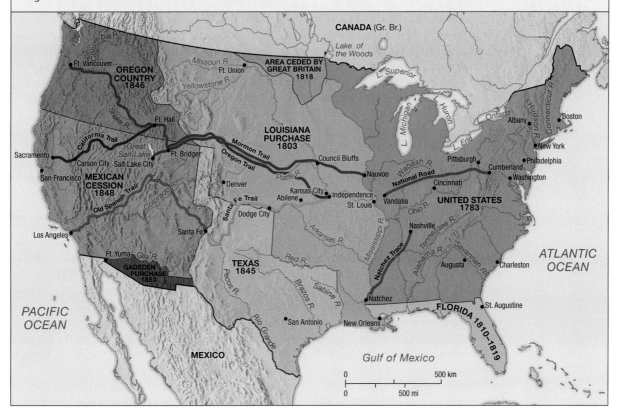

these "Texicans" had proved neither loyal to Mexico nor interested in adopting Mexican ways. Led by Sam Houston, in 1836 they rose in rebellion, captured Mexico's president in battle, and forced him to grant Texas independence. The new "Lone Star Republic" then requested annexation by the United States.

At first the U.S. government was hesitant to take this step, knowing it might lead to war with Mexico; but in the 1840s an expansionist nationalism began to reshape American policy. Inspired by self-righteous optimism, many Americans had long seen themselves as God's instruments in building a New World society free from the problems and corruption of the Old. Now they came to see it as their divine right, or **manifest destiny**, to expand and control the whole continent. In 1844, they chose James Polk, a committed expansionist, as president. The next year Congress approved the annexation of Texas.

Polk proceeded to fulfill his expansionist goals. In 1846 he settled a dispute over the Pacific Northwest (then called the Oregon territories) by agreeing to divide it with Britain along the 49th parallel, bringing the region south of that line under U.S. control. That same year the Mexican-American War began, driven both by American expansionism and Mexican resentment over the annexation of Texas. It ended two years later in American victory. By the Treaty of Guadalupe Hidalgo in 1848 the northern half of Mexico, from Texas to California, became the American Southwest. In less than half a century, the United States had almost quadrupled its size, and the federal republic now spanned the continent "from sea to shining sea."

But expansion intensified two grave social rifts that already divided the nation. In acquiring Mexico's land the United States acquired the Mexicans who lived there, and in expanding westward it claimed the homelands of numerous Amerind nations. Mexicans were subjected to vicious stereotypes and ethnic discrimination, often treated as aliens in their own ancestral lands. Amerinds were driven from their lands and slaughtered in wars or herded onto reservations. The brutal treatment of these people, victims of manifest destiny, contradicted the presumption that Americans were shaping a superior society unstained by the Old World's sins.

Even more divisive was the issue of slavery, which had confounded the republic from its inception. By the time of the Mexican-American War, slavery had caused increasing bitterness and mistrust between North and South. The acquisition of vast new lands, and the question of whether slavery would be extended to them, helped transform this divisive dilemma into a violent conflict.

The United States expands under the principle of "manifest destiny"

The Mexican-American War adds extensive territories to the United States

North Against South

Increasing disparities between North and South compounded the dispute over slavery. For decades, owing partly to regional differences and partly to Britain's Industrial Revolution, the North and South had developed in different directions. The North was beginning to industrialize: factories and businesses helped cities grow. Northerners looked to the federal government for measures to support these new industries, such as tariffs to protect them against foreign competition. Nationalistic northerners increasingly took pride in the growth and strength of their nation, identifying less with their region or states than with the United States as a whole.

The South, meanwhile, as the main supplier of cotton for textile mills in Europe and New England, had remained an agrarian society based on plantations and slaves. Enormous

Sectional interests differentiate North and South

demand for cotton and the exploitation of slave labor provided southern planters with a healthy income to support their aristocratic lifestyle; they had little need for industry or interest in urbanization. Slaves manufactured what was needed on the plantations, and the South's cities were small, primarily ports from which cotton and other agricultural products were shipped. Southerners opposed tariffs because they increased the cost of imports, particularly manufactured goods from England and luxury items from France. They, too, were proud of their nation, but were even more attached to their states, promoting states' rights over the interests of the country as a whole.

An 1884 lithograph of a cotton plantation on the Mississippi River.

Though they dominated southern politics, planters were but a small minority of southern males. In 1860, only 25 percent of southerners owned slaves, and most owned only two or three. The majority of the South's white people owned no slaves at all but supported the slave system because it was the foundation of the southern economy. In the South, slaves represented wealth, and many families who did not have them aspired to purchase them. Moreover, southern culture was patriarchal, and poorer men bowed to the wishes of the planters who dominated society. Farmers who opposed slaveholding would not be allowed to use the planter's dock for shipping goods downriver, or be able to call on the planter for help in time of drought or flood. Finally, planters and farmers may have been far apart in wealth and social standing, but their white skin gave them a common interest in keeping slaves in their place and in reinforcing racial barriers.

Increasingly, then, northern industrialism conflicted with southern agrarianism, while northern nationalism clashed with southern sectionalism. As the interests and cultures of North and South diverged, slavery became the flashpoint. In the first half of the nineteenth century, a worldwide antislave movement had led to global prohibition of the slave trade, abolition of slavery throughout the British Empire, and the rise of a vocal abolitionist movement in the northern states. Southern whites, however, seeing their lifestyle as dependent on slavery, passionately defended this ancient institution.

Slavery becomes the principal issue dividing North and South

Although the federal government lacked authority to outlaw slavery in the existing states, northern politicians tried to keep it from spreading to the western territories (Map 28.2). Southern slave states, fearful that their influence would decline as they became increasingly outnumbered by northern and western free states, resisted these efforts and began to think that they might be better off outside the union. An elaborate compromise in 1850 helped postpone the break (see "Four Perspectives on the American Union"). But in 1860 former Illinois Congressman Abraham Lincoln, running on a platform that opposed the expansion of slavery into the new territories, was elected president in a vote that divided along sectional lines. By the time he took office the next March, seven southern states had formally seceded, claiming the right to freely withdraw from the union, much as they had freely joined it seven decades earlier. When Lincoln, a dedicated unionist, asserted that the southern states were in rebellion and made clear his intent to crush this secession by force, four more states seceded, joining the other seven in a new Confederate States of America. The War Between the States had begun.

Since industrial technology helped decide its outcome, the U.S. Civil War (1861–1865) was in many ways the first truly modern war. It involved mass production of weapons, the use of railways to move supplies and troops, the sending of messages by telegraph, and the use of ironclad ships and early types of submarines, trench warfare,

An ironclad warship of the Union Navy during the American Civil War.

Map 28.2 Slavery and Civil War in the United States, 1820–1865

The enslavement of African Americans, taken for granted by the Constitution of 1787, eventually tore the young republic apart. Note the sharp geographic division between southern "slave states" and northern "free states." Southern states, fearful that Congress would eventually contain a majority of free states and then would vote to outlaw slavery throughout the nation, insisted that for each free state admitted to the Union after 1815, one slave state must be admitted to balance voting in the Senate. This compromise broke down in the early 1850s and led quickly to civil war. Why did the compromise fail as the United States expanded westward?

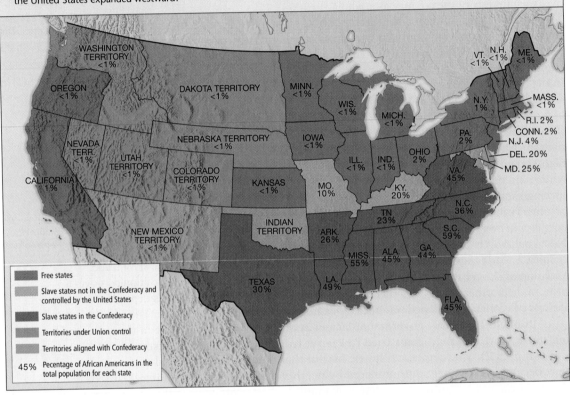

Legend:
- Free states
- Slave states not in the Confederacy and controlled by the United States
- Slave states in the Confederacy
- Territories under Union control
- Territories aligned with Confederacy
- 45% Pecentage of African Americans in the total population for each state

The Civil War affects the United States profoundly

repeating rifles, and early machine guns. Although the South had talented generals and brave soldiers, the North's industrial wealth and power secured its victory.

The northern triumph in the Civil War had several crucial results. It preserved the union, establishing conclusively that the United States was a single nation, not an association of autonomous states. It ended slavery, provisionally through Lincoln's Emancipation Proclamation issued during the war and permanently by the thirteenth constitutional amendment, ratified in 1865. By resolving the threat of disunity and ensuring the predominance of northern economic interests, the war also removed the last obstacles to the growth of American industry.

The Civil War did not, however, resolve the status of liberated slaves. Northern efforts at **Reconstruction**, designed to reintegrate the South into the union, deeply embittered southern whites, while providing southern blacks with little means to secure their

Document 28.1 Four Perspectives on the American Union

In 1850 the Missouri Compromise, carefully crafted in 1820 to preserve the balance between free and slave states in the federal system of the United States, fell apart over the question of the disposition of the vast territories acquired in the Mexican-American War (the Mexican Cession). Did this mean that the American Union was headed for dissolution over the issue of slavery in the newly acquired territories? Four of the leading statesmen of the day offered these perspectives between 1850 and 1858.

In 1850 Senator Henry Clay of Kentucky, "the Great Compromiser," offered yet another compromise designed to save the Union. His Compromise of 1850 tilted toward the South, admitting California as a free state at the expense of permitting the extension of slavery to New Mexico and Utah. Arguing for his proposal, Clay raised the specter of Southern secession:

Mr. President, I am directly opposed to any purpose of secession, of separation. I am for staying within the Union and fighting for my rights—if necessary, with the sword—within the bounds and under the safeguard of the Union . . . Here I am within it, and here I mean to stand and die . . . within it to protect myself . . . Will there not be more safety in fighting within the Union than without it? . . . The dissolution of the Union and war are identical and inseparable; they are convertible terms . . .

I conjure gentlemen, whether from the South of the North, by all they hold dear in this world, by all their love of liberty, by all their veneration for their ancestors, by all their regard for posterity, by all their gratitude to Him who has bestowed upon them such unnumbered blessings, by all the duties which they owe to mankind and all the duties they owe to themselves, by all these considerations I implore them to pause—solemnly to pause—at the edge of the precipice before the fearful and disastrous leap is taken in the yawning abyss below which will inevitably lead to certain and irretrievable destruction.

SOURCE: Henry Clay, "Compromise Resolutions," 31st Congress, 1st Session, February 6, 1850.

Four weeks later, Senator John C. Calhoun of South Carolina responded to Clay's appeal with a warning that the South would secede from the Union unless the North agreed to extend slavery to all the new territories, and to a constitutional amendment restoring the balance of power between North and South:

The prospect, then, is that the two sections in the Senate, should the efforts now made to exclude the South from the newly acquired territories succeed, will stand before the end of the decade twenty Northern states to twelve Southern (considering Delaware as neutral), and forty Northern senators to twenty-eight southern. This great increase of senators, added to the great increase of members of the House of Representatives and electoral college on the part of the North, which must take place over the next decade, will effectually and irretrievably destroy the equilibrium which existed when the government commenced . . . What was once a constitutional federal republic is now converted, in reality, into one as absolute as that of the Autocrat of Russia, and as despotic in its tendency as any absolute government that ever existed . . .

How can the Union be saved? . . . The North has only to will it to accomplish it: to do justice by conceding to the South an equal right in the acquired territory, and to do her duty by causing the stipulations relative to fugitive slaves to be faithfully fulfilled; to cease the agitation of the slave question; and to provide for the insertion of a provision in the Constitution, by an amendment, which will restore to the South in substance the power she possessed of protecting herself before the equilibrium between the sections was destroyed by the action of this government . . . At all events, the responsibility of saving the Union rests on the North and not on the South . . .

SOURCE: John C. Calhoun, "Either Slavery or Disunion," 31st Congress, 1st Session, March 4, 1850.

(continued)

Document 28.1 *continued*

Three days after Calhoun's speech, Senator Daniel Webster of New Hampshire rose to answer him. His lengthy address, known to history as The Seventh of March Speech, confounded antislavery forces in New England by urging northerners to accept the Compromise of 1850:

Mr. President, I wish to speak today, not as a Massachusetts man, but as an American . . . I speak today for the preservation of the Union. Hear me for my cause . . .

But I will state these complaints, especially one complaint of the South, which has in my opinion just foundation: and that is that there has been found . . . among individuals and among the legislatures of the North, a disinclination to perform, fully, their constitutional duties in regard to the return of persons bound to service who have escaped into the free states. In that respect, it is my judgment that the South is right and the North is wrong . . .

I hear with distress and anguish the word "secession," especially when it falls from the lips of those who are patriotic, and known to the country, and known all over the world, for their political services. Secession! Peaceable secession! Sir, your eyes and mine are destined never to see that miracle. The dismemberment of this vast country without convulsion! . . . Who is so foolish, I beg everybody's pardon, as to expect to see any such thing? . . . No, Sir! No, Sir! I will not state what might produce the disruption of the Union; but, Sir, I see as plainly as I see the sun in heaven what that disruption itself must produce; I see that it must produce war . . .

Sir, I may express myself too strongly, perhaps, but there are impossibilities in the natural as well as in the physical world, and I hold the idea of a separation of these States, those that are free to form one government, and those that are slave-holding to form another, as such an impossibility. We could not separate the States by any such line, if we were to draw it. We could not sit down here today and draw a line of separation that would satisfy any five men in the country . . .

And now, Mr. President, instead of speaking of the possibility or utility of secession, instead of dwelling in those caverns of darkness, instead of groping with those ideas so full of all that is horrid and horrible, let us come out into the light of day; let us enjoy the fresh air of Liberty and Union . . . Never did there devolve on any generation of men higher trusts than now devolve upon us, for the preservation of this Constitution and the harmony and peace of all who are destined to live under it . . .

SOURCE: Daniel Webster, "The Seventh of March Speech," 31st Congress, 1st Session, March 7, 1850.

The Compromise of 1850 became law, but it did not end the debate over slavery and secession. As the decade moved along, the Kansas-Nebraska Act of 1854 repealed the Missouri Compromise and laid northern territories open to slavery, while the Supreme Court's 1857 ruling in the case of *Dred Scott v. Sandford* held that even free blacks were not entitled to citizenship, and that Congress had no power to prohibit the extension of slavery anywhere in the United States. Responding to the widening gulf between North and South over these matters, Abraham Lincoln, a candidate for a Senate seat in Illinois, spoke these prophetic words on June 16, 1858:

"A house divided against itself cannot stand." I believe this government cannot endure, permanently, half slave and half free. I do not expect the Union to be dissolved; I do not expect the house to fall; but I do expect it will cease to be divided. It will become either all one thing, or all the other. Either the opponents of slavery will arrest the further spread of it and place it where the public mind shall rest in the belief that it is in the course of ultimate extinction, or its advocates will push it forward till it shall become alike lawful in all the states, old as well as new, North as well as South . . .

SOURCE: Abraham Lincoln, "Speech to the Republican State Convention at Springfield, Illinois," June 16, 1858.

rights and welfare in the long run. Many former slaves, most of whom had no land and little money or education, eventually became **sharecroppers**, farming the lands of white landowners in return for half their harvest. Beginning in the 1880s and 1890s, once Reconstruction had ended, African Americans were systematically deprived of the vote and segregated in public places by notorious **Jim Crow laws** that institutionalized racial discrimination in the southern states.

Industry, Immigration, and Overseas Commitments

In the North, spurred by the immense wartime demand for manufactured goods, industry in the 1860s began growing at a phenomenal rate. Exploiting extensive natural resources—including coal, iron, cotton, timber, waterpower, minerals, and oil—and supported by a government clearly sympathetic to their needs, American capitalists and consumers created an industrial superpower over the next half century. America's numerous rivers and lakes, and especially its new railways, linked the nation. Food for the rapidly growing workforce was supplied by American farmers, some of whom transformed the Great Plains into wheat and corn fields that fed the nation.

Labor came from within the country, as Americans left farms to take new jobs in the cities, but especially from abroad, as millions of Europeans were drawn by America's promise of freedom and prosperity. Immigration soared in the 1840s with the failure of Ireland's potato crop, the sole source of sustenance for most of that island's population, and the resulting mass migration of a million starving people. By 1900 tens of thousands of people came each year from southern and eastern Europe. Between 1860 and 1914 almost 30 million immigrants arrived in the United States, a mass migration unprecedented in world history. Many immigrants took factory jobs, swelling the population of the great northern cities, while others worked in mines and built railways. Laboring long hours, often for low wages, these immigrant laborers helped transform the American nation into an industrial giant.

U.S. economic expansion attracts a huge number of immigrants

But immigrants were not always warmly welcomed. Many Americans resented the newcomers and their unfamiliar customs, beliefs, and languages. America's Protestant majority, alarmed by the numbers of incoming Irish, Italian, and Polish Catholics, as well as Russian Jews, often treated these new groups with hostility. Concerns that low-paid immigrant workers were taking jobs from Americans who had been in the country longer sparked ethnic conflicts in the industrial North and violent hostility to Chinese workers in the West. **Nativism**, as anti-immigrant sentiment was called, led to the enactment in the 1880s of a ban on immigrants from China, and in the 1920s of strict numerical limits on those from southern and eastern Europe.

Nativism develops as a reaction to massive immigration

The massive numbers of foreigners further complicated the nation's racial problems. Many new arrivals, themselves victims of nativist bigotry, sought to boost their status by adopting racist attitudes toward the former slaves, who remained at the bottom of the social and economic structure. At the same time, white supremacist groups such as the Ku Klux Klan, a secret, nativist, racist group first organized in the South, directed violent fury against Catholics and Jews as well as against African Americans.

Despite these tensions, the United States was becoming a world power. Although Americans traditionally avoided overseas commitments, some of them were eager to join the imperialist ventures that Western industrial nations engaged in toward the

U.S. anti-immigration poster: Laborers of many ethnic groups build a wall to keep out Chinese immigrants.

end of the nineteenth century. In 1898, aroused by Spanish efforts to crush a revolt in Cuba, one of the last colonies in Spain's once-great empire, the United States fought and won the Spanish-American War. Cuba gained independence from Spain but effectively became an American protectorate, while Puerto Rico and the Philippine Islands were transferred from Spain to the United States, essentially as colonies. Born of revolt against colonial control, America now had its own colonial empire.

The United States becomes a world power

By the early twentieth century, the United States was a unified, wealthy nation with the world's largest industrial economy, an abundant supply of resources and food, and a vast, diverse population marked by regional, racial, and ethnic tensions. Despite these concerns, it was on its way to becoming the planet's most powerful and influential nation.

The Consolidation and Expansion of Canada

North of the United States, during the nineteenth century, Canada also emerged as a vast new nation. Although its development in some ways paralleled that of the United States, Canada avoided violent upheavals. Yet it also experienced ethnic strife, the product of a colonial heritage that was both French and British.

French and British Colonization of Canada

In the seventeenth century, while England was establishing colonies along the Atlantic coast, French explorers, trappers, and traders were creating a huge empire to the North and West. Unlike the British to the South, however, the French did not come in large numbers, numbering no more than 90 thousand by the mid-1700s.

Britain takes Canada from France in 1763

The events of the Seven Years War (1756–1763), also called the French and Indian War in North America, were disastrous for France, depriving it of its North American empire, much of which was taken over by Britain. Later, the American Revolution (1775–1783) cost Britain its original colonies but left it in control of Canada, to which thousands of British loyalists fled from the new United States. These immigrants, anxious to remain British subjects, gave Canada for the first time a sizable English-speaking population.

Canada is divided into two colonies

Accustomed to British ways, the newcomers soon pressed for their own representative assembly, similar to those that had existed in their former colonies. Fearful of conflict between them and the French Canadians, in 1791 Britain's Parliament divided Canada into two colonies, giving each an elected assembly and an appointed governor. The French Catholic area (later called Quebec) became Lower Canada, since it lay in the lower valley of the Saint Lawrence River, while the English Protestant region (later called Ontario) became Upper Canada (Map 28.3). Unrecognized were Amerind nations, whose interests were dismissed by the British. Some, like the Inuit, lived in remote northern latitudes in which Europeans had no interest. Others, like the Huron, saw their claims pushed aside by British military power.

Dominion, Expansion, and Ethnic Anxieties

By 1837, however, severe tensions between the two colonies, and between the governor and assembly within each colony, produced violent revolts. Fearful that each might declare independence, or perhaps be annexed by the expansive American republic to the

Map 28.3 The Expansion of Canada, 1867–1873

Canada became a self-governing dominion of the British Empire in 1867. Suspecting that the United States might feel that its philosophy of "manifest destiny" entitled it to expand northward, Prime Minister John A. MacDonald purchased the largely empty Northwest Territories from the trading companies that owned them. Then Canada's Parliament admitted Manitoba, British Columbia, and Prince Edward Island as additional provinces. Observe that MacDonald's actions changed Canada from a small, Atlantic-oriented country to the second largest nation on earth, spanning the continent and exceeding the United States in size. What challenges might arise from such rapid expansion into largely empty lands?

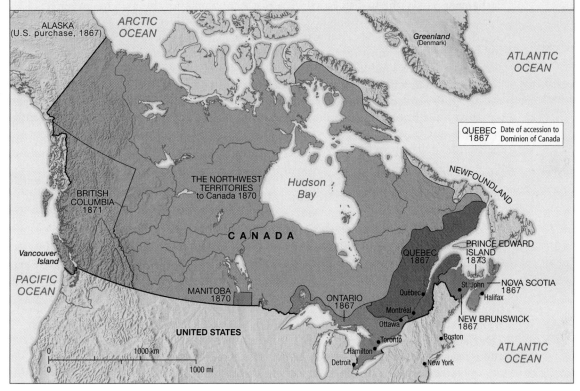

South, the British sent the respected Lord Durham to examine the situation. His 1839 *Report on the Affairs of British North America* became the blueprint for **dominion government** in a number of British colonies. This "Durham Report" called for self-governance by cabinets and prime ministers accountable to elected assemblies, and for federation of adjacent colonies into larger and stronger dominions. In response to these recommendations, Parliament's Canada Act of 1840 united the two colonies under a single two-house legislature. Although Britain retained control of trade and foreign policy, Canadians henceforth ran their own internal affairs.

Canada becomes a single colony in 1840

In the 1860s, two key Canadian leaders, appalled by the U.S. Civil War and anxious to prevent a similar conflict in Canada between people of French and British heritage, developed a compromise plan for nation building. One was George-Étienne Cartier (*zhorzh-Āt-YEN kart-YĀ*), committed to preserving French-Canadian culture; the other was John A. MacDonald, dedicated to fostering Canadian nationalism in a unified nation. At several key conferences in 1864 they helped write a Canadian constitution that combined a British-style parliamentary government with a federal union like that of the United States. The constitution secured British political structures while allowing the French-speaking province of Quebec enough autonomy to protect its heritage. To reduce the potential for the kind of states' rights conflicts that had torn apart the United States, the Canadians agreed that any powers not listed in the constitution would belong to the federal government rather than to the provinces. In 1867, Britain's Parliament passed the British North America Act, which put this system into effect, creating the Dominion of Canada. It included not only Upper and Lower Canada, now called Ontario and Quebec, but also two former maritime colonies, New Brunswick and Nova Scotia. In most respects an independent nation, Canada retained its allegiance to the British monarch, represented by a governor-general.

Prime Minister John A. MacDonald spearheads Canadian expansion

MacDonald, who served as prime minister for most of the period between 1867 and 1891, expanded the country with breathtaking speed (Map 28.3). In 1869 he negotiated with the British Hudson Bay Company to buy the Northwest Territories, an enormous expanse of wilderness and Amerind land stretching across the northern part of the continent. The province of Manitoba, established on some of this land, was added in 1870 to the federation. In 1871, MacDonald persuaded the large western colony of British Columbia to become a Canadian province; two years later he did the same with the small eastern colony of Prince Edward Island. By 1873 the Dominion of Canada, like the United States, extended from ocean to ocean.

MacDonald's great achievement, however, was not just to acquire vast tracts of land but also to link them into a unified nation. The key to unity was construction of the Canadian Pacific Railway, completed in 1885, a magnificent engineering feat that not only connected the East with the West but also opened up the country's interior. In the years that followed, thousands came to Canada from central and northern Europe: some settled in eastern industrial cities such as Toronto and Montreal; others took westbound trains to Canada's plains, which became a fertile grain-producing region. The Canadian economy thrived, aided by the explosive growth of American industry and its need for the natural resources that Canada could provide.

As in the United States, however, expansion heightened tensions within Canada. As more and more English-speaking provinces were added to the dominion, French Canadians in Quebec came to feel increasingly alienated from the rest of the country and concerned that their political and economic influence was declining. In the twentieth century they sought to enhance their status, some by having large families to increase their numbers, and others by forming a separatist movement and threatening to secede. Despite its internal tensions and dual culture, however, Canada remained a united country.

The Revolutions of Latin America

Despite ethnic tensions and regional strife, in the nineteenth century the United States and Canada both secured national unity, territorial expansion, and economic growth. In the rest of the Americas, however, people were less fortunate. They revolted against Portugal and Spain, gained independence, and created a number of new nations that shared a Latin American cultural heritage. But many of these nations were ruled by **caudillos**, strong and often unscrupulous personalities, and they failed to achieve either enduring institutional stability or sustained economic growth.

By the early 1800s, the Spanish and Portuguese empires in the western hemisphere had existed for more than three hundred years. They had endured many challenges and crises but had shown resilience in the face of changing times. Their sudden collapse, between 1808 and 1824, was set in motion by Napoleon's conquest of the Iberian Peninsula.

Preconditions for Revolution

The rebellions that erupted in Spanish America early in the nineteenth century were grounded in animosity between two kinds of Spaniards (Chapter 19). *Criollos*, Spaniards born in America, were distrusted by the Spanish kings, who had never met them and could not directly control them through their families and property. *Peninsulares*, Spaniards born in the Iberian peninsula, thus monopolized the highest offices in the Americas, but they had little interest in the Spanish Empire other than the wealth they could extract from it and take back with them to Spain. Of 170 viceroys in Spanish America, only four had been born there—all to high-ranking Spanish officials living temporarily in America. Most key positions in the military and the Church likewise went to *peninsulares*. *Criollos*, excluded from these posts by the place of their birth, resented the arrogance of the *peninsulares*. Similar prejudices irritated those born in Portuguese Brazil.

In the eighteenth century, these grievances were reinforced by the ideas of the French Enlightenment. Only a few Latin Americans could read pamphlets written by French *philosophes* such as Voltaire and Rousseau, but those who did came to consider their exclusion from high position not only unfair but irrational. Such ideas undermined the traditional acceptance of Iberian rule.

Criollos resent discrimination by peninsulares

Enlightenment ideas had this subversive effect even under the governance of an enlightened absolutist. Carlos III, who ruled Spain from 1759 until 1788, was a modern king who considered himself a servant of his people. He instituted reforms in administration, financial management, and imperial commercial policies, aiming to modernize his empire and improve the lives of its citizens. Although these reforms succeeded in many respects, their tendency to centralize authority in Madrid alienated *criollos*, who were accustomed to considerable local autonomy. They responded by demanding more radical changes than Madrid was willing to permit. By the early nineteenth century, many Spanish Americans considered their government unresponsive to their needs and indifferent to their opinions.

Yet many more remained loyal to Spain. The benefits of Carlos III's reforms were real, and at the time of his death in 1788 the Spanish Empire had never been more effectively governed or more prosperous. The success of the American Revolution inspired a few radicals by proving that colonies could defeat their mother country, but potential rebels had little support prior to 1808. Spain and Portugal had ruled their American colonies for more than three centuries without professional military garrisons, except in a few areas where they were needed to guard against foreign invasion or Amerind raids. In all those years there was not a single uprising that suggested irreconcilable differences with Madrid or Lisbon.

There had, however, been uprisings. More than fifty Amerind revolts took place between 1740 and 1780, culminating in a large-scale rebellion between 1780 and 1783

Despite occasional uprisings, Iberian America remains essentially content with colonial status that claimed more than 100 thousand lives. Its leader, an Amerind who called himself Tupac Amaru II after the last Sapa Inca, called for specific reforms, including the removal of corrupt colonial officials, the end of forced labor service, and better working conditions in mines. But neither he nor his followers sought to challenge the legitimacy of Spanish colonial rule or to expel Spain from America, and Carlos III gave them no chance to change their minds. A Spanish army was quickly dispatched to Lima to put down the Tupac Amaru Rebellion.

Similarly, the 1781 *comunero* revolt in New Granada protested specific issues, in this case significant tax and price increases designed to raise funds to defend the region against possible British attack. Royal authorities deceived a rebel army of several thousand men by appearing to agree to reforms even as they assembled a loyal force. This army then caught the rebels by surprise and defeated them.

Neither the Amerind revolts nor the taxpayer rebellions were directed against Spanish rule. Spain's authority in America remained unquestioned, and few thought that open revolt would stand any chance of military success. In ruling a far-flung empire with a very small number of professional soldiers and considerable political skill, Spain enjoyed great success that might have lasted even longer had it not been for Napoleon Bonaparte.

The Napoleonic Wars alter the relationship between Iberian kingdoms and their colonies

Most Latin American nations owe their liberation to a chain of events set in motion by Napoleon. His armies invaded Portugal in November 1807 and Spain in March 1808 because those kingdoms had violated France's Continental System. When France removed King Carlos IV from the Spanish throne, *criollos* saw a startling opportunity: they could carry out conservative revolutions, breaking away from the puppet regime that Napoleon had established in Madrid while claiming loyalty to the true king of Spain. Since the Spanish American empire until recently had been the king's personal possession, rather than part of a centralized state, there was significant public sympathy for efforts to "defend" the deposed king's colonial possessions against a French conqueror.

In 1810 matters came to a head, as town meetings in major cities such as Caracas and Buenos Aires formally refused allegiance to the French puppet regime and appointed **juntas** (*HOON-tahs*), or provisional governments, to rule on behalf of imprisoned King Carlos. The juntas, however, did not gain the support of the few Spanish military units stationed in the Americas. These local garrisons usually made it clear that they would neither serve the French usurper nor support any moves toward independence. Yet these units were so small that they could not stifle all talk of revolution.

Regional Character of the Spanish American Revolutions

The 1810 uprisings against Spanish rule occurred within regional contexts that eventually helped shape the boundaries of the new nations. As of 1776, Spain's American empire was administered through four viceroyalties—New Spain, Peru, New Granada, and La Plata (Map 28.4)—further subdivided into twelve *audiencias* located in major cities such as Mexico City, Lima, Caracas, Bogotá, and Buenos Aires. Viceroys attempted to ensure compliance with royal edicts throughout a viceroyalty, while *audiencias* could more easily supervise and execute laws on a regional level.

Revolutions in Iberian America occur regionally

When revolutions broke out in 1810, some were spearheaded by local elites in major cities such as Caracas and Buenos Aires, while others were opposed by elites in similar

Map 28.4 Iberian America in 1810

The Spanish American and Portuguese American Empires covered three-quarters of the land surface of the western hemisphere in 1810. Notice that nearly all of this territory was divided into five enormous viceroyalties, ruled by viceroys who were the personal representatives of their kings. When King Jōao VI of Portugal was forced to flee to Brazil, and King Carlos IV of Spain was thrown into a dungeon by Napoleon Bonaparte, the viceroys lost much of their leverage over their colonists, and Spanish and Portuguese Americans began to talk seriously about independence. How did the overthrow of these kings help to stimulate the independence movements?

Disputed by Great Britain, Spain, and Russia

Effective frontier of Spanish Settlement

ATLANTIC OCEAN

VICEROYALTY OF NEW SPAIN

Mexico City • • Veracruz

Havana

CUBA

SAINT DOMINGUE (HAITI)

JAMAICA

PUERTO RICO

SANTO DOMINGO

• Guatemala

Caribbean Sea

Caracas •

Bogotá •

VICEROYALTY OF NEW GRANADA

GUIANA

Galápagos Islands

Amazon R.

PACIFIC OCEAN

VICEROYALTY OF BRAZIL

Lima • VICEROYALTY OF PERU

Bahia

Paraná R.

São Paulo • • Rio de Janeiro

VICEROYALTY OF RÍO DE LA PLATA

Santiago •

Buenos Aires • • Montevideo

AUDIENCIA OF CHILE

Spanish colony
Viceroyalty of New Spain
Viceroyalty of New Granada
Viceroyalty of Peru
Audiencia of Chile
Viceroyalty of Río de la Plata
Portuguese colony
Viceroyalty of Brazil
Disputed territory
Disputed by Great Britain, Spain and Russia

0   1000 km
0   1000 mi

Islas Malvinas (Falkland Islands)

Cape Horn

cities, such as Mexico City and Lima. In either case, initial fighting took place within the region controlled by that city, and not across Spanish America as a whole. Formidable topographical barriers, such as the Andes Mountains, the Atacama Desert, and the dense rain forests of Central America, worked to regionalize conflict further.

These conditions meant that the revolutions were fought and won in one region at a time, rather than as a general war for independence of the kind that took place in Britain's North American colonies. It also meant that newly independent governments would begin building new nations at different times, in different regions, under different circumstances, with populations that did not consider themselves "Latin Americans," but citizens of individual regions.

Independence Movements in South America

In northern South America, fighting focused on Venezuela. There a wealthy young *criollo* named Simón Bolívar became the improbable hero of Latin American liberation. Educated in Europe, Bolívar considered himself a child of the Enlightenment and an admirer of the reforms of the French Revolution. Both the 1812 Spanish Constitution of Cádiz and the 1787 Constitution of the United States inspired him with a vision of what a liberated Spanish America might look like, as the story at the beginning of this chapter indicates. Bolívar exploited that inspiration to dominate the movement for Spanish American independence.

Simón Bolívar.

An outstanding horseman although not a professional soldier, Bolívar had a shaky grasp of military strategy, but he was a bold leader who never knew when he was beaten. He lost most of his battles, but persevered, winning the *last* battles and thereby gaining final victory. Along the way he got vital support from the black cowboys of the Venezuelan backlands, superb fighters whose ruthless tactics destroyed the Spaniards. He marched his men across the Andes into what is today Colombia and won the battle of Boyacá in 1819, an astonishing feat still studied in military academies. He drafted laws, wrote constitutions for more than one Spanish American country, and created institutions of government. Bolívar did not win independence by himself, but like George Washington in British North America, he proved an indispensable leader (see "Excerpt from Simón Bolívar: The Jamaica Letter").

Bolívar and San Martín lead the independence movements

Farther south, the rebel junta in Buenos Aires found itself ignored by Madrid. Argentina is more than eight thousand miles from Spain, and the Spanish kings never appreciated its potential. So the junta, freed from having to defend itself, set out to export revolution to the surrounding Spanish colonies. Crucial to its efforts was an Argentine-born professional military officer, José de San Martín (*hō-SĀ dā sahn mahr-TĒN*), who in 1810 was serving with Spanish forces fighting Napoleon in Europe.

San Martín returned to Buenos Aires and embraced the revolutionary cause. He was convinced that the key to Spanish domination of the continent was the colony of Peru; rebel victory there, he believed, would guarantee independence for all of Spanish South America. San Martín asked the junta for a post in western Argentina, from which he raised an army and conquered Chile after a dangerous crossing of the Andes. Then he invaded Peru by sea, aided by a first-rate mercenary sailor, Thomas Lord Cochrane, an adventurous British aristocrat who hated authority and loved money and war. Together they gave revolutionary forces a foothold in Peru. Bolívar then used that position to complete the liberation of Spanish South America by 1824 (Map 28.5).

Document 28.2 Excerpt from Simón Bolívar: The Jamaica Letter

. . . It is a grandiose idea to think of consolidating the New World into a single nation, united by pacts into a single bond. It is reasoned that, as these parts have a common origin, language, customs, and religion, they ought to have a single government to permit the newly formed states to unite into a confederation. But this is not possible. Actually, America is separated by climatic differences, geographic diversity, conflicting interests, and dissimilar characteristics . . .

Among the popular and representative systems, I do not favor the federal system. It is over-perfect, and it demands political virtues and talents far superior to our own. For the same reason I reject a monarchy that is part aristocracy and part democracy, although with such a government England has achieved much fortune and splendor . . . Do not adopt the best

system of government, but the one that is most likely to succeed . . .

When success is not assured, when the state is weak, and when results are distantly seen, all men hesitate; opinion is divided, passions rage, and the enemy fans these passions in order to win an easy victory because of them. As soon as we are strong and under the guidance of a liberal nation which will lend us her protection, we will achieve accord in cultivating the virtues and talents that lead to glory. Then will we march majestically toward that great prosperity for which South America is destined . . .

SOURCE: Simon Bolivar, "The Jamaica Letter," in Vicente Lecuna and Harold A. Bierck, Jr., editors, *Selected Writings of Bolivar*, volume I (New York: Columbia University Press, 1951).

Failure and Eventual Success in Mexico

Spain's most valuable possession in the Americas was Mexico, called New Spain. Its *criollo* elite was just as resentful of peninsular domination as its counterparts in Caracas and Buenos Aires, and perhaps with greater reason, since *peninsulares* were more likely to settle in New Spain than in any other Spanish American colony. But when a radical priest, Father Miguel Hidalgo (*mih-GWEL hih-DAHL-gō*), organized a peasant and Amerind rebellion in the fall of 1810, he failed to gain *criollo* support. A revolt of the poor and the colored carried little attraction for the wealthy and white. Hidalgo was captured and executed by Spanish loyalist forces in 1811. His successor, another priest named José María Morelos (*mō-REH-lōs*), followed him to the firing squad four years later.

Mexican independence did not appear likely, but a liberal revolt in Spain in 1820, forcing the king to call a representative parliament, changed the situation dramatically. When this news reached New Spain, conservative *criollos* and *peninsulares*, both alarmed at the idea of a progressive government in Spain, united against Spanish rule. Important officers of Mexico's Spanish garrison joined the cause, led by Agustín de Iturbide (*ē-TUR-bē-dā*), who assured conservatives that the new nation would remain a Catholic monarchy (with Iturbide himself as emperor) and that there would be neither revenge nor discrimination against *peninsulares*. These reassurances ensured the revolution's success, and New Spain became independent Mexico in 1821.

Social revolutions fail in Mexico, but a conservative uprising succeeds

From Colony to Empire in Brazil

The final important new Latin American nation was Brazil, which had been ruled by Portugal, not Spain. In 1807, hours before Napoleon's occupation of Lisbon, the Portuguese prince regent and his court escaped to Brazil on British ships. Their arrival, which brought

Map 28.5 Independent Latin American Nations After 1825

Once independence was achieved, three of the five Spanish American viceroyalties (Map 28.4) split into multiple individual states. Gran Colombia, the former Viceroyalty of New Granada, hung together until 1830, after which it divided into Venezuela, Colombia, and Ecuador. The Viceroyalty of the Rio de la Plata split into the United Provinces (or Argentina), Bolivia, Paraguay, and Uruguay. The Viceroyalty of New Spain became Mexico but lost its southern portion to the United Provinces of Central America, which later subdivided further. Note that the Viceroyalties of Peru and Brazil remained largely intact. What factors might account for the ability of these two regions to remain united?

European royalty to American shores for the first time, was not without its comic side. Society women of the colonial capital, Rio de Janeiro, flocked to dockside to welcome the court and observe the latest European fashions. The lengthy shipboard voyage, with insufficient fresh water for bathing, had led to infestations of lice, so the women on board had shaved their heads to get rid of the critters. When the ladies of the court disembarked, the colonial matrons, at first astonished, promptly went home to shave their heads, imitating what they assumed was fashionable among European royalty.

Humorous misunderstandings aside, the transfer of the monarchy to Brazil was a shocking event, as if King George III had decided in 1770 to run the British Empire from Boston. Prince Regent Jõao (*ZHWOW*), who became King Jõao VI in 1816, fell in love with Brazil, judging that its size and resources made it potentially much stronger than Portugal. When Napoleon's defeat restored Portugal's independence, Jõao stalled for years, but by 1821 he was forced to return or lose the throne. Before leaving for Portugal, he appointed his son Pedro regent of Brazil and told him not to return to Portugal to become king in his turn, but to declare Brazil independent, keeping both countries under the rule of the same royal family. When called to Portugal in 1822, Pedro obeyed his father, formally separating Brazil from Portugal. Resistance from Portuguese troops in Brazil was fierce but brief.

The Portuguese Court heads for exile in Brazil

Thus by 1825, all but a few tiny areas of Latin America were independent of Europe. The difficult task of nation building, already under way, aimed to construct strong and stable societies on the foundations laid during the independence period.

Mexico from Santa Anna to Díaz

Mexico was unfortunate. By the time it gained independence in 1821, 11 years of fighting had wrecked its mines, destroyed its businesses, and impoverished its peasants. More than 500 thousand of its 6 million people had perished. Its leader, Iturbide, was an unprincipled adventurer whose misrule as Emperor Agustín I ended in 1823. The next year he was executed, as various caudillos who had dominated the revolutionary years vied for power.

The victor was Antonio López de Santa Anna, who claimed to establish a republic but pushed Mexican political development in a strongly authoritarian direction. He worked hard to strengthen executive power in ways that would make it immune to elections, limits on terms of office, or the actions of other branches of government. When congress, for example, objected to his dictatorial rule, he dismissed it by force and replaced its elected legislators with men whose careers and salaries depended on his generosity. Santa Anna excelled during the revolution against Spain but later lost half his country to the United States in the Mexican-American War of 1846–1848. By the time he was overthrown in 1854, he had crippled Mexico's prospects for balanced government.

Mexico's early development emphasizes strong executive power

La Reforma

La Reforma, the revolutionary movement that overthrew Santa Anna's dictatorship, was in trouble from the outset. Composed of politicians and lawyers influenced by the Enlightenment and by nineteenth-century liberalism, it sought to reduce the privileges of the country's conservative churchmen, landowners, and military leaders. In 1857, when the reformers instituted a liberal constitution, the military rebelled and the government was forced to flee Mexico City. The fugitive reform government, led by President Benito Juárez (*WAH-rez*), a lawyer and a Zapotec Indian, fought a three-year civil war—the War of the Reform—against the conservative forces.

Juárez established his rump government in Veracruz, a stronghold of liberalism and Mexico's main seaport. From there he could control shipping into and out of Mexico and secure the customs duties that formed the bulk of government revenues in a nation without income or property taxes. He then used the money to purchase weapons abroad while denying arms shipments to his enemies. Even more important for Mexico's future, Juárez issued the Reform Laws, which created an institutional framework on the foundation laid by the Constitution of 1857. Juárez offered a government of laws rather than one of privilege and force, and his vision and his economic stranglehold prevailed. By 1860 the war was over and he was back in Mexico City.

Juárez wins a civil war and defeats French intervention

Then Juárez blundered, refusing to honor the debts his former opponents owed to foreign banks. His refusal was legally justified, but it provided French Emperor Napoleon III with an excuse for invading Mexico to collect the debts and installing a puppet regime under Maximilian von Habsburg. The Maximilian Affair provoked a five-year guerrilla war in a country already devastated by civil strife. Juárez and his government won again when France withdrew in 1867, but Mexico was bankrupt, and the formerly liberal Juárez found himself ruling as a dictator until his death in 1872 in a vain effort to rebuild his shattered nation.

Social Structure and the Porfiriato

The dramatic events of Juárez's rule had little impact on Mexico's social structure. The country's governance systems and its mostly rural society remained colonial. Its native peoples lived in isolated villages called pueblos linked by dirt roads or by no roads at all, largely unchanged since the days of Cortés. Huts were constructed of adobe or split reeds, and usually shared among people, pigs, chickens, and dogs. Schools were nearly nonexistent, and most Amerinds could neither read nor speak Spanish.

Poverty and prosperity coexist in Mexico

By contrast the capital, Mexico City, had wide, well-swept, and well-lit streets and a population that by 1850 exceeded 170 thousand. Many schools and churches dotted its residential districts, and lovely public parks provided recreational opportunities for the well-to-do. Yet even in urban areas, desperate poverty existed side by side with the obvious wealth enjoyed by a privileged few.

Ladies of high social station led pampered lives, presiding over luxurious homes, discussing literature or the opera with friends, and attending balls and theatrical performances regularly. But most Mexican women were far less fortunate. In rural areas they kept house and worked long hours in the fields; in towns and cities they worked in textile mills, in restaurants, or in wealthy households as servants.

The Porfiriato begins to modernize Mexico

Mexicans' lives changed little until 1876, when Porfirio Díaz (*DĒ-ahz*), a general who had supported the constitutional forces, emerged as a military hero intent on saving his country from chaos. He ruled Mexico until 1911 in the **Porfiriato,** a period of political repression and rapid economic development. The massive foreign investment he attracted from England, Belgium, Germany, France, and the United States caused critics to accuse him of selling the nation's resources to foreign exploiters, while supporters praised his modernization of a backward land. His government paved roads, extended power lines, laid railways, and developed water and sewage systems. His notorious "rural guards," a ruthless government police force, stamped out banditry and crime with on-the-spot executions. Corpses of hanged men dangled from trees along country roads as a warning to would-be criminals.

None of these efforts, however, brought real help to the lower classes. Rural laborers continued to be plagued by poor nutrition, low wages, rates of infant mortality that approached 80 percent in some areas, and a life expectancy of 30 years. Most were tied to the farms through debts that kept them and their descendants virtually enslaved in menial jobs. In 1910, as Mexico approached the centenary of Hidalgo's 1810 revolution, 50 percent of all the nation's dwellings were classified as unfit for human habitation by Mexico's admittedly lax standards. Only 20 percent of the population was defined as "literate," and many of those could do little more than sign their names.

By then Díaz was in his 80s, but his reluctance even to discuss a successor helped create a liberal coalition dedicated to his overthrow. The coalition united behind Francisco Madero (*mah-DĀ-rō*), a wealthy landowner's son, who believed that democracy could cure all of Mexico's ills. His opportunity to test his belief came in 1911, when Díaz was forced to resign in the face of a bloody revolution. But that revolution was social as well as political, and Mexico's problems were not easily solved.

Women in nineteenth-century Mexico making sacks for coffee.

Argentina and Chile: Contrasts in The Southern Cone

Two new nations dominated South America's Southern Cone, so called because the continent's southern portion is cone-shaped. Argentina endured decades of dictatorship before developing durable institutions and modernizing its economy and society. By 1914 it was reasonably prosperous. Chile, in contrast, enjoyed stable government for sixty years without being plagued by caudillos. But its deeply rooted social inequalities combined with its economic volatility to imperil its institutions in the Revolution of 1891.

Argentina from Rivadavia to Rosas

At the time of independence, Argentina was a sparsely populated agricultural land with a literate elite clustered in Buenos Aires, the nation's principal seaport. The city's residents, known as **porteños** (*pōr-TĀN-yōs*) or "port dwellers," considered themselves superior to the illiterate **gauchos** (cowboys) of the backlands and the ranchers who dominated the country's agrarian economy. Bernardino Rivadavia (*rē-vah-DAH-vē-ah*), a *porteño* who led the government in the 1820s, attempted to provide Argentina with such basic institutions as a parliament, postal service, national bank, budget office, and judiciary. But like Bolívar and Juárez, he was influenced by the Enlightenment, which had little impact on the uneducated majority of Argentines. He offended them with his policies of religious toleration, encouragement of immigration, and political centralization, and their rebellion in 1827 forced him into exile.

Porteños and gauchos dominate different portions of Argentina's economy

Rivadavia had institutionalized Argentina before its citizens were ready for modern government. His successor, Juan Manuel de Rosas (*RŌ-sahs*), was both a clever executive and a brutal gaucho, a man whose business and administrative skills were offset by

Rosas reverses Rivadavia's efforts at institutionalization

a tendency to use violence as a tool of governance. Unlike Mexico's Santa Anna, Rosas was a man of genuine ability; but like Santa Anna, he retarded his nation's political development by dismissing legislatures rather than working with them to create balanced government. His overthrow in 1852, led by a Brazilian-financed coalition of rivals, opened the path to modernization.

Modernization: Society, Women, and the Economy

After a decade of strife between Buenos Aires and rural backlands was settled by compromise, Argentina entered a period of dramatic change. Its newly stabilized government promoted public works and addressed issues such as the status of Amerinds and women, education, immigration, and economic expansion.

Under a succession of presidents of high ability, the country built railways and telegraph lines, installed a sewer system in Buenos Aires, and laid a transatlantic, suboceanic cable. Argentina's flatness made it ideal for railroads, and their rapid development opened the interior to settlement. The gaucho disappeared in the 1880s, replaced by immigrants who rode the new trains to previously remote regions of the country.

The Argentine army subjugates native peoples

Once there, the new arrivals worked land previously belonging to Amerinds. As recently as 1876, an Amerind raid within sixty miles of Buenos Aires had carried off five hundred prisoners and 300 thousand head of cattle. In 1879, however, the Argentine army, which had grown significantly during a recent war with Paraguay, embarked on what was called the "conquest of the wilderness." Soldiers swept across western and south central Argentina, killing many Amerinds and confining the survivors to reservations. This campaign against the Amerinds was similar to those undertaken in the same years by Chile and the United States. Now Argentina's interior lands lay open to white development.

The cosmopolitan elite that encouraged the conquest of the wilderness also felt the country could not fully modernize until women learned to read and write. In Spanish America prior to 1810, women had been the preservers of traditional Spanish culture, passing on to their children European Catholic attitudes about religion, morality, and proper conduct. Now Argentina's leaders wanted modern, progressive attitudes instilled in the nation's youth. If women were going to transmit such attitudes, the men reasoned, they would have to be educated.

Schooling for women was a difficult struggle despite strong presidential leadership. Conservatives feared that educated women would become too independent and abandon their traditional roles of child rearing and homemaking. In fact middle-class women seemed to be doing just that, creating a feminist movement that in the late nineteenth century began agitating for equal access to higher education. By 1914 Argentina had the most advanced education for both men and women in Latin America, but opportunities for women remained limited. Educated in separate, single-sex schools, women studied a more limited curriculum and thus could not enter the male-dominated professions of law, medicine, and engineering. This educational situation did not improve significantly until the 1940s.

Argentina becomes a major agricultural exporter

Meanwhile, agriculture remained the foundation of Argentine prosperity. The country's export economy had initially centered on sheep: in the 1850s the United States purchased huge quantities of Argentine wool, and by 1880 sheep outnumbered people in Argentina by 30 to one. Although wool exports declined after the U.S. Civil War, because of a high protective tariff instituted in the United States in 1867, that decline coincided with an agricultural revolution that by 1890 made Argentina a principal world producer of wheat, corn, barley, and oats.

Then, after 1900, Argentine cattle ranching was revitalized by new technologies developed by Chicago meat-packing companies such as Armour and Swift. Chilling beef for transport rather than freezing it improved the texture and flavor, creating a huge new market in Europe. Chilled beef soon became Argentina's most profitable export, tying the nation's economic fortunes to its European markets. By 1914, Argentina's per capita income rivaled those of Germany, Belgium, and Holland, and its foreign trade exceeded Canada's.

Argentina's prosperity attracted a huge number of immigrants from Spain, Italy, and Germany, nearly six million between 1871 and 1914, more than half of whom became permanent residents. These immigrants almost overwhelmed a country whose population in 1869 had been only 1.8 million. One result was a dramatic increase in Argentina's literacy rate, from 22 percent in 1869 to 65 percent in 1914, since most European immigrants could read and write.

The booming economy, however, did not benefit all. Argentine landowners and commercial leaders remained extremely wealthy, while 80 percent of the workers (most of them foreign-born) lived with their families in one-room tenements or shacks. Because of the country's agricultural revolution, they enjoyed a more nutritious diet than did the laboring classes in Mexico and Chile, but the country's social structure perpetuated the economic and political subordination of the immigrant population. Even the immigrants who settled the interior did so not as landowners but as hired workers on the estates of the wealthy. Moreover, Argentina's political structure, in which most authority resided in the executive, was not designed to be responsive to the needs of an immigrant population.

Argentina's economic expansion attracts immigrants

Immigrant hotel, Buenos Aires.

Chilean Institutionalization

The executive dominance characterizing Argentine government was also present in Chile, Argentina's western neighbor. The remotest of Spain's former colonies, Chile in 1825 had a population of only half a million people, most living in rural areas. Mining was the basis of its economy, and most miners worked in dangerous conditions and lived in desperate poverty. Clearly Argentina had a more desirable location, but Chile quickly developed governmental institutions that achieved political stability following independence.

This was accomplished by Diego Portales (*pōr-TAH-lez*), a businessman-turned-politician who dominated Chilean politics in the 1830s. Portales considered it his duty to impose order on a disorganized and illiterate population, but he wanted a strong state to rest on stable institutions rather than personal loyalties. He succeeded so thoroughly that Chile avoided caudillismo altogether. The Constitution of 1833, which he wrote, provided for an indirectly elected president and congress, with suffrage limited to property-holding, literate males over age 25. This document furnished Chile with a highly centralized government in which municipal and provincial authorities were subject to direct control by the president.

Portales initiates Chilean institutionalization

Portales' successful institutionalization of Chile was envied throughout Latin America. Chile's first three presidents each served two complete five-year terms, but this stability was achieved by manipulating elections at all levels and retaining the loyalty of the military through pay raises and professional advancement. Then in 1857 the Conservative

Party, which had elected the first three presidents, split over the issue of religious toleration for non-Catholics, and the Liberals, who favored toleration, came to power in the election of 1861.

The Liberals took control at a time of significant change. Chilean wheat farmers had prospered greatly during the California gold rush of 1849, as Chile was the only wheat-producing country on the Americas' Pacific coast and sold enormous quantities of grain to feed California's booming population. Increased tax receipts financed gas lighting for Santiago, Chile's largest city, which grew to a population of 150 thousand by 1875. Chile also attracted British financiers, whose Pacific Steam Navigation Company dispatched passenger ships as far as Seattle and Liverpool, England. In 1874 the company's gross tonnage made it the equal of the entire U.S. Navy.

Prosperity also made possible Chile's national railway network. In a country shaped like a 3,200-mile-long shoestring, with an impassable desert in the North, dense forests in the South, the Andes Mountains in the East, and the Pacific Ocean in the West, oxcarts were inadequate for modern development. New railways, however, provided rapid, inexpensive transportation for agricultural products, mineral wealth, and manufactured goods. They fostered the creation of a national economy linking all parts of Chile. Following Chile's decisive victory over its northern neighbors in the War of the Pacific (1879–1883), its new national economy took off.

Social Stratification and Inequality

The War of the Pacific brings tremendous benefits to Chile

The source of conflict in the War of the Pacific was the nitrate-rich regions to the North of Chile, owned by Peru and Bolivia but developed primarily by Chileans. When Europeans began seeking nitrate for fertilizer and explosives, Peru and Bolivia became aware of the valuable resources they had formerly ignored. Their efforts to tax Chilean mines in violation of treaty agreements and to prevent Chile from seizing all the nitrate fields led to war. Chile's victory over its rivals made it the dominant military power on South America's western seaboard, deprived Bolivia of its seacoast, and launched a lengthy economic boom grounded in the lucrative nitrate fields.

Yet a booming economy did little to alter Chile's rigid social stratification. Plenty of jobs became available, but pay was low and working conditions horrible. The rich became richer, as mining companies and landowners profited from improved transportation systems. In some respects Chile was progressive: professional schools were opened to women in 1879, and Latin America's first female doctor and lawyer were both Chileans. But these high-profile advances obscured the lack of meaningful opportunity for women and men of modest means. Chile's population was less than 3 million in 1895, and most Chileans were impoverished.

Chilean social inequality excludes many from nitrate-based prosperity

Devastating public health conditions only made matters worse. Malnutrition and disease cut Chile's average life expectancy to 35 years in 1900. Only the wealthiest sections of Santiago and Valparaiso had clean water and sewage systems, while the working poor lived in squalor, with up to eight people in one unventilated 15-by-25-foot room. Typhoid fever raged unchecked through city slums, and in the early 1900s Chile's suicide rate was the highest on earth.

While the poor suffered, much of the country's newfound wealth went into the military. Previously small, the Chilean army grew tremendously during the War of the Pacific, and the government used it in 1883 to subjugate the Araucanian (*ar-ow-KAH-ne-uhn*) Amerinds in the far South, who had retained their independence since the Spaniards arrived. Peruvian and Bolivian bitterness over the war's outcome led to border disputes that kept the Chilean military on alert. The army hired German officers to modernize Chilean military education, while the navy expanded using increased appropriations from a national budget flush with unprecedented surpluses.

One unanticipated effect of this military expansion was the Revolution of 1891, in which both parties to a political dispute called on armed support. President José Manuel Balmaceda (*bahl-mah-SĀ-dah*) alienated Conservatives by pushing an ambitious program of public works and social reform, at the same time antagonizing Liberals by increasing executive power at the expense of Congress. In 1890 Congress refused to pass Balmaceda's budget, but he announced that he would spend the money anyway. This action split the military: the army sided with Balmaceda, and the navy sided with Congress, which voted in January 1891 to depose the president.

An Araucanian chief.

An eight-month civil war followed, but given Chile's long coastline the outcome was never in doubt: a government opposed by the navy could not survive. The army's German supervisors went over to the navy's side, and Balmaceda committed suicide one day after his presidential term expired. The Revolution of 1891 ended any chance for the restoration of a strong presidency in Chile. Thereafter Congress dominated government in this most institutionally stable of all Latin American republics.

The Revolution of 1891 ensures legislative domination in Chile

Brazil's Experiment with Empire

After independence, Brazil charted a course different from those of the other new nations of Latin America. In 1822, when Prince Regent Pedro declared independence from Portugal, he effectively established a European monarchy in the Americas. As Emperor Pedro I, however, he quickly ran into problems. Brazil was a constitutional monarchy, but Pedro was temperamentally autocratic. The country's *criollo* elite resented the peninsular-born Portuguese whom Pedro trusted and promoted to high office. Then Brazil lost an entire province (afterward known as independent Uruguay) in a disastrous war with Argentina (1825–1828). With that Pedro lost the confidence of his subjects, and in 1831 he abdicated in favor of his young son, who reigned nearly sixty years as Emperor Pedro II.

The Long Reign of Pedro II

Brazil adopts a four-branch system of government

Unlike his father, Pedro II had the right temperament to rule a nation like Brazil. Tall and rangy, with a long beard, domed forehead, and gentle manner, he was a well-read, contemplative man who considered himself an enlightened monarch. The Brazilian Constitution of 1824 provided for four branches of government: executive, legislature, judiciary, and *poder moderador* (moderative power), the last of these giving the emperor a veto over legislation, the right to dissolve Congress, and power to appoint governors, judges, and bishops. The moderative power was designed to give the emperor authority to reconcile disputes between branches and prevent extreme swings of the electorate in one direction or another. Pedro II exercised that power judiciously, balancing liberals with conservatives and steering a moderate political course. His conduct was largely responsible for the longevity of the Brazilian Empire.

Brazil's modernization began in the 1850s, facilitated by the development of banks and credit, and by an immense boom in coffee production as coffee drinking became popular

Pedro II.

in Europe and North America. Bankers raised capital for massive public works improvements, including telegraph lines, railways, and a transatlantic cable linking Brazil to Europe. By 1870 Rio de Janeiro was a thriving metropolis of 600 thousand, four times the size of Mexico City, with paved streets, gas lighting, and a vibrant social life.

Brazil's interior, however, remained mostly undeveloped, largely because its dense rain forests, steep mountain ranges, and turbulent rivers made travel there nearly impossible. When the transatlantic cable was completed in 1874, Pedro II could communicate with London almost immediately, while sending a letter from his palace in Rio to the upper Amazon could take months. Brazil's advantages of size and natural resources were thus offset by difficulties of access. Nevertheless, by 1876 the country was so successful, and Pedro so widely respected, that he was given the honor of helping to ring the Liberty Bell in Philadelphia on the centennial of the U.S. Declaration of Independence.

Slavery, Society, and Imperial Collapse

The future of Pedro's monarchy, however, was threatened by the question of slavery. After the United States ended slavery in 1865, Brazil was the world's last independent nation to permit it. The Atlantic slave trade had been suppressed, but Brazil's huge slave population did not need imports to sustain itself. Under international pressure for abolition, in 1871 the country enacted the Law of the Free Womb, freeing all children born of slave mothers on or after September 28, 1871. This was a gradual emancipation that would have ended slavery only over the course of decades, and even that limited intent was evaded. For years slave owners registered the birthday of slave babies as September 27, 1871.

Outrage over slavery undermines the Emperor's authority

Amid widespread moral outrage, culminating in the army's reluctance to pursue fugitive slaves, Pedro sailed for Europe to have surgery early in 1888. In his absence, his daughter, Princess Isabel, signed the Golden Law of May 13, 1888, emancipating all slaves in Brazil immediately and without compensation to landowners. In so doing, she brought Brazil into line with international expectations and basic human decency.

But she also signed the empire's death warrant. Emancipation without compensation alienated Brazilian landowners, as their bank loans, which had used slaves as collateral, were now jeopardized. Others too were disaffected. Pedro's dedication to religious toleration had already alienated the Catholic Church, and in Congress an active republican minority opposed his monarchy. Princess Isabel was widely unpopular, and the army turned against the regime when the high command's pay and benefits were reduced in 1889. As troops occupied the government buildings, no one stepped forward to defend the monarchy. Pedro II abdicated quietly and went into exile in Europe, where he died in 1891. This bloodless revolution ended the western hemisphere's only successful monarchy, initiating a transition to what seemed a stable republic.

European immigration changes Brazil

To some extent, slavery and the empire had been undermined by economic and social changes, inspired by the coffee boom and increased immigration from Europe. Paid workers proved 50 percent more efficient than slaves in cultivating coffee, reducing the utility of slave labor. Moreover, as prosperity and warm weather attracted huge numbers of immigrants from Portugal, Spain, Italy, Germany, and Russia, Brazil was Europeanized. Immigrants brought European concepts, labor unions, and political parties—and a European love of soccer—and they overwhelmed the native and black populations. In 1890, 44 percent of Brazil's population was white; in 1940 the figure had risen to 63 percent.

The shift resulted not only from European immigration but also from high mortality rates among black people.

Regrettably, with a flood of literate immigrants the government saw no need to educate the Brazilian-born lower classes; its failure to modernize primary education retarded social mobility throughout the twentieth century. A small but growing feminist movement—an outgrowth of the crisis over slavery in the 1870s—began working to secure basic rights for women, including education, voting rights, and access to professional careers. But their efforts often met resistance from many of the men who had worked with them to end slavery, continuing to delay meaningful advances for women and the poor.

Chapter Review

Putting It in Perspective

By 1820, most regions in the Americas had achieved independence from Europe's colonial powers, and by 1900, the new nations had diverged widely. The United States, with its durable constitution, abundant natural resources, and unprecedented immigration, succeeded in surmounting sectional strife to grow into a stable and prosperous industrial giant. Similarly, Canada, aided by Britain's desire to keep it from being annexed by its expansive southern neighbor, established enduring institutions and a thriving economy while expanding across the continent.

Mexico, once Spain's largest and wealthiest colony, experienced caudillismo, social strife, territorial loss, and foreign intervention, and failed to sustain either stability or prosperity. Argentina, after some initial turmoil, developed stable political institutions. Chile and Brazil enjoyed decades of stability, although military interventions at the end of the 1800s signaled upheavals ahead. Several smaller states, plagued by chronic instability and caudillismo, moved from government to government with little continuity.

Nonetheless, in the course of the nineteenth century, the Americas had undergone an incredible transformation. A host of new nations, large and small, had replaced the vast European empires that earlier ruled these lands. Although they separated themselves politically from Europe, these new nations adopted European ideas and welcomed millions of European immigrants. But despite their independence and innovations, the peoples of the western hemisphere experienced uneven levels of prosperity and were often vexed by problems derived from their European heritage.

Reviewing Key Material

KEY CONCEPTS

manifest destiny, 702	junta, 712
Reconstruction, 704	La Reforma, 717
sharecropper, 707	Porfiriato, 718
Jim Crow laws, 707	*porteño*, 719
nativism, 707	gaucho, 719
dominion government, 709	*poder moderador*, 723
caudillo, 710	

KEY PEOPLE

Simón Bolívar, 699, 714	Antonio López de
Abraham Lincoln, 703	Santa Anna, 717
John A. MacDonald, 709	Benito Juárez, 718
King Carlos III, 711	Porfirio Díaz, 718
Tupac Amaru II, 712	Bernardino Rivadavia, 719
Napoleon Bonaparte, 712	Juan Manuel de Rosas, 719
José de San Martín, 714	Diego Portales, 721
Miguel Hidalgo, 715	Emperor Pedro II, 723
King Jõao VI, 717	

ASK YOURSELF

1. How did the doctrine of manifest destiny affect the growth of both the United States and Canada?
2. How did the victory of the North in the Civil War facilitate the economic development of the United States?
3. Why did many Latin American revolutions have conservative roots? In what ways were they based on European ideas?

4. How did caudillismo rather than institutionalization affect the independent development of Mexico and Argentina?
5. How did immigration affect the national development of Argentina, Brazil, and the United States?

GOING FURTHER

Adelman, J. *Republic of Capital: Buenos Aires and the Legal Transformation of the Atlantic World*. 1999.

Bailyn, B. *The Ideological Origins of the American Revolution*. 1992.

Bauer, K. J. *The Mexican-American War, 1846–1848*. 1976.

Bushnell, D., and N. Macaulay. *The Emergence of Latin America in the Nineteenth Century*. 1995.

Collier, S., and W. Sater. *A History of Chile*. 1994.

Da Costa, E. V. *The Brazilian Empire: Myths and Histories*. 2005.

Davis, D. *Slavery and Human Progress*. 1984.

Foner, E. *Reconstruction: America's Unfinished Revolution, 1863–1877*. 1988.

Fox, G. *Hispanic Nation: Culture, Politics, and the Construction of Identity*. 1997.

Haring, C. *Empire in Brazil*. 1947.

Kinsbruner, J. *Independence in Spanish America*. 1994.

Lynch, J. *Simón Bolívar: A Life*. 2006.

Martin, G., ed. *The Causes of Canadian Confederation*. 1990.

McPherson, J. *Battle Cry of Freedom: The Civil War Era*. 1988.

Meyer, M., and W. Sherman. *The Course of Mexican History*. 2002.

Morris, R. *Founding of the Republic*. 1985.

Nugent, W. *Crossing: The Great Transatlantic Migrations, 1870–1914*. 1992.

Pike, Douglas. *Australia*. 1969.

Rock, D. *Argentina 1516–1987*. 1987.

Rodriguez, J. *The Independence of Spanish America*. 1998.

Rodriguez, J. *The Origins of Mexican National Politics*. 1997.

Stevens, D. *Origins of Instability in Early Republican Mexico*. 1991.

Telles, E. *Race in Another America: The Significance of Skin Color in Brazil*. 2004.

Voss, S. *Latin America in the Middle Period, 1750–1920*. 2002.

Key Dates and Developments

1789	Adoption of the United States Constitution
1791	Canada Divided: Upper and Lower Canada
1803	U.S. purchases Louisiana Territory from France
1807–08	Napoleon invades Portugal and Spain Portuguese Prince Regent Jõao flees to Brazil
1810	Latin American revolutions begin
1818	Chile gains independence
1819	Bolívar wins the Battle of Boyacá
1820	San Martín lands in Peru
1821	Iturbide leads Mexico to independence
1821–27	Rivadavia tries to institutionalize Argentina
1822	Meeting between Bolívar and San Martín in Ecuador Pedro I proclaims Brazilian independence
1824	Bolívar completes liberation of Spanish America
1824–54	Santa Anna dominates Mexico
1831–89	Pedro II Reigns as Emperor of Brazil

1833	Chilean Constitution, drafted by Portales
1839	Durham Report on the Affairs of British North America
1840	Canada Act unites Upper and Lower Canada
1846–48	Mexican-American War
1854–72	La Reforma in Mexico
1861–65	Civil War in the United States
1862–67	French Intervention in Mexico
1867	British North America Act creates Dominion of Canada
1876–1911	The Porfiriato in Mexico
1879–83	War of the Pacific
1888	Abolition of slavery in Brazil
1889	Overthrow of the Brazilian empire
1898	Spanish-American War

CHAPTER 29

Confrontation and Adaptation in Eastern and Southern Asia, 1770–1914

Asians Confront Western Technology
In the nineteenth century Asians confronted and adapted to Western impacts and technologies. This color print shows Japanese observing an American ironclad steamship.

In 1793, at China's bustling seaport of Tianjin (*t'YEN-JIN*), a large warship arrived from a distant land. Aboard was an assortment of diplomats, scientists, artists, musicians, and translators, led by Lord George Macartney, representing Britain's King George III. Hoping to persuade China's leaders to open their ports to British goods, Macartney's mission brought six hundred cases of his country's finest wares, including textiles, carpets, cutlery, pottery, clocks, scientific gadgets, and musical instruments.

The mission, however, soon ran into problems. Macartney, a proud English aristocrat, refused to perform the kowtow, a humble bow that involved touching one's forehead to the floor, and thus he was at first denied an audience with China's Qianlong (*ch'YEN LŌNG*) Emperor. The Chinese treated the British goods as tribute from an inferior nation, while Macartney, observing conspicuous poverty and crude weapons, concluded that China was backward and weak. When finally allowed to visit Qianlong at his splendid summer palace, Macartney was shown pavilions full of exquisite Chinese commodities, and learned of the ruler's disdain for Western products. "Our celestial empire possesses all things in prolific abundance," the emperor proclaimed in a letter to King George III. China had "no need to import the manufactures of outside barbarians."

South and East Asia

Six decades later, in 1853, a similar encounter occurred in Japan. Here the visitors were Americans, arriving in ironclad steam-powered warships, with a letter from their president insisting that Japan open its ports to trade with the United States. After several days of awkward standoff, Japanese officials agreed to take the letter to Japan's military leader, the shogun. The visitors departed but promised to return the next year. Awed by America's warships with their large guns, but faced with strong resistance from his samurai warriors to the American demands, the shogun agreed in 1854 to open two small ports to U.S. trade. At the agreement's ceremonial signing, Japanese sumo wrestlers entertained their Western guests, while Japanese officials went for rides on a scale-model steam-powered train, brought from America to impress them.

These two encounters exemplify Asian responses to increasing Western intrusions during the nineteenth century. Accustomed to regarding Westerners as inferior "barbarians," Asians tried first to limit these intrusions, then to exploit them by selectively adapting Western commerce, ideas, and weapons, hoping to strengthen themselves to resist the outsiders. The result was a century of confrontation and adaptation in Asia.

Instability and Endurance in China

In the nineteenth century the Chinese empire, which long had dominated East Asia (Map 29.1), endured a series of disasters that shattered its power and prestige. In part, these calamities resulted from poverty, corruption, and discontent in China. In part, they stemmed from the intrusions of Western merchants, missionaries, and military forces, which helped to undermine China's central authority and destabilize Chinese society.

FOUNDATION MAP 29.1 East and South Asia Around 1800

At the end of the eighteenth century, China remained East Asia's dominant power, with neighboring nations paying it tribute in return for protection and trade. Notice, however, that Spain ruled the Philippines, and that Western commercial interests controlled parts of India and Indonesia. Why did China and Japan seek to minimize connections with the West?

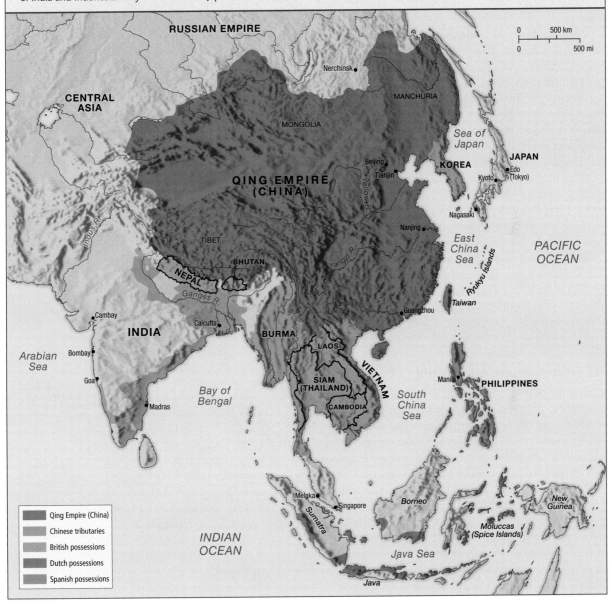

RUSSIAN EMPIRE

0   500 km
0   500 mi

Nerchinsk

CENTRAL
ASIA

MANCHURIA

MONGOLIA

Sea of
Japan

JAPAN

Beijing
Tianjin

KOREA

Kyoto Edo
(Tokyo)

QING EMPIRE
(CHINA)

Nagasaki

Nanjing

East
China
Sea

PACIFIC
OCEAN

TIBET

BHUTAN

Ryukyu Islands

NEPAL

Ganges R.

Guangzhou

Taiwan

Cambay

Calcutta

INDIA

BURMA

Arabian
Sea

Bombay

LAOS

Goa

VIETNAM

SIAM
(THAILAND)

Manila

PHILIPPINES

Madras

Bay of
Bengal

CAMBODIA

South
China
Sea

Melaka

Singapore

Borneo

New
Guinea

Sumatra

Moluccas
(Spice Islands)

INDIAN
OCEAN

Java Sea

Java

Indus R.

Yellow R.

Yangzi R.

Legend:
- Qing Empire (China)
- Chinese tributaries
- British possessions
- Dutch possessions
- Spanish possessions

China's Internal Problems

After conquering China in the mid-1600s and establishing the Qing (*CHING*) dynasty, China's Manchu rulers presided over a long era of stability and prosperity, leading most Chinese to accept the rule of the outsiders from Manchuria (Chapter 21). By the early 1800s, however, both stability and prosperity in China were on the wane.

One key factor in China's instability was population growth. Agricultural advances, including cultivation of fast-growing rice from Southeast Asia and sweet potatoes from the Americas, along with irrigation and forest clearing to bring more land under cultivation, produced abundant food in the early Qing era. But this abundance also helped double China's population, from about 150 million in the mid-1600s to more than 300 million by the early 1800s, while the growth in farmland and food production failed to keep pace. Countless impoverished peasants, lacking sufficient land to support themselves and their families, joined rebel groups that sought to gain land and food by attacking the estates of large landowners.

Southeast Asian and American crops spur Chinese population growth

A second contributing factor was bureaucratic corruption. Local officials often enriched themselves through bribes and extortion, taxing the peasants far beyond what the state required and then pocketing the excess themselves. This practice, aptly called the "squeeze," sapped the common people's scant resources, while the emperor and his favorites drained the imperial treasury to live in lavish splendor.

Such developments bred widespread discontent, especially in southern and western China, where corruption and poverty were acute. One result was the White Lotus Rebellion (Chapter 21), a vast peasant uprising that disrupted much of western China from 1796 to 1804. Another was growing disenchantment with the Qing government, once more regarded by many Chinese people as a foreign regime.

Poverty and corruption fuel Chinese discontent with Qing regime

The Opium Trade and Its Impact

Meanwhile Western influence in China was beginning to grow. Since the mid-1700s, the Chinese government had limited trade with Westerners (mostly Dutch and British merchants) to the large southern port of Guangzhou (*GWAHNG-JŌ*), which the British called Canton. Even there this trade was restricted and controlled by the **Cohong**, the city's merchant guild, a group of Chinese firms authorized by the imperial government to conduct commerce with foreigners. Despite these restrictions, the British developed a lucrative trade, buying Chinese products and then selling them in the West at huge profit. But the trade was one-sided: Europeans readily bought China's tea, silk, and porcelain, but since the Chinese bought little in return, the foreigners had to pay for their purchases mostly in silver. In 1793, frustrated by these restrictions and the growing silver drain, Britain sent the Macartney mission, described at the start of this chapter, to urge the Chinese to buy more British goods. But the British made little headway, as China's emperor insisted that his realm already possessed "all things in prolific abundance." (See "Excerpts from Qianlong's Letter to King George III")

Chinese trade restrictions frustrate the British

There were, however, several things that China did not possess in prolific abundance. One was industrial technology: the machines and weapons that would soon make little Britain mightier and wealthier than enormous China. Another was **opium**, an addictive

Document 29.1 Excerpts from Qianlong's Letter to King George III

In 1793, in an effort to get China to reduce its restrictions on foreign trade, Britain's King George III sent a mission under Lord Macartney to meet with China's Qianlong Emperor. The emperor's condescending response, disdaining the British as barbarians from a remote island whose goods China had no need for, reflected China's attitude toward outsiders at the end of the eighteenth century.

You, O King, live beyond the confines of many seas, nevertheless, impelled by your humble desire to partake of the benefits of our civilisation, you have dispatched a mission respectfully bearing your memorial . . .

I have perused your memorial: the earnest terms in which it is couched reveal a respectful humility on your part, which is highly praiseworthy. In consideration of the fact that your Ambassador and his deputy have come a long way with your memorial and tribute, I have shown them high favour and have allowed them to be introduced into my presence. To manifest my indulgence, I have entertained them at a banquet and made them numerous gifts . . .

Our dynasty's majestic virtue has penetrated unto every country under Heaven, and Kings of all nations have offered their costly tribute by land and sea. As your Ambassador can see for himself, we possess all things. I set no value on objects strange or ingenious, and have no use for your country's manufactures . . .

You, O King, from afar have yearned after the blessings of our civilization . . . I have already taken note of your respectful spirit of submission, have treated your mission with extreme favour and loaded it with gifts . . .

Yesterday your Ambassador petitioned my Ministers to memorialise me regarding your trade with China, but his proposal is not consistent with our dynastic usage and cannot be entertained. Hitherto, all European nations, including your own country's barbarian merchants, have carried on their trade with our Celestial Empire at Canton. Such has been the procedure for many years, although Our Celestial Empire possesses all things in prolific abundance and lacks no product within its own borders. There was therefore no need to import the manufactures of outside barbarians in exchange for our own produce. But as the tea, silk and porcelain which the Celestial Empire produces, are absolute necessities to European nations and to yourselves, we have permitted, as a signal mark of favour, that foreign *hongs* [merchant firms] should be established at Canton, so that your wants might be supplied and your country thus participate in our beneficence. But your Ambassador has now put forward new requests which completely fail to recognise the Throne's principle to "treat strangers from afar with indulgence," and to exercise a pacifying control over barbarian tribes, the world over. Moreover, our dynasty, swaying the myriad races of the globe, extends the same benevolence towards all. Your England is not the only nation trading at Canton. If other nations, following your bad example, wrongfully importune my ear with further impossible requests, how will it be possible for me to treat them with easy indulgence? Nevertheless, I do not forget the lonely remoteness of your island, cut off from the world by intervening wastes of sea, nor do I overlook your excusable ignorance of the usages of our Celestial Empire. I have consequently commanded my Ministers to enlighten your Ambassador on the subject, and have ordered the departure of the mission . . .

SOURCE: Emperor Qian Long, *Letter to George III, 1793*, Chinese Cultural Studies, http://academic.brooklyn.cuny.edu/core9/phalsall/texts/qianlong.html. From E. Backhouse and J. O. P. Bland, *Annals and Memoirs of the Court of Peking* (Boston: Houghton Mifflin, 1914) 322–331.

narcotic drug, made from poppies that grew profusely in India, which produced a sense of euphoria when ingested or smoked. Although opium was illegal in China, the British smuggled it in by sea from India, and its addictive properties soon created a growing demand among the Chinese people. Opium thus gave the British a pernicious but profitable way to redress the trade imbalance.

And redress it they did. From 1800 to 1840 the amount of opium smuggled each year into China increased more than tenfold, from fewer than four thousand 130-pound chests in 1800 to more than 40 thousand in 1840. Its value soon exceeded that of all Chinese goods sold to the British, shifting the trade balance in Britain's favor and causing silver to flow *out* of China—a serious problem for China since its taxes were paid mainly in silver. The spread of opium addiction, moreover, weakened China's army and bureaucracy and created a public health crisis in its urban slums. No wonder many Chinese perceived the British not just as "barbarians" but also as "foreign devils."

To confront the opium crisis, in 1839 China's Daoguang (*DOW-GWAHNG*) Emperor, who reigned from 1821 to 1850, dispatched a conscientious commissioner named Lin Zexu (*LIN DZUH-SHOO*) to Guangzhou to halt the opium trade. Lin Zexu used drastic measures, confiscating and destroying more than 20 thousand chests of British opium and sending Britain's Queen Victoria a letter threatening to execute opium-smuggling "barbarians" by "decapitation or strangulation" (see "Lin Zexu's Letter to Queen Victoria"). Enraged at the destruction of what they insisted was their "private property," and maintaining that China had no authority to prosecute British subjects, the British merchants appealed to their home government, which in turn sent warships to blockade Guangzhou.

Lin Zexu oversees de-
struction of British
opium.

The resulting conflict, known as the First Opium War (1839–1842), was a humiliation for China. The British, with modern warships and well-armed troops, easily defeated China's outmoded forces, occupied Chinese ports, and even sent a 70-ship armada led by an iron-hulled steamship up the Yangzi River to demonstrate their naval superiority (Map 29.2).

The Treaty of Nanjing (1842), which ended the war, required China to abolish the Cohong monopoly, pay Britain a huge indemnity, and cede it the island of Hong Kong (southeast of Guangzhou). It also gave the British full commercial access to five major Chinese ports and exempted British subjects from Chinese jurisdiction. Before long the French and Americans, eager to get in on the China trade, pressured the Qing regime to grant them similar rights.

These Western intrusions proved catastrophic for China. The opium trade, although still illegal, expanded to more than 60 thousand chests a year by the 1850s, intensifying China's public health crisis. A cruel new commerce called the **coolie trade** emerged, as Western merchants hired or kidnapped Chinese workers and shipped them abroad to serve as laborers in places such as Cuba, Peru, and California. These involuntary migrants, disparagingly called "coolies," helped fill a labor shortage created by the banning of the slave trade (Chapter 30), working in mines and building railways that added to the wealth of the West. But wages were so low and working conditions so brutal that "coolies" were often little better off than slaves.

Discredited by defeat and weakened by rampant opium use in its army, the Qing regime found it harder than ever to deal with widespread discontent. Its problems were compounded in 1850 when the prudent and frugal Daoguang Emperor died, leaving the throne to his dissolute 19-year-old son, who reigned from 1850 to 1861 as the Xianfeng (*shē-YAN FUNG*) Emperor. From a traditional Chinese perspective, as floods and famines ravaged the land, the Qing dynasty appeared to have lost the Mandate of Heaven.

Document 29.2 Lin Zexu's Letter to Queen Victoria

In 1839 Commissioner Lin Zexu, the Chinese official tasked with stopping the smuggling of opium by British subjects into China, composed a letter to Britain's Queen Victoria demanding British aid in ending this practice, warning that persons who persisted in this illegal commerce would be liable to execution under Chinese law.

The kings of your honorable country . . . have always been noted for their politeness and submissiveness . . . For this reason the Celestial Court in soothing those from afar has redoubled its polite and kind treatment . . .

But after a long period of commercial intercourse, there appear among the crowd of barbarians both good persons and bad, unevenly. Consequently there are those who smuggle opium to seduce the Chinese people and so cause the spread of the poison to all provinces . . . His Majesty the Emperor, upon hearing of this, is in a towering rage . . .

Suppose there were people from another country who carried opium for sale to England and seduced your people into buying and smoking it; certainly your honorable ruler would deeply hate it and be bitterly aroused. We have heard heretofore that your honorable ruler is kind and benevolent. Naturally you would not wish to give unto others what you yourself do not want . . .

Suppose a man of another country comes to England to trade, he still has to obey the English laws; how much more should he obey in China the laws of the Celestial Dynasty?

Now we have set up regulations governing the Chinese people. He who sells opium shall receive the death penalty and he who smokes it also the death penalty. Now consider this: if the barbarians do not bring opium, then how can the Chinese people resell it, and how can they smoke it? The fact is that the wicked barbarians beguile the Chinese people into a death trap. How then can we grant life only to these barbarians? He who takes the life of even one person still has to atone for it with his own life; yet is the harm done by opium limited to the taking of one life only? Therefore in the new regulations, in regard to those barbarians who bring opium to China, the penalty is fixed at decapitation or strangulation. This is what is called getting rid a harmful thing on behalf of mankind.

Now we . . . have received the extraordinary Celestial grace of His Majesty the Emperor, who has redoubled his consideration and compassion. All those who from the period of the coming one year (from England) or six months (from India) bring opium to China by mistake, but who voluntarily confess and completely surrender their opium, shall be exempt from their punishment. After this limit of time, if there are still those who bring opium to China then they will plainly have committed a willful violation and shall at once be executed according to law, with absolutely no clemency or pardon. This may be called the height of kindness and the perfection of justice . . .

After receiving this dispatch will you immediately give us a prompt reply regarding the details and circumstances of your cutting off the opium traffic. Be sure not to put this off . . .

SOURCE: Lin Zexu [Lin Tse-Hsü], *Letter of Advice to Queen Victoria*. Chinese Cultural Studies, http://academic.brooklyn.cuny.edu/core9/phalsall/texts/com-lin.html. From Ssuyu Teng and John Fairbank, *China's Response to the West* (Cambridge, MA: Harvard University Press, 1954).

The Taiping Rebellion and China's Disintegration

But who would gain Heaven's Mandate? For a while it looked to be Hong Xiuquan (*HŌNG shē-Ō choo-WAHN*), a tempestuous young man from southern China, who led a vast uprising called the **Taiping Rebellion** (1850–1864). Fueled by anti-Manchu hostility and Western religious ideas, this massive revolt, together with natural disasters and other uprisings, produced colossal devastation in China.

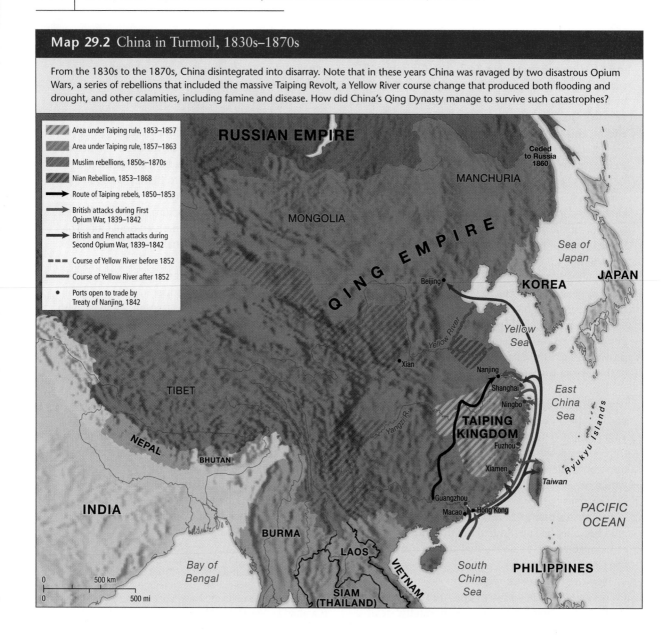

Map 29.2 China in Turmoil, 1830s–1870s

From the 1830s to the 1870s, China disintegrated into disarray. Note that in these years China was ravaged by two disastrous Opium Wars, a series of rebellions that included the massive Taiping Revolt, a Yellow River course change that produced both flooding and drought, and other calamities, including famine and disease. How did China's Qing Dynasty manage to survive such catastrophes?

Legend:
- Area under Taiping rule, 1853–1857
- Area under Taiping rule, 1857–1863
- Muslim rebellions, 1850s–1870s
- Nian Rebellion, 1853–1868
- Route of Taiping rebels, 1850–1853
- British attacks during First Opium War, 1839–1842
- British and French attacks during Second Opium War, 1839–1842
- Course of Yellow River before 1852
- Course of Yellow River after 1852
- Ports open to trade by Treaty of Nanjing, 1842

Hong Xiuquan blends Hakka and Christian ideals

Hong, who belonged to an oppressed minority called Hakka, initially aspired to a career in China's civil service. In 1837, however, after three times failing the civil service exams, he became very ill. By his own account he lapsed into a 40-day coma, during which he had visions. Later, influenced by Christian writings and Western Protestant missionaries, he concluded that he had been taken up to heaven, given a new heart that made him the younger brother of Jesus Christ, and commanded by God to smite the foreign devils who were destroying China. Inspired by this experience, Hong formed a new faith that embraced puritanical Christian values, banning opium, alcohol, adultery, gambling, and foot binding. Defying China's patriarchal traditions and social stratification, his "Society of God Worshipers" also stressed ideals popular among the Hakka, such as gender equality, communal property, and an end to social classes. It thus attracted many poor and oppressed men and women.

In 1850, concluding that the foreign devils he must smite were China's Manchu rulers, Hong Xiuquan assembled a devout and highly disciplined militia, made up of both men and women, who were treated as equals. By 1853 they had defeated a large Manchu army, captured the city of Nanjing, and declared it the capital of a new realm called the Taiping (*TĪ-PING*) Kingdom. For the next decade it ruled much of central China.

Although Taiping means "Great Peace," the Taiping Rebellion brought horrific violence, as Taiping forces fought Manchu armies in a bloody civil war that lasted until 1864. Revolts among Muslims in southern and western China added to the chaos, as did the Yellow River's sudden change of course in 1852, causing drought and famine in its former path and devastating floods in its new one. This wreckage in turn sparked an uprising called the Nian Rebellion, in which starving peasants, led by secret rebel bands called Nian, seized a large segment of northeastern China, terrorizing landlords and attacking towns with a quick-striking cavalry militia. Taking advantage of this turmoil, Britain and France launched a Second Opium War (1856–1860) to further impose their will on the Qing regime. From 1850 to 1864, as rebellions, famine, disease, and war took perhaps 20 million lives, China's once-illustrious empire fell into disarray.

Revolts, disasters, and foreign incursions devastate China

The Dynasty's Survival and Regional "Self-Strengthening"

The Qing dynasty nonetheless survived. Chinese Confucian officials, terrified by the rebels, rallied to its support, while the Taiping Kingdom was weakened by internal conflicts. Furthermore, after 1860, having won the Second Opium War and forced the Qing regime to grant them new privileges, the Western powers supported its survival in order to protect their gains. The regime itself, desperate to restore order, allowed some officials to form regional armies to combat the rebels. One of these armies, led by an eminent Confucian named Zeng Guofan (*DZUNG GWŌ-FAHN*), defeated the Taiping forces in 1864 and, after Hong Xiuquan committed suicide, massacred his followers in Nanjing. Another regional army, formed by Zeng's talented protégé Li Hongzhang (*LĒ HŌNG-JAHNG*), crushed the Nian rebels four years later, and the Muslim revolts in the West were finally quelled in the 1870s.

The dynasty thus endured, but momentum shifted to the regional leaders, who now had their own armies and officials. Distressed by China's vulnerability to the Western powers, they worked to modernize its industry and military in a series of efforts that came to be called "self-strengthening." Before his death in 1872, for example, Zeng Guofan built shipyards, military schools, and munitions factories, and he sent young men to America to study Western science and engineering. Li Hongzhang created his own industrial empire of railways, factories, and mines. He made numerous international contacts, negotiating treaties with Britain and France, buying warships built in the West, and using Western experts to help run his railways and mills. As head of his own army and China's leading industrialist, he amassed great power and wealth.

Regional "self-strengthening" efforts adapt Western ideas

The Empress
Dowager Cixi.

Corruption and
conservatism hamper
China's modernization

Although they often acted on their own, most regional leaders for the time being supported the imperial government, dominated from 1861 to 1908 by a capable but unscrupulous woman called Cixi (*TSUH-SHĒ*). Formerly one of emperor Xianfeng's many concubines, she had borne him a son in 1856 and, after Xianfeng died in 1861, used her status as the new child emperor's mother to become China's regent and effective ruler. Fourteen years later, when her son the emperor (rumored to have been weakened by syphilis acquired in sexual debaucheries) died at age 19, she intrigued to keep her power by placing her four-year-old nephew on the throne.

Known as the Empress Dowager (widow empress), Cixi worked tenaciously from 1861 until her death in 1908 to preserve her own power and that of the Qing regime. To restore stability after the rebellions, she and her officials granted tax relief, repaired roads and canals, and built grain storage facilities to protect against famine. But she also used her position to enhance her lavish lifestyle and prevent social or political change, at least until her last few years.

China thus failed to modernize quickly enough to resist continued Western intrusion. The Chinese bureaucracy's traditional disdain for foreign goods and ideas hampered efforts to buy Western weapons and build industries that might compete with the West. Corruption and greed among Chinese leaders also diverted funds and resources needed for modernization. Cixi, for example, used money intended for updating China's navy to finance lavish personal projects, including an extravagant houseboat made of solid marble, so heavy it could not float. Even Li Hongzhang, the most notable of the "self-strengthening" regional leaders, took bribes and seemed more eager to enhance his wealth and power than to strengthen China.

Subordination and Resistance in India

In the mid-nineteenth century, while Western intrusions were contributing to China's disintegration, Western domination was helping unite and transform the Indian subcontinent. The British enterprise in India, at first primarily commercial, expanded and solidified into outright political control. One result was that India's distinct cultures were subordinated by the British, who sought not only to exploit the subcontinent but also to impose Western ideas and ways. Another result was that many of India's autonomous states were consolidated into a huge British colony, administered largely by British-educated Indian professionals, some of whom would later lead the quest for a united, independent India.

Commercial Connections and Cultural Conflicts

Unlike China, but somewhat like Europe, India historically was not a unified state, but rather an assortment of independent realms, connected by commerce, common cultural values, and the Hindu religion. In the sixteenth century, however, much of the subcontinent had come under the Mughal Empire, an Islamic regime that initially allowed the native cultures and faith to flourish, but later oppressed them and subjected them to Muslim domination (Chapter 17).

Then, in the eighteenth century, as the Mughal regime declined, large parts of the subcontinent came under the sway of the British East India Company, a commercial venture that held a monopoly of Britain's trade with southern Asia (Chapter 22). In some regions, which it had conquered using **sepoys** (*SĒ-poyz*)—Indian soldiers who were trained and commanded by the British—the company's rule was direct. In other areas, which it administered through pacts with Indian princes, the company exercised its influence indirectly.

At first the expansion of British influence mattered little to most people in India. Foreign domination was nothing new to them: in the Mughal era they had accepted alien rule as long as the rulers tolerated Indian cultures and beliefs. And the British East India Company, whose major concern was trade, initially was quite tolerant. Indeed, the company seemed less oppressive than the most recent Mughal rulers, who had imposed harsh taxes and restrictions on India's non-Muslim majority. So in the early years of company control, common people across the subcontinent were scarcely aware of their new overlords from a distant land.

The British East India Company gains influence in India

In the nineteenth century, however, the British presence had significant consequences. First, cheap slave-grown cotton from America and inexpensive cotton clothes from England's textile mills ended India's traditional dominance of the global market for cotton and cotton goods. Second, the British started imposing Western values on India. They took steps to abolish such practices as **sati** (*suh-TĒ*), a custom by which upper-caste Hindu widows were sometimes burnt to death on their husband's funeral pyre, and **thagi** (*thuh-GĒ*), the work of professional bandits (or "thugs") who attacked and strangled travelers as a religious ritual. Dismissive of Indian institutions, British reformers sought to establish Western-style educational and judicial systems in India. One of them, historian Thomas Babington Macauley, even asserted that "a single shelf of a good European library is worth the whole native literature of India."

British industry and commerce have growing impact on India

Meanwhile, to protect their commercial and strategic interests, the British expanded their direct control over other parts of India (Map 29.3). During the Napoleonic Wars (1799–1815), for example, fearing a possible French attack on the Indian subcontinent, the British seized the state of Mysore (*mī-SOR*) in southern India (1799). Several years later they invaded the lands of the Maratha (*mah-rah-TAH*) Confederacy in western and central India, finally annexing them in 1818. In 1839–1849, to counterbalance Russian expansion in Central Asia, the British took control of the Sind and Punjab (*pun-JAHB*) regions in northwest India. By the 1850s, the British dominated most of the Indian subcontinent.

Britain expands direct control over much of India

The Indian Revolt of 1857

Over the years, as the British role in India expanded, Britain's government had become concerned that the company, a commercial enterprise, was wielding too much political and military power. Reacting to reports of plunder and abuse of Indians by company officials, the British Parliament passed an India Act in 1784, setting up a board of control to oversee the company's operations. Parliament then restricted the company's commercial monopoly in 1814 and ended its privileged status altogether in 1833. More and more, control of India was shifting from the company to the crown, that is, from the officers of the British East India Company to the leading officials of the British royal government.

The expansion of British rule, combined with British insensitivity to Indian ways, led to the Indian Revolt of 1857. Begun as an insurrection by Indian sepoy soldiers against their British commanders, it is also known in Britain as the "Sepoy Mutiny."

Indians revolt against British domination

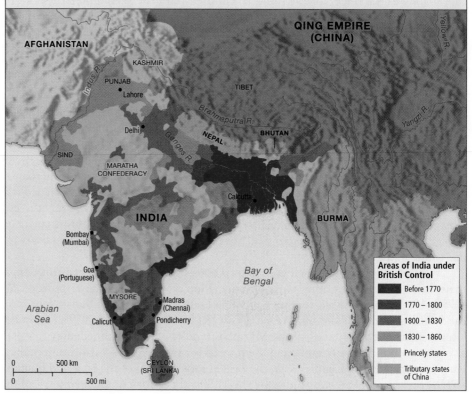

Map 29.3 Growth of British Power in India, 1770–1860

Between 1770 and 1860 the British extended their rule over most of the Indian subcontinent. Notice that in 1770 the British role in India was still primarily commercial, with the British East India Company controlling several coastal regions, but by 1860 almost all of India was under the direct or indirect dominion of Britain's imperial government. How did British rule help unite India and pave the way for Indian nationalist movements?

Areas of India under British Control

- Before 1770
- 1770 – 1800
- 1800 – 1830
- 1830 – 1860
- Princely states
- Tributary states of China

The revolt was triggered by British introduction of accurate new rifles for the sepoys and by rumors that, to use the cartridges for these rifles, they would have to bite off a protective wrapping greased with the fat of cows or pigs. Both Hindu soldiers (who considered cows sacred) and Muslim soldiers (who considered pork unclean), upset that they might violate their religious laws by tasting a forbidden substance, refused to use the new cartridges. Although the British eventually withdrew the order that sepoys must bite off the wrapping, they chained and imprisoned many sepoys for refusing to follow this order.

Enraged at this treatment of their comrades, hundreds of sepoys rampaged across the Ganges River valley, killing their British officers and many other Britons, including women and children. Others in northern India, including former landowners and regional rulers who had been displaced by the British, joined in the rebellion. Horrified by the slaughter of their own people, British officials responded by ruthlessly crushing the revolt in 1858, burning whole villages and executing rebels by hanging them or shooting them with cannons. Superior weapons, and the loyalty of sepoys brought from elsewhere in India, helped the British prevail.

After the revolt the British enterprise in India, begun as a commercial venture, was fully converted into imperial rule. Determined both to assert full control and provide more effective governance, Britain abolished the East India Company, imposing crown rule through a viceroy who governed in the name of the British monarch. Many Indian soldiers, their loyalty no longer trusted, were replaced with British troops. Local Indian rulers were formally subordinated to Britain's Queen Victoria, who in 1876 was declared Empress of India by the British Parliament.

British troops crushing Indian Revolt.

The Rise of Indian Nationalism

In strengthening its control over India, however, Britain inadvertently aided the rise of Indian nationalism. By unifying India's diverse states under direct and indirect British rule, for example, and by creating a uniform civil service, along with a network of roads, railways, and telegraph lines, the British helped unite the subcontinent politically and economically. And by encouraging Indians to learn British ways to reinforce this rule, the British helped to foster a growing sense of Indian national unity.

Since the eighteenth century, a number of Indians had studied English language and ways, partly to participate in commerce and partly to incorporate Western science and technology into India's long tradition of mathematical and scientific expertise. Now the British, eager to instill their ideals in Indian leaders and officials, further encouraged such study, helping to develop a British-educated, English-speaking Indian elite. Many of its members attended British universities and then returned to play leading roles in Indian society.

In time some members of this elite formed an Indian nationalist movement. In learning British ways they also learned Western liberal and nationalist ideals, which they adapted to India. If liberal ideals such as freedom and self-rule were vital to the British people, reasoned these Indian leaders, should not such ideals also apply to the people of India? If European nationalists took great pride in their historic institutions and beliefs, should not Indians do likewise?

Indian elites adapt Western liberal and nationalist ideas to India

In 1885, a group of British-educated Indian leaders convened the first session of what came to be called the Indian National Congress. Based on earlier regional political associations in India, and modeled in part on British political parties, the Congress pushed for greater involvement of Indians in their own governance. Over the next several decades, faced with British resistance, it became increasingly assertive, developing into a full-blown nationalist movement. One faction, led by Gopal Krishna Gokhale (*GŌ-kuh-lā*), a highly respected educator and moderate political leader, called for greater Indian autonomy within the British Empire. Another faction, led by Bal Gangadhar Tilak (*TĒ-lahk*), a prominent mathematician and radical nationalist whom the British at one point deported for sedition, pressed for full independence. Later, under the inspirational leadership of Mohandas Karamchand Gandhi (Chapter 32), the Indian National Congress led a sustained non-violent struggle for a united, independent India.

Indian National Congress pushes for Indian self-rule

Restoration and Adaptation in Japan

Japan, like China and India, was forced to deal with Western intrusions during the nineteenth century. As in China and India, these intrusions resulted in humiliation and internal upheaval. Unlike China and India, however, Japan avoided Western economic and political domination. It did not, however, avoid Western cultural and technological influence. Indeed, in order to defend itself from Western powers, Japan modified many of its traditional ways and institutions, borrowing ideas and technologies from its Western antagonists. As the Asian nation that most successfully resisted Western rule, Japan also became the most fully Westernized of the major Asian nations.

The Tokugawa Shogunate and the Western Challenge

By the mid-nineteenth century, Japan had experienced more than two hundred years of self-imposed isolation under the Tokugawa family, whose leaders ruled from the city of Edo as shoguns. In theory the shogun was merely Japan's highest military official, appointed by the emperor to command the imperial armies. In practice, however, as overlord of the daimyo (regional warlords) and samurai warriors, the shogun was far more powerful than the emperor, who reigned in the ancient city of Kyoto as a godlike religious figure lacking political power.

Japan minimizes Western connections for two centuries

Since the early 1600s, to protect Japan from European influence, the Tokugawa shoguns had banned most contact with Westerners, except for limited commercial and cultural connections with the Dutch, who were allowed to operate a small trading post near the southern port of Nagasaki (*NAH-gah-SAH-kē*). For over two centuries, then, Japan had preserved and developed its culture without much Western intrusion.

Americans press Japan to open trade

In the 1850s, however, a new Western power, the United States of America, decided to do business with Japan. As American whaling ships and merchant vessels increasingly traveled the Pacific, the U.S. government came to see Japan as a potential refuge for stranded whalers and refueling point for American steamships on their way to and from Chinese ports. In 1853, as described at the start of this chapter, an American squadron with ironclad steamships arrived near Edo and transmitted to the shogun a letter calling for open trade relations.

U.S. forces in Japan, 1853.

This naval visit, led by Commodore Matthew Perry, triggered a crisis in Japan. On one hand, Japanese law forbade most contact with Westerners under penalty of death; on the other hand, the Americans had superior ships with powerful guns that Japan could not match. When Perry returned with a larger force in 1854 and insisted on a response, the shogun tried to compromise, agreeing to open two small ports to trade with the United States.

This compromise satisfied no one. It went too far for many defiant samurai, who had wanted to fight the Americans and felt that their shogun dishonored his country by dealing with "barbarians." But it did not go far enough for the Americans and other Western powers, who soon forced Japan to sign unequal treaties, like those imposed on China, that opened more ports to Western trade and exempted Westerners in Japan from Japanese jurisdiction. By 1859, not only the Americans, but also the Dutch, Russians, British, and French, had imposed such treaties, fully opening Japan to Western trade and Western influence.

Western powers impose trade treaties on Japan

Civil War and Meiji Restoration

The shogun's submission to Western demands created a distressing dilemma for many samurai warriors. They believed that his action had betrayed Japan and compromised his moral authority, but, according to their samurai code, they were honor-bound to serve him loyally. If they defied him they would dishonor themselves, and for the samurai dishonor meant death.

To resolve this dilemma, some of the samurai launched a movement to "honor the emperor" and "expel the barbarians." Inspired by Yoshida Shoin (*YŌ-shē-dah SHŌ-ēn*), a passionate young patriot who had earlier tried to hide on one of Perry's ships to study Americans first hand, these samurai declared that their ultimate loyalty was not to the shogun but to the emperor, the shogun's divine overlord and rightful Japanese ruler. In their view they could best honor the emperor by defying the shogun and fighting the foreign devils.

Although Yoshida was beheaded in 1859 for plotting to murder an agent of the shogun, in the 1860s Yoshida's admirers helped to trigger a series of civil wars in which some daimyo and their samurai remained loyal to the shogun, while others sought to overthrow him and restore the emperor to full political power. The Western powers, perplexed by these upheavals, responded to occasional attacks on their ships by shelling some coastal fortresses, but did not intervene directly. Finally, in 1868, the forces supporting the emperor prevailed, defeating the shogun and abolishing his office.

To emphasize the end of the shogunate, the victorious samurai had the young emperor Mutsuhito (*moot-soo-HĒ-tō*), who had recently inherited the throne, move from Kyoto to the shogun's former palace at Edo. That city, replacing Kyoto as Japan's imperial capital, was renamed Tokyo, or "eastern capital." Since Mutsuhito's reign was given the title Meiji (*MĀ-jē*), meaning "Enlightened Rule," he was called the Meiji Emperor, and the re-establishment of the emperor as head of Japan's government came to be known as the Meiji Restoration.

Rebellious samurai depose shogun and restore emperor

Meiji Emperor in samurai attire.

Centralization and Western Adaptations

Japan's government, however, was actually run by the emperor's advisors, a gifted group of young samurai drawn from the factions that had defeated the shogun. They soon decided that, to protect their country from the West, they must unite and adapt to Western ways: in order to "expel the barbarians" Japan must first emulate them. During the long Meiji reign (1867–1912), Japan pursued both centralization and selective adaptation of Western ideas and technologies.

Aware of the recent humiliations imposed by the West on India and China, the Meiji regime moved quickly to concentrate its power and unite Japan in the face of the foreign threat. The regime required the various daimyo warlords to surrender their troops and domains to the emperor and then to move to Tokyo and become imperial officials. The regime also moderated Japan's rigid class distinctions, curtailing samurai class privileges and ending regular stipends to the samurai. The regime then began in 1873 to create a new military system, based on French and German models, replacing the old class-based samurai armies with a large army made up mainly of commoners drafted into service. Armed with modern rifles rather than samurai swords, the new army was controlled by the central government, rather than by local lords.

To strengthen Japan, the Meiji regime adapts Western ideas

Some samurai rebel against the end of class privilege

Although most daimyo and samurai accepted these reforms, knowing they could not face the Western threat as separate forces with outmoded weapons, some were deeply distressed at the loss of their honored status. In 1877, after the regime ordered the samurai to discard the fabled swords that symbolized their status, about 40 thousand samurai staged a mass revolt led by Saigo Takamori (*SĪ-gō tah-kah-MAW-rē*), a heroic warrior who had helped defeat the shogun in 1868. Saigo fought bravely, but he and his forces could not overcome the new army's superior size and weaponry. Defeated and branded a traitor, Saigo regained his honor by committing seppuku, the samurai suicide ritual, and thus became a romantic symbol of the glorious samurai era that had come to an end.

Japan adapts Western ways to fit its culture

In the ensuing decades, anxious to replicate the power and wealth of the industrial West, Japan adapted many Western ways to fit its East Asian society. To spur industrial growth, for example, the government built railways, textile mills, factories, and mines, then sold them to wealthy families to raise money. Thus arose the **zaibatsu**— distinctive Japanese family-owned conglomerates, each typically having its own banks, shipping lines, railways, mines, factories, and retail outlets. To provide the knowledge needed for industrial society, the Meiji regime established a new system of mandatory education, modeled on those in America and France, combining Western-style technical knowledge with traditional Japanese literature and learning. In 1889 the regime adopted a Western-type constitution, establishing a two-house parliament and a cabinet, while reserving vast authority for the emperor, to whom the cabinet and military were directly responsible. Culturally, the Japanese imitated Western forms of dress, dining, architecture, art, and entertainment, blending them with traditional Japanese styles.

By the 1890s, then, Japan was emerging as a blend of East and West, a Western-style industrial power on the edge of Asia. Two ominous factors were also beginning to emerge. One was the absence in the new constitution of effective checks on the power of the military, which reported directly to the emperor, enabling it at times to act without approval of the civilian government. Another was the reality that the Japanese islands, so favored by climate and rich in beauty, lacked large deposits of mineral resources—such as iron and petroleum—that were essential for industry. These two factors would dominate Japanese policies for the next half century, as Japan embarked on increasingly audacious efforts, from 1894 until 1945, to gain control of such resources through military expansion.

The Impact of Imperialism in Asia

Japan was not the only power seeking to expand in Asia. In the nineteenth century the British, French, and Dutch, exploiting China's declining ability to protect the smaller nations to its South from outside intervention, increasingly brought these nations under imperial control. Then, in the 1890s, after Japan exploited China's weakness in a war for control of Korea, these and other European powers forced the Qing regime to grant them zones in China for economic exploitation. For a time it seemed as if the "foreign devils" would dismantle the celestial empire.

Southeast Asia and the West

Mainland Southeast Asia, the region east of India and south of China, was so strongly influenced by both these cultures that it was often called "Indochina." Its various states, although politically autonomous, derived their main beliefs and institutions from the Indian and Chinese traditions. Most of these states also paid tribute to China and looked to it for protection. For centuries this region, populated mainly by Buddhist village farmers who grew rice in the hot, rainy climate, attracted scant attention from European visitors, most of whom focused on the profits they could make by trading with India, the East Indies, and China (Map 29.4).

From 1771 until 1802, however, a massive revolt called the Tay-Son Rebellion rocked Vietnam, Southeast Asia's easternmost state, leading a young prince named Nguyen Anh (*'n-GIH-un AHN*) to seek outside assistance (Chapter 21). The French, hoping to regain some influence in Asia after their ouster from India by the British, provided him with soldiers and weapons, helping him crush the revolt and found the Nguyen dynasty (1802–1945). Reigning until 1820 as Emperor Gia Long (*jē-AH LAWNG*), he did not promote trade with France but did allow the French to send some Catholic missionaries, who in time attracted a number of Vietnamese converts.

In the 1850s, alarmed at the growing number of Catholics in this largely Buddhist land and angered by a French priest's alleged involvement in a plot to overthrow him,

Southeast Asian states pay tribute to China

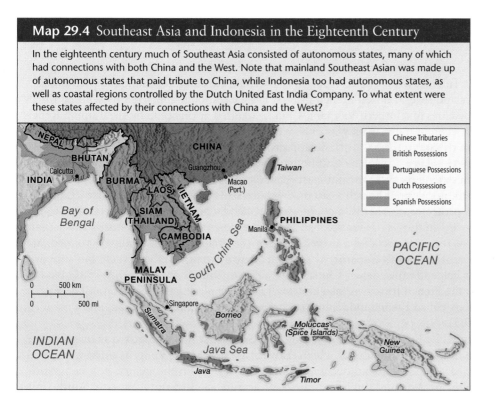

Map 29.4 Southeast Asia and Indonesia in the Eighteenth Century

In the eighteenth century much of Southeast Asia consisted of autonomous states, many of which had connections with both China and the West. Note that mainland Southeast Asian was made up of autonomous states that paid tribute to China, while Indonesia too had autonomous states, as well as coastal regions controlled by the Dutch United East India Company. To what extent were these states affected by their connections with China and the West?

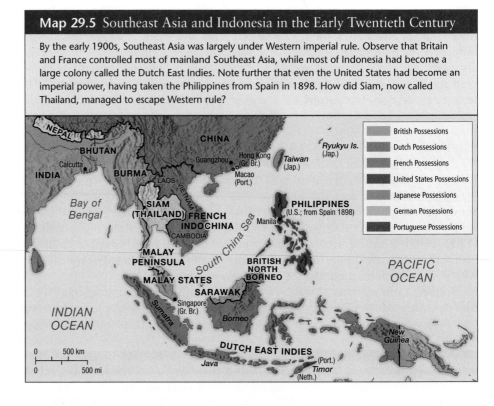

Map 29.5 Southeast Asia and Indonesia in the Early Twentieth Century

By the early 1900s, Southeast Asia was largely under Western imperial rule. Observe that Britain and France controlled most of mainland Southeast Asia, while most of Indonesia had become a large colony called the Dutch East Indies. Note further that even the United States had become an imperial power, having taken the Philippines from Spain in 1898. How did Siam, now called Thailand, managed to escape Western rule?

Emperor Tu Duc, who reigned from 1847 to 1883, executed thousands of Vietnamese Catholics and several dozen French priests. France responded in 1858 by sending forces to occupy cities in southern Vietnam. China, engulfed at this time by the Taiping Rebellion and Second Opium War, was unable to help Vietnam, despite the fact that it had long paid tribute to China for trade and protection.

Five years later a revolt in Cambodia, Vietnam's western neighbor, allowed France to further extend its sway in Southeast Asia. Despite the fact that Cambodia's king neither sought nor desired French assistance, France sent in troops and proclaimed Cambodia a French **protectorate**, that is, a country controlled by an outside power claiming to provide security. In the 1870s France also sent forces to combat rebels in northern Vietnam; in 1883 it, too, was declared a protectorate by the French. China finally responded, at the behest of Vietnam's emperor, by sending an army to attack the French, but superior weapons helped France defeat China in the Franco-Chinese War of 1883–1885. Finally, in 1893, the French took over neighboring Laos, completing the formation of a large new colony called French Indochina, encompassing Vietnam, Cambodia, and Laos (Map 29.5).

> France exploits China's weakness to expand in Southeast Asia

Meanwhile Britain was also moving into Southeast Asia. To guard their sea route between India and China, over which traveled such valuable items as opium, tea, and silk, in 1819 the British had occupied Singapore, a port on the straits, between mainland Southeast Asia and the East Indies, connecting the Indian Ocean and South China Sea. In the 1870s, as France expanded its control over Vietnam and Cambodia, the

British extended their influence northward from Singapore, to protect that port. They took over several small sultanates on the southern Malay peninsula, soon a key source of industrial resources such as tin, and later rubber—after rubber trees were planted there by the British who smuggled seeds from Brazil. In the 1880s, anxious to prevent the French from expanding toward British India, Britain conquered and annexed the kingdom of Burma, a country today called Myanmar (*mē-AHN-mar*), rich in oil and teakwood.

In all Southeast Asia only Thailand, then called Siam, escaped colonization in the nineteenth century, partly because neither Britain nor France was willing to let the other gain control there. Two talented Thai kings, Rama IV (1851–1868) and Rama V (1868–1910), cleverly exploited the British-French rivalry to keep Thailand independent. To further reinforce their realm against Western intrusion, these kings centralized the state bureaucracy, established an educational system, and introduced such technologies as printing presses, railways, and telegraphs. Modernized by its monarchs and spared the disruption of Western imperial rule, Thailand emerged as Southeast Asia's most stable and prosperous nation.

Thailand exploits Western rivalries to maintain its independence

Indonesia and the Dutch

The East Indies, a long string of islands today known as Indonesia ("Indian Islands"), stretching from Southeast Asia toward Australia, had a past that paralleled in many ways that of the Indian subcontinent. Like India, Indonesia included many diverse realms, most of which had been influenced by Hinduism and Buddhism; like India, by the sixteenth century, Indonesia had come largely under Muslim control. In the seventeenth and eighteenth centuries, much as parts of India came under the sway of the British East India Company, parts of Indonesia came to be controlled by the Dutch United East India Company, a similar state-sponsored enterprise that monopolized trade between the Netherlands and East Indies from 1602 until 1799.

In the nineteenth century, the Kingdom of the Netherlands expanded Dutch influence in Indonesia, first by forging agreements with various local rulers and then by requiring Indonesian villagers to set aside one-fifth of their land for cultivation of export crops such as sugar, pepper, coffee, tea, and tobacco. By collecting these globally popular products as a form of taxation, and then selling them abroad at huge profits, the Dutch gained vast wealth while most Indonesians continued to live in great poverty. By the early twentieth century, as the islands also began supplying industrial resources such as rubber, tin, and oil, the Dutch ruled most of Indonesia as a large and lucrative colony called the Dutch (or Netherlands) East Indies.

Indonesia is subjected to Dutch commerce and control

Japan Versus China in Korea

Meanwhile, noting China's weakness in the face of Western intrusions, Japan had begun to expand and carve out its own Asian empire. As early as 1872, influenced by expansionist advisors, the new Meiji regime in Tokyo laid claim to the Ryukyu (*rē-YOOK-yoo*) Islands, a chain of small isles south of Japan, the largest of which is Okinawa (*ō-kē-NAH-wah*). The Chinese, who had long received tribute from the Ryukyu king, refused to recognize this new Japanese claim. So Japan responded by moving the king to Tokyo in

Japan exploits China's weakness to annex Ryukyu Islands

1879, proclaiming him a Japanese nobleman, and declaring that the Ryukyu chain was officially part of Japan (Map 29.6). The Qing regime in China, facing France's challenge in Southeast Asia and not yet fully recovered from the calamities of the 1850s and 1860s, could do little more than protest.

Tonghak Revolt in Korea blends Eastern and Western beliefs

Far more troubling to the Qing regime was the Japanese challenge in Korea, a former Chinese colony and longtime tributary that had copied much of its culture from China. So similar to China was Korea, in fact, that in the 1860s it had even experienced its own variant of China's Taiping Rebellion. In 1860 an impetuous young man named Cho'e Che-u (*CHEH CHĀ-OO*), having repeatedly failed the Korean civil service exams, claimed that he was commanded by God to start a new religion. Known as Tonghak ("Eastern Learning"), this messianic creed combined Buddhist, Daoist, Confucian, and Christian ideas, calling for creation of an earthly righteous kingdom in which all would be equal under God. Its radical egalitarianism attracted numerous poor Korean peasants, who rose in a mass revolt against oppressive landlords and state officials. In 1864, however, Korean authorities crushed the revolt, beheading Cho'e Che-u and killing thousands of his followers. But the Tonghak creed was not entirely suppressed.

In the 1870s, eager to industrialize, Japan began to covet Korea's natural resources, which included sizable deposits of coal and iron. In 1875, in a move reminiscent of the U.S. opening of Japan two decades earlier, the Meiji regime sent a fleet to Korea, hoping to force the Koreans to trade with Japan. The overmatched Koreans, advised by their Chinese overlords to negotiate with the Japanese, agreed the next year to let them conduct commerce at three Korean ports.

Japanese inroads in Korea trigger conflict with China

In the 1880s, however, anxious to forestall any further expansion of Japanese influence in Korea, still regarded by China as a tributary and protectorate, Chinese industrialist Li Hongzhang decided to take action. Using his private army, which he had refused to disband after crushing the Nian Rebellion, he sent troops into Korea under the command of a talented protégé named Yuan Shikai (*yoo-AHN shur-KĪ*). Then, in 1894, as tensions increased between China and Japan, the Tonghak Revolt resurfaced, threatening to topple the Korean government. Seeing this unrest as a golden opportunity to expand their influence in Korea, the Japanese sent in troops to help crush the revolt. Quickly these troops came into conflict with the Chinese forces already in Korea.

Japan defeats China in conflict over Korea

The resulting war between China and Japan, known as the Sino-Japanese War (1894–1895), was the first direct test of each country's modernization program. The conflict proved painful for China. Corrupt Chinese officials had purchased inferior weapons from the West, pocketing what they saved by not buying higher-priced arms. Chinese commanders, moreover, had not learned how to use the new weapons or employ new naval methods. The Japanese, better led and better equipped, defeated the Chinese at sea, then overran Korea and the southern part of the Chinese province of Manchuria. As Japanese forces moved toward Beijing, China's capital, the Qing regime agreed to terms, recognizing Korea as fully independent and ceding to Japan both the island of Taiwan and southern Manchuria's Liaodong (*lē-OW DŌNG*) Peninsula (Map 29.6).

The Scramble for Chinese Concessions

Western powers pressure Japan to give up gains in Manchuria

Stunned by Japan's decisive victory, and by its acquisition of so much Chinese territory, Russia, France, and Germany quickly intervened, pressuring Japan to return the Liaodong Peninsula, its newly gained foothold in Manchuria. Once Japan complied,

Map 29.6 Japanese Expansion in Asia, 1867–1912

During the reign of the Meiji Emperor (1867–1912), Japan created its own colonial empire in East Asia. Notice that Japan annexed the Ryukyu Islands in 1879, acquired Taiwan in the Sino-Japanese War (1894–1895), and gained southern Sakhalin Island, a protectorate in Korea, and influence in Manchuria as a result of the Russo-Japanese War (1904–1905). What key factors facilitated Japan's imperial expansion?

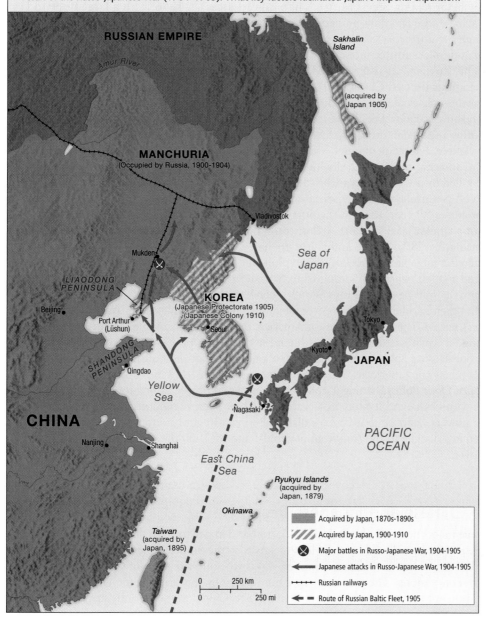

RUSSIAN EMPIRE

Amur River

Sakhalin Island
(acquired by Japan 1905)

MANCHURIA
(Occupied by Russia, 1900-1904)

Vladivostok

Mukden

LIAODONG PENINSULA

Beijing

Port Arthur (Lüshun)

Sea of Japan

KOREA
(Japanese Protectorate 1905)
(Japanese Colony 1910)

Seoul

Tokyo

Kyoto

JAPAN

SHANDONG PENINSULA

Qingdao

Yellow Sea

CHINA

Nanjing

Shanghai

Nagasaki

East China Sea

PACIFIC OCEAN

Ryukyu Islands
(acquired by Japan, 1879)

Okinawa

Taiwan
(acquired by Japan, 1895)

Legend:
- Acquired by Japan, 1870s-1890s
- Acquired by Japan, 1900-1910
- ⊗ Major battles in Russo-Japanese War, 1904-1905
- ← Japanese attacks in Russo-Japanese War, 1904-1905
- ▸▸▸▸ Russian railways
- ◂■ Route of Russian Baltic Fleet, 1905

0   250 km
0   250 mi

however, it became clear that this **Triple Intervention** was meant not to protect China's territorial integrity but to advance the intervening powers' imperial ambitions in China.

First to move in were the Russians, who were building the **Trans-Siberian Railway**, a 5,800-mile railroad stretching from European Russia to Russia's Pacific coast. Intended as a great new trade route linking East and West, it was also designed to aid Russian industry by providing access to Asia's natural resources. In 1896, with a large bribe to Li Hongzhang, the Russians gained China's consent to build a segment of this railway through the northeast Chinese province of Manchuria, saving them hundreds of miles of track and huge sums of money.

This Russian advance sparked a three-year **scramble for concessions**, in which European nations pressed China for special privileges, called concessions, that would allow their economic exploitation of key regions of China (Map 29.7). Seeking to gain industrial resources such as coal and iron while opening extensive markets for their textiles and other industrial goods, Westerners imposed their will on the Qing regime. In 1897, for example, France demanded and received railway and mining privileges in southern China, adjacent to French Indochina. Later that year, after two German missionaries were killed by a Chinese anti-Christian mob in northeastern China's Shandong (*SHAHN-DŌNG*) peninsula, Germany seized the Chinese port of Qingdao (*CHING-DOW*), then negotiated a 99-year lease on the port and mineral rights to the whole region. Soon Russia got a similar lease on Port Arthur (now Lüshun) at the southern tip of the Liaodong Peninsula. By 1899 France and Germany had extended their concessions, Britain had extracted a huge new concession to exploit the Yangzi River valley, and even Italy had secured a small concession along China's eastern coast. For a while it looked as if much of China would be divided into Western concessions.

But then another Western power, flexing its newfound muscles in Asia, came to China's rescue. The United States of America, despite its anticolonial origins, in 1898 had acquired its own East Asian possession, taking the Philippine Islands from Spain in the brief but decisive Spanish-American War. Concerned that the European concessions in China might cut Americans out of the Chinese trade, in 1899 the United States proclaimed an **Open Door Policy**, issuing a note to each imperial power calling for free and equal trade with China and for the preservation of China's territorial integrity. One by one the other powers, worried that China's dismemberment might lead to wars among them, agreed in principle to the American demands, and by 1900 the scramble for concessions was over.

The Chinese and Japanese Response

The events of the 1890s brought humiliation and anger to both China and Japan. The Chinese were humiliated by their loss to Japan in the Sino-Japanese War, and angered at the Western powers, which had claimed rights to exploit regions of China in their scramble for concessions. The Japanese were humiliated by the Triple Intervention, which forced them to return the Liaodong Peninsula to China, and especially angered at the Russians, who had subsequently moved into Manchuria themselves.

Both Asian nations reacted by waging war against Western powers: China's Qing dynasty supported an internal anti-Western uprising, and Japan's Meiji leaders started a

China agrees to let Russia build railway through Manchuria

China forced to grant Western powers economic exploitation zones

U.S. Open Door Policy helps deter dismemberment of China

Cartoon depicting U.S. Open Door Policy.

Map 29.7 East and South Asia in the Early Twentieth Century

By the early twentieth century, China had lost its dominant role in East Asia. Observe that most of the neighboring regions and states had come under Western or Japanese rule, and China itself had been forced to grant concessions (economic exploitation zones) to Western countries and Japan. Why was China unsuccessful in resisting Western and Japanese expansion? How did China manage to avoid total Western colonization?

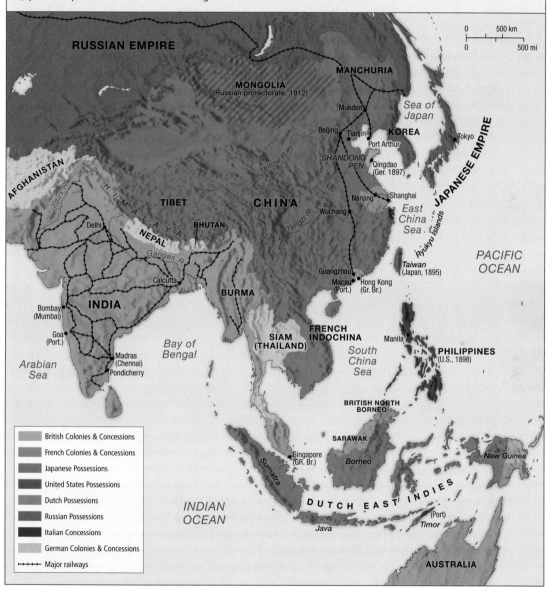

conflict with Russia. China's efforts proved futile, leading to a series of last-ditch reforms that failed to save the regime, while Japan's were successful, bringing new status and global respect to the island nation. By 1912 Japan had emerged as East Asia's foremost power, while China's ancient celestial empire was gone, overthrown by revolution and replaced by a republic.

The Boxer Uprising in China

In 1898, amid the Western scramble for concessions, China experienced devastating floods, renewing the widespread perception that the Qing dynasty had lost Heaven's Mandate. That same year Empress Dowager Cixi, determined to maintain her power, blocked an effort begun by her nephew, the emperor, to institute Western-style reforms. She then arrested him, declared that he was too ill to rule, and once again proclaimed herself regent, even though her nephew was by this time 27 years old. The next year, angered at the foreign powers partitioning her empire, she aligned with a secret martial arts society that launched an extensive anti-Western rebellion.

Boxer Uprising attacks Western interests in northern China

The Society of Righteous and Harmonious Fists, whose members were called Boxers, blamed the floods on the Europeans, saying that they had upset the sacred Earth by violating it with their railways, mines, and telegraph poles. By reciting a magic oath three times, then breathing through clenched teeth and foaming at the mouth, the Boxers believed they could make themselves impervious to Western bullets. In early 1900, with Cixi's tacit consent, they went on a rampage in northern China, smashing railways and telegraph lines, burning down Christian churches and convents, slaying thousands of Chinese Christians, and killing a few hundred Europeans. In June, as the Boxers invaded Beijing and laid siege to the Legation Quarter, a section of the city housing foreign embassies, Cixi and her regime formally declared war on the imperialist powers—Britain, France, Germany, Russia, Japan, and the United States.

Western forces combat Boxer Uprising.

The Boxer War was short and bloody. For two months the Western embassy guards, who numbered less than five hundred, held out against about 200 thousand rebels, who quickly found that they were not immune to Western bullets. Meanwhile the Western powers and Japan assembled a force of 30 thousand soldiers, who then stormed Beijing and lifted the siege, bringing the war to an end.

Incredibly, the empress dowager managed to hold on to power. Having fled Beijing in a peasant cart to the ancient city of Xi'an, she called on the foreigners to help her put down the revolt, pretending that she had not backed the rebels and declared war on the West. Her rival Li Hongzhang, who had opposed the war and remained on good terms with the Western powers, persuaded them to go along with her pretence. Eager to restore order and exploit the concessions they had won from Cixi's regime, and seeing no viable alternative to her continued rule, the invading nations agreed to the fiction that they had merely assisted her in crushing the rebels.

The Russo-Japanese War

Russia occupies Manchuria during the Boxer Uprising

In the midst of the chaos in China, the Russians sent troops to Manchuria to protect their railway interests from the Boxers. This Russian action further angered the Japanese, already irate at having been forced to give China back the Liaodong Peninsula. Now, fearing that Russia's presence in Manchuria would hinder their access to its ample coal and iron deposits, which they considered crucial to their industrial growth, the Japanese resolved to force the Russians out.

There followed several years of diplomatic maneuvering by both Japan and Russia. Having boosted its status with the Western powers by joining them in crushing the Boxers, Japan played skillfully on growing Western fears of Russian expansion and even concluded an "Anglo-Japanese" alliance with Britain in 1902 (Chapter 31). Bowing to international pressures, Russia agreed to evacuate its troops from Manchuria by the end of 1903.

But the Russian troops did not actually withdraw. Instead, they began to extend their influence into northern Korea through a commercial enterprise, supposedly designed to exploit Korean timber resources, but actually formed by Russian expansionists with the support of Russia's tsar. Then, as the deadline for troop withdrawal neared, Russia offered to negotiate with Japan to divide Manchuria and Korea into Japanese and Russian economic exploitation zones.

Russians resist Japanese pressure to withdraw from Manchuria

Japan, however, sensing that Russia merely meant to stall and keep its troops in Manchuria, secretly prepared for war. On February 8, 1904, in a pre-dawn surprise strike, Japanese torpedo boats devastated the Russian Pacific fleet, based at Port Arthur. Thus began the Russo-Japanese War (1904–1905). Having destroyed Russian sea power in the region, the Japanese landed troops in Korea and Manchuria, where they defeated the Russians in several big land battles. Russia then sent its large Baltic fleet, stationed near Saint Petersburg, on a six-month journey all the way from Europe around Africa to East Asia. But the Japanese navy, with ample time to prepare, ambushed and destroyed the Russian fleet off Japan's southwest coast in May 1905 (Map 29.6).

Japan attacks Russia and wins Russo-Japanese War

In August, American-sponsored peace talks at Portsmouth, New Hampshire, brought the war to an end. The defeated Russians returned Manchuria to China, while Japan gained primary influence in Korea, a leasehold on the Liaodong Peninsula, railway rights in southern Manchuria, and the southern half of Sakhalin (*SAH-kuh-LĒN*) Island (north of Japan). Five years later, Japan formally annexed Korea, transforming it into a colony of the Japanese Empire.

The Russo-Japanese War, although fought only in East Asia, had a profound global impact. Shattering the myth of European superiority, Japan demonstrated that Western ways and weapons could be used to defeat a Western imperial nation. Japan's victory thus gave hope to millions of Asians and Africans who had come under European rule. It also convinced the Japanese that military expansion was a good way to gain access to industrial resources. And it showed them that staging a surprise attack was a good way to fight a great power.

Negotiators at Portsmouth peace talks.

The End of the Chinese Empire

China, meanwhile, was belatedly trying to imitate Japan's modernization. Both to help her regime survive and to relieve the people's poverty, which she had witnessed during the Boxer War as she fled Beijing in a peasant cart, Empress Dowager Cixi at last agreed to allow reforms. From 1901 until 1908 her regime worked to replace the age-old Confucian civil service exams with a new Western-style education system and to create an imperial parliamentary system similar to those in Germany and Japan. After Li Hongzhang died in 1901, she also provided his protégé, the ambitious Yuan Shikai, with the means to modernize China's military forces.

These reforms, designed to save the dynasty, may have hastened its end. Since the time of the Taiping rebellion, when regional leaders were allowed to form their own armies, some had led the "self-strengthening" movement and grown used to acting with considerable autonomy. Now that the regime, with its reforms, seemed to be trying to regain the initiative, regional leaders resisted. Even Yuan Shikai, rather than upgrading the entire Chinese army, focused on expanding and improving the forces directly loyal to him, making him a potential threat to the regime. Thus, after both Cixi and her nephew the emperor died in 1908, the regents of the new emperor, a three-year old boy called Puyi, forced Yuan Shikai to retire.

Chinese Revolution blends anti-Manchu fervor with Western ideologies

By this time a revolutionary movement, aimed at replacing the Qing regime with a parliamentary republic, was gaining support in China. The movement's main spokesman was Sun Yixian (*SUN Ē-shē-AHN*), also known abroad as Sun Yatsen (*YAHT-SEN*) and in China as Sun Zhongshan (*JONG-SHAHN*). A peasant from southern China, he had lived in Hawaii as a youth with his brother, become a Christian, and studied Western medicine in British Hong Kong. Blending anti-Manchu hatred of the "foreign" Qing regime with Western-style liberal and nationalist ideals, he had returned to China to press for political change. But his activism had upset the imperial authorities, and in 1896 he had fled abroad to avoid arrest. For the next 15 years he had traveled the world promoting a democratic Chinese revolution. Then, while in Denver, Colorado, in October 1911, he learned that a rebellion had begun in China.

The revolt started quite by chance. At Wuchang (*WOO-CHAHNG*), a provincial capital in central China (Map 29.7), a group of rebel conspirators were discovered by police after accidentally blowing up their own hideout with a bomb. On October 10, 1911, as the police began to round up the conspirators, those who were not immediately arrested seized a local weapons arsenal, prompting the regional governor to panic and flee. Large-scale riots soon broke out at various places in China, while disaffected regional leaders did little to aid the regime. In December, Sun Yixian returned and declared a Chinese revolutionary republic.

Revolt leads to end of Qing dynasty and creation of Chinese Republic

Meanwhile, in desperation, the young emperor's regents summoned Yuan Shikai from retirement, seeing him as the only one in China with the military skills and experience to restore order. But rather than crushing the rebels, Yuan negotiated with both them and the regents. As a result of these talks, the boy ruler Puyi formally abdicated his throne on February 12, 1912, and in March Yuan Shikai became president of a new Chinese Republic, conceived as a Western-style parliamentary regime. Sun Yixian emerged as the leader of its main political opposition party. China's celestial empire, having dominated East Asia for over two thousand years, thus came to an end.

Chapter Review

Putting It in Perspective

Before 1800, Asian peoples had few direct contacts with the Western world. Commercial connections were limited to places such as Nagasaki in Japan, Guangzhou in China, and various footholds established by the British East India Company in India and its Dutch counterpart in Indonesia. Most Asians were unaware that Westerners existed, and those Asians who did know about them tended to regard them as "barbarians," aliens from inferior cultures who came to Asia seeking to acquire some of the riches of Eastern civilizations.

In the nineteenth century, however, the dynamic changed. The Europeans, empowered by new technologies and weapons, extended their control over India, Indonesia, and much of Southeast Asia, while intruding extensively in China. By the century's end, most of southern Asia and much of eastern Asia had come under the direct or indirect influence of the Western powers. Of the major Asian nations, only Japan and Thailand escaped this fate, and they did so in part by adopting Western ideas and technologies.

Western incursions intensified the internal problems of many Asian societies, helping to subvert their traditional economies and values. China was ravaged by opium addiction, foreign wars, and disastrous internal rebellions. Japan was shaken by civil war and subjected to sweeping social changes. India was rocked by rebellion and transformed by British rule. Southeast Asia was colonized and exploited by France, while Indonesia was similarly exploited by the Dutch. By the early twentieth century, Asians were adapting some of the ways of the West, not only because these ways were imposed by Western imperialists but also because, as the Japanese showed, Asians could adapt Western ways to resist and defeat the West.

Reviewing Key Material

KEY CONCEPTS

Cohong, 730
opium, 730
coolie trade, 732
Taiping Rebellion, 733
sepoys, 737
sati, 737
thagi, 737
zaibatsu, 742
protectorate, 744
Triple Intervention, 748
Trans-Siberian Railway, 748
scramble for concessions, 748
Open Door Policy, 748

KEY PEOPLE

Lin Zexu, 732
Hong Xiuquan, 733
Zeng Guofan, 735
Li Hongzhang, 735
Cixi, 736
Gopal Krishna
   Gokhale, 739
Bal Gangadhar Tilak, 739
Matthew Perry, 740
Yoshida Shoin, 741
Meiji Emperor, 741
Saigo Takamori, 742
Emperors Gia Long and
   Tu Duc, 743, 744
Kings Rama IV and
   Rama V, 745
Cho'e Che-u, 746
Yuan Shikai, 746
Sun Yixian (Sun Yatsen), 752

ASK YOURSELF

1. What factors and events contributed to China's instability from 1796 to 1864? How and why did the Qing dynasty survive?
2. How did India's commercial connections with Britain lead to India's subjugation? How did Indians respond? Why and how did British policies expedite Indian resistance to British rule?
3. What factors account for the fall of the Tokugawa shogunate and the Meiji Restoration in Japan? What factors account for the rise of Japanese imperialism under Meiji rule?
4. How did China and Japan respond to Western intrusions? Why was Japan more successful in its efforts than China? How did Western influence contribute to the end of the Chinese empire?
5. How did people in each key Asian country adapt Western ways and ideas to fit their Asian cultures and to resist or challenge Western influence and control?

GOING FURTHER

Bays, Daniel H. *China Enters the Twentieth Century*. 1978.
Beasley, W. G. *The Meiji Restoration*. 1972.
Bergere, M. C. *Sun Yat-Sen*. 2000.
Bose, Sugata. *The Indian Ocean Rim: An Inter-Regional Arena in the Age of Global Empire*. 2003.

Chang Hsin-pao. *Commissioner Lin and the Opium War.* 1964.

Craig, Albert M. *Choshu in the Meiji Restoration.* 1961.

Curtain, Philip. *The World and the West: European Challenge and Overseas Response in the Age of Empire.* 2000.

Duus, P. *The Rise of Modern Japan. 2nd ed.* 1998.

Ebrey, Patricia B., et al. *East Asia: A Cultural, Social, and Political History.* 2006.

Edwards, Michael. *British India, 1772–1947.* 1968.

Esherick, J. *The Origins of the Boxer Uprising.* 1987.

Fay, Peter Ward. *The Opium War, 1840–1842.* 1975.

Ferguson, N. *Empire: The Rise and Demise of the British World Order.* 2003.

Gillard, David. *The Struggle for Asia, 1828–1914.* 1977.

Hibbert, C. *The Dragon Wakes: China and the West, 1793–1911.* 1970.

Huber, T. *The Revolutionary Origins of Modern Japan.* 1981.

Hunter, J. *The Emergence of Modern Japan.* 1989.

Janson, M. B., ed. *The Emergence of Meiji Japan.* 1995.

Keene, D. *Emperor of Japan: Meiji and His World.* 2000.

Masani, Zareer, ed. *Indian Tales of the Raj.* 1988.

McClain, J. L. *Japan: A Modern History.* 2002.

Michael, Franz H. *The Taiping Rebellion.* 1972.

Polachek, James M. *The Inner Opium War.* 1992.

Preston, D. *The Boxer Rebellion.* 2001.

Reischauer, E. *Japan: The Story of a Nation.* 1981.

Schirokauer, C., and D. N. Clark. *Modern East Asia: A Brief History.* 2004.

Spence, J. D. *God's Chinese Son: The Taiping Heavenly Kingdom of Hong Xiuquan.* 1996.

Spence, J. D. *The Search for Modern China. 2nd ed.* 1999.

Taylor, Jean G. *Indonesia: Peoples and Histories.* 2003.

Têng, S. Y. *The Taiping Rebellion and the Western Powers.* 1971.

Totman, C. *The Collapse of the Tokugawa Bakufu, 1862–1868.* 1980.

Wakemann, F., Jr. *The Fall of Imperial China.* 1975.

Waley, Arthur. *The Opium War Through Chinese Eyes.* 1968.

Wild, A. *East India Company.* 2000.

Wilson, George M. *Patriots and Redeemers in Japan.* 1992.

Wolpert, S. *A New History of India. 5th ed.* 1997.

Key Dates and Developments

Date	Event	Date	Event
1771–1802	Tay-Son Rebellion in Vietnam	1877	Samurai Rebellion in Japan
1793	Macartney mission to China	1883–1885	Franco-Chinese War over Vietnam
1799	Dissolution of Dutch United East India Company	1885	Formation of the Indian National Congress
1839–1842	First Opium War	1889	Japanese Constitution
1850–1864	Taiping Rebellion in China	1894–1895	Sino-Japanese War and Triple Intervention
1853–1854	Perry's visits to Japan	1896–1899	Scramble for concessions in China
1856–1860	Second Opium War	1899–1900	Open Door Policy
1857–1858	Indian Revolt	1900	Boxer Uprising in China
1859	French occupation of southern Vietnam	1902	Anglo-Japanese alliance
1860–1864	Tonghak Revolt in Korea	1904–1905	Russo-Japanese War
1868	Meiji Restoration in Japan	1911–1912	Chinese Revolution: End of Chinese Empire
1876	Britain's Queen Victoria declared Empress of India		

The Transformation of West Asia and Africa, 1800–1914

- Changing Patterns in West Asia and North Africa

- Changing Patterns in Sub-Saharan Africa

- The Age of Imperialism in Africa

- The Impact of Empire on Africa

- Chapter Review

The Opening Of The Suez Canal

In the nineteenth century, as reflected in this image of the ceremonial opening of the Suez Canal in 1869, new global commercial and imperial connections contributed to the transformation of West Asia and Africa.

In 1819 the Zulu, a small southeast African clan, fought a ferocious two-day battle against a neighboring clan. Outnumbered nearly two-to-one, the Zulu emerged victorious, using new tactics devised by Shaka (*SHAH-kuh*), their innovative young ruler. Rather than throwing long spears from a distance, a traditional tactic typically producing few casualties, the Zulu attacked with short stabbing spears at close range, systematically slaughtering their enemies. Under Shaka the Zulu would create a mighty empire, defeating all who resisted their expansion.

Africa and West Asia

Six decades later Shaka's nephew, Zulu king Cetshwayo (*kech-WAH-yō*), fought a war against outsiders from Britain. At first the Zulu did well, killing more than a thousand British soldiers in one 1879 battle. But later that year the British attacked Cetshwayo's capital, Ulundi. The Zulu, with 15 thousand warriors, had a three-to-one edge, but the British had an even bigger advantage: a dozen artillery pieces, and several Gatling machine guns, capable of firing three thousand rounds per minute. The Zulu fought bravely, but could not get close to the British, who used their deadly weapons to mow down their foes from 75 yards away. The British then burned the Zulu capital, leaving behind a field of corpses to mark the bloody Battle of Ulundi.

These two conflicts reflect dramatic changes that occurred in Africa and West Asia during the nineteenth century. At the century's outset, connections and conflicts in these regions typically fit long-established patterns. Most of North Africa and West Asia belonged to the Ottoman Empire, a multinational realm created several centuries earlier. Much of sub-Saharan Africa was organized into clans led by local chiefs, sometimes dominated by a regional kingdom. Along the coasts were seaports, trading towns that conducted commerce in gold, ivory, and other commodities, as well as in African slaves.

During the nineteenth century, however, the slave trade was suppressed and replaced by new commercial enterprises. Several new regional powers, including the Zulu, also emerged early in the century. But the biggest changes came toward the century's end, when European powers, driven by new industries and ideologies (Chapter 27), carved up Africa among them, using new weapons against which neither Ottomans nor Africans initially had much defense. By the early 1900s, the Ottoman Empire was a shrunken remnant of a once-great realm, while most of Africa had been divided into European colonies. As a result, the economic, social, cultural, and political patterns that had long existed in these regions were substantially transformed.

Changing Patterns in West Asia and North Africa

Since the seventh century, West Asia and North Africa had been linked religiously and culturally by Islam. To Muslims, in fact, North Africa was the **Maghrib** (*MUH-grib*), Arabic for "the West," since it was the western part of the Islamic world. And to Muslims

West Asia, which (along with Egypt) was known in Europe as the Near East—now widely called the **Middle East**—was the center of Islamic civilization.

Since the early 1500s, most of West Asia and North Africa had also been linked politically by the vast empire of the Ottoman Turks (Map 30.1). From their capital at Constantinople, which the Turks also called Istanbul, Ottoman sultans had ruled their multinational realm with a blend of pragmatism, flexibility, and toleration (Chapter 17). Straddling parts of Europe, Asia, and Africa, and sitting astride the trade routes connecting the three continents, the Ottoman Empire long had been one of the world's largest, wealthiest, and mightiest realms.

By the late 1700s, however, the once-mighty Ottomans had fallen on hard times, as Russia repeatedly defeated them and took away chunks of territory. Lagging behind Europe militarily and industrially, in the 1800s the Ottomans tried to reform their realm but failed to halt its disintegration. North Africa gained freedom from Ottoman dominion, only to come increasingly under European rule.

Scene from Russian-Turkish conflict, 1787.

Reform and Rebellion in the Ottoman Empire

In the late 1700s, seeking to reverse his realm's decline, Sultan Selim (*seh-LĒM*) III, reigning from 1789 to 1807, initiated reforms designed to centralize his administration and modernize his military. In 1798–1799, however, his armies were unable to stop the occupation of Egypt by French forces under Napoleon Bonaparte. Although the French troops were withdrawn to fight elsewhere in 1801, and Egypt thus nominally returned to Ottoman sway, the sultans regained no real control of the region.

In 1805, impressed with the success of Napoleon's French armies, Selim ordered a restructuring of Ottoman forces. This reorganization, however, threatened the privileged status of the Janissaries, the elite slave soldiers who had long formed the premier corps of the Ottoman army, and they responded with a fierce rebellion in Ottoman southeast Europe. Selim survived this mutiny, in part by retracting his reforms. But in 1807 another armed revolt resulted in his imprisonment and eventual strangulation.

French occupation of Egypt spurs Ottoman reform efforts

The empire's troubles continued under Selim's cousin, Sultan Mahmud (*mah-MOOD*) II, who reigned from 1808 to 1839. Defeat by Russia in 1812 cost the Ottomans more land in southeast Europe and strengthened Russian influence there. Buoyed by the success of the Russians, with whom they shared a common Christian Orthodox faith, the Greeks rebelled against the sultan in 1821. Although at first contained by Ottoman forces, the rebellious Greeks eventually gained independence with help from the Russians, who once again defeated the Ottomans in 1828–1829 (Chapter 26).

Russians help Greeks gain independence from Turks

Faced with his realm's disintegration, Mahmud initiated a new set of reforms. In 1826 he began a comprehensive military reorganization, which once again prompted a Janissary rebellion. This time, however, the regime rose to the challenge: Mahmud waged war against the Janissaries, and when they refused to submit he had cannons fired repeatedly into their barracks, massacring them by the thousands. He then abolished the Janissary corps and began developing a new army trained in European techniques, equipped with modern firearms, and based on mass conscription like armies in the West. Mahmud also brought law and education under state control, thus undermining the influence of the ulama (*oo-lah-MAH*), the learned religious leaders, steeped in Islamic law, who traditionally dominated law and education in most Muslim countries.

FOUNDATION MAP 30.1 Africa and West Asia Around 1800

In the early 1800s, as in the previous three centuries, the Ottoman Empire connected West Asia and North Africa. Note, however, that no such empire connected sub-Saharan Africa, which instead encompassed various small African states, a number of coastal seaports, and numerous stateless societies, with people living in farming villages organized into clans ruled by local chiefs. What commercial connections linked parts of Africa into the global economy?

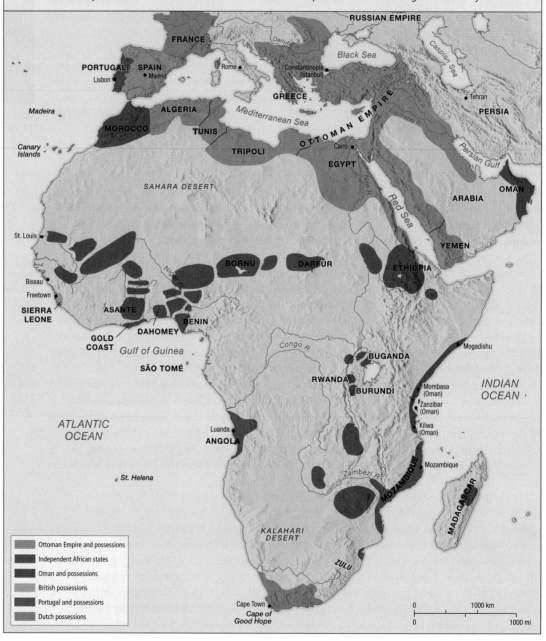

Legend:
- Ottoman Empire and possessions
- Independent African states
- Oman and possessions
- British possessions
- Portugal and possessions
- Dutch possessions

The Tanzimat and the Young Turks

Mahmud's successors followed with the **Tanzimat** (*tahn-zē-MAHT*), or "reorganization," a sweeping set of reforms, enacted from 1839 to 1876, designed to modernize and Westernize the Ottoman Empire (see "Excerpts from the Tanzimat Rescripts"). An admirer of Britain and France, Grand Vizier (chief minister) Mustafa Reshid (*reh-SHED*)—awarded the honorary title pasha (*pah-SHAH*) and hence called Reshid Pasha—avidly promoted the reforms. They established regional representative assemblies, a secular school system, a more equitable tax structure, and a new set of laws modeled in part on France's Napoleonic Code. The Tanzimat also included a further restructuring of the military and a promise of equal rights for all men in the empire, including its non-Muslims (mostly Christians and Jews). Although the reforms applied mainly to men, the new liberal atmosphere they fostered allowed the formation of several schools for women and increased participation by women in literature, art, and society.

Tanzimat reforms adapt Western ideas to Ottoman society

The Tanzimat, enforced by a new system of state law courts rather than the ulama, enraged the Islamic elite by ending its traditional control of law and education. But the reforms impressed the British and French, who began to see the Ottomans as increasingly enlightened and liberal, and thus worthy of protection against reactionary Russia. In 1854–1856, Britain and France joined with the Turks to defeat the Russians in the Crimean War (Chapter 27).

The Tanzimat culminated in 1876 with the proclamation of a liberal constitution by Sultan Abdulhamid (*ahb-dul-hah-MED*) II (1876–1909), followed the next year by the summoning of a Turkish Parliament. Within a few years, however, unwilling to accept the limitations these institutions placed on his authority, Abdulhamid shut down the parliament and suspended the constitution. Increasingly despotic, he then ruled with an iron fist, imposing strict censorship and employing a system of secret police to repress dissent.

Discontent nonetheless continued to grow. Defeat in another war with Russia (1877–1878) humiliated the Ottomans and cost them control of more lands in southeast Europe (Map 30.2). Influenced by liberal and nationalist ideals, some Turkish college students plotted against the sultan in 1889. Then, when their plot was discovered, they fled to Paris and started preparing a new revolution. These youthful reformist rebels, later called **Young Turks**, collaborated with dissident Ottoman army officers to rebel in 1908, forcing Abdulhamid to restore the constitution and parliament. The next year they deposed him in favor of his mild-mannered brother, who as Sultan Mehmet V (1909–1918) basically let the Young Turks run the show. They fostered industrialization and promoted Turkish nationalism, hoping to emulate the West's power and wealth by adapting its industries and ideologies. But they also joined with Germany in the Great War, a disastrous decision that led to the end of the Ottoman Empire.

The Transformation of Egypt

Meanwhile, the Ottoman decline had enabled ambitious North African leaders, still under Ottoman control, to assert autonomy. Chief among these was Muhammad Ali, a former soldier in the Ottoman army sent to resist Napoleon's invasion of Egypt in 1798–1799. In a chaotic power struggle following France's 1801 withdrawal, Muhammad Ali rose to prominence, and in 1805 was appointed Ottoman viceroy in Egypt. From then until 1848

Document 30.1 Excerpts from the Tanzimat Rescripts

The Tanzimat, a reform designed to modernize and strengthen the Ottoman Empire in the mid-nineteenth century, was embodied in several rescripts issued by the Ottoman sultans. They aimed to establish more equitable systems of law, taxation, education, and military service, and to guarantee the rights and security of all Ottoman subjects, without regard to race, language, class, or religion.

THE RESCRIPT OF GÜLHANE (3 NOVEMBER 1839) All the world knows that in the first days of the Ottoman monarchy, the glorious precepts of the Kuran and the laws of the empire were always honored. The empire in consequence increased in strength and greatness . . . In the last one hundred and fifty years a succession of accidents and . . . causes have arisen which have brought about a disregard for the sacred code of laws . . . , and the former strength and prosperity have changed into weakness and poverty; an empire in fact loses all its stability so soon as it ceases to observe its laws . . .

Full of confidence, therefore, in the help of the Most High, and certain of the support of our Prophet, we deem it right to seek by new institutions to give to the provinces composing the Ottoman Empire the benefit of a good administration.

These institutions must be principally carried out under three heads, which are:

1. The guarantees insuring to our subjects perfect security for life, honor, and fortune.
2. A regular system of assessing and levying taxes.
3. An equally regular system for the levying of troops and the duration of their service . . .

From henceforth . . . the cause of every accused person shall be publicly judged . . . , and so long as a regular judgment shall not have been pronounced, no one can secretly or publicly put another to death . . .

Each one shall possess his property of every kind, and shall dispose of it in all freedom . . . These imperial concessions shall extend to all our subjects, of whatever religion or sect they may be; they shall enjoy them without exception . . .

RESCRIPT OF REFORM (18 FEBRUARY 1856) The guarantees promised on our part by the [Rescript] of Gülhane, and in conformity with the Tanzimat, to all the subjects of my Empire, without distinction of classes or of religion, for the security of their persons and property and the preservation of their honour, are today confirmed and consolidated . . .

Every distinction or designation tending to make any class whatever of the subjects of my Empire inferior to another class, on account of their religion, language, or race, shall be for ever effaced . . .

As all forms of religion are and shall be freely professed in my dominions, no subject of my Empire shall be hindered in the exercise of the religion that he professes . . .

. . . All the subjects of my Empire, without distinction of nationality, shall be admissible to public employments, and qualified to fill them according to their capacity and merit . . .

All the subjects of my Empire, without distinction, shall be received into the Civil and Military Schools of the Government if they otherwise satisfy the conditions as to age and examination . . .

Steps shall also be taken for the formation of roads and canals to increase the facilities of communication and increase the sources of the wealth of the country. Everything that can impede commerce or agriculture shall be abolished.

SOURCE: Boğaziçi University, Atatürk Institute of Modern Turkish History (http://www.ata.boun.edu.tr/) (translator unknown) http://coursesa.matrix.msu.edu/~fisher/hst373/Gulhane.html

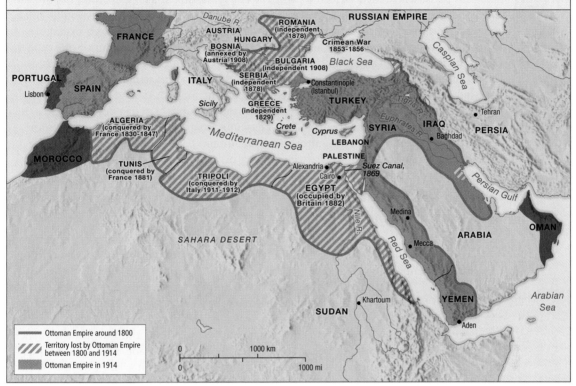

Map 30.2 The Diminishing Ottoman Empire, 1800–1914

Although declining in power and prestige, in 1800 the Ottoman Empire was still an extensive realm, encompassing a wide variety of cultures in southeast Europe, West Asia, and North Africa. Observe, however, that by 1914 it was confined mostly to West Asia, having lost control of North Africa and most of southeast Europe. What factors and developments helped set the stage for Ottoman decline?

he was effectively Egypt's ruler, transforming its economy, building a powerful military, and starting a dynasty that would reign until the 1950s.

Moving to assert his authority, Muhammad Ali disposed of all potential opposition. He massacred the Mamluks, the class of slave soldiers who had served for centuries as Egypt's ruling elite, and brutally repressed several peasant revolts. He also dispossessed the old landowners, converting their estates into state property and making himself the country's main landlord.

Muhammad Ali then proceeded to transform Egypt's agriculture and commerce. He compelled the peasants to give up subsistence farming, in which they produced mainly food for their own consumption, and instead to grow **cash crops**, commodities that when harvested could be sold for money to purchase food and other things they needed. The most valuable cash crop was cotton, which grew very well in the Nile River valley and produced healthy profits for the regime when sold to industrial Europe. Muhammad Ali then used these profits to create a modern army and navy, to start a Western-style public school system, and to begin to industrialize Egypt by building factories and textile mills.

By the 1830s, as a result, Muhammad Ali had amassed greater wealth and power than his overlord, the Ottoman sultan. Eager to assert his new military might, the Egyptian leader fought two wars against the Ottomans. In the first conflict (1831–1833), his (possibly adopted) son Ibrahim (*ib-rah-HĒM*) Pasha seized much of Syria and then governed it for most of the decade. In the second war (1838–1841), Ibrahim's forces again defeated the Ottomans, whose fleet defected to Egypt's navy. It looked as if Egypt might gain full independence. But the European powers, fearful that a powerful new Egypt would replace the weak Ottomans astride the east-west trade routes that brought vital goods and resources to Europe, intervened. They forced Muhammad Ali to end Ibrahim's rule in Syria and to continue Egypt's nominal submission to the Ottoman sultan.

In economic affairs, Europeans also thwarted Egypt's industrialization. To protect their industrial preeminence, the British compelled Muhammad Ali to remove the protective tariffs he had placed on imports of Western industrial goods. Egypt's new industries then could not compete with inexpensive European imports that flooded local markets and undercut local producers. Thus, although Muhammad Ali did much to modernize Egypt, quintupling its commerce and vastly enhancing his own wealth, he was stymied in his efforts to transform his country into an independent industrial power.

Commerce and culture in Cairo, Egypt, in the 1800s.

The Suez Canal and Its Impact

Muhammad Ali's grandson, Abbas Hilmy (*ah-BAHSS HILL-mē*) I, viceroy in Egypt from 1848 to 1854, was a conservative Muslim who sought to undo his grandfather's reforms. Distrusting Europeans and resenting their influence in Egypt, he closed the Western-style schools and factories started by Muhammad Ali, and even opposed a French plan to construct one of the century's great engineering marvels: a canal for sea-going ships across the Isthmus of Suez.

Eager to gain a greater share of the commerce between Asia and Europe, the French had long dreamed of building a canal to shorten the east-west trade routes, over which traveled such valuable items as spices, tea, and cotton. The all-water route around Africa, pioneered in the late 1400s by the Portuguese, not only was long and treacherous but also had come to be dominated by the Dutch and British. Having occupied Egypt in 1798–1799, Napoleon Bonaparte explored the possibility of building a Suez Canal. But at the time the task seemed too daunting, given the region's hot, arid climate and the need to conscript tens of thousands of laborers, working with picks and shovels, to dig a trench roughly thirty feet deep, two hundred feet wide, and one hundred miles long.

The development of steam-powered excavators and dredgers during Europe's Industrial Revolution, however, made a canal project possible by the time of Sa'id Pasha (*sah-ĒD pah-SHAH*), a French-educated, pro-Western Egyptian leader who replaced Abbas Hilmy and reigned from 1854 to 1863. Construction was begun in 1859 by the Suez Canal Company, organized under the leadership of Ferdinand de Lesseps (*duh LESS-ups*), a former diplomat who had been France's consul in Egypt in the 1830s. Beset by labor problems and a cholera epidemic, the project took ten years.

The delays, however, did not dampen the excitement in Egypt on November 17, 1869, when the Suez Canal was officially opened (see page 755). A grand ceremony, presided over by Sa'id's successor Ismail (*iss-MAH-ēl*) and French Empress Eugenie (*oo-zhā-NĒ*), and witnessed by dignitaries from Africa, Asia, and Europe, featured a parade of steam

Industrial advances facilitate construction of Suez Canal

Suez Canal enhances connections between East and West

and sailing ships moving through the wonderful new waterway. The canal cut travel time from Europe to Asia in half, from more than a month to less than two weeks, substantially lowering east-west shipping costs and bolstering global commerce and industry. It also seemed to promise a flourishing future for Egypt, which owned 44 percent of the Suez Canal Company shares. But only six years later, his regime deep in debt, Ismail sold these shares to the British—a disaster for Egypt that within a decade would subvert its long-held hopes for independence (see "Global Trade and the Occupation of Egypt," below).

The Suez canal.

The Origins of Arab Nationalism in West Asia

Northeast of Egypt, the Muslim lands of Palestine, Lebanon, Syria, and Iraq, as well as parts of Arabia, had likewise long been provinces of the Ottoman Empire. In the nineteenth century, however, the Arab peoples of these regions gradually grew restive under Turkish rule. Inspired by Egypt's resurgence, influenced by Western connections, and troubled by Turkish reforms, some of these Arabs began to dream of self-rule, sowing seeds of Arab nationalism that would sprout in the twentieth century.

Egypt was both an example and impetus for Arab nationalism in West Asia. As an Arab country that had begun to modernize and assert its autonomy, Egypt provided a model of what other Arab lands could hope to accomplish. Moreover, by conquering and ruling Lebanon and Syria in the 1830s, Egypt connected them through its commerce with the industrial West. Western links were strengthened several decades later by Lebanon's Maronite Christians, members of an ancient Lebanese church affiliated with Roman Catholicism, who worked with Western educators to establish schools in Lebanon, including a French Jesuit college. By the century's end, such connections had helped to expose many Arabs to Western notions of nationalism and liberalism, and some had started to agitate against Turkish control.

Enhanced connections with the West promote Arab nationalism

Meanwhile the Turkish Tanzimat, by strengthening Ottoman administration and granting legal equality to non-Muslims, was producing an anti-Turkish reaction among other Arabs. Fearful of being engulfed by Ottoman Westernization and secularization, some Arab Muslims started pushing for political autonomy, and eventually for full independence from Ottoman rule.

Ottoman reforms provoke anti-Turkish Arab nationalism

The Plight of the Maghrib

West of Egypt, the Maghrib encompassed four North African Muslim countries, sometimes collectively called the Barbary States (possibly because Berbers were their original ethnicity). In the early 1800s, three of them—Tripoli (today part of Libya), Tunis, and Algeria—were autonomous provinces of the Ottoman Empire (Map 30.2), recognizing its sultan as overlord but running their own affairs. Only Morocco, on Africa's northwest coast, was fully independent, an Islamic kingdom with a dynasty dating from the 1600s. Like Egypt, these countries hoped to benefit from the Ottoman decline; like Egypt, these countries found their hopes thwarted by outside interference.

The Barbary States provoked this interference by profiting from piracy. For centuries the notorious Barbary pirates had preyed on Mediterranean shipping, and their rulers collected tribute from countries trying to buy immunity from piracy. But in 1801 the ruler of Tripoli, incensed that the upstart Americans refused his demands for higher tribute,

United States and Britain suppress North African piracy

declared war on the United States. The Americans won the Tripolitan War (1801–1805), ending Tripoli's tribute system. Ongoing efforts by the British and American navies, culminating in British bombardment of Algeria in 1816, terminated the tribute extortions of the other North African states.

Although diminished by such efforts, piracy persisted, giving France a pretext for invading Algeria. In 1827 Algeria's ruler, angered by unpaid French debts, supplied another pretext when he smacked the French consul with a fly swatter. The French regime of Charles X, eager to employ the many jobless veterans of the Napoleonic Wars and hoping for a quick victory to revive its flagging fortunes, invaded Algeria in July of 1830—three weeks before Charles himself was deposed by France's July Revolution (Chapter 26).

Algerians valiantly resist French takeover, but fail

The French soon conquered northern Algeria, but their hopes for quick victory were dashed by Abdelqadir al-Jazairi (*ab-dul-KAH-dur al-jah-ZAH-ih-rē*), a young Algerian leader who took charge in 1832. He created a new state in the interior, rallying his people in a spirited resistance that forced France for a time to make concessions. The French, however, eventually launched a massive assault, devastating Algeria and compelling Abdelqadir to surrender in 1846. Highly respected nonetheless by friend and foe alike, he came to be known as the "father of modern Algeria."

France's conquest of Algeria marked the beginning of the end of North African autonomy. In 1835, taking advantage of the turmoil, the Ottoman sultan sent forces to reoccupy Tripoli, henceforth subjecting it to direct Ottoman rule. Tunis survived as an autonomous Ottoman province, and Morocco as an independent state, until they were engulfed by a series of changes that affected the whole continent, including Africa south of the Sahara Desert.

Changing Patterns in Sub-Saharan Africa

At the start of the nineteenth century, several economic and political patterns prevailed south of the Sahara. Along the coastlines and the desert's southern edge were urban centers and independent kingdoms, many of which were involved in trading slaves and commercial goods. In the interior, most Africans lived by farming and herding, typically in agrarian villages governed by village elders and clan chiefs. Then some patterns started changing. The slave trade was outlawed, resulting in efforts to replace it with new economic enterprises, as well as in efforts to continue it illegally by procuring captives from East Africa. These commercial changes coincided with the rise of some new regional states, altering Africa's political landscape.

The Banning of the Slave Trade

From the sixteenth through eighteenth centuries, the western coastal regions of Africa, and the nearby interiors, were ravaged by the Atlantic slave trade (Chapter 23). Millions of Africans, mostly men and boys, were shipped overseas, robbing these regions of labor and talent, upsetting the gender balance, and wreaking havoc on family and economic structures. Some Africans nonetheless gained power and wealth by selling slaves to Europeans, often in return for firearms, which were then used to conquer other Africans and acquire more captives.

By 1800, however, a growing international movement sought to outlaw the slave trade and eventually end slavery itself. Haiti's successful slave rebellion in the 1790s, along with numerous failed slave revolts, terrified slave owners and highlighted the dangers of their enterprise. The European Enlightenment, culminating in the American and French revolutions, had promoted notions of liberty and equality that hardly harmonized with human bondage. Increasing numbers of Christian missionaries and anti-slave abolitionists had also begun condemning slavery and the slave trade as appalling moral evils.

Global antislavery movement arises by 1800

Among the most compelling early abolitionists was Olaudah Equiano (ō-*LOUD-ah ek-wē-AH-nō*), a former slave who claimed to have been kidnapped from West Africa at age 11, shipped across the Atlantic to the West Indies, then sold to a Virginia plantation owner and later to an English sea captain. After gaining some education and purchasing his freedom, he eventually wrote his memoirs, publishing them in England in 1789. Although historical research has cast doubt on his African origins, his personal account of the evils of slavery was convincing to many of his contemporaries. His book sold widely in Europe and America, strengthening the anti-slavery movement, ably led in Britain by William Wilberforce, a devout Christian member of parliament.

Equiano memoir spreads anti-slavery sentiment

Olaudah Equiano.

Meanwhile, Britain's industrial revolution was producing new machines run by moving water or steam, reducing demand for human muscle, and was showing that paid workers using machines were far more productive than slaves. Industrialists, moreover, were coming to see Africa mainly as a source of raw materials rather than forced labor. Slavery was coming to be seen as neither morally defensible nor economically efficient.

In 1803, responding to such perceptions, Denmark outlawed the slave trade, followed in 1807 by Great Britain. They were joined in 1808 by the United States, and during the next decade by Sweden, France, and the Netherlands. After 1815, British ships, with help from Americans and others, patrolled the West African coast, stopping slave ships, arresting slave traders, and freeing their human captives. These efforts did not end slavery: owning slaves was still legal in the Americas, millions of slaves were already there, and Spain and Portugal permitted legal slave trade until the 1840s. But the efforts to end commerce in human captives did help to transform African economic patterns.

New Economic Patterns

One result of the banning of the slave trade was the development of new commercial activities to replace it. Eager to continue trade with Europe for textiles, tobacco, alcohol, and guns, enterprising Africans soon provided products to fill the slave trade's void. Some of these products, such as gold and ivory, had for centuries been part of African commerce. Production of these items, and of commodities such as coconuts and cloves, increased with the slave trade's decline.

Meanwhile, Europe's industrial revolution was giving other items a new commercial significance. One was raw cotton, grown in Egypt and East Africa to help supply Europe's booming textile mills. Another was gum arabic, a substance extracted from certain West African trees, which was used to make glues and dyes for these textile mills. A third was palm oil, a thick, greasy fluid used in making candles and soaps. As it also became the leading lubricant for Europe's industrial machines, it emerged as one of West Africa's main commercial exports, until it was replaced by petroleum in the twentieth century.

Supplying products for industry strengthens slavery within Africa

Ironically, however, cotton and cloves were grown on slave plantations, while gum arabic and palm oil production also involved slave labor. Male slaves, for example, were given the difficult and dangerous work of climbing lofty palm trees, cutting down heavy palm nuts, and then, after female slaves had extracted the oil by pummeling the palm nuts, conveying the bulky liquid downstream using huge log dugout canoes. Paradoxically, then, the banning of the overseas slave trade helped strengthen slavery within Africa.

Another ironic outcome of the slave trade's prohibition was the fact that it resulted, not in an immediate end of the outlawed commerce, but rather in its relocation from West to East Africa. To avoid the British and American ships patrolling the Atlantic coast, many slave traders transferred their activities to Africa's eastern shores, where coastal city-states had long conducted lucrative slave commerce with countries around the Indian Ocean and Arabian Sea. East African slave merchants were happy to add to their business by selling captive Africans to traders bound for the Americas, where slavery was still practiced even though the slave trade was illegal.

Captives freed from a slave ship, East Africa, 1884.

The Atlantic slave trade thus persisted for decades after it was banned. In fact, by decreasing the supply of slaves on the market and making their transport more dangerous, the ban on the slave trade helped to increase the market value of slaves. Traders willing to take the risk could therefore buy slaves in East Africa, transport them to the Americas, and reap a huge profit if they avoided detection. Between 1800 and 1870, despite ongoing efforts to suppress the slave trade, at least a million more captives were shipped from Africa to the Americas—an average of over a thousand per month during these seven decades.

Indeed, as long as slavery itself was legal, there was a demand for slaves and thus profit in illegal slave trade. Slavery was outlawed in 1833 in all British possessions, and 15 years later in French colonies, but it was legally practiced in the United States until 1865, in Cuba until 1886, and in Brazil until 1888. Only when slavery itself was banned did the demand decline, eventually curtailing the commerce that brought misery to many million Africans.

The Rise of New Regional States

Changing trade patterns were accompanied by the rise of various new regional states (Map 30.3). In West Africa, an extensive new Islamic domain called the Sokoto (*sō-KŌ-tō*) Caliphate arose in the interior, while several new settlements for returning former slaves were established on the Atlantic coast. In East Africa, the island municipality of Zanzibar emerged as the center of a huge trading empire, and several smaller commercial realms developed farther inland. In South Africa, the new Zulu Kingdom created by Shaka, described at the start of this chapter, was challenged by the rise of other new states, including some formed by intruders of European ancestry.

West Africans historically blend Islam with local faiths

THE SOKOTO CALIPHATE. West Africa's most dynamic new state arose from a movement to strengthen and purify Islam as practiced in that region. For centuries Islam had flourished among the ruling classes and educated people who lived in West African cities, but in rural areas the farmers and herders often retained their age-old polytheistic beliefs. Muslim rulers long had tolerated these traditional religions, partly because they were thoroughly entrenched and partly because they enhanced these rulers' power by portraying them as

Map 30.3 Africa in the Mid-Nineteenth Century

From the 1820s through the 1870s, Africa experienced numerous changes. Notice that a number of new states emerged, including the Fulani and Tukulor Empires and Republic of Liberia in West Africa, and the Zulu Kingdom and Boer Republics in southeastern Africa. Note also that, although Britain and other powers banned the slave trade early in the 1800s, it was still conducted through mid-century by Portugal, Spain, Zanzibar, and various illegal traffickers. What factors contributed to the emergence of new African states? Why did the slave trade continue to operate even though it had been banned?

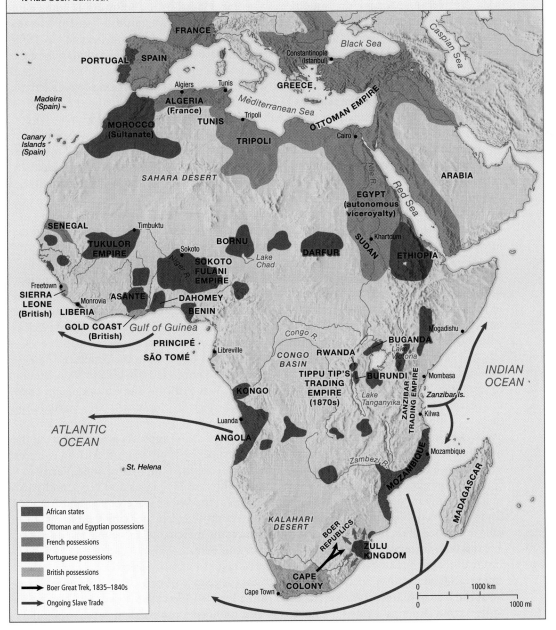

Legend:
- African states
- Ottoman and Egyptian possessions
- French possessions
- Portuguese possessions
- British possessions
- → Boer Great Trek, 1835–1840s
- → Ongoing Slave Trade

0 1000 km
0 1000 mi

semi-divine (Chapter 13). As a result, religious practice in West Africa often blended local customs and traditional beliefs with superficial allegiance to Islam.

In the 1700s, however, the **Fulani** (*FOO-LAH-nē*), a pastoral people from West Africa's grasslands, were attracted to Sufism—perhaps because this form of Islamic mysticism (Chapter 12) provided a communal spirituality and elaborate ritual that adapted well to their rural lifestyle. By 1800 Usman dan Fodio (*oos-MAHN dahn fō-DĒ-ō*), a charismatic Fulani mystic, had clashed with local rulers, whom he accused of betraying Islam by tolerating "paganism" among their people. Hailed by his followers as both caliph (successor to the prophet Muhammad) and "commander of the faithful," in 1804 he declared a "jihad of the sword," a holy war to defend Islam against "unbelievers." In 1809, after Usman's inspired armies had won a series of battles, the caliph's headquarters were established at a new town called Sokoto.

Thus was born the Sokoto Caliphate, which presided over a domain often called the Fulani Empire, for a time the region's largest state and—next to Brazil and the United States—one of the world's largest slaveholding societies. After Usman died in 1817 his son, Muhammad Bello, continued to expand the realm for the next few decades, extending its sway over local rulers while granting them considerable autonomy. Schools and mosques were built to reinforce Islam, while the old rural religions were rigorously suppressed. The caliphate lasted almost a century, successfully resisting outside intrusions, before finally coming under British control in the early 1900s.

Sokoto's success inspired the formation of other "jihad states" in West Africa, the largest of which, called the Tukulor Empire, arose in the 1850s. Racked by revolts, it disintegrated in the 1880s and fell to the French soon thereafter.

LIBERATED SLAVE STATES AND AMERICAN CONNECTIONS. In coastal West Africa, the banning of the slave trade led to the creation of several new homelands for liberated slaves. Some of their citizens were captives freed from slave ships intercepted in transit by European navies enforcing the ban on the slave trade. Others were former slaves from the Americas who moved back to Africa, contributing to transatlantic cultural connections.

In 1787, British abolitionists, along with liberated slaves from the Americas, had founded a settlement they named Freetown in Sierra Leone (*sē-AIR-uh lē-ōN*), a site that for centuries had been an outpost for trade between West Africans and Europeans. In 1808, the year after Britain's Parliament prohibited the slave trade, the British navy started using the site as a base from which to combat this commerce, and as a destination for African captives that British sailors liberated from intercepted slave ships. As a result, during the next half-century, perhaps 100 thousand **recaptives**, people from various African cultures who had been freed from slave trading vessels, were resettled in Sierra Leone. Partly to create a community out of people with so many different languages and ways, and partly to increase the influence of English culture in Africa, the British government and Anglican Church worked diligently to transform recaptives into English-speaking Christians. In time a number of them and their descendants became merchants, missionaries, doctors, and lawyers, forming a Europeanized West African elite.

A different sort of experiment began in 1821, just south of Sierra Leone, when the American Colonization Society, established several years earlier to bring liberated slaves from the United States to Africa, acquired some land on West Africa's coast. The first settlers from America arrived the next year and founded a town called Monrovia (after

Margin notes:

Fulani launch a "holy war" to purify West African Islam

Fulani cavalry uniform.

Freed slaves in Sierra Leone blend African and European ways

Freed slaves in Liberia bring American ideals to Africa

U.S. President James Monroe), which in time became the capital of a new nation called Liberia. After being governed for several decades by the American Colonization Society, and battling with African neighbors who profited from slavery and the slave trade, Liberia proclaimed independence in 1847, with a constitution modeled on that of the United States. The American connection was also personified by Liberia's first president, Joseph Jenkins Roberts, a free-born black American from Virginia.

As nations throughout the Americas abolished slavery during the nineteenth century (Chapter 28), freed slaves also settled elsewhere on Africa's coast. At a French fort and Catholic mission on the Gulf of Guinea, for example, a freed slave settlement was formed in 1849 at a place called Libreville (*LĒ-bruh-vill*)—the French equivalent of Freetown— that was influenced by French culture and Catholicism. Liberated slaves from Latin America also came back to Africa in chartered ships, bringing Latin American styles and cultural values. As a result of these resettlements, coastal West African cities exhibited elements of Western culture, including European languages, Christian religions, and fashions in architecture and dress transplanted from the Americas.

French and Latin American freed slaves blend African and Western ways

African-American cultural connections worked in both directions. Although thousands of former slaves returned to Africa, most of those born in the Americas stayed there. They became an influential **African diaspora**: descendants of transplanted Africans who enriched American societies with features from their African cultures. They infused American Christianity, for example, with elements of African spirituality, such as spirited worship, exuberant music, and visions of heaven as a place for reunion with departed loved ones. Popular Latin dances, such as mambo and conga, arose out of African roots. And striking new forms of music, including especially jazz, combined African rhythms with European harmonies and instrumentation.

African diaspora blends African and American cultures

THE ZANZIBAR COMMERCIAL EMPIRE. As slave trading shifted from Africa's western shores to its eastern coast, the East African island of Zanzibar emerged as the center of this traffic. About twenty miles off east central Africa's coast, Zanzibar had been established as a trading post in the late 1600s by Arabs from the Persian Gulf sultanate of Oman. Under the energetic rule of Sa'id ibn Sultan (*sah-ĒD ib'n sool-TAHN*), also called Sa'id Sayyid (*sah-ĒD SĪ-yid*), who reigned from 1806 to 1856, Zanzibar grew into a powerful commercial empire that controlled a number of coastal cities and parts of the interior. So wealthy did it become, in fact, that Sa'id Sayyid moved his headquarters from Oman to Zanzibar in 1828.

Zanzibar commerce connects and exploits much of East Africa

Zanzibar's empire was built on commerce interconnected with slavery. The island's main exports were slaves, captured in the African interior by warriors; cloves and co- conuts, produced on slave plantations; and ivory, from elephant and rhinoceros tusks carried from inner Africa by caravans of slaves. Eventually, under British pressure, the sultan restricted East Africa's coastal slave trade, which was formally suppressed in 1857. The use and sale of slaves in the East African interior, however, continued into the 1870s.

In the interior, enterprising merchants also formed personal empires based on the Zanzibar trade. Most famous was Tippu Tip, a part-Arab, part-African entrepreneur who used European guns to control and exploit the upper Congo River basin in the mid-1800s. He gained great wealth but disrupted the whole region, killing much of its wildlife in his relentless hunt for ivory. Northwest of Lake Victoria, in what is now Uganda, a

Ivory tusks, Zanzibar.

centuries-old small realm called Buganda grew into a prominent regional power, enriched by such destructive but profitable pursuits.

THE ZULU KINGDOM AND THE BOER REPUBLICS. In southeastern Africa, beyond the reach of Zanzibar's commercial realm, a different sort of empire emerged in the early 1800s. Unlike the other new sub-Saharan states, it was a warrior kingdom based on military innovation and capability in combat. Created by the Zulu, one of many Bantu-speaking South African peoples (Chapter 13), this kingdom became the region's dominant power until it was challenged by two new republics formed by descendants of Dutch colonists.

Led by Shaka, the brilliant warrior king depicted at the start of this chapter, the Zulu carved out a sizable realm by conquest, killing thousands and scattering many others who fled in the face of their assaults. Shaka, who reigned from 1816 to 1828, organized Zulu youth into regiments and trained them in Zulu traditions, building their loyalty both to him and to their people. His innovations also helped transform South African warfare from a relatively restrained rite in which warriors threw light spears at each other from a distance, into a fierce form of close combat in which disciplined soldiers equipped with ox-hide shields and short stabbing spears systematically slew their foes.

Shaka was ruthless, but his detractors may have amplified his reputation for cruelty. The assertion that his wars depopulated whole regions, for example, was later made by Westerners eager to discredit the Zulu and colonize these regions. The claim that Shaka mourned his mother's death in 1827 by having numerous women killed, so their sons would share his grief, may have been advanced by his half-brother and successor Dingane (*din-GAH-neh*) to justify his assassination of Shaka in 1828. Dingane's reign (1828–1840) was marked by internal conflicts among the Zulu, and by intrusions into their lands of Dutch South Africans called Boers.

The Boers, later called **Afrikaners** (*af-rih-KAH-nurz*), were descendants of Dutch and other European immigrants who had settled in southernmost Africa, near the Cape of Good Hope, after the Dutch East India Company founded a station there for Asia-bound ships in 1652 (Chapter 23). Far from the liberal ideals of the European Enlightenment and Atlantic Revolutions, the Boers had developed a society based on farming, ranching, slavery, racism, and rigid Calvinist values. Perceiving themselves as God's chosen race in the wilderness, they dismissed local Africans as godless, sub-human heathens. As *trekboers* (Dutch for "wandering farmers"), the colonists had organized patriarchal pastoral communities, speaking a language called Afrikaans (a South African variant of Dutch) and clashing repeatedly with neighboring South Africans.

In 1806, during the Napoleonic Wars, the British seized the Cape of Good Hope from the Dutch (then under French dominion) who formally ceded it to Great Britain in 1814. At first the Boers, used to being left alone, paid little heed to the new regime in what was now the British Cape Colony. Soon, however, many were upset by Britain's relatively liberal attitude toward black South Africans. In 1835, a few years after Britain banned slavery throughout its empire (including the Cape Colony), thousands of Boers began the **Great Trek**, a mass migration northeast from the Cape Colony into South Africa's interior. Over the next two decades, comparing themselves to Biblical Hebrews entering the "Promised Land," they set up two independent republics: the Orange Free State (in the Orange River region) and Transvaal (north of the Vaal River).

Zulu kingdom connects much of southeastern Africa by conquest

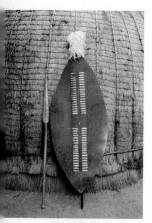

Zulu shield and spears.

Relations between Boers and Zulu got off to a disastrous start. In February 1838, alarmed by the intrusion of white settlers into Zulu territory, Zulu king Dingane invited a group of Boers to his village and then had them all killed. In December a new Boer leader, Andries Pretorius (*pruh-TOOR-ē-oos*), heading a force armed with muskets and cannons, avenged these killings by routing the Zulu at the Battle of Blood River—so named because the water ran red with the blood of three thousand slain Zulu. Pretorius went on to become the first president of Transvaal, whose capital was later named Pretoria in his honor.

After gaining British recognition in the 1850s as independent Boer republics, the Orange Free State and Transvaal had little contact with the outside world. Later in the century, however, the discovery in this region of vast deposits of diamonds and gold would shine a global spotlight on the Boers, engulfing them in a wave of imperialism that swept across the whole continent.

Boers prevail in conflicts with Zulu

The Age of Imperialism in Africa

For more than four centuries, from the mid-1400s through the mid-1800s, contact between Africans and Europeans was limited largely to the African shorelines. Some Europeans had ventured inland to capture and transport slaves, but Africans had conducted most such operations. Europeans during this era did little to colonize Africa: as late as 1875, European possessions in Africa included only the British Cape Colony, Portuguese Angola and Mozambique, French Algeria, and various small coastal outposts. Outsiders had made very few inroads into the African interior (Map 30.3).

In the last few decades of the nineteenth century, however, this situation changed. Between 1880 and 1914, armed with new technologies, impelled by new ideologies, and inspired by age-old motives such as curiosity and greed, Europeans brought most of Africa under their colonial control, increasing their holdings from under 10 percent to over 90 percent of the African continent (Map 30.4).

Sketches by famed explorer and missionary, Dr. David Livingstone.

Factors that Facilitated Imperialism

As noted in Chapter 27, the Industrial Revolution provided Europeans with the wealth and technology to dominate the world, and with the motivation to seek control of natural resources found outside of Europe that were needed for industry. As further explained in that chapter, nationalism and racism were also factors in European imperialism, which to some extent was inspired—or at least justified—by a desire to impose Western ideals upon Asians and Africans. With respect to Africa, however, several additional factors fostered European imperialism.

One such factor was the interaction between exploration and journalism. Seeking fame and fortune, and stirred by scientific curiosity, nineteenth-century Western explorers sought out Africa's natural wonders. They traced the courses of the Niger and Congo Rivers, found the sources of the Nile, and sighted such marvels as Mount Kilimanjaro (*kill-uh-mun-JAH-rō*), Lake Tanganyika (*tan-gun-YĒ-kah*), and Victoria Falls (Map 30.4). The popular press in Europe and America, where such natural wonders were previously

Explorers and journalists enhance Western interest in Africa

Map 30.4 Colonization of Africa, 1880–1914

In the late nineteenth and early twentieth centuries, European powers claimed control of almost all of Africa, dividing up the continent and forming new boundaries with little regard for traditional cultures, states, and commerce. Notice that by 1914 the only remaining independent African states were Ethiopia and Liberia. How and why did these two African states remain independent while the rest of Africa was colonized?

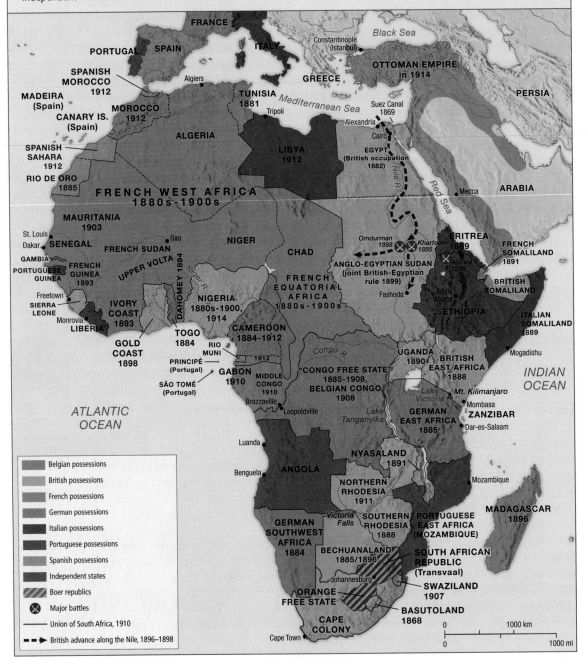

unknown, eagerly reported the explorers' adventures. By arousing public interest in Africa, and by conveying detailed knowledge of the African interior, these exploits helped lay the foundations for European colonial expansion.

Another factor that facilitated imperialism was advanced medical knowledge, which helped Europeans to survive in tropical Africa. For centuries it was called the "white man's graveyard," since most Europeans who went into the interior died within a few years from diseases such as malaria, spread to humans by Africa's abundant mosquitoes. But in the early 1800s chemists isolated **quinine**, an alkaloid substance derived from cinchona (*sing-KŌ-nuh*) trees, found mainly in South America's Andes Mountains, the bark of which had been used for some time to treat symptoms of malaria. Once doctors found that quinine could prevent, not just treat, this often-fatal disease, Europeans in Africa started taking it while still healthy, vastly reducing (but not totally eliminating) their chances of getting malaria. Quinine was also used to make a beverage known as "tonic water," which Europeans mixed with gin, creating the "gin and tonic."

Quinine enables more Europeans to survive in Africa

A third factor that favored Europeans was their monopoly on the most modern weapons. For centuries Africans had bought guns from Europeans, often trading slaves for firearms. But the weapons that Africans acquired were old-style muskets, inaccurate, unreliable, and slow, as they had to be loaded by pushing the projectile down the barrel. As Western weapons-makers perfected new rifles that could quickly be reloaded and re-fired by using a cartridge inserted in the breech (a chamber behind the barrel), Europeans mostly kept these **repeating rifles** out of African hands. The same was true of the new rapid-fire machine guns, including the hand-cranked Gatling gun, first used in the U.S. Civil War, and the fully automatic Maxim gun invented in the 1880s, each of which fired hundreds of rounds per minute. By the late 1800s, the imperialists had a vast firepower advantage, frequently making African resistance futile.

Modern weapons give Europeans advantage over Africans

Maxim gun.

Even when Africans did get modern weapons, they often faced other obstacles. One was a lack of ammunition, which they could only get by defeating or dealing with Europeans. A second was the fact that most Africans were farmers, unable to leave fields long untended to fight lengthy wars and vulnerable to European crop-destroying "scorched-earth" tactics. A third was the willingness of some Africans to ally with the outsiders, in order to gain an advantage over neighboring African foes.

The Colonization of the Congo Basin

An American newspaper's publicity stunt helped start the European contest for colonies in Africa. In 1871 Henry Morton Stanley, a British-born journalist employed and financed by the *New York Herald*, conducted a highly publicized search for Dr. David Livingstone, a noted explorer and missionary presumed lost in central Africa. Finally finding the physician, ailing and frail, in a village by Lake Tanganyika, Stanley reportedly greeted him, "Doctor Livingstone, I presume,"—soon a celebrated salutation throughout the Western world. Five years later Stanley led another expedition, jointly sponsored by the *Herald* and the *London Daily Telegraph*, which followed the Congo River from its sources to its mouth.

Stanley's search for Livingstone boosts Western interest in Africa

Enthralled by these adventures, and by dreams of owning his own African colony, Belgium's King Leopold II in 1878 hired the reporter-turned-explorer to set up trading posts in the Congo basin. Within a few years, after signing trade treaties with hundreds of Central African leaders, Stanley claimed the region for European investors headed by Leopold II, who ruthlessly exploited its resources and brutalized its people.

In 1880 the French, concerned that the claims of Leopold and Stanley might exclude them from Central Africa, sent a mission to the region just north of the lower Congo River. Anxious also to protect French settlements in nearby Gabon, the French concluded their own treaties with local African rulers. The groundwork was thus laid for a group of colonies collectively called the French Congo, later consolidated as French Equatorial Africa (Map 30.4).

Global Trade and the Occupation of Egypt

Suez Canal halves east-west shipping distance, boosting global trade

Meanwhile, in northeast Africa, the 1869 opening of the Suez Canal focused global attention on Egypt. By cutting in half the shipping distance between West and East, the canal gave a boost to both global trade and the new coal-powered steamships, whose usefulness in the east-west trade had been limited by the costs and burdens of carrying enough coal for the long route around South Africa. Britain, with its numerous steamships and extensive trade with India, soon became the canal's main user, and began to take special interest in Egyptian affairs.

Britain's interest was further enhanced by the imprudent policies of Ismail, who governed Egypt from 1863 to 1879, and was granted the title khedive (*keh-DĒV*), or "prince," by the Ottoman sultan. To finance his ambitious modernization projects, which included roads, industries, and railways in addition to the Suez Canal, Ismail borrowed huge amounts of money from European creditors, increasing Egypt's national debt by 1,400 percent. In an effort to avoid bankruptcy, as noted above, in 1875 he decided to sell his 44 percent interest in the canal. When the French unwisely declined to buy these shares, British Prime Minister Benjamin Disraeli jumped at the chance to do so, and Britain thereby became one of the canal's key shareholders.

British occupy Egypt to protect their canal interests

In 1876, concerned that Khedive Ismail might still default on his loans, Britain and France compelled him to let foreigners manage his finances. But foreign fiscal control, resulting in high taxes and military pay cuts, offended nationalist Egyptian army officers, who soon rebelled against the khedive. The Ottomans removed him in 1879, but the rebellion continued. Finally, in 1882, to protect their investments and secure the canal, the British sent an army to occupy Egypt and crush the insurrection. Although their stated intent was to stay only a year or so until order was restored, the British remained in Egypt for decades and maintained control of the canal until 1956.

The Imperial Scramble

At Berlin Conference Europeans set rules for colonizing Africa

Before long other European powers, fearful that Africa might be partitioned before they secured their shares, scrambled to get colonies of their own. Seeking to set some ground rules, German chancellor Otto von Bismarck hosted a conference at Berlin in 1884–1885. Here the powers agreed that, rather than merely negotiating treaties with local African leaders, a European nation must henceforth establish "effective occupation" to lay claim to a region. This provision meant that the European country must actually colonize the area, establishing a military and political presence as well as an economic one. The powers also promised to suppress slavery in the lands they controlled and to keep these lands open to trade with other countries.

Pledging to abide by these rules, Belgium's King Leopold II expanded his control of the Congo region, establishing a "Congo Free State" under his personal rule. Obsessed, however, with producing a profit by exploiting the region's rich resources—ivory, palm oil, copper, and especially rubber—Leopold instead made Congo a hell on earth. Beginning in the 1890s, when the newly invented inflatable tire sparked a global rubber demand, his agents imposed rubber quotas through forced labor. His private army enforced his rule through flogging, torture, hostage-taking, village burning, murder, and mutilation—including the widespread cutting off of hands. According to some accounts, more than half the region's estimated 30 million people perished under Leopold's rule, due to wars, rebellions, killings, starvation, and disease. After 1900, reports of these atrocities provoked international outrage, prompting Belgium's parliament to take over the region from Leopold in 1908. His worst abuses were curtailed, and the region became a colony called the Belgian Congo.

Belgium's King Leopold II ruthlessly exploits Congo region

Meanwhile other European powers, operating on the basis of the Berlin agreements, carved up almost all the rest of Africa. Britain and France were the biggest empire builders, dividing up most of the northern half of Africa between them, while Britain also set up a sizable domain in the South. Germany took control of Cameroon and Togo on the Gulf of Guinea, and established protectorates over German East Africa, today called Tanzania (*tan-zuh-NE-uh*), and German Southwest Africa, now the Republic of Namibia (*nuh-MIB-ē-uh*). Italy took much of Somaliland in East Africa, Eritrea (*er-uh-TRE-uh*) on the Red Sea, and Tripoli in North Africa, while Portugal and Spain expanded and consolidated earlier colonial holdings. By 1914, the only independent states in Africa were Liberia, the small West African republic created by former American slaves, and Ethiopia, the ancient Christian kingdom in East Africa south of the Red Sea (Map 30.4).

The Roots of African Resistance

Ethiopia preserved its independence with Western weapons and anti-Western national fervor, providing a model for African resistance to colonial control. In the 1890s, after Italy sought to impose a protectorate over his country, Ethiopian King Menilek (*MEN-uh-leck*) II (1889–1913) raised a 100 thousand–man army to confront the intruders. Fired by national pride, and armed with modern rifles supplied by the French to thwart their Italian rivals, the Ethiopians defeated an Italian force of 15 thousand men at Adowa (*AH-duh-wuh*) in 1896. This stunning victory showed the world that Africans, when armed with modern weapons and inspired by nationalist zeal, could hold their own against European armies.

Ethiopians routing Italians at Adowa.

Other Africans also sought to resist the Europeans. In the Sudan region south of Egypt a radical anti-Western Muslim movement emerged in the 1880s. It was led by a charismatic Muslim mystic who claimed to be al-Mahdi ("the divinely-inspired one"), a messianic leader many Muslims believed God would send to restore the true faith and herald the end of time. Early in 1885, al-Mahdi and his armies captured Sudan's capital, Khartoum (*kar-TOOM*), massacred its British-led Egyptian garrison, and set up headquarters across the Nile River at Omdurman.

Mahdi movement clashes with British interests in Sudan

But the British later got revenge. In the 1890s they set out to amass a string of possessions linking northern and southern Africa—from Cairo, Egypt, to the Cape of Good Hope—and to connect the continent by constructing a "Cape to Cairo" railway. They thus decided to subdue Sudan, then controlled by **Mahdists**, disciples of al-Mahdi, who had died in 1885. So in 1896 a British force led by General Horatio Kitchener began moving south from Egypt, armed with modern weapons and building a railway as it went. In September 1898, when Kitchener arrived at Omdurman, his 25 thousand–man army met a force of about 40 thousand Mahdist warriors. Inspired by religious zeal, but lacking modern weapons, the Mahdists repeatedly charged the British positions, but were killed by a continuous barrage of fire from machine guns, repeating rifles, and cannons. Unlike the Ethiopians, who had modern weapons, the Mahdists were destroyed.

Several weeks later an odd episode almost triggered war between Britain and France. A small French expedition, traveling overland from the West, had arrived in July at Fashoda (*fah-SHŌ-duh*) on the Nile, four hundred miles south of Omdurman, and claimed the whole region for France. When Kitchener, delayed by the Battle of Omdurman, arrived at Fashoda in September, he encountered the French expedition. Having got there first, the French insisted the land was theirs, sparking a brief war scare between the two powers. Eventually, however, aware that Britain had a much larger army on the scene, France's government backed down and ordered its small force withdrawn. Britain thus gained control of the entire Nile Valley.

Diamonds, Gold, and Diversity in South Africa

British expansion in South Africa, meanwhile, was resisted by the Boers. Imperialism there was tied to precious minerals, located largely in lands claimed by Boers (Map 30.5), attracting global interest and bringing to the region a growing diversity of peoples.

The history of South Africa, long seen as remote from the centers of global power and wealth, was altered forever in 1867 when a Boer farmer, living near the Orange Free State's southwest border, saw some children playing with small sparkling stones. Intrigued, he took one of these glimmering pebbles to a nearby town, where it was appraised as a diamond. Within a few years, thousands more of these precious gems were found, and thousands of outsiders, driven by "diamond fever," poured into the region.

In 1871, allegedly to protect local Africans from oppression by racist Boers, the British annexed the diamond field area, angering the Boers, who considered it theirs. Britain then imposed its own oppression on the local Africans, using modern weapons to demolish African armies—including those of Zulu King Cetshwayo, as described at the start of this chapter. By 1888 a British company called De Beers Consolidated Mines, founded by an English entrepreneur named Cecil Rhodes, had gained control of the entire South African diamond business, making Rhodes one of the world's richest men.

But diamonds were only one aspect of South Africa's riches. An even more spectacular discovery was made in Transvaal, along a ridge called the Rand, where immense deposits of gold were found in 1886. Soon fortune-seekers intent on mining gold came in large numbers to Transvaal from Europe, Australia, and America, while laborers were brought from all over Africa and India to work the gold and diamond mines. The region's population thus became increasingly multicultural and multiracial.

Diamond mine in South Africa.

Discovery of diamonds fuels conflicts between British and Boers

Gold discovery brings people from around the world to Transvaal

Map 30.5 The Struggle for South Africa, 1867–1910

In the late 1800s and early 1900s, the British took over most of southern Africa, conquering the Zulu and other African peoples, and engaging in a long struggle with two Boer republics, Orange Free State and Transvaal. Note that, after Britain won the South African War (1899–1902), the former Boer republics were united with the British Cape Colony, Natal, and Zululand in 1910 to form the Union of South Africa, dominated by its British and Boer inhabitants. What factors fueled the British desire to control the two Boer republics? What tactics did the British use to subdue them?

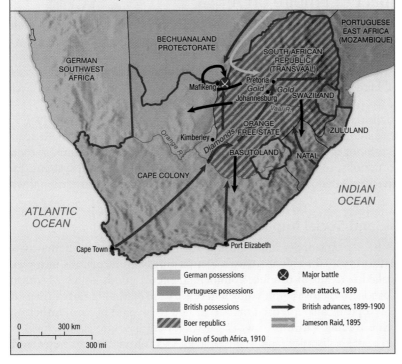

Deeply resenting the diverse newcomers, the Boers restricted their rights. In 1895 Cecil Rhodes, by then prime minister of Britain's Cape Colony, sent a small force led by his agent Jameson to invade Transvaal, hoping to spark a revolt among the newcomers that would topple its Boer regime. No such rebellion ensued, and the Boers repulsed the raid, but tensions between them and the British continued to escalate until war broke out in 1899.

The South African War (1899–1902), known in Britain as the Boer War, pitted the world's mightiest power against two small Boer republics, but the conflict was resolved neither easily nor quickly. Armed with modern rifles and resolved to defend their realm, the Boers battled the British with guerrilla tactics. Finally the frustrated British sent a huge army under General Kitchener, who broke the Boers' resistance by forcing their women and children into concentration camps, burning their homes, and using scorched-earth tactics that ravaged the lands of both Boers and local Africans.

The Boers surrendered in 1902, but their defeat was only a temporary setback. Eventually their Afrikaner descendants dominated the Union of South Africa, formed in 1910 when Britain gave a measure of self-rule to the region's white minority. Within decades this white minority, descended mainly from Boer and British settlers, imposed a racist regime upon the region's large black African majority (Chapter 37).

Boer forces in South African War.

The Impact of Empire on Africa

Before the coming of colonialism, Africans had a variety of political, economic, religious, and social systems. Some lived in large kingdoms or thriving urban centers, with powerful rulers, commercial economies, educated elites, Islamic institutions, and often warrior nobilities. Many others, however, lived in villages led by elders and chiefs, raised crops and tended herds, worshiped local deities, and centered their lives on patriarchal families and clans.

Imperialism transforms African societies

Imperialism had a transformative impact on these traditional systems. Eager to exploit Africa's human and natural resources, and smugly assuming that African institutions were inferior to their own, Europeans consciously sought to impose their own economic outlooks, social structures, religious views, and political systems. European influence thus permeated Africa, mixing, and often clashing, with traditional ways of life.

Economic and Social Implications

Colonial rule transforms Africa's agrarian economy

Economically, Africans under imperial rule often had to adapt to a new way of life. The Europeans transformed some of Africa's best pastures and farmlands into plantations, then compelled Africans to produce commercial export goods—such as cotton, palm oil, coconuts, cocoa, and cloves—on lands where Africans had long raised their own animals and food. Europeans also imposed taxes that had to be paid in cash, rather than in food or goods, thus forcing Africans to work for wages on plantations, in mines, or on railways, often at great distance from their village. And colonial borders created by imperialists, often without regard for grazing lands, clan domains, or African ethnic and linguistic boundaries, disrupted traditional economic, social, and political patterns, resulting in regional conflicts that endure to this day.

Colonial rule undermines African family and social structures

These developments carried sweeping implications for African societies. Traditional African social structures, based on patriarchal families and clans, were undermined as men had to work far from their villages, leaving their wives and children to tend crops and livestock alone. In colonial society at large, a new hierarchy arose, with Europeans on top, Western-educated Africans in the middle, and exploited African workers at the bottom. Clan structures broke down, family ties were destroyed, and long-held customs and traditions were forgotten.

Colonial rule alters African women's roles

Women's lives were particularly affected. Mass production of inexpensive clothes by Europe's textile mills and garment industries, for example, destroyed the market for handmade clothing, one of the few trades traditionally open to African women. And the mass relocation of men from African villages forced women to work in the fields while also performing their customary household and caregiver duties. At the same time, with so many men gone from the villages, women started playing a more prominent role in local governance, running the village and making key decisions while the men were away. And some African women even had a chance to get an education and acquire new skills, in schools and missions started by Europeans.

The Impact of Western Ideals and Institutions

Traditional African ways were thus blended with new ideas, promoted by Christian missionaries who built churches and hospitals, and by European educators who set up Western-style schools. Some Africans, learning to read and write European languages, eventually formed educated elites that, while still subordinate to Europeans, attained substantial wealth and power over other Africans. Many Africans converted to Christianity, the faith of their foreign rulers. Even more, however, adopted Islam, which had deeper roots in Africa and fewer ties to colonialism than the white man's Christian creed.

Africans being baptized as Christians.

In seeking to impose law and order, and thus protect their political and commercial interests, Europeans also introduced new concepts of administration and justice, based on centralized bureaucracies and judicial systems. Some Europeans initially tried governing through local African rulers; other Europeans imported and appointed their own administrative officials; but most eventually trained African lawyers, managers, soldiers, and police to run the colonies under European supervision. In many areas, the old African order of elders, clans, councils, and kings was blended and assimilated into Western-style government bureaucracies, staffed by Africans but controlled by European imperialists.

Africans blend traditional cultures with Western and Muslim ways

African Resistance to Colonial Rule

Although Africans were often defenseless against Western weaponry, they were not necessarily passive or compliant. Many resisted the alien occupation, fighting fiercely to protect their customs and ways. The Zulu, for example, battled the Boers in numerous wars and were beaten by the British in 1879 only after years of stalwart struggle. The Mahdist warriors of Sudan massacred a British-Egyptian force at Khartoum in 1885 and then fought courageously until they were finally crushed at Omdurman in 1898 by Kitchener's superior weapons. And in repulsing the Italians in 1896, the Ethiopians showed that African soldiers equipped with modern rifles could defeat European troops.

Eventually, the realties of colonial rule provided new motives and methods for African resistance. The brutality of European imperialism, by nature oppressive and exploitative, helped unite Africans against the outsiders. As Africans learned European ideals, they began to use these ideals against their Western rulers. Africans who adopted liberal and Christian values, for example, pointedly called on the Europeans to end their oppression of Africans and treat them with Christian compassion. Africans who studied in Europe or America often came home inspired by notions of nationalism and democracy, and began insisting that they also applied to Africa. Africans who fought in European wars returned with skills and training useful in forming African liberation armies. In the twentieth century, these factors helped to build independence movements across the African continent.

Africans adapt Western weapons and ideals to combat European rule

Chapter Review

Putting It in Perspective

Nineteenth-century connections and conflicts transformed West Asia and Africa, imposing new economic, political, social, and cultural patterns. The international slave trade was banned, and eventually abolished, with various new kinds of commerce taking its place. Traditional subsistence farming, long the foundation of most African economies, was replaced in many regions by cash crops such as cotton and cloves, by increased production of items such as palm oil, coconuts, and ivory, and by the mining of valuable minerals such as diamonds and gold.

In West Asia and North Africa, as the Ottoman realm sought to halt its decline by adapting some Western ways, it alienated Arab Muslims and proved unable to maintain control of its North African dominions, which eventually came under European sway. In sub-Saharan Africa new states emerged, forged by religious fervor, commercial connections, or military might, but they likewise were overwhelmed by the advance of European imperialism.

In West Asia and North Africa, Islamic cultural and social structures continued, but they increasingly coexisted with new Western-style laws and education systems. Throughout sub-Saharan Africa, however, traditional clan and village societies were replaced by structures imposed by Europeans and staffed with Western-educated Africans. European languages, Christian religious values, and Western ideologies such as liberalism and nationalism also influenced many Africans. These Africans, adapting Western ideals and modern weapons into their African heritage, in the twentieth century would lead the liberation of Africa from European rule.

Reviewing Key Material

KEY CONCEPTS

Maghrib, 756
Middle East, 757
Tanzimat, 759
Young Turks, 759
cash crops, 761
Fulani, 768

recaptives, 768
African diaspora, 769
Afrikaners, 770
Great Trek, 770
quinine, 773
repeating rifles, 773
Mahdists, 776

KEY PEOPLE

Shaka, 756, 770
Cetshwayo, 756, 776
Sultan Mahmud II, 757
Mustafa Reshid Pasha, 759
Sultan Abdulhamid II, 759
Muhammad Ali, 759
Ibrahim Pasha, 762
Khedive Ismail, 762
Abdelqadir al-Jazairi, 764
Olaudah Equiano, 765
William Wilberforce, 765
Usman dan Fodio, 768

Joseph Jenkins Roberts, 769
Sa'id ibn Sultan (Sa'id Sayyid), 769
Tippu Tip, 769
Dingane, 770
Henry Morton Stanley, 773
King Leopold II, 773, 775
King Menilek II, 775
al-Mahdi of Sudan, 775
Horatio Kitchener, 776
Cecil Rhodes, 776

ASK YOURSELF

1. Why and how did the banning of the slave trade impact the African economy? In what ways did the ban help to reinforce both slavery and the slave trade?
2. How did the new regional states that emerged in Africa in the early nineteenth century differ from each other, in terms of both their origins and their operations?
3. How did Ottoman decline, and Turkish attempts at reform, influence the various regions of West Asia and North Africa? What were the main elements and impacts of Egypt's modernization? Why did Egypt and the rest of North Africa fail to gain independence?
4. How and why did each of the main regions of Africa come under European control in the late nineteenth century? How did some Africans seek to resist this control?
5. What were the main effects of imperialism on African cultures and societies? In what ways did imperialism undermine Africa, and in what ways did it help to foster African resistance?

GOING FURTHER

Achebe, Chinua. *Things Fall Apart*. 1958.
Ahmad, Feroz. *The Young Turks*. 1969.

Ajayi, J., and M. Crowder, eds. *A History of West Africa.* 1985.

Alpers, Edward. *Ivory and Slaves in East Central Africa.* 1975.

Boahen, A. Adu. *African Perspectives on Colonialism.* 1987.

Cleveland, W. L. *A History of the Modern Middle East.* 2000.

Collins, R., ed. *Historical Problems of Imperial Africa.* 1994.

Coquery-Vidrovitch, C. *African Women: A Modern History.* 1997.

Curtain, Philip. *The World and the West: European Challenge and Overseas Response in the Age of Empire.* 2000.

Delius, Peter, *The Land Belongs to Us.* 1984.

Findley, C. V. *Bureaucratic Reform in the Ottoman Empire.* 1980.

Flint, John E. *The Cambridge History of Africa.* Vol. 5. 1976.

Guy, J. *The Destruction of the Zulu Kingdom.* 1979.

Hopkins, A. G. *An Economic History of West Africa.* 1973.

Hothschild, Adam. *King Leopold's Ghost.* 1998.

Julien, Charles A. *A History of North Africa.* 1970.

Kinross, J. P. D. B. *The Ottoman Centuries.* 1977.

Lapidus, I. *A History of Islamic Societies.* 1988.

Law, Robin. *From Slave Trade to "Legitimate" Commerce.* 1996.

Lewis, David Levering. *The Race to Fashoda.* 1995.

Lovejoy, Paul. *Slow Death for Slavery.* 1993.

MacKinnon, Aran. *The Making of South Africa.* 2003.

Marcus, Harold. *A History of Ethiopia.* 1994.

Miers, S., and R. Roberts. *The End of Slavery in Africa.* 1988.

Mitchell, T. *Colonizing Egypt.* 1988.

Northrup, David. *Africa's Discovery of Europe, 1450–1850.* 2002.

Omer-Cooper, John D. *The Zulu Aftermath.* 1966.

Packenham, Thomas. *The Scramble for Africa, 1876–1912.* 1991.

Robinson, R., and J. Gallagher. *Africa and the Victorians.* 1969.

Rodney, Walter. *How Europe Underdeveloped Africa.* 1981.

Rotberg, Robert I., ed. *Africa and Its Explorers.* 1970.

Sheriff, Abdul. *Spices and Ivory in Zanzibar.* 1987.

Shillington, Kevin. *History of Africa.* Rev. ed. 2005.

Thompson, Leonard. *A History of South Africa.* 1995.

Toledano, E. *State and Society in Nineteenth Century Egypt.* 1990.

Vandervort, B. *Wars of Imperial Conquest in Africa.* 1998.

Vatikiotis, P. J. *The History of Modern Egypt.* 1991.

Warwick, Peter, ed. *The South African War.* 1980.

Wesseling, H. L. *Imperialism and Colonialism.* 1997.

Worden, Nigel. *A History of Modern South Africa.* 1995.

Key Dates and Developments

Date	Development	Date	Development
1798–1801	French occupation of Egypt	1871	Stanley's search for Livingstone
1803–1818	Banning of the slave trade	1875	British purchase of Egyptian canal shares
1804–1809	Formation of Fulani Empire (Sokoto Caliphate)	1878–1884	Stanley's acquisition of Congo region for Leopold II
1805–1848	Transformation of Egypt under Muhammad Ali	1882	British occupation of Egypt
1806–1856	Commercial empire in Zanzibar under Sa'id Sayyid	1884–1885	Berlin Conference on Africa
1816–1828	Zulu conquests under King Shaka	1885–1908	Leopold II's brutal rule of "Congo Free State"
1821	Formation of freed slave settlement in Liberia	1885–1914	Scramble for colonies in Africa
1830–1847	French conquest of Algeria	1886	Discovery of gold in South Africa
1835	Beginning of the Boers' Great Trek	1896	Ethiopian defeat of Italians at Adowa
1839–1876	The Tanzimat: Reforms in the Ottoman Empire	1898	British massacre of Sudanese Mahdists at Omdurman
1867	Discovery of diamonds in South Africa	1899–1903	South African War (Boer War)
1869	Opening of the Suez Canal		

The Great War and the Russian Revolutions, 1890–1918

Over The Top

U.S. infantry goes "over the top," emerging from a trench on the Western Front of the Great War in 1918. Trench warfare became the most memorable feature of this traumatic, bloody conflict (page 792).

- The Path to War and Revolution

- Deadlock and Devastation, 1914–1916

- Year of Revolution, 1917

- Year of Decision, 1918

- Chapter Review

It was Sunday, June 28, 1914. Archduke Franz Ferdinand, Crown Prince of Austria-Hungary, paid a state visit to Sarajevo (*sah-rah-YĀ-vō*), capital of the Austrian province of Bosnia. As his motorcade entered the city, a terrorist seeking to free Bosnia from Austria threw a bomb at Franz Ferdinand's car. The assassin's aim was off, and the bomb blew up the car behind the Archduke's. Enraged, Franz Ferdinand shortened his visit by several hours. As he was leaving the city, however, his car took a wrong turn and stalled on a small side street. Watching from a nearby café was another assassin, who walked up to the car and murdered the Archduke and his wife with a revolver. Within five weeks all Europe was at war.

**Allied and
Associated Powers
(Red)**

**Central Powers
(Tan)**

Neutrals (Green)

At the palace of Versailles in France, precisely five years after the shots at Sarajevo, European leaders met in solemn assembly to sign a treaty formally ending the conflict triggered by those shots, then known as the Great War. It had killed more than nine million people, devastated much of Europe, helped spark momentous revolutions in Russia, and spread fear across the globe. The experience was so horrifying that the peacemakers at Versailles hoped not merely to end the Great War, but to abolish war forever.

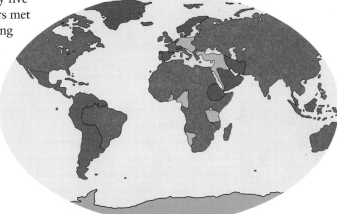

The Path to War and Revolution

In 1890 Europe stood at the peak of world power. Industrial modernization and the technologies it generated gave Britain, France, and Germany unprecedented wealth and dominion, with global empires encompassing much of Africa and Asia. Italy and Belgium also gained African colonies, as industrial nations competed for possessions and access to raw materials. But the Russian, Austrian, and Ottoman Empires, for centuries dominant in Eastern Europe and beyond, had been slow to industrialize, and they had fallen behind. Liberalism and nationalism also threatened these three multinational realms, as their various peoples pressed for greater freedom and autonomy. After 1890 rivalries among all these powers intensified as each sought to improve its status and security. Europe divided into powerful and hostile alliances, leading to a series of crises that eventually culminated in catastrophic conflict.

The Diplomatic Revolution of 1890–1907

In 1890 Europe was also at peace. The wars of Italian and German unification, fought decades earlier, had altered the balance of power in favor of a newly unified Germany. But under Chancellor Otto von Bismarck, that new nation had emerged as a conservative power, maintaining its position by preserving the status quo. France, humiliated and hoping to regain Alsace and Lorraine, provinces lost to Germany in the Franco-Prussian War (1870–1871), was kept isolated and powerless by Bismarck's skillful diplomacy. He engineered a series of alliances designed to isolate France and keep Austria and Russia from fighting each other in the Balkans.

Between 1879 and 1882, at Bismarck's initiative, Austria, Italy, and Germany put aside past animosities to sign the **Triple Alliance**, a defensive pact in which each promised to assist the others in the event of unprovoked attack by a third party (Map 31.1). Then, in 1887, a Reinsurance Treaty with Russia gave Germany additional leverage in the Balkans: in the event of war in that region, Germany would oppose whichever nation it considered the aggressor. Since neither Russia nor Austria alone could win a war against Germany, Austro-Russian tensions in the Balkans were effectively frozen in place. Moreover, since Italy, Austria, and Russia were each allied with Germany, France was left isolated on the continent with no anti-German allies. These twin pillars of Bismarck's diplomacy—isolation of France and prevention of Balkan war—kept Europe at peace throughout the 1870s and 1880s.

Bismarck's Alliances maintain peace in Europe

William II, Kaiser of Imperial Germany.

REVERSAL OF BISMARCK'S DIPLOMACY. But starting in 1890, Bismarck's efforts were undone by a new German Kaiser. William I died in March 1888 at age 91; his son Frederick III died three months later of throat cancer. The throne thus passed to 29-year-old William II, a brash young man who dismissed Bismarck in 1890, regarding him as out of touch with contemporary problems. The new Kaiser wanted to play the leading role in German foreign affairs.

This prospect was dangerous for Germany because, although quick-witted, William II was an erratic ruler with no temperament for the hard work required of a monarch who wished to govern as well as reign. Lacking Bismarck's ruthlessness and skill, William took ill-considered actions that quickly compromised Germany's dominant position in Europe. He and his new ministers felt that Germany's Reinsurance Treaty with Russia (1887) violated the spirit of the Triple Alliance of 1882 (Germany, Austria-Hungary, and Italy) by making it unclear whether Germany would support Austria or Russia in a Balkan war. They therefore refused to renew the Reinsurance Treaty when it expired in 1890.

The decision for nonrenewal destroyed both of Bismarck's pillars. With one stroke it tilted Germany toward Austria in the Balkans and prompted Russia, which considered nonrenewal a hostile act, to seek an alliance with France. This ended France's isolation and compromised Germany's dominant position in Europe. War became a realistic possibility, and if it occurred, Germany would have to fight a two-front war against Russia in the East and France in the West.

Germany unwittingly initiates a Diplomatic Revolution

The implications of the Franco-Russian alliance, initiated in 1891 and formalized in 1894, were not lost on William II, but he blamed Germany's weakened position on his enemy's intrigues rather than learning from his mistake. Certain of the purity of his motives, he was insensitive to how they were perceived by other governments. Thus in 1898, when he authorized a huge naval expansion so that Germany's fleet could rival Britain's and ensure German access to its overseas colonies, he was astounded to learn that London feared this buildup. As an island nation that had to import food, Britain responded with its own massive increase in naval production. The hugely expensive naval arms race that followed embittered both sides.

Abandoning their historic avoidance of peacetime alliances, the British also started seeking allies to counter the German threat. That threat was, from Britain's perspective, a global one. In 1902 Britain and Japan, both alarmed by German and Russian expansionism in East Asia, concluded an alliance. Now Japan's large Pacific fleet could protect the British Empire in Asia, relieving Britain's Grand Fleet for action in European waters.

FOUNDATION MAP 31.1 European Alliances and Crises, 1905–1914

The Diplomatic Revolution of 1890–1907 divided Europe into two approximately equivalent alliance systems: the Triple Alliance and the Triple Entente. Observe that the Triple Alliance occupied a central position on the continent, surrounded by the nations of the Triple Entente. Between 1905 and 1914, a series of international crises, clustered in southeastern Europe and North Africa, brought Europe ever closer to armed hostilities. Yet between 1905 and 1913, each of these crises was settled peacefully. How did this succession of peaceful resolutions actually make war more rather than less likely in 1914?

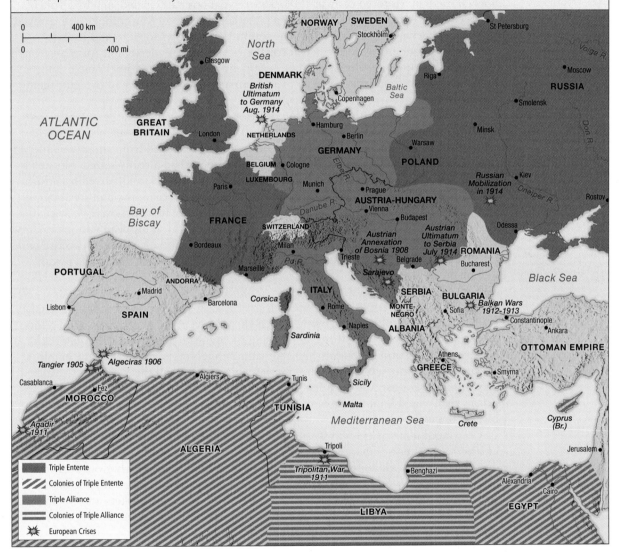

Even more unprecedented was the Entente Cordiale (*ahn-TAHNT kord-YAL*), or "Cordial Alliance," of 1904, in which longtime enemies Britain and France agreed to respect each other's African domains and consult one another should a third party (such as Germany) threaten the peace.

Stunned by these developments, but considering Franco-British animosities too deep to permit genuine partnership, German leaders resolved to test the Entente by provoking a crisis. In 1905 Kaiser William II visited the North African sultanate of Morocco, which France had been trying, over German objections, to make into a French protectorate. There he gave a highly provocative anti-French speech. Fearing war with Germany, France reluctantly submitted its Moroccan policy to an international conference at Algeçiras (*al-jeh-SĪ -russ*) in Morocco early in 1906. Thirteen nations participated, and by a vote of 10–3 the Act of Algeçiras granted France a preferential status in Morocco. France received solid British backing, while Germany was supported only by Morocco and Austria-Hungary. A stinging diplomatic defeat for the Germans, it underscored Austro-German isolation and mutual dependence, since even their ally Italy voted for France. And rather than separating Britain and France, Germany's belligerence had brought them closer together.

As Germany's international position deteriorated, that belligerence grew. German leaders perceived the empire to be encircled by the Franco-Russian Alliance (which its own diplomatic ineptness had done so much to create), excluded from choice colonies in Asia and Africa that the older British and French empires had already seized, blocked by the British Grand Fleet from access to the colonies it did possess, and barred by British merchants and contracts from markets to which its rapidly expanding industrial might entitled it. Sensing its increasing isolation, Germany became more assertive with each rebuke. Meanwhile this assertiveness continued to cause other European nations to draw together. In 1907 Britain and Russia, each aligned with France, concluded an accord with each other. This development, unthinkable only a few years earlier, was made possible by dramatic developments in Russia.

Germany's sense of isolation intensifies its assertive conduct

RUSSIA AND ITS CHALLENGES. In the early 1900s, Russia suffered from many internal problems. Rapid population growth, which shrunk the average peasants' land allotments, threatened their self-sufficiency. Rising nationalism among non-Russian nationalities, which constituted roughly half the realm's inhabitants, threatened the empire's cohesion. Its slowness to industrialize left it lagging far behind the West and threatened its great power status. And its ruler, Tsar Nicholas II (1894–1917), rigidly opposed to reforms that would limit his powers, lacked the decisiveness needed to exercise those powers effectively.

Convinced nonetheless that Russia must modernize in order to survive, Sergei Witte (*VIT-tuh*), Minister of Finance from 1892 to 1903, promoted industrialization through government action. He borrowed vast funds from abroad (particularly from Russia's new ally, France) to support new enterprises and build railways, especially the monumental trans-Siberian line, which provided access both to Asian markets and to Siberia's abundant resources, including timber and oil. His policies brought impressive increases in Russia's state revenues and industrial output.

Russia wrestles with the dilemma of modernization

But his policies also destabilized Russia. As thousands of peasants moved to cities to work in factories, their dislocation strained the social structure. Uprooted from their villages, crowded into urban slums, and compelled to work long hours at low wages in dangerous, monotonous jobs, Russian factory workers soon became a powerful force for change. Poor harvests and a weak economy added to the general discontent, as did the empire's efforts to "russify" its ethnic minorities by forcing them to adopt Russian language and ways.

As social unrest increased, various revolutionary groups emerged. *Liberals* wanted a Western-style parliamentary regime, complete with a constitution and capitalist economy. *Socialist revolutionaries*, rejecting Western capitalism, wanted a socialist revolution based on the peasant masses. *Marxists*, or *social democrats*, saw the industrial working class as the backbone of a socialist revolution that would transfer ownership of the means of production to the workers. In the early 1900s, growing social unrest was manifested in student demonstrations, industrial strikes, peasant uprisings, and political assassinations that rocked the Russian Empire. Minister of Interior Viacheslav Plehve (1902) and the tsar's uncle, Grand Duke Sergei (1904) were blown to bits by bomb-throwing assassins. Industrial growth, intended to build Russia's wealth and power, seemed to be tearing it apart.

A textile mill in Tashkent, Russian Central Asia, around 1900.

The Russo-Japanese War (1904–1905) complicated the unrest (Chapter 29). At first Japan's attack prompted a patriotic surge that quieted revolutionary activity. But when military setbacks began to discredit the tsarist regime, factory workers rebelled against extended work hours and pressures to boost production for war. In January 1905, a sincere but naive Orthodox priest organized a massive workers' march in Saint Petersburg. The marchers called for shorter workdays, expanded civil rights, and an end to the war. Although they carried icons and sang patriotic hymns, imperial troops opened fire on them, slaughtering several hundred.

Bloody Sunday, as this event was labeled, stunned Russia's people and undermined support for Nicholas II. Within months Russia was engulfed in revolution, as strikes and demonstrations spread throughout the land. By October 1905, as massive general strikes—in which all workers, rather than just those in a particular industry, walked off the job—shut down major cities, Saint Petersburg was controlled by a council, or **soviet**, of elected workers' delegates.

Threatened by these events, the tsar ended the war and issued an "October Manifesto," promising a constitution and an elected parliament, or **Duma**. This action satisfied liberals, splitting the opposition and helping to save the regime. Radicals and socialists continued to rebel, but tsarist forces, reinforced by loyal troops returning from the war, eventually crushed the remnants of the revolt.

The Revolution of 1905 forces Nicholas II to make political concessions

The tsar thus survived the Russian Revolution of 1905 by agreeing to share power with the Duma. His new constitution, however, severely restricted this parliament, and his government shut it down when it seemed too radical. In 1907 his prime minister imposed a new electoral system that ensured a loyal majority. The revolution thus did little to limit the regime's power. But it gave Russian workers a brief taste of freedom, taught them how to organize soviets, and provided revolutionaries with experience that they would put to use in revolutions to come.

The war and revolution also helped Russia and Britain overcome their longstanding animosity. Russia's defeat by Japan convinced the British that Russia was less dangerous than Germany, and Russia's reformed government seemed superficially similar to Britain's parliamentary monarchy. Mutually fearful of Germany's growing power, in 1907 the two countries signed an Anglo-Russian Entente, reconciling their claims to colonies and spheres of influence in Asia.

The Crises of 1908–1913

The Triple Entente
balances the Triple
Alliance

The Anglo-Russian Entente completed the **Diplomatic Revolution of 1890–1907**, creating a **Triple Entente** (Britain, France, and Russia) to offset the Triple Alliance of Germany, Austria-Hungary, and Italy. Europe had moved in 17 years from a continent dominated by Germany to one balanced precariously between equal alliance systems. This development was dangerous not only to Germany but also to European peace. Power relationships among nations are safest when they are *imbalanced*: war is unlikely when one side clearly dominates the other. When equilibrium exists, however, either side may be tempted to test its luck. Such would be the case in Europe after 1907.

In 1908 a crisis arose over Austria's decision to annex the Balkan provinces of Bosnia and Herzegovina (*her-tseh-gō-VĒ-nah*), which it had administered since 1878 but which technically were owned by the declining Ottoman Empire. Claiming it had prior Russian approval, Austria annexed the provinces in October. Russia, however, perceiving itself as protector of the provinces' Slavic peoples, voiced strong objections and demanded that Austria give part of these provinces to Serbia, a neighboring Slavic nation long supported by Russia. But Germany, supporting Austria, forced Russia to back down by threatening war. Though resolved without war, this **Bosnian Crisis of 1908–1909** tied Austria even closer to Germany and provoked Russia into funding an immense eight-year military buildup designed to prevent similar humiliations.

A series of crises both
frightens and reassures
Europe

In 1911 came a Second Moroccan Crisis, prompted by German discontent with the first one's outcome in 1906. Watching in frustration as France slowly took over Morocco in violation of the Act of Algeçiras, Germany sent a gunboat to the Moroccan port of Agadir. The Germans later said they were trying to obtain French concessions elsewhere in Africa in return for German recognition of a French protectorate over Morocco, but that aim initially was not clear. War seemed a real possibility, and France's ally Britain starkly warned Germany not to treat Britain "as if she were of no account in the Cabinet of Nations." War was avoided when France agreed to cede Germany a large slice of French Equatorial Africa. But the crisis frightened Britain and France into concluding a 1912 naval agreement, pledging each to defend the other's interests in case of war. Once again, Germany's belligerence had further united its foes.

Italy, meanwhile, eager to expand its African holdings, took Tripoli from the Ottomans during a war fought in 1911–1912. Emboldened by the Ottomans' poor performance in this war, four small Balkan nations then formed an anti-Turkish alliance. Much to the world's surprise, the Balkan allies drove the Ottomans from the Balkans in the First Balkan War (1912), but then fought among themselves over the spoils in the Second Balkan War (1913). Since the European powers assembled a conference to prevent these wars from spreading and arranged a compromise to safeguard the interests of Austria and Russia, these events actually reassured Europe. By the end of 1913, Europeans felt confident that any future crisis could be managed by negotiation, which had resolved every recent confrontation.

The Crisis of July 1914

Franz Ferdinand's
murder provokes a
European crisis

In June 1914, as described at the beginning of this chapter, Archduke Franz Ferdinand, heir to the throne of Austria-Hungary, visited Sarajevo, the capital of Bosnia, to observe military maneuvers. The visit angered Serbs and Bosnians, embittered by Austria's annexation of Bosnia in 1908. When the Archduke and his wife were murdered on June 28 by Gavrilo Princip (*PRIN-chip*), a Bosnian assassin trained and equipped in Serbia, the Serbian government was widely seen as responsible. Although Franz Ferdinand was not popular in Austria, in a Europe ruled mostly by monarchs, the assassination of a crown prince was a very serious matter. The general expectation was that Austria would somehow punish Serbia.

Austria decided to go to war against Serbia but was uncertain of how Russia, Serbia's protector, might respond, and therefore asked for assurance of German support. Assuming that Tsar Nicholas II would sympathize with the family of the murdered Franz Ferdinand, and therefore considering Russian intervention unlikely, Kaiser William II promised to back any action Austria might take. This guarantee was the infamous **"blank check,"** a document that would allow Austria to lead Germany and the rest of Europe into war. Austria prepared a ten-point ultimatum, or set of strict demands, the refusal of any one of which would justify Vienna in breaking off diplomatic relations as a prelude to war. The harsh ultimatum was actually designed to prove unacceptable to Serbia and make war inevitable. But Serbia's reply was conciliatory, impressing even Germany's Kaiser with its effort to keep peace. It fell short of total acceptance, however, so on July 25 Austria broke off relations.

In light of Serbia's moderate response, European opinion, which three weeks earlier might have supported Austria, now swung firmly to the Serbian side. Britain, preoccupied with a dangerous crisis over Irish Home Rule (Chapter 27), assumed that Germany would be receptive to a conference like the one that had contained the Balkan Wars. This time, however, Germany was more interested in confrontation than cooperation. On July 28, Austria declared war on Serbia, and Russia, overcoming any sympathy the Tsar may (or may not) have felt for Franz Ferdinand, prepared to fight in support of the Serbs. France resolved to stand by Russia, and Britain warned the Germans that it might not be able to stay neutral in a Franco-German war. Sobered by these developments, Germany sought on July 30 to restrain Austria, but it was too late. The need to move large numbers of troops on railways placed European armies on rigid timetables. This necessity was particularly pressing in Germany, which, threatened with a war on two fronts, planned to defeat France in six weeks and then turn to deal with Russia, whose less-developed transport system would slow its mobilization for war.

Needing to move before its enemies could prepare, Germany declared war against Russia on August 1 and France on August 3 (Map 31.2). The next day, as Germany's army invaded neutral Belgium on the way to attacking France, Britain, like Germany a guarantor of Belgian neutrality, entered the war on the side of France and Russia. All the great powers of Europe except Italy were now at war.

The July Crisis of 1914, unlike its predecessors, resulted in war for several reasons. Austria wanted to end Serbian ethnic agitation. Germany wanted to back its Austrian ally, assuming it would be better to risk war now than to wait until Russia completed its military buildup. Russia wanted to avoid humiliation like that of 1908–1909. France wanted to avenge the loss of Alsace-Lorraine and support its Russian ally. Britain wanted to avoid a French defeat that would give Germany control of France's ports on the English Channel. And all military leaders wanted to mobilize before their enemies did so. None of these "wants," however, made war inevitable. European nations had freedom of choice, and could have opted against war in 1914. They did not.

Archduke Franz Ferdinand (left) and Emperor Franz Josef of Austria-Hungary.

Germany's unconditional support of Austria leads to war in Europe

European powers choose war over peace

Map 31.2 The Great War in Europe and Southwest Asia, 1914–1918

The Great War quickly became stalemated late in 1914. The Central Powers exploited their central position on the continent to attack on different fronts at different times, but trench warfare, barbed wire, and machine guns all favored the defensive posture of the Triple Entente. Note that German forces conquered an amount of Russian territory equivalent in size to all of Germany and Austria-Hungary combined. Despite this achievement, why did the Central Powers fail to win the war?

Deadlock and Devastation, 1914–1916

Why didn't the European nations decide against war? First, the military capabilities of the rival alliances were so closely matched that each side was willing to take a chance on victory. Second, each nation's leaders expected to win quickly, in the sort of victorious flurry that had characterized European warfare since the defeat of Napoleon. None of them expected the war to do what it did—come close to destroying European civilization. This helps explain why they were all willing to roll the dice at a time when their forces were so closely balanced. Third, many people in each country actually welcomed the prospect of war as an escape, in the words of poet Rupert Brooke, "from a world grown old and cold and weary," and believed it would be a purification that would create a stronger, cleaner world. So hundreds of thousands of young men, cheered by their families and sweethearts, marched off to war in August 1914, grateful for the opportunity to prove themselves, rejoicing with Brooke: "Now God be thanked who has matched us with His hour!"

The most famous recruiting poster ever devised, featuring the face of British Field Marshal Lord Kitchener.

Stalemate on the Western Front

Reality set in quickly, and reality was devastating. Belgian resistance slowed the German army, the British arrived in France more quickly than anticipated, and Russia mobilized with unusual speed to attack Germany in the East. But Germany's strategy for dealing with a two-front war was unrealistic in any case, as it relied for success on more top-flight combat divisions than the German army possessed. The Kaiser's forces won some impressive victories, bringing them close to Paris. But at the Marne River, having mobilized the city's taxis to transport their troops, the French outflanked the Germans and forced them to retreat. By mid-September the opposing armies were stalemated.

Both sides anticipate a short, victorious war

This deadlock in the West produced a "race to the sea," eight weeks in which each side attempted to outflank the other. It ended in mid-November at the English Channel. Meanwhile, in the East, a premature Russian advance into East Prussia, designed to relieve pressure on the French in the West, succeeded in doing that but ended in disaster. German Generals Paul von Hindenburg and Erich Ludendorff isolated and destroyed the entire Russian Second Army, ending the threat of invasion and saving Austria, which was being defeated farther south by the Russians.

In just a few months of warfare, losses were appalling. In three months France had lost 306 thousand soldiers, 3 percent of its military-age males, and more than the United States would later lose during all of World War II. Germany, with a military-age population three times larger than France's, had lost 241 thousand men. Farther east, Russia and Austria had suffered catastrophic losses, with 1.5 million Russian and 1.268 million Austrian troops killed or captured. Russia's huge population could replace those losses, but Austria's could not. So the danger to Germany and Austria stemmed not only from Germany's failure to defeat France quickly but also from the destruction of the cream of the Austro-Hungarian armies. To prevent total collapse on the Eastern Front in 1915, Germany transferred sizable forces eastward and held the defensive in the West.

Dead soldiers in a trench on the Western Front.

That defensive gave the Great War its most morbid characteristic: **trench warfare**. From the English Channel to the Franco-Swiss border, the Germans dug an elaborate system of parallel and angled trenches that the French could neither outflank nor pierce.

The Western Front stalemates into trench warfare

France, perplexed, built trenches of its own. For the next three years each of these opposing systems prevented any meaningful breakthrough and frustrated generals schooled in attacking rather than defending.

Trenches had been used before. In the American Civil War, Confederate General Robert E. Lee had employed so many of them that his men called him "the King of Spades." But prior to 1914, trenches had been dug to fortify positions for a battle or siege and then abandoned when it was over. In the Great War, trenches became permanent installations. Their permanence was attributable to barbed wire, which slowed offensives to a crawl, and especially to the machine gun. Capable of firing 11 rounds a second through water-cooled barrels, machine guns swept the entire field in front of a trench, cutting off attackers at the knees. Eventually offensive technology would be developed to neutralize these factors. For the moment, however, bewildered commanders launched repeated attacks "over the top" of the trenches (see page 782), sending soldiers surging into the barbed-wire traps of "no-man's land" between opposing lines in the vain hope of achieving a breakthrough.

Trench warfare consumed soldiers' lives at unprecedented rates, transforming war from violence carrying the prospect of glory into violence of unending degradation (see "Charles Hamilton Sorley, 'When You See Millions of the Mouthless Dead'"). Men lived and died in ditches eight feet deep, standing in stagnant water, plagued by rats and vermin, and often living next to the decaying corpses of their comrades. The optimism of the nineteenth century died on the Western Front, as trenches scarred both the landscapes of northeastern France and the psyches of the men who occupied them.

Efforts to Break the Stalemate

As casualties relentlessly mounted, each side added allies and sought to break the stalemate. Germany and Austria-Hungary, joined by Bulgaria and Ottoman Turkey in a coalition called the Central Powers, employed mass attacks and artillery bombardments,

Document 31.1 Charles Hamilton Sorley, "When You See Millions of the Mouthless Dead"

The poetry of the Great War captured in vivid, unforgettable imagery the shocking hopelessness of the gruesome slaughters on the Western Front. Charles Hamilton Sorley was killed in action in 1915, but not before he had written what many have called the saddest poem of the war.

When you see millions of the mouthless dead

Across your dreams in pale battalions go,

Say not soft things as other men have said,

That you'll remember. For you need not so.

Give them no praise. For, deaf, how should they know

It is not curses heaped on each gashed head?

Nor tears. Their blind eyes see not your tears flow.

Nor honour. It is easy to be dead.

Say only this, "They are dead." Then add thereto,

"Yet many a better one has died before."

Then, scanning all the o'ercrowded mass, should you

Perceive one face that you loved heretofore,

It is a spook. None wears the face you knew.

Great Death has made all his forevermore.

SOURCE: website.lineone.net/~nusquam/mouthles.htm

supplemented on land by poison gas and at sea by German submarine warfare. Britain, France, and Russia, joined by Britain's ally Japan and other nations in a combination called the Allied Powers, relied heavily on mass attacks and a British naval blockade of Germany. Hoping to gain Austrian territory in a peace settlement, Italy joined the Allies in 1915, abandoning its prewar alliance with Germany and Austria.

OFFENSIVES IN THE EAST AND SOUTHEAST. As 1915 began, General Erich von Falkenhayn (*FAHL-ken-hīn*), chief of the German General Staff, argued against a defensive posture in the West. Noting Britain's ability to draw reinforcements from Canada and Australia, he wanted to defeat France before these reinforcements made an impact. But although Falkenhayn outranked Hindenburg and Ludendorff, they, not he, had won Germany's only decisive victory in 1914, and they demanded an offensive in the East. So in the West Falkenhayn settled for smaller attacks using chlorine gas, a fearsome new weapon that, when inhaled, stimulated fluid production in the lungs to cause death by drowning. Eventually used by both sides, poison gas was limited in its usefulness by shifting winds, which sometimes blew the gas back on the side releasing it, and by the development of gas masks. It nonetheless killed tens of thousands of horses, on which all armies depended for transport, and heightened the impersonal doom of trench warfare.

Poison gas fails to break the stalemate

Hindenburg's insistence on an eastern offensive was logical. A victory there would prevent Austria's collapse and possibly force Russia, frighteningly short of rifles and artillery shells, to seek a cease-fire. From May to September 1915, the Central Powers' offensive captured more than 750 thousand Russian prisoners. This offensive saved the Austrian army but did not prevent the Russians from withdrawing into their vast interior. There they raised reinforcements to replace their dead and captured, hoping their increasing output of industrial weapons would eventually enable them to turn back the Germans. As in France in 1914, Germany won major victories in the East but lacked the overwhelming superiority required to win the war. Italy's entry on the side of the Allies further reduced German prospects. It also tied down Austrian forces in bloody, debilitating fighting for the remainder of the war.

If the Central Powers could not break the stalemate in the West or East, perhaps the Allies could break it in the southeast. Turkey's entry into the war late in 1914 on the side of the Central Powers had closed Russia's southern seaports, since Turkey controlled entry to the Black Sea through the Dardanelles Straits. Winston Churchill, Britain's First Lord of the Admiralty, proposed an expedition to force the Straits open and force Turkey out of the war. On April 25, 1915, an improvised landing force of Britons, Australians, and New Zealanders went ashore on the Gallipoli (*gah-LIH-pō-lē*) peninsula. It quickly found itself pinned on the beaches under Turkish artillery fire from defensive positions coordinated by Captain Mustafa Kemal (*moo-STAH-fah keh-MAHL*), who would go on to rule Turkey after the war. The British did not have sufficient troops for a full-scale invasion, and they had underestimated the effectiveness of Turkish resistance. By January 9, 1916, the invaders evacuated the Gallipoli peninsula. Both sides suffered losses in the hundreds of thousands, and the stalemate continued.

The Allied landing at Gallipoli fails

THE WAR AT SEA. By the end of 1915, although the Central Powers held a strong position in the heart of Europe, their impressive offensives had failed to defeat any of their enemies. Germany, moreover, was increasingly deprived of food and supplies by a tight British naval blockade. The British Grand Fleet outmatched the German High Seas

Troops from Australia and New Zealand at Gallipoli.

Fleet in both equipment and seamanship. It could maintain a tight blockade regardless of the number of merchant vessels sunk by German **U-Boats** (submarines), a number that ranged from fifty to one hundred per month but failed to stop supplies from reaching Britain.

U-Boat warfare damages Germany's relations with the United States

British naval efforts were therefore primarily defensive, forcing Germany to take the initiative or slowly starve. U-Boat warfare raised German hopes but proved frustrating: rules of the sea required that a submarine give warning before launching torpedoes and allow crews and passengers to be rescued. Since this process exposed and endangered these small boats, they often ignored it, casting Germany in the role of an outlaw nation. The sinking of neutral vessels by mistake caused diplomatic crises, as did the sinking in 1915 of the British passenger liner *Lusitania*. That ship was carrying more than a thousand American passengers as well as a cargo of contraband munitions destined for Britain. The heavy loss of life almost forced the United States to break diplomatic relations with Germany, which thereafter temporarily restricted its U-Boat raids.

The Lusitania while it was still afloat.

THE VERDUN, SOMME, AND BRUSILOV OFFENSIVES. By early 1916, the balance of forces was shifting to favor the Allies. Tremendous Russian industrial expansion provided adequate modern equipment for the tsar's armies; France had mobilized unprecedented numbers of women for factory work, releasing thousands of men for combat duty; and Britain, whose army in 1914 had seven combat divisions, now fielded seventy. Made confident by this increase in offensive power, Allied generals planned to attack German lines north of the river Somme in northern France. But they overestimated their own strength and underestimated German defensive capability. Meanwhile Falkenhayn struck first, unleashing an offensive against the French at Verdun, a fortress in eastern France.

Verdun was selected for its symbolic significance: as a fortress town since Roman times, it represented France's will to resist. Falkenhayn, not realizing how much French factory work had been shifted to women, believed that France must be running short of military-age men. By besieging Verdun, he meant not to capture it but to force France to defend it by sending in more and more men. Eventually France would either lose Verdun or spread its remaining forces so thin that Germany could break through elsewhere on the Western Front.

Germany attacked Verdun on February 21 with a bombardment so enormous that the roar of the guns was heard in England. For a few days it seemed the town would fall, but the French, deciding it must be held, appointed General Philippe Pétain (*PĀ-tan*) to hold it. Pétain entrenched his men in fortifications to wait out the shelling. Eventually, unprotected German infantry moved forward and were shot down. By the end of June each side had lost more than 200 thousand killed and wounded, and Verdun's crater-scarred landscape resembled the surface of the moon.

Devastated landscape, Northern France.

Falkenhayn's failure at Verdun would cost him his command in August, but on July 1 he was still in charge as the Allies opened their offensive on the River Somme in northern France. They, too, placed their faith in overwhelming artillery fire, but nothing worked as expected. The British Army alone lost 20 thousand dead in the first eight hours, the largest one-day loss in British military history. By August 1 the combatants combined had lost more than 350 thousand men, and the front lines had scarcely moved. The Somme offensive finally ended on November 19, after more than 1.2 million men had been killed or wounded.

Finally the lessons of trench warfare began to sink in. Throwing huge numbers of cloth-clad soldiers at positions protected by barbed wire and machine guns produced carnage without altering the tactical situation in any useful way. The foot soldiers cursed their generals; a popular analysis of the fighting is entitled *Lions Led by Donkeys*. But without technology that could overcome trenches, the generals had few options. Frustrated by their inability to break the stalemate, they could think of nothing more creative than to propel more and more men into the devastation of trench warfare. None of the generals yet advised his government to seek a negotiated peace, although deadlocked wars in centuries past had been settled by negotiation.

The deadlock in the West did not, however, prevent movement in the East. Falkenhayn had attacked Verdun freely because he thought the 1915 German assault had ruined Russia's offensive capability. He was mistaken. In June 1916, Russian General Alexei Brusilov (*broo-SĒ-loff*) launched an offensive that henceforth bore his name. Brusilov's offensive split the Austrian Seventh Army in two, took 400 thousand prisoners, and cost the Central Powers a million casualties. He lacked the rail and road systems to follow up his victories, but he pushed Austria to the brink of collapse and achieved the greatest territorial gain since the beginning of trench warfare. The Central Powers were running out of manpower and resources. It was time for statesmen to find a way to make peace.

The 1916 offensives devastate the Western Front

Austro-Hungarian soldiers wearing gas masks.

The War Against Germany's Colonies

Colonial issues did not, in themselves, cause the Great War. That conflict erupted over purely European issues. But colonial disputes had contributed significantly to the rising tensions between the new German Empire and the longer-established empires of France and Britain. Once war broke out, Germany was forced to fight on two fronts, leaving it unable to defend its overseas possessions adequately. Military actions by forces from Britain, France, Belgium, Japan, Australia, and New Zealand picked off those possessions one by one, making the Great War a truly global war long before the 1917 intervention of the United States.

JAPAN OCCUPIES GERMANY'S PACIFIC EMPIRE. In Asia, the Anglo-Japanese Alliance of 1902 obligated Japan to come to Britain's aid if its possessions were attacked by a third party. On August 1, 1914, London informed Tokyo that it did not expect to ask for Japan's intervention. Three days later Japan declared itself neutral. But by August 6 Britain was having second thoughts. The Royal Navy wanted to blockade the German port of Qingdao on China's Shandong Peninsula while simultaneously hunting German warships and armed merchant ships in order to keep Pacific sea lanes safe for British commerce. These goals could not be achieved without sending additional British ships to the Pacific, and those ships were needed in the Atlantic. Britain therefore asked Japan for help in capturing or sinking armed German merchant ships, while German warships and the blockade of Qingdao would be handled by the Royal Navy.

This arrangement was limited collaboration, inconsistent with neutral status. On August 7–8 the Japanese cabinet decided to declare war on Germany and to move to eliminate German influence in China and the Pacific. This action frightened China, which feared Japanese more than European expansionism. Britain, recognizing Japan's intent to

Japan's entry creates a global war

partition China, then urged Japan to remain neutral. But Tokyo argued that Japanese public opinion demanded war with Germany and that the government could not resist the will of the people. Neither claim was fully true, but with Britain preoccupied with Germany in Europe, on August 23 Japan entered the war on its own terms (Map 31.3).

Japan moved at once against the German garrison at Qingdao, ignoring China's neutrality in doing so. Sixty thousand Japanese soldiers, with one British and one Indian battalion, laid siege to the city in early September. Qingdao's main defenses were designed to deal with an attack by China similar to those of the Boxer Rebellion, so they faced landward, but the Japanese, British, and Indians struck from seaward positions. Even so, it took until November 7 for the invaders to force the garrison of three thousand German marines to surrender. By that time all of Germany's Pacific holdings

Map 31.3 The Great War in Asia, 1914–1918

When Britain asked Japan for assistance in tracking down armed German merchant vessels, Japan took the opportunity to declare war on Germany and occupy German possessions in East Asia and the Pacific. Notice that Australia and New Zealand occupied other German holdings on behalf of the British Empire. Farther west, India made significant contributions in men, horses, and supplies to the Allied war effort. Why was Britain more prepared than Germany to fight a global war on a global scale?

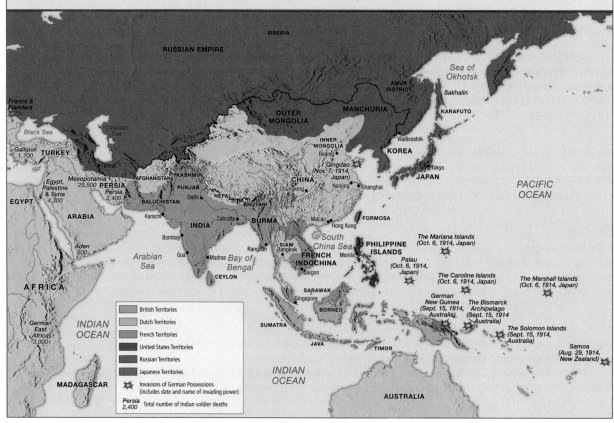

had been overrun. New Zealand troops occupied Samoa without resistance on August 29, and on September 15 the Australians accepted the surrender of all of German New Guinea and the Solomon Islands, where the Germans were led by an artillery captain who had no guns and an equestrian instructor who had no horses. Obviously Germany had never intended to defend the region vigorously. German defenses were no better in the Caroline Islands, the Marshall Islands, the Mariana Islands, and the island of Palau, all of which fell to the Japanese on October 6. Japan's entry into the Great War thereby allowed it to conquer territories which could form an outer defense perimeter for the Japanese Empire in the event of a future conflict with a Pacific power such as the United States.

An ammunition factory in India.

India makes an enormous contribution to the Allied war effort

India's small participation in the siege of Qingdao proved to be only the beginning of a major military commitment made by Britain's most valuable imperial possession. No fighting took place on the subcontinent, but 850 thousand Indian soldiers fought beside the British in Asia, Africa, and Europe. Nearly 50 thousand died in those actions. India also contributed 150 thousand horses and mules, 11 thousand camels, 75 thousand tons of timber, and 550 million rounds of ammunition. The extent of this assistance made Britain's refusal to grant meaningful autonomy to India after 1918 very difficult for Indians to accept.

DEVASTATION IN AFRICA. Germany's African colonies were not particularly valuable in themselves; they were table scraps left to the Germans after the British and French Empires had eaten their fill. But they could serve as staging areas for attacks on British and French interests, and their six important wireless stations could relay messages from Germany to its ships around the world. Britain and France wasted no time in attacking Germany in Africa.

The easiest Allied victory came in the West African territory of Togo (Map 31.4). Surrounded by the British Gold Coast and French West Africa, it fell to a joint invasion on August 27, 1914. The West Central African colony of Kamerun proved harder for the Allies. A combination of skillful German resistance, difficult topography, and the impossibility of fighting during the five-month season of torrential rains delayed Allied victory into 1916. By that time German Southwest Africa had already surrendered, in July 1915, to a joint force of 60 thousand Britons and Boers.

That left German East Africa, a sprawling colony as large as France, with a defense force of fewer than three thousand men commanded by Colonel Paul von Lettow-Vorbeck, a veteran of the Boxer Rebellion who had no intention of surrendering to the British or to anyone else. Lettow launched raids into British East Africa (Kenya) and Uganda in 1914, raising the German flag beneath Mount Kilimanjaro and causing an uproar among Britain's colonists. His forces repelled a joint British-Indian offensive that November, after which he confined his efforts to guerrilla warfare, fighting and quickly withdrawing. After German resistance collapsed in Southwest Africa, experienced troops from that conflict arrived in East Africa and embarked on a 1916 campaign under the command of General Jan Christiaan Smuts, a master of unconventional warfare who had repeatedly frustrated the British in the Boer War.

Smuts launched a multinational offensive from four different colonies at once, using British forces from Kenya and Nyasaland, Belgian troops from the Congo, and Portuguese soldiers from Mozambique, hoping to encircle Lettow and end the fighting in

Map 31.4 The Great War in Africa, 1914–1918

Germany's African colonies were lightly defended and could never have affected the fighting in Europe, but each of them contained at least one wireless station that could relay communications from Germany to German ships around the world. The Allies wanted to destroy these stations, and also to remove these colonies from German control. Observe that the stiffest fighting occurred in German East Africa, where forces under Colonel Paul von Lettow-Vorbeck remained in the field until after the armistice was signed in 1918. Why would the Allies have had such difficulty overcoming German resistance in East Africa?

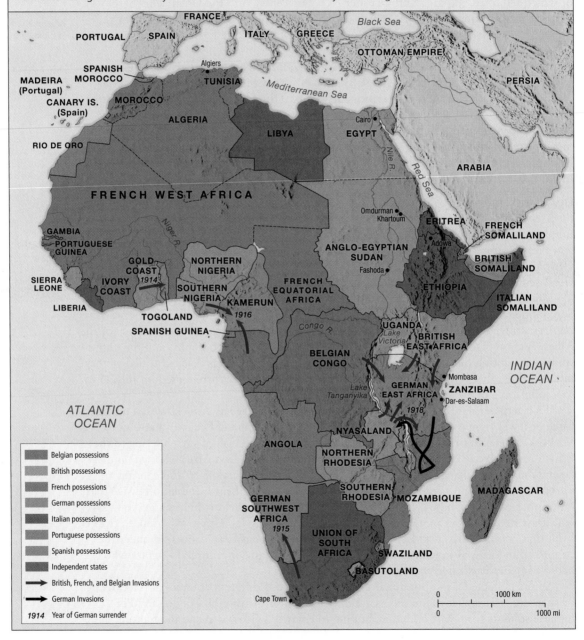

Africa. Lettow, however, now commanded more than 16 thousand men, most of them native Africans who had enlisted in his cause and knew the terrain better than Smuts. Lettow divided his German-African forces, broke out southward into Mozambique, moved northward again around Lake Nyasa, and ended up in northern Rhodesia, where he finally surrendered his command on November 25, 1918. His bloodied but undefeated troops had fought the British as recently as November 12, one day after the Armistice had been signed in France.

The battles over Germany's colonies devastated much of Africa. Campaigning in Kamerun lasted two years and wrecked much of the countryside. East Africa was ravaged by the constant fighting between Germany and Britain, which resulted in burned villages, loss of crops and stored food, and the drafting of more than 100 thousand Africans to serve as soldiers and porters. Nearly 10 percent of Africans drafted died, mostly from malnutrition and disease. To make matters worse, the global influenza pandemic of 1918 killed over 3 percent of the entire population of east, west, and central Africa. To Europeans, Africa was a sideshow to the main war, but to Africans, it was everything they had. By 1918 they responded to the Allied victory with little more than exhaustion and relief.

The Great War creates chaos in Africa

Civilian Life During the Great War

War's hardship lay heaviest on the soldiers, but noncombatants suffered too, although in different ways. By the end of 1916, the war had disrupted civilian life in all warring nations. Food, clothing, and critical raw materials were distributed on a priority basis, with military needs taking precedence. Inevitable shortages at home were handled through rationing, which restricted each person or family to a fixed quantity of each item per month or year. Many families lost members to military service, while those remaining at home were often required to work up to 72 hours a week in war plants.

Women workers in a British shipyard.

Since Britain was not invaded, its people suffered least, but their lives were not easy. Britain imported much of its food, and U-Boat raids jeopardized both agricultural and industrial imports. The British avoided malnutrition through strict rationing, and Germany's inability to sink the entire British merchant marine allowed imports to reach England, but the island nation's birth weights declined, and vitamin deficiencies afflicted many children. British soldiers were probably the war's best-fed troops, but at the expense of provisions for people at home.

In France, the huge casualty lists of 1914 led to the drafting of most able-bodied men and their replacement in factories and on farms by women. France lost a higher percentage of men aged 18 to 25 than any other warring nation, leaving many women without spouses and depressing the birthrate for the next two decades. German occupation of northeastern France cost that nation 80 percent of its prewar industry. New factories were established farther south, but the French people suffered severe shortages of manufactured consumer goods for the duration of the war.

France uses women in factories and on farms

Germany suffered tremendously, largely because of the slow strangulation imposed by the British blockade. Having counted on swift victory, the Kaiser's regime had no plans for allocating resources or feeding people at home in a lengthy war. Resource allotment was eventually handled by a central government agency, as the German economy shifted all production priorities to the war effort. More than a million women joined the industrial workforce, leaving children in the care of grandparents or aunts and necessitating rapid overhauling of workplaces—for example, through installation of women's lavatories on factory floors. Long hours of wartime work ruined the health of many malnourished women, unaccustomed to strenuous physical labor.

The British blockade causes malnutrition in Germany

Malnutrition was the principal challenge facing the German home front. Germany in 1913 imported one-third of its food supply. The British blockade cut off food imports, and the harvests of 1916 and 1917 were unusually poor due to fertilizer shortages and terrible weather. In the "turnip winter" of 1916–1917, turnips and other vegetables usually fed to livestock became main dishes on German dinner tables. Bread was made from one part flour and two parts sawdust, occasionally mixed with powdered limestone. Rations declined to one thousand calories per day, although 2,280 is the average required for adult health. About 750 thousand Germans died of malnutrition between 1914 and 1918, while many others fell to disease, their immune systems weakened by lack of food, the rationing of soap to one small bar per month, and the rationing of coal, which lowered household temperatures to levels dangerous in Germany's chilly climate.

In Russia, the government encouraged wartime sacrifice by banning the sale of vodka. At first the results were beneficial: criminal cases in Russia's capital declined 80 percent, and the incidence of poverty dropped by 75 percent as savings deposits grew. But consumption of tea and sugar increased tremendously, and by 1916 vodka-starved Russians had begun drinking varnish and cologne. Russian farmers kept pace with food demand, but soldiers at the front were fed first. Russia's railway system eventually proved unable to supply both soldiers and cities in a country partially occupied by enemy forces, triggering cataclysmic revolutions in 1917.

Year of Revolution, 1917

The year 1917 proved pivotal for both sides. The Allies gained a long-term advantage with the entry on their side of the United States. But mutinies in France and revolutions in Russia hurt the Allied cause in the short run, giving the Germans an apparent edge going into 1918.

The United States Enters the War

The United States tries to remain neutral

Woodrow Wilson, president of the neutral United States, tried to end the war late in 1916 by asking both sides to state the terms they needed to ensure their future security. The request was modest, but results were disappointing: each alliance presented uncompromising demands that were mutually exclusive. Reelected in November 1916 on the slogan "He kept us out of war," Wilson watched uneasily, fearing that unless the conflict ended soon, he would be unable to keep America out much longer.

On January 31, 1917, Wilson's apprehensions grew stronger. The Germans, faced with continuing military stalemate and starving from Britain's blockade, resumed unrestricted submarine warfare. The Kaiser's advisors argued that U-Boats could strangle Britain and end the war quickly; they minimized the consequences of a break with the United States, whose small army would need months of expansion and training, and whose soldiers would have to be ferried to Europe in troop ships that U-Boats could sink. Their argument was desperate rather than logical, but the longer the stalemate lasted, the weaker the Central Powers became and the more willing they were to grasp at any possible solution.

America's reaction to Germany's unleashing of its U-Boats startled Berlin. On February 26, 1917, Wilson asked Congress for permission to arm merchant ships. Three days later the U.S. government published the **Zimmermann Note**, an intercepted effort by German diplomat Arthur Zimmermann to bribe Mexico into an alliance against the United States by offering to return Texas, New Mexico, and Arizona, lost in the Mexican-American War of 1846–1848, in the event of German victory. Public outrage over this offer and persistent U-Boat attacks against American shipping led Wilson to ask Congress for a declaration of war on April 2, 1917. Congress complied four days later, but not until 1918 did large numbers of U.S. soldiers, transported across the Atlantic by naval convoys for protection against German U-Boats, arrive in France. When they did, however, they brought new energy that helped defeat the Germans.

Germany's U-Boat warfare brings the United States into the war

Anti-German propaganda.

Mutinies in the French Army

In the meantime, however, widespread mutinies rocked France's war-weary armies. Following the failure of an April 1917 offensive, nearly half the units in the French army refused to participate in further attacks.

The French government took the mutinies seriously because they were national in scope, involving civilian as well as military discontent. French soldiers lived in terrible conditions, ate inadequate food, and received almost no leave time. Their families endured high prices, long workweeks, and grinding anxiety over loved ones at the front. Both soldiers and families suffered from the stress of an apparently endless war. The government responded by suppressing strikes at home, naming the controversial, passionately anti-German, 76-year-old Georges Clemenceau (*klā-mahn-SŌ*) as prime minister, and appointing as army chief General Pétain, hero of Verdun. Pétain improved the food, granted regular leaves, and punished thousands of mutinous soldiers. Most important, he suggested that future attacks would be mounted only if they had legitimate prospects of success. Building on his reputation as a general who never asked men to sacrifice their lives needlessly, he gradually restored discipline and ended the crisis.

France limits the impact of mutinies

The French mutinies were a lost opportunity for the Germans. Unaware of the French protests, German commanders Hindenburg and Ludendorff, having reoriented German strategy eastward after replacing Falkenhayn in 1916, concentrated on the Eastern Front throughout 1917. That shift may have saved the French army.

The Russian Revolutions

Nothing, however, could save the Russian monarchy, battered by German advances and by the breakdown of Russia's wartime food supply system. In March 1917, food shortage sparked a spontaneous revolt that overthrew the tsarist regime. For the next eight months, an ineffective transitional regime sought vainly to restore order and maintain the war effort, but it was overthrown in November by Marxist revolutionaries, committed to removing Russia from the war and establishing a socialist society.

STRESSES AND STRAINS OF THE GREAT WAR. The Great War was disastrous for Russia from the outset. In the war's first month, as Germany invaded France, the Russians had rushed to relieve their French allies by attacking Germany from the East. By prompting the Germans to divert troops from France, this assault helped the French hold on. But the unprepared and poorly led Russians were badly defeated by the Germans and never fully recovered.

As the war continued and supplies of rifles, munitions, and food ran low, Russia's situation went from bad to worse. Russian forces fought well against Austria, but they were no match for the Germans, whose 1915 offensive pushed deep into the tsarist empire. Huge numbers of refugees, fleeing the German advance on foot, overwhelmed Russian roads and towns, undermining morale and further slowing the flow of supplies.

In August of that year, faced with a series of defeats, Tsar Nicholas II made a fateful decision: he assumed command of the Russian armies himself. His goals were to raise the soldiers' morale with his presence at the front, and to signal friends and foes that Russia would stay in the war despite its crippling setbacks. But the tsar's lack of military expertise soon made him a liability, and his absence from the capital left him reliant on his wife, Empress Alexandra, for governmental administration. And she was distracted and increasingly discredited by her connections with a dissolute Siberian "holy man" called Rasputin, who was apparently able to heal her son Alexis, heir to the Russian throne.

Russia staggers under the war's burdens

THE FALL OF THE RUSSIAN MONARCHY. Alexis had hemophilia, a congenital condition that kept his blood from clotting, so even the slightest cut or bruise could cause him to bleed to death. But Rasputin, apparently through prayer, seemed to be able to stop the bleeding. Seeing him as a savior sent by God, Alexandra came to trust him fully and rely on his advice.

Unfortunately for the monarchy's public image, Rasputin also led a life of public drunkenness and debauchery. Moreover, Alexandra herself was originally from Germany, the hated enemies' homeland. And to protect her son, his condition was kept secret, so the public did not know why Rasputin enjoyed her favor. As she systematically replaced effective ministers with unscrupulous incompetents favored by Rasputin, Russia's internal order disintegrated. The result was scandal: while the tsar was at the front, it seemed, a treacherous German woman and her depraved friend were ruining Russia.

Rasputin and Alexandra prove unable to lead Russia effectively

As the situation deteriorated, even loyal monarchists lost faith in the regime. Despite all efforts, the Duma could overcome neither the blunders of Russian officials nor the skills of German armies. Finally, in December 1916, a reactionary Duma deputy and two relatives of the royal family decided to murder Rasputin. First they fed him wine and pastries laced with cyanide poison. Then, when he remained unfazed, they shot him, clubbed him till he was unconscious, and drowned him in a canal.

The murder, of course, changed little. The Germans were still advancing, the inept ministers were still in office, internal order was still breaking down, and the distraught empress continued to hold power. Even as she conducted seances to communicate with her departed advisor, patriotic Russians and dedicated Duma deputies began to look for ways to replace their failing leaders with a more capable regime.

Meanwhile a far deeper and broader revolt was taking shape among the Russian masses. By this time runaway inflation, sparked by the printing of excess currency to pay for the war effort, had eroded people's meager incomes, while the hardships of continued conflict had pushed them to the breaking point. In the villages, from which most able men had long since been sent to the front, the remaining overstrained peasants refused to sell their grain in return for the worthless currency. Cities started running out of bread, and as work hours increased to meet war demands while purchasing power fell, large numbers of urban workers went out on strike. At the front, where millions of Russian troops had been killed, wounded, or captured, soldiers began questioning both the war and their orders. Pushed beyond all patience, the masses were beginning to move.

Early in 1917 tensions exploded in Russia's capital, renamed Petrograd (Peter's city) during the war because Petersburg sounded too German. On March 8, International Women's Day, exasperated female textile workers started a mass demonstration. They were joined by throngs of women who were waiting in long lines for bread and by striking men from the city's other industries. By the next day the whole city was on strike, and rioters controlled the streets. Away at the warfront, Nicholas responded by closing down the Duma, which he somehow blamed for the uproar, and by ordering local troops to disperse the demonstrators. On March 11 they did so, shooting into the rioting crowds and effectively clearing the streets. But that night the tormented troops, upset at being ordered to shoot their own people, resolved not to do it again, and some started to mutiny. On March 12 the rioting resumed, but when soldiers were ordered to fire at the crowds they shot their officers instead.

The tsar's authority had evaporated. On March 15, pressed by several Duma deputies and army officers, he renounced the throne for himself and his sickly son. Nicholas's brother, next in line, wisely refused to accept it. The imperial Russian monarchy silently ceased to exist.

DUAL POWER AND THE BOLSHEVIK CHALLENGE. In the midst of the revolution, two important bodies emerged to dominate developments for the next eight months. One was the **Provisional Government**, a temporary cabinet composed largely of Duma leaders, which assumed power until a new constitution could be enacted. Another was the **Petrograd Soviet**, made up of deputies elected by workers and soldiers, modeled on the soviet of 1905.

The Provisional Government, led by liberals, proclaimed democratic rights and freedoms for all, and promised to hold elections for a constituent assembly that would decide the future form of rule. But it alienated peasants by postponing major land reforms. It failed to fully restore internal order, or to solve Russia's economic problems. Most disastrously, it kept Russia in the war, determined to press on to victory despite the suffering of the people.

The Petrograd Soviet, led by socialists who believed Russia too economically primitive for a socialist regime, agreed to let the Provisional Government manage matters for the time being. Backed by strong popular support, however, the Soviet sought to shape policy, creating an ambiguous situation that Russians called "dual power." As the Petrograd Soviet called for broad reforms and peace "without annexations or indemnities," local soviets, elected by workers, soldiers, and peasants, sprang up all over Russia.

Following these events from afar was Vladimir Ilich Ulianov (*ool-YAH-noff*), better known as Lenin. Fifteen years earlier, as a rising socialist leader, he had challenged the orthodox Marxist view that industrial workers would eventually unite and create a

The Russian monarchy breaks under the strain of war

Burying the fallen, Petrograd, March 1917.

Dual centers of power cause chaos in Russia

Lenin.

Lenin's Bolsheviks appeal
to ordinary Russians

The Bolsheviks take
power in Russia

socialist revolution. The workers, he argued, would not do this on their own: they would merely form unions and settle for better wages and working conditions. Revolution, he asserted, must instead be made by a dedicated group of professional revolutionaries, acting as the workers' "vanguard." His views had split Russian Marxists into two factions: his supporters, who called themselves **Bolsheviks** ("those in the majority"), and their opponents, called Mensheviks ("those in the minority"). Having fled Russia to avoid arrest by tsarist police, Lenin had been attending a conference of European socialists in Switzerland when the Great War broke out. Switzerland was neutral in the conflict, and as part of its neutrality, it prohibited political leaders and men of military age who were citizens of the nations at war from leaving the country. Lenin was trapped in Switzerland along with other Russians in exile.

Now, suddenly, Russia was in revolution, and Lenin could not be part of it. His frustration grew as he learned that Soviet leaders, including some of his Bolsheviks, had let the Provisional Government take power rather than launching a socialist rebellion. In a sealed train provided by the Germans, who helped him return in hopes that his presence would weaken Russia's war effort, Lenin made his way to Petrograd in April. Once there, he stunned his socialist colleagues by demanding an immediate end to the "imperialist war" and the overthrow of the Provisional Government. He also called for the **nationalization** of all Russian land—the forced transfer of private property to state control. Later he simplified his views into slogans appealing to the Russian masses: "Peace!" "Land!" "Bread!" and "All power to the Soviets!"

Although Soviet leaders considered Lenin's ideas too radical, the workers found them attractive, and support for the Bolsheviks began to grow. So did their upper ranks. In May, Leon Trotsky, a brilliant Marxist orator and organizer who had helped lead the soviet of 1905, returned from exile in New York. Though a longtime political opponent of Lenin, he now joined him in pushing for immediate revolution, adding immensely to the energy and effectiveness of the Bolshevik leadership.

Confusion followed. In July radical workers and sailors, inspired by Lenin's ideas and angered at the Soviet's refusal to take power, rose in rebellion in Petrograd. Lenin at first tried to stop the uprising, believing that the Bolsheviks were not yet ready to take power, and then reluctantly gave it his support. But the "July Days" revolt failed when Soviet leaders rejected its demands, and forces loyal to the Provisional Government, influenced by rumors that Lenin was a German agent, disarmed the rebels and arrested some Bolshevik leaders. When Lenin himself fled to Finland, it appeared that the Bolshevik movement would collapse.

THE BOLSHEVIK TRIUMPH. In September, however, the Bolsheviks were rescued by actions of Russian conservatives. Eager to strengthen the Provisional Government and shut down the Soviet, General Lavr Kornilov (*kor-NĒ-loff*), the army's commander-in-chief, began sending troops toward Petrograd. But Russia's Prime Minister, Alexander Kerensky, fearing a right-wing coup, fired the general and called on the people to "save the revolution." Bolshevik leaders, including Trotsky, were released from prison and quickly took charge of the resistance, in which Bolshevik sailors and railway workers defeated the "Kornilov mutiny."

Suddenly the Bolsheviks were heroes. As their support among workers grew, they gained a majority in the Petrograd Soviet and elected Trotsky as its chair. Lenin returned in October, and together they planned a new revolution, timed to coincide with an All-Russian

Congress of Soviets, convening in the capital on November 7, 1917. Early that morning, Bolshevik Red Guards seized the city's railway stations and other strategic locations. By afternoon, most of Petrograd was in their hands. That evening, with 390 of the 650 delegates, the Bolsheviks took control of the Congress of Soviets. When Mensheviks and others walked out in protest, Trotsky rhetorically relegated them to the "dustbin of history." The next day the Bolsheviks completed their coup by storming the headquarters of the Provisional Government.

Moving quickly to implement their program, the Bolsheviks formed a Soviet government, with Lenin at its head. They issued a Decree on Peace, declaring an end to the war, and a Decree on Land, authorizing peasants to divide up nobles' estates. They nationalized banking and foreign trade, and urged workers to take control of factories. After several weeks of fighting, they defeated the remnants of the Provisional Government, took charge of Moscow, and spread their power to other Russian cities. In November they permitted previously planned elections for the constituent assembly, but when it became clear they could not control the assembly, they shut it down in January 1918 after it met for only one day. They also adopted the Western calendar, moved the capital to Moscow, began to repress the Orthodox church, and officially started calling themselves Communists.

The Bolsheviks move to fulfill their promises

Further actions by the new regime underscored its radical nature. It declared equal status for all Soviet citizens, without regard to social class or gender, making Soviet Russia the first major country to provide legal equality and full voting rights to all women. It also proclaimed equality for Russia's many ethnic minorities, some of whom, including Finns, Estonians, Latvians, Lithuanians, and Poles, gained independence at the end of the Great War. And, determined to get Russia out of the war and fulfill their Decree on Peace, Russia's new rulers began seeking a separate peace with Germany.

Bolshevik poster extolling the revolution.

Year of Decision, 1918

As 1918 began, the Soviet decision to seek peace appeared to give Germany the advantage in the Great War. The Allies, it is true, stood to gain eventually from the arrival of fresh American troops, but few had arrived thus far. In the meantime, by making peace with Russia, the Germans could move half a million battle-tested troops from the Eastern to the Western Front, giving them a huge advantage in northern France. It seemed that they might break the stalemate and win the war before the Americans could make much difference.

Barely noticed in all the upheaval was the use at the Battle of Cambrai in northern France, in November–December 1917, of a new technology that might favor the Allies. The British sent three hundred ungainly machines into combat and won a limited but highly significant victory. The perplexed Germans called these machines "power-driven mechanized vehicles on treads that destroy trenches." The more succinct British called them "tanks."

Russian Withdrawal from the War

On March 3, 1918, German and Soviet officials signed the Treaty of Brest-Litovsk, ending Russia's participation in the Great War. In a calculated risk of dazzling magnitude, the Bolsheviks gave Germany two-thirds of Russia west of the Ural Mountains in return for peace. Lacking an army capable of stopping the Germans, and anxious to maintain worker support by keeping his 1917 promises, Lenin explained that the Bolsheviks needed peace to consolidate their power.

The Treaty of Brest-Litovsk gave the Germans access to huge supplies of timber, oil, and grain from western Russia, but more important, it freed fifty combat-ready divisions for immediate transfer to the Western Front. There Ludendorff and Hindenburg were preparing a Great March Offensive, designed to batter the Allies into submission. The Americans were starting to arrive in force: 300 thousand had debarked by March, and 1.3 million would land in France by August. But these raw recruits were not as militarily valuable as the 500 thousand battle-toughened Germans transferred from east to west. If the war lasted until 1919, the influx of fresh Americans would eventually alter the balance in favor of the Allies, but no such alteration seemed possible in 1918.

The Treaty of Brest-Litovsk enables Germany to fight on one front

The Great March Offensive and Influenza Pandemic

The Great March Offensive began well for the Germans: 76 German divisions overran 28 British divisions, pushing them back toward Paris. Desperate to avoid catastrophe, the British agreed to serve under the French General Ferdinand Foch (*FŌSH*), whose appointment as overall commander of Allied forces on April 3, 1918, saved the situation by giving one man unconditional authority to allocate reserves.

Foch's efforts to stiffen Allied resistance were aided by Americans and by the flu. By late May, German forces stood only 56 miles from Paris, but there they were blocked by inexperienced American troops at Belleau Wood. This unexpected U.S. victory startled the Germans. Driven to the limits of their endurance, they soon fell victim to one of history's deadliest afflictions: the great influenza pandemic of 1918.

This disease, which incapacitated half a million German soldiers in June, was much more deadly than the varieties of flu that today kill more than 36 thousand Americans each winter. Sweeping the globe in 1918, it struck down young and old, healthy and infirm, killing perhaps as many as 50 million people. Infected with catastrophic fevers and severe respiratory infections, many sufferers literally drowned in their own blood and fluids. Advancing German troops, exposed to the elements in an unusually wet spring and malnourished because of the British blockade, proved far more susceptible than well-fed Allies quartered in trenches, houses, and barns.

A pandemic of influenza kills many millions throughout the world

Unity of command enabled the Allies to exploit the German plight. On July 18, Foch committed Allied reserves to a surprising counteroffensive. The German lines shuddered and fell back. After four years of brutal war, they lacked the manpower reserves to blunt the Allied assault, and in technological development they had fallen fatally behind. Technology, which in 1914 had favored the defensive, now provided the attacker with the tank as a means of destroying trenches. The Allies had produced more than a thousand quality tanks, while the Germans had built about fifty inferior ones.

Bulgaria's surrender dooms the Central Powers

Ludendorff tried unsuccessfully to stabilize his front, but German forces were demoralized by defeat, weakened by disease, terrified by Allied tanks, and disheartened by the prospect of continuing American arrivals. Foch threw everything he had into a broad-front assault on September 26; two days later Ludendorff's nerve cracked, and he decided to ask the Kaiser to seek an armistice. One day after that, Germany's ally Bulgaria asked for an armistice on the Balkan Front. With Bulgaria out of the war, Allied forces could drive northwest from the Balkans into Austria-Hungary, defenseless there since it had committed all its troops to the Italian Front. Austria's collapse would open a "back door" into Germany, which lacked sufficient reserves to defend a new front. Bulgaria's surrender was the final blow. The war in Europe was nearly over.

Decision in Southwest Asia

In Southwest Asia, the Great War was ending as well. In entering the war on the side of the Central Powers, the Ottoman Empire had committed itself to more than its limited infrastructure and industrial base could support. An Ottoman attack on Russia through the Caucasus Mountains in December 1914 proved decidedly ill advised, as more than 30 thousand Turks died of frostbite and the Russians counterattacked successfully. The campaign was disastrous not only for the Ottomans but for their Armenian subjects.

An Ottoman grenade with a fuse made from rope.

The Russian army's counteroffensive included a division of Christian Armenians, who reportedly massacred the inhabitants of several Turkish villages. This alleged atrocity, coupled with the April 1915 declaration of a secessionist Armenian government backed by the Russians, caused many Turks to doubt the loyalty of people of Armenian descent. Between 1915 and 1918, according to many historians, half a million Armenians were deported to Mesopotamia, while more than a million were murdered outright or died of disease and starvation during forced marches across desert regions. The scholarly and political disputes over how many were killed and whether or not these actions constituted **genocide**, the deliberate and systematic destruction of an entire race or ethnic group, pale beside the immensity of the human tragedy that befell the Armenians.

The Turkish victory at Gallipoli in 1915 did not cure the vulnerability of the Empire. Continuing warfare in the Caucasus brought many casualties and little gain. In 1916 Hussein ibn Ali, Sherif of Mecca, protector of the Holy Places of Islam, placed himself at the head of an Arab revolt that immediately threatened Ottoman control of Palestine and Arabia. A British liaison officer, Colonel T. E. Lawrence, offered tactical advice to the Arabs and rode into history as "Lawrence of Arabia." But the heavy fighting against the Ottomans was done by an army of Britons, Australians, and New Zealanders based in Egypt, and an army of Indians fighting in Mesopotamia.

Indian and British forces in Mesopotamia took Baghdad in 1917 and Mosul the following year, threatening Ottoman petroleum resources (Map 31.5). In Palestine, the Egyptian-based army of General Allenby took Jerusalem in December 1917 and by September 1918 was confronting Turkish forces at Megiddo, the "Armageddon" referred to in the Bible. Allenby's forces won the battle at Megiddo, broke through Turkish lines, and forced the Ottoman Empire to sign an armistice on October 30. Together with Bulgaria's surrender in September, this left Germany and Austria-Hungary isolated and desperate.

The Ottoman Empire collapses

The Path to the Armistice

Ending the war formally took until early November. The Kaiser decided to ask for a truce on the basis of the Fourteen Points, a plan for a just peace outlined by Wilson in January 1918 (see "Woodrow Wilson: The Fourteen Points"). But for Wilson, who had

Map 31.5 The Great War in Southwest Asia, 1917–1918

The Ottoman Empire, attacked from three sides, finally cracked under the strain in 1918. Note that Indian and British troops, moving up the Tigris and Euphrates valleys, conquered Mesopotamia and compromised Ottoman petroleum supplies. An Arab army in Palestine and Syria weakened the southern flank and helped British forces, moving north from Egypt, to break through at Megiddo and force the Ottomans to capitulate on October 30, 1918. Why did the Ottoman Empire, known for a century as the "Sick Man of Europe," succeed in holding out for so long?

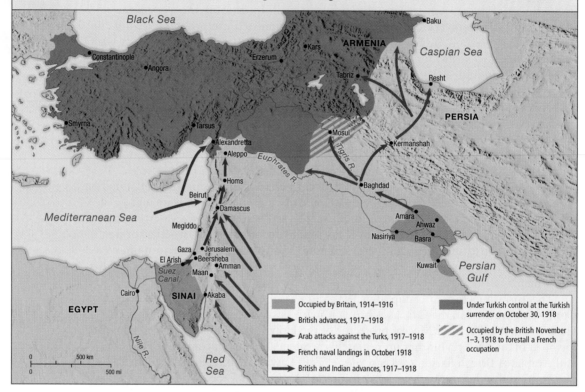

led America into the war "to make the world safe for democracy," no government led by an emperor could be sufficiently democratic. On October 16 he issued conditions that implied that the Kaiser should abdicate. William II, outraged, resisted until November 9. By then Austria-Hungary had also surrendered, and Germany's army continued to retreat toward its own frontier.

Now the weakening of German morale proved decisive. Sailors of Germany's High Seas Fleet mutinied when admirals asked them to put to sea to fight the British Grand Fleet and go down with honor. Faced with desertion and civil war, the German High Command informed the Kaiser that the army would no longer defend his regime. Disbelieving to the last, William went into exile in neutral Holland, where he lived quietly until 1941, dying a year after Nazi Germany invaded and subjugated the country that had welcomed him.

Armistice talks were proceeding as William left. Having appealed for a truce on the basis of the Fourteen Points, the German government was appalled at the severity

Document 31.2 Woodrow Wilson, The Fourteen Points

In January 1918, U.S. President Woodrow Wilson outlined what he hoped would be viewed as the foundation upon which a just and lasting peace might be established. His outline became known as the Fourteen Points.

I. Open covenants of peace, openly arrived at, after which there shall be no private international understandings of any kind but diplomacy shall proceed always frankly and in the public view.

II. Absolute freedom of navigation upon the seas, outside territorial waters, alike in peace and in war . . .

III. The removal, so far as possible, of all economic barriers and the establishment of an equality of trade conditions among all the nations consenting to the peace and associating themselves for its maintenance.

IV. Adequate guarantees given and taken that national armaments will be reduced to the lowest point consistent with domestic safety . . .

VII. Belgium, the whole world will agree, must be evacuated and restored, without any attempt to limit the sovereignty which she enjoys in common with all other free nations . . .

VIII. All French territory should be freed and the invaded portions restored, and the wrong done to France by Prussia in 1871 in the matter of Alsace-Lorraine, which has unsettled the peace of the world for nearly fifty years, should be righted . . .

IX. A readjustment of the frontiers of Italy should be effected along clearly recognizable lines of nationality.

X. The peoples of Austria-Hungary, whose place among the nations we wish to see safeguarded and assured, should be accorded the freest opportunity to autonomous development.

XI. Rumania, Serbia, and Montenegro should be evacuated; occupied territories restored; Serbia accorded free and secure access to the sea; and the relations of the several Balkan states to one another determined by friendly counsel among historically established lines of allegiance and nationality . . .

XII. The Turkish portion of the present Ottoman Empire should be assured a secure sovereignty, but the other nationalities which are now under Turkish rule should be assured an undoubted security of life and an absolutely unmolested opportunity of autonomous development, and the Dardanelles should be permanently opened as a free passage to the ships and commerce of all nations under international guarantees.

XIII. An independent Polish state should be erected which should include the territories inhabited by indisputably Polish populations, which should be assured a free and secure access to the sea, and whose political and economic independence and territorial integrity should be guaranteed by international covenant.

XIV. A general association of nations must be formed under specific covenants for the purpose of affording mutual guarantees of political independence and territorial integrity to great and small states alike.

of the terms actually offered. Germany was required to evacuate all occupied territory, abandon German territory west of the Rhine River, repudiate the Treaty of Brest-Litovsk, surrender all its ships and massive amounts of military equipment, and agree to **reparations**, payments to compensate the Allies for war damages. These terms were imposed on a nation devastated by the influenza pandemic and literally starving from the effects of the British blockade, a continuing act of war for which no ending date was set.

The Great War is ended by an armistice

That condition transformed the truce into an outright surrender. An **armistice** is a temporary cessation of hostilities between warring powers; but the continuing blockade, weakening Germany's ability to resist with each passing day, effectively made it impossible for Germany to resume fighting. When bells rang throughout Europe and America at 11:00 a.m. Greenwich Mean Time on November 11—the eleventh hour on the eleventh day of the eleventh month of 1918—they tolled not merely an armistice, but the actual end of the Great War.

Chapter Review

Putting It in Perspective

With the end of the Great War, later called World War I, Europe's long nightmare seemed over. The conflict's crushing impact had fallen mostly on Europe, which at the close of 1918 lay demoralized, devastated, and in many ways transformed. The royal houses of Germany, Austria-Hungary, and Russia had been overthrown, and the Ottoman Sultan would soon follow. Austria-Hungary and the Ottoman Empire had broken apart, the former into small national states, the latter into a Turkish national state and regions that became virtual colonies of Britain and France. Marxism had come to power in Russia, frightening capitalist nations everywhere and heightening postwar anxieties. The war had toppled dynasties and changed the way in which Europe was organized.

For more than nine million people, the organization of Europe was irrelevant: they were dead. The casualty lists dwarfed even those of the Napoleonic Wars. But for many who had not served at the front, the death toll was less devastating than the living human wreckage. Men without limbs and without faces haunted the cities of Europe, surviving hideous wounds that in earlier wars would have killed them on the battlefield. Tens of thousands suffered from shell-shock, a debilitating psychological condition stemming from prolonged exposure to artillery bombardment. Civilians, particularly in Germany, had suffered terribly from malnutrition and exposure, factors that fed the enormous death tolls in the influenza pandemic. The result was a demographic void, an absence of healthy young men between the ages of 18 and 35 that would scar Europe for two generations.

The physical destruction of land and property was unprecedented. Trench warfare wrecked vast areas of northeastern France. Unexploded shells and munitions lay in fields across Europe, maiming curious children into the 1960s. Livestock had been blown to bits or butchered for food in colossal numbers; replacing them would take decades. The task of rebuilding was daunting.

Finally, the prospect of another such war altered the perspectives of traumatized Europeans. Nearly everyone agreed that such a catastrophe must never be allowed to happen again, but how could it be prevented? Could the nations of Europe bury their hatreds along with their dead and learn to work together for stability and peace? The answers to these questions were not immediately apparent, and in the silence created by their absence, the nightmare lived on.

Reviewing Key Material

KEY CONCEPTS

Triple Alliance, 784	trench warfare, 791
Bloody Sunday, 787	U-Boats, 794
soviet, 787	Zimmermann Note, 801
Duma, 787	Provisional Government, 803
Diplomatic Revolution of 1890–1907, 788	Petrograd Soviet, 803
Triple Entente, 788	Bolsheviks, 804
Bosnian Crisis of 1908–1909, 788	nationalization, 804
	genocide, 807
blank check, 789	reparations, 809
	armistice, 810

KEY PEOPLE

Franz Ferdinand, 783, 788	Kaiser William II, 786
Otto von Bismarck, 783	Tsar Nicholas II, 786

ASK YOURSELF

1. How was the European balance of power transformed by the Diplomatic Revolution of 1890–1907?
2. Why wasn't the Crisis of July 1914 resolved peacefully, as so many earlier crises had been?
3. Why was the Great War so much more protracted than earlier wars in the nineteenth century? Why was it so much more deadly?
4. How did the strains of modernization and war weaken the Russian monarchy? Why did the Bolsheviks triumph in Russia in 1917?
5. Why did the Allies eventually win the Great War?

GOING FURTHER

Barry, John. *The Great Influenza*. 2003.

Beckett, Ian. *The Great War, 1914–1918*. 2001.

Eksteins, Modris. *Rites of Spring: The Great War and the Birth of the Modern Age*. 1989.

Ferguson, Niall. *The Pity of War*. 2000.

Ferro, Marc. *The Great War, 1914–1918*. 1993.

Fitzpatrick, Sheila. *The Russian Revolution, 1917–1932*. 2nd ed. 1994.

Florinsky, Michael. *The End of the Russian Empire*. 1961.

Fromkin, David. *Europe's Last Summer*. 2004.

Fussell, Paul. *The Great War and Modern Memory*. 1977.

Gatrell, Peter. *Government, Industry and Rearmament in Russia, 1900–1914*. 1994.

Gilbert, Martin. *The First World War: A Complete History*. 1996.

Hasegawa, Tsuyoshi. *The February Revolution: Petrograd, 1917*. 1981.

Holquist, P. *Making War, Forging Revolution*. 2002.

Joll, James. *The Origins of the First World War*. 2nd ed. 1992.

Keegan, John. *The First World War*. 1999.

Langer, William. *European Alliances and Alignments, 1871–1890*. 1977.

Neiberg, Michael. *Fighting the Great War: A Global History*. 2005.

Stevenson, David. *Cataclysm: The First World War as Political Tragedy*. 2004.

Strachan, Hew. *The First World War: To Arms*. 2001.

Tuchman, Barbara. *The Guns of August*. 1962.

Wohl, Robert. *The Generation of 1914*. 1979.

Key Dates and Developments

1890–1907 The Diplomatic Revolution	**1916** Battle of Verdun The Somme Offensive The Brusilov Offensive
1894–1917 Reign of Nicholas II in Russia	
1904 Anglo-French Entente	**1917** Fall of the Russian monarchy (March) United States enters the war Mutinies in the French army Bolshevik Revolution in Russia (November)
1904–1905 Russo-Japanese War	
1905 Russian Revolution of 1905	
1907 Anglo-Russian Entente	**1918** Treaty of Brest-Litovsk Great March Offensive Global influenza pandemic Armistice (November 11)
1908–1914 European crises	
1914 The Great War begins Deadlock develops on Western Front	
1915 Italy enters the War Sinking of the *Lusitania* Landing at Gallipoli	

Anxieties and Ideologies of the Interwar Years, 1918–1939

- Western Society and Culture in an Age of Anxiety

- Democracy, Depression, and Dictatorship

- New Varieties of Nationalism in Africa and Asia

- Chapter Review

An Age Of Anxiety

Anxieties abounded in the interwar years, as long-held standards of behavior, art, and science seemed to disappear. This famous "surrealist" painting, *The Treachery of Images*, proclaims in French that "This is not a pipe"—making the point that perceptions of "reality" can be deceiving. It is, after all, a *painting*, not a pipe (see page 817).

In December 1918, Woodrow Wilson was greeted in Paris by seas of flags and flowers, and then warmly cheered by enormous crowds as he rode through town in an open carriage. Earlier that year, declaring his objectives in the Great War, the American president had listed Fourteen Points (page 809) that he thought should be the basis for a peace settlement. They included such idealistic goals as open peace talks, freedom of the seas, free trade, arms control, and **national self-determination**—the right of each nationality to freely decide its own political status. In November, Germany had agreed to a war-ending armistice based on his Fourteen Points. Now, as he arrived for the Paris Peace Conference that would shape the postwar world, Wilson was the man of the hour, a prophet whose idealism fed people's hopes for an enduring peace fair to victor and vanquished alike. The hopes and dreams of a war-weary world rested on his shoulders.

Dictatorships

Western Democracies, Colonies, Dominions

Soon, however, world events dampened these hopes and dreams. At the peace conference, beginning in January 1919, Allied leaders, bent on punishing defeated foes, resisted Wilson's idealism. Britain and France sought to weaken Germany by imposing huge reparations payments. The Italians demanded lands secretly promised them when they joined the war, and then went home enraged when Wilson and others rejected their demands. In April, in Amritsar, India, troops under British command shot hundreds of anti-British protesters, dimming hopes for self-determination in Europe's Asian colonies. In May, Chinese students in Beijing, angered that the conference permitted Japan to take over German claims in China, began a mass movement heralding the rise of Chinese nationalism and communism. In June, outside Paris, at the palace of Versailles, subdued German delegates signed a harsh treaty imposed by the conference, while flags across Germany flew at half mast to mark the nation's resentment. In September, back in Washington, exhausted by futile efforts to promote the Versailles Treaty to his own country, Wilson suffered a paralyzing stroke.

Animosities enduring from the war—and from the peace imposed at Paris—would contribute two decades later to a Second World War. In the interwar era (1919–1939), nations East and West were torn by cultural and social changes, the global economy was rocked by depression, and radical new ideologies reshaped Europe, Africa, and Asia. So unsettling was this era that later observers called it the Age of Anxiety.

Western Society and Culture in an Age of Anxiety

The Great War devastated Europe, physically and emotionally. The lands where it was fought, strewn with mines and scarred by trenches, would take decades to recover, while the loss in human potential caused by its countless casualties was incalculable. Prewar faith in progress, driven by new technologies, died in the trenches as new technologies helped produce inhuman slaughter. As hope and idealism gave way to fatalism and cynicism, challenging new ideas, combined with social and cultural changes, added to the anxieties of the interwar years.

The Rise of Relativism and Relativity

Especially unsettling was a growing attitude of **relativism**, the view that truth and morality vary from one person, group, or situation to another. People in the West had long presumed that absolute standards of truth and morality existed, and that human reason, aided by divine revelation, could distinguish fact from falsehood and good from evil. But by the 1920s, with faith in Western ideals shaken by the war, many were coming to feel that all certainties had vanished. Much as "beauty is in the eye of the beholder," what was true for one person might be false for another, and what was wrong in some cultures or conditions might be acceptable in others.

Relative thinking challenges traditional morality

To some extent, nineteenth-century ideologies (Chapter 27) had laid the foundations for twentieth-century relativism. Marxism, for example, held that human society was based on class struggle, and that violent rebellion was not a moral evil but a necessary part of that struggle. Indeed, to many Marxists and followers of other ideologies, a statement's truth or an action's morality depended on whether or not it advanced their cause. Social Darwinists, who applied Darwin's notion of "survival of the fittest" to human societies, also saw struggle as essential, but they, unlike Marxists, claimed that the strong must naturally prey on the weak. Truth and morality were superseded by the struggle for survival, which justified almost any action advancing one's nation or race. Even imperialism and the Great War, both of which involved mass carnage, were seen by Social Darwinists as components of this natural struggle.

Freud asserts that behaviors are induced by unconscious drives

In the twentieth century, new understandings of human psychology further challenged conventional attitudes about truth and morality. Austrian psychiatrist Sigmund Freud (*FROID*), disputing the idea that human behavior is based on rational decisions, held that people are driven by unconscious instincts and impulses that conflict with the conscious mind. Freud's ideas—including his focus on human drives for sexual pleasure, his rejection of religious scruples, and his concept of a death wish that clashes with self-preservation instincts—suggested that, since human behaviors are induced by unconscious urges, there can be no absolute moral standards.

Einstein asserts that measurements of time and space are relative

Another form of relative thinking revolutionized physics, whose laws had seemed so constant since the time of Isaac Newton. In 1905 and 1916 Albert Einstein, a German scientist of Jewish descent, published his theories of **relativity**, asserting that measurements of time, space, and motion vary with the perspectives of observers (see "Einstein on Relativity"). To explain his concepts, Einstein used illustrations based on moving trains. If a man drops a stone from a moving train, for example, he will see the stone fall in a straight line (ignoring wind resistance), but an observer on the ground will see the stone fall in a curve. Similarly, if a bird flies by in a straight line, the man on the train will see it flying with a different speed and direction than observed by the person on the ground. The stone's path and the bird's speed and direction are thus relative to the location and movement of the two observers.

In his famous formula $E=mc^2$ (energy equals mass times the speed of light squared), Einstein proposed that matter could be converted into energy, asserting that each atom of matter contains enormous energy in its nucleus. By the 1940s, scientists would split

Albert Einstein.

Document 32.1 Einstein on Relativity

In 1905 and 1916 Albert Einstein published his special and general theories of relativity, revolutionizing science by asserting that measurements of time, space, and motion are relative to the location and movements of observers. In the excerpts below, he uses examples based on moving trains to help demonstrate his theories.

It is not clear what is to be understood . . . by "position" and "space." I stand at the window of a railway carriage which is travelling uniformly, and drop a stone on the embankment, without throwing it. Then, disregarding the influence of the air resistance, I see the stone descend in a straight line. A pedestrian who observes the misdeed from the footpath notices that the stone falls to earth in a parabolic curve. I now ask: Do the "positions" traversed by the stone lie "in reality" on a straight line or on a parabola? . . . With the aid of this example it is clearly seen that there is no

such thing as an independently existing trajectory . . . , but only a trajectory relative to a particular body of reference . . .

. . . In order to attain the greatest possible clearness, let us return to our example of the railway carriage supposed to be travelling uniformly . . . Let us imagine a raven flying through the air in such a manner that its motion, as observed from the embankment, is uniform and in a straight line. If we were to observe the flying raven from the moving railway carriage, we should find that the motion of the raven would be one of different velocity and direction, but that it would still be uniform and in a straight line . . .

SOURCE: Albert Einstein, *Relativity: The Special and General Theory* (1920) III. "Space and Time in Classical Mechanics" (http://www.bartleby.com/173.3); V. "The Principle of Relativity (In the Restricted Sense)" (http://www.bartleby.com/173.5).

---

the atoms of radioactive elements, such as uranium and plutonium, to release their nuclear energy and develop atomic bombs (Chapter 33). In showcasing science's vast creative and destructive powers, scientists helped to further blur distinctions between good and bad.

Einstein asserts that matter can be converted into energy

All these new ideas added to the age's uncertainties. If truth and morality varied according to one's situation and psychology, if time and space varied according to one's perspective, and if even solid-looking matter was made up of energy particles, how could humans ever trust their judgments? Human judgments, after all, had led to the Great War.

Technology and Popular Culture

Meanwhile, as new ideas transformed people's perspectives, new technologies transformed their everyday lives. In the 1920s, especially in the West, the growing use of radios, phonographs, movies, telephones, electric appliances, and automobiles gave rise to whole new forms of popular culture. Radios, for example, enabled sports fans to follow their favorite teams, feeding a growing frenzy for spectator sports. Radios and phonograph records helped millions enjoy new forms of popular music, including blues and jazz. And millions went to movies each week—especially after 1927, when films with sound, pioneered by an immensely popular American movie called *The Jazz Singer*, began replacing silent films.

New technologies transform Western popular culture

Telephones, refrigerators, and washing machines made life easier for many; but the most influential new mass-market product was the automobile. To make production more efficient, American auto maker Henry Ford used the **assembly line**, making vehicles by conveying them in a continuous flow through a series of work stations that each performed a single function. This system enabled Ford to mass-produce millions of inexpensive cars, known as Model Ts, at prices affordable to ordinary people, including his own well-paid workers.

Mass-produced cars and trucks foster regional and global connections

As other manufacturers, following Ford's lead, used assembly lines to package foods and make appliances, mass-produced goods and vehicles transformed Western societies. Roads were paved and expanded to accommodate cars and trucks, and dotted with gasoline stations, supplying fuel from oil-rich regions such as Texas, the Dutch East Indies, and the Persian Gulf. Rural residents drove cars to town to shop or attend movies, while city people used cars for weekend drives to the countryside or beach. Farmers plowed fields with motorized tractors, while townsfolk ate produce brought daily by motor trucks. Nations were knit together by new technologies, as autos reduced distances and expanded regional contacts, while radio programs, newscasts, movies, and sports reached millions, helping to foster a sense of national culture.

Cars on Daytona Beach, Florida in the 1920s.

New technologies also were used to build political support. Radio transmitted "fireside chats" by British Prime Minister Stanley Baldwin and U.S. President Franklin Roosevelt, as well as fiery speeches by Italian dictator Benito Mussolini and Germany's Adolf Hitler. In the 1920s, movies such as *Battleship Potemkin*, by Soviet film pioneer Sergei Eisenstein, rallied support for communism by exalting Russia's revolutionary past; in the 1930s, films such as *Triumph of the Will*, by German female filmmaker Leni Riefenstahl, showcased mass glorification of Hitler.

Changes in the Role of Women

Expanding roles for women affect fashions and social conduct

Riefenstahl's filmmaking career was but one example of the new roles played by women in the postwar West. Following the Great War, women in Britain, Germany, Poland, Russia, and America received voting rights, partly in response to decades of activism promoting women's suffrage and partly in recognition of the work done by women who took jobs in industry when the men were off at war. Although most women gave up these jobs after the war, some stayed on to pursue careers in industry and business formerly closed to women, while those returning to the home often did so with a new assertiveness based on their wartime work experience.

Changing women's roles were also reflected in new fashions and behaviors. Freeing themselves from confining corsets that accentuated breasts and hips, some young women became "flappers," sporting short hair, short skirts, and straight-fit styles emphasizing boyish figures. Liberated by automobiles from parental supervision, single young women and men went on dates to movies and dances, smoked cigarettes in public, and in cars engaged in sexual conduct their parents surely would have frowned on.

Measuring women's shorter swimsuits in the 1920s.

Architecture, Art, and Literature

New trends and technologies also affected architecture, art, and literature. By the early twentieth century, growing use of cranes, elevators, structural steel, and reinforced concrete helped architects design larger and taller buildings than before. Devising new styles based on simplicity and function, architects such as Germany's Walter Gropius and his

Bauhaus (*BOUW-house*) school created elegant but practical structures in cities from America to India. Cities became assortments of cubic structures, from large block-shaped buildings to soaring urban skyscrapers.

New art forms were likewise inspired by new urban realities and by global connections forged in the imperial age. Before the Great War some European artists, influenced by Japanese art that disregarded perspective and realism, experimented with impressionism, depicting impressions made on the painter by scenes from nature and modern urban life. Inspired by cubic urban structures and by African art forms, Spanish-French painter Pablo Picasso created **cubism**, an artistic style using geometric shapes to produce bold images. After the war German artist Otto Dix used ghastly images to capture war's nightmare and postwar social decadence, while Picasso and others embraced **surrealism**—art that sought to challenge perceptions (see page 812) or to portray Freud's unconscious world of drives, fantasies, and dreams. As artists depicted subjective impressions instead of objective reality, artistic standards, like moral norms and scientific measurements, were revolutionized by relativism.

New literary methods also violated traditional standards. In his novel *Ulysses* (1922), for example, Ireland's James Joyce used a stream of consciousness technique, later adopted by others, to depict the free and ungrammatical flow of a character's inner thoughts and impressions. And American poet e. e. cummings shunned such conventions as rhyme, meter, and capitalization.

Other writers and poets reflected the age's anxieties. In a two-volume work, *The Decline of the West* (1918 and 1922), German educator Oswald Spengler claimed that Western Civilization, having undergone cycles of growth and development like other great cultures before it, was now in decline and decay. In the 1929 novel *All Quiet on the Western Front*, German author Erich Maria Remarque depicted the ordeals of a group of young men who joined the German army in the Great War expecting to find honor and glory but instead finding only death, degradation, mutilation, and madness. In *The Waste Land* (1922), British-American poet T. S. Eliot provided bleak, grotesque images of desolation, death, and despair. And in *The Second Coming* (1921), Irish poet W. B. Yeats cogently captured the era's pervasive pessimism:

Things fall apart; the center cannot hold;

Mere anarchy is loosed upon the world,

The blood-dimmed tide is loosed, and everywhere

The ceremony of innocence is drowned;

The best lack all conviction, while the worst

Are full of passionate intensity.

A cubist painting by Pablo Picasso.

Global connections and urban realities impact architecture and art

Literature and poetry reflect new techniques and global anxieties

Democracy, Depression, and Dictatorship

Yeats's pessimism proved prophetic. In the interwar years, efforts to achieve an enduring peace proved elusive. Hopes gave way to resentments, prosperity gave way to depression, and democracies gave way to dictatorships—often driven by men and ideologies full of passionate intensity.

The Versailles Settlement

In 1919 the victorious powers—led by U.S. President Woodrow Wilson, British Prime Minister David Lloyd George, and French Premier Georges Clemenceau (*klā-mahn-SŌ*)—dominated the Paris Peace Conference cited at the start of this chapter. Excluded from the conference were the defeated powers, Germany and its allies, as well as the new Soviet Russia. The result was a settlement devised and imposed by the victors.

Great War victors impose harsh treaties on the vanquished

Although the victors imposed a treaty on each defeated country (Germany, Austria, Hungary, Bulgaria, and Ottoman Turkey), the centerpiece of the postwar settlement was the Treaty of Versailles with Germany. A compromise between Wilson, who had promised a just peace, and his allies, who sought retribution for their suffering and reward for their hard-won triumph, it formally blamed the Germans for the war and forced them to pay huge reparations for war damage. Germany also had to reduce its army to 100 thousand men, surrender land to Belgium, France, and Poland, demilitarize its Rhineland region bordering Belgium and France, and give up all its overseas colonies. When the treaty was signed on June 28, 1919, exactly five years after the shots at Sarajevo that triggered the Great War, the starved, exhausted Germans bitterly resented the harsh pact forced upon them.

Treaties form League of Nations, but U.S. fails to join

At Wilson's insistence, the treaties also created the **League of Nations**, an international organization designed to maintain peace by cooperation among its members, intended eventually to include most of the world's nations. It opened in 1920 but was weakened by the absence of Wilson's own country. The U.S. Senate, wary of foreign commitments, rejected Wilson's dream by failing to ratify the Versailles Treaty. The world's richest nation thus was not a member of the League.

Britain and France manage former German and Ottoman possessions

Former German colonies and Ottoman provinces became **League of Nations mandates**, lands entrusted to victorious nations such as Britain, France, or Japan, allegedly to help prepare the people for self-rule. This formula allowed the victors to take over the possessions of the vanquished, including Arab lands in the Middle East, while paying lip service to Wilson's notion of national self-determination.

Democracy and Dictatorship in Eastern Europe

Meanwhile, following the collapse of the Russian, German, and Austro-Hungarian empires during the Great War, numerous new nations emerged in Eastern Europe, formed by nationality groups long subject to these realms. The former Russian regions of Finland, Estonia, Latvia, and Lithuania became independent states. The Austro-Hungarian Empire was replaced by the smaller nations of Czechoslovakia, Austria, Hungary, and Yugoslavia, the last of which united the former empire's southernmost domains with its initial war enemy, Serbia. A new Poland, made up of lands from each of the three old empires, was linked to the Baltic Sea by a "Polish Corridor" that divided East Prussia from the rest of Germany. Prewar Romania doubled its size with territories taken from Russia and Austria-Hungary (Map 32.1).

Arab delegates at the Paris Peace Conference.

The rise of these new nations at first appeared a triumph for democracy. All had democratic institutions, including elected parliaments and written constitutions defining people's rights. Even Hungary, after a short-lived communist regime in 1919, became a constitutional monarchy, as did Yugoslavia. But all had serious problems that soon subverted democracy.

FOUNDATION MAP 32.1 Europe and the Middle East in the 1920s and 1930s

In the wake of the Great War, numerous new nations and dependencies emerged in Eastern Europe and the Middle East. Notice, from the prewar boundaries that are superimposed on this postwar map, that most of the new nations and dependences were carved out of the territories of the old German, Austrian, Russian, and Ottoman Empires, all of which had ceased to exist due to war and revolution. Why were most of these new nations and dependencies plagued by political, social, and economic anxieties?

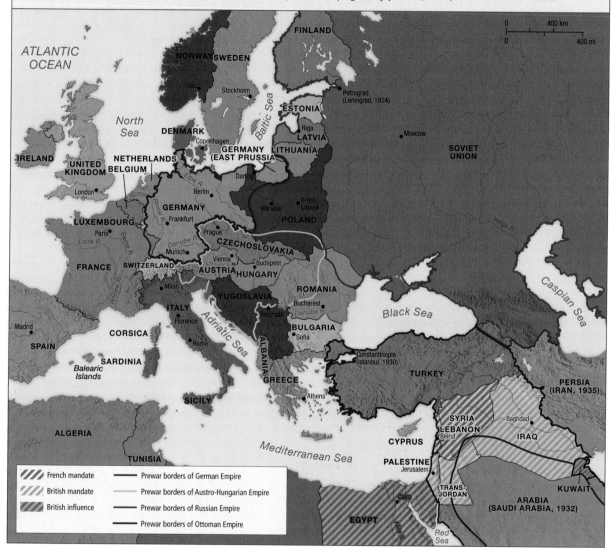

One major problem was the existence of dissatisfied ethnic minorities. Eastern Europe's nationalities were so intermingled that most of the new nations—although based on the ideals of national self-determination—included many people who differed in language and loyalty from the majority. Poland and Czechoslovakia, for example, each contained many Germans, who often felt more loyal to Germany than to the county where they lived.

Ethnic unrest and unemployment unsettle new democracies

Another problem was unemployment, especially among former soldiers, some of whom formed bands of angry outcasts. With few skills other than fighting, they roamed the streets assaulting passers-by and staging periodic protests.

Fear of communism aids the rise of dictatorships

The biggest problem, however, was fear of communism. Living in the shadow of Soviet Russia, a huge realm that sought to promote communist revolutions in other countries, most of the new nations soon deemed democracy too weak to combat the Soviet challenge. Fearful of Soviet power, and of communist inroads among their own working classes, they restricted democratic rights and cracked down on dissent. By the early 1930s, all the new nations except Finland and Czechoslovakia were ruled by **dictators**, leaders who wielded total control, dominated weak elected institutions, and used the army and police to suppress dissent.

Fascism in Italy

Democracy's biggest setback in the 1920s came not in Eastern Europe but in Italy, a parliamentary monarchy and victor in the Great War. Many Italians felt betrayed by Allied leaders, who had secretly promised Italy some lands ruled by Austria when Italy joined the war, but failed at Versailles to fully honor this promise, on the grounds that secret agreements violated Wilson's Fourteen Points.

Anger at Allied "betrayal" and economic crises unsettle postwar Italy

Compounding Italian resentment was a postwar economic crisis. High unemployment, especially among war veterans, led to widespread working-class unrest, and Italian communists exploited this unrest to promote crippling strikes. When Italy's parliamentary democracy proved unable to control the situation, many Italians supported a new movement pledging to combat communism and restore order.

Mussolini and his Fascists exploit crises to gain power

This movement's leader was a combative ex-journalist named Benito Mussolini. A former socialist, he had become a nationalist while serving as a corporal in the Great War. Irate at the Allied snub of Italy in 1919, he formed a "fighting band," or *fascio di combattimento* (FAH-shō dē com-bat-ē-MEN-tō), of former soldiers like himself committed to fighting communism and advancing Italian nationalism. The term *fascio*, a bundle of rods like the ones carried by ancient Roman officials as symbols of their power, gave the movement its name. **Fascism**, an ideology that promoted belligerent nationalism and repressive dictatorship, subjected individual rights to the goals of the nation and its leader.

Mussolini, a bald, burly, swaggering showman, sent his black-shirted fighting squads into the streets to beat up communists and socialists. These "Blackshirts" broke strikes and burned labor union headquarters, adding to the public crisis. In October 1922 Mussolini organized a "March on Rome" to intimidate the government. When King Victor Emanuel III, fearing civil war, refused to declare martial law so the army could fight the fascists, the prime minister and cabinet resigned. Anxious to restore order, the king then appointed Mussolini prime minister, confident that Italy's constitutional structure would keep him from gaining too much power.

The king was soon proven wrong. Granted emergency powers to restore order, Mussolini used them to enact a law giving two-thirds of the seats in parliament to the party getting the most votes in an election. In 1924 elections, rigged by fascist thugs who threatened to beat up anyone who voted against fascism, his party got the votes it needed to govern alone. By the late 1920s the fascists were the only party left.

Benito Mussolini.

Although he destroyed democracy, Mussolini was very popular. In place of political divisions he offered unity, efficiency, and popular programs. His "corporate state" divided the economy into 22 areas, each supervised by a "corporation" made up of business, labor, and government leaders, thus combining private ownership with economic controls. He boasted of making trains run on time—although travelers frequently found them as late as ever. He provided public spectacles, including fiery speeches during which he often stripped to the waist and thumped his barrel chest as the crowd chanted "Duce" (*DOO-chā*), Italian for "leader." In the 1930s, as the world was rocked by economic depression, his fascist methods were emulated elsewhere—most ominously, in Germany.

Economic controls and popular diversions sustain Mussolini's dictatorship

The Great Depression and Its Global Impact

By 1929, although suppressed in Italy and most of Eastern Europe, democracy remained strong in Western Europe and America. During the next decade, however, a disastrous economic depression threatened its survival even there.

The Great Depression of the 1930s was triggered by events in America, where an economic boom in the 1920s created an illusion of endless prosperity. Confident consumers bought autos, appliances, and other goods, frequently on credit. As businesses flourished, more and more people bought stocks, or shares in commercial enterprises. Often they did so "on margin," paying 10 percent of the stock's current price, borrowing the rest from their brokers, then selling the stock when prices rose, repaying their brokers and pocketing the profits. Everyone, it seemed, was making money.

All was well as long as prices rose. But in 1929, fears that stocks were overpriced led many investors to sell. The resulting decline in demand for stocks drove prices down, starting a chain reaction. As brokers lost money, they demanded full payment from their clients for stocks purchased on margin; to get the money, the clients had to sell stocks at a loss, further driving prices down. On October 24 ("Black Thursday") and October 29 ("Black Tuesday"), the bottom fell out of the New York Stock Exchange, with many stocks losing half their value.

The 1929 Stock Market Crash shattered consumer confidence. Shaken Americans simply stopped buying, decreasing demand for goods, so manufacturers cut production and laid off many workers. Now without incomes, they could not buy goods, furthering the downward spiral. Banks were caught in the middle: ruined stock investors and laid-off workers could no longer make payments owed to banks for loans and mortgages, while cash-strapped depositors sought to withdraw all their money. Having loaned that money to others, from whom they could not collect, many banks were forced to close, robbing many people of their life savings.

Stock Market Crash shatters American prosperity

Other banks survived by demanding full repayment of loans made to European firms that had borrowed heavily from U.S. banks to finance the Great War and postwar recovery. To come up with the money, these firms laid off workers, resulting in mass unemployment—especially in Germany, where U.S. loans had been used extensively to finance reparations payments to France required by the Versailles Treaty.

Further American actions globalized the Great Depression. In 1930, desperate to protect declining U.S. industries from foreign competition, Congress passed the Smoot-Hawley Tariff, placing huge duties on imports from other countries. Despite a signed appeal from a thousand American economists, warning that this measure would ruin the

American actions globalize Great Depression

Bread line during the Great Depression.

world economy, President Herbert Hoover signed it into law. Globally sold goods, such as beef from Argentina, coffee from Brazil and Indonesia, and sugar from Brazil and the Caribbean, thus lost their American markets, causing economic crises in these countries. Many regimes responded with their own **economic nationalism**, erecting tariff walls and trade barriers to protect their national industries and products from international competition. The result was bitter friction among nations and further devastation of the world economy.

The Great Depression thus became a global calamity. From 1929 to 1932, worldwide industrial production dropped by 38 percent. In industrial countries unemployment ranged from 20 percent to 33 percent. Thousands lost homes as banks foreclosed on mortgages unpaid by jobless workers. In the United States, able-bodied people in the prime of life waited in line for rations of bread or sold apples for nickels on street corners; others committed suicide, or abandoned their families to become wandering, rootless "hoboes."

Depression and farming crisis deepen global suffering

The suffering was worsened by a global agricultural crisis. Responding to food shortages in Europe during and after the Great War, North American farmers had expanded their output of wheat and other grains. But in the 1920s, as farming rebounded in Europe and agricultural advances brought higher crop yields, the resulting grain surplus caused prices to fall sharply. Then, in the 1930s, high rates of urban unemployment decreased demand for food, damaging agricultural economies and ruining farmers everywhere.

Depression undermines support for capitalism and democracy

Capitalism and democracy were shaken. Support for radical movements grew the world over, as desperate people opted to sacrifice freedom for economic stability. Even in places with long traditions of political and economic freedom, people increasingly looked to government for solutions.

The New Deal in the United States

In America, where the crisis began, President Hoover was ill-equipped to deal with the Depression. A staunch believer in free markets, he refused to support federal unemployment relief or direct intervention in the economy. Instead he sought vainly to restore consumer confidence by promising that prosperity was "just around the corner." As suffering mounted, he lost the 1932 election to Franklin D. Roosevelt, an engaging Wilsonian idealist who promised "a New Deal for the American people."

Surprising even supporters, Roosevelt proved a tireless activist whose infectious optimism and eloquence, enshrined in such memorable phrases as "the only thing we have to fear is fear itself," made him one of America's most effective presidents. Using government programs to relieve misery, increase buying power, and promote economic recovery, he infused new hope into the nation and created a consensus on behalf of activist government.

Roosevelt uses government intervention to combat Depression

Roosevelt proposed and Congress enacted numerous ambitious measures. A huge public works program, launched to provide jobs for the unemployed, built or rebuilt schools, highways, bridges, and public buildings throughout the country. Subsidies to farmers helped them leave some fields unfarmed, reducing overproduction, which had undermined farm profits by driving prices down. Banks were regulated, deposits insured by the government, and buying stock on margin prohibited. A Civilian Conservation Corps sent jobless young men into rural areas to plant millions of trees and build hydroelectric dams on rivers such as the Tennessee and Columbia. Most enduring of all was the Social Security system, through which the government provided pensions for the aging and later also the disabled.

The results of all this legislation were mixed. On one hand, Roosevelt's vigorous federal intervention may have saved American capitalism: the crisis was so severe that massive government spending was probably the only way to get money into circulation and reinvigorate industrial production. On the other hand, the New Deal did not end the Depression. Slow production gains were reversed by a 1937 recession. What ended unemployment in America was not the New Deal but World War II, which put millions to work producing war materials and serving in the armed forces.

The Civilian Conservation Corps at work, 1937.

But the impact of Roosevelt's activism outweighed its failures. Vastly expanding the federal bureaucracy, his policies provided a new vision of democratic governance, summarized eloquently by Roosevelt himself: "Better the occasional errors of a government that cares about its citizens than the constant omissions of a government frozen in the ice of its own indifference." The New Deal abolished child labor, set minimum wages and maximum work hours, and guaranteed workers the right to bargain collectively. Its measures and its methods, which mobilized the government in support of the common people, endured and affected American society long after the Great Depression was over.

Roosevelt was both loved and hated to a degree unmatched by other elected leaders. A wealthy man, he was reviled by the rich as a traitor to his class, while inspiring in ordinary people an affection so powerful it transcended politics. He styled himself "the champion of the forgotten man," and that description, endorsed by millions, gave him the moral authority to lead his nation through the Great Depression and Second World War.

Roosevelt's activism restores American hope

Democracy and Socialism in Western Europe

Unlike America, which before the Depression was averse to government activism and supremely self-confident, Western Europe had a history of social legislation (Chapter 27) and deep insecurities flowing from the Great War. Western European voters were thus more open than Americans to socialistic experiments.

Britain's new Labour Party, which had socialist ideals and labor union roots, twice won elections in the 1920s under Ramsay MacDonald, illegitimate son of a poor Scottish woman, who became Britain's first socialist prime minister. Assuming that role for a second time in 1929, MacDonald like Hoover had to deal with the Great Depression. In 1931, as the crisis worsened, MacDonald formed at the king's request a coalition government of Labourites, Conservatives, and Liberals, abandoning radical socialism and splitting his own party. The new coalition adopted economic nationalism and cut spending on social programs, but these steps did not end the Depression. In 1935 the British turned to Stanley Baldwin, whose calm manner reassured them, but the economy did not recover until Neville Chamberlain, who replaced Baldwin as prime minister in 1937, increased defense spending and introduced a military draft.

France in the interwar years, obsessed with recovery from the Great War and fearful of German resurgence, was beset by short-lived governments averaging less than a year. When depression hit in the early 1930s, fascist groups formed across the country, declaring democracy too weak to deal with the crisis, while scandals undermined the government's moral legitimacy.

Western Europeans try various methods to restore prosperity

In response came the Popular Front, a coalition of leftist parties that won the 1936 elections under Socialist Leon Blum. Elated workers launched a series of strikes that forced the new government to grant 12 percent wage increases, paid vacations, and a 40-hour workweek. But these progressive measures backfired, reducing production and scaring investors into withdrawing money from France's economy. The ensuing economic downturn undermined the Popular Front, and in 1937 Blum was voted out by the National Assembly. A series of weak coalition governments followed, leaving France ill equipped to meet the challenge of a resurgent Germany.

In Norway and Sweden, depression brought less misery than elsewhere. Popularly elected socialist governments provided "cradle to grave" health and welfare benefits, supported by high taxes. Scandinavian socialism thus presented a viable democratic alternative to dictatorial communism, practiced in Soviet Russia.

Communism in Russia

When Bolshevik communists seized power in Russia in 1917, their aim was to spark an international revolution against world capitalism. When no such upheaval occurred, however, they slowly transformed Marxist internationalism into Soviet nationalism: rather than working toward a worldwide workers' rebellion, they focused on strengthening Soviet Russia as a socialist fatherland, combining communism's global goals with Russia's national agenda.

Civil war, won by communists, devastates Russia

THE RISE OF SOVIET NATIONALISM. The first step toward Soviet nationalism came in March 1918 when, ignoring pleas from his own party to launch an international communist crusade, Soviet leader V. I. Lenin withdrew Russia from the Great War through the Brest-Litovsk Treaty with Germany. This action, designed to give the Soviets time to consolidate control in Russia, instead set off a Russian civil war. In it a new "Red Army," capably created from scratch by Soviet War Commissar Leon Trotsky, fought the "White" armies, a coalition of anticommunist Russians. The Allied Powers, hoping to get Russia back into the war against Germany, also sent troops to aid the Whites. But the various White armies were unable to coordinate their attacks, and Allied interest in Russia waned once the Great War ended. By early 1921, the Reds had emerged victorious.

But the Reds had little to celebrate. After the Great War and Russian civil war, Russia was totally ravaged. Since 1913, its industrial production had dropped 80 percent, and agricultural output had been cut in half. Millions had perished from combat, disease, and starvation, capped by catastrophic famine in 1921.

Soviet poster from 1920s: "Bridge to a bright future."

Ever the realist, Soviet leader Lenin that year took another step back from global communist revolution, instituting a New Economic Policy (NEP) that used capitalist techniques to strengthen his communist nation. Although the Soviet state kept control of foreign trade and major industries, which it had nationalized, NEP allowed smaller businesses (which made up most of the economy) to operate as private enterprises. Instead of seizing grain from peasants, as it did during the civil war, the regime imposed a tax in kind—a fixed percentage of the harvest payable in grain. Peasants could sell what was left on the open market, giving them a potent (yet capitalistic) incentive to produce. Communist Russia also opened trade with capitalist countries such as Britain and Germany, acting like a traditional nation-state rather than a revolutionary regime. In 1922,

Lenin implements New Economic Policy to rebuild Russia

as if to mark this transition, a new constitution formally created a federal state called the Union of Soviet Socialist Republics (USSR), or the Soviet Union.

That same year Lenin, only 52, suffered the first of several strokes that finally took his life in 1924. As he became increasingly incapacitated, many saw War Commissar Leon Trotsky, Lenin's most capable colleague, as the likely new Soviet leader. But other communists, annoyed by Trotsky's arrogance and fearful that he might use his control of the Red Army to become a military dictator, formed a coalition against him. The coalition came to be dominated by Joseph V. Djugashvili (*joo-GAHSH-vē-lē*), General Secretary of the Soviet Communist Party, who called himself the "Man of Steel": Stalin.

Stalin was a crude but effective organizer, good at getting things done. As general secretary, he set the party's agenda, ran its daily affairs, and appointed its local managers. While others grappled with major issues, he dealt with organizational affairs, quietly amassing power by staffing the party structure with his supporters. He also positioned himself as Lenin's heir by creating a cult to the late leader, marked by a marble mausoleum in Moscow and by the renaming of Petrograd (formerly Saint Petersburg) as Leningrad.

Joseph Stalin.

In 1925, after it defeated Trotsky and deposed him as War Commissar, the anti-Trotsky coalition crumbled. Afraid that Stalin was gaining too much power, his former allies turned against him. But they were too late: with his control of the party, Stalin deftly ousted his adversaries, and by 1928 he had become the Soviet dictator.

Stalin's rise to dictatorship marked the triumph of Soviet nationalism. His defeated foes, as Marxist internationalists, saw the NEP as a tactical retreat and were eager to resume the quest for world revolution. But Stalin, as a Soviet nationalist, insisted on **socialism in one country**, a program that focused on strengthening the USSR, while requiring communists everywhere to put off world revolution and support the Soviet state.

After defeating his rivals, however, Stalin grew impatient with the NEP. At first it had been successful, restoring production to prewar levels by the mid-1920s, but by 1928 economic progress had slowed. Fearful that the capitalist powers would soon move to crush his country, with its weak industrial base, Stalin decided that the USSR could not survive without rapid industrial growth.

Stalin also decided that, to support this growth, he needed control of the Soviet grain harvest. Under the NEP, like farmers in the West, Soviet peasants found that an oversupply of grain drove prices down. So rather than selling their grain at a loss, the peasants had begun to hoard it, hoping to push prices back up. These actions infuriated Stalin, who badly needed grain to feed urban factory workers and to sell abroad for machines to build his industrial base.

STALIN'S REVOLUTION. Stalin's response was the "Stalin Revolution," a mass campaign to reorganize farming and rapidly expand industry. It began in 1928 with the First Five Year Plan, an economic blueprint that set ambitious targets and timetables for Soviet industrial and agricultural output. On paper it looked like a rational approach, but in practice it produced a frenzied and forcible mobilization of the entire society.

The agricultural reform, called collectivization, created a monstrous catastrophe. To gain control of the grain, Stalin forced peasants onto **collective farms**, multi-family farms supposedly owned by their members but actually run by the state, which took all the grain it needed to support industrialization. When farmers fought collectivization, realizing it would cost them control of the harvest, Stalin's regime called them "enemies of the people" and sent troops with machine guns to destroy them. As civil war swept Soviet Ukraine in the early 1930s, millions of resisters were shot or sent to prison camps in Siberia, where they were made to mine that region's resources under inhuman conditions. As the state's need for grain increased, moreover, it took most of the harvest, leaving farmers less than they needed for survival. The resulting forced famine killed five to ten million people.

Appalled by such atrocities, even loyal communists began to see Stalin as a murderous monster. Fearful that they might plot against him, in the mid-1930s the Soviet dictator turned his repression against the party itself. The People's Commissariat for Internal Affairs, known by its Russian initials NKVD, arrested numerous communists and charged them with fabricated crimes, such as collaborating with enemy countries or supporting Trotsky, whom Stalin had driven into foreign exile in 1929. During the **Great Purges**, Stalin's systematic efforts to eliminate opponents in 1936–1938, dozens of party and military officials were placed on trial, forced to make false confessions, and summarily shot. Millions of other people were arrested and shipped to Siberia. Finally, in 1940, a Stalin henchman, using an ice axe, murdered Trotsky in Mexico.

By this time, Stalin had managed to both industrialize the USSR and terrorize its people into submission. Through superhuman sacrifices by Soviet workers, combined with machinery purchased abroad using grain taken from the farmers, the Soviet Union had become an industrial giant. But Soviet society scarcely resembled the "worker's paradise" envisioned by early socialists. Workers and peasants, in whose name the revolution was made, now lived in fear of the Stalin regime, working long hours in dismal factories and on collective farms under oppressive state control. To make their nation an industrial power they paid a terrible price.

To Stalin, however, there had been no choice: in order to survive, the Soviet Union had to overcome its backwardness as quickly as possible. In a 1931 speech, responding to requests that he slow the pace of industrialization, he used Russian nationalism and fear of foreigners to justify his frantic approach:

> No, comrades . . . , the pace must not be slackened . . . To slacken the pace would mean to lag behind; and those who lag behind are beaten . . . Old Russia . . . was ceaselessly beaten for her backwardness . . . She was beaten because to beat her was profitable and went unpunished . . . We are fifty or a hundred years behind the advanced countries. We must make good this lag in ten years. Either we do it or they crush us.

The Soviet dictator was paranoid, obsessed with real and imagined foes, but his speech proved prophetic. Ten years later, in 1941, his newly industrialized nation would face his ultimate fear: a massive invasion by a resurgent Germany.

National Socialism in Germany

Germany's path to dictatorship, like Russia's, was marked by economic woes, fears and resentments of foreigners, and a desire to strengthen the nation against outside interference. After more than a decade of democracy, in the 1930s Germany came under the

Stalin's industrialization and terror regiment Soviet society

Industrial power prepares Soviets to resist foreign attack

Giant Soviet steel mill of the 1930s.

control of a nationalist, racist, and militarist movement known as National Socialism, supporters of which were called **Nazis**.

THE FAILURE OF GERMAN DEMOCRACY.

German democracy, initiated in the wake of the Great War, faced obstacles from the outset. One was an overabundance of political parties, making it hard for any to win a majority of seats in the Reichstag (*RĪKS-tahk*), Germany's elected assembly. Governing cabinets thus were usually multi-party coalitions, and the chancellors who headed these cabinets often found it hard to keep their coalitions together. Another was the fact that many Germans detested the Weimar (*VĪ-mar*) Republic (named for the city where its constitution was drafted in 1919) for accepting the hated Versailles Treaty and the crippling reparations payments.

War reparations and multiple parties weaken German democracy

By 1923, unwilling to further offend the German people by raising taxes to fund the reparations, the cash-starved Weimar government simply stopped making payments. When France responded by occupying Germany's industrial Ruhr Valley, German workers struck in protest; France in turn closed off the region, preventing delivery of food and goods to the striking workers. The government, forced by public opinion to pay the strikers unemployment benefits, printed vast amounts of paper money, resulting in horrific inflation. By August, a loaf of bread cost millions of times what it had earlier that year, and workers were paid with bales of worthless bills. Millions of Germans thus lost their life savings.

During this crisis, an obscure rabble-rouser made his first bid for power. Adolf Hitler, an embittered young Austrian who had fought bravely in the German army during the Great War, had since become leader of the **National Socialist German Workers' Party**, a fringe group later called the Nazis. A spellbinding speaker, he trumpeted the myth that "undefeated" Germany had been "stabbed in the back" by traitors who accepted the peace terms, and he urged Germans to rearm and avenge the humiliation of Versailles. In November 1923 he launched a *putsch* (attempted power grab) in a Munich beer hall, firing a shot into the ceiling to signal the start of his rebellion.

German woman fuels stove with worthless money during inflation crisis.

Hitler and Nazis try to grab power during inflation crisis

But German democracy survived the 1923 crisis. The "Beer Hall Putsch" was quickly crushed and Hitler was jailed for a year, while the Reichstag found a strong leader in Gustav Stresemann (*SHTRĀ-zuh-mahn*). A pragmatic nationalist, Stresemann raised taxes, cut government spending, revalued the currency, and negotiated long-term low-interest loans from the United States (which could not collect war debts from its allies unless Germany paid them reparations). The inflation ended, payments resumed, and France withdrew from the Ruhr. In 1925 Stresemann negotiated the Locarno Treaties with France, Belgium, Poland, and Czechoslovakia, agreeing that Germans would not use force to change the 1918 borders, and in 1926 he brought Germany into the League of Nations. By the time he died in 1929, Germany seemed stable and prosperous, and Hitler's Nazis had faded into insignificance.

Then came the Great Depression. As struggling American banks called in their loans, the German economy collapsed. Millions of Germans, frightened and unemployed, began voting for extremist parties. Hitler's promises to rearm Germany, renounce Versailles, and expel the Jews, whom he blamed for Germany's suffering, struck a responsive chord—as did German Communist Party promises of a full-employment workers' state. By 1932 the Nazis and Communists were two of the Reichstag's largest parties. In January 1933,

Great Depression strengthens support for communism and Nazism

when German capitalists and nationalists, terrified of a communist takeover, opted to support the Nazis as a lesser evil, Hitler was appointed chancellor, heading a coalition of Nazis and small right-wing parties.

HITLER AND THE THIRD REICH.   Having come to power by democratic means, Hitler quickly destroyed German democracy. In February 1933, when the Reichstag building burned down, he obtained emergency powers to deal with the crisis. Accusing communists of setting the fire (although some evidence pointed to the Nazis), Hitler got the Reichstag to ban the Communist Party. Then he proceeded to dissolve the other parties one by one. By July Germany was a one-party state, which Hitler called the Third Reich (Third Empire).

Hitler becomes chancellor and destroys German democracy

The Nazis then regimented the rest of German society. Labor unions were dissolved into the Reich Labor Front, an organization of labor and management delegates dominated by Nazi agents. Protestant leaders were intimidated by Hitler's popularity, while the Vatican, fearing Nazi oppression of German Catholics, made a pact with Hitler ensuring the Church's rights in Germany if it avoided politics. Youth groups were absorbed into the Hitler Youth (for boys aged 9–18) and League of German Girls. A Ministry of Propaganda, headed by Josef Goebbels (*GEH'r-bulz*), took control of newspapers, magazines, radio stations, and film studios. Within months the Nazis controlled almost every aspect of German life.

Hitler promotes nationalism, racism, and anti-Semitism

Although the Third Reich was a dictatorship, with strict controls and concentration camps to confine dissenters, Hitler was popular with Germans. He united them as one, with himself as their *Führer* (leader). He restored their national pride, lost after the Great War, declaring them a **"Master Race"** descended from ancient Aryans and destined to dominate "subhuman Slavic races" by conquering **Lebensraum** (*LĀ-behnz-raowm*)—living space for Germany's growing population—in Poland and the USSR (see "Excerpts from Hitler's *Mein Kampf*").

Hitler exploited people's fears by promoting anti-Semitism, anti-Jewish hostility long present in Christian Europe. But his attacks were racial, not religious: he vilified Jews as an impure race that must not be allowed to pollute the German Master Race through intermarriage or illicit sex. Nazi laws deprived Jews of German citizenship and forbade Jews under penalty of death from having sexual relations with "pure" Germans. On *Kristallnacht* (the Night of Broken Glass), November 9–10, 1938, Nazis instigated anti-Jewish riots, burning synagogues across Germany, destroying thousands of Jewish-owned shops, and killing nearly one hundred Jews. Mass Jewish emigration, prompted by such actions and promoted by Nazis seeking to make Germany *Judenrein* (free of Jews), reduced its Jewish population from 560 thousand in 1933 to under 300 thousand in 1939.

Synagogue being burned during Kristallnacht.

Hitler borrows to build Germany, based on future war

Hitler, meanwhile, restored German prosperity, putting jobless men to work building tons of military equipment and great highways (*Autobahnen*) on which to transport it. He urged women to leave the work force, to free up jobs for men and enlarge the Master Race by having Aryan babies. He financed his costly projects with ten-year government bonds, vowing to repay them by plundering nations later conquered by Germany. His plans were thus based on a new European war to restore German dominance and reverse the shameful verdict of Versailles. That conflict, later called World War II, would not be long in coming.

Document 32.2 Excerpts from Hitler's Mein Kampf

In Mein Kampf (My Struggle), which he composed in prison after the failed "Beer Hall Putsch" of 1923, Adolf Hitler set forth his racist ideology, describing "Aryans" as a "superior" race that was meant to subjugate others, and identifying Jews as the "enemy of mankind." He called on Germans to expand eastward to conquer land in Russia, denouncing its "Bolshevism" and "Jewish rule."

. . . Nature's restricted form of propagation and increase is an almost rigid basic law . . .

The stronger must dominate and not blend with the weaker . . . Only the born weakling can view this as cruel . . .

The fox is always a fox, the goose a goose, the tiger a tiger . . . [Y]ou will never find a fox who . . . might, for example, show humanitarian tendencies toward geese, as similarly there is no cat with a friendly inclination toward mice . . .

No more than Nature desires the mating of weaker with stronger individuals, even less does she desire the blending of a higher with a lower race . . .

Historical experience . . . shows with terrifying clarity that in every mingling of Aryan blood with that of lower peoples the result was the end of the cultured people . . .

[I]t is no accident that the first cultures arose in places where the Aryan, in his encounters with lower peoples, subjugated them and bent them to his will . . .

As long as he ruthlessly upheld the master attitude, not only did he really remain master, but also the preserver and increaser of culture . . .

. . . The great leaders of Jewry are confident that . . . the Jews will devour the other nations of the earth . . .

[T]he Jew knows very well that he can undermine the existence of European nations by a process of racial bastardization . . .

And again the National Socialist movement has the mightiest task to fulfill.

It must open the eyes of the people . . . and it must remind them again and again of the true enemy of our present-day world . . . It must call eternal wrath upon the head of the foul enemy of mankind as the real originator of our sufferings.

It must make certain that . . . the mortal enemy is recognized and that the fight against him becomes a gleaming symbol . . . to show other nations the way to the salvation of an embattled Aryan humanity . . .

Only an adequately large space on this earth assures a nation of freedom of existence . . .

[W]e National Socialists must . . . secure for the German people the land and soil to which they are entitled on this earth . . .

And so we . . . stop the endless German movement to the south and west, and turn our gaze toward the land in the east . . .

If we speak of soil in Europe today, we can primarily have in mind only Russia and her vassal border states. Here Fate itself seems desirous of giving us a sign. By handing Russia to Bolshevism, it robbed the Russian nation of that intelligentsia which . . . guaranteed its existence as a state . . . For centuries Russia drew nourishment from this Germanic nucleus . . . Today it . . . has been replaced by the Jew. Impossible as it is for the Russian by himself to shake off the yoke of the Jew . . ., it is equally impossible for the Jew to maintain the mighty empire forever. He himself is no element of organization, but a ferment of decomposition . . . And the end of Jewish rule in Russia will also be the end of Russia as a state . . .

SOURCE: Adolf Hitler, *Mein Kampf*, translated by Ralph Manheim (Boston: Houghton Mifflin, 1971) 284–286, 295–296, 638–640, 643, 652, 654–655.

New Varieties of Nationalism in Africa and Asia

While Stalin blended nationalism with communism, and Hitler combined nationalism with racism, Africans and Asians adapted the notion of national self-determination to fit their own conditions and cultures. As a result, in the interwar years, new forms of nationalism arose across Africa and Asia.

Nationalism and Anticolonialism in Africa

African nationalism arises in resistance to colonial rule

The Great War and Versailles settlement aided African nationalism, which was rooted in **anticolonialism**, or resistance to colonial rule. Taught by their European rulers to use European weapons against other Europeans, and exposed to Wilsonian ideals of national self-determination, Africans concluded they could use these weapons and ideals to fight European rule. Since the Europeans were still better armed, however, Africans found open revolt futile—especially after the French slaughtered the Baya people, who rebelled in 1928–1931 against forced railway labor in French Equatorial Africa (Map 32.2). Interwar African nationalism thus aimed for eventual rather than immediate independence.

African workers and farmers strike against Europeans

Some African workers and farmers, seeking better working conditions or higher prices for their crops, went on strike against European employers. Strikes in British-held regions in the Gold Coast and the Northern Rhodesian copper belt achieved only modest gains, but in the 1930s Gold Coast cocoa farmers forced a significant price increase by withholding their produce from the markets. Nationalists led these protests, learning from them the prospects and limitations of collective action.

In the Belgian Congo, nationalism grew out of religion. Simon Kimbangu (*kim-BAHN-goo*) founded his own church in 1921 and proclaimed himself prophet. He taught that God would deliver the Congo peoples from Belgian bondage, and that in the meantime they need not pay taxes. The exasperated Belgians threw him in prison (where he died in 1951), but his church included future nationalist leaders such as Joseph Kasa Vubu (*kah-sah-VOO-boo*), who became the first president of independent Congo in 1960.

Africans devise religious and cultural forms of nationalism

African and non-African intellectuals developed other forms of nationalism. In the 1920s Marcus Garvey of Jamaica founded the Universal Negro Improvement Association, advocating "Africa for the Africans" and the end of European rule. Garvey was based in New York, and he never visited Africa, but his movement inspired several young Africans who led the anticolonial struggle after 1945. A culture-based alternative was offered by the Négritude movement, an association of French-speaking writers in West Africa and the Caribbean who celebrated African cultural traditions and their differences from European cultures. One such scholar, Léopold Senghor (*SONG-or*), became the first president of independent Senegal in 1960.

In South Africa the **African National Congress** (ANC), founded in 1912 by educated black professionals to combat white racial repression, made little headway in the interwar years. Later, however, as anticolonialism swept Africa after World War II, ANC became the continent's strongest nationalist organization.

Marcus Garvey.

Secular and Islamic Nationalism in the Middle East

By destroying the Ottoman Empire, which dissolved in defeat in 1918, the Great War helped foster several forms of nationalism in the Middle East. Turkey, the empire's main successor state, adopted a Western-style secular nationalism, promoting loyalty to nation above religion, while others in the region sought to merge nationalism with Islamic, and often anti-Western, ideals.

Mustafa Kemal fosters modernization and secular nationalism in Turkey

In a 1919–1923 revolt, Turkish nationalists led by war hero Mustafa Kemal defeated and expelled the Ottoman sultan, who at Allied insistence had given up most of the realm's non-Turkish regions, and created a Republic of Turkey in the region that was left (Map 32.3). As president and virtual dictator until he died in 1938, Kemal moved to

Map 32.2 Africa in the 1920s and 1930s

Although nationalist liberation movements arose and spread among Africans during the interwar years, most of Africa remained under European colonial rule. Note that France, Britain, and South Africa governed Germany's former colonies as League of Nations mandates, that Egypt gained independence but remained under strong British influence, and that Ethiopia lost independence when it was invaded and occupied by Italy in 1935–1936. How did the Great War help to promote African nationalist movements? Why did these movements have limited success during the interwar years?

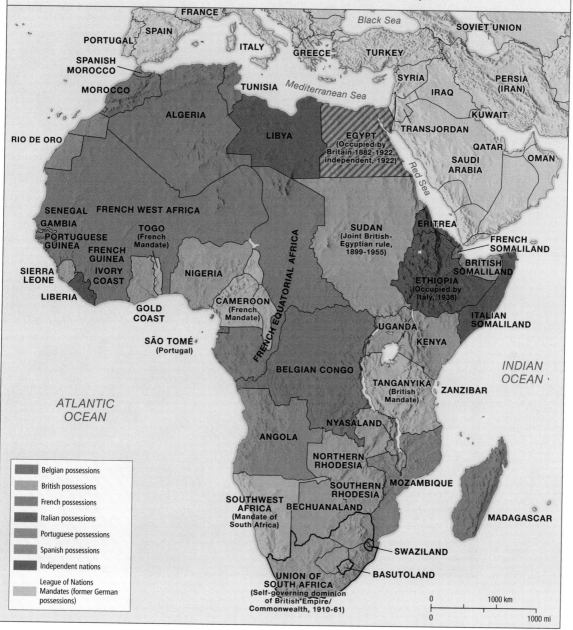

Map 32.3 The Middle East in the 1920s and 1930s

The interwar era brought major changes to the Middle East. Observe that after the Ottoman Empire's collapse some of its former lands became French and British mandates, others eventually became part of Saudi Arabia, and what was left became the Republic of Turkey, with a new capital at Ankara. Note also that in 1930 the old capital, Constantinople, was formally renamed Istanbul (a name that Turks had long used for the city); that Egypt, occupied by Britain since 1882, became an independent monarchy in 1922; and that Persia, ruled by Reza Shah Pahlavi from 1925 to 1941, was renamed Iran in 1935. How did tensions between secular and Islamic nationalism affect the Middle East in the interwar era?

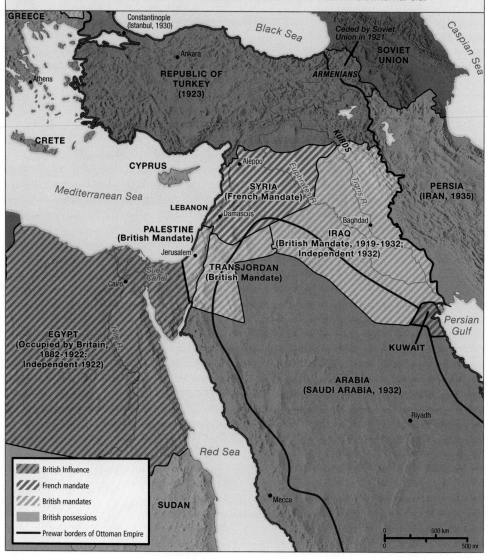

modernize industry and westernize Turkish society, convinced that failure to do so had caused the Ottoman collapse. Determined to reduce Islam's role, and to have his people identify themselves as Turks more than as Muslims, he replaced Islamic schools with secular ones, Arabic script with the Latin alphabet, and Islamic law (Shar`ia) with Western-style legal codes. He abolished the sultanate and caliphate, took the name Atatürk ("father of Turks"), and made Turkey a modern secular nationalistic state.

Kemal Atatürk promotes shift from Arabic to Latin script.

Hoping to hasten economic development by doubling the talent pool, Kemal expanded opportunities for women, who between 1900 and 1920 had gained access to secondary education and factory jobs. Building on these foundations, his reforms banned polygyny, granted gender-neutral access to divorce, gave women the right to vote, and guaranteed their rights to education and employment.

Kemal's secular policies sent shock waves across the Middle East. In Persia Reza Shah Pahlavi (*PAH-luh-vē*), a military man who took power and reigned as shah (king) from 1925 to 1941, sought to imitate Kemal's reforms. He built railways and industries, reformed the legal system, and renamed his country Iran (after the ancient Aryans who had settled there). He even sought to end the seclusion and veiling of women, but stiff opposition from the country's powerful Shi'ite Muslim clerics limited his success.

Reza Shah Pahlavi tries to modernize and secularize Iran

Elsewhere other Muslims, deeply offended by such secularism, responded with forms of nationalism tied to Islamic identity. In Egypt, which became an independent monarchy in 1922, the Society of Muslim Brothers, a militant Islamic nationalist group devoted to resisting secularism, emerged in 1928. In formerly Ottoman Syria and Palestine, nationalism took a pro-Islamic anti-Western tone against France and Britain, which during the war had promised independence to Arabs in these regions but then ruled them as League of Nations mandates. France further upset Muslims by carving from its Syrian mandate an area called Lebanon with a large Christian population, hoping to form a Christian-dominated nation. Britain likewise angered Muslims by letting many Jews settle in its Palestine mandate, based on a wartime promise to help Jews form a national homeland there. Although Britain and France withdrew in the 1940s, their actions inflamed hatreds and resentments that plague the region to the present day.

Other Muslims embrace Islamic and anti-Western nationalism

In Iraq, made up of three former Ottoman provinces where Britain had a League of Nations mandate, the British tried to create a Muslim nation. After forming a monarchy in 1921 under King Faisal (*FĪ-sul*), son of Hussein ibn Ali, Sherif of Mecca, who had led the Arab Revolt against the Ottomans in the Great War, Britain recognized Iraqi independence in 1932. But Iraq's contentious religious and ethnic groups, including Shi'ite Muslim Arabs, Sunni Muslim Arabs, and Kurds, complicated efforts to achieve any sense of national unity.

French and British mandates create problems in Lebanon, Palestine, and Iraq

More successful were the efforts in Arabia of Abdul Aziz ibn Saud (*sah-OOD*), leader of a strict Muslim sect called Wahhabism (Chapter 22), who in the 1920s defeated other Arabs and in 1932 formed the Kingdom of Saudi Arabia. To create a Saudi national identity in a desert land dominated by Arab tribes, he imposed Wahhabism as the national form of Islam. He also forged links with each tribe by marrying more than 240 women, divorcing most of them after two weeks and sending them back to their tribes pregnant and laden with gifts. Ibn Saud was prolific—by 2000 the House of Saud had more than 6,700 princes—but his gifts were modest, usually an ornately woven robe and a couple of goats, since his wealth was at first quite limited.

Ibn Saud uses Wahhabism and royal marriages to unite Arabia

Then Charles Crane, founder of the Crane Plumbing Company in the United States, sent an engineer to Arabia to search for the world's most precious liquid: water. After 18 months, he reported to Crane that Arabia is a limestone shelf with no underground water; then he resigned and went to work for Standard Oil of California. The engineer had found not water but oil, which was on its way to replacing coal as the world's main fuel. By 1950 Saudi oil reserves were known to be the richest on earth, and Saudi Arabia was on its way to becoming one of earth's richest nations.

Nationalism and Nonviolence in India

Indian nationalism grew out of British imperial rule, which united the diverse subcontinent and created a British-educated Indian elite influenced by Western notions of nationalism and democracy. In 1885, members of this elite had formed the Indian National Congress, a nationalist body advocating self-rule for India (Chapter 29). After Indian troops fought for Britain in the Great War, Woodrow Wilson's call for national self-determination raised hopes that the Allies would grant India self-government as a matter of both gratitude and principle.

But the British were loath to let their lucrative colony go. They increased the role of Indians in its governance but imposed laws making Indians accused of anti-British activity liable to imprisonment without trial, sparking demonstrations across India. In April 1919 in Amritsar (Map 32.4), a British commander ordered Indian soldiers under his command to fire repeatedly on demonstrators, killing almost four hundred and wounding more than a thousand. The Amritsar Massacre shattered hopes for peaceful transition to Indian self-rule and left India on the brink of rebellion.

At this point an unusual leader emerged. Son of a prosperous Hindu merchant, Mohandas K. Gandhi (1869–1948) had studied law in England and practiced it in South Africa. There, evicted from a "whites only" train car and barred from "whites only" hotels, he identified with South Africa's oppressed racial minorities. In time he developed **satyagraha** (*sut-YAH-gruh-huh*), or "truth force," a nonviolent way to combat oppression by refusing to cooperate with oppressors (see "Gandhi on Nonviolent Resistance"). Returning to India, he promoted this concept as a rising leader of the Indian National Congress.

Gandhi with spinning wheel.

In 1920, following the Amritsar Massacre, Gandhi led a national boycott, urging Indians not to buy British products, pay British taxes, or participate in British institutions. In 1922, when some of his followers defied him and turned to violence, Gandhi was arrested for inciting insurrection. Distressed, after two years in jail he withdrew from politics to work among the poor. But in 1930, outraged by British imposition of a heavy tax on salt, he re-emerged to lead a mass nonviolent resistance campaign. Since most Indians, unlike Westerners, still lacked refrigeration, they needed salt to preserve their food, so he urged them to get their own salt from seawater. Under his leadership some 50 thousand Indians staged a sensational Salt March, walking two hundred miles to the seaside salt flats, where they peacefully endured brutal beatings ordered by British officials.

When reports of these beatings prompted an international outcry, British authorities, seeing that their use of force was futile, negotiated with Gandhi. The resulting Government of India Act, passed by Britain's parliament in 1935, gave India a constitution calling for an elected two-house national legislature. It was not full independence—the British still controlled the government's executive branch—but it was a major step toward self-rule.

Map 32.4 India Between the Wars, 1919–1939

British domination of India continued in the interwar years. Note that Britain ruled much of India directly, but other parts indirectly through treaties with rulers of Indian "princely states." Note also that, in the wake of the 1919 Amritsar Massacre, Mahatma Gandhi's nonviolent resistance campaigns, including the 1930 Salt March, compelled Britain to grant India a measure of self-rule by the late 1930s. Why did many Indian Muslims resist the idea of a united and independent India?

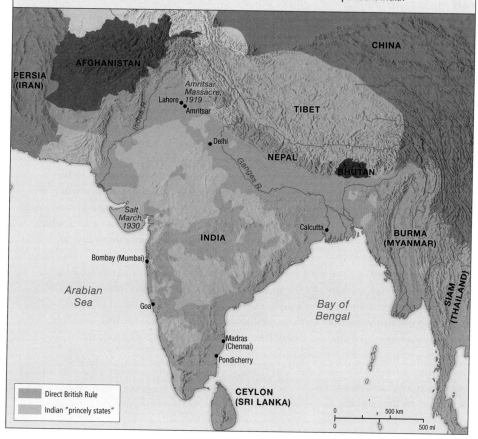

One key factor in Gandhi's success was his conversion of Indian nationalism from an aim of the elite into a movement of the masses, who affectionately called him Mahatma ("great-soul"). Sparsely dressed in hand-woven cloth he spun on a small spinning wheel, he identified with the outcastes and poor, inspiring in them dignity and pride. Another factor was his clever exploitation of Britain's self-interest. Realizing that imperial rule relied on Indian cooperation, he promoted noncooperation, seeking to convince the British that continuing their control would be more trouble and expense than letting go. A third factor was his aptitude for public relations and seizing the moral high ground. Reports of Indian nonviolence in the face of brutal beatings by imperial troops helped win sympathy in Britain for Indian self-rule.

Gandhi's mass appeal and moral standing undermine British rule

Document 32.3 Gandhi on Nonviolent Resistance

In his efforts to lead India to independence from British rule, Mohandas K. Gandhi adopted an approach, very much in contrast with Hitler's, that opposed oppression with nonviolent resistance, portraying it as the ultimate in strength and courage, while scorning violence and retaliation as forms cowardice and weakness.

. . . I believe that non-violence is infinitely superior to violence, forgiveness is more manly than punishment . . .

Strength does not come from physical capacity. It comes from an indomitable will . . . We in India may in a moment realize that one hundred thousand Englishmen need not frighten three hundred million human beings. A definite forgiveness would, therefore, mean a definite recognition of our strength. With enlightened forgiveness must come a mighty wave of strength in us . . .

I am not a visionary. I claim to be a practical idealist. The religion of non-violence is not meant merely for the . . . saints. It is meant for the common people as well. Non-violence is the law of our species as violence is the law of the brute. The spirit lies dormant in the brute, and he knows no law but that of physical might. The dignity of man requires obedience to a higher law—to the strength of the spirit.

I have therefore ventured to place before India the ancient law of self-sacrifice. For *satyagraha* and its offshoots, non-cooperation and civil resistance, are nothing but new names for the law of suffering . . .

Non-violence in its dynamic condition means conscious suffering. It does not mean meek submission to the will of the evil-doer, but it means the pitting of one's whole soul against the will of the tyrant. Working under this law of our being, it is possible for a single individual to defy the whole might of an unjust empire . . .

Non-violence is not a cover for cowardice, but it is the supreme virtue of the brave. Exercise of non-violence requires far greater bravery than that of swordsmanship. Cowardice is wholly inconsistent with non-violence. Non-violence . . . is a conscious deliberate restraint put upon one's desire for vengeance. But vengeance is any day superior to passive, effeminate, and helpless submission. Forgiveness is higher still. Vengeance too is weakness. The desire for vengeance comes out of fear of harm, imaginary or real. A dog barks and bites when he fears. A man who fears no one on earth would consider it too troublesome even to summon up anger against one who is vainly trying to injure him . . .

Non-resistance is restraint voluntarily undertaken for the good of society. It is, therefore, an intensively active, purifying, inward force. It is often antagonistic to the material good of the non-resister . . . It is rooted in internal strength, never weakness . . .

SOURCE: Mohandas K. Gandhi, "The Gita and Satyagraha," in *Gandhi: Selected Writings*, selected and introduced by Ronald Ducan (New York: Harper and Row, 1971) 48–49, 55.

Muslim League, fearing Hindu rule, leads separatist movement

Gandhi's success, however, was incomplete, for he failed to fully calm the fears of India's Muslim minority. The 1937 elections held under the new constitution gave the Hindu-dominated Indian National Congress most of the legislative seats. Concerned that Indian independence would result in oppression of Muslims by the Hindu majority, Muhammad Ali Jinnah, leader of an association called the Muslim League, turned it into a separatist movement. But violent clashes between Hindus and Muslims then strengthened British imperialists, who portrayed these clashes as proof that India was not ready for self-rule. Indian independence was delayed until 1947.

Nationalism and Communism in China

China, too, was profoundly affected by nationalist reaction against foreign intervention, by ideas adapted from the West, and by internal divisions. But China's divisions were based not on religion, as in India and the Middle East, but on ideology, as nationalists and communists fought over China's future.

THE RISE OF NATIONALIST CHINA. The father of Chinese nationalism was Sun Yixian (*SUN Ē-shē-AHN*), also called Sun Yatsen, a Western-educated Chinese doctor who had emerged in the early 1900s as a leader of the revolution against the imperial regime. When that regime fell in 1912, however, realizing that he lacked military support, Sun stepped aside in favor of former general Yuan Shikai, who became president of a new Chinese Republic (Chapter 29). Sun then formed the Guomindang (*GWŌ-MIN-DONG*), or "National People's Party," a nationalist and democratic political organization that proceeded to win a majority of the seats in 1913 parliamentary elections.

Sun Yixian forms the Guomindang as Chinese Nationalist Party

But Yuan Shikai, a military man with imperial ambitions, soon outlawed the Guomindang, closed down the parliament, and schemed to make himself emperor. He was thwarted, however, by rebellion in the South, and humiliated when Japan used the Great War to seize the Shandong peninsula, a key coastal region in northeast China earlier leased by Germany.

Yuan Shikai bans Guomindang and bids to become emperor

When Yuan died suddenly in 1916, China dissolved into chaos. Although his regime still functioned in Beijing under his former aides, in the provinces his governors and generals emerged as regional warlords, collecting taxes and commanding armies that fought each other and pillaged the land. China's "Warlord Era" lasted from 1916 to 1928.

Regional warlords rule China after Yuan Shikai's death

Meanwhile Sun, having fled abroad in 1913, returned to China in 1917 to rebuild the Guomindang. The Russian Revolution, occurring that same year, provided inspiration and support. Lenin's equating of imperialism with capitalism, and Soviet pledges to back Asian independence movements, found ready reception in China—especially after May 4, 1919, when news reached Beijing that the Paris Peace Conference had ignored China's pleas and Wilson's principles to let Japan keep control of the Shandong peninsula. The resulting **May Fourth Protests**, a series of anti-Western demonstrations that spread quickly across China, laid the groundwork for nationalist revolution.

Allied snub and May Fourth protests fuel Chinese nationalist fervor

Communism was also gaining in appeal. In Shanghai in 1921, Chinese Marxists founded the Chinese Communist Party, aiming to secure with Soviet support a socialist future for China. In 1924, at Soviet urging, the Chinese Communist Party joined the Guomindang, linking communism with nationalism against capitalism and imperialism in a common effort to liberate China from the warlords and the West. Aided by Soviet agents, Sun reshaped the Guomindang as a Soviet-style revolutionary party with activist groups, or cells, in major cities. He also published an influential work, *The Three Principles of the People*, calling for nationalism, democracy, and "people's livelihood," often equated with socialism.

Chinese communists and nationalists combine in effort to unite China

After Sun's death in 1925, however, power in the Guomindang passed to its military wing, led by Sun's disciple Jiang Jieshi (*jē-AHNG jē-EH-SHUR*), also called Chiang Kaishek (*jē-ANHG KĪ-SHEK*). Sun had tapped Jiang, who had studied Red Army methods in Moscow, to form a Guomindang army that could conquer the warlords. In 1926, having trained a large force, Jiang set out on a "Great Northern Expedition," moving north from his party's southern base to unite China under Guomindang rule (Map 32.5). He was supported in this effort by nationalists and communists alike.

After Sun dies, Jiang Jieshi and the army dominate Guomindang

Map 32.5 Nationalist China and Expansionist Japan, 1926–1937

The interwar years were marked by turmoil in China. Note that during the Great Northern Expedition (1926–1928), which Chinese Nationalists launched to unify China, they allied with warlords and foreign capitalists and started to attack China's communists, who eventually survived by fleeing to Yan'an on the fabled Long March (1934–1935). Why and how did Japan use China's weakness to create a Japanese puppet state in Manchuria?

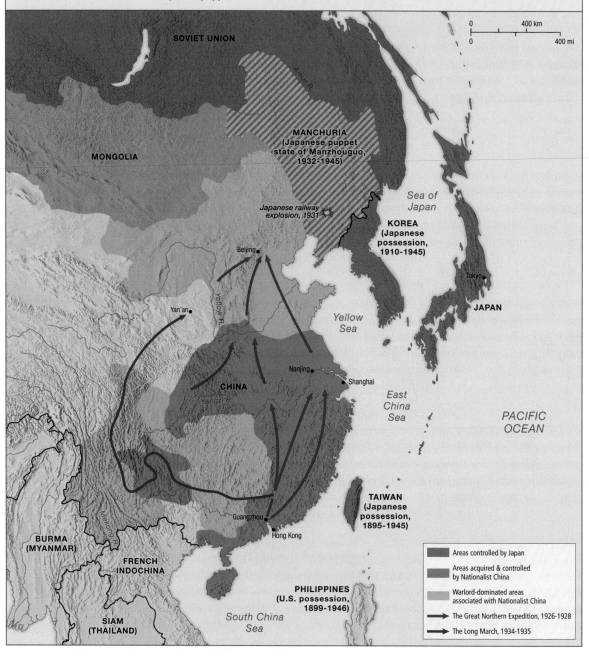

On their way north, however, in 1927, Jiang and his troops visited Shanghai. Long a center of Western capitalist commerce, this port city teemed with poorly paid dock and factory workers, living in squalor and working long hours in unsafe conditions. Communists from Shanghai and elsewhere organized these workers, raised their national awareness, and persuaded them to take over the city to welcome Jiang as a liberator. But Jiang, in collusion with the capitalists, instead stunned the city by using his army to massacre Shanghai communists.

Jiang turns against communists and massacres them in Shanghai

Jiang had reasons for staging this **Shanghai Massacre**. He was concerned that the communists, whose numbers were growing, might soon dominate his movement. He was alarmed by recently discovered evidence that the Soviets planned to use his revolution to bring China under communist control. He was impressed by the power and wealth of Western capitalists, whose help he could use in rebuilding China. And he was shaped by his background: as a soldier, like Yuan Shikai, he believed in using force against potential foes.

Jiang resumed the Great Northern Expedition, but his allies and aims had changed. He sided with Western capitalists, married a wealthy American-educated woman in 1927, and later became a Christian. Rather than attacking warlords, he cut deals with them, letting them maintain regional rule if they recognized his regime. By 1928, it seemed, Jiang was master of China, president of a Nationalist regime with its capital at Nanjing.

Jiang "unites" China by cutting deals with warlords and West

Despite its parliamentary institutions and Western ties, however, "Nationalist China" was a one-party state with limited strength. Jiang's power came from his army, his ties with the warlords, and appointment of his cronies as key officials to run China's economy. While Jiang focused on his military, these "bureaucratic capitalists" worked to modernize and industrialize China, while also gaining great wealth for themselves.

NATIONALISTS VERSUS COMMUNISTS. Jiang's dominion in China was far from complete. He controlled the cities and army, the standard centers of strength. But the masses of people neither lived in cities nor served in the army. Most were peasants who lived in villages with their extended families, tilling the soil as they had for ages. Shattered by the slaughter at Shanghai, the remnants of China's communists turned to these peasants to form the foundations of a new revolution, under the influence of a gifted young Marxist named Mao Zedong (*MAOW zuh-DŌNG*).

Jiang has little influence over Chinese peasant masses

Raised among peasants and inspired by both Sun and Lenin, Mao had become a communist, but he had trouble relating to urban factory workers. In his native province, however, he saw peasants organize themselves to combat landlords and warlords. Rejecting the orthodox Marxist view that revolution must arise with the urban proletariat, in 1927 he published a radical report claiming that peasants could lead China to socialism. Unlike Jiang, who allied with the rich and strong, Mao looked to the poor and weak to help him transform society. But like Jiang, Mao felt the future must be shaped by force. "A revolution is not a dinner party," he wrote. "A revolution is an insurrection, an act of violence by which one class overthrows another."

Mao Zedong advocates peasant socialist revolution

During the next four years, Mao and his comrades worked to mobilize peasants in south central China, forming a small "Chinese Soviet Republic" with its own institutions and army. But Jiang then sought to crush this movement with a series of military attacks. In October 1934, facing imminent defeat, Mao and about 100 thousand supporters decided to escape. With the Nationalist army in full pursuit, they fled on foot across mountains, plains, and rivers to the wilds of the West and North, fighting constant battles in a

Communists flee on "Long March" from Jiang's attacks

six thousand–mile retreat, later hallowed in communist legend as the **Long March** (Map 32.5). A year later, about 20 thousand communist survivors reached the relative safety of the remote northwest.

Mao and communists rebuild in remote Yan'an

There, protected by the region's rocks, hills, gullies, and isolation, Mao rebuilt his movement. Based in the town of Yan'an, he promoted socialism among the region's rural people, operating clinics, shops, and schools in caves to shield them from Nationalist attacks. His programs eventually won him broad support among China's peasants, vastly increasing his following. Meanwhile, in 1936, Jiang was forced by one of his warlords to negotiate a truce with the communists, so China could deal with a growing foreign threat: the military expansionism of imperial Japan.

Nationalism and Militarism in Japan

More than any other Asian nation, Japan had imitated the West in focusing on industry and military might. By defeating Russia in 1905, Japan had also emerged as Asia's dominant power. But the island nation, for all its ambitions, did not have the fuel and raw materials to sustain an industrial economy and modern military. Japan thus sought to extend its sway over nearby Asian regions rich in resources.

One such region was Korea, occupied by Japan in the Russo-Japanese War and formally annexed in 1910. Mixing modernization with repression, Japan built roads, factories, hospitals, and schools, but also exploited Korea's resources and undermined its culture, forcing Koreans to speak Japanese and take Japanese names.

Japan expands into Korea and Shandong to gain resources

The Great War gave Japan new opportunities for growth. Using as a pretext its 1902 alliance with England, Japan declared war on Germany in 1914 and then seized China's Shandong peninsula, an iron-rich region the Germans had leased, as well as a number of German-held Pacific islands. Japan also profited commercially from the war, selling materials and supplies to the European Allies. In 1919 the Allies rewarded Japan, recognizing its rights in Shandong and giving it League of Nations mandates to govern the islands it had taken.

Industry and democracy grow in Japan in 1920s

Despite a postwar recession and a 1923 Tokyo earthquake that took 130 thousand lives, in the 1920s Japan experienced real economic growth. Japanese *zaibatsu*—private industrial empires, such as Mitsui and Mitsubishi, that made and sold products ranging from textiles to steamships—emerged among the world's largest commercial conglomerates. By the 1930s, owing to urban industrial expansion, almost half Japan's people lived in cities, up from only 12 percent in the 1890s. And many adopted a new urban culture, ignoring old Shinto and Buddhist values while embracing such modern amusements as movies, magazines, and sports.

In these years Japan also became more democratic. In 1925 the vote was extended to all men over 25, quadrupling the electorate, but still excluding women, who would not get voting rights until two decades later. New social legislation lifted restrictions on labor unions, limited work hours, and initiated a national health insurance program. By 1926, at the accession of Emperor Hirohito (1926–1989), Japan seemed to be evolving into a stable capitalist democracy.

Japanese youths in samurai dress reflect rising militarism.

But looming on the horizon were several threatening clouds. One was a growing population, which rose from 40 million in the 1890s to 70 million in the 1930s, deepening demand for resources and space—thus adding to expansionist pressures. Another was the growth of foreign trade, which made Japan wealthy but also dependent on markets in the West.

Most ominous was the rise of **militarism**, an exaltation of the armed forces that promoted military might as central to the nation's character. Enthused by Japan's victory over Russia and success in the Great War, many Japanese revered their military, expecting it to secure land and resources while stressing traditional samurai values of courage, honor, loyalty, and toughness. Furthermore, since the constitution gave the civilian government little control over the armed forces, military leaders could often act unhindered on their own.

Need for resources and space fuels Japanese militarism

Adding to these anxieties was the Great Depression, which devastated Japan. In the early 1930s, as Western nations imposed import quotas and tariffs, Japanese exports steeply declined, greatly reducing profits and wages and causing mass unemployment. In 1931, moreover, disastrous crop failure brought starvation to the countryside. As civilian leaders proved unable to ease their distress, many in Japan looked to the military for solutions.

Depression, Western tariffs, and crop failure devastate Japan

And the military looked to Manchuria, where Japan had based troops since the war with Russia. A huge Chinese province rich in coal and iron, it had ample land to provide food and space for Japan's growing population. In September 1931, some Japanese officers conspired to blow up a Japanese-owned railway in Manchuria and blame the act on Chinese terrorists. Citing a need to defend Japan's interests, the Japanese army then attacked Chinese forces and proceeded to conquer Manchuria, creating there in 1932 a Japanese puppet state called Manzhouguo (*man-JOO-gwō*).

Japanese army creates puppet state in Manchuria

The "Manchuria Incident" was disastrous for Japanese democracy. The civilian government, unable to restrain the military, resigned in futility at the end of 1931. A new prime minister, vainly seeking to restrain the armed forces, was murdered by a militarist the next May. Concluding that only the military could control its own, the emperor then made an admiral prime minister, ending civilian rule. Soon the new government started suppressing left-wing political parties and eventually all opposition.

Military leaders come to rule Japan in 1930s

The Manchuria Incident was also a blow to world peace. In 1933, when the League of Nations censured Japan for aggression in Manchuria, the Japanese withdrew from the League and grew more aggressive. In 1936 they signed the Anti-Comintern Pact, an agreement to collaborate with Nazi Germany against international communism. The next year, as Japan began a new arms buildup, its forces in Manchuria triggered a war with China. This was later merged with conflicts in Europe into a Second World War.

Japan exits the League and signs pact with Nazi Germany

Chapter Review

Putting It in Perspective

During the two decades that followed the Great War, Woodrow Wilson's dream of national self-determination turned into a nationalistic nightmare. The Versailles settlement, a compromise between Wilsonian ideals and Allied retributions, frustrated the hopes of both winners and losers, while cultural changes and new ideologies heightened global anxieties. In the 1920s, faced with economic and political instability, Italy and most of Eastern Europe turned from democracy to dictatorship. In the 1930s, shaken by the Great Depression, America and Western Europe retreated into economic nationalism, depriving other nations of Western markets and globalizing the crisis. Russia and Germany both became brutal dictatorships, Stalin's based on Soviet nationalism and Hitler's on nationalistic racism.

Meanwhile, anti-Western anxieties and nationalistic ideologies fueled anticolonialism in Africa, secular and Islamic nationalism in the Middle East, nonviolent resistance in India, conflicts between nationalists and communists in China, and expansive militarism in Japan. By the late 1930s, it was clear that the Great War had not been "the war to end all wars," as Wilson and others had hoped. Instead it had only been the First World War, soon to be surpassed in brutality and breadth by a second global conflict.

Reviewing Key Material

KEY CONCEPTS

national self-
   determination, 813
relativism, 814
relativity, 814
assembly line, 815
cubism, 817
surrealism, 817
League of Nations, 818
League of Nations
   mandates, 818
dictators, 820
fascism, 820
economic nationalism, 822
socialism in one country,
   825

collective farms, 825
Great Purges, 826
Nazis, 827
National Socialist German
   Workers' Party 827
Master Race 828
Lebensraum, 828
anticolonialism, 830
African National
   Congress, 830
satyagraha, 834
May Fourth Protests, 837
Shanghai Massacre, 839
Long March, 840
militarism, 841

KEY PEOPLE

Woodrow Wilson, 813, 818
Sigmund Freud, 814
Albert Einstein, 814
Henry Ford, 815
Sergei Eisenstein, 816
Leni Riefenstahl, 816
Pablo Picasso, 817
David Lloyd George, 818
Georges Clemenceau, 818
Benito Mussolini, 820
Herbert Hoover, 822
Franklin D. Roosevelt, 822
Ramsay MacDonald, 823
Stanley Baldwin, 823
Leon Blum, 824
V. I. Lenin, 824
Leon Trotsky, 824
Joseph Stalin, 825

Adolf Hitler, 827
Gustav Stresemann, 827
Simon Kimbangu, 830
Marcus Garvey, 830
Mustafa Kemal, 830
Reza Shah Pahlavi, 833
King Faisal, 833
Abdul Aziz ibn Saud, 833
Mohandas K. Gandhi, 834
Muhammad Ali
   Jinnah, 836
Sun Yixian (Sun
   Yatsen), 837
Yuan Shikai, 837
Jiang Jieshi (Chiang
   Kaishek), 837
Mao Zedong, 839

ASK YOURSELF

1. Why did the Paris Peace Conference of 1919 fail to provide a just and lasting peace? Why did the Treaty of Versailles cause so much disappointment and resentment?

2. Why was there so much turmoil in Western culture in the interwar years? Why did so many new democracies fail to survive?

3. Why and how did the U.S. Stock Market Crash of 1929 result in a global depression? What impact did the depression have on political changes in America, Western Europe, Germany, and Japan?

4. How did Mussolini, Stalin, and Hitler gain power? What methods and concepts did each use to control and strengthen his country?

5. What were the origins, ideals, and accomplishments of the nationalist movements emerging between the wars in Africa, the Middle East, and Asia? How and why did these nationalist movements differ from one another?

GOING FURTHER

Bosworth, R. J. B. *Mussolini*. 2002.
Brendon, Piers. *The Dark Valley: A Panorama of the 1930s*. 2000.
Brown, Judith M. *Gandhi: Prisoner of Hope*. 1989.
Bullock, Alan. *Hitler: A Study in Tyranny*. 1964.
Bullock, Alan. *Hitler and Stalin: Parallel Lives*. 1993.
Burleigh, M. *Third Reich: A New History*. 2000.
Cleveland, W. L. *History of the Modern Middle East*. 2nd ed. 2000.
Dirlik, A. *The Origins of Chinese Communism*. 1989.
Dulffer, J. *Nazi Germany 1933–1945*. 1996.
Eastman, L. *The Abortive Revolution: China Under Nationalist Rule, 1927–1937*. 1974.
Evans, R. J. *The Coming of the Third Reich*. 2004.
Eyck, Erich. *History of the Weimar Republic*. 1962.
Fenby, J. *Generalissimo: Chiang Kai-shek and the China He Lost*. 2003.
Fitzpatrick, S. *Stalin's Peasants: Resistance and Survival in the Russian Village After Collectivization*. 1995.
Freund, Bill. *The Making of Contemporary Africa*. 1999.
Galbraith, John Kenneth. *The Great Crash, 1929*. 1965.
Gandhi, Mohandas K. *An Autobiography*. 1957.
Irokawa, Daikichi. *The Age of Hirohito*. 1995.
Kater, M. *The Hitler Youth*. 2004.

Kershaw, Ian. *Hitler: Nemesis*. 2000.

Kindelberger, C. P. *The World in Depression, 1929–1939*. 1986.

Kuromiya, H. *Stalin's Industrial Revolution, 1928–1932*. 1988.

Lee, Stephen J. *European Dictatorships, 1918–1945*. 2nd ed. 2000.

Lewin, Moshe. *The Soviet Century*. 2005.

Lin Yu-sheng. *The Crisis of Chinese Consciousness: Radical Anti-traditionalism in the May Fourth Era*. 1979.

Mango, A. *Ataturk: Biography of the Founder of Modern Turkey*. 2000.

Mann, Michael. *Fascists*. 2004.

Masselos, Jim. *Indian Nationalism*. 1991.

McElvaine, R. *The Great Depression: America, 1929–1941*. 1984.

Medvedev, Roy. *Let History Judge: The Origins and Consequences of Stalinism*. 1989.

Mee, Charles L. *The End of Order: Versailles, 1919*. 1980.

Mehta, V. *Mahatma Gandhi and His Apostles*. 1977.

Mussolini, Benito. *Fascism: Doctrine and Institution*. 1968.

Paxton, R. O. *The Anatomy of Fascism*. 2004.

Payne, Stanley G. *A History of Fascism, 1914–1945*. 1995.

Sato, Barbara. *The New Japanese Women: Modernity, Media, and Women in Interwar Japan*. 2003.

Schram, S. *Mao Tse-tung: A Political Biography*. 1966.

Service, Robert. *Stalin: A Biography*. 2004.

Sheridan, James E. *China in Disintegration, 1912–1949*. 1975.

Shirer, William. *The Rise and Fall of the Third Reich*. 1960.

Snow, Edgar. *Red Star Over China*. 1938.

Sontag, R. J. *A Broken World, 1919–39*. 1971.

Spielvogel, J. *Hitler and Nazi Germany*. 5th ed. 2005.

Stephenson, Jill. *Women in Nazi Germany*. 2001.

Thurston, R. W. *Life and Terror in Stalin's Russia*. 1996.

Tucker, R. *Stalin in Power, 1928–1941*. 1990.

Volkogonov, Dmitri. *Stalin: Triumph and Tragedy*. 1996.

Whittam, J. *Fascist Italy*. 1995.

Wolpert, S. *Congress and Indian Nationalism*. 1988.

Key Dates and Developments

Year	Development		Year	Development
1918–1921	Reds prevail in Russian Civil War		1929	U.S. Stock Market Crash triggers Great Depression
1919	Paris Peace Conference formulates Treaty of Versailles		1930	Smoot-Hawley Tariff globalizes Great Depression
1919	Amritsar Massacre kills hundreds in India		1930	Gandhi organizes Salt March in India
1919	May Fourth Protests fuel nationalism in China		1930–1933	Civil war and forced famine kill millions in Soviet Ukraine
1919–1923	Kemal overthrows Ottoman sultan, creates Republic of Turkey		1931	Japanese army conquers Manchuria
1920	U.S. Senate fails to ratify Versailles Treaty		1932	Ibn Saud forms Kingdom of Saudi Arabia
1921	Lenin initiates New Economic Policy		1932	Iraq granted independence under King Faisal
1922	Mussolini takes power in Italy		1933	Hitler comes to power in Germany
1923	Inflation crisis rocks Germany		1934–1935	Mao leads Long March in China
1923	Tokyo Earthquake kills 130,000		1935	Persia is renamed Iran
1925	Reza Shah Pahlavi becomes ruler of Persia		1935	Britain grants India limited constitution
1925	Locarno Treaties stabilize Central Europe		1936	Germany and Japan sign Anti-Comintern Pact
1927	Jiang Jieshi massacres Chinese communists in Shanghai		1936–1938	Stalin conducts Great Purges in Russia
1928	Stalin launches First Five Year Plan			

World War II and the Holocaust, 1933–1945

Japanese Attack On Pearl Harbor, 1941

A motor launch rescues a sailor from the water alongside the burning American battleship *West Virginia* during the Japanese attack on Pearl Harbor, December 7, 1941. The Japanese attack converted a major war in Europe into World War II, a truly global war (page 858).

On September 2, 1945, a solemn ceremony took place on board the *Missouri*, a United States Navy battleship anchored in Tokyo Bay, Japan. Thousands of uniformed military personnel lined the decks as General Douglas MacArthur, commander of American forces in the Pacific, read the terms of surrender. Then, conspicuous in their formal civilian attire of top hats and tails, representatives of the Japanese Empire stepped forward to sign the surrender papers. The entire ceremony took only a few minutes to end history's bloodiest war.

Allied Nations in Red

Axis Nations in Tan

Neutral or Occupied Nations in Green

World War II was over. Sixty million people lay dead, the majority of them noncombatants caught in the gruesome clutches of a total war that made few distinctions between soldiers and civilians. In some respects, the war settled issues left unfinished from the Great War of 1914–1918. In other respects, it opened a new era in the evolution of the modern world. For many of those living at the time, 1945 signified a genuine turning point in history, both a completion of the past and an irrevocable break with it. They would carry the trauma of World War II with them the rest of their lives.

The Road to War

In the 1930s, most Europeans were trying to put the trauma of the Great War behind them. But to Adolf Hitler, Chancellor of Nazi Germany, that war had never really ended. He had come to power pledged to renew it, and the conflict he started would, until December 1941, be justifiably known as Hitler's War.

The Nazi worldview demanded huge additional territories, as *Lebensraum*, or "living space," for the German Master Race (Chapter 32). That space, according to Hitler, could be found to Germany's east, on the fertile plains of Poland and European Russia (Map 33.1). Gaining it would require victory in a war for mastery of Europe. France must be defeated, since it would never permit such German expansion without a fight, but Britain, Hitler hoped, could be bought off with a promise to respect the British Empire. The Soviet Union would, of course, fight to save itself, but Slavs, whom Nazis considered subhuman, would be no match for the Aryan armies. Victory was not certain but was likely.

Hitler's program requires a major war

Germany Prepares, 1933–1936

Hitler's initial moves as chancellor mixed aggression with caution. Recognizing German military inferiority resulting from the Versailles Treaty, he worked to improve Germany's international position while confusing its enemies. In 1933 Germany withdrew from the League of Nations, protesting its members' failure to agree on mutual disarmament while they kept Germany disarmed. Simultaneously, however, Hitler negotiated a ten-year nonaggression pact with Poland and renewed a 1926 economic treaty between

Hitler implements a two-track foreign policy

FOUNDATION MAP 33.1 Europe in 1933

Despite its defeat in the Great War, Germany still dominated Europe politically and economically. Note that despite being cut in two by the Polish Corridor and having its western frontiers demilitarized, Germany remained a centrally located nation, well placed to resume its struggle for continental supremacy. Why were its former opponents, Russia, France, and Britain, unable to keep Germany under control?

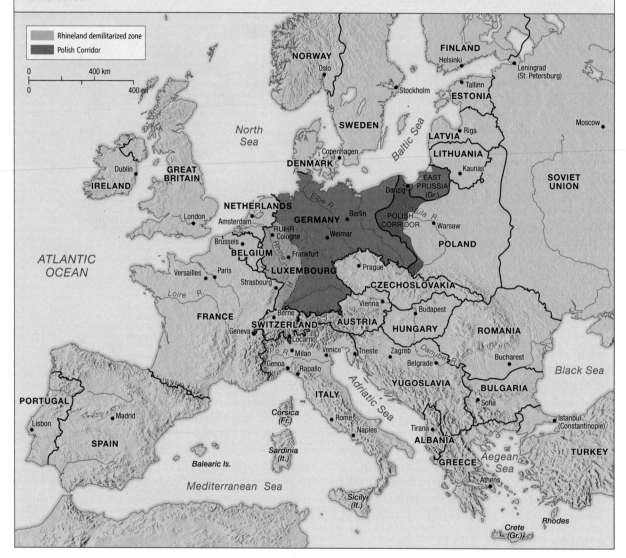

Germany and Soviet Russia. This combination of combativeness with reassurance allowed observers to see what they wanted to see.

Hitler's double game was derailed in the summer of 1934, when he overreached by authorizing the Austrian Nazi Party to attempt to overthrow the Austrian government. The rebels succeeded in assassinating Austria's chancellor, Engelbert Dollfuss, but then spent the rest of the evening drinking in Viennese bars and were soon arrested. Benito Mussolini's forces mobilized on Italy's Austrian frontier, sending a clear signal that Italy would not tolerate German intervention in Austrian affairs. Hitler quickly backed down, claiming he had had nothing to do with the assassination, but his international image had clearly been damaged, and his relationship with Europe's senior fascist dictator, Mussolini, was shaky.

Then Hitler's luck improved. In 1935 Mussolini invaded Ethiopia, hoping to avenge Italy's defeat at Adowa in 1896 (Chapter 30) by conquering that nation and beginning the construction of what he called the "New Roman Empire." The League of Nations, to which Italy belonged, promptly placed economic sanctions on Italy—an embargo that banned all exports to Italy except oil. Unable to purchase munitions and industrial equipment from League members, Italy turned to Germany, which as a nonmember could sell to Rome without penalty. Hitler thus was able to build a friendship with Mussolini while demonstrating the weakness of the League.

That same year, Germany formally denounced the Treaty of Versailles (Chapter 32) and proceeded to rearm and create an air force. An angry France discussed anti-German measures with Britain, but received no encouragement. Three months later the reason for British reluctance was revealed: Hitler had purchased British silence by negotiating a naval agreement limiting Germany's fleet to 35 percent the size of Britain's. Hitler's double game had succeeded again. The following year, he dramatized the inability of Britain and France to deal with his increasing power by remilitarizing the Rhineland, again in defiance of Versailles' terms. Once more the victors of 1918 did nothing, in part because they believed that their citizens would not be willing to go to war to prevent Germany from rearming territory that everyone recognized was German in the first place. But the impression of weakness in the democracies was unmistakable.

Outmaneuvering Britain and France, Germany remilitarizes the Rhineland

Civil War in Spain, 1936–1939

British and French ineffectiveness was further highlighted by their response to the outbreak of civil strife in Spain. There a revolution in 1931 had exchanged a monarchy for an unstable republic. In February 1936 a leftist coalition won the Spanish general election; five months later, a group of conservative, fascistic military officers led by General Francisco Franco rose in revolt, invading Spain from its own Mediterranean and North African colonies. The leftist parties rallied to the republican cause as Spain plunged into a catastrophic civil war.

The Popular Front government found itself less well equipped than its rebellious army. Seeking to purchase weapons abroad, it was turned down by Paris and London, who sought to confine the crisis by committing all nations to a policy of nonintervention. This policy benefited the rebels not only because they possessed more and better weapons than the government, but also because two of the three nations that violated the nonintervention agreement—Italy and Germany—backed Franco. The fascist dictatorships, claiming to defend Europe against Bolshevism, sent troops and equipment to the rebels, while Soviet Russia actually confirmed fascist charges by aiding the Spanish Republic. Britain and France merely stood by and watched the Spanish government collapse.

In a material sense, interventionist aid was overrated. The Soviets, more than a thousand miles from Spain, sent not weapons but technicians and advisors. Some of them

Spanish Civil War poster.

helped, but others meddled in disputes within the Spanish Communist Party and actually weakened the republican cause. Germany sent planes that destroyed cities such as Guernica to test the effects of terroristic bombing on civilian populations. But in general Hitler held back, hoping that a prolonged civil war might weaken his enemy France, which was divided over whether to intervene militarily on behalf of the Spanish Republic. Only Italy intervened in strength, sending more than 50 thousand soldiers and significant quantities of weapons. But what the rebels really needed was an embargo on arms sales to republican forces, which in effect they got when Britain and France refused to sell arms to either side.

The democracies respond inadequately to the civil war in Spain

To most of the world, the lesson of the Spanish Civil War appeared to be that the democracies were afraid to confront the dictators, even though Britain and France might hide behind the moral superiority of nonintervention. Toward the end of the 1930s, the principal questions facing Europe seemed to be when and where—and even if—the democracies would stand up to the dictators.

Germany's Eastward Expansion

Italy joins Germany in the Rome-Berlin Axis

German intervention in Spain sealed Hitler's friendship with Mussolini, leading to a German-Italian alliance called the Rome-Berlin Axis. This fascist partnership seemed potentially stronger than the Anglo-French alliance, which lacked the American and Russian support it had enjoyed during the Great War. Along with Germany's earlier remilitarization of the Rhineland, the Axis gave Hitler the foundation he needed to take the initiative in European diplomacy. From February 1938 through March 1939, Germany acted while Britain and France reacted.

Germany's eastward expansion was implemented one step at a time, with careful attention to its flanks and rear. Geography dictated that Austria, on its southern flank, be handled first. In 1919, Austria had tried to unite with Germany rather than stand alone as a feeble remnant of the once-mighty Habsburg Empire. But that union, known as *Anschluss* (*AHN-schloose*), never had a chance because the victorious powers thought Germany should be penalized rather than rewarded for losing the war. Austrian and German interest in *Anschluss* persisted, though, and after Hitler came to power in Germany in 1933, an Austrian version of the Nazi Party grew rapidly and worked toward union. In Vienna, Chancellor Kurt von Schuschnigg quietly sought to maintain Austrian sovereignty without needlessly antagonizing Hitler. This effort ended in February 1938 when Hitler ordered Schuschnigg to accept Austrian Nazis into his cabinet or face war. Hitler himself had begun in 1933 with only three Nazis in a cabinet of 11; clearly he meant to gain control of the Austrian government in a similar way.

Schuschnigg stalled for nearly a month. Then he announced, with four days' notice, a nationwide referendum on Austrian independence. Furious, Hitler ordered an immediate invasion, which succeeded without bloodshed because Austrian forces were instructed by their government not to resist (Map 33.2). German tanks and jeeps, caught with insufficient oil in their crankcases, broke down in embarrassing numbers on the road to Vienna, but nothing could dampen Hitler's joy at proclaiming the union of his homeland and his Third Reich.

Still Britain and France did nothing. They had no alliance with Austria, and their people were unlikely to support a war to prevent German-speaking Austrians from becoming Germans. Hitler had used the self-determination clauses of the Treaty of Versailles to

Map 33.2 German Territorial Expansion, 1938–1939

National Socialist foreign policy was based on the conquest of *Lebensraum*, or living space, in Poland and Russia. Notice the dates of Germany's successive actions, as Hitler's government moved from west to east. Why were these actions necessary in this sequence before Germany could proceed to conquer *Lebensraum*?

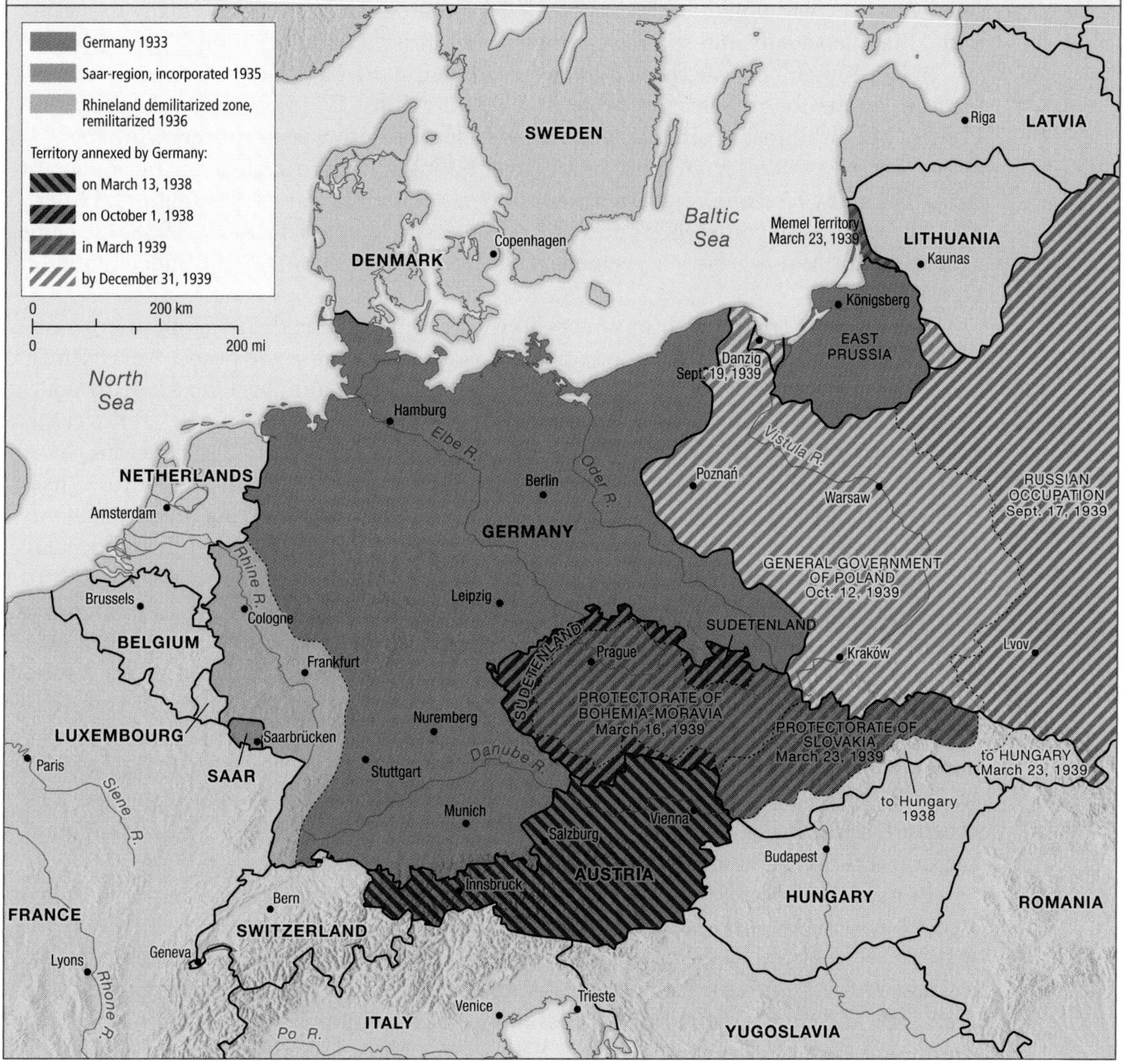

Legend:
- Germany 1933
- Saar-region, incorporated 1935
- Rhineland demilitarized zone, remilitarized 1936

Territory annexed by Germany:
- on March 13, 1938
- on October 1, 1938
- in March 1939
- by December 31, 1939

0   200 km
0   200 mi

Labels on map: North Sea, SWEDEN, Riga, LATVIA, Baltic Sea, Memel Territory March 23, 1939, LITHUANIA, Kaunas, DENMARK, Copenhagen, Königsberg, EAST PRUSSIA, Danzig Sept. 19, 1939, Hamburg, Elbe R., NETHERLANDS, Amsterdam, Berlin, Oder R., Poznań, Warsaw, RUSSIAN OCCUPATION Sept. 17, 1939, Vistula R., GERMANY, Rhine R., Brussels, Cologne, BELGIUM, Leipzig, Frankfurt, GENERAL GOVERNMENT OF POLAND Oct. 12, 1939, SUDETENLAND, Prague, Kraków, Lvov, LUXEMBOURG, Saarbrücken, Nuremberg, Paris, SAAR, Stuttgart, Danube R., PROTECTORATE OF BOHEMIA-MORAVIA March 16, 1939, PROTECTORATE OF SLOVAKIA March 23, 1939, to HUNGARY March 23, 1939, Munich, Salzburg, Vienna, to Hungary 1938, Budapest, Seine R., AUSTRIA, Innsbruck, Bern, FRANCE, SWITZERLAND, HUNGARY, ROMANIA, Lyons, Geneva, Rhône R., ITALY, Venice, Trieste, Po R., YUGOSLAVIA

his advantage. But Czechoslovakia was next on his list, and that nation had an alliance with France.

Again Hitler argued for self-determination. The western border region of Czechoslovakia, called the Sudetenland (*soo-DĀ-ten-land*), was populated mainly by Germans, and Hitler claimed Germany's right to annex the area. Throughout the summer of 1938, Hitler

After annexing Austria, Hitler turns on Czechoslovakia

pressured the Czechs to cede him the Sudetenland, and the Sudeten Nazi Party increased the pressure by staging provocations and incidents. But the Czechs, counting on French support, stood firm. They knew that as the Sudetenland contained most of Czechoslovakia's frontier fortifications against Germany, the rest of the nation would be defenseless without the region. British Prime Minister Neville Chamberlain, desperate to avert another European war that would doubtless involve his country, flew twice to Germany to meet with Hitler personally. But still the German leader insisted on annexation.

In late September war seemed likely, a fact that worried not only German military leaders (who thought Germany would lose a war against Czechoslovakia, Britain, and France) but also most ordinary Germans, who lacked enthusiasm for renewing the Great War. Mussolini, having no intention of taking Italy into such a war but reluctant to see Germany lose one, suggested a four-power conference at the last minute. Hitler agreed, hosting the conference himself in Munich on September 28–29, 1938. He came away with an Anglo-French agreement that Germany would annex the Sudetenland on October 1.

The Munich Conference gives the Sudetenland to Germany

The Munich Treaty, with its concessions to Germany, was the triumph of appeasement, a policy of giving in to a potential aggressor to maintain the peace. Appeasement arose not out of cowardice but of a sincere desire to avoid another Great War by addressing German concerns over the severity of the Treaty of Versailles. Its fatal weakness was that the Nazi government was not so much interested in these concerns, which it viewed as pretexts, as in what could be gained by the threat of force or by force itself. Czechoslovakia rightly believed that it had been sold out to a bullying dictator. Chamberlain wrongly believed that he had secured "peace in our time"; what he had gained was peace for six months. On March 15, 1939, Germany invaded the remainder of Czechoslovakia, which was now a purely Slavic country with almost no German population. Clearly Hitler's intention was not to pursue self-determination or to adjust genuine grievances but to expand Germany eastward. Poland would be next on the list.

The Munich Conference of 1938. Front row, from left to right: Chamberlain, Daladier, Hitler, Mussolini, Italian foreign minister Ciano.

Temporarily the initiative passed to Britain and France, which issued a guarantee of Polish independence on March 31. But this commitment did not impress Hitler, who could not imagine that Britain and France would fight to defend a nation with a weak army when they had sold out Czechoslovakia, a well-fortified country with a strong one. His cynicism made him miss the point: the democracies now knew that his self-determination rhetoric was fake, and at last they took action.

Pressure on Poland increased until, on August 23, Germany shocked the world by signing a nonaggression pact with the Soviet Union. Germany agreed to divide Poland with the Soviets and to grant the Soviet Union other favorable adjustments along its western borders. In return, the Soviets guaranteed Germany regular shipments of grain, oil, and timber. British blockades had caused crippling shortages of food and supplies in Germany during the Great War, so this **Nazi-Soviet Pact** effectively rendered Germany blockade-proof by giving it access to Russian food and resources. Hitler assumed this agreement would convince Britain and France that it was useless to fight over Poland, but when Germany invaded that country on September 1, London and Paris demanded German withdrawal by September 3 (see "Address by Führer and Reich Chancellor Adolf Hitler to the German Reichstag"). When the deadline expired, Britain and France declared war on Germany, beginning what would later be known as World War II.

Document 33.1 Address by Führer and Reich Chancellor Adolf Hitler to the German Reichstag

For months we have been suffering under the torture of a problem which the Versailles *Diktat* created—a problem which has deteriorated until it becomes intolerable for us. Danzig was and is a German city. The Corridor was and is German. Both these territories owe their cultural development exclusively to the German people. Danzig was separated from us, the Corridor was annexed by Poland . . . You know the proposals that I have made to fulfill the necessity of restoring German sovereignty over German territories. You know the endless attempts I made for a peaceful clarification and understanding of the problem of Austria, and later of the problem of the Sudetenland, Bohemia, and Moravia. It was all in vain . . .

I am determined to solve (1) the Danzig question; (2) the question of the Corridor; and (3) to see to it that a change is made in the relationship between Germany and Poland that shall ensure a peaceful co-existence . . . I am asking of no German man more than I myself was ready throughout four years at any time to do. There will be no hardships for Germans to which I myself will not submit. My whole life henceforth belongs more than ever to my people. I am from now on just the first soldier of the German Reich. I have once more put on that coat that was the most sacred and dear to me. I will not take it off again until victory is secured, or I will not survive the struggle . . . If our will is so strong that no hardship and suffering can subdue it, then our will and our German might shall prevail.

SOURCE: The archives of the Avalon Project at the Yale Law School, http://www.fcit.usf.edu/holocaust/resource/document/HITLER1.html

Hitler's War, 1939–1941

From September 1939 until December 1941, world leaders usually called the new conflict "the European War." In the newspapers, on radio broadcasts, and in everyday conversation, however, it was known as "Hitler's War." Adolf Hitler's actions had started the war, his ideology inspired it, and his leadership guided Germany to unprecedented territorial domination. By July 1940, German forces occupied most of the continent and intimidated the few neutral nations that remained. Europe's future appeared to be one of subjugation to the Master Race.

Germany's invasion of Poland begins World War II

From Poland to France

German conquest of Poland took only four weeks, featuring a new tactic called **Blitzkrieg**, or "lightning war." Striking more rapidly than the enemy was nothing new in warfare; what made Blitzkrieg so effective was the radio, which permitted instant communication between armored units on the ground and dive-bombers in the air. The resulting coordination of modern mechanized units threw the more conventional Polish forces into disarray and gave the Germans a reputation for machine-like efficiency despite the fact that most of their transportation, like that of other European armies in 1939, was still handled by horses. After three weeks, fulfilling the terms of the Nazi-Soviet Pact, the Soviets invaded from the East to help Germany complete the division of Poland (Map 33.3). The USSR proceeded to improve its borders in the Baltic region, taking territory from Finland in the Russo-Finnish War (November 1939–March 1940), and absorbing the Baltic States of Estonia, Latvia, and Lithuania in July 1940 through nonaggression pacts and internal subversion.

Blitzkrieg enables Germany to conquer Poland quickly

German mechanized warfare.

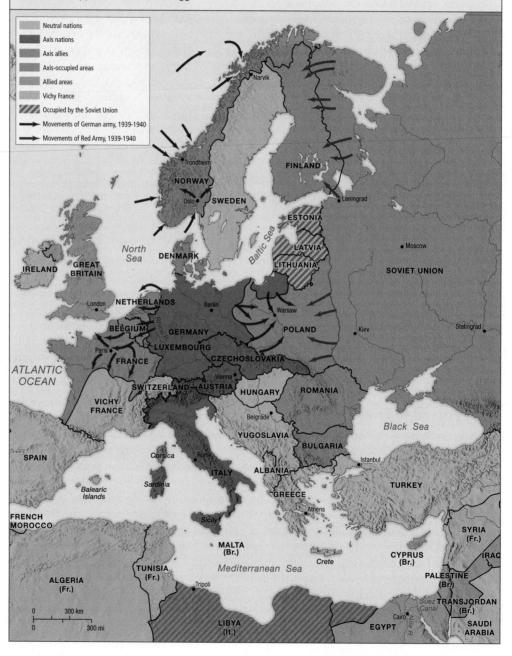

Map 33.3 Hitler's War in Europe, 1939–1940

Once Germany had secured its southern and eastern flanks by absorbing Austria and Czechoslovakia (Map 33.2), Hitler was free to initiate a European war. Observe that Germany and the Soviet Union collaborated to conquer Poland, and that Soviet support left Germany free to turn westward against Norway, the Netherlands, Belgium, Luxembourg, and France. How might Hitler's strategy have changed had the Soviet Union not supported his westward aggression?

Neutral nations
Axis nations
Axis allies
Axis-occupied areas
Allied areas
Vichy France
Occupied by the Soviet Union
Movements of German army, 1939-1940
Movements of Red Army, 1939-1940

While the Soviets were occupying additional land, Germany was engaged in the so-called Phony War, a quiet seven-month period in which Hitler first tried to convince Britain to withdraw from the war, and then, having failed in this effort, looked for a strategy that would defeat France. Attacking westward in spring of 1940, Germany broke the French lines by driving armored units through the dense Ardennes Forest on the Franco-Belgian border. The French high command, having observed the effectiveness of Blitzkrieg in Poland, was for some reason unprepared for such tactics in France and had stationed no reserve forces with which to counter a possible breakthrough. Meanwhile the British Expeditionary Force, trapped against the English Channel at Dunkirk, narrowly escaped to England when Hitler ordered a 48-hour halt for tank maintenance. France surrendered on June 24, 1940. General Charles de Gaulle, French Minister of War, flew to London and announced the formation of the Free French movement in hopes of attracting French volunteers to continue the fight against Germany, but few heard his radio broadcast of June 18 and even fewer responded to his call.

Hitler receiving news of France's surrender.

The fall of France shocked the world. Until then the war had been a series of sideshows that, although important in themselves, could not settle the conflict. But France was a different matter. Nazi Germany had achieved in six weeks what Imperial Germany had been unable to accomplish in more than four years between 1914 and 1918. Hitler was master of most of the European continent, and any future challenge to his rule would necessitate an invasion of Europe from abroad. The French army had been considered the bastion of democracy against fascist aggression; its amazingly swift collapse demoralized those throughout the world who yearned for Hitler's defeat. Many feared that the Third Reich, as Hitler had boasted, really would last a thousand years.

The conquest of France makes Germany master of Europe

The Battle of Britain

Yet Britain remained undefeated, and its morale showed no signs of weakening. Winston Churchill had replaced Neville Chamberlain as prime minister just before the Nazi attack on France. Passionately anti-German, referring to Hitler as a "bloodthirsty guttersnipe" and invariably pronouncing "Nazi" to rhyme with "nasty," Churchill employed his remarkable rhetorical skills to inspire his island nation and rebuild its confidence in ultimate victory (see "Address of Winston Churchill to Parliament, June 4, 1940"). In this mission he was indirectly aided by Hitler, who had no coherent plan for defeating Britain. Everyone, including Churchill, knew that if the German army landed in England it would win the war; but everyone also knew that Britain's Royal Navy was powerful enough to prevent an invasion. The unavoidable logic in this thinking led Hitler into the unusual tactic of trying to destroy Britain's Royal Air Force so that his own **Luftwaffe** (the German air force) could keep the Royal Navy bottled up in port while the German army invaded.

Fires burn in London during the Battle of Britain.

This approach produced the Battle of Britain, a contest between air forces that the British won between August and November 1940. They used a new detection system called "radar," invented in Britain in 1938, to direct their fighters against incoming German raiders. Their pilots performed with such efficiency and heroism that Churchill claimed, "Never in the field of human conflict was so much owed by so many to so few."

Britain frustrates Germany's bid for air superiority

Document 33.2 Address of Winston Churchill to Parliament, June 4, 1940

. . . I have, myself, full confidence that if all do their duty, if nothing is neglected, and if the best arrangements are made, as they are being made, we shall prove ourselves once again able to defend our Island home, to ride out the storm of war, and to outlive the menace of tyranny, if necessary for years, if necessary alone. At any rate, that is what we are going to try to do. That is the resolve of His Majesty's Government—every man of them. That is the will of Parliament and the nation. The British Empire and the French Republic, linked together in their cause and in their need, will defend to the death their native soil, aiding each other like good comrades to the utmost of their strength. Even though large tracts of Europe and many old and famous States have fallen or may fall into the grip of the Gestapo and all the odious apparatus of Nazi rule, we shall not flag or fail. We shall go on to the end, we shall fight in France, we shall fight on the seas and oceans, we shall fight with growing confidence and growing strength in the air, we shall defend our Island, whatever the cost may be, we shall fight on the beaches, we shall fight on the landing grounds, we shall fight in the fields and in the streets, we shall fight in the hills; we shall never surrender; and even if, which I do not for a moment believe, this Island or a large part of it were subjugated and starving, then our Empire beyond the seas, armed and guarded by the British Fleet, would carry on the struggle, until, in God's good time, the New World, with all its power and might, steps forth to the rescue and the liberation of the Old.

SOURCE: Robert Rhodes James, editor, *Winston S. Churchill: His Complete Speeches, 1897–1963*, Volume VI (1935–1942), (New York: Chelsea House Publishers, 1974), 6230–6231.

The German Invasion of Russia

Frustrated by a war against an enemy he couldn't invade, Hitler turned east to fulfill the Nazi quest for living space in European Russia. He had promised his generals that he would not fight a two-front war, but since neither Britain nor Germany was capable of invading the other, he could plausibly claim that action on the British front was stalled. Besides, if Hitler's drive for living space was going to succeed, Germany would have to fight the USSR at some point. Hitler assumed that the Russians, a Slavic people scorned by the Nazis as "subhumans," would quickly fall to the Master Race.

Germany invades Russia to fulfill Hitler's ideological dream

The invasion of Russia began on June 22, 1941, and it took the Soviet government completely by surprise (Map 33.4). Washington and London had repeatedly given Moscow intelligence data concerning Nazi troop movements, but Stalin had dismissed them as capitalist lies designed to break up the Nazi-Soviet alliance. He apparently suffered a nervous collapse when the invasion began and emerged 11 days later shaken and grim. By July 16 German armored units had broken the Red Army's lines, taken more than a million prisoners, and penetrated deep into Russia.

The main problem facing Germany was the immensity of the Soviet Union, amounting to one-sixth of the land surface of the globe. The primitive state of local roads slowed the German advance, but even had that advance been swifter, Germany did not have enough soldiers to achieve victory over a country so large. In addition, the Red Army, substantially larger than the German, drew on huge manpower reserves. German forces made their task much more difficult by treating non-Russian ethnic groups, which had initially welcomed them as liberators from Communist oppression, as Slavic subhumans. Finally, Hitler and his high command failed to define a single principal objective, choosing instead to drive simultaneously for the cities of Leningrad, Moscow, and Kiev.

Map 33.4 Germany's Invasion of the USSR, 1941

Frustrated by his inability either to conquer Britain or to force it out of the war, Hitler turned on the Soviet Union in June 1941, intent on fulfilling the Nazi objective of acquiring *Lebensraum*. Note that numerous German thrusts enabled them to occupy immense areas of western Russia but left Moscow unconquered and most of the Soviet Union free of German control. Why was Germany unable to defeat the Soviet Union in 1941?

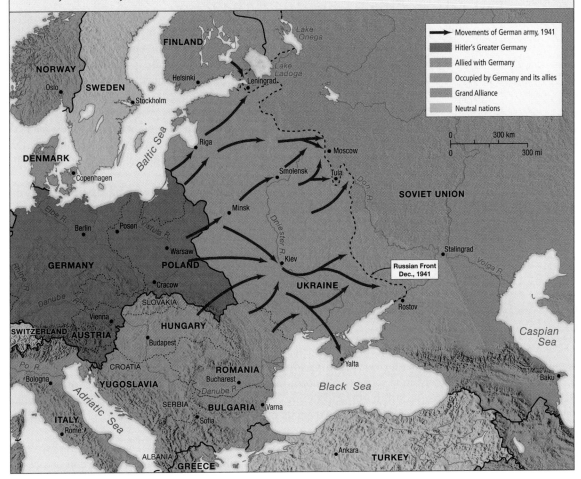

Moreover, Soviet resistance proved more persistent than Germany had anticipated. By November Kiev had been taken, Leningrad was besieged but could not be completely surrounded, and furious fighting engulfed the western approaches to Moscow. Acting out of sheer desperation, and believing a spy's report that Japan would move against the Americans, British, and Dutch in the Pacific rather than against Soviet Siberia, Stalin in late November transferred 250 thousand Siberian troop reserves west to the Moscow front, under Georgi Zhukov (*gay-ŌR-gē ZHOO-kawf*), his most successful commander. The resulting Soviet counteroffensive in early December caught the Germans off guard and unprepared for winter conditions. The supposedly subhuman Russians then handed

A Soviet counteroffensive surprises the German army

the German army a stinging defeat. The Germans stiffened and held their positions throughout the winter, but Hitler's chain of Blitzkrieg victories was over, and anti-Nazi forces gained new hope.

East Asia and the Pacific, 1937–1942

Meanwhile, events in East Asia and the Pacific were transforming Hitler's conflict into a Second World War. Japan had fought on the winning side in the Great War but had been treated with condescension by its allies after 1919. The Japanese government's request that the Versailles Treaty include a racial equality clause had been rejected by Britain, France, and the United States. At the Washington Naval Conference of 1921, Japan was forced to accept a treaty that limited it to only three large naval ships for every five built by the United States and five built by Britain. In 1924, the United States Congress passed discriminatory immigration legislation that permitted 53,000 British immigrants to enter each year, but only 100 Japanese. Japan concluded that its former allies thought little of its wartime support.

Suffering economically from the Great Depression (Chapter 32), Japan decided in 1931 to secure the natural resources it needed for its rapidly developing industrial capability by conquering China's resource-rich province of Manchuria. Six years later, on July 7, 1937, Japanese army units from Manchuria, staging provocative maneuvers in China, clashed with Nationalist Chinese troops at the Marco Polo Bridge, not far from Beijing.

The New Order in East Asia

Japanese aggression and atrocities endanger Asia

Japan followed up this incident by conquering northeast China, hoping to quickly force the Nationalists to accept peace terms. But Chinese president Jiang Jieshi (Chiang Kaishek), faced with overwhelming force, refused to surrender or to mount an all-out resistance. Determined to press forward, the Japanese struck south, capturing Shanghai in a bloody three-month battle and taking Nanjing in December. Japanese troops then went on a rampage in Nanjing, massacring as many as 200 thousand people and raping thousands of women.

The international outcry that followed this **"Rape of Nanjing"** energized Chinese resistance to Japanese military occupation. It also inadvertently produced further atrocities. Hoping to satisfy their soldiers and prevent future international condemnation over mass rapes, the Japanese set up "comfort stations" near the front lines, forcing young Korean girls to serve as "comfort women," whom Japanese soldiers repeatedly raped each day. But the outcry over Nanjing did not slow Japan's advance. By the end of 1938 the Japanese had conquered most of eastern China (Map 33.5). Declaring a "New Order in East Asia," they portrayed themselves as liberators who were cleansing the region of Western imperialists and creating a prosperous new economic sphere dominated by Asians.

Still the Chinese refused to submit. The Chinese Communists, from their northwestern base at Yan'an, mounted an effective guerrilla campaign that tormented Japanese troops, sabotaged their systems of transport and supply by blowing up trucks and trains, and won the allegiance of many Chinese peasants. Meanwhile the Nationalists, whose

The Rape of Nanjing.

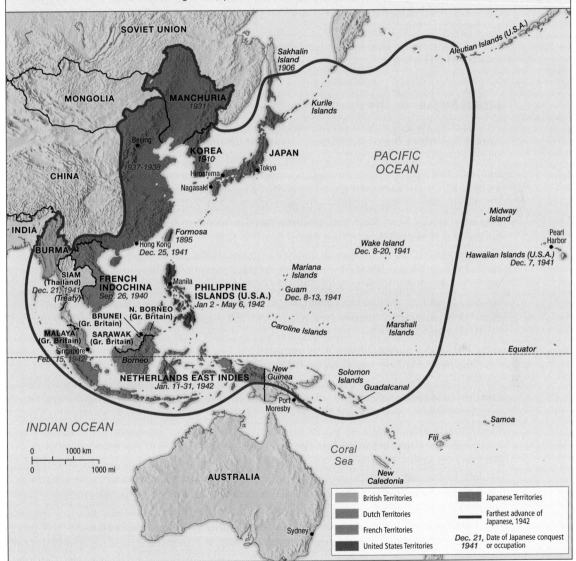

Map 33.5 Japanese Conquests, 1937–1942

From its island base, Japan in fewer than fifty years created an empire and expanded it to the line shown on the map. Notice that this expansion was achieved at the expense of Britain, China, the United States, France, and the Netherlands. None of the first three countries was willing to accept Japanese domination of the region, and Japan's strength was inadequate to force them to do so. What disadvantages did Japan face as a result of its rapid expansion?

inability to stop the invaders was rapidly eroding their public support, retreated to central China and hoped that Japan would make a major mistake.

A few years later, their hopes were fulfilled. In 1940, after France surrendered, the French colony of Indochina was left unprotected. Attracted by that region's assets and awed by Nazi success, the Japanese joined the Axis, allying with Germany and Italy in the Tripartite Pact. Japan then began moving troops into Indochina. Hoping to force them to withdraw, the United States imposed an embargo in 1941, depriving Japan of American supplies, including oil. But this embargo only confirmed Japan's conviction that it must possess its own sources of fuel and raw materials.

Japan decides to gain resources through conquest

Acting on this conviction, the Japanese planned a bold and spectacular operation: a campaign to conquer British Singapore and Malaya, the oil-rich Dutch East Indies, and the Philippine Islands, an American commonwealth. The action would start with a surprise assault on the U.S. Pacific fleet, based in the Hawaiian Islands at a naval station called Pearl Harbor.

Japan Strikes in the Pacific

Recognizing its inability to defeat the United States militarily, Japan gambled that a rapid takeover of the western Pacific would shock the Americans and leave them unwilling to spend the time, blood, and money required to retake it. If this hoped-for scenario did not materialize, Tokyo was left with no plausible alternative to defeat. This desperate gamble led Japan to one of the most brilliant tactical victories of the war.

Japan attacks Pearl Harbor to eliminate the U.S. Pacific Fleet

In late November 1941 an invasion fleet headed southward from Japan. Simultaneously Japan's First Air Fleet, an innovative grouping of eight aircraft carriers into a single attack force, left northern Japan heading east. In a carefully coordinated multi-pronged assault spread across thousands of miles of the Pacific, the southern force attacked Guam, Wake Island, Hong Kong, Malaya, and the Philippines on December 7–8, while the First Air Fleet attacked Pearl Harbor. American forces, anticipating the southern but not the eastern thrust, were caught unprepared in the greatest military disaster in American history (see page 844). All eight American battleships anchored in the harbor were either sunk or disabled, and more than three thousand casualties were inflicted. Japanese losses were minimal.

The Pearl Harbor attack boosted Japanese morale, but they lost their gamble. Rather than accepting Japan's actions, U.S. President Franklin Roosevelt obtained a declaration of war from Congress, and American resolve strengthened around the cry "Remember Pearl Harbor!" Four days after the attack, Germany and Italy declared war on the United States. They were under no obligation to support Japan, but Hitler hoped to encourage the Japanese to engage the United States in a lengthy war that would distract America for years. He assumed that the American public would demand an all-out effort against Japan and that U.S. forces would make little impact on the war in Europe until after Germany defeated Soviet Russia. Therefore, Hitler believed, his declaration of war would be without practical effect but would further heighten the morale of the Japanese.

The Allies decide to deal with Germany before Japan

Hitler was wrong on several counts. First, Germany did not defeat Russia. Second, Roosevelt, Churchill, and their military advisors agreed to pursue the defeat of Germany first, making the war against Japan secondary. Finally, the Japanese did not need German encouragement. By May 1942 they had conquered every one of their objectives in an astonishing display of military boldness and skill. When the Philippines finally surrendered to Japan on May 6, 1942, Tokyo controlled the western Pacific, threatened Australia, and was poised to strike against the three American aircraft carriers that, being at sea on maneuvers, had not been destroyed at Pearl Harbor (Map 33.5).

End of the Japanese Advance

Admiral Isoroku Yamamoto (*ih-sō-RŌ-koo yah-mah-MŌ-tō*), architect of the Pearl Harbor strategy, designed another two-pronged plan to destroy the carriers. A massive eight-carrier strike force would leave Japan bound for Midway Island, the only remaining American military possession west of Hawaii. On route, four of the eight carriers would separate from the main body and head northeast, threatening an invasion of Alaska. Yamamoto reasoned that Admiral Chester Nimitz, commanding what remained of the U.S. Pacific Fleet, would be compelled to divide his forces to counter the threat, and his carriers would be isolated and sunk one by one.

But Nimitz, whose intelligence section was reading Japanese naval codes, knew that Midway was the principal target and did not divide his forces. The Americans were still outnumbered by four carriers to three, but a squadron of off-course American dive-bombers accidentally found the Japanese carriers. They took them by surprise and destroyed all four. The Midway disaster ended Japan's string of victories and virtually guaranteed its ultimate defeat.

Japan's strategy fails at Midway

North Africa and Europe, 1942–1943

In the winter of 1941–1942, assuming that Japan would tie down the Americans in the Pacific for several years, Hitler renewed his attack on the Soviet Union by driving southeast toward the oil-rich Caucasus region. That strategic decision was opposed by many of his military advisors. Some encouraged continuing pressure on Moscow, in hope of cracking Soviet resistance there. Others, like Field Marshal Erwin Rommel, begged Hitler to push from North Africa through the Suez Canal and the Middle East, eventually linking up with Japan in the Persian Gulf and Indian Ocean. Such a strategy would deprive Britain of its oil and might force it into a compromise peace.

Erwin Rommel, the "Desert Fox".

The Battle for North Africa

Rommel, one of the century's finest battlefield commanders, was in North Africa because of Italian military errors. Mussolini had become overconfident after Germany's defeat of France and committed his finest troops to Italy's African colony of Tripoli in an effort to push Britain out of Egypt. Instead the British forces, outnumbered ten to one, invaded Tripoli and humiliated the Italians by forcing huge numbers of them to surrender. Fearful that Mussolini would abandon the struggle, Hitler decided to send Rommel at the head of two tank divisions, the "Afrika Korps," to reverse Italy's failure.

The North African desert turned out to be ideal terrain for tanks. German forces quickly pushed the British back into Egypt (Map 33.6). London naturally reinforced its position in order to defend the Suez Canal, but when Rommel asked for more troops and equipment, as well as for a strategic decision to turn North Africa into a principal combat area, Hitler denied both requests. In both 1941 and 1942 Hitler focused on *Lebensraum* and the Soviet Union rather than the Middle East, thereby missing a reasonable chance at forcing Britain out of the war. Rommel, undersupplied and undermanned, proved tactically brilliant in desert warfare but unable to overcome Britain's material superiority.

The British War Cabinet determined to preserve that superiority. In summer of 1942, Britain's Eighth Army received its new commander, General Bernard Law Montgomery,

Germany loses in North Africa

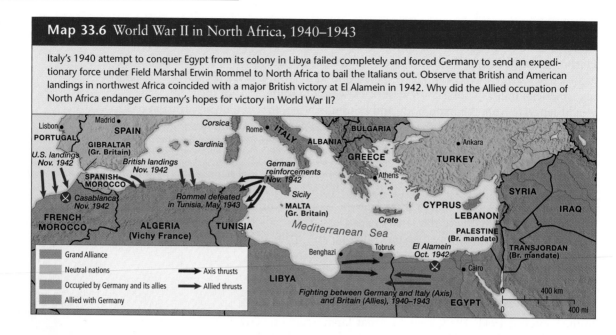

Map 33.6 World War II in North Africa, 1940–1943

Italy's 1940 attempt to conquer Egypt from its colony in Libya failed completely and forced Germany to send an expeditionary force under Field Marshal Erwin Rommel to North Africa to bail the Italians out. Observe that British and American landings in northwest Africa coincided with a major British victory at El Alamein in 1942. Why did the Allied occupation of North Africa endanger Germany's hopes for victory in World War II?

a feisty Scot who believed in rigorous training and crushing material advantage. That October he attacked and defeated the Afrika Korps. Simultaneously, U.S. forces, having waited nearly a year to engage the Germans, landed in Morocco and Algeria. Caught between the British and Americans, Rommel's troops fought skillfully but hopelessly. Ironically, now that it would do no good, Hitler insisted on reinforcing Rommel—over the latter's explicit objections. When the Afrika Korps surrendered on May 13, 1943, an additional 250 thousand German soldiers needlessly became prisoners of war.

Stalingrad and Kursk

By mid-1943 the war in the east had also turned against Germany. Hitler's decision to drive toward the Caucasus was ill-advised, dragging the German army into a house-to-house battle for the large city of Stalingrad. In November 1942, a Soviet counteroffensive penetrated a weak point in the German lines and encircled the city (Map 33.7). German forces trapped there were forbidden to try to break out until the armies invading the Caucasus could be withdrawn; otherwise more than a million men would have been captured. By the time the withdrawal was completed, it was too late to save Stalingrad. The German Sixth Army, reduced from 220 thousand to 90 thousand freezing, starving men, surrendered on February 2, 1943. It was the turning point of the war for the Soviet Union, and Stalin ordered night-long fireworks over Red Square in celebration.

The Red Army takes the strategic initiative at Kursk

Germany still held the strategic advantage, however, and proved it by attacking the Soviets near Kursk in July. The week-long fight was the largest tank battle in history until the Ramadan War between Egypt and Israel in 1973; astronauts can still see, from outer space, a large reddish-brown spot near Kursk, the rusting remains of thousands of destroyed tanks. When the battle was over, the Germans had lost and the Soviets had

Map 33.7 Soviet Victories at Stalingrad and Kursk, 1942–1943

Unable to take Moscow in 1941, the Germans turned south to the oil fields of the Transcaucasus in 1942. Their defeat at Stalingrad was a principal turning point in the war. But notice that the Red Army was unable to take the offensive until after the German defeat at Kursk in 1943 in the largest tank battle of the war. How did the Red Army then proceed to expel the Germans from Russia?

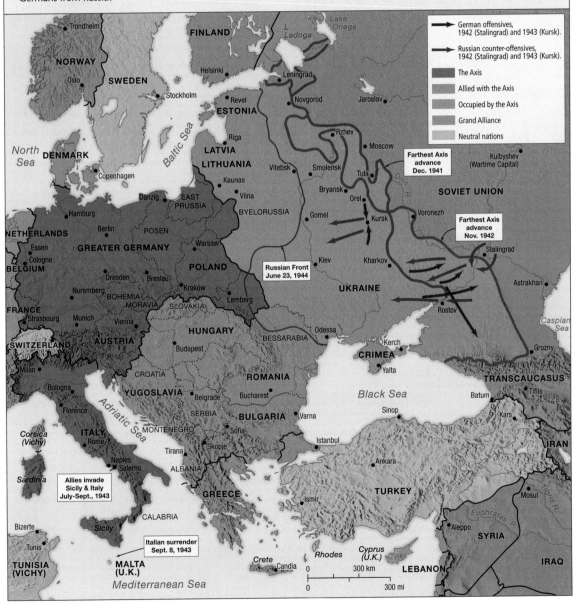

gained the initiative. Like the Midway defeat for the Japanese, for the Germans Kursk marked the end of expansion.

Civilian Life in World War II

Many of the hardships the Great War imposed on civilians (Chapter 31) returned to plague the home fronts in World War II. Rationing reappeared as a means for managing shortages of food, fuel, clothing, and vital raw materials. Tens of millions labored six or seven days a week in defense plants. Once again, women took up work on farms and in factories as men were drafted. But new burdens appeared in the early 1940s to intensify civilian suffering.

Female welder at a munitions plant, 1942.

In Britain, Germany, Japan, Poland, and Russia, aerial bombing destroyed homes and burned whole sections of cities. Air raids in the Great War had been sporadic and ineffective, but now they were relentless and devastating. People huddled behind drawn curtains in darkened rooms during nighttime blackouts, which plunged entire cities into darkness to make them less visible to bombers. Others crammed into underground shelters for protection. Sometimes there was no escape: in Hamburg, Dresden, and Tokyo, massive incendiary bombing created firestorms that raised surface temperatures to over 2,000 degrees. Some people caught outside shelters were trapped in asphalt as streets melted; others were boiled alive when they dove into canals to escape the heat; still others were melted into tiny pools of liquid fat.

Ground warfare was no less destructive. In Russia, advancing Germans totally destroyed more than 19 thousand villages, often burning the inhabitants alive in synagogues or churches. When Soviet forces invaded Germany in 1945, they retaliated by crucifying German farmers on barn doors and raping and mutilating women. Japanese soldiers in Manila in 1944 slaughtered the patients and staff of entire hospitals and threw babies against walls to break open their skulls. In the Great War, British propaganda had accused Germans of atrocities against Belgian civilians, but most such accusations were fictional; in World War II, the brutality was both factual and unimaginable.

Many civilians caught in war zones did not survive. Tens of millions perished in China and Russia as battlefields shifted back and forth across major cities. The city council of Benghazi in North Africa posted street signs in both English and German; Benghazi changed hands five times in two years, each change more destructive than the one before. Even in places without armed conflict, death was never far away from civilians. In Bengal in eastern India, shipping shortages and British administrative failures combined in 1943 to produce a famine that killed 1.5 million people. Compared with those who suffered such horrors, civilians enduring shortages and lengthy workweeks seemed fortunate indeed.

Resistance to Nazi Rule

World War II produces intense civilian suffering

In Nazi-occupied Europe, as nations were systematically plundered to feed and enrich the conquerors, civilians suffered extensively from cold, malnutrition, and deprivation. These hardships, combined with Nazi treatment of conquered nationalities as inferior peoples, provoked desperate resistance to German rule.

Underground resistance organizations developed quickly in France, Yugoslavia, Greece, and Czechoslovakia, where rugged terrain aided concealment. Britain encouraged these groups by sending agents behind enemy lines and, in Yugoslavia, through air drops of men carrying money and weapons. Countries with level terrain, like Belgium and Holland, could not create complex resistance networks. But in Poland, a country with few mountains, an underground Home Army recruited 300 thousand men and women between 1940 and 1944. These organizations carried out sabotage and spread anti-German propaganda in an effort to keep hope alive.

Yet the resistance movements did not seriously weaken Nazi control. When underground agents assassinated Reinhard Heydrich, Reich Protector of Bohemia and Moravia, in Prague in 1942, brutal Nazi retaliation served as a warning to all resisters. More than 1,300 Czech men, women, and children from two nearby villages were murdered, and the villages themselves were bulldozed and burned to the ground. Germany monopolized the heavy equipment required to conduct modern warfare; without such materiel, the Polish Home Army was cut to pieces when it revolted in Warsaw in August 1944. The Red Army, a few miles away, did not intervene, seeing an advantage to German slaughter of anticommunist Poles.

Resistance movements fail to cripple the German occupation of Europe

Nazi Mass Murder

For millions of Jews and other innocent civilians, Nazi occupation meant mass murder. Before the war, in Germany itself, Nazi anti-Semitism had been characterized by vandalism, legal harassment, persecution, and beatings. But the German conquests of 1939–1940, and invasion of Russia in 1941, brought millions of Jews under Nazi control. In the summer of 1941 Hitler and the German leadership, obsessed with the Nazi vision of racial purification, decided to exterminate them all.

Extermination Camps

The methodology of mass murder evolved between 1939 and 1941. In September 1939, the Nazi regime started systematically killing people it considered unproductive or inferior. This euthanasia campaign killed more than 120 thousand mental patients, disabled people, terminally ill people, and severely wounded soldiers. A public outcry embarrassed the government and drove the slaughter underground in 1941, but two years of murder had created a variety of extermination methods and an experienced corps of professional killers. In the following years, both the methods and the murderers were used throughout Europe against Jews and others the Nazis considered unworthy of life. Hitler was indifferent to moral considerations and unafraid of the condemnation of other nations. Referring to the slaughter of the Armenians in the Great War (Chapter 31), he observed on more than one occasion, "Who today remembers the Armenians?"

Initially, Jews were shot or gassed with carbon monoxide in the back of vans. Those methods, however, proved time-consuming and wasteful. By the fall of 1941 Germany had begun to experiment with mass gassings in detention-camp buildings disguised as showers. Zyklon-B, a high-potency insecticide, proved effective in murdering hundreds of people at a time. On December 8, 1941, gassings in trucks with Zyklon-B began at

Nazi Germany embarks on a policy of genocide

Jewish Hungarian women at Auschwitz-Birkenau.

Chelmno in Poland, the first of six designated extermination sites. Five others followed, all in Poland, including the largest and most infamous, Auschwitz-Birkenau, at which more than two million people were murdered (Map 33.8). By the end of the war nearly six million Jews had perished from gas, brutalization, malnutrition, exposure, and disease in what later became known as the Holocaust.

On January 30, 1942, in a villa in the Berlin suburb of Wannsee (*VAHN-sā*), Reinhard Heydrich, who was then head of the Security Service of the Nazi SS (Hitler's elite bodyguard), convened a conference of Nazi officials from across Europe to discuss the "Final Solution to the Jewish Question": mass murder. Heydrich's deputy and "Jewish specialist," Adolf Eichmann, an expert in train scheduling, explained how Jews from throughout Europe would be transported to camps in Poland. The journeys would take days in unheated and unventilated boxcars without sanitary facilities; food and water would be minimal or unavailable. Many Jews would die before reaching the camps; once there, the rest would die through overwork, exposure to cold, malnutrition, or outright murder. If any objections to this plan were raised at Wannsee, the minutes of the conference do not record them.

Nazi racial doctrine defined Jews as "race defilers" who schemed to destroy the Master Race through intermarriage and seduction. Many of those who assisted in the Holocaust, however, knew little of these ideas. For most ordinary Germans, as well as the Dutch, French, Latvians, Poles, Romanians, Ukrainians, and others who helped them, Jews were outsiders despised for various reasons—as killers of Christ, moneylenders, rivals for economic or educational advantage, or practitioners of mysterious rituals. Some Jews had been assimilated into Europe's dominant cultures, but many remained in cohesive communities and were feared and resented. The Holocaust was conceived and planned by fanatical racists seeking to "purify" Europe of Jews and make it safe for the "Master Race," but it was carried out by ordinary people who did not like Jews and thought little of anyone who did. Some of those involved in the killings were sadists and criminals, but just as often they were otherwise normal people who behaved with unspeakable cruelty out of fear, a desire to conform and obey orders, a sense of their own superiority, or in the hope of gaining some sort of advantage.

The Implementation of Mass Murder

Beginning early in 1942, occupied Europe was "combed" of Jews from west to east. Of those who reached the camps alive, most were gassed within a few hours of arrival. The strongest were selected for forced labor on minimal rations; some were chosen for medical experiments, others for service as prostitutes. By early 1943 most Polish Jews had been gassed at Treblinka or Auschwitz, and the few German Jews remaining after years of persecution were also dead. Much of the richness and beauty of European Jewish culture went with them.

In the rest of Europe, chances for survival varied widely from country to country. Most Dutch Jews were killed at Auschwitz, although some, like Anne Frank, a young Dutch girl whose diary was later found and published throughout the world, were moved from one camp to another. Nearly all the Jews of Denmark survived, protected by Danish authorities and eventually smuggled by boat into neutral Sweden. Italians considered exterminating Jews abhorrent, and not until Germany occupied much of Italy following Mussolini's overthrow in 1943 were most Italian Jews shipped to Auschwitz.

Map 33.8 The Holocaust in Europe, 1941–1945

In pursuit of its racist ideology, Nazi Germany created an intricate network of detention facilities, transit sites, and death camps across Europe. More than six million Jews were murdered, and they were not the only group processed through this system. Note that Soviet POWs, Polish Catholics, Sinti and Roma peoples, Serbians, homosexuals, Jehovah's Witnesses, and handicapped or politically undesirable Germans were also exterminated. What might account for the widely varying numbers of Jewish deaths from one country to another?

Legend:

- Greatest extent of Axis power, 1942
- *1,000* Estimates of Jewish deaths in the "final solution"
- ■ Main concentration camp, founded before 1940
- ■ Main concentration camp, founded from 1940
- ● Camp built for implementation of "final solution" from 1941
- ✖ Euthanasia center
- ◉ Transit camps for deportations to Auschwitz
- ▲ Mass murder site
- ▫ Major ghetto

Total Deaths from Nazi Extermination Policies

European Jews	6,183,000
Soviet POWs	3,000,000
Polish Catholics	3,000,000
Serbians	700,000
Sinti and Roma	250,000
Germans (political prisoners, resisters, and handicapped)	150,000
Homosexuals	12,000
Jehovah's Witnesses	2,500
TOTAL	**13,297,500**

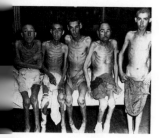

Concentration camp
survivors.

Russian, Romanian, Latvian, and Lithuanian Jews were systematically exterminated, while Hungarian Jews were protected by Admiral Nicholas Horthy's pro-German dictatorship until he was forced to resign in 1944. Hundreds of thousands of them were then murdered. By that time, however, the Red Army was moving into Poland, where it liberated the death camps one by one. In advance, however, the Germans evacuated remaining prisoners to Germany by atrocious "death marches," in which tens of thousands died of maltreatment and cold. The survivors were imprisoned in camps in Germany, such as Dachau, Buchenwald, and Bergen-Belsen, where tens of thousands more, ill and malnourished, perished, including Anne Frank, who died in March 1945.

Jews were the primary targets of Nazi extermination policies, but they were not the only ones. Sinti and Roma people from Hungary and Romania, often called Gypsies, were depicted by Nazis as inferior racial stock, placed in camps, and often killed. In occupied Poland, those with college degrees, including doctors, lawyers, Catholic clergy, and military officers, were systematically shot in order to deprive the Poles of future leadership. Soviet and other Slavic prisoners of war were treated brutally; more than 90 percent of them died from overwork, starvation, and sadistic medical experiments. Homosexuals were singled out for isolation, persecution, and murder. Had Germany won World War II, none of the groups of people listed here would have survived.

The Question of Responsibility

In the face of the scale of Nazi atrocities, not fully known until the war's end, people around the world anguished over the question of responsibility: could anyone have done anything to prevent these horrors? The Allied governments protested and publicized the atrocities, but their broadcasts reached few Germans and were not widely believed even in Britain and America. World War I atrocity propaganda had largely been proven false, and most people assumed that the atrocities said to be committed in this war were also false. The Allies, after all, were hardly neutral observers. After Pope Pius XII died in 1958, some suggested that this head of a neutral state and moral leader of global stature, who knew the details of the Nazi program through the Vatican's diplomatic network, should have spoken out against Nazi crimes. But there is no reason to believe that large numbers of German Catholics would have refused to cooperate with their government even had the Pope asked them to do so. Some suggested that the Allies should have bombed the camps, but by 1944, when Allied planes first came within bombing range of Auschwitz, the vast majority of Jews who would perish in the Holocaust were already dead. Moreover, had the camps been bombed, the Nazis would have found other ways to carry out their murderous agenda. In short, Roosevelt's consistently articulated position still seems the most practical: the best way to stop the killings was to win the war and destroy the Nazi regime.

Responsibility for the Holocaust rests with Nazi Germany

When British and American troops liberated Buchenwald and Bergen-Belsen in spring of 1945, the films they made there shocked the world. Starving people sitting beside mounds of decaying corpses, bulldozers pushing heaps of naked bodies into mass graves, and the hollow-eyed stares of the barely living were shown in newsreels for months. One consequence of the Holocaust, as Hitler had intended, was the virtual destruction of Jewish culture in Europe. An unintended result was widespread pressure for the establishment of a Jewish state in Palestine as a place of refuge. Yet nothing could replace the hopes and lives destroyed in history's most extensive and appalling genocide.

The Defeat of Germany, 1944–1945

By late summer of 1943, defeat of the Nazis seemed possible. In the Soviet Union, encouraged by its victories at Stalingrad and Kursk, the Red Army began the gradual liberation of Soviet soil. In Italy, a successful Allied landing and Mussolini's overthrow gave Germany a second front to defend. But much of Europe was still under Nazi occupation, and the Germans would not be defeated easily.

American soldiers wade ashore at Omaha Beach in Normandy on D-Day, June 6, 1944.

Squeezing Germany Between West and East

At a meeting that November in Tehran, the capital of Iran, Churchill, Roosevelt, and Stalin agreed on a third front: an Anglo-American invasion of France, across the English Channel, scheduled for May 1944 under the direction of U.S. General Dwight D. Eisenhower. Stalin promised to support this risky but necessary undertaking with a massive eastern offensive to distract Germany and relieve the pressure on Allied beachheads. When the landings occurred in Normandy on **D-Day**, June 6, 1944, they surprised the German military, which expected the invasion to come ashore near Calais, only 19 miles by ship from England (Map 33.9). Despite fierce resistance on Omaha Beach, the Allies held their ground. Stalin's promised eastern drive began on June 22 (the third anniversary of the invasion of Russia) and achieved surprising gains. In mid-August, as Soviet pressure in Poland combined with an Allied breakout from Normandy, it appeared likely that the war in Europe would end in 1944.

The Allies attack Germany from East and West

Unexpectedly, however, the Germans regrouped and stabilized both fronts. Field Marshal Walther Model, known as "the Führer's Fireman," shuttled from one side of Germany to the other shoring up shattered lines. In Italy, the Allied invasion was stalled by difficult terrain, German defensive skills, and the poor performance of some American generals. Although it failed, a desperate German winter offensive in the west reminded Allied leaders that Germany's army remained intact and powerful.

The fighting finally ended with a crushing display of Allied superiority in manpower and materiel. The Red Army's January 1945 offensive tore huge gaps in the German lines and probably would have ended the war within weeks had Stalin been less sensitive to the concerns of his allies. At a February conference in Yalta, a southern Soviet resort town, the three Allied leaders—Churchill, Roosevelt, and Stalin—formally agreed to divide both Germany and its capital, Berlin, into military occupation zones at the close of the war. A Soviet conquest of Berlin at a time when British and American forces had not yet set foot on German soil might have worried and embarrassed the western Allies.

Allied Victory in Europe

On March 7, 1945, the Americans and British finally crossed the Rhine and broke into Germany itself. Montgomery's British forces drove across the North German plain, American troops under Generals Omar Bradley and George Patton pierced central and southern Germany, and in the east, the Soviets resumed their offensive in mid-April.

Map 33.9 The Allied Victory in Europe, 1944–1945

Between June 6, 1944 (the date of the invasion of Normandy), and May 8, 1945, Germany was squeezed from west and east. The bulk of the fighting was done by the Red Army, against which Germany deployed 80 percent of its forces, and which occupied most of Eastern Europe on its path toward Germany. Observe that the Eastern Front was twice the length of the Western Front. How might this disparity in deployment of soldiers and resources have affected Stalin's expectations of what Russia might gain from its victorious efforts?

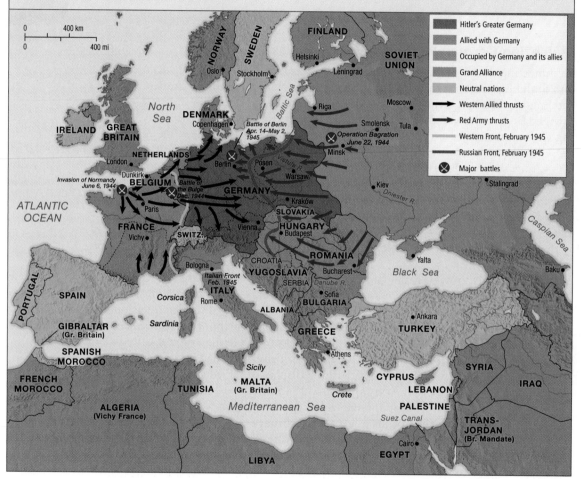

Outnumbered and outgunned, its tanks driven by 60-year-old veterans of the Great War and its fortifications manned by 13-year-old boys, the German army cracked. Roosevelt's death from a stroke on April 12 deprived him of the satisfaction of seeing the war end. On April 30 Roosevelt's principal antagonist, Adolf Hitler, shot himself in his Berlin bunker as Soviet troops took the city one street at a time. Germany surrendered in the west on May 8 and in the east the next day, ending the Second World War in Europe.

The Defeat of Japan

As Germany's dreams of European domination collapsed, Japan's strategy for creating an empire by expelling Western powers from East and Southeast Asia also failed. That strategy was grounded in the assumption that the United States, once defeated at Pearl Harbor and in the Philippines, would never commit the money and troops necessary to conquer Japan. But the American government, capitalizing on widespread fury at Japan's surprise attack in 1941, made those commitments without hesitation. Once mobilized, the U.S. economy and industrial base, much larger than those of the Japanese Empire, secured the eventual U.S. victory.

The American Strategy

In the Pacific war, unlike the war in Europe, most of the combat took place at sea or following the amphibious landing of soldiers from troop ships, and nearly all the fighting was done by Japanese and Americans. Late in 1942 the Americans, ready to take the offensive following their victory at Midway, had to choose a route along which to approach Japan. A northern route across tiny Pacific islands would rely on the U.S. Navy, but its military arm, the U.S. Marine Corps, might be too small for the land fighting required. A southern approach utilizing Australia and the Dutch East Indies would rely on the army rather than the navy, and American policymakers leaned in this direction. But such a choice would center on General Douglas MacArthur, a brilliant egomaniac whose defense of the Philippines had made him a hero in the United States but whose arrogance made him deeply unpopular with superiors and subordinates alike.

The solution was to choose the southern route but divide command between Admiral Nimitz and General MacArthur. This interservice compromise defied logic and led to mass duplication of resources and effort, but it thoroughly frustrated the Japanese, who were caught between two related yet independent offensives, each too powerful for them to defeat (Map 33.10). Japan's conquests had given it vast deposits of raw materials, but Japanese military industries benefited very little from them. Relentlessly, American submarines and surface vessels sank Japanese ships attempting to transport such materials.

Still, the Americans faced difficulties. Amphibious assaults upon Pacific islands proved deadly. Large parts of the Pacific remained unmapped in the early 1940s, and generals coordinating landings with tidal variations had to rely on guesswork provided by Pacific islanders. Once ashore, ground forces faced well-entrenched, skillful Japanese infantry totally dedicated to their cause and willing to follow the ancient samurai code (Chapter 14) by dying to the last man. Poisonous insects and reptiles, stifling heat and drenching rains, and tropical fevers and diseases added to the burden of fighting. American and British forces fighting Japanese troops in the jungles of Burma and New Guinea suffered similarly.

The Americans attack the Japanese Empire by northern and southern routes

The Japanese Empire Contracts

Gradually the Americans pushed the Japanese back. The names of battles on formerly unfamiliar Pacific islands became, for Americans, a litany of sacrifice; for the Japanese, the battles brought hostile forces ever closer to the Japanese home islands. During most of the war only medium-range bombers were available, and they were hardly

Map 33.10 World War II in the Pacific, 1942–1945

Between 1942 and 1945, Japan was attacked by British forces in Burma, by Chinese forces in China, and by American forces in the central and southern Pacific. Note that the Americans, unable to agree on a northern or a southern path to Japan, proceeded along both paths at the same time. The conquest of the Marianas in summer 1944 brought the Japanese home islands within range of American bombers, which then subjected Japan to a devastating bombing campaign, culminating in the use of atomic weapons. How did the intervention of the Soviet Union, which occurred at the same time as the atomic explosions, affect Japan's desire to continue the war?

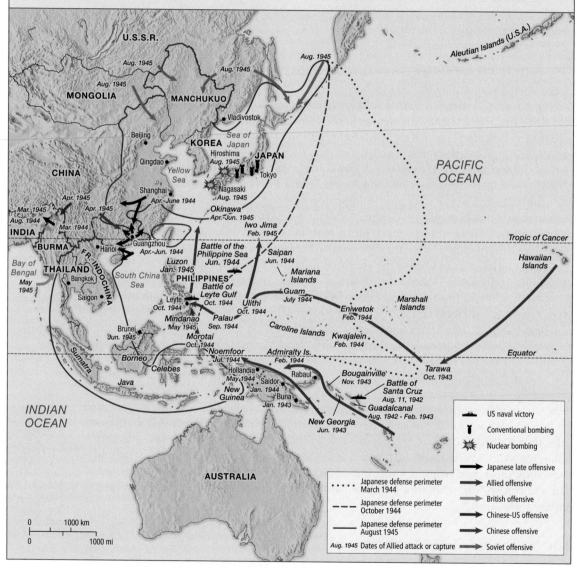

adequate to cover the vastness of the Pacific. But in late 1944 the United States introduced the B-29 Superfortress. With its pressurized cabin, the B-29 could fly at altitudes up to 35 thousand feet, putting it well beyond the range of enemy fighters and anti-aircraft weapons. Now, as MacArthur's forces retook the Philippines, aided by the U.S. Navy's decisive victory in October at Leyte Gulf, attention shifted to the capture of two islands. Iwo Jima would place B-29s within range of Japan's home islands, and Okinawa could serve as a staging area for an amphibious assault upon Japan itself.

A U.S. Marine receives communion from a Catholic chaplain atop Mount Suribachi on Iwo Jima.

The fighting for Iwo Jima, a desolate volcanic island defended by 20 thousand Japanese, began in February 1945 and lasted three hellish weeks. The Japanese dug in and died to the last man. They killed six thousand Americans and wounded 25 thousand more, making this the only Pacific battle in which American casualties (31 thousand) exceeded Japanese (21 thousand). The campaign for Okinawa lasted nearly three months (April–June 1945), but in that action Americans killed 110 thousand Japanese while losing seven thousand of their own. In both battles, but especially at Okinawa, Japanese fighter pilots flew suicide missions, deliberately crashing their planes into American ships. These "kamikaze" fighters, named for the "divine winds" that thwarted the thirteenth-century Mongol attacks on Japan (Chapter 15) sank 55 ships and terrified Americans, who considered them evidence of unrelenting Japanese fanaticism. In fact, they were evidence of desperation. As most of Japan's best pilots were already dead, aviation fuel to train replacements was unavailable, and first-time pilots were usually killed at once by experienced Americans, Japan's leaders decided to send them to their deaths in a way that might inflict some real damage.

> Gruesome combat engulfs Iwo Jima and Okinawa

Kamikaze warfare and Japanese unwillingness to surrender in the face of certain death made Americans dread an amphibious landing on Japan. Aerial bombing, its advocates hoped, might force the Japanese into surrendering before a landing would be necessary. In February 1945 General Curtis LeMay, commanding the 20th U.S. Air Force, employed clusters of incendiary bombs in an effort to burn as much of Japan as possible. On March 9 a raid on Tokyo by 279 B-29s destroyed 40 percent of the city in three hours, killing 89 thousand civilians and demolishing 267 thousand buildings. By summer Japan's six largest cities were devastated, with two million buildings destroyed, 260 thousand people killed, and 9 to 13 million more made homeless. LeMay's practice of dropping leaflets announcing his next target in advance produced panic. As millions of workers fled to the countryside, Japan's war economy, already deprived of raw materials, shut down.

> Aerial bombing destroys Japan's largest cities

Atomic Weapons

Some Japanese leaders realized there was no point in fighting on. In early July Japan approached the USSR, still neutral in the Pacific war, with a request to inform the Americans of Japan's wish to surrender, so long as the emperor could be retained as head of state and symbol of national unity. Stalin, who had agreed at Yalta to declare war on Japan three months after Germany's defeat, passed the information to Harry Truman, president since Roosevelt's death in April. But the United States had insisted throughout the war on unconditional surrender, and by the time Japan's request reached Truman, he had learned of a fearsome new weapon that he hoped would make it unnecessary to invade Japan, bargain over surrender terms, or bring the Soviets into the Pacific war.

The effects of the atomic bomb on Hiroshima.

This weapon was the atomic bomb, a secret project initiated in 1942 with the intent of harnessing the immense power released by splitting the atoms of radioactive elements, a process called nuclear fission. American, British, and expatriate European scientists, working at sites in the United States, finally developed a workable device, successfully tested at Alamogordo, New Mexico, on July 16, 1945. Its enormous explosive power, equivalent to 20 thousand tons of dynamite in a single bomb, made it the most potent weapon yet developed. Its use against civilian targets raised serious ethical concerns among some of the scientists who helped create it, but there is no evidence that the United States government viewed it as anything other than a weapon of great power that would save lives by ending the war quickly.

The United States uses atomic weapons against Japan

After Alamogordo the Americans possessed enough fissionable material for only three bombs, and Truman ordered two of them sent immediately to the Pacific island of Tinian, where two specially configured B-29s with handpicked, highly skilled crews were waiting. On August 6 the first atomic bomb used in warfare fell on **Hiroshima**, destroying most of the city and instantly killing between 70 thousand and 80 thousand people. Thousands more died from burns and radiation sickness within weeks. On August 8 the USSR, fulfilling Stalin's Yalta promise, declared war on imperial Japan. On August 9 the Americans, having heard no response to their demands for immediate Japanese surrender, dropped a second bomb on Nagasaki, killing 35 thousand people and leveling much of the city. The emperor then intervened and forced a Japanese surrender. With the signing of a formal surrender aboard the U.S. battleship *Missouri* in Tokyo Bay on September 2, history's deadliest war officially ended.

The Legacy of World War II

The Great War, now called World War I, had brought drastic political changes, but those that followed World War II were even more shattering. Nazism, fascism, and Japanese militarism were abolished, replaced eventually by political systems imposed by the conquerors. Italy and Japan remained intact, while Germany and Austria were temporarily divided among four occupying powers—Britain, France, the Soviet Union and the United States. The occupations lasted until 1955 in Austria and 1990 in Germany. The war in Europe was followed by more than four decades of hostility and tension between the USSR and its former allies, a debilitating and dangerous global confrontation known as the Cold War (Chapter 34). The League of Nations, now defunct, was replaced by a United Nations composed of all powers that had declared war against the Axis. It soon expanded to include the losers (although divided Germany remained outside until 1973), and it became a forum for Cold War disputes. The Grand Alliance of Britain, the United States, and the Soviet Union broke apart because of distrust between communism and capitalism, and between Stalin and everyone else.

The war's enormous devastation requires massive reconstruction

Terrible devastation complicated recovery efforts. Japanese cities, the largest of them almost totally destroyed, were rebuilt rapidly with American aid, largely because of Japan's importance as a potential Western ally in the Cold War. But Europe was divided between Soviet and Western zones of occupation and influence, and within those zones by national boundaries and ethnic hatreds. Millions of displaced persons, having lost their homes or countries, roamed the continent, seeking villages and towns that no longer existed, searching for relatives and loved ones killed in battle, murdered in the Holocaust, buried by collapsing buildings, crushed by tanks, or simply lost. Cities were clogged with corpses and rubble (Dresden, Germany, was not cleared of rubble until 1965), while hunger, disease, and poverty gripped the demoralized survivors. "Europe is a charnel-house," said Churchill, and Harry Truman, having ridden through Berlin on his way to a conference in July 1945, arrived at his destination trembling. He had fought in the Great War and seen terrible suffering, he commented, but nothing like this. In the Second World War, 60 million people perished, two-thirds of them in China and the Soviet Union combined.

These terrors were eventually overcome, however, in part because of other aspects of the war's legacy. The Cold War encouraged the Western allies to help rebuild the roads and bridges of their friends and former foes. The Allies' task was assisted by the unprecedented authority the war had conferred on modern governments. To win the war, democracies such as Britain and America had employed such authoritarian techniques as seemed necessary for survival. Afterward, peacetime regimes retained that centralization of power, and they were able to work quickly to bring recovery and stability.

Eventually those aspects of wartime governance were institutionalized or replaced, but other legacies of the war, particularly in scientific and medical fields, had an even more extensive and enduring impact on human life. Radar, which had saved Britain in 1940, was now enhanced through microwave technology, making possible not only the postwar microwave oven but also tiny radar sets on aircraft, which in turn made postwar commercial aviation viable. Passenger aircraft came to be powered by jet engines, first used in wartime Germany and then modified in Britain and America for peacetime use. The world's first computer, which filled a huge room at the University of Pennsylvania after coming online in 1945, foreshadowed an information age previously unimaginable. Eventually, artificial earth satellites made possible intercontinental telephone and television communication, accurate weather forecasting, and Internet transmissions; they were placed in space by ballistic missiles, a technology developed by Germany during the war.

Medically, wartime advances proved tremendously helpful to humanity. The development of penicillin ushered in the age of antibiotics; together with sulfa drugs used to treat previously fatal infections, it saved the lives of many soldiers and allowed generations of children to grow up in relative freedom from life-threatening infectious disease. Residents of the tropics likewise benefited from the development of synthetic atebrine, providing better treatment for malaria. The creation of the potent insecticide DDT for use in the jungles of Asia and the South Pacific sharply reduced outbreaks of malaria and typhus after the war ended. In addition, battlefield perfection of techniques of blood transfusion rendered significant benefits to civilians after 1945.

Wartime medical advances offer peacetime benefits

So the world survived, and some of it prospered after its emergence from the destruction of war. Europe, torn apart by the two world wars (together sometimes called the Thirty Years War of 1914–1945), eventually attained unprecedented levels of stability and affluence, as did Japan and other parts of Asia. The war contributed to the fatal weakening of European overseas empires and exerted a direct impact on the decolonization movements that succeeded after 1945. The horrifying destruction of the war years gave way to rebuilding and rapid economic growth, and the technological and medical improvements of those years benefited nearly everyone. These benefits do not diminish the incalculable costs, both financial and human, of the savage conflict we call World War II, but they do testify to humanity's immense capacity for survival and growth, even in the most agonizing circumstances.

One aspect of the war's legacy, however, threatened to destroy not only what had managed to survive but also the very existence of human life on the planet. Nuclear power offered tremendous potential benefits in terms of energy and peaceful uses of radiation, but the mushroom clouds over Hiroshima and Nagasaki cast a shadow of fear over the postwar years. The Cold War that followed World War II was darkened from its outset by that shadow.

Chapter Review

Putting It in Perspective

In the 1930s it had seemed unlikely that democracy could survive. The anxieties of the 1920s, culminating in the Great Depression, made many believe that only powerful authoritarian governments could deal with the issues left by the Great War. Italy and Japan, which had fought on the winning side, and Germany and Russia, which had lost, shared deep dissatisfaction with the war's results and installed such dictatorships in an effort to reassert their claims. Democracies like Britain and France tried in vain to appease these dictators, while the world's largest democracy, the United States, withdrew from European affairs. In such a climate, rulers like Hitler, Mussolini, and Stalin flourished.

Eventually, however, the dictatorships grew impatient with appeasement. Germany started a major war in 1939 in pursuit of living space in the east and a racial paradise for the "Master Race." Italy joined the struggle in 1940, hoping to profit from Germany's victory over France at little cost to itself. Japan attempted to secure raw materials for its industrialized economy by conquering China and expelling Europeans and Americans from their holdings in the central and western Pacific. By early 1942, these Axis powers appeared to be winning what by then was known as World War II.

But the dictators had overreached. The Soviet Union, itself a dictatorship, had at first appeased Hitler through the Nazi-Soviet Pact of 1939, but two years later found itself invaded by Germany. Its enormous reserves of manpower and huge expanses of territory proved too much for the German army to handle. Britain survived the defeat of France in 1940 and refused to surrender. Its command of the Atlantic sea lanes and the courage and skill of its fighter pilots saved it from German invasion. Finally, Japan's attack on Pearl Harbor brought the United States into the war. America's tremendous industrial capacity enabled the nation to fight major wars on two fronts, supply its allies with huge quantities of war materiel, and carry out the research and development required to produce atomic weapons. The devastating combination of Russia, Britain, and the United States provided the Grand Alliance with the overwhelming force necessary to win World War II.

The legacy of the war was mixed. Widespread destruction, the deaths of 60 million people, and the use of massive aerial bombing and atomic weapons marked World War II as the most terrible conflict in human history. But the war also brought dramatic scientific, technological, and medical advances that extended human life expectancy and improved the quality of life for billions of people. Out of the appalling suffering came hope for a better future and widespread resolve to avoid a third world war.

Reviewing Key Material

KEY CONCEPTS

Lebensraum, 845
Anschluss, 848
Nazi-Soviet Pact, 850
Blitzkrieg, 851

Luftwaffe, 853
Rape of Nanjing, 856
D-Day, 867
Hiroshima, 872

KEY PEOPLE

Douglas MacArthur, 845, 869
Adolf Hitler, 845
Benito Mussolini, 847
Francisco Franco, 847
Neville Chamberlain, 850
Winston Churchill, 853
Georgi Zhukov, 855
Josef Stalin, 854
Jiang Jieshi, 856
Franklin Roosevelt, 858
Isoroku Yamamoto, 859
Chester Nimitz, 859

Erwin Rommel, 859
Bernard Law
    Montgomery, 859
Reinhard Heydrich, 863
Adolf Eichmann, 864
Anne Frank, 864
Pope Pius XII, 866
Dwight Eisenhower, 867
Walther Model, 867
Omar Bradley, 867
George Patton, 867
Harry Truman, 871

ASK YOURSELF

1. Why did Germany absorb Austria and Czechoslovakia before invading Poland in 1939? What did Hitler's government hope to accomplish?

2. Why was Germany unable to conquer the Soviet Union?
3. Why did Japan attack the United States in 1941?
4. What strategies did the Allied powers use to defeat the Axis forces between 1942 and 1945? What factors made these strategies effective?
5. How and why did Germany murder millions of Europeans during World War II?

GOING FURTHER

Dallek, Robert. *Franklin D. Roosevelt and American Foreign Policy, 1932–1945*. 1979.

Dower, John. *War Without Mercy: Race and Power in the Pacific War*. 1986.

Erickson, John. *The Road to Berlin: Stalin's War with Germany*. 1983.

Glanz, David, and Jonathan House. *When Titans Clashed: How the Red Army Stopped Hitler*. 1998.

Hilberg, Raul. *The Destruction of the European Jews*. 2001.

Ienaga, Saburo. *The Pacific War, 1937–1945*. 1978.

Iriye, Akira. *The Origins of the Second World War in Asia and the Pacific*. 1987.

Keegan, John. *The Second World War*. 1990.

Kershaw, Ian. *Hitler*. 2 volumes, 1998 and 2001.

Prange, Gordon. *At Dawn We Slept: The Untold Story of Pearl Harbor*. 1981.

Rhodes, Richard. *The Making of the Atomic Bomb*. 1986.

Taylor, Telford. *Munich*. 1984.

Watt, D. C. *How War Came*. 1989.

Weinberg, Gerhard. *The Foreign Policy of Hitler's Germany*. 2 volumes, 1970 and 1980.

Weinberg, Gerhard. *A World At Arms*. 1994.

Yahil, Leni. *The Holocaust*. 1990.

Yamamoto, Masahiro. *Nanking: Anatomy of an Atrocity*. 2000.

Key Dates and Developments

1937	Japan invades China
1938	Germany annexes Austria Munich Conference: Germany annexes Sudetenland
1939	Germany takes Czechoslovakia Nazi-Soviet Pact Germany invades Poland; Britain and France declare war
1940	Germany conquers Norway, Holland, Belgium, and France Battle of Britain
1941	Germany invades the Soviet Union Japan attacks Pearl Harbor
1942	Japan conquers Dutch East Indies and Philippines

	Extermination of European Jews and others begins United States defeats Japan at Midway Island Allies invade North Africa
1943	USSR defeats Germany at Stalingrad Allies invade Italy
1944	Normandy invasion and Soviet offensive in the east
1945	United Nations Organization established Germany surrenders Atomic bombing of Hiroshima and Nagasaki Japan surrenders

East Versus West: Cold War and Its Global Impact, 1945–Present

Atomic Explosion

The mushroom cloud of a nuclear blast, such as this U.S. atomic bomb test in 1946, was a terrifying symbol of the Cold War, a 45-year struggle between capitalist West and communist East affecting the entire world.

July 24, 1945, was not a good day for Joseph Stalin.

Eight days earlier, arriving in Germany for a conference at Potsdam with British Prime Minister Churchill and U.S. President Truman, the Soviet leader had been in a dominant position. His country, after all, was the main contributor to the Allies' victory over Germany: Soviet troops had fought the most crucial battles, and Soviet peoples had borne the brunt of the bloodshed. Stalin's Red Army, occupying Eastern Europe and eastern Germany, was the world's mightiest military force. Even Truman, anxious to get Soviet help in the ongoing war against Japan, was initially very respectful toward the Soviet dictator.

As the conference proceeded, however, Truman grew increasingly assertive. At the meeting on July 24, he joined Churchill in sternly rebuking Stalin for Soviet repression in occupied Eastern Europe. Then, as the session ended, Truman quietly informed the Soviet leader that America had a new weapon of "unusual destructive force." Stalin's response, a vague assertion that it should be "put to good use against Japan," was so indifferent that Churchill wondered if the Soviet leader understood the weapon's significance.

NATO Countries

Communist Countries

Stalin indeed understood. His spies had kept him informed of U.S. efforts to build an atomic bomb, which on July 16 had been successfully tested in New Mexico. He knew this new weapon would make it harder to get concessions from his Western allies, who now had less need of his help in defeating Japan. He knew the American bomb would offset his Red Army's might in any postwar contest for global preeminence. And he knew he was no longer the world's most powerful man—henceforth that distinction belonged to Truman, an untested newcomer on the world stage. That night, in his private quarters, Stalin ordered his lieutenants to accelerate Soviet efforts to develop atomic weapons. Later, back in Russia, he gathered his top scientists, slammed his fist on a table, and demanded: "Comrades, build me a bomb. The Americans have destroyed the balance of power."

The ensuing nuclear arms race, the Red Army's continuing occupation of Eastern Europe, and American determination to stop the spread of Soviet communism fueled an intense 45-year East-West struggle that affected the whole world. The West, known to foes as the "imperialist camp" and friends as the "free world," included the capitalist democracies of Western Europe and North America, led by the United States. The East, also called the "communist bloc," included the communist countries of Eastern Europe and Asia, led by the USSR. Americans and Soviets confronted each other globally—through threats, propaganda, espionage, the arms race, and support for opposing sides in regional conflicts—but they did not engage in hot combat (armed warfare) directly against one another. The struggle between these two "superpowers" thus was called the Cold War.

Origins of the Cold War

The Cold War was rooted in ideological conflict between communism and capitalism and in distrust between East and West stemming from their struggle against Nazi Germany. In central and Eastern Europe, at the end of World War II, the Soviet Union pursued objectives that proved incompatible with those of its wartime Western allies.

Capitalism and communism have conflicting goals and ideals

Communism and capitalism had always been hostile. Communists openly aimed to destroy world capitalism, with its emphasis on individualism and competition, and replace it with a global community based on collectivism and cooperation. Stalin had postponed, but by no means abandoned, this goal, while building Soviet socialism and resisting the Nazis. Capitalists, for their part, were determined to stop the spread of communism, which they saw as a mortal threat to Western freedom and prosperity.

East-West tensions evolve during struggle against Nazis

Even their joint struggle against Nazism had been fraught with distrust. Capitalists resented the Nazi-Soviet pact of 1939, which had enabled Germany, with Soviet agreement, to overrun Poland and much of Western Europe. Communists were upset that the Western allies delayed their main anti-German offensive until June 1944, three years after the Nazi invasion of the Soviet Union, by which time the Soviets had driven out the Germans at an appalling price. Since the war cost the USSR 25–30 million lives, while Britain and America together suffered fewer than a million fatalities, the Soviets felt they had endured more than their share of suffering. And since the Red Army had freed Eastern Europe from Nazi control, the Soviets felt they had earned the right to decide that region's future.

Soviet and Western postwar goals prove incompatible

Furthermore, by 1945, the whole western part of the USSR was devastated. Faced with massive rebuilding projects, and anxious to prevent future invasion, Stalin had several key goals: Germany must be militarily incapacitated so it could not strike again; it must make huge reparations payments to rebuild the USSR; and the Soviets must be shielded against future attack by a buffer zone of friendly countries in Eastern Europe. While noting the Soviet need for security and reconstruction, however, the Western powers opposed massive reparations, and wanted free elections in Germany and Eastern Europe—which might well result in leaders unfriendly to the Soviet Union. Western goals were thus incompatible with Stalin's.

The Yalta and Potsdam Conferences

In February 1945, while Allied armies were still fighting Germans, Stalin met with U.S. President Franklin Roosevelt and British Prime Minister Churchill at the southern Soviet city of Yalta to plan the postwar peace. By then the Red Army, in driving out the Germans, had occupied much of Eastern Europe, including most of Poland. Furthermore, although in Europe the end of the war was in sight, in Asia it was not, so Roosevelt and Churchill were willing to bargain for Soviet help against Japan.

Stalin, Roosevelt, and Churchill at Yalta.

Western Allies make concessions to Soviets at Yalta

Consequently, at Yalta, Stalin got much of what he wanted. His allies agreed to let Poland be ruled by a Soviet-sponsored government, which the Soviets had already installed, and to let the USSR keep the eastern part of prewar Poland, annexed in 1939. In return, Poland was to be compensated with territory from Germany, moving Polish borders westward (Map 34.1). Stalin promised to let Poles elect their own leaders (a commitment he

FOUNDATION MAP 34.1 European Boundary Changes and Occupation Zones, 1945–1955

The end of World War II brought major territorial changes to Europe. Observe that the USSR kept lands it had earlier claimed in Eastern Europe, including the entire eastern part of prewar Poland, and that Poland was compensated with lands from prewar Germany, while the rest of Germany and Austria were divided into occupation zones. Note further that by 1949 the British, American, and French zones in Germany had merged to form capitalist West Germany; the Soviet zone had become communist East Germany; and Soviet-sponsored communist regimes ruled Poland, Czechoslovakia, Hungary, Romania, and Bulgaria. Why did Germany's occupation and division continue throughout the Cold War, even though Austria's ended in 1955?

would not keep) and in a secret agreement pledged to declare war on Japan three months after the war in Europe ended (a commitment he would honor precisely). He also cleared the way for the **United Nations** (U.N.), an international peacekeeping body created to replace the defunct League of Nations, by dropping his earlier demand that, since the USSR consisted of 16 (later 15) Soviet republics, it should have 16 seats in the U.N. General Assembly

Allies divide Germany into occupation zones

The allies agreed to divide Germany temporarily into occupation zones: a Soviet sector in the East, and British, American, and French zones in the West. But Roosevelt and Churchill, judging that reparations imposed on Germany after World War I had aided Hitler's rise, resisted Stalin's demand for reparations, so action on that issue was postponed. Otherwise, the Soviet leader had reason to be pleased with the Yalta accords.

Much had changed, however, by the next Allied meeting, held in Germany at Potsdam in summer 1945. Roosevelt had died in April, and was replaced by Harry Truman, a blunt, combative man who disliked communists as much as Nazis and had once said he hoped that war between them would "kill as many as possible." Germany had surrendered in May, removing the main reason for Allied cooperation, which was further strained by Soviet repression in occupied Eastern Europe. And, in the midst of the Potsdam talks, Churchill was replaced as prime minister by Clement Attlee, a mild-mannered socialist whose Labour Party won a stunning electoral upset by pledging to improve British workers' lives and decrease Britain's global commitments.

Postwar America emerges as leader of the Western world

Attlee's pledge to reduce Britain's international role meant that the United States would henceforth be the Western world's main leader. Emerging from the war with immense wealth and power, Americans had boundless faith in capitalist democracy and contempt for Soviet socialism. And, as details arrived in Potsdam about the atomic bomb, successfully tested in New Mexico as the conference began, Truman and his aides saw little need for further concessions to the communists.

Americans, strengthened by A-bomb, resist Soviets at Potsdam

So the Americans stood up to Stalin at Potsdam. They agreed to let him take reparations from Germany, but only from the less-developed Soviet-occupied zone, whose factories would be disassembled and sent east by rail. Truman demanded free elections in Eastern Europe, which Stalin resisted, knowing that these would likely install anti-Soviet regimes. And, as noted at the start of this chapter, the president told the Soviet leader about the awesome new U.S. atomic weapons—then hastened to use them against Japan soon after the conference concluded.

Truman later said that he used the atomic bombs to end the war without an invasion of Japan, which would have cost thousands of American lives. Historians have since asserted, however, that he also had other goals: to demonstrate American strength to the Soviets and to end the war before the Soviets could occupy part of Japan, much as they had occupied eastern Germany and most of Eastern Europe.

Divided Europe: The "Iron Curtain"

Soviet authority in Eastern Europe by then was becoming entrenched. From 1945 to 1948, determined to secure his buffer zone of countries friendly to the USSR, Stalin used coercion and rigged elections to establish Soviet-dominated "satellite" regimes in Poland, Romania, Bulgaria, Hungary, and Czechoslovakia, forming a coalition called the **Soviet bloc**.

Document 34.1 Churchill's Iron Curtain Speech

In 1946, former British Prime Minister Winston Churchill traveled to the United States, anxious to enlist American support in what he foresaw as a growing struggle against the spread of communism. On March 5, at Westminster College in Fulton, Missouri, with President Harry Truman behind him, Churchill dramatically sounded the alarm, using the image of an "iron curtain" to highlight the division of Europe into communist East and capitalist West.

The United States stands at this time at the pinnacle of world power. It is a solemn moment for the American democracy. For with this primacy of power is also joined an awe-inspiring accountability to the future . . .

A shadow has fallen upon the scenes so lately lighted by the Allied victory. Nobody knows what Russia and its Communist international organization intends to do in the immediate future, or what are the limits, if any, to their expansive and proselytizing tendencies . . . It is my duty, however, . . . to place before you certain facts about the present position in Europe.

From Stettin in the Baltic to Trieste in the Adriatic, an iron curtain has descended across the Continent. Behind that line lie all the capitals of the ancient states of central and eastern Europe. Warsaw, Berlin, Prague, Vienna, Budapest, Belgrade, Bucharest, and Sofia, all these famous cities and the populations around them lie in what I might call the Soviet sphere, and all are subject, in one form or another, not only to Soviet influence, but also to a very high and increasing measure of control from Moscow . . . The Communist parties, which were very small in all these eastern states of Europe, have been raised to preeminence and power far beyond their numbers and are seeking everywhere to obtain totalitarian control. Police governments are prevailing in nearly every case . . .

Whatever conclusions may be drawn from these facts—and facts they are—this is certainly not the liberated Europe we fought to build up. Nor is it one which contains the essentials of a permanent peace . . .

SOURCE: *The New York Times*, March 6, 1945, page 4.

He failed, however, to establish control over Yugoslavia, where communists gained and exercised power independent of the Soviet Union.

The West, meanwhile, having largely demobilized its forces following the war, increasingly felt threatened by Soviet power. The massive Red Army, renamed the Soviet Army in 1946, remained in occupation of Manchuria, northern Korea, northern Iran, Eastern Europe, and above all eastern Germany, where it continued to station hundreds of thousands of soldiers. Judging that only America could block further Soviet expansion, former Prime Minister Churchill, speaking in Missouri in March 1946, evoked the image of a Europe divided by a line running from its northern to southern coasts (see "Churchill's Iron Curtain Speech"). "From Stettin in the Baltic to Trieste in the Adriatic," he declared, with President Truman behind him, "an iron curtain has descended across the Continent." East of that line, Churchill went on, lay countries imprisoned by communism.

Postwar Soviet expansion worries Western leaders

The iron curtain imagery, combined with Soviet belligerence, helped to arouse the Americans. They demanded that Stalin withdraw his troops, as he had previously promised, from occupied northern Iran; faced with forceful U.S. pressure, he eventually complied. Later that year, the Americans declared their intent to keep forces in western Germany indefinitely and to unite most of western Germany by merging their occupation zone with Britain's.

Churchill's speech helps persuade Americans to counter Soviet expansion

The Truman Doctrine and Marshall Plan

In the following year, 1947, major U.S. initiatives sought to counter communism's spread. In March, reacting to a communist insurgency in Greece and to Soviet pressures against Turkey, President Truman proclaimed a new policy, soon called the **Truman Doctrine**. Henceforth, he avowed, the United States must "support free peoples who are resisting attempted subjugation by armed minorities or by outside pressures"—leaving no doubt that he meant communist minorities and pressures from Soviet Russia. And it soon became clear that American aid would go far beyond Greece and Turkey: in June Secretary of State George Marshall announced a massive program of U.S. economic aid to all of war-torn Europe. Although billed a "European Recovery Program," the **Marshall Plan** was designed to preclude communist expansion by strengthening Europe economically, thus advancing America's Cold War strategy.

Americans adopt global strategy based on containment of communism

In July George F. Kennan, a policy planner in the U.S. State Department, gave the new American strategy a name. In the journal *Foreign Affairs*, in an article signed "Mr. X" (since he lacked official permission to use his real name), Kennan promoted "a long-term, patient but firm and vigilant containment of Russian expansive tendencies," claiming that communism, if so contained, would eventually collapse. **Containment of communism** hence became the central aim of U.S. Cold War policy. Over the next four decades, America provided political, economic, and often military support to almost any regime anywhere resisting Soviet influence, while the Soviets similarly aided forces resisting Western domination.

The Berlin Blockade and NATO

Stalin reacted angrily to the U.S. initiatives. Realizing that Marshall Plan aid would boost American influence in Europe, he ordered his Eastern European satellites to reject it and later formed a Council for Mutual Economic Assistance (Comecon) to advance their economic development. He also ordered them to rid their regimes of all remaining non-communists. Accordingly, in February 1948, communists took full control of Czechoslovakia, completing consolidation of the Soviet bloc. Stalin also feared that the West would use the Truman Doctrine and Marshall Plan to rebuild and reunify Germany, threatening Soviet security. This perception was enhanced in June 1948, when France merged its German occupation zone with the British-American sector, uniting all western Germany, which was also given a unified currency. On June 24, Stalin retaliated by blocking all road and rail routes from western Germany to Berlin.

Stalin's blockade of Berlin triggers major Cold War crisis

Thus began the Berlin blockade, the Cold War's first great crisis. The German capital, like the whole country, had been divided into occupation zones by the four wartime allies (Map 34.1, inset). But since Berlin lay inside Soviet-occupied eastern Germany, ninety miles behind the "iron curtain," the city's British, French, and American sectors, collectively called West Berlin, depended upon food and supplies delivered from western Germany. Without such supplies, 2.5 million West Berliners could not long survive. The Western allies, Stalin figured, would have to either abandon Berlin or make concessions elsewhere to get him to reopen the routes.

American-British airlift overcomes Berlin blockade

Truman, however, rejected both these options, along with a proposal for a U.S. armored force to fight its way to Berlin through Soviet-occupied eastern Germany. Instead he opted, with British support, to supply West Berlin by air. For the next 11 months, American and

British cargo planes flew food and supplies around the clock into West Berlin. Anxious to avoid an all-out war with the world's only nuclear power, the Soviets chose not to forcibly interrupt the airlift. They quietly ended the blockade in May 1949.

By then it was obvious that Stalin's blockade had backfired. Rather than abandoning Berlin, the Americans instead abandoned their historic avoidance of peacetime military alliances. In April 1949, the United States, along with Canada, Iceland, and nine European nations, formed an alliance called **NATO** (North Atlantic Treaty Organization), designed to protect Western Europe against Soviet expansion. Warning that an "attack against one" member would be considered "an attack against them all," the alliance thereby served notice to the Soviets that any attempt to expand in Europe would mean war with the United States. Implicit in this warning was a nuclear threat: since popular resistance in Western democracies to a peacetime draft made it hard for NATO nations to match Soviet Army troop strength, the alliance would rely on U.S. nuclear weapons to deter a Soviet attack.

The Berlin airlift.

NATO Alliance commits United States to defend Western Europe

The Global Confrontation

By 1949, then, deadlock had developed in Europe: communists controlled the east, relying on the Soviet Army's might, and NATO defended the west, backed by the U.S. nuclear arsenal. At the center of the standoff was Germany, where two separate states were created that year: a capitalist West Germany in the zones occupied by Britain, America, and France, and a communist East Germany in the Soviet sector.

Soon, however, communist advances elsewhere expanded the East-West stalemate into a global confrontation. The rise of communist regimes in China and North Korea, and later in North Vietnam and Cuba, was met by forceful U.S. efforts to stop further communist expansion. New leaders emerging in both East and West failed to solve the standoff, while both sides developed horrific new weapons that put the whole world at risk.

Cold War standoff in Europe grows into global confrontation

New Realities and New Leaders

On August 29, 1949, far ahead of Western expectations, the USSR tested an atomic bomb over the northern Pacific, abruptly ending America's nuclear monopoly. Scarcely a month later, on October 1, 1949, a communist government took control in China, the world's most populous nation, sending shock waves throughout the Western world. In June 1950, a communist regime established by the Soviets in North Korea abruptly invaded non-communist South Korea. Suddenly the Soviets had the bomb, and a relentless Red tide seemed to be engulfing the globe (Map 34.2).

Communist triumph in China stuns and alarms the West

The unnerved Americans, resolving to stem the communist tide, chose to defend South Korea. The ensuing Korean War (1950–1953), described in Chapter 35, pitted an American-led United Nations coalition against Soviet-supplied communist forces, threatening to spark a new global conflict. But the United States, anxious not to weaken its defenses in Europe by pursuing an all-out Asian war, confined its campaign to Korea, even when Communist China sent hundreds of thousands of volunteer troops to help the North Koreans. And the USSR, although it gave arms to its communist allies, avoided

Communists stalemate American–led coalition in Korean War

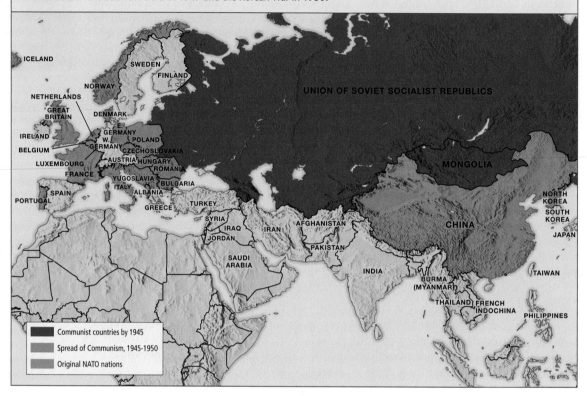

Map 34.2 Communist Expansion in Eurasia, 1945–1950

In the wake of World War II, communism spread quickly across Eurasia. Notice that, between 1945 and 1950, the Soviets consolidated Communist control in occupied Eastern Europe and North Korea, while communist regimes also came to power in Yugoslavia, Albania, and China, adding to the impression of a "Red tide" sweeping the globe. How did this impression influence the formation of NATO in 1949 and the Korean War in 1950?

direct involvement. In July 1953, unwilling to risk another world war, both sides settled for a truce in Korea that simply sustained the stalemate.

By this time both the Americans and the Soviets had new leaders. In January 1953, General Dwight Eisenhower, the Allied commander in Western Europe during World War II, replaced Harry Truman as U.S. president. In March came the death of Joseph Stalin, followed by a succession struggle that resulted eventually in the rise of a new Soviet Communist Party leader named Nikita Khrushchev (*kroosh-CHOFF*).

To cut defense costs, United States relies on global nuclear threat

Eisenhower, a popular war hero who had led the 1944 Normandy invasion, was committed both to combating communism and to cutting U.S. defense costs, which had become immense. Seeking simultaneously to save money and strengthen U.S. defenses, his administration decided to reduce its armed forces and deter the Soviets mainly with nuclear weapons—a policy called "massive retaliation." By arming its new B-52 long-range jet bombers with hydrogen bombs (newly developed nuclear weapons that were many times more powerful than the original atomic bombs), the United States could respond to a Soviet Army attack in Europe by dropping these "H-bombs" on the USSR. Faced with this threat, presumably, the Soviets would dare not attack, and America could avoid the huge expense of stationing numerous U.S. troops in Europe and Asia. The policy provided, in the words of one American official, a "bigger bang for the buck."

Rather than making the world safer, however, the new U.S. policy merely accelerated the arms race. Determined to neutralize the American atomic threat, the Soviets produced their own H-bombs and long-range bombers that were capable of hitting the United States. Soon Britain and France, doubting that America would really risk its own annihilation to defend Western Europe, were developing and enlarging their own atomic forces. By 1960 there were four nuclear powers and thousands of nuclear weapons, posing a threat to humanity's survival should there be an all-out global war.

Soviets develop and expand nuclear forces to counter U.S. threat

Khrushchev, meanwhile, proved a formidable foe. The self-educated son of impoverished peasants, he was a firm believer in the virtues of Soviet socialism, which had enabled him to rise from obscurity to enormous power. He was convinced that communists could win a prolonged global contest against capitalism, partly by strengthening Soviet power and partly by supporting the global movement against Western colonialism.

Decolonization and Global Cold War

The Cold War coincided with an era of **decolonization**, a process (described in Chapters 35 and 37) whereby colonized peoples in Asia and Africa gained independence from Western imperial domination (Map 34.3), often through nationalistic "liberation movements." Communists since V. I. Lenin, depicting Western imperialism as an outgrowth of industrial capitalism and colonized peoples as allies of socialists in a global struggle against capitalist imperialists, had encouraged such movements. Now Khrushchev and his successors actively supported them, and aided former colonies emerging from Western domination, hoping thereby to undermine the West and win friends for the USSR. To counter Soviet advances, the West in turn aided anticommunist elements in regions emerging from colonialism. Nationalists in Asia and Africa, and even in Latin America, exploited the East-West rivalry to obtain weapons and resources from one side or the other, further globalizing the Cold War.

Soviets aid Asians and Africans emerging from Western colonialism

The superpowers sought allies wherever they could find them, often ignoring ideology to do so. One example was India, freed from British rule in 1947 but split into two hostile states. The Republic of India, a Hindu-led Western-style democracy, took economic aid from the USSR, which hoped to expand its influence in South Asia. Pakistan, a Muslim military dictatorship, got both military and economic assistance from the United States, which wanted a strong ally in the region to help resist Soviet inroads. Another example was the former Dutch East Indies, which became independent Indonesia in 1949. The Soviets supported Sukarno, a nationalist who led the new nation until the mid-1960s, ignoring the fact that he was more mystical and Muslim than Marxist. The Americans supported his successor Suharto, a military dictator who seized power in 1967, overlooking his regime's antidemocratic oppression and rampant corruption.

Asians, Africans, and Latin Americans exploit global Cold War rivalry

Similar situations emerged in the Middle East and Africa. The USSR, anxious to gain influence and undermine the West, aided Arab nationalists in Egypt, Algeria, and elsewhere—despite the fact that they were monotheistic Muslims who had no use for atheistic communism. The United States, anxious to encourage pro-Western Arab forces and

Soviets and West aid opposing sides in Asian and African conflicts

Map 34.3 Decolonization and Cold War Clashes, 1945–1970s

The Cold War became closely interconnected with anticolonial struggles in Africa and Asia. Observe that, between 1945 and the 1970s, almost all colonial and mandate regions in Africa and Asia gained independence from their former Western rulers. How did this decolonization, combined with Soviet efforts to win allies in these regions, help to foster Cold War clashes and conflicts throughout Africa and Asia?

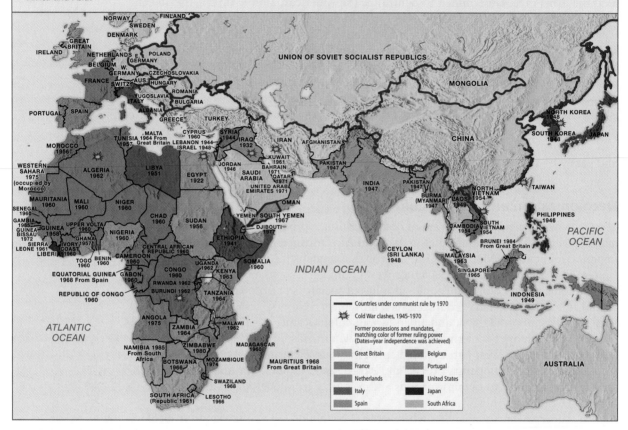

secure oil supplies, supported oil-rich Persian Gulf regimes—despite the fact that they were undemocratic and openly oppressive. In central Africa, when Belgium abruptly freed its Congo colony in 1960, the Soviets supported its new president, pan-African nationalist Patrice Lumumba—prompting the Americans to consider him a communist and oppose him.

Asia, Africa, and Latin America become Cold War battlegrounds

In general, then, while aiding the cause of decolonization and frustrating the West, Soviet support for anticolonial nationalists did little to advance the communist cause. Although happy to take Soviet aid, these nationalists, anxious not to trade freedom from Western rule for Soviet domination, rarely joined the communist camp. Two major exceptions were Vietnam, where a communist-led insurgency ended French colonial rule in 1954, and Cuba, where a regime came to power in 1959 that soon proved anti-American and pro-Marxist. In the 1960s these two nations became major Cold War battlegrounds.

Peaceful Coexistence and Its Problems

By then Khrushchev's efforts to strengthen his own empire had tarnished his anti-imperial image. In 1955, when NATO admitted West Germany, he responded by forming the **Warsaw Pact**, a Soviet-led alliance of East European communist states (Map 34.4). It counterbalanced NATO and also rationalized continued Soviet Army presence in Eastern Europe. In 1956, when the Hungarians sought to leave the Soviet bloc, Khrushchev

Soviets consolidate control over Eastern Europe

Map 34.4 Divided Europe: NATO vs. Warsaw Pact, 1955–1991

From 1955 to 1991, Europe was divided into hostile alliance systems. Note that NATO consisted mainly of Western nations, led by the United States, and the Warsaw Pact embraced the Soviet Union and its Communist satellites in Eastern Europe. What were the similarities and differences between these two alliances?

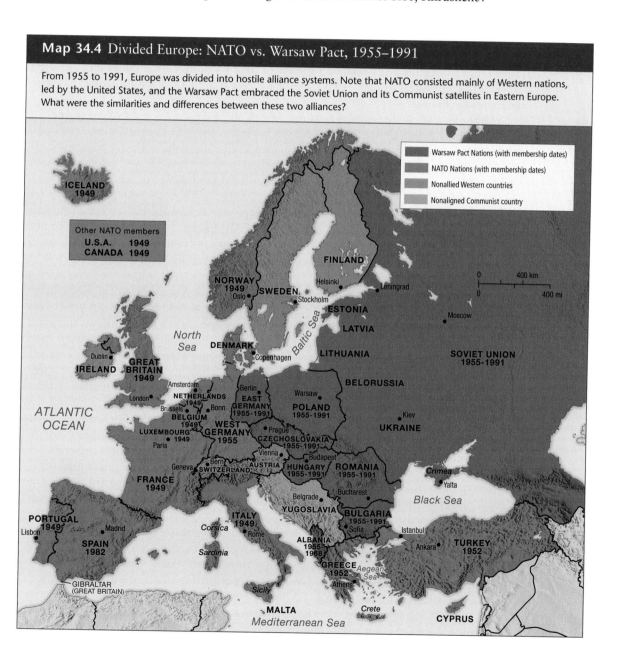

brutally repressed their rebellion with troops and tanks. This episode, which showed the world how the Soviets enforced their own imperial rule, undermined their reputation as supporters of national liberation.

Soviets develop nuclear-armed rockets capable of striking America

Even more alarming to the West were Soviet advances in weapons and rockets. In 1957, the Soviets successfully tested an **ICBM** (intercontinental ballistics missile), an unmanned rocket that could hit America with nuclear warheads from the USSR. The Soviets also beat the Americans into outer space, launching *Sputnik* (*SPOOT-nēk*), the world's first artificial earth satellite, in 1957, and sending cosmonaut Yuri Gagarin (*gah-GAH-rēn*) into orbit in 1961.

Soviet feats spark rocket and space race with America

These spectacular Soviet accomplishments stunned the Americans. Shocked that Soviet technology suddenly seemed superior to their own, they soon built their own fleet of ICBMs and embarked on an expensive space race that in 1969 would land U.S. astronauts on the moon.

Early Soviet rocket.

Although such achievements restored American pride, they could not overcome America's new vulnerability. Protected from invasions by wide oceans, Americans had historically assumed that wars were mostly fought elsewhere. Now Soviet possession of ICBMs, and periodic passes of Soviet earth satellites over the United States, made it painfully clear that Soviet rockets could reach the American homeland. Never again could Americans feel fully secure.

Khrushchev, nonetheless, had no desire to wage war against the United States. Acutely aware that a nuclear conflict could destroy the USSR, he rejected the communist premise that capitalism made war inevitable. Instead he pressed for "peaceful coexistence" between East and West, confident that, if war could be avoided, communism would eventually prevail as the superior system.

Khrushchev calls for "peaceful coexistence" between East and West

Eager to make the Soviet model more attractive to the rest of the world, Khrushchev worked to remove the worst abuses of the Stalinist system and to provide a better life for Soviet peoples. In 1956, in an emotional "secret speech" in the middle of the night to a Communist Party Congress behind locked doors, he detailed and denounced the crimes of his paranoid predecessor (see "Khrushchev on Peaceful Coexistence and on Stalin's Crimes"). Stunned delegates wept openly as Khrushchev blamed Stalin for imprisoning, torturing, exiling, and murdering countless innocent people, including many loyal communists.

Khrushchev denounces Stalin's crimes and eases internal oppression

The speech, a poorly kept secret that soon leaked out and was published in the West, was reinforced by other efforts Khrushchev made to break with the Stalinist past. He relaxed Stalin's censorship, reduced internal oppression, freed many political prisoners, and launched ambitious efforts to improve food and housing, with the stated goal of matching Western living standards by the 1970s. Although these reforms fell short of providing either freedom or prosperity, they did demonstrate that the Soviet system was becoming less harsh.

Khrushchev's trip to America paves way for Paris summit meeting

In 1959, to bolster his peacemaker image, Khrushchev made a 12-day trip to America. He toured U.S. cities, met with politicians and entertainers, explored an Iowa cornfield, and even sought to visit California's new Disneyland theme park—but was prevented from doing so by security concerns. His buoyant personality did much to ease American anxieties: this ebullient man, who so obviously enjoyed life, hardly seemed the sort who would start a nuclear war. He and Eisenhower discussed ways to reduce world tensions, and planned to meet again at a **summit conference**, a face-to-face meeting of the world's

Document 34.2 Khrushchev on Peaceful Coexistence and on Stalin's Crimes

In February 1956, at the 20th Congress of the Soviet Communist Party, Soviet leader Nikita Khrushchev delivered two momentous speeches. In a public address at the beginning of the Congress, he called for peaceful coexistence with the West, revising the Marxist-Leninist doctrine that capitalistic imperialism made war inevitable. In a secret speech in the middle of the night at the end of the conference, he denounced Joseph Stalin and the crimes of the Stalin era. The secret eventually leaked out, and the speech was published in the West. While proving less paranoid than his predecessor, however, Khrushchev ended neither the Cold War nor Soviet repression.

EXCERPTS FROM KHRUSHCHEV'S REPORT TO THE 20TH PARTY CONGRESS . . . For the strengthening of world peace, it would be of tremendous importance to establish firm, friendly relations between the two biggest powers of the world, the Soviet Union and the United States . . . We want to be friends with and to cooperate with the United States in the effort for peace and security of the peoples as well as in the economic and cultural fields. We pursue this with good intentions, without holding a stone behind our back . . . If good relations are not established between the Soviet Union and the United States, and mutual distrust exists, this will lead to an arms race on a still greater scale and to a still more dangerous growth of the forces on both sides . . .

The principle of peaceful coexistence is gaining increasingly wider international recognition. And this is logical, since there is no other way out of the present situation. Indeed, there are only two ways: either peaceful coexistence or the most devastating war in history. There is no third alternative . . .

As will be recalled, there is a Marxist-Leninist premise which says that while imperialism exists wars are inevitable. While capitalism remains on earth the reactionary forces representing the interests of the capitalist monopolies will continue to strive for war gambles and aggression, and may try to let loose war. But there is no fatal inevitability of war. Now there are powerful social and political forces, commanding serious means capable of preventing unleashing of war by the imperialists and—should they try to start it—of delivering a smashing rebuff to the aggressors and thwarting their adventuristic plans . . .

EXCERPTS FROM KHRUSHCHEV'S SECRET SPEECH . . . After Stalin's death the Central Committee of the Party began explaining concisely and consistently that it is impermissible and foreign to the spirit of Marxism-Leninism to elevate one person, and to transform him into a superman possessing supernatural characteristics akin to those of a god . . . Such a belief about a man, and specifically about Stalin, was cultivated among us for many years . . .

Stalin originated the concept of enemy of the people. This term . . . made possible the usage of the most cruel repression . . . against anyone who disagreed with Stalin . . . This led to glaring violations of revolutionary legality, and to the fact that many entirely innocent people . . . became victims.

. . . It became apparent that many party, Soviet and economic activists, who were branded . . . as enemies, were actually never enemies, spies, wreckers, etc . . . ; they were only so stigmatized, and often no longer able to bear barbaric tortures they charged themselves (at the order of the investigative judges-falsifiers) with all sorts of grave and unlikely crimes . . . Many thousands of honest and innocent Communists have died as a result of this monstrous falsification of cases . . .

. . . Stalin was a very distrustful man, sickly suspicious . . . This sickly suspicion created in him a general distrust even toward eminent party workers who had known him for many years. Everywhere and in everything he saw enemies, "two-facers," and "spies." Possessing unlimited power, he indulged in great willfulness and choked a person morally and physically . . .

SOURCES: *The New York Times*, February 15, 1956, page 10; United States Congress, *The Congressional Record*, 84th Congress, 2nd Session, vol. 102 (1956), pages 9389, 9391, 9392, 9394, 9395.

most powerful leaders, the following year in Paris. By early 1960, as Soviet and Western officials prepared for the Paris summit, the Cold War's end seemed in sight.

Such hopes, however, were dashed in May 1960, when an American U-2 spy plane, sent to take reconnaissance photos on the eve of the summit, crashed in the USSR. Assuming the pilot was dead, America issued a false claim that the craft was a weather plane accidentally flown off course. Khrushchev, who for four years had been angered by such spy flights over his country, now revealed that the U-2 pilot had been captured alive, and demanded an American apology. But Eisenhower, who admitted publicly that he had authorized the mission, refused to repent.

Khrushchev's anger at U-2 Affair ruins Paris summit

This **U-2 Affair** doomed the Paris summit. Blaming Eisenhower for endangering the peace, Khrushchev in Paris again demanded an apology. When none was forthcoming, he vehemently denounced the Americans and refused to negotiate. The summit ended in shambles, as did several years of work toward peaceful coexistence. Giving up on Eisenhower, whose presidency was nearing its end, Khrushchev waited to encounter the next American president.

Berlin, Cuba, Vietnam, and MAD

Khrushchev and Kennedy clash about Berlin at Vienna

John F. Kennedy, who took office in January 1961, was handsome, rich, and eloquent but inexperienced in foreign affairs and eager to show his strength as a Cold Warrior. When he met Khrushchev at a summit conference in Vienna, Austria, that June, the Soviet dictator bullied the new president about Berlin. Since 1949 more than two million people had escaped communist East Germany by crossing from East Berlin to West Berlin. To stop this outflow, Khrushchev demanded that the Western powers abandon the city. Failure to do so, he threatened, would result in war. Kennedy was shaken but refused to back down, and went home expecting the worst.

Summer 1961 was filled with foreboding, as Kennedy announced a military buildup, bracing for another Berlin blockade and perhaps even war. In August, however, the communists stunned the world by building a barbwire barrier to seal off the border between East and West Berlin. Then, in the next few months, they replaced the barbwire with a wall.

Berlin Wall, built by communists, symbolizes global East-West divide

Much to Berliners' dismay, Kennedy did not try to stop construction of the wall, since it posed no real threat to the West. Indeed, by stopping the human outflow, the wall enabled the Soviets to accept continued Western presence in Berlin, eventually easing the crisis. But the Berlin Wall, which stood 28 years as an unsightly symbol of communist oppression, further undermined the Soviet image. As Kennedy later claimed in a stirring speech to a huge crowd in West Berlin: "Freedom has many difficulties and democracy is not perfect. But we have never had to put a wall up to keep our people in."

Khrushchev, meanwhile, faced an even deadlier dilemma. As Kennedy accelerated the arms race by ordering production of a thousand new ICBMs, the Soviets, with fewer than a dozen, lagged far behind. The USSR did not have the wealth to build huge numbers of expensive missiles and at the same time fund Khrushchev's plans to improve the domestic economy.

Khrushchev responds to U.S. missile buildup by placing Soviet missiles in Cuba

The Soviet leader's attention turned to Cuba, ninety miles from American shores, where Fidel Castro, an anti-American revolutionary, had taken power in 1959. After the United States tried unsuccessfully to unseat him by landing armed anti-Castro Cubans in Cuba at the "Bay of Pigs" in April 1961 (Chapter 36), Castro began pressing for Soviet protection against another U.S. attack. In response, in spring 1962, Khrushchev came up with a perilous plan. He would secretly place Soviet mid-range nuclear missiles in Cuba, where they could target the United States. He could thus protect Castro, counter the U.S. missile buildup, and save the Soviet Union the huge cost of building numerous new ICBMs. Once the missiles were in place in Cuba, he planned to reveal their presence, and perhaps use them as leverage to secure withdrawal of Western forces from Berlin.

But in October 1962, before the Soviets had completely installed their missiles, American spy planes discovered their presence in Cuba. Kennedy demanded their removal and had the U.S. Navy blockade Cuba to halt further weapons shipments, provoking a superpower confrontation called the **Cuban Missile Crisis**. For several days the world watched in terror as the Soviets and Americans teetered on the brink of war. But Khrushchev chose not to challenge the blockade and Kennedy resisted pressure to bomb or invade Cuba. Finally, in return for a public U.S. promise not to invade the island, Khrushchev agreed to remove the missiles. Privately, Kennedy also pledged to remove from Turkey American mid-range missiles that were aimed at the USSR.

Stepping back from the brink of catastrophe, Kennedy and Khrushchev sought to reduce tensions, and in 1963 they agreed to a treaty banning all nuclear tests except those held underground. The Nuclear Test Ban Treaty helped curb atmospheric pollution from nuclear tests but did little to stop the arms race, since the agreement did not ban production of new weapons.

In November of that year, while in Dallas, Texas, President Kennedy was shot and killed by an assassin. His successor, Lyndon Johnson, sent increasing numbers of U.S. troops to Vietnam, divided after French defeat in 1954 into communist North Vietnam and anticommunist South Vietnam. For the next decade the Vietnam War (Chapter 35) was a central Cold War battleground, with Americans fighting in South Vietnam against a communist insurgency backed by the North, which was aided with supplies and weapons by the Soviets and Chinese communists.

Meanwhile the arms race accelerated. In 1964, plagued by domestic and foreign failures, Khrushchev was displaced by a group of his former subordinates, led by a new party boss named Leonid Brezhnev. Blaming the Cuban Missile Crisis on Soviet weakness, the new regime pursued a relentless naval and nuclear buildup. By the 1970s, both superpowers had built thousands of nuclear bombs and missiles—so many that the world lived in terror of a superpower conflict that would incinerate hundreds of millions in an atomic inferno. But the horror of such a war may have helped to prevent it: knowing that an all-out conflict could annihilate both sides along with much of the world, each side sought to avoid one. This "balance of terror" was also known as Mutual Assured Destruction, aptly abbreviated as **MAD**.

United States blockades Cuba and Soviets agree to remove missiles

Cartoon of Khrushchev and Kennedy fighting on "Cuban cliff."

U.S. troops sent to South Vietnam to fight communists

Brezhnev regime replaces Khrushchev and accelerates arms race

The West in the Cold War Era

Despite extreme international tensions, the nations of the West achieved unparalleled prosperity during the Cold War. Western Europeans emerged from the ashes of World War II, rebuilt their economies with substantial U.S. help and, as they lost their colonial empires, sought to strengthen their commerce and status through European unity.

Americans used their abundant wealth and resources to cover costly Cold War endeavors, while dealing with troublesome domestic divisions and serious societal changes.

The Revival of Western Europe

Western Europeans lose colonies but regain prosperity

The Cold War era was not easy for Western Europeans. Having long dominated the globe, they now found themselves dependent on America for military and economic support. Europe's Asian and African colonies, guided by growing nationalism, armed with modern weapons, and sometimes backed by Soviet support, increasingly claimed independence (Chapters 35 and 37). Faced with such claims, Britain, Belgium, and the Netherlands reluctantly released their colonies, while France and Portugal sought for years to hold on to theirs. Eventually, however, such efforts proved futile: by 1975, almost all of Asia and Africa were independent, and Europe's once-great global empires were gone (Map 34.3). The era of European domination was over.

Western Europe nonetheless survived and thrived. Aided by the U.S. Marshall Plan and protected by NATO, Europe's capitalist democracies enjoyed enormous economic expansion in the 1950s and 1960s. To foster growth, governments intervened in the economy, using planning commissions to set goals, supplying funds and tax incentives to businesses, and even controlling key industries. To improve the status of the working classes, and thus counter the appeal of communism, the governments expanded social programs, providing health insurance, unemployment compensation, old-age pensions, public housing, and family allowances to help parents care for children. They thus combined elements of socialism with capitalist economies.

Western Europeans unite to increase economic strength

To strengthen themselves economically, and decrease their dependence on America, European nations also began to unite in their own self-interest. Led by France and West Germany, in 1957 six of them formed the European Economic Community (EEC), also called the **Common Market**, reducing tariffs on one another's goods to foster commercial growth. EEC expansion was slowed in the 1960s by French president Charles de Gaulle, a fervent nationalist who blocked Britain from joining, concerned that British participation would dilute French influence. De Gaulle also withdrew French forces from NATO's joint command, asserting France's military independence but keeping France in the alliance.

In the 1970s, however, the European Community (EC), created in 1967 by merging the EEC with several other agencies, again began to expand. By 1973 de Gaulle was gone, as were most of Europe's colonies, and an economic downturn had brought high unemployment and working class unrest. Anxious, therefore, to increase its markets and resources, the EC welcomed Britain, Ireland, and Denmark as members. By the 1980s, when three more nations were added, the EC encompassed more than 300 million people and over a quarter of the world's trade.

European Economic Community grows into European Union

Further integration and expansion followed. In 1993 the EC was incorporated into a new European Union (EU), which launched a common currency called the euro, replacing numerous old national currencies with a single monetary system. By 2007, the EU had grown to 27 nations (Map 34.5) with half a billion people, embracing even former Soviet satellites that had by then gained independence. In 2005, however, voters in France and the Netherlands, fearful that their countries could lose their political autonomy, refused to ratify a negotiated European Constitution, sidetracking efforts to augment Europe's economic integration with greater political unity.

Map 34.5 Growth of the Common Market and European Union, 1957–2007

Founded in 1957, the European Economic Community (EEC), also called the Common Market, connected six Western European nations into a powerful and prosperous economic free-trade zone. Notice that, having merged with other agencies in 1967 to form the European Community (EC), it added six new members in the 1970s and 1980s. Note also that in 1993, a few years after the USSR disintegrated, the EC became part of a new European Union (EU), which added nations from the former Soviet bloc and grew to 27 members by 2007. What were the main advantages of Common Market membership? Why did some members resist efforts at political integration?

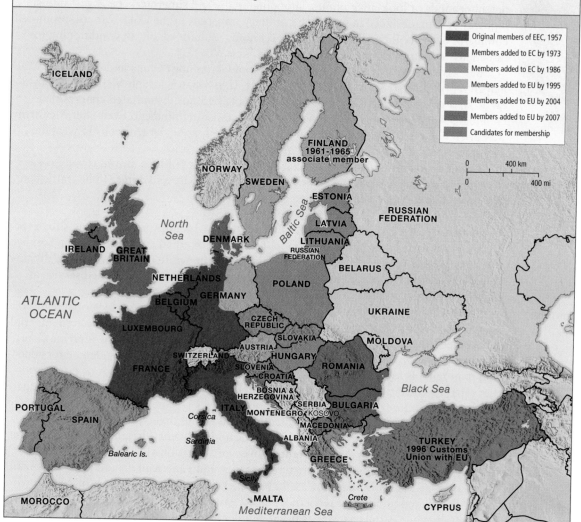

- Original members of EEC, 1957
- Members added to EC by 1973
- Members added to EC by 1986
- Members added to EU by 1995
- Members added to EU by 2004
- Members added to EU by 2007
- Candidates for membership

Affluence and Anxieties in America

As Western Europeans dealt with their diminished status after World War II, America enjoyed unprecedented influence and affluence. But pressing Cold War concerns, along with deep divisions in American society, also produced intense anxieties in the "land of plenty."

Global commerce and Cold War spending enhance American affluence

Rows of look-alike houses in suburban America.

Urban problems and fear of communism foster American anxieties

America in the Cold War years experienced unparalleled abundance. A huge global and domestic demand for U.S. consumer goods, following years of shortage during World War II, combined with massive Cold War defense spending to generate an economic boom. As purchasing power more than doubled between 1945 and 1970, Americans rushed to buy houses, cars, and televisions, which soon replaced radios as the main form of home entertainment. Improved roads and incomes helped millions move from crowded cities, with closely packed dwellings and street-front stores, to sprawling suburbs, with neat neighborhoods of look-alike homes, shopping malls, and supermarkets. A vast interstate highway system, designed in part to aid military transport in the Cold War era, promoted commerce and mobility, while a changing economy and affordable air conditioning fostered mass migration to the sunny South and West.

But anxieties persisted in America. The rise of Communist China and the Korean War helped set off a "Red Scare" in the early 1950s. U.S. Senator Joseph McCarthy, using a tactic later called "McCarthyism," made sweeping and unsubstantiated charges that communists had infiltrated government, industry, and entertainment. Even after McCarthy was discredited in 1954, fear of communism persisted, as Soviet triumphs in weaponry and space seemed more threatening with each Cold War crisis.

Urban problems added to the sense of insecurity. As millions moved to suburbs, decaying inner cities became breeding grounds of drug abuse and crime, while traffic congestion and industrial pollution fouled the air and water.

THE AMERICAN CIVIL RIGHTS MOVEMENT. Furthermore, African Americans, long subject to racial discrimination, began to press more forcefully for equal civil rights. In the South, black people had for years been segregated by law from white people, systematically denied the right to vote, placed in separate and poorly funded schools, denied service at restaurants, and restricted to designated restrooms and drinking fountains.

Civil rights movement combats American racism

By the 1950s, however, widespread reaction against racism, fueled by global revulsion against Nazi racist atrocities and by Asian and African struggles against Western imperialism, compelled America to confront its own racial divide. In 1954 the U.S. Supreme Court, faced with overwhelming evidence that schools for white children provided better education than schools for black children, ruled in the case of *Brown v. Board of Education* that separate education was inherently unequal, and soon ordered schools to desegregate "with all deliberate speed."

Black American Rosa Parks on a Montgomery bus.

In 1955 a black boycott of segregated buses in Montgomery, Alabama, brought to the fore Dr. Martin Luther King, Jr., a magnetic and eloquent African American minister who emerged as leader of the **civil rights movement**, a nationwide campaign for racial equality. Combining appeals to Christian morality and American democratic ideals with tactics used by India's Mahatma Gandhi (Chapter 32)—including protest marches, civil disobedience, and nonviolent resistance—King gained a mass following and broad support among white people as well as black people. With the backing of President Lyndon Johnson, a former Southern segregationist who now committed his administration (1963–1969) to fighting racism and poverty, the U.S. Congress passed a 1964 Civil Rights Act banning discrimination in jobs and public services, a 1965 Voting Rights Act ensuring black citizens the right to vote, and an array of antipoverty programs.

Ongoing racial and ethnic tensions deepen U.S. social unrest

Racism and racial tension nonetheless endured. Legal segregation had been banned, but across the country white people still resisted sharing neighborhoods and schools with African Americans. In the mid- to late 1960s, a series of violent upheavals in many U.S. cities made it clear that racial divisions and inequalities persisted. As America grew increasingly diverse, people of Asian, Latin American, and Amerind backgrounds, who also experienced discrimination, similarly sought to gain equality by using the methods and ideals of the civil rights movement.

Segregated facilities in America.

DIVISIONS IN AMERICAN SOCIETY. Racial and ethnic tensions were not the only anxieties afflicting Cold War America. Protests against an unpopular war, along with changing attitudes toward sex, gender, and family, also reflected deep divisions in American society.

From 1965 to 1973, U.S. combat forces fought in the debilitating Vietnam War (Chapter 35). At first the conflict, perceived as part of the global struggle against communism, enjoyed broad public support. Within a few years, however, increasing troop call-ups and mounting casualties convinced many Americans that the war was going badly and that claims to the contrary by U.S. leaders were lies. By 1967 an antiwar movement was staging public protests demanding U.S. withdrawal.

The antiwar movement attracted many members of the **baby boom** generation, Americans born during a huge surge in births following World War II. Raised in affluence and influenced by a youth culture that combined opposition to racism and violence with relaxed attitudes toward sex and drugs, many baby boomers joined both civil rights protests and antiwar protests. Many young men also resisted the draft, which made them liable to military service, and some even left the country. In 1968, as civil rights leader Martin Luther King and antiwar candidate Robert Kennedy (the late president's brother) were assassinated, and riots disrupted the presidential nominating conventions, U.S. society seemed to be dissolving into chaos.

Antiwar movement heightens unrest among American youths

That same year, after promising to end the Vietnam War and to restore "law and order," Richard Nixon, a crafty politician and Cold Warrior, was elected president. By gradually reducing the U.S. role in Vietnam, he restored some stability, but riots resumed in 1970 when he expanded the war to Cambodia. In 1973 he suspended the draft and secured a U.S. withdrawal from the war, easing domestic tensions. But the Watergate scandal, exposing Nixon's efforts to hide his awareness of a break-in by some of his staff at the offices of his political foes in Washington's Watergate hotel complex, created further turmoil, leading to his disgrace and resignation in 1974.

Antiwar protesters with flowers confront U.S. soldiers.

By then America was undergoing a social revolution. In the 1960s, a new women's rights movement, building on the efforts of the earlier crusade that helped women obtain voting rights, inspired millions of women to pursue careers—such as law, public service, medicine, and management—hitherto open mainly to men. Divorce rates doubled between 1960 and 1980, as women who could earn a living felt less constrained to remain in unhappy marriages and as divorce and remarriage became more socially acceptable. Sexual relations outside of marriage likewise became more acceptable, as more and more couples cohabited without marriage or as a prelude to marriage. Abortions increased in the 1970s and 1980s, especially after a 1973 Supreme Court decision, in the case of *Roe v. Wade*, supported abortion rights for women. Alarmed by such developments, religious conservatives sought to outlaw abortion and restore "traditional family values," a set of moral standards condemning sex outside of marriage, denouncing homosexual relationships, and asserting that a wife's main career should be that of homemaker and mother.

Changing women's roles and sexual standards challenge U.S. society

The Soviet Bloc

Khrushchev visiting factory in communist Albania.

Life in the Soviet bloc contrasted sharply with life in the West. Stalin, desperate to rebuild his war-torn country following World War II, re-imposed a harsh police state to control Soviet society while ruthlessly exploiting his new Eastern European satellites. Khrushchev, hoping to set a more attractive example, eased repression and tried to improve people's lives, ending Stalin's worst abuses and investing heavily in housing, agriculture, and consumer goods. But a series of poor harvests undercut his agricultural advances and the Cuban crisis settlement ruined his bid to overtake America without a costly arms race. The Brezhnev regime (1964–1982), while taking modest measures to improve living standards, cracked down on dissent and spent huge sums on a massive arms buildup. By the 1970s the USSR had surpassed America in numbers of long-range missiles, but its domestic economy still lagged far behind.

Life Under Communist Rule

Communism did many things for its people. It supplied a wide range of social services, including free health care, day care for children, subsidized housing, low-cost food and consumer goods, cheap public transport, quality education, guaranteed employment, and extensive pensions. Soviet society was among the world's most literate, while Soviet scientists and athletes ranked with the world's best. As the USSR and its satellites grew increasingly urban and industrial, more and more people enjoyed concerts, ballets, movies, sports, television, and even Western imports such as rock music and jazz.

Communism supplies social services but not freedom or abundance

But communism provided neither freedom nor Western-style prosperity. Stalin's successors softened his system but continued to control both society and economy. Although censorship was relaxed in the Khrushchev era, artists, writers, and the state-run media were still expected to emphasize the country's successes in science, sports, and space, while ignoring such failures as its shortage of quality goods and housing. A centralized economy, with a succession of five-year plans that set specific quotas for every industry and enterprise, helped the regime focus resources on the arms race, but it also regimented the rest of society. From central Europe to the Pacific, people in the Soviet bloc lived in cramped, dingy apartments and waited in long lines to buy drab produce grown on dismal collective farms and shoddy goods made in industries plagued by alcoholism and absenteeism.

Market in Soviet Central Asia, early 1960s.

Nor did Soviet communism create the classless society Marxists had envisioned. While the masses endured a dreary existence, a privileged elite of high officials and their families enjoyed superior housing and medical care, fancy vacations and country homes, and access to special stores selling luxury items such as caviar and imported liqueurs. Soviet women often held jobs in areas dominated by men in the West, such as medicine and engineering, but Soviet wives were still expected to shop, cook, and clean for their husbands and families. By the 1970s, communist idealism had given way to cynicism and careerism, while aging Soviet rulers focused mainly on maintaining control.

"Classless" communist societies produce new privileged elites

Similar conditions prevailed in other communist countries, which typically had their own planned economies, privileged elites, and drab living conditions. The contrast was especially striking in the divided nations of Korea and Germany, where people in the communist part endured poverty and oppression, while those in the capitalist part grew increasingly prosperous. But even in Communist China, where mass experiments meant to improve life instead provoked mass suffering, prosperity proved elusive until the 1980s and 1990s, when new leaders added capitalist incentives to communist controls (Chapter 35).

Challenges to Soviet Authority

In the USSR, communist control meant suppressing dissenters who dared to criticize or defy the regime. Aleksandr Solzhenitsyn (*sōl-zhih-NĒT-sin*), a brilliant Russian author who had spent years in a Stalinist prison camp, was accused of treason for writing *The Gulag Archipelago*, an account of the prison camp system, and exiled abroad in 1974. Andrei Sakharov (*SAH-kha-roff*), an eminent nuclear physicist who helped develop the Soviet H-bomb in the 1950s but in the 1960s became an outspoken critic of Soviet human rights abuses, was confined in 1980 to a city in central Russia to keep his message from the outside world. Other prominent dissidents were harassed by Soviet secret police, imprisoned on false charges, or confined in psychiatric wards. Nonetheless, despite such repression, a network of dissident writers and human rights activists operated throughout the Brezhnev years, secretly typing and circulating works exposing Soviet failings.

Soviets vainly struggle to suppress internal dissent

The Soviets also struggled to keep their satellites in line. In Czechoslovakia in 1968, for example, a communist reformer named Alexander Dubček (*DOOB-chek*) introduced "socialism with a human face," lifting most restrictions on speech, press, and foreign travel. After watching warily for months, the USSR sent in troops and tanks to crush the reform movement, eventually removing Dubček and installing a repressive regime. The Soviet invasion of Czechoslovakia was justified by an assertion, later called the **Brezhnev Doctrine**, that the USSR had the right to intervene in other communist countries to protect the global interests of socialism, as defined by Soviet leaders. In 1981, after an independent trade union called Solidarity staged strikes and protests in Poland, the Soviets again threatened to intervene in a satellite country. But Poland's communist regime imposed martial law (emergency military rule) to restore order and outlawed the dissident union, thereby making a Soviet invasion unnecessary.

Soviets control their satellites with force and fear

Clearly, then, the Soviet bloc was sustained by the threat of force. To millions of Eastern Europeans, and to non-Russians who made up half the USSR's population, the Soviet bloc was merely a replica of the old tsarist Russian empire, with Marxism serving as a new pretext for Russian imperial ways. Envious of Western affluence and aware that Europe's empires in Asia and Africa had crumbled, many Soviet subjects dreamed of the day that the Soviet empire would likewise fall apart. Somewhat to their surprise, that day was not long in coming.

The End of the Cold War Era

By the late 1960s the Cold War was taking its toll on both superpowers. Through enormous efforts, the Soviets had managed to surpass the United States in numbers of ICBMs and to hold their vast empire together. But their economy was stagnant, and their comradely ties with Red China had given way to bitter rivalry, sparking deadly border clashes in 1969. The Soviet leaders thus agreed to hold talks with the Americans, mired in the Vietnam War and facing their own stalled economy, in an effort to ease anxieties and control the nuclear arms race.

Détente and Its Demise

Cold War costs and nuclear fears prompt efforts at détente

The result of these negotiations was an era of **détente** (*dā-TAHNT*), a relaxation of international tensions, during the 1970s. Early in the decade, when Soviet-American talks to end the arms race bogged down, President Nixon reached out to Communist China, paying it a historic visit in February 1972. This trip not only opened dialogue between China and America, bitter foes for over two decades; it also raised Soviet fears of Chinese-American cooperation, thus prompting Soviet leaders to work out agreements with the United States. As a result, in May 1972 in Moscow, Brezhnev and Nixon signed treaties limiting the numbers of offensive and defensive missiles each side could have and endorsed several scientific and cultural agreements. The next year U.S. involvement in Vietnam ended and Brezhnev visited the United States. In 1975, after a dramatic orbital docking of American and Soviet space vehicles raised hopes for joint scientific endeavors, the two superpowers joined 33 other countries in signing the Helsinki Accords, a comprehensive set of agreements to stabilize Europe's security. Once again, the Cold War seemed to be ending.

Clashes in Africa and Islamic world undermine efforts at détente

Détente, however, had its limits. Hampered by the huge costs of their armed forces and atomic arsenals, the Soviets were eager to end the arms race, but not their global efforts to spread communism. The USSR thus kept aiding Vietnamese communists, even after U.S. withdrawal, while also sending military aid to African Marxists in Ethiopia and Angola, and to Arab Muslims fighting Israel in the Middle East (Map 34.6). U.S. attempts to promote human rights provisions of the Helsinki Accords, especially those allowing Soviet bloc citizens access to Western publications and broadcasts, angered the Soviets, who saw such efforts as schemes to destabilize their bloc with anti-Soviet propaganda. A new arms control pact, signed in 1979, went unratified by the U.S. Senate after the USSR, to support a client regime endangered by revolt, invaded neighboring Afghanistan at the end of that year. This Soviet assault, beginning a lengthy Soviet-Afghan War (1979–1989), dealt a death blow to détente.

"Stop the arms race" poster, 1978.

Seeing the Soviets' Afghan incursion as a threat to vital U.S. oil shipments from the Persian Gulf, President Jimmy Carter, whose administration (1977–1981) had previously worked to end the arms race, now initiated anti-Soviet sanctions and a new American arms buildup. But U.S. voters, upset by a flagging economy and by Carter's inability to secure the release of American hostages seized in Iran in 1979, voted him out of office in 1980, electing instead an ardent anticommunist who opposed reconciliation with the Russians.

Alarmed by Soviet aggressiveness, America intensifies the arms race

Ronald Reagan came to the presidency in 1981 with an optimistic faith in America and deep distrust of the USSR, which he famously labeled an "evil empire." Asserting that the Soviets would cheat on any arms agreement, he and his advisors denounced détente and intensified the arms race, hoping thereby to bankrupt the USSR. Imitating Soviet support for anti-Western liberation movements, the Reagan administration aided anticommunist insurgents in Angola, Ethiopia, Nicaragua, and Afghanistan, and even supplied modern anti-aircraft missiles to Afghan rebels fighting Soviet forces. The Cold War and arms race thus resumed with full force.

Map 34.6 Cold War Clashes of the 1970s and 1980s

Despite efforts to achieve détente between the superpowers in the 1970s, the Cold War continued and grew more intense in the 1980s. Note that East and West remained locked into hostile alliances, and that Cold War clashes persisted in Africa and Asia during these decades. How did Soviet support for anti-Western movements and U.S. aid to anticommunists fuel conflicts and confrontations in various parts of these continents?

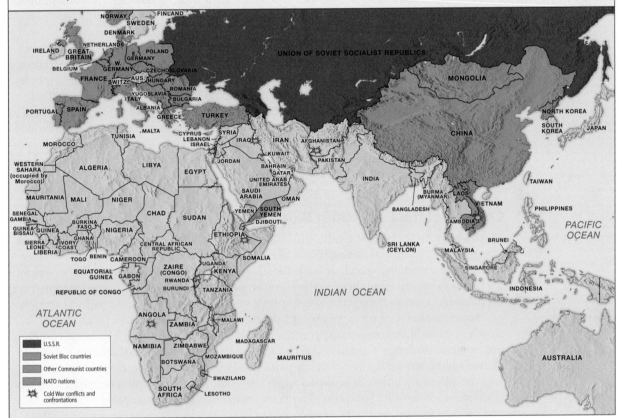

The Gorbachev Revolution

In Moscow, however, Leonid Brezhnev's death in 1982 opened the way for a major policy shift. His last years had been marred by economic stagnation, the rise of the anti-Soviet Solidarity union in Poland, and failures in the Afghan War, in which ragged rebel guerrillas were humbling the mighty Soviet Army and draining Soviet resources. Like Brezhnev himself, his immediate successors were aging and ailing bureaucrats, both of whom died before they could have much impact. But in 1985 power passed to a young, energetic new Soviet leader named Mikhail Gorbachev (*GOR-buh-CHOFF*), who was eager to make changes.

Keenly aware of the Soviet system's shortcomings, Gorbachev promoted *perestroika* (*p'YEH-reh-STRAW-ē-kah*), "restructuring" of Soviet society. To boost economic output, he experimented with Western-style profit and market incentives, granted greater autonomy for farmers and factory managers, and launched a drive against drunkenness

Gorbachev seeks "restructuring" and improvement of Soviet economy by restricting alcohol sales. To improve government performance he combated corruption, encouraged *glasnost* (*GLAHSS-nōst*), or open discussion of the USSR's problems, and eventually allowed limited democratic elections.

Gorbachev seeks reduced global tensions to ease strain on Soviet economy

To free up resources for his reforms and reduce the strain of military expenses and support for Cold War clients, Gorbachev also sought to ease international tensions. He held a series of summit meetings with Ronald Reagan who, despite his anticommunism, decided he could deal with the new Soviet leader, and the two signed a 1987 treaty eliminating mid-range missiles.

Their efforts to reduce long-range weapons, however, were thwarted by Reagan's ambition to build an elaborate space-based missile defense system, officially called **SDI** (Strategic Defense Initiative) but widely known as "Star Wars" (after a popular film series in which futuristic space weapons were used to fight an evil empire). Reagan depicted SDI as a "peace shield" that would render nuclear missiles obsolete by making it possible to intercept them in space before they neared their targets. But the Soviets saw it instead as a weapon that would free the United States to attack the USSR without fear of retaliation. Gorbachev therefore denounced SDI, postponing his pursuit of further arms accords until after Reagan was replaced in 1989 by George H. W. Bush, a cautious president less wedded to SDI.

Collapse of the Communist Bloc

Gorbachev withdraws from Afghan War and renounces use of force

Meanwhile Gorbachev took other striking steps. In 1988 he began withdrawing Soviet troops from Afghanistan, acting to end the war that he called a "bleeding wound." Later that year, in a stunning speech at the United Nations, he called on all countries to renounce the use of force and announced massive Soviet military cuts. And in 1989 he disowned the Brezhnev Doctrine, inviting Eastern European nations to pursue their own paths to socialism.

Poland and Hungary ease repression and proclaim free elections

Since the threat of force was what held the Soviet empire together, Gorbachev's words and deeds had huge consequences for the Soviet bloc. Eastern European communist regimes, no longer sure they could count on the Soviets to help them crush dissent, started taking steps to gain public support. The Polish government, for example, legalized the Solidarity union, suppressed since 1981, and created a new senate based on free elections, soon won by Solidarity. The Hungarian communists scheduled free elections and, hoping to impress voters, tore down barbwire borders barring escape to the West, thereby opening a hole in the iron curtain.

East Germany opens its borders; Berliners tear down Berlin Wall

East Germans then proved especially creative. Thousands of them, hearing the news from Hungary, hastily decided to "vacation" there, then escaped to the West through the open borders with their families and portable possessions. When East Germany's communist rulers reacted by banning trips to Hungary, East Germans went to Czechoslovakia instead, and pressured the Czechs into providing them with trains to West Germany. Embarrassed by this spectacle, with no support from the Soviets and with anticommunist rallies arising throughout East Germany, the communist East German regime took a daring gamble. On November 9, 1989, it officially opened East Germany's borders with the West, hoping that East Germans would be less likely to relocate if they could freely go back and forth. But the gamble quickly failed, as exultant Berliners soon began tearing down the wall that divided their city.

Berlin Wall's fall sparks democratic revolts throughout Eastern Europe

The fall of the Berlin Wall and the Soviet failure to stop it inspired uprisings in the other Soviet satellites. By the end of 1989 most of Eastern Europe had moved toward independence, often with little bloodshed. The violent exception was Romania, where communist dictator Nicolae Ceausescu (*chow-SHESS-koo*) used his police to massacre protesters, until his forces finally rebelled and killed him on Christmas day.

In free elections held in East Germany in March 1990, voters overwhelmingly chose candidates who favored German unification. That summer, in return for a huge West German loan to support the struggling Soviet economy, Gorbachev agreed not to resist German reunification. In October 1990 Germany was reunited, with West Germany's government taking over eastern Germany, where the former communist regime simply ceased to exist. The next month, an agreement by the superpowers and 22 other nations to reduce their military forces in Europe added another indication that the Cold War was over.

Reunified Germany and force reduction pact mark end of Cold War

Disintegration of the USSR

Then came the collapse of the USSR itself. As the nation's economy, hampered by bad harvests and bureaucratic stagnation, continued to decline, Gorbachev's popularity with his people plummeted. Using the new openness he allowed, they spoke out against him and his system. Furthermore, inspired by events in Eastern Europe, the country's fifteen 15 Soviet Socialist Republics, each dominated by a different nationality, began demanding national independence. By late 1990 all 15 had proclaimed some form of autonomy—including even Russia, the largest Soviet republic, encompassing three quarters of the USSR's territory and over half its people (Map 34.7).

Cartoon of Gorbachev and Soviet breakup.

Hoping to halt the USSR's disintegration, in January 1991 the Soviets sent forces into Latvia and Lithuania, two small Soviet republics that had declared outright independence. Scrambling to save the situation, Gorbachev then promoted a new "union treaty" designed to give the republics internal autonomy while preserving the overall union in foreign and military affairs. The treaty, however, enraged communist hardliners, who wanted to preserve strong centralized control and thus saw the treaty as a betrayal of Soviet interests and principles.

Gorbachev tries to sustain USSR as republics assert independence

On August 19, 1991, the day before the treaty was scheduled to be signed, eight hard-liners, including the defense minister and head of security police, attempted an ill-conceived coup. Visibly fortified with vodka, they publicly declared a state of emergency and ordered troops to occupy major cities. Having earlier detained Gorbachev, however, they failed to arrest Boris Yeltsin, outspoken head of the Russian republic. Climbing atop a tank in front of the Russian parliament building in Moscow, Yeltsin boldly urged mass resistance to the coup. Soon thousands gathered in support, defying police and military forces assembled on the scene. When commanders, unsure of their troops' loyalty and anxious to avoid a bloodbath, decided the next day not to order an assault, the coup leaders had no way to assert control. Within a few days they gave in, ending the abortive "vodka putsch" and letting Gorbachev resume his duties.

Hard-line coup attempt foiled by Yeltsin, head of Russian republic

But momentum had by this time passed to Yeltsin and the heads of the other republics, who each asserted more independence following the coup. Gorbachev strove to devise a new union treaty, hoping to preserve some Soviet authority, but few paid any attention. After several months, Russia and many other republics formed a Commonwealth of Independent States, a loose coalition with no central control, and agreed to dissolve the USSR. On December 25, 1991, when Gorbachev reluctantly resigned his post, the once-mighty Soviet Union ceased to exist.

Soviet Union crumbles as Russians and others withdraw

Map 34.7 Disintegration of the Communist Bloc, 1989–1992

In 1989 revolts in Eastern Europe brought independence to former Soviet satellites, and in 1990 the republics making up the USSR also began to assert autonomy. Notice that, despite Soviet leader Gorbachev's efforts to preserve the Soviet Union, by the end of 1991 it had disintegrated into 15 separate countries, most of which formed a Commonwealth of Independent States. Note also that Yugoslavia split apart in 1991–1992, and that Mongolia abandoned communism in 1992, leaving China, North Korea, Vietnam, and Cuba as the only remaining communist countries. How did the Eastern European revolts of 1989 help to trigger the USSR's disintegration two years later?

The World Transformed

In a few years, then, the global situation had completely changed. The Soviet bloc was gone, Germany was reunited, and the USSR had split into 15 separate states. Communism survived in China and Cuba, as well as Vietnam and North Korea, but none of these regimes could approach the might of the former Soviet Union. In Asia, Africa, and Latin America, anti-Western regimes and rebels could no longer look for Soviet support, leaving them thus vulnerable to the impositions of America, the sole surviving superpower. The communists had lost the Cold War.

Post-Soviet Russia tries democracy but soon becomes repressive

Russia still had formidable forces, but it lacked political and economic stability throughout the 1990s. Yeltsin, who served as president from 1991 to 1999, was plagued by ill health and by challenges to his authority from the Russian parliament and from Chechnya, a small southern region that sought to break from Russia and form a separate republic. His successor, Vladimir Putin, a former officer in the Soviet security police, sought to crush the Chechnya revolt and suppress internal dissent, silencing critics and taking control of the media and provincial governors. In the early twenty-first century, while

Russia's democratic freedoms waned, its economic clout increased, owing to global demand for its vast oil and natural gas resources.

Europe, no longer divided between communism and capitalism, moved toward even greater unity, as former Soviet satellites joined NATO and the European Union (Map 34.8). The breakup of Yugoslavia into smaller republics in 1991 led to bloody ethnic wars in

European Union and NATO admit former Soviet satellites

Map 34.8 Twenty-First Century Europe: Fragmentation and Integration

In the late twentieth and early twenty-first centuries, Europe experienced both increased fragmentation and increasing integration. Observe that the breakups of the USSR, Yugoslavia, and Czechoslovakia created many new independent European nations, while the expansion of NATO and the European Union connected many European nations militarily and economically. Why did French and Dutch voters refuse to ratify a new European Constitution in 2005, thereby slowing efforts to increase Europe's political integration?

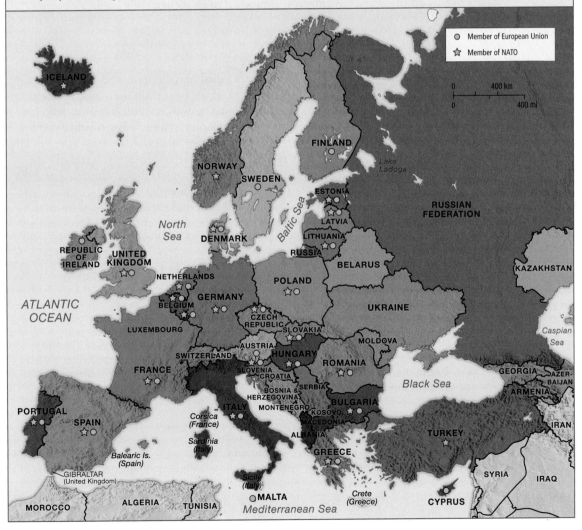

Bosnia (1992–1995) and Kosovo (1998), but NATO involvement eventually brought a fragile peace to the region.

United States faces severe global challenges despite unrivaled power and wealth

The United States, emerging from the Cold War as the world's only superpower, enjoyed unrivaled influence and prosperity throughout the 1990s. But an economic downturn in 2000, and the subsequent failures of several large U.S. corporations, showed that American capitalism faced serious problems. So did American security. After Islamic terrorists, angered at U.S. policies in the Middle East, used hijacked airliners to kill thousands of Americans in September 2001 (Chapter 37), the nation felt newly vulnerable to terrorist attacks. A U.S. invasion of Iraq two years later divided America and damaged its global standing, since Iraq had not been directly involved in the September attacks, and since American-led occupying forces failed for years to stabilize Iraq.

The end of the Cold War thus brought neither peace nor global stability. The terrifying and traumatic superpower struggle was over, but conflicts over beliefs and resources, intensified by clashes between cultures, continued to challenge the world.

Chapter Review

Putting It in Perspective

The Cold War divided the world into two immense armed camps, led by competing superpowers, driven by conflicting ideals, and characterized by contrasting political and economic systems. The capitalist West and communist East struggled for supremacy through a series of crises, any of which could have led to all-out war, all the while striving to avoid such war since it would destroy them both and much of the world. Stalemated in Europe, they battled for influence in Asia and Africa, where conflicts in such places as Korea, Vietnam, Cambodia, Ethiopia, Angola, and Afghanistan took millions of lives. For four decades humanity endured both the ongoing dread of unlimited war and the ongoing reality of limited wars occurring somewhere in the world.

Humanity nonetheless survived the Cold War. America achieved great prosperity while leading the West against Soviet communism, but also was torn by internal divisions regarding race, gender, morality, and the U.S. role in the world. Western Europeans, while losing their colonies and looking to America for defense against the Soviet Union, overcame age-old divisions to unite militarily and economically.

The Soviets relied mainly on armed force, sacrificing prosperity in order to sustain their vast military might, while using the constant threat of force to keep subject peoples in line. When Gorbachev, hoping to refocus Soviet resources on economic growth, acted to reduce the armed forces and remove the threat of force, the Soviet empire crumbled and the Cold War came to an end.

The Cold War had extensive global impact. It compounded anticolonial conflicts, aggravated regional upheavals, and complicated efforts to achieve stability in Asia, Latin America, Africa, and the Middle East. The next three chapters discuss these efforts and upheavals.

Reviewing Key Material
KEY CONCEPTS

United Nations, 880
Soviet bloc, 880
Truman Doctrine, 882
Marshall Plan, 882
containment of
    communism, 882
NATO, 883
decolonization, 885
Warsaw Pact, 887
ICBM, 888

summit conference, 888
U-2 Affair, 890
Cuban Missile Crisis, 891
MAD, 891
Common Market, 892
civil rights movement, 894
baby boom, 895
Brezhnev Doctrine, 897
détente, 898
SDI, 900

KEY PEOPLE

Joseph Stalin, 877
Harry Truman, 877
Winston Churchill, 877
Clement Attlee, 880
George Marshall, 882
George F. Kennan, 882
Dwight Eisenhower, 884
Nikita Khrushchev, 884
Sukarno, 885
Suharto, 885
Patrice Lumumba, 886
Yuri Gagarin, 888
John F. Kennedy, 890
Fidel Castro, 890
Lyndon Johnson, 891

Leonid Brezhnev, 891
Charles De Gaulle, 892
Martin Luther
  King, Jr., 894
Richard Nixon, 895
Aleksandr Solzhenitsyn, 897
Andrei Sakharov, 897
Alexander Dubček, 897
Jimmy Carter, 898
Ronald Reagan, 898
Mikhail Gorbachev, 899
George H. W. Bush, 900
Nicolae Ceausescu, 901
Boris Yeltsin, 901
Vladimir Putin, 902

ASK YOURSELF

1. Why did the Cold War begin? How did the differing ideals, actions, and perspectives of Soviet and Western leaders contribute to the onset of the Cold War?
2. Why did the Cold War expand into a global confrontation? Why did the USSR aid anticolonial movements and former European colonies? Why did such aid often fail to advance the spread of communism?
3. What were the main Cold War crises? Why did each occur, and how was it resolved? Why did efforts at peaceful coexistence in the 1950s and détente in the 1970s fail to end the Cold War?
4. How did life in the Soviet bloc differ from life in the West during the Cold War? What problems and divisions beset Soviet and Western societies?
5. What major strategies did each side adopt in the Cold War? What were the major strengths and weaknesses of the Soviet bloc and of the West? Why did the West prevail in the Cold War?
6. What actions and decisions by Soviet and Western leaders led to the end of the Cold War and the disintegration of the Soviet empire?

GOING FURTHER

Alperovitz, Gar. *Atomic Diplomacy*. Rev. ed. 1985.
Beschloss, Michael. *The Crisis Years, 1960–1963*. 1991.
Brown, D. *Globalization and America Since 1945*. 2003.

Chafe, W. H. *The Unfinished Journey: America Since World War II*. 5th ed. 2003.
Crockatt, R. *The Fifty Years War*. 1995.
Dobbs, M. *Down with Big Brother: Fall of the Soviet Empire*. 1997.
Dockrill, M. *The Cold War, 1945–1963*. 1988.
Frankel, M. *High Noon in the Cold War: Kennedy, Khrushchev, and the Cuban Missile Crisis*. 2004.
Fursenko, A., and T. Naftali. *Khrushchev's Cold War*. 2006.
Gaddis, J. L. *The Cold War: A New History*. 2005.
Garthoff, R. *Détente and Confrontation*. 1985.
Gleason, A. *Totalitarianism: Inner History of the Cold War*. 1995.
Halle, Louis J. *The Cold War as History*. 1994.
Hitchcock, W. *The Struggle for Europe: The Turbulent History of a Divided Continent, 1945–2002*. 2003.
Hunt, Michael. *The World Transformed, 1945–Present*. 2004.
Isserman, M., and M. Kazin. *America Divided*. 2000.
James, H. *Europe Reborn: A History, 1914–2000*. 2003.
Judge, E., and J. Langdon. *The Cold War: A History Through Documents*. 1999.
Judge, E., and J. Langdon. *A Hard and Bitter Peace: A Global History of the Cold War*. 1996.
Khrushchev, Nikita. *Khrushchev Remembers*. 1970.
Kotkin, S. *Armageddon Averted: The Soviet Collapse, 1970–2000*. 2001.
LaFeber, W. *America, Russia, and the Cold War, 1945–1992*. 2002.
Lapidus, Gail. *Women, Work, and Family in the Soviet Union*. 1982.
McCormick, J. *Understanding the European Union*. 2005.
Pagden, A., ed. *The Idea of Europe*. 2002.
Paterson, T., et al. *American Foreign Relations*. 6th ed. 2004.
Perkins, Ray. *The ABCs of the Nuclear Arms Race*. 1991.
Reynolds, David. *One World Divisible: A Global History Since 1945*. 2000.
Rifkin, J. *The European Dream*. 2004.
Rosen, Ruth. *The World Split Open: How the Modern Women's Movement Changed America*. 2000.
Roskin, M. G. *The Rebirth of Eastern Europe*. 2001.
Schaller, M., et al. *Present Tense: The United States Since 1945*. 2004.
Shipler, D. K. *Russia: Broken Idols, Solemn Dreams*. 1983.
Suny, Ronald. *The Soviet Experiment*. 1998.

Taubman, William. *Khrushchev: The Man and His Era.* 2003.

Turner, H. *The Two Germanies Since 1945.* 1987.

Urwin, D. *The Community of Europe.* 1995.

Walker, M. *The Cold War: A History.* 1993.

Westad, O. A. *The Global Cold War.* 2005.

Whitfield, Stephen. *The Culture of the Cold War.* 1991.

Wilkenson, J., and H. Stuart Hughes. *Contemporary Europe: A History.* 10th ed. 2004.

Yergin, Daniel. *Shattered Peace.* 1977.

Zubok, V., and C. Pleshakov. *Inside the Kremlin's Cold War.* 1997.

Key Dates and Developments

Year	Event	Year	Event
1945	Yalta and Potsdam conferences	1962	Cuban Missile Crisis
1947	Truman Doctrine and Marshall Plan	1965–1973	Direct U.S. involvement in Vietnam
1948–1949	Berlin blockade and airlift	1968	Soviet invasion of Czechoslovakia
1949	NATO Treaty, communist victory in China	1972	Nixon's China visit; Soviet-American arms control pact
1950–1953	Korean War	1979–1989	Soviet involvement in Afghan War
1955	Warsaw Pact	1989	Fall of Berlin Wall, revolutions in Eastern Europe
1957	Soviet ICBM and Sputnik, European Common Market	1990	Reunification of Germany
1960	U-2 Affair	1991	Disintegration of USSR
1961	Berlin Wall erected	1993	Formation of European Union

The Upheavals of Asia, 1945–present

Modern Urban Asia

The era following World War II brought massive upheavals in Asia. Asians threw off Western domination, engaged in bloody regional conflicts, and transformed age-old rural ways of life by creating modern urban societies with global connections, as illustrated by this photo of Osaka, Japan.

On September 2, 1945, the day Japan's surrender formally ended World War II, a small, frail man addressed a huge crowd in the Southeast Asian city of Hanoi. "All men are created equal," he proclaimed in Vietnamese. "They are endowed by their creator with certain inalienable rights; among these are life, liberty, and the pursuit of happiness." Noting that this "immortal statement" was from the U.S. Declaration of Independence, he went on to assert: "In a broader sense, this means: All the peoples of the earth are equal from birth; all the peoples have a right to live, to be happy and free." The speaker, known as Ho Chi Minh (*HŌ-CHĒ-MIN*), was declaring independence for his nation, Vietnam.

South and East Asia

Vietnam, like many Asian lands, had endured both Western imperialism and Japanese aggression. It had been part of France's Indochina colony since the 1800s and of Japan's empire since 1941. Now, however, Ho Chi Minh hoped that Vietnam could avoid the return of French colonial control by declaring independence and appealing to American ideals of freedom and human rights. But France, determined to regain great power status after World War II, wanted to restore imperial rule. Furthermore, since Ho Chi Minh was communist, and France became part of America's anticommunist alliance, Indochina's quest for independence soon got caught up in the Cold War, bringing Southeast Asia over three decades of almost constant conflict.

Ho Chi Minh's declaration and the ensuing conflicts exhibit the ideals and global connections fueling upheavals in Asia after World War II. Adapting for their own purposes Western ideals such as democracy, nationalism, and socialism, Asians sought to escape Western domination, only to become enmeshed in global Cold War politics. India gained independence but divided into separate Hindu and Muslim nations, one courted by the Soviets and the other by the Americans. Japan arose from the ashes of defeat, with American help, to become a capitalist stronghold in Asia. China endured a brutal civil war won by communists, who then combined calamitous experiments in socialist mass mobilization with bitter hostility toward the West. Korea and Indochina became the Cold War's bloodiest battlegrounds, torn by civil wars that emerged as international conflicts between communism and capitalism. By the early twenty-first century, although many Asians continued to be plagued by sweeping social changes and persistent poverty, economic growth and the end of the Cold War finally brought stability and prosperity to much of Asia.

Independence and Conflict in India and Pakistan

After decades of struggle for independence, the Indian subcontinent (Map 35.1) was freed from British rule in 1947. But with independence came partition, as the former British colony was split into two hostile states: the Republic of India, a huge Hindu-dominated democracy, and a somewhat smaller Islamic Republic of Pakistan, which

FOUNDATION MAP 35.1 East and South Asia in 1945

Following Japan's defeat in World War II, many of Asia's prewar rulers sought to maintain or restore the power they had before the war. Note that the British still ruled India, the Nationalists reclaimed control of China, the French sought to reassert imperial rule in Indochina, and the Dutch did the same in Indonesia. Note also, however, that within a decade these regimes would all be replaced. What factors and movements challenged the positions of Asia's prewar rulers?

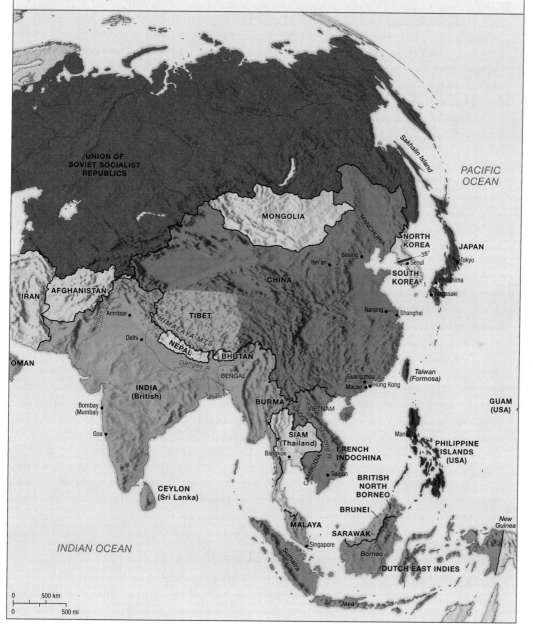

became a dictatorship. As both states grappled with poverty and population growth, they remained bitter foes. Their ongoing clashes were aggravated by Cold War politics and later by each nation's development of atomic weapons.

Independence and Partition

In the 1930s, under Mahatma Gandhi's leadership, Indians had compelled Britain to grant them some autonomy (Chapter 32). By the 1940s, however, two key obstacles limited further progress. One was the Muslim League, representing India's large Islamic minority, which feared repression by the Hindu majority if India became independent—despite Gandhi's pledges to honor Muslim rights. Another was World War II, which heightened tensions between India and Britain, especially after Britain committed India to war without consulting Indian leaders. Dismayed, Gandhi and his followers planned a new anti-British campaign, but were arrested in 1942 by the British government of Winston Churchill. A passionate opponent of Indian independence, Churchill in 1931 had found it "nauseating" that "seditious" Gandhi negotiated "half-naked" with British officials.

India gains independence, but Muslim Pakistan splits off

The end of the war in 1945 brought India new hope and new problems. British voters swept Churchill's government from office that summer, and his successors, intent on reducing Britain's overseas obligations, began moving to grant India self-rule. But the Muslim League, led by Muhammad Ali Jinnah, organized protests against a united India and pressed for a separate Islamic state. When these protests fueled violent clashes between Hindus and Muslims, threatening mass chaos, Britain reluctantly agreed to partition the subcontinent. On August 15, 1947, two separate new independent nations emerged: the Republic of India and the Islamic Republic of Pakistan (a name meaning "Land of the Pure"), itself divided into East and West sections on opposite sides of northern India. Saddened by his country's "vivisection," Gandhi refused to rejoice, predicting instead that "rivers of blood" would flow.

Mass relocation and violence mar Indian independence

Gandhi's prediction proved prophetic. Since Hindu and Muslim populations were often intermingled, the partition left millions of Muslims in Hindu-dominated India, and numerous Hindus in Islamic Pakistan. Fearing repression, many of these people moved. Muslims left India for East or West Pakistan, while Hindus fled these lands in the other direction. In chaotic mass migrations, marred by bloody clashes and forcible expulsions, hundreds of thousands were killed. All-out war erupted in the northern region of Kashmir, claimed by both Pakistan and India (Map 35.2). Although eventually divided by a 1949 truce, Kashmir remained a source of bitter conflict between the two new nations. By this time Gandhi was gone, murdered in 1948 by a militant Hindu who resented the Mahatma's efforts to accommodate Muslims. The "rivers of blood" that Gandhi had foreseen thus included his own.

India: Democracy, Progress, and Problems

Gandhi slain, but his ally Nehru leads non-aligned, democratic India

The Republic of India adopted a parliamentary system modeled on Britain's, with democratic rights guaranteed for all citizens, regardless of sex, religion, or caste. Until 1964 it was led by Jawaharlal Nehru (*juh-wuh-har-LAHL NĀ-roo*), Gandhi's longtime associate, who as prime minister used state-run industries and modernizing reforms to pursue

Map 35.2 India and Pakistan Since 1947

In 1947, after decades of resisting British rule, India finally achieved independence. Observe, however, that owing to the efforts of India's Muslim separatists, the former British colony was split into two hostile states—Hindu-dominated democratic India and Muslim Pakistan—that contended for control of Kashmir in the north and remained bitter foes for decades. Note also that in 1971 East Pakistan rebelled and, with Indian assistance, became an independent nation known as Bangladesh. Why was there such hostility between Pakistan and India? What impact did Cold War politics have upon their hostility?

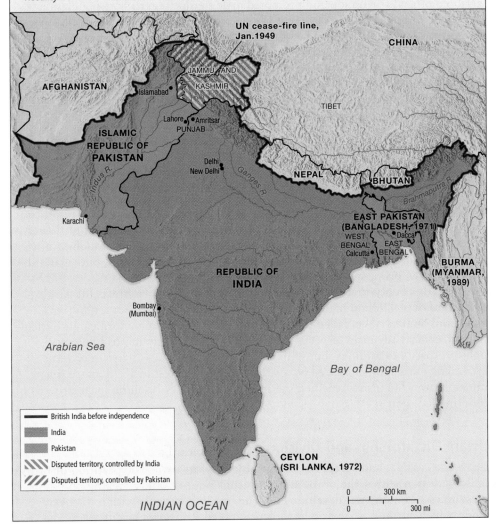

prosperity. Principled and conscientious, he achieved modest success, but massive poverty and population growth continued to burden the new nation.

In foreign affairs, Nehru practiced nonalignment, rejecting U.S. pressures to join the anticommunist camp and accepting substantial Soviet aid. India thus in the 1950s became a leader of the **nonaligned nations**, a group of countries (also including Indonesia,

Egypt, and Yugoslavia) that refused to side with either superpower, hoping thus to get aid from both while avoiding Cold War commitments.

Indira Gandhi improves agriculture and curbs population growth

In 1966, two years after Nehru's death, his daughter Indira Gandhi (no relation to the Mahatma) became prime minister and then dominated India for almost two decades. Talented and tenacious, she initiated programs to provide the poor with housing and land. She also supported the **Green Revolution**, a global agricultural movement that used synthetic fertilizers and scientifically developed high-yield crops to enhance farm output. She attacked official corruption and promoted male sterilization to slow population growth. These unpopular efforts brought her electoral defeat in 1977, but in three years voters returned her to office when her successors proved ineffective. Increasingly rigid and self-righteous, she was challenged by the nation's Sikhs, a religious minority whose faith combined elements of Hinduism and Islam. In 1984, after some Sikhs turned to violence in pushing for political autonomy, she ordered an attack on the Sikhs' Golden Temple at Amritsar, killing more than 450 people. Several months later her own Sikh guards murdered her in retribution.

Indian foreign minister meeting with Soviet and Chinese officials, 1962.

Indira Gandhi's son Rajiv Gandhi, a former airline pilot who replaced her as prime minister, focused the next five years on enhancing India's military strength and technological know-how—efforts that helped India eventually become a nuclear power and world leader in computer technology. But Rajiv was tainted by charges that he took financial kickbacks from a Swedish firm that sold India weapons, and his government was voted out in 1989. Two years later, while campaigning for return to office, he and 16 others were blown apart by a woman, with a bomb in a basket of flowers, who allegedly had ties to another violent separatist movement. Sonia Gandhi, Rajiv's Italian-born widow, later became a prominent force in Indian politics, but legally she could not become prime minister due to her foreign origins.

Agricultural advances and technology increase Indian prosperity, but poverty persists.

By the early twenty-first century, then, India was a land of contrasts. Its surging population of over a billion made it by far the world's largest democracy, but its guarantees of human rights failed to satisfy religious and ethnic minorities. Its agricultural and technical advances, especially its leading role in computer technology, brought prosperity to millions, but millions of others continued to live in poverty. India's military strength, enhanced by a successful nuclear test in 1998, made it a prominent power but also intensified the regional instability resulting from strife with neighboring Pakistan.

Persistence of poverty in India.

Pakistan: Dictatorship and Division

Pakistan, meanwhile, had severe internal problems of its own. The partition of British India left Pakistan with some of the subcontinent's poorest lands, lacking both mineral resources and industrial development. The ongoing struggle with India over Kashmir, which erupted into periodic violence, taxed Pakistan's resources and increased the influence of its army. Although it had parliamentary institutions, Pakistan by 1958 had become a military dictatorship, remaining thereafter largely under dictatorial rule.

Pakistan becomes military dictatorship and U.S. Cold War ally

Yet the Cold War gave Pakistan a major advantage. The United States, intent on containing communism by forming alliances with countries near the communist bloc, allied with Pakistan's repressive regime, giving it extensive economic and military aid.

In the 1960s the people of East Pakistan, separated from West Pakistan by more than a thousand miles (Map 35.2), grew discontented with the dictatorship that ruled them from the west. Sharing West Pakistan's Muslim faith but differing in language and culture, East Pakistan's Bengali people voted in 1970 for autonomy. The next year, however, the regime in West Pakistan used tanks and troops to slaughter Bengalis rioting for self-rule. Then, after millions of refugees fled East Pakistan to India, Indira Gandhi's government sent forces to help the Bengalis defeat Pakistan's army. East Pakistan thus in 1971 became a new nation called Bangladesh (East Bengal), which after independence continued to be torn by poverty and instability.

East Pakistan rebels and becomes independent Bangladesh

What was left of Pakistan, in the west, fared better, benefiting from American military and economic aid. But the Pakistani army's political involvement repeatedly frustrated efforts at civilian rule, while widespread corruption impeded attempts to achieve stability and prosperity. Zulfikar Ali Bhutto (*BOO-tō*), for example, who ruled the country through martial law during the 1970s, was arrested by his foes for electoral fraud and executed in 1979. His daughter Benazir Bhutto, the first woman to head a modern Muslim country, served twice as prime minister (1988–1990 and 1993–1996), and was twice dismissed on charges of corruption.

Tensions with volatile neighbors also troubled Pakistan. In the 1980s, during the Soviet-Afghan War, Pakistan became a base for Afghan anti-Soviet rebels and for U.S. efforts to supply them with weapons. In 1998, after India tested its first nuclear weapons, Pakistan exploded its own atomic device, raising fears of nuclear war between the bitter foes. In 2001, after an Afghanistan-based Muslim terrorist group attacked the United States in September, Pakistan supported a U.S. invasion of Afghanistan—fueling violent unrest in Pakistan, where many Muslims shared the terrorists' antipathy toward America. Pakistani President Pervez Musharraf (*moo-SHAH-ruf*), a military man who had seized power in 1999, sought to forcibly suppress unrest. But his harsh repression only prompted more violence, including terrorist bombings and the assassination of Benazir Bhutto in 2007 as she sought a return to power.

Afghan wars, atomic race with India, and unrest unsettle Pakistan

Revival and Resurgence of Japan

While India and Pakistan dealt with internal and external strife, Japan, whose major cities were reduced to rubble in 1945 by American bombs, emerged from the ashes of World War II to become a U.S. Cold War ally and an economic powerhouse. Restructured with American help along democratic and capitalistic lines, Japan came to rival the West in productivity and prosperity. Japan's economy, however, remained dangerously dependent on foreign markets and imported natural resources, while its society still struggled with contrasts between its Eastern traditions and its modern Western values.

Global commerce conducted at Japanese shipyard.

Japan's Economic Miracle

Japan's recovery was aided by postwar U.S. occupation, lasting from 1945 until 1952. Determined to rid Japan of militarism, Americans strove to remake the island nation into a capitalist democracy. Under General Douglas MacArthur, who served as occupation commander, they helped Japan devise and implement a democratic constitution and

U.S. occupation and support promote Japanese prosperity and democracy

Tokyo war crimes tribunal.

bill of rights that granted the vote and legal equality to both men and women. Japan's armed forces were limited in size, and its emperor was reduced to symbolic status. A war crimes tribunal set up by MacArthur tried and executed Japan's top wartime leaders but was relatively lenient to lower-ranking officials. The *zaibatsu*, huge Japanese industrial conglomerates that had been central to the war effort, were broken into smaller firms. Workers were encouraged to form unions with full rights to bargain and strike. Large estates owned by wealthy landlords were divided into small farms and sold at low cost to former tenants. Education was restructured along American lines, with a new emphasis on individualism challenging Japan's traditional collectivist approach.

Japan also gained from the Cold War. As the Soviet-American struggle intensified, and communism spread to nearby North Korea and China, U.S. leaders came to see Japan as a bulwark against Asian communism. America thus treated Japan more as an ally than as a defeated foe, opening U.S. markets to Japanese products and giving Japan's people extensive economic aid. A 1951 treaty committed America to defend Japan militarily, allowing U.S. forces to maintain bases on Japanese soil. Thus protected from foreign attack, and limited by its constitution to a small military force, Japan was able to focus its energies on economic growth.

Cold War divisions help Japan become a bastion of capitalist democracy

Japan's economic approach, blending market capitalism with central government planning, soon became a model for the rest of Asia. In collaboration with business, the government's Ministry of International Trade and Industry (MITI) set production goals and quotas, granted cooperating firms low taxes and interest rates, and shielded these firms from foreign competition with tariffs and import controls. Japanese government and business thus worked together, competing in the global market almost like one huge enterprise, sometimes described as "Japan, Incorporated."

These efforts nourished Japan's "economic miracle." With solid government support, broad access to Western markets, and strong traditions of employee loyalty and hard work, Japanese enterprises flourished. Some, such as Sony, Nissan, Toyota, and Honda, became global conglomerates, ranking among the world's largest and best-known corporations. They rewarded their workers with good pay and benefits, job security, and company-sponsored health and recreation programs. By the 1980s, Japan's living standards were among the world's highest, and its economy was second only to America's.

A science class in Japan.

Problems amid Prosperity

For all its success, however, Japan faced serious problems. Some stemmed from its dependence on global commerce, others from a clash between its Westernized culture and traditional values.

Japan depends on global trade and energy imports

Because it lacked mineral resources and relied on foreign trade, Japan was vulnerable to actions by its trading partners, especially the United States. American efforts to protect U.S. business from growing imports of low-cost Japanese goods, including a 10 percent import surcharge imposed in 1971, underscored Japan's reliance on U.S. markets and its vulnerability to U.S. economic protectionism. In 1973, oil-producing Arab nations placed an embargo on petroleum shipments to America and its allies because they supported Israel in a war against Arab countries (Chapter 37). This embargo created critical shortages in Japan, highlighting its almost total dependence on foreign fuels and raw materials. A severe economic downturn in the 1990s, combined with increased competition from other Asian nations, Europe, and America, further damaged Japanese economic confidence.

Meanwhile, Western culture's pervasive impact continued to subvert Japan's traditions, including Shinto and Buddhist religious practice. Furthermore, although Japan's crime rate remained lower than crime rates in the West, Japanese cities nonetheless suffered from similar industrial blights—slums, traffic jams, urban sprawl, and air pollution. Even Japanese democracy, modeled on that of the West, was marred by corruption and scandal, intensified by the longtime rule of the Liberal Democratic Party, which held power from 1955 until 1993.

Western impacts and urban blight mar Japan's traditional culture

In gender matters, too, Japan was torn between tradition, which assigned women a submissive role, and modern expectations, which promoted equality. Japanese women now had full legal rights and growing employment opportunities, but Japan's corporations still often put them in subordinate positions, with lower salaries and fewer chances for advancement than men. Meanwhile, the male-dominated Japanese government for decades concealed World War II atrocities against women by Japanese troops, including the use of Korean "comfort women" as sex slaves for Japanese soldiers (Chapter 33). In 1993 the government finally apologized, after women who survived these abuses came forth to publicize them, but some Japanese leaders continued to deny or minimize the extent of such wartime atrocities.

Japanese women gain legal rights but male dominance persists

These problems, however, could not diminish the impact of Japan's achievements after World War II. Within a few decades, with help from its former foes, the island nation had emerged from defeat and devastation to become one of the world's most prosperous and influential countries.

Conflict and Division in China and Korea

While Japan was rising from the ashes, China and Korea, freed at the end of World War II from Japanese occupation, were plunging into conflict and chaos. In 1946 a civil war broke out between the Chinese Communist Party and China's Nationalist government, widely discredited by rampant corruption and poor performance in the war against Japan. In a stunning Cold War triumph for global communism, the communists emerged victorious in 1949, controlling the Chinese mainland, while the Nationalists survived by moving their regime to the island of Taiwan off China's southeast coast. Then, in 1950, Asian peace was shattered again by conflict in Korea, which became a Cold War battleground. Three years of futile fighting left Korea, like China, with two hostile regimes, one communist and one nationalist.

Communist soldiers study artillery during Chinese civil war.

Civil War in China: Communists Versus Nationalists

On the surface, during China's long war against Japan (1937–1945), Chinese Nationalists and communists were allegedly united against the common foe. In reality, however, they waged simultaneous struggles against Japan and each other. Expanding from Yan'an, their remote northwestern base, the communists waged effective guerilla war, tormenting the Japanese troops who occupied northern and eastern China. The Nationalists, meanwhile, hampered by corruption and incompetence, retreated from the Japanese, while striking out

China's communists gain popular support during war against Japan sporadically against the communists. By 1945 the communists, by vigorously resisting the invaders, had greatly enhanced their prestige, while the Nationalists under Jiang Jieshi (Chiang Kaishek) had lost much support.

Japan's defeat and U.S. aid restore Nationalist rule in China

When Japan surrendered in 1945, both sides in China scrambled for position. The Nationalists, aided by American vehicles, planes, and ships, soon reoccupied most of the territory vacated by Japan. Jiang seemed once again the master of China. Manchuria, however, was still occupied by Soviet troops, who had moved in at the end of the war.

Hoping to avoid a Chinese civil war, which the Soviets could exploit, the United States negotiated a truce between China's communists and Nationalists, getting both to endorse a coalition government. The deal, however, was doomed. The communists, distrusting America as the capitalist world's leader and the Nationalists' main supporter, accepted the truce only to buy time. And Jiang Jieshi, with a huge army and access to U.S. arms, still intended to crush his communist foes. By mid-1946 the truce had broken down, and China was engulfed in civil war.

Initially the Nationalists did well. Because they controlled China's cities, railways, factories, and mines, they were able to dominate industry and transportation. Their three-million-man army outnumbered the communist forces by at least three to one. And their modern American weapons and vehicles gave the Nationalists a big edge over the communists, whose rifle supply was limited and who moved mainly on foot. By mid-1947, the Nationalists had moved across northern China and captured the communist headquarters at Yan'an (Map 35.3).

Communists benefit from guerilla tactics and broad peasant support

But the communists were far from beaten. During the long war against Japan, they had honed their guerrilla tactics, learning to fight a better-armed foe by avoiding direct combat and relying on subversion and sabotage. In their years at Yan'an they had won over the peasants by giving them land and abolishing social classes. The Nationalists controlled the cities and railways, but the communists were aided and supplied by village peasants, who made up most of China's population.

War refugees, China, 1949.

Communist commander Lin Biao (*LIN b'YOW*) retreated with his "People's Liberation Army" to Soviet-occupied Manchuria, where he gained access to Soviet weapons and those left behind by Japan. Determined to crush his foes, Jiang pursued the communists into Manchuria, extending his supply lines and leaving his forces vulnerable. A communist counterattack, aided by peasants who disrupted the Nationalists' supply lines and dug trenches to trap their tanks, turned the tide in 1948. The communists won victory after victory, taking Beijing in January of 1949 and Nanjing in April. By summer the Nationalist forces were in full flight.

Divided China: Taiwan and the People's Republic

But communism's triumph proved incomplete. The Nationalists fled to the island of Taiwan, where they were protected by the seas and the U.S. Navy. Ruling only Taiwan, they nonetheless called their regime the Republic of China, claimed with American support to be China's legitimate government, and even held China's United Nations seat until 1971. Led by Jiang Jieshi, who ruled the island under martial law until his death in 1975, they dreamed of restoring their rule over China's mainland. But by 1987, when Taiwan finally lifted martial law and began moving toward democracy, this dream had long since disappeared. The future of mainland China lay in communist hands.

Map 35.3 Communist Victory in China, 1948–1949

In the early stages of the Chinese Civil War, the Nationalists, with a much larger army and modern equipment, seemed to have the advantage over the communists. Notice, however, that after retreating into Manchuria early in the war, the communists turned the tables in 1948 and, with the aid of their peasant supporters, began a counterattack that defeated the Nationalists in 1949. What factors contributed to communist victory, and why was it incomplete? How and why did the Nationalist regime survive?

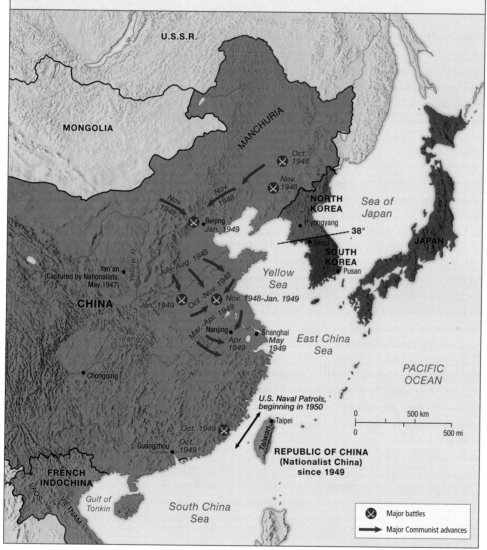

The communists, meanwhile, moved to consolidate their power. On October 1, 1949, at a grand ceremony in Beijing, their longtime charismatic leader Mao Zedong proclaimed a new regime called the People's Republic of China. The world's most

Communists create People's Republic and ally with USSR

populous country, its half-billion people constituting over a fifth of all humanity, was now under communist control.

Much to the dismay of the Western powers, which refused to recognize the new regime and called it simply "Red China," early in 1950 Mao and his comrades concluded a treaty of friendship and alliance with the Soviet Union. But even as China's new rulers moved to transform their country along communist lines, their efforts were diverted by a complex conflict in Korea.

Occupation, Partition, and Conflict in Korea

Soviet and U.S. occupation zones result in divided Korea

Like China, Korea emerged in 1945 from Japanese occupation only to be divided between communists and nationalists. In the waning days of World War II, after entering the war against Japan, the Soviets invaded northern Korea. As the war ended, the United States, anxious to keep its Soviet allies from taking all of Korea, insisted on dividing it at the 38th parallel of latitude into U.S. and Soviet occupation zones. In the north, within a few years, the USSR installed a Soviet-style government led by Kim Il-sung, a capable, ruthless communist who had been active in anti-Japanese resistance. In the south, under U.S. influence, a right-wing nationalist named Yi Sung-man, widely known as Syngman Rhee, emerged in 1948 as president. The superpowers then removed their troops, leaving the country split into hostile states.

Communist North Korea invades South Korea in 1950

The fragile peace did not last long. On June 25, 1950, with a large, Soviet-equipped army, North Korea launched a massive invasion across the 38th parallel, quickly overrunning most of the south (Map 35.4). But America, stunned by communism's recent triumph in China, was not about to let another country "go communist." After promoting a United Nations resolution calling for military support for South Korea, the Americans helped create a U.N. military force. Anxious to show that the new United Nations—unlike the old League of Nations—could resist aggression, 15 other countries joined in this effort, the U.N.'s first military action.

American–led U.N. forces drive communist armies deep into North Korea

Led by America's General Douglas MacArthur, the U.N. force soon reversed the war's momentum. In September, with a surprise amphibious landing at the port of Inchon behind the lines of North Korean forces, MacArthur divided them and drove them from the south. In October, expanding beyond his initial objective of liberating the south, MacArthur pushed into North Korea, aiming to drive out the communists and unite the country. By November he occupied most of the north and seemed on the verge of victory.

Communist Chinese troops help North Korea drive back U.N. forces

But again the war's momentum changed. As MacArthur's forces approached the Yalu River, which separates Korea from China, the Communist Chinese began to fear that he might invade their land. In late November, without declaring war, they started sending in thousands of Chinese troops to aid the North Koreans. Caught off guard, the U.N. forces retreated, barely escaping to the south, where they regrouped and continued the war.

As a stalemate soon developed, not far from the 38th parallel, the frustrated MacArthur demanded authority to attack Communist China. But his superiors, anxious to avoid an all-out Asian war, opted to limit the conflict to Korea and seek a negotiated truce. In 1951, when he openly questioned this policy, MacArthur was relieved of his command. The war dragged on in debilitating deadlock until July 1953, when an

Map 35.4 The Korean War, 1950–1953

The Korean War began in summer of 1950, when Communist North Koreans invaded and overran much of South Korea. Note, however, that in the fall an American-led United Nations coalition drove them back deep into the North, only to have the momentum change again in November, when communist Chinese forces came to the aid of the North Koreans. Note also that, after a lengthy and debilitating deadlock, the fighting finally ended in 1953 with a truce that left Korean split into two hostile states. Why did the communist Chinese intervene in the Korean War? Why did they call their forces "volunteers"?

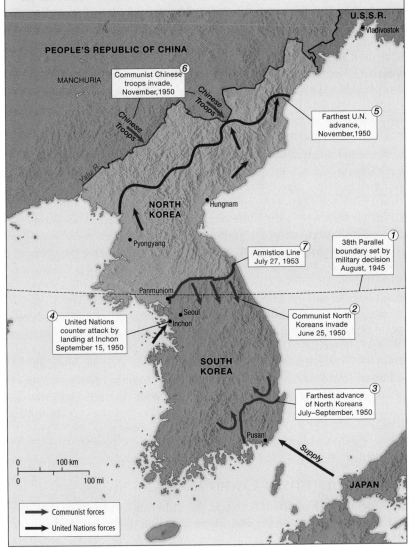

U.S.S.R.

Vladivostok

PEOPLE'S REPUBLIC OF CHINA

MANCHURIA

⑥ Communist Chinese troops invade, November,1950

Chinese Troops

Chinese Troops

Yalu R.

⑤ Farthest U.N. advance, November,1950

NORTH KOREA

Hungnam

Pyongyang

⑦ Armistice Line July 27, 1953

① 38th Parallel boundary set by military decision August, 1945

Panmunjom

④ United Nations counter attack by landing at Inchon September 15, 1950

Seoul
Inchon

② Communist North Koreans invade June 25, 1950

SOUTH KOREA

③ Farthest advance of North Koreans July–September, 1950

Pusan

Supply

JAPAN

0   100 km
0   100 mi

→ Communist forces
→ United Nations forces

armistice finally ended the fighting. Over two million people had been killed, including numerous Korean civilians, while countless other Koreans suffered from disease, dislocation, and the death of loved ones as their country was ravaged. And yet Korea remained divided, separated by a heavily patrolled demilitarized zone (DMZ), two and a half miles wide, along the armistice line.

Divided Korea: Communist North, Capitalist South

In the North Kim Il-sung ruled a Stalin-style communist police state for the next four decades. The regime's planned economy, state-run industries, and collective farms reflected its Soviet roots. Relentlessly hostile to South Korea and America, it maintained good relations with both Communist China and the USSR, even when these two countries eventually became bitter rivals. After Kim Il-sung died in 1994, his son Kim Jong-il continued the repressive regime. An eccentric recluse with a love of fast cars and a mortal fear of air travel, the younger Kim moved to develop nuclear weapons, despite a faltering economy and widespread famine.

Korean child receiving food aid.

In the South Syngman Rhee, whose American-backed regime was authoritarian and corrupt, ruled as dictator until 1960, when he was ousted by a student-led uprising. The next year, however, the military seized control, and it retained power for the next three decades. General Park Chung-hee, who served as president from 1961 until his assassination in 1979, combined political repression with strong support for industry and economic growth. By the 1980s, with U.S. help and access to global markets, South Korea had become a capitalist powerhouse, with automaker Hyundai and electronics giant Samsung among the world's leading corporations.

Repressive regimes rule South Korea, but U.S. backing helps bring prosperity

The regime nonetheless remained repressive, rigging elections, censoring the press, and suppressing dissent. In 1980 Kim Dae-jung, leader of the democratic opposition, was arrested and condemned to death. Under U.S. pressure, the regime reduced his sentence to 20 years in prison, and later let him go to America for medical care. In 1987, as South Korea prepared to host the 1988 Summer Olympic Games in its capital, Seoul, student-led protests captured world attention, compelling the government finally to allow free elections.

Seoul, South Korea's modern capital.

Democratic reforms followed, but corruption scandals and a short but severe Asian economic downturn in 1997 plagued the new democracy. Elections that year brought to power the widely admired Kim Dae-jung, who improved the economy, reduced corruption, and even reached out to the communist North, meeting with North Korean leader Kim Jong-il in the year 2000. By the twenty-first century, despite ongoing corruption problems, South Koreans lived in a prosperous and democratic society.

Radicalism and Pragmatism in Communist China

The Chinese were less fortunate than South Koreans. After driving out the Nationalists in 1949, the communists formed a socialist government based on the Soviet model, with Mao Zedong as Chairman of the party's Central Committee, and his comrade Zhou Enlai (*JŌ EN-LĪ*) as the government's premier. The regime labored mightily to transform the country and improve people's lives, but its efforts also brought mass upheavals and extensive suffering.

Early Radical Reforms

Seeking to remake China in accord with their communist vision, Mao and his comrades initiated radical reforms and mobilized mass campaigns designed to end corruption and instill new selfless socialist values. They transferred land from landlords to peasants, encouraged peasants to share farm animals and tools, and killed many thousand former landlords and others labeled "enemies of the people." In another radical break with the past, the new regime promoted equality for women, easing access to day care for children so mothers could work outside the home. A 1950 Marriage Reform Law allowed women to inherit property and seek divorces, while inviting young people to choose their own spouses—thus undermining the age-old practice by which parents arranged their children's marriages. In the next five years, several million women divorced the men they had earlier been compelled to wed.

Following the Soviet Union's example, China's communists also centralized control over information, education, and the economy. They directly managed the media, which they used to mobilize support for the party and attack practices they deemed harmful to society, such as drug abuse, corruption, prostitution, and religion. To educate the masses and instill communist ideals, the regime took control of schools and colleges and required teachers to follow a curriculum imposed by communist authorities. And in 1953, with Soviet assistance, the government initiated a Five-Year Plan, designed to promote heavy industry and collectivize farming. By the mid-1950s the Chinese communists seemed to be creating a Soviet-style socialist society.

But Mao's vision differed radically from the Soviet model. Whereas Soviet communism, in line with Marxist doctrine, was based on the urban proletariat, Mao's revolutionary goals were founded on the rural peasants. Inspired by his peasant background and disdain for urban elites (Chapter 32), Mao intended to create a rural, egalitarian, socialist society. Moreover, while Soviets strove to transform society through economic planning and socialist programs, Mao sought to do so by changing the people themselves, using media control and mass campaigns to mold people's minds, alter their attitudes, and mobilize the masses for heroic achievements.

Communist China's radical reforms seek to aid peasants and women

Landowner trial, China, 1950s.

China adopts Soviet-style central planning and control

Mao's peasant socialism and mass campaigns diverge from Soviet model

The Great Leap Forward and Its Failure

Although the Five-Year Plan fostered real economic growth, for Mao, the rural revolutionary, it was too urban, timid, slow, and bureaucratic—too much like the Soviet system of centralized control by an elite managerial class. By 1958 he was ready to try something new. So that year he launched the Great Leap Forward, a sensational campaign of mass mobilization designed to rapidly reshape China into a model rural socialist society. Small collective farms were combined into huge communes of five thousand families, many of which had collective work brigades, communal dining halls, day-care facilities, and even their own small factories. Industry was decentralized and moved from cities to communes, where peasants produced goods in rural workshops and steel in small backyard furnaces. China's future, Mao insisted, must be fashioned by the rural masses, not by urban technocrats and bureaucrats. "Twenty years in a day" was his slogan, and the Chinese people strove valiantly to meet his ambitious goals.

Great Leap Forward forms huge rural communes throughout China

Poor performance and natural disasters ruin Great Leap Forward

But the Great Leap Forward turned into a great catastrophe. Lack of industrial expertise resulted in shoddy goods, backyard furnaces produced inferior steel, and pressures to meet unrealistic goals led communes to overstate the size of their harvests, creating a massive food shortage. In 1960 a nationwide drought, regional typhoons, and torrential rains helped turn the tragedy into a horrendous famine, killing an estimated 20–30 million people.

Chinese split with Soviets and develop nuclear weapons

This catastrophe, moreover, fueled a growing rift between China and the USSR, which had been giving the Chinese substantial aid. In 1960 the Soviets, offended by Mao's rejection of their model and loath to use their limited resources to support his disastrous Great Leap Forward, abruptly cut off aid. The Chinese, offended by Soviet leader Khrushchev's efforts at "peaceful coexistence" with the West (Chapter 34), increasingly renounced these efforts as collaboration with communism's enemies. By 1963 the two communist giants were openly vilifying each other. In 1964 China tested an atomic bomb, adding to the fears of Soviet leaders, who were aware that Mao seemed to see nuclear war as a viable option.

Meanwhile moderate Chinese leaders, including Premier Zhou Enlai, were trying to repair the damage resulting from Mao's radical experiment. In 1960 these moderates abandoned the Great Leap Forward, relaxed the pace of change, began dismantling the communes, and reduced the role of Mao Zedong. Respecting Mao's earlier achievements, they let him remain party chairman, but otherwise eased him into semi-retirement.

The Great Proletarian Cultural Revolution

Mao's youthful Red Guards conduct a new radical mass campaign

But Mao, the legendary "Great Helmsman" who had piloted the communists to power, refused to sail quietly into the sunset. Late in 1965, aided by Defense Minister Lin Biao and the People's Liberation Army, Mao launched his most spectacular venture: the Great Proletarian Cultural Revolution.

Mao's "Little Red Book."

Seizing control of the media and denouncing the moderates as followers of the "capitalist road," he urged young people to form **Red Guards**, radical militias aimed at restoring Maoist revolutionary fervor. Millions of high school and university students responded enthusiastically. The young Red Guards then went on a rampage, attacking all traces of capitalist elitism in China. They disrupted businesses and closed down universities, forcing managers and professors to labor in the fields with the peasants. The Red Guards also held mass rallies to glorify their leader, waving copies of his "Little Red Book," *Quotations from Chairman Mao*, a collection of sayings they could recite by heart (see "*Quotations from Chairman Mao*"). This spectacle marked the high point of the cult of Mao and the ultimate expression of his radical populism in action. But it also echoed China's past: indeed, as Mao basked in mass exaltation, he almost seemed to have assumed the Mandate of Heaven, enjoying the regal status once reserved for Chinese emperors.

Cultural Revolution creates chaos, ruins economy, and isolates China

Like the Great Leap Forward, however, the Great Proletarian Cultural Revolution was a catastrophic failure: it created mass chaos, set the economy back years, and isolated China from the outside world, which watched in spellbound anxiety. Finally, in 1970, the radicalism subsided, schools and businesses reopened, and stability was restored. By 1971 the moderates were back in power and Lin Biao was dead, reportedly killed in a plane crash as he fled toward the Soviet Union following a failed attempt to

Document 35.1 Quotations from Chairman Mao

The "Little Red Book" of *Quotations from Chairman Mao* was a central symbol of China's Great Proletarian Cultural Revolution, with youthful Red Guards committing it to memory and waving it zealously at mass rallies in support of Mao. Here are some excerpts that provide a flavor of what was called Mao Zedong Thought.

A revolution is not a dinner party, or writing an essay, or painting a picture, or doing embroidery; it cannot be so refined, so leisurely and gentle, so temperate, kind, courteous, restrained and magnanimous. A revolution is an insurrection, an act of violence by which one class overthrows another.

Every Communist must grasp the truth, "Political power grows out of the barrel of a gun."

. . . There are two winds in the world today, the East Wind and the West Wind . . . I believe . . . today that the East Wind is prevailing over the West Wind. That is to say, the forces of socialism have become overwhelmingly superior to the forces of imperialism.

The revolutionary war is a war of the masses; it can be waged only by mobilizing the masses and relying on them.

The atom bomb is a paper tiger which the U.S. reactionaries use to scare people. It looks terrible, but . . . the outcome of a war is decided by the people, not by . . . new types of weapon.

Every comrade must . . . understand that as long as we rely on the people, believe firmly in the inexhaustible creative power of the masses and hence trust and identify ourselves with them, we can surmount any difficulty, and no enemy can crush us while we can crush any enemy.

There is an ancient Chinese fable called "The Foolish Old Man Who Removed the Mountains." It tells of an old man who lived . . . long ago and was known as the Foolish Old Man of North Mountain. His house faced south and beyond his doorway stood . . . two great peaks . . . obstructing the way. With great determination, he led his sons in digging up these mountains hoe in hand. Another greybeard, known as the Wise Old Man, saw them and said derisively, "How silly of you to do this! It is quite impossible for you few to dig up these two huge mountains." The Foolish Old Man replied, "When I die, my sons will carry on; when they die, there will be my grandsons, and their sons and grandsons, and so on to infinity. High as they are, the mountains cannot grow any higher and with every bit we dig, they will be that much lower. Why can't we clear them away?" Having refuted the Wise Old Man's wrong view, he went on digging every day, unshaken in his conviction. God was moved by this, and he sent down two angels, who carried the mountains away . . . Today, two big mountains lie like a dead weight on the Chinese people. One is imperialism, the other is feudalism. The Chinese Communist Party has long made up its mind to dig them up. We must persevere and work unceasingly, and we, too, will touch God's heart. Our God is none other than the masses of the Chinese people. If they stand up and dig together with us, why can't these two mountains be cleared away?

SOURCE: Quotations from Chairman Mao Tse-tung. 2. Classes and Class Struggle, 5. War and Peace, 6. Imperialism and All Reactionaries Are Paper Tigers, 8. People's War, 12. Political Work, 14. Relations between the Army and the People, 21. Self-Reliance and Arduous Struggle. http://art-bin.com/art/omaotoc.html

seize power for himself. According to a mythical but widely circulated account, when Mao learned that Lin Biao was escaping after his act of betrayal, the Great Helmsman stretched out his arm toward his former comrade's flight path, and at that instant Lin Biao's plane exploded. Such was the power attributed to Mao Zedong.

China's Opening to the West

Mao's era, however, was approaching its end. The aging chairman again faded into the background as moderate comrades sought to end China's isolation. Premier Zhou Enlai, a gifted diplomat and nimble opportunist who retained his premier's post throughout the Cultural Revolution, now engineered a stunning change in Chinese foreign policy. He helped open his communist country to the capitalist West.

China's change of course was preceded by a dangerous deterioration in Chinese-Soviet relations. In 1967, Red Guards on the rampage denounced the Soviet Union and besieged its Beijing embassy. In 1968, the Soviets invaded Czechoslovakia and proclaimed the Brezhnev Doctrine, asserting the USSR's right to intervene in other communist countries (Chapter 34). China reacted in horror, fearing it might be the next Soviet target. In 1969, Communist China and the Soviet Union fought several brief but deadly undeclared border wars along their lengthy frontier. Hoping to offset the threat from their Soviet neighbor, Chinese leaders started looking to improve relations with the West.

The Americans, meanwhile, moved to exploit the hostility between China and the USSR. They began to seek dialogue with Communist China, whose existence the United States had never formally recognized. In 1971 the United States lifted restrictions on American travel to China. The Chinese then invited the U.S. table tennis team to play in Beijing, where the team was warmly welcomed by Zhou Enlai himself. This "Ping Pong diplomacy" helped pave the way for a secret visit to Beijing that summer by President Nixon's national security advisor (and later secretary of State) Henry Kissinger, followed by a dramatic announcement from Nixon himself that he would soon visit China. Later that year the United Nations recognized Communist China, giving it the seat previously held by the Nationalists on Taiwan.

Nixon's visit to China in February 1972, parts of which were televised around the world, featured meetings with Zhou and Mao, attendance at banquets and a ballet, a presidential trip to China's Great Wall, and a joint statement pledging both sides to work for improved relations. The visit did not, however, result at once in formal relations between the two countries, since the Chinese insisted that America first break relations with Taiwan. Only in January 1979, when America finally did so (while continuing military and economic support for Taiwan), were full diplomatic relations established between the United States and the People's Republic.

Deepening Soviet-China split marked by bloody border clashes

Communist China opens dialogue with America and gains U.N. seat

China hosts U.S. president, and later establishes diplomatic relations

China After Mao: Economic Freedom, Political Repression

By then the People's Republic had new leaders. In 1976 Zhou Enlai and Mao Zedong both died, and a new power struggle arose between radicals and moderates. Led by Mao's widow Jiang Qing (*jē-AHNG CHING*), a group of radicals, later called the **Gang of Four**, sought to seize power and renew the Cultural Revolution. They were defeated and imprisoned by moderates under Deng Xiaoping (*DUNG shē-YOW PING*), an aging pragmatist who had survived the Long March (Chapter 32). Deng had worked to restore the economy after the Great Leap Forward, but then was denounced as a "capitalist road" follower and expelled from leadership during the Great Proletarian Cultural Revolution. Back in power as vice premier in 1977, Deng ran the country through his protégés, whom he placed at the head of the government and the Communist Party.

Nixon in China.

Deng and his protégés gradually liberalized the economy. Breaking with Mao's radical collectivism, they allowed small profit-oriented private businesses, experimented with free enterprise in special economic zones, and sent Chinese students abroad to study business, science, and technology in Japan, America, and Europe. Using capitalist-style incentives and claiming it was "glorious" to "get rich," the regime allowed peasants to farm small family plots and sell what they produced in open markets. China's new leaders also patched up relations with the USSR, while continuing to woo the West with prospects of lucrative trade—even as they flooded global markets with inexpensive shoes, toys, bikes, watches, and clothes, made in Chinese factories using low-cost Chinese labor. These efforts increased China's stability and prosperity, tripling average family income by the 1990s.

Deng and pragmatists liberalize economy and pursue global trade

But the moderates did not bring China freedom or democracy. After initially easing repression, Deng and his comrades in the 1980s faced growing demands for greater democratization. These demands increased until spring 1989, when idealistic students staged mass demonstrations in Beijing's vast Tiananmen Square, calling for more democracy and less corruption. Fearing that such demonstrations could trigger mass unrest, the leaders chose to suppress them. On June 4, 1989, the regime trucked in troops from the provinces, used tanks and artillery to clear the square, and killed hundreds, if not thousands, of demonstrators.

Tiananmen Square Massacre reinforces political repression

The Tiananmen Square Massacre shocked the world, but it did no long-term damage to China's economy or foreign trade. Eager to exploit the massive market of more than a billion Chinese, the West concluded that sanctions against China would do more harm than good. Even after Deng Xiaoping died in 1997 at age 92, his colleagues continued to combine economic liberalization with political repression. Under Jiang Zemin (*jē-AHNG zuh-MIN*), president of the People's Republic from 1993 to 2003, China expanded its domestic market economy and international trade, while sternly suppressing dissent.

Chinese pragmatists suppress dissent while liberalizing commerce

By the early twenty-first century, then, China had achieved both political stability and economic growth. Its great urban centers sported skyscrapers, traffic congestion, air pollution, countless cell phone users, and a wide array of businesses large and small. Not everyone shared the new prosperity: party officials and their families grew rich through commercial connections, but workers in some businesses lost their jobs due to capitalist competition, and peasants in remote areas still lived in great poverty. Gender disparities resurfaced, as parents seeking to improve family incomes pulled daughters out of school to work in Chinese industry, where they were less likely than men to be promoted and more apt to be laid off. The new China had become a modern economic power, but it scarcely resembled the egalitarian peasant socialist society envisioned by Mao Zedong.

The old and the new in Shanghai, China.

The Agonies of Southeast Asia and Indonesia

South of China, upheavals also marked the postwar era in the former French colony of Indochina, embracing Vietnam, Laos, and Cambodia, and in the former Dutch East Indies, now called Indonesia. As people in these regions sought freedom from foreign rule, their efforts were entangled in the global Cold War struggle between communism and capitalism, spawning wars, rebellions, and genocide. Only after the Cold War's end did these lands achieve some stability.

Vietminh, France, and the First Indochina War

Indochina's strife was rooted in the era of French colonial rule, lasting from the mid-1800s until World War II. During this era, France governed the masses of Buddhist village farmers through an elite minority of urban, French-educated, Vietnamese Catholics. An independence movement aimed at ending French rule arose, led by a Vietnamese nationalist who took the name Ho Chi Minh ("he who brings enlightenment").

Ho Chi Minh fights to free Indochina from France and then Japan

As a young man, after leaving Vietnam to work as a cook on a steamship, Ho Chi Minh traveled widely and lived for six years in France. There, dismayed by France's refusal to give colonists the same rights as French citizens and attracted by the anti-imperialism of Russia's Marxist leaders, he became communist. After sojourns in the USSR and China, he returned to Vietnam, where in 1930 he formed the Indochinese Communist Party. In 1941, as Japan occupied Indochina, Ho joined other nationalists to form a coalition called **Vietminh**, the Vietnamese Independence Brotherhood League, which then conducted guerrilla war against Japanese occupation forces. As described at the start of this chapter, on the day Japan surrendered to the Allies in September 1945, Ho Chi Minh proclaimed independence for Vietnam.

France tries to restore imperial rule after World War II

But France had other ideas. Eager to restore their national pride and great power status, undermined by four years of German occupation (1940–1944), the French sought to resurrect their old colonial empire. Needing a strong France to counter Soviet power in Europe, Britain and America tacitly supported this effort.

Vietminh forces defeat France in First Indochina War

The result was the First Indochina War (1946–1954), a debilitating conflict between the French and Vietminh. The Vietminh commander, former history teacher and gifted strategist Vo Nguyen Giap (*VŌ 'n-GIH-un z'YAHP*), used guerrilla tactics to wear down the French until he had amassed, with Chinese help, a sizable, well-equipped army. Then, in spring 1954, as the French wearied of war, he trapped and defeated them in northern Indochina at a place called Dien Bien Phu (*dē-YEN bē-YEN FOO*) (Map 35.5).

Geneva Accords split Indochina into Laos, Cambodia, North Vietnam, and South Vietnam

Meanwhile, French leaders met in Geneva, Switzerland, with Indochinese delegates and key officials from Britain, America, the USSR, and China in talks aimed at ending the Indochina War. In July 1954, they produced the **Geneva Accords**, an agreement to end French rule in Indochina and divide the former colony into Laos, Cambodia, North Vietnam, and South Vietnam. Laos and Cambodia would have neutral regimes, aligned with neither the communist East nor the capitalist West. North Vietnam would be ruled by Vietminh (led by Ho Chi Minh and the communists), and South Vietnam would soon have an anticommunist Catholic president named Ngo Dinh Diem (*'n-GŌ DIN dē-YEM*). But Vietnam's partition into North and South was meant to be temporary: the Geneva Accords called for elections in 1956 to unite the country.

Those elections, however, were not held. The United States, fearing that Vietminh's prestige and popularity would ensure its victory, thus bringing all Vietnam under communist rule, backed efforts by Ngo Dinh Diem to prevent the vote. Anxious to counter communism, the United States opted to prevent elections the communists might win. America thus became the main supporter of an unpopular and increasingly dictatorial South Vietnamese regime.

Vietnam, America, and the Second Indochina War

Diem's regime, moreover, was neither strong nor stable. By relying on colonial structures the French had created and giving government jobs to the Catholic minority, Diem alienated both nationalists and Buddhists. Taking advantage of Diem's unpopularity, communists in South Vietnam formed a nationalist coalition called the National Liberation Front and guerrilla units called **Viet Cong**. By 1963, South Vietnam was in chaos, with Viet Cong leading a full-fledged insurgency against Ngo Dinh Diem, and with Buddhist monks burning themselves to death on city streets to protest his repressive rule.

The Americans, having formerly supported Diem with military aid and advisors, finally conspired against him with his army, which killed him in November 1963. South Vietnam thus came under military rule, but even the army could not restore stability.

Capitalizing on the chaos, in 1964 communist North Vietnam started sending armed units south to support the Viet Cong. That same year, in the nearby Gulf of Tonkin, U.S. surveillance ships reported being shot at by North Vietnamese patrol boats. Although North Vietnam denied these reports, which were never verified, the U.S. Congress passed a Gulf of Tonkin Resolution authorizing President Lyndon Johnson to take "all necessary measures . . . to prevent further aggression." It turned out to be a license to wage war. As American forces arrived the next year in large numbers, South Vietnam's insurgency became an international conflict.

For several years the war intensified, as America sent more and more troops while North Vietnam, supplied with arms and aid by the Soviets and Chinese, funneled in forces along the "Ho Chi Minh Trail," a crude network of pathways through neutral Laos and Cambodia (Map 35.5). Advanced American weapons and mass bombing, exceeding all the firepower used in World War II, caused extensive damage and countless casualties but failed to crush the communists.

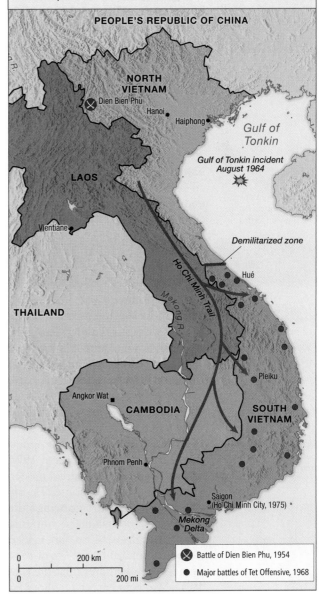

Map 35.5 Vietnam, Laos, and Cambodia, 1954–1975

After France lost the First Indochina War (1946–1954), its Indochina colony was divided into North Vietnam, South Vietnam, Laos, and Cambodia. Note, however, that despite massive U.S. military support for South Vietnam, North Vietnam won the Vietnam War (1964–1975) and united all Vietnam under communist control. How did these developments help bring communists to power in Laos and Cambodia?

PEOPLE'S REPUBLIC OF CHINA

NORTH VIETNAM
Dien Bien Phu
Hanoi
Haiphong
Gulf of Tonkin
Gulf of Tonkin incident August 1964

LAOS
Vientiane
Demilitarized zone
Ho Chi Minh Trail
Hué
Mekong R.
THAILAND
Pleiku
Angkor Wat
CAMBODIA
SOUTH VIETNAM
Phnom Penh
Saigon (Ho Chi Minh City, 1975)
Mekong Delta

0   200 km
0   200 mi

⊗ Battle of Dien Bien Phu, 1954
● Major battles of Tet Offensive, 1968

U.S. soldiers in
Vietnam.

Then, in early 1968, communist commander Vo Nguyen Giap surprised the Americans with simultaneous attacks throughout South Vietnam during celebrations of the Lunar New Year, known in Vietnam as *Tet*. Militarily this **Tet Offensive** was a failure for North Vietnam, as U.S. forces soon regained all the ground taken in the initial attacks. But the offensive undermined American morale. Stunned that the battered communists could launch a major assault, and shocked by televised images of the violence, Americans concluded that victory was not in sight, as their leaders had claimed. In March, his credibility shaken, President Johnson announced he would not seek reelection. The spring and summer of 1968 were marked by antiwar protests and violence across the United States (Chapter 34). In November, Americans elected a new president, Richard Nixon, who promised an honorable end to the Vietnam War.

Nixon initiated **Vietnamization**, a process that transferred the fighting to South Vietnam's army, while gradually withdrawing U.S. troops and negotiating with the North. But he also enlarged the conflict into a Second Indochina War, invading Cambodia in 1970 to destroy bases and supply lines used by communist forces in South Vietnam. In 1972, when negotiations stalled, he renewed massive bombing of North Vietnam. Nixon's tactics achieved his goal, an agreement with North Vietnam, signed in Paris in January 1973, suspending the conflict and providing for withdrawal of all U.S. forces.

But Nixon's tactics also left the region in chaos. In 1974, with the Americans gone, North Vietnam again began sending forces south, and in early 1975 it launched an all-out offensive. By April the communists had conquered the South, uniting Vietnam under their rule. That same year communist regimes took power in Laos and Cambodia, ending the Second Indochina War.

The Cambodian Catastrophe

But Southeast Asia's agony did not end. In 1975, Cambodia's new ruling communist party, the **Khmer Rouge** (*kuh-MER ROOZH*), or "Red Khmer" (Khmer is the ethnicity to which most Cambodians belong), launched a radical mass campaign inspired by China's Great Proletarian Cultural Revolution. Led by Pol Pot, a Maoist fanatic determined to create an agrarian communist society, the Khmer Rouge sought to de-urbanize Cambodia, seizing city dwellers at gunpoint and herding them to the countryside to work the fields. Urban professionals, including bankers, lawyers, doctors, teachers, and others who dared resist, were executed en masse, while thousands more died of overwork and starvation. Over the next few years, according to outside estimates, up to two million of Cambodia's seven million people may have died in this genocidal slaughter.

Then Cambodia's catastrophe became more complex. Taking advantage of the chaos, communist Vietnam in 1978 invaded communist Cambodia, replacing Pol Pot's Khmer Rouge regime with a moderate communist state called the People's Republic of Kampuchea (*KAHM-poo-CHĒ-uh*), the local ethnic name for Cambodia. But in 1979, alarmed by Vietnam's growing influence, communist China invaded communist Vietnam to punish it for invading communist Cambodia.

China's invasion was brief. Vietnam's army, with battle-tested troops and modern weapons supplied by Soviets or captured from Americans, rebuffed the Chinese forces. The Chinese soon withdrew, but their invasion heartened Pol Pot and others opposing Cambodia's new regime, many of whom had fled to neighboring Thailand. These assorted rebels, including Khmer Rouge and other Cambodian nationalists, conducted civil war against Cambodia's Vietnam-backed regime throughout the 1980s. Displaying both the complexity and cynicism of Cold War politics, communist Russia and communist Vietnam supported the Cambodian regime, while their main foes—communist China and capitalist America—backed the Cambodian rebels, including the murderous Khmer Rouge.

In the early 1990s, when the United Nations negotiated a truce and sent in peacekeepers, Cambodia finally regained some stability. Following national elections in 1993, it officially became a constitutional monarchy under King Norodom Sihanouk (*SĒ-uh-NOOK*), who had fled Cambodia before the 1970 U.S. invasion. In 1997, repudiated even by former supporters, Pol Pot was arrested and convicted of treason; he died the next year under house arrest. Cambodia's nightmare seemed to be over at last.

U.N. truce and elections finally stabilize Cambodia

Indonesia Between East and West

Indonesia, the three-thousand-mile-long island chain to the south of Indochina, also experienced both European imperialism and Japanese occupation. Before World War II, as the Dutch East Indies, it was exploited for its spices, coffee, oil, and rubber. After the war, led by a romantic revolutionary nationalist named Sukarno, it became an independent nation, buffeted between East and West.

Sukarno, the "father of modern Indonesia," was a poor schoolteacher's son who completed a degree in civil engineering before founding the Indonesian Nationalist Party in 1927. A compelling speaker whose outlook on life combined nationalism, Islam, and Marxism with Indonesian mysticism and magic, he sought to blend these incompatible ideals into an independence movement through the power of his own personality. Imprisoned and later exiled by the Dutch, he returned to his homeland in 1942 to serve as an advisor to the Japanese, who had occupied Indonesia, while urging them in vain to grant his people independence. When the war ended in 1945, Sukarno declared Indonesia independent. The Dutch sought to reassert control, but after four years of futile fighting they gave up, and in 1949 Indonesia became an independent republic (Map 35.6).

Sukarno leads Indonesia to independence from Dutch

Sukarno and his revolutionary colleague, Muhammad Yamin, formulated the **Panca Sila**, or Five Pillars, as the basis for the development of independent Indonesia. Similar in some ways to Sun Yixian's *Three Principles of the People* (Chapter 32), Panca Sila tried to unify Indonesian peoples on a foundation of nationalism, internationalism, government by popular consent, social justice, and belief in one God. Panca Sila, however, could not transcend the differences among Muslim and Christians, rich and poor, and Indonesia's numerous ethnicities. Genuine national unity thus eluded Indonesia, as deep-seated poverty and religious tensions continued for decades to cause widespread suffering.

Pro-Sukarno rally, Indonesia.

In foreign affairs, like India's Nehru, Sukarno emerged as a leader of the nonaligned nations, rejecting alliance with either East or West. In 1955, at the Indonesian city of Bandung (*BAHN-doong*), he hosted a conference of 29 nations, mostly from Asia and Africa, that likewise identified with neither the Western capitalist world nor the Soviet bloc. In a stirring speech, Sukarno used Indonesia's cultural and religious diversity as a model for how new nations, emerging from colonial control, could put aside their differences and unite to advance common interests. Eventually, however, attracted by Soviet aid, Sukarno led his nation into the Soviet camp. This abandonment of nonalignment

Sukarno first joins non-aligned nations, then sides with Soviets

Map 35.6 East and South Asia in the Early Twenty-First Century

By the early twenty-first century, virtually all of East and South Asia had gained freedom from foreign domination, and many of its nations had attained some stability and prosperity. Note, however, that serious tensions persisted in North Korea, Pakistan, Indonesia, and elsewhere, that millions of Asians remained very poor, and that a catastrophic tsunami off the Indonesian coast killed over 200 thousand people in 2004. What factors contributed to Asia's increasing prosperity? What factors help to explain the persistence of poverty amidst this growing prosperity?

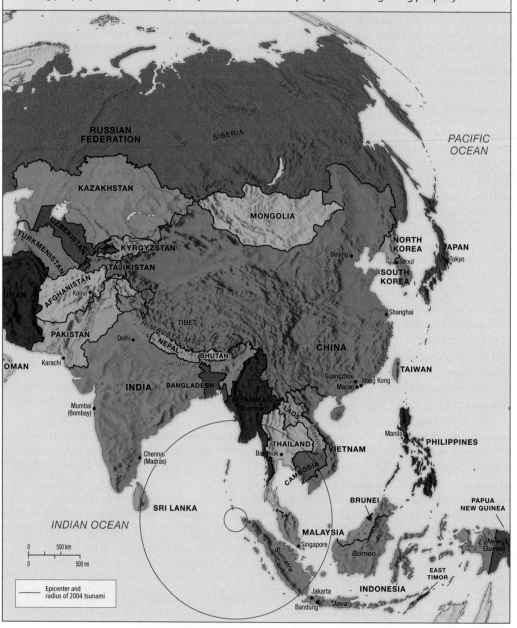

enmeshed Indonesia in the Cold War and made Sukarno an enemy of the United States, while his new ally, the USSR, considered Indonesia relatively unimportant and invested few resources there.

Sukarno's policies thus led Indonesia into a dead end. Between 1965 and 1967, a military strongman named General Suharto turned the country around, launching a violent anticommunist crusade that killed more than 300 thousand people and filled Indonesia's rivers with headless corpses. Suharto ousted Sukarno in 1967, then ruled for three decades as a staunch pro-Western and anti-Soviet dictator. The Western democracies overlooked his regime's corruption and repression.

Suharto ousts Sukarno and leads brutal pro-Western dictatorship

By the 1990s, however, the Cold War was over, the USSR was gone, and the aging dictator was in trouble. With 200 million people, his nation was the world's fourth most populous country. But despite Indonesia's rich resources and economic potential, most of its people lived in poverty and resented the vast wealth amassed by Suharto and his family. Concerned by the growing popularity of Islamist fundamentalism (Chapter 37), Suharto reached out to Muslims, making the pilgrimage to Mecca in 1990 and periodically visiting the tombs of Indonesian Muslim saints. But in return he expected Muslims to accept clear separation between religion and his government, a distinction rejected by Islamist fundamentalists. In 1996 he repressed violent protests by students and Islamic leaders. Then an Asian financial crisis the next year undermined the Indonesian economy, and in 1998 a popular uprising forced Suharto to step down.

Muslim protests and financial crises finally force Suharto out

In 1999 a new government was elected democratically, but ongoing unrest, as well as regional tensions between Christians and Muslims, quickly undermined it. Two years later, Indonesia's assembly replaced the country's president with Megawati Sukarnoputri, the legendary Sukarno's daughter. After Pakistan's Benazir Bhutto, she was the second woman to lead a modern Muslim nation—and the world's most populous Muslim nation at that.

As president, however, Megawati Sukarnoputri faced numerous problems, including a weak economy and an armed Islamist rebellion in the northwest. In 2002 a terrorist car bomb exploded at a nightclub on the Indonesian island of Bali, killing more than two hundred people and injuring at least three hundred others. In 2003, resolving to stabilize her country, she launched an all-out military attack on the Islamist rebels, but in September of 2004, faced with widespread unemployment and charges of corruption, she was voted out of office. Three months later a massive undersea earthquake off the country's western coast unleashed a colossal tsunami (Map 35.6) that killed more than 200 thousand Indonesians and wrecked many coastal cities on the island of Sumatra. Rich in resources and diversity, but plagued by poverty and problems, twenty-first century Indonesia faced a promising but challenging future.

Poverty, terrorism, and a deadly tsunami add to Indonesian instability

Changes in Asian Societies

Sweeping economic and social changes accompanied Asia's upheavals in the wake of World War II. Eager to escape foreign domination by acquiring wealth and power, Asian nations expanded their industry and technology, exploiting Cold War rivalries to get aid from the Soviets or from the West. Industry and technology fostered urbanization, as millions of Asians moved from rural villages to industrial cities. These transitions in turn brought changes in family and gender roles, presenting new challenges and opportunities for Asian societies.

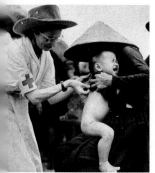

Inoculation of Asian
child in the 1950s.

Industry, Technology, Population, and Urbanization

In the decades after World War II, aware that industry, technology, and commerce had brought wealth and power to the West, Asian nations sought to expand in these areas. At first the Cold War aided their efforts: eager to support Asian friends, Americans provided Japan, Taiwan, and South Korea with economic assistance and access to Western markets, while Soviets aided India and initially Communist China. In time, however, Asians developed their own economic approaches, typically combining market capitalism with central government planning.

Japan led the way with this approach, creating by the 1970s an economic powerhouse that was the envy of Asia. By the 1980s Taiwan and South Korea had imitated Japan's success. After abandoning Mao's disastrous anti-urban experiments, China, too, achieved substantial economic growth by blending central state control with open market incentives, while India used a similar combination to attain global leadership in electronics and computer technology.

Meanwhile modern medicines and inoculations, increasingly available to ordinary Asians, helped accelerate Asian population growth. Death rates declined markedly, especially among children, while traditional Asian preference for large families initially kept birth rates high. Eventually government efforts to promote smaller families, such as China's rigorous "one child per family" campaign, reduced birth rates through contraception and abortion, combined with economic incentives for limiting family size. Despite such efforts, however, Asia's population more than doubled in the second half of the twentieth century, from under 1.5 billion in 1950 to over 3.5 billion in 2000—by which time nearly 60 percent of the earth's people lived in Asia.

The attraction of the large cities, which offered not only industrial jobs but also educational and cultural opportunities, combined with population growth to promote mass urbanization. Tens of millions of Asians moved from rural villages to large urban areas, despite the anti-urban efforts of Mao Zedong and Pol Pot. Millions of the new city-dwellers found jobs in industry and commerce; but since there were not enough such jobs to go around, millions of others joined a vast urban underclass of destitute people dwelling in sordid slums and shanties. Yet the mass migrations to the cities continued, as percentages of Asians in urban areas tripled, from under 15 percent in 1945 to roughly 50 percent by the early twenty-first century—by which time Asia had at least eight cities with metropolitan populations exceeding ten million people.

Rural Asia also experienced great changes. Policies promoted by both capitalist and communist regimes, for example, gave land to small farmers, curtailing such traditional practices as tenant farming and absentee landlordism. Fast-growing, high-yield "miracle rice," developed in the 1960s, together with synthetic fertilizers, vastly expanded the output of Asian farmers, accelerating the Green Revolution. In time village life was also enhanced by more and more clinics and schools, while new technologies, such as radios, televisions, and wireless phones, connected even small remote settlements with the outside world.

Changing Family and Gender Roles

Asia's upheavals also affected the traditional Asian family. The partition of India and Pakistan, wars in Korea and Vietnam, and violent mass campaigns in China and Cambodia tore apart millions of families, destroying their homes, dividing their loyalties, and

Asian populations increase greatly despite efforts to curb growth

Asian cities grow rapidly as people seek urban jobs

High-yield crops and new technologies begin to transform rural Asia

Urbanization undermines traditional Asian families

causing mass dislocation. But urban growth played an even more disruptive and transformative role. For when rural Asian families moved to cities, they frequently did so in stages, with one spouse moving first to find employment, then often living there alone for a time and sending money back to the village. Since whole clans rarely moved to the city at once, large extended families, long dominant in villages, typically gave way to smaller nuclear families in cities. Government birth control programs, along with urban crowding, also led city couples to keep families small.

Childbirth education in southern Asia.

In cities, moreover, new institutions assumed many of the family's traditional roles. In cities, for example, education meant public schools teaching academic subjects (such as calculating, reading, and writing), rather than families passing on practical skills (such as farming, carpentry, spinning, and weaving) as in the traditional village. In cities, care for the sick and elderly was supplied by public clinics and government pension programs rather than by the family. In cities, social discipline was furnished by courts and police, who punished offenses (such as loitering or urinating in public) that were not crimes in the village, where heads of families resolved conflicts and punished offenders. In cities, recreation occurred at public settings such as taverns, teahouses, movies, concerts, and sporting events, while in villages it often meant visiting with one's extended family. In cities, worship took place at temples, or did not take place at all (especially in communist countries where religion was discouraged), while in villages it typically occurred at family shrines. Urbanization thus diminished the family's role in many Asian people's lives.

Urban institutions, schools, and clinics take on traditional family roles

Urbanization also affected traditional gender roles. When men moved to the city to find jobs, their wives often stayed behind to run the household, and thus grew accustomed to heading the family by the time they rejoined their husbands. When women moved to the city to find jobs, they acquired greater independence and gained a new status as family wage earners by sending money they earned back to the village. When families were reunited, men often tried to reassert their family authority, sometimes reacting to their reduced status by abusing their wives and children. But traditional patriarchal dominance nonetheless gradually waned.

In the meantime, Asian women acquired political and civil rights, along with greater reproductive and economic freedom. Political reforms in most Asian countries gave women the right to vote, along with legal rights and educational opportunities that in theory (though often not in practice) made them equal to men. Access to government-provided contraceptives and abortions also helped women control the timing of pregnancies and family size. Economic pressures to enhance family income, combined with exposure to Western media depicting women in professional roles, encouraged Asian women to seek jobs outside the home and even to pursue careers in such areas as business, medicine, and law.

Asian women gain legal rights and greater economic opportunities

Asian women did not, however, gain full equality with men. In most Asian societies, women who worked outside the home, often with lower pay and less potential for advancement than men, were still expected to fulfill traditional roles in the household, and even in the workplace. In Japanese corporations, for example, women were often expected to serve tea to male executives, while female political leaders were rare in Japan, Korea, and Taiwan. Elsewhere in Asia, however, talented and ambitious women—such as Indira and Sonia Gandhi in India, Benazir Bhutto in Pakistan, Jiang Qing in China, and Megawati Sukarnoputri in Indonesia—played very prominent and highly visible roles.

Many Asian women still treated as subordinate by men

In villages across Asia, patriarchal attitudes persisted. In many cases parents still arranged marriages, the bride's family still supplied a dowry, and wives were still seen as their husband's property. On occasion, as in times gone by, an Indian or Pakistani husband who was unhappy with his wife might abuse or even kill her so he could seek a new wife. By the late twentieth century, however, such practices had become increasingly rare.

Sometimes practices intended as progressive, when combined with traditional patriarchal attitudes, had unintended results. In China, for example, the "one child per family" program and ready access to abortion, combined with the age-old preference for male children and new technologies that can identify sex before birth, led many families to abort girls or sell their newborn daughters on the black market. A gender imbalance thus developed among Chinese children, with boys outnumbering girls in some places by 10 percent or more. Illegal commercial networks sold many orphaned Chinese girls into domestic servitude or urban prostitution.

Still, despite the resilience of some traditional attitudes and behaviors, the transformation of Asian societies was profound. By the early twenty-first century, instead of living in villages in patriarchal families and producing their own food and goods, most Asians lived in urban areas in small nuclear families and worked for wages with which they bought food and goods. Asia's upheavals and urbanization had brought mass trauma and distress, but Asians in the process had acquired new wealth, new technologies, new outlooks and attitudes, and new ways of life.

Indian women receiving military training.

Chapter Review

Putting It in Perspective

In the decades after World War II, global connections contributed to conflicts in Asia, as efforts to gain independence from the West and implement new ideals, combined with Cold War ideologies and tensions, produced dramatic and often violent upheavals. The bloody partitioning of India, Mao's catastrophic mass campaigns in China, disastrous wars in Korea and Indochina, deadly repressions and revolts in Indonesia, and Pol Pot's genocidal policies in Cambodia killed many millions of people and shattered millions of lives. Rapid transformation from rural to urban societies created mass dislocation, disrupting and altering traditional family and gender roles.

Eventually, however, global connections helped Asian nations gain varying degrees of stability and prosperity. Japan and South Korea flourished, capitalizing on global commerce by blending market capitalism with central state planning. India used Soviet and Western aid, modern agricultural science, and global leadership in electronic technology to reduce poverty and instability. China, after years of

disastrous turmoil, achieved stability and economic growth by combining authoritarian governance with open market incentives and global trade. By the early twenty-first century, although population growth and regional hostilities continued to cloud Asian horizons, Asia's growing political and economic strength suggested that Asians may well have largely put their upheavals behind them.

Reviewing Key Material
KEY CONCEPTS

nonaligned nations, 911	Viet Cong, 927
Green Revolution, 912	Tet Offensive, 927
Red Guards, 922	Vietnamization, 928
Gang of Four, 924	Khmer Rouge, 928
Vietminh, 926	Panca Sila, 929
Geneva Accords, 926	

KEY PEOPLE

Ho Chi Minh, 908, 926	Benazir Bhutto, 913
Jawaharlal Nehru, 910	Pervez Musharraf, 913
Indira Gandhi, 912	Douglas MacArthur, 913
Rajiv Gandhi, 912	Jiang Jieshi (Chiang
Sonia Gandhi, 912	Kaishek), 916
Zulfikar Ali Bhutto, 913	Lin Biao, 916

ASK YOURSELF

1. How were each of the major Asian nations affected by the rivalry between communism and capitalism during the Cold War? Why did the Cold War have such a devastating impact on Asia?

2. Why was British India divided into two separate countries when it gained independence in 1947? Why was there so much ongoing hostility between India and Pakistan?

3. What combination of factors made possible Japan's economic miracle? How did each of the other Asian nations seek to imitate Japan's success?

4. What was Mao Zedong's vision for China, and how did he seek to implement it? Why did his efforts to implement his vision fail, and why were they so traumatic for China?

5. How did technology, urbanization, and population growth impact traditional family and gender roles in Asia? Why was this impact so profound?

GOING FURTHER

Baxter, C. *Bangladesh: From a Nation to a State*. 1997.

Beeson, M., ed. *Contemporary Southeast Asia*. 2004.

Benson, Linda. *China Since 1949*. 2002.

Bhasin, K., et al., eds. *Against All Odds: Essays on Women, Religion and Development from India and Pakistan*. 1994.

Borthwick, Mark, ed. *Pacific Century*. 1992.

Brass, P. *The New Cambridge History of India: The Politics of Independence*. 1990.

Brown, Judith. *Nehru*. 1999.

Cummings, B. *Korea's Place in the Sun*. 1997.

Dreyer, June T. *China's Political System*. 5th ed. 2005.

Ebrey, Patricia B., et al. *East Asia: A Cultural, Social, and Political History*. 2006.

Evans, R. *Deng Xiaoping and the Making of Modern China*. 1993.

Fitzgerald, F. *Fire in the Lake*. 1970.

Gamer, R. E. *Understanding Contemporary China*. 2002.

Ganguly, S., ed. *South Asia*. 2006.

Gordon, A. *Postwar Japan as History*. 1993.

Hardgrave, R. and S. Kochanek. *India: Government and Politics*. 1986.

Harrison, S., et al. *India and Pakistan: The First 50 Years*. 1999.

Jones, H., *Indonesia: The Possible Dream*. 1971.

Karnow, S. *Vietnam: A History*. 2nd ed. 1997.

Kaufman, B. *The Korean War*. 1986.

Kingsbury, D. *Southeast Asia: A Political Profile*. 2nd ed. 2005.

Kingston, J. *Japan in Transformation, 1952–2000*. 2001.

Lee Feigon. *China Rising: The Meaning of Tiananmen*. 1990.

Liang Heng and J. Shapiro. *After the Revolution*. 1986.

McCargo, D. *Contemporary Japan*. 2nd ed. 2004.

Meisner, M. *Mao's China, and After*. 1986.

Merrill, John. *Korea: The Peninsular Origins of the War*. 1989.

Neher, C. *Southeast Asia: Crossroads of the World*. 2nd ed. 2005.

Olson, J., and R. Roberts. *Where the Domino Fell: America and Vietnam, 1945–1995*. 4th ed. 2004.

Reischauer, E., and M. Jansen. *The Japanese Today*. 2nd ed. 2004.

SarDesai, D. *Southeast Asia: Past and Present*. 2nd ed. 1989.

Schirokauer, C., and D. Clark. *Modern East Asia*. 2004.

Schoppa, R. K. *Revolution and Its Past: Identities and Change in Modern Chinese History*. 2nd ed. 2006.

Shaplen, R. *Bitter Victory*. 1986.

Spence, J. *Mao Zedong*. 1999.

Spence, J. *The Search for Modern China*. 1990.

Steinberg, D. *In Search of Southeast Asia*. 2nd ed. 1985.

Stueck, W., ed. *The Korean War in World History*. 2004.

Tao Jie et al., eds. *Holding Up Half the Sky: Chinese Women Past, Present, and Future*. 2004.

Terrill, R. *The New Chinese Empire*. 2003.

Tinker, H. *South Asia: A Short History*. 1990.

Vatikiotis, M. *Indonesian Politics Under Suharto*. 1993.

Vickers, A. *A History of Modern Indonesia*. 2005.

Wasserstrom, J., and E. Perry, eds., *Popular Protest and Political Culture in Modern China*. 2nd ed. 1994.

Key Dates and Developments

1945–1952	U.S. occupation of Japan
1946–1949	Chinese Civil War and communist victory
1946–1954	First Indochina War
1947	Independence and division of India and Pakistan
1949	Independence of Indonesia
1950–1953	Korean War
1958–1960	Great Leap Forward in China
1960–1963	Split between China and USSR
1964–1975	Vietnam War/Second Indochina War
1966–1969	Great Proletarian Cultural Revolution in China
1969	Border wars between China and USSR
1971	Independence of Bangladesh from Pakistan

1972	Nixon's visit to China
1973	U.S. withdrawal from Vietnam
1975–1977	Cambodian genocide
1978–1997	Deng Xiaoping's economic reforms in China
1984	Assassination of Indira Gandhi in India
1989	Tiananmen Square Massacre in China
1998	Testing of nuclear weapons by India and Pakistan
2000	Meeting of North and South Korean leaders
2004	Tsunami devastates Indonesia and much of southern Asia
2005	North Korea claims to have developed nuclear weapons
2007	Assassination of Benazir Bhutto in Pakistan

CHAPTER 36

Reform and Revolution in Latin America, 1914–Present

- Latin America and the World Since 1914

- Democracy and Dictatorship in Latin America

- Six Regional Transitions

- Chapter Review

Juan And Evita Perón

Juan and Evita Perón ride through Buenos Aires in June 1951. Evita is wearing her trademark mink coat to ward off the chill of the Argentinian winter. The Peróns were Latin America's ultimate power couple, the most skillful politicians Argentina had ever seen (page 949).

Salvador Allende (*eye-YEHN-dā*), president of Chile, entered his office at the Moneda Palace in Santiago at 6 a.m. Tuesday, September 11, 1973. That was an unusually early arrival for a man who customarily handled paperwork until late in the evening, but this was an unusual day. A military conspiracy was attempting to overthrow his freely elected Marxist government, and Allende wanted to organize resistance as rapidly as possible. By late morning, however, planes were bombing the palace, tanks were clearing the streets of the government's defenders, and the conspirators were offering Allende safe passage out of the country. The president chose instead to remain at his post, and shortly after 2 p.m., as infantry began to storm the palace, Salvador Allende committed suicide, using a pistol given him by Cuba's president Fidel Castro.

Latin America

Allende's death was only the beginning of the Chilean tragedy. The military regime that replaced him turned Santiago's soccer stadium into a detention, torture, and execution center in the weeks following September 11. Opponents of the regime disappeared by the thousands. Political parties were abolished, the constitution was suspended, and Chilean democracy was extinguished. An authoritarian dictatorship clamped its iron fist around the throat of a nation that, at the outset of the twentieth century, had been widely considered a model of representative government. The explanation of these events is found not solely in Chile's domestic history but in the global situation to which Latin America was connected in the twentieth century.

Latin America and the World Since 1914

The principal nations of Latin America entered the twentieth century in varying stages of political and economic development. For each of them, the century's first four decades proved turbulent. World War II and the Cold War that followed it ended isolationism in the United States and made isolation unworkable throughout the Western Hemisphere. Quickly, every major nation of Latin America became part of a wider and more complex global system.

In the process, Latin American concerns were often subordinated to superpower rivalries. The United States supported brutal military dictatorships in Argentina, Brazil, and Chile in the 1960s and 1970s, largely out of fear that those countries would otherwise fall to international communism. The Soviet Union maintained close ties with Cuba, a communist regime after 1959, as a means of encouraging communist development in other Latin American states.

As the Cold War waned and eventually ended, so did many oppressive Latin American regimes that had been supported by either the United States or the Soviet Union. Argentina in 1983, Brazil in 1985, and Chile in 1990 all returned to democratic rule. But the fundamental problems of modernization, poverty, and inequality that had been ignored during the Cold War remained unsolved and largely unaddressed. In the final years of the twentieth century, they reemerged to present young democracies with daunting difficulties and to call into question the long-term stability of Latin America.

Connections: Latin America in the Global Economy

When Latin America won independence from Spain and Portugal in the 1820s, the new nations found it difficult to establish links to the world economy. Mexico emerged from the independence period economically devastated, while South American countries found that their remoteness from Europe reduced opportunities for transatlantic trade once the colonial connection was gone. Landowners and manufacturers responded by producing crops and goods for localities and regions rather than for foreign markets.

By 1900, however, the situation had changed dramatically. European industrialization rapidly increased demands for the resources and food that Latin America could provide. Coffee and rubber from Brazil, tin from Bolivia, copper and nitrates from Chile, sugar from Cuba, wheat and beef from Argentina, and wool from Argentina and Uruguay were shipped to Europe and the United States. In return, Latin Americans purchased large quantities of European-made clothing, tools, and machines. This developing commercial relationship stimulated foreign investment in Latin America, particularly in railways, roads, bridges, and mines. Foreign control of important sectors of the economy became a sensitive political issue in Mexico, Chile, Bolivia, Peru, and other nations in the opening years of the twentieth century.

Despite this concern, Latin America's integration into a global import-export economy led to rapid growth and prosperity. Brazilian and Argentine elites grew tremendously wealthy, and their investments in commercial enterprises attracted large numbers of immigrants from Europe to fill labor shortages. Immigration stimulated urbanization and the development of a working class committed to unionization. These immigrants remained excluded from political power because they could not vote until they became citizens, and citizenship, considered not a right but a privilege, was granted to very few. Political elites gained the support of the increasingly prosperous middle classes by granting them access to the political system. Then both upper and middle classes worked together to keep the working classes relatively powerless.

The Great Depression upset this comfortable collaboration. Global demand for Latin American commodities and foodstuffs declined drastically, ending decades of growth and undermining confidence in political leaders who failed to control the damage (Map 36.1). Middle-class citizens broke with upper-class political elites and supported military takeovers, which were attempted in eight Latin American nations between 1929 and 1933. Military and civilian governments alike tried to limit the impact of the Depression by promoting economic diversification through industrialization. If Latin American nations could produce more of their own industrial goods, the new governments reasoned, they would be less affected by global economic fluctuations. New industries would also provide additional manufacturing jobs for their urban working classes.

Countries with small domestic markets and economies built around the production of one or two commodities found industrialization difficult. These included the tin-centered

European industrialization stimulates Latin American economies

A coffee bar in Buenos Aires in 1950.

Latin America suffers during the Great Depression

FOUNDATION MAP 36.1 Commodity Production in South America, 1900

As the twentieth century began, South America's productivity made it a valuable trading partner with Europe, North America, and Asia. Notice the concentrations of commodities: rubber in the Amazon basin of Brazil, coffee in southern Brazil, cattle and sheep in Argentina and Uruguay. What factors account for such concentrations?

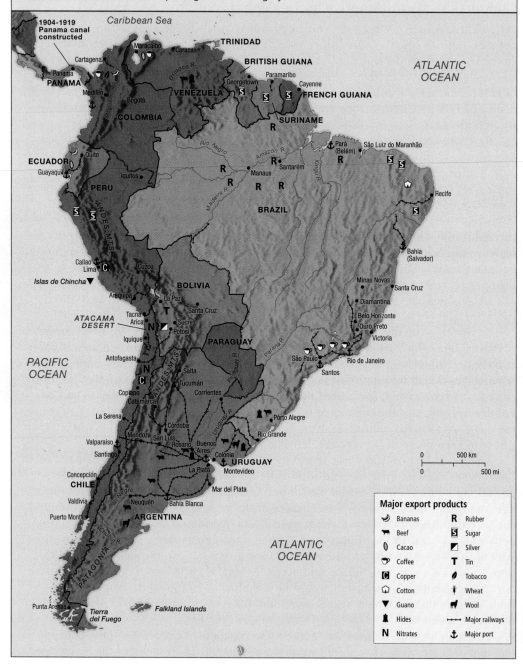

Major export products			
🍌	Bananas	R	Rubber
🍖	Beef	S	Sugar
🥥	Cacao	◣	Silver
☕	Coffee	T	Tin
C	Copper	◊	Tobacco
🏠	Cotton	⚱	Wheat
▼	Guano	🐄	Wool
🏺	Hides	••••	Major railways
N	Nitrates	⚓	Major port

economy of Bolivia, the coffee- and banana-based economies of Central America, and the oil-dominated economy of Venezuela. More diversified economies in nations with larger populations were more successful. Argentina, Brazil, and Mexico were able to manufacture their own products to replace those previously imported from Europe or the United States, while Chile applied industrial technologies to improve output in its copper and nitrate mines. As a result of the growing number and importance of these manufacturing jobs, the working classes became increasingly strong and assertive, forming labor unions and offering a new power base for populist politicians. Juan Perón in Argentina, Getúlio Vargas in Brazil, Arturo Alessandri in Chile, and Lázaro Cárdenas in Mexico all appealed to workers and created urban-based coalitions that competed for power with traditional agricultural and landed elites.

These populist leaders were unable, however, to build solid economies. By the 1960s Latin America was no longer completely dependent on fully industrialized nations, but it relied on them for some commodities and could be adversely affected by changes in the global economy over which it had no control. Machine tools and large capital equipment still had to be imported, and if global market prices of exports like copper, coffee, beef, and grain declined, so would Latin America's ability to pay for those imports. Increasing exports would only depress world prices and further reduce the region's ability to pay. When such developments occurred, industrial workers suffered greatly, and their unions responded to deteriorating economic conditions with strikes, demonstrations, and in Argentina and Uruguay, urban terrorism.

Populist leaders build urban coalitions

As public order came apart, military regimes took control in Brazil (1964), Chile (1973), and Argentina (1976). In itself, these developments were nothing new. Ever since Latin America won its independence, its military leaders had claimed and exercised the right to overthrow incompetent or corrupt civil governments. But these new regimes, unlike previous ones, did not act quickly to return power to civilians. Instead they abolished political parties and civil rights, imprisoned and tortured their political opponents, and based their continued control on their ability to restore economic prosperity. Excluding the working classes from political and economic influence, the military governments built partnerships with multinational corporations, refinanced their debts, and stimulated their economies by borrowing enormous sums abroad. Between 1970 and 1980, Latin America's foreign debt soared from $27 billion to $231 billion, with interest payments alone rising from $2 billion to $18 billion.

Loading coffee at a dock in Columbia.

Massive debt incapacitates Latin American economies

For a time refinancing and borrowing worked, and news of the Brazilian and Chilean "economic miracles" encouraged foreign banks to lend them even more money. But during the global economic downturn of 1980–1983, the debt-ridden nations found themselves caught between rising interest payments and a sharp reduction in export earnings. International lenders such as the World Bank and the International Monetary Fund offered help in refinancing massive debt, but only if the debtor nations reformed their economies, cut government expenditures, and welcomed additional foreign trade and global investment. Latin America accepted these conditions, but enormous sums flowed out of the region to repay the debt to the industrialized world, leading to a decade of declining economic output. Discredited military dictators retired and handed the debt problem over to civilian governments willing to accept political accountability and leave office once their terms expired. Though the debt problem remained unsolved, Latin America's connections to global financial markets were rebuilt.

Conflict: Latin America and Global War

When the Great War broke out in 1914, few Latin Americans thought their region would be affected. They assumed that the assassination of the Archduke and the crisis between Austria-Hungary and Serbia were European issues with no serious implications for the Western Hemisphere. But soon two battles took place nearby: in autumn 1914 the German Pacific Squadron defeated the British in a naval battle off Coronel, Chile, and then, on December 8, that squadron was destroyed by more British warships at the Battle of the Falkland Islands off the Argentine coast. More significantly, Britain's naval blockade of Germany, and Germany's retaliation by U-Boat warfare, made Atlantic shipping risky, especially for nations like Chile and Argentina, traditional suppliers of copper, nitrates, wheat, and beef to many European nations.

But the Great War did not seriously affect Latin America until the United States became a combatant in April 1917. After that, Brazil actively participated on the Allied side and earned a seat at the Paris Peace Conference in 1919. Chile's copper and nitrates found a willing buyer as the United States began expanding a small army into a huge force destined for battle in Europe. Chilean prosperity was intense but short lived: the end of the war in November 1918 also ended sizable United States orders for Chilean resources. Most other Latin American nations were relieved as the return to peacetime conditions in the Atlantic reestablished their access to European markets. In sum, the Great War left Latin America on the sidelines, permitting the region to avoid the trauma and death experienced in Europe and, to a lesser extent, in the Middle East and Africa.

European issues affect
Latin America

Two decades after the Armistice, the outbreak of World War II placed Latin America in a very different situation. During the 1930s, Germany and Italy demonstrated an interest in the Western Hemisphere. German money financed the Nacista Party in Chile, an imitation of the German National Socialist Party. Germany also underwrote nationalistic German organizations in cities with large German populations, such as São Paulo, Brazil, and Buenos Aires, Argentina, and, in the United States, New York, St. Louis, Cincinnati, and Milwaukee. Italy provided small sums of money and plenty of advice to the fascistic Integralista Party in Brazil. These activities had limited effects, but Nazi and fascist ideologies clearly threatened the entire Western Hemisphere.

Germany's aggression against Austria and Czechoslovakia in 1938 led the hemisphere's foreign ministers, meeting in Lima, Peru, to sign a declaration of hemispheric unity against subversion inside the hemisphere or invasion from outside. The outbreak of war in September 1939 led to a more extensive declaration, creating a neutrality zone extending 300 miles off the coasts of North and South America and providing for inter-American economic coordination. After France, Holland, and Denmark were conquered by Germany in 1940, their colonies in the West Indies and South America became potential bases for German attacks or sabotage against the Panama Canal. The United States was authorized by all hemispheric nations to establish a protectorate over those colonies.

Mexican workers help
the U.S. economy in
wartime

Japan's attack on Pearl Harbor brought the United States into the war, and most Latin American nations cooperated closely with their northern neighbor. Mexico sent a squadron of fighter pilots to fly in the Philippines in 1944, and 250 thousand Mexicans enlisted in the U.S. armed forces. Tens of thousands of *braceros*, or immigrant workers, entered the United States to work in factories in place of U.S. citizens called to active duty. Panama worked closely with the United States to protect the Panama Canal. Chile resumed its Great War role as a valued supplier of copper and nitrates. But the most significant Latin American roles in World War II were played by two South American powers that had long been rivals: Brazil and Argentina.

Brazil made several crucial contributions to the Allied war effort. Its government leased to the United States a large tract of land in Natal, where Brazil juts eastward into the South Atlantic, only 1,900 miles from West Africa. There the United States constructed a huge air base that by 1944 was the busiest in the world. Transatlantic air travel was impossible in World War II because of limited fuel capacities, so U.S. troops and cargo for the invasion of Europe were shuttled from air bases in the United States to Panama, then to Natal, then to West Africa, and then to England. In return for the leasing rights to Natal, the United States gave Brazil a complete steel plant, transplanted immediately after the war from western Pennsylvania to a site in southeastern Brazil named Volta Redonda. The Brazilian government then built South America's largest steel industry around it. Brazil also supplied the Allies with rubber, a vital raw material, after Japan took control of most of the world's rubber by occupying the sprawling rubber plantations of Southeast Asia.

In addition to these material contributions, Brazil played an active combat role in the war. When Germany declared war on the United States in December 1941, Washington had made no meaningful preparations to defend commercial shipping along the country's eastern seaboard. During the first five months of 1942, German U-Boats went unchallenged as they sunk U.S. ships. Brazil then sent its own submarines to patrol the seaboard and the Caribbean, freeing U.S. submarines for action against Japan. Brazilians also sent a 25 thousand–soldier infantry division into combat in Italy in 1944. The Brazilian Military Cemetery in central Italy testifies to the scale of Brazil's effort.

Brazil plays an active role in World War II

Argentina's position in World War II was very different from that of Brazil. The Argentine army overthrew the civilian government in 1943 in order to prevent a declaration of war against Germany. Most Argentine officers had been posted to Germany for military training in the 1920s and 1930s, and they were convinced that the German Army was invincible. Although it became difficult to maintain that belief in 1943, Argentina remained neutral until April 1945, when it declared war on Germany and Japan in order to qualify for membership in the newly established United Nations Organization. After the war ended, Argentina permitted tens of thousands of German bureaucrats, soldiers, and war criminals to enter the country under assumed names to escape Allied military courts. These policies earned Argentina the hostility of the U.S. government for the next decade, while its archrival Brazil prospered economically and was seriously considered for a permanent seat on the United Nations Security Council.

Argentina's policies irritate the United States

Connections and Conflict: Latin America and the United States

Late in his presidency, Porfirio Díaz of Mexico lamented: "Poor Mexico! So far from God. So close to the United States." Latin America's geographic proximity to the United States has been a source of connections and conflicts for two centuries. The **Monroe Doctrine** of 1823 committed the United States to defend the newly created Latin American states against any European efforts at recolonization. For the next fifty years, the United States was deeply involved in its own westward expansion (or manifest destiny) and its bloody Civil War. Thereafter, the United States began constructing commercial links with its southern neighbors, spearheaded by entrepreneurs like Minor Cooper Keith, who built

U.S. President Theodore Roosevelt running a steam shovel during construction of the Panama Canal, 1906.

railways across Central America and helped create the United Fruit Company, and W. R. Grace and Company, which underwrote telegraph networks, financed the Brazilian rubber industry, and sold manufactured goods throughout Latin America.

Then, in 1895, revolution broke out in Cuba, one of Spain's few remaining Western Hemispheric colonies. The United States expressed outrage at Spain's brutal suppression of Cuban revolutionaries, but was also tempted by the prospect of seizing some of Spain's Caribbean possessions as a prelude to building a canal across Central America. Two months after an explosion of unclear origin destroyed its battleship *Maine* in Havana harbor in February 1898, the United States declared war on Spain. By August 1898 the war was over, leaving the victorious United States in possession of Guam, the Philippines, and Puerto Rico. Cuba became independent in principle, although the Platt Amendment, passed by the U.S. Senate in 1901, gave Washington unprecedented rights of intervention there.

Building on the Platt Amendment, U.S. President Theodore Roosevelt extended the right of intervention to the entire Caribbean basin. His 1904 **Roosevelt Corollary** to the Monroe Doctrine asserted the right to intervene in the internal affairs of nations when Washington found evidence of "chronic wrongdoing," including an inability to pay debts, keep order, or dispense justice. Between 1901 and 1928, the United States intervened militarily in Mexico, Central America, and the Caribbean more than fifty times. This aggressive behavior, called **gunboat diplomacy**, infuriated Latin Americans and helped bring to power military dictators who promised to maintain order and protect the investments of United States citizens and companies.

In the late 1920s, this policy began to change. Reuben Clarke, legal counsel to the U.S. Department of State, argued in a 1928 memorandum that gunboat diplomacy and the Roosevelt Corollary violated the intent and spirit of the Monroe Doctrine by destabilizing weaker states and making foreign intervention more rather than less likely. Five years later, Theodore Roosevelt's distant cousin Franklin became president of the United States and committed that country to "the policy of the good neighbor" with respect to Latin America. In one of his folksy "fireside chat" radio addresses, Franklin Roosevelt observed that while a good neighbor does not remain indifferent to dangers threatening the house next door, neither does he break the door down whenever his neighbor does something he does not like. Roosevelt's **Good Neighbor Policy** ushered in a new era of U.S. policy toward Latin America, in which the United States claimed it would respect the laws of its neighbors, refrain from military or political influence in their affairs, and restrict itself to economic investment and diplomatic persuasion. Interestingly, however, United States intervention in Latin America actually increased during Roosevelt's presidency. The forms of engagement were more subtle and respectful, and connections were preferred to conflicts, but the engagement remained active and strong.

Latin American support for the United States during World War II seemed to solidify the Good Neighbor Policy. But the end of World War II did not end global conflict. Serious tensions developed between capitalist and communist states, taking the form of a long struggle known as the Cold War (Chapter 34). At first, Latin America played a minor role in this confrontation. The principal capitalist nation was the United States, a country so powerful that no state in the Western Hemisphere was willing to oppose it openly. In Argentina, President Juan Perón spoke vaguely of a "Third Way" between

The United States gains an empire through the Spanish-American War

Gunboat diplomacy gives way to the Good Neighbor Policy

Workers at a banana plantation owned by the United Fruit Company, Nicaragua.

capitalism and communism but never attempted to implement his ideas. Other nations of Latin America supported the United States through the Organization of American States, a hemispheric association dominated by Washington.

Then, in 1958, Cuban guerrillas led by Fidel Castro mounted a serious challenge to that island's dictator, Fulgencio Batista (*full-HEHN-see-yō bah-TEE-stah*). The United States, viewing Castro as an honest, idealistic young hero, gave him some support by embargoing arms shipments to Batista. But after Castro came to power in January 1959, U.S. President Dwight Eisenhower discovered that Castro was far more radical than he had suspected. Castro quickly imposed his own dictatorship, shooting thousands of Batista's supporters and nationalizing industries and United States–owned corporations.

Fidel Castro and supporters, February 1959.

Castro's leftist policies immerse Cuba in the Cold War

The United States responded vigorously to Castro's leftist policies. It trained a paramilitary force of Cuban exiles to invade the island and overthrow Castro, but that force was disastrously defeated in an April 1961 landing at the Bay of Pigs in southern Cuba. The invaders were captured, the U.S. role was exposed, and a triumphant Castro drew closer to the Soviet Union, proclaiming himself a communist.

Soviet premier Nikita Khrushchev called Cuba an "unsinkable aircraft carrier in the Caribbean" and supplied the island with oil and machinery, but he feared a second U.S. invasion. Addressing this and other concerns, including the U.S. superiority in nuclear weapons and the continued western presence in Berlin, Khrushchev in 1962 placed medium-range ballistic missiles in Cuba. When U.S. spy flights revealed their presence, President John F. Kennedy placed a naval quarantine line around Cuba and demanded their removal. The Cuban Missile Crisis lasted 13 days and brought the world to the edge of nuclear war, but ended peacefully when Khrushchev removed the missiles in return for Kennedy's public pledge not to invade Cuba and private pledge to withdraw obsolete U.S. missiles from Turkey.

The Cuban Missile Crisis brings the world to the brink of war

The Cuban Missile Crisis affected the Cold War profoundly (Map 36.2). Kennedy and Khrushchev, shaken by their brush with catastrophe, installed direct electronic communication between the White House and the Kremlin and signed a limited nuclear test ban treaty in 1963. Later that year Kennedy was murdered by an assassin linked to a pro-Castro organization, and in 1964 Khrushchev was removed by Soviet leaders exasperated by his adventurism in placing the missiles in Cuba in the first place. Castro remained in control of Cuba into the twenty-first century, protected by Kennedy's pledge and by the U.S. realization that it could, after all, survive in the same hemisphere with a communist state.

But Cold War issues continued to affect relations between Latin America and the United States. In 1965 the Johnson administration landed Marines in the Dominican Republic to suppress a reformist revolution that Washington wrongly believed to be communist. Between 1970 and 1973, the Nixon administration waged economic warfare against the freely elected Marxist government of Salvador Allende in Chile, destabilizing it and giving the Chilean armed forces a reason for overthrowing it, as described in this chapter's opening. And in the 1980s, the Reagan administration confronted a grass-roots leftist governing coalition in Nicaragua, the **Sandinista Front for National Liberation**, which overthrew dictator Anastasio Somoza in 1979 and established close ties with Cuba and the Soviet Union. The United States tried unsuccessfully to arm counterrevolutionary forces and isolate Nicaragua within the hemisphere. However, the Sandinista government

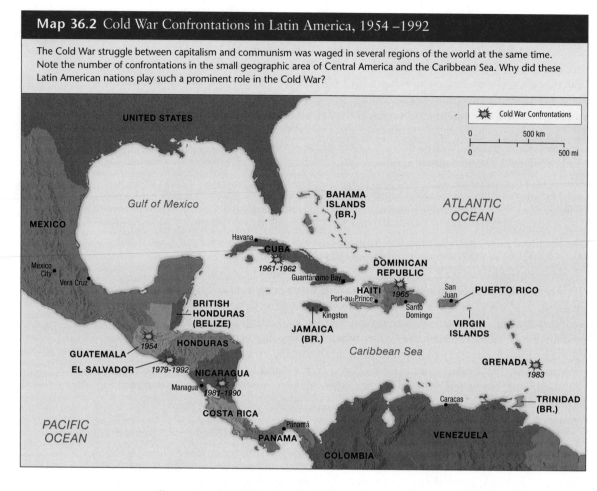

Map 36.2 Cold War Confrontations in Latin America, 1954 –1992

The Cold War struggle between capitalism and communism was waged in several regions of the world at the same time. Note the number of confrontations in the small geographic area of Central America and the Caribbean Sea. Why did these Latin American nations play such a prominent role in the Cold War?

was eventually removed in 1987, not by subversion but by losing a free election and quietly withdrawing into political opposition.

U.S. attitudes toward Latin America change when the Cold War ends

The end of the Cold War in 1990 and the collapse of the Soviet Union the following year removed the communist-capitalist confrontation from the troubled relationship between Latin America and the United States. In this more relaxed international atmosphere, economic and cultural connections that had remained strong but submerged during the Cold War suddenly resurfaced. U.S. and global investment in Brazil, Chile, and Mexico flourished, enhanced by the establishment of the **North American Free Trade Area** (NAFTA) linking Canada, Mexico, and the United States in 1993. Washington supported other efforts to lower trade barriers across Central and South America. Immigration into the United States from Latin American countries increased greatly, and people of Hispanic descent became the largest U.S. minority population group in 2005. In the process, U.S. cuisine, music, and entertainment became latinized to an extent inconceivable only twenty years earlier.

These developments laid the foundation for a more productive and mutually respectful relationship between the United States and Latin America. The regional and global conflicts of the twentieth century gave way to the potentially beneficial connections of the twenty-first. For the first time, interhemispheric relations were largely determined not by those states' responses to events set in motion by external forces but by their own reactions to each other.

Democracy and Dictatorship in Latin America

During the twentieth century, Latin America nations were faced with the same choice between dictatorship and democracy that confronted Europe, Asia, and Africa. Argentina, Brazil, and Chile experienced different types of dictatorships before democratizing near the end of the century. In Mexico, a political and social revolution between 1910 and 1920 changed the nation's governing structures and replaced one-man rule with one-party rule.

Argentina: The Failure of Political Leadership

Argentina's nineteenth-century political system (Map 36.3) was dominated by an elite of wealthy merchants, large estate owners, and military officers (Chapter 28). Reformers created a political movement, the Unión Cívica Radical (**UCR**, or Radical Civic Union), which rebelled several times between 1890 and 1910 in an effort to crack this elite's power. Finally, in 1916, a change in Argentina's election laws made possible a reasonably honest election, which was won by the UCR candidate, Hipólito Yrigoyen (*hih-PŌ-lē-tō ear-ih-GŌ-yen*).

Yrigoyen was an effective candidate but a poor president. His UCR promoted working-class wage increases and improvements in working conditions. But in 1919, as wages stagnated while food prices rose as a result of increased demand from war-ravaged Europe, Argentina was swept by strikes. Yrigoyen's government broke the strikes, shooting hundreds of demonstrators in the capital city of Buenos Aires and alienating its working-class supporters. This action permanently weakened the UCR, and a coalition of conservatives and military leaders overthrew the government in 1930. This coalition ruled Argentina for the next 13 years, reversing progress toward democracy. Then the Argentine army took over the government in 1943, and two years later Colonel Juan Domingo Perón (*peh-RŌN*) had emerged as the nation's leader.

The UCR fails to improve the condition of Argentine workers

PERÓN'S APPEAL TO ARGENTINES. Juan Perón was a modern-day *caudillo*, ruling through a combination of charm, magnetism, and cunning. He understood that the UCR had recognized the growing political leverage of the Argentine middle and working classes and that Yrigoyen had alienated the working class through strikebreaking and indifference. Perón, resolving not to make the same mistake, built a political power base within the working class.

Juan Perón builds a working-class political base

Perón's affection for working people was both genuine and calculated. He showered them with benefits: minimum-wage and maximum-hours legislation, paid vacations, the "thirteenth month" (a Christmas bonus of one month's pay), and, most important, the security of knowing that their welfare was foremost in his mind. While addressing his beloved *descamisados* (*dez-cah-mē-SAH-dōz*, or "shirtless people," Argentina's manual laborers), Perón would take off his own shirt and tie and stand before them bare-chested, flashing his magnificent smile and assuring them of his affection for them. They repaid him

Map 36.3 Argentina

Argentina is the second largest nation in South America and is five times the size of France. Observe that the country extends for two thousand miles from north to south. What impact would this have on Argentina's climate?

- ⊙ National capitals
- ★ Provincial capitals

Document 36.1 Eva Perón Discusses Why She Joined Juan D. Perón

The people's enemies were and remain Perón's enemies.

I have seen them approach him with every kind of malice and lie.

I want to denounce them definitively.

Because they will be the eternal enemies of Perón and of the people, here and every place in the world where the flag of justice and liberty is raised. We have defeated them, but they belong to a race that will never die definitively.

Perón's enemies . . . I have seen them up close and personal.

I never remained in the rearguard of his battles.

I was in the front line of combat, fighting the short days and the long nights of my zeal, infinite like the thirst of my heart. And I carried out two tasks—I don't know which was more worthy of a small life like mine, but my life in the end—one, to fight for the rights of my people, and the other, to watch Perón's back.

In this double duty, immense for me, armed with nothing but my ardent heart, I met the enemies of Perón and my people.

They are the same!

Yes! I never saw anyone from our race—the race of the people—fighting against Perón.

But I did see the others. They cannot be near the people or the men whom the people elect to lead them.

And they definitely cannot be the leaders of the people.

The leaders of the people must be fanatics for the people.

If not, they grow dizzy at the top—and they do not return!

SOURCE: Eva Perón, *In My Own Words: Evita* (New York: New Press, 1996), 55–57.

with their loyalty and their votes, providing him with the margin of victory in the elections of 1946 and 1951. Perón thereby built a strong base of support that lasted for decades after he was driven out of office in 1955.

Perón was ably assisted by his wife Evita (*AY-VĒ-tah*), an exceptionally shrewd politician known for her fur coats and platinum-colored hair (see page 937). A mediocre film actress and radio "weather girl," María Eva Duarte met Colonel Perón in 1943 and married him two years later (see "Eva Perón Discusses Why She Joined Juan D. Perón"). More radical than he in her political thinking, perhaps because of her own impoverished childhood, Evita encouraged lower-class resentment for the wealthy, while her magnificent wardrobe inspired the poor to think that if a destitute girl like her could become rich, one day they might do the same. This blend of anger and hope made her the idol of millions of Argentines. When she died of cancer in 1952 at age 32, two million people attended her funeral. And, at a time when only twenty million people lived in Argentina, a petition with six million signatures was presented to Pope Pius XII, asking for her canonization as a Catholic saint.

Evita Perón becomes Latin America's most influential female leader

When Perón fell from power in 1955, the causes were of his own making: gross mismanagement of agricultural policy and the squandering of Argentina's huge postwar credit balances. In addition, in a bitter quarrel with the Catholic Church over its refusal to make Evita a saint, he decided to penalize it by legalizing divorce. The military leaders who sent Perón into exile in Spain thought they were rid of a typical Latin American dictator, despite his two victories in free elections and his undeniable personal popularity.

Perón dominates Argentine politics even after his overthrow

They were mistaken. The succession of military and civilian governments that followed Perón proved even less capable of handling Argentina's problems. Meanwhile, the exiled former president urged his followers to cast blank ballots in Argentine elections to demonstrate support for him. The totals were high enough to embarrass the government: in one case, the winner actually ran second to "blank." Perón's support *grew* while he was exiled, as younger people who could not remember his mistakes fell in love with his legend. "Peronism without Perón" haunted Argentine politics as the destabilization caused by blank ballots led to military dictatorships, which in turn were fought bitterly by urban terrorist groups like the **Montoneros** (*mawn-tawn-AIR-ōz*).

Urban terrorism plagues Argentina and Uruguay

Urban terrorism became a disturbingly common feature of Latin American political life in the late 1960s. Argentina's Montoneros, Uruguay's **Tupamaros** (*too-pah-MAH-rōz*), and less effective bands in other South American states robbed banks, dynamited power plants, and kidnapped and murdered government officials. These groups stood far to the political left, considering traditional communist parties to be tools of the establishment. The Montoneros hated the police, the military, executives of large companies, and U.S. and European diplomats, all of whom they characterized as oppressors. When several Montoneros kidnapped and killed an Argentine general in 1970, the army realized it had to come to terms with Perón. Only he seemed to have the personal prestige to stabilize the country, and they expected his return would split the Montoneros, some of whom considered him an oppressor, while others fondly remembered his kindness to the working class.

ARGENTINE ARTISTRY: JORGE LUÍS BORGES. As social and political difficulties wracked Argentina, the nation's most famous literary figure entered the final decades of his exceptionally creative life. Jorge Luís Borges (*HOAR-hā loo-EES BOAR-hāz*, 1899–1986), born in Buenos Aires, was of mixed Argentine-English ancestry and spoke English as his first language. Educated in Geneva, Switzerland, he moved back to Buenos Aires in 1921 and quickly became an influential literary figure. From 1937–1946 he worked as a cataloguer at a branch of the Buenos Aires Municipal Library, a job that bored him but that gave him ample opportunity to hide in the stacks and read. Like Einstein in the patent office in Bern, Switzerland (Chapter 32), his mundane work gave him time to think and write.

In 1946 Borges was fired by Perón because of his anti-Peronista political leanings. During the Perón years, he wrote many of the short stories that earned him an international reputation as a master of that craft. When Perón was overthrown, Borges became director of the National Library of Argentina; with 900 thousand books at his disposal, he promptly went blind from an eye condition inherited from his father's side of the family. He continued to write, however, and had won virtually every significant literary award in the world, except for the Nobel Prize for Literature, by the time of his death in 1986.

Borges had his opinions about Argentina's political turbulence, and those opinions got him into trouble with Perón, but they seldom appear in his poetry or fiction. Most of his stories embrace universal themes: the search for meaning in life, the relationship between time and space (again reminiscent of Einstein), and the concept of infinity. Borges' fiction suggests that there is no such thing as material substance; the sensible world consists exclusively of ideas, which themselves exist only as long as they are perceived within people's minds. The human search for meaning in an infinite universe is futile. Since material things do not exist, time is not restricted by them, and there are multiple strands of time coexisting at once, some intersecting and others paralleling each other.

All of this might seem overly philosophical, but Borges' short stories, few of which are more than six pages long, are both fascinating and haunting. In *The Aleph*, a man finds in a cellar a small, bright sphere in which all the places in the world, seen from every conceivable angle, coexist at once. In *The Book of Sand*, a peddler of bibles sells a man a book that has neither beginning nor end, and no page of which, once examined, ever appears again. In *The Other*, Borges himself, seated on a bench by the Charles River in Cambridge, Massachusetts, in 1969, discovers to his horror that the man seated next to him is also Borges, seated on a bench by the Rhône river in Geneva sometime between 1914 and 1921. This master of short fiction lived in Argentina during times of upheaval, but in many ways stood apart from his society, writing vividly of abstract concepts that his words made concrete.

Jorge Luis Borges in front of the National Library, Buenos Aires.

ARGENTINA AFTER PERÓN. Borges was not the only Argentine dismayed when, in 1973, after months of negotiations, the 78-year-old Perón returned triumphantly from exile to become president again. But his death the next year left the presidency to his fourth wife, Isabel, who had run as his vice president in 1973. Mystified by the duties of the presidency, she began consulting astrologers. In 1976, as inflation rose to 4,640 percent per year, she was removed by the military. The new military dictatorship waged a "**dirty war**" against Peronists, Montoneros, and Communists, imprisoning people without trial, torturing them to death, and disposing of the bodies in unmarked graves. More than 25 thousand people disappeared this way between 1976 and 1978.

The Argentine military dictatorship wages war against leftists

Every Thursday morning between 1977 and 1983, the **Mothers of the Plaza de Mayo** (*MĪ-yō*) marched around that square in front of the Casa Rosada, the presidential residence in Buenos Aires, to protest the disappearance of their husbands and children. At first the regime ignored them and the economy turned prosperous. But in 1982 the military leadership broke off negotiations with Great Britain over the future of the Falkland Islands (which Argentines call the Malvinas), claimed by both countries since 1833. Argentine soldiers invaded the islands on April Fool's Day, 1982, quickly finding that the joke was on them. Rather than let the rocky, windswept islands go, British Prime Minister Margaret Thatcher launched a massive military expedition to retake them. The British won the Falklands War, Thatcher was triumphantly reelected, and the Argentine military dictatorship collapsed.

Borges protested the "dirty war" and ridiculed the Falklands conflict, calling it "two bald men fighting over a comb." He welcomed the restoration of civilian government in 1983 as Raúl Alfonsín (*ahl-fahn-SĒN*) of the UCR was elected president. Generals who had conducted the "dirty war" were put on trial and convicted, but lower-ranking officers were exempted in 1987 to avoid the threat of a military revolt. Meanwhile the trauma of those whose relatives "disappeared" continued to haunt Argentine society. Yet Perón's political successors won office in their own right and proved to be ordinary politicians, neither magical nor charismatic.

Brazil's currency devaluation wrecks the Argentine economy

Argentina's most vexing problem after 1990, however, was neither the military nor the Peronistas but the economy. Burdened with a huge foreign debt, a commercial system that failed to modernize after World War II, and a legacy of bitterness between management and labor, Alfonsín was unable to control triple-digit inflation and a shrinking

Gross Domestic Product (GDP). In 1991 Argentina, Brazil, Paraguay, and Uruguay established **MERCOSUR**, the "Common Market of the South," in an effort to imitate the success of the European Community. But in 1999 Brazil devalued its currency, raising the cost of Argentine products in Brazil and creating in Argentina a massive trade deficit. The following year the Argentine currency collapsed. Argentines were forbidden to take money out of the country, banks closed for indefinite periods, and one of the world's potentially richest nations resorted to barter for ordinary transactions. Modest stability returned late in 2002, but Argentina's underlying economic problems remained, calling into question not only the nation's financial health, but also the long-term survival of its democracy.

Brazil: Development and Inequality

Brazil emerged from the Great War as South America's most powerful and prosperous nation (Map 36.4). But this prosperity depended on high world market prices for two principal commodities, rubber and coffee. In the early 1920s, competition from Southeast Asia cut world rubber prices by 95 percent and bankrupted many Brazilian rubber planters. Then, in 1929, staggering political and economic mismanagement caused coffee prices to collapse. The next year, politically progressive military officers joined forces with politicians resentful of Brazil's powerful coffee-growing states, São Paulo, Minas Gerais, Rio de Janeiro, and Rio Grande do Sul, to overthrow the Brazilian Republic in the Revolution of 1930. Now an unimposing provincial governor from southern Brazil, Getúlio (*jeh-TOO-lē-yō*) Vargas, began a 24-year reign as that nation's most capable twentieth-century leader.

Pressures on Brazilian coffee and rubber lead to revolution

GETÚLIO VARGAS AND MODERNIZATION. Brazil's presidents had long been weak, and real power rested with governors and strongmen of the country's most important states. Vargas surprised everyone, however, by moving swiftly to remake Brazil. He removed the governors of every state except one, replacing them with federal "interventors" reporting directly to him. This move provoked an armed rebellion in the state of São Paulo, which the army suppressed after four months' intense fighting. By defeating the Paulista Revolt of 1932, Vargas discredited advocates of state power and strengthened the central government. He used his opportunity to press for extensive bridge and road projects and to grant women the vote in 1932, endorsing the demands of the Brazilian Federation of Feminine Progress and its suffragist founder, the botanist Bertha Lutz.

Brazil was then drawn into the global upheavals of the 1930s by its large Italian and German immigrant communities. The Integralistas, a fascist organization led by Plínio Salgado, a well-to-do young politician who altered his appearance to resemble Adolf Hitler's, fought in the streets with the communist-dominated National Liberation Alliance. Vargas used fears of a radical takeover to move against both extremes and suspend constitutional guarantees in 1937. He replaced democratic government with a military-backed dictatorship called the *Estado Nôvo* (*ess-TAH-dō Nō-vō*), or New State.

With Congress exiled and democratic processes discarded, Vargas could act as he pleased. His new state included elements of fascism, but Vargas was a pragmatist indifferent to ideology. He saw the world heading for war and seized the opportunity to position Brazil advantageously on the side of the United States.

Using the *Estado Nôvo*'s centralized executive powers, Vargas aggressively pursued economic development. Labor and management were placed under state control, appointments to civil service positions were based on merit, and the federal government created a number of state-owned manufacturing enterprises. Most of the groundwork

Vargas uses his dictatorial authority to remake Brazil

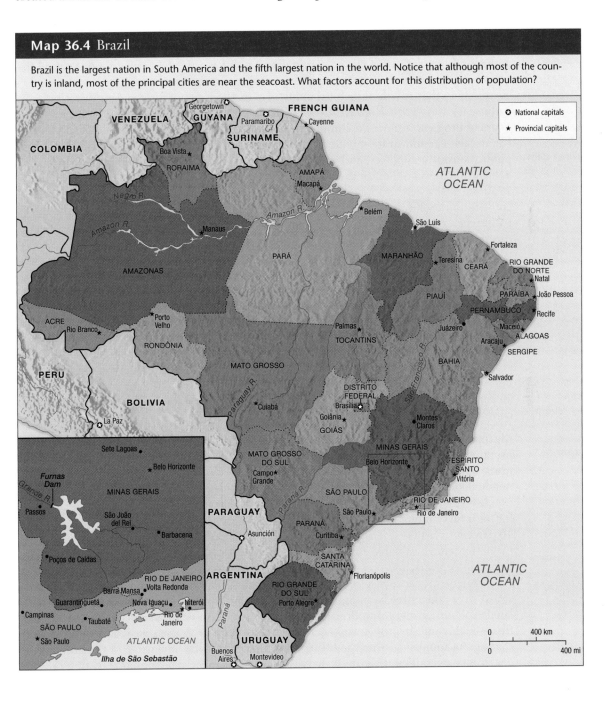

Map 36.4 Brazil

Brazil is the largest nation in South America and the fifth largest nation in the world. Notice that although most of the country is inland, most of the principal cities are near the seacoast. What factors account for this distribution of population?

Rio de Janiero in the 1940's.

Kubitschek's program modernizes Brazil at the cost of massive inflation

for Brazil's remarkable economic expansion of the late 1950s was laid under the Estado Nôvo. But even a smooth political operator like Vargas could not conceal the fact that Brazilians fighting for democracy in Europe were governed by dictatorship at home. In October 1945 the military returned from the war, removed Vargas from office, and sent him back to his ranch in southern Brazil. Free elections followed.

MODERNITY AND ITS STRESSES, 1954–1964. Vargas' legacy was both personal and substantive. An engaging, warm-hearted man who had always cared deeply for Brazil's land and people, he was also a clever, manipulative politician. He had recognized the need to modernize Brazil by developing its transportation network, improving its harbors, and encouraging the growth of its local industries. In 1955 one of his protégés, Juscelino Kubitschek (*hoo-seh-LĒ-nō KOO-bih-check*), won the presidency with the slogan "Fifty Years of Progress in Five," a commitment to build on the foundations Vargas had laid. Kubitschek's administration built roads, bridges, and hydroelectric plants, erected immense public-housing complexes, and granted extensive subsidies to developing industries such as steel and automobiles. In the process, however, inflation spiraled out of control, and by 1960 Brazilians were working harder than ever, yet enjoying *less* purchasing power. Brazil's constitution prohibited its presidents from seeking immediate reelection, and although Kubitschek remained personally popular, he was replaced in 1960 by a popular young candidate, Jânio Quadros (*HAH-nē-ō KWAH-drōss*).

Quadros, the energetic reforming mayor of São Paulo, won the election by appealing to Vargas' political opponents. But in Brazil presidential and vice-presidential races are separate, and the vice president elected in 1960, João Goulart (*ZHWOW goo-LAHRT*), was a Vargas supporter and, in the eyes of many, a dangerous leftist. When Congress refused to enact Quadros' huge budget and the impulsive president resigned, the Brazilian military considered deposing Goulart. This standoff was broken by a compromise, but Goulart proved less successful at running the economy than he was at plundering it through graft, corruption, and cronyism. By April 1964 the army overthrew him and replaced him with a military government. For modernized Brazil, this action seemed to belong to an earlier age, and when it was not followed by the long-established practice of returning control to civilians, Brazilians were shocked.

The Brazilian military installs a two-decade dictatorship

MILITARY RULE, 1964–1985. The 21-year dictatorship that followed was notorious for its brutal violation of human rights. The regime abolished freedom of speech, freedom of the press, and free elections, and systematically tortured and killed its opponents. But an economic boom between 1967 and 1974 helped the new government greatly, promoting foreign investment in the northeast and the Amazon valley and making vast sums available for highways and industrial development. Brazil's economy grew at an average rate of 10 percent over that seven-year period. By 1974, manufactured goods exceeded coffee as the nation's most valuable export. Purchasing power rose for nearly all classes of Brazilians during those years, and prosperity encouraged many to overlook the military oppression.

Military rule creates an economic boom

Brazil's experience inspired imitation, as both Chile (in 1973) and Argentina (in 1976) were taken over by military dictatorships that revoked human rights and stimulated economic growth. But Brazil's economy began to slow down in 1975, when a killing frost—highly unusual for Brazil—devastated the coffee crop and sent world coffee prices soaring. As competitors such as Nigeria and Colombia took advantage of the situation, Brazil lost a significant share of the world coffee market. The global recession of

1974–1975, brought on by an Arab oil embargo (Chapter 37), also depressed the prices of Brazilian exports. At the same time, the country's huge foreign debt was burdened by rising interest rates. The military regime, having borrowed heavily abroad to finance its economic reforms, was now unable to pay the installments. Inflation reached 100 percent by 1980, hurting the middle and working classes and the poor, and strikes swept through Brazilian factories.

BRAZILIAN ARTISTRY: PELÉ. Before, during, and after the two decades of military rule, the aspect of everyday life that most united Brazilians was their national sport: soccer. The game was introduced to Brazil in 1894 by Charles Miller, a Brazilian teenager of English descent. Only whites could play in organized leagues until 1923, but by the 1930s the sport was fully integrated. It quickly became a national obsession, punctuated by Brazilian victories in the World Cup tournaments of 1958, 1962, 1970, 1994, and 2002.

The appeal of soccer was grounded in several factors. There was no other organized sport in Brazil to compete with it. It could be played on any level stretch of ground, without expensive apparatus: all that was needed was a ball and a couple of orange crates to mark the goals. It rewarded improvisation and individual skill, and the rhythms of soccer reminded many Brazilians of their most popular dance, the samba. By 1950, when Brazil hosted the World Cup tournament, Rio de Janeiro boasted the world's largest soccer stadium, seating 175 thousand people, with standing room for 42 thousand more. Every Brazilian city supported numerous soccer clubs.

Brazilian soccer stars were adored like movie stars in Hollywood, and many of them either adopted "stage names" or went by a single name. Leônidas, the "Black Diamond," invented the bicycle kick in the 1930s; the maneuver involves performing a backward half-somersault while kicking the ball in the opposite direction, over your head or shoulder. The fabled Mané Garrincha, whose legs were deformed by vitamin deficiencies and malnutrition, capitalized on his disabilities to dribble the ball through and around baffled defenders; he was a mainstay of the World Cup championship teams of 1958 and 1962. But the most famous soccer artist of the twentieth century was Edson Arantes do Nascimento, whose friends called him Pelé. Born in 1941, he played on all three Brazilian World Cup championship teams between 1958 and 1970.

The Brazil side that won the 1958 World Cup, with Garrincha (first from left) and Pelé (third from left) in the front row.

Pelé had every skill required not only for success but for stardom. Joseph Page says it best: "He had it all: speed, mobility, a sense of oneness with the ball, uncanny vision, a fearsome shot off either foot, and, the crowning touch, an audacious, instinctive creativity." Pelé was both an amazingly productive goal-scorer and a marvelous passer who made all his teammates look spectacular. Films of his games show a man who dominated the field as though the sport had been invented for his personal fulfillment. Beyond this, his sunny disposition and expansive personality made him the ideal ambassador for soccer, a star who loved people and would talk with anyone. An artist with a soccer ball and a captivating person, Pelé and his exceptional teammates gave Brazilians ample reason to feel proud during the difficult decade of the 1960s.

RETURN TO DEMOCRACY . . . AGAIN. By the late 1970s, economic problems encouraged Brazilians to question the government on other grounds. Its human rights policy alienated the powerful Catholic Church, which denounced the government through the National Council of Brazilian Bishops and supported striking workers. Even former supporters of the military dictatorship began calling for a return to civilian rule, and the regime had

Economic pressures force the military to return power to civilians little choice but to liberalize. Gradually it eased restrictions on personal liberties, and in 1985 Brazil held its first free presidential election since 1960.

Civilian rule was welcomed throughout the country, but the two-decade military dictatorship had traumatized everyone. The people no longer viewed the army as an impartial guarantor of good government, though a younger group of generals tried to reassure civilians that the military would no longer intervene in politics. Yet the new civilian leaders proved no more capable of handling the economy than their military predecessors. Inflation exceeded 200 percent in both 1985 and 1990, wiping out the economic gains of 1967–1974.

In 2000, of Latin American nations, only Argentina's economic situation was worse. Then in 2002 the Brazilian presidency was won by Luís Inacio da Silva (*ē-NAH-sē-ō dah SEAL-vah*), who called himself Lula. A former auto mechanic, he was the first president in Brazilian history to come from a nonprivileged background, and his career as a labor organizer and leftist politician led wealthy Brazilians to view him as a dangerous radical. But once in office, Lula and his economic team rescued Brazil from the brink of financial default, revised the public pension system, and made significant progress in reforming the nation's antiquated, inequitable tax structure. His practical policies raised the possibility that Brazil might begin to close the gap between rich and poor and reach its economic potential.

Chile: Socialism, Militarism, and Democracy

For Chile, the early decades of the twentieth century were disruptive. The country's institutional framework had come apart in the Revolution of 1891 (Chapter 28), and politicians in Chile's capital of Santiago had been unable to reassemble it. The country was troubled by wildly fluctuating copper and nitrate prices after World War I. Reformers such as Arturo Alessandri tried to modernize but were periodically replaced by military regimes that proved no more capable of stabilizing the nation.

The Great Depression cripples Chile

In the 1930s, the Great Depression devastated Chile. Exports of copper and nitrates, as well as their prices on the world market, declined steeply. The military regime, unable to cope with the social chaos caused by the Depression, called Alessandri back to office in 1932. He drastically reduced government spending, and the gradual global economic recovery in the mid-1930s helped stabilize Chile's economy. But the nation's rigid class structure, dominated by ancient families of Basque origin, kept the majority of its citizens on the edge of poverty. World War II temporarily eased social tensions by increasing demand for Chile's minerals, but the end of the war reduced that demand and plunged the "shoestring republic," one of the planet's most geographically isolated nations, into the Cold War.

CHILE AND THE COLD WAR. At first Chile seemed an unlikely place for Cold War confrontation. Despite the country's deep class divisions, which seemed ripe for Marxist analysis, neither Moscow nor Washington considered the country particularly important until a Marxist economics professor named Salvador Allende began running for president every six years, from 1952 through 1970.

Allende, a dumpy, bespectacled man, preached a message of social equality and redistribution of wealth that caught the imaginations of many lower-class Chileans. After Fidel Castro's revolution in Cuba, the United States came to view an Allende victory as a potential propaganda disaster for capitalism. Such an event would be the first instance of a Marxist candidate winning a truly free election, and would stamp communism as the "wave of the future" in Latin America. Chile therefore took on a significance out of all proportion to its actual status in international affairs. In 1964 the United States poured millions of dollars into the campaign of Allende's opponent, Eduardo Frei (*FRĪ*). Frei won the election, but his moderate reform programs did not achieve the "Revolution in Liberty" he had promised. The next elections, in 1970, were widely viewed as a showdown between capitalism and Marxism.

Once again the United States spent heavily to influence the outcome, but this time, in a three-way race, Allende won the presidency by a narrow margin. He promised that at the end of his six-year term he would leave office willingly and turn power over to his legal successor. Yet communist governments did not permit free elections, and although Allende was a Socialist, much of his support came from communists. The Chilean military, recalling its unsuccessful efforts to govern the country in the 1920s and 1930s, initially supported Allende as the rightful president, preventing would-be revolutionaries from taking action.

Chilean miners drill for nitrates with jackhammers.

ALLENDE'S MARXIST EXPERIMENT. The United States, however, was determined to remove Allende from office. The Nixon administration cut off Chile's sources of credit and pressured foreign lenders to call in their debts. At the same time, Allende miscalculated drastically. He authorized huge wage increases for Chilean workers, hoping that a sharp increase in the demand for manufactured goods would stimulate industrial production. All it stimulated was runaway inflation, which rose to 566 percent annually by 1973. In rural areas, landless Amerind and mestizo peasants seized lands from their owners and refused Allende's demands that they return them. By mid-1973 Chile was plagued by a series of strikes, the most serious of which were two work stoppages by truckers, indispensable movers of goods and services in that oddly shaped land. The military had backed Allende for nearly three years despite strong U.S. pressure, but it finally decided to remove him after the second truckers' strike.

Allende's election leads to U.S. destabilization efforts

On September 11, 1973, Chilean air force planes bombed the Moneda Palace, and as tanks shelled the building and infantry broke in, Allende committed suicide. More than two thousand people died in the bloodiest military takeover in South American history. Power passed to a four-man *junta* composed of chiefs of the Chilean armed services. The dominant member, General Augusto Pinochet (*ō-GOOSE-tō pē-nō-SHAY* or *pē-nō-SHET*), had supported Allende until his final month in office. Pinochet, following the model of the Brazilian military dictatorship, refused to return power to civilian officials and ruled Chile for 17 years.

CHILEAN ARTISTRY: PABLO NERUDA. Watching these events in horror was Pablo Neruda, Chile's finest poet and the 1971 winner of the Nobel Prize for Literature. Born in Santiago in 1904, Neruda began writing poetry at the age of nine. Three years later he met the Chilean poet Gabriela Mistral, herself a Nobel Prize winner, who encouraged his ambitions and urged him to read British and American poets. Neruda soon discovered the writings of the American Walt Whitman, who became the major influence on his work.

After completing his education, Neruda joined the Chilean foreign service in 1927 and was posted to several South and East Asian and Eastern European countries, where he became, as he later recalled, "a citizen of the world." By the 1930s he was a dedicated communist, and was in Spain during the Spanish Civil War, when as a Chilean diplomat he looked on as the international brigades of volunteers entered Madrid to assist the leftist Spanish Republic against the Fascists of General Francisco Franco (see "Pablo Neruda, 'The Arrival in Madrid of the International Brigades'"). Returning to Chile in 1938, he left the foreign service and became a professional writer and poet, as well as an active communist politician.

Neruda remained a communist until Nikita Khruschev's Secret Speech in 1956 (Chapter 34) disillusioned him and forced him to critically examine his earlier adherence to Marxism. But he never lost his sympathy for the condition of the working classes in Chile and elsewhere, and he used his 1971 Nobel acceptance speech to call attention to their plight. Only Borges matched him in international fame among Latin American writers, and the two men were friends for many years, despite their disagreements about many current issues. Ill with heart disease for years, Neruda died sud-

---

Document 36.2 Pablo Neruda, "The Arrival in Madrid of the International Brigades," translated by Jodey Bateman.

One morning in a cold month
In an agonizing month, spotted with mud and smoke
A month that wouldn't get on its knees, a sad
besieged, unlucky month
When from beyond my wet window panes you could
hear the jackals
Howling with their rifles and their teeth full of blood
then
When we didn't have more hope than a dream
of more gun powder, when we believed by then
That the world was full of nothing but devouring
monsters and furies,
Then, breaking through the frost of that cold
month in Madrid, in the early morning mist
I saw with my own eyes, with this heart which looks out
I saw the bright ones arrive, the victorious fighters

From that lean, hard, tested rock of a brigade.
It was the troubled time when the women
Carried an emptiness like a terrible burning coal,
And Spanish death, sharper and more bitter
than other deaths
Filled the fields which until then had been honored by
wheat.

Through the streets the beaten blood of men had joined
With water flowing out of the destroyed hearts of houses
The bones of dismembered children, the piercing
Silence of women in mourning, the eyes
Of the defenseless closed forever,
It was like sadness and loss, like a spat-upon garden
Comrades,
Then

I saw you,
And my eyes even now are full of pride
Because I saw you arriving through the
Morning mist, coming to the pure brow of Spain
Silent and firm
Like bells before daybreak
So solemn with blue eyes coming from far, far away
coming from your corners, from your lost homelands,
from your dreams
Full of burning sweetness and guns
To defend the Spanish city where freedom was trapped
About to fall and be bitten by beasts.

Brothers, from now on
Your purity and your strength, your solemn story
Will be known by child and man, by woman and old one,
May it reach all beings who have no hope, may it
descend into the mines corroded by sulphuric air,
May it climb the inhuman stairways to the slave
May all the stars, all the wheat stalks of Spain and the
world
Write your name and your harsh struggle
And your victory, strong and earthy as a red oak tree.

Because you have given new birth by your sacrifice
To the lost faith, the empty soul, the confidence in the
earth
And through your abundance, your nobility, your deaths,
Like through a valley of hard, bloody rocks
Passes an immense river of doves
Made of steel and hope.

www.motherbird.com/arrival_brigades.html

denly on September 23, 1973, twelve days after the overthrow of Allende, whom he had supported vigorously.

PINOCHET'S BRUTAL DICTATORSHIP. In a series of violent outbreaks during the first five months of the military dictatorship, Neruda's home was looted and vandalized after his death. This was only one way in which Pinochet's government attacked its opponents. Suspects were beaten, tortured, held without bail or notification to families, and in many cases simply disappeared. Some were buried in mass graves in remote areas; others were thrown alive out of airplanes over the Pacific, after having their bellies slit open so the bodies would not float. The regime, acting on its belief that authoritarian government was superior to popular sovereignty, set out to destroy Chilean democracy, declaring all political parties illegal, dissolving Congress, and suspending the constitution.

Pinochet installs a brutal military dictatorship

Pinochet turned Chile's economy over to economists from the University of Chicago, and in the late 1970s Chile experienced impressive prosperity. Social programs were either slashed or abolished, and the lower classes were placed on what amounted to an austerity program. Inflation declined to 32 percent in 1978 and 10 percent in 1982. Chile's economy grew at an average rate of 7 percent from 1976 through 1981, although purchasing power declined and the gap between rich and poor widened dramatically.

In 1980 Pinochet drew up a new constitution extending his presidential term to 1990. But a recession in the early 1980s dampened public enthusiasm for his regime, and the Latin American financial crisis of 1982, brought on by Mexico's decision to default on its foreign debt, hit the Chilean economy hard. Unemployment soon reached 30 percent of the work force, and the regime was forced to confront urban demonstrations on the 11th of each month, beginning on September 11, 1983, the tenth anniversary of the takeover.

Anti-Pinochet poster, 1977.

As the economy slowly recovered, international pressure on the regime mounted. Pope John Paul II, for example, visited Santiago in 1986 and refused to appear in public with Pinochet. The Pope, who advocated democracy in Poland and other Soviet bloc nations, could not appear to endorse the man who had destroyed Chilean democracy. The United States continued to support the dictatorship because of Pinochet's anticommunist policies, but most European states urged Pinochet to step down.

In 1988, apparently convinced of his own popularity, Pinochet held a special election: a "yes" vote would retain him in office until 1997, while a "no" vote would call for a return to civilian rule. Opposition forces created an alliance called the *Concertación* (*kahn-sair-tah-sē-ŌN*), which orchestrated television advertisements complete with rock music proclaiming "The Moral Supremacy of the No." The alliance also rented a large network of computers to monitor the election for vote fraud. By a 55–43 percent margin, "no" defeated "yes," and after some cautious bargaining, Pinochet accepted the verdict. His democratically elected successors were committed to restoring democracy, working for social justice, and promptly investigating human rights abuses that had occurred during the military dictatorship. By 2007, Chile's democratic institutions had been reinvigorated, and the nation's economy was the most stable in South America.

Mexico: The Legacy of the Revolution

Mexico, which had been dominated by dictators for most of the nineteenth century (Chapter 28), changed dramatically early in the twentieth (Map 36.5). The dictator Porfirio Díaz had worked hard from 1876 to 1910 to modernize the nation, attracting foreign

Map 36.5 Mexico

Mexico stretches 2,100 miles from northwest to southeast. Although it is nearly four times the size of France, it is the smallest of the three nations of North America. Observe the short distance (only 150 miles) across the Isthmus of Tehuantepec, separating the Gulf of Mexico from the Pacific Ocean. Why is this short distance significant for Mexican trade?

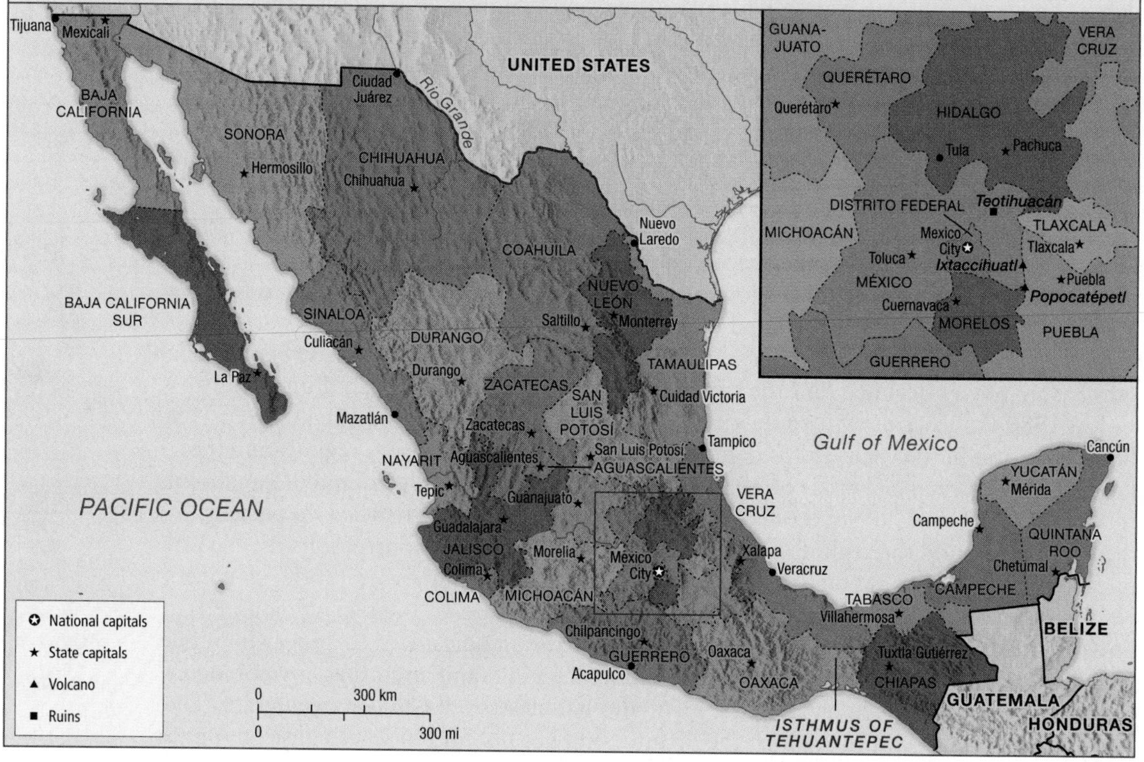

investment, building a large railway network, and working closely with scientists and technicians to develop an industrial base. But social and political repression remained, with most Mexican peasants working as a landless class and voting rights limited to a very small number of property-owning men. Many educated Mexicans believed that economic modernization could not succeed without social and political reform. Díaz was driven out in a violent revolution in 1911, and the leader of the rebels, Francisco Madero, became president of Mexico.

THE REVOLUTION OF 1910–1920. In 1911 it appeared that the Mexican Revolution was over, but it lasted nine more years. Madero, focusing on political democracy, underestimated the severity of Mexico's social and economic problems. Rival leaders Emiliano Zapata and Pancho Villa (*VĒ-yah*) took up arms against him on behalf of vast numbers of impoverished Mexicans. In 1913, elements in the Mexican army that had previously supported the Díaz dictatorship took advantage of these divisions to overthrow and murder Madero. Mexico then endured seven years of turbulence, civil war, and U.S. intervention before the revolution finally ended in 1920.

The Mexican Revolution developed into a more radical social movement than observers had expected in 1910. The Constitution of 1917 provided a means for far-reaching land redistribution to the peasants. It also placed severe restrictions on the Catholic Church (whose leadership, like that of the military, had supported Díaz), and granted unprecedented rights to organized labor. If implemented completely, it would revolutionize the ownership of property and the exercise of power in Mexico. But it was so radical that even its partial implementation brought on recurring cycles of rebellion, civil war, and political assassination, with displaced elites fighting radical reformers for control of the country.

Mexico embarks on a social revolution

In the midst of this chaos, the government commissioned some of Mexico's most prominent artists to paint educational murals on the walls of public buildings. The purpose was to display great events in Mexican history to the three out of four adults who, in 1920, could not read, but the consequence was to create an artistic school known as Mexican muralism. Its chief practitioners—José Clemente Orozco, David Alfaro Siqueiros, and Diego Rivera—quickly became famous throughout the world for their strikingly innovative use of vivid colors and dramatic techniques. Rivera's wife, Frida Kahlo, while not herself a muralist, also became a powerful nationalistic artist in her own right. Together their work publicized the sufferings and achievements of Mexican historical figures as well as populist themes.

Dream of a Sunday Afternoon in the Alameda Central by Diego Rivera (1947). Frida Kahlo is to the left of the figure of death.

Rivera's highly realistic and colorful murals conveyed a clear social message—that it was time to return the Amerind to the mainstream of Mexican society. Rivera and Kahlo, as well as Siqueiros, were communists, and their leftist politics and social activism typified the radicalism of many who experienced the Mexican Revolution. It was that sort of radicalism that those who wished to institutionalize the Revolution hoped to channel into stabilizing activities.

INSTITUTIONALIZATION: THE PRI. The development of the Institutional Revolutionary Party, or **PRI,** ended social and political turmoil. Claiming to embody the true spirit of the Mexican Revolution, it was so successful in winning elections that it was nicknamed the "Factory of Presidents." The PRI's corporate structure guaranteed representation for peasants, workers, middle class, and military, thus tying it closely to the principal elements of Mexican society. With widespread support, the PRI found it easy to elect candidates, but it also resorted to vote fraud in those few instances when popularity was not enough. From 1929 to 2000, its dominance gave Mexico one of Latin America's most politically stable governments.

The PRI brings stability without genuine democracy

This political stability, however, concealed serious social and economic inequalities. Even though the Constitution of 1917 had been designed to alleviate poverty, by 1929 most Mexican peasants still had no hope of owning enough land to feed their families. During the presidency of Lázaro Cárdenas (1934–1940), this situation was partially corrected. Cárdenas nationalized foreign oil companies and transferred farmland from large landowners to collective farms, similar in some respects to those in Soviet Russia. He became the most popular president in Mexican history, a revolutionary icon whose faded photograph still hangs on the walls of dwellings throughout Mexico.

POLITICAL AND ECONOMIC STRAINS. The Cárdenas presidency marked the most radical phase of the Mexican Revolution. When World War II began and Mexico sided firmly with the United States, radicalism and even egalitarianism were suppressed. In the immediate postwar years, the PRI restrained all domestic opposition and increased its power through corruption and favoritism. When Fidel Castro seized power in nearby Cuba and attempted to export communism to other Latin American countries, Mexico reacted sharply, fearing both communist action and U.S. reaction. Mexican apprehension grew even stronger in the 1980s, when leftist rebellions in Nicaragua and El Salvador sent refugees fleeing into Mexico, threatening to destabilize a nation for which political stability, won with such difficulty, had become an end in itself.

Mexico maintains good relations with the United States

Mexican relations with the United States remained close. In 1963 the Kennedy administration agreed to return a disputed border region to Mexico. Thirty years later, the creation of the North American Free Trade Area appeared highly beneficial to the Mexican economy, which had grown consistently between 1958 and 1973 but had been depressed since the mid-1980s by low crude oil prices. A U.S. loan of $20 billion (repaid with interest two years later) lent support to Mexico's economy in the mid-1990s, and NAFTA, which reduced tariffs between the United States, Mexico, and Canada, promised to stimulate economic growth for all its participants.

These developments might have worked to the PRI's advantage, but the party was damaged by three scandalous events. First, President Gustavo Díaz Ordaz ordered the army and police to shoot hundreds of student demonstrators in Mexico City just before the 1968 Olympic Games. The students had been protesting the authoritarian nature of Mexico's allegedly democratic government, and this "Tlatelolco Massacre" proved that they were right. The slaughter undermined PRI's reputation and credibility. Second, revelations that Carlos Salinas (*sah-LĒ-nahss*), president from 1988 to 1994, had embezzled hundreds of millions of dollars from the federal treasury forced him to flee the country following the end of his term. The scandal spotlighted PRI corruption and cost the party much of the legitimacy it had earned through more than six decades of reasonably competent rule. Third, the PRI candidate for president claimed to have won the 1994 election despite the widespread belief that Cuahtémoc (*kwah-TĀ-mock*) Cárdenas, son of Lázaro, had actually won, and that the PRI had stolen the election through massive vote fraud. By the late 1990s the PRI was under serious challenge.

Scandals bring down the PRI

For the first time since the 1920s, other parties presented competitive alternatives to the PRI, and in 2000 one of them, the Partido del Acción Nacional (PAN, or National Action Party), elected its presidential candidate, Vicente Fox, in the most stunning Mexican political upheaval in eighty years. Mexico then embarked on a transition from one-party government to multiparty democracy, the outcome of which depended largely on Fox's success or failure as the first non-PRI president since 1929.

Fox had a difficult time in office. The PRI remained in control of Congress, blocking most of his initiatives. Extensive illegal immigration to the United States troubled relations between the two neighbors. Even NAFTA, which had been implemented with such high hopes, fell victim to globalization of the world economy. Although many jobs from the United States relocated to Mexico because of its cheap labor, many more relocated from Mexico to China, where labor was even less expensive.

Six Regional Transitions

By the early twenty-first century, the principal nations of Latin America had begun to emerge from long, difficult struggles with their authoritarian heritage. Argentina, Brazil, Chile, and Mexico had developed democratic institutions and had committed their societies to making those institutions work. The region seemed more politically stable than at any other time since the era of independence. Yet it still faced critical social and economic transitions, six of which are considered here.

Gender Roles

For centuries, Latin American women were largely confined to the home and the care of children, placing them outside the public sphere. The Spanish and Portuguese conquests had brought the Iberian concept of **machismo,** the praise of masculine virility and power, into Amerind societies already dominated by men. Iberian-American women were expected to be models of spiritual and moral superiority and purity, models that do not allow active participation in the sometimes corrupt aspects of public life.

A Peruvian couple, late 19th century.

Women such as Evita Perón broke with this model in some ways, but not in others. Evita exercised immense influence in Argentina between 1945 and 1952, but that influence derived largely from her ability to depict herself as "the mother of the people," thereby retaining traditional feminine attributes while projecting her energies into the public sphere. When she fell ill with uterine cancer, her physician was too embarrassed to disclose to her the true severity of her illness, because it was a female disorder—and Evita, observing the same convention, never asked about her condition until it was too late.

Evita Perón's example reveals one dimension of the challenge facing Latin American women. In the twentieth century, they gained access to higher education and pursued careers in various professions, including medicine and law. But while they began to play public roles in areas such as human rights, education, and economic security, they did not address issues such as workplace equality and reproductive rights. Many Latin American women remain uncomfortable with those and similar issues, in part because action in such matters requires a level of political activism that might compromise the spiritual and moral purity associated with womanhood.

Latin American women face systemic challenges

Inequality

Latin American societies were highly stratified, with tremendous inequalities of wealth between upper and lower classes. In the sixteenth century, Iberian social structures were imposed upon Amerind societies that were themselves hierarchical. The Spanish and Portuguese kings simply replaced the Aztec and Inca emperors, and Iberian conquistadors replaced Amerind nobles. After independence, Iberian-descended owners of large landed estates and prosperous merchants and bankers formed a new aristocracy based on wealth. They restricted their ranks by limiting other groups' access to higher education and legally barring them from land ownership.

These inequalities continue to trouble Latin America in the twenty-first century. Although Mexico and Argentina allow access to higher education based on merit, Brazil, the region's largest and potentially most prosperous country, continues to view higher education as solely for privileged elites. Fewer than 1 percent of adult Brazilians have college or university degrees, a figure that demonstrates how difficult it is for lower-class Brazilians to attain upward social mobility.

Amerinds from Tierra del Fuego, Chile.

Debt

To reduce debt, Latin American nations struggle to increase economic productivity, but the two aims often work against each other. Argentina, Brazil, and Mexico, in particular, are burdened with huge indebtedness to foreign lenders, most of it occurring recently. As the new civilian governments took charge of their nations' economies, they took responsibility for existing debts but also increased them. In the 1990s, Latin American nations finally began to achieve some prosperity, as massive foreign investment reduced inflation and produced solid economic growth. Yet the region remains highly vulnerable to fluctuations in global demand for its exports, as well as to sharp swings in world financial markets: Mexico's financial system crashed in 1994, and Argentina's in 2000.

During this economic turmoil, international agencies such as the International Monetary Fund and the World Bank lent large sums to Latin American countries to help them cover interest payments on existing debt. This new money came with conditions: recipients were required to open their economies to foreign investment, reduce inflation, and minimize government's role in economic life. The last of these promoted democratization by encouraging military leaders, most of them wedded to governmental control of the economy, to turn their powers over to civilians. But it also increased the size of the debt it was helping to service. Without significant increases in economic productivity, Latin American debt will continue to weigh heavily on the region.

Debt continues to hamper Latin American economies

Population

The prospects for sustainable economic growth and meaningful social change in Latin America are profoundly affected by population growth. Demand for resources, availability of jobs, and provision of adequate social services are all population dependent. In the 1960s it was frequently stated that Latin America's "population explosion" would doom the region to perpetual poverty if drastic measures were not taken to control the size of families. In 1970 the average number of children per Latin American family was six. Three decades later, access to contraception and improvements in education for women had helped reduce the number of children per family in nations such as Mexico and Brazil to 2.5.

Yet because children and youth constitute such a large proportion of Latin American populations, in coming years millions will be ready for the workplace but unable to find employment. This situation will have a negative impact on Latin American productivity and ability to pay interest on debts. It will also promote emigration. Progress has been made in controlling population growth, but decades of sustained effort will be required to stabilize that growth at economically beneficial levels.

The skyline of Sâo Paulo, Brazil's largest city.

Demographic pressures hinder Latin America's development

Poverty

The four transitions already discussed must be successfully completed if Latin America is to emerge from the cycle of poverty that has plagued it for centuries. Poor people cannot afford to educate women, cannot struggle effectively against inequality and for social justice, and cannot contribute to their nations' efforts to reduce indebtedness. Nor can the poor be counted on to reduce population growth, since many of them see large numbers of children as insurance for old age, not as obstacles to economic advancement. As long as Latin American elites, who control the productive capacities of their nations, fail to grasp the importance of distributing wealth and purchasing power more equitably, their societies will remain poverty ridden and weak. Poverty, in turn, will negate the best efforts of democratic governments to modernize those societies and improve living standards.

Religion

As Latin America entered the twenty-first century, its religious allegiance was changing significantly for the first time in nearly five hundred years. The Iberian conquest installed Catholicism as the only religion permissible under colonial rule. Iberian Catholicism, rich in tradition and ritual, proved attractive to Amerinds, whose own religious practices were often highly ritualized. Until the 1960s, no other religion enjoyed a significant following in Latin America.

Then reforms in the Roman Catholic Church diminished its appeal to Latin Americans. The Second Vatican Council, held from 1962 to 1965, brought together Church officials and theologians from around the world to try to modernize Catholicism in response to total war, the Holocaust, the emergence of Marxism, and other upheavals of the twentieth century. The Council's changes in the Catholic Mass, designed to simplify the worship service and increase popular participation through the use of local languages, troubled many Latin Americans who cherished the complex rituals they had known since childhood. Some turned to evangelical Protestant Christianity, which since the early 1970s has been growing rapidly in Latin America, in part because it provides the ceremony and mystery that many Latin American Catholics expect in their religious services.

Latin American Catholicism begins to lose some of its influence

In addition to simplifying the Mass, Catholicism addressed the appeal of Marxists like Cuba's Castro and Chile's Allende by advocating improvement in the conditions endured by the poor. Latin American bishops and cardinals were expected to take the side of the poor against the wealthy elites, and to stand firmly for social and economic justice. Theologians from Mexico and Brazil developed a concept of **liberation theology**, which held that Jesus of Nazareth had preached not only a message of love but also a message of opposition to unjust government. Liberation theologians urged cooperation between Catholics and Marxists against Latin American upper classes that kept the poor impoverished. That message was sometimes dangerous to deliver, as evidenced by the assassination of Roman Catholic Bishop Oscar Romero of El Salvador by a right-wing death squad in 1980.

Despite such risks, liberation theology flourished from 1968 through 1979, but after that a new Catholic leader, Pope John Paul II (1979–2005), restrained its practitioners. The new pope, who supported anti-Marxist liberation throughout Eastern Europe, was not unmoved by cries for justice. But he believed that the Catholic faith and Marxism, which denies that anything spiritual can exist, could never be reconciled, and that cooperation between the two was shortsighted and dangerous. Catholicism's abandonment of liberation theology nonetheless disappointed many Latin American Catholics. Efforts by Catholics and evangelical Protestants to develop a theology that addresses Latin American realities testify to religious transitions ongoing in the region.

Mayan ceremony on the steps of a Catholic church, Mexico.

Chapter Review

Putting It in Perspective

Latin American countries passed through many dramatic changes during the twentieth century. Each of the region's main nations—Argentina, Brazil, Chile, and Mexico—endured either violent revolutions or brutal military dictatorships. Each entertained fresh hopes for the consolidation of democracy as the century ended. Cuba played a surprisingly significant role during the Cold War because of Fidel Castro's Communist revolution, but its ability to destabilize the region waned with the end of that conflict and the Soviet Union's collapse. By the early twenty-first century, Latin America seemed politically stable, poised to fulfill its sizable potential and improve living standards for its hundreds of millions of people.

Latin American societies remained profoundly traditional, however, burdened with inequitable social hierarchies and with deeply held convictions about the subordinate role of women and the irrelevance of higher education for both men and women. Important progress had been made in limiting the pace of population growth, an achievement that required the alteration of long-standing religious beliefs and social conventions, but economic and social inequalities remain as challenges to prosperity.

Reviewing Key Material

KEY CONCEPTS

braceros, 942	Montoneros, 950
Monroe Doctrine, 943	Tupamaros, 950
Roosevelt Corollary, 944	"dirty war", 951
gunboat diplomacy, 944	Mothers of the Plaza de
Good Neighbor Policy, 944	Mayo, 951
Sandinista Front for	MERCOSUR, 952
National Liberation, 945	*Estado Nôvo*, 952
North American Free	*Concertación*, 959
Trade Area (NAFTA), 946	PRI, 961
UCR, 947	machismo, 963
descamisados, 947	liberation theology, 965

KEY PEOPLE

Salvador Allende, 938, 956	Getúlio Vargas, 952
Theodore Roosevelt, 944	Arturo Alessandri, 956
Franklin Roosevelt, 944	Augusto Pinochet, 957
Fidel Castro, 945	Porfirio Díaz, 959
Hipólito Yrigoyen, 947	Lázaro Cárdenas, 961
Juan Perón, 947	Oscar Romero, 965
Evita Perón, 949	

ASK YOURSELF

1. In what ways were Juan Perón's presidencies beneficial to Argentina, and in what ways were they harmful? What circumstances undermined Argentine stability after Perón was gone?

2. How did Getúlio Vargas attempt to modernize Brazil? How successful was he? What obstacles prevented further success?

3. How did the Cold War, and the Castro regime in Cuba, affect Latin American stability? Why did Salvador Allende's government appear so disturbing to the United States?

4. Why did military regimes in Argentina, Brazil, and Chile eventually relinquish power to civilians?

5. How did the Institutional Revolutionary Party stabilize Mexican politics?

GOING FURTHER

Andrews, George. *Afro-Latin America, 1800–2000*. 2004.

Constable, Pamela, and Arturo Valenzuela. *A Nation of Enemies: Chile Under Pinochet*. 1991.

Hahner, June. *Emancipating the Female Sex: The Struggle for Women's Rights in Brazil, 1850–1940*. 1990.

Harding, Rachel. *A Refuge in Thunder: Candomblé*. 2000.

Kaufman, Edy. *Crisis in Allende's Chile: New Perspectives*. 1988.

Knight, Alan. *The Mexican Revolution*. 1986.

Loveman, Brian. *Chile: The Legacy of Hispanic Capitalism*. 1999.

Meyer, Michael, and William Sherman. *The Course of Mexican History*. 6th ed. 1999.

Pablos, Julia. *Women in Mexico: A Past Unveiled*. 1999.

Pérez, Louis, Jr. *Cuba: Between Reform and Revolution*. 1995.

Rock, David. *Argentina, 1516–1987*. 1987.

Skidmore, Thomas. *Brazil: Five Centuries of Change.* 1999.

Skidmore, Thomas. *The Politics of Military Rule in Brazil, 1964–1985.* 1988.

Szulc, Tad. *Fidel: A Critical Portrait.* 1986.

Taylor, Diana. *Disappearing Acts: Spectacles of Gender and Nationalism in Argentina's "Dirty War."* 1997.

Thomas, Hugh. *Cuba: The Pursuit of Freedom.* 1971.

Turits, Richard. *Foundations of Despotism: Peasants, the Trujillo Regime, and Modernity in Dominican History.* 2003.

Womack, John, Jr. *Zapata and the Mexican Revolution.* 1968.

Woodward, Ralph. *Central America: A Nation Divided.* 1999.

Key Dates and Developments

Argentina

1916	Yrigoyen (UCR) elected president
1930	Military coup overthrows President Yrigoyen
1943	Military coup overthrows President Castillo
1946–1955	First presidency of Juan D. Perón
1952	Death of Evita Perón
1973–1974	Second presidency of Juan D. Perón
1976–1983	Military dictatorship and "dirty war"
1982	Argentina defeated by Britain in Falklands War
1983	Raúl Alfonsín elected president
2000	Argentine currency collapses

Brazil

1919	Brazil participates in Paris Peace Conference
1921	World rubber prices collapse
1929	World coffee prices collapse
1930	Revolution brings Getúlio Vargas to power
1930–1945	First presidency of Getúlio Vargas
1937	Creation of the *Estado Nôvo*
1942	Brazil declares war on Germany
1946	Volta Redonda steel plant opens
1950–1954	Second presidency of Getúlio Vargas
1958, 1962, 1970, 1994, 2002	Brazil wins Soccer World Cup
1964–1985	Military dictatorship
1967–1974	Brazilian "Economic Miracle"
1975	Freeze destroys Brazilian coffee crop
1985	Democracy returns
2002	Luís Inacio de Silva ("Lula") elected president

Chile

1920–1924	First presidency of Arturo Alessandri
1932–1938	Second presidency of Arturo Alessandri
1964–1970	Presidency of Eduardo Frei / United States begins to intervene in Chilean politics
1970–1973	Presidency of Salvador Allende
1973	Overthrow and suicide of Allende
1973–1990	Augusto Pinochet's military dictatorship
1988	Referendum rejects Pinochet's rule
1998–2000	Pinochet arrested in Britain
2000	Socialist Ricardo Lagos elected president

Mexico

1910–1920	The Mexican Revolution
1928	Creation of the "Official Party" (PRI in 1945)
1934–1940	Presidency of Lázaro Cárdenas
1963	U.S. returns El Chamizal to Mexico
1968	Tlatelolco Massacre
1993	Creation of NAFTA
2000	Vicente Fox elected as first non-PRI president since 1924

Post-Colonial Challenges in Africa and the Middle East, 1939–Present

- The Context of African Decolonization

- The Transformation of Africa After 1945

- Challenges Facing Independent Africa

- The Transformation of the Middle East

- Chapter Review

Signing Of The Camp David Accords

U.S. President Jimmy Carter looks on approvingly as Egyptian President Anwar al-Sadat (at left) and Israeli Prime Minister Menachem Begin (at right) sign the Camp David Peace Accords in Washington, March 26, 1979. The peace treaty between Egypt and Israel split the anti-Israeli coalition in the Middle East and marked the beginning of a new era in that region (page 989).

On a sweltering late summer afternoon in September 1961, a small plane crashed in the newly independent nation of Congo. It was carrying United Nations Secretary General Dag Hammarskjöld (DAHG HAH-mur-shuld) to a meeting with the prime minister of a province attempting to secede from Congo. Hammarskjöld, who died in the crash, was working to negotiate a peaceful settlement of the year-old Congo Crisis. Although he died a hero to the Western world, many black Africans viewed him as a paternalistic white European who was seeking to maintain European influence in the newly emerging nations of Africa.

Forty years later, on a cool, late summer morning in September 2001, the United Nations Secretary General led a hushed General Assembly in a moment of silence for nearly three thousand people killed the previous week by planes crashed deliberately in a terrorist attack on the United States. Unlike Dag Hammarskjöld, this Secretary General was not characterized as a paternalistic white European. He was Kofi Annan (*KŌ-fē AHN-ahn*), a black African from Ghana, a nation independent for only four years at the time of Hammarskjöld's crash.

During those 40 years, the nations of Africa and the Middle East had changed dramatically. Although they broke colonial ties with the West, they continued to struggle with resentments and problems developed under colonial rule and in the decades that followed. The emergence of independent nations in Africa and Southwest Asia, and their efforts to meet the challenges of modernization, could now be seen as watershed developments, filled with meaning for the entire world.

The Context of African Decolonization

Europe's nineteenth-century "scramble for Africa" (Chapter 30) had been accomplished with the assistance of advanced technology and modern weapons that, with few exceptions, Africans did not possess. In 1910, the possibility that Africans might once again administer their own affairs appeared remote. The global wars of 1914–1918 and 1939–1945 changed that situation, giving Africans hope that they might be able to break free from their colonial ties to European nations.

The Impact of World War II

Italy's 1935 invasion of Ethiopia, a country whose two millennia of independence had made it a symbol of African resistance to outside rule, combined with Nazi Germany's fanatical racism to convince most Africans to oppose fascism during World War II. African volunteers fought for France and Britain, and when African soldiers led by British officers liberated Ethiopia from Italy in 1941, all Africa rejoiced. Africans even came to hope that their contributions to an eventual Allied victory might help end colonial rule throughout the continent.

Africa participates
actively in World War II

Africa's support for the Allied cause was significant. Britain recruited sizable numbers of volunteers in its colonies through village chiefs, while French General Charles de Gaulle's Free French movement (Chapter 33) drafted more than 100 thousand men in French West Africa alone. Even more crucial to the Allied effort was Africa's resource base, particularly after Japan took resource-rich Southeast Asia in 1941–1942. Africa provided the Allies with large quantities of cotton, palm oil, tin, rubber, coffee, tea, and cocoa. These contributions, which assisted both Allied armies and Allied populations at home, gave Africans a well-deserved sense of importance, earning them the indebtedness of the British and French.

The contributions, however, were not completely beneficial for Africans. Many African soldiers died in combat or returned home maimed, while European exporters paid African producers low fixed prices for their products, which were then sold in Europe at inflated wartime rates. As manufactured goods from Europe were sold in Africa at equally inflated prices, the war left the average African producer materially worse off than before. To Africans in 1945, colonialism offered few benefits.

Workers load bundles of sisal leaves onto open wagons, British East Africa, 1940s.

Africa derives advantages from World War II

Africa did gain some long-term advantages from the war. The Allies built airports and improved harbor facilities throughout West Africa, turning Freetown in Sierra Leone into a vital Atlantic port, and developing Accra in the Gold Coast as a staging area for the movement of troops to North Africa. In South Africa, the local manufacture of clothing, tools, and machinery was stimulated by wartime reductions in European imports, and by the end of the war manufacturing replaced mining as the principal element in the country's economic base. Although these industries were owned by whites, they provided a framework of modernization that could be used by independent nations if and when colonialism ended.

The war also furnished Africans who fought it with perspective and increased self-respect. All notions of white racial superiority vanished as Europeans destroyed themselves and devastated Europe. African soldiers who witnessed the liberation of German death camps saw for themselves the terrifying consequences of belief in a master race. Never again would African military veterans willingly accept white colonial domination.

European attitudes also changed as a result of the war, and this change benefited parts of Africa. Charles de Gaulle, for example, knew that France's colonies had given him a base of support without which his Free French movement would have collapsed. He convened a conference of delegates from throughout French Africa at Brazzaville in the French Congo in 1944. There he listened to African aspirations for autonomy within the empire, and explicitly guaranteed major economic, social, and political reforms for African peoples under French rule. As provisional president of France from 1944 to 1946, he fulfilled those commitments. At the same time the British government, its financial resources depleted by the war, began withdrawing from South Asia and laid plans for movement toward self-government for Britain's African colonies.

European Preparations for Colonial Autonomy

Decolonization in Asia in the first decade after the war did not guarantee that it would follow quickly in Africa. Nationalist movements in Asia dated back to at least 1900, and independence there was earned only after long, grinding struggles. In contrast, most of sub-Saharan Africa's colonial territories lacked nationalist movements in 1945 (Map 37.1). Nonetheless, Britain and France knew from the Asian example that nationalism was a

FOUNDATION MAP 37.1 Africa in 1945

At the end of World War II, the map of Africa had changed very little from what it had looked like in 1919. Notice that most of the continent remained under European colonial rule. Only four independent nations existed: Egypt (partially occupied by British troops), Ethiopia, Liberia, and the Union of South Africa. How would the sweep of decolonization across the continent alter the map of Africa?

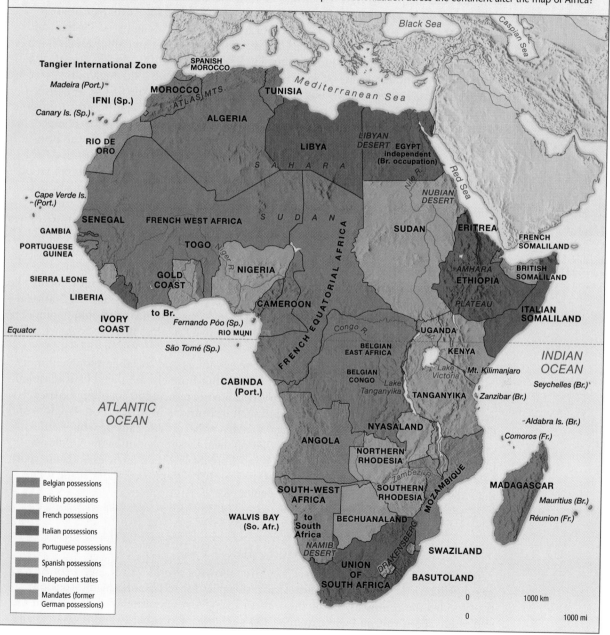

Tangier International Zone

Madeira (Port.)

SPANISH MOROCCO

MOROCCO

IFNI (Sp.)

Canary Is. (Sp.)

ATLAS MTS.

TUNISIA

Black Sea

Caspian Sea

Mediterranean Sea

ALGERIA

RIO DE ORO

LIBYA

LIBYAN DESERT

EGYPT independent (Br. occupation)

SAHARA

Nile R.

Red Sea

NUBIAN DESERT

Cape Verde Is. (Port.)

SENEGAL

FRENCH WEST AFRICA

SUDAN

SUDAN

ERITREA

FRENCH SOMALILAND

GAMBIA

PORTUGUESE GUINEA

TOGO

Niger R.

NIGERIA

AMHARA

ETHIOPIA

BRITISH SOMALILAND

SIERRA LEONE

GOLD COAST

LIBERIA

CAMEROON

PLATEAU

ITALIAN SOMALILAND

Equator

IVORY COAST

to Br.

Fernando Póo (Sp.)

RIO MUNI

FRENCH EQUATORIAL AFRICA

Congo R.

UGANDA

KENYA

INDIAN OCEAN

São Tomé (Sp.)

BELGIAN EAST AFRICA

Lake Victoria

Mt. Kilimanjaro

Seychelles (Br.)

CABINDA (Port.)

BELGIAN CONGO

Lake Tanganyika

TANGANYIKA

Zanzibar (Br.)

Aldabra Is. (Br.)

ATLANTIC OCEAN

NYASALAND

Comoros (Fr.)

ANGOLA

NORTHERN RHODESIA

MADAGASCAR

SOUTH-WEST AFRICA

Zambezi R.

SOUTHERN RHODESIA

MOZAMBIQUE

Mauritius (Br.)

WALVIS BAY (So. Afr.)

to South Africa

BECHUANALAND

Réunion (Fr.)

NAMIB DESERT

DRAKENSBERG

SWAZILAND

UNION OF SOUTH AFRICA

BASUTOLAND

Belgian possessions

British possessions

French possessions

Italian possessions

Portuguese possessions

Spanish possessions

Independent states

Mandates (former German possessions)

0   1000 km

0   1000 mi

dagger pointed at the heart of colonialism. Colonial officials hoped that the appeal of nationalism could be reduced by granting local autonomy to African colonies while retaining final control in London and Paris.

Britain and France revise their policies toward Africa

Immediately after the war, in an effort to reshape its empire, Britain developed a complex colonial policy. Its sense of urgency was heightened by the **Fifth Pan-African Congress**, held in Manchester, England, in late summer of 1945. At that gathering, nationalist leaders such as Jomo Kenyatta of Kenya, Léopold Senghor of Senegal, and Kwame Nkrumah (*KWAH-mā un-KROO-mah*) of Gold Coast announced their intention of creating independence movements. Hoping to prevent this, Britain launched a serious effort to modernize its colonies economically and socially. Although only 4 percent of African teenagers were attending secondary schools in 1960, the British established colonial universities and improved roads and port facilities. They restructured local government on a democratic basis, thereby forcing nationalist politicians to compete for public support against local chiefs, who could be more easily controlled by the British. In 1948, the white racist National Party won a startling electoral victory in South Africa and implemented its ruthless **apartheid** system of institutionalized racial discrimination. These events frightened London: British settlers in East and Central Africa might be inspired to treat their African majorities similarly, which in turn would increase the appeal of Marxist nationalist movements among Africans. London granted those settlers considerable local autonomy in an effort to prevent South African influence from spreading northward.

Kwame Nkrumah, Ghanaian independence leader and first president of the country.

Like Britain, France initiated a broad program of economic stimulation in its African colonies, hoping to prevent there the development of nationalist movements like the Vietminh in Indochina (Chapter 35). African representation in the French National Assembly was increased, and a new "French Union" was designed to promote joint consideration of policies and programs for the entire empire. Unlike Britain, however, France did not envision local autonomy.

Belgium and Portugal prohibit political activity in their African colonies

Even Belgium planned for more aggressive economic and social development in its colonies, Ruanda-Urundi and the Belgian Congo. But Brussels continued its traditional policy of obstructing the formation of an African elite, refusing to encourage African access to European universities or to build such institutions in Africa. Both Belgium and Portugal also prohibited all local political activity, either by Africans or white settlers, expecting to prevent the development of nationalism by simply outlawing politics entirely. Portuguese repression, implemented more rigorously than its Belgian counterpart, held off the independence of its African empire until 1975, more than a decade longer than any of the more flexible European democracies.

The Transformation of Africa After 1945

Africa changed dramatically in the fifty years following World War II. In North Africa, in sub-Saharan Africa, and in South Africa, struggles for independence and freedom transformed the continent. Throughout these years, African nationalists hoped that the end of European rule and white domination would bring prosperity and dignity to all parts of the continent. Independent existence, however, proved far more challenging than they had anticipated.

African Nationalism and the Cold War

The tendency of European and American governments to view decolonization in the context of the Cold War complicated their responses to African independence movements. France, which had been defeated in Indochina by the Vietminh (Chapter 35), was particularly concerned about communist influence. Since Sékou Touré, Kwame Nkrumah, and several other African nationalist leaders were Marxists, and since revolutionary organizations such as Algeria's FLN received weapons and supplies from Soviet bloc nations, including Czechoslovakia, most French prime ministers before de Gaulle assumed that Moscow was controlling African nationalist movements. Many American, Belgian, British, and Portuguese officials held the same assumption.

This conclusion was partly true. The Soviet Union was committed to the destruction of European colonialism in Africa and Asia and routinely offered independence movements verbal support, especially at the United Nations. Moscow also provided weapons and supplies to nationalist movements, insofar as possible. But to be a Marxist, particularly in a colonial setting, was significantly different from being a communist and accepting direction from the Soviet Union.

Many African nationalists viewed Marxism as an attractive alternative to capitalism. Instead of the apparent chaos of a capitalist marketplace, Marxism offered the stability of an economy controlled by the government. Instead of competition, Marxism offered cooperation, which was highly regarded in traditional African societies. Instead of inequality of wealth, Marxism held that wealth should be distributed "to each according to his needs." These aspects of Marxism were appealing, and they did not require acceptance of communism. Indeed, to accept direction from the Soviet Union seemed to many nationalists to be exchanging one set of European masters for another.

A Marxist poster exhorting Africans and other colonial peoples to rise up against Western powers.

African nationalist leaders often complicated the situation further by accepting aid from both the Soviets and the Americans during the Cold War. Nkrumah of Ghana, Julius Nyerere of Tanzania, Kenneth Kaunda of Zambia, and Jomo Kenyatta of Kenya were skilled at using superpower competition to their advantage, as was the Egyptian nationalist leader Gamal Abdel Nasser. Both Moscow and Washington lobbied for the support of newly independent nations in the United Nations General Assembly, and too easily assumed that governments not openly supportive were aligned with the other side. Once the Cold War ended, it was easier to understand the reality of the situation. African nationalist leaders had been acting in what they believed to be the interests of their own new nations, not in the interests of ideologies like communism and capitalism, and not in the interests of white, non-African nations like the United States and the Soviet Union.

North Africa

The Second World War brought German, Italian, British, and American troops to North Africa, throwing that region into turmoil and destabilizing the French and Italian colonial possessions of Morocco, Algeria, Tunisia, and Libya. When Italy lost the war, it also lost Libya (Map 37.2). Morocco and Tunisia were French protectorates, enjoying some degree of local autonomy under native rulers. The Sultan of Morocco and the Bey of Tunis, widely perceived as French puppets, were caught between governors from Paris and local independence movements. But the French war in Indochina distracted colonial

Map 37.2 Decolonization in Africa and Asia, 1941–1985

In 1945, only four African states were independent (Map 37.1). Note that by 1985, nearly the entire continent was self-governing. Most African nations gained independence during the period 1957–1965, a time characterized by British prime minister Harold Macmillan as one in which "winds of change" gusted across Europe's colonial possessions. Comparing Africa with the Middle East and Asia, what does this map tell you about patterns of decolonization?

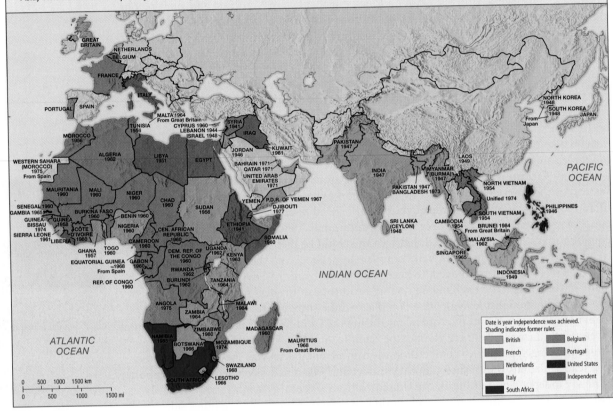

officials and nationalists alike until 1954, when Algeria took the lead in the struggle for independence in North Africa.

Algeria liberates itself through armed struggle

Algeria was technically not a colony, but a department of France, much as Hawaii is part of the United States. 90 percent of its residents were Arab or Berber Muslims, but 10 percent were Europeans, many of them descendants of French settlers from the 1830s. On the day World War II ended in Europe, May 8, 1945, a victory parade in the Algerian town of Sétif was disrupted by fights between Algerian nationalists and French soldiers. Eighty-eight French and more than a thousand Algerians died. Combat veterans such as Ahmed Ben Bella and Belkacem Krim responded by forming a secret nationalist organization, the *Front de Libération National*, or FLN. France's defeat in Indochina by the Vietminh gave the FLN confidence to launch the All Saints' Day Rising on November 1, 1954, a coordinated revolt in 45 Algerian cities signaling the beginning of Algeria's struggle for independence.

That struggle quickly earned the name "the dirty war." The FLN, which never numbered more than 20 thousand, was unable to oppose French army units in conventional warfare, so it used terrorist tactics, planting bombs in schools, post offices, and restaurants, often near windows so that survivors would be blinded by flying glass. The French responded with systematic torture of suspects, a strategy that caused increasing numbers of Algerians to support independence. Each side massacred innocent people connected with the other. By 1958 France had 750 thousand soldiers stationed in Algeria, but they could not discover and disarm every underground FLN operative. The great majority of Algerian Muslims resisted the French at every turn, sabotaging their military bases, cutting the throats of their sentries at night, and concealing and protecting FLN fighters during French military sweeps and searches.

On May 13, 1958, when the French National Assembly created a cabinet committed to negotiating with the FLN, the French army in Algeria, which was dedicated to keeping Algeria French, revolted. It seized control of the department from civilian authorities and threatened to invade France itself unless a government was formed that would keep Algeria French. Blackmailed by its own military, the Assembly turned to France's only hero of World War II, Charles de Gaulle. Invested with emergency powers for six months, de Gaulle pushed through a new French constitution providing for a strong presidency, ran successfully for that office, and used his position to address not only the Algerian war but also the future of the French Empire itself.

De Gaulle's policy toward Algeria astonished nearly everyone. By mid-1959 Algerian Muslim resistance had convinced him that they would never accept continued French rule, and he was not willing to station a million-man army there to guarantee it. The only alternative was to negotiate Algerian independence, and when de Gaulle's attitude became known, the army revolted in 1960 and 1961, attempting to remove the president and cancel the negotiations. Both times de Gaulle put down the revolt, persuading most French people to support his plan for disengagement while ordering rank-and-file soldiers to arrest or shoot their officers in defense of the government's authority. De Gaulle survived an organized campaign of assassination attempts and successfully removed France from Algeria in 1962.

The rest of North Africa was already free. France, overextended in Algeria, had freed Morocco and Tunisia in 1956, while Egypt, technically independent since 1922, became fully so when British troops evacuated the Suez Canal Zone in 1955. Only Spanish Morocco, also known as Western Sahara, remained as a last vestige of European imperialism north of the Sahara.

The new nations adopted differing styles of governance. Morocco remained a monarchy, as did Libya until 1969. In that year King Idris was overthrown in a conspiracy led by Colonel Muammar al-Qaddafi (*kuh-DAH-fē*), who ruled as a military dictator into the twenty-first century. The father of Tunisian independence, Habib Bourguiba (*boor-GĒ-buh*), ruled Tunisia as "president for life" until driven out in 1989; his replacement was no more democratic. The Egyptian revolution of 1952 that overthrew King Farouk brought the army to power under Gamal Abdel Nasser (1952–1970), Anwar al-Sadat (1970–1981), and Hosni Mubarak (since 1981). In Algeria, the FLN ruled alone until 1988, when an opposition movement of Islamist fundamentalists weakened it to the point that the military was forced to step in, an action that provoked widespread atrocities as fundamentalists then fought the military. North Africa's difficulties since in-

Members of a women's section of the FLN at a rally supporting Algerian independence.

Issues of governance arise in North Africa

dependence have been primarily political; the region has by and large achieved economic stability and has escaped the health crises and extensive poverty common in sub-Saharan Africa.

Sub-Saharan Africa

South of the Sahara, hopes for new beginnings flourished in the late 1950s. The success of independence movements in North Africa inspired Africans farther south to press harder for self-determination. Between 1957 and 1965, one former colony after another gained its freedom. In the following decades, however, the hopes that accompanied independence dimmed. Climatic changes caused severe droughts just south of the Sahara, and as the desert expanded southward, millions were displaced and malnourished. In the 1980s, an incurable disease called AIDS (Acquired Immune Deficiency Syndrome) infected tens of millions of Africans, mostly south of the Sahara. By 1995, nations such as Uganda, Botswana, and Zimbabwe were experiencing population reductions, as life expectancy for men fell into the upper 30s. Africans south of the Sahara had overcome colonialism, but not poverty and disease.

BRITAIN'S RETREAT FROM EMPIRE. Britain's African empire slipped away more slowly than France's. Beginning in 1947, London gradually surrendered control over the Gold Coast. There the dynamic nationalist leader Kwame Nkrumah became secretary of the United Gold Coast Convention, modeled to some extent on the successful Indian National Congress. Nkrumah led a series of strikes against British rule in the late 1940s, for which he spent several years in prison. In 1951, after his party won a majority in the Gold Coast legislature, he was released. He then conducted painstaking negotiations with British authorities and became prime minister when the Gold Coast became independent as the new nation of Ghana in 1957. By that time, failure in the 1956 Suez Crisis (discussed later in this chapter) had convinced London that it could not retain all its far-flung possessions. Ghana's independence opened the floodgates. The West African colony of Nigeria gained freedom in 1960, while Sierra Leone and The Gambia followed in 1961.

A pro-independence demonstration in Ghana.

Britain liberates its African colonies

In British East Africa, four colonies (Kenya, Uganda, Tanganyika, and Zanzibar) followed separate paths to become three independent nations. Nationalists led by Julius Nyerere (*nē-eh-RĀ-rā*) formed the Tanganyikan African Nationalist Union (TANU) in 1954, using Nkrumah's Gold Coast Convention as a model. Nyerere brought different African peoples together through use of the Swahili language, for centuries the language of East African trade. TANU won a majority in 1958 parliamentary elections, and Tanganyika gained independence in 1961, merging in 1964 with the offshore island sultanate of Zanzibar to create Tanzania. In neighboring Uganda, the Uganda People's Congress led a political alliance that gained freedom for the colony in 1962.

Kenya's independence movement was the last to succeed in British East Africa. Oppression of Africans by white settlers in the lush Kenyan highlands provoked a rural uprising there in 1952, led by an organization called Mau Mau (*MAOW MAOW*). This organization sought sweeping redistribution of white-owned lands to Kenyans rather than political independence, and most Kenyan nationalists disapproved of its violent tactics. Mau Mau burned white settlers' crops and farmhouses, and British troops fought

Julius Nyere, first president of Tanzania.

back, killing more than 10 thousand rebels in 13 years and imprisoning nationalist leaders in the mistaken belief that Mau Mau was a top-down political movement rather than a grassroots uprising. By 1955 Mau Mau was defeated, but London turned against the settlers whose oppression had caused the uprising. Nationalist leader Jomo Kenyatta, released from prison in 1961, led his party to victory in parliamentary elections, and Kenya became independent in 1963.

In British Central Africa, 200 thousand white settlers in Southern Rhodesia imposed apartheid-style segregationist laws modeled on those of South Africa. In 1953 London permitted the white settlers to create the Federation of Rhodesia and Nyasaland, which these settlers hoped would become a state like South Africa, with enough economic power to suppress nationalist movements by force. More extreme racist legislation followed, while nationalists organized strikes and demonstrations that quickly turned violent.

Mau Mau sympathizers in detention camp, early 1952.

In 1960 British prime minister Harold Macmillan, in a speech in Cape Town, South Africa, referred to the "wind of change" that was sweeping across Africa. The wind, of course, was African nationalism, and Britain was forced to acknowledge it. In 1964 Northern Rhodesia, led by Kenneth Kaunda, won its independence as Zambia, and Nyasaland, led by Sir Hastings Banda, became independent Malawi. But white settlers in Southern Rhodesia, trying to prevent a similar development in that region, declared independence from Britain in 1965 as a white-supremacist state. Supported by South Africa, but condemned by Britain and most of the rest of the world, Rhodesia held out against several separate African nationalist movements until 1980. Then a peace settlement enabled a black-majority government to assume power in the renamed state of Zimbabwe.

British prime minister Macmillan speaks of a "wind of change"

FAILURE OF THE FRENCH COMMUNITY. The Algerian war and de Gaulle's election as president called into question the future of the French Empire in Africa. France's new constitution, adopted in 1958, guaranteed all French colonies the right to self-determination, which might consist of independence or continued affiliation with France in the newly created "French Community." De Gaulle hoped that, given a choice between total independence and continued ties with France, the colonies would choose the latter. Initially all did so except Guinea, whose nationalist leader, the militant Marxist trade unionist Sékou Touré (*SĀ-koo too-RĀ*), campaigned vigorously against the Community, convincing 95 percent of voters to cast ballots against it.

A literacy class in French West Africa, 1950s.

De Gaulle responded to Touré's victory angrily, granting Guinea immediate independence and immediately withdrawing all French economic aid and equipment. Filing cabinets were shipped back to France, telephones were torn from walls, and lightbulbs were removed from their sockets. All Guineans who had worked for the French government, as soldiers or civil servants, were fired at once and denied pensions. De Gaulle may have expected that these actions would force Guinea to come back to the French Community, but Touré turned to the Soviets and Nkrumah's Ghana for help, and the new nation became a symbol of African defiance of colonialism. But its economy, always fragile, collapsed.

The French then hoped that Guinea's example would discourage other nationalist movements, but it did just the reverse. As Touré gained folk hero status, and British West Africa moved rapidly toward independence, the French Community was obviously failing. Between 1958 and 1960 all of France's African colonies except Djibouti (*jih-BOO-tē*) voted for

The French Community fails

independence. Disappointed, de Gaulle nevertheless reacted realistically, no doubt with the trauma of Algeria's fight for independence in mind. Agreements with the new states guaranteed continued French economic domination, a relationship later described as **neocolonialism**. For the rest of the century, France exercised extensive influence over its former empire, sending in the military to defend its commercial interests when political instability threatened.

CHAOS IN BELGIUM'S EMPIRE. In central Africa, Belgium owned three colonies: the Congo, Rwanda, and Urundi. The Congo, most notably, was rich in diamonds and other precious minerals. In 1959, mild pressure from the new Congolese National Movement, headed by an educated labor union leader named Patrice Lumumba, brought an offer of independence from the Belgian government, which was frightened by the prospect of Algerian-style war. But Belgium had done little to prepare the Congolese to rule themselves; there were only 16 university-educated Congolese in the entire colony. No sooner had independence been celebrated on July 1, 1960, than the new country fell apart.

Belgium's sudden withdrawal throws the Congo into chaos

Lumumba, who became prime minister, governed energetically, but he had no real political organization or associates whose talents matched his own. Moreover, the tribal nature of Congolese society proved a hindrance to national rule. Tribes in the Congo were much more important than political movements, and each tribe distrusted the others. Lumumba's tribal power base was in the countryside, but he had to rule from the capital city, Leopoldville, where his backers were outnumbered by tribal supporters of the president, Joseph Kasa Vubu. Both rivals were astonished when the resource-rich province of Katanga seceded from Congo less than a week after independence was declared. The Congolese army promptly mutinied; its soldiers, divided by tribal loyalties of their own and trained by their Belgian officers to consider nationalists like Lumumba and Kasa Vubu barbarians, now refused to obey the new leaders. Soldiers imprisoned their officers and began molesting black and white citizens alike. In response, Belgium intervened militarily to protect Belgian nationals. It also supported Katanga's secession, hoping it would further weaken Lumumba's position and justify the return of Belgian control.

Lumumba and Kasa Vubu, surrounded by chaos, sought U.N. intervention against Belgium but then discovered that Secretary General Dag Hammarskjöld, a Swede, insisted on negotiating with Katanga as though it were independent. The Congolese leaders suspected a European plot to recolonize Congo, and on July 14, 1960, they appealed to the Soviets to intervene. Although the two men acted jointly, the United States, which had been suspicious of Lumumba's leftist sympathies, concluded that he was a communist holding Kasa Vubu hostage. When U.N. troops arrived in Leopoldville the next day, they moved quickly to block the Soviet Union and the Marxist government of Guinea from any influence in the Congo.

Had the U.N. entered Katanga and expelled Belgian forces, the secession would have collapsed. Instead Katangese secession ruined prospects for a truly independent Congo and took the lives of both Lumumba and Hammarskjöld. Lumumba and Kasa Vubu fired each other (although neither had the authority to do so), and in the resulting turmoil, Lumumba ended up in the hands of Katangese soldiers, who murdered him in January 1961. As recounted at the opening of this chapter, Hammarskjöld, flying between Leopoldville and Katanga in a tireless effort to bring about a settlement, was killed that September in a plane crash.

Finally, at the end of 1962, the United Nations disarmed Belgian forces in Katanga and ended the secession. By that time Colonel Mobutu Sese Seko (*muh-BOO-too SĀ-sā SĀ-kō*) had emerged as a military strongman backed by the United States, which hoped to use him to control Congo's mineral resources. In November 1965 he overthrew the Congolese government and embarked on a 32-year military dictatorship of the unfortunate country, which he renamed Zaire.

The other two Belgian colonies gained independence in 1962 under the names Rwanda and Burundi. The Hutu and Tutsi peoples, dominant in Rwanda and Burundi, respectively, had been wary of each other since German and Belgian colonial officials had designated the Tutsi as the (allegedly) more advanced of the two ethnic groups and had favored them over the Hutu. In 1994, a plane carrying the president of Rwanda was shot down by missiles fired from a Rwandan military base. This proved to be the signal for a deliberately orchestrated genocide, in which Hutu paramilitary formations, backed by some Rwandan army units, massacred more than 500 thousand Tutsi. U.N. peace-keeping forces were pulled out, and since characterizing the conflict as genocide would have required intervention under international law and the United Nations Charter, that word was avoided in all official reports. The only outside forces remaining were two hundred soldiers from Ghana who had been sent to Rwanda as monitors for upcoming elections; they remained at their posts and saved thousands who would otherwise have been slaughtered.

Ethnic rivalries cause genocide in Rwanda

The Rwandan catastrophe quickly spilled over into neighboring Zaire, where Mobutu's dictatorship was crumbling as he neared death from cancer. Rwandan government forces, in pursuit of fleeing Hutu militias, crossed the border into eastern Zaire and linked up with movements resisting Mobutu. In 1997 Mobutu fled into exile, and resistance forces proclaimed the Democratic Republic of Congo. But Congo's enormous mineral wealth attracted military intervention against the new government from Angola, Rwanda, Uganda, and Zimbabwe, and eastern Congo exploded into a multinational conflict that by 2007 had killed more than 3.8 million people in the bloodiest conflict since World War II. Various attempts were made to end the fighting, but none have proved workable.

PORTUGAL'S UNIQUE DECOLONIZATION. The Portuguese Empire in Africa proved remarkably resistant to the impulse toward independence, at least for a time. Portugal was a poor country by European standards, and its government considered its African colonies vital to the Portuguese economy. There would therefore be no peaceful road to independence.

In 1961 the colonies of Angola, Mozambique, and Portuguese Guinea erupted in violent demonstrations against colonial rule. Antônio Salazar's fascist government (1932–1968) dispatched most of the Portuguese army to its colonies to suppress the fighting, but it did not end. As the fighting continued throughout the 1960s, Portuguese forces were gradually horrified by their own brutalities against people fighting for the sort of freedom Portuguese themselves would have cherished. By April 1974 the discontent of Portuguese soldiers had convinced several members of the military high command that Portugal could not win these wars. During one of its periodic reports to the government in Lisbon concerning the progress of the fighting, the high command overthrew that government and granted independence to the Portuguese Empire, effective in

The Portuguese army supports decolonization

April 1975. Civil wars between Marxist and non-Marxist nationalists broke out in Angola and Mozambique, with Marxists taking power in both countries and retaining control until after the Soviet Union's collapse in 1991.

From Apartheid to Freedom in South Africa

The struggle against colonialism took place all over the continent, but for decades the attention of Africans and non-Africans alike was fixed on South Africa, an autonomous British dominion until 1961, when it declared full independence. South Africa had fought against Germany and Japan in World War II under a coalition government headed by General Jan Christiaan Smuts, but his defeat by Daniel Malan's National Party in 1948 ushered in a new and disturbing era. Malan campaigned on a platform of apartheid, or strict racial segregation, under which white South Africans systematically discriminated against black South Africans (who made up the majority of the population) and people of mixed racial background (whom white South Africans called "Coloreds"). Sexual relations between whites and either blacks or Coloreds were absolutely prohibited under the Immorality Act. Blacks and Coloreds were denied the right to vote, were limited to menial occupations, and mostly lived in poverty. Police brutality against these oppressed groups was systematized and encouraged by the government and its supporters.

The National Party introduces apartheid in South Africa

Staggered by the regime's ruthlessness, blacks fought back through strikes and protests organized by the **African National Congress**. The ANC formed an alliance with the outlawed South African Communist Party, and the government promptly suppressed both organizations. ANC leaders such as Nelson Mandela and his law partner Oliver Tambo were removed from society, Mandela to a life prison term and Tambo to exile. Another resistance leader, Steve Biko, one of the founders of the Black Consciousness Movement, died in 1977 from brain injuries he received while in police custody.

Police beating anti-apartheid demonstrators in Durban, South Africa, 1959.

Antigovernment riots and police atrocities called the world's attention to this Nazi-style governance, as did *Cry, the Beloved Country*, a devastating fictional indictment of apartheid written in 1948 by a white South African politician, Alan Paton. White resistance to apartheid also came from the speeches of Helen Suzman, a member of parliament. The U.N. repeatedly censured South Africa, its athletes were banned from the Olympic Games, and it was increasingly isolated and condemned.

Eventually apartheid collapsed from a combination of internal and external pressures. By the late 1980s, internal opposition from blacks, Coloreds, and moderate whites increased, while international economic sanctions gravely weakened the country's economy. In 1989, prime minister F. W. de Klerk opened negotiations with the ANC, releasing Mandela in 1990 and working with him to end apartheid in 1993. With all South Africans finally allowed to vote, Mandela was elected president in 1994, and South Africa began a long-overdue transition to multiracial democracy.

A significant stage in that transition was official recognition that the apartheid system had provoked violence and crime on all sides. Central to this recognition was the creation of an innovative Truth and Reconciliation Commission, which held public hearings and granted amnesty to anyone willing to confess his or her crimes. This made the atrocities of the past a matter of public record, which the government considered an indispensable condition for multiracial cooperation. The amnesties proved controversial, because they permitted torturers and murderers to escape punishment, but for many the public testimony allowed healing to begin. In the early twenty-first century South Africa looked to a difficult future, but with a degree of national unity not thought possible in 1990.

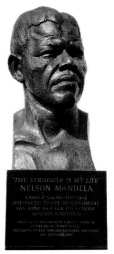

Challenges Facing Independent Africa

Throughout Africa and across the globe, the destruction of European colonialism stimulated excitement and hope, particularly among the young. Within Africa, young nationalists and idealists set to work building free and independent states. From the United States, young people came to Africa as part of the Peace Corps, a volunteer program created by President John F. Kennedy that builds infrastructure and improves education in developing nations. For a few years, the future of Africa seemed bright.

Nelson Mandela.

But nearly a century of colonial rule had molded African realities in ways agreeable to Europeans but often obstructive to Africans. The Cold War, with its superpower competition for the allegiance of newly formed countries, brought foreign pressures to nations like the Congo. Many African leaders proved poorly trained, corrupt, overwhelmed by the magnitude of the task facing them, or a combination of all three.

Politics: Democracy or Dictatorship?

Before the Europeans arrived, African societies were organized along tribal lines. Clan lineage and collective tribal decision-making were determining factors in setting policy, and kings or emperors, despite their exalted titles, usually ruled more by consultation than by force. In contrast, European colonial governments were top-down dictatorships administered from cities thousands of miles away. Dismissing captive peoples as inferior, they ruled through a blend of paternalism, patronage, and brutality. By 1945, most living Africans were unfamiliar with pre-imperial governing structures. Colonial despotism was the only form of government they had ever known.

The problems of the new nations were compounded because their boundaries had been drawn by European imperialists and were completely unsuited to African realities. Cutting across village, clan, and tribal communities, the lines looked neat and crisp on maps of Africa but left local populations bewildered and divided. When independence arrived, peoples speaking different languages, practicing different customs, worshiping different gods, and observing different traditional structures of social organization were expected to unify and to participate in European-style, multiparty democracies.

European imperialism holds back the growth of African democracy

Independence movements committed to popular sovereignty and parliamentary governance struggled with these African realities. Trying to reconstruct ethnic and tribal communities, politicians formed parties based more on those communities than on political or economic policies. This structure made parliamentary compromise difficult and allowed authoritarian leaders to assert that multiple parties destroyed national unity instead of promoting it. From this argument, it was a short step to one-party dictatorship, and this step was taken by Kwame Nkrumah in Ghana, Sir Hastings Banda in Malawi, Sékou Touré in Guinea, and Emperor Bokassa I in the Central African Republic. Other rulers, like Jomo Kenyatta in Kenya, Kenneth Kaunda in Zambia, and Julius Nyerere in

The opening of parliament in newly independent Ghana, 1957.

Tanzania, endorsed democratic ideals and permitted some criticism of the government, but ruled for decades as authoritarian leaders.

One-party, one-man rule marked the early years of independent Africa. Pluralistic politics gradually emerged in several nations in the 1990s, but only after the death or removal of the leaders listed above. In other countries, the fall of one dictator simply led to the rise of another. Political difficulties proved a long-lasting legacy of imperial rule.

Economic Underdevelopment

European economic exploitation of Africa was as destructive as its political domination. The imperialists plundered the continent of its mineral wealth and agricultural commodities. They forced African farmers to turn their land over to the production of valuable crops for export. As the cultivation of basic foodstuffs was neglected, a continent that had always been able to feed itself turned into a net importer of food. Development of local industries was not permitted; Europe's interest lay in exploiting its colonies, not in modernizing them. Colonial Africa was a net exporter of wealth to the industrialized world.

African economies are unprepared for independence

Independent African nations, led by elites often educated in Europe or North America, eagerly set out to industrialize. They hoped a North Atlantic model of modernization would enable Africans to replace European manufactured goods with locally made products, thus ending the export of African wealth to developed countries. For a number of reasons, this did not happen.

First, independent African societies contained too few educated people to industrialize on their own. Britain, France, Italy, Belgium, and Portugal had educated young Africans not for the challenges of independence but for the service of colonialism. The small number of trained Africans that European schools produced could not modernize their countries without massive expert assistance from the developed world.

Second, European technology and equipment were indispensable to African industrialization, and Europeans made them available at outrageous prices, payable not in African currencies (worthless in Europe) but in African minerals and commodities. This arrangement perpetuated the old colonial trading patterns and European economic control.

African infrastructure was designed for Europe's convenience

Third, African roads, railways, and telegraph and telephone lines were designed not for independent states but for colonies. Rail lines and roads ran from interior farming communities or mining districts directly to seaports, from which African wealth could be efficiently shipped to Europe or North America. Seldom did roads link one inland community with another. Electronic communications were equally European-oriented: a resident of Nairobi, Kenya, could place a telephone call to London relatively easily, but to call Mogadishu in the neighboring country of Somalia required routing to London, then to Rome (since Somalia had been an Italian colony), and from there to Mogadishu. Again the old colonial infrastructure perpetuated neocolonialism and hindered the development of relations between independent African nations.

One-product economies make African development difficult

Fourth, many new nations were burdened with economies dominated by one crop or one mineral. Zambia's copper, Ghana's cacao, Gabon's timber, and Sierra Leone's diamonds absorbed so much of the productive capacity, financial investment, and human talent of those countries that economic diversification seemed both impractical and undesirable. It was easier and more profitable to continue supplying those products to the developed world than it would be to convert to a balanced economy which, even if it could be achieved, might actually leave the country less prosperous than before.

These and other factors impeded the growth of healthy economies and tempted African leaders with the prospect of riches. Those who continued neocolonialism and assisted the developed world in exploiting African agricultural and mineral wealth were handsomely rewarded for their services. Corrupt, manipulative dictators kept their populations in poverty while placing their illegal gains in Swiss bank accounts and living in luxury in the midst of squalor. It is not surprising that in some of the newly independent nations, corrupt regimes were overthrown and immediately replaced by governments that were even more dishonest. Only in the 1990s did many African countries begin to develop the foundations of modern economies.

Social Challenges: Poverty, Ignorance, Disease

Underlying the economic difficulties of the newly liberated nations was a fundamental, sobering reality: Africa, a continent rich in the cultures and traditions of its peoples, was impoverished in areas indispensable to modernization. Its crops and minerals were subject to global market shortages and surpluses that African nations could not control. Deposits of coal, the cheapest fuel available for early-stage industrialization, were conspicuously absent from most African nations, and those few countries with significant oil reserves, like Algeria, Libya, and Nigeria, discovered after independence that those fields were still the property of multinational oil companies. Much of Africa's mineral wealth had already been taken away by Europeans, and as the Sahara Desert crept farther south following post-1950 changes in rainfall patterns, even a renewable resource like food became increasingly scarce. Africa's poverty, whatever its causes, was an undeniable fact, one with which all of its newly liberated nations would have to cope.

Dealing with poverty was made especially difficult by the low educational levels of most Africans. A few elite Africans had been educated in Europe and the United States, but the vast majority had not, and a significant minority had never been educated at all. African primary and secondary schools were clearly inferior to European and American schools, and most African students who attended them did so only long enough to learn how to read, write, and do basic arithmetic. These problems stemmed in part from imperial powers' indifference to the education of ordinary Africans and in part from the overwhelmingly rural character of most African societies, which made formal education less useful than backbreaking daily labor. The inadequate education of most Africans placed the already troubled new nations at an even more serious disadvantage.

As the decades turned over and the generation that had won independence aged and died, educational deficiencies were to some degree remedied, while poverty often deepened. Then a massive continental health crisis devastated many of Africa's weakest societies: the global spread of HIV/AIDS, a condition first identified in the Belgian Congo in 1959 that destroys the immune system and leaves the body open to lethal infections. It is most deadly in impoverished countries with poor health care systems, and it has devastated Malawi, Uganda, Zimbabwe, and South Africa. By 2007 between 25 and 30 percent of adults in eastern, southern, and central Africa were HIV-positive, and average life expectancy had fallen by four to ten years. Because most of its victims are young adults, HIV/AIDS kills or weakens the most economically productive sector of

Exporting cotton in Sudan, 1960s.

A satellite photograph of a dust storm over Morocco in 2003.

Serious social problems confront African nations

the population and leaves many young children orphaned. The burden it places on African health care systems is catastrophic.

All of these challenges are formidable obstacles for African nations hoping to modernize. Only insofar as Africa makes political and economic progress will it be able to create a stable framework for addressing poverty, ignorance, and disease.

The Transformation of the Middle East

The Second World War transformed the regions in which it was fought and the people who contributed to the war effort. For the Middle East the war's most dramatic consequence was the creation of Israel, an entirely new state whose presence focused Arab hostilities in the region and elevated regional conflicts to global significance.

The State of Israel and the Palestinian Conflict

In the nineteenth century, European Jews were divided over their prospects in modern national states dominated by Christians. Some hoped to assimilate by becoming secularized and adopting nationalism as a sort of substitute religion. Others, the **Zionists**, followed journalist Theodor Herzl's belief that Jews would always be outsiders in Christian Europe; only a state of their own would afford them genuine security. After witnessing the anti-Semitic hatred heaped upon Captain Dreyfus (Chapter 27), Herzl concluded that escape from Europe was the only rational strategy for Jews. His Zionist movement unsuccessfully sought territory for a Jewish homeland in remote locations such as Uganda and Wyoming, but Palestine, the ancestral home of the Jewish people, became the movement's preferred objective.

Zionism seeks a homeland for the Jewish people

Zionism's problem was that Palestine, part of the Ottoman Empire until 1918 and a British mandate after that, was populated by a Jewish minority and an Arab majority. Jewish nationalism was therefore bound to oppose Arab nationalism in the Middle East, and since Britain considered Arab friendship vital to the preservation of its connection to India and its exploitation of Persian Gulf oil, prospects for creation of a Jewish state seemed unlikely.

The **Balfour Declaration**, issued in 1917 by British Foreign secretary Arthur Balfour to gain Jewish support for the Allied side in World War I, placed Britain on record in support of a Jewish homeland in Palestine, provided the rights of existing Arab residents were not infringed. This clause, however, negated the entire document. Local Arab communities resisted the immigration of Jews from Europe and America, and during World War II many Arabs quietly sympathized with Nazi war aims. If Germany won the war, Arabs understood, it would take Palestine from the defeated British and expel the Jews. But Germany lost, and knowledge of the Nazi extermination of millions of European Jews heightened Zionism's appeal to Jews and swung American public opinion in favor of the creation of a Jewish state in Palestine. In 1945 the World Zionist Congress demanded that Palestine be opened to one million Jews, while U.S. President Harry Truman asked Britain to admit 100 thousand displaced Jews from war-torn Europe into Palestine. Several Arab states responded with warnings that they would use military force to oppose the creation of a Jewish state in Palestine.

Britain vainly sought a peaceful solution even as Jewish terrorist groups like the Irgun (*ear-GOON*) destabilized Palestine with bombings and murders in an effort to force the British out. In 1947 the United Nations recommended ending the mandate by partitioning Palestine into two states, one Palestinian and one Jewish (Map 37.3). Arab leaders rejected this solution, demanding that all Palestine be constituted as one state led by Arabs. More than 700 thousand Palestinian Muslims and Christians fled the country as the State of Israel was proclaimed on May 14, 1948. The new nation guaranteed Jews throughout the world a safe haven from future persecution. It was immediately attacked by seven Arab states, led by Egypt.

The Arab-Israeli War of 1948–1949 transformed the Middle East. Israeli forces outnumbered those of their enemies, and since Israeli independence was immediately recognized by both the U.S. and USSR, Israel could purchase modern weapons from both America and communist-dominated Czechoslovakia. Israeli victory in 1949 left the Arab states with humiliated armies and governments that had lost credibility with their own people. Arab monarchies in Syria (1949), Egypt (1952), and Iraq (1958) were overthrown by military conspiracies dedicated to secularization, modernization, and eventual victory over Israel. Meanwhile more than half a million Palestinians suffered in impoverished refugee camps in Jordan, deprived of clean water, decent shelter, and hope for the future.

The failure of Israel, the Arab states, and the U.N. to solve this refugee problem created the **Palestinian Question**. In 1949 the U.N. estimated that 726 thousand refugees were living in makeshift camps. Unlike displaced persons in Europe and India after 1945, these people were neither resettled in foreign lands nor returned to their own. Most remained in the filthy camps, where they lived as stateless persons for generations. By 2000, some of those born in the camps immediately after the 1948–1949 war had become grandparents, presiding over extended families whose members knew no other life. In 1949 one of the refugees assassinated King Abdullah of Jordan, widely considered the most moderate and realistic of the Arab leaders. The teeming camps became breeding grounds of hatred for all such moderates, as well as for Israel and its allies, especially the United States.

Young women members of the Irgun receiving military training in the 1940s.

The War of 1948–1949 creates the Palestinian Question

Arab Nationalism and the Arab-Israeli Wars

Egypt, as the most powerful Arab state, led the anti-Israeli coalition, and its 1952 revolution against King Farouk posed a serious threat to the Jewish state. A military dictatorship, installed under the leadership of Colonel Gamal Abdel Nasser, aimed for a more modern, secular regime that could avenge the humiliation of 1948–1949 and destroy Israel. Nasser was hailed as a champion of Arab nationalism, but he was much more than that. He was a charismatic, messianic figure who aspired to nothing less than the unification of all Arabs under his leadership.

This pan-Arabism would be difficult to achieve, because the states in which Arabs lived had long engaged in internal tribal, regional, and religious conflict. With the exception of Israel, all Middle Eastern and North African states that became independent after 1945 were Arab, but most of their populations were neither exclusively Arab in ethnicity nor exclusively Sunni Muslim in religion. Lebanon was torn by civil strife in 1958, in 1975–1976, and throughout the 1980s. Yemen was divided into two states for two

Map 37.3 The Arab-Israeli Conflict, 1947–2007

The proclamation of the State of Israel on May 14, 1948, was immediately followed by Israel's War of Independence against several Arab nations. Other Arab-Israeli wars followed in 1956, 1967, and 1973. Observe that the United Nations Partition Plan of November 1947 (see enclosure) established two states in the British mandate of Palestine, one Jewish and one Arab, as well as an international zone surrounding Jerusalem. But this plan was invalidated by the War of Independence, and Israel's borders were further modified by its occupation of the Sinai Peninsula, Gaza, the West Bank, and the Golan Heights in 1967. The continuing Israeli-Palestinian conflict focuses on the establishment of the type of Palestinian state originally conceptualized in the Partition Plan of 1947. How do the territories occupied by Israel in 1967 continue to affect Arab-Israeli relations?

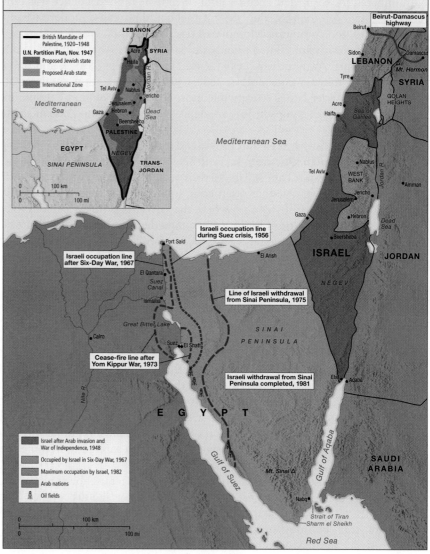

decades after 1962, with North Yemen backed by Saudi Arabia and South Yemen supported by Egypt and the Soviet Union. After gaining independence in 1956, the Sudan's northern region, Islamic and Arabic-speaking, struggled against its non-Islamic, non-Arabic southern region. After fighting its brutal war for liberation from France in 1954–1962, Algeria endured severe civil strife between its secularist military government and a cohesive, well-financed Islamist fundamentalist movement.

Despite these obstacles, Nasser worked toward unification. Barely surviving an assassination attempt in 1954 launched by Islamist fundamentalists opposed to the new regime's secularism, the new Egyptian leader fostered pan-Arab nationalism throughout the Arab world. This pan-Arabism led him to smuggle arms to Algeria's anti-French rebels and to establish close ties with the Soviet Union, which increasingly backed Arab nationalism to gain influence in the Middle East. In 1956, troubled by Nasser's policies, the United States cut off funding for the Aswan High Dam, an Egyptian power project designed to control the yearly flooding of the Nile.

Nasser attempts to unite the Arab world

Nasser responded by seizing the Suez Canal from the British, a daring move that delighted Arab nationalists (see "Speech by President Gamal Abdel Nasser of Egypt, September 15, 1956"). International attention quickly focused on the region when in November 1956 an Israeli attack on Egypt across the Sinai Peninsula was accompanied by a joint Anglo-French effort to retake the Canal. But neither Britain nor France had consulted the United States, and President Dwight Eisenhower opposed their military action, fearing that the real winners in a prolonged struggle would be the Soviets and their Arab nationalist allies. Interestingly, the USSR also opposed the Anglo-French

The Suez Crisis makes Nasser a hero

Document 37.1 Speech by President Gamal Abdel Nasser of Egypt, September 15, 1956

In these decisive days in the history of mankind, these days in which truth struggles to have itself recognized in international chaos where powers of evil domination and imperialism have prevailed, Egypt stands firmly to preserve her sovereignty . . . Egypt nationalized the Egyptian Suez Canal Company. When Egypt granted the concession to de Lesseps [in the 1860s] it was stated in the concession between the Egyptian Government and the Egyptian Company that the Company of the Suez Canal is an Egyptian company subject to Egyptian authority. Egypt nationalized this Egyptian company and declared freedom of navigation will be preserved.

But the imperialists became angry. Britain and France said Egypt grabbed the Suez Canal as if it were part of France or Britain. The British Foreign Secretary forgot that only two years ago he signed an agreement stating the Suez Canal is an integral part of Egypt. Egypt declared she was ready to negotiate.

But as soon as negotiations began, threats and intimidations started . . .

We believe in international law. But we will never submit. We shall show the world how a small country can stand in the face of great powers threatening with armed might. Egypt might be a small power, but she is great inasmuch as she has faith in her power and convictions . . .

We shall defend our freedom and independence to the last drop of our blood. This is the staunch feeling of every Egyptian. The whole Arab nation will stand by us in our common fight against aggression and domination. Free peoples, too, people who are really free will stand by us and support us against the forces of tyranny . . .

SOURCE: *The Suez Canal Problem, 26 July–22 September 1956*, U. S. Department of State Publication No. 6392 (Washington, 1956), 345–351.

action, fearing precisely the opposite: a swift Egyptian defeat. Britain and France, having alienated both superpowers, were forced to agree to a cease-fire and eventual withdrawal. The Suez Crisis made Nasser an Arab hero, while convincing Britain that it would be unable to hold its African empire in the long term. It also emboldened the Israelis, whose armored forces had performed brilliantly against their Egyptian counterparts.

For the next decade Nasser pursued his dream of Arab unity. In 1958 Syria's Arab nationalist government joined with Egypt to create the United Arab Republic (UAR), marking the high point of pan-Arabism. That July, however, the king of Iraq was assassinated in a military coup and the United States was frightened into sending marines to Lebanon to stop what appeared to be Nasser's plan to unite the entire region. But the marines were greeted on Lebanon's beaches by startled sunbathers and soft-drink vendors; no Nasserites could be located. Iraq, like Saudi Arabia, realized that joining the UAR meant sharing its oil revenues with Egypt and petroleum-poor Syria; it stood aside, and in 1961 a military coup in Damascus ended Syria's partnership with Egypt. Disappointed, Nasser turned inward, intent on building socialism at home.

Arab unity appeared dead, but Nasser's Egypt remained indispensable to Arab efforts against Israel. Egypt's defeats in 1948–1949 and 1956 only strengthened Nasser's resolve to modernize his armed forces in order to stand a chance of defeating Israel. The problem was that after the events of 1956 cut Nasser off from Western aid, this modernization depended on military assistance from the Soviet Union, whose equipment was inferior to Israel's. Egyptian military leaders failed to assess the weapons situation realistically and advised Nasser poorly.

In 1963, Israel's decision to draw water from the Jordan River (Map 37.3) revitalized Nasser's cause. At Arab summits he hosted in January and September 1964, participants established the **Palestine Liberation Organization (PLO)**, a coalition of more than thirty anti-Israeli organizations dedicated to Israel's destruction and its replacement by a secular Palestinian state. Now the Palestinian Question was attached to Egypt's foreign policy. In 1966 a radical wing of Syria's Ba'ath Party took power in Damascus and pressed Egypt for war with Israel. Nasser, whose armed forces still lacked adequate offensive weaponry, decided to ally with Syria in hopes of restraining its new radical regime. But he miscalculated drastically.

The Six-Day War changes the Middle East

Border clashes between Syria and Israel triggered a crisis in the spring of 1967. Fearing an Israeli attack on Egypt, Nasser blockaded Israeli shipping at the mouth of the Gulf of Aqaba. Israel responded on June 5 with a devastating predawn air strike, destroying Egypt's air force on the ground. It followed up with a shattering armored offensive that took the Sinai Peninsula, East Jerusalem, the West Bank of the Jordan River, and Syria's Golan Heights.

In the short run that brief, dramatic campaign, which came to be called the Six-Day War of June 1967, closed the Suez Canal for eight years and ended Nasser's goal of Arab leadership. Secular military dictatorships like his had come to power promising to defeat Israel; when they failed to do so, they lost their legitimacy in the view of Muslim traditionalists. In the long run, the lands occupied by Israel during the war became a crucial obstacle to regular relations between Israel and its Arab neighbors. Sinai was returned to Egypt in 1981–1982, but by then Israelis had begun building settlements in

Palestinian areas of the occupied West Bank, seeming to signal Israel's intent to control those lands indefinitely.

Following Nasser's sudden death in 1970, his successor, Anwar al-Sadat, expelled Soviet advisors and joined Syria in a surprise attack on Israel on October 6, 1973, the Jewish holy day of Yom Kippur and the tenth of Ramadan, Islam's holiest month. This Yom Kippur/Ramadan War ended in Arab defeat, but only after massive U.S. aid made up for initial Israeli setbacks. Arab oil-exporting nations embargoed oil shipments to nations supporting Israel, more than doubling the price of gasoline and plunging Europe, America, and Japan into severe recessions. Sadat's initial victories won him great respect in Egypt and gave him the leverage to break the cycle of warfare in the Middle East.

In 1977, convinced that continued tension with Israel would permanently impoverish Egypt, Sadat opened peace talks with the Jewish state. After the conclusion of peace in 1979 (see page 968), Egypt eventually regained the Sinai. But this peace also cracked the anti-Israeli coalition, leading to Egypt's expulsion from the League of Arab States and to Sadat's 1981 assassination by Islamist fundamentalists. His successor, Hosni Mubarak, nonetheless maintained Egypt's peace with Israel.

Anwar al-Sadat.

Egypt and Israel make peace

The Development of Islamist Fundamentalism

Egypt's startling decision to make and maintain peace with Israel astounded the Islamic world. The foundation of the State of Israel and the inability of Islamic countries in the Middle East to destroy it produced anguished soul-searching among Muslims. Once again, Islamic regimes confronted the reality and the consequences of Western technological supremacy. As Ira Lapidus demonstrates in his superb work, *A History of Islamic Societies*, Islamic responses were developed in the centuries-old context of Islamic connections and conflicts with the West.

NINETEENTH-CENTURY ISLAMIC RESPONSES. In the nineteenth century, **Islamic modernism** developed in reaction to the challenges posed by technologically advanced European societies. Many educated Muslims appreciated Western achievements and political values. These elites wanted to reshape Islam along European social and political lines, forming secular nationalist states to replace multinational states like the Ottoman Empire.

Islamic modernism held that if Muslims wished to compete militarily with European powers, they would have to centralize power in national states, establish Western-style education, industrialize their economies, and employ European military techniques and technologies. The Young Turks, during the last decade of the Ottoman Empire, were the first such modernist group to exercise power, preparing the way for Kemal Atäturk's later creation of a secular Turkish state.

Islamic reformism was a different response, developed by Sufi brotherhoods, tribal and religious leaders, and many farmers and merchants. They advocated a revitalization of Islam itself, both religiously and socially. Reformist scholars argued for the purification of Islamic beliefs and rituals in the light of proper understanding of the Qur'an and Shari`ah. They contended that corrupt forms of Islam should be abolished, by force if necessary. Non-Muslim practices and peoples should not be tolerated. True

Islamic modernism and reformism seek to change the nature of Islamic states

An Islamic school in Morocco.

Muslims must emphasize theological purity, moral rightness, and unwavering commitment to the creation of a righteous Islamic society throughout the world. Wahhabism (Chapter 22) was a reformist movement that eventually succeeded in creating a new nation, Saudi Arabia.

Modernism and reformism were not mutually exclusive. One could preach a return to the principles of early Islam while simultaneously recommending educational and technological modernization. Reformism in colonial areas could be transformed into resistance to foreign rule. But in the 1970s, Muslims found neither modernism nor reformism adequate to deal with existing realities. In this context, they developed a third response: **Islamic revival**.

ISLAMIC REVIVAL SINCE THE 1970s. After the Yom Kippur/Ramadan War of 1973 and Egypt's subsequent decision to make peace with Israel, Islamic revival spread rapidly throughout the Muslim world. In a religious context, Islamic revival was similar to Islamic reformism, embracing various movements designed to emphasize personal religious devotion and purify Islamic practice. But in a cultural context Islamic revival went further, denouncing Western values such as materialism, individualism, moral relativism, religious tolerance, sexual permissiveness, greater freedom for women, drug culture, and rock music. Islamic revival movements believe that these values and practices undermine Muslim family life and religious authority.

Islamic revival challenges Western values

Attacking Western values and stressing Islamic fundamentals, including the Qur'an and sayings of the Prophet, these movements are often described together in the West as **Islamist fundamentalism**. But in practice they vary widely. Some are tolerant, others intolerant; some are democratic, others authoritarian; some are peaceful, others revolutionary; some are open to dialogue with the West, others are not. Islamist fundamentalist movements view moderate Muslim regimes as corrupt, excessively cooperative with the West, and insufficiently devoted to the purification of Islamic religious practice. Such movements seek to remove moderate regimes from power, and thus are dedicated to political as well as religious change. But some of these groups are devoted to peaceful, evolutionary political change, while others are *jihadist* (Chapter 11), using violence as the principal tool for bringing change about.

ISLAMIC REVOLUTION IN IRAN. In 1979, the removal of the secular, modernizing Shah of Iran by traditionalists backing a conservative Shi'ite cleric, the Ayatollah Ruhollah Khomeini (*eye-ah-TŌ-lah roo-HŌ-lah hō-MĀ-nē*), brought Islamist fundamentalists to power. The Shah, a Sunni Muslim ruling a largely Shi'ite country, had been widely criticized for modernization's impact on traditional Iranian society. Drug use, alcohol consumption, and Western styles of dress and conduct deeply offended many Shi'ites, whose form of Islam was puritanical. But the Shah had also been protected by the United States, and his removal was accelerated by three foreign policy concerns: American support for Israel, the failure of secular regimes like his to destroy the Jewish state, and the frustration caused in the Muslim world by Egypt's peace with Israel. Ayatollah Khomeini proclaimed an Islamic Republic, in which religious leaders would exercise all executive, legislative, and judicial authority. Iran's opposition to the role played by the United States in the Middle East put it on a collision course with Washington, and a crisis erupted in 1979 when Iranian militants broke

Iran's Islamic Revolution challenges traditional Muslim regimes

Map 37.4 The Middle East Since 1945

The independence of the United Arab Emirates in 1971 ended European colonial rule in the Middle East. Notice the central geographic position of Iraq, mirroring the central position of Mesopotamia in ancient times. Since 1948 the region has been plagued by frequent wars: the various Arab-Israeli wars (Map 37.3), the Iran-Iraq War of 1980–1988, the Persian Gulf War of 1991, and the American invasions of Afghanistan in 2001 and Iraq in 2003. What accounts for the continuing turmoil in this region?

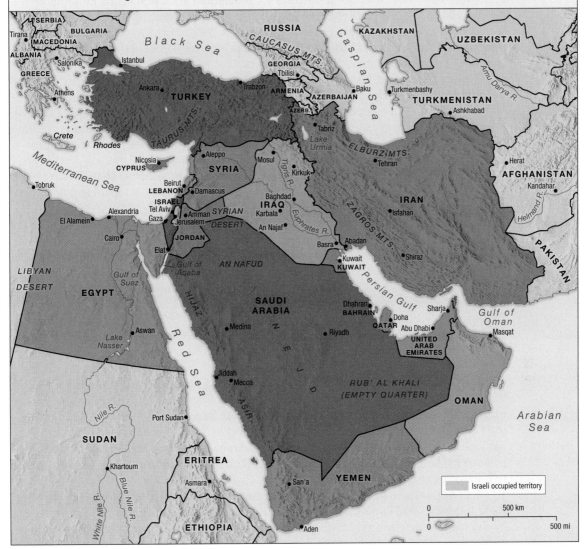

into the U.S. Embassy in Tehran and captured 52 embassy personnel whom it claimed were spies. This violation of diplomatic immunity caused a crisis lasting until the hostages were released in 1981 and poisoned U.S.-Iranian relations for decades thereafter.

ANTI-ISRAELI AND ANTI-WESTERN TERRORISM. We begin this section with a direct disclaimer. Terrorism is a highly sensitive subject in the modern world, and there are those who maintain that to attempt to understand the motives of terrorists, or the factors that make terrorism seem attractive to certain people, is to defend or approve of terrorism. This attitude is misguided. To understand an action or a condition is not the same as approving of it. To decide not to attempt to understand an action or a condition, because to do so may be controversial, is an act of willful ignorance. This section contains observations about the nature of terrorism and the conditions that help to nourish it. Those observations are provided in the hope that readers will understand terrorism, not that they will approve of it.

Although peace with Egypt brought Israel unprecedented military security, it also encouraged the growth of groups that fought Israel through terrorism, since Arab states could no longer hope for success through conventional military means. Terrorist attacks stem not from power but from the lack of it. States or organizations that lack the military, economic, or diplomatic resources to fight powers they consider oppressors sometimes turn to terrorism as a means of striking back. The Irgun, a Jewish organization, had resorted to terrorism after World War II in an effort to drive the British out of Palestine. Terrorism is therefore not a philosophy, an ideology, or a form of government: it is a tactic used by the weak against the strong.

Terrorism takes root in the Middle East

Israel's overwhelming military superiority in the Middle East, together with Egypt's departure from the anti-Israeli coalition, led some who felt powerless to turn to terrorism. Groups such as Islamic Jihad, Hezbollah (*HEZ-buh-lah*), and Hamas (*hah-MAHS*) carried out attacks on Israeli forces in Lebanon, parts of which were occupied by Israel in 1982 in an effort to expel Palestinian organizations that had taken refuge there under Syrian protection. One year later, suicide bombers killed 241 U.S. Marines and 58 French soldiers sent to Lebanon in an effort to pacify that country by separating Israeli forces from Palestinians and Syrians.

Terrorist groups such as these justified their actions by pointing to Israel's prolonged occupation of the territories taken in the 1967 war, in violation of a United Nations Security Council resolution. Frustrations on both sides led to abusive behavior and provocations. The poverty of the refugee camps bred despair, religious extremism, and support for radical action against Israel and its principal supporter, the United States. Islamic states such as Iran and Syria openly supported terrorist activities, while moderates in the Palestinian Arab community were overcome by those preaching hatred. As terrorist groups flourished, those endorsing peaceful paths to change were marginalized.

Terrorist attacks were intended to force Israel to withdraw from the occupied West Bank territories and make concessions to the Palestinians, but the growth of terrorism had no noticeable effect on Israeli policy. In 1988, Palestinian groups shifted their focus to attacking Israeli soldiers and civilians in the occupied territories. This **Intifada** (*in-ti-FAH-dah*), or "shaking off," was designed both to damage Israel's occupying forces and to call world attention to injustices against Palestinians. It caused significant physical and psychological trauma in Israel, but did not bring about an Israeli withdrawal. In the 1990s, events in the Persian Gulf temporarily sidetracked the *Intifada*, but it later returned at the same time that a global wave of terrorist attacks occurred.

Persian Gulf Wars and Global Terrorism

Islamist fundamentalism defined as enemies not only non-Islamic states but also all secularized Arab states, including Iraq, ruled since 1972 by Saddam Hussein, a military dictator whose socialistic Ba'ath Party had taken power in a 1968 coup. Believing that Iran had been weakened militarily by its break with America, Saddam in 1980 attempted to seize an Iranian waterway linking his country to the Persian Gulf. The ensuing Iran-Iraq War dragged on for eight years, killing nearly two million soldiers and civilians and severely straining both countries' economies. It ended in 1988 with modest territorial gains for Iraq.

Two years later, Saddam tried to make up for the war's economic losses by seizing the oil-rich nation of Kuwait, claimed for decades by Iraq as its nineteenth province. But his ambitions were thwarted by the United States, which organized a 32-nation U.N. coalition, supported by Saudi Arabia and other Arab nations fearing Iraqi expansionism. In early 1991, in the **Persian Gulf War**, the coalition expelled Iraq from Kuwait. Its success greatly heightened U.S. leverage in the Middle East. That leverage, coupled with Israeli restraint in the face of Iraqi efforts to draw Israel into the war and split the coalition, shattered the longstanding Arab refusal to recognize Israel's right to exist. Saudi Arabia, which for decades had poured money into the anti-Israeli cause, now stated that Israel had earned the right to be treated as a good neighbor and cut off funding for the PLO, which had backed Iraq in the Persian Gulf War.

Iraq's seizure of Kuwait leads to regional conflict

Left without financial backing, in 1993 PLO leader Yasir Arafat signed a peace agreement with Israeli Prime Minster Yitzhak Rabin (*rah-BĒN*) in Washington on the White House lawn. Under its terms, Israel accepted the necessity of creating a Palestinian state and the PLO recognized Israel as a legitimate nation. Peace between Israel and Jordan followed in 1994, and it appeared that the troubled Middle East might be on the verge of a solution to the vexing Palestinian Question.

A U.S. tank in front of burning oil wells during the Persian Gulf War.

Then violence and extremism again shattered the possibility of peace. An Israeli extremist, outraged at these developments, assassinated Rabin at a peace rally in 1995. The next year, terrorist groups found a safe haven in Afghanistan, where the Taliban came to power. This ultrafundamentalist movement subjected its citizens to the full rigors of seventh-century Islamic law, characterized by mutilation and execution for offenses that elsewhere were punished by imprisonment or fines. Under Taliban rule, women were banned from employment and denied an education. Throughout the 1990s, militant fundamentalists organized and trained in Afghanistan for actions throughout the Middle East. Terrorists orchestrated attacks on Israelis, worked to undermine the Egyptian government, murdered thousands in Algeria, carried out assaults on U.S. embassies and ships, and solidified Iran's Islamic Republic.

Al Qaeda attacks the United States

In 2000, negotiations in America over Palestinian statehood came close to reaching an agreement but ultimately failed. A tragic sequence of events followed. The *Intifada* was renewed on the West Bank, while in Israel a new hard-line government opposed further concessions to the Palestinians. Then, on September 11, 2001, came a dramatic attack on the United States. Members of a terrorist network called Al Qaeda (*AHL KĪ-dah*) hijacked four commercial airliners and deliberately crashed them into both towers of the World Trade Center in New York City (collapsing both buildings), the Pentagon in Washington, and an open field in Pennsylvania (the last crash resulting from an apparent struggle between passengers and hijackers). Aghast at its vulnerability and the deaths of almost three thousand Americans, the United States promptly declared war against terrorism. In October 2001, American forces attacked Afghanistan and removed its Taliban government, which had furnished bases to Al Qaeda.

Two years later, a coalition of forces led by the United States invaded Iraq, destroyed the Ba'athist regime, and captured Saddam Hussein. Washington's stated objective was to establish a democratic government in Iraq, thereby removing it as a possible base for terrorist attacks. Since Iraq apparently was not involved in the 2001 attacks on America, however, the Iraq War of 2003 proved highly controversial, and it increased hatred of America throughout the Islamic world. Countries seen as supporters of the American-led invasion, including Spain, Indonesia, Britain, and Saudi Arabia, were themselves attacked by terrorists.

The destruction of Ba'athist Iraq, moreover, left Iran as the Persian Gulf's main power, dramatically altering the balance of forces in Islamic Southwest Asia. In 2005, as Iraq under U.S. occupation struggled to form a democracy acceptable to its Shi'ite, Sunni Arab, and Kurdish populations, Iranian voters elected as president Mahmoud Ahmadinejad (*ahk-mah-DĒ-nih-jahd*). The new president was an Islamist fundamentalist whose desire to develop a uranium-enrichment program far more sophisticated than that required to make nuclear fuel for peaceful purposes led many to conclude that he hoped to build nuclear weapons and destroy Israel.

More than half a century after the end of World War II and the establishment of Israel, peace had not come to the Middle East.

Chapter Review

Putting It in Perspective

In the early twenty-first century, the problems of Africa and the Middle East seemed overwhelming. Some of Africa's problems had natural causes, such as the severe droughts of 1970–1990 that pushed the Sahara farther south, and the catastrophic AIDS epidemic that reduced populations in sub-Saharan Africa. Others, however, were legacies of colonialism, which left most African nations without the industrial resources required for modernization and unfamiliar with the functioning of modern democratic societies. Although many of these new nations were dangerously unstable, the former colonial powers of Europe often washed their hands of Africa after independence, reducing aid to minimal levels. Rapid population growth meant that most families lived in poverty and frustrated efforts to improve literacy rates and public health. These enormous problems undermined the hopes Africans once held for the benefits of decolonization and independence.

The Middle East faced a different set of challenges. Terrorist attacks against Israel, the United States, and other lands perceived as their supporters marked the resurgence of an Islamist fundamentalism that was amplified by anti-Western resentments and failure to resolve the Palestinian Question. In the face of this resurgence, Islamic societies had to choose: would they continue efforts to modernize, secularize, and democratize, even if such changes proved incompatible with their traditional values and cultures? Or would they pursue the antimod-ernist and antimaterialistic philosophies that were still powerfully attractive to many Muslims? Would they find a way to coexist in peace with Israel? Or would they persist in efforts to destroy the Jewish state? On the answers to such questions rest the future stability and prosperity of the Middle East and the world.

Reviewing Key Material

KEY CONCEPTS

decolonization, 971	Palestinian Question, 986
Fifth Pan-African Congress, 973	Palestine Liberation Organization (PLO), 989
apartheid, 973	Islamic modernism, 990
neocolonialism, 979	Islamic reformism, 990
African National Congress (ANC), 981	Islamic revival, 991
Zionists, 985	Islamist fundamentalism, 991
Balfour Declaration, 985	Intifada, 993
	Persian Gulf War, 994

KEY PEOPLE

Dag Hammarskjöld, 970, 979	Nelson Mandela, 981
Kofi Annan, 970	Theodor Herzl, 985
Charles de Gaulle, 971	Gamal Abdel Nasser, 986
Jomo Kenyatta, 973	Anwar al-Sadat, 990
Léopold Senghor, 973	Ayatollah Ruhollah Khomeini, 991
Kwame Nkrumah, 973	Saddam Hussein, 994
Julius Nyerere, 977	Yasir Arafat, 994
Sékou Touré, 978	Yitzhak Rabin, 994
Patrice Lumumba, 979	
Mobutu Sese Seko, 980	

ASK YOURSELF

1. How and why did World War II lead to the decolonization of Africa?
2. How and why did Britain and France differ in their attitudes toward African nationalism?

3. How were Arab nationalism and the Palestinian Question connected?
4. How does Islamist fundamentalism affect the conflict between modernity and tradition in the Islamic world?

GOING FURTHER

Ansprenger, F. *The Dissolution of the Colonial Empires.* 1989.

Berman, Bruce, and John Lonsdale. *Unhappy Valley: Conflict in Kenya and Africa.* 1992.

Cooper, Fred. *Africa Since 1940.* 2000.

Davidson, B. *The Black Man's Burden: Africa and the Curse of the Nation-State.* 1992.

Dekmejian, R. H. *Islam in Revolution: Fundamentalism in the Arab World.* 1995.

Dubow, S. *Racial Segregation and the Origins of Apartheid in South Africa.* 1989.

El Khazen, M. *The Breakdown of the State in Lebanon, 1967–1976.* 2000.

Esposito, J. L., ed. *The Iranian Revolution: Its Global Impact.* 1990.

French, Howard. *A Continent for the Taking.* 2004.

Goodman, David. *Fault Lines: Journeys into the New South Africa.* 1999.

Hargreaves, J. D. *Decolonization in Africa.* 1988.

Keddie, N. R. *Modern Iran: Roots and Results of Revolution.* 2003.

Keddie, N. R. *Women in Muslim Societies: The Long Path of Change.* 2004.

Long, D. E. *The Kingdom of Saudi Arabia.* 1997.

Louis, W. R., and R. Owen. *Suez 1956: The Crisis and Its Consequences.* 1989.

Mamdani, Mahmood. *When Victims Become Killers: Colonialism, Nativism, and the Genocide in Rwanda.* 2001.

Mandela, Nelson. *Long Walk to Freedom.* 1994.

Musallam, A. M. *The Iraqi Invasion of Kuwait.* 1996.

Polk, W. R. *The Arab World Today.* 1991.

Shillington, Kevin. *History of Africa.* 1995.

Smith, C. *Palestine and the Arab-Israeli Conflict.* 1988.

Throup, D. W. *Economic and Social Origins of Mau Mau.* 1987.

Waterbury, J. *The Egypt of Nasser and Sadat.* 1983.

Key Dates and Developments

African Independence

1935	Italy invades Ethiopia
1941	Liberation of Ethiopia
1944	Brazzaville Conference
1945	Fifth Pan-African Conference
1948	National Party wins South African elections
1951	Independence: Libya
1956	Independence: Morocco, Tunisia, the Sudan Suez Crisis
1957	Independence: Ghana
1958	Independence: Guinea All-African People's Conference in Ghana
1960	Independence: Senegal, Mauritania, Mali, Upper Volta, Ivory Coast, Chad, Central African Republic, Gabon, Togo, Dahomey, Cameroon, Congo, Nigeria, Somalia Congo Crisis
1961	Murder of Lumumba; Death of Hammarskjöld Independence: Tanganyika
1962	Independence: Algeria, Uganda, Rwanda, Burundi
1963	Independence: Kenya Nelson Mandela imprisoned in South Africa
1964	Independence: Zambia, Malawi Creation of Tanzania
1965–1980	White supremacist government in Southern Rhodesia
1966	Independence: Botswana, Lesotho
1968	Independence: Swaziland
1974	Revolution in Portugal
1975	Independence: Guinea-Bissau, Angola, Mozambique
1977	Independence: Djibouti
1980	Independence: Zimbabwe
1990	Independence: Namibia
1993	Release of Nelson Mandela
1994	Free elections in South Africa

The Middle East Since 1945

1946	Independence of Transjordan
1948	Foundation of the State of Israel
1948–1949	First Arab-Israeli War
1949	Revolution in Syria
1952	Revolution in Egypt (Nasser)
1956	Suez Crisis
1958	United Arab Republic (Egypt and Syria) Revolution in Iraq
1964	Formation of the Palestine Liberation Organization
1967	Six-Day War
1968	Ba'athist Revolution in Iraq
1970	Death of Nasser
1973	Yom Kippur/Ramadan War
1979	Peace between Egypt and Israel Islamic Republic proclaimed in Iran
1980–1988	Iran-Iraq War
1981	Assassination of Sadat
1982	Israel invades Lebanon
1988	First Palestinian *Intifada*
1990	Iraq invades Kuwait
1991	Persian Gulf War
1993	Oslo Accords: Israel recognizes PLO
1994	Peace between Jordan and Israel
1995	Assassination of Rabin
2000	Second Palestinian *Intifada*
2001	September 11 terrorist attacks against U.S. United States invades Afghanistan
2003	United States invades Iraq

African diaspora "Dispersed" or transplanted Africans and their descendants.

African National Congress An organization founded in South Africa in 1912 by educated African professionals to combat white racial oppression.

Afrikaners Descendants of Dutch and other European immigrants who settled in southernmost Africa near the Cape of Good Hope after 1652; also called Boers.

Ahimsa Nonviolence toward all living things, a principle followed by the Jains of India.

Almoravids Berber followers of a militantly puritanical sect of Islam who believed that in order to conduct successful wars against unbelievers, Muslims must first purify their own souls.

Amerinds Anthropological term for American Indians, used to distinguish them from the Indians of South Asia.

Ancestor worship Veneration of a family's departed relatives and forebears, originally practiced in ancient China.

Animism The belief that spirits exist that can either help or harm human beings.

Anschluss Union of Austria with Germany, carried out by Hitler in 1938.

Anticolonialism Resistance to colonial rule.

Apartheid A system of institutionalized racial discrimination established in South Africa in 1948.

Archaic Period An era in ancient Greece, from 700 to 500 B.C.E., during which city-states matured and population growth resulted in a shortage of farmland, leading Greeks to develop colonies around the Mediterranean world.

Aristocracy Rule by a class of well-born families.

Armistice A temporary cessation of hostilities between warring powers.

Artistic Realism An artistic style pioneered by Giotto, emphasizing detail, depth, and perspective to replace stylized rigidity with lifelike portraits.

Asceticism The practice of extreme self-denial and renunciation of all possessions.

Assassins A Shi'ite sect of killers known as *hashashin*, or "hashish users."

Assembly line A process by which products are manufactured in continuous flow through a series of stations that each perform a separate function.

Augustus One who rules with majesty and grandeur; a title Rome conferred on Octavian.

Baby boom A huge surge of births in the United States in the two decades following the end of World War II.

Balance of power A situation in which key nations offset each other's strengths, so that none is strong enough to impose its will on the others.

Balfour Declaration Issued in 1917, this statement placed Britain on record in support of a Jewish homeland in Palestine.

Bantu The West African word for "people"; a group of related languages; tribes of West Africans who migrated throughout much of Africa over a number of centuries.

Bastille A large prison and arsenal in eastern Paris whose capture in 1789 by supporters of the National Assembly frightened King Louis XVI into capitulating to the French Revolution.

Bill of Rights A written document specifying the rights that King William III and Queen Mary of England were required to endorse in 1689 as conditions of their rule.

Bishops Christian Church officials presiding over districts known as dioceses.

Blank check Issued in July 1914, a guarantee that Germany would support any action Austria might take against Serbia in the aftermath of the assassination of Austrian Archduke Franz Ferdinand.

Blitzkrieg "Lightning war," an innovative German tactic based on radio coordination between armored units and dive-bombers; instrumental in Germany's defeat of Poland in 1939.

Bloody Sunday A day in January 1905 on which a massive, peaceful workers' demonstration was fired on by imperial Russian troops, killing several hundred.

Bolsheviks Literally, "those in the majority" in the Russian Social Democratic Party after 1903; led by Lenin, they seized power in the October Revolution of 1917 and later became the Soviet Communist Party.

Bosnian Crisis of 1908–1909 A serious international crisis that tied Austria closer to Germany and provoked an immense eight-year military buildup in Russia.

Boston Tea Party A protest in 1773 by Britain's colonists in Boston against a tax levied on tea.

Boyar class An aristocracy that played a significant role throughout much of Russian history.

Braceros Mexican immigrant workers who began entering the United States in 1942 to work in factories replacing U.S. workers drafted during World War II.

Brezhnev Doctrine The assertion in 1968, following the Warsaw Pact's invasion of Czechoslovakia, that the Soviet Union had the right to intervene in other communist countries to protect the global interests of socialism, as defined by Soviet leaders.

Bridewealth In Africa, a payment from the groom to the parents of the bride to compensate them for the loss of their daughter and assure them that he would treat her well.

Bubonic plague A deadly contagion typically carried from rodents to humans by fleas.

Caesaropapism The vesting of all spiritual and political authority in a single person in the Byzantine Empire.

Calico Indian cotton cloth that came from Calicut on India's Malabar Coast.

Caliph Successor of Muhammad, the Messenger of God.

Capitalism An economic system based on competition among private enterprises.

Cash crops Commodities that when harvested could be sold for money to purchase food and other necessities.

Cassava A large hardy root plant from the American tropics, native to Brazil and used as a food staple in Africa; also called manioc.

Castes Exclusive and restrictive hereditary occupational groupings, based on birth and ranked in hierarchical order.

Caudillos Latin American leaders who ruled as strong personalities and often failed to develop stable and enduring political and economic institutions.

Celibacy Abstinence from marriage and sex.

Chan (Zen) Buddhism A belief system teaching that meditation is the only path to enlightenment and stressing love of nature, simplicity of life, and individual self-discipline.

Charter companies Trading associations protected by royal monopoly.

Chinampas Large latticework platforms of layered mud and lake plants floating on the surface of a Mexican lake and designed for cultivation of crops.

Chosen people The belief that the Jewish people were chosen by the one true God to be his people.

City-States Independent urban political domains that controlled the surrounding countryside.

Civil rights movement A nationwide campaign for racial equality in the United States in the twentieth century.

Civil service exams Chinese examinations requiring applicants for the state bureaucracy to demonstrate comprehensive knowledge of the Confucian classics.

Civilizations Very large complex societies, or regional groups of complex societies, with widely shared or similar customs, institutions, and beliefs.

Classical Period The era from 500-338 B.C.E., in which classical Greek philosophy, art, and drama flourished.

Cohong Merchant guild of Guangzhou (Canton); a group of Chinese firms authorized by the imperial government to conduct commerce with foreigners.

Collective farms In Soviet Russia, multifamily farms supposedly owned by their members but actually run by the state.

Collective liability A Russian practice whereby all members of a community were jointly responsible for taxes and other obligations, and were considered liable for the actions of everyone in the community.

Committee of Public Safety A group of officials given broad powers in 1793-1794 to protect France from foreign and domestic enemies.

Common market The European Economic Community, a coalition of nations agreeing to reduce tariffs on each other's goods to expedite commercial growth.

Communists Revolutionary socialists who promoted violent overthrow of the existing political and social order.

Compromise of 1867 A bargain granting Hungarians autonomy by dividing the Habsburg Monarchy into self-governing Austrian and Hungarian sections.

Concertación A Chilean democratic alliance that successfully defeated General Augusto Pinochet's referendum on continuation of military rule in 1988.

Concubines Women who are not the main wife of a man (commonly a ruler) but are kept by him for sexual purposes.

Confucianism A system of thought in China based on humane conduct and familial respect.

Congress system An ongoing mechanism devised by Prince Metternich to enable Europe's major powers to hold periodic meetings to preserve order.

Conservatives People who sought to retain the structures and ways of the past.

Containment of communism A United States Cold War policy based on George Kennan's assertion that communism, if contained geographically and prevented from expanding, would eventually collapse.

Continental system Napoleon's insistence that all European countries dominated by France boycott British goods.

Coolie trade The hiring or kidnapping of poor Chinese workers to serve as cheap labor in places such as Cuba, Peru, or California.

Cosmic mission theory The Aztec theory that the sun must be nourished with an invisible elixir found only in beating human hearts.

Cossacks A diverse assortment of frontier adventurers dwelling in the steppe lands north of the Black and Caspian Seas.

Cottage industry A system under which peasants would make products in their own cottages and sell them to merchant capitalists.

Council of the Indies A board established by King Carlos I of Spain in 1524 to supervise every aspect of government in Spanish America.

Covenant A binding agreement between the God of Israel and his chosen people.

Criollos White people of European ancestry born in Spanish America.

Cuban missile crisis A grave confrontation between the United States and the Soviet Union over the presence of Soviet nuclear missiles in Cuba.

Cubism An artistic style using geometric shapes to produce bold images.

Cultural adaptation The process by which hominids used their intellectual and social skills to adjust to their surroundings and improve their chances for survival.

Cultures Unique combinations of customs, beliefs, and practices that distinguish societies from each other.

Cuneiform Wedge-shaped writing developed by the Sumerians.

Daimyo Hereditary regional warlords who dominated segments of Japan.

Daoism A naturalistic Chinese philosophy calling on people to live in harmony with nature.

D-Day June 6, 1944, the day on which the Allies invaded France to begin to liberate Western Europe from German occupation.

Decolonization A process whereby colonized peoples in Asia and Africa gained independence from Western imperial domination, often through nationalistic "liberation movements."

Deism A rational religion that viewed God not as a divinity deeply involved in human affairs, but as a master mechanic or "great watchmaker" who created the universe as a vast machine, established the laws by which it operated, and then mostly left it alone.

Democracy Rule by the entire body of citizens.

Descamisados "Shirtless ones," Argentina's manual laborers who formed the base of support for President Juan D. Perón.

Détente A relaxation of international tensions.

Dharma The faithful performance of the duties pertaining to one's caste or station in life; such performance determines one's fate in the next life.

Dictator Originating in Rome, a term to characterize a tyrant.

Dictators In the twentieth century, leaders who wielded total control, dominated weak elected institutions, and used the army and police to stifle dissent.

Diplomatic Revolution of 1890–1907 The process whereby Bismarck's diplomacy was reversed and Germany was encircled by France, Russia, and Britain.

Dirty war The Argentine military government's repression, torture, and murder of Peronists, Montoneros, and Communists from 1976 to 1978; also used to describe the French-Algerian War of 1954–1962.

Dominion government A compromise whereby large British colonies such as Canada and Australia were granted self-government while technically remaining dominions of the British Empire.

Domostroi "Household Order," a manual advising Russians on running their families.

Dowry A bridal endowment of money or property.

Duma A Russian council or parliament.

Dutch learning Western techniques of shipbuilding, weaponry, art, sciences, music, and medicine, transmitted to Japan by the Dutch.

Dynastic cycle A four-phase cycle in China during which a dynasty emerges, rules well for a time, then rules poorly and is overthrown by a new dynasty.

Economic nationalism The creation of tariff walls and trade barriers to protect a country's industries and products from international competition.

The elect In Calvinist Christianity, people chosen beforehand by God for salvation.

Eleven Years' Tyranny The period between 1629 and 1640 when King Charles I ruled England without calling Parliament.

Enclosures The practice by English landowners of fencing or hedging off large tracts of land to pasture their sheep or to implement new farming methods.

Enlightenment A European intellectual movement, inspired by boundless faith in human reason, that sought by using reason to achieve progress in all areas of human endeavor.

Enterprise of the Indies Columbus's detailed plan for a westward maritime expedition to discover a shorter route from Europe to East Asia.

Estado Nôvo "New State," a military-backed dictatorship established by Getúlio Vargas in Brazil in 1937.

Estates general A nationwide assembly of representatives from the three estates of French society.

Eunuchs Castrated men who ran the ruler's palace and guarded his concubines.

Farming villages Small settlements of homes in a compact cluster, surrounded by lands on which the villagers raised food.

Fascism An ideology that promoted belligerent nationalism and repressive dictatorship, subjecting individual rights to the goals of the nation and its leader.

Fatimid An Egyptian Shi'ite dynasty that broke away from Abbasid rule and established a separate caliphate along the Nile River in 929.

Fatwa A legal opinion from the highest Islamic legal authority.

Fifth Pan-African Congress A meeting in Manchester, England, in 1945 in which several African nationalists announced their intention to create independence movements.

Five Pillars The basic religious tenets of Islam.

Floating world Japanese urban amusement areas offering men escape from austerity in indulgent nightlife.

Foot binding A process in which the feet of Chinese girls were tightly wrapped with strips of cloth to make them sexually attractive to men.

Foragers Those who subsist by gathering wild plant foods and hunting wild animals.

Fresco Painting on walls when the plaster was still wet so the colors would penetrate it.

Fronde A rebellion of French nobles between 1648 and 1653 attempting to reverse the trend toward royal absolutism.

Fulani A pastoral West African people who became enchanted with Sufism and founded the Sokoto Caliphate in 1809.

Gang of Four A group of Chinese radicals who sought to seize power after Mao's death in 1976 in order to renew the Cultural Revolution.

Gauchos   Cowboys of the Argentine backlands.

Geneva Accords   A multinational agreement reached in 1954 to end French colonial rule in Indochina.

Genocide   The deliberate and systematic destruction of an entire race or ethnic group.

Glorious Revolution   A cooperative effort by the English Parliament and an invasion force from the Netherlands to overthrow King James II in 1688.

Golden Horde   A large Mongol khanate that ruled over Russia and part of Central Asia in the thirteenth and fourteenth centuries.

Good neighbor policy   United States President Franklin Roosevelt's 1933 commitment that the United States would respect the laws of its Latin American neighbors and refrain from military or political involvement in their affairs.

Gothic architecture   A style of European church architecture that produced impressive churches with pointed arches, towering walls, and stained glass windows.

Grand vezir   Chief minister to the sultan of the Ottoman Empire.

Great ice age   An immense stretch of time marked by frigid glacial stages when enormous ice masses called glaciers spread across much of the globe.

Great Khan   The main successor of Genghis Khan, direct ruler of all Mongol lands in East Asia and overlord of all other Mongol realms.

Great purges   Stalin's systematic effort to eliminate his opponents in 1936–1938.

Great Trek   A mass migration of Afrikaners northeast from Cape Colony into South Africa's interior, beginning in the 1830s.

Greco-Roman culture   A blending of Roman culture with that of the Greeks.

Green revolution   A global agricultural movement that used synthetic fertilizers and scientifically-developed high-yield crops to enhance farm output.

Guerrilla warfare   Raids by small roving bands of warriors that aim to disrupt armies rather than defeating them in open battle.

Guilds   Associations formed to promote the commercial and professional interests of a particular occupational group, such as merchants, shoemakers, or weavers.

Guillotine   A scaffold devised to release a heavy blade that instantly beheaded its victims.

Gunboat diplomacy   Aggressive behavior by the United States toward Latin American nations.

Haiku   Concise 17-syllable Japanese poems organized in three successive lines of five, seven, and five syllables.

Hammurabi's Code   A compilation of early Mesopotamian laws.

Hellenic   The culture developed by Greeks.

Hellenistic   The culture resulting from the blending of Greek, Persian, Egyptian, and Indian customs and societies.

Heresy   A religious opinion contrary to accepted Christian Church doctrine.

Hieroglyphics   Ancient Egyptian writing system based on pictographs.

Hiroshima   The Japanese city that was the first to be destroyed by atomic bombing in 1945.

Holy fools   Radical religious ascetics in Muscovy who renounced all worldly goods, wore few clothes, and uttered cryptic phrases that many Russians considered prophetic.

Hominid   A term scientists apply to human beings and their two-legged pre-human predecessors.

Homo sapiens   "Wise human," a term designating the species that includes all modern people.

Humanism   An outlook emphasizing the value of humans and their activities rather than focusing on faith and spirituality.

ICBM   Intercontinental Ballistics Missile, an unmanned rocket that can be launched from one continent to hit targets on another continent.

Iconoclasm   The destruction of religious images known as icons in the Byzantine Empire.

Icons   Stylized wooden paintings depicting Christian holy persons, venerated as sources of grace and often displayed in Orthodox churches.

Ideologies   Comprehensive systems of thought intended to explain and transform society in accordance with certain political, social, and cultural ideals.

Il-khans   Southwest Asian Mongol rulers or "subordinate khans."

Imperialism   The use of military force (or the threat of such use) to establish European colonies in Africa, India, and Southeast Asia, and to open up countries such as China to Western commercial exploitation.

Indo-European   A family of languages from India, Iran, and Europe that share many common features.

Indulgence   In the Christian Church, a remission of the punishment due for sins that were sacramentally forgiven; designed to reduce or eliminate suffering in purgatory.

Industrialization   A momentous shift from a rural agrarian economy to an urban manufacturing economy.

Inflation   A situation in which money declines in value and the prices of goods and services rise.

Inquisition   A judicial institution within the Christian Church that prosecuted people it identified as heretics.

Intifada   "Shaking off," an uprising designed to damage Israeli occupation forces and to call world attention to injustices perpetrated against Palestinians.

Irish Home Rule   A quest to gain domestic autonomy for Ireland.

Islamic modernism   A nineteenth century reaction to the challenges posed by technologically advanced European societies; modernists wanted to reshape Islam along European social and political lines.

Islamic reformism A nineteenth century reaction to the challenges posed by technologically advanced European societies; reformists wanted to revitalize Islam by purifying it religiously and socially.

Islamic revival A 1970s reaction to the continued existence of the State of Israel; revivalists denounced materialistic Western values as subversive of Muslim family life and religious authority.

Islamist fundamentalism A generic term for movements dedicated to political as well as religious change that view moderate Muslim regimes as excessively cooperative with the West.

Isma'ilis A branch of Shi'ite Islam claiming direct descent from Isma'il, the last publicly seen imam.

Janissaries Ottoman infantry composed of slaves who were Christian-born converts to Islam and were totally dependent on the sultan.

Jatis Regional subcastes in India, each identified with a certain trade, a specific locale, and often a particular god or goddess.

Jihad In Arabic, a "struggle" or "striving" by Muslims to uphold, defend, or spread their faith.

Jim Crow laws Post-Reconstruction laws that sanctioned racial discrimination in the southern United States.

Jingoism Belligerent popular nationalism based on warlike pride in a country's colonial conquests.

Jujitsu A Japanese form of hand-to-hand combat using holds, blows, and throws to disable an opponent.

Junkers East Prussian noble families who furnished officers for the Prussian army.

Junta Provisional governments appointed in Spanish America to rule on behalf of the imprisoned King Carlos IV; later used as a generic term for provisional military governments throughout the region.

Kabuki A form of Japanese drama in which elaborately made-up and costumed men performed both male and female roles using elaborate and seductive gestures.

Kamikaze "Divine winds," storms that sunk Mongol invasion fleets that attacked Japan in 1274 and 1281.

Kana A writing system using simplified Chinese characters to create a phonetic Japanese alphabet.

Karma One's fate or destiny in the next incarnation, as determined by performance of dharma in this life.

Khan A Central Asian regional overlord who exercised broad authority but was expected to consult regularly with a council of tribal leaders and gain its approval for his decisions.

Khanates Vast autonomous regions of the Mongol Empire.

Khmer Rouge "Red Khmer," the Cambodian Communist Party that took power in 1975 and slaughtered nearly two million people.

Khoisan Unique languages, distinguished by clicking sounds, spoken by the indigenous inhabitants of southern Africa.

Kinship group An extended family comprising grandparents, parents, siblings, aunts, uncles, cousins, and other relatives.

Knights Armed mounted warriors whose code of conduct entailed strict devotion to their overlords and to the Christian Church.

Kremlin A fortified area in central Moscow housing churches, palaces, and government headquarters.

Laissez faire A French term meaning "let them do as they choose," asserting that governments should not intervene in economic affairs.

La Reforma The Mexican revolutionary movement that overthrew Santa Anna in 1854 and then attempted to implement democratic reforms and a liberal constitution.

League of Nations An international organization (1919–1945) designed to maintain peace by cooperation among its members.

League of Nations mandates Lands entrusted to specified nations, mostly Britain or France, allegedly to help prepare the people for self-rule.

Lebensraum The Nazi concept that "living space" for the German Master Race must be conquered from Poland and Russia.

Legalism A Chinese philosophy advocating strict enforcement of stringent laws by a powerful authoritarian state.

Liberalism An ideology based on liberty, calling for constitutional governments with restricted powers, elected legislatures, and safeguards protecting people's rights.

Liberation theology A Catholic theological concept holding that Jesus of Nazareth preached not only a message of love, but also a message of opposition to unjust government; developed by theologians from Mexico and Brazil.

Limited monarchy An English alternative to royal absolutism in which nobles and the middle classes worked together to restrict the authority of the ruler.

Long Count calendar A complex calendar used by the Olmec and Maya peoples to date events according to cycles.

Long March The 6,000-mile retreat of the Chinese Communists from southern to northwestern China, enabling them to escape destruction by Nationalist forces and to rebuild their movement.

Loyalists Colonists in British North America who opposed the revolt against their mother country.

Luddites English workers between 1811 and 1816 bent on breaking machines they blamed for taking their jobs.

Luftwaffe The name for the German Air Force between 1935 and 1945.

Machismo The Iberian concept of the exaltation of masculine virility and power.

MAD Mutual Assured Destruction, a policy of nuclear deterrence based on the assumption that since nuclear war would destroy both sides, neither side would be foolish enough to start one.

Magna Carta   The "Great Charter" issued by King John of England in 1215, affirming nobles' rights and placing the king firmly under the law.

Mahabharata   The world's longest epic poem, telling of a legendary war between related families in ancient India.

Mahdists   Disciples of Muhammad Ahmed, a Sudanese mystic who claimed to be al-Mahdi, "the divinely-inspired one," and who fought the British to establish a radical anti-Western Islamic regime in the 1880s.

Mahgrib   The Muslim term for North Africa, meaning "the West," since it was the western part of the Islamic world.

Malabar coast   India's southwestern seaboard, home to several Portuguese, Dutch, and British commercial centers in the sixteenth and seventeenth centuries.

Mandarins   A Portuguese rendition of a Southeast Asian term for government ministers, used to refer to a Chinese scholar-bureaucrat class recruited through extremely rigorous civil service examinations.

Mandate of Heaven   A Chinese ruler's right to rule, provided that he governed justly and humanely.

Manifest Destiny   The belief by many people in the United States that their country had a god-given right to expand and control the entire continent of North America.

Manors   Large European landed estates owned by nobles and worked by peasant farmers.

Maratha   A Hindu nationalist movement founded to resist Mughal rule in India.

March of the Women   A march in 1789 by six thousand hungry French women that forced King Louis XVI to move from Versailles to Paris.

Maroons   Runaway slaves who established independent wilderness communities in the Americas, where they maintained many African customs.

Marshall Plan   A United States economic aid program, also called the European Recovery Program, designed to preclude communist expansion by strengthening Europe economically after World War II.

Master race   The Nazi assertion that Germans are descended from ancient Aryans and are destined to dominate "subhuman" or inferior races.

May Fourth protests   A series of anti-Western demonstrations that spread quickly across China in 1919, laying the groundwork for nationalist revolution.

Medieval   Referring to the Middle Ages, the period from the fall of Rome through the fourteenth century in Europe.

Mercantilism   A policy designed to create a condition in which a country's trading exports exceeded its imports in value.

Mercosur   The "Common Market of the South," established by Argentina, Brazil, Paraguay, and Uruguay in 1991.

Mesoamerica   Territory that comprises Mexico and northern Central America.

Mestizos   People of mixed descent in Iberian America.

Metropolitan   The head bishop of the Russian Orthodox Church.

Middle East   A modern term used to refer to West Asia and Egypt.

Middle Passage   The name given to the voyage westward across the Atlantic from West Africa during which slaves bound for the Americas suffered terrible hardships.

Militarism   An exaltation of the armed forces, coupled with the assertion that military might is central to a nation's character.

Mitima   The Inca practice of integrating conquered peoples through resettlement.

Moksha   Liberation from the cycle of death and reincarnation in Hinduism.

Monarchy   Rule by one person.

Monasticism   A religious movement in which especially devout men and women withdrew from secular society to live in religious communities, where life was characterized by prayer and self-denial.

Monotheism   Belief in a single god.

Monroe Doctrine   Issued by United States President James Monroe in 1823, it committed the United States to defend the newly created Latin American states against any European efforts at recolonization.

Montoneros   An Argentine urban terrorist group in the 1960s and 1970s.

Mosque   An Islamic house of worship.

Mothers of the Plaza de Mayo   Women who marched in front of Argentina's executive mansion each Thursday between 1977 and 1983 to protest the disappearance of their husbands and children.

Movable type   A method of printing using small metal blocks for each letter, arranged in a frame to print one page and then rearranged and reused to print other pages.

Mummification   An elaborate process for preserving the bodies of prominent people after death.

Mystery religions   Southwest Asian belief systems that addressed directly the problems of human weakness, divine redemption, and eternal life.

Napoleonic Code   Napoleon's codification of French laws that guaranteed all male citizens equality before the law.

Nation   A political community united by its people's sense of common heritage and culture.

National self-determination   The right of each nationality to freely decide its own political status.

National Socialist German Workers Party   A fascist, anti-Semitic, racist mass movement whose supporters were often called Nazis.

Nationalism   An intense devotion to one's own cultural-linguistic group and to its embodiment in a unified, independent state.

Nationalization   The takeover of private properties or enterprises by the national state.

Nativism   Domestic opposition to immigration from Asia and southern and eastern Europe into the United States.

NATO   North Atlantic Treaty Organization, an alliance concluded in 1949 and designed to protect Western Europe against Soviet expansion.

Natural law   A Roman vision of legal principles applicable to all societies regardless of time or circumstances.

Nawabs   Local Indian princes whom the British called "nabobs."

Nazis   Nickname for supporters of the National Socialist German Workers Party, a fascist, anti-Semitic, racist mass movement led by Adolf Hitler.

Nazi-Soviet Pact   Non-aggression pact between Germany and the Soviet Union in 1939 whereby Germany granted the USSR part of Poland and several other territorial adjustments in return for grain, oil, and timber; also called the Molotov-Ribbentrop Pact.

Neanderthals   An extinct group of large-brained hominids whose remains were first discovered in 1856 in Germany's Neander Valley.

Neocolonialism   Continued economic domination of former colonies by the power that had ruled them before they gained political independence.

Neolithic   The period between 10,000 and 3,000 B.C.E., during which people developed better tools, domesticated plants and animals, cultivated crops, herded livestock, and established permanent settlements; also known as the New Stone Age.

Ninety-five Theses   A set of propositions challenging the Christian Church's power to forgive sins and grant indulgences; issued by Martin Luther in 1517.

Nirvana   A state of infinite tranquility and peace.

Nonaligned nations   A group of countries in the 1950s that refused to side with either the United States or the Soviet Union.

North American Free Trade Area   Known as NAFTA, an economic agreement linking Canada, the United States, and Mexico in 1993.

North German Confederation   The unification of all states in North Germany following Prussia's victory over Austria in 1866.

Nuclear families   Families made up only of parents and their children.

Old believers   Those who rejected Patriarch Nikon's changes in Russian Orthodox practices and openly defied church and state leaders in the seventeenth century.

Oligarchy   Rule by a select few.

Open Door policy   Proclaimed by the United States in 1899, calling for free and equal trade with China and for the preservation of China's territorial integrity.

Opium   An addictive narcotic drug made from a certain kind of poppy.

Pale of Jewish Settlement   A broad band of lands along Russia's western borders where Jews were allowed to reside, although they were increasingly subjected to assorted legal limitations and abuses.

Paleolithic   The period of the earliest and longest stage of human cultural development; also known as the Old Stone Age.

Palestine Liberation Organization   "PLO," founded in 1964; a coalition of more than thirty anti-Israeli organizations dedicated to Israel's replacement by a secular Palestinian state.

Palestinian question   A refugee problem created by the displacement of Palestinians during the Israeli War for Independence of 1948–1949 and never settled thereafter.

Panca Sila   "Five Pillars" proposed by Ahmed Sukarno and Muhammad Yamin as the basis for the development of independent Indonesia.

Papal primacy   The doctrine that the pope has authority over the entire Christian Church.

Paris Commune   A revolutionary government that governed Paris from March to May 1871, opposing the national government of France.

Pastoral nomads   People who raise livestock for subsistence and move occasionally with their herds in search of fresh grazing grounds.

Patriarchal   A type of society dominated by males who served as heads of households and as community leaders.

Pax Mongolica   The "Mongolian Peace" that advanced the flow of goods and ideas among Eurasian peoples.

Pax Ottomanica   "Ottoman peace," the stability, prosperity, and peace that accompanied Ottoman rule.

Pax Romana   "Roman peace," a time of stability and prosperity beginning in the reign of Caesar Augustus.

Peninsulares   White residents of Spanish America who had been born in Spain.

People of the Book   Islamic term for Jews and Christians, peoples who possess their own scriptural texts.

People of color   A term applied in Saint-Domingue to former slaves and persons of mixed racial heritage who were legally free but were treated by whites as socially inferior.

Persian Gulf War   A 1991 conflict in which a 32-nation coalition expelled Iraq from Kuwait and shattered the long-standing Arab refusal to recognize Israel's right to exist.

Petrograd Soviet   A council of deputies elected by workers and soldiers in the capital of Russia in 1917; it struggled for power against the Provisional Government.

Philosophes   Eminent French thinkers who dominated the Enlightenment in the eighteenth century.

Physiocrats   The leading economic thinkers of the Enlightenment who were convinced that increased production and trade would enhance national wealth.

Poder moderador   "Moderative power" under the Brazilian Empire, giving the emperor authority to reconcile disputes between branches of government and prevent radical swings of the electorate in any extreme direction.

Polis   The Greek word for city-state.

Polygyny   The practice by which a man took more than one wife.

Polytheistic   The practice of worshiping more than one god.

Pope   The bishop of Rome, who headed the Christian Church and claimed to be the vicar, or agent, of Christ on earth.

Porfiriato   A period of political repression and rapid economic development in Mexico during the dictatorship of Porfirio Díaz.

Porteños   "Port dwellers" in Buenos Aires, Argentina, who considered themselves superior to illiterate gauchos.

Predestination   The belief that God long ago decided everyone's eternal fate.

PRI   The Institutional Revolutionary Party, claiming to embody the true spirit of the Mexican Revolution of 1910.

Prime Minister   The British system, initiated in 1721, in which the same person exercises both legislative and executive leadership by serving as leader of both Parliament and the royal government.

Printing press   A machine used to print pages set in movable type.

Proletariat   A large class of landless laborers who moved to cities and entered the industrial work force.

Protectorate   A country controlled by an outside power claiming to provide security.

Provisional Government   A temporary cabinet composed largely of Duma leaders after the tsar of Russia was overthrown in 1917.

Purdah   The seclusion of married women through their confinement to certain rooms of the house.

Pure Land Buddhism   A belief system that claimed that humans could not achieve enlightenment by their own efforts and must rely instead on faith in the Buddha of Infinite Light who ruled the Western Paradise, or "Pure Land."

Purgatory   In Christian belief, a place of suffering that purified the soul so it could enter heaven.

Puritanical   Referring to people who uphold an austere moral code and simple religious practices.

Puritans   Calvinist Christians who considered Anglicanism too much like Roman Catholicism and developed their own simplified church in England.

Quinine   An alkaloid substance derived from the bark of cinchona trees and used to prevent and treat malaria.

Quipu   A piece of wood with knotted cords dangling from it that served the Inca as a means of sending messages.

Qur'an   The holy book of Islam.

Race   A concept that divides human beings into categories based on external characteristics, especially skin color.

Racism   The belief that race was the main determinant of human traits and abilities, with some races seen as superior to others.

Ramayana   A great Indian epic poem based on Vedic oral traditions.

Rape of Nanjing   The Japanese Army's massacre and abuse of hundreds of thousands of Chinese in Nanjing in December 1937.

Recaptives   People from various West African cultures who had been freed from slave trading vessels and were then resettled in Sierra Leone.

Reconquista   The Christian reconquest of Iberia from the Muslims.

Reconstruction   Efforts by the Northern United States to reintegrate the South into the Union following the Civil War.

Red Guards   Radical paramilitary units striving to restore Maoist revolutionary fervor by attacking all vestiges of capitalist elitism in China.

Reign of Terror   The actions of French revolutionary tribunals in condemning and executing hundreds of thousands of people believed to be opposed to the French Revolution.

Relativism   The view that truth and morality vary from one person, group, or situation to another.

Relativity   Einstein's assertion that measurements of time, space, and motion vary with the movements and perceptions of observers.

Reparations   Payments by a country defeated in war to compensate for war damages.

Repeating rifles   Weapons that can quickly be reloaded and refired by inserting cartridges into the breech.

Republic   A flexible form of government by elected representatives.

Residencia   A thorough audit of a Spanish colonial official's conduct during his term of office.

Romanticism   A rejection of the rationalism of the Enlightenment, emphasizing emotion, passion, exuberance, heroism, and the beauty of nature.

Roosevelt Corollary   United States President Theodore Roosevelt's 1904 amplification of the Monroe Doctrine, asserting a U.S. right to intimidate or overthrow Latin American governments that did not behave acceptably.

Royal absolutism   A system of governance in which the ruler's authority is said to come directly from God, and in which no earthly institution may override that authority.

Sacraments   In the Christian Church, sacred rites believed to bestow the graces needed for salvation.

Salon   Regular gatherings during the Enlightenment where eminent thinkers and writers mingled with political and social leaders.

Samsara   The belief that each being has an eternal spiritual core which is reborn, or "reincarnated," into a new body after the old one dies.

Samurai Japanese warriors who provided military service to their lords and eventually became Japan's dominant class.

Sandinista Front for National Liberation A leftist coalition that overthrew Nicaraguan dictator Anastasio Somoza in 1979 and established close ties with Cuba and the Soviet Union.

Sans-culottes The urban working poor during the French Revolution, who wore ordinary trousers instead of the culottes, or knee-breeches, worn by the nobles.

Sapa Inca The Inca emperor, who claimed to rule by divine right because of his direct descent from Inti, the sun god.

Sati A practice in India whereby a widow cremated herself on her dead husband's funeral pyre.

Satrapy One of twenty provinces of the Persian Empire.

Satyagraha "Truth force," Gandhi's nonviolent way to combat oppression by refusing to cooperate with oppressors.

Schism A division of the Christian Church into separate, competing churches.

Scholar gentry An educated Confucian elite class supported by both official posts and large rural estates.

Scholasticism A system of study combining Christian faith with ancient Greek philosophy, especially that of Aristotle.

Scramble for concessions The period from 1896–1899 during which European nations pressed China for special privileges, called concessions, that would allow them to exploit key regions of China.

SDI Strategic Defense Initiative, or "Star Wars," an elaborate space-based missile defense system on which United States President Ronald Reagan authorized research and development in the 1980s.

Sea Peoples Assorted marauders of unknown origins who ravaged eastern Mediterranean lands in the thirteenth and twelfth centuries B.C.E.

Semitic A language family that includes Arabic, Hebrew, and the languages spoken by ancient Akkadians, Babylonians, and Phoenicians.

Sepoys Indian soldiers trained and commanded by the British.

Seppuku The practice of ritual suicide by which a defeated samurai warrior in Japan could restore his honor.

Serfs Peasants bound to the manor and under the control of its lord.

Service state Tsar Peter I's reform of Russian government, requiring all nobles to serve in either the military or the bureaucracy.

Shah The Persian word for king.

Shamanism A form of religion in which spiritual leaders called shamans performed elaborate rituals to communicate with spirits, heal the sick, forecast the future, and influence events.

Shanghai massacre Jiang Jieshi's slaughter of Chinese Communists in Shanghai in 1927.

Sharecroppers Americans who farmed lands supplied by a landowner, to whom they then were required to pay half their harvest.

Shari`ah The holy law of Islam.

Shi'ites The minority of Muslims, following the "Party of Ali" (*Shi'at Ali*).

Shinto The "way of the kami," a nature-based Japanese religion.

Shogun The commander-in-chief of Japan's armed forces and the real ruler of the nation.

Sikh An Indian belief system that blends and synthesizes Hindu and Islamic elements.

Silk Road A network of trade routes named for the precious Chinese fabric it conveyed.

Simony The sale of offices in the Christian Church.

Slavery An institution in which some people owned other human beings and subjected them to involuntary service.

Socialism An ideology based on equality, calling for redistribution of income, improved working conditions, and the political empowerment of workers.

Socialism in One Country Stalin's program that focused on strengthening the USSR while requiring communists everywhere to postpone world revolution and support the Soviet state.

Socratic dialogue Rigorous questioning and analysis of ethical issues, as practiced by the Greek philosopher Socrates.

Soviet Russian word for "council," referring to elected bodies of workers' delegates in 1905 and 1917; later used to refer to the regime that ruled Russia from 1917 until 1991.

Soviet Bloc A post-World War II coalition of Soviet-dominated "satellite" regimes in Poland, Romania, Bulgaria, Hungary, East Germany, and Czechoslovakia.

Stateless societies Independent African villages and federations of villages ruled by local patriarchs and chiefs.

States Territorial entities ruled by a central government.

Struggle of the Orders A bitterly divisive social contest between patricians and plebeians in the Roman Republic.

Stupa A massive domed edifice constructed of stone, used as a temple for Buddhist pilgrimage and worship.

Sufism A mystic strain of Islam that advocates direct union with God through prayer, contemplation, and religious ecstasy.

Summit conference A face-to-face meeting of the world's most powerful leaders.

Sunni The majority of Muslims, claiming to follow the Sunna, the traditional practices of the Prophet.

Surrealism Art that sought to challenge perceptions or to portray Freud's unconscious world of drives, fantasies, and dreams.

Swahili A language widespread in East Africa; the name of Bantu-Arabic East African culture.

Table of Ranks Tsar Peter I's fourteen-level organizational ladder, requiring state officials and military officers to work their way up through a series of promotions based on performance rather than heredity or prestige.

Tahuantin-suyu "Empire of the Four Quarters," the official name of the Inca Empire.

Taiping Rebellion A vast uprising in China between 1850 and 1864, fueled by anti-Manchu hostility and Western religious ideas.

Tanzimat "Reorganization," a sweeping set of reforms enacted from 1839 to 1876 and designed to modernize and Westernize the Ottoman Empire.

Tatar yoke The era of Mongol domination of Russia.

Tennis Court Oath A pledge taken in1789 by representatives in France's National Assembly not to disperse until France obtained a written constitution.

Tet Offensive A surprise attack on South Vietnamese and United States forces launched by the Viet Cong in 1968 and coinciding with Tet, the Vietnamese Lunar New Year.

Thagi The work of professional bandits or "thugs" who attacked and strangled travelers in India as part of a religious ritual.

Three Religions A Vietnamese belief system blending Mahayana Buddhism, Confucianism, and Daoism.

Tlaxcallan Confederacy An alliance of several city-states opposed to the Aztec Empire.

Trans-Siberian Railway A 5,800-mile railroad stretching across Russia from west to east.

Treaty of Tordesillas A 1494 agreement between the Portuguese and Spanish designed to divide the world between them.

Trench warfare A brutalizing, degrading form of combat in which soldiers lived and died fighting in ditches eight feet deep; caused by the stalemate on the Western Front during the Great War.

Triangular trade A three-cornered Atlantic trade, centered on the sale and labor of African slaves, connecting Europe, West Africa, and the Americas.

Tribes Large associations of villages, bands, or clans that share a common language and often a common leader.

Triple Alliance The alliance of Austria-Hungary, Germany, and Italy (1882–1914).

Triple Entente The alliance of Britain, France, and Russia (1907–1914).

Triple Intervention The combination of Russia, France, and Germany that pressured Japan to renounce the Liaodong peninsula in Manchuria in 1895.

Truman Doctrine U. S. President Harry Truman's 1947 proclamation that the United States must "support free peoples who are resisting attempted subjugation by armed minorities or by outside pressures."

Tsar A Russian version of the title "caesar" used by Roman and Byzantine emperors, first used in Russia by Grand Prince Ivan III.

Tupamaros An Uruguayan urban terrorist group in the 1960s and 1970s.

Turtle ships Innovative Korean ships whose decks were protected with iron plating.

Twelfth Imam Also called the "Hidden Imam," a messianic Muslim leader who vanished in the ninth century C.E.; Shi'ites believe he will return to create a religious kingdom and usher in a period of prosperity and peace enduring until the Last Judgment.

Tyranny The illegal seizure of power by someone who had no right to exercise it.

U-boats German term for "Under-the-Sea-Boats," or submarines.

UCR Radical Civic Union, an Argentine reform movement that became the nation's largest political party in the early twentieth century.

Umma A purely Islamic community.

United Nations An international peace-keeping body designed to replace the defunct League of Nations in 1945.

Universal male suffrage Voting rights for all men.

University An educational institution in which scholars from various fields helped students become experts and then granted them degrees to certify their expertise.

Upanishads Philosophical and religious texts composed by learned writers over many centuries, beginning in late Vedic India.

Urdu An Indian language written with the Persian alphabet and employing many Persian terms.

Urfi State laws used by the Ottoman sultan without restriction from Islamic legal authority.

U-2 Affair The crash of an American spy plane in the USSR on May 1, 1960 that became an international incident and was used to cancel a summit conference in Paris.

Vaccination The process of immunizing people against disease by injecting them with a weak dose of the disease so that they can build immunity to it.

Varnas Classes in Aryan Indian society, based on the functions fulfilled by their members.

Vassals Subordinate warlords who swore allegiance and pledged military service to a higher lord.

Vedic The culture of Aryan India.

Vernacular literature Literature written in the everyday language spoken by common people.

Viceroy "Vice-king," an official responsible for the execution of the monarch's orders in a large subdivision of the empire or realm.

Viet Cong "Vietnamese Communists," a nickname given to the paramilitary guerrilla units of the National Liberation Front of South Vietnam.

Vietminh The Vietnamese Independence Brotherhood League, a coalition of nationalists formed in 1941 and led by the Indochinese Communist Party in a struggle to liberate Vietnam from colonial rule.

Vietnamization A process by which the United States transferred responsibility for fighting the Vietnam War to the army of South Vietnam.

Wahhabism The austere, deeply puritanical brand of Islam practiced in Saudi Arabia since the 1740s.

Warsaw Pact A Soviet-led alliance of East European communist states designed to counterbalance NATO.

Westernization The adoption by non-Western nations of Western-style industries, technologies, institutions, and ideologies.

Women's suffrage Voting rights for all women.

Xiongnu Warlike Turkish nomads from the Central Asian steppes who threatened China from the north.

Yin and yang A Chinese principle emphasizing the balancing and blending of natural forces.

Yoga A school of classical Hindu philosophy emphasizing meditation and self-knowledge.

Young Turks Young reformist rebels who collaborated with dissident Ottoman army officers in 1908 to force the sultan to restore the constitution and parliament.

Zaibatsu Large Japanese conglomerates that each owned a diverse array of industries, businesses, banks, and resources.

Zemski sobor A specially convened "Assembly of the Land" made up of delegates from Muscovy's various classes.

Zemstvo An assembly elected in each Russian county and province after 1864 and charged with caring for local needs such as roads, schools, medicine, and emergency food supplies.

Zen (Chan) Buddhism A belief system teaching that meditation is the only path to enlightenment and stressing love of nature, simplicity of life, and individual self-discipline.

Ziggurats Massive brick towers that ascended upward in a series of tiers, typically topped by shrines that could be used for religious ceremonies.

Zimmermann Note An effort by a German diplomat to bribe Mexico into an alliance against the United States in 1917; intercepted and decoded by the British, it outraged public opinion in the neutral United States.

Zionists Followers of Theodor Herzl's conviction that Jews would always be outsiders in Christian Europe and that they should therefore seek the establishment of a Jewish state.

Zoroastrianism A Persian belief system including the concepts of free will and a Last Judgment.

Cover Sequoyah (1770–1843) and his Cherokee alphabet, Courtesy of the Library of Congress; Islamic calligraphy, Patrick Ben and Luke Snyder/Lonely Planet Images; El Castillo Pyramid Chichen Itza, Yucatan, Mexico, Peter Adams/JIA/CORBIS; Buddha Sakyamuni, The Art Archive/Musée Guimet Paris/Dagli Orti; D'Espanol y Mulata produce Morisca/Breamore House, Hampshire, England; Tomb of Nebamun, © Copyright The British Museum/Art Resource, NY; Tondo of St. Mamai, c. 1000/Courtesy of the Library of Congress; The NEMESIS destroying Chinese war junks in Anson's Bay, The Art Archive/Eileen Tweedy; Rhinos in Chauvet Cave, French Ministry of Culture and Communication, Regional Direction for Cultural Affairs—Rhone-Alps, Regional Department of Archaeology; International Space Station, NASA; "Parade on Tsarina's Meadow", Vsesoiuznyi Muzei A.S. Pushkina; Bronze head, Kim Sayer © Dorling Kindersley; Spanish Civil War poster, Courtesy of the Library of Congress.

Chapter 1 p. 1, Chauvet cave paintings: horses, Ministere de la Culture et de la Communication. Direction Regionale des affaires Culturelles de Rhone–Alpes, Service Regional de l'Archeologie; **p. 4,** Representative hominid tools, Howard S. Friedman/Pearson Education/PH College Corbis/Bettman; **p. 9,** Venus of Willendorf, © Archivo Iconografico, S.A./CORBIS; **p. 15,** Indians plant corn, Courtesy of the Library of Congress; **p. 18,** Potters and pottery, EMG Education Management Group.

Chapter 2 p. 23, Sumerian Ziggurat, World Tourism Organization: Iraq; **p. 25,** Assyrian King Sargon and a high official, John Serafin/Pearson Education Corporate Digital Archive; **p. 28,** Clay tablet, Courtesy of the Library of Congress; **p. 34,** Assyrian warrior, EMG Education Management Group; **p. 36,** The hanging gardens of ancient Babylon, EMG Education Management Group; **p. 39,** Mummy Case of Lady Takhenmes, Peter Anderson © Dorling Kindersley, Courtesy of the Bolton Metro Museum; **p. 42,** Sphinx and Cheops Pyramid at Giza near Cairo, Egypt/Egyptian Tourist Authority; **p. 43,** Statues of Ramses II at Abu Simbel, Dominique Roger/Egyptian Tourist Authority; **p. 44,** Wall painting showing Nubians presenting gifts and food offerings, © The British Museum; **p. 48,** A recreation of the ancient walled city of Jerusalem, Israel Ministry of Tourism, North America.

Chapter 3 p. 54, Early Indian sculpture, Andy Crawford © Dorling Kindersley, Courtesy of the National Museum, New Delhi; **p. 58 (top),** General view of Mohenjodaro, Embassy of Pakistan; **p. 58 (bottom),** Seal of Mohenjodaro, Embassy of Pakistan; **p. 59,** Dancing girl, Mohenjo-daro, Embassy of Pakistan; **p. 63,** Two relief panels from the stupa of Bharhut, Courtesy of the Library of Congress; **p. 65,** Vishnu and Lakshmi, Courtesy of the Government of India Tourist Office, New York; **p. 75,** The Great Stupa at Sanchi, Dale William/Government of India.

Chapter 4 p. 80, Cross-section illustration of the tomb of Qin Shihuangdi showing the Terra Cotta Army, Richard Bronson, © Dorling Kindersley; **p. 83 (top),** China, Ningxia, Shapotu, Yellow River/Eddie Gerald, © Dorling Kindersley; **p. 83 (bottom),** Yangshao pottery from Banpo, China/Courtesy of the Library of Congress; **p. 85,** Chariot burial from the royal Shang tombs near Anyang/National Archives and Records Administration; **p. 86,** Chinese writing on a piece of bone, Laurence Pordes, © Dorling Kindersley/Courtesy of The British Library; **p. 89,** Bell from Zhou Dynasty, Alan Hills, © The British Museum; **p. 90,** Confucius surrounded by his disciples, Courtesy of the Library of Congress; **p. 96,** China's Great Wall, Jupiter Images; **p. 97,** Cave 323, Mogao Grottoes, Dunhuang, China./© www.dunhuanghun.com Dunhuang Academy. All rights reserved; **p. 101,** Model of a Han era house, Courtesy of the Library of Congress; **p. 104,** Bactrian camel, camelus bactrianus/ Dave King, © Dorling Kindersley.

Chapter 5 p. 107, Pueblo Bonito, Chaco Canyon, New Mexico/ Courtesy of the Library of Congress; **p. 109,** Clovis points from sites New Mexico, Arizona, and Colorado/National Archives and Records; **p. 112,** Totem Park, Brockton Point, Gunter Marx, © Dorling Kindersley, Courtesy of Stanley Park, Totem Park, Vancouver, British Columbia; **p. 114,** Ancient Ruins in the Canyon de Chelly, Arizona/Timothy O'Sullivan National Archives and Records Administration, Presidential Library; **p. 115,** Monk's Mound in Cahokia, Otis Imboden, Jr./NGS Image Collection; **p. 118,** Colossal Olmec, Demtrio Carrasco © CONACULTA-INAH-MEX. Authorized reproduction by the Instituto Nacional de Antropologia e Historia; **p. 121,** Venus calendar, Sachsische Landesbibliothek; **p. 122,** Pyramid of the Moon, Mike Peters/Pearson Education Corporate Digital Archive; **p. 124,** Atlantis de Tula, Hidalgo/Andrew Sacks, Embassy of Mexico; **p. 129,** Chimu society woven polychrome textile panel, © Judith Miller/Dorling Kindersley/Arte Primitivo.

Chapter 6 p. 133, Frieze showing Persian palace guard/© The British Museum; **p. 139,** Clay cylinder with text, Alan Hills and Barbara Winter/© The British Museum; **p. 143,** Iran, Persepolis: Eugene Gordon, Dorling Kindersley Media Library; **p. 144,** Silver goat from 5th century B.C., Alan Hills and Barbara Winter/© The British Museum; **p. 145,** Ruins of the entrance to the palace of Darius, Iranian Embassy; **p. 151,** Part of a mosaic illustrating the Battle of Issus, Soprintendenza alle Antichita della Campania, picture by Raymond V. Schoder.

Chapter 7 p. 156, Greek athletes on a glazed Athenian vase, National Archives and Records Administration; **p. 159 (top),** Fresco from the Palace of Knossos, Crete/Hirmer Verlag/Pearson Education U.S. ELT; **p. 159 (bottom),** Agamemnon's mask, Prentice Hall School Division; **p. 163,** Ancient Greek figurine of a warrior, Nick Nicholls/© The British Museum; **p. 164,** Pericles; Statesman of Greece, Courtesy of the Library

pter 23 **p. 556**, Njinga of Ndongo, By permission of The British Library; **p. 561**, View of El Mina, Courtesy of the Library of Congress; 2, Ingenio azucarero, Brazil/Courtesy of the Library of Congress; **p. 564**, Diagram of slave ship, Courtesy of the Library of Congress; **p. 565**, e Janeiro slave market, The Bridgeman Art Library International; **p. 567**, 1830's engraving of Timbuktu, Courtesy of the Library of Congress; 9, Benin bronze head, Kim Sayer, © Dorling Kindersley; **p. 571**, Don Alvaro, King of Kongo/Courtesy of the Library of Congress; **p. 572**, of Kilwa, Courtesy of the Library of Congress; **p. 576** (top), Fort at Cape Town, National Archives of South Africa; **p. 576** (bottom), Slave e, 1784/Courtesy of the Library of Congress.

pter 24 **p. 581**, Hall of Mirrors at Versailles, Daniel Thierry/French Government Tourist Office; **p. 584**, Richelieu, Courtesy of the Library ongress; **p. 585**, Louis XIV, Max Alexander, © Dorling Kindersley, Courtesy of Etablissement public du musée et du domaine national de illes; **p. 589**, "An Officer and a Soldier," Courtesy of the Library of Congress; **p. 591**, Oliver Cromwell, Dorling Kindersley, © The Wallace ction, London; **p. 593** (top), Copernicus's heliocentric view of the universe/Courtesy of the Library of Congress; **p. 593** (bottom), Title page *Novvum Organum*, Courtesy of the Library of Congress; **p. 594**, Galileo's view of moon, Courtesy of the Library of Congress; **p. 595**, Title from Hobbes' *Leviathan*, 1651/Courtesy of the Library of Congress. Rare Book and Special Collection Division; **p. 598** (top), Page from rot's *Encyclopedia*, Courtesy of the Library of Congress; **p. 598** (bottom), Voltaire, Courtesy of the Library of Congress; **p. 601**, Summer ence of Habsburgs, Peter Wilson/© Dorling Kindersley, Courtesy of Schloss Schonbrunn, Vienna.

pter 25 **p. 606**, St. Basil's Cathedral, Leslie Deeb/Pearson Education/PH College; **p. 609**, Vasnetsov's "The Walled City," Demetrio asco, © Dorling Kindersley; **p. 611**, 16th century engraving from Sigmund, Freiherr von Herberstein "Rerum Moscoviticarum commentarii," /Courtesy of the Library of Congress; **p. 617**, Interior of the Cathedral of the Virgin of Smolensk, Demetrio Carrasco, © Dorling Kindersley; 19, Cossack maiden's shirt, Greek National Tourism Organization; **p. 621**, Traditional wooden house, Siberia/Eric Baccega, Nature Picture ary; **p. 623** (top), W. Holl's engraving of Peter the Great, Courtesy of the Library of Congress; **p. 623** (bottom), The first "Winter Palace," . Engraving by A. Zubov, 1717; **p. 626**, Carta of Imperial Russia, Courtesy of the Library of Congress. Rare Book Collection, Law Library; 29 (top), "Peoples of the Empire"/Courtesy of the Library of Congress; **p. 629** (bottom), Title page from "Vedomosti," newspaper/Courtesy e Library of Congress.

pter 26 **p. 633**, The destruction of the king's statue in New York, Courtesy of the Library of Congress; **p. 636**, Gun powder holder, tesy of the Library of Congress; **p. 638**, The Repeal, Courtesy of the Library of Congress; **p. 639**, The Boston Tea Party, Courtesy of the ary of Congress; **p. 641**, Surrender of British troops at Yorktown, Courtesy of the Library of Congress; **p. 642**, Reveil du Tiers Etat, Courtesy e Library of Congress; **p. 643**, A paper "assignat," Chas Howson/© The British Museum; **p. 645**, Execution of Louis XVI, Courtesy of ibrary of Congress; **p. 647** (top), Clothing of Sans Culottes, Mark Hamilton/© Dorling Kindersley; **p. 647** (bottom), Small painting of oleon, Dorling Kindersley/© The Wallace Collection, London; **p. 649**, The Rosetta stone, © The British Museum; **p. 653**, Toussaint verture, Courtesy of the Library of Congress; **p. 655**, Napoleonic forces in battle, Dorling Kindersley/© The British Museum.

pter 27 **p. 663**, Power looms, David Lyons/© Dorling Kindersley, Courtesy of the Boott Cotton Mills Museum, Lowell, Massachusetts; 66, Flyer spinning frame, Dave King/© Dorling Kindersley, Courtesy of the Science Museum, London; **p. 668**, The Crystal Palace Courtesy of ibrary of Congress; **p. 670**, Stuttgart Street scenes, Courtesy of the Library of Congress; **p. 671** (top), Carting, drawing, and boxing cotton, 835/Courtesy of the Library of Congress; **p. 671** (bottom), Mill worker in mule spinning room, Fiskeville, RI, 1909/Lewis Hine, Courtesy of ibrary of Congress; **p. 672**, Urban squalor, Courtesy of the Library of Congress; **p. 673**, Karl Marx, Courtesy of the Library of Congress; 76 (top), Beethoven sonata, Courtesy of the Library of Congress; **p. 676** (bottom), Liberty Leading the People, Dagli Orti (A) Picture Desk/ al Collection; **p. 681**, Suffragists parade, April 5, 1917/Courtesy of the Library of Congress; **p. 684**, Otto von Bismark, National Archives Records Administration; **p. 686**, Aleksei Venetsianov's "Harvesting Summer," 1827/National Archives and Records Administration; **p. 688**, century images from Tbilisi, Georgia, Ukrain/Courtesy of the Library of Congress; **p. 689**, Italian immigrants at Ellis Island, Courtesy of the ary of Congress; **p. 692**, Pears' Soap ad/*Collier's*, October 4, 1899; **p. 694**, Valparaiso Docks, Chile, 1914/ Courtesy of the Library of Congress.

pter 28 **p. 698**, Constitution of the United States of America, Courtesy of the Library of Congress; **p. 703** (top), Cotton plantation, Cour- of the Library of Congress; **p. 703** (bottom), Ironclad war ship, Courtesy of the Library of Congress; **p. 707**, Anti-immigrant cartoon, Cour- of the Library of Congress; **p. 714**, Simon Bolivar, 1783–1830/Courtesy of the Library of Congress; **p. 719**, Mexican laborers, Courtesy of Library of Congress; **p. 721**, Immigrant hotel in Buenos Aires, Courtesy of the Library of Congress; **p. 723** (top), Araucanian Indian, Courtesy e Library of Congress; **p. 723** (bottom), Dom Pedro II of Brazil, Courtesy of the Library of Congress.

pter 29 **p. 727**, Japanese view American steamship, Courtesy of the Library of Congress; **p. 732**, Destroying opium, Courtesy of the Library Congress; **p. 736**, The Empress Cixi (Old Buddha)/Courtesy of the Library of Congress; **p. 739**, The Great Revolt of 1857, Bobby Kohli/© ling Kindersley; **p. 740**, American marines in Japan, 1853/Courtesy of the Library of Congress; **p. 741**, Japanese Emperor, Japan National rist Organization; **p. 748**, Open Door Policy, Courtesy of the Library of Congress; **p. 750**, Boxer Rebellion, Courtesy of the Library of gress; **p. 751**, Theodore Roosevelt with Japanese and Russian officials, Courtesy of the Library of Congress.

Chapter 30 p. 755, Opening of the Suez Canal, Courtesy of the Library of Congress; p. 757, Keppen's "Battle of Kinburne," 1855/From "A. V. Suvorov" (Moscow: "Izobraztiel'noe iskusstvo," 1986); p. 762, 19th century Cairo, © Dorling Kindersley; p. 763, Suez Canal, Jon Spaull/© Dorling Kindersley; p. 765, Equaino-Jason Young, Courtesy of the Library of Congress; p. 766, African slave trade, Courtesy of the Library of Congress; p. 768, Fulani uniform, Ray Moller/© Dorling Kindersley, Courtesy of the Powell-Cotton Museum, Kent; p. 769, African elephant tusks, © Dorling Kindersley; p. 770, Zulu shield and spears, Roger de la Harpe/© Dorling Kindersley; p. 771, Illustrations from David Livingstone's journals, Courtesy of the Library of Congress; p. 773, Soldier with Maxim machine gun, ca. 1885/Brian Delft, © Dorling Kinder; p. 775, Abyssinians routing Italian troops, Private Collection/Archives Charmet/The Bridgeman Art Library; p. 776, Diamond mining at Kimberley, National Archives of South Africa; p. 778, Afrikaners during South African War, National Archives of South Africa; p. 779, African being baptized, National Archives of South Africa.

Chapter 31 p. 782, "Over the Top," National Archives and Records Administration; p. 784, William II, Kaiser of Imperial Germany/Taber Prang Art, Courtesy of the Library of Congress; p. 787, Interior of a textile mill in Tashkent, Courtesy of the Library of Congress; p. 789, Emperor Francis Joseph and Archduke Ferdinand, National Archives and Records Administration; p. 791 (top), Recruiting poster with portrait British War Minister General Kitchener, Andy Crawford/Dorling Kindersley, © Imperial War Museum, London; p. 791 (bottom), Dead German soldiers from the Battle of La Basse, National Archives and Records Administration; p. 793, ANZAC troops at Gallipoli, National Archives and Records Administration; p. 794 (top), The Lusitania, Courtesy of the Library of Congress; p. 794 (bottom), War-devastated landscape in Northern France, National Archives and Records Administration; p. 795, Austro-Hungarian troops defend the Eastern Front, National Archives and Records Administration; p. 797, An ammunition factory in India, British Information Services; p. 799, Women workers at a naval ship-building yard, Courtesy of the Library of Congress; p. 801, Knight of Civilization takes on the Kaiser, Courtesy of the Library of Congress; p. 803, Burial day of the victims of the Revolution. March 23, 1917, Petrograd/Courtesy of the Library of Congress; p. 804, Lenin, Courtesy of the Library of Congress; p. 805, A Kravchenko (d. 1940) Fund of Freedom." From Baburina, "Rossiia-20 vek: istoriia strany v placate." Panorama, Moscow, Russia; p. 807, Antique Turkish Tufenjieff grenade with rope fuse, Gary Ombler/© Dorling Kindersley/Courtesy of Imperial War Museum, London.

Chapter 32 p. 812, Rene Magritte's "La Trahison des Images," Los Angeles County Museum of Art, Purchased with funds provided by the Mr. and Mrs. William Preston Harrison Collection; p. 814, Albert Einstein, Courtesy of the Library of Congress; p. 816 (top), Cars along Daytona Beach in the 1920's, Courtesy of the Library of Congress; p. 816 (bottom), Washington D.C. beach scene, 1920's/Courtesy of the Library of Congress; p. 817, A Picasso painting, John Heseltine/© Dorling Kindersley; p. 818, Prince Faisel with Lawrence of Arabia, National Archives and Records Administration; p. 820, Benito Mussolini, Courtesy of the Library of Congress; p. 822, Bread line during the Great Depression, 1930's/Courtesy of the Library of Congress; p. 823, CCC enrollees placing sandbags on the levee at Cates Landing, Tennessee during 1937 flood/National Archives and Records Administration; p. 824, Baburina, "Rossia—20 vek: istoriia strany v placate." Panorama, Russia; p. 825, Joseph Stalin, Courtesy of the Library of Congress; p. 826, The "City of Iron"—Magnitogorsk, circa 1939/National Archives and Records Administration; p. 827, A Berlin woman starting the morning fire with marks/Courtesy of the Library of Congress; p. 828, Synagogue being burned during Kristallnacht (November 9–11, 1938), D. O. W./U. S. Holocaust Memorial Museum; p. 830, Marcus Garvey, Courtesy of the Library of Congress; p. 833, Turkish President Mustafa Kemal Ataturk, Turkish Tourism and Information Office; p. 834, Mohandas Gandhi, Courtesy of the Library of Congress; p. 840, Yearning for Military Heroes: Japanese patriotic society members dressed as samurai, approx. 1925/National Archives and Records Administration.

Chapter 33 p. 844, Pearl Harbor Attack, 7 December 1941/National Archives and Records Administration; p. 847, Spanish Civil War poster, Courtesy of the Library of Congress; p. 850, Munich Conference, 1938/National Archives and Records Administration; p. 851, World War II, National Archives and Records Administration; p. 853 (top), Adolf Hitler receiving news of France's surrender, National Archives and Records Administration; p. 853 (bottom), The London Blitz, British Information Services; p. 856, Chinese condemned for collaboration with Japanese, Courtesy of the Library of Congress; p. 859, Erwin Rommel, National Archives and Records Administration; p. 862, Woman factory worker, Courtesy of the Library of Congress; p. 864, Jewish Hungarian women at Auschwitz-Birkenau, Poland/Photo by Bernhard Walter; source: National Archives and Record Administration; p. 866, German concentration camp, 1945/Courtesy of the Library of Congress; p. 867, D-Day, Normandy Omaha Beach troops landing/Courtesy of the Library of Congress; p. 871 (top), U. S. Marines at Iwo Jima/National Archives and Records Administration; p. 871 (bottom), View of atomic bomb damage to Hiroshima, Japan/National Archives and Records Administration.

Chapter 34 p. 876, Baker Day explosion of the fifth atomic bomb at Bikini, National Archives and Records Administration; p. 878, Crimea Conference with Churchill, Roosevelt, and Stalin/U. S. Army Photograph; p. 883, Berlin airlift/Courtesy of the Library of Congress; p. 888, Model of Soviet A1 rocket, © Dorling Kindersley; p. 891, Political cartoon by Guernsey Le Pelley, Courtesy of the Library of Congress; p. 894 (top), Aerial view of Levittown, New York/National Archives and Records Administration; p. 894 (bottom), Rosa Parks, Courtesy of the Library of Congress; p. 895 (top), Segregation, Russell Lee/Courtesy of the Library of Congress; p. 895 (bottom), Female anti-war demonstrator, S. Sgt Albert and R. Simpson/National Archives and Records Administration; p. 896 (top), Khrushchev visits Albanian factory/Courtesy of the Library of Congress; p. 896 (bottom), Soviet outdoor market, Courtesy of the Library of Congress; p. 897, Anti-Stalin poster, Courtesy of the Library